EXPERIENCING LAW SERIES™

EXPERIENCING PROFESSIONAL RESPONSIBILITY

Michael P. Maslanka
UNT Dallas College of Law

Michael Kagan
University of Nevada, Las Vegas
William S. Boyd School of Law

Nancy Ann Dao
University of West Los Angeles School of Law

WEST
ACADEMIC
PUBLISHING

© 2023 LEG, Inc. d/b/a West Academic
   860 Blue Gentian Road, Suite 350
   Eagan, MN 55121
   1-877-888-1330
West, West Academic Publishing, and West Academic are trademarks of West Publishing Corporation, used under license.

Printed in the United States of America

ISBN: 978-1-68561-809-4

Professor Maslanka

Dedication:

To the memory of my parents, Dorothy and Frank, who taught me right from wrong.

Acknowledgments:

My boundless gratitude to Research Assistant (now sister lawyer) Rossina Ortega and to Research Assistant and UNT Dallas Law graduate Carmen Coreas. This book was published because of their diligence and commitment. Thanks go to our high school intern, Shreya Lokhande, for her industry (Gen Z to the rescue!) and Stewart Caton (Professor of Practice/Law Liberian), who was always already to research all issues, no matter how obscure. And to the students (yes, each of them) from whom I am always learning. Thanks to Louis Higgins and Danny Buteyn and the outstanding team at West Academic. On a personal note, my drivers and friends Sebagadis Taddessa and Amarjitpal Gill, were and are indispensable parts of my daily life. My gratitude to Lola for being a nonjudgmental part of my life. I want to thank my law school mentors, Professor Jay Mootz and Leticia M. Saucedo. Finally, to my co-authors Michael Kagan and Nancy Ann Dao for their invaluable perspectives. While it may not take a bustling city to write a book, it certainly takes a caring village.

Professor Kagan

Dedication:

To the students of the UNLV Immigration Clinic, past, present, and future.
You inspire me to be a better lawyer.

Professor Dao

Dedication:

To all law students, who dream of changing the world. "Có công mài sát có ngày nên kim."

Summary of Contents

PART VI. THE LAWYER AS BUSINESSPERSON AND ENTREPRENEUR

PART VII. YOUR CAREER AS A LAWYER

Table of Contents

PART II. A LAWYER'S DUTIES TO THE CLIENT

PART III. THE LAWYER BEFORE TRIAL

PART IV. THE LAWYER AT TRIAL

PART V. THE LAWYER AS TRANSACTIONAL ADVOCATE

PART VI. THE LAWYER AS BUSINESSPERSON AND ENTREPRENEUR

PART VII. YOUR CAREER AS A LAWYER

Table of Cases

The principal cases are in bold type.

EXPERIENCING PROFESSIONAL RESPONSIBILITY

Why Study Professional Responsibility?

All law schools require this course. The American Bar Association (ABA) started mandating Professional Responsibility (PR) as a course in the aftermath of the Watergate scandal in the late 1960s and early 1970s that culminated in the resignation of then President Richard M. Nixon. The legal profession was shocked that so many lawyers were implicated in the scandal from conception to cover-up. Thus, the outcry for the mandatory teaching of ethics in law schools. In fact, each aspiring lawyer is now required to pass the MPRE (Multistate Professional Responsibility Exam) which is based largely on the Model Rules of Professional Responsibility (Model Rules) promulgated by the ABA. Like the Uniform Bar Examination, the MPRE is a standardized examination. All of its questions will be multiple choice. This course and our book will help you successfully navigate this requirement to becoming barred.

But PR as a course is so much more and so is, we believe, our book. Its purpose is also to bridge the gap between law school and what you will experience in your practice. Scholarship confirms that there is a disconnect. Professor Deborah Jones Merritt and researcher Logan Cornett make this point in *"Building A Better Bar: The Twelve Building Blocks of Minimum Competence*, Institute for the Advancement of the American Legal System, December 2020.

Their research highlighted the following:

1) Upon reflection, new lawyers remarked that PR was their most important law school course because, as practicing lawyers, it is the subject matter that arises most often in their practices regardless of its nature. And yet, they believe that their PR classes did not prepare them for practice.

2) New lawyers possess a general sense that they are unable to make decisions consistent with professional ethics, often because matters go "sideways" so quickly in practice. In short, new lawyers feel they need to be better able to think ethically on their feet.

3) New lawyers experience difficulty reconciling their roles as zealous advocates of their clients—glamorized in media—with their roles as officers of the court.

4)   New lawyers are concerned that their personal beliefs and life experiences will not fully integrate with their professional lives. 60% of new lawyers view "social consciousness/community involvement" as an important element of their practice and 62.1% believe that a "commitment to justice and the rule of law" are likewise necessary elements of lawyering. Many readers of our book will be Gen Z (born between 1995 and 2010) for whom social justice will be an important facet of their professional lives.

5)   In her recent article *#FortheCulture: Generation Z and the Future of Legal Education* (Michigan Journal of Race and the Law 2020), Professor Tiffany D. Atkins observes "In addition to social justice activism, Gen Zers also feel very strongly about diversity. Based on their exposure to different cultures through social media and their own social circles, Gen Zers expect to live, work and learn among people who are different than them."

The changing demographics of the United States demonstrate that they are right. The 2020 Census notes that 44.9 million persons who live in the United States are foreign born. What does this mean to the reader of this book? Professional norms need to adapt to the diversity of the population that the legal profession serves.

In short, a PR course needs to address these concerns, not just prepare students for the MPRE and the Bar Exam. We've written a book specifically designed to help train you in how lawyers actually experience PR as it unfolds in their daily legal practices. We include the following key features:

> ➤   **Cases and Materials/X-Ray Questions**

Case selections are less focused on Supreme Court cases with their concurrences and dissents and more focused on the typical issues, temptations, and dilemmas that lawyers experience. To assist your understanding, each case is preceded by a section called "X-Ray Questions." These are designed to help you in coming to a deeper and more profound understanding of the case from both theoretical and practical vantage points. It is worth noting that—unlike most law school courses—many of the cases in this book are here mainly to illustrate how a court applies a rule or principle. Only a minority of the cases in this book established a new rule of law. We compliment these case selections with "*Scenarios*" which give concrete illustrations of the Rules under discussion and with a "*Let's Chart It!*" feature that flowchart concepts.

➤ **Deconstruction Exercise/Rule Rationale**

Mastering PR also requires an understanding and application of textual analysis and rule rationale. Why did the drafters of the Model Rules use a certain word or phrase in lieu of other words or phrases? As one of your authors tells PR classes "doctors use scalpels and lawyers use words." We will therefore perform a textual analysis of the rules. In addition, know this: the lawyer who knows the rule and the reason for the rule, will always—in a legal firefight—possess a strategic and tactical advantage over a lawyer who only knows the rule. We will look at the reasons for the rule and—at times—whether the reasons are still valid or whether the rule is a candidate for change. These skills are portable to all of your other law school classes.

➤ **Scenarios/Leaning into Practice/Beyond the Cite**

Scenarios are short and contextually driven fact patterns that illustrate a point under discussion or challenge you to apply a rule or use your judgment/discretion in resolving an ethical dilemma. Leaning into Practice takes scenarios a step further and illustrates how ethical considerations will impact your daily practice of law. Finally, Beyond the Cite delves into human nature as it interacts with PR, considerations as important as the rules themselves.

➤ **Cultural Competence and Three Dimensional World Challenges**

These materials recognize and discuss the multiracial and multicultural aspects of practice. The client base that lawyers must serve is changing, and lawyers must adapt and change with it in order to fulfill their professional responsibilities. Thus, our book deals with cross cultural issues in client interviewing, negotiations, and trial arguments. These materials are interspersed throughout the book.

➤ **Your Life, Your Career**

We hope that each of you will look back on your professional careers and say, "what a wonderful way to have spent my life." We discuss candidly the pressures of practice and provide suggestions on dealing effectively with them. But know this: while we owe duties to our clients, and we owe duties to the legal system, we also owe duties to ourselves, our consciences, and our spirits.

We aspire to impart with a comprehensive and integrated view of PR, not a mere siloed understanding. When the semester is completed, you will possess unified understanding of how the concepts, the rules, and the caselaw interact and interlock with one another. Law is not a linear study; rather, it is a vibrant ecosystem. The rules create an ethical ecosystem and PR invites you to practice using the judgment and discretion that are the hallmarks of an effective lawyer— to learn how to start thinking like lawyers.

We are profoundly grateful that your professor adopted our book. Please reach out to us with any considered critiques, questions, or thoughts. We are looking forward to accompanying you on your professional journey which starts now.

MICHAEL P. MASLANKA
Dallas, Texas

MICHAEL KAGAN
Las Vegas, Nevada

NANCY ANN DAO
Santa Ana, California

PART I

The Lawyer and Forming the Attorney-Client Relationship

CHAPTER 1

Formation of the Relationship

Coming Attractions

Why do we start a professional responsibility casebook with the formation of the attorney-client relationship (ACR)? There are other worthwhile candidates as entry points—the self-regulation of the legal profession, admission as a member of the bar, and the duty to maintain client confidences—are all, by way of example, important topics and worthwhile candidates for the first substantive chapter. But we elected to start where all ethical issues begin in practice: When a potential client walks in the door. A lawyer's ethical obligations depend on what happens at that point.

If an ACR is created, then *all* ethical obligations are triggered under the Rules and common law. The chart below shows one flowchart path to when some obligations are triggered but no ACR is formed; namely, when there is a consultation between a member of the public and a lawyer about a legal matter, but the person only remains a "prospective client." In that situation, the lawyer assumes only limited, albeit important, ethical obligations involving the confidentiality of information and the maintenance of the attorney-client privilege.

What circumstances, then, trigger the formation of an ACR, a graduation from prospective status to actual client status? The most typical is an explicit agreement between the lawyer and a person or an entity. While this explicit agreement is often reduced to writing, it need not be (except for when a contingency fee is the means of lawyer payment). Nor does there even need to be an exchange of something of value for lawyer services in order to form an ACR.

A second way to create an ACR is through a lawyer's conduct; in other words, an implicit agreement. Think back to 1L contracts. If a party "reasonably" concludes that an agreement is formed because of the conduct (manifestations in contract law lingo) of another, then a contract is, in fact, formed. We will see this in the *Togstad* case. A lawyer's manifestation in this regard can include giving apparent authority to form an ACR to an administrative assistant or a paralegal. These concepts are not embodied in the Rules but rather in the *Restatement of the Law Third*, The Law Governing Lawyers, Section 14.

Finally, the third way of ACR formation is a court mandated order that a lawyer represent a litigant. Constitutional Law principles sometimes accord criminal defendants a right to legal representation. In this regard, courts also possess both statutory powers as well an inherent authority to require a lawyer to form an ACR.

There are also special variations of the formation of an ACR. For example: A policyholder of an insurance contract is sued. If there is coverage, his insurance company appoints a lawyer to represent the insured and pays the legal fees of the appointed lawyer. Is the client the insurance company or the insured? This is the third-party payor scenario and raises a question we will see repeatedly: who is the client? This is not the only situation in which the basic question of client identity is raised. Another example is when officers of a corporation or public institution confronts a legal problem. Who does the corporation's lawyer in that setting actually serve? Is it the officer—whom the lawyer deals with daily and whose conduct might be the subject of the suit—or is it the company or entity as an institution? What if the lawyer ends up talking to employees who have significant legal issues that may implicate the company? Can the lawyer represent a flesh and blood person, and also the entity? Finally, what about a client with diminished capacity, often because of advanced age or perhaps because of minority status? Who is the client? The individual of diminished capacity? The family? Those with power of attorney? Who calls the shots in this scenario?

Section 1.   The Formation (or Not) of the Attorney-Client Relationship

We start where you will start as a lawyer: Meeting with a potential client. If so, one of two events will result: you will form an (ACR), or you won't. If the first, then all of the Rules will apply to your conduct. If the second, you will still owe a duty of confidentiality to the prospective client; that is, you may not reveal or use what the prospective client told you in discussions about forming the ACR. Also, you must protect the attorney-client privilege which prevents disclosure of your dealings from the prying eyes of third parties such as other lawyers or the government. No one would consult with a lawyer to discuss potential representation if they thought the lawyer would not preserve their confidences.

Finally, we will introduce you here to the concept of a conflict of interest. What if the lawyer learns information from the prospective client, decides not to represent the person or entity, and is later asked to bring a claim against the prospective client or to engage in negotiations adverse to the prospective client? Has the receipt of confidential information by the now prospective client disqualify the lawyer from taking on the representation? Can this possibility be planned for? We will tackle these questions shortly. For now, work through the following chart, so you can get a sound footing on the ACR formation.

Let's Chart It!

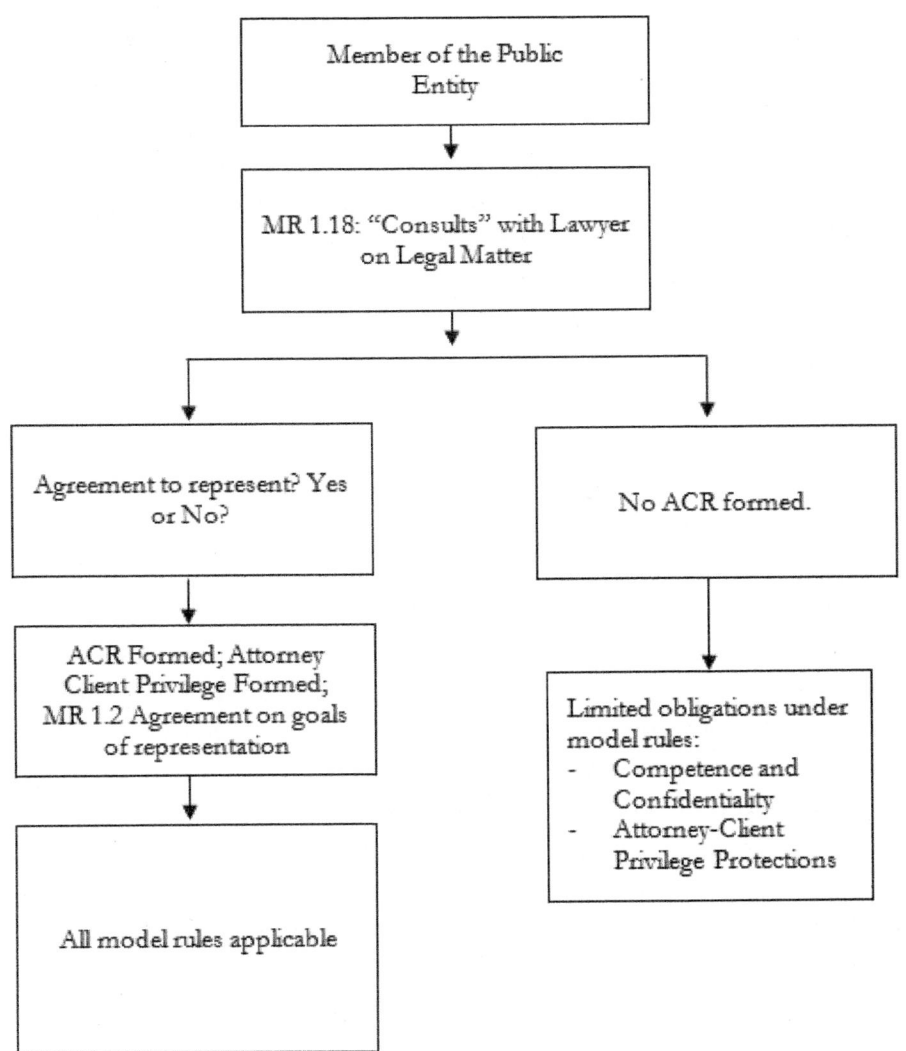

We will expand on the substance of the chart shortly. But before we do, let's explore an issue that is often inextricably intertwined with ACR formation—namely, agreement between the lawyer and the client on the professional services to be rendered. A task that requires clarity on the part lawyer's part as the following hypothetical illuminates.

Section 2.   Setting Goals with New Clients

When a new client walks into a lawyer's office, it is easy to miss something obvious. Typically, when we think about the formation of an ACR, we think about things like confidentiality. For a prospective client to tell a lawyer about her problem, she has to reveal confidences, which the lawyer has to protect much like the information she learns about her existing conflicts. We also have to think about screening for conflicts of interest, as we will learn later. There is an entire rule focusing on these concerns, explicitly for prospective clients.

When a new client walks in the door, a lawyer will think about whether she wants to offer to represent this client, and what her fee should be. The client might ask whether she wants this person as her lawyer. And if they agree, the lawyer might issue an engagement letter, as we will discuss later in this Chapter.

Who sets the goals? A first, easily forgotten step in establishing an Attorney-Client Relationship is to clearly define the client's objectives. If we focus just on confidentiality, conflicts of interest, and the mechanics of formalizing an ACR, we are still leaving out something very obvious, and yet something very easy to neglect: Why does this person want a lawyer to begin with? What is the problem she is trying to solve, or the goal she is trying to achieve?

One of the most important rules of legal ethics is that the client, not the lawyer, sets the objectives of a representation. Rule 1.2(a) says "a lawyer shall abide by a client's decisions concerning the objectives of representation." When we study attorney-client communication, we will learn that there is an important distinction between objectives and means. Clients do not control, say, what strategy to use in questioning a witness in a deposition. Lawyers should consult and communicate with their clients about such tactical choices, but the client does not get to dictate them. But clients do get to decide the ultimate objectives. So, while a client doesn't get to decide who to depose first in a lawsuit, a client does get to decide why am I in this lawsuit to begin with, and what kind of outcome do I want to pursue from it?

Many ethical problems in legal practice, including many malpractice cases, have their roots in a failure by the lawyer to make sure there is a clear understanding of the client's objectives. There are many reasons why this might happen. But an important one is structural, built into the practice of law for many lawyers.

Law practices are built around specific areas of legal practice. So, a law firm might specialize in real estate transactions, or family law, or criminal defense. This makes sense for lawyers, because the law is so vast. To be competent at what they do, lawyers need to be able to specialize in certain areas of practice that they can master, because no lawyer is an expert on everything. Sometimes this kind of narrow focus is actually imposed by law on a legal practice. For example, many public defender offices are established by local or state law which only allows them to represent people on criminal matters.

The trouble, though, is that life is complicated. Clients' problems don't always fit neatly into a single area of expertise. Consider a lawyer who helps a small restaurant owned by a married couple. A lawyer who does this work might be an expert on small business organization and may acquire a great deal of knowledge about tax, employment law, maybe even real estate. Already, that is quite a lot for a single lawyer to master. But imagine that the married couple begin to fight. Their relationship sours, and divorce looms. That divorce might pose a huge threat to the business, but the lawyer may also know little about divorce law.

The business of law matters here, too. Much like any business, law firms acquire knowledge about how they can deliver a particular product at a profit. They learn from experience about the kind of resources required for particular types of cases, and the kind of fee structure that can make such service affordable for clients and still profitable for an attorney. Lawyers in a specialized field typically know that one type of approach to a legal problem will generate far more work over a long period of time than another approach. And so, they may want to organize their legal practice around one type of case, but not another.

For example: When Immigration and Customs Enforcement arrests and detains a person in order to deport them, she can hire a lawyer to defend herself. Yet a lawyer has a choice about what kind of representation to offer. A lawyer in this situation can defend the person against deportation. Or the lawyer can represent the person only in seeking bond to get out of detention, or both. If the lawyer is only representing the person in the bond case, then the person might actually be unrepresented on the question of whether she should ultimately be allowed to stay in the country. The bond case and the deportation case are likely to be handled by the same Immigration Judge in the same court, sometimes in a hearing held on the same day. If this is confusing, that is in a sense the point. Clients in this situation often express confusion about why the lawyer they thought they hired showed up for one hearing, but not for the other. But for the lawyer, it probably makes a great deal of sense, and a great deal of difference for her legal practice. Bond cases can usually be resolved in a few weeks. But fighting a deportation case might take years.

The potential for misunderstanding between lawyers and clients is vast. It can often be corrected through clear communication. But in the real world of legal practice, that does not always happen. As you begin to build your legal careers, think about the steps that you can take to avoid this pitfall. Consider this as you think about the following scenario.

LEANING INTO PRACTICE

The following story is fictional but is based on a real malpractice case. As you read it, you will probably notice that there are probably several ethical problems with the lawyer's conduct. But focus on where they started. Think about whether the lawyer came to an understanding with the client about the objective of the representation at the beginning of the relationship.

Julie and Her Old Boss

In 2008, Julie Taylor was 55 years old. She had worked most of her career in medical billing, for a variety of doctor's offices. By this point in her career, she was very happy to be working for Dr. Robert Talen, a dermatologist. She started working for him in 2005.

Dr. Talen was generally beloved by his staff. One reason for this was money. Dr. Talen had an informal practice of giving his staff "loans" when they had financial needs. Sometimes it was to help buy a house. Sometimes it was to pay emergency bills. Dr. Talen would have the employee sign a loan agreement imposing repayment terms. But in every previous case that anyone could remember, he would not actually collect. When Julie came to work for him, other staff told her about this practice. They told her it was a kind of employment perk, that it was part of what made Dr. Talen wonderful.

But in 2008, the financial crisis struck. Julie's husband lost his job, which hurt their finances. Julie went to Dr. Talen to ask for a loan. Sure enough, he gave her $30,000, and had her sign a loan agreement. And, sure enough, when

---

the first payment came due, she did not pay, and Dr. Talen did not do anything about it.

But then, as the financial crisis rolled on, Dr. Talen's medical practice began to suffer, too. In 2009, he had to lay off staff, including Julie. And not only that: He started demanding that Julie repay the loan.

Julie was in a panic. With her savings, she and her husband could pay their household bills, but not the $30,000 debt. And she was angry. She felt that Dr. Talen was treating her differently than all of his other employees.

One of Julie's friends told her that she needed to go see a lawyer and recommend someone: Bill Wendall. "I know someone who went to him with a debt problem like yours, and he solved it. I think," her friend said. Julie went to Bill Wendall's office. The sign on the office said, "Wendall and Partners, Attorneys. Bankruptcy Lawyers."

Julie explained her problem to Bill. He was warm and understanding. She felt a lot of shame about her financial troubles, and Bill told her that many people were going through the same thing. He also told her, "This problem can be solved. Trust me." He told her that he charged $1,000, "for a case like yours." She wrote him a check. He gave her a thick pack of papers, asking for lots of financial information from her and her husband. He told her to fill it out and to come back for a second appointment.

When Julie got home, she looked at the packet. It was a bankruptcy application. She became confused. She hadn't thought of bankruptcy as an option. She didn't know much about what that might mean, but it scared her. She wasn't sure. But Bill Wendall seemed to know what he was doing, and her friend had recommended him. She planned to ask him more about bankruptcy at the next appointment, but she didn't fill out the packet yet.

Before Julie saw Bill Wendall again, she was served with a Complaint. Dr. Talen was suing her to collect on her debt to him. Julie was even more scared than before. The Complaint had a deadline on it, too. She had to respond to the court, and she didn't know how. It seemed that her problems were only getting worse.

Julie brought the Complaint to her next appointment with Bill Wendall. He again calmed her down. "I'm not surprised they're trying this," he said. "We can help you respond to it." He said they would file an Answer to the Complaint in court, and that would start a lawsuit that would go on for a long time. "Meanwhile, we really need that packet filled out. Can you fill that out, and call us when it's done?"

Julie left, feeling relieved. Bill Wendall filed an Answer to the lawsuit by Dr. Talen, and the lawsuit proceeded. Julie still wasn't sure she wanted to file for bankruptcy, and so she waited to hear news about her lawsuit. But over the following months, she didn't hear anything. She sent Bill Wendall an email but got an out of office message. She called, and his secretary said he was on vacation.

Finally, Julie's friend told her that she could look her own case up on the court's website. When she did that, she was shocked. She saw, from just a week earlier, that a "default judgment" had been entered against her. Apparently, there had been a hearing, and Bill Wendall had not shown up.

Angry, Julie called Bill on the phone. He took her call, and it was the last time they spoke. "Ma'am, I think you misunderstood," he said. "I am very sorry for your situation. But I offered to help you with your bankruptcy case, but you never came back to me with the information. I even filed the Answer as a favor to you, to help you. I can't defend a lawsuit like this for just $1,000. You would have had that default judgment much earlier if I hadn't done that favor. But I can't help you if you don't help me."

SOLUTIONS: THE LAWYER SHOULD HAVE, WOULD HAVE, COULD HAVE. . .

Clearly, many things went wrong in Julie's case. But as you think about where the problems with her lawyer started, think about how the lawyer understood the client's objectives, and how Julie herself understood her own problem. Most important, think about what you might have done differently if you were the lawyer.

Think for a moment about Bill Wendall's statement at the end, that, "I can't defend a lawsuit for just $1,000." That's not unreasonable, in a certain way. Litigation is extremely expensive. But how does that interact with the rule that the client controls the objectives of the representation? Does a client get to impose on a lawyer to pursue something that the lawyer doesn't want to pursue? Of course not.

Although client's set the objectives, lawyers can and should advise clients about objectives. Lawyers can, and should, tell clients what might be realistic and unrealistic. Lawyers can, and should, also tell clients what the difficulty level might be for pursuing different objectives. Perhaps Objective A is achievable but would likely require years of litigation and much higher legal fees. Perhaps Objective B isn't as good but could be achieved quickly and at lower cost. It is important to have this discussion at the outset of an Attorney-Client Relationship, and usually to then memorialize the client's choice in the engagement letter. Also remember, in most situations, if the client wants to pursue a goal that an attorney thinks is unachievable, the attorney could just decline representation, or insist on a higher up-front fee.

Section 3. Screening Potential Client and L.A.S. (Lawyer Avoidance Syndrome)

X-Ray Questions

Even when the goals of the client are fully understood by the lawyer, trouble lurks if the lawyer should never have taken on the client in the first place. As you read this excerpt from a book by lawyer Walt Bachman ask yourself honestly whether you could foresee the issues he describes arising in your practice. Ask yourself about the last time you did not trust your intuition ("gut feeling") and a decision went away. Are there tells (in poker a "tell" is when a player unconsciously reveals what they are thinking through physical mannerisms or verbal phrasing) you can think of a potential client showing?

Why do lawyers—especially new lawyers—take on what turn out to be problem clients? They are flattered that a person wants to retain them; or they worry that if they don't take this gig then another one may not come along, or they think they need fees generated. (By the way, these are natural feelings to have, as your authors can attest.) And lawyers sometimes take on such representation even though their better instincts warn them not to. so. Bachman explains, in forming a troubled ACR, one taken for poor reasons or despite one's better judgment, can lead to trouble. (As professional salespersons remark, "the best sale you make is often the one you did not make.") Consider MR 1.4: Communication, "A lawyer shall:

(2) reasonably consult with the client about the means by which the client's objectives are to be accomplished;

(3) keep the client reasonably informed about the status of the matter;

(4) promptly comply with reasonable requests for information; and

(5) consult with the client about any relevant limitation on the lawyer's conduct when the lawyer knows that the client expects assistance not permitted by the Rules of Professional Conduct or other law."

Simply put, you can end up violating MR 1.4 because you do not want to deal with the client as a person or deal with the client's legal issue or both. Consider tasks in your life you should not have taken on but, against your better judgment, did. What was the result? Most likely, you put off doing the task of dealing with the person, didn't you? In a word: procrastination. This all too human trait arises in the legal profession as well, and you will experience it (as we all have or will) in what Bachman calls "Lawyers' Avoidance Syndrome" or L.A.S.

BEYOND THE CITE

By: Walt Bachman, Law v. Life: What Lawyers Are Afraid to Say about The Legal Profession 26–29 (1995).

It also became apparent to me during my ethics enforcement (Bachman, at one point in his career, worked as a Grievance Prosecutor for the State Bar of Minnesota) years that those who are tormented by what might be termed the Lawyers' Avoidance Syndrome are less likely to be deterred by threat of discipline or cured by psychological counseling, particularly in extreme cases, than almost any other type of conduct. Lawyers' Avoidance Syndrome— LAS—is a most resistant strain of affliction.

I recall one otherwise good lawyer who was placed on formal probation following a number of client complaints, the only principal condition being that he returned telephone calls from clients inquiring about their cases within 48 hours. He was later disbarred when a single client produced records showing more than twenty successive unanswered long-distance calls over several months. Under order of the state Supreme Court to return telephone calls, he still lacked the ability to do so even upon painful disbarment. I found that lawyers who had both chronic neglect and drinking problems could more readily stop drinking through treatment than cease harmful procrastination. While neurotic procrastinators are present in all fields of work, lawyers with LAS are in a position to do extreme damage to themselves and others. I would venture to guess that this problem is at the core of many cases of what is diagnosed as depression or anxiety.

From the episode I suffered myself and as often pained observer of the misery caused by this syndrome, I have noted that LAS progresses in severity through four distinct stages of behavior.

LAS Stage One: Phobic Delay. The LAS pattern always beings with the equivalent of putting the client's file in the back of the cabinet. The key to distinguishing LAS behavior from the prudent prioritizing of any busy lawyer's workload is the linkage of the delay with something specific the lawyer wishes to avoid, rather than with the overall crush of time pressures. It is the difference between setting aside a filed because it requires several hours of uninterrupted time to conduct legal research or review documents, for example, and setting aside the file because you dislike the very idea of talking with Dan Doberman again or because you regret having accepted a case in an unfamiliar area. The former is ordinarily delay and the latter is Stage One LAS.

LAS Stage Two: [Truths.] Sooner or later, the delaying lawyer will be contacted by someone about the case, most commonly the client, who will call to ask some version of "How's my case coming along?" One of the telltale symptoms of LAS is the immediate knotting of the lawyer's stomach that accompanies this call, an indicator that personal guilt, and not mere unpleasantness at facing a disgruntled client, is rearing up. The response is often a white lie citing something the lawyer needs to do but hasn't yet done: "I've been working in the law library on a thorny legal issue in your case" or "I've sent document demands to the lawyer for the other side" or "It's in the mail." For many lawyers, reaching this stage is sufficient to overcome the block that led to inaction, and they feel compelled to go to the law library, draft the document demand, or put "it" in the mail in order to make their statements "true."

LAS Stage Three: [Falsehoods.] The foundation for this stage is normally the failure to follow through on pervious white lie promises. Two characteristics separate this stage from Stage Two. First, the lawyer typically starts to place false blame on others. ("Doggone, that blasted lawyer hasn't gotten back to me let on those document requests" or "I can't understand why they haven't responded to my letter" or "It must have been lost in the mails.") Second, by now there is likely to be written documentation of the lawyer's avoidance conduct, such as client letters innocently regurgitating earlier false assertions by the lawyer.

By the time Stage Three LAS has been reached, it is impossible to exaggerate the lawyer's daily emotional suffering. One otherwise completely decent and likable small-town lawyer, who was disbarred solely for chronic Stage Three-type conduct, told me: "You will never know what it's like to be me, to get up in the morning and be ashamed to look at myself in the mirror while shaving." For some, disbarment itself afforded real emotional relief from the hellish pain of responsibility for harmful, of unintended, conduct they were literally unable to control.

LAS Stage Four: Invented Lawsuits. As bizarre as it may seem, the crazy culmination of extreme LAS is the lawyer's creation of wholly fictitious lawsuits, stages of lawsuits, or even settlements. It is as though the false world the lawyer has created in Stages One through Three has become reality.

While highly unusual, there have been cases in which a divorce lawyer informed a client his or her divorce was final when, in actuality, the lawyer's LAS had led the case to languish in limbo, thereby creating unwitting bigamists. Other lawyers have paid a fictious "settlement" out of their own funds (or funds diverted from partner accounts or other clients' trust accounts), rather than disclose chronic inaction. Such lawyers are not only disbarred, but often prosecuted as felons and bankrupted by subsequent lawsuits. While these cases form an infinitesimal fraction of the practicing bar, they depict the tragically self-destructive extremes of LAS, where in most cases there is no underlying nefarious intent on the part of the lawyer. [. . . .]

Section 4. Duties Owed to Prospective Clients

Not all persons who consult you for legal services will become clients. If these persons/entities and the lawyer do not form an ACR, they remain as prospective clients. As you saw on the chart there are duties still owed by the lawyer, even to a prospective client. These duties include maintaining confidences disclosed in discussion involving potential representation. But there is more. We asked previously what happens if a lawyer consults with a person, no ACR is formed, but subsequently a different person consults with the same lawyer about representing the person in the matter in which the prospective client sought representation. Would that second representation be allowed? Here is how we determine the answer: ask whether the information learned from the prospective client would give an unfair advantage to the new potential client.

We will first look at maintaining the confidences of a prospective client, and then turn to the conflict issue which could lead to the lawyer being disqualified from representing the new client.

A. Prospective Client and Protecting Confidences

This duty is imposed upon a lawyer because a potential client would not even seek out legal assistance if the person/entity thought that what was disclosed could be revealed or used by the lawyer. Thus, MR 1.18. which is set out in the following opinion, requires that a lawyer maintain confidences of a prospective client even though no ACR was formed. (Also, the attorney-client privilege applies to the consultation with the prospective client as well.)

Model Rule 1.18(a)(b): Duties to Prospective Client

(a)   A person who consults with a lawyer about the possibility of forming a client-lawyer relationship with respect to a matter is a prospective client.

(b)   Even when no client-lawyer relationship ensues, a lawyer who has learned information from a prospective client shall not use or reveal that information, except as Rule 1.9 would permit with respect to information of a former client.

Deconstruction Exercise/Rule Rationale

Note that the operative verb in the first line is "consults." Why? Action verbs are often used in the rules in order to encompass the broadest range of scenarios. Other candidates could have been "met with" or "discuss" but they would constrict coverage, not expand it. After all, would contact via a lawyer's website be included within the scope of these words? Arguably not. Note too, the strategic use of a small word with a large impact—"or." The rule prohibits not only revealing confidential information to others but from using the information for any reason whatsoever. The rule is designed therefore to encourage a person to fully and completely explain all aspects of a potential legal issue. Why? So that the lawyer can decide whether to take on the representation and also for the prospective client to know that the lawyer will hold those confidences dear.

Cases and Materials

X-Ray Questions (*Cicero*)

The following case is based on a sports scandal involving a college football team. A person was accused of unlawfully selling sports memorabilia; the team involved was the Ohio State University and their coach, Jim Tressel. The person accused went to see a local lawyer about legal representation after the FBI raided his home and seized various memorabilia items. The lawyer, apparently for purposes of self-aggrandizement, emailed Tressel to tell him what the authorities had done based on his interview of the prospective client. The lawyer also told Tressel that the person was in serious jeopardy. The Ohio State Supreme Court considered that MR 1.18 was violated. It concluded that a one-year suspension from the practice of law was warranted.

What was the Court's reasoning for finding a violation of MR 1.18? Note that the lawyer told the coach to keep "confidential "the information in the emails he sent. And it appears that the coach did so. The lawyer took precautions to ensure that the information did not spread beyond Tressel. So, why a one-year suspension—that is, he cannot practice law and make a living for a full year. Do you consider this an overly harsh punishment? After all, no one was harmed by the sharing of the information. Should a "no harm, no foul" rule be in place?

Finally, this case introduces you to two new concepts. First is MR 8.4(c) which is part of a general, catch all rule prohibiting certain forms of misconduct (namely, dishonesty, fraud, deceit, or misrepresentation). Why do the Rules contain such a provision? Isn't it redundant of the other, more specific rules. We will encounter MR 8.4(c) again. Second, you will see how a court reasons out the discipline to be imposed. Discipline, unlike with malpractice claims, is designed to deter future rule violations and to rehabilitate the lawyer. (By contrast, a malpractice claim is designed to make a damaged plaintiff whole for the lawyer's negligence or breach of fiduciary duty to the client). So, what was your answer on whether the discipline was fair in this case? Does your opinion change by knowing that in 2019, the lawyer was permanently disbarred—effectively capital punishment for a legal career. *Disciplinary Counsel v. Dougherty and Cicero*, 157 Ohio St. 3d 486 (Ohio 2019). Was his disbarment inevitable or is that 20/20 hindsight?

Disciplinary Counsel v. Cicero

Supreme Court of Ohio, 2012.
134 Ohio St.3d 311.

LANZINGER, J.

Respondent, Christopher T. Cicero of Columbus, Ohio, Attorney Registration No. 0039882, was admitted to the practice of law in Ohio in 1988. On June 13, 2011, relator, disciplinary counsel, filed a complaint with the Board of Commissioners on Grievances and Discipline. The complaint charged Cicero with professional misconduct based on his communicating information that he had received from a prospective client to a third party. Relator alleged that Cicero's conduct violated Prof. Cond. R. 1.18 (prohibiting a lawyer from using or revealing information learned during discussions with a prospective client) and 8.4(h) (prohibiting a lawyer from engaging in conduct that adversely reflects on the lawyer's fitness to practice law).

A panel of the Board of Commissioners on Grievances and Discipline heard testimony, reviewed the evidence, and made findings of fact and conclusions of law. The panel concluded that Cicero had violated Prof. Cond. R. 1.18 and 8.4(h) and recommended that this court suspend his license to practice law in Ohio for six months. The board adopted the panel's findings and recommended sanction, and further recommended that the costs of the proceedings be taxed to Cicero.

Cicero filed objections to the board's report. For the reasons that follow, we overrule those objections, accept the board's findings of fact and misconduct, and suspend Cicero from the practice of law in Ohio for one year.

Misconduct

Factual Background

On April 1, 2010, federal law enforcement officials raided Edward Rife's house and seized $15,000 to $20,000 worth of Ohio State University football memorabilia as part of a drug-trafficking investigation. Rife testified that on April 2, the day after the raid, he and Joseph Epling, a former partner in Rife's tattoo business, met with Cicero to discuss his criminal case. Cicero and Epling testified before the panel and denied that an April 2 meeting occurred, but both testified that Cicero and Epling had a phone conversation on April 1 during which they discussed the raid on Rife's home.

On the afternoon of April 2, Cicero sent an e-mail to Jim Tressel, who was then the head coach of the Ohio State University football team. In the e-mail, Cicero alerted Tressel to a possible association between Rife and team members and provided general information about Rife's background and the raid on Rife's home.

Rife retained Stephen Palmer to represent him in the criminal case, and Palmer discussed a possible plea deal and ten-year prison sentence with Rife. Rife testified that he became unsatisfied with Palmer and scheduled another meeting with Cicero to discuss his case. This meeting took place on April 15.

Although Cicero denies giving any legal advice, the panel found that Cicero did express legal opinions during this meeting. First, the panel found that Cicero assured Epling, who was also present at the meeting, that he did not need to hire a lawyer. The panel believes Cicero gave this advice to clear away any potential conflict so he could represent Rife. Second, Cicero admitted that he advised Rife that he could not get the Ohio State memorabilia back if the federal government believed that Rife had purchased it using drug money. This was advice that the panel considered to be of a legal nature and within the particular expertise of a criminal-law attorney. Third, Cicero testified that he told Rife that a person in Rife's situation faces two choices: "You either can sit in the county jail for a long period of time, or you can start cooperating with the federal government and become a snitch." Rife testified that although he never specifically asked for the information, he gave at the April 15 meeting to be kept confidential, he assumed that it would be. He never gave Cicero permission to reveal to Tressel any information discussed. The panel found that Cicero should have treated the information from Rife as confidential, but instead, he planned to forward the information he learned to Tressel, and he did not disclose to Rife this intent.

On the morning of April 16, Cicero sent a second e-mail to Tressel. As the e-mail reveals, Cicero revealed specifics of Rife's case that he had learned the previous day:

- I had Eddie Rife in my office for an hour and a half last night.

- What I tell you is confidential.

- He told me [a former player] gave him some type of MVP trophy—but I don't [sic] know the year.

- He told me he has about 15 pairs of cleats (with signatures), 4–5 jerseys—all signed by players, the 2009 Wisconsin game ball (whoever that was awarded to).

- He told me he has about 9 rings Big Ten Championship.

- He will not talk publicly about this.

- If he retains me, and he may, I will try to get these items back that the government now wants to keep for themselves.

- Just passing this info on . . . especially now that I actually talked to Mr. Rife.

(Emphases added.) Later that day, Cicero sent another e-mail to Tressel in which he disclosed further information about Rife:

He is in really big trouble. The federal government has told him that his best offer is to take 10 years in prison. *He wanted my opinion yesterday on his situation.*

- I have to sit tight and wait to see if he retains me, but at least he came in last night to do a face to face with me.

- One correction from my first email to you . . . he did confirm to me that he put out on the street the government took 70,000 from his house, but he made that up so other associates of his would think it; so they wouldn't [sic] do a home invasion on him and his family. But, he had that much cash just lying around.

- Take care. I will keep you posted as relevant information becomes available to me. *Just keep our emails confidential.* Thank you.

(Emphases added.) Cicero testified that he did not intend to tell Tressel that Rife might retain him and that he was not referring to Rife when he said, "If he retains me, and he may," but Cicero did admit that the e-mails are written in a way that the only person Cicero could be referring to is Rife.

Legal Analysis

Prof. Cond. R. 1.18 sets forth a lawyer's duties to a prospective client. It provides:

(a) A person who consults with a lawyer about the possibility of forming a client-lawyer relationship with respect to a matter is a prospective client.

(b) Even when no client-lawyer relationship ensues, a lawyer who has learned information from a prospective client shall not use or reveal that information, except as Rule 1.9 would permit with respect to information of a former client.

(c) A lawyer subject to paragraph (b) shall not represent a client with interests materially adverse to those of a prospective client in the same or a substantially related matter if the lawyer received information from the prospective client that could be significantly harmful to that person in the matter, except as provided in paragraph (d). If a lawyer is disqualified from representation under this paragraph, no lawyer in a firm with which that lawyer is associated may knowingly undertake or continue representation in such a matter, except as provided in paragraph (d).

(d) When the lawyer has received disqualifying information as defined in paragraph (c), representation is permissible if:

> (1) both the affected client and the prospective client have given informed consent, confirmed in writing, or:

> (2) the lawyer who received the information took reasonable measures to avoid exposure to more disqualifying information than was reasonably necessary to determine whether to represent the prospective client; and

>> (i) the disqualified lawyer is timely screened from any participation in the matter and is apportioned no part of the fee therefrom; and

>> (ii) written notice is promptly given to the prospective client.

We agree with the board that relator has proved by clear and convincing evidence that Rife was a prospective client of Cicero. As the panel found, the two discussed the possibility of a client-lawyer relationship; Cicero admitted this in his e-mails to Tressel, and Rife testified as to the discussion. Rife's testimony was corroborated by Palmer, who testified that Rife had told him soon after the meeting with Cicero that Cicero had quoted him a fee. Rife met with Cicero on April 15 to discuss his case, and Cicero offered legal advice in response to Rife's questions.

Cicero argues that Epling's presence during the April 15 meeting indicates that Epling, rather than Rife, was his client. We find this argument unpersuasive. While Prof. Cond. R. 2.3 does permit a lawyer to provide an evaluation of a matter affecting a client for the use of a third party, the record is clear that Epling was not a client of Cicero during the events in question. Epling testified that Cicero told him he did not need a lawyer for representation in relation to the raid on Rife's home. Epling stated, "I knew I didn't need a lawyer because I wasn't involved." Furthermore, Cicero's e-mails to Tressel clearly indicate that Cicero believed that Rife was a prospective client.

Because relator has established that Rife was a prospective client of Cicero, we must next consider whether Cicero improperly revealed information learned during his consultation with Rife. Prof. Cond. R. 1.18(b) states that information that an attorney receives from a prospective client should not be revealed, except as permitted under Prof. Cond. R. 1.9(c), which states:

A lawyer who has formerly represented a client in a matter shall not thereafter do either of the following:

(1) use information relating to the representation to the disadvantage of the former client except as these rules would permit or require with respect to a client or when the information has become generally known;

(2) reveal information relating to the representation except as these rules would permit or require with respect to a client.

In his objections to the board's report, Cicero argues that the information he communicated to Tressel was "generally known" and that the communication was therefore permitted by Prof. Cond. R. 1.9(c)(1). A close examination of the April 16 e-mails, however, reveals that Cicero disclosed not only generally known information—for example, that Rife's home had been raided by federal agents—but also a number of specific details about Rife's case that Cicero could only have learned during his consultation with Rife. This information does not fall into the "generally known" exception of Prof. Cond. R. 1.9(c). Cicero violated Prof. Cond. R. 1.18(b) when he disclosed to Tressel confidential information about Rife's case learned during the April 15 meeting.

We note that this is the first case in which we have had the occasion to determine whether an attorney violated Prof. Cond. R. 1.18 by revealing the confidences of a prospective client. We also recognize that the Official Comments to the rule indicate that the protection afforded by the rule is limited in scope:

Prospective clients, like clients, may disclose information to a lawyer, place documents or other property in the lawyer's custody, or rely on the lawyer's advice. A lawyer's discussions with a prospective client usually are limited in time and depth and leave both the prospective client and the lawyer free (and sometimes required) to proceed no further. Hence, prospective clients should receive some but not all of the protection afforded clients.

Not all persons who communicate information to a lawyer are entitled to protection under this rule. A person who communicates information unilaterally to a lawyer, without any reasonable expectation that the lawyer is willing to discuss the possibility of forming a client-lawyer relationship, is not a "prospective client" within the meaning of division (a).

While we recognize that some limitations on the rule's protection to prospective clients may be justified, those limitations do not come into play here. Indeed, this case goes to the very heart of confidentiality between a prospective client and an attorney. Before obtaining representation, clients must meet with attorneys, and attorneys often must obtain sensitive information before they can decide whether to represent a client. Prospective clients trust that their confidences will be protected when they engage in an initial consultation with an attorney. Cicero's almost immediate dissemination of the detailed information that Rife provided on April 15 directly violated that trust. This conduct violates Prof. Cond. R. 1.18, as well as Prof. Cond. R. 8.4(h), which prohibits a lawyer from engaging in conduct that adversely reflects on the lawyer's fitness to practice law.

Cicero argues that the evidence on the record does not clearly and convincingly prove the violations found by the board. He asserts that Rife was an unreliable witness and that the panel did not explain why it accepted Rife's testimony over his own. Cicero's argument is unavailing. "Unless the record weighs heavily against a hearing panel's findings, we defer to the panel's credibility determinations, inasmuch as the panel members saw and heard the witnesses firsthand." *Cuyahoga Cty. Bar Assn. v. Wise*, 108 Ohio St.3d 164, 2006-Ohio-550, 842 N.E.2d 35, ¶ 24, citing *Cincinnati Bar Assn. v. Statzer*, 101 Ohio St.3d 14, 2003-Ohio-6649, 800 N.E.2d 1117, ¶ 8. The panel did explain why it chose not to believe Cicero's testimony, stating, "Respondent's testimony at the hearing was at times disingenuous and not credible." Furthermore, Cicero's own testimony and the e-mails he sent to Tressel form a sufficient basis for a finding that he violated Prof. Cond. R. 1.18(b).

We therefore hold that relator has proved by clear and convincing evidence that Cicero violated Prof. Cond. R. 1.18 and 8.4(h).

Sanction

When imposing sanctions for attorney misconduct, we consider relevant factors, including the ethical duties that the lawyer violated, and the sanctions imposed in similar cases. *Stark Cty. Bar Assn. v. Buttacavoli*, 96 Ohio St.3d 424, 2002-Ohio-4743, 775 N.E.2d 818, ¶ 16. We also weigh evidence of the aggravating and mitigating factors listed in BCGD Proc.Reg. 10(B). *Disciplinary Counsel v. Broeren*, 115 Ohio St.3d 473, 2007-Ohio-5251, 875 N.E.2d 935, ¶ 21. Because each disciplinary case is unique, we are not limited to the factors specified in the rule but may take into account "all relevant factors" in determining what sanction to impose. BCGD Proc.Reg. 10(B).

The board found as a mitigating factor that Cicero has an excellent reputation among judges and attorneys for professional integrity and competence. But the board found five aggravating factors. First, Cicero has a prior disciplinary offense for which he was suspended from the practice of law in Ohio for one year. See *Disciplinary Counsel v. Cicero*, 78 Ohio St.3d 351, 678 N.E.2d 517 (1997). Second, the board concluded that Cicero acted with a selfish motive, because his reason for disclosing to Tressel his possible attorney-client relationship with Rife was self-aggrandizement. Third, the board stated that Cicero's "testimony at the hearing was at times disingenuous and not credible." Fourth, the board stated that Cicero refused to acknowledge the wrongful nature of his misconduct. Fifth, the board concluded that the disclosure of the information about the Ohio State memorabilia caused Rife and his family to be subjected to criticism and harassment by the news media and others for causing harm to the Ohio State football program.

Cicero argues that only his prior disciplinary record should qualify as an aggravating factor. Recognizing that the panel was in the best position to evaluate the demeanor and credibility of the witnesses, we accept its findings in regard to the additional four aggravating factors and consider them in our determination of the appropriate sanction.

As noted above, we have not yet addressed a case in which an attorney has violated Prof. Cond. R. 1.18. Cicero argues for a six-month stayed suspension, citing *Disciplinary Counsel v. Yurich*, 78 Ohio St.3d 315, 677 N.E.2d 1190 (1997); *Disciplinary Counsel v. Shaver*, 121 Ohio St.3d 393, 2009-Ohio-1385, 904 N.E.2d 883; *Geauga Cty. Bar Assn. v. Psenicka*, 62 Ohio St.3d 35, 577 N.E.2d 1074 (1991); and *Columbus Bar Assn. v. Boggs*, 39 Ohio St.3d 601, 529 N.E.2d 936 (1988). Relator correctly points out, however, that none of these cases involved any aggravating factors. And in the other case cited by Cicero, *Disciplinary Counsel v. Kimmins*, 123 Ohio St.3d 207, 2009-Ohio-4943, 915 N.E.2d 330, ¶ 18, in which the respondent received a one-year stayed suspension, we found fewer aggravating factors and more mitigating factors and explicitly noted that there was an absence of a dishonest or selfish motive.

Relator cites *Columbus Bar Assn. v. Dye*, 82 Ohio St.3d 64, 694 N.E.2d 440 (1998), in which we imposed a two-year suspension. Dye, however, involved more than disclosure of confidential client information. The violations in Dye included collecting an illegal or clearly excessive fee, accepting and continuing representation of a client when the attorney's independent professional judgment regarding another client would be adversely affected, and failing to return the remainder of a fee. Id. at 66–67. Clearly, the violations in Dye were more numerous than in the present case.

Because the facts of this case fall between those in the cases cited by Cicero and those cited by relator, we hold that a one-year suspension is proper. This sanction comports with the severity of Cicero's violations and takes into account both the mitigating and aggravating factors. Cicero is hereby suspended from the practice of law in Ohio for one year. Costs are taxed to Cicero.

Judgment accordingly.

SOLUTIONS: THE LAWYER SHOULD HAVE, WOULD HAVE, COULD HAVE. . .

Although Cicero was not retained to be Rife's attorney, he owed ethical obligations to Rife as a prospective client. These were to keep all information he learned from the communication as confidential. Doing so is a fundamental duty of a lawyer as we will explore in a later chapter discussing Model Rule 1.6. For now, understand this: the duty to keep secret what you are told by a prospective client is just as important as keeping secret what you are told by a client with whom you form an ACR. This rule applies whether unconsented disclosure is to one person or to one hundred. While there will be exception to keeping confidences, rest assured that currying favor with someone in power is not one of them.

B. The Prospective Client and Disqualification

The preceding case dealt with an outright violation of MR 1.18. The following case deals with a lawyer who is subject to disqualification from a lawsuit in the following timeline: Lawyer A meets with prospective client (ABC Company) and is asked to submit a proposal in order to represent it in a lawsuit (this process is a/k/a "a beauty contest") against XYZ Company. ABC Company selects a different lawyer, Lawyer Z; the rejected lawyer (A) then ends up representing XYZ Company in the lawsuit brought by ABC that A and ABC had discussed.

Model Rule 1.18(d)(2)(i)(ii): Duties to Prospective Clients

(d) When the lawyer has received disqualifying information as defined in paragraph (c), representation is permissible if:

(1) both the affected client and the prospective client have given informed consent, confirmed in writing, or:

(2)   the lawyer who received the information took reasonable measures to avoid exposure to more disqualifying information than was reasonably necessary to determine whether to represent the prospective client; and

> (i)   the disqualified lawyer is timely screened from any participation in the matter and is apportioned no part of the fee therefrom; and

> (ii)   written notice is promptly given to the prospective client.

Deconstruction Exercise/Rule Rationale

Here, the rule deals with the lawyer who, especially in a small town or mid-sized city with a somewhat limited potential client pool, might be unable to represent a person or entity because the lawyer met with a prospective client, no ACR was formed, and then the lawyer later retained by a new client involving the same matter and whose interests are thus likely adverse to those of the prospective client. MR 1.18 seeks to harmonize the needs of the prospective client who provided confidential information with the needs of the public to have its choice of lawyers. The Rule strikes a balance allowing representation if the lawyer took "reasonable measures" to make sure that the lawyer does not learn so much in the initial consultation that—should an ACR not be formed—the new client would not have an unfair advantage. Now, a different lawyer in the same firm can handle the matter provided that the contact lawyer is screened off from other lawyers regarding the confidential information learned in the consultation. The purpose of the rule? To ensure that the contacted lawyer does not infect the other firm lawyers with knowledge gained in the consultation. The case we selected to illuminate this rule sets out exactly what is a "reasonable measure."

Cases and Materials

X-Ray Questions (*SkyBell*)

This is a Silicon Valley case interpreting MR 1.18, which California adopted in 2018. It involves a dispute between two competitors over the increasingly lucrative video doorbell market; that is, a home or apartment's doorbell doubles as a video camera. A firm was asked by one of the major doorbell makers to make a pitch for business. The firm devoted substantial time and effort in doing so. It failed. While this firm was not elected, it ended up representing the company that the prospective client was planning on suing. The firm made an appearance in the lawsuit on behalf of the competitor. The prospective client who had rejected the firm as its counsel, not surprisingly moved to disqualify the firm. The trial court granted the motion. Why? What was the court's reasoning?

Pay special attention to the firm that was ultimately selected to represent the prospective client. Does anything about the selection suggest that perhaps the decision on whom to retain was already made by the prospective client despite the trappings of a beauty contest? Why would a prospective client do so? How could the law firm have protected itself from disqualification if it was not awarded the business? The firm gambled everything on winning the beauty contest. Like in the casino it put all its chips on one number and one color. It therefore lost not one time, but twice. The court expounds on these prophylactic measures in some detail; list them. Why didn't the firm take advantage of the measures to avoid disqualification? Consider the last paragraph of the opinion and the court's language. In a dispute between a lawyer and a prospective client, the court places the burden upon the lawyer to establish that denial of the motion to disqualify counsel is warranted. Why?

SkyBell Techs., Inc. v. Ring, Inc.

United States District Court for the Central District of California, 2018.
2018 U.S. Dist. LEXIS 217502.

I.   BACKGROUND

A.   SkyBell Conducts a "Beauty Contest"

SkyBell is in the business of manufacturing and selling smart video doorbells. (Declaration of Joseph F. Scalisi ("Scalisi Decl."), Docket No. 48-2 ¶ 2.) In mid-2017, SkyBell decided to research the possibility of enforcing its patent portfolio against its various competitors, including Ring. (*Id.* ¶ 4.)

In October 2017, SkyBell approached Travis Jensen ("Jensen"), a partner in Orrick's Silicon Valley office, about potentially representing it in such litigation. (*Id.* ¶ 5; Declaration of Travis Jensen ("Jensen Decl."), Docket No. 53-1 ¶ 2.) Jensen immediately requested that a conflicts check be run against the Orrick conflicts database, and he determined that no conflict existed in a potential representation of SkyBell in patent litigation. (Jensen Decl., Docket No. 53-1 ¶ 3.)

In his supplemental declaration supplemental submitted the day of the hearing, Jensen asserts that he told SkyBell's outside patent counsel to provide him no more information than necessary to conduct a conflicts search. (Jensen

Supp. Decl. ¶ 4.) In his supplemental declaration submitted the day of the hearing, Jensen asserts that he told SkyBell's outside patent counsel to provide him no more information than necessary to conduct a conflicts search. (Jensen Supp. Decl. ¶ 4.)

After advising SkyBell of the absence of conflicts, Jensen had an introductory call with Joseph Scalisi ("Scalisi"), SkyBell's Chief Executive Officer, Robert Mahan ("Mahan"), SkyBell's Chief Financial Officer, and two of SkyBell's outside patent attorneys on November 1, 2017. (*Id.* ¶ 4; Scalisi Decl., Docket No. 48-2 ¶ 6.) The call lasted approximately one hour, and the following five topics were discussed: (1) the key patents to be enforced against Ring; (2) the reasons SkyBell believed Ring to be infringing; (3) issues concerning validity and the prior art; (4) SkyBell's financial position; and (5) settlement strategy. (Scalisi Decl., Docket No. 48-2 ¶ 7.) Following the call, SkyBell sent Jensen various materials, including tear-downs of the Ring products SkyBell believed to be infringing. (*Id.* ¶ 8.)

Around the time of the initial November 1, 2017, call, SkyBell asked Jensen to prepare a written proposal for Orrick to represent SkyBell in an action to enforce SkyBell's patents against one or more possible defendants. (Jensen Decl., Docket No. 53-1 ¶ 5.) According to Jensen, he understood that Orrick was bidding against other firms in a competitive pitch process or "beauty contest," and that SkyBell would evaluate Orrick's proposal along with proposals from multiple other law firms in order to determine which firm to retain. (*Id.*) Jensen also understood that the fee arrangement would be a competitive aspect of the bidding process, and that Orrick would have to be creative in its fee proposal to win the pitch. (*Id.*) Jensen and an associate in Orrick's New York office, Tyler Miller ("Miller"), prepared a nearly 40-page proposal and enforcement strategy document (the "Written Proposal") to represent SkyBell. (*Id.* ¶¶ 6–7; Scalisi Decl., Docket No. 48-2, Ex. A.)

Included in the Written Proposal is a 12-page section regarding Orrick's strategic analysis and recommendations for SkyBell's patent enforcement campaign. (Scalisi Decl., Docket No. 48-2, Ex. A at 12–23.) Four of these pages specifically address Orrick's recommendations and proposed strategy for enforcement against Ring. (*Id.* at 16–19.) There are also separate sections detailing Orrick's understanding of SkyBell's strategic business objectives and current goals for its patent enforcement campaign, SkyBell's patent portfolio, the possible venue options, and the economics and players in the video doorbell market. (*Id.* at 5–10.) Additionally, three pages include Orrick's fee proposal and budget. (*Id.* at 31–33.) Finally, the remaining pages include general background information on Orrick's Intellectual Property Group, biographies of the proposed team, venue statistics, an executive summary, a table of contents, and heading pages separating the sections. (*Id.* at 1–4, 11, 24–30, 34–37.) The Written Proposal identifies three potential Orrick attorneys to work on the matter: Jensen, Miller, and Johannes Hsu in Orrick's Orange County office, and around November 13, 2017, Jensen also identified Chris Ottenweller in Orrick's Silicon Valley office as a possible team member. (Jensen Decl., Docket No. 53-1 ¶ 15.) Each page of the Written Proposal is labeled privileged and confidential. (Scalisi Decl., Docket No. 48-2, Ex. A.)

Jensen sent the Written Proposal to Scalisi on November 8, 2017, and the next day, he met with Scalisi, Mahan, and one or more of SkyBell's outside patent attorneys at SkyBell's office in Irvine, California. (*Id.* ¶ 17; Scalisi Decl., Docket No. 48-2 ¶¶ 9–10.) The meeting lasted approximately three hours, and during the meeting, Jensen explained Orrick's proposed strategy and budget, discussed the five topics identified above, and answered questions from SkyBell's representatives. (Scalisi Decl., Docket No. 48-2 ¶¶ 9, 11; Jensen Decl., Docket No. 53-1 ¶ 17.) Following the meeting, Jensen sent SkyBell a proposed written engagement letter, which SkyBell never signed. (Jensen Decl., Docket No. 53-1 ¶ 18.)

Ultimately, SkyBell decided not to retain Orrick and selected another law firm to represent it. (*Id.* ¶ 19.) However, SkyBell and Orrick continued to have discussions about Orrick potentially representing SkyBell in IPR challenges or acting as shadow counsel. (Scalisi Decl., Docket No. 48-2 ¶ 13.) On January 5, 2018, SkyBell filed the instant patent infringement action against Ring. (Compl., Docket No. 1.) SkyBell alleges that it is the sole owner of U.S. Patent Nos. 9,055,202; 9,179,109; 9,179,107; 9,743,049; and 9,160,987 (the "patents-in-suit"), and that various Ring products and services infringe the patents-in-suit. (First Amended Complaint ("FAC"), Docket No. 27 ¶¶ 4, 16–36.) After the case was filed, Jensen emailed Scalisi noting its filing, and as recently as March 2018, Jensen sent Scalisi emails related to the case, including patent cases that might be of relevance. (Scalisi Decl., Docket No. 48-2 ¶¶ 13–14.)

B. Clement Roberts Joins Orrick

Ring retained Clement Roberts ("Roberts") to represent it in the instant action on January 5, 2018. (Declaration of Clement S. Roberts ("Roberts Decl."), Docket No. 54-2 ¶ 1.) At that time, Roberts was a partner at Durie Tangri, LLP. (Id.) According to Ring's founder and Chief Executive Officer, Jamie Siminoff, Roberts was chosen because of his longstanding and close relationship with

Ring. (Declaration of Jamie Siminoff ("Siminoff Decl."), Docket No. 54-1 ¶¶ 1–4.) For the first five months after being retained, Roberts and his team spent more than 1,500 hours working on the matter. (Roberts Decl., Docket No. 54-2 ¶ 2.) This work included, among other things, drafting an answer and counterclaims, as well as conducting multiple settlement discussions with SkyBell's counsel. (*Id.* ¶ 2; Answer, Docket No. 33.)

On June 1, 2018, Roberts joined Orrick's San Francisco office. (Declaration of Larry Low ("Low Decl."), Docket No. 53-2 ¶ 15.) The next business day, Roberts notified SkyBell's counsel that he had joined Orrick. (Declaration of Marc C. Fenster ("Fenster Decl."), Docket No. 48-1, Ex. C at 16–17 (pagination per docket).) Roberts also notified SkyBell's counsel that Orrick had implemented an ethical screen prior to him joining the firm, and provided details of the screen. (*Id.* at 15.)

C. Orrick's Ethical Screen

On May 30, 2018, after Roberts informed Orrick of his decision to join the firm, but before he joined, Orrick implemented an ethical screen to ensure that any attorney or staff member who was involved in the pitch to SkyBell (the "SkyBell Screened Group") was screened from any attorney or staff member who would be working on the Ring litigation (the "Ring Litigation Group"). (Low Decl., Docket No. 53-2 ¶¶ 7–16.) The SkyBell Screened Group includes: two attorneys substantively involved in preparing the Written Proposal, one marketing director who helped assemble and format the Proposal, five management personnel who reviewed and approved the Proposal and alternative fee budget, and four attorneys who received the Proposal or had discussions with Jensen. (*Id.* ¶ 14.) The Ring Litigation Group includes Roberts and five other Orrick attorneys. (*Id.* ¶ 15.) At least two of the attorneys in the Ring Litigation Group worked at Orrick at the time of the pitch. (Mot., Docket No. 48 at 7.) The ethical screen implemented by Orrick consists of the following:

1. A prohibition on members of the SkyBell Screened Group from working on the Ring patent litigation;

2. A prohibition on members of the SkyBell Screened Group and the Ring Litigation Group communicating about either the pitch or the litigation, and a special caution to avoid such communication at firm events, meetings, or other gatherings;

3. A prohibition on members of each group possessing or reading materials from the other group relating to the pitch or the litigation;

4.   A plan for periodic reminders; and

5.   A requirement that any exception to the rules must be authorized by the Risk and Compliance counsel (no exceptions have been made to date and there are no planned exceptions), and a plan for updating the screened groups as necessary.

(Opp'n, Docket No. 53 at 7–8; Low Decl., Docket No. 53-2 ¶ 13; Fenster Decl., Docket No. 48-1, Ex. C at 15 (pagination per docket).) Additionally, Orrick gathered and quarantined all correspondence and documents related to the pitch from the SkyBell Screened Group and placed them in a restricted cabinet on Orrick's network, which can be viewed by only five attorneys at Orrick in the Risk and Compliance department and two attorneys working on the opposition brief to the instant motion. (Low Decl., Docket No. 53-2 ¶¶ 9–12; Opp'n, Docket No. 53 at 8.)

Immediately upon joining Orrick, Roberts was made part of the screen, as were the other five Orrick attorneys in the Ring Litigation Group immediately upon joining the case. (Low Decl., Docket No. 53-2 ¶ 15.) Each member of the Ring Litigation Group submitted a declaration stating that they were not involved in the pitch to SkyBell, that they have not received information from the SkyBell Screened Group, and that they do not work in the same office as Jensen. (Roberts Decl., Docket No. 54-2 ¶ 3; Declaration of Alyssa Cardis ("Cardis Decl."), Docket No. 54-3 ¶¶ 3–4; Declaration of Don Daybell ("Daybell Decl."), Docket No. 54-4 ¶¶ 3–4; Declaration of Michael C. Chow ("Chow Decl."), Docket No. 54-5 ¶¶ 3–4; Declaration of Joong Youn Cho ("Cho Decl."), Docket No. 54-6 ¶¶ 3–4; Declaration of Andrew J. Kim ("Kim Decl."), Docket No. 54-7 ¶¶ 3–4.) Additionally, none of the members of the SkyBell Screened Group are being apportioned any part of the fees from the Ring litigation matter. (Low Decl., Docket No. 53-2 ¶ 16.)

III. DISCUSSION

A.   The New California Rules of Professional Conduct

On March 30, 2017, the Board of Trustees of the State Bar of California filed a request for approval of comprehensive amendments to the California Rules of Professional Conduct with the California Supreme Court. On May 10, 2018, the Supreme Court issued Administrative Order 2018–05–09, S240991, approving 69 new and amended rules. The Board of Trustees adopted the new and amended rules after a comprehensive review process and public comment period. The new version of the Rules of Professional Conduct approved by the Supreme Court officially goes into effect on November 1, 2018.

The new version of the California Rules of Professional Conduct differs from the old version of the Rules in several major respects. Relevant to the present motion, the new version contains a rule with no corresponding prior counterpart, *Rule 1.18*, regarding duties to prospective clients. The old version of the Rules is silent with regards to duties owed to prospective clients, and instead contains *Rule 3–310*, which concerns avoiding the representation of adverse interests to both current and former clients.

SkyBell and Orrick dispute which version of the California Rules of Professional Conduct should apply. SkyBell argues that the new version of the Rules, specifically Rule 1.18, should not apply because the new Rules do not go into effect until November 1, 2018, and were not in effect at the time Orrick obtained SkyBell's confidential information or when the conflict of interest arose. (Mot., Docket No. 48 at 19; Reply, Docket No. 57 at 9.) In contrast, Orrick argues that it is simply an administrative matter for the State Bar that the new Rules do not officially go into effect until November 1, 2018, and that there is no existing contingency that will prevent their implementation. (Opp'n, Docket No. 53 at 11.) Orrick argues that the new Rules will inevitably go into effect fewer than sixty days from the date of the hearing on this motion. (Id.) Additionally, Orrick argues that there is no dispute about how the California Supreme Court feels about the ethical issue underlying the motion, regarding a firm undertaking a representation adverse to a former prospective client, because the Court told us in May when it approved the new version of the California Rules of Professional Conduct. (*Id.* at 11–12.)

As stated above, California law governs motions to disqualify. See *Rodriguez*, 563 F.3d at 967. Because the Court must apply California law in determining matters of disqualification, the Court "must follow the reasoned view of the [California] [S]upreme [C]ourt when it has spoken on the issue." *In re Cty. of L.A.*, 223 F.3d at 995. While there is no California case law discussing the newly approved *Rule 1.18*, the Court deems the Supreme Court's approval of the new Rule as the best indicator of the California Supreme Court's position on the ethical issue. Therefore, even though the new version of the Rules is not technically in effect, the California Supreme Court has made clear that the new Rules are the correct ethical standard and most in line with current judicial thinking on matters of attorney ethics. Accordingly, the Court analyzes the present motion under the new California Rules of Professional Conduct, which includes the new *Rule 1.18*.

B. Application of New *California Rule of Profession Conduct 1.18*

Rule 1.18 of the new California Rules of Professional Conduct sets forth the duties owed to a prospective client. The Rule provides:

(a) A person who, directly or through an authorized representative, consults a lawyer for the purpose of retaining the lawyer or securing legal service or advice from the lawyer in the lawyer's professional capacity, is a prospective client.

(b) Even when no lawyer-client relationship ensues, a lawyer who has communicated with a prospective client shall not use or reveal information protected by Business and Professions Code section 6068, subdivision (e) and rule 1.6 that the lawyer learned as a result of the consultation, except as rule 1.9 would permit with respect to information of a former client.

(c) A lawyer subject to paragraph (b) shall not represent a client with interests materially adverse to those of a prospective client in the same or a substantially related matter if the lawyer received from the prospective client information protected by Business and Professions Code section 6068, subdivision (e) and rule 1.6 that is material to the matter, except as provided in paragraph (d). If a lawyer is prohibited from representation under this paragraph, no lawyer in a firm with which that lawyer is associated may knowingly undertake or continue representation in such a matter, except as provided in paragraph (d).

(d) When the lawyer has received information that prohibits representation as provided in paragraph (c), representation of the affected client is permissible if:

(1) both the affected client and the prospective client have given informed written consent, or

(2) the lawyer who received the information took reasonable measures to avoid exposure to more information than was reasonably necessary to determine whether to represent the prospective client; and

(i) the prohibited lawyer is timely screened from any participation in the matter and is apportioned no part of the fee therefrom; and

(ii) written notice is promptly given to the prospective client to enable the prospective client to ascertain compliance with the provisions of this rule.

1. SkyBell is a Prospective Client

As an initial matter, SkyBell is a prospective client within the meaning of *Rule 1.18(a)*. SkyBell, through its authorized representatives Scalisi, Mahan, and the two outside patent attorneys, consulted Jensen as part of the beauty contest for the purpose of determining whether to retain Orrick to represent it in patent litigation. (Scalisi Decl., Docket No. 48-2 ¶¶ 6, 9; Jensen Decl., Docket No. 53-1 ¶¶ 4, 17.)

2. Orrick Received Confidential Information Material to the Matter

Orrick does not dispute that during the November 1, 2017 phone call, and November 9, 2018 meeting the following confidential information was disclosed and discussed: (1) the key patents to be enforced against Ring; (2) the reasons SkyBell believed Ring to be infringing; (3) issues concerning validity and the prior art; (4) SkyBell's financial position; and (5) settlement strategy. (Scalisi Decl., Docket No. 48-2 ¶¶ 7, 11; Opp'n, Docket No. 53 at 16.) Instead, Orrick argues that these were not "material" disclosures, and that most of the information is already public. (Opp'n, Docket No. 53 at 16.) Orrick argues that because SkyBell has already filed suit and served its infringement contentions, it has already disclosed the key patents to be enforced against Ring and the reasons SkyBell believes Ring to be infringing. (*Id.*) Orrick also argues that the prior art is public in nature and therefore not confidential. (*Id.*) Additionally, Orrick argues that SkyBell's financial position will be the subject of discovery in this case and likewise is not confidential under the circumstances. (*Id.*) Further, Orrick suggests that information regarding SkyBell's settlement strategy is not material because the parties have already engaged in settlement discussions, but assumes, for purposes of the motion, that SkyBell's settlement strategy is material. (*Id.* at 16–17.)

It is clear that Orrick received confidential information from SkyBell within the meaning of Cal. Bus. & Prof. Code § 6068(e)(1)7 and new California Rule of Professional Conduct 1.6, and Orrick concedes this fact in the opposition. (Opp'n, Docket No. 53 at 16–17.) While Orrick argues that most of this information is already public or will be discoverable in this case, Comment [5] to new *Rule 1.9*, regarding duties to former clients, makes clear that "[t]he fact that information can be discovered in a public record does not, by itself, render that information generally known[.]" Therefore, the fact that some of this information is publicly available in court filings does not change the fact that it was all information that Orrick acquired by virtue of its discussions with SkyBell regarding the potential representation. Nor does it matter that some of this information was already served as part of SkyBell's infringement contentions or may be discoverable because this does not strip it of its confidential nature at the time the information was divulged. Furthermore, Orrick's argument that this information is not material to the matter is inconsistent with its position, discussed below, that this same information was reasonably necessary for it to determine whether to represent SkyBell in this matter. Therefore, pursuant to new *Rule 1.18(c),* Orrick may not represent a client with interests materially adverse to SkyBell in the same matter, given that Orrick received confidential information from SkyBell that is material to the matter, unless it qualifies for one of the exceptions set forth in subsection (d).

3. Orrick Did Not Take Reasonable Measures to Avoid Exposure to More Information than Was Reasonably Necessary to Determine Whether to Represent SkyBell

The exception set forth in new *Rule 1.18(d)(2)* provides that when a lawyer has received material confidential information from a prospective client, representation of a client with interests materially adverse to the prospective client is not permissible unless "the lawyer who received the information took reasonable measures to avoid exposure to more information than was reasonably necessary to determine whether to represent the prospective client." Additionally, Comment [3] to *Rule 1.18* states that "[i]n order to avoid acquiring information from a prospective client that would prohibit representation as provided in paragraph (c), a lawyer considering whether or not to undertake a new matter must limit the initial interview to only such information as reasonably appears necessary for that purpose." SkyBell argues that Orrick took no measures to avoid exposure to more information than was reasonably necessary to determine whether to represent SkyBell. (Mot., Docket No. 48 at 20.) SkyBell argues that Orrick placed no limitations on the information that was to be shared whatsoever, and to the contrary, Orrick encouraged SkyBell to be as open as possible with information related to the potential lawsuit against Ring. (*Id.*; Scalisi Decl., Docket No. 48-2 ¶ 15 ("During our communication with Orrick, we were never informed that we should withhold any information concerning our planned lawsuit until it had decided to take the case. Indeed, we were encouraged to provide all of the information we had, and we complied where possible."). Additionally, SkyBell argues that the information provided to Orrick during the pitch process went far beyond what was reasonably necessary for it to determine whether to represent SkyBell. (Mot., Docket No. 48 at 19.) SkyBell argues that Orrick crossed this benchmark, at the earliest, when it informed SkyBell that it had cleared conflicts, and at latest, when it prepared the nearly 40-page Written Proposal aimed at gaining SkyBell's business. (*Id.*)

In response, Orrick argues that it was reasonable for Jensen to receive the information he did from SkyBell in the circumstances of the pitch process. (Opp'n, Docket No. 53 at 17.) Orrick argues that it was reasonable for Jensen to believe that SkyBell was advised by independent counsel as to the scope of disclosures it should be making as part of the pitch process. (*Id.*) Additionally, Orrick argues that it needed to develop a strong understanding of the facts and merits of the case to prepare a proposal and structure the fees. (*Id.*) Orrick argues that its Written Proposal included a proposed alternative fee arrangement, and in order to determine whether this arrangement would be feasible, Orrick required fairly extensive information from SkyBell. (*Id.*) Orrick argues that it is common for lawyers pitching patent cases to receive extensive disclosures. (*Id.* at 17–18.) Moreover, Orrick concedes that while it of course wanted the work, it first needed to evaluate the potential matter to make sure the fees made sense. (*Id.* at 18.) In support of its opposition, Orrick puts forth the expert declaration of Stephen S. Korniczky ("Korniczky Decl."). (Korniczky Decl., Docket No. 53-3.) Korniczky is an experienced patent attorney and trial lawyer and has participated in hundreds of pitches for patent litigation in his career. (*Id.* ¶¶ 2–7.) Korniczky opines that the level of interaction that occurred between Orrick and SkyBell during the pitch process was entirely typical for patent litigation. (*Id.* ¶ 21.) Additionally, Korniczky states that it is inconsistent with his experience that a law firm needs no more than the information needed for an initial conflict check to determine whether to accept an engagement. (*Id.* ¶ 22.)

The Court finds that Orrick failed to take reasonable measures to avoid exposure to more information than was reasonably necessary to determine whether to represent SkyBell. *Rule 1.18(d)(2)* not only requires that the information received by the attorney be reasonably necessary to determine whether to represent the prospective client, but it also states that the attorney must take "reasonable measures" to avoid or limit exposure to this information. Likewise, Comment [3] to the Rule states that the attorney "must limit the initial interview" to receive only information that is reasonably necessary. The Rule explicitly contemplates that the attorney take some type of affirmative step or act to limit or avoid exposure to more information than is necessary.

Crediting Jensen's supplemental declaration, Orrick did take reasonable steps with regard to the information it received for purposes of a conflicts check.

However, no further steps were taken after Orrick advised that the conflicts had been cleared. A one-hour telephone conversation and a three-hour in person meeting then ensued.

It is not enough that the information the attorney received, in hindsight, was reasonably necessary to determine whether to represent the prospective client. There must be some type of preceding or concurrent affirmative act that is carried out by the attorney to limit the disclosure. Scalisi states in his declaration that during the communications between Orrick and SkyBell, SkyBell's representatives were never informed by Orrick that they should withhold any information and were actually encouraged to provide all of the information they could. (Scalisi Decl., Docket No. 48-2 ¶ 15.) While Orrick claims that it was reasonable for it to believe that SkyBell was well-advised by independent counsel as to the scope of the disclosures it should be making, this does not constitute an affirmative act on the part of Orrick to limit its exposure. (Opp'n, Docket No. 53 at 17.)

At oral argument, Orrick contended that if it only acquired reasonably necessary information, it necessarily took measures to ensure that it only received necessary information. Orrick also argued the any caution would be so vague and meaningless as to have no practical force whatsoever. The Court rejects both points.

First, Orrick's formulation of the Rule, as requiring disqualification only if the "the exposure [went beyond] information . . . reasonably necessary to determine whether to represent the prospective client," completely omits any reference to the "reasonable measures" requirement. (Opp'n, Docket No. 53 at 13.) Orrick's analysis likewise overlooks this aspect of the Rule. The "reasonable measures" requirement is integral to the Rule. It acts as a prophylactic to ensure that both the attorney and the prospective client are aware of the limitations on the disclosure of confidential information.

Second, the contention that a caution would have been meaningless ignores the sophisticated environment in which the discussions took place. It also ignores Jensen's statement that he in fact gave a cautionary instruction in soliciting information for a conflicts check. He told SkyBell's outside patent counsel to "limit the information he provided to me about the potential representation only to the information I needed to run a conflicts check." (Jensen Supp. Decl. ¶ 4.) The language which Jensen used was neither vague nor talismanic boilerplate, and presumably at least Jensen thought he was communicating effectively. There is no reason why a similar warning could not have been given before Jensen embarked on a far less structured interchange in the course of his subsequent telephone call and meeting where the possibility of receiving confidential information was open ended. A warning was not given; Jensen's own conduct demonstrates that it could have been and should have been.

In his Supplemental Declaration, Jensen raises a second point for the first time:

> Although I do not remember the exact dates of all my discussions with SkyBell about a potential contingency arrangement, I recall that, at the time SkyBell shared confidential information with me, SkyBell knew that there was no guarantee Orrick would be able to accept the matter on a contingency basis.

(Jensen Supp. Decl. ¶ 7.) No similar statement appears in Jensen's original declaration. While the Written Proposal does not contain a contingent fee option, there is no mention in the Fee Proposal and Budget Section that such an arrangement is unlikely or even off the table. To the contrary, Orrick states that it "does have experience with a variety of alternative fee arrangements and would be willing to discuss such an arrangement if of interest to SkyBell." (Written Proposal, p. 31.) Again, Jensen's Supplemental Declaration comes after the Court issued its tentative and distinguished the present situation from Vaccine Center discussed next.

In support of its position, Orrick cites an unpublished, out-of-district authority applying a nearly-identical Nevada rule regarding duties to prospective clients, *Vaccine Ctr., LLC v. GlaxoSmithKline LLC*, No. 2:12-cv-01849-JCM-NJK, 2013 U.S. Dist. LEXIS 53902, 2013 WL 1787176 (D. Nev. Apr. 25, 2013). (Opp'n, Docket No. 53 at 17–18.) In Vaccine, the court found that an attorney "took reasonable measures to avoid exposure to more disqualifying information than was reasonably necessary to determine whether to represent [a] prospective client." 2013 U.S. Dist. LEXIS 53902 [WL] at *1. In reaching this conclusion, the court focused on the fact that the attorney made clear to the prospective client from the outset that his firm did not normally take cases on a contingency basis, but that he would review any material or documents in order to assess whether it would be economically viable to represent the client. Id. In its tentative, the Court distinguished Vaccine Center.

While Orrick argues that the financial and settlement disclosures in this case were similarly reasonable for Orrick to obtain under the circumstances, the present case is distinguishable because unlike the attorney's preliminary statements in Vaccine that there was a significant possibility that his firm would not ultimately take the case, Orrick placed no such preliminary limitation on Orrick's representation of SkyBell. (Tentative Order Granting Motion to Disqualify, pp. 13–14.) Given that Orrick cited Vaccine Center in its opposition, one must wonder why it did not marshal the facts, if available, concerning reasonable measures to bring itself within the analysis in Vaccine Center.

The Court concludes that in light of the contradictory showing before the Court, Orrick has not presented substantial evidence that at each stage of the discussions with SkyBell it took effective and "reasonable measures to avoid exposure to more information than was reasonably necessary." Orrick does not qualify for the exception set forth in new *Rule 1.18(d)(2)*.

Furthermore, while there is support for Orrick's position that the information it received from SkyBell was necessary for it to prepare a competitive pitch and participate in the beauty contest, it is a separate matter whether the substantial disclosures that occurred were reasonably necessary for Orrick to determine whether to represent SkyBell in the patent litigation against Ring. The Korniczky Declaration lends support to the fact that in the patent litigation context, prospective clients have come to expect law firms participating in a beauty contest to conduct a substantial legal and factual analysis and offer a detailed legal strategy as part of trying to win the representation, which requires some disclosure of confidential information, especially if the law firm is proposing an alternative fee arrangement. (Korniczky Decl., Docket No. 53-3 ¶¶ 9, 12, 13–16.) Korniczky concludes that, as a result, "it is common in the industry for a firm to receive [confidential] information as part of a pitch process in order to evaluate the litigation." (*Id.* ¶ 16.) However, simply because the disclosure of some or a substantial amount of confidential information is common practice among firms engaging in beauty contests for patent litigation does not mean that the firms necessarily need all of this confidential information to determine whether they would accept the engagement. Presumably, most firms have already determined that they would represent a client if selected before expending significant time and resources to participate in lengthy and extensive pitch processes. Orrick even concedes as much, despite adding the qualification that it needed access to SkyBell's confidential information to ensure that the fees made sense before it could know for sure. (Opp'n, Docket No. 53 at 18.) Moreover, Orrick's communications with SkyBell went well beyond an "initial interview," as Jensen continued to communicate with SkyBell until as recently as March 2018, five months after the initial November 1, 2017, phone call took place. (Scalisi Decl., Docket No. 48-2 ¶ 14.) It is a close question whether the information Orrick received was reasonably necessary for it to determine whether to represent SkyBell. Nonetheless, the Court need not decide this issue because it has already determined that Orrick did not take any reasonable measures to avoid exposure to such information. Therefore, Orrick does not qualify for the exception set forth in new *Rule 1.18(d)(2)*. Accordingly, pursuant to new *Rule 1.18(c)*, Orrick may not represent Ring in the instant matter against SkyBell.

As noted by both Orrick and SkyBell, a variety of policy considerations are implicated by this motion. (Opp'n, Docket No. 53 at 23–25; Reply, Docket No. 57 at 15–18.)

Orrick argues that the Court must consider Ring's right to the counsel of its choosing and that Roberts was chosen because of his close relationship with Ring. (Opp'n, Docket No. 53 at 23–24; Siminoff Decl., Docket No. 54-1 ¶¶ 1–4.) Orrick argues that disqualifying Roberts would substantially disrupt this litigation because Ring would be forced to retain new lead counsel that would have to get up to speed regarding the defense of SkyBell's claims and Ring's own affirmative counterclaims. (Opp'n, Docket No. 53 at 24.) Orrick also argues that the Court must consider the possibility that tactical abuse underlies the motion, and the potential for abuse by plaintiffs in inviting large swathes of firms to pitch in an effort to conflict them out of representing potential defendants. (*Id.* at 24–25.) Additionally, Orrick argues that a rigid approach to disqualification would limit attorney mobility, which has become common practice, and unfairly punish Roberts for electing to join Orrick. (*Id.* at 25.)

SkyBell, on the other hand, argues that allowing Orrick to obtain SkyBell's material confidential information regarding the Ring litigation and then turn around and represent Ring in the same matter would undermine the important policy considerations in preserving public trust in the integrity of the bar and the fairness of the judicial process. (Reply, Docket No. 57 at 15–16.) Additionally, SkyBell argues that there is no evidence to suggest any tactical abuse, given that it was genuinely interested in potentially hiring Orrick to represent it and could never have predicted that Ring's lead counsel would ultimately join Orrick. (*Id.* at 16.) Moreover, SkyBell argues that Orrick and Roberts were aware of the conflict of interest and potential for disqualification before Roberts joined the firm, and they cannot now complain that they will be disqualified for a conflict of their own making. (*Id.* at 18.)

"Disqualification motions involve 'a conflict between the clients' right to counsel of their choice and the need to maintain ethical standards of professional responsibility.' " *Kirk*, 183 Cal. App. 4th at 792 (quoting *SpeeDee Oil*, 20 Cal. 4th at 1145). The Court must consider the "client's right to chosen counsel, an attorney's interest in representing a client, the financial burden on a client to replace disqualified counsel, and the possibility that tactical abuse underlies the disqualification motion." Id. (quoting *SpeeDee Oil*, 20 Cal. 4th at 1145). Additionally, the Court must consider that "increased mobility of lawyers between firms calls for a less rigorous application of the disqualification rules." *In re Cty. of L.A.*, 223 F.3d at 996–97 ("The changing realities of law practice call for a more functional approach to disqualification than in the past."). However, "the most egregious conflict of interest is representation of clients whose interests are directly adverse in the same litigation." *SpeeDee Oil*, 20 Cal. 4th at 1147 ("Such patently improper dual representation suggests to the clients—and to the public at large—that the attorney is completely indifferent to the duty of loyalty and the duty to preserve confidences."). Thus, "[t]he paramount concern must be to preserve public trust in the scrupulous administration of justice and the integrity of the bar." *Kirk*, 183 Cal. App. 4th at 792 (quoting *SpeeDee Oil*, 20 Cal. 4th at 1145). "The important right to counsel of one's choice must yield to ethical considerations that affect the fundamental principles of our judicial process." Id. (quoting *SpeeDee Oil*, 20 Cal. 4th at 1145).

The situation before the Court raises serious ethical concerns about firms obtaining substantial confidential information from a prospective client while participating in a competitive pitch process, and after failing to be selected, turning around and representing the other side in the same matter. To be sure, the present circumstances could not have been reasonably anticipated by either side. However, the fundamental problem is still present and no less serious. While prospective clients in the patent litigation context may have come to expect law firms seeking to represent them to offer detailed proposals that require the disclosure of confidential information, it is the responsibility of the firms that participate to ensure that they are aware of and abiding by appropriate ethical standards. Orrick did not do so in this case. It obtained considerable confidential information from SkyBell, failed to take reasonable measures to limit or condition this disclosure in any way, and now seeks to represent the adverse side in the same matter. While disqualification may seem like a drastic result from Orrick's perspective, Orrick was aware that disqualification was a risk when Roberts joined the firm, and SkyBell should not be the one to pay for Orrick's failure to meet the ethical requirements here. Therefore, policy considerations weigh in favor of disqualification.

IV. CONCLUSION

For the foregoing reasons, the Court grants the motion to disqualify.

At the hearing, Ring asked the Court to stay the proceeding for thirty days to allow for transition to new counsel. SkyBell does not object. (Skybell's Supplemental Brief, p. 7, Docket No. 67.) The Court stays the matter, and sets a status conference for October 15, 2018, at 11:30 a.m. The parties shall submit a joint report seven days in advance.

Ring also asked for a determination that its present counsel be permitted to transfer its work product to new counsel. There is no evidence that Roberts or any member of the Ring Litigation group has interacted with anyone on the Orrick team which pitched the representation to Skybell or otherwise been tainted by joining Orrick. SkyBell partially acquiesces in the request and does not object to transfer of work product created prior to Orrick's assumption of the representation. (*Id.*) SkyBell is directed to file a response within seven days.

SOLUTIONS: THE LAWYER SHOULD HAVE, WOULD HAVE, COULD HAVE. . .

Orrick started off on the right foot by performing a conflict check to determine whether it currently represented or had represented any of the parties. And, in doing so, it just obtained "name, rank and serial number"—that is, the basic information-to make this determination. So far, so good. But Orrick's duty was a continuing one, requiring it—*before* being retained—*not* to learn confidential information at the risk of disqualification if ultimately not selected. Why take the chance? There is tremendous pressure at firms to produce billable hours. One's judgment can become clouded in these circumstances. Moreover, a beauty contest is sometimes designed with the potential client knowing, well in advance, whom it plans to select and is conceivably taking an opportunity to shop for free advice. The bottom line: law firms should engage in a realistic risk/reward analysis prior to deciding to go full tilt for the business.

BEYOND THE CITE

Obligations to Prospective Clients: Confidentiality, Conflicts and "Significantly Harmful" Information, Formal Opinion 492, June 9, 2020.

The ABA offers some guidance to law firms in the position in which Orrick found itself:

> ➤ Identify conflicts of interest before undertaking representation in any matter. Every lawyer "should adopt reasonable procedures, appropriate for the size and type of firm and practice, to determine whether there are actual or potential conflicts of interest." Rule 1.7, Comment. These procedures should be designed to identify any conflict at the earliest practicable point in discussions with a would-be client as to whether the lawyer may undertake the representation and before the representation is undertaken. These procedures should be followed in the case of all new matters, even where the lawyer previously has represented or is currently representing the client in other matters."

> ➤ Limit information from a would-be client to that which is necessary to check for conflicts. When obtaining the preliminary information before undertaking the representation, the lawyer should obtain from the would-be client only information sufficient to determine whether a conflict or potential conflict of interest exists and whether the new matter is one within the lawyer's capabilities and one in which the lawyer is willing to represent the would-be client. The would-be client should be cautioned at the outset of the initial conversation not to volunteer information pertaining to the matter until after the lawyer has had an opportunity to determine whether a conflict of interest exists and whether the lawyer is capable and willing to undertake the representation if the client elects to use the lawyer's services."

LEANING INTO PRACTICE

The issues in *Skybell* arise in high stakes litigation between fierce business competitors as well as in more typical types of litigation. Consider this hypothetical.

Nicole Lawyer is a personal injury attorney representing plaintiffs. Her email is on the State Bar website. On a Monday morning she receives an email from Malik Prospective Client:

Dear Nicole:

I saw your email on the State Bar website, so I thought I would email you. I see that you are certified in personal injury law, and I am sure that is the type of lawyer that I need. I was driving on the highway, and I was rear-ended by three cars. I was in the second car. I think this is called a daisy chain car wreck (At least that's what the internet says.) I have a lot of pain in my back, and my knee hurts a lot!!! I guess I need to be honest, though, with you. Before the accident, I had three boilermakers at the local bar. Do you think anyone will find out? Will it hurt the amount of any money I am entitled to? Thanks in advance, Nicole. You can reach me at the following phone number!

Regards,

Malik

It turns out Nicole was in court Monday morning and therefore did not check her email. She had a previously set meeting with Joe Hurt, a potential new client, in the courthouse cafeteria and went there right after court. She still had not checked her emails from the morning. In her interview with Joe, he told Nicole that he was injured in a multiple car wreck case, that he was not at fault, and that he wanted to hire Nicole to represent him. Joe also gave Nicole a police report detailing the facts of the accident. She agreed to represent him and went back to her office to send an engagement letter to him. Before she did so, she checked her email and read Malik's email. She did not respond right away and instead read the police report. Guess what? That's right: the police report established that it was Malik's car that hit Joe's car. This chain of events raised serval questions in Nicole's mind:

First, is what she was told by Malik confidential information that she could not use or disclose? We will work on this rule, which is MR 1.6, in a short while, but this will serve as an introduction to the concept of confidentiality.

Second, is Nicole now precluded from representing Joe in a lawsuit against Malik? Can Nicole use the information disclosed by Malik in representing Joe? Why or why not?

Third, if Nicole cannot represent Joe, can she accept the representation of Malik?

C.   Prospective Client and Conflict Waivers

One way a law firm can insulate itself from the granting of a disqualification motion is by using a prospective waiver. In short, the prospective client agrees in advance to waive any conflict that might arise in the future.

Cases and Materials

X-Ray Questions (*Galderma*)

A general or broad advance conflict waiver will ordinarily be unenforceable. More often than not, a broad advance waiver is ineffective mainly because the majority of prospective clients are not sophisticated enough to understand the material risks from the open-ended language in the waiver. The *Galderma* case will show, however, that a broad advance waiver is appropriate when a client is a highly sophisticated one who is a regular user of legal services; represented by its own counsel; and the waiver is sufficiently detailed to inform the client of the material risks associated for the client in waiving future conflicts. Note that the waiver here, provides that the firm agrees to disqualification if it seeks to represent any other client with an "interest materially and directly to yours (i) in any matter substantially related to our representation of you and (ii) with respect to any matter where there is a reasonable probability that confidential information you furnished to us could be used to your disadvantage." This provision seems reasonable. Why would Galderma balk when V & E represented a company that had sued Galderma involving a matter unrelated to the subject matter of (V & E) representation of it?

This case also explains further the important concept of "informed consent" that permeates practice. In the following case, V & E argued that Galderma gave informed consent to waive any future conflicts that is, to allow V & E to represent any entitles or persons adverse, in certain respects, to Galderma. Have you heard of this concept which also arises in the medical profession? The definition of "informed consent" is set out in MR 1.0(e).

> **Model Rule 1.0(e):** "Informed consent" denotes the agreement by a person to a proposed course of conduct after the lawyer has communicated adequate information and explanation about the material risks of and reasonably available alternatives to the proposed course of conduct.

Why do we have the concept of informed consent? Essentially informed consent is a P.A.C.—the lawyer explains to the client the Pros, Alternatives, and Cons of any proposed course of action. Why did the court find that the P.A.C. was satisfied here? Do you think the General Counsel of Galderma carefully read the waiver and analyzed its implications or did he merely just consider it so much boiler plate that would never be invoked by (V & E)? Do you think V & E went through the P.A.C. analysis with the GC? What role did the relative legal sophistication of the GC play in the court's decision to uphold the waiver? Why?

Notice that the court develops a sliding scale analysis. Less legally sophisticated client, less likely a waiver will be upheld; more legally sophisticated client, more likely to be upheld. Note too that the waiver did not apply "to any matter that is substantially related to our representation of you." Why was this language inserted? Why is it important? Finally, there is another section of the Model Rules (MR 1.8(h)) dealing with prospective waivers. This rule is triggered when a lawyer asks a client, at the inception of the ACR, to waive any future claims of malpractice. This is only permissible if the client is independently represented by their own lawyer in making such an agreement. There, that was the case. Should not an individual or an entity be allowed to strike whatever deal they want to strike? Is this rule not this an overly paternalistic mindset? Why though is this mindset reflected in the Rules?

Galderma Laboratories, L.P., Galderma S.A., and Galderma Research & Development, S.N.C. v. Actavis Mid Atlantic LLC

United States District Court, N.D. Texas, Dallas Division, 2013.
927 F. Supp. 2d 390.

ED KINKEADE, DISTRICT JUDGE.

Before the Court is Plaintiffs Galderma Laboratories, L.P., Galderma S.A., and Galderma Research & Development, S.N.C.'s (collectively "Galderma") Motion to Disqualify Vinson & Elkins, LLP (Doc. No. 18). The Court conducted a hearing on this motion on October 28, 2012. The Court has reviewed the motion, the parties' briefs, the appendices and supplemental appendices. Additionally, the Court has reviewed the Executive Summaries filed by each party (Docs. No. 54 & 55), has considered the parties' arguments at the hearing on October 28, 2012, and the applicable law. The Court DENIES Galderma's Motion (Doc. No. 18) because Galderma gave informed consent to Vinson & Elkins's ("V & E") representation of clients directly adverse to Galderma in matters that are not substantially related to V & E's representation of Galderma.

I. Factual Background

Galderma is a worldwide leader in the research, development, and manufacturing of branded dermatological products. Galderma is headquartered in Fort Worth where it employs approximately 240 people. Galderma and its affiliates have operations around the world, employing thousands of people and reporting worldwide sales of 1.4 billion euros for the year 2011 alone.

As a complex, global company, Galderma routinely encounters legal issues and the legal system. Galderma has its own legal department to address these issues. The legal department is headed by its Vice President and General Counsel, Quinton Cassady. Mr. Cassady is a lawyer who has practiced law for over 20 years and has been general counsel for Galderma for over 10 of those years. In addition to an inhouse legal department, Galderma, through Mr. Cassady, frequently engages outside counsel to assist with a wide range of issues. Over the past 10 years, Galderma has been represented by large law firms including DLA Piper, Paul Hastings, and Vinson & Elkins, LLP ("V & E"). Galderma also engages smaller law firms as needed.

In 2003, Galderma and V & E began its attorney-client relationship. V & E sent Galderma an engagement letter. As part of the engagement letter, V & E sought Galderma's consent to broadly waive future conflicts of interest, subject to specific limitations identified in the engagement letter. The waiver contained in the engagement letter is as follows:

We understand and agree that this is not an exclusive agreement, and you are free to retain any other counsel of your choosing. We recognize that we shall be disqualified from representing any other client with interest materially and directly adverse to yours (i) in any matter which is substantially related to our representation of you and (ii) with respect to any matter where there is a reasonable probability that confidential information you furnished to us could be used to your disadvantage. You understand and agree that, with those exceptions, we are free to represent other clients, including clients whose interests may conflict with ours in litigation, business transactions, or other legal matters. You agree that our representing you in this matter will not prevent or disqualify us from representing clients adverse to you in other matters and that you consent in advance to our undertaking such adverse representations.

On behalf of Galderma, Mr. Cassady signed that he understood and, on behalf of Galderma, agreed to the terms and conditions of engaging V & E, including the waiver of future conflicts of interest.

Beginning in 2003, Galderma engaged V & E for legal advice relating to employee benefit plans, Galderma's 401(k) plan, health care benefit programs, employment issues, and other issues relating to the administration of such programs. V & E continued to advise Galderma on employment and benefits issues into July of 2012.

In June 2012, while V & E was advising Galderma on employment issues, Galderma, represented by DLA Piper and Munck Wilson Mandala, filed this intellectual property lawsuit against Actavis Mid Atlantic, LLC ("Actavis"). At that time, V & E had already represented various Actavis entities in intellectual property matters for six years. Without any additional communication to Galderma, V & E began working on this matter for Actavis, and in July 2012, V & E filed Actavis's answer and counterclaims.

In July 2012, Galderma received a copy of Actavis's answer and counterclaims, and became aware that V & E was representing Actavis. After brief discussions in late July between Mr. Cassady and V & E, Galderma asked V & E to withdraw from representing Actavis. On August 6, 2012, V & E chose to terminate its attorney-client relationship with Galderma rather than Actavis. On that same day, V & E stated that it would not withdraw from representing Actavis, because Galderma had consented to V & E representing adverse parties in litigation when it signed the waiver of future conflicts in the 2003 engagement letter. Galderma then brought this motion to disqualify.

II. Galderma's Motion to Disqualify

Galderma now moves to disqualify V & E from representing Actavis in the underlying patent litigation. The briefing of the parties has been wide-ranging, but at oral arguments, counsel acknowledged that the crux of the issue is this: whether or not Galderama, a sophisticated client, represented by in-house counsel gave informed consent when it agreed to a general, open-ended waiver of future conflicts of interest in V & E's 2003 engagement letter. Galderma argues that its consent was not "informed consent" when its own, in-house lawyer signed the agreement on its behalf because V & E did not advise Galderma of any specifics with regards to what future conflicts Galderma may be waiving. V & E argues that in this case, because Galderma is a highly sophisticated client who is a regular user of legal services and was represented by its own counsel, the waiver language is reasonably adequate to advise Galderma of the material risks of waiving future conflicts, despite being general and open-ended.

[. . . .]

(Editor's Note: This case introduces you to Model Rule 1.7 that we will study in depth. MR 1.7 deals with conflicts of interest that arise when a lawyer deals with a current client. Here, the lawyer has an interest—waiver of a future conflict—that could possibly be at odds with the prospective needs of the lawyer's client.)

1.   ABA Model Rules and Applicable Comments

One source for determining how to apply the Model Rules is the comments to the Model Rules. The comments do not add obligations to the Model Rules but provide guidance for practicing in compliance with the Rules. *Id.* Preamble, cmt. 14. The text of each Rule is authoritative, but the Comments are intended as guides to interpretation. *Id.* Preamble, cmt. 21.

The Comments to Rule 1.7, governing current client conflicts, recognize that a lawyer may properly request a client to waive future conflicts, subject to the test in Rule 1.7(b). *Id.* 1.7, cmt. 22. The effectiveness of the waiver is generally determined by the extent to which the client reasonably understands the material risk that the waiver entails. *Id.*

When dealing with a waiver of future conflicts, a specific waiver of a particular type of conflict has the greatest likelihood of being effective. *Id.* A general and open-ended waiver will ordinarily be ineffective, because the client will likely not have understood the material risks involved. *Id.* Consent using a general or open-ended waiver is not per se ineffective, but considering the entire spectrum of clients, a general and open-ended waiver is likely to be ineffective because the vast majority of clients are not in a position to understand the material risks from the open-ended language of the waiver itself.

The same comment highlights that consent to a general, open-ended waiver is more likely to be effective when dealing with a narrow set of circumstances. If the client is an experienced user of the legal services involved and is reasonably informed regarding the risk that a conflict may arise, that consent is more likely to be effective. *Id.* The consent is particularly likely to be effective when the client is independently represented by other counsel in giving consent and the consent is limited to future conflicts unrelated to the subject of the representation. *Id.*

The comments to Rule 1.0, which defines "informed consent," mirror the comments to Rule 1.7. For consent to be "informed," the lawyer must take reasonable steps to ensure that the client or other person possesses information reasonably adequate to make an informed decision. *Id.* R. 1.0, cmt. 6. Ordinarily, this requires communication that includes a disclosure of the facts and circumstances giving rise to the situation, any explanation reasonably necessary to inform the client or other person of the material advantages and disadvantages of the proposed course of conduct and a discussion of the client's or other person's options and alternatives. *Id.* The more experienced the client is in legal matters generally and in making decisions of the type involved, the less information and explanation is needed for a client's consent to be informed. *Id.* When dealing with a client who is independently represented by other counsel in giving the consent, generally the client should be assumed to have given informed consent. *Id.* Just like Rule 1.7, Rule 1.0 shows there is a vast difference in what type of disclosure is necessary to ensure that a client has reasonably adequate information to make an informed decision, depending on the sophistication of the client and, importantly, whether or not the client is represented by an independent lawyer.

2. ABA Committee on Ethics and Professional Responsibility Formal Ethics Opinions

The ABA's Standing Committee on Ethics and Professional Responsibility has also issued a formal ethics opinion dealing expressly with informed consent to future conflicts. ABA Comm. on Ethics & Prof'l Responsibility, Formal Op. 05–436 (2005) [hereinafter ABA Formal Op. 05–436]. As amended in February 2002, Rule 1.7 permits a lawyer to obtain effective informed consent to a wider range of future conflicts than would have been possible under the Model Rules prior to their amendment. *Id.* Prior to the 2002 Amendment of the Model Rules, informed consent was limited to circumstances in which the lawyer was able to and did identify the potential party or class of parties that may be represented in the future matter. *Id.*; ABA Comm. on Ethics & Prof'l Responsibility, Formal Op. 93–372 (1993) (withdrawn) [hereinafter ABA Formal Op. 93–372]. Additionally, informed consent may have been limited further by the need to identify the nature of the likely future matter. ABA Formal Op. 05–436; ABA Formal Op. 93–372. Relying on Comment 22, the Committee opined that, following the amendment, open-ended, general informed consent was likely to be valid if the client is an experienced user of legal services. ABA Formal Op. 05–436. The opinion gave significant weight to the sophistication of the client and its use of independent counsel, factors which previously had not been relevant to informed consent. See ABA Formal Op. 05–436 (Opinion 93–372 does not vary its conclusions as to the likely effectiveness of informed consent to future conflicts when the client is an experienced user of legal services or has had the opportunity to be represented by independent counsel in relation to such consent). The Committee concluded that because Comment 22 supported the validity of a general, open-ended waiver in particular circumstances, the limits on effective consent established in ABA Formal Opinion 93–372 were no longer consistent with the Model Rules. ABA Formal Op. 05–436.

C.   Burden of Proof

On a motion to disqualify, the movant bears the ultimate burden of proof. Galderma must establish that there is a conflict of interest under the applicable ethics standards and if so, that disqualification is the proper remedy. See *Forsyth v. Barr*, 19 F.3d 1527, 1546 (1994) (placing the burden of establishing a conflict on the client seeking disqualification). V & E does not dispute the concurrent representation of Galderma and Actavis establishes a conflict of interest under the Model Rules. V & E argues that Galderma gave informed consent for V & E to represent clients adverse to it in litigation, which waives any right to claim a conflict of interest. Absent informed consent, there is no question that V & E's contemporaneous representation of Actavis and Galderma is a current client conflict on an unrelated matter. See *In re Dresser*, 972 F.2d at 545; MODEL RULES OF PROF'L CONDUCT R. 1.7 (2010).

With regards to allocating the burden of proof, the issue of "informed consent" is similar to the issue of exceptional circumstances that the court addressed in *In re Dresser*. See *In re Dresser*, 972 F.2d at 545. On the issue of exceptional circumstances, the court noted that it would be the attorney's burden to show a reason why the court should allow the otherwise impermissible dual representation. *Id.* Other courts considering informed consent in this context have also concluded that shifting the burden is appropriate, so that the attorney bears the burden of showing informed consent. See *Celgene Corp. v. KV Pharmaceutical Co.*, No. 07–4819, 2008 WL 2937415, at *6 (D.N.J. July 29, 2008); *El Camino Res., Ltd. v. Huntington Nat'l Bank*, 623 F.Supp.2d 863, 869 (W.D.Mich.2007). Because, absent informed consent, there is no question that V & E's contemporaneous representation of Actavis and Galderma is a current client conflict on an unrelated matter, Galderma need prove nothing more to establish a violation of Model Rule 1.7. V & E has raised the issue of informed consent in response to the otherwise established violation. Because V & E has raised the issue in its defense, the Court concludes that V & E has the burden to show that Galderma gave informed consent. Because the Court concludes that Galderma gave informed consent, the Court need not address whether Galderma has proved that disqualification of V & E is warranted.

D.   Whether or Not Galderma Gave Informed Consent to the Waiver of Future Conflicts

To meet its burden of showing informed consent, V & E must show that it provided reasonably adequate information for Galderma to understand the material risks of waiving future conflicts of interest. MODEL RULES OF PROF'L CONDUCT R. 1.0, cmt. 6 (2010). Two related questions in this test form the analysis. The first question is whether the information disclosed is reasonably adequate for a client to form informed consent. If the waiver does, the second question is, whether or not the disclosure is reasonably adequate for the particular client involved in this case. The focus of the first question is on what information is being disclosed, and the focus of the second question is on circumstances pertaining to the client.

1. Whether V & E's Disclosure Is Reasonably Adequate for a Client to Form Informed Consent

Rule 1.0 provides three basic factors to help determine whether a disclosure is reasonably adequate to allow for informed consent. See id., 1.0(e). Rule 1.0(e) identifies that informed consent is characterized by: 1) agreement to a proposed course of conduct, 2) after the lawyer has communicated adequate information and explanation about the material risks, and 3) the lawyer has proposed reasonably available alternatives to the proposed course of conduct. *Id.* The language of the agreement is a primary source for determining whether or not a particular client's consent is informed. See *Celgene Corp.*, 2008 WL 2937415, at 8 (July 29, 2008 D.N.J.).

The waiver language at issue in this case is found in V & E's 2003 engagement letter. First, the 2003 engagement letter identifies a course of conduct with regard to concurrent conflicts of interest. Second, the engagement letter includes an explanation of the material risk in waiving future conflicts of interest. Third, the letter explains an alternative course of conduct for Galderma. All of these favor a finding that Galderma's agreement manifested informed consent.

First, the Court examines the language for whether or not the parties agreed to a course of conduct with regard to conflicts of interest. The letter, in relevant part, states:

> We recognize that we shall be disqualified from representing any other client with interests materially and directly adverse to yours (i) in any matter which is substantially related to our representation of you and (ii) with respect to any matter where there is a reasonable probability that confidential information you furnished to us could be used to your disadvantage. You understand and agree that, with those exceptions, we are free to represent other clients, including clients

whose interests may conflict with yours in litigation, business transactions, or other legal matters.

These sentences, the bulk of the waiver language, identify a course of conduct for the parties. The course of conduct identified is that V & E is given wide ranging freedom to represent other clients, including those whose interests conflict with Galderma. The outer boundaries of the parties agreed course of conduct is defined in the previous sentence. Despite V & E's freedom to represent other clients with conflicting interests, V & E would not be able to represent a client in a material and directly adverse manner where the adverse representation is substantially related to the representation of Galderma, or there is a reasonable probability that confidential information Galderma furnished could be used to its disadvantage. The course of conduct identified in the waiver language provides for broad freedom for V & E to represent clients with whom it would otherwise have a conflict of interest, limited by specifically identified situations.

Galderma argues the waiver is open-ended and vague, which makes it unenforceable. First, an open-ended waiver is not per se unenforceable. See MODEL RULES OF PROF'L CONDUCT R. 1.7, cmt. 22 (2010) (allowing for the validity of open-ended waivers). Second, simply because a waiver is general, does not mean it is vague. The waiver language in the contract signed by Galderma provides a framework for determining in the future, when a conflict arises, whether or not V & E will be disqualified.

Galderma maintains that the provisions of the waiver must be more specific so that a person who reads the waiver can know whether the parties anticipated a particular party or a particular type of legal matter. Naming a potential party and the nature of a future matter were requirements identified by the ABA Committee on Ethics prior to the 2002 amendments. ABA Formal Ethics Op. 93–372. The amendments, for the first time specifically included guidance on informed consent to future conflicts of interest. ABA Formal Ethics Op. 05–436. The 2002 amendments, which support the validity of general, open-ended waivers, permit informed consent to a wider range of future conflicts that would have been possible prior to the amendments. *Id.* Because the 2002 amendments changed the standard for when a client's waiver of future conflicts is effective, and in response to those changes, the ABA subsequently withdrew Formal Opinion 93–372, a lawyer is no longer required to meet the limitations established in ABA Formal Ethics Opinion 93–372 to obtain informed consent from all clients. See ABA Formal Op. 05–436. While specifying a particular party or type of legal matter does make it more likely that the waiver will be effective for a wider range of clients, using a general framework for determining a course of conduct does not render the waiver unenforceable. The waiver language supports a finding of informed consent because it provides a course of conduct by which the parties can manage future conflicts relating to the attorney-client relationship.

Second, the Court looks to see whether or not the waiver language includes any explanation of the material risk of waiving future conflicts of interest. Waiver language that informs the client of the material risk of waiving future conflicts supports a finding of informed consent. See MODEL RULES OF PROF'L CONDUCT R. 1.0(e) (2010); *Celgene*, 2008 WL 2937415, at 8. V & E waiver language in this case informs Galderma that if they agree, Vinson and Elkins representation of Galderma, "will not prevent or disqualify us from representing clients adverse to you in other matters." The previous language explains that V & E is not necessarily disqualified when representing another client with interests "materially and directly adverse to [Galderma]." The waiver explains that agreeing to the waiver risks V & E advocating for another client directly against Galderma. This is exactly the risk of which Galderma now claims they were not informed. This language explains the material risk in waiving future conflicts, and so this language also supports a finding of informed consent.

Third, the Court looks to see whether the waiver language contains any explanation of reasonably available alternatives to the proposed course of conduct. When the waiver language includes explanation of alternatives to the course of conduct, this also supports a finding that the client gave informed consent. See MODEL RULES OF PROF'L CONDUCT R. 1.0(e) (2010); *Celgene*, 2008 WL 2937415, at 8. In this case, the alternative course of conduct is for Galderma to hire other counsel. The waiver language tells Galderma, "You are free to retain any other counsel of your choosing." Elsewhere, the engagement letter tells Galderma that V & E's representation of Galderma is based on the parties' mutual consent. The language in the waiver and the agreement as a whole identifies at least one alternative; Galderma need not engage V & E on this matter if they do not wish to consent to the proposed terms and conditions. This language, although the least clear of the three factors, also supports a finding of informed consent.

[. . . .]

The Court concludes that the waiver in the 2003 engagement letter is reasonably adequate to allow clients in some circumstances to understand the material risk of waiving future conflicts of interest. The language discloses a course of conduct for determining when V & E will be disqualified, explains the material risk that V & E may be directly adverse to the client, and explains an alternative, that the client need not hire V & E if it does not wish to consent. The Court must next examine Galderma's sophistication and whether Galderma was independently represented in the waiver to determine whether or not the disclosure provided was reasonably adequate to allow Galderma to understand the material risks of waiving future conflicts. *Id.* R. 1.0, cmt. 6 & R. 1.7, cmt. 22.

2. Whether V & E's Disclosure is Reasonably Adequate for Galderma to Form Informed Consent

For the general, open-ended waiver to be valid in this case, V & E must still establish that the disclosure was reasonably adequate to allow Galderma to understand the material risks involved. The communication necessary to obtain informed consent varies with the situation involved. *Id.* R. 1.0, cmt. 6. The principal considerations at this point in the analysis are the sophistication of the parties and whether the client was represented by counsel independent of the law firm seeking the waiver. See RESTATEMENT (THIRD) LAW GOVERNING LAWYERS § 122, cmt. c(i) (2000).

a. The Client's Sophistication

The parties have disagreed sharply as to whether or not the client's sophistication is relevant to resolving this issue. Galderma argues that the sophistication of the client is not relevant, whereas V & E argues that a client's sophistication is a critical factor.

The Comments to the Model Rules and the ABA Committee on Ethics Opinions state that client sophistication is indeed relevant. A lawyer need not inform a client of facts or implications already known to the client. MODEL RULES OF PROF'L CONDUCT R. 1.0, cmt. 6 (2010); RESTATEMENT (THIRD) OF LAW GOVERNING LAWYERS § 122, cmt. c(i) (2000). Thus, the client's existing knowledge affects whether the disclosure in a case is reasonably adequate. Additionally, a client is also sophisticated when "the client . . . is experienced in legal matters generally and in making decision of the type involved. . . ." MODEL RULES OF PROF'L CONDUCT R. 1.0, cmt. 6 (2010). Normally, such persons need less information and explanation than others. *Id.* The comments to Model Rule 1.7, specifically dealing with conflicts of interest, also consider the knowledge and experience of the client in determining whether or not a client's consent is effective. See MODEL RULES OF PROF'L CONDUCT R. 1.7, cmt. 22 (2010). Since the addition of these Comments to the Model Rules, the Committee on Ethics has also changed its position, concluding that the effectiveness of client consent does vary with the client's level of sophistication. ABA Formal Op. 05–436 (withdrawing its prior Formal Op. 93–372 as now inconsistent with the Model Rules). Under the 2002 changes to the Model Rules, a sophisticated client need not be provided as much information for the disclosure to be reasonably adequate for the client to give informed consent.

Galderma is highly sophisticated client. Galderma describes itself as one of the world's leading dermatology companies. In 2011, Galderma and its affiliates reported worldwide sales of 1.4 billion euros, which is approximately 1.87 billion dollars. Galderma is involved in extensive research as part of its normal operations, having filed approximately 5,500 patent applications and patents. Galderma operates worldwide with either R & D centers or manufacturing centers in France, Sweden, Canada, Brazil, Japan, and the United States.

Galderma is also sophisticated in its legal experience. Galderma is presently involved in approximately a dozen different lawsuits, many involving large, complex patent disputes. Galderma litigates in state and federal courts across the country, including Texas, New York, Massachusetts, Florida, Georgia, Illinois, Wisconsin, and Delaware. In doing so, Galderma routinely retains different, large law firms to advise the corporation on various matters across the country including, DLA Piper, Paul Hastings, and V & E. Galderma is experienced in retaining large, national law firms and has signed waivers of future conflicts as part of engaging a national law firm on at least two other occasions, including as recently as February of 2012. Quinton Cassady, who signed the 2003 V & E engagement letter, is the same person who signed engagement letters with DLA Piper which also contained waivers of future conflicts. In one case, Mr. Cassady even initialed the future conflicts waiver portion of an engagement letter. The record in this case demonstrates that Galderma is a client who is highly sophisticated in both legal matters generally and in making decisions to retain large, national firms. This level of sophistication weighs in favor of finding informed consent in this case.

[. . . .]

b.   Independent Counsel

Another related, but different factor the Court considers is whether the client is represented by independent counsel. A client represented by independent counsel needs less information and explanation than others for its consent to be informed. MODEL RULES OF PROF'L CONDUCT R. 1.0, cmt. 6 & R. 1.7, cmt. 22 (2010); ABA Formal Op. 05–436. For the purposes of determining informed consent, the effect is the same whether that independent lawyer is inside the client's organization or is other, outside counsel. RESTATEMENT (THIRD) OF LAW GOVERNING LAWYERS, § 122, cmt. c(i) (2000). The importance of this factor is obvious. The ultimate test for determining whether a client gave informed consent is whether the disclosure is reasonably adequate to allow a client to understand the material risks involved. MODEL RULES OF PROF'L CONDUCT R. 1.0, cmt. 6 & R. 1.7, cmt. 22 (2010). When the client has the benefit of its own lawyer, who is bound by and familiar with the same ethical obligations of the lawyers seeking a waiver, less disclosure is needed to reveal to the independent counsel and its client the consequences of agreeing to the proposed waiver of future conflicts. Another lawyer, who is familiar with the ethical requirements of practicing law, is inherently more informed than even the most sophisticated lay person. The comments to the Model Rules reflect the importance of this factor, going so far as to say that "generally a client . . . who is independently represented by other counsel in giving the consent should be assumed to have given informed consent." *Id.* R. 1.0, cmt. 6 (emphasis added).

Galderma has its own legal department. Galderma has a general counsel with over 20 years of experience practicing law, who is a member of both the Texas state bar and the federal bar. Galderma relies on its general counsel, Mr. Cassady, and the corporate legal department to give competent legal advice pertaining to complex legal matters. Mr. Cassady, as an inside counsel, is still lawyer independent from V & E, advising Galderma on whether or not Galderma should give its consent. See RESTATEMENT (THIRD) OF LAW GOVERNING LAWYERS, § 122, cmt. c(i) (2000).

Mr. Cassady claims now that he did not intend to consent to V & E representing a generic drug manufacturer when he signed the 2003 engagement letter. The language in the Model Rules is clear; informed consent turns on an objective standard of reasonable disclosure and reasonable understanding. See MODEL RULES OF PROF'L CONDUCT R. 1.0 & 1.7 (2010). Mr. Cassady's current declaration that he did not actually intend for Galderma to consent does make a general waiver invalid because when a sophisticated party is represented by independent counsel a general, open-ended waiver is still likely to be reasonably adequate disclosure.

Galderma argues that existing case law holds that even a sophisticated client, represented by its own independent counsel cannot give informed consent based on general, open-ended waiver language. The national standard set by the ABA Model Rules and the Restatement (Third) of the Law Governing

Lawyers do not take such a position, and the cases cited by Galderma are distinguishable in critical ways.

Galderma argues that the rationale of a pair of cases out of California persuasively demonstrate why V & E's waiver language is not sufficient for a client to form informed consent. See *Visa U.S.A., Inc. v. First Data Corp.*, 241 F.Supp.2d 1100 (N.D.Cal.2003); *Concat, L.P. v. Unilever, P.L.C.*, 350 F.Supp.2d 796 (N.D.Cal.2004). Galderma's reliance is misplaced for several reasons. First, the *Concat* court relying on Visa U.S.A., held that to obtain informed consent, the prospective waiver must disclose the nature of the subsequent conflict. *Concat, L.P.*, 350 F.Supp.2d at 820. There is no requirement under the current Model Rules that all prospective waivers must disclose a specific nature of a subsequent conflict to be valid. See MODEL RULES OF PROF'L CONDUCT R. 1.7 (2010).

Second, the *Concat* court found that the waiver language was not sufficient to form informed consent, because it did not name a specific party like the advance waiver in *Visa U.S.A., Inc.* See *Concat* 350 F.Supp.2d at 821. The *Visa U.S.A., Inc.* court relied, in part, on Formal Opinion 93–372, which stated that the closer the lawyer who seeks a prospective waiver can get to circumstances where not only the actual adverse client but also the actual potential future dispute is identified, the more likely the prospective waiver is ethically permissible. *Visa U.S.A., Inc.*, 241 F.Supp.2d at 1107. While still true, a disclosure, identifying a particular client no longer a requirement for every client to form informed consent. See ABA Formal Op. 05–436 (withdrawing and expanding on ABA Formal Op. 93–372). Critically, nothing in either case suggests the courts examined the national standard for informed consent in light of the changes to the Model Rules and the new comments, on which the parties have focused in this case. Because of that court's reliance on ABA Formal Opinion 93–372, which the ABA has since withdrawn, and because ABA Formal Opinion 05–436 expanded the situations for which a waiver provides a basis for informed consent, the difference between *Visa* and *Concat* is no longer persuasive for whether a particular waiver is insufficient to form the basis of informed consent. See ABA Formal Op. 05–436 (stating that Opinion 93–372 concludes informed consent is limited to circumstances in which the lawyer is able to and does identify the potential party or class of parties that may be represented in the future matter(s), and Opinion 93–372 is no longer consistent with the Model Rules).

[. . . .]

supervise the investigators but merely signed their contract. At the time, he said, that seemed like "a reasonable accommodation for a longtime client," but was, in retrospect, "a mistake." Boies also suggested that he believed Weinstein's investigators were not hired to bully Times reporters but to find out the truth of the allegations they were checking out.

Moreover, according to Boies, the Times knew from the moment it hired Boies Schiller that the firm has some clients whose interests diverge from those of the newspaper. According to Boies' statement, the firm specifically said at the time of its engagement that it "needed to be able to continue to represent clients adverse to the Times on matters unrelated to the work we were doing for the Times." In fact, Boies said, Boies Schiller's engagement letter with the Times included a clause acknowledging the conflicts issue.

He quoted the agreement: "We have explained and you have agreed that as a result of the types of clients the firm advises and the types of engagements in which we are involved, we may be requested to act for other persons on matters which are not substantially related to the engagement, where the interests of the other persons, and the firm's representation of them, may be against the client's, including adversity in litigation."

If you work at a big firm, you know how common this sort of "advance conflict waiver" has become as law firms have sprawled into giant, far-flung operations. The Third Restatement of the Law Governing Lawyers permits lawyers to ask clients for open-ended consent to conflicts. The American Bar Association's Model Rules of Professional Conduct similarly allow lawyers to request advance waivers from clients.

Both the ABA and the Restatement caution, however, that advance waivers may not amount to informed consent. "If the consent is general and open-ended, then the consent ordinarily will be ineffective, because it is not reasonably likely that the client will have understood the material risks involved," the ABA said in a note to its conflicts rule. "On the other hand, if the client is an experienced user of the legal services involved and is reasonably informed regarding the risk that a conflict may arise, such consent is more likely to be effective, particularly if, e.g., the client is independently represented by other counsel in giving consent and the consent is limited to future conflicts unrelated to the subject of the representation."

Broadly speaking, there are two different ways to think about advance conflict waivers, depending on what you think of the balance of power between clients and outside lawyers. In one view, advance waivers reflect the modern marketplace for legal services, in which sophisticated clients shop for different law firms to handle different sorts of cases. From that perspective, the waivers benefit clients because law firms will accept discrete assignments without having to worry they're ceding future opportunities to work for rival clients.

But you could conversely argue that law firms take advantage of clients by getting them to sign open-ended waivers that don't specifically anticipate all of the ways outside counsel can end up across the table from them. That seems to be the Times' point in firing Boies.

Oddly, considering their wide use, advance conflict waivers rarely flare up in public controversies. Before the Boies episode, the most notable case involving an advance waiver was probably Mylan's bid for a preliminary injunction barring Kirkland & Ellis from representing a competitor, Teva, in a hostile bid for the generic drugmaker. Kirkland had obtained an advance conflict waiver from Mylan, which it represented in a handful of regulatory cases, in large part because of the law firm's longtime client relationship with Teva. But when Teva launched a takeover offer for Mylan, Mylan said the conflict waiver didn't encompass a hostile takeover. It moved to disqualify Kirkland from advising Teva, arguing that the firm had had access to confidential Mylan product information. After a federal magistrate sided with Mylan, Kirkland stepped aside.

U.S. District Judge Ed Kinkeade of Dallas had a more permissive view of advance conflict waivers in 2013's Galderma Laboratories v. Actavis. The judge denied Galderma's motion to bounce Vinson & Elkins from defending Actavis in a patent case, holding that Galderma gave informed consent to V&E when it signed an open-ended conflicts waiver that said, in part, "You agree that our representing you in this matter will not prevent or disqualify us from representing clients adverse to you in other matters and that you consent in advance to our undertaking such adverse representations."

Let's Chart It!

The foregoing concept is illustrated on this chart.

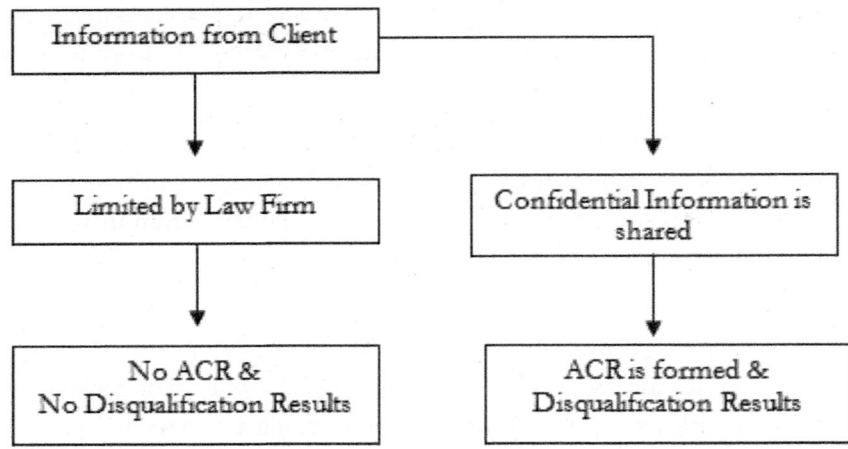

LEANING INTO PRACTICE

You are setting up your practice and are establishing a website. Draft a disclaimer on how to defeat a claim that an ACR was formed because a member of the public contacted your law firm through its website. Research website disclaimers from ethics opinions of the state or local bar associations. Draft a disclaimer that best fits your needs when you are in practice and explain why you drafted it the way that you did.

Section 5. The Attorney-Client Relationship Formation

Now that we have worked through the concept of a prospective client, and ethical issues surrounding the same, let's return to the formation of an ACR. Recall it can be formed as a conscious decision of a lawyer and a person or an entity. But sometimes it can be formed by conduct by a lawyer forming an ACR without fully intending to do so. As in dealing with the ambiguities of prospective client interactions, we will see that the law places the burden on the lawyer to ensure clarity on whether formation of an ACR occurred. We will also begin our explanation of the rules that lawyers must adhere to which are triggered by ACR.

Let's Chart It!

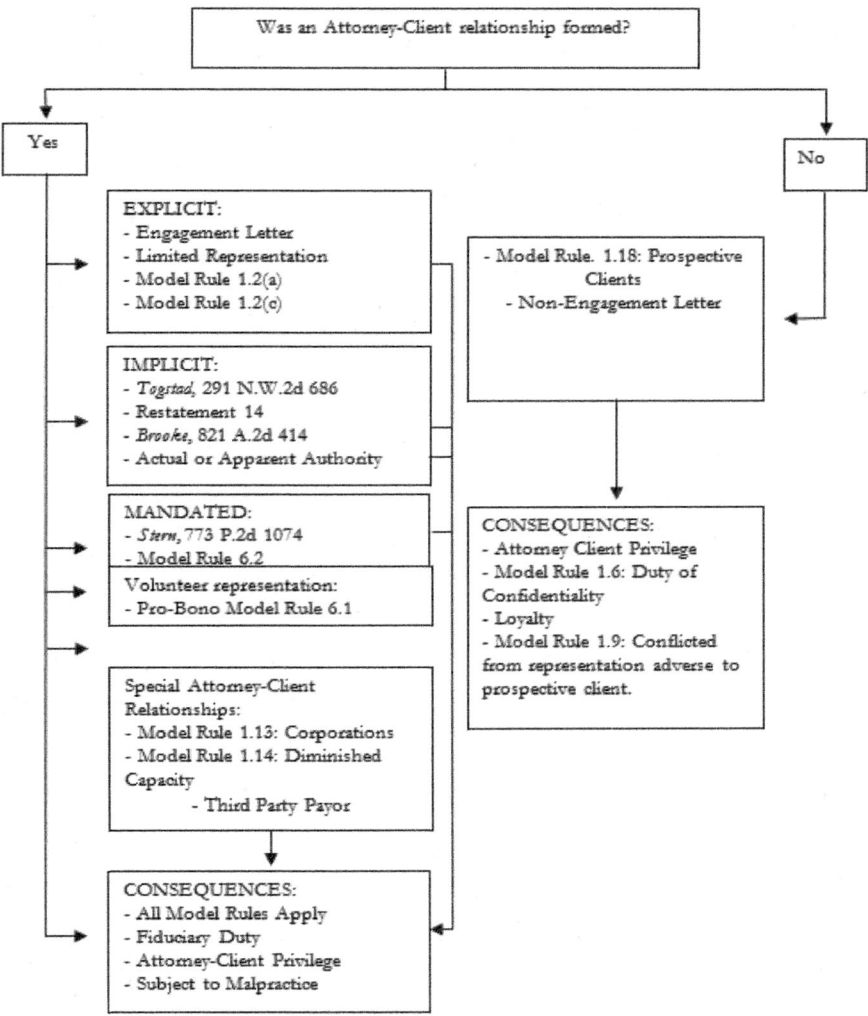

A. Explicit Formation

An explicit formation is the most basic type of ACR and the one with which you are most familiar. This type of agreement is usually reduced to writing. What terms should an ACR encompass? We will see that some can be agreed to while others—no matter how clear the informed consent—cannot. Moreover, even in an explicit agreement some terms—as you will recall from 1L contracts—contain implied terms. We see this with MR 1.2.

Model Rule 1.2(a) allocates the division of duties and rights between the lawyer and the client. Generally speaking, the client determines the objective of a representation and makes major ultimate decisions whether to settle or plea bargain; whether to testify; whether to seek a jury or a judge as the trier of fact. By contrast, is the duty of the lawyer, as we discussed at the outset of the book, to understand these objectives and best devise a means of achieving them and to communicate that to the client.

Model Rule 1.2: Scope of Representation and Allocation of Authority Between Client and Lawyer

(a)   a lawyer shall abide by a client's decisions concerning the objectives of representation and, as required by Rule 1.4 [communication], shall consult with the client as to the means by which they are to be pursued. A lawyer may take such action on behalf of the client as is impliedly authorized to carry out the representation. A lawyer shall abide by a client's decision whether to settle a matter. In a criminal case, the lawyer shall abide by the client's decision, after consultation with the lawyer, as to a plea to be entered, whether to waive jury trial and whether the client will testify.

(b)   A lawyer shall not counsel a client to engage, or assist a client, in conduct that the lawyer knows is criminal or fraudulent, but a lawyer may discuss the legal consequences of any course of conduct with a client or assist a client to make a good faith effort to determine the validity, scope, meaning, or application of the law.

(c)   A lawyer may limit the scope of the representation if the limitation is reasonable under the circumstances and the client gives informed consent.

Deconstruction Exercise/Rule Rationale

This rule contains a fair amount to unpack. What is the most important word in (a)? Recall that doctors have scalpels and lawyers have words. Here, that word is "abide," which means "to bear patiently." *Abide*, MERRIAM-WEBSTER.COM, https://www.merriam-webster.com/dictionary/abide (last visited June 17, 2021). The selection means that the client makes ultimate decisions even though the lawyer disagrees with these decisions and, in fact, asserts excellent reasons for the client *not* to do what she wants to do. Please work with your professor and classmates in discussing what other words could have been selected, list them and then ask why they do not fit this goal.

The rule also uses the word "impliedly." This word was selected for the sake of efficiency; after all, a lawyer must contact counsel opposite to try and settle the matter or make arrangements for depositions to be taken. While a client could require that all decisions or contacts be run first by the client for approval, such a micromanaging arrangement would be impossible in practice and a lawyer very unlikely to enter into an ACR with that client if this were a term that the client insisted on. (Think L.A.S. infecting the ACR.) We will return to the "impliedly" concept later as we will see in MR 1.6 and Confidentiality.

We also see in MR 1.2 that sometimes porous line between counseling a client about a proposed course of action that would be unlawful (ok) and assisting the client in engaging in that course of action (not ok). Note the use of the disjunctive "or" between "criminal" and "fraudulent." As with the use of "or" elsewhere, this disjunctive expands a Rule's coverage.

Another key word choice used in MR 1.2 and throughout the Rules is: "knowingly." The word constricts coverage instead of expanding coverage. MR 1.0(f) defines it as "actual knowledge of the fact in question." A person's knowledge may be inferred from circumstances." A lawyer cannot take an ostrich-like attitude of self-delusion when the truth is right in front of the lawyer. Still, the reach of the Rule is intended to focus on lawyer knowledge—whether implicit or explicit—so that one cannot violate the rule by mere negligence. The negligence concept is limited to claims for malpractice, not rule violation.

X-Ray Questions

While the client makes the ultimate decision on whether to settle her case, does not the lawyer have an equal right to be paid for his services? This Opinion Letter poses that dilemma and sides with the client. Why? What professional value is the Opinion Letter seeking to uphold? Is there a way for the lawyer to both take on the case and still ensure getting paid? If so, what is it?

BEYOND THE CITE

THE STATE BAR OF CALIFORNIA STANDING COMMITTEE ON PROFESSIONAL RESPONSIBILITY AND CONDUCT FORMAL OPINION NO. 2009–176

ISSUE

In a lawsuit prosecuted by Attorney A against Defendant, Client has a statutory right to seek an award of attorney's fees. Attorney B, Defendant's counsel, makes a settlement offer, conditioned on Client's waiver of his statutory right to attorney's fees, that is insufficient to compensate Attorney A for her fees. (1) May Attorney A bar the settlement notwithstanding Client's desire to accept it?

STATEMENT OF FACTS

Client engages Attorney A to prosecute a lawsuit against Defendant under [ABC Law]. In addition to creating substantive claims, [ABC Law] is a "fee shifting statute," granting a successful plaintiff a right to seek an award of attorney's fees. Client and Attorney A enter into a written fee agreement that is legally valid and ethically compliant. The fee agreement provides that Attorney A shall be paid a one-third contingent fee or the statutory award [under ABC Law], whichever is greater.

Attorney A has previously represented, and currently represents, others pursuing claims under [ABC Law] against Defendant. Attorney B, counsel for Defendant, has handled many of these matters and is responsible for defending Client's lawsuit. In the past, after settling claims under [ABC Law], the plaintiffs have filed motions for attorney's fees. As a result, on Attorney B's recommendation, Defendant has decided to make fee-waiver settlement offers in lawsuits under the Act generally, and Attorney B has conveyed such offers. [These fee waivers provide that the plaintiff agrees not to seek statutory fees under ABC Law.]

Extensive motion practice and pretrial discovery ensue in Client's lawsuit. Attorney B recommends to Defendant to make a fee-waiver settlement offer of $20,000, and Defendant accepts the recommendation. Attorney B conveys the settlement offer to Attorney A. If Client were to accept the settlement offer, Attorney A would receive far less than the value of the time she has invested in Client's lawsuit. The reasonable value of her services totals $100,000, [and would be recoverable under ABC Law].

In light of the evidence revealed in discovery, Attorney A believes Client's case to be winnable at trial and the fee-waiver settlement offer to be less than the potential value of Client's claim. Attorney A advises Client regarding her analysis of the merits, likelihood of success at trial, potential damages award, and the practicalities of litigation. Client, weary of litigation, decides the settlement offer is adequate and instructs Attorney A to accept it.

DISCUSSION

[. . . .]

An Attorney May Not Bar Settlement

The first question presented by the factual scenario is whether Attorney A may bar the $20,000 fee-waiver settlement offered to Client by Defendant through Attorney B, notwithstanding Client's desire to accept the offer. The answer is no.

Subject to rules, statutory provisions, and judicial decisions governing fees and fee agreements, a lawyer has a contractual right to the compensation specified in the fee agreement with a client. We consider here a situation in which Attorney A has such a contractual right to the greater of a one-third contingent fee or the statutory attorney's fee and has rendered services fairly valued at an amount much greater than the $20,000 fee-waiver settlement offer that Client wishes to accept.

In the factual scenario, it is to Attorney A's own personal advantage to press Client's case to conclusion in hopes of securing a victory and assurance of payment under the fee-shifting provisions of the Act. Attorney A, however, may not veto a settlement that Client wishes to accept in order to benefit herself. Instead, Attorney A is obligated to inform Client of Defendant's settlement offer and to consummate the settlement in accordance with Client's wishes even if it reduces the likelihood of recovering the full value of her services.

[. . . .]

What other decisions are solely in the decision-making purview of the client? Let's say that a client is convicted of murder and sentenced to death. While his lawyers rationally believe that there are excellent arguments to avoid the death penalty, the client wishes to die. Assuming client competence, this too is the client's decision as the lawyers for a defendant discovered in *Red Dog v. State*, 625 A.2d 245 (Del. 1993), where the Delaware Supreme Court gently admonished them on their ethical obligations to "abide" when they sought to spare their client from the death penalty. The decisions on whether to testify would also be included in these ultimate client decisions.

This of course is not to say that a lawyer, during the ACR, abandons his or her role as a counselor. MR 2.1 specially contemplates that a lawyer can refer to non-legal considerations as well as legal ones in advising a client absent client instruction otherwise. But the final call is always with the client, not the lawyer.

Let's continue with the allocation of responsibility between lawyer and client looking at MR 1.2(c) and how it works in tandem with the rule dealing with client communication, MR 1.4.

Model Rule 1.2(c)

(c)   A lawyer may limit the scope of the representation if the limitation is reasonable under the circumstances and the client gives informed consent.

Deconstruction Exercise/Rule Rationale

What are the key words? Start with "may" which is a permissive word as opposed to some of the rules we study which use a mandatory "shall." Then ask what word does "may" or "shall" modify? Here it is: "limit." So, a lawyer and a client may modify the ACR to cover only certain areas or topics. That right exists but is not an unrestricted right. As you have learned in your other courses, no right is 100% unrestricted. There will always be speed bumps to its exercise. Just as when we study the duty of a lawyer to "zealously represent" a client, there are limits imposed upon the lawyer. Here, it is that the exercise of the right be "reasonable" under the circumstances.

Scenario No. 1: The Case of the Lawyer Who Requires Veto Power over Settlement

A lawyer places the following in the engagement letter with a client: "Lawyer will explain the pros and cons of any settlement offer made to Client; however, Client agrees that lawyer shall have veto power over client's decision whether to accept what lawyer considers to be an unacceptable offer. This is impermissible because it infringes, in contravention of MR 1.2, on the absolute right of the client whether to settle and, if so, for how much or how little. The needs of the lawyer are therefore subordinate to the desires of the client.

Scenario No. 2: The Case of the Overly Demanding Client

The client asks her lawyers to draft non-competition agreements for her employees banning them, if they leave employment, from competing for at least one year after departure. The client tells the lawyer, "Look, only spend three hours max on drafting the agreements. No more." The lawyer knows, based on his experience, that such agreements, in order to be competently done and thus enforceable, require at least 20–25 hours of work because interviews need to be conducted to ascertain job duties, to understand the nature of the client's competitive environment, and to go through several drafts. The lawyer's duty to preform competent work under MR 1.1 trumps his duty to abide by his client's wishes.

X-Ray Questions (*Limited Scope Engagement Letter*)

Here is the start of an engagement letter. Why is the scope of the representation the opening paragraph? Does it concern you, at first glance, that the letter also states what is not part of the scope? Do you believe a client will be offended? Why is there language that the lawyer will withdraw from representation if the client asks for unethical action? After all, nothing untoward has yet occurred. Note how the last paragraph contemplates and preempts issues arising in the three sample scenarios above.

BEYOND THE CITE

This agreement_____ (Lawyer) and _____ (Client) on the terms and conditions set forth below.

1. Limited Scope of Engagement—Negotiation. _____ hereby retains and authorizes _____ to provide advice, counsel, and representation with respect to certain employment-related legal claims _____ has against _____. The _____ shall represent _____ in settlement negotiations with _____ or until such representation is otherwise terminated in accordance with the terms of this Agreement.

_____ shall perform all legal services. _____ shall make all assignments of personnel for performance of legal services. Further, legal assistants and law clerks may perform certain services on _____ behalf under _____ supervision.

This engagement is limited to _____ representation of _____ in connection with the negotiation of a settlement with _____. Accordingly, I will not represent _____ in any other matter unless a new representation agreement is executed by the parties with respect to such new matter.

[. . . .]

Client acknowledges that lawyer has ethical obligations contained in the Rules of professional conduct which lawyer has discussed with Client. Client agrees that if she insists that lawyer violate one or more of these rules, that Lawyer will withdraw from representation and client agrees to assist with such withdrawal.

The engagement letter can serve both as an exercise in ethical conduct as well as a prophylactic against malpractice claims. This is why a lawyer explains what services she will "not" perform on behalf of a client. By way of example, look at *Smookler v. Kronish Lieb Weiner & Hellman LLP*, 2006 N.Y. Misc. LEXIS 3982 (N.Y. Sup. Ct. Jan. 11, 2006). There the defendant law firm was retained to represent the plaintiff in the formation of a business. Eschewing generic language that it would represent the plaintiff in "matters relating to the formation of the business," the engagement letter specifically stated what the lawyer would do in assisting on the formation but also on what it would specifically *not* do such as advise and consult. On the other issue it turns out that there were regulatory issues that landed the plaintiff into trouble and the plaintiff sued the firm for malpractice. Because of the language in the letter, summary judgment was granted to the firm on the malpractice claim.

As you learned in 1L torts, there is no liability absent a breach of duty or where there is no duty undertaken (or where specifically disavowed when the law permits) there is no liability.

B. Implicit Formation

An implicit ACR need not be the product of a lengthy conversation as we will see in *Togstad*. The ACR can be formed from a short conversation in an informal meeting—at a party, with your randomly assigned seat mate on an airplane, or on an internet chat room or lawyer's website. There are several issues to examine but the essential foundation is that the non-lawyer reasonably believes an ACR was formed because the person's legal issue was discussed, and the lawyer manifested an outward willingness to be that person's lawyer. Again, a concept you learned in 1L contracts matters; the issue is not what is subjectively believed but rather what is outwardly manifested by the lawyer.

The formation of an ACR is not in the Model Rules but rather is embodied in *Restatement of the Law Governing Lawyers*. For ease of reference, the *Restatement* citation is below:

§ 14. Formation of a Client-Lawyer Relationship

A relationship of client and lawyer arises when:

(1) a person *manifests* to a lawyer the person's intent that the lawyer provides legal services for the person; and either

    (a) the lawyer *manifests* to the person consent to do so; or

(b)   the lawyer fails to manifest lack of consent to do so, and the lawyer *knows or reasonably should know* that the person *reasonably relies* on the lawyer to provide the services; or

(2)   a tribunal with power to do so *appoints* the lawyer to provide the services.

Deconstruction Exercise/Rule Rationale

This provision encompasses each of the ways that an ACR can be formed (R/S1) plus (1)(a) is explicit formation. Now, (1) plus 1(b) is implicit formation with a prospective client manifesting consent, the lawyer not manifesting consent but acting in such a way that the prospective client walks away from a meeting with the reasonable belief that an ACR was formed. Put another way, the lawyer does or says something that leads the prospective client to conclude that the lawyer is, in fact, manifesting a desire to form an ACR.

Back to the chart and the concept of a prospective client. The Model Rules do cover the concept of a prospective client. As the comment to Model Rule 1.18 on prospective clients makes clear a prospective client relationship is created when a person consults with a lawyer on a legal matter. The surest way to stop a prospective client from claiming to be an actual client is to send a non-engagement letter or email to the person stating that the lawyer will not represent him. This way, the prospective client does not morph into an actual client—essentially moving from the right-hand column to the left-hand column of our chart—because the person(s) cannot claim that they reasonably believed or concluded that an ACR was formed. Any expectation that an ARC was formed is unreasonable.

Cases and Materials

X-Ray Questions (*Togstad*)

In *Togstad*, you will see how the confusion over whether there was or was not the formation of an ACR came back to bedevil Miller, the lawyer with whom Togstad met. When Togstad left Miller's office, she was essentially a ticking time bomb because an ACR was formed without Miller even being aware. This case demonstrates a lesson of great importance for lawyers: it is your duty to disabuse a prospective client that an ACR was formed.

As you read the opinion consider how it was that the paths of Miller and Togstad, intersected. After all, as you will see, Miller was not a personal injury lawyer, so why did he even meet with Togstad? What did he have to gain from the interaction? Can you see yourself acting as Miller did in accepting a meeting with someone you do not know but are merely introduced to? Miller and Togstad had a conversation but different recollections of it. Do you think varying recollections are common in life, and thus, the practice of law. What is the consequence in this case that flows from their conflicting memories? Why was it an important difference here? Shouldn't Togstad bear some—even a minimal responsibility for reaching out to Miller after their meeting when she did not hear from him? Is this another example of how the Rules have a bias favoring clients and prospective clients?

John R. Togstad, et al. v. Vesely, Otto, Miller & Keefe and Jerre Miller

Supreme Court of Minnesota, 1980.
291 N.W.2d 686.

PER CURIAM.

This is an appeal by the defendants from a judgment of the Hennepin County District Court involving an action for legal malpractice. The jury found that the defendant attorney Jerre Miller was negligent and that, as a direct result of such negligence, plaintiff John Togstad sustained damages in the amount of $610,500 and his wife, plaintiff Joan Togstad, in the amount of $39,000. Defendants (Miller and his law firm) appeal to this court from the denial of their motion for judgment notwithstanding the verdict or, alternatively, for a new trial. We affirm.

In August 1971, John Togstad began to experience severe headaches and on August 16, 1971, was admitted to Methodist Hospital where tests disclosed that the headaches were caused by a large aneurism on the left internal carotid artery. The attending physician, Dr. Paul Blake, a neurological surgeon, treated the problem by applying a Selverstone clamp to the left common carotid artery. The clamp was surgically implanted on August 27, 1971, in Togstad's neck to allow the gradual closure of the artery over a period of days.

The treatment was designed to eventually cut off the blood supply through the artery and thus relieve the pressure on the aneurism, allowing the aneurism to heal. It was anticipated that other arteries, as well as the brain's collateral or cross-arterial system would supply the required blood to the portion of the brain which would ordinarily have been provided by the left carotid artery. The greatest risk associated with this procedure is that the patient may become paralyzed if the brain does not receive an adequate flow of blood. In the event the supply of blood becomes so low as to endanger the health of the patient, the adjustable clamp can be opened to establish the proper blood circulation.

In the early morning hours of August 29, 1971, a nurse observed that Togstad was unable to speak or move. At the time, the clamp was one-half (50%) closed. Upon discovering Togstad's condition, the nurse called a resident physician, who did not adjust the clamp. Dr. Blake was also immediately informed of Togstad's condition and arrived about an hour later, at which time he opened the clamp. Togstad is now severely paralyzed in his right arm and leg and is unable to speak.

Plaintiffs' expert, Dr. Ward Woods, testified that Togstad's paralysis and loss of speech was due to a lack of blood supply to his brain. Dr. Woods stated that the inadequate blood flow resulted from the clamp being 50% closed and that the negligence of Dr. Blake and the hospital precluded the clamp's being opened in time to avoid permanent brain damage. Specifically, Dr. Woods claimed that Dr. Blake and the hospital were negligent for (1) failing to place the patient in the intensive care unit or to have a special nurse conduct certain neurological tests every half-hour; (2) failing to write adequate orders; (3) failing to open the clamp immediately upon discovering that the patient was unable to speak; and (4) the absence of personnel capable of opening the clamp.

Dr. Blake and defendants' expert witness, Dr. Shelly Chou, testified that Togstad's condition was caused by blood clots going up the carotid artery to the brain. They both alleged that the blood clots were not a result of the Selverstone clamp procedure. In addition, they stated that the clamp must be about 90% closed before there will be a slowing of the blood supply through the carotid artery to the brain. Thus, according to Drs. Blake and Chou, when the clamp is 50% closed there is no effect on the blood flow to the brain.

About 14 months after her husband's hospitalization began, plaintiff Joan Togstad met with attorney Jerre Miller regarding her husband's condition. Neither she nor her husband was personally acquainted with Miller or his law firm prior to that time. John Togstad's former work supervisor, Ted Bucholz, made the appointment and accompanied Mrs. Togstad to Miller's office. Bucholz was present when Mrs. Togstad and Miller discussed the case.

Mrs. Togstad had become suspicious of the circumstances surrounding her husband's tragic condition due to the conduct and statements of the hospital nurses shortly after the paralysis occurred. One nurse told Mrs. Togstad that she had checked Mr. Togstad at 2 a.m., and he was fine; that when she returned at 3 a. m., by mistake, to give him someone else's medication, he was unable to move or speak; and that if she hadn't accidentally entered the room no one would have discovered his condition until morning. Mrs. Togstad also noticed that the other nurses were upset and crying, and that Mr. Togstad's condition was a topic of conversation.

Mrs. Togstad testified that she told Miller "Everything that happened at the hospital," including the nurses' statements and conduct which had raised a question in her mind. She stated that she "believed" she had told Miller "About the procedure and what was undertaken, what was done, and what happened." She brought no records with her. Miller took notes and asked questions during the meeting, which lasted 45 minutes to an hour. At its conclusion, according to Mrs. Togstad, Miller said that "he did not think we had a legal case; however, he was going to discuss this with his partner." She understood that if Miller changed his mind after talking to his partner, he would call her. Mrs. Togstad "gave it" a few days and, since she did not hear from Miller, decided "that they had come to the conclusion that there wasn't a case." No fee arrangements were discussed, no medical authorizations were requested, nor was Mrs. Togstad billed for the interview.

Mrs. Togstad denied that Miller had told her his firm did not have expertise in the medical malpractice field, urged her to see another attorney, or related to her that the statute of limitations for medical malpractice actions was two years. She did not consult another attorney until one year after she talked to Miller. Mrs. Togstad indicated that she did not confer with another attorney earlier because of her reliance on Miller's "legal advice" that they "did not have a case."

On cross-examination, Mrs. Togstad was asked whether she went to Miller's office "to see if he would take the case of (her) husband." She replied, "Well, I guess it was to go for legal advice, what to do, where shall we go from here? That is what we went for." Again, in response to defense counsel's questions, Mrs. Togstad testified as follows:

> Q   And it was clear to you, was it not, that what was taking place was a preliminary discussion between a prospective client and lawyer as to whether or not they wanted to enter into an attorney-client relationship?
>
> A   I am not sure how to answer that. It was for legal advice as to what to do.
>
> Q   And Mr. Miller was discussing with you your problem and indicating whether he, as a lawyer, wished to take the case, isn't that true?

A   Yes.

On re-direct examination, Mrs. Togstad acknowledged that when she left Miller's office she understood that she had been given a "qualified, quality legal opinion that (she and her husband) did not have a malpractice case."

Miller's testimony was different in some respects from that of Mrs. Togstad. Like Mrs. Togstad, Miller testified that Mr. Bucholz arranged and was present at the meeting, which lasted about 45 minutes. According to Miller, Mrs. Togstad described the hospital incident, including the conduct of the nurses. He asked her questions, to which she responded. Miller testified that "(t)he only thing I told her (Mrs. Togstad) after we had pretty much finished the conversation was that there was nothing related in her factual circumstances that told me that she had a case that our firm would be interested in undertaking."

Miller also claimed he related to Mrs. Togstad "that because of the grievous nature of the injuries sustained by her husband, that this was only my opinion and she was encouraged to ask another attorney if she wished for another opinion" and "she ought to do so promptly." He testified that he informed Mrs. Togstad that his firm "was not engaged as experts" in the area of medical malpractice, and that they associated with the Charles Hvass firm in cases of that nature. Miller stated that at the end of the conference he told Mrs. Togstad that he would consult with Charles Hvass and if Hvass's opinion differed from his, Miller would so inform her. Miller recollected that he called Hvass a "couple days" later and discussed the case with him. It was Miller's impression that Hvass thought there was no liability for malpractice in the case. Consequently, Miller did not communicate with Mrs. Togstad further.

On cross-examination, Miller testified as follows:

Q   Now, so there is no misunderstanding, and I am reading from your deposition, you understood that she was consulting with you as a lawyer, isn't that correct?

A   That's correct.

Q   That she was seeking legal advice from a professional attorney licensed to practice in this state and in this community?

A   I think you and I did have another interpretation or use of the term "Advice". She was there to see whether or not she had a case and whether the firm would accept it.

Q   We have two aspects; number one, your legal opinion concerning liability of a case for malpractice; number two, whether there was or wasn't liability, whether you would accept it, your firm, two separate elements, right?

A   I would say so.

Q   Were you asked on page 6 in the deposition, folio 14, "And you understood that she was seeking legal advice at the time that she was in your office, that is correct also, isn't it?" And did you give this answer, "I don't want to engage in semantics with you, but my impression was that she and Mr. Bucholz were asking my opinion after having related the incident that I referred to." The next question, "Your legal opinion?" Your answer, "Yes." Were those questions asked and were they given?

MR. COLLINS: Objection to this, Your Honor. It is not impeachment.

THE COURT: Overruled.

THE WITNESS: Yes, I gave those answers. Certainly, she was seeking my opinion as an attorney in the sense of whether or not there was a case that the firm would be interested in undertaking.

Kenneth Green, a Minneapolis attorney, was called as an expert by plaintiffs. He stated that in rendering legal advice regarding a claim of medical malpractice, the "minimum" an attorney should do would be to request medical authorizations from the client, review the hospital records, and consult with an expert in the field. John McNulty, a Minneapolis attorney, and Charles Hvass testified as experts on behalf of the defendants. McNulty stated that when an attorney is consulted as to whether he will take a case, the lawyer's only responsibility in refusing it is to so inform the party. He testified, however, that when a lawyer is asked his legal opinion on the merits of a medical malpractice claim, community standards require that the attorney check hospital records and consult with an expert before rendering his opinion.

Hvass stated that he had no recollection of Miller's calling him in October 1972 relative to the Togstad matter. He testified that:

A   —when a person comes into me about a medical malpractice action, based upon what the individual has told me, I have to make a decision as to whether or not there probably is or probably is not, based upon that information, medical malpractice. And if, in my judgment, based upon what the client has told me, there is not medical malpractice, I will so inform the client.

Hvass stated, however, that he would never render a "categorical" opinion. In addition, Hvass acknowledged that if he were consulted for a "legal opinion" regarding medical malpractice and 14 months had expired since the incident in question, "ordinary care and diligence" would require him to inform the party of the two-year statute of limitations applicable to that type of action.

This case was submitted to the jury by way of a special verdict form. The jury found that Dr. Blake and the hospital were negligent and that Dr. Blake's negligence (but not the hospital's) was a direct cause of the injuries sustained by John Togstad; that there was an attorney-client contractual relationship between Mrs. Togstad and Miller; that Miller was negligent in rendering advice regarding the possible claims of Mr. and Mrs. Togstad; that, but for Miller's negligence, plaintiffs would have been successful in the prosecution of a legal action against Dr. Blake; and that neither Mr. nor Mrs. Togstad was negligent in pursuing their claims against Dr. Blake. The jury awarded damages to Mr. Togstad of $610,500 and to Mrs. Togstad of $39,000.

On appeal, defendants raise the following issues:

(1) Did the trial court err in denying defendants' motion for judgment notwithstanding the jury verdict?

(2) Does the evidence reasonably support the jury's award of damages to Mrs. Togstad in the amount of $39,000?

(3) Should plaintiffs' damages be reduced by the amount of attorney fees they would have paid had Miller successfully prosecuted the action against Dr. Blake?

(4) Were certain comments of plaintiffs' counsel to the jury improper and, if so, were defendants entitled to a new trial?

1. In a legal malpractice action of the type involved here, four elements must be shown: (1) that an attorney-client relationship existed; (2) that defendant acted negligently or in breach of contract; (3) that such acts were the proximate cause of the plaintiffs' damages; (4) that but for defendant's conduct the plaintiffs would have been successful in the prosecution of their medical malpractice claim. See, *Christy v. Saliterman*, 288 Minn. 144, 179 N.W.2d 288 (1970).

This court first dealt with the element of lawyer-client relationship in the decision of *Ryan v. Long*, 35 Minn. 394, 29 N.W. 51 (1886). The Ryan case involved a claim of legal malpractice and on appeal it was argued that no attorney-client relation existed. This court, without stating whether its conclusion was based on contract principles or a tort theory, disagreed:

> [I]t sufficiently appears that plaintiff, for himself, called upon defendant, as an attorney at law, for "legal advice," and that defendant assumed to give him a professional opinion in reference to the matter as to which plaintiff consulted him. Upon this state of facts the defendant must be taken to have acted as plaintiff's legal adviser, at plaintiff's request, and so as to establish between them the relation of attorney and client.

Id. (citation omitted). More recent opinions of this court, although not involving a detailed discussion, have analyzed the attorney-client consideration in contractual terms. See, *Ronnigen v. Hertogs*, 294 Minn. 7, 199 N.W.2d 420 (1972); *Christy v. Saliterman*, supra. For example, the Ronnigen court, in affirming a directed verdict for the defendant attorney, reasoned that "(u)nder the fundamental rules applicable to contracts of employment the evidence would not sustain a finding that defendant either expressly or impliedly promised or agreed to represent plaintiff." 294 Minn. 11, 199 N.W.2d 422. The trial court here, in apparent reliance upon the contract approach utilized in Ronnigen and Christy, supra, applied a contract analysis in ruling on the attorney-client relationship question. This has prompted a discussion by the Minnesota Law Review, wherein it is suggested that the more appropriate mode of analysis, at least in this case, would be to apply principles of negligence, i. e., whether defendant owed plaintiffs a duty to act with due care. 63 Minn.L.Rev. 751 (1979).

We believe it is unnecessary to decide whether a tort or contract theory is preferable for resolving the attorney-client relationship question raised by this appeal. The tort and contract analyses are very similar in a case such as the instant one, and we conclude that under either theory the evidence shows that a lawyer-client relationship is present here. The thrust of Mrs. Togstad's testimony is that she went to Miller for legal advice, was told there wasn't a case, and relied upon this advice in failing to pursue the claim for medical malpractice. In addition, according to Mrs. Togstad, Miller did not qualify his legal opinion by urging her to seek advice from another attorney, nor did Miller inform her that he lacked expertise in the medical malpractice area. Assuming this testimony is true, as this court must do, see, *Cofran v. Swanman*, 225 Minn. 40, 29 N.W.2d 448 (1947), we believe a jury could properly find that Mrs. Togstad sought and received legal advice from Miller under circumstances which made it reasonably foreseeable to Miller that Mrs. Togstad would be injured if the advice were negligently given. Thus, under either a tort or contract analysis, there is sufficient evidence in the record to support the existence of an attorney-client relationship.

Defendants argue that even if an attorney-client relationship was established the evidence fails to show that Miller acted negligently in assessing the merits of the Togstads' case. They appear to contend that, at most, Miller was guilty of an error in judgment which does not give rise to legal malpractice. *Meagher v. Kavli*, 256 Minn. 54, 97 N.W.2d 370 (1959). However, this case does not involve a mere error of judgment. The gist of plaintiffs' claim is that Miller failed to perform the minimal research that an ordinarily prudent attorney would do before rendering legal advice in a case of this nature. The record, through the testimony of Kenneth Green and John McNulty, contains sufficient evidence to support plaintiffs' position.

In a related contention, defendants assert that a new trial should be awarded on the ground that the trial court erred by refusing to instruct the jury that Miller's failure to inform Mrs. Togstad of the two-year statute of limitations for medical malpractice could not constitute negligence. The argument continues that since it is unclear from the record on what theory or theories of negligence the jury based its decision, a new trial must be granted. *Namchek v. Tulley*, 259 Minn. 469, 107 N.W.2d 856 (1961).

The defect in defendants' reasoning is that there is adequate evidence supporting the claim that Miller was also negligent in failing to advise Mrs. Togstad of the two-year medical malpractice limitations period and thus the trial court acted properly in refusing to instruct the jury in the manner urged by defendants. One of defendants' expert witnesses, Charles Hvass, testified:

> Q: Now, Mr. Hvass, where you are consulted for a legal opinion and advice concerning malpractice and 14 months have elapsed (since the incident in question), wouldn't and you hold yourself out as competent to give a legal opinion and advice to these people concerning their rights, wouldn't ordinary care and diligence require that you inform them that there is a two-year statute of limitations within which they have to act or lose their rights?

> A: Yes. I believe I would have advised someone of the two-year period of limitation, yes.

Consequently, based on the testimony of Mrs. Togstad, i.e., that she requested and received legal advice from Miller concerning the malpractice claim, and the above testimony of Hvass, we must reject the defendants' contention, as it was reasonable for a jury to determine that Miller acted negligently in failing to inform Mrs. Togstad of the applicable limitations period.

[. . . .]

Affirmed.

SOLUTIONS: THE LAWYER SHOULD HAVE, WOULD HAVE, COULD HAVE. . .

To avoid the lawsuit, Miller should have sent Togstad a non-engagement communication. In telling her that he would not represent her. This is an effective tool because it eliminates any reasonable expectations per the Restatement, that an ACR was created. The following Leaning into Practice teaches you fluency in the mindset and the language of such communications.

LEANING INTO PRACTICE

Review these non-engagement communication insertions and decide whether they should be included in non-engagement communication. Explain your answer.

   i)   At the end of the communication, "please let us know if you have any questions."

   1)   "We urge you to seek other counsel as soon as possible because your potential claim has a statute of limitations which means that it just be brought within a certain period of time or be lost."

   2)   Same as above but the communication states that "the statute of limitations is 300 days."

   3)   While you arguably have a valid claim, we are not interested at this time in representing you."

   4)   "Our decision not to represent you should not be taken as being our opinion on whether you have a valid claim."

   5)   "We are enclosing the original documents and tape recording that you left with us."

   6)   We are troubled from an ethical standpoint by the fact that you made a surreptitious tape recording."

7)   "If you can find and provide corroborating witnesses or evidence to us, we may be interested in filing a lawsuit on your behalf."

8)   "Thank you for meeting with us about your claim of sexual harassment."

9)   "Thank you for bringing your original diary and original tape recording to our meeting. Because we will not be representing you, we are returning it in the same envelope."

ii)   In the TV series Breaking Bad, the corrupt attorney Saul Goodman tells meth dealers Walter White and Jesse Pinkman: "Put a dollar in my pocket! You want attorney-client privilege, don't you? . . . Put a dollar in my pocket. Make it official." When they give him some spare cash from their pockets, he announces: "You are now officially represented by Saul Goodman and Associates!" But let's clear up any misunderstanding. The exchange of money is not necessary to form an attorney-client relationship. That is a myth, but it is repeated in the TV shows and movies every so often. Many attorneys represent clients pro bono or on contingency, in which case no money will be exchanged at the outset of the relationship. A payment might be relevant because it could be evidence of a contract, but it is not necessary. A lawyer needs to beware that behavior that might lead a reasonable person to conclude that he or she is agreed to do legal work might create an ACR, and that will in turn trigger far more extensive obligations.

Cases and Materials

X-Ray Questions (*Brooke*)

In *Brooke*, a lawyer drafted a will for a sometime client who was also a longtime friend. But my making himself a beneficiary of the will, the lawyer violated a Model Rule on personal conflicts of interest (MR 1.8). The violation hinged on whether, as we have discussed, whether an ACR was formed. How did the court reason out that an ACR was arguably formed? What reasoning did the court use in rejecting the defense that there is a "friendship" exception to ACR formation? Is this the right holding? After all, you have relatives and close friends who will need legal advice and therefore seek your counsel. What harm, if any, would result if such an exception were grafted onto the rules?

Attorney Grievance Commission of Maryland v. John A. Brooke

Court of Appeals of Maryland, 2003.
821 A.2d 414.

RAKER, JUDGE.

[. . . . .]

(Editor's Note: John Brooke was a lawyer and very close friends, for a period of some twenty years, with John C. Sherpinski. By way of example, Brooke owned a home on the Eastern shore of Maryland and Sherpinski kept his boat at the home. Brooke had previously done legal work for him. Shortly before he died, Sherpinski asked Brooke to draft a will for him and Brooke, along with his admin assistant, put together a generic will. The beneficiary of the will? Brooke. Doing so is a violation of a conflicts rule we will study, MR 1.8(c), which prohibits a lawyer drafting a will and also making himself its beneficiary. Brooke defended based on his argument that there was no attorney-client relationship and thus, though as a lawyer he was subject to the rule of professional conduct, he did not violate any rule of professional conduct. The following is how the appeals court, in reviewing the decision below, dealt with this argument.)

We turn first to respondent's contention that the hearing judge erred in concluding that an attorney-client relationship existed between respondent and the testator with respect to the will. The record contains clear and convincing evidence that an attorney-client relationship was established between respondent and Mr. Sherpinski with respect to the preparation of the will.

Our predecessors have noted that "[w]hat constitutes an attorney-client relationship is a rather elusive concept." *Attorney Grievance Comm'n v. Shaw*, 354 Md. 636, 650, 732 A.2d 876, 883 (1999) (quoting *Folly Farms I, Inc., v. Trustees*, 282 Md. 659, 670, 387 A.2d 248, 254 (1978)). The question of whether an attorney-client relationship exists has arisen in a variety of circumstances. For example, this Court has considered whether the relationship exists in the context of agency and principal such that the lawyer bound the purported client to a particular transaction, *see Brown v. Hebb*, 167 Md. 535, 175 A. 602 (1934); whether a lawyer engaged in a business partnership was in an attorney-client relationship vis-a-vis his partners, *see Attorney Grievance Comm'n v. Kramer*, 325 Md. 39, 599 A.2d 100 (1991); and whether an attorney-client relationship exists for purposes of a claim against the Client Security Trust Fund. *See Folly Farms I*, 282 Md. 659, 387 A.2d 248. *See also, McCormick on Evidence* § 88, at 352 (5th ed.1999) (referring to the relationship in the context of the evidentiary privilege in attorney-client communications).

The Supreme Judicial Court of Maine, in *Board of Overseers of the Bar v. Mangan*, 763 A.2d 1189 (2001), in a disbarment disciplinary proceeding, recently considered whether an attorney-client relationship existed between the attorney and a purported client. The court reiterated its definition of "client," stating that "the term 'client' includes one who is either 'rendered professional legal services by a lawyer, or who consults a lawyer with a view to obtaining professional legal services from him.' " *Id.* at 1192 (quoting *Board of Overseers of the Bar v. Dineen*, 500 A.2d 262, 264 (Me.1985)). Although an attorney-client relationship ordinarily rests on contract, the contract need not be express and may be implied from the conduct of the parties. *See Shaw*, 354 Md. at 650–51, 732 A.2d at 883; *Healy v. Gray*, 184 Iowa 111, 168 N.W. 222 (1918). It is not necessary to the relationship that a retainer be requested or paid. *See Shaw*, 354 Md. at 650, 732 A.2d at 883. This Court has stated that the lack of any explicit agreement or payment arrangement did not preclude the formation of an attorney-client relationship. In *Attorney Grievance Comm'n v. James* we stated:

> "Although an agreement upon the amount of a retainer and its payment is rather conclusive evidence of the establishment of the attorney-client relationship, the absence of such an agreement or payment does not indicate conclusively that no such relationship exists. Indeed, the payment of fees is not a necessary element in the relationship of attorney and client. The services of an attorney to the client may be rendered gratuitously but the relationship of attorney and client nonetheless exists."

355 Md. 465, 476–77, 735 A.2d 1027, 1033 (1999) (quoting *Central Cab Co. v. Clarke*, 259 Md. 542, 549–50, 270 A.2d 662, 666 (1970)). Many courts have adopted the following standard to assess whether the relationship has been established: An attorney-client relationship is said to have been created when (1) a person seeks advice or assistance from an attorney; (2) the advice or assistance sought pertains to matters within the attorney's professional competence; and (3) the attorney expressly or impliedly agrees to give or actually gives the desired advice or assistance. *See Board of Overseers of the Bar v. Mangan*, 763 A.2d 1189, 1192–93 (Me.2001); *State v. Gordon*, 141 N.H. 703, 692 A.2d 505, 506 (1997); *DeVaux v. American Home Assur. Co.*, 387 Mass. 814, 444 N.E.2d 355, 357 (1983); *Kurtenbach v. TeKippe*, 260 N.W.2d 53, 56 (Iowa 1977); *Sheinkopf v. Stone*, 927 F.2d 1259, 1264 (1st Cir.1991).

The Restatement (Third) of the Law Governing Lawyers addresses the formation of an attorney-client relationship as follows:

"A relationship of client and lawyer arises when:

(1) a person manifests to a lawyer the person's intent that the lawyer provide legal services for the person; and . . .

(b) the lawyer fails to manifest lack of consent to do so, and the lawyer knows or reasonably should know that the person reasonably relies on the lawyer to provide the services. . . ."

Restatement (Third) of the Law Governing Lawyers § 14 (2000). The commentary describes the means by which an attorney-client relationship may be formed without an express agreement by the lawyer:

"Like a client, a lawyer may manifest consent to creating a client-lawyer relationship in many ways. The lawyer may explicitly agree to represent the client or may indicate consent by action, for example by performing services requested by the client. An agent for the lawyer may communicate consent, for example, a secretary or paralegal with express, implied, or apparent authority to act for the lawyer in undertaking a representation."

Restatement (Third) of the Law Governing Lawyers § 14, cmt. (e). See also *DeVaux*, 444 N.E.2d at 357–58 (stating that jury could find formation of attorney-client relationship based on conduct of attorney's secretary, even absent any conduct by attorney himself). An attorney-client relationship, therefore, does not require an explicit agreement. The relationship may arise by implication from a client's reasonable expectation of legal representation and the attorney's failure to dispel those expectations.

Respondent characterizes the interaction between Mr. Sherpinski and himself as "a product of their long-standing friendship" rather than a professional, attorney-client relationship. He identifies the close friendship, the brevity of the discussion, the lack of any other recent legal work by respondent on Sherpinski's behalf, and the lack of any agreement or appointment.

The evidence of close friendship does not negate the existence of an attorney-client relationship. Although an attorney providing assistance to a friend does not necessarily enter into an attorney-client relationship, it has never been the case that social interaction precludes an attorney from providing legal services to a client. *See Attorney Grievance Comm'n v. Sait*, 301 Md. 238, 482 A.2d 898 (1984) (finding no attorney-client relationship between attorney and family friend where attorney told friend he could not provide legal advice and counseled securing alternate representation).

It is undisputed that respondent had performed legal work for Mr. Sherpinski in the past. On September 8, 1999, Mr. Sherpinski sought advice and assistance from respondent. The discussion occurred in respondent's law office, out of the presence of other people. The subject of the discussion was the drafting of a will, a matter within respondent's professional competence. The respondent's secretary drafted the will using respondent's legal forms. The will designated respondent as Mr. Sherpinski's personal representative. Perhaps most compelling, when contacted by the police following the discovery of Mr. Sherpinski's remains, respondent informed them that he was Mr. Sherpinski's attorney. There is no indication that the legal relationship of attorney-client, which previously existed between respondent and Mr. Sherpinski, was ever terminated. Judge McCurdy's finding that an attorney-client relationship existed when the will was created was supported by clear and convincing evidence. Accordingly, this exception is overruled.

Respondent's second exception to the hearing judge's proposed conclusions of law relies on the faulty premise that no attorney-client relationship existed. He argues that because there was no attorney-client relationship, his interaction with Mr. Sherpinski did not amount to the practice of law. Respondent further claims that he did not engage in the practice of law because:

> "[h]e did not do anything which required legal knowledge or skill, apply legal principles, exercise his professional judgment as a lawyer in connection with Mr. Sherpinski's will, interpret any documents, give any legal advice, or apply legal principles to any complex problem."

To determine whether an individual has engaged in the practice of law, the focus of the inquiry should "be on whether the activity in question required legal knowledge and skill in order to apply legal principles and precedent." *Attorney Grievance Comm'n v. Hallmon*, 343 Md. 390, 397–98, 681 A.2d 510, 514 (quoting *In re Discipio*, 163 Ill.2d 515, 206 Ill.Dec. 654, 645 N.E.2d 906, 910 (1994)). "Where trial work is not involved but the preparation of legal documents, their interpretation, the giving of legal advice, or the application of legal principles to problems of any complexity, is involved, these activities are still the practice of law." *Id.*, 681 A.2d at 514 (quoting *Lukas v. Bar Ass'n of Montgomery County*, 35 Md.App. 442, 448, 371 A.2d 669, 673, cert. denied, 280 Md. 733 (1977)).

In the present case, the respondent's conduct was directly related to the preparation of a legal document and advice related thereto. As indicated above, the conduct was taken within the scope of an attorney-client relationship. Thus, respondent's exception is without merit and is overruled.

Respondent's final exception is without merit. As stated, the hearing judge properly found respondent in violation of Rule 1.8(c). A violation of the Rules of Professional Conduct may be a basis for finding a violation of Rule 8.4. Respondent argues that finding him in violation of both Rule 1.8(c) and Rule 8.4 constitutes double punishment for the same conduct. This argument ignores this Court's repeated assertion that the purpose of sanctioning an attorney's conduct is to protect the public rather than to punish the errant attorney. *See Attorney Grievance Comm'n v. Powell*, 369 Md. 462, 474, 800 A.2d 782, 789 (2002). Furthermore, the finding of a rule violation is a separate matter from the imposition of the sanction. The severity of the sanction imposed will depend on the particular facts and circumstances of each case; "the gravity of misconduct is not measured solely by the number of rules broken but is determined largely by the lawyer's conduct." *See Attorney Grievance Comm'n v. Briscoe*, 357 Md. 554, 568, 745 A.2d 1037, 1044 (2000) (quoting *Attorney Grievance Comm'n v. Milliken*, 348 Md. 486, 519, 704 A.2d 1225, 1241 (1998)). The hearing judge's conclusion that respondent violated Rule 8.4 was supported by clear and convincing evidence.

(Editor's Note: All Bar Associations, as part of being a self-regulated profession, investigate grievances against lawyers as opposed to a regulatory board that is generally appointed by the governor of a state. The lawyer has due process rights and grievances are, after investigation and no resolution, often litigated in state court with the Bar as the prosecutor as we see in this case. Here Brooke argued that the suspension from practice sought by the Bar was excessive in light of several mitigating factors: his lack of prior disciplinary sanctions; that this matter involved only a single act of misconduct; that he was unaware of Model Rule 1.8(c); and that there was evidence that he exercised undue influence upon Mr. Sterpinski. The court was unmoved and imposed a suspension from the practice of law.)

SOLUTIONS: THE LAWYER SHOULD HAVE, WOULD HAVE, COULD HAVE. . .

Under ABA Model Rule 1.8(c), if a lawyer is related to the client, the lawyer is permitted to prepare a will giving the lawyer a substantial gift. (Naturally, in such circumstances, the lawyer becomes open to claims that undue influence was exercised in dealing with the relative.) In Brooke's case, the lawyer should have avoided drafting the will for his friend. Brooke should have told him to seek another lawyer to draft the will. His failure to do so resulted in the formation of an ACR and a violation of MR 1.8(c).

> This case also illustrates a fundamental principal of practice; namely, the less you must explain, the better off you will be. Brooke could have easily suggested another lawyer; prevented this lawsuit; and enriched his relationship with another member of the bar who could possibly refer work to him. While it was likely difficult to say "no" to a close friend, prudence and ethics dictate another path.

LEANING INTO PRACTICE

Consider this hypothetical. You have your own personal injury practice, and you employ a receptionist/paralegal. One day, a person calls and says that she was injured in a fall at the entry to a grocery store because ice was allowed to accumulate and cause a dangerous condition. The receptionist/paralegal is under strict written instructions from you that he is never to enter into an ACR and if he does, he will be terminated. He, though, tells the caller to inform the store in writing of the incident; to write a letter to you setting out what occurred; and arranges for a medical examination by a doctor used by your firm. The letter to you is written but he misfiles it, you never see it, and the limitations period runs. You are sued for malpractice. Can you obtain a summary judgment of the malpractice lawsuit based on the lack of an ACR? After all, malpractice requires the violation on of a duty and if no ACR was formed, then no duty was breached and there is no claim.

The answer is "no." These facts are taken largely from *DeVaux v. Am. Home Assurance Co.*, 444 N.E. 2d 355 (Mass. 1983). While the employee didn't have actual authority to enter into an ACR, the prospective client had a reasonable belief that there was an ARC based on apparent authority. Thus, there was a sufficient dispute of material fact for the issue of ACR formation to be submitted for a jury determination. Recall from your 1L year that apparent authority "results from conduct (or lack of conduct) by the principal (that's you) which causes a third person reasonably to believe that a particular person . . . has authority to enter into negotiations or to make representations as his agent." Here, the plaintiff claims the lawyer placed his (staff person) in a position where prospective clients might have reasonably believed that the staff person had the authority to establish the attorney-client relationship."

C. Mandated Representation

Model Rule 6.2: Accepting Appointments

A lawyer shall not seek to avoid appointment by a tribunal to represent a person except for good cause, such as:

> (a)   representing the client is likely to result in violation of the Rules of Professional Conduct or other law;

> (b)   representing the client is likely to result in an unreasonable financial burden on the lawyer; or

> (c)   the client or the cause is so repugnant to the lawyer as to be likely to impair the client-lawyer relationship or the lawyer's ability to represent the client.

Deconstruction Exercise/Rule Rationale

The third method for ACR creation is court mandated representation. This form of ACR, as we see in our flow chart, requires that a lawyer adhere to the identical ethical obligations as in the other two ways of formation. Mandated representation is an option possibly in both criminal and civil cases.

Let's take criminal matters first. As you learned in your Con Law class, the United States Supreme Court held in 1963 that the Sixth Amendment guarantees an indigent defendant legal representation in a criminal case. *Gideon v. Wainwright*, 372 U.S. 335 (1963). (By the way, we will see how Con Law intersects with PR through this book. Next up: whether there is a Constitutional right to perjury). Thus, a lawyer must be appointed to represent indigent defendants accused of crimes if imprisonment is a possibility. Because the Court considers legal representation of indigents a fundamental right, it is imposed upon the states through the Fourteenth Amendment.

What about the appointment of a lawyer to an indigent person in a civil case? 28 U.S.C. 1915(e)(1–2) provides that: "The court may request an attorney to represent any (person claiming *in forma pauperus* status) unable to employ counsel and may dismiss the case if the allegation of poverty is untrue, or if satisfied that he action is frivolous or malicious." But in *Mallard v. United States District Court*, 490 U.S. 296 (1989), the Court held that this section does not authorize a federal court to require an unwilling lawyer to represent an indigent litigant in a civil case.

But there are two other sources empowering a court to appoint a lawyer for an indigent civil litigant: a court's inherent authority and a lawyer's duty as an officer of the court. We will see these concepts later in this book, but we introduce them to you now.

A court's inherent authority is based on the need for a default power, apart from a statutory grant of authority, to manage a court's docket and ensure that justice is meted out to those appearing before it. The concept of "officer of the court" is one of a professional duty imposed upon lawyers in their role as professionals. In short, a lawyer's duty to serve—not only the client—but also the legal system used by the client. These dual concepts empower a court to appoint a lawyer to represent an indigent civil litigant. For an extensive discussion and analysis of these concepts read *Bothwell v. Republic Tobacco Co., et al*, 912 F. Supp. 1221 (D. Neb. 1995).

Cases and Materials

X-Ray Questions (*Stern*)

In the following case, Ronald Stern was an in-house attorney for a company. He was appointed by a court to represent a criminal defendants. Lawyers usually choose which client to represent. However, for Stern, as an officer of the court in Colorado, he was appointed to represent this indigent defendant when the public defender was conflicted from representation. Even after great efforts by Stern to withdraw from the case, the Supreme Court of Colorado ruled that in order to withdraw from such court appointments, Stern must make a sufficient showing that he is incompetent under MR 1.1, not just merely asserting incompetence with a conclusory assertion. As one of your authors likes to say in class, a conclusion is like a doughnut with sprinkles on it—pretty, available, appetizing but without any national value. What did the court say about his showing of purported incompetence?

The Colorado Supreme Court adopts a ruling from the Alaska Supreme Court that "(a)lthough not all attorneys are competent in criminal law, lack of experience in criminal cases will not always justify an attorney's refusal to represent an indigent criminal defendant." Why did the court adopt this language? What is the overarching point that the court is making? The court sets out a burden shifting scheme for determining whether a lawyer's competence objection is meritorious. What is it? Do you agree? Finally, consider the idea of an officer of the court. This might make more sense, some argue, if a lawyer's legal education is publicly financed. But it is not so limited. Why? Because a lawyer owes an ethical duty not only to the client but also to the legal system as well. What is your opinion? We will consider these ethical duties to the legal system in future chapters and how they are in tension with our ethical duties of zealous representation.

Ronald S. Stern v. The County Court in and for the County of Grand and Judge Scotty P. Krob

Supreme Court of Colorado, 1989.
773 P.2d 1074.

ROVIRA, JUSTICE.

The question presented in this case is whether the trial court abused its discretion by appointing an attorney with limited experience in criminal matters to represent a criminal defendant. We conclude that the trial court did not abuse its discretion. Accordingly, we affirm.

I.

Appellant, Ronald S. Stern, has been a licensed attorney in the State of Colorado since 1974. Stern practices law in Grand County, Colorado, a rural community with a relatively small population. A limited number of attorneys practice law in Grand County, and only two or three of them routinely practice criminal law. Stern's practice includes civil litigation, but he has limited experience in trying criminal cases.

In December 1986, Stern was appointed by Judge Scotty P. Krob of the County Court in and for the County of Grand to represent an indigent criminal defendant charged with second degree assault, a class 4 felony, and two misdemeanors. The Colorado Public Defender was unable to represent the defendant because of a conflict of interest.

Shortly thereafter, Stern moved to withdraw, contending that he was incompetent to represent the defendant and was prevented from doing so by C.P.R. DR6–101(A). Stern asserted that he was incompetent because he had not voluntarily represented a criminal defendant for eleven years and had "read no cases, rules, or other materials having to do with criminal law or procedure in the same period of time." He also alleged that undertaking the representation would "constitute legal malpractice and would not constitute effective assistance of counsel as required by the Sixth Amendment to the Constitution of the United States." The county court denied Stern's motion, stating: "Having received the motion it is hereby denied. The Court would refer counsel to those rules regarding association of co-counsel, if necessary."

Stern then commenced an action in district court pursuant to C.R.C.P. 106. In his complaint, he restated his reasons for seeking leave to withdraw and sought an order requiring the county court to grant his motion to withdraw. After considering the answer and affidavit of Judge Krob1 submitted by the attorney general and briefs submitted by both parties, the district court dismissed Stern's complaint. In its order, the district court ruled:

> Upon review of the pleadings filed herein the plaintiff's request for judgment on the pleadings will be granted and this Court will rule on this matter based on the pleadings and judicial notice of the Plaintiff's considerable competence in those areas of the civil law in which this Court sees the plaintiff on a regular basis. . . .

> As noted in the memorandum filed by the Defendant on 2–17–87 the case law has recognized the obligation of the lawyer to educate himself and certainly this plaintiff is very capable of accomplishing that task. Based on the law cited by Defendant, the Plaintiff's complaint is dismissed.

Stern appealed to the court of appeals, but the county court requested that the case be certified to this court pursuant to section 13–4–109, 6A C.R.S. (1987), and C.A.R. 50. On September 9, 1987, we accepted jurisdiction.

II.

In *Gideon v. Wainwright*, 372 U.S. 335, 83 S.Ct. 792, 9 L.Ed.2d 799 (1963), the United States Supreme Court held that the sixth amendment's guarantee of counsel is a fundamental right "made obligatory upon the States by the Fourteenth Amendment," and therefore the fourteenth amendment requires appointment of counsel for indigent defendants in state court. In *Argersinger v. Hamlin*, 407 U.S. 25, 92 S.Ct. 2006, 32 L.Ed.2d 530 (1972), the Court held that "absent a knowing and intelligent waiver, no person may be imprisoned for any offense, whether classified as petty, misdemeanor, or felony, unless he was represented by counsel at his trial." *Id.* at 37, 92 S.Ct. at 2012 (footnote omitted). Consequently, an attorney must be provided to represent indigent defendants accused of crimes if imprisonment is to be imposed.

In Colorado, the state public defender is charged with the responsibility of representing indigent defendants. When the public defender cannot represent an indigent defendant because of a conflict of interest, the burden of representation must be placed elsewhere. In Grand County, the county court has placed this burden on the private bar.

A trial court's power to appoint counsel to represent an indigent defendant "cannot be questioned. Attorneys are officers of the court and are bound to render service when required by such an appointment." *Powell v. Alabama*, 287 U.S. 45, 73, 53 S.Ct. 55, 65, 77 L.Ed. 158 (1932). "The professional obligation to respond to the call of the court is an incident of the privilege to practice law and does not offend constitutional commands." *Daines v. Markoff*, 92 Nev. 582, 555 P.2d 490, 493 (1976); see also *Branch v. Cole*, 686 F.2d 264, 266–67 (5th Cir.1982); *State ex rel. Wolff v. Ruddy*, 617 S.W.2d 64, 65 (Mo.1981); *Smith v. State*, 118 N.H. 764, 394 A.2d 834, 837 (1978).

The Ethical Considerations of the Code of Professional Responsibility, which represent the objectives toward which an attorney should strive, describe the responsibility of the profession to the community:

> Historically, the need for legal services of those unable to pay reasonable fees has been met in part by lawyers who donated their services or accepted court appointments on behalf of such individuals. The basic responsibility for providing legal services for those unable to pay ultimately rests upon the individual lawyer, and personal involvement in the problems of the disadvantaged can be one of the most rewarding experiences in the life of a lawyer. Every lawyer, regardless of professional prominence or professional workload, should find time to participate in serving the disadvantaged. The rendition of free legal services to those unable to pay reasonable fees continues to be an obligation of each lawyer. . . .

C.P.R. EC2–25.

The American Bar Association Standards for Criminal Justice (Standards) have offered a solution to the problem of finding counsel to represent indigent criminal defendants. The Standards suggest that "[t]he legal representation plan for each jurisdiction should provide for the services of a full-time defender organization and coordinated assigned-counsel system involving substantial participation of the private bar." Standards for Criminal Justice § 5–1.2 (1986).

According to the Standards, the purposes of a "mixed" system include the following: the contribution of private attorneys to the knowledge of public defenders; the existence of a "safety valve" that prevents the caseload pressures on each group from becoming overly burdensome; the assurance that private attorneys will have a continued interest in the welfare of the criminal justice system; and the fact that private attorneys are "essential if full-time defenders are to avoid conflicts of interest in representing codefendants." Standards for

Criminal Justice § 5–1.2 commentary at 10 (1986). Although the responsibility for providing "legal representation is shared by the bar with society as a whole," "the bar should play a major role in ensuring the provision of legal representation." Standards for Criminal Justice § 5–1.1 commentary at 7 (1986).

The Standards also recommend a standard for an attorney's eligibility to serve as appointed counsel:

> Assignments should be distributed as widely as possible among the qualified members of the bar. Every lawyer licensed to practice law in the jurisdiction, experienced and active in trial practice, and familiar with the practice and procedure of the criminal courts should be included in the roster of attorneys from which assignments are made.

Standards for Criminal Justice § 5–2.2 (1986). The comments to this standard provide:

> [T]he standard rejects the notion that every member of the bar admitted to practice in a jurisdiction should be required to provide representation. The practice of criminal law has become highly specialized in recent years, and only lawyers experienced in trial practice, with an interest in and knowledge of criminal law and procedure, can properly be expected to serve as assigned counsel. While it is imperative that assigned counsel possess advocacy skills so that prompt and wise reactions to the exigencies of a trial may be expected, this alone is not deemed sufficient. There must also be familiarity with the practice and procedure of the criminal courts and knowledge in the art of criminal defense.
>
> It is critical, however, that the assigned-counsel system be administered in a manner that attracts participation from the largest possible cross-section of members of the bar and affords opportunities for inexperienced lawyers to become qualified for assigned cases. Accordingly, those responsible for administering assigned-counsel programs should continuously canvass the bar to make certain that all who display a willingness to serve are permitted to do so. . . . Where interested attorneys lack sufficient experience and skill in criminal defense, there are a variety of procedures that can help them qualify for assigned cases.

Standards for Criminal Justice § 5–2.2 commentary at 27–28 (1986) (footnotes omitted).

Finally, with respect to the function of defense counsel, the Standards have described the "Trial lawyer's duty to administration of justice" as follows:

(a)   The bar should encourage through every available means the widest possible participation in the defense of criminal cases by experienced trial lawyers. Lawyers active in general trial practice should be encouraged to qualify themselves for participation in criminal cases both by formal training and through experience as associate counsel.

(b)   All qualified trial lawyers should stand ready to undertake the defense of an accused regardless of public hostility toward the accused or personal distaste for the offense charged or the person of the defendant.

(c)   Qualified trial lawyers should not assert or announce a general unwillingness to appear in criminal cases.

Standards for Criminal Justice § 4–1.5 (1986). The comments to Standard 4–1.5 provide:

Wide participation in the defense of criminal cases is important to the health of the administration of criminal justice and to the fulfillment of the bar's obligation to ensure the availability of qualified counsel to every accused. However, lawyers and judges are unanimous in acknowledging that not every lawyer licensed to practice is actually able to try a case in court effectively. Though only a fraction of all criminal cases go to trial, the judgment and experience of a trial lawyer are also essential in the process of negotiation leading to a disposition without trial. But the nature of a trial lawyer's experience in civil trial practice is such as to qualify the lawyer for participation in criminal practice if additional training and experience in criminal law and procedure is acquired. Such training is, of course, available through the large number of continuing legal education programs sponsored by state and local bars and by private organizations. "On the job" experience can be appropriately gained by assigning lawyers with little or no criminal trial experience to act as associate counsel to lawyers who are more experienced in the criminal courts.

By encouraging the significant number of lawyers who are now active only in the civil courts to obtain training and experience in criminal practice, and to make themselves available and willing to undertake the defense of criminal cases, the bar will take a significant step toward making certain that competent counsel is provided. At the same time, the participation in the criminal justice system of lawyers whose practice is largely in the civil courts will help avert the undesirable professional isolation of criminal trial specialists. The civil lawyer's familiarity and acquaintance with the procedures and problems of the administration of criminal justice may also encourage the lawyer to play a larger role in the reform and improvement of the criminal law and its processes.

The highest tradition of the American bar is found in the obligation, in the lawyer's oath, never to reject "from any consideration personal to myself, the cause of the defenseless or oppressed." A lawyer has the duty to provide legal assistance "even to the most unpopular defendants." . . . The sure way to guarantee adherence to this tradition of denying no defendant competent legal representation is for all trial lawyers to prepare themselves to act in criminal cases.

Standards for Criminal Justice § 4–1.5 commentary at 19–21 (1986) (footnotes omitted).

With these considerations in mind, we address the arguments presented in this case.

A.

Stern argues that he is incompetent to handle criminal cases; therefore, he is prohibited from representing the defendant in this case by C.P.R. DR6–101(A)(1). C.P.R. DR6–101(A)(1) provides: "A lawyer shall not: (1) Handle a legal matter which he knows or should know that he is not competent to handle, without associating with him a lawyer who is competent to handle it."

The Alaska Supreme Court has addressed this argument in *Wood v. Superior Court*, 690 P.2d 1225 (Alaska 1984), and *DeLisio v. Alaska Superior Court*, 740 P.2d 437 (Alaska 1987). In *Wood*, an attorney who had not handled a criminal case for approximately eleven years was appointed to represent a criminal defendant. The attorney refused to accept the appointment, and the trial judge found him in contempt. The attorney appealed, arguing, among other things, that he was not competent in criminal matters and that he could not provide effective assistance of counsel.

On appeal, the court said that, although not all attorneys are competent in criminal law, lack of experience in criminal cases will not always justify an attorney's refusal to represent an indigent criminal defendant. *Wood*, 690 P.2d at 1230.

> [I]t is all too obvious that 'in some instances an appointed lawyer who prepares diligently will nevertheless be unable to prepare himself sufficiently to be competent to represent the defendant,' and that in those instances the appointed lawyer should not bear primary responsibility for the case. The American Bar Association's Committee on Ethics and Professional Responsibility suggests that attorneys finding themselves in this situation should ask the court to appoint, 'as associate or co-counsel, an additional lawyer who is competent to handle the matter in question.'

Id. at 1230 (quoting ABA Comm. on Ethics and Professional Responsibility, Informal Op. 1216 (1972)) (citations omitted).

The court rejected the argument that an attorney's statement that he or she is incompetent automatically excuses the attorney from providing representation and concluded that "[a] showing that an attorney is not competent must be made to the court." *Id.* at 1232. With respect to the attorney who appealed in that case, the court held:

> [The attorney] himself stated that he had handled some criminal cases until 1973. [The trial judge] pointed out that in working for the Court System as a law clerk [the attorney] had dealt with criminal matters. On this record we cannot say that he was not competent to practice criminal law or that indigent defendants represented by him would necessarily have received ineffective assistance of counsel.

> *Id.*

In *DeLisio*, 740 P.2d 437 (Alaska 1987), the Alaska Supreme Court was again faced with the argument, made by an attorney who was appointed to represent an indigent defendant, that he was incompetent to handle a criminal case. The court quickly disposed of this argument, stating:

> [W]e reject [the attorney's] contention that he is incompetent to represent a criminal defendant. At the contempt hearing before [the trial judge, the attorney] stated that he had not handled a criminal case of any magnitude for at least fifteen years. He acknowledged, however, that he had served as a court-appointed criminal defense attorney from 1962 to 1963, had worked as a prosecutor for a year and a half, and had handled occasional criminal appointments between 1965 and 1967 or 1968. While criminal practice and

procedure ha[ve] undoubtedly changed since [the attorney] was active in the criminal bar, the assertion that an attorney with [his] trial experience is unable to provide adequate representation is at best disingenuous and need not be seriously considered.

DeLisio, 740 P.2d at 438 (footnote omitted).

We believe that when an attorney who is appointed to represent a criminal defendant believes that he is incompetent to handle the case, he has the burden of proving his incompetence to the court. If the attorney carries this burden, the trial court must decide whether the attorney is capable of becoming competent on his own or whether the appointment of co-counsel is necessary until such time as the attorney becomes competent.

Here, Stern made no sufficient showing that he is incompetent beyond merely asserting that this is true. In addition, we note that if Stern had met his burden of showing that he is incompetent, the district court believed that he is "very capable of accomplishing th[e] task [of becoming competent]." Accordingly, we believe that the trial court did not abuse its discretion in appointing Stern.

B.

Stern also argues that he cannot provide effective assistance of counsel as required by the United States and Colorado Constitutions. U.S. Const. amends. VI & XIV; Colo. Const. art. II, § 16. Therefore, according to Stern, he should be allowed to withdraw. We reject Stern's argument because it is premature to assert ineffective assistance of counsel before representation has occurred.

In *United States v. Cronic*, 466 U.S. 648, 104 S.Ct. 2039, 80 L.Ed.2d 657 (1984), the trial court appointed a young lawyer with a real estate practice to represent a criminal defendant indicted on mail fraud charges involving the transfer of over $9,400,000 in checks. The court allowed the attorney only 25 days for pretrial preparation, even though it had taken the government over four and one-half years to investigate the case and it had reviewed thousands of documents during that investigation.

After being convicted on 11 of the 13 counts in the indictment, the defendant appealed, arguing that he received ineffective assistance of counsel in violation of the sixth amendment. The Supreme Court disagreed, holding that the defendant "can therefore make out a claim of ineffective assistance only by pointing to specific errors made by trial counsel." *Id.* at 666, 104 S.Ct. at 2050 (footnote omitted). Applying this standard to the facts of this case, it is clear that

Stern's claim that he cannot provide effective assistance of counsel is premature because he has provided no representation and a claim of ineffective assistance of counsel can only be asserted by pointing to specific errors made by trial counsel after representation has occurred.

We addressed a similar argument in *People v. District Court*, 761 P.2d 206 (Colo.1988). In District Court, an attorney, who was appointed to represent an indigent defendant in a criminal case, filed a motion to withdraw and a motion to dismiss the charges against the defendant based on the limitation on fees payable to court-appointed counsel for indigent defendants. The attorney argued, and the district court agreed, that the limitation on the total fee he could be paid for representing an indigent defendant violated the defendant's right to effective assistance of counsel. This court reversed, concluding:

> The district court's dismissal of the charges on the basis of a prospective denial of [the defendant's] right to effective assistance of counsel was premature because it is inconsistent with Strickland's demand that an aggrieved defendant demonstrate actual substandard performance and prejudice resulting therefrom.

Id. at 210 (referring to *Strickland v. Washington*, 466 U.S. 668, 104 S.Ct. 2052, 80 L.Ed.2d 674 (1984)). Likewise, Stern's assertion that he cannot provide effective assistance of counsel to his appointed client is premature because it is inconsistent with Strickland's requirement that an aggrieved defendant demonstrate actual substandard performance and prejudice resulting from his attorney's performance.

Accordingly, the trial court's order is affirmed.

VOLLACK, J., does not participate.

SOLUTIONS: THE LAWYER SHOULD HAVE, WOULD HAVE, COULD HAVE. . .

Stern's argument that he cannot provide effective assistance of counsel was rejected by the court because it was premature to assert ineffective assistance of counsel before the actual representation commenced. Stern would be allowed to withdraw if he later makes a factually and sufficient showing that he was incompetent. Simply stating the lack of experience in criminal cases did not justify Stern's refusal to representation. If that was a normalized excuse, then lawyers could invoke it at any time would they not? What would the effect be?

LEANING INTO PRACTICE

The following are scenarios on whether an ACR was formed. These exercises will help hone your sensitivity to the issue of the formation, sometimes inadvertent, of an ACR.

1)   You are talking to a close friend. He explains a legal issue that he is confronting. You listen carefully but say nothing. At the end of the recitation the friend says, "are you interested in taking my case?" and you say "I don't think so." Has an ACR been formed?

2)   Joe Lawyer is General Counsel of a company. He tells you that his company needs a lawyer that does securities regulation work which you do not do. So, Joe hires Lola Lawyer for this purpose. But from time to time, Joe calls you to get your take on whether Lola is proceeding along the right path in a general sense. You answer the questions even though Joe's company is not paying you. And, in fact, Lola is doing a great job and you inform him. Has an ACR been formed between you and Joe's company? Why or why not?

3)   Lupe Civilian comes to visit Emmy Lawyer at her firm, the Sorrow and the Pity. Emmy is a partner there. Lupe tells Emmy that she wants to sue her former business partner, Juan Civilian for breach of fiduciary duty. Emmy performs a conflicts check and finds there is none. There is no further discussion of the potential lawsuit substance except that from time-to-time Lupe curses about Juan. but Emmy says, "let me show you around." Emmy shows her the mock courtroom, the large law library and introduces her to some new associates and tells Lupe, "They would work on your case." Lupe tells Emmy, "You have a great firm. You are the ones for me." Emmy validates the parking and Lupe drives off. Has an arguable ACR been formed?

4)   Eddie is a complete stranger to Lola Lawyer. Lola, on a Monday docket call, goes to the courthouse, Eddie goes up to Lola and says, out of the blue, "You look like a lawyer. My girlfriend Nina and I have been charged with two burglaries, but I did the first one alone. Are you a lawyer?" Lola says, "yes I am a lawyer and I specialize in criminal defense." Eddie says, "what should I do?" Lola responds "beats me. But heck you could go to jail for a

while! Go talk to the public defender. You look like a deadbeat who can't pay me." Was an arguable ACR formed?

5) Same facts but Eddie speaks in a hushed tone to Lola, invites Lola to speak with him in an alcove away from the main lobby, and then tells her his story. Lola asks some questions on the details of the indictment, asks how much he can afford in fees, and asks questions on the evidence against him.

Is an arguable ACR formed?

6) Isabella Civilian is at a party. She learns from the host that Joe Lawyer specializes in insurance claims. She goes up to Joe and says "Hi! I understand that you specialize in insurance claims! Boy, have I got a doozy for you! Bet you've heard a lot, but my issue is really oddball! Mind if I tell you about it?" Joe is a polite sort and listens to her and occasionally takes a sip of his martini and nods. She tells him "my roof blew off in that winter storm we had in February and I filed a claim and, well, the insurance company said it was an act of God and I said, 'oh no you can't get out of it that easily' and I told them they misread the policy (Isabella explains why in some detail; she got her law degree on Google) and then they said I was wrong and told me why. And I told them they were wrong (Isabella then launches into what she said to them) What do you think? Can you help me?" Joe says "I am not really in a position to advise you on this issue. Good luck!" Later, Isabella finds a lawyer who sues the insurance company for wrongful denial of a claim. Turns out the insurance company retains Joe to defend the lawsuit. Was an ACR formed? If so, what do you think might be the representation consequences to the litigants?

X-Ray Questions

Sometimes art can better portray a legal idea than all the opinions and law review commentary ever could. Here is a brief excerpt from one of William Lashner's novels about the ethically challenged lawyer Victor Carl. Do you agree with how he describes the role of a lawyer. Why? Is this role the same or different from what you imagined in coming to law school? Why? Is the role the same or different from how you imagined it to be before coming to law school?

BEYOND THE CITE

By: William Lashner, "*Past Due*," HarperTorch, 2004.

This is from the novel "Past Due" by William Lashner. The client is a man named Joey Cheaps, who was murdered; his lawyer is thinking:

"Joey Cheaps might have been a sad sack, no account who still owed me my fee, but he was a client. That means something to be a client. It means he gets my loyalty, whether he deserves it or not. It means he gets my absolute best for the price of an hourly fee. It means in a world where every person has turned against him there is one person who will fight by his side for as long as there is a battle to be fought. And the final battle, as far as I could see, was just beginning. So, I couldn't just ignore what had happened. I couldn't just ignore that my client was dead, that his killer was free, that his past had risen to swallow him whole. My life was imploding in on itself like the fizzling core of an atomic bomb, but a client was dead, and something had to be done. Yes, something had to be done."

D. Special Attorney-Client Relationships

Introduction

We have covered the three types of ACRs. While different in origin, each share a common attribute; they are clear on the identity of the client. The following three ACRs share the opposite trait: they are not always clear on the identity of the client. As we saw in *Togstad*, the responsibility to ensure the ACR clarity falls squarely upon the lawyer. So, too, with the following three special types of ACR: when a person other than the client pays the legal fees; when a lawyer represents an entity, such as a corporation, and an employee of same (often labeled "constituent"); and, finally, when a client evinces possible "diminished capacity" to make legal decisions and to provide directions to counsel.

1)   *Third-Party Payor*

Third-Party Payor is one type of special attorney-client relationship. Lawyers are sometimes asked to represent a client where the legal fees are paid by a third-party payor. Third party payor usually occurs with a family member or friend, an indemnitor in such cases of liability for insurance company, or with a co-client or with a third-party funder in the business of financing litigation. To whom does an attorney owe a duty of loyalty and confidentiality when he accepts legal fees from a third-party payor?

Let's take a look at Model Rule 1.8(f), dealing with the circumstances that must exist in order for a lawyer to allow third-party payment:

> ➤ The client gives informed consent;

> ➤ There is no interference with the lawyer's independence or professional judgment or with the client lawyer relationship; and

> ➤ Information relating to representation of a client is protected as required by Rule 1.6, the rule on confidentiality that extends between lawyer and client and prohibits disclosure of confidential information to the third-party payor absent informed consent of the client.

Lawyers are prohibited from accepting or continuing representation when the lawyer sees that the third-party payor will interfere with the lawyer's independent professional judgment. It is also important for the lawyer to obtain informed consent from the client regarding the third party paying for the lawyer fees. Third-party payors can have different interests in the case outcomes than the actual client. But they are paying the lawyer's fees, they believe they are the attorney's boss—wrong! The lawyer owes the duty of loyalty and confidentiality to the client, not to the third-party payor.

Cases and Materials

X-Ray Questions (*Yellow Cab Corp.*)

Here we see several issues. Why did the court consider the insurance company (insurer) to also be a client, albeit a secondary one, with the insured (the taxi company) as the primary? Do the lawyer's duties to each differ or are they the same? What are the practical considerations for a lawyer in this situation? This case also introduces you to a concept of a conflict of interest involving a former client of a lawyer. Here, the conflict arose when the law firm that was representing the cab company and the insurance company split into two different firms; one of the new firms was asked to sue its former client, the insurance company; and the insurance company sought to disqualify the firm. What standard was used by the court in making that decision? This question is resolved by Model Rules 1.9 and 1.10 which will both be discussed in depth later.

Nevada Yellow Cab Corp. v. Eighth Jud. Dist. Ct. ex rel. Cnty. of Clark

Supreme Court of Nevada, 2007.
152 P.3d 737.

OPINION

PER CURIAM.

This original petition for a writ of mandamus challenges a district court order disqualifying counsel for petitioner Nevada Yellow Cab Corporation in an insurance bad faith action against Insurance Company of the West (ICW). ICW had previously retained the firm Vannah Costello Canepa Riedy & Rubino (VCCRR) to represent its insureds in tort actions brought by third parties. In one such case, VCCRR was retained by ICW to represent Yellow Cab. VCCRR was subsequently replaced by new counsel, and the case settled in the middle of trial for more than double the policy limits, with Yellow Cab required to contribute a substantial amount toward the settlement.

Petitioner Robert Vannah was a VCCRR partner at the time that VCCRR represented Yellow Cab, although he did not personally work on the case. After ICW terminated VCCRR, the firm dissolved. Vannah and others formed a new firm, and an associate who had performed substantial work on Yellow Cab's representation in the tort action joined Vannah at his new firm.

Yellow Cab subsequently hired Vannah and his new firm, petitioner Vannah Costello Vannah & Ganz (VCVG), to sue ICW for bad faith based on ICW's pretrial rejection of a policy-limits offer. ICW moved to disqualify Vannah and his new firm, and the district court granted its motion.

In concluding that writ relief is not warranted in this case, we expressly adopt the majority rule that counsel retained by an insurer to represent its insured represents both the insurer and the insured in the absence of a conflict. Thus, an attorney-client relationship existed between ICW and the associate who had previously defended Yellow Cab, who was now employed by Vannah's new firm. As the district court did not manifestly abuse its discretion in determining that disqualification was warranted, based upon this former representation, the substantial relationship between the two representations, and the adversity of Yellow Cab's and ICW's positions in the bad faith case, we deny this petition.

FACTS

From 1998 to 2001, the law firm of Vannah Costello Canepa Riedy & Rubino (VCCRR) was one of the Southern Nevada firms retained by real party in interest Insurance Company of the West (ICW), primarily to defend its insureds in civil lawsuits filed by third parties. Almost all of VCCRR's work on these matters was performed by partner Michael Rubino and associate Denise Cooper Osmond. VCCRR also apparently represented ICW in two first-party matters, one an underinsured motorist coverage claim by an insured, handled by Rubino and Osmond, and one an uninsured motorist coverage claim that later generated a bad faith claim, handled only by Rubino. Notably, after the bad faith allegation was made in the latter case, ICW reassigned the case to new counsel.

In 1999, ICW retained VCCRR to defend its insured, Yellow Cab, in a personal injury lawsuit stemming from an accident between one of Yellow Cab's drivers and the plaintiff, Heather Nash. Yellow Cab had an ICW liability policy with limits of $500,000 and a self-insured reserve of $50,000. From January 1999 to November 2002, Rubino and Osmond defended Yellow Cab in the matter and regularly updated ICW on the litigation's status. Apparently, during this time period, the complaint and an answer were filed, the NRCP 16.1 conference was held, and some discovery, including document production and several depositions, occurred.

In November 2002, without Yellow Cab's consent, ICW terminated VCCRR and retained a different law firm to assume Yellow Cab's representation. Shortly before trial, the plaintiff offered to settle for the policy limits; ICW instructed counsel to reject the offer. In March 2003, after the first few days of trial went poorly for Yellow Cab, the case settled for $1.3 million, $800,000 more than Yellow Cab's $500,000 policy limit. Yellow Cab was required to pay $500,000 toward the settlement.

In 2003, VCCRR split into two firms, Vannah Costello Vannah & Ganz (VCVG), and Canepa Riedy & Rubino; Vannah and Osmond stayed with the former firm, and Rubino went with the latter firm. Also, in June 2003, Yellow Cab retained Vannah to file a bad faith action against ICW based on the *Nash* lawsuit, particularly its failure to accept the plaintiff's policy-limits offer shortly before trial and its subsequent settlement for more than double the policy limits after trial commenced. Since the firm split, VCVG represents Yellow Cab on a regular basis in all of its legal matters.

After ICW retained counsel to defend the bad faith action, its counsel notified Vannah of a perceived conflict of interest. ICW's counsel asked Vannah to research the issue and requested that Vannah's firm withdraw. About a month later, ICW's counsel spoke with Vannah, who explained that he did not believe a conflict existed and that he would not withdraw unless ordered to do so.

Shortly thereafter, ICW and Yellow Cab discussed mediation and agreed in principle to the idea. In its correspondence on this matter, ICW reiterated its belief that a conflict existed and specifically stated that its consent to mediation did not waive its right to seek disqualification of Vannah's firm if mediation failed. Deciding on a mediator and scheduling took almost a year, and the mediation was not held until July 2005.

After the mediation failed, ICW filed the underlying motion to disqualify Vannah and VCVG. Yellow Cab, Vannah, and the firm opposed the motion. At the hearing, the district court judge concluded that the "potential conflict" was too great and granted the motion. This writ petition followed. An answer was ordered and has been timely filed, and oral argument was held.

DISCUSSION

In deciding this petition, we first resolve the threshold issue of whether ICW waived any conflict by waiting until two years after the complaint was filed to seek disqualification. We then consider whether the district court appropriately determined that a conflict existed under the applicable ethical rule's three-part analysis: first, whether ICW is a former client; second, if so, whether the former representation of ICW is substantially related to VCVG's current representation of Yellow Cab; and third, whether the two representations are adverse. Finally, we determine whether the district court manifestly abused its discretion in concluding that disqualification was warranted. Because ICW did not waive any conflict and the district court's disqualification decision was well within its discretion, we deny the petition in this case.

. . . .

Existence of a conflict

The issue of whether Vannah and his firm have a conflict of interest in representing Yellow Cab in the bad faith action is primarily resolved by our rules of professional conduct governing conflicts with former clients and imputed disqualification of law firms. At the time of the underlying proceedings, these rules were identified as SCR 159 and 160; following comprehensive amendments to the rules of professional conduct after this petition was filed, they are now Nevada Rules of Professional Conduct 1.9 and 1.10. For ease of reference, and since the former version of the rules apply to this case, we use the older terminology.

Under SCR 159, which governs conflicts based on former representation, a lawyer may be disqualified from representing a client against a former client if the current representation is substantially related to the former representation. Thus, for a potentially disqualifying conflict to exist, the party seeking disqualification must establish three elements: (1) that it had an attorney-client relationship with the lawyer, (2) that the former matter and the current matter are substantially related, and (3) that the current representation is adverse to the party seeking disqualification. Under SCR 160, the disqualification of a lawyer practicing in a firm is generally imputed to other lawyers in the firm.

The parties do not dispute that the third element is satisfied—that Vannah's current representation of Yellow Cab in the bad faith action is adverse to ICW. Thus, the existence of a conflict turns on the first and second elements: whether ICW is a former client and whether the current and former representations are substantially related.

Whether ICW is a former client

With respect to the relationship between an insurer and counsel the insurer retains to defend its insured, the majority rule is that counsel represents both the insurer and the insured in the absence of a conflict. This rule requires that the primary client remains the insured. . . but counsel in this situation has duties to the INSURER as well. While the insured is the primary client, counsel generally learns confidential information from both the insured and the insurer and thus owes both of them a duty to maintain this confidentiality; and, since counsel generally offers legal advice to both the insured and the insurer, counsel owes a duty of care to both. FINALLY, AS MOST States, including Nevada, have a rule that permits joint representation when no actual conflict is present, courts that have adopted a dual-representation principle in insurance defense cases reason that joint representation is permissible as long as any conflict remains speculative.

While we have not directly addressed this issue in our prior opinions, we have implicitly recognized that an attorney-client relationship exists between a medical malpractice insurer and the lawyer it retains to defend its insured doctor. Also, in considering whether the insurer can assert an attorney-client or work product privilege for documents prepared during the representation of an insured, we have presumed that an attorney-client relationship exists between the insurer and counsel it retained for its insured. We now expressly adopt the majority rule concerning the relationship between an insurer and counsel retained by the insurer to defend its insured. In the absence of a conflict, counsel represents both the insured and the insurer. Thus, the first element in this matter's conflict analysis—requiring an attorney-client relationship—is met.

Substantial relationship between former and current matters

Determining whether a conflict exists, then, depends upon whether the second element of the conflict analysis is met, that is, whether Vannah's prior representation of ICW is substantially related to the underlying bad faith case. In *Waid v. District Court*, we recently adopted a three-part test to determine whether two representations are substantially related. A district court presented with a disqualification motion based on a former representation should

> (1) make a factual determination concerning the scope of the former representation, (2) evaluate whether it is reasonable to infer that the confidential information allegedly given would have been given to a lawyer representing a client in those matters, and (3) determine whether that information is relevant to the issues raised in the present litigation.

We noted in *Waid* that a superficial resemblance between the matters is not sufficient; "rather, the focus is properly on the precise relationship between the present and former representation."

Yellow Cab, Vannah and VCVG contend that no substantial relationship exists between the current bad faith action and any prior representation of ICW because the *Nash* settlement was completely handled by another firm, after Vannah's former firm was terminated. The district court disagreed, and we conclude that it did not manifestly abuse its discretion in doing so.

With respect to the *Waid* test's first prong, concerning the scope of the prior representation, the documents before us support a finding that Vannah's former firm was responsible for defending the *Nash* litigation from its inception in January 1999 until November 2002, only four to five months before trial, and that associate Denise Osmond participated extensively in this representation. Considering the second prong, the district court could have reasonably inferred that Osmond obtained confidential information concerning ICW's handling of Nash's claim during this three-year period. Finally, the way that ICW handled Nash's claim against Yellow Cab is the precise subject of the underlying litigation. Thus, the district court did not abuse its discretion in concluding that the two matters are substantially related, that Osmond has a conflict under SCR

159, and that this conflict is imputed under SCR 160 to Vannah and the rest of the firm, VCVG.

Whether disqualification was warranted

We have previously recognized that a district court must undertake a balancing test in determining whether disqualification is warranted in a particular situation and should weigh the prejudices that the parties will suffer based on the district court's decision, consider the public interest in the administration of justice, and discourage the use of such motions for purposes of harassment and delay:

> Courts deciding attorney disqualification motions are faced with the delicate and sometimes difficult task of balancing competing interests: the individual right to be represented by counsel of one's choice, each party's right to be free from the risk of even inadvertent disclosure of confidential information, and the public's interest in the scrupulous administration of justice. While doubts should generally be resolved in favor of disqualification, parties should not be allowed to misuse motions for disqualification as instruments of harassment or delay.

One purpose of disqualification is to prevent disclosure of confidential information that could be used to a former client's disadvantage. Here, ICW perceived a conflict almost immediately after the complaint was filed, but then it waited two years to seek disqualification, thus providing ample opportunity for disclosure of the information it ostensibly sought to protect. ICW's apparent acquiescence in VCVG's representation of Yellow Cab for two years, with no protection for its assertedly confidential information, arguably detracts from its current insistence that this information be held inviolate.

But the district court is more familiar with this case than we are, and it had the best opportunity to evaluate whether disqualification was warranted. We have repeatedly pointed out that a district court's discretion in such matters is broad and that its decision will not be set aside absent a manifest abuse of that discretion. We are not persuaded that the district court manifestly abused its broad discretion in disqualifying Vannah and his firm in this case, and thus, we deny the petition.

CONCLUSION

Having considered the petition, the answer, the documentation submitted by the parties, and the oral argument held in this matter, we are not persuaded that the district court manifestly abused its discretion in disqualifying Vannah and his firm. Accordingly, we deny the petition.

MAUPIN, C.J., concurring.

This is indeed a close case. As noted by the majority, Insurance Company of the West (ICW) waited two years after appreciating the perceived conflict before formally seeking disqualification. One can understand the firm's intransigence in refusing to voluntarily withdraw based upon a good faith belief that it held no confidential information that could compromise ICW's defense in the bad faith litigation. But, because the issue is close, and because the district court could reasonably conclude that ICW's former insurance defense counsel gained some knowledge generally about ICW's internal claims policies, I cannot conclude that the district court manifestly abused its discretion in its ruling of disqualification.

X-Ray Questions

Litigation financing as a business? It is here now! The following opinion letter from California addresses ethical issues arising from its arrival. If your case was big enough, would you consider such financing? Before reading the opinion, ask yourself what ethical dilemmas are presented. Is this development a passing fade or a permanent fixture?

BEYOND THE CITE

THE STATE BAR OF CALIFORNIA STANDING COMMITTEE PROFESSIONAL, RESPONSIBILITY AND CONDUCT FORMAL OPINION NO. 2020–204

The question posed before the Committee was straightforward: what ethical obligations arise when a lawyer represents a client whose case is being [sponsored] by a third- party litigation funder? Here are the key points:

- Some states have outright bans on this practice, referred to by terms originating in Medieval England: "champerty and maintenance." They were developed to prevent feudal lords from financing other individuals' legal claims against the financier's political or personal enemies. While some states enact bans on the practice, others—such as California permit the practice—provided that a lawyer adheres to the rules of professional responsibility when they arise in the ACR. But the bans are not slowing the industry growth. The American Lawyer is entitled "Big Law's Share of the Litigation Funding Pie Skyrocketed in 2021" by Dan Packle (March 2022) describes the rise of this practice, noting that litigation funders initiated 426 new funding arrangements in 2021 as compared to 312 in 2020. One source estimates it as a $17 billion dollar industry with 52% of that money being spent in the United States. Insurance Journal, December 13, 2021. But the practice is not only for large pieces of litigation notes The National Law Review, "What Every Lawyer Should Know About Litigation Funding" by Paul M. Coppola September 11, 2022, but also for, say, a typical automobile accident because liability, damages and insurance coverage are either known or capable of a reasoned estimate. Against this rising tide, the California Bar issued its guidance.

- The ethical duties for lawyers arise on several fronts according to the California Bar.

➢ Competence (MR 1.1) and Communication (MR 1.4)

The Opinion is clear: "To the extent the client's ability to accomplish its objectives depends on the client's ability to fund the litigation or fund the client's personal expenses while proceeding with the litigation, the lawyer's representation of the client may involve advising the client as to whether litigation funding would assist in accomplishing the client's goals." Moreover, the lawyer, in giving advice in this area, must do so competently either acquiring the knowledge to advise or by retaining a person to advise that the lawyer has vetted and can vouch for. This foreshadows our discussion of competence in Chapter 4.

- The importance of exercising independent judgment on behalf of the client cannot be stressed too much. There is a temptation to give the one who pays you what they want in terms of means or result or appear to do so. The client must therefore be told of the temptation and must give their informed consent to the use of a funder after an explanation by the lawyer of the P.A.C. (Pros, Alternatives, Cons) and this explanation, consist with MR 2.1: Advisor, must be candid, direct, unvarnished, and not vague, wishy-washy and euphemistic.

> • Finally, the opinion sets out that a lawyer's duties are not dictated by the terms of the funding agreement, and makes an insightful comparison—especially for our purposes—to the insurance contract between the insurance company and the insured when the company retains the lawyer; namely, that the insured is the primary/principal client and if there are any limitations on the lawyer in the insurance contract, the lawyer must advise he client early on and always follow the client's directives (say as to how much to settle for), not that of the insurance company.

X-Ray Questions

The following is a common occurrence for those who practice criminal law. A father and a mother pay a lawyer to defend their child. Who is the client in this situation and why? What are the conditions upon which such an arrangement is permissible? As a threshold matter, why are any conditions necessary? Pay special attention to the principal that a lawyer owes a duty of undivided loyalty to the client; that the lawyer must always exercise independent judgment on the client's behalf; and that the lawyer must "abide" by the client's decisions on the goals of representation, not those of another.

BEYOND THE CITE

NEW YORK STATE BAR ASSOCIATION COMMITTEE ON PROFESSIONAL ETHICS FORMAL OPINION 1063 (6/29/15)

The inquirer agreed to represent an 18-year-old client ("Son") in a criminal defense matter. When the inquirer initially met Son at the Town Court, the Son's divorced parents ("Mother" and "Father") were present. Although only Son signed a retainer agreement, each of the client's parents paid one-half of the retainer. The inquirer continues to represent Son.

Recently, inquirer agreed to represent Mother in two matters against Father. One is a custody dispute against Father (not involving Son). The other is a support matter against Father in which Son is among the subjects of the support sought. Opposing counsel has protested that, having taken money from Father, it is a conflict of interest for inquirer to represent Mother adverse to Father.

OPINION

[. . . .]

It is well-established that when a lawyer accepts payment from a third party to represent a client, the third-party payor is not a client merely by virtue of paying the lawyer's fee. See N.Y. State 716 (1999) (when an insurance company retains a lawyer to represent a policyholder, the client is the policyholder, not the insurance company). See generally American Law Institute, Restatement Third, The Law Governing Lawyers, § 14, cmt. c (2000) (paying a lawyer does not by itself create a client-lawyer relationship with the payor if the circumstances indicate that the lawyer was to represent someone else).

[. . . .]

A lawyer who accepts payment from third parties may therefore wish to inform such persons that the lawyer does not represent them and has no duties to them. The lawyer should also avoid giving legal advice to the third-party payor, and should make clear that the lawyer will not share confidential information with the third-party payor absent informed consent from the client See Rule 1.8(f)(3) (lawyer shall not accept fees from third party unless "the client's confidential information is protected as required by Rule 1.6").

Rule 1.8(f) recognizes that, when the lawyer accepts payment of his or her fee from a third party, the interest in being paid might affect the lawyer's independent professional judgment on behalf of the client. Consequently, it prohibits the lawyer from accepting such compensation unless:

1. the client gives informed consent;

2. there is no interference with the lawyer's independent professional judgment or with the client-lawyer relationship; and

3. the client's confidential information is protected as required by Rule 1.6.

If these three conditions are fulfilled, the Rules permit the third party payment. See N.Y. State 1000 (2014), in which compliance with Rule 1.8(f) operates to permit payment even by one whose interests are adverse or potentially adverse to those of the client. (Indeed, Opinion 1000 points out that, where legal fees are paid by an indemnitor such as an insurance company, the interests of the indemnitor are often contrary to those of the client.)

Model Rule 1.13: The Entity v. The Individual as a Client

(a)   A lawyer employed or retained by an organization represents the organization acting through its duly authorized constituents.

. . . .

(f)   In dealing with an organization's directors, officers, employees, members, shareholders or other constituents, a lawyer shall explain the identity of the client when the lawyer knows or reasonably should know that the organization's interests are adverse to those of the constituents with whom the lawyer is dealing.

(g)   A lawyer representing an organization may also represent any of its directors, officers, employees, members, shareholders or other constituents, subject to the provisions of Rule 1.7. If the organization's consent to the dual representation is required by Rule 1.7, the consent shall be given by an appropriate official of the organization other than the individual who is to be represented, or by the shareholders.

Deconstruction Exercise/Rule Rationale

Model Rule 1.13 guides the duties of a lawyer who is retained or employed by an organization or corporation. A company can only act though, as you learned in Business Associations, through its employees, often called constituents. Who is the client? Is it the CEO, officers, or employees? Or is it the organization? We will see this quandary play out into a disaster in *Baldwin*.

The lawyer must therefore clarify the lawyer's role when dealing with the organization's directors, officers, employees, if the lawyer reasonably knows that the organization's interest is adverse to these constituents. The lawyer must explain the identity of the client and that the lawyer is representing the organization and not those individuals.

The lawyer should therefore consider implementing the following:

➤   Advise the constituents that you are the organization's lawyer, not their lawyer

➤   Remind the constituents that there is a potential conflict of interest and that you cannot represent them, especially if it is their conduct that is being challenged

> ➤ Advise constituents to obtain independent representation

> ➤ Refrain from providing legal representation for that individual, which as you have learned includes asking and answering questions to avoid the formation of an ACR with the constituent

> ➤ Tell them that the attorney-client privilege is inapplicable to any discussion with them in their individual capacity for their individual conduct as opposed to their conduct as constituents.

It is therefore good lawyering to advise those employees that the organization is the client, remind them that they are not the client, and anything they say adverse to the organization will not be protected. Now, a lawyer may represent both the organization and the employee or constituent if there is no possible conflict of interest, either actual or perceived. In these circumstances it is mandatory that a Joint Representation Agreement be reviewed with both the entity and the individual and that true informed consent—the PAC: Pros, Alternatives and Cons—is provided to each lawyer's client.

X-Ray Questions

The following is a sample Joint Representation Agreement. It deals with a lawyer who seeks to represent both an entity as well as individuals employed by an entity. Why does it state that both the individual and the entity acknowledge that their interests are aligned? If this is not true, then why would a lawyer be unable to represent both concurrently? Can a lawyer simply assume that the acknowledgment is sufficient to allow joint representation, or should a lawyer make an independent assessment of the accuracy of these representations? Why or why not? Would it be wise for a lawyer to simply give the agreement to each prospective client and ask each of them to read the agreement and to sign if neither has any questions? Why or why not? What do you think should be required in explaining the agreement? Any provisions surprise you? Do you not see the need for some of them?

BEYOND THE CITE

JOINT REPRESENTATION AGREEMENT

COMPANY and EMPLOYEE (collectively: "Defendants") have been named as Defendants in a lawsuit styles Plaintiff v. COMPANY and EMPLOYEE, as a case No. _____ in the Court of _____; and

WHEREAS COMPANY and EMPLOYEE each desire to retain ATTORNEY to act as counsel for each of them with regard to the defense of this Lawsuit;

Editor's Note: This section helps the clients understand who the lawyer is representing in this case: to wit: Paragraphs 1 through 6 set out the foundation for the joint representation; namely, that the manager is innocent of the allegations and has so represented to the corporation. But the key is that while facts do not change, they sometimes come to light and those facts or allegations may lead to a misalignment between the interests of the company and the individual. And as with any agreement there needs to be a contingency in place for what occurs if this misalignment comes to pass. These paragraphs explain what will occur if so. It is essential that the lawyer is transparent to both manager and company because each, upon the signing the agreement, becomes a client.

NOW THEREFORE, it is mutually agreed as follows:

1. Based upon all facts presently known to the Defendants, including information supplied by EMPLOYEE, Defendants believe that Plaintiffs claims are unmeritorious. Neither COMPANY nor EMPLOYEE perceives or is aware of any present existing or potential conflict between them with respect to the defense of this Lawsuit; and both COMPANY and EMPLOYEE specifically waive any actual or potential conflict that may exist, and consent to joint representation of both Defendants by ATTORNEY.

2. EMPLOYEE acknowledges that he may now or in the future retain separate counsel if he desires to do so.

3. COMPANY and EMPLOYEE agree to advise ATTORNEY and each other immediately at any time any actual or perceived conflict between them arises.

4. If ATTORNEY, COMPANY, or EMPLOYEE perceives any actual or potential conflict in the future, EMPLOYEE agrees that ATTORNEY will withdraw with respect to representing EMPLOYEE. EMPLOYEE consents to ATTORNEY continuing to represent COMPANY following the termination of representation of EMPLOYEE, because of perceive conflict of interest or otherwise.

5. COMPANY and EMPLOYEE agree that the interests of EMPLOYEE appear to be identical with the interest of the COMPANY. ATTORNEY will not assert in behalf of

EMPLOYEE any position that ATTORNEY believes is inconsistent or in conflict with the representation of COMPANY. EMPLOYEE acknowledges that, if he wishes to assert in his own behalf any position that is inconsistent or in conflict with a position asserted in behalf of COMPANY, he must retain separate counsel. EMPLOYEE agrees that, if COMPANY asserts any position in its own behalf that is inconsistent or in conflict with a position asserted in behalf of EMPLOYEE, ATTORNEY may withdraw from representing EMPLOYEE and continue to represent COMPANY.

6.   The interest of EMPLOYEE appearing at the time of the execution of this Agreement to be identical with the interest of COMPANY, COMPANY will undertake to pay attorney's fees incurred in the representation of EMPLOYEE by ATTORNEY. In the event that EMPLOYEE becomes represented by attorneys other than ATTORNEY, EMPLOYEE shall be responsible for payment of attorney's fees for such separate counsel, absent any specific agreement otherwise by COMPANY.

Editor's Note: The Employee and Company's interests must be consistent, but sometimes, as it turns out, now each party has their own interest in the matter and the parties understand that they can retain their own separate counsel. The attorney also withdraws from representation for the Employee and may continue to represent the Company. Paragraph 7 is an example of transparency and contemplates a possible future event but does not now preclude the joint representation.

7.   COMPANY and EMPLOYEE acknowledges that, under some circumstances, COMPANY as Principal may have a duty to indemnify EMPLOYEE as Agent for liability for actions taken within the scope of employment; and under some circumstances, EMPLOYEE may have a duty to indemnify COMPANY for liability for certain actions beyond the scope of employment. At the time of execution of this Agreement, COMPANY is not aware of any facts suggesting that EMPLOYEE's actions were beyond the scope of employment COMPANY and EMPLOYEE each acknowledge that each will determine whether insurance or indemnification coverage may exist for either of them, with respect to any claim made in the Lawsuit or with respect to the cost of defense; and if any such coverage exists, COMPANY and

EMPLOYEE agree promptly to advise ATTORNEY and each other.

Editor's Note: Paragraph 8 is key. Why? Recall that Lawyer has two clients and must be candid with both. By way of example, what if Manager tells the Lawyer right before Manager's deposition that he is guilty of the allegations and demands that Lawyer not tell his employer (the Lawyer's other client). Imagine the ethical pickle that results without paragraph 8.

8. COMPANY and EMPLOYEE each agree that attorney-client communications with regard to any Defendant may be disclose in the course of representation to and among all other Co-Defendants represented by ATTORNEY, during or after representation; and COMPANY and EMPLOYEE further agree not to disclose any such attorney-client communications except as provided in this paragraph, and to maintain the privilege of attorney-client communications.

9. EMPLOYEE acknowledges that he has been advised, prior to executing this Agreement, that he has the option of retaining separate counsel, that he has freely chosen to execut3ed this Agreement without any encouragement or solicitation, and that no other representation have been made to him regarding the retention of ATTORNEY other than those set out in this Agreement.

Model Rule 1.7: Conflict of Interest: Current Clients

(a) Except as provided in paragraph (b), a lawyer shall not represent a client if the representation involves a concurrent conflict of interest. A concurrent conflict of interest exists if:

(1) the representation of one client will be directly adverse to another client; or

(2) there is a significant risk that the representation of one or more clients will be materially limited by the lawyer's responsibilities to another client, a former client or a third person or by a personal interest of the lawyer.

(b) Notwithstanding the existence of a concurrent conflict of interest under paragraph (a), a lawyer may represent a client if:

(1)   the lawyer reasonably believes that the lawyer will be able to provide competent and diligent representation to each affected client;

(2)   the representation is not prohibited by law;

(3)   the representation does not involve the assertion of a claim by one client against another client represented by the lawyer in the same litigation or other proceeding before a tribunal; and

(4)   each affected client gives informed consent, confirmed in writing.

Let's Chart It!

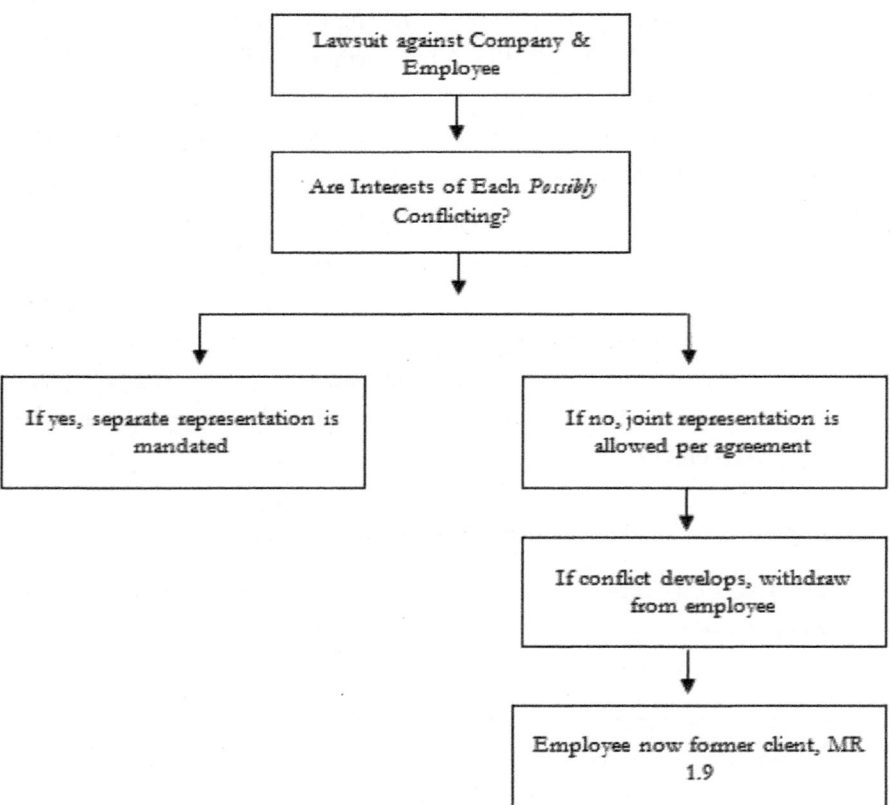

Deconstruction Exercise/Rule Rationale

This rule deals with concurrent representation; that is, the lawyer is representing not one client, but two, at the same time and in the same matter. The representation is thus concurrent. Such representation is forbidden if the two clients are or can be directly adverse to one another. (Note that a conflict can exist even if there is only a possibility that the client has different goals and objective that could result in an actual on going conflict). This situation arises, by way of example, when one client seeks to cast blame for the event in question on the other client and therefore shift liability and/or responsibility for damages. Thus, their interests are "directly" adverse to one another. Litigation is a zero-sum game and the less that Client A must pay in damages, the happier Client A is and, similarly, the less co-client B must pay, the happier that Co-client B is. For one to win, the other must lose. It is impossible to represent both. Note that in (b) the language of a "significant" risk that a lawyer's duty of undivided loyalty would likely be impaired by representing "one" or more clients than the lawyer cannot undertake the representation. The key modifying word is "significant" which is not defined in the Rules but whose dictionary definition is "sufficiently great or important to be worthy of attention." Finally, the ultimate purpose of the Rule is to ensure that a lawyer gives undivided loyalty to the client. But for this to occur the identity of the client must be pellucid. The following case highlights what occurs when the lawyer is confused about the identity of her client and thus unsure where her loyalties should reside.

Cases and Materials

X-Ray Questions (*Baldwin*)

This case is the result of the Penn State football scandal. A former coach, Jerry Sandusky was accused of child molestation at the Penn State football facility and elsewhere. A criminal complaint was made, and Sandusky was indicted and convicted. But Penn State itself came under criminal investigation as well. Did university officials know or suspect that Sandusky was engaged in harmful conduct? Did they take an ostrich-like attitude of self-delusion about the crimes? Could they have done more to prevent or uncover the criminality? A former grand jury was investigating, therefore, possible criminality of not only Penn State but also of its leaders. In this situation, it was critical for an attorney to know the identity of her client. But General Counsel for Penn State, a former Pennsylvania Supreme Court Justice, did not see it that way. She failed to appreciate that the executives could be facing jail time as *individuals*, in addition to the university being liable through this segment of the case (we will return to the rest of the opinion later in the book when discussing her lack of competence), ask yourself why she acted the way that she did and made the decisions that she did. If she had read MR 1.7 do you think she would have understood the perilous predicament that she and the executives were facing? Better yet, why did no one in her office of lawyers tell her that separate counsel for the school and its executives was the only course of action given the inherent and irreconciled conflicts? Do you understand why a Joint Representation Agreement would not work in this scenario?

Office of Disciplinary Counsel v. Cynthia A. Baldwin

Supreme Court of Pennsylvania, 2020.
225 A.3d 817.

JUSTICE DONOHUE.

In this matter, we consider the request of the Petitioner, the Office of Disciplinary Counsel ("ODC"), to impose discipline in the form of a public censure on Respondent, Cynthia A. Baldwin ("Respondent"), in connection with her representation of Pennsylvania State University ("Penn State") and three of its administrators during grand jury proceedings investigating matters relating to child abuse accusations against Gerald A. Sandusky ("Sandusky"), a former assistant football coach at Penn State. On November 21, 2017, the ODC filed a Petition for Discipline against the Respondent, charging her with violations of Rules 1.1, 1.6(a), 1.7(a) and 8.4(d) of the Pennsylvania Rules of Professional Conduct relating to her joint representation of Timothy Curley ("Curley"), Penn State's Athletic Director, Gary Schultz ("Schultz"), Penn State's former Senior Vice-President for Finance and Business, and Graham Spanier ("Spanier"), Penn State's president (collectively "Individual Clients") as well as Penn State (collectively with Individual Clients, the "Clients"). In its findings and recommendations, the Disciplinary Board of the Supreme Court of Pennsylvania ("Disciplinary Board") concluded that Respondent "failed to protect her clients' right to competent counsel and entitlement to unfettered loyalty, which serious misconduct contributed to criminal charges against her clients, and ultimately caused certain charges to be quashed, thereby prejudicing the administration of justice." Disciplinary Board's Report and Recommendations, 3/18/2019, at 48 (hereinafter, the "Disciplinary Board Report"). The Disciplinary Board recommended discipline in the form of a public censure by this Court. We impose discipline in the form of a public reprimand.

II. Factual and Procedural History

A. Grand Jury Presentment

The facts underlying the ODC's Petition for Discipline against the Respondent are ultimately intertwined with Presentment No. 29, issued by the

Thirty-Third Statewide Investigating Grand Jury on October 26, 2012 (hereinafter, the "Grand Jury Presentment"). We provide this summary of facts to provide context for our discussion and analysis of these disciplinary proceedings.

In 2009, the Office of Attorney General ("OAG") presented allegations of Sandusky's repeated sexual abuse of children to a statewide investigating grand jury. Of relevance here, the ensuing investigation uncovered two instances of abuse that took place on the Penn State campus, one in 1998 and a second in 2001.

The 1998 incident involved an eleven-year-old boy. Grand Jury Presentment at 6. Sandusky took the victim to the East Area Locker Room on Penn State's campus, where they wrestled and then used exercise machines. *Id.* Sandusky then insisted that they shower together. *Id.* Sandusky put his arms around the victim and squeezed him, making the boy very uncomfortable. *Id.* When Sandusky took the victim home, his mother asked why his hair was wet and became concerned upon learning of the joint shower. *Id.* The next morning, she filed a report with the University Police Department. *Id.* Centre County Children and Youth Services were also notified, but it referred the case to the Pennsylvania Department of Public Welfare, citing a conflict of interest due to its involvement with the Second Mile Foundation, a charity established by Sandusky in the 1970's that focused on assisting boys between the ages of eight and eighteen. *Id.* at 7.

Tom Harmon was the Chief of Police of the University Police Department in 1998. As his department's investigation proceeded, Chief Harmon kept Schultz, who oversaw the University Police Department as part of his administrative position at Penn State, updated on its progress. *Id.* at 8. Schultz, in turn, kept Curley and Spanier apprised of the investigation's progress, primarily through email messages. *Id.* at 9. On June 9, 1998, Schultz sent Curley an email, on which Spanier was copied, informing him that the Centre County District Attorney had decided not to pursue criminal charges against Sandusky. *Id* at 10. The police report of the investigation was not filed in the usual location. Instead, it was assigned an administrative number, which made it difficult, if not impossible, to access the report without that number. *Id.* at 11.

The Grand Jury Presentment also reported that in 2001, Michael McQueary, then a graduate assistant for the football team, witnessed Sandusky with a young boy in a locker room shower on the University's main campus. *Id.* at 12. McQueary reported this incident to head football coach Joseph V. Paterno, *id.* at 13, who testified to the grand jury that McQueary described

Sandusky as fondling or doing something of a sexual nature to a young boy in the shower. *Id.* Paterno further testified that in turn he relayed this information to Schultz and Curley. *Id.* at 14. Seven to ten days later, Schultz and Curley met with McQueary. *Id.* at 16. McQueary told the grand jury that he described to Schultz and Curley the sexual nature of what he had witnessed. *Id.*

Schultz then decided upon a plan that involved three parts. First, Curley would meet with Sandusky, tell him that they were aware of the 1998 incident, advise him to seek professional help, and prohibit him from ever again bringing boys into campus facilities. *Id.* at 15–16. Second, the chair of Second Mile would be notified. *Id.* And third, the matter would again be reported to the Pennsylvania Department of Public Welfare for investigation, as had been done in 1998. *Id.* Curley responded that he would prefer not to report the matter to the public welfare department so long as Sandusky was cooperative with their efforts. *Id.* at 16–17. Spanier was advised of the modified approach and agreed with the decision not to report the matter to an outside agency. *Id.* at 17–18. Curley then executed the revised two-part plan, conducting separate meetings with Sandusky and a Second Mile representative. *Id.* at 18–19.

B.   Grand Jury Subpoenas to the Clients

On December 28, 2010, Respondent received a telephone call from the OAG regarding a grand jury investigation of multiple claims of child abuse against Sandusky. N.T. 5/23/18, at 366. The OAG asked Respondent to accept service of four subpoenas (which she later did), one for documents directed to Penn State and three for testimony from Curley, Schultz, and Paterno. *Id.* at 367. The subpoena duces tecum was directed to Penn State and requested "any and all records pertaining to Jerry Sandusky and incidents reported to have occurred on or about March 2002, and any other information concerning Jerry Sandusky and inappropriate contact with underage males both on and off University property. Response shall include any and all correspondence directed to or regarding Jerry Sandusky." Subpoena No. 1179, Attachment. The subpoenas to Curley, Schultz and Paterno were directed to them personally, without reference to Penn State or their employment titles. Subpoena No. 1176 (Curley); Subpoena No. 1178 (Schultz); Subpoena No. 1177 (Paterno). These three subpoenas indicated that the witnesses were to appear to testify before the grand jury on January 12, 2011, just nine days later. *Id.* Curley and Schultz were not served with a subpoena duces tecum.

Respondent first met with Curley in connection with his grand jury testimony in Spanier's office. N.T. 5/23/18, at 371. Respondent later testified that:

> I explained to them [Curley and Spanier] about the grand jury, how it was, that it wasn't like a regular courtroom, how many people were on, that there would be thirty-some people on it, and what they were doing, that it was an investigating grand jury because they really didn't know what a grand jury was, and I—I did explain that [Curley] could have a personal attorney to go with him to the grand jury, and that, you know, he shouldn't be nervous, just tell the truth, that's what all of this is about. . ."

Id. at 371. Respondent further testified that Spanier, in Curley's presence, instructed Respondent to go with Curley to the grand jury; that she told them she was general counsel and could not be Curley's personal attorney; that nothing Curley said would be confidential; and that Curley could retain a personal attorney. According to Respondent, Curley said that he did not know any lawyers. *Id.* at 372.

Respondent and Curley then met privately in Respondent's office. Respondent later indicated that they discussed what she had explained to him at the meeting in Spanier's office and reviewed his recollection of events involving Sandusky. *Id.* at 373–74. With respect to the 2001 incident, Respondent said that "basically he told me yes, he knew about this incident, and it had been described as horseplay." *Id.* Respondent's sole private conversation with Schultz before his grand jury testimony followed, and by Respondent's account, Schultz's recollections were in line with Curley's. *Id.* at 375. Respondent indicated that "[Schultz] told me the same thing that [Curley] told me, that it had been described as horseplay." *Id.* Respondent testified that neither Curley nor Schultz told her that a sex act had taken place between Sandusky and the boy in the shower, *id.* at 376, but the record does not reflect whether or not she specifically asked either of them whether one had occurred. During these meetings with Curley and Schultz, there was no discussion regarding the 1998 incident, as Respondent had no knowledge at that time that any such event had taken place. Both Curley and Schultz denied having any documents relating to Sandusky's activities. *Id.* at 377.

Based on these meetings, Respondent determined that their stories were consistent, as they "told me the same thing." *Id.* at 375. She further decided that the interests of Curley and Schultz were consistent with Penn State's interests.

Accordingly, she made the judgment that she could represent them both before the investigating grand jury during their questioning. *Id.* at 378.

On the morning of January 12, 2011, Respondent accompanied Curley and Schultz to interviews with an OAG representative. Report and Recommendations of the Hearing Committee Report ("Hearing Committee Report"), Exhibit D (interview notes). Later that day, she then accompanied each of them to their appearances before the investigating grand jury. In his grand jury testimony, Curley testified that in 2001, Paterno contacted him (and Schultz) and requested an immediate meeting regarding an incident reported to him by McQueary. N.T. (grand jury), 1/12/2011 (Curley testifying), at 4–5. Paterno informed them that McQueary had seen Sandusky in the shower with a child and was "uncomfortable" with what he had observed. *Id.* at 5. According to Curley, when he and Schultz later met with McQueary, McQueary told them that Sandusky and the boy "were horsing around, that they were playful, and that it just did not feel appropriate." *Id.* at 7. Curley insisted that neither McQueary nor Paterno told them, in any form, that there was any sexual conduct involved, including anal intercourse. *Id.* Curley testified that he did not inform campus police of the incident because he did not think that what had been reported was a crime. *Id.* at 12.

Curley testified that he promptly advised Spanier regarding the incident. *Id.* at 8. He stated that he reported the incident to the executive director of the Second Mile Foundation and instructed Sandusky to refrain from bringing young people into the athletic facilities at Penn State. *Id.* at 10–11. Curley acknowledged that there was no follow up investigation into the 2001 report by McQueary. *Id.* at 13. He denied having any knowledge of the 1998 incident involving Sandusky. *Id.* at 13–14.

Also accompanied by Respondent, Schultz testified before the grand jury that he attended a meeting with Paterno and Curley regarding the 2001 incident. Schultz indicated that Paterno had been informed by a graduate student of disturbing and inappropriate behavior by Sandusky in the shower. N.T. (grand jury), 1/12/2011 (Schultz testifying), at 5. Schultz also stated that he and Curley met with McQueary. *Id.* at 9–10. Unlike Curley, Schultz maintained that after talking to both Paterno and McQueary, he was of the view that what had occurred was sexual in nature. He told the grand jury:

> Q.   Did you, nevertheless, form an impression about what type of conduct this might have been that occurred in the locker room?

A.   Well, I had the impression that it was inappropriate. Telling you what kind of thing I had in my mind without being clear, without him telling me, but, you know. I had the feeling that there was perhaps some kind of wrestling around activity and maybe [Sandusky] might have grabbed the young boy's genitals or something of that sort is kind of the impression that I had.

Q.   Would you consider that to be inappropriate sexual conduct?

A.   Oh, absolutely. Well, I don't know the definition of sexual, but that's certainly inappropriate for somebody to do.

Q.   We can all agree that an adult male under no circumstances other than a doctor should be grabbing the genitals of a young boy?

A.   I agree completely with that.

Id. at 22–23.

Schultz testified that between himself, Curley and Spanier, it was agreed that Sandusky would be instructed to never again bring children into the football building. *Id.* at 11. Unlike Curley, Schultz further testified that it was his recollection that the three administrators agreed to request the same child protection agency that had investigated the 1998 incident be contacted regarding the 2001 events. *Id.*

The grand jury did not question Curley as to whether he was in possession of any documents relating to Sandusky. When asked if he had any such documents, Schultz responded as follows:

Q.   Do you believe that you may be in possession of any notes regarding the 2002 incident that you may have written memorializing what occurred?

A.   I have none of those in my possession. I believe that there were probably notes taken at the time. Given my retirement in 2009, if I even had them at that time, something that old would have probably been destroyed. I had quite a number of files that I considered confidential matters that go back years that didn't any longer seem pertinent. I wouldn't be surprised. In fact, I would guess if there were any notes, they were destroyed on or before 2009.

Id. at 16.

Schultz did not deny knowledge of the 1998 incident involving Sandusky, though he could not recall the specifics of what had occurred. He indicated that the matter was turned over to a Commonwealth-affiliated (rather than a local) child protection agency for investigation and that no charges were ever filed. *Id.* at 11. He testified that he kept Spanier advised as matters proceeded in 1998, as "it would have been a routine way of handling things, that I would have kept him informed [regarding the 1998 and 2001 incidents]." *Id.* at 17–18.

On March 22, 2011, OAG investigators interviewed Spanier, who was accompanied by Respondent. N.T. 5/23/18, at 386–87. On March 24, 2011, a subpoena was issued to Spanier for testimony before the grand jury on April 13, 2011. Subpoena No. 92 (Spanier). Respondent interviewed Spanier, found his testimony to be consistent with that of Curley and Schultz (even though their testimony was inconsistent with each others), and thus determined that she could accompany Spanier during his grand jury testimony. N.T., 5/23/18, at 387–88. Before the grand jury with respect to the 2001 incident, Spanier recalled that on one occasion Curley and Schultz sought his advice regarding a matter involving Sandusky "with a younger child . . . horsing around in the shower." N.T. (grand jury), 4/13/2011 (Spanier testifying), at 14. Spanier denied that Curley or Schultz told him that the horseplay could have been sexual in nature. *Id.* at 25–26. He indicated that he instructed them to inform Sandusky that he should not bring children under eighteen years of age into the locker room facilities and to contact the board chair of the Second Mile Foundation. *Id.* at 16–17. Spanier denied any knowledge of the 1998 incident. *Id.* at 34–35 ("I'm not aware of allegations against Mr. Sandusky in 1998. . . .").

On November 7, 2011, the Commonwealth charged Curley and Schultz with one count each of perjury and failure to report suspected child abuse. Hearing Committee Report, Exhibits Q, S. Respondent advised Curley and Schultz to retain private counsel and, at their request, made arrangements for them to do so. N.T., 5/23/2018, at 395. She also advised Spanier to hire private counsel. *Id.* at 396. Newly retained personal counsel for Curley and Schultz notified Respondent by letter that their clients each considered her to have been his personal attorney before the investigating grand jury and that they did not waive any claim of attorney-client privilege. *Id.*, Exhibits K(f), K(g), M. By letter dated June 22, 2012, Respondent, through counsel, denied the invocations of the attorney-client privilege by Curley and Schultz, insisting that as counsel for Penn State, she had acted solely in a corporate capacity with them before the grand jury and not in any individual capacity. *Id.*, Exhibit K(h).

In a letter dated December 19, 2011, counsel for the OAG advised Respondent that Penn State's continuing failure to provide documents in response to the subpoena duces tecum was concerning, and implicitly threatened the university with contempt of court "and any other appropriate measures applicable to obstruction against the institution and those individuals responsible for these decisions." N.T., 5/23/2018, at 402. Respondent was subsequently served with a subpoena to testify before the grand jury on October 26, 2012. Subpoena No. 883 (Baldwin). Four days prior to Respondent's grand jury testimony, the supervising judge of the grand jury held a conference to discuss privilege issues raised by private counsel for Schultz and Curley. Hearing Committee, Exhibit M. To resolve any conflicts, counsel for the OAG, Frank Fina ("Fina"), agreed not to ask Respondent any questions that implicated confidential communications. *Id.* at 11–12. Meanwhile, counsel for Penn State agreed to waive any attorney-client privileges, except to the extent that such privileges existed between Respondent and Curley and/or Schultz. Hearing Committee Report, Exhibits K(e), K(h).

During her grand jury testimony, Respondent stressed that she had made every effort to comply with the subpoena duces tecum, but that the three administrators had lied to her about the existence of multiple documents that reflected their detailed knowledge and participation in the 1998 and 2001 incidents.

> Q. Did they [Schultz, Curley, and Spanier] ever in any way, shape, or form disclose to you when you were asking them for this material anything about 1998 or 2001 and the existence of e-mails from those events?
>
> A. Never.
>
> Q. We also know that Mr. Schultz had a file regarding Jerry Sandusky in his office; and that in that file were documents related to his retirement agreement.
>
> There were drafts and other documents related to his employment and his retirement and then there were handwritten notes and e-mails pertaining to the 1998 crimes of Mr. Sandusky and the 2001 crimes of Mr. Sandusky.
>
> Again, same question, did he ever reveal to you the existence of that Sandusky file or any of its contents?
>
> A. Never. He told me he didn't have anything.

N.T. (grand jury), 10/26/2012 (Respondent testifying), at 20. In other portions of her testimony, Respondent, in response to questions posed by counsel for the OAG, revealed the contents of numerous communications between herself and Curley, Schultz and Spanier. *See, e.g., id.* at 22.

On November 1, 2012, four days after Respondent testified before the investigating grand jury, several new charges were filed against Curley and Schultz, including endangering the welfare of children, obstruction of justice and conspiracy to commit obstruction of justice. Hearing Committee Report, Exhibits P, Q, R, S, T. On the same date, charges were filed against Spanier, including perjury, failure to report suspected child abuse, obstruction of justice, endangering the welfare of children and conspiracy to commit obstruction of justice. *Id.,* Exhibit U.

In 2014, Curley, Schultz and Spanier filed motions to preclude Respondent from testifying in the criminal trials in Dauphin County. Hearing Committee Report, Exhibit W. The trial court denied the motions, but the Superior Court reversed and quashed all of the perjury, obstruction of justice and related conspiracy charges. *Curley,* 131 A.3d at 1007; *Schultz,* 133 A.3d at 328; *Spanier,* 132 A.3d at 498. The Superior Court concluded that Respondent, during her grand jury testimony, had breached the attorney-client privilege. *Curley,* 131 A.3d at 1007; *Schultz,* 133 A.3d at 326; *Spanier,* 132 A.3d at 498. In its ruling, the Superior Court barred Respondent from testifying against Curley, Schultz or Spanier. *Curley,* 131 A.3d at 1007; *Schultz,* 133 A.3d at 328; *Spanier,* 132 A.3d at 498. The OAG did not appeal these rulings, but rather entered into plea bargains with Curley and Schultz, pursuant to which each pleaded guilty to one count of endangering the welfare of children. Spanier's case proceeded to trial, which resulted in a guilty verdict on one count of endangering the welfare of children. Curley and Schultz both testified for the Commonwealth.

C. Disciplinary Proceedings

On November 24, 2014, the ODC initiated disciplinary proceedings by filing a Petition for Discipline against Respondent, charging her with violations of Rules 1.1, 1.6(a), 1.7(a) and 8.4(d) of our Rules of Professional Conduct. The Hearing Committee conducted an evidentiary hearing and produced a thorough report that reviewed the evidence and made findings of fact and recommendations. The Hearing Committee determined that Respondent represented Curley, Schultz and Spanier in a personal capacity during their grand jury testimony. Hearing Committee Report at 39–42. The Hearing Committee, however, determined that Respondent did not violate Rule 1.7(a), as she had conducted a reasonable investigation into the interests of Penn State and the Individual Clients with respect to the grand jury investigation and had, based upon that investigation, reasonably concluded that the interests of Penn State and the individuals were consistent. *Id.* at 42–44. The Hearing Committee further concluded that Respondent did not violate Rule 1.1, as she had provided competent representation of Curley, Schultz and Spanier. *Id.* at 44–45. Further, Respondent did not violate RPC 1.6(a), as her testimony before the grand jury fell within exceptions to that rule and did not improperly reveal protected information about her representation of the individuals. *Id.* at 44–64. Because Respondent had not engaged in misconduct, the Hearing Committee determined that her actions were not prejudicial to the administration of justice, and therefore Respondent had not violated Rule 8.4(d). *Id.* at 65.

Both parties filed exceptions to the Hearing Committee's report. Respondent took issue with the Hearing Committee's determination that she represented Curley, Schultz and Spanier in their individual capacities, while the ODC filed exceptions to its rulings related to violations of Rules 1.1, 1.6(a), 1.7(a) and 8.4(d). On March 18, 2019, the Disciplinary Board issued a report reversing the determinations of the Hearing Committee. The Disciplinary Board agreed with the Hearing Committee that Respondent had represented the three administrators in their personal capacities before the grand jury but concluded that she failed to recognize the multiple conflicts of interest between her clients. Disciplinary Board Report at 28–30, 33–37. The Board further determined that Respondent did not exercise the legal knowledge, skill, thoroughness and preparation reasonably necessary for the representations of Curley, Schultz and Spanier before the grand jury. *Id.* at 30–33. She further failed to maintain the confidentiality of communications between herself and her clients. *Id.* at 37–42. Finally, the Disciplinary Board found that Respondent's conduct prejudiced the administration of justice. *Id.* at 42–43. The Disciplinary Board found that Respondent poses no danger to the public or the profession and that her character remains of the highest quality. The Disciplinary Board concluded that public censure, rather than a public reprimand, is the appropriate remedy in this case. *Id.* at 48.

Respondent poses two questions for this Court's consideration:

1. Did the [ODC] establish by clear and convincing evidence that [Respondent] committed disciplinary violations of Rules 1.1, 1.6, 1.7 or 8.4 of the Rules of Professional Conduct?

2. Was there any legitimate basis to impose any form of discipline upon [Respondent] in the absence of any aggravating factors, multiple mitigating factors and no prior disciplinary history?

Respondent's Brief at 2.

III. Analysis

A.   Respondent was Personal Counsel to Curley, Schultz and Spanier

We first consider the ODC's contentions that Respondent violated Rules 1.1 and 1.7, which provide as follows:

. . . .

Rule 1.7. Conflict of Interest: Current Clients

(a)   Except as provided in paragraph (b), a lawyer shall not represent a client if the representation involves a concurrent conflict of interest. A concurrent conflict of interest exists if:

(1)   the representation of one client will be directly adverse to another client; or

(2)   there is a significant risk that the representation of one or more clients will be materially limited by the lawyer's responsibilities to another client, a former client or a third person or by a personal interest of the lawyer.

(b)   Notwithstanding the existence of a concurrent conflict of interest under paragraph (a), a lawyer may represent a client if:

(1)   the lawyer reasonably believes that the lawyer will be able to provide competent and diligent representation to each affected client;

(2)   the representation is not prohibited by law;

(3)   the representation does not involve the assertion of a claim by one client against another client represented by the lawyer in the same litigation or other proceeding before a tribunal; and

(4)   each affected client gives informed consent.

Pa.R.P.C. 1.1, 1.7. To evaluate these claims by the ODC, we must first decide the nature of the representation that existed between Respondent and Curley, Schultz and Spanier during the time period immediately before and during their grand jury testimony. Curley, Schultz and Spanier insist that Respondent represented them in their individual capacities without limitation. Respondent, in contrast, posits that she represented them only in a representative capacity in their roles as employees and representatives of Penn State.

We begin with Respondent's testimony at the evidentiary hearing before the Hearing Committee, where she offered the following testimony regarding the events leading to her decision to accompany Curley and Schultz at the grand jury for their interviews and testimony:

A. I—I did explain that Tim could have a personal attorney go to go with him to the grand jury, . . . and Graham said, "Well, Cynthia, you go with him, you can go with him, you go with him." And I said, "well, yes, but I can't be his personal attorney because I'm general counsel," and I said—and I said to him, I said, "You know, Tim, that if I go with you, nothing that you say would be confidential," that— and—and I know that the testimony has been I said I have to tell the board of trustees, but I said, "Just like we're talking here to Graham, Graham could know, the board of trustees could know," and I said to him, you, "If you want a personal attorney, you know, just call someone." He said, "I don't know any lawyers." After that discussion, then he went downstairs to my office.

Q. Did Mr. Curley understand the instructions you gave him, based on your understanding?

A. Oh, yes.

Q. Okay. Did Mr. Curley ask you to be his personal counsel?

A. No.

Q. Did at some point in time you speak to Mr. Schultz—

A. I did.

Q. —about your representation of him?

A. When he came back from vacation.

Q. And what did you discuss with Mr. Schultz?

A. I discussed the same thing with him. I went through what we in the office called the corporate *Miranda*, and that is, I told him that I could go in with him, he could get personal counsel, I could go in with him, but he knew that I was general counsel of Penn State, that nothing he told me would be confidential as to my client, Penn State, and that I needed to know what he was going to tell me to determine whether there was any conflict with the client. Gary told me the same thing that Tim told me.

Q.   Did Mr. Schultz ask you to represent him in any type of personal capacity?

A.   No.

Q.   Did Mr. Curley or Mr. Schultz raise any concern about complying or cooperating with the investigation?

A.   None.

Q.   Now, a lot has been made about these *Upjohn* warnings. Do you know what the *Upjohn* warnings are?

A.   Yes.

Q.   Do you believe you gave them?

A.   Yes.

Q.   Was your inquiry about whether a conflict existed between these individuals and the university satisfied?

A.   Yes.

Q.   Can you explain to the Panel?

A.   Well, the fact is, is that there was no way that I was going in if there was a conflict between Penn State and what they were telling me. They both said that [what they had been told back in 2001 about Sandusky's contact with a youth] was horseplay, that it was wrestling around, and that's what they knew. Okay? And there was—that, therefore, no conflict with the university, and so, that was the reason that I—I went in with them, and—and they were—because it was explained to me that this was about the Sandusky investigation, and Penn State had an obligation to cooperate, I mean, there was no way that the university wasn't going to cooperate with this, and that—and they were executives of the university, so—

N.T., 5/23/2018, at 371–379.

Immediately prior to Curley's and Schultz's testimony before the grand jury, the grand jury supervising judge asked Respondent who she represented. She responded as follows:

OAG: Judge, we're here on Notice 29. We have some witnesses to be sworn, Mr. Curley and Mr. Schultz.

Judge: Represented by?

Respondent: My name is Cynthia Baldwin, general counsel for Pennsylvania State University.

Judge: Will you be providing representation for both of those identified witnesses?

Respondent: [Schultz] is retired but was employed by the university and [Curley] is still an employee.

N.T. (grand jury), 1/12/2011, at 7–8. In this exchange, Respondent did not plainly indicate either that she viewed herself as representing these administrators solely in an agency capacity or that she represented them in their personal individual capacities. The supervising grand jury judge, in the presence of Respondent, then advised Curley and Schultz of their rights as grand jury witnesses.

As witnesses before the Grand Jury, you're entitled to certain rights and subject to certain duties which I am now going to explain to you. All of these rights and duties are equally important and it's important that you fully understand each of them.

First, you have the right to the advice and assistance of a lawyer. This means you have the right to the services of a lawyer with whom you may consult concerning all matters pertaining to your appearance before the Grand Jury.

You may confer with your lawyer at any time before, during and after your testimony. You may consult with your lawyer throughout your entire contact with the Grand Jury. Your lawyer may be present with you in the Grand Jury room during the time you're actually testifying and you may confer with her at that time.

You also may at any time discuss your testimony with your lawyer and except for cause shown before this Court, you may disclose your testimony to whomever you choose, if you choose.

You also have the right to refuse to answer any question pending a ruling by the Court directing you to respond if you honestly believe there are proper legal grounds for your refusal. In particular, you have the right to refuse to answer any question which you honestly believe may tend to incriminate you.

Should you refuse to answer any question, you may offer a reason for your refusal, but you're not obliged to do so. If you answer some questions or begin to answer any particular question, that does not necessarily mean you must continue to answer your questions or even complete the answers you have started.

Now, any answers you give to any question can and may be used against you either for the purpose of a Grand Jury Presentment, Grand Jury Report or a Criminal Information.

In other words, if you're uncertain as to whether you may lawfully refuse to answer any question or if any other problem arises during the course of your appearance before the Grand Jury, you may stop the questioning and appear before me, either alone or in this case with your counsel, and I will rule on that matter whatever it may be.

Id. at 8–10. Spanier later received the same instructions.

Immediately thereafter, at the outset of Curley's grand jury testimony, the following exchange occurred between Curley and counsel for the OAG:

Q.   You have counsel with you?

A.   Yes, I do.

Q.   Would you introduce her, please?

A.   My counsel is Cynthia Baldwin.

N.T. (grand jury), 1/12/2011 (Curley testifying), at 3. Respondent did not object to this statement or offer any clarification regarding the nature of her representation of Curley, including in particular no statements indicating, or even suggesting, that she represented Curley only in a representative capacity in his role as the athletic director of Penn State.

Likewise, Schultz's testimony began with the following question and answer:

Q.   You are accompanied today by counsel, Cynthia Baldwin; is that correct?

A.   That is correct.

N.T. (grand jury), 1/12/2011 (Schultz testifying), at 3. Again, Respondent offered no response or disagreement with this testimony and offered no indication that she represented Schultz only in his capacity as an administrator and representative of Penn State.

In April 2011, the outset of Spanier's grand jury testimony began as follows:

Q.   Sir, could you give us your name for the record, please?

A.   Graham Spanier.

Q.   Sir, you're represented by counsel today?

A.   Yes.

Q.   Could you just identify counsel?

A.   Cynthia Baldwin sitting behind me.

N.T. (grand jury), 4/13/2011 (Spanier testifying), at 3. As with Curley's and Schultz's similar testimony, Respondent did not object or otherwise respond in an effort to advise the grand jury that she represented Spanier in an agency capacity as a result of his position as the current president of Penn State.

Based upon the entirety of the evidence of record, we agree with the conclusions of both the Hearing Committee and the Disciplinary Board that Respondent represented Curley, Schultz and Spanier in their personal capacities at the time of their grand jury testimony. The Hearing Committee found as follows:

> Respondent very clearly sought to ensure that there was no conflict between their interests and the interests of [Penn State]. She said that she could not go in with them to the Grand Jury proceedings unless she was sure that there was no conflict between them and [Penn State]. Her *Upjohn* or *Miranda* warnings, as they were referred to, expressly provided that she can concurrently represent employees of [Penn State] while representing [Penn State] if their interests align. Indeed, [Amy McCall], [Penn State's] former associate general counsel, confirmed that the *Upjohn* warnings were given and the conflict examination made in order to determine if they could also represent the individual employees in matters in which they were representing [Penn State], and if this could not be done, then the employees were advised to get their own counsel. She acknowledged that it was common practice for the [Penn State] office of general counsel to provide joint representation to university employees when their interests were aligned.

> Respondent clearly determined on the basis of what these individuals told her that their interests were aligned with [Penn State's] such that she could represent them. Based upon this conclusion, she told them that she could accompany them to their Grand Jury testimony. While she clearly advised them that they could engage separate counsel, she never told them they needed separate counsel because she could not represent them or that if they did not get separate counsel, they would be unrepresented.

We do not find that her admonitions to at least Mrs. Curley, Schultz and Spanier that their conversations with her were not privileged from disclosure to [Penn State] in any way undermines the conclusion that she represented the individual employees. It is merely the appropriate advice to give one of multiple clients: Where an attorney represents multiple clients in the same matter, it is in fact imperative that they be advised whether their communications with her are privileged from each other or shared jointly. She never told them that their conversations with her were not privileged from disclosure to third parties because she did not represent them; nor did she tell them that [Penn State] was free to authorize the disclosure of her conversations with them to third parties because she did not represent them individually. Instead, all of her statements in this regard were wholly consistent with her representing them jointly with [Penn State].

Hearing Committee Report at 39–40 (emphasis in original).

In its report, the Disciplinary Board added the following relevant findings:

Mr. Curley, Mr. Schultz and Dr. Spanier were subpoenaed in their personal capacities. They were aware that Respondent was Penn State's General Counsel. Respondent informed each of them that they could have other counsel if they so desired and that she could not represent them if their stories were not consistent and not aligned with Penn State's interests. After hearing their stories, Respondent agreed she could accompany them to the grand Jury. Respondent never advised them that she solely represented them in their capacities as agents of Penn State, nor did she advise them that she did not represent them in their personal capacities. There is no writing memorializing discussions regarding the nature of the representation and inherent conflicts and no writing indicating the individuals gave informed consent.

At the grand jury, each Individual separately identified Respondent on the record as their counsel. They did not identify Respondent as Penn State's counsel nor did they indicate that her representation of them was limited to their status as employees of Penn State. Respondent did not contradict or limit their declarations. . . . She allowed them to testify under oath that she was their counsel without limitation, and she did not correct these statements. The evidence supports the conclusion that Respondent agreed to represent Mr. Curley, Mr. Schultz, and Dr. Spanier as their personal attorney (and) that they understood this to be the agreement.

It follows that Respondent did not understand the nature of her representation of Mr. Curley, Mr. Schultz and Dr. Spanier, as she maintains that her representation of the individuals was solely in their capacities as agents of Penn State. In the face of the indicia of her representation of the individuals in a personal capacity, we find no evidence that Respondent at any time stated to any of them, that she solely represented them in their capacities as agents of Penn State. Any intention on Respondent's part to limit her representation of Mr. Curley, Mr. Schultz and Dr. Spanier to one only in their capacity as agents of Penn State was ineffective, because Respondent never told them she was so limiting her representation, and Mr. Curley, Mr. Schultz and Dr. Spanier had no basis upon which to conclude that she was doing so.

Disciplinary Board Report at 29–30.

As indicated, the present record of disciplinary proceedings fully supports these findings. In further support of our determination that Respondent represented Curley, Schultz and Spanier in their individual capacities is the guarantee under Pennsylvania law that witnesses offering testimony before a grand jury are entitled to the presence of their counsel. As far back as *In re Groban's Petition*, 352 U.S. 330, 77 S.Ct. 510, 1 L.Ed.2d 376 (1957), the United States Supreme Court recognized that a witness testifying before a grand jury remains protected by the privilege against self-incrimination. *Id.* at 333, 77 S.Ct. 510. Further, in *Commonwealth v. McCloskey*, 443 Pa. 117, 277 A.2d 764 (1971), this Court held that a grand jury witness must be advised/warned that he is entitled to come before the court accompanied by counsel and obtain a ruling as to whether he should answer a question that may incriminate him.

Such a warning gives full recognition to the delicate position of a witness before an investigating grand jury. He has been summoned to testify, and he is subject to contempt proceedings should he refuse to testify without justification. The question of when a witness has 'reasonable cause to apprehend danger' and hence can exercise his right against self-incrimination is not always clear. As was stated in *Jones v. United States*, 342 F.2d 863 (D.C. [Cir.] 1964).

If . . . [a witness] answers incriminating questions he may make it certain . . . that he will be indicted. And testimony before the grand jury may be used . . . to impeach his testimony at trial. If he refuses to testify at all, or to answer some questions on the ground that answers might incriminate him, the grand jury may draw conclusions. If he refuses to answer questions that are not incriminating, he may be guilty of contempt.

Id. at 868. Determining what is an incriminating statement is not always clear to a layman. We thus conclude that a subpoenaed witness who has given testimony before an investigating grand jury without the above warning has been denied his right against self-incrimination.

Id. at 777; *see also id.* at 780 (" 'A potential defendant who is brought before the grand jury without an attorney at his side is almost helpless.") (Eagan, J. concurring and dissenting). As recited, Curley, Schultz and Spanier received the warning in Respondent's presence. It is impossible to conclude in light of the seriousness and solemnity of the warnings administered by the supervising judge that the Individual Clients believed anything other than their personal interests were being protected by Respondent. Likewise, knowing she was the only attorney present with the Individual Clients when the warnings were administered, it cannot be fathomed that Respondent did not understand that she was representing them personally.

Were we to conclude that Respondent did not represent Curley, Schultz and Spanier, as Respondent argues, it would amount to a determination that these three witnesses effectively waived their rights to counsel before the grand jury. The record contains no indication that any such waivers occurred. Instead, the record unequivocally establishes that the Individual Clients reasonably believed that Respondent was representing them personally and individually.

[. . . .]

Pa.R.P.C. 1.7

By agreeing to undertake the concurrent representation of Penn State, Curley, Schultz and Spanier, Respondent committed multiple violations of Pa.R.P.C. 1.7. Rule 1.7 requires attorneys to avoid conflicts of interest in the representation of multiple clients. A conflict of interest exists under Rule 1.7(a)(1) when the representation of one client is materially adverse to the interests of another client or where there is a "significant risk" that the representation of one client will be materially limited by the lawyer's responsibilities to another client as proscribed by Pa.R.P.C. 1.7(a)(2). A client may waive a conflict of interest, but only upon providing informed consent. Pa.R.P.C. 1.7(a)(2). In the present circumstance, the Disciplinary Board properly concluded that Respondent's concurrent representation of Penn State and Curley, Schultz and Spanier "undoubtedly created a significant risk that her ability to consider, recommend or carry out an appropriate course of action for each client could be materially limited by her representation of Penn State." Disciplinary Board Report at 34. According to the Disciplinary Board,

> Respondent understood that the grand jury was investigating Sandusky regarding alleged child abuse, and that Mr. Curley, Mr. Schultz and later Dr. Spanier would be questioned about what they knew. It is difficult to believe that Respondent, a seasoned attorney, did not perceive the danger in her representation of all of these clients. *Id.*

We agree with these observations of the Disciplinary Board. As noted, Respondent now claims that she did not know of any potential conflicts because Curley, Schultz and Spanier lied to her. Even to the extent that this is true, it does not account for the "significant risks" of substantial conflicts of interest with her representation of Penn State. As indicated, at the time that the grand jury served testimonial subpoenas on Curley, Schultz and Spanier, it also served Penn State with a subpoena for documents related to Sandusky matters. Its investigation had expanded beyond the criminal conduct of Sandusky into new territory, namely an investigation of the possible criminal conduct of Penn State and its highly ranking representatives. Under Rule 1.7, Respondent could not represent both Penn State and members of its senior leadership without full disclosure of all possible conflicts in order to obtain informed consent, and Penn State documents, especially the trove of emails stored on its computer servers, were the tangible source of information regarding potential conflicts among the four clients. Reliance on painfully cursory interviews with senior leadership to conclude the absence of a conflict was a disservice to Penn State. Proper conflicts analysis required intensive investigation of the actions of said senior leadership. Respondent knew, or clearly should have known, that any wrongdoing by officers of the university would expose Penn State to criminal and/or civil liability. It was obviously in Penn State's interest to avoid these pitfalls and thus, if necessary, to disassociate itself from these individuals. With knowledge of actual wrongdoing by its representatives, as evidenced by available records, Penn State could have avoided the pitfalls of the joint representation.

Respondent also failed to recognize the likelihood of conflicts of interests between Curley, Schultz and Spanier. Respondent reasonably should have recognized the substantial risk that the representation of one of the Individual Clients could be materially limited by the responsibilities to each of the other

Individual Clients. Spanier, by virtue of his position as President of the University, faced potential criminal liability and was entitled to personal counsel who would seek to isolate him from first level decisions. Schultz and Curley likewise were entitled to personal counsel who would develop a defense unconstrained by consideration of the other's defense given their varying levels of decision making. In *Pirillo v. Takiff*, 462 Pa. 511, 341 A.2d 896 (1975), this Court upheld a decision by the supervising judge of a grand jury to disqualify an attorney and his associate from representing twelve witnesses subpoenaed to appear before the grand jury. In support of the ruling, the Court stated that

> [t]he multiple representation interfered with the individual witness's right to effective counsel. For example, if witness A has information about witness B's criminal conduct, one attorney could not represent both. It may be in A's best interest for counsel to advise A to cooperate. However, this could operate to the detriment of B.

Id. at 899; *see also In re Philadelphia Investigating Grand Jury XII*, 529 Pa. 471, 605 A.2d 318, 320 (1992) (holding that the representation of multiple grand jury witnesses is inappropriate where each witness was a potential defendant and the testimony of each witness might incriminate one or more of the other witnesses).

Discrepancies between the testimonies of Curley, Schultz and Spanier materialized before any of the three testified before the grand jury, evidencing actual conflicts of interest. As noted herein, prior to the grand jury testimony of Curley and Schultz on January 12, 2011, both witnesses were interviewed, accompanied by Respondent, by an OAG investigator. The notes of these interviews reveal important differences in their recollection of events and, critically, they reveal a divergence from what Respondent reported that these individuals told her when she met with them to determine whether she had a conflict of interest in representing them along with Penn State.

Curley's interview notes are relatively consistent with his original description of events when he met with Respondent. Curley indicated that (1) with respect to the 2001 incident, there was no indication that sexual acts had occurred, and that "it seemed to be something that could have been misconstrued and was inappropriate behavior at best;" (2) he did not report the 2001 incident to the police department "because he informed Spanier;" and (3) he had no knowledge of the 1998 incident or any other such matter involving Sandusky." Investigation Notes at 1.

Schultz stands in sharp contrast. Contrary to Curley's recitation and Respondent's version of Schultz's original disclosures to her, Schultz told the

OAG investigator (1) that while McQueary's description of the 2001 incident was vague, "it was his impression based upon the information that he was provided that there was inappropriate sexual conduct between Sandusky and a minor;" (2) McQueary had related that "Sandusky may have grabbed genitals;" (3) he was aware of the 1998 incident involving Sandusky and a child and that he "was sure that Spanier knew of the 1998 incident." *Id.*

Both witnesses offered testimony before the grand jury that was substantially identical to these recited interview summaries. The conflicts of interest revealed by these revelations are obvious. Contrary to Respondent's testimony that her interview with Schultz did not result in any report of sexual acts by Sandusky (and thus no knowledge of possible criminal wrongdoing), Schultz revealed in both his OAG interview and before the grand jury that he believed and understood that one or more sexual acts had in fact occurred. Curley was consistent with his denial of any knowledge (much less involvement) in the 1998 incident, but Schultz was not. To the contrary, Schultz not only indicated that he knew about the 1998 incident, he also testified that Spanier was unquestionably aware of it. In his later grand jury testimony, Spanier, also represented by Respondent, testified that he lacked any knowledge or information relating to the events in 1998.

The substantial risk of disqualifying conflicts that should have been apparent from the outset of the service of grand jury subpoenas on the Individual Clients became actual conflicts at least as early as the OAG interviews preceding the grand jury testimony. Respondent failed to take any actions in response to this information, resulting in multiple violations of Rule 1.7. After their interviews and prior to their grand jury testimony, Respondent should have advised Curley and Schultz that she could not represent either of them and obtained a continuance until independent counsel could be obtained by them. She also could not subsequently represent Spanier because Schultz's recollection of events linked him (and Penn State) to knowledge of the 1998 incident, which Spanier consistently (including in his grand jury testimony) denied. The interviews and grand jury testimony of Curley and Schultz also implicated Spanier with knowledge of Sandusky's activities. Although it should have been clear at the time of the service of the subpoena that the Individual Clients needed personal counsel, the information obtained in the interviews preceding Curley, Schultz and Spanier's grand jury testimony cried for the conclusion that each required experienced personal counsel. The best interests of one or all of them may have been an offer to cooperate but this advice would or could have been detrimental to the other concurrently represented clients. Concurrent representation of Penn State, Curley and Schultz was patently improper and violative of Pa.R.P.C. 1.7.

[. . . .]

We hereby impose discipline in the form of a public reprimand, to be administered by the Disciplinary Board. Respondent is ordered to pay the costs of investigation and prosecution in this matter.

SOLUTIONS: THE LAWYER SHOULD HAVE, WOULD HAVE, COULD HAVE. . .

Baldwin should have asked herself a simple question to avoid the thicket she ended up in: "Is there a possibility that the university and the executives would point fingers at one another as to whom was to blame for Sandusky being allowed to engage in his criminal conduct?" If the answer was "yes" or "maybe", then she cannot represent both. No amount of informed consent or carefully drafted Joint Representation Agreements will cure this dilemma caused by these answers. The is a non-consentable conflict. A lawyer cannot reasonably believe that she could represent both. The Comments to the Rule spell out that the test of allowable concurrent representation be what would an objective, non-involved lawyer make of the multiple representation from an ethical standpoint.

LEANING INTO PRACTICE

In *U.S. v. Upjohn Company*, the U.S. Supreme Court held that attorney-client privilege applies when a lawyer representing the corporation conducts interviews with company employees about possible misconduct, but the lawyer must warn the employee being interviewed that the lawyer does not represent the employees, and that the employee can obtain their own legal counsel. This warning is sometimes called the Corporate *Miranda* Warning.

Imagine this scenario. Rafael Lawyer was hired by ABC Company's Board of Directors to investigate allegations that the company had engaged in a price fixing conspiracy. Rafael is instructed to interview all top executives. Rafael meets with the CFO but failed to give this warning. The CFO reveals that he has been involved in possible criminal conduct related to the price fixing. The CFO claims other executives knew about it, but the other executives deny this. Based upon what you have learned thus far, what is the consequence of Rafael not giving the *Upjohn* warning? Recall the lessons learned in the formation of the ACR.

It can be difficult to explain to longtime associates and contacts at an entity that they need to get their own lawyers. In some instances, the lawyer has worked closely with them; and has perhaps developed a personal friendship. Imagine you are in the position of Attorney Baldwin. Prepare an outline of how you plan on breaking it to them that they will need to get their own lawyers. What are your true goals as a lawyer, not as a friend? What will you say? Will you take a direct or an indirect approach? Why? Keep in mind that transparency is the key to these conversations as to many issues you will confront in experiencing PR, not the issue confronting Brooke.

2)   *Model Rule 1.14: Clients with Diminished Capacity*

This is one of the more challenging ACRs and—with an aging population—one that will become ever more common. (The rule deals as well with minors and adults suffering from diminished capacity as the result of an organic injury.) An increasing number of law schools are offering courses in elder law. Model Rule 1.14 provides guidance to lawyers on this type of attorney-client relationship.

Model Rule 1.14: Client with Diminished Capacity

(a)   When a client's capacity to make *adequately* considered decisions in connection with a representation is diminished . . .the lawyer shall, as far as reasonably possible, *maintain* a normal client-lawyer relationship with the client.

(b)   When the lawyer reasonably believes that the client has diminished capacity, is at risk of *substantial* physical, financial or other harm unless action is taken and cannot *adequately* act in the client's own interest, the lawyer *may* take reasonably necessary protective action, including consulting with individuals or entities that have the ability to take action to protect the client and, in appropriate cases, seeking the appointment of a guardian ad litem, conservator or guardian.

(c)   Information relating to the representation of a client with diminished capacity is protected by Rule 1.6. When taking protective action pursuant to paragraph (b), the lawyer is impliedly authorized under Rule 1.6(a) to reveal information about the client, but only *to the extent reasonably necessary* to protect the client's interests.

Deconstruction Exercise/Rule Rationale

> Under MR 1.14, why did the drafters insert *adequately* before *considered*? They could have left the word off as a modifier or could have inserted a different modifier such as *thoroughly* or *exhaustively*.

> We see the use of the word *maintain*. What does the use of this word suggest to you? Does it suggest that a lawyer with a client with diminished capacity must be ready to adapt to a client's changing circumstances?

> When the lawyer *reasonably* believes that the client has diminished capacity, is at risk of *substantial* physical, financial or other harm unless action is taken and cannot adequately act in the client's own interests, the lawyer *may* take reasonably necessary protective action, including consulting with individuals or entities that have the ability to take action to protect the client and, in appropriate cases, seeking the appointment of a guardian ad litem conservator, or guardian.

The answer to all three questions is that the orientation for lawyers of the drafters was to treat clients with diminished capacity as much as possible like any other client and not to presume that they are unable to manage their legal affairs.

We see here another small word in addition to "or"—but also with an oversized impact—namely, the word "may." Why did the drafters use this word as opposed to "shall"? Both were equally available to the Rule drafters. Because a lawyer is expected in this Rule—and in most of the Rules—to use their best judgment, in selecting from a variety of options—in order to best serve the needs of the impaired client. We also see the phase "impliedly authorized" that pops up in other Rules as well. Why? What is its utility? A client cannot sometimes, if impaired, decide on their own and therefore the lawyer becomes the default decision maker. (Or, the lawyer makes certain decisions, as we previously discussed, because not all decisions can efficiently or effectively be run by the client.) Finally, there is a new phrase used in this rule that we will see again—"to the extent reasonably necessary." In MR 1.14 this phrase is coupled with the release and use of the client's confidential information and will be used again when we study MR 1.6 that deals with confidential information in general. The phrase is used very surgically because it requires a nuanced approach to decision making as opposed to a "green light" approach.

Scenario No. 1: The Case of the Older Man; the Younger Woman Lover; and a Changed Will

Isabella Lawyer has represented Juan Carlos Client for many years and prepared his initial estate plan. In recent years, Isabella has interacted with Juan Carlos on several social occasions and has noticed signs of diminished capacity. Juan Carlos has asked Isabella to redo his estate plan to essentially disinherit his children and to make Lola, Juan Carlos's much younger companion, the sole heir. Isabella is very troubled by the request. What inquires, if any, should she make regarding her client? Should she ask Juan Carlos? What if he says that he is in love, that he and Lola are moving in together and it is not for Isabella to judge? What if Isabella reasonably concludes however that Lola is exerting an undue influence on Juan Carlos and that Juan Carlos is at substantial risk of being swayed by such influence? Should Isabella change the will as her client directs?

Scenario No. 2: The Case of the Damaged Brain and a Lawyer's Loyalty

John Client is involved in a serious car accident which results in damage to his brain and a change in his personality. He changed from being deeply cautious and conservative to risk embracing and reckless, with episodes of mania, an increase in risky personal conduct, and an attitude of let's live today because tomorrow we may die. Recently John's relatives have told him: "we love you so much. We are worried about you and the way you act. We have hired a lawyer and plan on going to court and asking that a conservator be placed in charge of your affairs." John says he wants to hire you to represent him. With his consent, you involve a close friend of John and a doctor who deals with brain trauma matters. You reasonably conclude based on the examination that a conservatorship is very likely in John's best interests. But you also reasonably conclude that if John were willing, the doctor could set up a supportive decision-making structure that, with the help of John's friend, could help improve his ability to make considered choices. You tell John that a conservatorship would not be so bad, but he says "Never! Never! Death before dishonor!" You reasonably believe that John's stance reflects his commitment to personal liberty, notwithstanding the risks involved that you have warned John about. Can you represent John in opposing the conservatorship?

Scenario No. 3: The Case of the Forward-Thinking Lawyer

Nadda Lawyer is meeting with Octavia Client. Octavia is wealthy. Currently she is competent. She tells Nadda though that she is concerned about ultimately suffering from dementia because early onset Alzheimer's disease afflicted several blood relatives. When that occurred, there were contentious disputes over money and assets. Octavia's goal is to avoid that scenario. Nadda discusses an advance authorization of the disclosure of confidential information, including Octavia's condition when, in Nadda's judgment, it would be appropriate to do so in order to represent Octavia. (Normally, as we will see when we study Model Rule 1.6, which is the rule on confidential information, a lawyer must not disclose a client's confidences unless a client provides consent.) Do you think that Nadda can ethically recommend this course of action? What is the upside or the downside for both Octavia and Nadda?

Cases and Materials

X-Ray Questions (*Szymkowicz*)

Here we see a lawyer become involved in an estate matter. The lawyer engaged in "joint representation" of both a mother (his original client) with a sizeable estate, and her son, a potential heir of the estate, who was seeking a power of attorney over the estate. There was evidence that the mother suffered from diminished capacity. What issues did the court see as posing a potential conflict of interest in the joint representation? While the interest of the mother and of the son were mostly aligned, there was not perfect alignment. In the counter view, what was the consequence of that fact? Can you envision that there are some things the mother might want that are not wanted by the son and vice versa? Does there need to be an actual conflict of interest between mother and son as to goals to preclude the lawyer from representing both concurrently or does there only need to be a potential conflict of interest? Can you tie this question into what we discussed in *Baldwin*? An issue here for a lawyer is who is the client: the family member or the mother?

In re John T. Szymkowicz, John P. Szymkowicz, Leslie Silverman, Robert King, Members of the Bar of the District of Columbia Court of Appeals

District of Columbia Court of Appeals, 2015.
124 A.3d 1078.

PER CURIAM:

The Board on Professional Responsibility concluded that respondent John T. Szymkowicz, his son respondent John P. Szymkowicz, and respondent Leslie Silverman did not violate any Rules of Professional Conduct in connection with their representation of Genevieve Ackerman. The Board further found that respondent Robert King violated only Rule of Professional Conduct 1.5(b), by failing to provide Ms. Ackerman with a written retainer agreement. The Board recommends that Mr. King be informally admonished. Mr. King does not contest that finding and recommendation. Bar Counsel challenges the Board's determinations that respondents did not violate Rule 1.7, which relates to conflict of interest, and Rule 8.4, which relates to dishonesty. We accept the Board's determinations with respect to Rule 8.4, but remand for further proceedings with respect to conflict-of-interest issues arising from respondents' representation of Ms. Ackerman.

I.

Except where noted, the following facts are undisputed. In May 2002, Ms. Ackerman, who was then eighty-five years old, executed a trust. The trust was intended to support Ms. Ackerman during her lifetime but also to provide support for her son, Dr. Stephen Ackerman. Trust assets included Ms. Ackerman's home on Plymouth Street, NW in Washington, D.C., an interest in a house on North Carolina Avenue, SE in Washington, D.C., and a condominium in Sea Colony, Delaware. Dr. Ackerman lived in the North Carolina Avenue house. Upon Ms. Ackerman's death, trust assets were to be divided equally between Dr. Ackerman and his sister, Mary Frances Abbott. The trust made monthly payments to Dr. Ackerman, which were to be treated as advances of Dr. Ackerman's share of the trust assets. Frank Abbott, Ms. Abbott's husband, was named trustee, and Ms. Abbott was named successor trustee. Revocation of the trust required approval of the trustee. The trust also contained a no-contest provision, providing that anyone who challenged the trust would lose beneficiary status under the trust.

In the summer of 2002, Dr. Ackerman retained the Szymkowiczes to challenge the trust. Dr. Ackerman contended that Ms. Ackerman wanted him to have the Sea Colony property, which therefore should be excluded from the trust assets. The Szymkowiczes subsequently filed suit ("*Ackerman I*") in Superior Court on behalf of Dr. Ackerman to remove Mr. Abbott as the trustee and to reform the trust by excluding the Sea Colony property from the trust assets. In connection with that lawsuit, Mr. J.T. Szymkowicz met with Ms. Ackerman and obtained an affidavit stating that Ms. Ackerman had intended to leave the Sea Colony property to Dr. Ackerman rather than placing the property into the trust, that she wanted to name Dr. Ackerman as a co-trustee, and that she wanted to eliminate the no-contest clause because she had not intended to include such a clause in the trust.

A number of health professionals evaluated Ms. Ackerman's condition in 2004. In January 2004, Dr. Lila McConnell, Ms. Ackerman's doctor, concluded that Ms. Ackerman had significant cognitive impairment and would likely be unable to participate in intense questioning. In June 2004, Dr. William Polk found that Ms. Ackerman suffered from mild dementia and depression but that her thoughts were "logical and organized" and that she had the "capacity to make health care and personal decisions for herself." Finally, Dr. Paulo Negro reported in August 2004 that Ms. Ackerman suffered from dementia and cognitive impairment and was "unable to exercise proper judgment."

In August 2004, Dr. Ackerman obtained a power of attorney (POA) from Ms. Ackerman. Ms. Ackerman had previously granted a POA to Ms. Abbott in 1999. Ms. Ackerman revoked Dr. Ackerman's POA in November 2004. Ms. Ackerman subsequently executed several additional documents granting a POA to Dr. Ackerman.

Ms. Ackerman's greatest desire was to restore peace to her family. In December 2004, Mr. J.T. Szymkowicz told Ms. Ackerman that Dr. Ackerman would drop his lawsuit in *Ackerman I* if she would revoke the trust entirely and transfer the trust assets back to herself. In May 2005, the Szymkowiczes began to also represent Ms. Ackerman. The same month, the Szymkowiczes filed a suit in Superior Court, on behalf of Ms. Ackerman, seeking to revoke the trust ("*Ackerman II*"). Dr. Ackerman did not drop *Ackerman I* after the filing of *Ackerman II*.

After holding a trial in May 2005, the trial court in *Ackerman I* ruled in favor of the Abbotts and the trust, finding that there was no basis to reform the trust and that the no-contest provision was valid and enforceable. *Ackerman v. Genevieve Ackerman Family Tr.*, 908 A.2d 1200, 1202 (D.C.2006). This court affirmed the trial court's judgment. *Id.* at 1201–04.

Ms. Ackerman was also evaluated by doctors in 2006. Dr. Negro concluded in March 2006 that Ms. Ackerman's ability to process complex information was limited, that Ms. Ackerman did not know which papers she had signed with respect to Dr. Ackerman's POA, and that Ms. Ackerman suffered from dementia. Dr. Richard Ratner agreed, based on observations in February and May 2006, that Ms. Ackerman showed some signs of dementia and that her memory was "problematic." Dr. Ratner concluded, however, that Ms. Ackerman was steady in her desire to grant a POA to Dr. Ackerman and in her belief that the Abbotts had not appropriately consulted Ms. Ackerman about her finances. Ultimately, Dr. Ratner concluded that Ms. Ackerman was competent to revoke the trust and grant a POA to Dr. Ackerman.

In March 2007, Mr. J.T. Szymkowicz withdrew from *Ackerman II* based on a concern that he might be called as a witness by the defense. It is unclear whether Mr. J.T. Szymkowicz withdrew from representing Ms. Ackerman altogether. At Mr. J.T. Szymkowicz's recommendation, Ms. Ackerman hired Ms. Silverman to represent Ms. Ackerman in *Ackerman II*. Toward the beginning of the representation, Ms. Silverman consulted Ms. Ackerman about the litigation for about an hour and a half. Mr. J.T. Szymkowicz and Dr. Ackerman were present at that meeting. Dr. Ackerman paid for Ms. Silverman's services from Ms. Ackerman's funds. In making decisions with regard to the representation, Ms. Silverman consulted with Dr. Ackerman, who held a POA for Ms. Ackerman. Ms. Silverman enlisted Mr. King to help represent Ms. Ackerman in *Ackerman II*.

After a trial in July 2007, the trial court in *Ackerman II* upheld the trust, concluding that Mr. Abbott, as trustee, had not approved revocation of the trust and that there was no basis for removing Mr. Abbott as trustee or ordering an accounting. At the trial, Ms. Ackerman could not remember that a trust had been executed, who had prepared the trust, that Dr. Ackerman had filed suit in *Ackerman I,* or that Mr. Abbott was the trustee. The trial court did not decide the disputed question whether Ms. Ackerman had capacity to file the lawsuit.

At various times during 2007, Dr. Ackerman, Mr. J.T. Szymkowicz, and Ms. Silverman worked to prevent Mr. Abbott from selling Ms. Ackerman's interest in the North Carolina Avenue property, where Dr. Ackerman was living. In addition, Mr. J.T. Szymkowicz drafted (1) a document assigning Ms. Ackerman's interest in the North Carolina Avenue property, as well as other interests, to Dr. Ackerman for $1; and (2) a new will pursuant to which Ms. Ackerman made Dr. Ackerman the personal representative of her estate and removed the trust as beneficiary. Mr. J.T. Szymkowicz sent those documents to Ms. Silverman as "draft models from which to work." Ms. Ackerman subsequently executed those documents.

In September 2007, Mr. Abbott filed suit in Superior Court seeking a declaration that Ms. Ackerman's interest in the North Carolina Avenue property was part of the trust property. The trial court granted the requested relief. Ms. Silverman noted an appeal on behalf of Ms. Ackerman, but that appeal was later dismissed because Ms. Silverman took no further action in the matter. Dr. Ackerman, represented by the Szymkowiczes, also appealed, and this court affirmed the trial court's ruling. *Ackerman v. Abbott,* 978 A.2d 1250 (D.C.2009).

In November 2007, Dr. Ackerman filed a pro se petition with the probate court alleging that Ms. Ackerman was incapacitated, because she was legally blind, and seeking to be named Ms. Ackerman's guardian and conservator. Dr. Ackerman later withdrew that petition. Meanwhile, Ms. Abbott filed a petition in March 2008 seeking to be named Ms. Ackerman's guardian and conservator. Although the probate court appointed an attorney to represent Ms. Ackerman in the matter, Dr. Ackerman also retained Mr. King to act as Ms. Ackerman's attorney in the matter. In June 2008, the probate court ruled that Ms. Ackerman had not been competent after 2004. The probate court further found that the POAs granted to Dr. Ackerman were invalid. The probate court nevertheless declined to appoint Ms. Abbott guardian or conservator, because the 1999 POA, which the court found to be valid, gave Ms. Abbott sufficient authority to manage Ms. Ackerman's affairs.

II.

After Ms. Abbott complained to Bar Counsel about respondents' actions, Bar Counsel brought charges against respondents alleging, in presently pertinent part, violations of Rules 1.5(b) (failure to provide engagement letter) (King), 1.6(a)(1) (revealing client confidences or secrets) (King and Silverman), 1.7(b)(2) (conflicting client interests) (Szymkowiczes), 1.7(b)(4) (personal-interest conflict) (King and Silverman), 1.16(a) (failure to withdraw) (all four respondents), 8.4(c) (dishonesty, fraud, deceit, and misrepresentation) (all four respondents), and 8.4(d) (serious interference with administration of justice) (all four respondents).

A.

Between October 2009 and March 2010, a twelve-day hearing was held before the Hearing Committee. At that hearing, Bar Counsel introduced evidence, including testimony from Ms. Abbott, in support of the conclusion that Ms. Ackerman was incompetent at all relevant times and that respondents knew or should have known that to be true. Bar Counsel also introduced evidence supporting a conclusion that Dr. Ackerman's interests and Ms. Ackerman's interests conflicted or at least potentially conflicted. Conversely, respondents introduced evidence to support the conclusion that, after appropriate inquiry, they reasonably determined that Ms. Ackerman had the legal capacity to make the decisions at issue. Respondents also introduced evidence in support of their positions that Ms. Ackerman's interests and Dr. Ackerman's interests were not conflicting and that respondents had adequately explained any potential conflicts to Ms. Ackerman.

With the exception of Mr. King's failure to obtain a written retainer agreement, the Hearing Committee found no Rule violations. The Hearing

Committee found that Ms. Ackerman was suffering from periodic memory loss that worsened over the period at issue. Nevertheless, the Hearing Committee concluded that Ms. Ackerman was capable of consulting with a lawyer and understanding the matters at issue in the proceedings. Moreover, the Hearing Committee concluded that the actions taken by respondents were in Ms. Ackerman's interests, as Ms. Ackerman perceived those interests, even though litigation costs reduced the value of the trust assets and some of respondents' actions, if successful, would have shifted assets from the trust to Dr. Ackerman. Specifically, the Hearing Committee concluded that respondents' actions were consistent with Ms. Ackerman's long-term interest in supporting Dr. Ackerman. Finally, the Hearing Committee concluded that in any event Bar Counsel had failed to show by clear and convincing evidence that respondents knew or should have known that Ms. Ackerman lacked the legal capacity to make the decisions at issue.

In reaching these conclusions, the Hearing Committee expressed doubts about the credibility of Ms. Abbott's testimony, finding that her anger toward respondents motivated her to press disciplinary charges, that she was biased against respondents, and that she had financial and other interests in preserving the trust.

With respect to Ms. Ackerman's mental status, the Hearing Committee concluded that the question was whether Ms. Ackerman had the capacity to make the particular decisions at issue. The Hearing Committee concluded that the medical evidence consistently indicated that, despite her limitations, Ms. Ackerman had the capacity to enter into contracts and to execute documents such as POAs and wills.

After reaching these general conclusions, the Hearing Committee made extensive specific findings with respect to its conclusions that respondents had not violated the Rules of Professional Conduct. Specifically, with respect to the conflict-of-interest charge arising from Mr. J.T. Szymkowicz's representation of both Ms. Ackerman and Dr. Ackerman, the Hearing Committee concluded that there was a potential for conflict of interest between Dr. Ackerman and Ms. Ackerman, but that Mr. J.T. Szymkowicz reasonably believed that he had obtained, and in fact did obtain, Ms. Ackerman's informed consent to the joint representation. The Hearing Committee also found that Ms. Ackerman's interests were not adversely affected by the joint representation, because both Dr. Ackerman and Ms. Ackerman wanted Dr. Ackerman to be financially supported. Finally, the Hearing Committee concluded that Mr. J.T. Szymkowicz's actions after March 7, 2007, did not raise a concern about joint representation, because Mr. Szymkowicz was no longer representing Ms. Ackerman.

With respect to the conflict-of-interest charge against Mr. J.P. Szymkowicz, the Hearing Committee found that Mr. J.P. Szymkowicz was a subordinate lawyer who reasonably relied on his father's representations that Ms. Ackerman had given informed consent to joint representation.

Finally, with respect to the conflict-of-interest charges against Ms. Silverman and Mr. King, the Hearing Committee concluded that both Ms. Silverman and Mr. King were entitled to rely on the apparently valid POAs Ms. Ackerman had executed in favor of Dr. Ackerman. Thus, no conflict of interest was created by Dr. Ackerman's payment of Ms. Silverman and Mr. King's fees or by Dr. Ackerman's management of the litigation on behalf of Ms. Ackerman.

B.

The Board agreed with the Hearing Committee's determination that Bar Counsel had failed to establish the alleged Rule violations at issue. Treating the issue as one of fact rather than law, the Board found ample support in the record for the Hearing Committee's conclusion that Ms. Ackerman had the legal capacity to make the decisions at issue. In any event, the Board concluded that the record supported the Hearing Committee's conclusion that respondents reasonably believed that Ms. Ackerman had the requisite capacity.

The Board further concluded that Mr. J.T. Szymkowicz had not violated the conflict-of-interest rule, because he had determined that the interests of Dr. Ackerman and Ms. Ackerman coincided. The Board also concluded that Mr. J.P. Szymkowicz justifiably relied on Mr. J.T. Szymkowicz's assurances that any potential conflict of interest had been adequately addressed with Ms. Ackerman. Finally, the Board concluded that Ms. Silverman and Mr. King did not commit conflict-of-interest violations. Specifically, although Ms. Silverman and Mr. King were paid by Dr. Ackerman and consulted with Dr. Ackerman in their representation of Ms. Ackerman, Ms. Silverman adequately determined that Ms. Ackerman's interests coincided with those of Dr. Ackerman.

Two Board members concurred separately. They concluded that Ms. Ackerman lacked capacity to make the decisions at issue or to give informed consent to the potential conflict between her interests and those of Dr. Ackerman. Nevertheless, they concurred in the Board's conclusion that respondents did not violate the rules at issue, because respondents took reasonable measures to determine Ms. Ackerman's competence and to obtain informed consent.

III.

"[T]he burden of proving . . . disciplinary charges rests with Bar Counsel, and [the Board's] factual findings must be supported by clear and convincing evidence." *In re Allen*, 27 A.3d 1178, 1184 (D.C.2011) (internal quotation marks omitted). We "shall accept the findings of fact made by the Board unless they are unsupported by substantial evidence of record. . . ." D.C. Bar R. XI, § 9(h)(1). Similarly, the Board must defer to the factual findings of the Hearing Committee if those findings are supported by substantial evidence. *See, e.g., In re Brown*, 112 A.3d 913, 917 (D.C.2015) (per curiam). We owe no deference to the Board's legal conclusions. *In re Yelverton*, 105 A.3d 413, 420 (D.C.2014), *petition for cert. filed*, No. 15–5001 (U.S. June 30, 2015).

A.

Bar Counsel challenges the Board's determination that respondents did not violate Rule 8.4(c) (dishonesty, fraud, deceit, and misrepresentation) and (d) (serious interference with administration of justice). Specifically, Bar Counsel argues that because respondents "knew Mrs. Ackerman had executed documents she was not competent to understand, their use of the documents was dishonest and interfered with the administration of justice." We find that there was sufficient evidence for the Board to conclude that Bar Counsel had failed to demonstrate by clear and convincing evidence that respondents violated Rule 8.4.

Bar Counsel introduced substantial evidence to support the positions that Ms. Ackerman was incompetent and lacked capacity to make the decisions at issue in this case and that respondents knew or should have known that to be true. But respondents introduced substantial evidence pointing in the opposite direction. We assume for current purposes that the ultimate question of Ms. Ackerman's competence or capacity is one of law, as to which this court would not owe deference to the Board or the Hearing Committee. *But cf. Butler v. Harrison*, 578 A.2d 1098, 1101 (D.C.1990) (court of appeals will reverse trial court's finding that party was competent to contract only if finding was clearly erroneous). In our view, however, the resolution of that question in the present case turns on the weight to be given to the underlying factual evidence presented by Bar Counsel and the contrary factual evidence presented by respondents. On that indisputably factual issue, we see no basis upon which we could appropriately disregard the conclusions of the Hearing Committee and the Board. *Cf., e.g., In re Nace,* 98 A.3d 967, 974 (D.C.2014) ("Where there is substantial evidence to support the agency's findings[,] the mere existence of substantial evidence contrary to that finding does not allow this court to substitute its judgment for that of the agency.") (brackets and internal quotation marks omitted).

Bar Counsel further argues that the Hearing Committee and the Board did not assess Ms. Ackerman's capacity with respect to each decision that she made, as required by *Butler,* 578 A.2d at 1100. To the contrary, we agree with the Board that "the Hearing Committee carefully analyzed whether Mrs. Ackerman had sufficient capacity at each of the discrete times she made decisions relevant to this case." Bar Counsel focuses in particular on respondents' actions in connection with Ms. Ackerman's 2007 assignment to Dr. Ackerman of interests in the North Carolina Avenue property and other assets. Specifically, Bar Counsel argues that respondents acted dishonestly in connection with that transaction, because they were aware—but did not disclose to the court—that Dr. Ackerman had already filed a guardianship petition claiming that Ms. Ackerman was incompetent. Dr. Ackerman's guardianship petition, however, rested not on an assertion that Ms. Ackerman lacked mental capacity but rather on an assertion that Ms. Ackerman could not adequately conduct her affairs because of her blindness. Any failure to disclose Dr. Ackerman's subsequently withdrawn guardianship petition thus does not in our view amount to dishonest conduct rising to the level of a violation of Rule 8.4(c).

B.

Bar Counsel also contests the Board's conclusion that respondents did not violate the conflict-of-interest rules. Our analysis of this issue differs significantly from that of the Board, and we conclude that the matter should be remanded to the Board for further consideration of the issue.

1.

Under Rule 1.7(b)(2), informed consent to joint representation is required if an attorney's representation of one client "will be or is likely to be adversely affected by representation" of the other client. In the Board's view, Mr. J.T. Szymkowicz correctly determined, after adequate inquiry, that Ms. Ackerman's interests and Dr. Ackerman's interests did not conflict. Thus, the Board concluded, the Szymkowiczes were not required to obtain informed consent from Ms. Ackerman to the joint representation. Whether the risks of joint representation are sufficient to require informed consent is a mixed question of law and fact. *Cf. Wages v. United States,* 952 A.2d 952, 960 (D.C.2008) (whether conflict of interest exists is mixed question of law and fact). We therefore defer to the Board's purely factual findings but decide de novo the ultimate question whether informed consent was required. *Cf., e.g., In re Martin*, 67 A.3d 1032, 1039 (D.C.2013) (court reviews de novo questions of law and ultimate fact). We conclude that informed consent was required.

We take as a given for these purposes the Board's conclusions that Ms. Ackerman had the legal capacity to make the decisions at issue; wanted to transfer her assets to Dr. Ackerman's control; wanted to provide for Dr. Ackerman, even to her financial detriment; did not want the trust to continue; did not want Mr. Abbott to continue as trustee; was willing to pursue litigation to achieve these objectives; and was aware of the risks and costs of litigation. Nevertheless, there was evidence (largely if not entirely undisputed) of numerous other circumstances indicating a risk of conflicting interests requiring informed consent to joint representation. For example, there was evidence that Ms. Ackerman had favorable feelings towards Mr. and Ms. Abbott; that Ms. Ackerman did not want litigation and wanted peace in the family; that Ms. Ackerman had granted Ms. Abbott a POA; that after granting Dr. Ackerman a POA, Ms. Ackerman promptly revoked that POA but then reversed course and again granted several POAs to Dr. Ackerman; that Ms. Ackerman agreed to the filing of *Ackerman II* with the understanding that Dr. Ackerman would drop *Ackerman I*, which Dr. Ackerman did not do; that the trust, which was primarily intended to support Ms. Ackerman, was running out of money to provide for Ms. Ackerman's care; and that Dr. Ackerman had indicated that, if the trust had to sell property, he wanted Ms. Ackerman's residence to be sold rather than the North Carolina Avenue property where Dr. Ackerman lived. Moreover, it is undisputed that Ms. Ackerman's capacity was to at least some degree diminished by dementia.

Thus, even if Dr. Ackerman's interests and Ms. Ackerman's interests generally coincided, there was evidence indicating a substantial risk that those interests did or might diverge in particular respects relevant to the conduct of the joint representation. Such risks are not unique to the present case. To the contrary, such risks are common where one lawyer represents multiple family members in estate-planning matters, which is why Comment [20] to Rule 1.7 states that disclosure and informed consent "are usually required" in that setting. *See also* D.C. R. Prof. Conduct 1.7, Comment [7] (Rule 1.7's "underlying premise is that disclosure and informed consent are required if there is any reason to doubt the lawyer's ability to provide wholehearted and zealous representation of a client or if a client might reasonably consider the representation of its interests to be adversely affected [by representation of another client]. . . . [I]f an objective observer would have any reasonable doubt on the issue, the client has a right to disclosure of all relevant considerations and the opportunity to be the judge of its own interests."); D.C. Leg. Ethics Op. 301 (2000) ("[I]f an objective observer can identify and describe concrete ways in which one representation may reasonably be anticipated to interfere with the other, then a cognizable conflict arises under our rules, and disclosure must be made and a waiver sought.") (internal quotation marks omitted); Carolyn L. Dessin, *Protecting the Older Client in Multi-generation Representations,* 38 Fam. L.Q. 247, 247, 268 (2004) ("Estate planning is a field in which attorneys often represent members of the same family of different generations. This frequently leads to situations in which the family members have conflicting, or at least potentially conflicting, financial interests. . . . Special concerns arise when one or more of the family members is in a declining physical or mental state as a result of aging. In that instance, an attorney must be even more sensitive to representing all of [the attorney's] clients zealously and avoiding conflicts of interest between [the attorney's] clients."); "A better approach is to inform fully each client about the potential for future conflict and obtain the informed consent of each client to the representation."); *cf. In re McMillan,* 940 A.2d 1027, 1036 (D.C.2008) ("The trial court could conclude on this record, as it did, that a lawyer who represented appellant's parents would have a conflict of interest in representing zealously the interests of their son upon whom they depended for support.").

In the circumstances of this case, we conclude that the Szymkowiczes could not properly represent both Ms. Ackerman and Dr. Ackerman without obtaining informed consent to the joint representation. Because it concluded that informed consent was not required, the Board did not decide whether informed consent was obtained. The Hearing Committee did conclude that Mr. J.T. Szymkowicz obtained Ms. Ackerman's informed consent. Nevertheless, "[r]ather than deciding [that] issue without the benefit of the Board's judgment, we leave [the issue] for the Board to consider on remand. . . ." *In re Hopkins,* 677 A.2d 55, 63 n. 17 (D.C.1996). We do, however, note several issues that may merit the Board's consideration: (1) whether, as Bar Counsel contends, respondents bear the burden of establishing that they obtained informed consent or whether instead Bar Counsel bears the burden in disciplinary proceedings of establishing the absence of informed consent; (2) whether, as the Hearing Committee appears to have assumed, the determination whether Ms. Ackerman gave informed consent should be made under the standard applicable to the determination whether a party had capacity to engage in a transaction; (3) whether Rule 1.7(b)(2) is violated whenever the requisite informed consent is not in fact obtained, or whether instead it is a defense under the Rule that the attorney reasonably but mistakenly believed that informed consent had been obtained; (4) the implications of Rule 1.14, which addresses the obligations of a lawyer representing a client with diminished capacity, a topic we discuss infra with respect to the conflict-of-interest charges against Ms. Silverman and Mr. King; and (5) the date on which the Szymkowiczes ended their representation of Ms. Ackerman.

2.

In determining that Dr. Ackerman's influence over Ms. Silverman and Mr. King did not raise a conflict-of-interest issue, the Board relied heavily on the conclusion that Dr. Ackerman's interests generally coincided with Ms. Ackerman's interests. We have already explained our disagreement with that approach. We have additional concerns, however, about the reliance Ms. Silverman and Mr. King placed on the fact that Dr. Ackerman had been granted POAs by Ms. Ackerman. Apparently in reliance on the POAs, Ms. Silverman and Mr. King took numerous significant steps in their representation of Ms. Ackerman without consulting Ms. Ackerman. To take just one example, Ms. Silverman discussed with Dr. Ackerman the assignment of the North Carolina Avenue property and other assets to Dr. Ackerman, and subsequently defended the validity of the assignment. Nevertheless, Ms. Silverman apparently did not discuss that assignment with Ms. Ackerman. The heavy reliance by Ms. Silverman and Mr. King on the POAs in this case is troubling for several reasons.

First, Ms. Ackerman's mental capacity was indisputably diminished to a degree. Under Rule 1.14(a), Ms. Silverman and Mr. King were required to, "as far as reasonably possible, maintain a typical client-lawyer relationship" with Ms. Ackerman. As the commentary to that Rule explains, that requirement applies even if a surrogate decisionmaker, such as a POA holder, exists. D.C. R. Prof. Conduct 1.14, Comment [2] ("The fact that a client suffers a disability does not diminish the lawyer's obligation to treat the client with attention and respect. Even if the person has a surrogate decision-maker, the lawyer should as far as possible accord the represented person the status of a client, particularly in maintaining communication."); *cf., e.g., Buras v. Ace Dynasty*, 731 So.2d 1010, 1012–13 (La.Ct.App.1999) ("[W]e are not persuaded that . . . the power of attorney executed by [the client] in favor of [the POA holder], disposed of [the lawyer's] responsibility to communicate with his client. . . ."). Relatedly, we agree with Bar Counsel that Rule 1.14, which is intended in substantial part to provide additional protections to clients with diminished capacity, is not properly read as generally altering the responsibility of attorneys to obtain the requisite informed consent before undertaking joint representation presenting a risk of conflicting interests. *Cf., e.g., Dayton Bar Ass'n v. Parisi*, 131 Ohio St.3d 345, 965 N.E.2d 268, 273 (2012) (per curiam) ("[W]hen taking actions authorized by [Rule 1.14], the lawyer must still determine whether the representation of one client will be directly adverse to the other and whether there is a substantial risk that the lawyer's ability to consider, recommend, or carry out an appropriate course of action for one client will be materially limited by the lawyer's responsibilities to another client.").

Second, although Comment [4] to Rule 1.14 states that an attorney can ordinarily look to a surrogate decision-maker for decisions on behalf of the client, the circumstances of this case were not ordinary. The holder of a POA generally has fiduciary obligations to the person who granted the POA. *See, e.g.,* Restatement (Third) of Agency §§ 1.04(7) (POA holder is agent), 8.01 (agent generally has fiduciary obligation to principal) (2008). Although this court does not appear to have addressed the issue, many states presumptively prohibit POA holders from relying on a POA to make property transfers to the POA holder. *See, e.g., Losee v. Marine Bank*, 286 Wis.2d 438, 703 N.W.2d 751, 752–53 (Ct.App.2005) (Wisconsin law "prohibits self-dealing not specifically permitted in the POA"); *see generally, e.g.,* Carolyn L. Dessin, *Acting as Agent Under a Financial Durable Power of Attorney: An Unscripted Role*, 75 Neb. L.Rev. 574, 612 (1996) ("Many states have held that an agent [including a POA holder] cannot make a gift of the principal's property to himself unless the governing instrument expressly gives the power to make gifts."). The fact that the transactions at issue involved self-dealing by Dr. Ackerman added to the risks of conflict created when Ms. Silverman and Mr. King took payment and direction from Dr. Ackerman while representing Ms. Ackerman. *Cf., e.g.,* Kenneth L. Jorgenson, *When a Beneficiary Asks You to Draft a Will*, 60-SEP Bench & B. Minn. 11, 12 (2003) ("A lawyer's disproportionate reliance upon a beneficiary for testamentary instructions begs conflict of interest claims and expands the opportunity for undue influence challenges."); Carolyn L. Dessin, *Protecting the Older Client in Multi-generation Representations*, 38 Fam. L.Q. 247, 264 (2004) (lawyer representing grantor of POA "must be careful to ascertain that he is carrying out [grantor's] wishes").

For these reasons, we conclude that there was a substantial risk of conflicting interests arising from Ms. Silverman's and Mr. King's connections to Dr. Ackerman while they were representing Ms. Ackerman. Because the Board concluded otherwise, it did not address whether Ms. Silverman and Mr. King obtained informed consent from Ms. Ackerman. We leave that issue to be addressed on remand.

For the foregoing reasons, we accept the Board's finding that Mr. King violated Rule 1.5(b) by failing to obtain a written retainer agreement; we accept the Board's recommendation that the Rule 1.5(b) violation by itself would warrant an informal admonition; we accept the Board's recommendation to dismiss the charged violations of Rule 8.4; and we remand the matter to the Board for further consideration of the conflict-of-interest charges against all respondents.

So ordered.

SOLUTIONS: THE LAWYER SHOULD HAVE, WOULD HAVE, COULD HAVE. . .

In discussing the risk of a joint representation, the court concludes "(s)uch risks are common where one lawyer represents multiple family members in estate-planning matters, which is why (informed consent)" is usually required in these situations. In other words, the clients need to know the pros and the cons of such joint representation, as well as the alternatives to joint representation. Often, the wise lawyer foregoes informed consent and solves the issue of whether to engage in joint representation by deciding to only represent one of the persons, not both.

Becoming a Professional

X-Ray Questions

This article is about Britney. It illuminates the issue of the twin—and often competing goals—of giving dignity and autonomy to the client with diminished capacity versus the need to care for their needs. This conflict harkens back to the use of the word "maintain" in MR 1.14. The rule says: "When a client's capacity to make adequately considered decisions in connection with a representation is diminished . . . the lawyer shall, as far as reasonably possible, maintain a normal client-lawyer relationship with the client."

Was a disservice done to Britney? Were people looking out for her best interests? Were the goals of the Rule met or were they perverted?

BEYOND THE CITE

By: Anna-Drake Stephens, *"Don't You Know That You're Toxic?"* A *Look at Conservatorships through the #FreeBritney Movement*, 45 LAW & PSYCHOL. REV. 223 (2020–2021).

"DON'T YOU KNOW THAT YOU'RE TOXIC?"

A LOOK AT CONSERVATORSHIPS THROUGH THE
#FREEBRITNEY MOVEMENT

Britney Spears, a famous singer and teen pop sensation during the 1990s and early 2000s, is no stranger to the spotlight. With her debut single of ". . .Baby One More Time" in 1998, Britney's musical career has spanned over two decades. She has performed world tours, completed a Las Vegas residency, guest-starred on television shows, and released nine studio albums. 3 In 2007 and 2008, her personal struggles became headline news photos of her driving with her son in her lap, shaving her head, and attacking a car with an umbrella covered almost every news outlet. Since then, Britney has been under a court-approved conservatorship that granted control over her life to her conservators. Today, Britney has once again found herself at the center of the spotlight, but for a different reason. This time, instead of people mocking her, people are coming out in support of the popstar. This article does not pick a side in the #FreeBritney movement, but instead reexamines the conservatorship process and begs the question of how the legal field can move forward from the attention on such a little known, or little cared for, area of the law.

I.   "SAY HELLO TO THE GIRL THAT I AM"—INTRODUCTION TO CONSERVATORSHIPS.

The idea of looking over someone who is disabled or incompetent is perhaps one of the oldest features of mental health law, going all the way back in time to the Romans. Conservatorship comes from "the state's parents patriae power, its duty to act as a parent for those considered too vulnerable to care for themselves." All fifty states and the District of Columbia have some kind of guardianship or conservatorship law. Each state has its own legal criteria, processes, and terminology for when a person is unable to care for themself. Depending on the terminology, the court appoints either a guardian or a conservator." Britney Spears lives in California, so this note will focus on California law. In California, the statute distinguishes between a guardian and a conservator. Under California law, a guardian is a person appointed over a minor, and a conservator is appointed over an adult. Despite the different names, the governing law on guardianships and conservatorships is similar.

California courts define conservatorship as a legal process where a judge appoints a person or an organization, called the conservator, to care for another adult who cannot take care of their self or their finances, called the conservatee. No conservatorship is granted "unless the court makes an express finding that the granting of the conservatorship is the least restrictive alternative needed for the protection of the conservatee.' " There are different conservatorships based on the needs of the conservatee." The most common type is a probate conservatorship, based on the California Probate Code. Probate Code Conservatorships can be general or limited. General conservatorships are for adults "who cannot take care of themselves or their finances." Limited conservatorships are for adults with developmental disabilities that do not need the higher level of care in a general conservatorship. If a conservatorship is needed immediately, a court can grant a temporary conservator until a general conservator is appointed. A temporary conservator is for a fixed period of time and can be a conservator "of the person, estate, or both." A temporary conservator's duties include the "care, protection, and support of the conservatee" as well as protecting the conservatee's finances and property.

A probate court can appoint a conservator of a person or a conservator of an estate. The conservator of a person is responsible for the conservatee's care and protection, living arrangements, and personal care. The conservator must get court approval for the health care and living arrangements of the conservatee and must report the conservatee's status to the court. The conservator of the estate is also responsible for the conservatee's finances, income, and assets. A conservator is appointed for an individual who cannot manage their own financial resources or is unable to resist fraud or undue influence. In determining who will be the conservator, the court looks to the best interests of the conservatee. There is an order of preference for conservatorships, starting with the spouse or domestic parent, adult child, parent, sibling, any other person prescribed in the law, or a public guardian.

To start the process of conservatorship, a person must file a petition and give proper notice to the required parties. A court investigator will then investigate the potential conservatee. Then, there will be a hearing where a judge will determine whether to grant or deny the conservatorship. A court may appoint more than one conservator of the person or estate. The court may also, upon request or on its own, order a review of the conservatorship. A conservatorship is usually permanent but can be amended or terminated. The judge may remove a conservator and appoint a new conservator. A conservator may also resign. If the conservatee recovers and is able to handle their own affairs, they can then petition the court to end the conservatorship. If this happens, the court will once again assign an investigator. If the judge ends the conservatorship, the conservator is released from all duties. The purpose of the conservatorship section of the California Probate Code is to "[p]rotect the rights of persons who are placed under conservatorship; . . . [p]rovide [for] the health and psychosocial needs of the proposed conservatee; . . . [c]onsider the best interests of the conservatee; . . . [and] [p]rovide for the proper management and protection of the conservatee's real and personal property."

Furthermore, the conservatee should be allowed to "remain as independent and in the least restrictive setting as possible." Conservatorship is a process of great trust and responsibility. A conservatee trusts that that the conservator will follow the law. The conservator should involve the conservatee in the decision-making process and make decisions that benefit the conservatee. A conservatee does not "necessarily lose the right to take part in important decisions affecting his or her property and way of life." The conservator should follow the conservatee's wishes and best interests. There are many alternatives to conservatorships, and a judge should consider all of the alternatives before placing someone under a conservatorship.

II. "ALL EYES ON ME IN THE CENTER OF THE RING"— INTRODUCTION TO BRITNEY'S CONSERVATORSHIP

A. "Oh Baby, Baby"—The beginning of Britney's Conservatorship

In 2007 and 2008, Britney had several public breakdowns. In 2008, she was twice put under a 5150 psychiatric hold for mental health evaluations. In California, a 5150 hold is the involuntary detainment of an adult for seventy-two hours in a psychiatric hospital when that adult is "evaluated to be a danger to others, or to himself or herself, or gravely disabled." One month after these psychiatric holds, Britney's father, Jamie Spears, filed a petition to become an emergency temporary conservator. On February 1, 2008, the judge granted Jamie's temporary conservatorship. The conservatorship became permanent before the year ended. Jamie was conservator of Britney's estate and person. An attorney, Andrew Wallet, was appointed as co-

conservator of the estate to help oversee Britney's finances. Finding that Britney could not appoint her own lawyer, the court appointed Samuel D. Ingham III to be her lawyer and help oversee the conservatorship. By March 2009, Britney was back on tour. Since being placed under conservatorship in 2008, Britney has released an album every two to three years, completed a successful Las Vegas residency, performed world tours, filmed a documentary, and guest-starred on various television shows. Now over a decade later, Britney is still under conservatorship.

In 2019, Britney's conservatorship underwent some changes. In January of that year, Britney announced via social media that she put her second Las Vegas residency on hold, basing this decision on her father's health. She did not post again on social media until April 2019. Shortly after that post, Britney checked into a mental health facility. She checked out on April 25, 2019. In March, Wallet stepped down as co-conservator citing "substantial detriment, irreparable harm and immediate danger" if he did not resign. Wallet, on top of his $426,000 annual salary as co-conservator of the estate, received $100,000 after his resignation. Wallet's resignation left Jamie as the sole conservator of the estate. Britney's mom intervened on May 6, filing a request to be updated on the details of Britney's conservatorship. On May 10, Britney appeared for a conservatorship hearing, which she usually did not attend. At this hearing, the judge ordered a 730 expert evaluation, a "comprehensive report prepared by a team of Britney's doctors and possibly a court-appointed medical professional." Later that month, Jamie filed a notice of intent to extend Britney's conservatorship to Hawaii, Louisiana, and Florida. In September, Jamie temporarily stepped down as conservator, reportedly due to health reasons, and left licensed fiduciary Jodi Montgomery as the temporary replacement.

B.   "*. . .Baby One More Time*"—*The Rise in the #FreeBritney Movement*

The phrase "Free Britney" first appeared in 2009 shortly after the conservatorship was granted. The #FreeBritney movement argues that a popstar who has released albums, toured, and completed a residency should not be under an arrangement meant to protect the elderly and those who are seriously disabled. The #FreeBritney movement experienced a resurgence in April 2019, after Britney checked herself into a mental health facility. Leading this new wave in the #FreeBritney movement was the podcast Britney's Gram. Declaring an emergency episode, the podcast hosts revealed an anonymous tip they received from a paralegal who worked in the office handling Britney's conservatorship. The voicemail informant said that what was happening was "disturbing, to say the least." The paralegal claimed Britney's father made her cancel the residency because she was not taking her medication. He also claimed that Britney had actually been in mental health care facility since January 2019. The anonymous voicemail said that Britney was "held against her will and her hospitalization as ordered by Jamie." According to the source, "this is not a decision she mad, at all." This voicemail and podcast reignited the #FreeBritney movement, leading to a nationwide conversation on conservatorships.

III. "A GUY LIKE YOU SHOULD WEAR A WARNING"— CRITIQUE OF CONSERVATORSHIPS

Conservatorships are often necessary, but the execution needs improvement. Too often, conservatorships are viewed as "harmless" and a way of extending the state's paternalism. While conservatorships are very hard to end, the process is relatively easy to begin. One state committee noted how "the appointment of . . . a conservator removes from a person a large part of what it means to be an adult: the ability to make decisions for oneself . . . [w]e terminate this fundamental and basic right with all the procedural rigor of processing a traffic ticket." As the American Civil Liberties Union (ACLU) described, "the ease with which disabled people can be stripped of their rights, and the extraordinary difficulties they face getting those rights back, is a systemic disability rights issue about which we have serious concerns." A conservatorship can be a "double-edged sword," used to protect an individual while at the same time removing their rights, which could lead to abuse of the conservatorship.

Conservatorships should be seen "as the most restrictive form of court intervention." Therefore, conservatorships should be the last resort, with the most minimal intervention option chosen first. In a conservatorship, the court strips the conservatee of her civil liberties. The conservator is then granted power over that individual, having the final authority on any decision. This transfer of power away from one person and to another person means that conservatorships can easily lead to abuse. Conservators, instead of helping, often steal, neglect, and abuse their conservatee.

Conservatorships are a huge responsibility, and most conservators are unprepared or untrained to take on this new role. One survey found that less than twenty-percent of courts gave instructions on the conservator's duties and responsibilities. Furthermore, most people who petition for a conservatorship are unaware of the alternatives. A conservatorship is a difficult job, which can cause friction and damage the relationships between the conservator, the conservatee, and the family involved.

Most problems involving conservatorships are with its "oversight and accountability." The court should be monitoring the conservatorship through reports, which the court should review in detail. In California, one year after the appointment of conservatorship and annually thereafter, the court must review the conservatorship. However, continued monitoring remains a problem for courts to enforce. Some courts may not follow up with the conservator. Or some courts may not consistently enforce their mandates. Additionally, not all states require that the report include the person's need for a continued conservatorship.

The ACLU has joined the conversation surrounding Britney and conservatorships, lending its support to Britney. The ACLU tweeted: "People with disabilities have a right to lead self-directed lives and retain their civil rights. If Britney Spears wants to regain her civil liberties and get out of her conservatorship, we are here to help her." According to the ACLU, "too often people with disabilities are stripped of virtually all of their civil rights through guardianships and conservatorships.'" The ACLU argues that "people with disabilities . . . are individuals with a full range of human experiences and preferences who have the right to exercise their civil liberties."

Nevertheless, there are some safeguards in place. The court can appoint a lawyer to advocate on behalf on the conservatee. The California Senate Committee on Judiciary in a 2015 report remarked that "[i]n theory the court-appointed counsel should be arguing on the proposed conservatee's behalf for a less-restrictive alternative to conservatorship whenever possible." There is, of course, the danger that the court-appointed lawyer fails to live up to his or her role as an advocate. Moreover, in California, the court is required to look at other, less restrictive alternatives before granting a conservatorship. In reality, however, conservatorships are put in place even when there are other alternatives available.

IV. "YOU'RE GOING TO HAVE TO SEE FROM MY PERSPECTIVE"—INSIDE BRITNEY'S CONSERVATORSHIP

Britney has not controlled her life for over a decade. She cannot make decisions, personal or financial; without approval from her conservators. Her conservatorship is "designed for people who cannot take care of themselves." The conservatorship allows her father to control "almost everything she touches—including her money, her health, and her daily routine. According to court findings, Jamie is in charge of "overseeing and coordinating Britney's business, costuming, personal, household stuff, and legal matters (touching upon entertainment, music, other business opportunities, family law issues, the litigation, trial and/or resolution of other disputes, and ongoing litigation and conservatorship matters.)

Also, Jamie is in charge of her business opportunities, her interviews, her car maintenance, and her children's custody. It is Jamie's responsibility to "pursue opportunities related to professional commitments and activities including but not limited to performing, recording, videos, tours, TV shows and other similar activities as long as they are approved by Ms. Spears's medical team." With the #FreeBritney movement, Britney's Instagram posts have received much attention. While there are many conspiracy theories and speculations surrounding her Instagram page, it is one of the only things Britney herself can control. Because of Britney's conservatorship, society, through her social media, has the opportunity to:

> watch[ ] someone at the limits of a very narrow, very prescribed world. It's as though all Spears can do, the only thing she has, is the ability to pace through the halls of her mansion and hit a mark, over and over and over again. And then, maybe, have someone else post the video online with a smartphone she's not allowed to use herself.

Critics have long questioned the payment for Britney's conservatorship team. The people who would help in deciding to end the conservatorship are the same people who profit off of it and oversee it. In 2015, Jamie made $130,000 annually. Elaine Renoire, president of the National Association to Stop Guardian Abuse, noted that "[a]s long as she is bringing in so much money and as long as the lawyers and conservators are getting paid, there is little incentive to end it . . . . Usually, the conservatorship just keeps going unless the conservatee makes a fuss or the family does." As of 2018, Britney was worth $59 million. She spent $1.1 million on legal and conservator fees that year.

While it is not uncommon for people under conservatorship to be productive, yet not considered to be legally competent, the secrecy of Britney's conservatorship adds to the suspicion of exploitation. Britney's father keeps the conservatorship details mostly private. Britney's family has also been quiet on the subject of her conservatorship. With the recent attention, the family members are speaking out more. In 2019, with the rise of the #FreeBritney movement, Britney's team began saying that the conservatorship was good for Britney. Her manager said in an interview that the conservatorship was not a "jail," but instead "help[ed] Britney make business decisions and manage her life in ways she can't do on her own. . . ." Her mother, on the other hand, has liked #FreeBritney social media posts, seemingly indicating her position. In July 2020, Britney's brother, Bryan, spoke on the conservatorship. He described how the conservatorship was great for Britney but noted the strain it put on the family. He also mentioned how Britney "[a]lways wanted to get out of [the conservatorship]," and expressed his concern on the reality of what would happen if the conservatorship ended.

Britney has also said little about the conservatorship and has not tried to change the structure of the arrangement. There were some exceptions to this silence at the very beginning of the conservatorship. One lawyer who Britney spoke to at the beginning said Britney was not comfortable with her father being conservator and opposed the conservatorship. Britney, herself, once commented on how her situation was "[t]oo in control . . . if I wasn't under the restraints I'm under, I'd feel so liberated. . . . Even when you go to jail, you know there's the time when you're going to get out. But in this situation, it's never-ending."

Britney's silence on the conservatorship, however, ended when her lawyer filed a court document stating that the conservatorship must be substantially changed. On August 1, 2020, Jamie refuted conspiracy theories and denied rumors that he had stolen from Britney's estate. On August 17, 2020, Britney requested to remove Jamie as sole conservator, stating that she was "strongly opposed" to her father returning as conservator of her person or estate. Britney filed to permanently replace her father with Jodi Montgomery. The Los Angeles County Superior Court in California extended the current conservatorship until February 1, 2021. Britney has also said in court documents that she is "vehemently opposed" to Jamie's motion to keep her conservatorship closed. For the conservatorship of the estate, court filings reveal that Britney instead preferred a corporate fiduciary to be appointed, requesting Bessemer Trust Company. On November 10, 2020, the judge appointed Bessemer Trust as co-conservator of the estate, but allowed her father to stay in his position. The judge stated she would consider future motions to reconsider Jamie's position or to remove Jamie completely. At this hearing, Ingram told the court that Britney is afraid of Jamie and will not perform again so long as Jamie is in charge. The #FreeBritney movement gathered outside the courthouse during this hearing with signs to show their support for Britney.

There is little doubt that this conservatorship was good for Britney in 2008. Britney needed help in early 2008, and the conservatorship provided that help. The conservatorship is credited with "rescuing [her] career-and her life." Britney's lawyer explained in one court filing how the early period of Britney's conservatorship "rescued her from a collapse, exploitation by predatory individuals and financial ruin." Even Britney's mother wrote in her book, "I shuddered to think . . . what depths of desperation we would have to plumb to regain charge of our child."

While conservatorships can be corrupted, there still might be a good reason why Britney is still under a conservatorship. Britney's mental condition or diagnosis is kept private. The media does not know how vulnerable she is, but the court does. And if Britney is "still at risk," then this conservatorship is functioning as it should. After all, the court must ensure that a person is not under a conservatorship unless it is needed. Former co-conservator Wallet once mentioned that he thinks Britney will always be under a conservatorship as "the conservatorship is in her best interests . . . [p]rotecting her assets is very important and for that the conservatorship has to stay in place because she is susceptible to undue influences." In Britney's case, there may be added pressure on the court to do the right thing as no California judge wants to make headline news of doing something wrong to Britney Spears. Still, a conservatee may recover enough so that a conservator is no longer needed, or is not needed as much. The conservatee may be able to make some sound decisions on her own. The question then becomes: at what point should the court loosen some restrictions and give a conservatee the chance to make her own decisions?

V. "MY LONELINESS IS KILLING ME"—THE PSYCHOLOGY OF AUTONOMY

Britney's lawyer has said that Britney is now "trying to regain some measure of personal autonomy." Autonomy is central to mental health law, as "there is considerable psychological value in allowing people to make choices for themselves." Conservatorships require a balancing of an individual's right to autonomy and an individual's need to be protected. This balancing can go beyond protection and interfere with autonomy. Autonomy is critical to psychological need to make decisions can be "profound." Therefore, putting someone under conservatorship is a very significant decision. As a California Probate Court case described it, "a conservatee may be subjected to greater control of his or her life than one convicted of a crime."

Being able to make a decision for oneself is a basic need. Personal choices involve commitment that reinforces achievement, allowing individuals to perform more effectively and feel greater satisfaction. When the government intervenes and denies an individual the right to make their own decisions, the results may be "counterproductive, ultimately frustrating the attainment of whatever goals government may think the individual should seek to achieve." Government intervention may also cause psychological damage. When individuals cannot make decisions, "they fail to develop those self-determining capabilities that are essential to mature, adult functioning." The loss of this right can reduce an adult to a child or nonperson, known as legal infantilization.

Moreover, the loss of autonomy can lead to a decrease in well-being. Autonomy is a "condition for flourishing." Individuals who cannot make decisions may have low self-esteem, withdrawal, and passivity. People under conservatorships are deprived of autonomy, and therefore are deprived of control over their lives. This control is necessary to well-being, and without this control, individuals can feel depressed. The value of autonomy on well-being can be seen in a wide variety of studies. One study with nursing home residents looked at the power of decision making. The residents were divided into two groups, and one group was allowed to make decisions while the other group made no decisions. The non-decision-making group debilitated seventy-one percent more that the decision-making group over a three-week period. On the other hand, the group that made decisions showed improvement, felt more active, and were generally happy. From this study, it can be concluded that removing autonomy does not necessarily benefit conservatees.

Being in control of one's environment is "an intrinsic necessity of life itself." It has been argued that decision making is essential to psychological development. Instead of legal infantilization, autonomy allows individuals to develop an act like adults. Moreover, the individual is treated as a human being, not an object. A court should consider the significance of the loss of autonomy and whether these negative effects outweigh the benefits. The psychological power of "autonomy requires that the government meet a high burden of justification" in granting a conservatorship.

VI. "NOW I'M STRONGER THAN YESTERDAY"—CONCLUSION

Britney Spears is only one of the many Americans who are under conservatorship. Britney is not the first celebrity to be placed under conservatorship, and she will not likely be the last. But she has brough attention to a little-known area of probate law. Through the rise of the #FreeBritney movement, conservatorships have become headline news. As the Britney's Gram podcast host described her story, "[m]any people fall victim to conservatorship abuse in this country, but sadly, they are often society's 'invisible.' [Britney] has shined a light on this larger issue, and hopefully that continues to be the case."

Because society will generally always care for the disabled, it is therefore important for everyone, including lawyers, to protect those in our society while still treating them with respect and dignity. Society's goodwill should not be imposed coercively. Conservatorships have the potential to be both necessary and proper. Nevertheless, all conservatorships carry with them the potential for abuse. Courts should strictly monitor conservatorships and seriously consider when some restrictions can be removed. The legal field must always keep in mind that a conservatorship is taking away someone's rights and personal liabilities and should always treat conservatorships as the last resort.

WHAT'S NEXT?

An integral part of forming the ACR is the determination of what fee, if any, to charge the client. There are a variety of options but they each share a core value: a fee must be both reasonable and earned. And, in the course of representation—starting at its inception—a lawyer is charged with very specific ethical obligations dealing with the custody of client property whether cash, cryptocurrency, or tangible property. The next chapter covers these obligations.

> To assess your understanding of the material in this chapter,
> click here to take a quiz.

CHAPTER 2

Fees and Property

Coming Attractions

Lawyers need to make a living. This basic fact sets up one of the most fraught subjects in the relationship between lawyers and their clients. A lawyer's interest in being paid for her work puts her in conflict with her client. It would be normal for two parties on opposite sides of a business transaction to hire lawyers to negotiate and manage the relationship, precisely because we understand there are adversarial interest involved in any relationship between someone selling services and her customer. And yet, here, the conflict of interests is actually inherent in the relationship between the client and her lawyer.

Lawyers' need to be paid creates challenges for how we conceive of lawyers' role in society in general. And it can be uncomfortable to talk about. As a profession, lawyers like to talk about their role in high minded terms. We pursue justice. We counsel clients. We defend people's rights. We help build productive partnerships. We resolve conflicts. We safeguard rule of law and the Constitution. It is hardly a secret that lawyers also need to pay their staff and keep our practices afloat, and that they often want to make a profit. But to emphasize these motives would suggest that lawyers might sometimes have cynical, self-interested motives. That is uncomfortable.

There are a number of ways in which lawyers are paid, from fees by the hour, to contingency fees, to working for a salary. Every single model, including providing free services *pro bono*, carries ethical pitfalls. There is a danger of violating professional rules in a manner that could lead to professional sanctions or a lawsuit by an aggrieved client. And there are questions that lawyers should ask themselves throughout their careers about the role of personal profit in their professional lives. There is no one right way for lawyers to think about the role of money in their lives. But to pretend that lawyers do not have their own personal interests at stake would be naïve, and ethically dangerous.

Section 1. Basic Fee Structure

The following flowchart sets out the general timeline of fee arrangements. We will also introduce you to the obligation for a lawyer to protect client property—whether it be money or tangible property entrusted by the client to your care.

Let's Chart It!

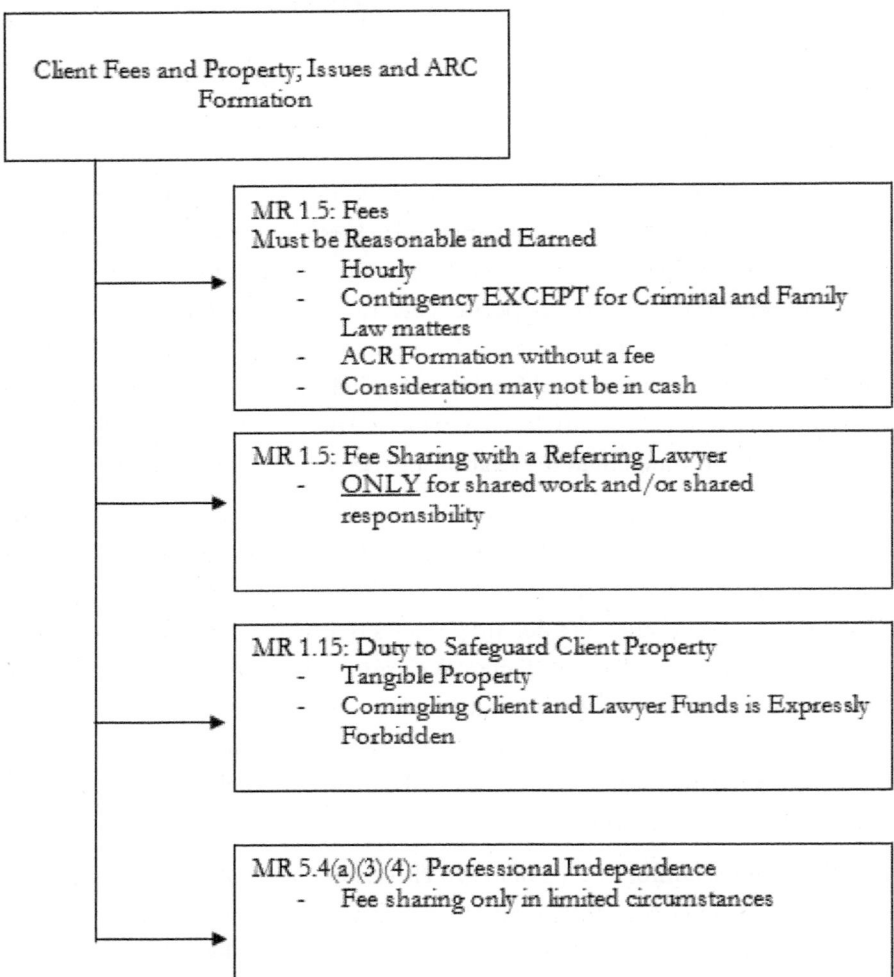

A. Hourly Fee Overview

Probably the most well-known way for lawyers to be paid is the hourly fee. Because it is so central to much legal practice, learning to keep track of time worked on client matters in 15-minute increments is a key skill that young lawyers need to learn. Productivity of attorneys is often measured in billable hours.

There are several ethics problems that arise in hourly billing. The most obvious is what is a fair hourly rate. But before we get to that problem, we need to highlight some more hidden features and challenges.

A first question to ask about any fee system is what kind of incentives it creates for the attorney. With hourly fees, attorneys have an incentive to do more work for a client. This can be a good thing, and it may be why hourly billing is typical in legal practice involving commercial and financially well-off clients. When paid by hour, a lawyer (or a law firm involving multiple lawyers) has an incentive to be as thorough as possible. If she does a bit more research to find helpful persuasive precedent or legislative history to add depth to a brief, she can be paid more. If she revises a draft contract just one extra time, improving subtle nuances in ways that reduce remote risks for her client, she can be paid more. As we will see, some other fee models do not incentivize lawyers to work harder for their clients in this way.

In ethical terms, the hourly system's incentive structure is both a feature and a bug. It encourages lawyers to go the extra mile (or the extra 15 minutes), which is fine if we assume that the most thorough possible legal work is always the goal. But maybe it isn't. From a consumer perspective, the client deserves to be able to assess whether the extra thoroughness is actually worth it. How much would an extra 5 hours of research into legislative history actually improve a client's chances of prevailing in court? That is often hard to say. Perhaps for some clients this is a minimal concern. Perhaps they are so wealthy that they are not sensitive to paying a bit more for the absolute best advocacy possible. Or perhaps the case is itself so high stakes that it is worth it to pay for every possible marginal advantage. But for clients on fixed budgets, the question whether the extra work is worth it is likely to loom large.

Add to this another problem: For a consumer to know whether an attorney's work is worth paying for, she would have to know how long the work is going to take. That is hardly easy, especially for people who do not frequently hire lawyers. Many young lawyers (and even some seasoned attorneys) habitually underestimate how long it will take to write a brief or draft a novel contract. It is important to keep in mind that unlike some other professions that often charge by the hour (think: therapists, plumbers, electricians), lawyers typically work out of sight of their clients. A thorough lawyer might spend two hours preparing for a 10-minute court hearing. A 15-minute telephone call might be followed by 15 hours of legal research and drafting. All that work may be legitimate and necessary. But a client can still easily and reasonably be shocked by the bill.

One thing is clear (mostly): In the words of an ABA ethics opinion: "In matters where the client has agreed to have the fee determined with reference to the time expended by the lawyer, a lawyer may not bill more time than she actually spends on a matter." ABA Formal Ethics Opinion 93–379. A lawyer may round up to the nearest 15-minute increment. That seems simple enough. But billing fraud—padding hours in order to charge clients more—is unethical. But that's really the easy question.

Cases and Materials

X-Ray Questions (*Clozel*)

In the following case, a court found proposed hourly fees for an attorney to be unreasonable. But it references many different factors. Was the hourly rate too high? Was the work excessive? Or both? Was the law firm here penalized precisely because they held themselves out as highly skilled, and if so, is that fair?

As you read this case pay special attention to the language used by the court: "simple task;" "defies imagination;" "inordinate amount of time;" "gross overreaching." Do you consider this strong language? Why do you think this language was used?

Thomas Clozel and Chine Labbe v. Hasan Jalisi and Azra Jalisi

Civil Court of the City of New York, 2012.
Index No. 11227/12.

FRANK P. NERVO, J:

Plaintiff moves for attorney fees pursuant to terms of a residential lease, having succeeded by default on a claim for return of a security deposit of $6,400 and treble damages. Plaintiff's counsel, Mayer Brown LLP, asserts it is due $126,026.88, after waiving certain costs, such as research fees from vendors, and its usual fees for services of administrative personnel and docket clerks at $110 to $125 per hour. A hearing on the motion was conducted on December 2, 2013. Given the fact that the items billed for, and the number of hours allegedly spent on them, is incredible, the court finds there is no basis to award any fee. . . .

Plaintiff submits a fourteen (14) page statement for counsel services. This statement demonstrates much duplicated effort, research on the most basic and banal legal principles that a client could reasonably expect counsel charging minimally $405 per hour would have prior knowledge of, not requiring review or oversight by a more senior associate, Jason I. Kirschner, at $615 per hour and a partner, Lee N. Abrams, at $895 per hour, all as unabashedly invoiced here. This is particularly egregious considering Mayer Brown LLP asserts it has attained a reputation as a "global law firm with a large litigation practice. . .routinely represent[ing] clients in connection with disputes arising from. . .landlord/tenant [matters]". For the sake of brevity, the court notes only the following as examples of the duplicative and unnecessary fees charged. . . .

February 15, 2012: Counsel Bridget P. Kessler "Researched. . .Civil Court procedural rules and pleadings requirements; researched New York law regarding security deposits and Real Estate licensing; drafted New York City Civil Court complaint seeking recovery of security deposit." Four and a half hours at $405 per hour: $1822.50. The court finds these are legal matters about which counsel is presumed to know and tasks that, even were they necessary, could have been performed within minutes. The court cannot discern any need to research the topic of real estate licensing, as it has nothing to do with the legal issue in question. In a nearly identical billing notation the next day, movant notes:

> February 16, 2012: "Researched. . .Civil Court procedural rules and pleading requirements; researched Maryland law regarding security deposits; researched New York state law regarding conversion of security deposits; drafted New York City Civil Court Complaint seeking recovery of security deposits."

Duplicating the effort of the prior day fails to make it any more warranted or valuable to the client, at a charge of $405 per hour for four hours, another $1620.00. The court will not award a fee for this simple task. While legal research may be billed for under appropriate circumstances, merely reading a court rule is not research.

On the following day, February 17, 2012, some part of four and a quarter hours was devoted to 'Revis[ing] a draft New York City Civil Court Complaint to recover security deposit; and on February 23, 2012, some part of an additional four and a half hours was spent again revising a draft complaint, albiet "based on additional factual information and legal research." However, after spending nearly five hours drafting the complaint, the substance of which could well have been pled by a summons with endorsed complaint, over the period February 24, 25, 27, and March 2, 2012 seven hours were spent exclusively on reviewing emails and documentation related to the security deposit in issue. Counsel asserts spending seven hours at $405.00 per hour, thus billing the matter $2835.00, reviewing documentation related to a one-time security deposit for which plaintiffs, as set forth in their eventual complaint, were in possession of a receipt. This is a grossly unnecessary amount of time for such a simple matter. Indeed, the basis upon which any attorney can actually occupy himself or herself over seven hours reviewing this nominal and uncomplicated material, in a simple case like this, defies imagination.

On March 12, 13, 14, and 27, 2012, counsel Kessler states that she spent four and three-quarter hours researching and discussing with her client and others trial strategy of the matter: $1923.75. This court cannot envision the inordinate circumstances under which any trial of this matter—had it gone to trial—would extend beyond sixty minutes, and preparation for that trial, in view of the time purportedly spent on the matter previously, would require much more than another sixty minutes. Thus, the court can find no reasonable basis for this excessive allocation of hours and the resultant fee.

July 18, 19 and 20, 2012 counsel Kessler spent the better part of two hours researching, drafting, reviewing, conversing, conferring, and discussing with others, then revising and serving the Notice of Inquest. The Notice of Inquest is a one-sided Blumberg form requiring the preparer to add the caption of the matter, check off two boxes, and answering a series of eight rather basic questions to assure compliance with pretrial procedures, all of which were correctly noted as "Not Applicable" in this case. To demand compensation for two hours of professional or non-professional time over three days to accomplish this essentially ministerial task, asserting it required researching, drafting, conversing, conferring and discussing of some sort, the court finds unbelievable. Further demonstrating the incredibility of this entire submission for counsel fees, on July 18, 2012, counsel Kessler billed for her "research regarding inquest" and "enforcing judgements," obviously before judgment was even entered, as well as the time a paralegal expended requesting a New York Practice Series book, presumably from the library of Mayer Brown, LLP. There is simply no justification for billing for such tasks. Again, this is not legal research; rather, it is simply becoming familiar with basic court procedures that an attorney is presumed to know.

July 28 and 29, 2012, counsellor Kessler's hourly rate rose to $475 per hour, required twenty six (26) hours over these two days to research a response to an order to show cause seeking vacatur of the default judgment, and the drafting of a memorandum of law. On July 31, 2012 that memorandum of law was drafted for the second time, and then revised at least twice on that same day over an additional eleven (11) hours, two of which purportedly required the undivided attention of more senior associate Jason I. Kirschner at $670.00 per hour. True, as part of this submission an attorney's affirmation was required, as well as an affidavit by the client and the compilation of some exhibits, and a hand full of emails did occur between various persons, however some of this was presumably accomplished on July 30th when associate counsel Kessler devoted an additional six (6) hours at $475.00 to this opposition. Ms. Kessler was further assisted in this endeavor by a Mary T. Barbetta, apparently a lay person, for four and a half (4.5) hours at $285.00 per hour, during which Ms. Barbetta created a table of authorities and reviewed the table of contents for the memorandum of law. Thus, at least fifty-two-and-one-half (52.5) hours of time were singularly devoted to preparing a simple opposition to an order to show cause seeking vacatur of a default judgment. This is a stunningly inordinate amount of time for such a simple task, and there is no basis to award compensation based on this incredible claim.

At the hearing of this motion on December 2nd, 2013 movant's counsel brought to the court's attention on more than one occasion that the representation by Meyer Brown LLP in this matter was "really, it was done as a favor" and "not looking to recover" anything from their clients, but rather as an accommodation for these clients. Consequently, it is apparent that the compensation anticipated by Mayer Brown LLP was that of good will which is, on many occasions, inestimable. While the Maryland fee statue and the loadstar analysis upon which movant relies provide for reasonable compensation of tenant's counsel in matters of this nature, the court will not countenance the gross overreaching evidenced under the facts and circumstances of this case in which the client is not even being billed for legal services.

To move any court to put its imprimatur of approval on such practices is simply intolerable. Under these circumstances, this court cannot and will not award any fees.

SOLUTIONS: THE LAWYER SHOULD HAVE, WOULD HAVE, COULD HAVE. . .

As stated by this court, "[t]his is a stunningly inordinate amount of time for such a simple task, and there is no basis to award compensation based on this incredible claim." The court obviously felt that the firm had poorly justified its bill. And then there is the fact that the legal fees were many times larger than the amount of money at stake for the client. These are the kinds of excessive bills that give lawyers a bad name.

LEANING INTO PRACTICE

The difficulty that legal consumers may have in anticipating legal bills is a major reason why legal practices that serve less wealthy clients often use flat fees instead of hourly fees. As we will see, flat fee models carry their own mix of advantages of disadvantages, but they at least make costs more predictable. But it is also worth asking whether the legal profession, or a single law firm, could improve the transparency and predictability of hourly fees. As one possibility, consider this provision in a state statute regulating hourly fees for auto mechanics:

Nevada Revised Statutes § 487.6877

If it is determined that additional charges are required to perform the repair authorized, and those additional charges exceed, by 20 percent or $100, whichever is less, the amount set forth in the estimate or statement required to be furnished pursuant [], the body shop or garage operator shall notify the owner and insurer of the motor vehicle of the amount of those additional charges.

In other words, in Nevada an auto mechanic must give a customer an estimate in advance of the costs of a repair. If the job turns out to require much more than the mechanic anticipated, the customer must be notified and consent. Interestingly, Nevada does not impose this safeguard on attorneys. Compare the far looser rule imposed on attorneys:

Model Rule 1.5(b)

(b)   The scope of the representation and the basis or rate of the fee and expenses for which the client will be responsible shall be communicated to the client, preferably in writing, before or within a reasonable time after commencing the representation, except when the lawyer will charge a regularly represented client on the same basis or rate. Any changes in the basis or rate of the fee or expenses shall also be communicated to the client.

Should the ABA and/or state bars consider tightening the provision by requiring attorneys to give clients binding estimates in advance of the costs for specific services, similar to the auto mechanic regulation? Even if not, if you were starting a law firm, would you adopt this practice or something like it for your firm?

BEYOND THE CITE

By: Walt Bachman, *The Almighty Billable Hour,* in *Law v. Life, What Lawyers Are Afraid to Say about the Legal Profession* 100–111 (1995).

The Almighty Billable Hour

Almost thirty years have elapsed since I last punched a time clock as a day laborer in my family's floral and gardening store. Yet I distinctly recall the vertical cardboard card with pre-printed lines given me every two weeks to log my work time. When inserted into the slot in the center of the time clock, the manila card was imprinted with the exact minute of my arrival or departure. The imprint was accompanied by a metallic ring that was duller than a cash register but resounded with more force and authority. As the two-week pay period progressed, the lines on the card became filled with the entries proving my labors, which were then converted arithmetically into a paycheck. At the end of a summer of work, I derived some measure of personal self-worth merely from the knowledge that I had created a stack of cards as tangible evidence.

A lawyers' time sheets, or time records, are far more detailed than my old timecards, which simply recorded the hours of my physical presence at the workplace. For every day I was engaged in the private practice of law, I recorded my time in 15-minute increments. Just as a gosling is imprinted to follow the first larger creature it encounters in life as its parent, even if that creature happens to be the barnyard golden retriever, I attempted to maintain the rules of logging time, I first learned, resisting efforts in later years to alter the mechanics or to computerize the process.

It is a mark if the indelible impression left by the first stage of the endlessly repeated administrivia of life that I have a clearer memory of the time sheets I used when I began practice than of my oldest child's first words or early birthday parties. Those first-time sheets were green, with pre-printed spaces to be filled in by hand indicating the client's name, the services provided, and the time spent.

Literally thousands of times, I wrote:

—"ABC Corporation: Telephone conference with client re summary judgment motion—15 minutes," or

—"Lincoln Jones: Legal research re statute of limitations—45 minutes," or

–"Universal Plastics, Inc.: Travel to and from courthouse and appearance before Judge Swanson on defendant's motion to compel discovery—two hours and 15 minutes."

At the end of each day, I gave these entries to my secretary, who in earlier days manually typed them on client billing sheets and in later days entered them into the law firm's computerized billing records.

The details of tracking time may vary from law firm to law firm. Some firms record time by bits as small as one-tenth of an hour, or even by the minute, whereas I was taught that any service worth the effort of recording the time deserved to be billed at a minimum of one-quarter of an hour. Some firms insist upon an elaborate description of the services provided, while some prefer unrevealing generalities like "legal services rendered." But these differences are all subsumed by the enshrined rule of modern American lawyering that a lawyer's worth is measured and a client is most often charged by a rate linked to the relentless tick of the clock: the billable hour.

It would be hard to overestimate the ascendant importance of billable hours in our legal profession. They are the litmus test of the worth and financial success of a lawyer or law firm. A lawyer who allows his or her annual billable hours to slip too low, or a firm that drops below the prevailing billable hour norms for its community, risks more than a decrease in income. Survival, of the lawyer within the firm or of the law firm itself, is at stake. Larger law firms exist today in an environment driven more by overall financial performance than by the quality of legal work generated or the reputation of its lawyers in the community. No one makes any meaningful effort to rank the quality of the lawyering done by these firms, but, for about the past ten years, national legal tabloids like *The Nation Law Journal* and similar local publication like *Minnesota's Journal of Law & Politics* have routinely published comparative rankings of law firms' financial performance. The surest way to move up or down in these rankings is to adjust the minimum number of billable hours expected of lawyers.

One fact predominates in any discussion of the role of billable hours over the past twenty years in American law practice: virtually every firm now requires its lawyers to bill substantially more hours than in the past. There has been a universal trend to increase the minimum floor of hours, the firm's "billable hours budge," for every lawyer, whether partner or associate. It is now standard for Wall Street firms to mandate minimum hours of 2,000 or more per year, and for other large firms around the country to require bulling approaching that amount.

Twenty years ago, there was much less emphasis on the billable hour, and the time commitment to law practice leeway given to individual lawyers was far wider. Lawyers with average billings of 1,500 hours per year often became partners; the same time sheet performance today would be considered grossly substandard. Across the country, lawyers; lives have been transformed by a ceaseless spiral of mandated workaholism.

The reasons for the universal increase in law firm work hours can be viewed from two perspectives: that of the managing partners and that of the beginning associate. The managing partners of any firm are responsible for its business functioning, its financial performance, its profitability for partners. The way most law firms bill their clients—a stated hourly rate times hours billed—circumscribes management options. Since the cost of operation, including rent, secretarial salaries, computer equipment, and supplies, are relatively fixed, profits can only be increased by raising either billing rates or billable hours.

From a business point of view, raising the lawyers' hours budget is preferable to hiking up rates because the change is invisible to clients. A firm that boosts the rate of the average partner from $190 to $200 per hour runs the risk of becoming less competitive in the local legal marketplace. Both current and potential future clients may take their legal work elsewhere to avoid the higher fees. Increasing the annual hours budge from 1,900 to 2,000 yields the same proportional rise in partners' profit, but without any detrimental effect upon competition between firms. Because costs are basically fixed, every extra hour worked and billed drops almost totally to the partners' bottom line.

But managing partners' financial woes extend far beyond a straightforward calculation of work hours times billing rates, due to another new development in the last generation—the "lateral" move of lawyers from firm to firm. In the 1960's, it was still considered improper for one law firm to hire a lawyer away from a competitive firm. Today, the hiring of laterals, both partners and associates, is one of the biggest sources of law firm growth. Every legal community is now constantly abuzz with gossip about the latest law firm defections and additions, and a firm's standing can fluctuate like the Down Jones average depending on the latest moves. "Did you hear that Schwartz left Pickering last month to head the probate department at

Trueblood? That makes three lost partners for Pickering in six months. If this keeps up, they're in real trouble."

While lawyers switch firms for many reasons, the lateral departures most dreaded by the managing partners are those involving the "most productive"—read "highest billing"—lawyers. To understand the inordinate financial impact of such a loss, consider a simplified hypothetical breakdown. If the average lawyer in a firm bills 1,800 hours per year, and the costs of operating the firm are about 50% of a total proceeds, 900 hours of effort goes to pay overhead. A partner billing at the rate of $200 per hour will contribute $350,000 to the firm's proceeds, $180,000 of which will pay costs and the same amount will be distributable through the partnership "pie." But a partner who bills, 2,400 hours will generate $480,000 in firm income for only slightly higher costs, say $200,00. The net return from the harder working partner would, in this example, be $280,000, or $100,000 more than the firm average. By working "only" 50% longer hours, the workaholic raises his or her contribution to partnership profits by about 65%. In other words, a partner's economic benefit to the firm is raised disproportionately by work habits that depart upwards from the firm's average.

Making calculations similar to this one, unhappy partners whose work habits are out of synch with others in their firm complain that their compensation is being dragged down. If entreaties to raise the firm's hourly budget are unsuccessful, or if the firm is unwilling to cut off a much larger slice of the compensation pie, the disaffected drone can jump laterally to another firm, typically one where the financial benefit of spreading the overhead among other like-minded time-grinders is maximized.

In this manner, the managing partners who permit their billable hours budget to fall out of line with the local competition risk far more than a slight imbalance in partners' income. The partnership itself can recede through erosion of its sized and, more importantly, loss of reputation, when lawyers jump laterally.

The other impetus for escalating work hours comes, ironically, from starting associates. Several years ago, when I was serving as a member of my law firm's management committee, I fielded numerous complaints from young lawyers about the pressures caused by the time demands of practice. Those with families were especially hard hit. Unlike the era when I began practice, when a (usually male) lawyer was seldom married to a working professional, by the 1980's most of our married young associates came from two-career homes. They almost uniformly urged me to hold the line on the billable hours budget and to resist boosting our hours requirements to match recent hikes by other firms.

Responding to these please, I supported a recruitment approach that differed from our competitors". Our firm decided to maintain its starting salary (then at $44,000, as I recall) and to emphasize that our billable hours budget was only 1,650 a year—at least 150 hours below that of firms that had increased their starting salaries to $50,000. We reasoned that the top law students would flock to a firm that offered a relatively high salary coupled with a more balanced and civilized lifestyle.

That year turned out to be the worst ever for our firm's recruitment efforts. Faced with crusting student loans of up to $75,000 to repay—and oblivious to the realities of the life they would face when billing 1,800 to 2,000 hours a year—candidates for associate positions opted in almost every instance for the higher salary instead of fewer work hours. By now, of course these same students, as young lawyers, are expressing misgiving about her harried and overworked lives. If only they had known as law students what they now know, my guess is most of them would gladly have scarified incremental dollars for a more balanced life. From hard-earned experience, I have come up with a rough rule of thumb for those who contemplate some form of life outside the practice of law, a life involving, say, marriage, children, hobbies or outside interests.

LESSON SEVEN: 10% of a lawyer's soul dies for every 100 billable hours worked in excess of 1,500 per year.

While one may quibble about the number or percentages, the conclusion that lawyering carried to excess is destructive to one's personal life is beyond reasonable dispute. The lawyer's professional life is filled with aggressive, manipulative, half-truthful and other destructive behaviors, most of which are necessary, if unfortunate, by-products of our adversary system. If one wishes to salvage a measure of humane existence from a life spent in the aggressive pursuit of other people's causes, one must keep billable hours below 1,500 a year. At 1,500 hours, there is time not only to attend Johnny's school pageant, play the clarinet, go fishing, or join a study group at the synagogue, but also find a sufficient respite from lawyering behaviors to offer a personal sanctuary or counterbalance.

Law students, who are accustomed to working long hours during law school, fail to appreciate the long-term significance of a lifetime regimen remised on 2,000 annual billable hours. Multiplying fifty weeks per year times forty hours, they conclude that 2,000 hours can be achieved by a work week less than the forty to fifty hours of their law school efforts. But that analysis ignores the difference between actual hours and billable hours, and also fails to comprehend the difference between the pressures of law school, which are basically intellectual, and the added strains that come with lawyerly responsibilities.

Young lawyers soon learn the distinction between hours spent working and billable hours. The ruth is that one needs to work 55–60 hours to bill forty. For starters, ordinary daily activities and pleasantries, such as greetings and chit-chat with co-workers and secretaries, coffee breaks, and bathroom breaks cannot be billed. When I punched a manual laborer's time clock, I was given credit for such time.

Paid holidays and vacations assume a different meaning to someone who's efforts are measured by annual billable hours. Young lawyers' friends who are in other fields of work are surprised to learn that law firms do not specify holidays, or the number of vacations days permitted. A starting associate may feel a kind of heady smugness when he or she says, "as long as I get my hours in, I can take as many holiday or vacation days as I want."

The reality is that it's harder to take a vacation from yourself than from a n employer. A billable hour system means that the cell door is open but a massive ball and chain remain invisibly attached. Come November, the associate who's hours are below budge—whether due to a dearth of work, a death in the family, attendance at career-enhancing legal education courses, or virtually any other reason—will be more likely to rescind that planned December vacation than if Scrooge himself were setting the work rules. As for holidays one came to expect as a given in law school, one soon learns that law firms are open and practicing hard on the days other employers give over to commemorating the deeds of national heroes, such as Martin Luther King, Lincoln, Washington, and Columbus. For an associate, these national holidays simply mean that he or she must send legal documents by fax or FedEx, rather than by U.S. mail.

Law students are largely unaware that the fastest-growing chunk of time commitments for practicing lawyers is the law-related *non*-billable hour. Lawyers are expected to spend an ever-increasing amount of time on a wide variety of non-recompensable duties: on law firm committees that do everything from manage the firm to select the office artwork; on recruiting and interviewing job applicants; on bar association and other professional activities; on attending continuing legal education course.

Another enormous time-gobbler for al lawyers is what is euphemistically referred to as "marketing," an area that has been dramatically altered during the past two decades. In 1970, the law firms with which interviewed assured me that the days were gone when lawyers were hired for their business or social contracts. A listing in the social register or membership in the poshest country club was irrelevant. The common pitch was: "We get and keep clients solely because of the quality legal work we do and the reputation that flows from that work." In those days, beginning lawyers were told not to worry about, or spend time on, attracting new clients. At that time, when the demand for sophisticated legal services outstripped supply, this message was more than recruiting hype. It was true.

The transformation of the legal marketplace withing the past twenty years has added to the work burdens of lawyers on a daily basis. From the outset, lawyers today are taught that attracting, obtaining, and keeping clients is required of everyone in the firm. The same large law firms that calmly assured the law students of the '60's and '70's that client-getting skills were completely unnecessary in their practice now inform even first-year associates that their marketing ability will be weighed heavily in considering admission to the partnership. Lawyers are expected to join clubs, give practicum seminars, write newsletters aimed at clients, and develop and follow up leads for new clients to an extent never before demanded. All of this time spent attracting and schmoozing clients translates to non-billable hours, which are simply added on top of the minimum work requirements of the firm.

Within the firm, a lawyer must be seen as causing the practice to grow, not merely improving his or her legal skills. A stunningly capable lawyer is less favored than a more mediocre marketing whiz. When I opted for law school over an MBA, I thought I was leaving the economically-driven hurly-burly of the business worlds for a dignified profession, a distinction becoming more and more blurred each year.

If law student recruits don't apprehend the true burden entailed in a 2,000 billable hour year, their lack of comprehension of the nature of a lawyer's life—especially a trial lawyer's—is even more critical.

Lawyers may be likened to verbal and psychological soldiers on the front lines of disputatious acrimony. They are just as in need of soulful R & R as any battle-weary grunt. That need goes beyond mere hours of work, just as solder's need to escape the battlefield has more to do with the character of the work than with the actual hours in battle. Indeed, some of the physical and emotions symptoms commonly reported by stressed-out lawyers are akin to those of post-traumatic stress syndrome in soldiers: the 3:00 a.m. awakenings, the traumatic fixations, the depression, the emotional exhaustion, the resort to mind-altering chemicals.

The cumulative impacts upon a lawyer of higher billable hour budgets, more non-billable practice-related commitments, and the intrinsically stressful character of the practice of law combine to deaden or destroy ethereal human qualities, or soul. Lawyers whose careers span this transformation from manageable profession to overworked business treadmill express disenchantment bordering on sullen hostility, often without a clear understand of the sources of their ennui.

Meanwhile, students who are racking up five-figure loans to pursue those big starting salaries have almost no meaningful concept of the life they will be expected to lead.

[. . . .]

B. Hourly Fees: Setting the Rate

We now turn to the fundamental question in hourly fees: How much is an hour of a lawyer's work worth? Of course, the answer is that it depends. Also, important to remember: A lawyer's hourly fee is not really just for the lawyer's work. It also pays his support staff, rent, etc. Nevertheless, lawyers' hourly rates are the subject of considerable public fascination, and occasional sarcasm given the eye-popping rates charges by at least a small number of lawyers.

For lawyers to make money solely by billing for their own work time requires accepting an obvious fiction: The lawyer's time is hardly the only cost involved in a law practice. What about office rent? Legal assistant and receptionist salaries? Electric bills? Obviously, those things must be paid for. But the same ABA opinion that says lawyers cannot falsely pad their hours also says that a lawyer cannot directly charge for the overhead required to keep a law office open. She may not, according to the ABA, directly charge a fee to cover the cost of staffing and equipping the office. A lawyer may charge extra fees for some costs—research fees, telephone calls, photocopying, etc.—but only "so long as the charge reasonably reflects the lawyer's actual cost for the services rendered." ABA Formal Ethics Opinion 93–379. In other words, a lawyer's time is often the only thing on which a law firm can directly turn a profit.

Model Rule 1.5(a)

A lawyer shall not make an agreement for, charge, or collect an unreasonable fee or an unreasonable amount for expenses. The factors to be considered in determining the reasonableness of a fee include the following:

(1)   the time and labor required, the novelty and difficulty of the questions involved, and the skill requisite to perform the legal service properly;

(2)   the likelihood, if apparent to the client, that the acceptance of the particular employment will preclude other employment by the lawyer;

(3)   the fee customarily charged in the locality for similar legal services;

(4)   the amount involved and the results obtained;

(5)   the time limitations imposed by the client or by the circumstances;

(6)   the nature and length of the professional relationship with the client;

(7)   the experience, reputation, and ability of the lawyer or lawyers performing the services; and

(8)   whether the fee is fixed or contingent.

Deconstruction Exercise/Rule Rationale

Note the sentence construction in the first line and the use of the disjunctive "or." It expands the reach of the rule. It means that merely stating an unreasonable fee, but never seeking to collect it, is still a violation.

LEANING INTO PRACTICE

Scenario: The Case of the Platinum Defense for a Brass DWI Charge

Potential client consults with a well-known lawyer on providing a defense to a DWI (Driving While Intoxicated) charge against his son. The lawyer candidly admits that he never handled a DWI, but the client retains him, nonetheless. No estimate of what fees could be expected is given to the client. The lawyer comes up with a creative defense after spending numerous hours researching DWI law. The defense is successful. Bills are then sent to the client which ultimately total $50,000 plus.

There is no question that the lawyer and his associates worked the hours billed. But the client files a grievance with the State Bar against the lawyer. The court holds that while the lawyer earned the fee it was not reasonable, in light of testimony that a simple DWI defense usually costs under $10,000. Of course, one might respond that most DWI defenses don't end in acquittal, so perhaps it was worth it. But the court emphasized that the client was not given any notice or reason to expect that fees would range so high.

Section 2.   Flat Fees

An obvious alternative to hourly fees is a flat fee. In short, with a flat fee the lawyer tells the client precisely how much the cost will be for the lawyer to perform a specific service. A lawyer can say, I charge X to process a routine bankruptcy, or Y to represent someone in a standard divorce. Flat fee arrangements are extremely common in many areas of legal practice that cater to people who are not wealthy and not frequent legal consumers. Family law, bankruptcy, criminal defense and immigration are prominent examples where flat fees are common. Nevertheless, a flat fee does not necessarily mean that the lawyer is being paid any less than she would be with an hourly rate. In theory, if one knows in advance how many hours of work a client-matter would require, a savvy lawyer could set a flat fee to be exactly the same as what she would be paid with an hourly rate.

A flat fee's great advantage is its transparency for the client. Unlike with hourly fee structures, a client should not be surprised by the bill if the attorney is working for a flat rate. A flat fee arrangement effectively shifts from the client to the attorney the burden to anticipate the amount of work that a case will require. This is appealing, both because it makes costs predictable, and because one would think that lawyers are in a better position than their clients to estimate in advance the work required.

Despite these advantages, flat fee arrangements do raise their own set of problems. First, what should happen if a matter resolves itself much faster and easier than anyone anticipated, but the client paid a high flat fee that envisioned a great deal more work? In Rule 1.5, the very first criteria involved in judging whether a fee is reasonable is "the time and labor required." If it turns out that very little lawyer labor was required, it can be difficult to justify keeping the fee. As a result, attorneys may need to give their clients' partial refunds.

There is a way in which this is actually unfair to attorneys who work regularly on a flat fee basis. An experienced attorney might know that a certain type of case on average takes about 20 hours of work. But an experienced attorney might also know that individual cases vary. Sometimes they might take 50 hours of work, and sometimes just 5 hours. If the attorney is always able to keep the fee for an average case, then this individual variation will even out over time, enabling the lawyer to keep costs predicable for clients. But if the attorney must refund the clients who end up with easy cases, while still being compelled to work extra time on the ones that turn out to be more complex, then the flat fee arrangement may become untenable. And that may not actually be a good result for the public.

One way around these problems is for attorneys to charge flat fees for more narrow parts of a matter, or to specify that there will be additional fees if certain things happen. So, for example, an attorney could charge a flat fee for only the initial phases of litigation, and charge additional fees for certain parts of discovery, for summary judgment, and for trial. Or, a lawyer could offer a hybrid fee—a flat fee, with triggers for additional fees if the work goes beyond a certain number of hours. But it should be noted that the more a flat fee becomes complex and contingent, the less it offers the advantages of transparency and predictability to clients.

Just as with hourly fees, we need to ask what incentives a flat fee creates for attorneys. With flat fees, an attorney has a financial incentive to take on a higher quantity cases, and to try to minimize the amount of work she needs to do for each one. Thus, the fear with flat fees would be that it will encourage mediocre or bare minimum legal work. For this reason, in the context of criminal defense, state and local governments that provide indigent defendants legal defense by paying flat fees have in some cases been successfully sued for systematically violating defendants' Sixth Amendment rights. This fear may be mitigated if the flat fee is high enough to compensate the attorney for thorough work. But if one of the appeals of flat fees is that is makes legal services more accessible to non-wealthy people, it would also seem predictable that market pressures will make it harder for lawyers to charge more.

The rules governing flat fees are heavily influenced by rules about advance fees. An advance is just that—an early payment, in advance of when it is earned. An advance fee payment can be made with hourly fees, as a way for the lawyer to be assured of payment. In this case, the advance payment must be held in trust by the attorney until it is actually earned. But a flat fee is something different—maybe. In theory, with a flat fee the attorney is setting a simple price for the service, regardless of how many hours it takes. But in practice flat fees ad advances can look similar. In both cases, the client pays a lump sum. As you read MR 1.15 and the following cases, consider whether the courts and the bar are adequately distinguishing flat fees and advances.

Model Rule 1.15: Safekeeping Property

(a)   A lawyer shall hold property of clients or third persons that is in a lawyer's possession in connection with a representation separate from the lawyer's own property. Funds shall be kept in a separate account maintained in the state where the lawyer's office is situated, or elsewhere with the consent of the client or third person. Other property shall be identified as such and appropriately safeguarded. Complete records of such account funds and other property shall be kept by the lawyer and shall be preserved for a period of [five years] after termination of the representation.

(b)   A lawyer may deposit the lawyer's own funds in a client trust account for the sole purpose of paying bank service charges on that account, but only in an amount necessary for that purpose.

(c)   A lawyer shall deposit into a client trust account legal fees and expenses that have been paid in advance, to be withdrawn by the lawyer only as fees are earned or expenses incurred.

(d)   Upon receiving funds or other property in which a client or third person has an interest, a lawyer shall promptly notify the client or third person. Except as stated in this rule or otherwise permitted by law or by agreement with the client, a lawyer shall promptly deliver to the client or third person any funds or other property that the client or third person is entitled to receive and, upon request by the client or third person, shall promptly render a full accounting regarding such property.

(e)   When in the course of representation, a lawyer is in possession of property in which two or more persons (one of whom may be the lawyer) claim interests, the property shall be kept separate by the lawyer until the dispute is resolved. The lawyer shall promptly distribute all portions of the property as to which the interests are not in dispute.

Deconstruction Exercise/Rule Rationale

Money of the client is the property of the client. The client owns it. Thus, the Bar looks with great disfavor on the lawyer playing fast and loose with the client's money because money—once gone—cannot always be recovered. It must be kept separate from the lawyer's property because the temptation at stake is too great and even a lawyer's negligence in handling the money—with no intent to steal—can lead to its loss. This rule also provides the other side of the fee equation, which is that a fee must not only be reasonable but also must be "earned." Here "earned" in the sense that the money becomes the property of the lawyer but only after the lawyer has performed the work for which the lawyer was retained.

Cases and Materials

X-Ray Questions (*In re Sather*)

If an attorney charges a flat fee and the case resolves more easily than expected, should the attorney give the client a refund? That is what the Supreme Court of Colorado held in *In re Sather.* But did the Colorado court really close the door entirely to flat fees?

In reading this case recall that a fee must, to be an ethical fee, satisfy two criteria: it must be earned and it also musts be reasonable. Apply this concept to the fee of the lawyer in this case. Was it both? Why or why not? What is the difference between a retainer fee and a flat fee? Focus on the difference in reviewing this case. We will study the point at which a fee is considered to be earned.

A few final questions. Look at the bolded language in Sather's fee agreement. Can you explain why that language, standing alone, is a violation of the Rules? The case also introduces you to MR 1.16 which deals with declining or terminating client representation, which is on the other end of the ACR formation spectrum. Here, the court explains that the structure of the fee agreement impedes the client's unrestricted right to end the ACR at any time and for any reason. How so?

In the Matter of Larry D. Sather

Supreme Court of Colorado, 2000.
3 P.3d 403.

JUSTICE BENDER delivered the Opinion of the Court.

I.   INTRODUCTION

In this attorney regulation proceeding, we address the conduct of the attorney-respondent, Larry D. Sather, who spent and failed to place into a trust account $20,000 he received as a "non-refundable" advance fee for a civil case. Because Sather treated these funds as his own property before earning the fee, Sather's conduct violated Colo. RPC 1.15(a). Sather labeled the $20,000 fee "non-refundable" even though he knew that the fee was subject to refund under certain circumstances, thereby violating Colo. RPC 8.4(c). After being discharged by his client, Sather failed to return all of the unearned portion of the $20,000 promptly, in violation of Colo. RPC 1.16(d).

In this original proceeding, we hold that an attorney earns fees by conferring a benefit on or performing a legal service for the client. Thus, under Colo. RPC 1.15 an attorney cannot treat advance fees as property of the attorney and must segregate all advance fees by placing them into a trust account until such time as the fees are earned. An attorney cannot label advance fees "non-refundable" because it misleads the client and risks impermissibly burdening the client's right to discharge his attorney, in violation of Colo. RPC 8.4(c) and 1.16(d).

After a hearing on the matter, the hearing board recommended that Sather be suspended for a year and a day as discipline for his violations of Colo. RPC 1.15(a), 1.16(d) and 8.4(c). We disagree with the board's recommendation. Because we have not previously explained that all advance fees, including "lump-sum" fees and "flat fees," must be placed into trust accounts and withdrawn only as the attorney performs services or confers benefits on the client, we do not impose a sanction on Sather for his violation of Colo. RPC 1.15(a). However, we agree with the hearing board that Sather be disciplined for violating Colo. RPC 1.16(d) and 8.4(c). Because Sather knowingly mishandled client funds and knowingly deceived a client, and in light of Sather's disciplinary history, we suspend Larry D. Sather for six months. Further, as a condition of reinstatement, Sather must demonstrate his fitness to practice by undergoing proceedings pursuant to C.R.C.P. 251.29, even though the term of the suspension is less than one year.

II. FACTS AND PROCEDURAL BACKGROUND

The hearing board found the following facts were established by clear and convincing evidence. Sather agreed to represent Franklin Perez in a lawsuit against the Colorado State Patrol and certain individual troopers. Perez alleged that the troopers violated his civil rights during a traffic stop on December 7, 1995. Almost a year after the stop, on November 15, 1996, Sather and Perez entered into a written agreement for legal services, captioned "Minimum Fee Contract." Sather drafted the agreement, the terms of which required Perez to pay Sather $20,000 plus costs to represent Perez in the case against the State Patrol. Sather testified that he had never charged this large an amount as a flat fee in a civil case.

The contract referred to the $20,000 alternatively as a "minimum fee," a "non-refundable fee," and a "flat fee." The contract stated that Perez understood his obligation to pay this fee "regardless of the number of hours attorneys devote to [his] legal matter" and that no portion of the fee would be refunded "regardless of the time or effort involved or the result obtained." The contract acknowledged Perez's right to discharge Sather as his attorney, but the contract informed Perez that in no circumstance would any of the funds paid be refunded:

IN ALL EVENTS, NO REFUND SHALL BE MADE OF ANY PORTION OF THE MINIMUM FEE PAID, REGARDLESS OF THE AMOUNT OF TIME EXPENDED BY THE FIRM.

The client has been advised that this is an agreed flat fee contract. The client acknowledges that the minimum flat fee is the agreed upon amount of $20,000, **regardless of the time or effort involved or the result obtained.**

(Emphasis in original.) Thus, the contract stipulated that Perez pay Sather $20,000 for his legal services; that he pay all legal costs incurred by Sather in the case; and that no funds would be refundable after Perez paid Sather the flat fee of $20,000.

Perez paid Sather $5,000 of the minimum fee on November 17, 1996. He paid the remaining $15,000 on December 16th. Sather spent the $5,000 soon after receiving the money. Sather kept the second payment of $15,000 for approximately one month before spending these funds. Sather did not place any of these funds in his trust account before spending them. Sather testified that he spent Perez's $20,000 because he believed he earned the fees upon receipt. Sather stated that while he could not cite a specific rule for this opinion, he thought it was a common practice in the legal community to treat flat fees as being earned on receipt.

Less than a month after agreeing to represent Perez, on December 6, 1996, Sather filed suit in Denver District Court on behalf of Perez against the State Patrol and three troopers. In addition to claims for tort and civil rights injuries, the complaint included a claim for attorney's fees. The Attorney General's Office, which represented the State Patrol and three troopers, negotiated with Sather and offered Perez a $6,000 settlement, which Perez refused. Sather then requested an extension of time to respond to a pretrial motion, which the court granted.

On April 21, 1997, in a matter unrelated to the Perez case, this court suspended Sather from the practice of law for thirty days, effective May 21, 1997. *See People v. Sather*, 936 P.2d 576, 579 (Colo.1997). As required, Sather notified Perez of his suspension and Perez responded on May 23, requesting an accounting of the hours Sather worked on his case. Perez requested that Sather provide the accounting by May 30, but Sather replied that he would be unable to provide this information until the third week of June. Thereafter, on June 4, 1997, Perez faxed Sather notice discharging him from his case because of the suspension.

Acting pro se, Perez received an extension of time to file a response to the State Patrol's motion after informing the court that he was seeking replacement counsel to handle the case. Then, on August 21, 1997, Perez wrote a letter to the Attorney General's Office, accepting the offer of $6,000 to settle all of his claims against the State Patrol and the troopers. In its findings of fact, the hearing board noted that the attorney for the Attorney General's office did not exert any pressure on Perez to settle the case and further noted that that the Attorney General's Office would have agreed to an extension of time had Perez needed it to obtain substitute counsel.

Sather provided the accounting requested by Perez on June 27, 1997. Sather claimed that his fees, his paralegal assistant's fees, costs and expenses in Perez's case as of the date of discharge totaled $6,923.64. At that time, Sather acknowledged that he should refund $13,076.36, the balance of the $20,000 paid by Perez.

Despite acknowledging his duty to return the unearned $13,076.36 to Perez, Sather did not refund any money to Perez because at the time of discharge he had spent Perez's funds. On September 3, 1997—three months after Perez discharged him—Sather paid Perez $3,000. Sather paid the remaining $10,076.36 on November 2, 1997. The hearing board found that this delay prejudiced Perez because he did not have access to his funds for almost five months.

At the time Sather and Perez entered into the flat fee agreement, Sather was involved in personal bankruptcy proceedings. Sather filed a Chapter 7 bankruptcy proceeding in U.S. Bankruptcy Court in March 1995, over a year before agreeing to represent Perez. Sather later converted this case to a Chapter 13 proceeding, and then attempted to reconvert the case to a Chapter 7 filing. At the time of the hearing, the bankruptcy case was still pending. During the representation, Sather never told Perez that he had declared bankruptcy. After discharging Sather, Perez hired an attorney to pursue a claim against Sather in the bankruptcy proceeding for a refund of the fees ($6,923.64) Sather charged for work on Perez's suit.

Much later, in June 1998, Perez and Sather agreed to an arbitration by the Colorado Bar Association concerning the amount of fees charged by Sather for his work. The arbitrator awarded Perez $2,100.00, which represented the cost to Perez to bring the arbitration action. The arbitrator did not award Perez any recovery of the fees Sather charged for work performed. Shortly before the hearing in this case, on November 17, 1998, Sather paid Perez the award.

After a hearing, the board recommended that Sather be suspended for a year and a day. The board found that Sather violated Colo. RPC 1.16(d) by failing to return Perez's funds for nearly five months after Perez discharged him. The board concluded that because Sather admitted that he knew he had an ethical obligation to refund any unearned fees to Perez, the characterization of Perez's fee as "non-refundable" constituted a material misrepresentation. Thus, Sather violated Colo. RPC 8.4(c) by engaging in conduct involving dishonesty, fraud, deceit, or misrepresentation.

In addition to these violations, the board found that Sather violated Colo. RPC 1.15(a) by negligently failing to keep his client's funds separate from his own. The board concluded that Sather's failure to adhere to this rule was negligent because a case addressing the issue was announced in close proximity to Sather's actions, and the board believed that Sather could have been unaware of the requirements for handling client funds. See *People v. Gilbert*, 921 P.2d 48, 49 (Colo.1996). Thus, the hearing board reasoned that Sather's failure to hold the $20,000 paid by Perez as separate from Sather's personal property resulted from a "negligent lack of attention to the case law," but there was not clear and convincing evidence showing that Sather knew or should have known that his conduct violated 1.15(a)'s requirement that client funds be segregated from the attorney's own funds.

The board concluded that the complaint did not allege that Sather's original fee of $20,000 was excessive or that the portion of the fee Sather claimed he earned, $6,923.64, was excessive in violation of Colo. RPC 1.5(a). Thus, the board did not consider whether Sather's fees violated Colo. RPC 1.5(a).

Sather was admitted to practice law in this state in 1976. He received a letter of admonition in 1983 for his failure to give an accounting of time spent and funds received in two cases. In 1996, Sather received a letter of admonition for failure to pay promptly a person he hired for investigative services. In 1997, Sather was suspended from the practice of law for thirty days for violations of

Colo. RPC 1.4 and 1.5 based on his failure to keep a client reasonably informed about a matter and for charging unreasonable fees. See *Sather*, 936 P.2d at 579. In 1993, Sather began experiencing personal problems due to the dissolution of his marriage, and he filed for bankruptcy in 1995. See *id.* at 578.

We note that this case arose under our previous attorney disciplinary system, which is no longer in place. See note 2, *supra*. Because we recognized the importance of this issue to the Colorado bar, we determined not to rely solely on the briefs filed in this court. We set this case for oral argument and directed the parties to brief the following questions:

1.   Whether under the facts of this case a violation of Colo. RPC 1.15(a) has been established.

2.   Whether under the facts of this case a violation of Colo. RPC 1.16(d) has been established.

3.   Whether under the facts of this case a violation of Colo. RPC 8.4(c) has been established.

In addition to setting this case for oral argument, we invited representatives of state professional organizations to submit amicus briefs on these issues. The Colorado Criminal Defense Bar and the Colorado Defense Lawyers Association submitted briefs as amici curiae.

III. DISCUSSION

Sather contends that under Colorado law it is unclear whether an attorney must deposit all advance fees—including flat fees—into a trust account until the fees are earned. Sather further argues that an attorney earns flat fees upon receipt and the fees are thus the attorney's property and not subject to the trust requirements of Colo. RPC 1.15. Sather's fee agreement also raises the issue of "non-refundable" fees.

In order to address the issues raised in this case, we examine first Colo. RPC 1.15's requirement that attorneys segregate their property and funds from their clients'. Second, we discuss when and under what circumstances a client's property or funds are earned by an attorney and may therefore be treated as the attorney's property. Thirdly, we address whether an attorney may charge a "non-refundable" fee.

A.   Colo. RPC 1.15 Requires Segregation of Attorney and Client Property

Initially, we address Colo. RPC 1.15(a), which requires that an attorney keep client funds separate from the attorney's own property:

> *In connection with representation, an attorney shall hold property of clients or third persons that is in an attorney's possession separate from the attorney's own property. Funds shall be kept in a separate account* maintained in the state where the attorney's office is situated, or elsewhere with the consent of the client or third person. . . . Complete records of such account funds and other property shall be kept by the attorney and shall be preserved for a period of seven years after termination of representation.

(Emphasis added.) In addition to this subsection of the rule, Colo. RPC 1.15(f)(1)9 requires that an attorney maintain client funds submitted to the attorney as advance fees in a separate trust account until the attorney earns the fees:

> (f)   Every attorney in private practice in this state shall maintain in a financial institution doing business in Colorado, in the attorney's own name, or in the name of a partnership of attorneys, or in the name of the professional corporation or limited liability corporation of which the attorney is a member, or in the name of the attorney or entity by whom employed:
>
> > (1)   A trust account or accounts, separate from any business and personal accounts that the attorney may maintain as an executor, guardian, trustee, or receiver, or in any other fiduciary capacity, into which trust account or accounts . . . any advance payment of fees that has not been earned shall be deposited . . . .

(Emphasis added.) Thus, Colo. RPC 1.15(a) and (f) indicate that an attorney has an obligation to keep clients' funds separate from his own, and that advance fees remain the property of the client until such time as the fees are "earned." *See also People v. Varallo*, 913 P.2d 1, 11–12 (Colo.1996) (disciplining attorney for failing to place unearned retainers in a separate account for the client); *People v. Brown*, 863 P.2d 288, 290 (Colo.1993) (finding violation in part where "respondent accepted a retainer from the client [and] deposited the retainer in the law firm's operating account although the retainer had not yet been earned").

The rule requiring that an attorney segregate funds advanced by the client from the attorney's own funds serves important interests. As a fiduciary to the client, one of an attorney's primary responsibilities is to safeguard the interests and property of the client over which the attorney has control. See *Olsen & Brown v. City of Englewood*, 889 P.2d 673, 675 (Colo.1995); Restatement (Third) of the Law Governing Lawyers § 56 cmt. (b) (Proposed Final Draft No. 1 1996) [hereinafter Draft Restatement]. Requiring the attorney to segregate all client funds—including advance fees—from the attorney's own accounts unless and until the funds become the attorney's property protects the client's property from the attorney's creditors and from misuse by the attorney. See *Gilbert*, 921 P.2d at 49–50; *People v. Shidler*, 901 P.2d 477, 479 (Colo.1995); *Iowa Supreme Court Bd. of Prof'l Ethics & Conduct v. Apland*, 577 N.W.2d 50, 56 (Iowa 1998); Model Rules of Professional Conduct Rule 1.15 commentary at 237 (3d ed.1996) [hereinafter Model Rules]. Thus, Colo. RPC 1.15(a) and (f) further the attorney's fiduciary obligation to protect client property.

In addition to protecting client property, requiring an attorney to keep advance fees in trust until they are earned protects the client's right to discharge an attorney. See Colo. RPC 1.16(d) cmt. ("A client has a right to discharge an attorney at any time, with or without cause, subject to liability for payment for the lawyer's services."). Upon discharge, the attorney must return all unearned fees in a timely manner, even though the attorney may be entitled to quantum meruit recovery for the services that the attorney rendered and for costs incurred on 410 behalf of the client. See Colo. RPC 1.16(d); *People v. Crews*, 901 P.2d 472, 474–75 (Colo.1995); *Olsen & Brown*, 889 P.2d at 677.

If an attorney suggests to a client that any pre-paid or advance funds are "non-refundable" or constitute the attorney's property regardless of how much or how little work the attorney performs for the client, then the client may fear loss of the funds and may refrain from exercising his right to discharge the attorney. See *Olsen & Brown*, 889 P.2d at 677; *In re Cooperman*, 187 A.D.2d 56, 591 N.Y.S.2d 855, 858 (1993), aff'd, 83 N.Y.2d 465, 611 N.Y.S.2d 465, 633 N.E.2d 1069 (1994). Because the unearned portion of the advance fees must be kept in trust and cannot be treated as the attorney's property until earned, the client will not risk forfeiting fees for work to be performed in the future if the client chooses to discharge his attorney. Thus, the requirement that the attorney place advance fees in trust protects the client's right to discharge his attorney.

B.　An Attorney Earns Fees by Conferring a Benefit on or Providing a Service for the Client

As we discussed, rule 1.15's requirement that an attorney hold in trust all unearned fees furthers important interests central to the attorney-client relationship. When a client pays an attorney before the attorney provides legal services, the crucial issue becomes whether funds are "earned on receipt" and may be treated as the attorney's property, or whether the fees are unearned, in which case the funds must be segregated in a trust account under Colo. RPC 1.15. As one publication aptly framed this dilemma:

> The basic question is, whose money is it? If it's the client's money in whole or in part, it is subject to the trust account requirements. If it is the lawyer's money, placing it into a trust account would violate the anti-commingling rule.

ABA/BNA *Lawyers' Manual on Professional Conduct* 45:109 (1993) [hereinafter ABA/BNA *Lawyers' Manual*]. We hold that an attorney earns fees only by conferring a benefit on or performing a legal service for the client. Unless the attorney provides some benefit or service in exchange for the fee, the attorney has not earned any fees and, with a possible exception in very limited circumstances, the attorney cannot treat advance fees as her property.

Funds given by clients to attorneys as advance fees or retainers benefit attorneys and clients. Some forms of advance fees or retainers appropriately compensate an attorney when the fee is paid because the attorney makes commitments to the client that benefit the client immediately. Such an arrangement is termed a "general retainer" or "engagement retainer," and these retainers typically compensate an attorney for agreeing to take a case, which requires the attorney to commit his time to the client's case and causes the attorney to forego other potential employment opportunities as a result of time commitments or conflicts. *See In re Scimeca*, 265 Kan. 742, 962 P.2d 1080, 1091–92 (1998); *In re Lochow*, 469 N.W.2d 91, 98 (Minn.1991); ABA/BNA *Lawyers' Manual, supra*, 45:110–11; Lester Brickman & Lawrence A. Cunningham, *Nonrefundable Retainers Revisited*, 72 N.C. L.Rev. 1, 6 (1993). Although an attorney usually earns an engagement retainer by agreeing to take the client's case, an attorney can also earn a fee charged as an engagement retainer by placing the client's work at the top of the attorney's priority list. Or the client may pay an engagement retainer merely to prevent the attorney from being available to represent an opposing party. *See* Alec Rothrock, *The Forgotten Flat Fee: Whose Money Is It and Where Should It Be Deposited?*, 1 Fla. Coastal L.J. 293, 357 (1999). In all of these instances, the attorney is providing some benefit to the client in exchange for the engagement retainer fee.

In contrast to engagement retainers, a client may advance funds—often referred to as "advance fees," "special retainers," "lump sum fees," or "flat fees"—to pay for specified legal services to be performed by the attorney and to cover future costs. *See Scimeca*, 962 P.2d at 1091; *Lochow*, 469 N.W.2d at 98; Model Rules, *supra*, Rule 1.5, commentary at 59; ABA/BNA *Lawyers' Manual*, *supra*, at 45:111. We note that unless the fee agreement expressly states that a fee is an engagement retainer and explains how the fee is earned upon receipt, we will presume that any advance fee is a deposit from which an attorney will be paid for specified legal services. See Draft Restatement, *supra*, § 50 cmt. (g) ("A fee payment that does not cover services already rendered and that is not otherwise identified is presumed to be a deposit against future services.").

Advance fees present an attractive option for both the client and the attorney. Like engagement retainers, advance fees allow clients to secure their choice of counsel. Additionally, some forms of advance fees, e.g., "lump sums" or "flat fees," benefit the client by establishing before representation the maximum amount of fees that the client must pay. See Rothrock, *supra*, at 354. In these instances, the client knows how much the total cost for legal fees will be in advance, permitting the client to budget based on a fixed sum rather than face potentially escalating hourly fees that may exceed the client's ability to pay. *See id.* So long as the fees are reasonable, such arrangements do not violate ethical rules governing attorney fees. See Colo. RPC 1.5 cmt. (endorsing the use of a "fixed amount" as the basis for a fee); Draft Restatement, *supra*, § 50 cmt. (g) (referring to "lump-sum" fees as complete payment for an attorney's services).

Advance fees benefit the attorney because the attorney can secure payment for future legal services, eliminating the risk of non-payment after the attorney does the work. See Rothrock, *supra*, at 354. Often, attorneys collect a certain amount from the client in advance of any work and deduct from that amount according to the hours worked or mutually agreed-upon "milestones" reached during representation (e.g., investigation, pretrial work and motions, negotiations, filings, handling a company's initial public offering, etc.). *See id.* at 355–56; Ariz. Ethics Op. 99–02 (1999). Attorneys often deduct costs from advance payments as they incur the costs, similar to the manner in which they deduct their fees as they are earned. Advance fees represent an alternative method of obtaining legal assistance that accommodates legitimate needs of both clients and attorneys, and by this opinion we do not intend to discourage these fee arrangements provided the fee agreements comply with the ethical principles discussed in this case.

In the case of both advance fees and engagement retainers, the attorney performs a service or provides a benefit to the client in exchange for the fee. We recognize that we have not previously explained the ethical principle that determines when an attorney may treat funds paid as engagement retainers or advance fees as property of the attorney. Because this principle is a crucial element of the attorney-client relationship, we make our interpretation of the underlying ethical principle explicit: an attorney earns a fee only when the attorney provides a benefit or service to the client. *See Gilbert*, 921 P.2d at 49 (finding violation of Colo. RPC where attorney "performed no services to earn the fees"); *Apland* 577 N.W.2d at 57 ("[A] lawyer cannot charge a fee for doing nothing") (quoting Brickman & Cunningham, *supra*, 72 N.C. L.Rev. at 17). Under Colo. RPC 1.15(a) and (f), all client funds—including engagement retainers, advance fees, flat fees, lump sum fees, etc.—must be held in trust until there is a basis on which to conclude that the attorney "earned" the fee; otherwise, the funds must remain in the client's trust account because they are not the attorney's property.

With respect to fees mutually agreed to be "earned on receipt," an attorney must describe in writing the nature of the benefit being provided to a specific client in order to claim some portion or all of an engagement retainer as earned when paid. *Cf.* Colo. RPC 1.5(b), cmt. (as amended, effective July 1, 2000) (requiring that all new fee agreements—and recommending that any changes in existing fee agreements—be explained to clients in writing). That is, an attorney cannot treat a fee as "earned" simply by labeling the fee "earned on receipt" or referring to the fee as an "engagement retainer." *See Wong v. Michael Kennedy, P.C.*, 853 F.Supp. 73, 81 (E.D.N.Y.1994). Rather, the attorney must explain in detail the nature of the benefit being conferred on the client, whether it is the attorney's guarantee of availability, prioritization of the client's work, or some other appropriate consideration. *See id.*; *Lochow*, 469 N.W.2d at 98.

Our holding that an attorney must keep advance fees in a separate trust account until the attorney performs legal services or otherwise confers a benefit on the client is consistent with our earlier cases. In *Gilbert*, we held that the respondent violated Colo. RPC 1.15(a) by failing to place $62 in filing fees and $600 in advance fees into a trust account. *See* 921 P.2d at 49. In *People v. Zimmermann*, we noted that the respondent's failure to deposit unearned advance fees, charged as "flat fees" by the attorney, violated DR 1–102(A)'s requirement that unearned retainers be placed in trust accounts. See 922 P.2d 325, 325–26 (Colo.1996). In *Varallo* we noted, "Depositing unearned retainers into [a] business operating account" violates the rule requiring that client funds be deposited into a trust account. See 913 P.2d at 11. In *Brown*, we disbarred the respondent in part because he placed retainer fees in an operating account before the fees were earned. *See* 863 P.2d at 290–91.

In sum, Colo. RPC 1.15 requires that attorneys segregate client funds, including those paid as advance fees, from the attorney's property. Engagement retainers are generally earned upon receipt and, so long as the basis of how the attorney earns this fee is clearly explained to the client in writing, they are the attorney's property. For other forms of advance fees, the attorney may transfer the funds to the attorney's personal or operating accounts only after earning the fees unless, within a very limited set of circumstances, the attorney and client have agreed in writing to allow the attorney to treat the unearned fees as property of the attorney. An attorney can earn fees only by providing services or conferring a benefit on the client, and the attorney must explain the nature of the services or benefit being conferred before he may treat advance funds as his own property.

C. "Non-refundable" Fees

Having discussed the ethical principle requiring that attorneys maintain in trust all advance fees until the attorney earns the fees, we address Sather's characterization of his fee as "non-refundable." Because fees are always subject to refund under certain conditions, labeling a fee "non-refundable" misleads the client and may deter a client from exercising their rights to refunds of unearned fees under Colo. 1.16(d). Thus, we hold that attorneys cannot enter into "non-refundable" retainer or fee agreements. As is the case with our holding that attorneys must place all unearned funds in trust until the attorney confers a benefit on or performs a service for the client, we have not previously made this prohibition explicit.

Some forms of advance fees called "non-refundable" fees are often treated by attorneys as earned on receipt and thus as the attorney's property. In these agreements, attorneys inform their clients that the non-refundable fee becomes earned on receipt and is the attorney's property irrespective of whether the attorney performs future legal services and regardless of the time the attorney devotes to the client's case. *See, e.g., Cooperman*, 611 N.Y.S.2d 465, 633 N.E.2d at 1070. These arrangements are controversial because attorneys treat funds as their own property before performing any legal services for the client:

> In the forefront of the debate on advance fee payments is the problem of the "non-refundable" retainer. A non-refundable retainer "allow[s] an attorney to keep an advance payment irrespective of whether the contemplated services are rendered." While widely used, this kind of arrangement is not immune to criticism.

ABA/BNA *Lawyers' Manual* at 45:110 (citations omitted); see also Model Rules, *supra*, Rule 1.5 commentary at 59.

A fee labeled "non-refundable" misinforms the client about the nature of the fee and interferes with the client's basic rights in the attorney-client relationship. Attorney fees are always subject to refund if they are excessive or unearned. See Colo. RPC 1.5(a); 1.16(d); Rothrock, *supra*, at 347. A fee agreement that suggests that advance fees are "non-refundable" undermines the client's understanding of her rights and may discourage a client from seeking refunds to which the client may be entitled. See Rothrock, *supra*, at 347.

In addition to misinforming the client, "non-refundable fees" may discourage the client from discharging his attorney for fear that the client will not be able to recover advance fees for which the attorney has yet to perform any work. *See Cooperman*, 611 N.Y.S.2d 465, 633 N.E.2d at 1072–73. Because the label is inaccurate and misleading, and discourages a client from exercising the right to discharge an attorney, we hold that attorneys may not enter into "non-refundable fee" agreements or otherwise communicate to their clients that the fees are "non-refundable."

We acknowledge that in some instances a client may agree with an attorney to allow the attorney to treat funds paid in advance of legal services or other consideration as property of the attorney and thus not subject to the trust account requirements. Although we do not address the exact contours of such an arrangement in this opinion and recognize that narrow exceptions to this rule may exist, we caution that at minimum such arrangements will be construed against the attorney and in favor of the client. *See Elliott v. Joyce*, 889 P.2d 43, 46 (Colo.1994). Furthermore, the attorney must expressly communicate to the client verbally and in writing that the attorney will treat the advance fee as the attorney's property upon receipt; that the client must understand the attorney can keep the fee only by providing a benefit or providing a service for which the client has contracted; that the fee agreement must spell out the terms of the benefit to be conferred upon the client; and that the client must be aware of the attorney's obligation to refund any amount of advance funds to the extent they are unreasonable or unearned if the representation is terminated by the client. Further, any arrangement that allows the attorney to treat unearned advance fees as his own property must protect the client's property interests in the funds and the client's right to discharge the attorney at any time without being penalized by "non-refundable" fees or retainers.

In the limited circumstances in which an attorney earns fees before performing any legal services (i.e., engagement retainers) or where an attorney and client agree that the attorney can treat advance fees as the attorney's property before the attorney earns the fees by supplying a benefit or performing a service, the fee agreement must clearly explain the basis for this arrangement and explain how the client's rights are protected by the arrangement. In either of these situations, however, an attorney's fees are always subject to refund if excessive or unearned, and an attorney cannot communicate otherwise to a client.

D.   Rulemaking

We have discussed at length three important principles of professional responsibility. First, we reviewed Colo. RPC 1.15's requirement that attorneys segregate client funds and property from their own. This requirement protects client property from attorneys' creditors and from abuse by the attorneys themselves. Second, we explained that an attorney may treat advance funds or other property submitted by the client in exchange for legal services or other benefits only when the attorney performs those services or confers the benefits. We agree with the Iowa Supreme Court that an attorney cannot earn a fee for doing nothing. See *Apland*, 577 N.W.2d at 57. Third, we stated that attorneys cannot characterize fees as "non-refundable" because an attorney's fees are always subject to refund if they are excessive or unearned and such a characterization misinforms a client and may discourage a client from seeking refunds to which he is entitled.

In addition to our overview of these important subjects, we examined two related areas in some detail. First, we reviewed how and when an attorney earns a fee upon receipt, as in the case of engagement retainers. Such fees are earned only when the attorney performs a service or provides an immediate benefit to the client. Second, we noted that in some limited circumstances, a client and her attorney may agree that the attorney may treat advance fees as her own property before performing the services paid for by the client. As we emphasized, attorneys in such arrangements must take particular care to protect the client's rights to discharge the attorney and to recoup unearned fees.

However, we also recognize that a substantial number of attorneys in this state may engage in conduct that would be affected by our discussion of these issues. For example, many attorneys collect flat fees in advance of performing work and place the fees in their operating accounts upon receipt. Because we acknowledge that our opinion concerning the proper disposition of such a fee has widespread practical implications and because we wish to provide practicing attorneys a full opportunity both to comment on any proposed rules and also to comport their practices to these ethical constraints, we are referring these issues to the Colorado Bar Association. We will request that the CBA solicit widespread comment from practicing attorneys and then draft proposed Rules that would implement the ethical principles that we today announce.

Until the court formally accepts and promulgates such Rules, we will not discipline attorneys for failing to place "flat fees" or similarly characterized fees into trust accounts until the attorney earns the fee, in violation of Colo. RPC 1.15(a). On the other hand, we will discipline attorneys who charge excessive fees, attorneys who fail to return unearned fees promptly and attorneys who characterize fees as non-refundable because attorney fees are always subject to refund if either excessive or unearned.

IV. DISCIPLINE OF ATTORNEY-RESPONDENT SATHER

Having examined the ethical principles applicable to this case, we address the board's recommendation that Sather be suspended for a year and a day. Because we have not previously made clear an attorney's obligation to deposit all forms of advance fees into trust accounts or explained the prohibition against "non-refundable" fees, we do not sanction Sather for violating these rules. For this reason, we do not accept the board's recommended sanction. Additionally, we assess the aggravating and mitigating circumstances of this case somewhat differently than did the board. Because Sather knowingly failed to return unearned fees and knowingly misrepresented the nature of the fees paid by a client, and in light of his disciplinary history, we hold that Sather be suspended for six months.

The hearing board concluded that Sather "negligently" violated Colo. RPC 1.15(a) by failing to keep client funds segregated from his own funds when he deposited the flat fee from Perez in his operating account before he earned the fees. As discussed, we acknowledge that our opinions have not made clear the requirement that under Colo. RPC 1.15 an attorney cannot treat as earned any advance fees for which the attorney has not provided a benefit or service to the client. We also note that Colo. RPC 1.15(f)—which requires that advance fees be kept in a client's trust account until the fees are earned and guides our interpretation of an attorney's responsibilities to safeguard client property under Colo. RPC 1.15—was not in effect at the time of Sather's conduct. Thus, although Sather violated this rule, we disagree with the board, and we do not discipline Sather for this violation.

Although we disagree with the board's conclusion that Sather's conduct warrants sanctions under Colo. RPC 1.15, we agree with the board's conclusion that Sather violated Colo. RPC 1.16(d) by only partially repaying Perez's advance fee three months after being discharged and paying the balance of the refund five months after being discharged. Once discharged from representing a client, an attorney "shall take steps to the extent reasonably practicable to protect the client's interests, such as . . . refunding any advance payment of fee that has not been earned." Colo. RPC 1.16(d). A discharged attorney must refund unearned fees in a timely fashion and failure to do so is a violation of Colo. RPC 1.16(d). *See Crews*, 901 P.2d at 474–75; *People v. Sigley*, 917 P.2d 1253, 1254 (Colo.1996) (finding violation of Colo. RPC 1.16(d) where respondent failed to return advance fees for seven months after discharge). Upon discharge, Sather acknowledged his obligation to return the unearned portion of the $20,000 to Perez, and Sather eventually returned the entire unearned amount of $13,076.36. Perez claimed that he was unable to retain alternate counsel because he did not have access to those funds after he discharged Sather, and the board concluded that his inability to use those funds caused harm to Perez. Because Sather only partially returned the unearned fees three months after being discharged and did not return the remainder of the unearned fees until five months after being discharged, we agree with the board that his conduct violated Colo. RPC 1.16(d).

We also agree with the board's determination that Sather violated Colo. 8.4(c) by materially misrepresenting to Perez the nature of the fee he paid. Colo. RPC 8.4(c) prohibits attorneys from engaging in conduct that involves "dishonesty, fraud, deceit, or misrepresentation." The fee agreement Sather drafted clearly expressed that the $20,000 was non-refundable, irrespective of the number of hours Sather spent on the case, and that "**IN ALL EVENTS, NO REFUND SHALL BE MADE OF ANY PORTION**" of the $20,000. (Emphasis in original.) Despite this strong language of the contract he drafted, Sather testified that he understood his ethical obligation to return any unearned portion of the fees in the event of discharge. We approve of the board's finding that Sather knowingly used misleading language to describe the fee arrangement and knowingly made a material misrepresentation to his client concerning the $20,000 advance fee. Thus, we accept the board's finding that Sather's conduct involved dishonesty, deceit, fraud and misrepresentation in violation of Colo. RPC 8.4(c).

Sather's conduct warrants suspension under the ABA *Standards for Imposing Lawyer Sanctions* (1991 & Supp.1992) [hereinafter ABA *Standards*]. In the absence of mitigating or aggravating factors, an attorney's conduct generally warrants suspension when the attorney knows or should know that he is dealing improperly with client property and causes injury or potential injury to a client. See *id.* at 4.12. Sather knew he was handling his client's property improperly when Sather failed to return promptly the unearned portion of Perez's advance fee. Sather's failure to refund the fees in a timely manner caused potential injury to Perez by subjecting the funds to claims from Sather's creditors. *See Shidler,* 901 P.2d at 479. Thus, Sather knowingly mishandled client funds and caused his client actual and potential harm, and his conduct therefore warrants suspension.

Sather's conduct also warrants suspension because he knowingly deceived a client and caused serious injury or potential serious injury to the client. See ABA *Standards, supra,* at 4.62. By his own admission Sather knew that, despite the fee agreement's boldface and repeated language to the contrary, he misrepresented the nature of the advance fee to Perez as "non-refundable" because fees are always subject to refund in the event they are unreasonable or unearned. See Colo. RPC 1.5(a); 1.16(d). Because Sather's conduct involved dishonesty, deceit, fraud and misrepresentation, it warrants suspension. *See also Sigley,* 917 P.2d at 1256.

As aggravating factors, the board considered Sather's prior disciplinary record, his selfish motive, the pattern of misconduct demonstrated, Sather's substantial experience in the practice of law, and his indifference to Perez's needs with respect to refunding the unearned advance fees. See ABA Standards, supra, at 9.22(a), (b), (c), (i), (j). Sather's prior disciplinary record contains incidents involving improper and "deceitful" fee practices. See *Sather,* 936 P.2d at 578–79. In addition, we note that Sather knowingly accepted a flat fee in a civil rights case without informing his client that he had filed for bankruptcy, which constitutes further evidence of a selfish motive. Sather has been an attorney in this state for over twenty years and has substantial experience in the practice of law. Thus, we agree with the board that Sather's prior disciplinary record, the pattern of misconduct demonstrated in the case, Sather's selfish motive, and his substantial experience in law are aggravating factors.

We disagree with the board, however, that Sather showed indifference to returning the unearned portion of the advance fee to Perez, and we do not consider this an aggravating factor. Sather acknowledged his obligation to refund the unearned fees to Perez, but failed to return the funds in a timely manner. This conduct, without more, does not constitute "indifference" towards his obligation to return the unearned fees, and we will not consider the acknowledgement of an ethical duty as justification for a harsher sanction. On the other hand, Sather was required to return the unearned fees and his acknowledgment of this duty does not justify a reduction in the sanctions to be imposed. Additionally, we want to encourage attorneys to acknowledge their duty to return unearned fees in the event they are discharged and we want attorneys to make efforts to return unearned fees even if the refund is untimely. Thus, we do not accept the board's conclusion that Sather was "indifferent" with respect to repaying Perez and we hold that Sather's acknowledgment of his obligation to repay Perez is neither an aggravating nor a mitigating circumstance.

As mitigating factors, the board considered that Sather experienced personal problems during the time period when the unethical conduct occurred, and that Sather cooperated with the regulation counsel. See ABA Standards, supra, at 9.32(c), (e). We agree with the board that these circumstances should be considered as mitigating factors.

Sather's conduct warrants suspension, which the ABA Standards suggests should not be for less than six months. See ABA *Standards, supra*, at 2.3. The board's recommendation of one year and a day may have been appropriate had we determined that, in addition to failing to return promptly unearned fees and making misrepresentations to his client, Sather should be sanctioned for violating Colo. RPC 1.15. See *Zimmermann*, 922 P.2d at 329–30 (imposing a one year and one day suspension where attorney recklessly mishandled client funds). However, because we do not discipline Sather for knowingly failing to place client funds into a trust account, we will impose a lesser sanction for his failure to return unearned fees and for knowingly making misrepresentations to a client. See *Sigley*, 917 P.2d at 1256 (imposing a thirty-day suspension where attorney failed to return unearned fees for seven months, had a conflict of interest with client, and knowingly deceived a client). Because Sather's disciplinary record reflects a history of inappropriate conduct with regard to fees, Sather should demonstrate his fitness to practice before being reinstated. See *Zimmermann*, 922 P.2d at 330 (requiring that attorney undergo reinstatement proceedings in order to protect public from recurring misconduct).

V. ORDER

It is hereby ordered that Larry D. Sather be suspended from the practice of law for six months. Because Sather's license has already been transferred to disability status, his suspension will begin immediately on the date we issue this opinion. We also order that Sather undergo reinstatement proceedings as set forth in C.R.C.P. 251.29 even though this section normally applies to suspensions of longer than one year. This requirement is in addition to the proceedings Sather must undergo to be reinstated from disability status. See

C.R.C.P. 251.30. We further order that, before petitioning for reinstatement, Sather pay the costs of this proceeding in the amount of $1,281.48 to the Attorney Regulation Committee, 600 Seventeenth Street, Suite 200 South, Denver, Colorado 80202.

SOLUTIONS: THE LAWYER SHOULD HAVE, WOULD HAVE, COULD HAVE...

We can all agree that Larry D. Sather's need for money put him into serious trouble. Sather should have put his $20,000 into a trust account, and not treated it as his own property before earning the fees. In addition, Sather should have returned all the unearned portion of the fees when he was discharged by his client because he had not yet earned it. Sather should not label advance fees "non-refundable" because it misleads the client into believing that the money—no matter how much work is done—is gone forever. Finally, on MR 1.16, the lawyer tried to crawl through the back window when he could not walk through the front door as one of your authors likes to say; that is, just as he cannot directly impede the unfettered right of the client to terminate him, so to he cannot indirectly do so through the non-refundable fee agreement he used.

Cases and Materials

X-Ray Questions (*In re Mance*)

The idea that an advance fee is merely a pre-payment of attorney work seems to undermine the idea of flat fees. Some courts have effectively prohibited any non-refundable advance fee. *See, e.g., Matter of Cooperman*, 633 N.E. 2d 1069 (N.Y. 1994). Such a rule seems to eliminate the concept of a flat fee, convert a flat fee as a simply hourly fees by other means. Other courts have clarified that while attorney's fees are by default the client's property until actually earned by the lawyer, there is room for attorneys and clients to contract around this.

Finally, pay close attention to the new concept of "fiduciary duty" that we will cover in depth in Chapter 4. When a lawyer enters into an ACR, it is a contractual relationship but also a fiduciary relationship as to the client. What is the difference? How does the court explain the nature of this duty? Do you recall the concept of the covenant of good faith and fair dealing from 1L contracts? If so, do you see a similarity?

In re Robert W. Mance, III

District of Columbia Court of Appeals, 2009.
980 A.2d 1196.

RUIZ, ASSOCIATE JUDGE:

This case presents us with the question whether a "flat fee" paid in advance for legal services is to be deemed an "advance[ ] of unearned fees" that is required to be treated as property of the client under Rule 1.15(d) of the D.C. Rules of Professional Conduct. The Board on Professional Responsibility ("Board") determined that a flat fee paid in advance of services being rendered becomes the attorney's property upon receipt, and, in the alternative, found that, even if the flat fee remains the client's property under Rule 1.15(d), the client in this case consented to having the fee treated as belonging to the attorney, as permitted by the rule. The Board recommends, however, that because respondent, Robert W. Mance, III, did commingle his funds (i.e., the flat fee) by placing part of it in a client trust fund, he should be sanctioned with a public censure. Respondent concurs with the Board's recommended sanction. Bar Counsel disagrees with the Board's interpretation of the rule and with its alternative finding of client consent, and urges the court to impose a harsher sanction of suspension on respondent than the public censure recommended by the Board. We agree with Bar Counsel, that for purposes of Rule 1.15(d), money paid by a client as a flat fee for legal services remains the client's property, and counsel may not treat any portion of the money otherwise until it is earned, unless the client has agreed otherwise. As we announce this interpretation of the rule for the first time in this case, however, we apply it prospectively, and we adopt the Board's recommendation that respondent receive a public censure for commingling funds.

I.   Factual Summary

On December 2, 2003, William Saunders retained respondent to represent his son, who was a suspect in a homicide case. Respondent told Mr. Saunders that his fee would be $15,000—with the initial installment of $7,500 to be paid up-front—and possibly an additional $5,000 for investigative services "depending on what was involved." The second installment of $7,500 was to be paid after Saunders's son turned himself in to the police. Without any further discussion about the fee, Mr. Saunders agreed and paid respondent the initial $7,500. Although they did not discuss how the money would be kept, respondent placed most of it, $6,010, in a client escrow account, and the rest in his operating account.

After having talked to the son, who said that he would not be ready to turn himself in for another month (in January 2004), respondent decided to wait until that time to take any action. Mr. Saunders, however, became frustrated with respondent, who appeared to him to be doing nothing on his son's behalf, and terminated his services in early January 2004. Respondent agreed to return the initial $7,500 payment, but did not do so until several months later because he did not have the funds readily available.

On May 27, 2004, Saunders filed a complaint with Bar Counsel claiming that respondent had failed to return the money as promised. After receiving the $7,500 from respondent a week later, however, Mr. Saunders told Bar Counsel that he wished to withdraw his complaint. It was not until Bar Counsel sent a letter to respondent two days later, on June 8, 2004, that he became aware that Mr. Saunders had filed a complaint against him.

Bar Counsel did not drop the case, as Mr. Saunders had requested. Instead, on July 27, 2005, Bar Counsel filed a Specification of Charges and Petition Instituting Formal Disciplinary Proceedings, which charged respondent with misappropriating client funds (Rule 1.15(a)); commingling his funds with client funds (Rule 1.15(a)); failing to maintain complete records of client funds (Rule 1.15(a) and D.C. Bar Rule XI § 19(f)); failing to treat an advance as client funds (Rule 1.15(d)); failing to take timely steps to surrender client funds (Rule 1.16(d)); and failing to deposit client funds in a specially-titled trust or escrow account (Rule 1.16(d)).

The hearing committee found that Rule 1.15(d) did not apply to a flat fee because it is not an "advance" but the agreed-upon fee regardless of how much (or how little) legal work was required; and that, in any event, Mr. Saunders had agreed that the $7,500 belonged to respondent upon receipt. However, the hearing committee concluded that respondent had commingled funds, in violation of Rule 1.15(a) because "[r]espondent had placed a portion of the $7,500 in an escrow account containing client funds. . . ." But, the hearing committee found respondent "did not fail to take timely steps to surrender client funds," noting that he "acted honorably, and after some delay, refunded his entire fee even though he had spent some time advising [the client] and [Mr.] Saunders." The hearing committee recommended a public censure.

Except as to the hearing committee's conclusion that respondent did not fail to promptly return the fee, the Board, with one member dissenting, adopted the committee's findings and conclusions, including the interpretation that Rule 1.15(a) does not require lawyers to treat "flat fees" as client funds. The Board accordingly dismissed four of the six charges, including the most serious one, misappropriation, and found that respondent had commingled funds, in violation of Rule 1.15(a), and that he failed to promptly return the fee, in violation of Rule 1.16(d). The Board agreed with the hearing committee's recommendation that respondent receive a public censure.

Before this court, Bar Counsel takes exception to the Board's interpretation of Rule 1.15(d) concerning advances on unearned fees, and to the Board's recommended sanction of public censure, arguing instead that respondent should be suspended for 60 days, with 30 days stayed in favor of one year of supervised probation.

Respondent agrees with the Board's interpretation of Rule 1.15(d) that a flat fee is not an advance on unearned fees. As to Rule 1.16(d), respondent argues that he "returned the fee as promptly as possible," and that "[t]here was no evidence of any purposeful intent to delay the return of the fee." He acknowledges that he commingled his fees in a client escrow account. Respondent does not take issue with the public censure recommended by the hearing committee and the Board, but argues that "suspension," as urged by Bar Counsel, "is not an appropriate sanction."

II.   Rule 1.15 and Flat Fees

Rule 1.15 provides:

(a)   A lawyer shall hold property of clients or third persons that is in the lawyer's possession in connection with a representation separate from the lawyer's own property. . . .

(d)   Advances of unearned fees and unincurred costs shall be treated as property of the client pursuant to paragraph (a) until earned or incurred unless the client gives informed consent to a different arrangement. Regardless of whether such consent is provided, Rule 1.16(d) applies to require the return to the client of any unearned portion of advanced legal fees and unincurred costs at the termination of the lawyer's services in accordance with Rule 1.16(d).

We hold that when an attorney receives payment of a flat fee at the outset of a representation, the payment is an "advance of unearned fees" and "shall be treated as property of the client . . . until earned unless the client consents to a different arrangement." Rule 1.15(d).

We begin our analysis by describing the nature of a flat fee. A flat fee is one that "embraces all work to be done, whether it be relatively simple and of short duration, or complex and protracted." *Iowa Sup.Ct. Bd. of Prof'l Ethics and Conduct v. Apland*, 577 N.W.2d 50, 55 (Iowa 1998) (quoting ABA Comm. on Ethics and Prof'l Responsibility, Informal Op. 1389 (1977)). A flat fee is different from an engagement retainer, which "is a fee paid, apart from any other compensation, to ensure that a lawyer will be available for the client if required." RESTATEMENT (THIRD) OF THE LAW GOVERNING LAWYERS § 34 cmt. e (2000); *see In re Sather*, 3 P.3d 403, 410 (Colo.2000) (en banc) ("In contrast to engagement retainers, a client may advance funds-often referred to as . . . 'flat fees'-to pay for specific legal services to be performed by the attorney and to cover future costs.") (citations omitted); see D.C. Legal Ethics Op. 264 (February 14, 2006) (an engagement retainer is a nonrefundable payment to assure the availability of the attorney whether services are performed or not). Engagement retainers are earned when received, but it may become necessary to refund even a portion of a retainer if the lawyer withdraws or is discharged prematurely. *See* RESTATEMENT (THIRD) OF THE LAW GOVERNING LAWYERS § 38 cmt. g (2000) ("A fee payment that does not cover services already rendered and that is not otherwise identified is presumed to be a deposit against future services.").

The primary rule concerning the amount of fees is that "[a] lawyer's fee shall be reasonable." Rule 1.5(a). We agree with the Colorado Supreme Court's holding in Sather that "an attorney earns fees only by conferring a benefit on or performing a legal service for the client." 3 P.3d at 410. "It simply makes no sense to permit lawyers to enter into fee agreements with clients stating that an advance payment such as a flat fee is earned upon receipt, when such payments are subject to being refunded to the extent unearned." Alec Rothrock, *The Forgotten Flat Fee; Whose Money is it and Where Should it be Deposited?*, 1 FLA. COASTAL L.J. 293, 347 (1999). Such a fee is earned "only to the degree that the attorney actually performs the agreed-upon services." *Id.* at 346. In sum, a flat fee is an advance of unearned fees because it is money paid up-front for legal services that are yet to be performed.

Here, the hearing committee found that that the $15,000 flat fee (with an additional $5,000 as required for third-party investigative services) was to compensate respondent for all the services that he would perform during the representation, from the inception of the case to its final disposition. Both Mr. Saunders and respondent testified that the first installment of $7,500 would cover respondent's efforts in assisting his client to turn himself in to the police, including contacting the government to find out about the charges against him, and possibly initiating discussions on a plea. Respondent was also expected to negotiate with the government over the terms of pretrial detention, as the client had said during an interview that he feared for his safety in jail as a result of his previous cooperation with the police in a drug case. Mr. Saunders promised to pay the second $7,500 after his son turned himself in, to compensate respondent for legal services to be rendered thereafter, which could have included a trial. Thus, when Mr. Saunders terminated the representation before the first milestone was met (before the client turned himself in to the police), respondent was obligated to return the initial payment—or the portion that he had not earned—because a lawyer "cannot earn a fee for doing nothing." *In re Sather*, 3 P.3d at 414 (citing *Apland*, 577 N.W.2d at 57).

A corollary to the rule that a flat fee is an advance of unearned fees, is that the fee must be held as client funds in a client's trust or escrow account until they are earned by the lawyer's performance of legal services. See Rule 1.15(d). In accepting this consequence of our interpretation, we recognize that there are competing interests:

> If the funds are entrusted until earned, the attorney bears the inconvenience and, in some cases, genuine hardship of a delay in enjoying payment. . . .

> If the funds are not entrusted until earned, the client suffers the risk that, if the funds are spent or attached by the lawyer's creditors, the client may obtain neither the agreed upon services nor the money in the form of a refund.

Rothrock, *supra* at 356 (quoting Lawrence A. Brickman, *Advance Fee Payment Dilemma: Should Payment be Deposited to the Client Trust Account or to the General Office Account?* 10 Cardozo L.Rev. 647, 669 (1989)). Upon consideration of these competing interests, we conclude that the client's interest in protecting the funds override that of the lawyer's in immediate access to them, and that the public is ultimately better served by requiring that the lawyer keep flat fees in a trust or escrow account. As the Iowa Supreme Court aptly noted:

> This approach (1) preserves the client's property from the reach of the lawyer's creditors, (2) preserves the client's property from possible misappropriation by the lawyer, and (3) enables the client to realistically dispute a fee where the funds are already in the lawyer's possession by disallowing a self help resolution by the lawyer and instead preserving the disputed funds intact until the dispute is resolved.

Apland, 577 N.W.2d at 56 (quoting Brickman, *supra* at 667).

Another important benefit to placing flat fees in a trust or escrow account is preservation of the client's right to choose his or her counsel, including the right to discharge an attorney. See D.C. Rule 1.7(b) cmt. 8 ("Clients have broad discretion to terminate their representation by a lawyer and that discretion may generally be exercised on unreasonable as well as reasonable grounds."). Since a flat fee is not owned by an attorney until it has been earned through the performance of services to the client, "the client will not risk forfeiting fees for work to be performed in the future if the client chooses to discharge his attorney." *In re Sather*, 3 P.3d at 410. With the flat fee protected, the client need not hesitate to exercise the right to discharge an attorney for fear that the attorney may keep the flat fee. *See id.* at 410 (citations omitted); Rothrock, *supra* at 359 ("[T]he client's absolute right to discharge the lawyer is impermissibly impaired if the lawyer cannot afford a refund and the client cannot afford to hire a new lawyer without one.").

Preserving the client's unfettered right to discharge an attorney protects the fiduciary relationship between lawyer and client. *See In re Cooperman*, 83 N.Y.2d 465, 611 N.Y.S.2d 465, 633 N.E.2d 1069, 1071 (1994) ("This unique fiduciary reliance, stemming from people hiring attorneys to exercise professional judgment on a client's behalf—'giving counsel'—is imbued with ultimate trust and confidence.") (citations omitted). A fee arrangement that "substantially alter[s] and economically chill[s] the client's unbridled prerogative to walk away from the lawyer" strikes at the "core of the fiduciary relationship." *Id.* at 1072. "To answer that the client can technically still terminate misses the reality of the economic coercion that pervades such matters." *Id.*

In this case, for example, respondent's delay in returning the flat fee hindered Mr. Saunders from obtaining new counsel after he became dissatisfied with respondent's performance. Although Mr. Saunders was eventually able to obtain new counsel for his son before he received the refund, he had told respondent when he terminated him that he needed the money back to hire a new attorney. The record does not reveal, however, what arrangement Mr. Saunders had with new counsel, and whether the delay in receiving the refund from respondent had any bearing on their arrangement. But it is reasonable to assume that in most cases where criminal representation is required, it is imperative that counsel be secured, and working on the client's behalf, at the earliest possible time.

We do not intend by our holding to discourage attorneys from charging flat fees, as we recognize the benefits of a flat fee arrangement for both the client and the attorney. For the client, it "eliminate[s] the uncertainty, anxiety and surprise often found with hourly rates, especially in protracted litigation. . . ." Rothrock, supra at 354. For the lawyer, it "reward[s] efficiency and enable[s] the attorney to concentrate on the representation instead of fighting with the client over monthly bills[, and] provide[s] certainty of payment. . . ." Id. We are not unaware that our holding could impose a financial hardship on solo practitioners and lawyers in smaller firms who rely on flat fees to maintain their practice. But we also note that, consistent with the general requirement that a lawyer must entrust flat fees in a trust or escrow account until earned, the client may consent otherwise (if properly informed, as we discuss infra), and the fee agreement may specify how and when the attorney is deemed to earn the flat fee or specified portions of the fee. See Rule 1.15(d); cf. Rothrock, supra, at 323 (Michigan rules allow the lawyer to withdraw fees according to milestones "based upon passage of time, the completion of certain tasks, or any other basis mutually agreed upon between the lawyer and client.") (citation omitted). Any such agreement, however, is subject to the overarching principle that an attorney's fees must be reasonable, and requires "return to the client of any unearned portion of advanced legal fees and unincurred costs." Rule 1.15(d); see Rule 1.16(d). Simply labeling a fee as something other than a flat fee or extreme "front-loading" of payment milestones in the context of the anticipated length and complexity of the representation will not excuse the lawyer from safekeeping the client's funds until it can reasonably be said that they have been earned in light of the scope of the representation.

We note that although this is the first time we have expressly addressed the applicability of Rule 1.15 to flat fees, our holding today is consistent with *In re Hallmark*, 831 A.2d 366 (D.C.2003), where we sanctioned a lawyer for failing to return unearned portions of a flat fee. In *Hallmark*, the attorney charged a flat fee for performing two discrete tasks, and there was a dispute over what services the lawyer had performed. We held there that, "[e]ven assuming that [Hallmark] was entitled to withhold a portion of the [flat] fee in compensation for [completing one of the tasks,] this does not justify the withholding of the entire fee amount as it is clear that she performed only part of the work." *Id.* at 372.

Although not many jurisdictions have had occasion to decide the precise issue of how flat fees are to be treated, we note that our holding is consistent with the clear precept that prevails around the country with respect to advances of unearned fees, including in our immediate neighbors, Maryland and Virginia. *See In re Sather*, 3 P.3d at 412; *Attorney Grievance Comm. v. Zuckerman*, 386 Md. 341, 872 A.2d 693, 711 (2005) ("[F]unds given to an attorney in anticipation of future services qualify as 'trust money'. . . ."); *In re Carpenter*, 755 N.W.2d 749, 749

(Minn.2008) (attorney transferred to inactive status after stipulating to various acts of misconduct including failure to deposit advance fees into a trust account); *State ex rel. Special Counsel for Discipline v. Fellman*, 267 Neb. 838, 678 N.W.2d 491, 496–97 (2004) (finding that "[t]he record in this case reveals no basis to find that the $1,100 was an engagement retainer belonging to [the attorney] upon receipt"); *In re Dawson*, 129 N.M. 369, 8 P.3d 856, 859 (2000) (holding that "a lawyer's claim that he or she charged a client a flat fee or retainer that is not refundable will not suffice to justify a failure to deposit unearned client funds in a trust account, a withdrawal of client funds from a trust account to pay fees that have not been earned, or a failure to promptly return unearned funds to a client upon termination"); *Marcus Santoro & Kozak, P.C. v. Wu*, 274 Va. 743, 652 S.E.2d 777, 781 (2007) ("An attorney who receives funds from a client for the future payment of legal fees for services not yet rendered holds those funds in trust."); *In re Blanchard*, 158 Wash.2d 317, 144 P.3d 286, 295 (2006) (attorney suspended for acts of misconduct, including failure to deposit advance fees into a trust account); *In re Gedlen*, 305 Wis.2d 34, 739 N.W.2d 274, 275–76 (2007) (attorney's license revoked for numerous acts of misconduct including failure to deposit advance fees in a trust account); *see also* Rule Regulating the Fla. Bar 5–1.1(b) ("Money or other property entrusted to an attorney for a specific purpose, including advances for fees, costs, and expenses, is held in trust and must be applied only to that purpose."); S.C. Rule of Prof'l Responsibility 1.15(c) ("A lawyer shall deposit into a client trust account unearned legal fees and expenses that have been paid in advance . . . ."); *cf. Smith v. Binder*, 20 Mass.App.Ct. 21, 477 N.E.2d 606, 608 (1985) (voiding nonrefundable retainer for public policy reasons); *In re Cooperman*, 611 N.Y.S.2d 465, 633 N.E.2d at 1072 ("[W]e hold that the use of a special nonrefundable retainer fee agreement clashes with public policy because it inappropriately compromises the right to sever the fiduciary services relationship with the lawyer.").

However, since we announce for the first time that under Rule 1.15(d) flat fees are an advance of unearned fees that belong to the client until earned by the lawyer (unless other reasonable arrangements have been made), we agree with the recommendation made by both the Board and Bar Counsel that our holding in this case should be prospective only. *See In re Sather*, 3 P.3d at 412 n. 11 (noting that "we are aware that many attorneys believe that they are adhering to the rules of professional conduct when they treat flat fees and other forms of advance fees as their own property, and we acknowledge that our holding today forecloses this widely-used practice. For these reasons, we make our holding prospective."). The rule's application to flat fees is not clear on its face and, as not only respondent but his expert testified, the understanding among lawyers with respondent's type of practice has been that flat fees belong to the lawyer upon receipt, and therefore need not be kept separately in a trust account. We are confident that the D.C. Bar Board of Governors, the Bar's relevant sections, and the Board and Bar Counsel will take steps to inform the Bar and provide attorneys with helpful guidance on how to conform their practice to the rule we announce in this opinion. Our purpose is not to discipline attorneys for inadvertent violations based on reasonable, but mistaken interpretations of the rules, but to make lawyers' obligations clear so that the interest of the public will be protected. *Cf. In re Haar*, 698 A.2d 412, 424 (D.C.1997) (mitigating sanction for negligent misappropriation because respondent believed "in good faith, although negligently, that he had an undisputed right" to withdraw money from the trust account to pay for his legal services).

III. Informed Consent

Although the default rule is that an attorney must hold flat fees in a client trust or escrow account until earned, we note that an attorney may obtain informed consent from the client to deposit all of the money in the lawyer's operating account or to deposit some of the money in the lawyer's operating account as it is earned, per their agreement. See Rule 1.15(d); *see also In re Sather*, 3 P.3d at 413–14. "Informed consent denotes the agreement by a person to a proposed course of conduct after the lawyer has communicated adequate information and explanation about the material risks of and reasonably available alternatives to the proposed course of conduct." D.C. Bar Rules—Terminology (2009). In order to ensure knowing client consent to a different arrangement concerning the treatment of flat fees, the Colorado Supreme Court has noted that

> the attorney must expressly communicate to the client verbally and in writing that the attorney will treat the advance fee as the attorney's property upon receipt; that the client must understand the attorney can keep the fee only by providing a benefit or providing a service for which the client has contracted; that the fee agreement must spell out the terms of the benefit to be conferred upon the client; and that the client must be aware of the attorney's obligation to refund any amount of advance funds to the extent that they are unreasonable or unearned if the representation is terminated by the client. *In re Sather*, 3 P.3d at 413. We agree, and add that the client should be informed that, unless there is agreement otherwise, the attorney must, under Rule 1.15(d), hold the flat fee in escrow until it is earned by the lawyer's provision of legal services.

Here, for example, if we assume our holding today applied to respondent, we would have to conclude that neither Mr. Saunders nor his son (the client) gave respondent the informed consent required to waive the requirements of Rule 1.15(d). Respondent admitted that he did not discuss the fee arrangement in detail with Mr. Saunders, and did not mention the option to deposit the advance payment in an escrow account. This was consistent with respondent's understanding that he had no obligation to do so. But, as a matter of fact, respondent did not communicate what a client would have needed to know to give informed consent. According to Mr. Saunders, respondent did not discuss with him how the initial payment of the flat fee was to be treated:

> [Attorney:] Did [respondent] discuss with you his belief that the $7500 was his money as soon as you gave it to him?

> [Mr. Saunders:] We didn't discuss that. I just figured that that was a lawyer's fee. So I didn't ask. I just figured that was the standard fee. That's what you paid for his service.

> . . . .

> [Attorney:] Do you know what an escrow account is?

> [Mr. Saunders:] I've got a faint idea what it is.

> [Attorney:] Did [respondent] discuss with you whether the money that you gave him would go into an escrow account or otherwise?

> [Mr. Saunders:] That never came up in our conversation.

In view of this testimony, we cannot agree with the Board's finding that "Mr. Saunders consented to an arrangement whereby the funds could be treated as the property of the attorney. . . ." At a minimum, a lawyer must explain to the client "the basis for this arrangement and explain[ed] how [the client's] rights are protected by the arrangement." *In re Sather*, 3 P.3d at 414. Where there is no discussion regarding the fee arrangement besides merely stating the overall fee, and no mention of the escrow account option, a client cannot be said to have a sufficient basis to give informed consent to waive the requirements of a rule designed to protect the client's interests.

IV. Sanction

"So long as the Board's sanction recommendation falls within the wide range of acceptable outcomes, it comes to us with a strong presumption in favor of its imposition. . . ." *In re Bingham*, 881 A.2d 619, 623 (D.C.2005). But "[i]n deciding whether to adopt the Board's recommendation, we must examine the 'nature of the violation, aggravating and mitigating circumstances, the absence or presence of our prior disciplinary sanctions, the moral fitness of the attorney, and the need to protect the legal profession, the courts, and the public.' " Id. (quoting *In re McLain*, 671 A.2d 951, 954 (D.C.1996)). "We also consider the number of clients prejudiced by an attorney's misconduct; the degree of vulnerability of the client prejudiced and the experience level of the attorney; and the time span of the misconduct; together with the Report and Recommendation of the [Board]." *In re Elgin*, 918 A.2d 362, 376 (D.C.2007) (citations omitted).

In light of the foregoing analysis of the applicability of Rule 1.15 to flat fees, respondent's actions would constitute misappropriation of client funds in violation of Rule 1.15(a); commingling of lawyer funds with those of the client in violation of Rule 1.15(a); failure to maintain complete records of client funds in violation of Rule 1.15(a) and D.C. Bar Rule XI § 19(f); failure to treat an advance as client funds in violation of Rule 1.15(d); failure to take timely steps to surrender client funds in violation of Rule 1.16(d); and failure to deposit client funds in a specially titled trust or escrow account, in violation of Rule 1.16(d). But because we have decided to apply our interpretation of Rule 1.15(d) prospectively, except for commingling and for failure to promptly return funds once respondent was terminated, respondent cannot be deemed to have committed the more serious violations of those provisions. *See Apland*, 577 N.W.2d at 56 (noting that the violations were "not intentional given the uncertainty at the time about whether such fees were subject to trust account requirements"). Therefore, the issue is what is the appropriate sanction for commingling (by depositing most of the flat fee respondent mistakenly, but in good faith, thought belonged to him in a client escrow account), and for failing to promptly return funds to the client once respondent agreed to do so.

We consider mitigating as well as aggravating factors. There are several factors that favor mitigation. Respondent fully cooperated with Bar Counsel during the proceeding. The hearing committee commented that it was "impressed with the seriousness with which [respondent] appeared to take these proceedings." As we have previously recognized, respondent has a "lengthy and well-reputed history of providing an important service" to the community by serving as one of the few members of the bar engaged in the practice of street crime defense. *In re Mance*, 869 A.2d 339, 342 n. 10 (D.C.2005). Any suspension has a greater impact on a solo practitioner, or a lawyer in a very small firm, than on a lawyer who is part of a larger practice where other attorneys can more easily step in during the period of suspension.

There are some aggravating factors. Respondent has a history of prior discipline: in 1996 and 2000, Bar Counsel informally admonished respondent for failing to provide a written retainer agreement as required by Rule 1.15(b); and in 2005, the court imposed a 30-day suspension on respondent, stayed in lieu of a one-year probation, for failing to protect his client's appeal rights in a criminal case. *See id.* We agree with the Board, however, that respondent's prior misdeeds, while not to be dismissed, do not implicate his moral character or integrity.

We also take into account that Mr. Saunders and his son were, to a degree, prejudiced by respondent's failure to promptly return the money. Mr. Saunders had told respondent that he needed the money to hire a new attorney. Mr. Saunders was, however, able to hire replacement counsel before he received the refund, and, once he did receive it, he withdrew his complaint and asked Bar Counsel to drop the disciplinary proceeding. Respondent also placed Mr. Saunders's money in jeopardy by commingling funds during a time when he was embroiled in a tax dispute with the D.C. government. But respondent did not, as the Board found, act dishonestly or attempt to misappropriate client funds.

In view of all these circumstances—which the Board considered in its report—we adopt the Board's recommended sanction of public censure, which is consistent with discipline imposed in similar cases. *See*, e.g., *In re Mitchell*, 727 A.2d 308, 314 n. 7, 315 (D.C.1999) (imposing public censure for various acts of misconduct, including violation of Rule 1.16(d)); *In re Goldberg*, 721 A.2d 627, 628 (D.C.1998) (per curiam) (imposing public censure for comingling); *In re Teitelbaum*, 686 A.2d 1037, 1039 (D.C.1996) (per curiam) (same); *In re Ingram*, 584 A.2d 602, 603–04 (D.C.1991) (per curiam) (public censure for commingling, failing to inform client of settlement, and failing to promptly deliver funds upon client's request).

Accordingly, Robert W. Mance, III, is hereby publicly censured.

So ordered.

SOLUTIONS: THE LAWYER SHOULD HAVE, WOULD HAVE, COULD HAVE. . .

The lawyer's main mistake was comingling client funds that should have been held separately. The court also lays down a new rule: A flat fee is an advance on unearned fees but expresses understanding that the lawyer could not have known this rule beforehand. A more disturbing aspect of this decision, however, is that it might be difficult for lawyers to use flat fees in a

> pure sense in the future. All that they can offer is an advance on hourly fees system. Put another way, it is fine for a lawyer, in the formation of the ACR, to ask for a deposit—especially in certain types of cases or when the lawyer is unfamiliar with the client. But the deposit money charged must be maintained in a separate account until the lawyer earns the money.

Section 3. Pro Bono and Salaried Free Legal Services

It is worth pausing briefly to consider pro bono legal services as a fee arrangement. When a lawyer is not paid for her work, we might think of that as a form of a flat fee, where the fee is set at $0. When a lawyer agrees to do that, she takes on the same problematic incentives of other flat fees. To be clear, attorneys often work extremely hard for pro bono clients, and for flat fee clients. They are ethically compelled to do so (duty of diligence), and are often highly, personally committed to their clients. Nevertheless, from a narrow financial point of view, a lawyer providing free services to a client has an incentive to limit their work so as to have more time to sell (for a fee) to other clients.

Pro bono legal services in which the attorney is not paid might be distinguished from legal aid programs where attorneys are paid salaries to deliver free services to members of the public. In that situation, the attorney's incentives are likely to depend on the specific employment arrangements of her organization. But the potential certainly exists for legal aid programs to take on too many cases, and to deliver mediocre legal work in each one.

Section 4. Contingency Fees

As we have seen, both hourly and flat fee arrangements carry with them significant problems in terms of the incentives they create for attorneys, and the barriers to legal services they may impose. The problems are especially acute for people and entities who lack the financial wherewithal to pay top dollar for legal services. In fact, some clients may not even have the capacity to pay a modest fee for legal representation. A common way out of these problems is the contingency fee. In these arrangements, a client agrees to give the attorney a share of the monetary relief she wins in a case, if any. Like other arrangements, contingency fee arrangements offer significant advantages, but also carry limitations and problems. In fact, contingency fees are specifically prohibited in certain contexts.

Model Rule 1.5(c): Fees

(c)   A fee may be contingent on the outcome of the matter for which the service is rendered, except in a matter in which a contingent fee is prohibited by paragraph (d) or other law. A contingent fee agreement shall be in a writing signed by the client and shall state the method by which the fee is to be determined, including the percentage or percentages that shall accrue to the lawyer in the event of settlement, trial or appeal; litigation and other expenses to be deducted from the recovery; and whether such expenses are to be deducted before or after the contingent fee is calculated. The agreement must clearly notify the client of any expenses for which the client will be liable whether or not the client is the prevailing party. Upon conclusion of a contingent fee matter, the lawyer shall provide the client with a written statement stating the outcome of the matter and, if there is a recovery, showing the remittance to the client and the method of its determination.

Deconstruction Exercise/Rule Rationale

Let's start with the advantages. One of the problems with hourly and flat fee arrangements is that they give lawyers incentives somewhat in tension with the interests of their clients. At their best, contingency fees perfectly align lawyers' interests with their clients, assuming the client's goal is to win as much money as possible. The more the client gets, the more the attorney gets. Because a client need not pay a cent unless she wins monetary compensation, clients who have meritorious claims but little ability to pay out of pocket can get access to representation. An attorney, who is presumably more expert than an average client, bears the burden to assess the likelihood of success and the amount of resources that would be required to litigate it. Contingency fees proliferate, especially in the field of torts law, for exactly these reasons.

A problem with contingency fees is that an attorney only gets paid at the end of the case. That becomes a thorny problem when a client switches attorneys midway through a case. Would it be fair for only the attorney who is retained at the very end to be rewarded because that is when a lucrative payout comes along, even if the work of an earlier attorney made that possible?

Under Rule 1.8(i), a "reasonable contingency fee" is allowed. But "A lawyer shall not acquire a proprietary interest in the cause of action or subject matter of litigation the lawyer is conducting for a client." But what is the difference? It is not entirely clear how to draw the line between a proprietary interest in litigation and a fee whereby the lawyer receives a percentage of an eventual award. The ABA Comment to the rule states that the purpose of the prohibition "is designed to avoid giving the lawyer too great an interest in the representation." Yet, from another perspective this is actually the virtue of contingency feels; they align attorney interests with their clients.

One question to ask yourself is why the organized bar seems somewhat more comfortable with contingency fees—which are explicitly permitted and regulated by MR 1.5(c)—while flat fees are shrouded in more ambiguity and ambivalence. As we have seen, courts often require a lawyer on flat fee to still "earn" the fee, which can obscure the difference between flat fees and hourly fees. But why is there no requirement that a lawyer on contingency "earn" every dollar? On a contingency, a lawyer who win a very large case could literally be paid millions of dollars without having to show that he really worked enough to earn every last penny. Is this different treatment of flat fees and contingency fees justified?

Cases and Materials

X-Ray Questions (*Brobeck*)

Contingency fee arrangements can sometimes lead to eye-popping fees for attorneys, arguably far out of proportion from the actual work required. By this perspective, the value of legal services can only be measured by the amount of time spent on a case—essentially, the hourly fee model as a norm. But that is not the only way to assess value of a professional service. Consider how the court determined the value of an attorney's work in the following case. Have you heard the phrase "bet the company case?" What does it mean? Do the Rules permit a higher than normal fee when the client may be faced with such a dilemma? In reading this case think back again to 1L contract and the lessons you learned about objective v. subjective intent in what he calls the "modern" view of "contract" formation. Was the law firm transparent in its dealing with the client? Why is it important to ask and answer that question?

Brobeck, Phleger & Harrison, a Partnership v. The Telex Corporation, a Corporation, and Telex Computer Products, Inc., a Corporation

United States Court of Appeals, Ninth Circuit, 1979.
602 F.2d 866.

PER CURIAM:

This is a diversity action in which the plaintiff, the San Francisco law firm of Brobeck, Phleger & Harrison ("Brobeck"), sued the Telex Corporation and Telex Computer Products, Inc. ("Telex") to recover $1,000,000 in attorney's fees. Telex had engaged Brobeck on a contingency fee basis to prepare a petition for certiorari after the Tenth Circuit reversed a $259.5 million judgment in Telex's favor against International Business Machines Corporation ("IBM") and affirmed an $18.5 million counterclaim judgment for IBM against Telex. Brobeck prepared and filed the petition, and after Telex entered a "wash settlement" with IBM in which both parties released their claims against the other, Brobeck sent Telex a bill for $1,000,000, that it claimed Telex owed it under their written contingency fee agreement. When Telex refused to pay, Brobeck brought this action. Both parties filed motions for summary judgment. The district court granted Brobeck's motion, awarding Brobeck $1,000,000 plus interest. Telex now appeals.

Telex was the plaintiff in antitrust litigation against IBM in the United States District Court for the Northern District of Oklahoma. On November 9, 1973 the District Court found that IBM had violated s 2 of the Sherman Act, 15 U.S.C. s 2 (Supp. IV 1974), and entered judgment for Telex in the amount of $259.5 million, plus costs and attorney's fees of $1.2 million. The court also entered judgment in the sum of $21.9 million for IBM on its counterclaims against Telex for misappropriation of trade secrets and copyright infringement.

On appeal, the Tenth Circuit reversed the entire judgment that Telex had won in the district court. *Telex Corp. v. International Business Machines Corp.*, 510 F.2d 894 (10th Cir. 1975). It also reduced the judgment against Telex on IBM's counterclaim to $18.5 million and affirmed the district court's judgment as modified.

Having had reversed one of the largest antitrust judgments in history, Telex officials decided to press the Tenth Circuit's decision to the United States Supreme Court. To maximize Telex's chances for having its petition for certiorari granted, they decided to search for the best available lawyer. They compiled a list of the preeminent antitrust and Supreme Court lawyers in the country, and Roger Wheeler, Telex's Chairman of the Board, settled on Moses Lasky of the Brobeck firm as the best possibility.

Wheeler and his assistant made preliminary phone calls to Lasky on February 3, 4, and 13, 1975 to determine whether Lasky was willing to prepare the petition for certiorari. Lasky stated he would be interested if he was able to rearrange his workload. When asked about a fee, Lasky stated that, although he would want a retainer, it was the policy of the Brobeck firm to determine fees after the services were performed. Wheeler, however, wanted an agreement fixing fees in advance and arranged for Lasky to meet in San Francisco on February 10th to discuss the matter further with Telex's president, Stephen Jatras, and Floyd Walker, its attorney in the IBM litigation.

The San Francisco meeting was the only in-person meeting between Lasky and the Telex officials on the subject of Brobeck's compensation. Jatras told Lasky that Wheeler preferred a contingency fee arrangement. Lasky replied that he had little experience with such arrangements but proposed a contingency fee of 5% Of either the judgment or settlement. Jatras thought there should be a ceiling and someone proposed that the ceiling be set at 5% Of the first $100 million. Jatras also proposed that anything due IBM on its counterclaim judgment be deducted before calculating the 5% Fee. Lasky rejected this, but suggested as a compromise that the amount of the counterclaim judgment be deducted if Telex received $40 million or less in judgment or settlement.

Lasky added that if there was to be ceiling on the contingent fee, there ought to be a minimum fee as well, and suggested that the minimum fee be $1 million. In his deposition, Jatras acknowledged that Lasky proposed a minimum fee, but disputed the other participants' account of the remainder of the discussion. According to Jatras, he told Lasky that Telex would not pay a minimum fee "unless we got something to pay it from." Lasky denied hearing such a proposal. The parties reached no final agreement at the San Francisco meeting. Jatras and Walker returned to Tulsa to discuss the meeting with the Telex management, while Lasky conferred with his partners.

The next day Walker drafted a memorandum to Jatras recounting the San Francisco meeting and including a proposed fee agreement. Jatras and Walker made some changes on the Walker draft agreement, and as modified, sent the proposed fee agreement to Lasky with a cover letter. The pertinent portion of this proposal, paragraph three, is set forth below:

Once a Petition for Writ of Certiorari has been filed with the Clerk of the United States Supreme Court then Brobeck will be entitled to the payment of an additional fee in the event of a recovery by Telex from IBM by way of settlement or judgment in excess of the counterclaim judgment; and, such additional fee will be 5% Of the first $100,000,000.00 of such recovery, the maximum contingent fee to be paid is $5,000,000.00 and the minimum is $1,000,000.00.

On the day he received the letter and proposed fee agreement, Lasky telephoned Jatras to tell him the proposal was not acceptable and that he would draft changes. Later that same day, Lasky sent to Jatras a letter in which he agreed to represent Telex and enclosed a memorandum agreement. This agreement, which Lasky had already signed, is set forth in full:

MEMORANDUM

1.   Retainer of $25,000.00 to be paid. If Writ of Certiorari is denied and no settlement has been effected in excess of the Counterclaim, then the $25,000.00 retainer shall be the total fee paid; provided however, that

2.   If the case should be settled before a Petition for Writ of Certiorari is actually filed with the Clerk of the Supreme Court, then the Brobeck firm would bill for its services to the date of settlement at an hourly rate of $125.00 per hour for the lawyers who have worked on the case; the total amount of such billing will be limited to not more than $100,000.00, against which the $25,000.00 retainer will be applied, but no portion of the retainer will be returned in any event.

3.   Once a Petition for Writ of Certiorari has been filed with the Clerk of the United States Supreme Court then Brobeck will be entitled to the payment of an additional fee in the event of a recovery by Telex from IBM by way of settlement or judgment of its claims against IBM; and, such additional fee will be five percent (5%) of the first $100,000,000.00 gross of such recovery, undiminished by any recovery by IBM on its counterclaims or cross-claims. The maximum contingent fee to be paid is $5,000,000.00, provided that if recovery by Telex from IBM in less than $40,000,00.00 gross, the five percent (5%) shall be based on the net recovery, i. e., the recovery after deducting the credit to IBM by virtue of IBM's recovery on counterclaims or cross-claims, but the contingent fee shall not then be less than $1,000,000.00.

4.   Once a Writ of Certiorari has been granted, then Brobeck will receive an additional $15,000.00 retainer to cover briefing and arguing in the Supreme Court.

5.   Telex will pay, in addition to the fees stated, all of the costs incurred with respect to the prosecution of the case in the United States Supreme Court.

Jatras signed Lasky's proposed agreement, and on February 28 returned it to Lasky with a letter and a check for $25,000 as the agreed retainer. To "clarify" his thinking on the operation of the fee agreement, Jatras attached a set of hypothetical examples to the letter. This "attachment" stated the amount of the fee that would be paid to Brobeck assuming judgment or settlements in eight different amounts. In the first hypothetical, which assumed a settlement of $18.5 million and a counterclaim judgment of $18.5 million, Jatras listed a "net recovery" by Telex of "$0" and a Brobeck contingency fee of "$0."

Lasky received the letter and attachment on March 3. Later that same day he replied:

> Your attachment of examples of our compensation in various contingencies is correct, it being understood that the first example is applicable only to a situation where the petition for certiorari has been denied, as stated in paragraph 1 of the memorandum.

No Telex official responded to Lasky's letter.

Lasky, as agreed, prepared the petition for certiorari and filed it in July 1975. He also obtained a stay of mandate from the Tenth Circuit pending final disposition of the action by the Supreme Court. In the meantime, Telex began to consider seriously the possibility of settlement with IBM by having Telex withdraw its petition in exchange for a discharge of the counterclaim judgment. Telex officials planned a meeting to discuss whether to settle on this basis, and Walker asked Lasky to attend in order to secure Lasky's advice on the chances that the petition for certiorari would be granted.

The meeting was held on September 5. Lasky told the assembled Telex's officials that the chances that the petition for certiorari would be granted were very good. Wheeler, however, was concerned that if the petition for certiorari was denied, the outstanding counterclaim judgment would threaten Telex with bankruptcy. Wheeler informed Lasky that Telex was seriously considering the possibility of a "wash settlement" in which neither side would recover anything and each would release their claims against the other. Lasky responded that in the event of such a settlement he would be entitled to a fee of $1,000,000. Wheeler, upon hearing this, became emotional and demanded to know from the others present whether this was what the agreement provided. Walker agreed that it had. Jatras said he didn't know and would have to read the correspondence.

Two days later Jatras wrote a memorandum for the Telex Board of Directors in which he stated:

"Lasky claims that his deal guarantees him $1 million fee in the event that Telex settles after the Petition for Writ is filed if the settlement is at least a 'wash' with the counterclaim judgment."

Wheeler doesn't agree that the Lasky interpretation is correct and has asked Jatras to review his notes and recollections of this matter. Jatras has done so and has no independent knowledge beyond the documents.

Having returned to San Francisco, Lasky, at Telex's request, prepared a reply brief to IBM's opposition to the petition for certiorari, and sent it to the Supreme Court on September 17th for filing. In the meantime, Wheeler opened settlement discussions with IBM. He telephoned Lasky periodically for advice.

On October 2 IBM officials became aware that the Supreme Court's decision on the petition was imminent. They contacted Telex and the parties agreed that IBM would release its counterclaim judgment against Telex in exchange for Telex's dismissal of its petition for certiorari. On October 3, at the request of Wheeler and Jatras, Lasky had the petition for certiorari withdrawn. Thereafter, he sent a bill to Telex for $1,000,000. When Telex refused to pay, Brobeck filed its complaint. On the basis of depositions and exhibits, the district court granted Brobeck's motion for summary judgment.

In a somewhat contradictory fashion, Telex contends on appeal that a number of genuine issues of fact exist with respect to Brobeck's motion for summary judgment but that none exists concerning its own motion. Telex argues that it, not Brobeck, is entitled to summary judgment, or alternatively, to go to trial to determine the meaning of the contract. Telex raises three contentions:

1) Brobeck was discharged by Telex, and therefore, Brobeck was limited to recovering the reasonable value of its services;

2) the correct interpretation of the contract requires resolution of disputed factual issues;

3) the fee awarded under the contract was so excessive as to render it unconscionable. We discuss each of these contentions in turn.

I

Discharge

Telex contends that, under California law, if a client who has retained an attorney on a contingent fee basis discharges the attorney before the contingency has occurred, the attorney is limited to recovering the reasonable value of the services rendered. *See Fracasse v. Brent,* 6 Cal.3d 784, 100 Cal.Rptr. 385, 494 P.2d 9 (1972). Telex contends there is a factual dispute as to whether Brobeck was discharged, and summary judgment was therefore inappropriate.

This contention borders on frivolousness. As Telex concedes, it never formally discharged Brobeck. Nor did it say or do anything from which an intent to terminate Brobeck prematurely could be inferred. Lasky, as agreed, prepared and filed the petition for a writ of certiorari. Even after the September 5, 1975 meeting with Telex, Lasky continued to render services to Telex. He prepared and filed a reply to IBM's response to the petition for certiorari, and during the settlement discussions with IBM, he advised Telex on the appropriateness of settlement when consulted by Telex officials.

Telex does not dispute these facts. It argues instead that "by relieving Brobeck of the task of pursuing the appeal (by its settlement with IBM), Telex discharged Brobeck as plainly as if the word 'discharge' was used." This analysis begs the question. Only if we assume that the wash settlement did not make the contingent fee clause operative is this line of reasoning persuasive. To make this assumption, however, we would have to adopt Telex's interpretation of the contract. This we cannot do. It is the very interpretation of the contract that is the central issue on this appeal, a matter to which we now turn.

II

Interpretation

Paragraph three of the memorandum agreement provided that Brobeck was entitled to an additional fee "in the event of a recovery by Telex from IBM by way of settlement or judgment of its claims against IBM." Telex contends that the wash settlement reached by IBM and Telex was not such a recovery because the contract contemplated that Brobeck would be entitled to its contingent fee only if Telex actually received money in settlement of its suit with IBM. Telex contends that as a result of this "ambiguity," what the parties actually intended the contract to mean, as evidenced by their words and conduct, is a factual matter that cannot be resolved on a motion for summary judgment.

Under California law, the determination of whether a written contract is ambiguous is a question of law that must be decided by the court. *Airborne Freight Corp. v. McPherson*, 427 F.2d 1283, 1285 (9th Cir. 1970) (interpreting California law); *Brant v. California Dairies, Inc.*, 4 Cal.2d 128, 133, 48 P.2d 13 (1935). Even if the written agreement is clear and unambiguous on its face, the trial judge must receive relevant extrinsic evidence that can prove a meaning to which the language of the contract is "reasonably susceptible." *Pacific Gas and Electric Co. v. G. W. Thomas Drayage Co.*, 69 Cal.2d 33, 37, 69 Cal.Rptr. 561, 442 P.2d 641 (1968). If the court finds after considering this preliminary evidence that the language of the contract is not reasonably susceptible of interpretation and is unambiguous, extrinsic evidence cannot be received for the purpose of varying the terms of the contract. *Airborne Freight Corp.*, 427 F.2d at 1286; *Pacific Gas & Electric Co.*, 69 Cal.2d at 39, 69 Cal.Rptr. at 565, 442 P.2d at 645. The case may then be disposed of by summary judgment. *Airborne Freight Corp.*, 427 F.2d at 1286; *See Parish v. Howard*, 459 F.2d 616, 619 (8th Cir. 1972), because interpretation of the unambiguous contract is solely a question of law. *Gardiner v. Gaither*, 162 Cal.App.2d 607, 614, 329 P.2d 22 (1958).

In performing our judicial function of interpretation, we note that "it is beyond question that every provision of a contract should be examined to determine the meaning and intention of the parties. . . . the meaning of words contained in a contract is to be determined not from a consideration of the words alone but from a reading of the entire contract." *Sunset Securities Co. v. Coward McCann, Inc.*, 47 Cal.2d 907, 911, 306 P.2d 777, 779 (1957). We seek to interpret the contract in a manner that makes the contract internally consistent.

Paragraph one of the agreement provided that:

1. Retainer of $25,000.00 to be paid. If Writ of Certiorari is denied and no settlement has been effected in excess of the Counterclaim, then the $25,000.00 retainer shall be the total fee paid; provided, however, that

Thus, paragraph one narrowly limits Brobeck's fee to its $25,000 retainer to one situation: where there has been no settlement in excess of the counterclaim And where the writ of certiorari has been denied. Telex would have us construe the agreement as if the conditions stated in this paragraph were fulfilled, which they were not. Rather, the language in paragraph one ("provided, however") clearly contemplated a different computation of the fee where the conditions in either of the succeeding two paragraphs were fulfilled.

Paragraph three began with the language "(o)nce a Petition for Writ of Certiorari has been filed with the Clerk of the United States Supreme Court . . . ." Thus, the filing of the petition for certiorari triggered the operation of paragraph three. The paragraph proceeds to outline the manner in which Brobeck's fee would be computed in the event of settlement. The fee was to be contingent on two ranges of settlement. For settlements of less than $100 million but greater than or equal to $40 million, Brobeck's fee would be 5% Of the "gross" recovery, i.e., the amount "undiminished by any recovery by IBM on its counterclaims or cross-claims." For any settlement of less than $40 million gross, the 5% Would be computed on the "net" recovery i.e., the recovery after deducting the credit to IBM by virtue of IBM's recovery against Telex "but the contingent fee shall not then be less than $1,000,000." Because the settlement reached with IBM was for less than $40 million gross, Brobeck was entitled to the $1 million contingent fee.

Telex argues that, because it received no money by virtue of the wash settlement with IBM, there was "no recovery by Telex from IBM by way of settlement or judgment of its claims against IBM," and therefore, the condition on which Brobeck would be paid was never fulfilled. Such a construction would create anomalies in the agreement that we cannot reasonably believe that the parties could have intended. First, Telex's requirement that it receive some cash by way of settlement of its claims against IBM could be satisfied by receipt of $1.00 from IBM. We agree with Brobeck that a construction of the contract that would condition the $1 million fee upon Telex's receipt of any amount of cash, no matter how slight, is untenable. Second, had Telex received $18.5 million from IBM in settlement of its antitrust claim, instead of receiving a discharge from its counterclaim judgment, it would have been in the same position as the wash settlement left it. Yet, Telex does not appear to dispute that in such a situation that Brobeck would be entitled to its $1 million fee. Telex's version of the agreement clearly exalts form over substance. Finally, Telex's construction of paragraph three is incompatible with paragraph two. Paragraph two provides that if the case is settled before the petition for a writ of certiorari is actually filed, then Brobeck could bill its services on an hourly basis not to exceed $100,000. It makes no sense to interpret paragraph three such that Telex pays less in attorney's fees where the petition is filed than when it is not. Not only would Brobeck have expended more time and effort where it actually completes and files the petition, but it also would have conferred on Telex the ability to use the completed petition as bargaining leverage in its negotiations with IBM. The substantial leverage that Telex gained by having filed a petition for certiorari is an explanation why Telex was willing to pay substantially more for a filed petition, and in fact, Telex appears to have benefited significantly by having filed the petition.

We conclude, therefore, that the contract was unambiguous on its face. As noted, however, California law allows a party to challenge a contract that is unambiguous on its face, *Pacific Gas & Electric Co.,* 69 Cal.2d at 39–40, 69 Cal.Rptr. at 565, 442 P.2d at 645, and accordingly, Telex presented extrinsic evidence to the district court to show that the contract was susceptible of its interpretation. The district court apparently concluded that this evidence was insufficient reasonably to support Telex's interpretation of the contract. Having carefully reviewed this evidence, taking the facts presented by Telex as true and resolving all doubts in its favor, *See Handi Investment Corp. v. Mobil Oil Corp.,* 550 F.2d 543, 546 (9th Cir. 1977), we agree with the district court. We find that this evidence, if anything, compels our interpretation of the contract.

Three persons were involved in the formation of the Telex-Brobeck agreement: Lasky, Jatras, Telex's president, and Walker, Telex's counsel. In their depositions, Lasky and Walker consistently agreed that the contract should be interpreted in the manner advanced by Brobeck: once the petition for certiorari was filed, Brobeck was entitled to collect at least $1 million unless Telex lost.

The extrinsic evidence advanced by Telex to support its interpretation of the contract consists almost exclusively of Jatras' belief that an additional fee would be paid only if there was a net recovery (i.e., a settlement in excess of the counterclaim judgment). Jatras claims that he expressed his belief to Lasky on several occasions.

To the extent that Telex is relying on Jatras' subjective belief to establish the meaning of the contract, we must disagree. Under the modern theory of contracts we look to objective, not subjective, criteria in ascertaining the intent of the parties. *See Meyer v. Benko,* 55 Cal.App.3d 937, 127 Cal.Rptr. 846 (1976). Even when we view Jatras's protestations as part of the objective circumstances surrounding the formation of the contract, we find that they do not make the contract reasonably susceptible to Telex's interpretation, because Jatras's words are contradicted by his later actions.

In reviewing the objective criteria, we rely heavily on the documents reflecting the negotiations between Telex and Brobeck. These documents more accurately reflect the parties' intent than the hindsight recollections of the parties. This is true particularly in this case because Jatras had no independent recollection of the negotiations. Two days after the stormy September 5 meeting,

Jatras wrote the previously quoted memorandum for the Telex Board of Directors in which Jatras stated:

> Wheeler doesn't agree that the Lasky interpretation is correct and has asked Jatras to review his notes and recollections of this matter. Jatras has done so and has no independent knowledge beyond the documents.

At his deposition, Jatras further stated that when Wheeler asked him at the September 5 meeting what the contract said, he told Wheeler that he did not know, and would have to review all the letters.

In particular, we address the significant differences between the paragraph three that was proposed by Jatras and rejected by Lasky, and the version of paragraph three that was proposed by Lasky and agreed to by Jatras. To highlight the distinctions we set them forth as follows, underlining the pertinent sections:

PARAGRAPH 3 REJECTED

"Once a Petition for Writ of Certiorari has been filed with the Clerk of the United States Supreme Court then Brobeck will be entitled to the payment of an additional fee in the event of a recovery by Telex from IBM by way of settlement or judgment In excess of the counterclaim judgment; and, such additional fee will be 5% Of the first $100,000,000.00 of such recovery, the maximum contingent fee to be paid is $5,000,000.00 and the minimum is $1,000,000.00."

PARAGRAPH 3 OF THE EXECUTED CONTRACT

"Once a Petition for Writ of Certiorari has been filed with the Clerk of the United States Supreme Court then Brobeck will be entitled to the payment of an additional fee in the event of a recovery by Telex from IBM by way of settlement or judgment Of its claims against IBM; and, such additional fee will be five percent (5%) of the first $100,000,000.00 gross of such recovery, undiminished by any recovery by IBM on its counterclaims or cross-claims. The maximum contingent fee to be paid is $5,000,000.00, provided that if recovery by Telex from IBM is less than $40,000,000.00, the five percent (5%) shall be based on the net recovery, i.e., the recovery after deducting the credit to IBM by virtue of IBM's recovery on counterclaims or cross-claims, But the contingent fee shall not then be less than $1,000,000.00."

From the above, it appears that the construction of the contract that Telex is presently advancing on appeal is the one contained in the version that was rejected by Brobeck. Telex explicitly proposed that Brobeck would be entitled to an additional fee in the event of a recovery in "excess of the counterclaim judgment." In other words, Telex proposed a contract whereby it would pay Brobeck only if Telex recovered an amount in excess of the amount owed on the counterclaim judgment. Brobeck, however, by excluding this limitation in its version sent Telex and to which the parties finally agreed, specifically rejected such a contract. We think that the only correct inference to be drawn from the omission of Telex's proposal in the final contract is that the parties agreed that Brobeck would be entitled to its additional fee in the event of a settlement between IBM and Telex, without regard to whether the amount of settlement was greater than the counterclaim judgment.

The events surrounding the cryptic "attachment" that Jatras sent to Brobeck after the contract was signed also belie Telex's interpretation of the contract. The first example in the series of eight hypotheticals supports Jatras's interpretation that the contingent fee would be paid only if there was a net recovery to Telex. Lasky, by a return letter, promptly disagreed with this interpretation, stating that it applied only in the situation when the petition for certiorari was denied. As Telex admitted in a request for admission:

> neither Mr. Jatras nor anyone else connected with defendants at any time wrote or spoke to Mr. Lasky concerning any statement in the letter of March 3, 1975, and particularly concerning the last paragraph
>
> . . . .

We regard Telex's inaction as acquiescing to Brobeck's interpretation of the contract.

Thus, we find that the extrinsic evidence offered by Telex did not make the contract reasonably susceptible to its interpretation. The contract remained unambiguous and disposition of the case by summary judgment was appropriate. *See Airborne Freight Corporation*, 427 F.2d at 1286.

III

Finally, Telex contends that the $1 million fee was so excessive as to render the contract unenforceable. Alternatively, it argues that unconscionability depends on the contract's reasonableness, a question of fact that should be submitted to the jury.

Preliminarily, we note that whether a contract is fair or works an unconscionable hardship is determined with reference to the time when the contract was made and cannot be resolved by hindsight. *Yeng Sue Chow v. Levi Strauss & Co.*, 49 Cal.App.3d 315, 325, 122 Cal.Rptr. 816 (1975).

There is no dispute about the facts leading to Telex's engagement of the Brobeck firm. Telex was an enterprise threatened with bankruptcy. It had won one of the largest money judgments in history, but that judgment had been reversed in its entirety by the Tenth Circuit. In order to maximize its chances of gaining review by the United States Supreme Court, it sought to hire the most experienced and capable lawyer it could possibly find. After compiling a list of highly qualified lawyers, it settled on Lasky as the most able. Lasky was interested but wanted to bill Telex on hourly basis. After Telex insisted on a contingent fee arrangement, Lasky made it clear that he would consent to such an arrangement only if he would receive a sizable contingent fee in the event of success.

In these circumstances, the contract between Telex and Brobeck was not so unconscionable that "no man in his senses and not under a delusion would make on the one hand, and as no honest and fair man would accept on the other." *Swanson v. Hempstead*, 64 Cal.App.2d 681, 688, 149 P.2d 404, 407 (1944). This is not a case where one party took advantage of another's ignorance, exerted superior bargaining power, or disguised unfair terms in small print. Rather, Telex, a multi-million corporation, represented by able counsel, sought to secure the best attorney it could find to prepare its petition for certiorari, insisting on a contingent fee contract. Brobeck fulfilled its obligation to gain a stay of judgment and to prepare and file the petition for certiorari. Although the minimum fee was clearly high, Telex received substantial value from Brobeck's services. For, as Telex acknowledged, Brobeck's petition provided Telex with the leverage to secure a discharge of its counterclaim judgment, thereby saving it from possible bankruptcy in the event the Supreme Court denied its petition for certiorari. We conclude that such a contract was not unconscionable.

The judgment of the district court is affirmed.

SOLUTIONS: THE LAWYER SHOULD HAVE, WOULD HAVE, COULD HAVE. . .

At first glance, the $1 million contingency fee paid by Telex might look a bit excessive. Looking closer, Telex was a multi-million corporation which had its own counsel to help it retain the best law firm. Without all the hard work that Lasky has put in the certiorari petition, IBM would not have been under pressure to reach a settlement with Telex. Therefore, Lasky's $1 million minimum fee was not unconscionable and excessive. Remember that MR 1.5(a)(4) is a guide in cases like this.

LEANING INTO PRACTICE

As a business model, contingency fees cannot fully solve the problem of access to legal representation for people without financial means. Contingency fee arrangements are only viable when there is enough money potentially to be won in a case, relative to the resources required to litigate it. Sometimes, a person has a great deal at stake, intense legal needs, but little or no money on the line directly. That would be the case, for example, with people needing immigration assistance. It may also be the case even when money is on the line, but not enough. For example, a person denied a relatively low wage payment might struggle to find an attorney to handle the case on contingency if the payment would be too low to compensate the attorney.

While for the most part contingency fees align lawyers' and clients' financial interests, there are some complex ways in which this may not always be the case. Lawsuits play out over time, with varying chances of prevailing, and with varying amounts of work required at different stages. The ABA, in Formal Opinion 94–389, permitted attorneys to raise contingency fee rates at later stages of litigation precisely because the amount of attorney work required increases as trial approaches.

In a typical tort case, a lawyer might realize that the case could produce a large award, eventually, but only after years of litigation and only with the risk of losing at trial. Such a claim may present an opportunity to settle earlier in the process for less. Objectively speaking, it is difficult to say which choice is better. The value of being paid with certainty sooner depends in large part of how much the plaintiff and attorney need closure immediately, and how well they can handle risk. Clients and their attorneys may not be similarly situated in this respect. A client might yearn for her day in court and thus resist settlement. Or a client might not be financially secure enough to fight in court for years. Lawyers, too, may have cash flow issues and might favor faster resolutions. Or an attorney might take many cases with high potential rewards and might be happy to win in only some of them, while individual clients might be less comfortable with that risk.

With contingency fees, attorney interests and client interests are only aligned with respect to winning money. The biggest problem with contingency fees is that money is not the only thing at stake in litigation. Clients may find litigation stressful and might want to resolve a case early when a lawyer wants to fight on for larger gain. Clients might be interested in forms of justice other than monetary compensation. Imagine a parent suing because her child was injured by industrial pollution. Some parents in this situation might want the offending company to be held accountable publicly, and to be forced to clean up the contamination. If the company offers a large monetary settlement but accepts not fault and demands a non-disclosure agreement, the parents' goals might be frustrated. But pursuing those goals might risk reducing the monetary reward on which the attorney's fee depends.

Model Rule 1.5(d): Fees

(d) A lawyer shall not enter into an arrangement for, charge, or collect:

(1) any fee in a domestic relations matter, the payment or amount of which is contingent upon the securing of a divorce or upon the amount of alimony or support, or property settlement in lieu thereof; or

(2) a contingent fee for representing a defendant in a criminal case

Deconstruction Exercise/Rule Rationale

The Model Rules prohibit contingency fees in two specific types of practice: Divorce cases and criminal defense. Why might these two areas of practice raise special concerns for contingency fee arrangements, and do these concerns justify an outright ban on the practice? Are there any other areas of legal practice where contingency fees should be banned? The Model Rules pointedly do not prohibit hourly fees or flat fees from any specific areas of practice. Only contingency fees are singled out this way.

Note that this is a mandatory rule. In the first line, it forbids entering into contingency fee arrangements in certain cases, even if the client consents in writing to the agreement. Why? The answer is that the incentives are all wrong. If the lawyer receives a percentage of the size of the martial estate, then the lawyer is incentivized to focus only on increasing the monetary award in the divorce, not to successfully facilitating resolution of the marriage, which likely involves many issues beyond money.

Section 5. Client Property

Lawyers frequently end up holding their clients' property, usually in the form of cash. We have already seen this issue in the context of fees. When a client pays a fee in advance of the lawyer doing any work, the excess money is actually the client's property. But that might be a more complex variety of the client property problem. As we saw in the *In re Sather* case, there could be at least some ambiguity about whether those funds really belong to the client or the lawyer. But often lawyers hold client property when there is no ambiguity about who it belongs to. This happens, for instance, when settlement checks are delivered to the attorney.

The rules about how to handle such funds are among the simplest that we will study in this course. Client and lawyer property must be kept separate. Period. Yet, the rule is violated, often. The reason for the violations probably relates to simple human temptation. Yet, there are a few wrinkles that arise. Especially: what happens if a third party comes forward with a claim that the client owes her money while the money is held by the attorney? We will look at those situations, too.

A. Keeping Funds Separate

1) Do Not Commingle Funds!

The basic rule is this: Lawyers may not commingle their own funds with their clients' funds. That means that lawyers must keep clients' money in a separate account, not just from their personal funds, but also from their law firm's funds. And the lawyer must keep copious, current records of the funds and all transactions drawn on them.

Model Rule 1.15: Client Property

(a)   A lawyer shall hold property of clients or third persons that is in a lawyer's possession in connection with a representation separate from the lawyer's own property. Funds shall be kept in a separate account maintained in the state where the lawyer's office is situated, or elsewhere with the consent of the client or third person. Other property shall be identified as such and appropriately safeguarded. Complete records of such account funds and other property shall be kept by the lawyer and shall be preserved for a period of [five years] after termination of the representation.

Deconstruction Exercise/Rule Rationale

Note that this rule includes two separate requirements. It is not enough for the lawyer to just keep good records of how much money she is holding for her client. They must also be held separately. The idea here is clearly to secure client property as much as possible against human temptation on the part of lawyers. If money were comingled, it would be harder to prevent lawyers from dipping into client funds if, say, their firm's cash flow was short for a month. It would start to seem in practice more like the attorney owed a debt to the client, to be paid later. But that is not the case. This money just does not belong to the attorney. The ABA Comment makes clear that the attorney in this case is holding the funds as a "professional fiduciary."

One clarification is important at the outset. We are talking here about lawyers acquiring client property through the practice of law. That's when these rules come into play. People who happen to be lawyers may also come into control of other people's property in other personal or business relationships. The ABA Comment notes lawyers might act as escrow agents, for example. Or a lawyer might serve as a fiduciary on a trust set up by someone in her family. In those situations, the duties required will be governed by the specific law on those specific situations. The fact that the person holding the property is an attorney is a peripheral detail.

2) *Client Trust Accounts: The Basics*

The basic way lawyers prevent the commingling of funds with their clients is through maintaining a separate Client Trust Account. That is simple enough, but there are some specific steps the attorney will need to follow to set up the account. Also important: The interest earned on the client funds belongs to the client and should be credited to the client's balance. The trust account gives rise to the one exception in which commingling funds is acceptable. A lawyer may add her own funds to the trust account to pay bank service charges—but for no other purpose. Lawyers should immediately notify clients when they receive funds on their behalf.

Some states require that the account be explicitly labeled with the bank. For instance, California's version of Rule 1.15 requires "identifiable bank accounts labeled 'Trust Account' or words of similar import." What this means is that checks drawn on the account will have a clear label, so it is clear that it is a payment from client funds. It also means that the account is transparently a trust account for anyone reviewing the records. That is a much better practice than simply having another bank account that only the law firm knows to be the Client Trust Account. Even in states where this labeling is not required, it is a very good idea. Once again, transparency is the guiding concept.

There are other safeguards that would be highly recommended and may be required in some states. For example, it may be unwise (and in some places prohibited) for the Client Trust Account to have an ATM card. The high duty of care required in safeguarding client property is better met by requiring checks or other transactions with written records. This helps ensure clearer record keeping (which a cash transaction at an ATM inherently does not), and also promotes more thoughtful decision-making by the attorney.

Cases and Materials

X-Ray Questions (*Barfield*)

Requiring Client Trust Accounts complying with rigorous record keeping rules is not the only approach the legal profession could take, in theory. We could instead just require lawyers to keep records of client's funds, and that they deliver these funds to their clients whenever required. A lawyer in this system might only be sanctioned if she fails to pay the client when required. But that is not the system that we have. Instead, a lawyer can be sanctioned for improper management of client funds even if a client has not been injured. Why does the bar take this approach?

In this case, the defense of the lawyer in this case was essentially "no harm, no foul." But the court rejected the defense. Why? She lost her ability to make a living as a lawyer. Years of school, years of likely paying off substantial student loan. Is disbarment too harsh a penalty when these facts are considered? What other system could be advised to discipline lawyers but not impose the equivalent of the death penalty upon them?

State of Nebraska Ex Rel. Counsel for Discipline of the Nebraska Supreme Court v. Jackie L. Barfield

Supreme Court of Nebraska, 2020.
305 Neb. 79.

PER CURIAM.

NATURE OF CASE

The respondent appeals from the report and recommendation of the referee in an attorney disciplinary action. The referee recommended disbarment for violations of Neb. Ct. R. of Prof. Cond. §§ 3–501.15 (safekeeping property) and 3–508.4 (rev. 2016) (misconduct) relating to the attorney's commingling of earned and unearned client payments and cash withdrawals and checks written from her attorney trust account to pay for business and personal expenses. The trust account also suffered several overdrafts. The respondent argues that suspension rather than disbarment is the appropriate discipline for her actions.

BACKGROUND

Jackie L. Barfield was admitted to the practice of law in the State of Nebraska in 1993, and at all times relevant was engaged in the practice of law in Omaha, Nebraska. Formal charges against her were filed by the office of the Counsel for Discipline of the Nebraska Supreme Court in February 2019.

The charges alleged that between October 2017 and April 2018, Barfield had written multiple personal checks and had made multiple cash withdrawals out of her attorney trust account. She had also paid insufficient-fund fees several times. Barfield admitted to writing personal checks and taking cash withdrawals from her attorney trust account, as well as having insufficient funds in that account, since at least 2013. Barfield was charged with violating §§ 3–501.15 (safekeeping property) and 3–508.4 (misconduct). Barfield, in her answer, admitted to the allegations.

In mitigation, Barfield pled that (1) any economic harm any person may have suffered from her acts was "of very brief duration," (2) she has been providing services to economically disadvantaged members of the public at lower-than-normal fees throughout her career, (3) she is a minister and religious leader providing "comfort and moral guidance to her small group of followers generally beneficial to the social moral fabric of her community," and (4) she has no prior serious disciplinary complaints except one related to an unpaid bill from a doctor, for which she was privately reprimanded approximately 20 years before. Pursuant to Barfield's motion, judgment on the pleadings was granted as to the facts, under Neb. Ct. R. § 3–310(L) (rev. 2014).

Neither party filed written exceptions to the referee's report that was issued after a hearing to determine the nature and extent of the discipline to be imposed, considering any aggravating and mitigating factors. The report set forth that Barfield had been without a business account for approximately 5 years and, since at least 2013, has been withdrawing cash and writing checks on her attorney trust account to pay for personal and business expenses. Barfield has paid insufficient fund charges since 2013 for at least 23 overdrafts on her attorney trust account.

The record reflects that previously, in May 2000, the Nebraska State Bar Association had privately reprimanded Barfield for failing to deposit into her trust account a check issued to honor a medical lien in relation to her client's settlement and for failing to promptly disburse a portion of the settlement funds designated for medical providers. The Counsel for Discipline had found in the private reprimand that Barfield violated provisions of the Code of Professional

Responsibility concerning general misconduct, neglect, and preservation of the identity of client funds.

BARFIELD'S TESTIMONY

Barfield testified at the disciplinary hearing. Barfield was not permitted to offer any other evidence concerning mitigation, due to her failure to comply with discovery deadlines.

Barfield explained that her business account had been closed approximately 5 years prior due to lack of funds. Rather than opening another business account, she used her trust account to pay business expenses. She did not open another business account until recently.

Barfield testified that for the past 5 years she had worked part time as a sole practitioner out of her daughter's home. She explained: "Well, the business expenses are home-related. And I practice out of Bellevue, which is my daughter's home, and so it's been difficult, and that's one of the reasons that I put things related to Barfield Law, I just put it in the trust account." She testified that she has had no support staff since she stopped practicing out of a stand-alone building approximately 5 years before the hearing.

Barfield testified that her retainers were generally small and had been earned sometimes even before they were deposited into the trust account. No client had ever complained about how their funds were handled. When asked whether her commingling and withdrawals had harmed her clients, she said:

Well, in reading some of the case law and—in my mind I didn't think it was, but in reading the case law, I understand since this case has started that even, you know, if you use it there's a possibility and so, yes, under those circumstances I do agree.

As for the overdrafts, Barfield explained that at least one of the overdrafts was due to a client's check bouncing—after she had withdrawn the deposit by making a check out to herself.

Barfield noted that since 2014, she has had several health concerns related to her knees and hips. She had been trying to wind up her practice in Nebraska in order to live permanently in Texas, where the weather was better for her health. But the winding up was taking longer than she thought, and she was traveling back and forth between a daughter's home in Texas and another daughter's home in Nebraska. The traveling had put an emotional strain on her, and she suffered from anxiety and migraines. In fact, she had suffered from "anxiety and everything" since she started practicing. Barfield testified that she had taken antidepressants "over the years" and had been prescribed medication for her anxiety.

With regard to the private reprimand approximately 20 years before, Barfield explained that the settlement payment to her client had been stopped due to an ongoing criminal matter in which the FBI was involved. This stop payment, in conjunction with her private practice being otherwise wound down after she accepted a position at a university, "threw my whole account off" and made it difficult for the doctor in question to contact her. Barfield left her job at the university after approximately 1 year of employment there and, in 2000, after taking another year to focus on her family and mental health, returned to private practice.

Barfield asked for any sanction short of disbarment. She stated that she now understood that she could not manage going back and forth between Texas and Nebraska anymore and would stay in Nebraska if allowed to continue to practice, stating:

[M]y intention is if I'm going to practice in Nebraska, I have to live in Nebraska. And the going back and forth is just too stressful. It's causing me a lot of anxiety and it puts you in the position of having to do more than you can handle.

Barfield testified that she served lower-income clients with the intention of giving back to her community. She explained, "I believe I focus so much probably on trying to do the best work for my clients, and I might have been hyper focused on that than what was going on in my life." Barfield testified that she never wished to harm her clients and believed she could properly manage a trust account in the future.

REFEREE'S RECOMMENDATION

The referee in his report noted that misuse of client trust accounts, even without obvious misappropriation, harms the reputation of the bar and that an appropriate sanction should be imposed that will deter others from such conduct. Barfield's conduct, the referee found, had tarnished the reputation of the bar.

The referee found that the duration and repetitive nature of Barfield's violations reflected negatively on Barfield's future fitness to practice law. Also, the referee considered Barfield's conduct to constitute both commingling and misappropriation that caused harm to her clients, reasoning:

[Barfield] admittedly left earned fees in her trust account without a clear accounting and separation until it was impossible to determine what money belonged to her and what belonged to her clients, thus commingling her money with client money. Additionally, [Barfield's] bank records show numerous overdrafts in her attorney trust account, which is clearly the misappropriation of client funds.

After considering sanctions imposed in similar cases, the referee concluded that the nature of Barfield's offenses "is of the gravest concern to the legal profession and the Court has consistently found these violations require disbarment, absent mitigation."

The referee found that Barfield had been cooperative throughout the investigation and disciplinary proceedings, which the referee considered a mitigating factor. The referee agreed with Barfield's counsel that Barfield's actions of readily admitting misconduct, acknowledging responsibility for her actions, and acknowledging that her violations have harmed the public reflected positively upon Barfield's attitude and character.

On the other hand, the referee stated that it appeared that Barfield failed to grasp the seriousness of her violations. The referee noted that Barfield had expressed that any economic harm was only of very brief duration. The referee also found that the lack of actual, or only minimal, harm was not a mitigating factor.

The referee also did not consider it as mitigating factors that there is no record of complaints from clients, attorneys, or courts against Barfield or that Barfield claimed to have modified her trust account practices, because she did so only after receiving notice of the disciplinary investigation. Lastly, the referee did not consider as mitigating any depression Barfield may have experienced, since she did not present any medical evidence that the depression was a direct and substantial contributing factor for her misconduct.

The referee found as an aggravating factor that this was not the first disciplinary action brought against Barfield concerning her trust account. Furthermore, the referee noted that Barfield's current misuse of her trust account was not an isolated incident but consisted of cumulative acts occurring over approximately 5 years.

The referee recommended disbarment with the following condition should Barfield apply for reinstatement: "[Barfield] should produce evidence satisfactory to the Court that she is fit to practice law; and further that the Counsel for Discipline has not been notified by the Court that [Barfield] has violated any disciplinary rule during her disbarment." The referee also recommended that Barfield be required to comply with the notification requirements of Neb. Ct. R. § 3–316 (rev. 2014) and that she be subject to punishment for contempt if she fails to do so. Finally, the referee recommended that Barfield be directed to pay costs and expenses in accordance with Neb. Rev. Stat. §§ 7–114 and 7–115 (Reissue 2012) and § 3–310(P) and Neb. Ct. R. § 3–323(B) within 60 days of any order imposing such costs and expenses.

ASSIGNMENT OF ERROR

Barfield disagrees with the referee's recommendation that she should be disbarred as a sanction for her misconduct.

STANDARD OF REVIEW

When no exceptions to the referee's findings of fact are filed by either party in a disciplinary proceeding, this court may, at its discretion, adopt the findings of the referee as final and conclusive.

Because attorney discipline cases are original proceedings before this court, we review a referee's recommendations de novo on the record, reaching a conclusion independent of the referee's findings.

ANALYSIS

Under § 3–310(L), we accept the findings of the referee as final and conclusive. In addition, Barfield admitted the allegations and, pursuant to Barfield's motion, judgment on the pleadings was granted. Barfield violated §§ 3–501.15 (safekeeping property) and 3–508.4 (misconduct). The only issue left to consider is the appropriate sanction.

Attorneys licensed to practice law in the State of Nebraska agree to operate under the supervision of the office of the Counsel for Discipline. A license to practice law confers no vested right, but is a conditional privilege, revocable for cause. Violation of any of the ethical standards relating to the practice of law or any conduct of an attorney in his or her professional capacity which tends to bring reproach on the courts, or the legal profession constitutes grounds for suspension or disbarment.

Under Neb. Ct. R. § 3–304, this court may impose one or more of the following disciplinary sanctions: "(1) Disbarment by the Court; or (2) Suspension by the Court; or 3) Probation by the Court in lieu of or subsequent to suspension, on such terms as the Court may designate; or (4) Censure and reprimand by the Court; or (5) Temporary suspension by the Court[.]" The goal of attorney discipline proceedings is not as much punishment as a determination of whether it is in the public interest to allow an attorney to keep practicing law. Providing for the protection of the public requires the imposition of an adequate sanction to maintain public confidence in the bar.

To determine whether and to what extent discipline should be imposed in an attorney discipline proceeding, we consider the following factors: (1) the nature of the offense, (2) the need for deterring others, (3) the maintenance of the reputation of the bar as a whole, (4) the protection of the public, (5) the attitude of the respondent generally, and (6) the respondent's present or future fitness to continue in the practice of law. Each attorney discipline case must be evaluated in light of its particular facts and circumstances. For purposes of determining the proper discipline of an attorney, we consider the attorney's actions both underlying the events of the case and throughout the proceeding, as well as any aggravating or mitigating factors. Furthermore, the propriety of a sanction must be considered with reference to the sanctions imposed in prior similar cases.

Barfield's use of her trust account as both a business account and a personal account violated the rule against commingling. Generally speaking, an attorney violates the rule against commingling when the funds of the client are intermingled with those of the attorney in such a way that their separate identity is lost and they may be used by the attorney for personal expenses or subjected to the claims of the attorney's creditors. Section 3–501.15(a) requires a lawyer to "hold property of clients or third persons that is in a lawyer's possession in connection with a representation separate from the lawyer's own property." Section 3–501.15(a) also requires that client "[f]unds shall be kept in a separate account maintained in the state where the lawyer's office is situated." The only exception is when the lawyer's own funds are deposited into a client trust account for the sole purpose of paying bank service charges on that account, and the exception applies only to deposits in the amount necessary for that purpose. Neither good faith nor ignorance of the rules prohibiting commingling client and personal funds provides a defense to a disciplinary charge that an attorney violated the rules against commingling.

This court considers commingling of client funds with an attorney's own funds to be a matter of gravest concern in reviewing claims of lawyer misconduct. The practice involves the inherent danger of unforeseen circumstances jeopardizing the safety of the client's funds. Even when the client suffers no loss, an attorney's commingling of client funds with personal funds is not a trivial or technical rule violation.

Because it is such a dangerous and unfortunately common basis for disciplinary action, there is a continuing need to send a clear and strong message deterring attorneys from commingling client and personal funds and from using client trust accounts as personal checking accounts. Commingling of client funds with personal funds, even when it does not involve obvious misappropriation, harms the reputation of the entire legal profession by undermining public confidence and trust in attorneys, in the courts, and in the legal system. Thus, we have repeatedly said that absent extraordinary mitigating circumstances, disbarment is the appropriate discipline in cases of misappropriation or commingling of client funds.

The burden is on the respondent to provide evidence to be considered for mitigation of the formal charges. Cooperation and remorse during disciplinary proceedings are mitigating factors, and it is undisputed that Barfield readily admitted her misconduct, fully cooperated in the investigation, acknowledged responsibility for her actions, and acknowledged that her violations harmed the public. Furthermore, Barfield testified that she provided legal services at a reasonable cost to those who could not otherwise afford such services. Continuing commitment to the legal profession and the community is a mitigating factor in an attorney discipline case, although we note that the record here is somewhat limited as to the level of Barfield's community involvement throughout her career.

Barfield further represents as a mitigating factor that there have never been any complaints against her for mishandling clients' cases or for failing to communicate or act. We have recognized that having no prior complaints is a mitigating factor, but we have not considered mitigating the lack of complaints in one area of conduct when there has been a past complaint in another area. Barfield's assertion ignores the prior complaint that resulted in the private reprimand in 2000.

Barfield does not argue that her mental or physical health is a mitigating factor. Regarding depression, we have said that in order to be a mitigating factor, the respondent must show (1) medical evidence that he or she is affected by depression, (2) that the depression was a direct and substantial contributing cause to the misconduct, and (3) that treatment of the depression will substantially reduce the risk of further misconduct. No such evidence was presented in this case. Neither, rightly, does Barfield argue that her lack of staff and her living situation, leading to her admittedly poor accounting practices, presented mitigating factors. Poor accounting practices are neither an excuse nor a mitigating circumstance in reference to commingled or misappropriated funds.

We have considered prior reprimands as aggravators, and we agree with the referee that the conduct resulting in the 2000 reprimand is an aggravating factor in this case. Because cumulative acts of attorney misconduct are distinguishable from isolated incidents, they justify more serious sanctions. We have said that cumulative acts of misconduct can, and often do, lead to disbarment. Barfield's description of her prior reprimand as a "misunderstanding of a debt owed to a medical provider," which occurred in the "distant past," does not remove it as an aggravating factor.

Moreover, we consider aggravating the fact that the acts of commingling presently at issue were both intentional and routine over the course of several years. During that time, Barfield used her trust account as both a business account and a personal account, regularly withdrawing cash or paying directly from the trust account her utilities, medical expenses, and store purchases.

Barfield asserts that the level of moral turpitude reflected in her commingling and misappropriation was dissimilar to other cases in which we have imposed disbarment, in that she "used her own funds from her trust account to pay day to day meager expenses because she lost her other accounts to write checks from," adding that "[s]he did not steal anybody's money." But we have repeatedly said that the fact that a client did not suffer any financial loss does not excuse an attorney's misappropriation of client funds and does not provide a reason for imposing a less severe sanction than disbarment. Further, Barfield fails to point to a case where the prolonged use of a trust account to pay meager, as opposed to lavish, expenses has led to a lesser sanction.

In numerous cases, we have imposed disbarment for commingling or misappropriation when the client did not suffer a financial loss, even when there were mitigating factors. In STATE EX REL. NSBA V. VEITH for example, the relator was disbarred because of several instances over the course of 8 months of having a deficient balance in his client trust account, which he subsequently attempted to remedy through personal loans to cover the deficiencies. The deficiencies were the result of transfers to his business account, and the transferred funds were used for salaries, office expenses, an upgraded computer system and law library, and a car.

We noted case law from other jurisdictions holding that the mere fact that an attorney's trust account balance falls below the amount deposited in and purportedly held in trust supports a finding of misappropriation, explaining that wrongful or improper intent is not an element of misappropriation. We found the proper sanction to be disbarment, despite no aggravating factors and several mitigating factors, including being in good standing and free from disciplinary complaint or penalty, cooperation with the investigation, remorse, a good reputation in the community, and the provision of many pro bono hours. We repeated that an attorney has a duty to keep separate and properly account for client trust funds and explained that an attorney may not use client trust funds to cover business expenses. We also disapproved of a prior trend toward lighter sanctions for such behavior, citing with approval another court's reasoning that imposing lighter discipline would " ' "stand out like an invitation to the lawyer who is in financial difficulty for one reason or another" ' " and that " ' "[t]he profession and the public suffer as a consequence." ' "

We have generally imposed the lesser discipline of suspension in cases of commingling or misappropriation only where (1) it involved an isolated incident or a limited number of incidents over a relatively isolated period of time, (2) there were multiple significant mitigating factors, and (3) there were no aggravating factors. Mitigating factors may overcome the presumption of disbarment in misappropriation and commingling cases only where they are extraordinary and, when aggravating circumstances are present, they substantially outweigh those aggravating circumstances.

Here, the mitigating factors of Barfield's cooperation, remorse, and efforts to provide affordable representation to the community, while laudable, are insufficient both to rebut the presumption of disbarment for commingling and to substantially outweigh the aggravating factors. This is not the first time Barfield has been disciplined in relation to her maintenance of her trust account, and she has for several years engaged in a continuous pattern of commingling client funds. Especially in light of the prior reprimand, Barfield's prolonged and persistent violation of the rule against commingling reflects a general failure to fully comprehend the serious nature of such conduct.

After balancing the relevant factors in comparison to other cases, considering the need to protect the public, considering the need to deter others, and considering the reputation of the bar as a whole, we agree with the referee that disbarment is the only appropriate sanction.

CONCLUSION

Barfield violated §§ 3–501.15 (safekeeping property) and 3–508.4 (misconduct). It is the judgment of this court that Barfield is disbarred from the practice of law in the State of Nebraska, effective immediately. She is directed to comply with § 3–316, and upon failure to do so, she shall be subject to punishment for contempt.

JUDGMENT OF DISBARMENT.

> ### SOLUTIONS: THE LAWYER SHOULD HAVE, WOULD HAVE, COULD HAVE. . .
>
> Barfield's argument essentially boiled down to this: no one was hurt by my using the trust account as a personal checking account. A violation of an ethical rule is nonetheless a violation no matter if harm befalls the client. Here though the punishment was swift: The professional equivalent of capital punishment. The Rules are often prophylactic by design, guarding against creating temptation. The way to avoid succumbing to temptation is to eliminate it from the environment in the first instance.

X-Ray Questions

While the practice of law is intellectually stimulating and emotionally rewarding, there are more mundane aspects that cannot be overlooked. Client trust accounts are one such aspect. Do you see yourself having challenges in performing the tasks described here by the State Bar of California? Which ones and why? Do you think that careless handling of other people's money can be tantamount to theft? Could failure to adhere to these concepts below lead to a criminal charge against a lawyer? If so, what?

> ## BEYOND THE CITE
>
> ### Handbook on Client Trust Accounting for California Attorneys
>
> State Bar of California, 2018.
>
> The following seven key concepts are all the background you need in order to understand your client trust accounting responsibilities.
>
> ### Key Concept 1: Separate Clients Are Separate Accounts
>
> Client A's money has nothing to do with Client B's money. Even when you keep them in a common client trust bank account (such as in an IOLTA account), each client's funds are completely separate from those of all your other clients. In other words, you are NEVER allowed to use one client's money to pay either another client's or your own obligations.
>
> When you keep your clients' money in a common client trust bank account, the way to distinguish one client's money from another's is to keep a client ledger of each individual client's funds (as required by rule 1.15(d)(3) and the recordkeeping standards under rule 1.15€). The client ledger tells you

how much money you've received on behalf of each client, how much money you've paid out on behalf of each client, and how much money each client has left in your common client trust bank account. If you are holding money in your common client trust bank account for 10 clients, you have to maintain 10 separate client ledgers. If you keep each client's ledger properly, you will always know exactly how much of the money in your common client trust bank account belongs to each client. If you don't, you will lose track of how much money each client has, and when you make payments out of your client trust bank account, you won't know which client's money you are using.

Key Concept 2: You Can't Spend What You Don't Have

Each client has only his or her own funds available to cover their expenses, no matter how much money belonging to other clients is in your common client trust bank account. Your common client trust bank account might have a balance of $100,000, but if you are only holding $10.00 for a certain client, you can't write a check for $10.50 on behalf of that client without using some other client's money.

The following example graphically illustrates this concept. Assume you are holding a total of $5,000 for four clients in your common client trust bank account as follows:

Client A $1000

Client B $2000

Client C $1,500

Client D $500

Total $5000

If you write a check for $1,500 from the common client trust bank account for Client D, $1,000 of that check is going to be paid for by Clients A, B and C. The funds you are holding in trust for them are being used for Client D's expenses. You should have a total of $4,500 for Clients A, B and C, but you only have $3,500 left in the trust account. In State Bar disciplinary matters, a finding of a failure to maintain a sufficient client trust account balance will support a finding of misappropriation.

Key Concept 3: There's No Such Thing As a "Negative Balance"

It's not uncommon in personal checkbooks for people to write checks against money they haven't deposited yet or hasn't cleared yet, and show this as a "negative balance." In client trust accounting, there's no such thing as a negative balance. A "negative balance" is at best a sign of negligence and, at worst, a sign of theft. (Don't think that because you have "automatic overdraft protection" on your client trust bank account and the check doesn't bounce, you have fulfilled your client trust account responsibilities.)

In client trust accounting, there are only three possibilities:

You have a positive balance (while you are holding money for a client);

You have a zero balance (when all the client's money has been paid out); or

You have a balance of less than zero (a so-called "negative balance") and a problem.

Key Concept 4: Timing Is Everything

It takes anywhere from a day to several weeks after you make a deposit before the money becomes "available for use." A client's funds aren't "available" for you to use on the client's behalf until they have cleared the banking process and been credited by the bank to your client trust bank account. (This is especially true when you receive an insurance company's settlement draft—which cannot clear until the company actually receives the draft at its home office during the bank collection process and honors the draft. Thus, insurance company settlement drafts will take longer to clear your account.) If you write a check for a client at any time before that client's funds clear the banking process and are credited to your client trust bank account, ordinarily either the check will bounce or you will be using other clients' money to cover the check.

The time it takes for client trust account funds to become available after deposit depends on the form in which you deposit them. Every bank has different procedures, so when you open your client trust bank account, get the bank's schedule of when funds are available for withdrawal. Depending on the instrument, you may have to wait as many as 15 working days before you can be reasonably confident that the funds are available. For example, even if you make a cash deposit, the money may not be available for use until the following day. If you deposit a personal check from an out-of-state bank, the money will take longer to be available. Either way, until the bank has credited a client's deposit to your client trust bank account, you can't pay out any portion of that money for that client.

You also need to know what time your bank has set as the deadline for posting deposits to that day's business and for paying checks presented to it. Otherwise, even when you have deposited cash, you may end up drawing on uncollected funds. For example, let's say your bank credits any deposit made after 3 p.m. on the following day, but stays open for business until 5 p.m. Your client arrives at 3:30 and gives you $5,000 in cash which you immediately deposit. At 4 p.m., you write a client trust bank account check to an investigator against that money. If the investigator presents the check for payment at the bank before it closes at 5 p.m., the check will either bounce or be covered by other clients' money.

You may be tempted to do your client a favor by writing a check to the client for settlement proceeds before the settlement check has cleared because you know there's money belonging to other clients in your client trust bank account to cover this client's check. Depending on the circumstances, your client may insist that you do this. Don't. If you do, you'll end up writing a check to one client using another clients' money. You shouldn't help one client at the expense of your obligations to your other clients. In other words, no matter how expedient or kind or convenient it seems, don't make payments on your clients' behalf before their deposited funds have cleared. Otherwise, sooner or later, you'll end up spending money your clients don't have.

Some banks offer an "instant credit" arrangement where the bank agrees to immediately credit accounts for deposits while the bank waits for the funds from another financial institution. Beware of this service because it is, in essence, a loan to the attorney that is deposited in the client trust bank account, and thus a commingling of funds. (An "instant credit" arrangement may also be offered as a form of overdraft protection.)

Key Concept 5: You Can't Play the Game Unless You Know the Score

In client trust accounting, there are two kinds of balances: the "running balance" of the money you are holding for each client, and the "running balance" of each client trust bank account.

A "running balance" is the amount you have in an account after you add in all the deposits (including interest earned, etc.) and subtract all the money paid out (including bank charges for items like wire transfers, etc.). In other words, the running balance is what's in the account at any given time. The running balance for each client is kept on the client ledger, and the running balance for each client trust bank account is kept on the account journal.

Maintaining a running balance for a client is simple. Every time you make a deposit on behalf of a client, you write the amount of the deposit in the client ledger and add it to the previous balance. Every time you make a payment on behalf of the client, you write the amount in the client ledger and subtract it from the previous balance. The result is the running balance. That's how much money the client has left to spend.

You figure out the running balance for the client trust bank account the same way. Every time you make a deposit to the client trust bank account, you write the amount of the deposit in the account journal and add it to the previous balance. Every time you make a payment from the client trust bank account, you write the amount in the account journal and subtract it from the previous balance. The result is the running balance. That's how much money is in the account.

Since "you can't spend what you don't have" (Key Concept 2: You Can't Spend What You Don't Have), you should check the running balance in each client's client ledger before you write any client trust bank account checks for that client. That way, if your records are accurate and up-to-date, it's almost impossible to pay out more money than the client has in the account.

Key Concept 6: The Final Score Is Always Zero

The goal in client trust accounting is to make sure that every dollar you receive on behalf of a client is ultimately paid out. What comes in for each client must equal what goes out for that client; no more, no less.

Many attorneys have small, inactive balances in their client trust bank accounts. Sometimes these balances are the result of a mathematical error, sometimes they are part of a fee you forgot to take, and sometimes a check you wrote never cleared or wasn't cashed.

Whatever the reason, as long as the money is in your client trust bank account, you are responsible for it. The longer these funds stay in the bank, the harder it is to account for them. Therefore, you should take care of those small, inactive balances as soon as possible, including, if necessary, following up with payees to find out why a check hasn't cleared.

If you take steps to take care of these small balances and are still unable to pay out the funds, you should consider whether the unclaimed monies escheat to the state pursuant to Code of Civil Procedure section 1518.

Key Concept 7: Always Maintain an Audit Trail

An "audit trail" is the series of bank-created records, like cancelled checks, bank statements, etc., that make it possible to trace what happened to the money you handled. An audit trail should start whenever you receive funds on behalf of a client and should continue through the final check you issue against them. Without an audit trail, you have no way to show that you have taken proper care of your clients' money, or to explain what you did with the money if any questions come up. The audit trail is also an important tool for tracking down accounting errors. If you don't maintain an audit trail, you will find it hard to correct the small mistakes, like errors in addition or subtraction, and the big mistakes, like miscredited deposits, that are inevitable when you handle money.

The key to making a good audit trail is being descriptive. Let's say you are filling out a deposit slip for five checks relating to three separate clients. All the bank requires you to do is write in the bank identification code for each check and the check amounts. This doesn't identify which client the money belongs to. If you include the name of the client and keep a copy or make a duplicate, you will know which client the check was for, which is the purpose of an audit trail. That will make it easy to answer any questions that come up, even years later.

By the same token, every check you write from your client trust bank account should indicate which client it's being written for, so that it's easy to match up the money with the client. That means you should NEVER make out a client trust bank account check to cash, because there's no way to know later who actually cashed the check. If you are handling more than one case for the client, indicate which matter the payments and receipts relate to on your checks and deposit slips.

A good audit trail, one that will make it easy for you to explain what happened to each client's money and to correct accounting errors, requires that you keep more than just the minimum records required by rule 1.15(d)(3) and the recordkeeping standards under rule 1.15(e) In the following list of elements of a good audit trail, records that are required by rule 1.15 are in bold.

A good audit trail should include:

- The initial deposit slip (or a duplicate copy or bank receipt). This should show the date the deposit slip was filled out; the amount of the deposit; the name or file number of the client on whose behalf the money was received; who the money came from; and the bank's date stamp showing the day the deposit was actually received.

- The bank statement which shows when the deposit was actually posted by the bank.

- The checkbook stub, which should show when payments were made, how much the payments were, to whom they were made and in connection with which client matter they were made.

- The cancelled check. In a good audit trail, the check should show the date the check was drawn; the amount of payment; who the check was made out to; the purpose of the check (or the matter it relates to); the order in which the check was negotiated (from the endorsements); and the date it was deposited for collection. (Regarding check imaging as a substitute for cancelled checks, see Section VII Recordkeeping, What Bank-Created Records Do You Have to Keep?)

- The bank statement which shows the date the trust account was actually charged for the check.

- Copies of the front and back of any executed drafts, especially insurance settlement drafts, received on behalf of a client.

Two final points: first, remember that interest earned on client funds belongs to the client. But sometimes there is no interest owed to the client because the amount of money held is too small or because the lawyer will be holding it for too brief a period of time. The legal profession has developed an innovation to use these funds to support legal aid programs: The IOLTA account. IOLTA stands for Interest on Lawyer Trust Accounts. Lawyers who handle nominal or transitory funds for their clients are required to have one of these accounts in most states.

An IOLTA account is a regular, interest-bearing bank account set up to be part of a pooled interest system. Unlike regular Client Trust Accounts, IOLTA accounts pool their interest and transfer it to a statewide trust fund that is used to support pro bono and legal aid programs. Usually, state bars identify specific banks that participate in the IOLTA system and provide attorneys with necessary documentation to register the account with the bank. Put another way, IOLTA is a financial instrument that mines interest from client funds that otherwise would not earn any, and then uses the proceeds for the public good.

Second point: lawyers must exercise proper care of a client's non-monetary property as well. Occasionally, lawyers come into possession of client property other than cash. Such property cannot be deposited in a trust account. But lawyers must handle the property following similar principles. Records must be copiously kept, and the property must be kept securely and separately from the attorney's personal and business assets. For paper securities and similar financial instruments, the ABA Comment to Rule 1.15 instructs lawyers to use a bank safe deposit box—essentially as close as one can get to a bank account.

If the nature of particular property makes the safe deposit box option impractical, a lawyer may have to get creative. One of the authors of this book once received a client's PlayStation, which was apparently his most prized possession. After some discussion in the office, the device was placed in a locked cabinet, separate from all the firm office equipment and supplies, with separate paper records signed by the attorney and office manager noting receipt, chain of custody and location of the object. The PlayStation was eventually returned to the client. The key principles to remember are reasonable security, record keeping, and no commingling.

B. Third Party Claims on Client Property

Perhaps the thorniest legal problem concerning client property held in trust by a lawyer is third party claims. In a typical situation, a lawyer might receive a large settlement payment for a client, only to have one of the client's creditors claim that all or some of the funds should be used to pay the client's debt. Lawyers in this situation must walk a difficult line. On the one hand, it is not the lawyer's role to judge the validity of the creditor's claim. To do so would probably clash with the lawyer's duty of loyalty to her client. But the lawyer cannot ignore a potentially valid claim, and just give the money to her client, potentially assisting her client in evading a creditor in the process.

Model Rule 1.15: Safekeeping Property

(d) Upon receiving funds or other property in which a client or third person has an interest, a lawyer shall promptly notify the client or third person. Except as stated in this rule or otherwise permitted by law or by agreement with the client, a lawyer shall promptly deliver to the client or third person any funds or other property that the client or third person is entitled to receive and, upon request by the client or third person, shall promptly render a full accounting regarding such property.

(e)   When in the course of representation, a lawyer is in possession of property in which two or more persons (one of whom may be the lawyer) claim interests, the property shall be kept separate by the lawyer until the dispute is resolved. The lawyer shall promptly distribute all portions of the property as to which the interests are not in dispute.

Deconstruction Exercise/Rule Rationale

The ABA Comment on this rule emphasizes that a lawyer must refuse to turn over property to a client if the third-party claim "is not frivolous." That means that a lawyer must make an initial assessment of the plausibility of the claim. Sometimes this will be obvious, such as if the creditor has a judgment lien or a pending lawsuit. But it may be less than that, such as if a creditor presents disputable evidence demonstrating a debt. Once a non-frivolous claim is presented, a lawyer's obligation is to notify the creditor of the receipt of funds, provide an accounting, and allow time for the creditor and client to resolve the claim. Remember, the lawyer is not required to resolve a dispute between her client and a third party, but rather to hold the funds in trust to allow the dispute to be resolved.

Cases and Materials

X-Ray Questions (*Taylor*)

The above analysis leaves this question unanswered: How much evidence of a valid third-party claim should be required for an attorney to be obligated to notify the supposed creditor and hold the funds in trust? The following two cases illustrate two different scenarios and reach opposite results. In one of them, the court was emphatic that the lawyer should have notified the third party. In the other, the court concluded that the had attorney had no obligation—but there was a dissent, suggesting that some judges may disagree. Given these outcomes, can you discern any clear factors to guide attorneys facing these problems?

State of Oklahoma, ex rel. Oklahoma Bar Association v. Michael C. Taylor

Supreme Court of Oklahoma, 2000.
4 P.3d 1242.

OPALA, J.

In this disciplinary proceeding against a lawyer, the issues to be decided are: (1) Does the record submitted for our examination provide sufficient evidence for a meaningful de novo consideration of the complaint and of its disposition? and (2) Is a thirty-day suspension an appropriate disciplinary sanction for respondent's breach of professional ethics? We answer both questions in the affirmative.

INTRODUCTION TO THE RECORD

¶ 2 The Oklahoma Bar Association [Bar] charged Michael C. Taylor [Taylor or respondent], a licensed lawyer from Tulsa, Oklahoma, with one count of professional misconduct. The parties' stipulation on file consists of stipulated facts, conclusions of law and agreed factors to be considered in mitigation of the discipline to be imposed. Left unresolved was the discipline to be recommended. Respondent admitted to having violated Rules 1.15(b)(c),3 5.3,4 8.1(b),5 and 8.4(a)(c),6 Oklahoma Rules of Professional Conduct [ORPC] and Rules 1.37 and 5.2,8 Rules Governing Disciplinary Proceedings [RGDP]. At the end of the hearing, the Professional Responsibility Tribunal [PRT or trial panel] directed the parties to offer a brief suggesting the discipline to be visited.

Following receipt of the parties' briefs and upon consideration of the stipulations and testimony on file the trial panel issued a report with its findings of fact and conclusions of law together with a recommendation for discipline. In accord with the parties' stipulations, the trial panel found that Taylor had violated ORPC Rules 1.15(b)(c), 5.3, 8.1(b), and 8.4(a)(c), and RGDP Rules 1.3 and 5.25.2. It recommended that Taylor be publicly censured and that he bear the costs of the proceedings.

THE CHARGES LODGED AGAINST THE RESPONDENT

¶ 7 The alleged misconduct occurred during respondent's representation of Shelby Deason and her two minor children [Deason or client], who were injured on 6 May 1998 in an automobile accident. From May through August of 1998 the Deasons received medical treatment from Dr. Gregg Alan Coker. On August 19 he sent to Prudential Insurance a final billing statement for his services in the amount of $890. Respondent settled the case with the insurer for $911.75.

¶ 8 On 2 November 1998 Prudential Insurance sent to Taylor three checks made payable to Dr. Coker, Taylor, and Deason totaling $911.75. Respondent did not notify Dr. Coker about the settlement checks. Instead, on November 9 respondent's employee (and wife), Mrs. Taylor, endorsed the names of Dr. Coker, Taylor, and that of the client on the three checks and deposited them in his trust account. Dr. Coker's name was signed without his knowledge or consent.

¶ 9 Dr. Coker's office manager (and wife), Kat Coker, would testify that on 10 December 1998 she was advised by Prudential Insurance that the Deason case had been settled and that payment had been sent to respondent. Mrs. Coker called respondent's office the same day to find out the status of the settlement check. She was informed by a temporary employee in respondent's office that they were waiting for Deason to sign the release. On 5 January 1999 she was again advised by the same employee that they were waiting on the client's signature before the funds could be disbursed.

¶ 10 Mrs. Coker's January 6 letter to Deason informed her that (a) respondent had been holding the settlement check for two months and that the physician's office had not been paid, (b) that respondent's employee told her they were trying to obtain her signature on the release so that funds could be disbursed, (c) and that unless Dr. Coker received full payment on January 20, a small claims action would be filed against Deason. A copy of the letter was sent to respondent. Two days later, Dr. Coker's office received an undated letter from respondent along with a check dated 9 November 1998 drawn on his trust account for $586.83 with a notation "part. pay Deason family." Respondent's letter neither addressed the two-month delay in sending payment nor explained how the settlement checks were negotiated without Dr. Coker's signature.

¶ 11 Mrs. Coker would testify that after checking with Prudential Insurance and determining that Dr. Coker was shown as a payee on the checks, she wrote (a) "VOID—NOT ACCEPTABLE" on respondent's letter and (b) "VOID" across the front of the respondent's check and returned both items to the latter. She again advised Deason that partial payment was not acceptable. On January 20 Dr. Coker received from Prudential Insurance copies of the negotiated settlement checks, discovering that three checks, not one, had been issued. The copies showed the endorsement of the payees' names on the back of the checks. Later that day Mrs. Coker called respondent's office and left a message that unless full payment was received by the end of the day, a complaint would be filed against him. Respondent did not comply with her demand.

¶ 12 On January 27 the Bar received from Dr. Coker a written grievance alleging (a) respondent failed to notify him upon receipt of settlement funds, (b) his office misrepresented the status of funds' disbursement, and (c) he forged Dr. Coker's signature on the settlement checks. The Bar advised the respondent by letter dated February 11 that a formal investigation had commenced and that he had 20 days to respond. When respondent did not timely answer, the Bar sent on March 15 a certified letter, informing him that failure to respond within five days would result in the issuance of a subpoena. In a letter to the Bar, dated March 15 but received March 17, respondent denied any wrongdoing, but failed, though he had been requested so to do, to address the applicability to his actions of ORPC Rules 1.15 and 8.1(a)(b)(c) and of RGDP Rule 1.4RGDP Rule 1.4.

¶ 13 In a March 15 letter to Dr. Coker, respondent tendered another check for $586.83 drawn on his trust account, stating that the amount represents the "net remainder" of the settlement proceeds. His letter explained that because an attorney's lien is superior to that by a physician, it was not "unlawful, unethical nor improper" to deposit the settlement check in the trust account and to pay the "appropriate and lawful costs and fees" due in the case. The letter did not explain (a) respondent's failure to send the November 9th check until some two months later, (b) the misrepresentations made by respondent's office regarding the status of the settlement distributions and (b) why Dr. Coker's signatures were placed on the back of the three checks without his authorization.

¶ 14 Respondent's June 21 letter to the Bar advised that he made four disbursements from the settlement proceeds for (a) an attorney's (referral) fee to Mark Harper ($101.97), (b) his counsel fee ($203.95), (c) costs (25.00) and (d) then "sent 100% of the remainder to Dr. Coker's office on the same day" ($586.83), referring to November 9, the day that respondent's checks were written and deposited to his operating account. In response to the Bar's query about the different signature styles on the back of the checks, respondent explained that because his bank would become concerned if all the endorsements on the checks appeared to be in the same handwriting, he avoided the problem by "altering the handwriting styles." This was done, he explained, not to perpetrate any fraud but merely to facilitate getting the funds deposited and then placed in the hands of the clients and medical providers. Respondent's letter failed to advise the Bar that although four checks were written on November 9, respondent's checks for attorney's fee and costs were deposited that day, but the checks to Dr. Coker and Harper were mailed some two months later. The letter also misrepresented to the Bar that these checks were sent the "same day" the respondent's check was deposited. According to respondent, the checks were being held until the settlement releases were either signed or authorized by his client.

¶ 15 Although respondent's letters to the Bar and to Dr. Coker disclaimed any wrongdoing in his handling of the settlement checks, he later stipulated that he had a duty (a) promptly to notify all interested parties that the funds had been received, (b) to obtain in writing the permission of all co-payees to endorse the checks and deposit them in his trust account, and (c) that if a dispute arose concerning their respective interests, to keep separate all funds until that dispute has been resolved.

IV

MISHANDLING OF FUNDS BELONGING TO A THIRD PARTY

¶ 16 The Bar has charged respondent with improperly managing the funds entrusted to him in violation of ORPC Rule 1.15(b) and (c). Rule 1.15 requires that lawyers who are entrusted with the property of clients and of third parties must hold that property with the care required of a "professional fiduciary." The basis for the rule is the lawyer's fiduciary obligation to safeguard trust property and to segregate it from the lawyer's own property, and not to benefit personally from its possession. Upon receiving funds in which a client (or third party) has an interest, a lawyer is required by ORPC Rule 1.15(b) to notify promptly the interested party. This notification allows the client (or third party) (a) the opportunity for an accounting and, if necessary, (b) the opportunity to dispute the respective interests before disbursement is made of the funds. Rule 1.15(c) requires an attorney to keep separate a client's (or third party's) funds in which the lawyer also has an interest until a proper accounting and severance of interests can be made or until any dispute over the quantum of interests is resolved.

¶ 17 We employ three different culpability standards when evaluating mishandling of client funds: 1) commingling, which takes place when client money is intermixed with the attorney's personal funds; 2) simple conversion, which occurs when a lawyer applies a client's money to a purpose other than that for which it was entrusted to the attorney and 3) misappropriation, the most serious infraction, which involves an act of conversion (or similar wrongful taking) when an attorney purposefully deprives a client of money by way of deceit and fraud. Complete separation of a client's money from that of the lawyer is the only way in which proper accounting can be maintained. The gravity of culpability in mishandling of funds ascends from the first to the last of the three categories. Each must be proved by clear and convincing evidence. A lawyer's mishandling of funds belonging to a third party is not to be treated differently from the approach we take to commingling, misappropriation or conversion of funds belonging to the lawyer's client. In each case, the lawyer violates the basic professional duty of trust, not only as counsel but also as fiduciary.

¶ 18 The record before us reveals that respondent (a) received three checks payable to Dr. Coker, respondent and to the client in November 1998; (b) failed to notify Dr. Coker of the checks until almost two months later, and (c) gave no legal excuse for the delay. On November 9 respondent's wife forged the signature of Dr. Coker on the back of the checks and deposited them in his trust account. On the same day he wrote two checks drawn on the trust account for his claimed fee and costs and deposited them in his operating account, (a) without first notifying Dr. Coker that the settlement checks had been received and (b) without giving Dr. Coker an opportunity to dispute the amount of the distribution. We find that respondent's (a) failure to notify promptly Dr. Coker of the receipt of the insurance checks (b) failure to hold the funds separate until the dispute over the respective interests in the funds (Dr. Coker's, the client's and Harper's) was resolved and (c) misleading (via his staff) Mrs. Coker about the distribution of the funds constituted a violation of ORPC Rule 1.15(b) and (c).

A THIRTY-DAY SUSPENSION IS AN APPROPRIATE SANCTION FOR RESPONDENT'S PROFESSIONAL MISCONDUCT

¶ 27 The primary purpose of disciplinary judicature is not to punish the delinquent lawyer but to protect the public by a thorough inquest into the respondent's continued fitness to practice law. Imposition of discipline is designed to foster these aims rather than to administer a purely punitive measure for a lawyer's professional dereliction.

¶ 28 While the PRT and the Bar recommend that respondent be publicly censured (and that he defray the costs of these proceedings), respondent suggests that his misconduct warrants a less severe discipline. He urges that we visit a private reprimand.

A.

Aggravation of Discipline

¶ 29 It would not be in keeping with our stewardship of public interest to visit in this case a mild form of discipline. When respondent received the settlement checks, he became a constructive trustee of Dr. Coker to the extent the physician may have had a legal claim to the money in respondent's hands. Respondent's breach of a fiduciary duty to Dr. Coker constitutes an aggravating factor that warrants a higher level of discipline. While the client did not join in the complaint by pressing for respondent's discipline, that aspect is without legal significance. Disciplinary judicature protects the public against lawyers whose professional misbehavior presents a risk to the served community as a whole—not just to individual clients or other complainants with standing as aggrieved persons.

¶ 30 Respondent's actions affected a third-party claim to the fund. By failing to hold separately funds that represent proceeds due his client as well as those of a third-party medical provider to whom the client was indebted and by diverting a portion of the funds to his personal account before any dispute could be resolved, respondent must be deemed to have commingled the funds he so withheld. This is particularly egregious where, as here, the respondent—without either notice to the third-party medical provider or any opportunity for an antecedent dispute resolution—deducts the fee quantum and costs due him, transfers it to his own account, and then for two months holds up the distribution to Dr. Coker (as well as to Harper) by misrepresenting the status of the funds' disbursement.

¶ 31 Moreover, respondent's breach of fiduciary duty was accompanied by total lack of candor in his failure to acknowledge the wrongfulness of his actions. He mistook the claimed superiority of his attorney's lien over that of the physician's as a license to breach the trust. In short, he failed to comprehend that, in the unfolded scenario, his fiduciary obligation included the physician as cestui que trust to the extent of the latter's interest in the recovered fund.

The Court also noted that the lawyer had failed to supervise nonlawyer staff, who included his wife, in handling the funds and was non-cooperative with the bar in the ensuing disciplinary proceedings.

SOLUTIONS: THE LAWYER SHOULD HAVE, WOULD HAVE, COULD HAVE...

Note the court's description of the lawyer as becoming a "constrictive trustee." Thus, the lawyer must act as a trustee would—meaning in the best interests of a third party. This is just one initial introduction to the duties an attorney owes to third parties. We will cover this important concept in our next chapter.

Cases and Materials

X-Ray Questions (*Klancke*)

This case involves a dispute over who would receive the proceeds of a large money judgment as a result of a fatality in a plane crash. A law firm became embroiled in the dispute because it received the monies and distributed to only one of those eligible. Those who did not receive the monies argued that the firm breached fiduciary various duties. What was the disagreement between the majority and the dissent? Do you see that the 2–1 vote could have gone the other way if there was a different panel of judges? What could the lawyers have done to try and insulate themselves from liability?

Kim Klancke, et al. v. Peter M. Smith, et al.

Colorado Court of Appeals, Div. V., 1991.
829 P.2d 464.

Opinion by JUDGE JONES.

Plaintiffs, Kim Klancke, Kirk Klancke, Kit Klancke, and Jill Klancke Cook (children), appeal from a summary judgment entered in favor of defendants, Peter M. Smith, Susan Y. Young, and Peter M. Smith and Susan Y. Young Law Offices, on claims of negligence and breach of fiduciary duty. We affirm.

This appeal arises out of a dispute over the disposition of proceeds recovered in a wrongful death action brought by Janet Klancke (Ms. Klancke) in federal district court. In that action, Ms. Klancke recovered a money judgment for the death of her husband, Calvin Klancke, who was killed in an airplane crash near Granby, Colorado, in 1986.

Plaintiffs are the surviving natural children of Calvin Klancke and are stepchildren of Ms. Klancke, who was Calvin Klancke's second wife.

Ms. Klancke retained defendants to prosecute her wrongful death claim. On June 16, 1986, defendant Smith filed a complaint in federal district court listing only Ms. Klancke as plaintiff.

While the wrongful death claim was pending, a dispute arose between the children and Ms. Klancke concerning the childrens' rightful share in the proceeds of any potential recovery. Ms. Klancke took the position that the children were required to prove their net pecuniary loss in order to share in the wrongful death recovery.

As a result of this dispute, three of the children retained separate counsel to represent their interests in the wrongful death action. The children concede that they at no time retained defendants to represent them in the wrongful death suit.

In June 1987, an attorney entered an appearance in the wrongful death action on behalf of certain of the children and filed motions regarding their participation in the action and sharing in any proceeds deriving therefrom.

In November of 1987, the federal district court issued two orders, in which it determined that, although the children are entitled to share in the proceeds of any recovery, under Colorado law, those proceeds may only be distributed to the surviving spouse in whose name the action was commenced.

On April 26, 1988, a jury awarded Ms. Klancke approximately $465,000 in her wrongful death action. On May 24, 1988, the judgment was satisfied when defendant Smith received payment and deposited the funds in his firm's trust account.

Before such satisfaction, the children filed a motion requesting the federal court to supervise distribution of the wrongful death proceeds, but that motion was denied on June 3, 1988. Subsequently, after deducting costs and attorney fees, defendant Smith distributed the wrongful death proceeds in their entirety to his client, Ms. Klancke.

Thereafter, the children commenced an action in the state court against Ms. Klancke for breach of trust and conversion. Summary judgment was entered in favor of the children in October 1989 in the approximate amount of $190,000. However, in August 1989, Ms. Klancke filed a petition for bankruptcy and an automatic stay was issued. Thereafter, the children brought this action against defendants.

Plaintiffs contend that the trial court erred in determining that defendants owed no duty to them, fiduciary or otherwise, to ensure that any wrongful death proceeds recovered were actually shared with or paid to them. We disagree.

An action for wrongful death did not exist at common law, but rather is entirely a creation of statute. Therefore, the proper method for distribution of monies recovered in connection with a wrongful death action must be derived exclusively from the terms of the wrongful death statute. *Clint v. Stolworthy*, 144 Colo. 597, 357 P.2d 649 (1960); *Campbell v. Shankle*, 680 P.2d 1352 (Colo.App.1984).

Colorado's wrongful death statute is set forth in § 13–21–201, et seq., C.R.S. (1987 Repl.Vol. 6A). The sections of the statute applicable here, §§ 13–21–201(1)(a) and 13–21–201(1)(b), provide that, within the first year from the date of death, the surviving spouse of the deceased has the exclusive right to bring the action. *See Campbell v. Shankle, supra.*

Section 13–21–203, C.R.S. (1987 Repl.Vol. 6A) provides that:

"All damages accruing under section 13–21–202 shall be sued for and recovered by the same parties and in the same manner as provided in section 13–21–201, and in every such action the jury may give such damages as they may deem fair and just . . . *to the surviving parties who may be entitled to sue. . . .*" (emphasis added)

Here, as in the *Campbell* case, the action was initiated within one year of the death at issue. Hence, the surviving spouse, here Ms. Klancke, had the exclusive right to sue under § 13–21–201 and she, therefore, was the party entitled to recover the damages awarded.

Although we agree that the children are entitled to a portion of the award, we conclude that defendant Smith satisfied his statutory duty by paying the settlement proceeds to his client, the surviving party entitled to sue and recover damages. *See* § 13–21–203; *Campbell v. Shankle, supra.* And, given the surviving spouse's express statutory right to receive the proceeds, we agree with the trial court's conclusion that the identity of the payor, in *Campbell* an insurance company, here an attorney, does not alter the result.

We also perceive no duty owed by defendants to the children based upon an attorney-client relationship.

The relationship of an attorney and client is based upon contract which may be implied by the conduct of the parties. *People v. Razatos*, 636 P.2d 666 (Colo.1981). However, to establish such a relationship based upon conduct requires a showing that a person seeks and receives legal advice from an attorney regarding the legal consequences of the person's past or contemplated actions. *People v. Morley*, 725 P.2d 510 (Colo.1986).

Here, the children concede that they did not retain defendants to represent them. The children also concede that no "express attorney-client" relationship existed between defendants and themselves. Furthermore, the record reveals a developing adversity between the children and Ms. Klancke, concerning which defendants could not ethically represent both sides. Under these circumstances, defendants' only client was Ms. Klancke.

An attorney is charged with a duty to act in the best interest of his or her client, and in fulfilling this obligation, the attorney is liable for injuries to third parties only for conduct that is fraudulent or malicious. *Schmidt v. Frankewich*, 819 P.2d 1074 (Colo.App.1991); *McGee v. Hyatt Legal Services, Inc.*, 813 P.2d 754 (Colo.App.1990).

Here, the trial court specifically found no evidence of fraud or malice on the part of defendants, and our review of the record leads us to conclude that the trial court was correct in its finding.

Summary judgment is proper upon a clear showing that no genuine issue of material fact exists and that summary judgment should be entered as a matter of law. C.R.C.P. 56(c); *Churchey v. Adolph Coors Co.*, 759 P.2d 1336 (Colo.1988).

We conclude that no genuine issues exist here regarding defendants' duty to the children, and that the trial court correctly applied the law to the undisputed facts. Accordingly, the trial court's entry of summary judgment was proper.

The judgment is affirmed.

PLANK, J., concurs.

JUDGE NEY dissenting.

I dissent from the majority's opinion which concludes that summary judgment in favor of defendant attorneys was appropriate merely because no attorney/client relationship existed between the defendants and the plaintiffs and, that therefore, the attorneys had no duty whatsoever to the plaintiffs. I would conclude that an attorney may, under circumstances as pled here, incur liability to non-clients.

Summary judgment is never warranted except on a clear showing that there exists no genuine issue as to any material fact and that the moving party is entitled to judgment as a matter of law. The moving party has the burden of establishing the lack of a triable factual issue and all doubts as to the existence of such an issue must be resolved against the moving party. Also, a party against whom summary judgment is sought is entitled to the benefit of all favorable inferences that may be drawn from the facts. *Churchey v. Adolph Coors Co.,* 759 P.2d 1336 (Colo.1988).

Here, it was undisputed that the attorney-defendants had no attorney/ client relationship with the plaintiffs. I, therefore, agree that the malpractice claims were properly decided against the plaintiffs.

However, the plaintiffs also pled a violation of a fiduciary duty, alleging that the attorneys, after full knowledge of the plaintiff's interest in the proceeds of the wrongful death action and with knowledge that their client would receive the proceeds subject to that interest, advised their client to resist plaintiff's claims and wrongfully transferred the proceeds to their client.

The Colorado Wrongful Death Statute, 13–21–201 C.R.S. (1987 Repl.Vol. 6A), grants a surviving husband or wife the exclusive right to initiate an action under the statute during the first year after the death of the spouse. However, pursuant to § 13–21–201(2), if such an action is brought by the surviving spouse, "the judgment obtained in said action shall be owned by such persons as are heirs at law of the deceased under the statutes of descent and distribution and shall be divided among such heirs at law in the same manner as real estate is divided according to said statute of descent and distribution." Therefore, under the facts here, the plaintiffs, owned fifty percent of the proceeds of the wrongful death action.

The plaintiffs pled, and there is evidence in the record to support the allegation, that the defendants in concert with their client wrongfully asserted that the plaintiffs would not be entitled to any portion of the proceeds unless they could prove their net pecuniary loss. There was evidence in the record from which it could be inferred that the defendants advised their clients to resist such payment. Such a position is directly contrary to Colorado law. *See Clint v. Stolworthy,* 144 Colo. 597, 357 P.2d 649 (1960).

Under the Wrongful Death Statute, a husband or wife who receives the proceeds of a wrongful death action holds such in the nature of a trust for the other owners. The attorney for a trustee has a fiduciary duty to the beneficiaries of that trust even though those beneficiaries are not the attorney's clients. *See Weingarten v. Warren,* 753 F.Supp. 491 (S.D.N.Y.1990).

Furthermore, an attorney who receives funds which he knows belong to parties other than his client may be held liable for dispersing such funds to his client if he has been put on notice of such wrongful distribution. *See Coppock v. Helfer*, 515 P.2d 488 (Colo.App.1973) (Not Selected For Official Publication).

To conclude, as the majority does, that attorneys who are in possession of property, which they know is owned by individuals other than their clients, are immune from liability to rightful owners for improper distribution of such property would place attorneys in a unique and preferred status contrary to sound public policy.

I, therefore, would reverse the summary judgment entered in favor of the defendants on the plaintiff's claim of breach of fiduciary duty.

SOLUTIONS: THE LAWYER SHOULD HAVE, WOULD HAVE, COULD HAVE. . .

When a lawyer has custody of money to which more than one person claims an ownership interest, the lawyer is well advised to hit the pause button and think before distributing. Perhaps the lawyer can seek the advice of ethics counsel from a firm or request an ethics opinion from the State Bar Association. Or, as you learned in 1L civ pro, file an interpleader suit and request that a court determine the ownership interests.

Becoming a Professional

X-Ray Questions

The challenges involved in the actual practice of law will change. That's a given. But will the rules on ethics need to change with the reality of practice? Remember that the lawyer who knows the rule and the reason for the rule will always—in a legal firefight—have an advantage over the lawyer who only knows the rules. Consider this in relation to the question of whether lawyers can accept new forms of currency for payment, analyzed below in the following piece from the North Carolina Bar Association.

BEYOND THE CITE

By: James M. McCauley, Sharon D. Nelson, and John W. Simek, *Is it Ethical for Lawyers to Accept Bitcoins and other Crypto Currencies?* **September, 2018.**

The Ethics Committee recently received an inquiry regarding the ethical implications of a lawyer receiving cryptocurrency (Bitcoin) as payment for legal fees or as payment for the benefit of a client or a third party. The inquiry was referred to a subcommittee for further review. Nebraska is currently the only jurisdiction that has issued an opinion on the ethical issues implicated by the multifaceted nature of cryptocurrency. The Virginia State Bar recently published an article referencing the Nebraska opinion and noting their concerns about the implications of cryptocurrency on a lawyer's professional responsibility. With permission from the authors and the Virginia State Bar, that article is republished here for our members' contemplation.

Cryptocurrency Baseline

Bitcoins are digital currency, and yes, lawyers are beginning to accept them from clients. They are also known as virtual currency or cryptocurrency since cryptography is used to control Bitcoin creation and transfer. They use peer-to-peer technology with no central authority or banks. The issuance of bitcoins and the managing of transactions are carried out collectively by the network.

Cryptocurrencies are created by a process called mining—by becoming a miner of cryptocurrencies, you make money (not much unless you are a major league miner). We won't go into all of the technology that is used to create and verify the transactions since it will probably make your head hurt. Mining is accomplished by executing complicated mathematic operations that take a lot of processing power. Hence the new phenomenon of cryptojacking in which miners hijack the computing resources of unknowing victims so they can mine cryptocurrencies. And yes, your network could be victimized and there is little chance you would know unless so much power is used that your network slows down.

Today there are a lot of different cryptocurrencies. Bitcoin is still one of the most well-known and popular. However, other cryptocurrencies such as Ethereum, Bitcoin Cash, Monero, Litecoin, Ripple, Dash, and others are gaining in popularity. They promise to scale better than Bitcoin and to provide stronger anonymous protections. As of April 26, 2018, the amazing number of different cryptocurrencies is 1,759 according to investing.com's current list located at https://www.investing.com/crypto/currencies. With all the various "flavors" of digital currencies, we're sure you'll find one to your liking.

All cryptocurrency transactions are recorded in a computer file called a blockchain, which is synonymous to a ledger that deals with conventional money. Users send and receive Bitcoin and other cryptocurrencies from their mobile device, computer, or web application by using wallet software. You can even use cloud services to host and manage your wallet(s). Frankly, we prefer to have direct control and keep our wallet(s) stored on local devices. Of course, don't forget to back up your wallet(s).

We won't get into all the technical and legal issues surrounding cryptocurrencies. Suffice it to say that these virtual currencies are here to stay and have value, although they remain extremely volatile. In the US, cryptocurrencies are regarded as property rather than cash, with all the consequent tax implications.

Ethical Issues

Let's deal with some of the ethical issues concerning the acceptance of cryptocurrencies.

Nebraska is the only state we are aware of that has issued an ethical opinion specifically for Bitcoin usage. Nebraska's opinion states that lawyers may accept payments in digital currencies, but must immediately convert them into US dollars. Any refund of monies is also made in US dollars and not in digital currency.

It is well known that an attorney can't access client funds until they are earned, hence the existence of trust accounts. Also, an attorney can accept property as payment, but there must be a valuation for the property. This is where accepting digital currencies could get a little muddy. The Virginia rules require that a fee for legal services must be "reasonable." If attorneys receive digital currency, they should immediately convert and exchange it to actual currency AND put it in their escrow account. This effectively (and actually) puts a value on the cryptocurrency, which is exactly the process described in the Nebraska opinion. As part of the reconciliation and billing process, the lawyer would just note wording stating the number of bitcoins or other cryptocurrency and the market value at conversion. What the Nebraska opinion did not address is the handling of transaction fees, which can be rather substantial. The majority of lawyers will use an exchange to convert the cryptocurrency into cash. Who pays the fee for this conversion? And what if the client insists that the lawyer hold an advanced fee payment in Bitcoin instead of converting it to US currency? If Bitcoin increases in value, who gets the windfall—the lawyer or the client? Who bears the risk if Bitcoin drops in value?

Criminal defense lawyers, of course, can face potential ethical and even criminal issues if clients pay them with assets they are determined to have acquired through illegal conduct. And yet, almost invariably, when we hear about lawyers accepting Bitcoin as payment, the lawyers involved are criminal defense attorneys. For all the talk of "privacy" and the frequent inability to prove the connection between illegal conduct and Bitcoin, it is clear that federal authorities believe the bitcoins are used to keep criminal activities financially untraceable. On the other hand, many legitimate businesses in the United States and Europe accept Bitcoin, including Dish Network, Overstock.com, and Expedia.

Holding Cryptocurrencies

What if the lawyer wants to keep the cryptocurrency for their own use? Can they just keep the cryptocurrency in their own electronic wallet and deposit cash in the trust account on behalf of their client? The answer to this question depends on whether the Bar considers bitcoins "funds" or "property" that a client entrusts to the lawyer. See Rule 1.15. Client "funds" belong in a trust account, but client "property" must be kept safe by the lawyer. Since a lawyer cannot deposit bitcoins in a trust account, describing it as "funds" is a problem.

When a client gives a lawyer bitcoins, it is "property," not actual currency, but Rule 1.15 requires a lawyer to safeguard client property. This means making sure your digital "wallet" is secure and backed up. If the lawyer wants to keep the bitcoins and give the client the equivalent value in cash, those funds must go into the trust account if the bitcoins were payment of an advanced fee. This would require the client's consent and would be subject to the business transaction rule under Rule 1.8(a), requiring that the terms of the transaction be fair and reasonable, confirmed in writing, and that the client be advised to seek independent counsel before entering into the agreement.

One legal ethicist, the late Professor Ronald D. Rotunda, disagreed with the Nebraska Bar's Ethics Opinion 17–03 that says the lawyer must convert the cryptocurrency immediately into US currency. *See, Bitcoin and the Legal Ethics of Lawyers,* dated November 6, 2017, on Justia's Verdict blog at bit.ly/2OzOFoT. Professor Rotunda correctly explains how Bar opinions have allowed that, subject to certain requirements, lawyers may accept from their clients' stock and tangible property in lieu of cash for payment of legal fees even if the stock or property might fluctuate in value after the lawyer has accepted it. In Rotunda's view, bitcoins are like gold in the sense that it is worth whatever people are willing to pay for them.

The Nebraska opinion requires that lawyers "mitigate the risk of volatility and possible unconscionable overpayment for services" by not retaining the digital currency and by converting it "into US dollars immediately upon receipt." To Rotunda, it is a business decision rather than an ethics decision if the client wants to shift the risk of volatility to the lawyer. If a client and lawyer agree to pay the lawyer with stock in lieu of currency, and the original value is reasonable at the time the parties contracted, the fact that the stock goes up or down in value does not make the acceptance of the stock unethical. The Bar opinions "look back" to the time that payment was accepted to determine whether the payment was "reasonable," and the lawyer may suffer a loss or a windfall, as the case may be. These opinions do not require that the lawyer sell the stock immediately to convert it to cash. In some initial public offerings, there may be "blackout periods" in which the lawyer is prohibited from selling the stock. That Bitcoin might drastically drop in value, resulting in the lawyer being underpaid, is not an ethics issue either, according to Rotunda. Lawyers are educated adults and can make the call to sell or keep the bitcoins and accept that risk.

Rotunda may have a point if the client pays the lawyer in bitcoins for past legal services. In that case, the lawyer has earned the fee and the bitcoins becomes the property of the lawyer. The lawyer can accept risk with respect to his or her own property. That the bitcoins cannot be deposited into a bank account is not an ethics issue if the bitcoins are payment toward an earned fee. Even if the client paid the fee in cash, a lawyer cannot deposit an earned fee in a trust account because that would be commingling. The ethics rules do not require the lawyer to deposit an earned fee in an operating account either. The lawyer could deposit the cash directly into a personal checking account.

If the client gives the lawyer bitcoins as an "advance fee," however, there are some problems. Rule 1.15 requires that a lawyer safe keep property that the client has entrusted to the lawyer. An "advanced fee" is property of the client until the lawyer has earned it, per Legal Ethics Opinion 1606. If Bitcoin plummets dramatically in value, and the client discharges the lawyer before the work is completed, the lawyer will not have kept safe sufficient funds or property to make a refund of the unearned fee as required by Rule 1.16(d); or, if the lawyer accepts Bitcoin in settlement of a client's claim, and Bitcoin loses value, the lawyer is unable to pay the client or to discharge third-party liens as required by Rule 1.15(b). The lawyer may discharge these obligations with other funds or property, but in doing so the lawyer would be making payments "out of trust" and not in compliance with the rules.

Another problem arises out of the fact that the Bar's regulation of trust accounts and recordkeeping has not kept pace with technology and does not contemplate cryptocurrency. Lawyers are required to keep records of trust account transactions that are auditable and verified through an approved financial institution's records and statements. No regulatory Bar is currently equipped to audit Bitcoin transactions and storage.

The Future

Unless some serious security measures are built into Bitcoin, we wouldn't recommend that you invest any serious wealth with the virtual currency. Certainly some virtual currencies are better protected than others, but you still might want to think long and hard about accepting Bitcoin or other cryptocurrency as lawyers. The bulk of people we know regard Bitcoin as "shady money," and they may well regard lawyers accepting Bitcoin as "shady lawyers." Will Bitcoin be legitimized one day in the eyes of average Joes and Janes? Maybe—but not soon.

Reprinted with permission of the Virginia State Bar.

As stated at the start of the book, learning professional responsibility is not a linear study, going from one rule to the next. It is an ecosystem in which various rules intersect to shape responses to various scenarios. But these rules were created for a reason, and it is worth remembering why we have them. Answer the questions posed as if there were no rules, and you are responsible for establishing them. So, consider the following two scenarios in which the client does not pay the fees agreed upon.

> ➢ Lola Lawyer represents XYZ Corporation in a lawsuit. As is customary in lawsuits in both federal and state court, a lawyer must move the court in order to withdraw as counsel in a lawsuit. Lola so moves and states in the motion that she and her client have irreconcilable differences and that the client will not be prejudiced by withdrawal at this stage of the litigation. She submits her affidavit in support of the motion under seal so only the Judge can see it. In it she details the fees that are not paid, attaches copies of emails and letters sent to the client in an effort to collect, as well as the engagement letter's provision on fees and payment. The party opposite files a motion to unseal the

affidavit so that it can read it. How should the court rule and why?

➤ Eddie Lawyer represents ABC Company in a lawsuit in which it is a defendant. ABC, despite repeated letters from him, is failing to pay his reasonable fees and reimburse him for expenses that he has paid for and for which ABC agreed to reimburse him. After many unsuccessful attempts at collection, he moves to withdraw, and states in the motion, in which counsel opposite is copied, that "ABC (representatives) have missed appointments on a number of occasions, failed to timely provide information necessary to the case, and made misrepresentations to its attorneys." In addition, he attaches several letters to the motion that he sent to the client including one that states, "your exposure as a defendant is in the tens of thousands of dollars." Is Eddie's conduct proper? Why or why not?

➤ Louise has lost her long-time husband, Brian, who recently died. Brian had a life insurance policy of $100,000 and Louise is the beneficiary. Louise goes to Tony Lawyer who Brian suggested she consult if anything should happen to him. Louise has all of Brian's papers and shows Tony some letters from the instance company asking for some standard documents, such as a death certificate, before paying Louise the $100,000. Tony Lawyer asks her to agree to a contingency fee agreement in which he would receive 20% of the $100,000 as his fee for helping her obtain the payout. He tells her that her choice of lawyer and payment method is hers and hers alone; that she is free to hire a different lawyer; and that he will accept no fee if he is unsuccessful in obtaining the insurance proceeds. Is Tony in violation of the Model Rules? Why or why not?

➤ Rosalinda Civilian and her three children eat at a new restaurant. The place has been open just a few days. They all get very ill from what they believe was poorly prepare food. Except for a few days of missed work and school, they all have recovered. Still Rosalind is upset and meets with Lola Lawyer about filing a lawsuit. Lola explains that damages will be minor, but she is just starting her practice and figures it will be good experience. Lola and Rosalinda execute a contingency fee agreement by which Lola will receive 33% of any recovery. She writes a demand letter to the restaurant. A week later, the restaurant offers her $250,000 to settle. Lola then finds out that the restaurant will have a grand opening in a few weeks and the announcement will be made that it is owned by a famous rock star, Lady Lauren, who is well known for her fear of any type of bad publicity. Rosalinda looks up contingency fees on the internet and demands that Lola change her fee structure to hourly. Lola refuses. Has Lola violated the Model Rules by deciding not to change the fee structure?

➤ Armando Lawyer represents Rowdy Client. Rowdy is arrested for firing off a gun on New Year's Eve. Because of Rowdy's past criminal record, he is sentenced to 6 months in the penitentiary. Rowdy asks Armando to take care of his rare gun collection for the 6 months. Armando agrees. But he lives in a very humid climate and takes no precautions to protect the guns from the weather. Armando offers him no advice, either. When Armando comes to retrieve his gun collection after serving time, he finds that they are all rusted and now are worthless. He files a grievance with the State Bar against Armando. Is the grievance likely to be sustained by the Bar? Why or why not?

WHAT'S NEXT?

The last two cases in this chapter explore a lawyer's obligations to a third-party resulting from the formation of an ACR. They transition us into the next chapter and an examination of other third-party obligations owed by a lawyer resulting from the formation. Sometimes, duties to our clients collide with these other duties. There will always be a tension between upholding the value of zealous representation with the value of adhering to behavioral norms that allow society to function effectively. The Rules and common law seek to strike a balance in resolving this tension. And, as future lawyers, consider whether that balance is properly struck.

Once we complete discussing these third person obligations, we will turn to the heart of the now formed ACR, obligations to the actual client, the person you represent. While the obligations differ, the central foundational elements of the ACR are identical—an attorney and a client; clarity on who is the actual client to whom duties are owed; a determination of goal(s) to be accomplished; consideration, if any, to be exchanged.

To assess your understanding of the material in this chapter, click here to take a quiz.

CHAPTER 3

Lawyer Obligations to Third Persons

Coming Attractions

Television shows and movies portraying lawyers advocating for their client have misled people into believing that lawyers *only* advocate for their clients. Not so. Lawyers wear many hats. Lawyers can be advocates, yes, but they also counsel and advise behind the scenes. And, most surprising of all, at least for television shows, lawyers owe ethical and legal obligations to third persons requiring them to be truthful and transparent with others in the course of client representation—sometimes even to the detriment of their clients. A lawyer owes obligations to third persons in both the course of representation but also obligations to third persons that are *not* in the course of representation, but rather in the course of being a professional with duties to the profession itself. The violation of these duties subjects the lawyer to discipline under the Rules in the same manner as a violation of a duty owed to a client. In short, no ACR does not equate with no obligation.

Let's Chart It!

This flow chart examines the multiple obligation that a lawyer has to third persons that are created because of the formation of an ACR. Once the ACR is formed—and the client's goals and expectations are established—the lawyer and the client must launch the ACR into the greater world, not just the insular confines of the ACR.

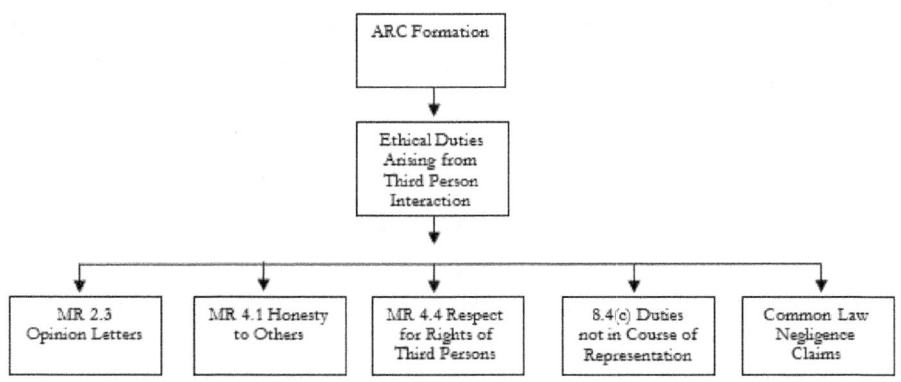

Section 1.   Opinion Letters

Model Rule 2.3: Evaluation for Use by Third Person

(a)   A lawyer *may* provide an evaluation of a matter affecting a client for the use of someone other than the client if the lawyer *reasonably believes* that making the evaluation is compatible with other aspects of the lawyer's relationship with the client.

(b)   When the lawyer knows or reasonably should know that the evaluation is likely to affect the client's interests *materially and adversely*, the lawyer shall not provide the evaluation unless the client gives *informed consent*.

(c)   Except as disclosure is authorized in connection with a report of an evaluation, information relating to the evaluation is otherwise protected by Rule 1.6.

Deconstruction Exercise/Rule Rationale

Subsection (a) uses the permissive word "*may*." While the lawyer must "abide" by a client's decision as to the objectives of a representation, a lawyer cannot just say anything that might help a client achieve her goals. In specific, a lawyer is not free to issue an opinion letter for a third person to rely on just because it assists the client. This is one of those times when a lawyer's judgment must act as a guardrail against a client's sometimes poor judgment.

Opinion letters span a broad spectrum from opinions on a client's financial solvency to whether a client is burdened by liens. This means a lawyer can be an evaluator by providing an opinion letter to a third person. Here, the lawyer's duty is to give information for the benefit of the third person who is considering doing business with the lawyer's client. This duty provides a fair and objective opinion on such matter. What should a lawyer do if a client asks for an opinion letter to help persuade a third person to do something, but it is the lawyer's honest opinion that it will not actually help the client? If the letter would impact her client "materially" and "adversely," the lawyer needs to hit the pause button and consult with the client and obtain the client's informed consent to send the letter. And because the letter will be relied upon by a third person the lawyer is undertaking a legal duty to provide an honest and complete opinion letter. If the client declines to provide all the information that the lawyer reasonably believes is necessary, the lawyer cannot send the letter or must identify what information was excluded from in the letter's preparation.

Cases and Materials

X-Ray Questions (*Greycas*)

This is an attorney malpractice case, but an unusual one. In this case, the plaintiff is not a former client. It actually was an entity that was considering giving a loan to the lawyer's client, who also was his brother-in-law). The loan company, not surprisingly, wanted assurances that the collateral involved (farm machinery) was free of liens. The lawyer gave false information to the loan company, taking at face value his brother-in-law's word that were none. Why was there a claim against the lawyer? After all, the lawyer was not representing the loan company. Would not the lawyer's good faith that the relative was telling the truth be a sufficient defense? Shortly we will read cases in which a lawyer admits to lying to a third person. When you read those cases and consider this, ask yourself: Is lying ever justified? Why do we lie? And, more fundamentally—what does it mean to "lie"? Should this case be treated differently? Finally, what claims did the court say could emerge from the lawyer's action or in this case inaction (not checking up on his brother-in-law's representation)?

Greycas, Inc. v. Theodore S. Proud

United States Court of Appeals, Seventh Circuit, 1987.
826 F.2d 1560.

POSNER, CIRCUIT JUDGE.

Theodore S. Proud, Jr., a member of the Illinois bar who practices law in a suburb of Chicago, appeals from a judgment against him for $833,760, entered after a bench trial. The tale of malpractice and misrepresentation that led to the judgment begins with Proud's brother-in-law, Wayne Crawford, like Proud a lawyer but one who devoted most of his attention to a large farm that he owned in downstate Illinois. The farm fell on hard times and by 1981 Crawford was in dire financial straits. He had pledged most of his farm machinery to lenders, yet now desperately needed more money. He approached Greycas, Inc., the plaintiff in this case, a large financial company headquartered in Arizona, seeking a large loan that he offered to secure with the farm machinery. He did not tell Greycas about his financial difficulties or that he had pledged the machinery to other lenders, but he did make clear that he needed the loan in a hurry. Greycas obtained several appraisals of Crawford's farm machinery but did not investigate Crawford's financial position or discover that he had pledged the collateral to other lenders, who had perfected their liens in the collateral. Greycas agreed to lend Crawford $1,367,966.50, which was less than the appraised value of the machinery.

The loan was subject, however, to an important condition, which is at the heart of this case: Crawford was required to submit a letter to Greycas, from counsel whom he would retain, assuring Greycas that there were no prior liens on the machinery that was to secure the loan. Crawford asked Proud to prepare the letter, and he did so, and mailed it to Greycas, and within 20 days of the first contact between Crawford and Greycas the loan closed and the money was disbursed. A year later Crawford defaulted on the loan; shortly afterward he committed suicide. Greycas then learned that most of the farm machinery that Crawford had pledged to it had previously been pledged to other lenders.

The machinery was sold at auction. The Illinois state court that determined the creditors' priorities in the proceeds of the sale held that Greycas did not have a first priority on most of the machinery that secured its loan; as a result Greycas has been able to recover only a small part of the loan. The judgment it obtained in the present suit is the district judge's estimate of the value that it would have realized on its collateral had there been no prior liens, as Proud represented in his letter.

That letter is the centerpiece of the litigation. Typed on the stationery of Proud's firm and addressed to Greycas, it identifies Proud as Crawford's lawyer and states that, "in such capacity, I have been asked to render my opinion in connection with" the proposed loan to Crawford. It also states that "this opinion is being delivered in accordance with the requirements of the Loan Agreement" and that

> "I have conducted a U.C.C., tax, and judgment search with respect to the Company [i.e., Crawford's farm] as of March 19, 1981, and except as hereinafter noted all units listed on the attached Exhibit A ("Equipment") are free and clear of all liens or encumbrances other than Lender's perfected security interest therein which was recorded March 19, 1981 at the Office of the Recorder of Deeds of Fayette County, Illinois."

The reference to the lender's security interest is to Greycas's interest; Crawford, pursuant to the loan agreement, had filed a notice of that interest with the recorder. The excepted units to which the letter refers are four vehicles. Exhibit A is a long list of farm machinery—the collateral that Greycas thought it was getting to secure the loan, free of any other liens. Attached to the loan agreement itself, however, as Exhibit B, is another list of farm machinery constituting the collateral for the loan, and there are discrepancies between the two lists; more on this later.

Proud never conducted a search for prior liens on the machinery listed in Exhibit A. His brother-in-law gave him the list and told him there were no liens other than the one that Crawford had just filed for Greycas. Proud made no effort to verify Crawford's statement. The theory of the complaint is that Proud was negligent in representing that there were no prior liens, merely on his brother-in-law's say-so. No doubt Proud was negligent in failing to conduct a search, but we are not clear why the misrepresentation is alleged to be negligent rather than deliberate and hence fraudulent, in which event Greycas's alleged contributory negligence would not be an issue (as it is, we shall see), since there is no defense of contributory or comparative negligence to a deliberate tort, such as fraud. See, e.g., *Cenco Inc. v. Seidman & Seidman*, 686 F.2d 449, 454 (7th Cir.1982) (Illinois law); cf. *Teamsters Local 282 Pension Trust Fund v. Angelos*, 762 F.2d 522, 528–29 (7th Cir.1985). Proud did not merely say, "There are no liens"; he said, "I have conducted a U.C.C., tax, and judgment search"; and not only is this statement, too, a false one, but its falsehood cannot have been inadvertent, for Proud knew he had not conducted such a search. The concealment of his relationship with Crawford might also support a charge of fraud. But Greycas decided, for whatever reason, to argue negligent misrepresentation rather than fraud. It may have feared that Proud's insurance policy for professional malpractice excluded deliberate wrongdoing from its coverage, or may not have wanted to bear the higher burden of proving fraud, or may have feared that an accusation of fraud would make it harder to settle the case—for most cases, of course, are settled, though this one has not been. In any event, Proud does not argue that either he is liable for fraud or he is liable for nothing.

He also does not, and could not, deny or justify the misrepresentation; but he argues that it is not actionable under the tort law of Illinois, because he had no duty of care to Greycas. (This is a diversity case and the parties agree that Illinois tort law governs the substantive issues.) He argues that Greycas had an adversarial relationship with Proud's client, Crawford, and that a lawyer has no duty of straight dealing to an adversary, at least none enforceable by a tort suit. In so arguing, Proud is characterizing Greycas's suit as one for professional malpractice rather than negligent misrepresentation, yet elsewhere in his briefs he insists that the suit was solely for negligent misrepresentation—while Greycas insists that its suit charges both torts. Legal malpractice based on a false representation, and negligent misrepresentation by a lawyer, are such similar legal concepts, however, that we have great difficulty both in holding them apart in our minds and in understanding why the parties are quarreling over the exact characterization; no one suggests, for example, that the statute of limitations might have run on one but not the other tort. So we shall discuss both.

Proud is undoubtedly correct in arguing that a lawyer has no general duty of care toward his adversary's client; it would be a considerable and, as it seems to us, an undesirable novelty to hold that every bit of sharp dealing by a lawyer gives rise to prima facie tort liability to the opposing party in the lawsuit or negotiation. The tort of malpractice normally refers to a lawyer's careless or otherwise wrongful conduct toward his own client. Proud argues that Crawford rather than Greycas was his client, and although this is not so clear as Proud supposes—another characterization of the transaction is that Crawford undertook to obtain a lawyer for Greycas in the loan transaction—we shall assume for purposes of discussion that Greycas was not Proud's client.

Therefore, if malpractice just meant carelessness or other misconduct toward one's own client, Proud would not be liable for malpractice to Greycas. But in *Pelham v. Griesheimer*, 92 Ill.2d 13, 64 Ill.Dec. 544, 440 N.E.2d 96 (1982), the Supreme Court of Illinois discarded the old common law requirement of privity of contract for professional malpractice; so now it is possible for someone who is not the lawyer's (or other professional's) client to sue him for malpractice. The court in Pelham was worried, though, about the possibility of a lawyer's being held liable "to an unlimited and unknown number of potential plaintiffs," *id.* at 20, 64 Ill.Dec. at 547, 440 N.E.2d at 99, so it added that "for a nonclient to succeed in a negligence action against an attorney, he must prove that the primary purpose and intent of the attorney-client relationship itself was to benefit or influence the third party," *id.* at 21, 64 Ill.Dec. at 548, 440 N.E.2d at 100. That, however, describes this case exactly. Crawford hired Proud not only for the primary purpose, but for the sole purpose, of influencing Greycas to make Crawford a loan. The case is much like *Brumley v. Touche, Ross & Co.*, 139 Ill.App.3d 831, 836, 93 Ill.Dec. 816, 819–20, 487 N.E.2d 641, 644–45 (1985), where a complaint that an accounting firm had negligently prepared an audit report that the firm knew would be shown to an investor in the audited corporation and relied on by that investor was held to state a claim for professional malpractice. In *Conroy v. Andeck Resources '81 Year-End Ltd.*, 137 Ill.App.3d 375, 389–91, 92 Ill.Dec. 10, 21–22, 484 N.E.2d 525, 536–37 (1985), in contrast, a law firm that represented an offeror of securities was held not to have any duty of care to investors. The representation was not intended for the benefit of investors. Their reliance on the law firm's using due care in the services it provided in connection with the offer was not invited. Cf. *Barker v. Henderson, Franklin, Starnes & Holt,* 797 F.2d 490, 497 (7th Cir.1986).

All this assumes that Pelham governs this case, but arguably it does not, for Greycas, as we noted, may have decided to bring this as a suit for negligent misrepresentation rather than professional malpractice. We know of no obstacle to such an election; nothing is more common in American jurisprudence than overlapping torts.

The claim of negligent misrepresentation might seem utterly straightforward. It might seem that by addressing a letter to Greycas intended (as Proud's counsel admitted at argument) to induce reliance on the statements in it, Proud made himself prima facie liable for any material misrepresentations, careless or deliberate, in the letter, whether or not Proud was Crawford's lawyer or for that matter anyone's lawyer. Knowing that Greycas was relying on him to determine whether the collateral for the loan was encumbered and to advise Greycas of the results of his determination, Proud negligently misrepresented the situation, to Greycas's detriment. But merely labeling a suit as one for negligent misrepresentation rather than professional malpractice will not make the problem of indefinite and perhaps excessive liability, which induced the court in Pelham to place limitations on the duty of care, go away. So one is not surprised to find that courts have placed similar limitations on suits for negligent misrepresentation—so similar that we are led to question whether, as suggested in *HGN Corp. v. Chamberlain, Hrdlicka, White, Johnson & Williams,* 642 F.Supp. 1443, 1452–53 (N.D.Ill.1986), these really are different torts, at least when both grow out of negligent misrepresentations by lawyers. For example, the Brumley case, which we cited earlier, is a professional-malpractice case, yet it has essentially the same facts as *Ultramares Corp. v. Touche, Niven & Co.,* 255 N.Y. 170, 174 N.E. 441 (1931), where the New York Court of Appeals, in a famous opinion by Judge Cardozo, held that an accountant's negligent misrepresentation was not actionable at the suit of a lender who had relied on the accountant's certified audit of the borrower.

The absence of a contract between the lender and the accountant defeated the suit in Ultramares—yet why should privity of contract have been required for liability just because the negligence lay in disseminating information rather than in designing or manufacturing a product? The privity limitation in products cases had been rejected, in another famous Cardozo opinion, years earlier. See *MacPherson v. Buick Motor Co.,* 217 N.Y. 382, 111 N.E. 1050 (1916). Professor Bishop suggests that courts were worried that imposing heavy liabilities on producers of information might cause socially valuable information to be underproduced. See *Negligent Misrepresentation Through Economists' Eyes*, 96 L.Q.Rev. 360 (1980). Many producers of information have difficulty appropriating its benefits to society. The property-rights system in information is incomplete; someone who comes up with a new idea that the law of intellectual property does not protect cannot prevent others from using the idea without reimbursing his costs of invention or discovery. So the law must be careful not to weigh these producers down too heavily with tort liabilities. For example, information produced by securities analysts, the news media, academicians, and so forth is socially valuable, but as its producers can't capture the full value of the information in their fees and other remuneration the information may be underproduced. Maybe it is right, therefore—or at least efficient—that none of these producers should have to bear the full costs. (Similar reasoning may explain the tort immunity, now largely abrogated, of charitable enterprises, and the tort immunities of public officers. See *Colaizzi v. Walker*, 812 F.2d 304, 308 (7th Cir.1987); *Carson v. Block*, 790 F.2d 562, 564 (7th Cir.1986).) At least that was once the view; and while Ultramares has now been rejected, in Illinois as elsewhere—maybe because providers of information are deemed more robust today than they once were or maybe because it is now believed that auditors, surveyors, and other providers of professional services were always able to capture the social value of even the information component of those services in the fees they charged their clients—a residuum of concern remains. So when in *Rozny v. Marnul*, 43 Ill.2d 54, 250 N.E.2d 656 (1969), the Supreme Court of Illinois, joining the march away from Ultramares, held for the first time that negligent misrepresentation was actionable despite the absence of a contract, and thus cast aside the same "privity of contract" limitation later overruled with regard to professional malpractice in Pelham, the court was careful to emphasize facts in the particular case before it that limited the scope of its holding—facts such as that the defendant, a surveyor, had placed his "absolute guarantee for accuracy" on the plat and that only a few persons would receive and rely on it, thus limiting the potential scope of liability. See *id.* at 67–68, 250 N.E.2d at 663.

Later Illinois cases, however, influenced by section 552 of the Second Restatement of Torts (1977), state the limitation on liability for negligent misrepresentation in more compact terms—as well as in narrower scope—than Rozny. These are cases in the intermediate appellate court, but, as we have no reason to think the Supreme Court of Illinois would reject them, we are bound to follow them. See *Williams, McCarthy, Kinley, Rudy & Picha v. Northwestern National Ins. Group*, 750 F.2d 619, 624 (7th Cir.1984). They hold that "one who in the course of his business or profession supplies information for the guidance of others in their business transactions" is liable for negligent misrepresentations that induce detrimental reliance. *Penrod v. Merrill Lynch, Pierce, Fenner & Smith,* 68 Ill.App.3d 75, 81–82, 24 Ill.Dec. 464, 469, 385 N.E.2d 376, 381 (1979); see also *Perschall v. Raney,* 137 Ill.App.3d 978, 983, 92 Ill.Dec. 431, 434, 484 N.E.2d 1286, 1289 (1985); Prosser and Keeton on the Law of Torts § 107, at p. 747 (5th ed. 1984). Whether there is a practical as distinct from a merely semantic difference between this formulation of the duty limitation and that of Pelham may be doubted but cannot change the outcome of this case. Proud, in the practice of his profession, supplied information (or rather misinformation) to Greycas that was intended to guide Greycas in commercial dealings with Crawford. Proud therefore had a duty to use due care to see that the information was correct. He used no care.

Proud must lose on the issue of liability even if the narrower, ad hoc approach of Rozny is used instead of the approach of section 552 of the Restatement. Information about the existence of previous liens on particular items of property is of limited social as distinct from private value, by which we mean simply that the information is not likely to be disseminated widely. There is consequently no reason to give it special encouragement by overlooking carelessness in its collection and expression. Where as in this case the defendant makes the negligent misrepresentation directly to the plaintiff in the course of the defendant's business or profession, the courts have little difficulty in finding a duty of care. Prosser and Keeton on the Law of Torts, supra, § 107, at p. 747.

There is no serious doubt about the existence of a causal relationship between the misrepresentation and the loan. Greycas would not have made the loan without Proud's letter. Nor would it have made the loan had Proud advised it that the collateral was so heavily encumbered that the loan was as if unsecured, for then Greycas would have known that the probability of repayment was slight. Merely to charge a higher interest rate would not have been an attractive alternative to security; it would have made default virtually inevitable by saddling Crawford with a huge fixed debt. To understand the astronomical interest rate that is required to make an unsecured loan a paying proposition to the lender when the risk of default is high, notice that even if the riskless interest rate is only 3 percent, the rate of inflation zero, the cost of administering the loan zero, and the lender risk-neutral, he still must charge an annual interest rate of 106 percent if he thinks there is only a 50 percent chance that he will get his principal back.

Proud argues, however, that his damages should be reduced in recognition of Greycas's own contributory negligence, which, though no longer a complete defense in Illinois, is a partial defense, renamed "comparative negligence." *Alvis v. Ribar*, 85 Ill.2d 1, 52 Ill.Dec. 23, 421 N.E.2d 886 (1981); see *Wolkenhauer v. Smith*, 822 F.2d 711, 717 (7th Cir.1987). It is as much a defense to negligent misrepresentation as to any other tort of negligence. *Luciani v. Bestor*, 106 Ill.App.3d 878, 889, 62 Ill.Dec. 501, 510, 436 N.E.2d 251, 260 (1982); *McAfee v. Rockford Coca-Cola Bottling Co.*, 40 Ill.App.3d 521, 526, 352 N.E.2d 50, 55 (1976); Prosser and Keeton on the Law of Torts, supra, § 108, at p. 750. On the issue of comparative negligence the district court said only that "defendant may have proved negligence upon the part of plaintiff but that negligence, if any, had no causal relationship to the malpractice of the defendant or the damages to the plaintiff." This comment is not easy to fathom. If Greycas was careless in deciding whether to make the loan, this implies that a reasonable investigation by Greycas would have shown that the collateral for the loan was already heavily encumbered; knowing this, Greycas would not have made the loan and therefore would not have suffered any damages.

But we think it too clear to require a remand for further proceedings that Proud failed to prove a want of due care by Greycas. Due care is the care that is optimal given that the other party is exercising due care. See *McCarty v. Pheasant Run, Inc.*, 826 F.2d 1554, 1557 (7th Cir.1987); *Davis v. Consolidated Rail Corp.*, 788 F.2d 1260, 1265 (7th Cir.1986) (both cases applying Illinois law). It is not the higher level of care that would be optimal if potential tort victims were required to assume that the rest of the world was negligent. A pedestrian is not required to exercise a level of care (e.g., wearing a helmet or a shin guard) that would be optimal if there were no sanctions against reckless driving. Otherwise, drivers would be encouraged to drive recklessly, and knowing this pedestrians would be encouraged to wear helmets and shin guards. The result would be a shift from a superior method of accident avoidance (not driving recklessly) to an inferior one (pedestrian armor).

So we must ask whether Greycas would have been careless not to conduct its own UCC search had Proud done what he had said he did—conduct his own UCC search. The answer is no. The law normally does not require duplicative precautions unless one is likely to fail or the consequences of failure (slight though the likelihood may be) would be catastrophic. One UCC search is enough to disclose prior liens, and Greycas acted reasonably in relying on Proud to conduct it. Although Greycas had much warning that Crawford was in financial trouble and that the loan might not be repaid, that was a reason for charging a hefty interest rate and insisting that the loan be secured; it was not a reason for duplicating Proud's work. It is not hard to conduct a UCC lien search;

it just requires checking the records in the recorder's office for the county where the debtor lives. See Ill.Rev.Stat. ch. 26, ¶ 9–401. So the only reason to backstop Proud was if Greycas should have assumed he was careless or dishonest; and we have just said that the duty of care does not require such an assumption. Had Proud disclosed that he was Crawford's brother-in-law this might have been a warning signal that Greycas could ignore only at its peril. To go forward in the face of a known danger is to assume the risk. See, e.g., *Davis v. Consolidated Rail Corp.*, supra, 788 F.2d at 1266–67 (Illinois law); *Phillips v. Croy*, 173 Ind.App. 401, 405, 363 N.E.2d 1283, 1285 (1977). But Proud did not disclose his relationship to Crawford.

The last issue concerns the amount of damages awarded Greycas. In estimating what Proud's negligence had cost Greycas, the judge relied heavily on the state court's finding that Greycas's lien was subordinate to other liens. Proud complains that it was wrong to give collateral estoppel effect to a finding in a case to which he was not a party. But we do not understand the district judge to have been using the judgment to prevent further inquiry into the question of Greycas's damages. The state court's judgment determining the priority of the liens was merely some evidence of the degree to which Proud's misconduct had injured Greycas; for the injury depended on the size of the perfected liens that were prior to its lien. No one tried to prevent Proud from proving, if he could, that the judgment in the state court was erroneous and that Greycas's lien had actually enjoyed the priority that Proud had represented it to have. Proud offered no such evidence. His attack on the state court judgment must fail.

We are aware that, with immaterial exceptions, see Fed.R.Evid. 803(23); Clayton Act § 5(a), 15 U.S.C. § 16(a), civil judgments are said not to be usable in subsequent proceedings as evidence of the facts underlying the judgment; for as to those facts, the judgment is hearsay. See 4 Weinstein's Evidence ¶ 803(22)[01], at 803–353 (1985); McCormick on Evidence § 318, at p. 894 (3d ed. 1984). Since judgments are often given conclusive effect in subsequent litigation, through the doctrines of res judicata and collateral estoppel, it is a little hard to understand why they should not be allowed to have merely evidentiary effect, if for some reason not all the requirements of res judicata or collateral estoppel are fulfilled. A practical reason for denying them evidentiary effect is, however, the difficulty of weighing a judgment, considered as evidence, against whatever contrary evidence a party to the current suit might want to present. The difficulty must be especially great for a jury, which is apt to give exaggerated weight to a judgment. The analytical difficulties posed by efforts to use a judgment as evidence are, however, the only good reasons offered for the rule (others are canvassed in McCormick on Evidence, *supra*, § 318, at p. 894), and as they are of less or no force where, as in this case, the trial is not to a jury, we are not sure the rule should apply in such cases. A further point is that a judgment, insofar as it fixes property rights, should be admissible as the official record of such rights, just like other documents of title, on which see Fed.R.Evid. 803(14); *Sanitary District v. U.S. Fidelity & Guaranty Co.*, 392 Ill. 602, 611–12, 65 N.E.2d 364, 368 (1946). That was the use made of it by Greycas and the district judge: the state court judgment fixed Greycas's rights, equivalent to title, in Crawford's farm machinery. In addition, there is always the catch-all exception to the hearsay rule to fall back on. See Fed.R.Evid. 803(24). "A [hearsay] statement not specifically covered by any of the foregoing exceptions but having equivalent circumstantial guarantees of trustworthiness" is admissible, subject to conditions that in fact are satisfied here.

There is still another path to the same conclusion: it should make no difference to Greycas's rights against Proud whether the state court judgment is erroneous. And if that is irrelevant, then the judgment is not being offered as hearsay at all. Greycas should not be penalized because a state court may have found the previous liens to be even more extensive than Proud's search, if he had conducted a search, would have revealed. If the injury to Greycas was a joint act of Proud and the state court, Proud is fully liable under conventional principles. If the state court judgment had been made up out of whole cloth— if there had been no prior liens when Greycas's lien was filed—then the search would have turned up nothing, and it could be argued therefore that Greycas would have gone ahead and have made the loan and have been burned just as badly as it was, but through no fault of Proud. But Proud was free to show this, since the state court judgment was put in merely as evidence of the status of Greycas's liens; and it was admissible for that purpose.

There are, finally, the discrepancies not only between Exhibit A and Exhibit B, but between those two exhibits on the one hand and the list of machinery attached to the state court's judgment fixing the priority of liens on the other. The judge resolved the first set of discrepancies by refusing to allow Greycas to claim damages with respect to any piece of machinery not on both lists. He resolved the second—and this is the focus of Proud's protest—on the basis of summaries prepared by Greycas's lawyers which purport to identify the same items on both lists, even though the items are sometimes called by different names (e.g., "sprayer" and "spreader"). Proud complains that the summaries did not meet the test for admissibility of summaries in the Federal Rules of Evidence. See Rule 1006. Such a complaint has a hollow ring in a bench trial. A district judge can be trusted in general, and in this particular instance, to give evidence its proper weight without regard to the technical rules of evidence, see McCormick on Evidence, *supra*, § 60, at pp. 153–54, which insofar as they relate to matters of probative force rather than to privilege are designed primarily for the control of juries. The summaries are basically just a matching of the descriptions in the two lists. They made it easier for the judge to compare the descriptions of each pair of items and decide whether they were probably referring to the same piece of machinery, only differently described. We can find no clear error in his comparisons.

Proud complains because the judge, in valuing the items, used the highest of three appraisals that Greycas had obtained before making the loan. The judge then subtracted 20 percent of that value, on the theory that that was the best estimate of the depreciation of the machinery between the date of the appraisal and the date of Crawford's default. He refused to use the price obtained at the auction, conducted six months after the default; that price was much lower. It is possible to argue that the appraisal the judge used was too high, or the 20 percent depreciation figure too low, or the auction price a better estimate of the value six months earlier; but such disagreements are rarely the stuff of clear error, and they are not here.

It may seem that the judge was, if anything, unduly generous to Proud, in giving Greycas only the value of the collateral on the date of default, rather than the unpaid principal of the loan. But for Proud's misrepresentations, Greycas would not have made the loan, so its damages are not just the collateral but the entire uncollectable portion of the loan together with the interest that the money would have earned in an alternative use. Evidently, though, Greycas has been able to recover some of its principal out of other assets of Crawford's estate; for it originally asked the district court for the unpaid balance of the loan, and only later amended its complaint to ask just for the value of the collateral on the date of the default. Of course, if Greycas had hopes of recovering out of the other assets of the estate more than the difference between the unpaid balance of the loan and the value of the collateral, there would be a serious question whether it had actually sustained the full damages that it is seeking in this action. It claims, however, that the other assets are worth less than this difference, and while Proud contests this claim, the district court did not commit clear error in taking Greycas's side in the dispute. We therefore conclude that the realizable value of Greycas's collateral on the date of Crawford's default was a real loss.

A final point. The record of this case reveals serious misconduct by an Illinois attorney. We are therefore sending a copy of this opinion to the Attorney

Registration and Disciplinary Commission of the Supreme Court of Illinois for such disciplinary action as may be deemed appropriate in the circumstances.

AFFIRMED.

SOLUTIONS: THE LAWYER SHOULD HAVE, WOULD HAVE, COULD HAVE. . .

Representation of a client does not empower a lawyer with a carte blanche to act in ways that harm a third person. Here, the lawyer undertook a duty (as you learned in 1L torts) to perform a competent job in checking for liens. And, fulfilling that duty would include checking lien records, not merely accepting the word of the client seeking the loan. The lawyer should have understood that there is no "client exception" to a competent discharge of the duty undertaken.

Section 2. Honesty to Others

Model Rule 4.1: Truthfulness in Statements to Others

In the course of representing a client a lawyer shall not knowingly:

(a) make a false statement of material fact or law to a third person; or

(b) fail to disclose a material fact to a third person when disclosure is necessary to avoid assisting a criminal or fraudulent act by a client, unless disclosure is prohibited by Rule 1.6.

Deconstruction Exercise/Rule Rationale

Contrary to popular stereotypes, you really should be able to trust a lawyer. Under MR 4.1, a lawyer has an ethical duty to be honest with others when acting on the client's behalf. The lawyer cannot lie, mislead, or misrepresent a material statement of fact or law to a third person. This means a lawyer is required to refrain from giving false statements and misrepresenting information to third persons.

The rule is drafted so that affirmative misrepresentations are prohibited as well as misrepresentations by silence. As Ben Franklin remarked, "half the truth is often the greatest lie." Are there exceptions to the rule. Traditional negotiation tactics are not prohibited, Comment 2 makes this clear: "Under generally accepted conventions in negotiation, certain types of statements ordinarily are not taken as statements of material fact. Estimates of price or value placed on the subject of a transaction or a party's intentions as to an acceptable settlement of a claim are ordinarily in this category . . ." Why? Because the drafters of the Rule knew that they could not change human nature nor dislodge negotiating tradition. Just as importantly, negotiating folds into a part of a lawyer's key skill set; namely, the ability and skill to persuade others. But caution: These permissible statements are usually subjective statements of opinion, not statements of objective, verifiable fact.

Notice the predicate to the application of this rule; namely the lawyer is dishonest to others in the "course of representing a client." But that is not really the end of a lawyer's duty of honesty. A lawyer must be honest in all dealings, not just those involving representation of a client.

Model Rule 8.4(c) covers this contingency:

It is professional misconduct for a lawyer to:

> (c) engage in conduct involving dishonesty, fraud, deceit, or misrepresentation.

Deconstruction Exercise/Rule Rationale

These are obligations to third persons that occur outside the course of representation. By way of examples, the failure to file tax returns; or violating the ethical rules of a relator (assuming the lawyer has a license in real estate as well); or committing consumer fraud if the lawyer owns a non-legal business, all fall into this category. Note that any of these violations, or similar ones, must be revealed by a bar applicant when applying to sit for the bar exam. Thus MR 8.4(c) is congruent and must be read in tandem with the requirement for bar admission set out in MT 8.1: Bar Admission and Disciplinary Matters that will be discussed later in the book.

Cases and Materials

X-Ray Questions (*Ausherman*)

In this case a lawyer sued Bank of America for the unlawful release of customer information. The lawyer stated that he knew the internal source at Bank of America who was releasing the information and would provide it as part of a settlement. The lawyer later testified that he did not know the identity of the "person" and admitted that he had lied in the course of settlement negotiations. The court was not pleased. Why did he say that he lied? Do you think zealous representation permits this conduct? Look at the court's rationale for rejecting the argument. MR 4.1 does not preclude standard negotiation techniques such as "puffery" that you might see with a salesperson at a car dealership. Do you believe the lawyer's conduct here is different? Why?

Earle Ausherman, et al. v. Bank of America Corporation

United States District Court, D. Maryland., 2002.
212 F.Supp.2d 435.

GRIMM, UNITED STATES MAGISTRATE JUDGE.

On May 28, 2002, this Court ordered Plaintiffs' counsel, Rodney R. Sweetland, III, to show cause why monetary sanctions, pursuant to Fed.R.Civ.P. 37(b),1 should not be imposed against him and/or his clients in connection with his failure to provide complete and non-evasive answers to ten interrogatories that he had been directed personally to answer by a previous court order. Paper No. 106.2 Whether sanctions should be imposed is now ripe for resolution. In this memorandum, I order—with considerable regret—but without reservation:

(1)   that Mr. Sweetland personally be sanctioned $8,649.25 pursuant to Rule 37(b);

(2)   that Mr. Sweetland be referred to this Court's disciplinary committee to determine what, if any, action should be taken in connection with the self-acknowledged untruths he communicated to Defendants' counsel in a letter dated April 24, 2002, which proposed settlement terms;

(3)   that the disciplinary committee further be asked to investigate certain representations made by Mr. Sweetland to this Court's clerk's office regarding the location of his principal place of practice in connection with his renewal application for membership in the bar of this Court;

(4)   that any Court orders previously issued that treated as confidential Mr. Sweetland's statements, or those of others, made either parol or in writing, in connection with his representation of Plaintiffs in this case be lifted to the limited extent that any such statements relate to or are referred to in the rulings made herein; and

(5)   that Evid. Rule 408 does not shelter Mr. Sweetland or any other counsel who would attempt to shield from the Court's scrutiny deliberately untruthful statements of material fact communicated to

opposing counsel in settlement negotiations relating to litigation pending in this Court.

Because these rulings involve highly important matters that concern the proper behavior of counsel who are entrusted with protecting the public's interests in fairly resolving matters in the litigation process, the background leading to this dispute and the basis for the rulings must be discussed in detail below.

BACKGROUND

The amended complaint asserts the claims of twenty-five plaintiffs, all represented by Mr. Sweetland, against Bank of America Corporation4; its related entity, Banc of America Auto Finance; and two unknown individuals, John Doe Number 1, alleged to be an unidentified employee of the Defendants, and John Doe Number 2, alleged to be an unidentified co-conspirator of John Doe Number 1 and who is not an employee of Defendants. Paper No. 21. The gravamen of the amended complaint is Plaintiffs' contentions that Defendants, through John Doe Number 1, improperly and without authorization, obtained consumer reports and/or investigative consumer reports regarding each Plaintiff and thereafter knowingly and willfully disseminated them to John Doe Number 2 and other unauthorized persons. Plaintiffs, who reside in twelve states and the District of Columbia, assert multiple causes of action against Defendants and the John Doe Defendants5 and seek recovery of a total of $6,250,000.00 in compensatory damages, $62,500,000.00 in punitive damages, and costs and attorneys' fees. Paper No. 21.

Defendants contend in numerous papers filed in this case and in Court hearings that an internal investigation failed to identify any employee responsible for the acts alleged to have been committed by John Doe Number 1 and, predictably and understandably, sought to discover the factual basis for Plaintiffs' numerous claims. This should have been an easy task, as such information clearly is discoverable under Rule 26(b)(1), but it was not.

Instead, at each turn, and in connection with each method of discovery employed, Defendants were unable to discover the factual bases of Plaintiffs' claims. What ultimately emerged from this time consuming, frustrating, and expensive process was that none of the Plaintiffs had personal knowledge of the facts underlying their claims. In fact, Plaintiffs were wholly ignorant that their credit information allegedly had been disseminated improperly to third persons until they received a letter from Mr. Sweetland informing them that Defendants had obtained their credit information and requesting their consent to become plaintiffs in this lawsuit.

Mr. Sweetland, in an effort not to divulge his own factual knowledge about Plaintiffs' claims, asserted the attorney client privilege and work product doctrine in responses to interrogatories and directed his clients not to answer questions concerning any factual information told to them by him. This tactic was rejected by the Court. Paper No. 58. Mr. Sweetland still refused, however, to provide this essential discovery, despite a succession of Court orders directing that he do so. See Papers Nos. 50, 58, 70, 106 and transcript of April 22, 2002, hearing, attached to this memorandum and order as Exhibit 1. This, in turn, led the Court reluctantly to order at an April 22, 2002, hearing that Mr. Sweetland personally be required to answer interrogatories regarding the factual bases of Plaintiffs' claims. Unfortunately, from the Court's perspective, Mr. Sweetland still did not answer completely and non-evasively the interrogatories that were ordered, as is required by Rule 37(a)(3). Paper No. 106. I therefore ordered, on May 20, 2002, that Mr. Sweetland be deposed and informed counsel that I would preside over the deposition to insure compliance with the Court's order. Id. This deposition took place on June 11, 2002.

During the deposition Defendants finally discovered that Mr. Sweetland first learned of the alleged improper conduct of Defendants during August 2000 from a former client, who "said that there was some large scale operation operating out of Bank of America selling credit reports to private investigators and anybody else who was interested." June 11, 2002, deposition of Rodney R. Sweetland, III at 14 ("Sweetland Deposition"). This client also told Mr. Sweetland that an employee of the Defendants was selling credit information to a third party and gave him the names of individuals whose credit reports had been obtained. Id. at 17–21. Mr. Sweetland's client, however, refused to disclose the names of the person(s) from whom he learned this information because he "didn't want to get them involved." Id. at 18. Mr. Sweetland, in turn, wrote to the individuals identified by his client as having their credit information obtained by John Doe Number 1, and twenty-five of them agreed to join in the pending lawsuit. Id. at 40, Exh. 4.

During his deposition, Mr. Sweetland also was questioned about a letter that he wrote to Defendants' counsel, dated April 24, 2002, in which he offered settlement terms to Defendants. Id. at 71–75. In brief, Mr. Sweetland's letter proposed that, in return for a payment of $75,000.00 per plaintiff, or a total of $1,875,000.00, he would provide Bank of America "with the name and other identifying information concerning an individual who may best be described as

John Doe # 3, the kingpin of the network which obtained credit reports from" Defendants. Id., Exh. 7. He continued, however, that he did not then know John Doe Number 3's identity and that he purposely would not discover this information so that he could not be compelled by court order to disclose it. Id. Specifically, he said:

> Please be advised that I do not at present know the identity of this individual. I have made confidential arrangements, however, to have that information provided to me once any possibility of my own deposition (or answering interrogatories) has passed. The source of the information will, not, for obvious, [reasons] provide me with any such information while I am subject to a court order. . . .

Id. Mr. Sweetland concluded relevantly: "I do not know how your clients wish to proceed against the people who penetrated their security, my understanding is that it will be relatively easy to unravel the situation once I provide you with John Doe # 3's identity." Id. Mr. Sweetland's statement that he could provide John Doe Number 3's identity, however, admittedly was untrue.

During his deposition, the following exchange took place between Mr. Sweetland and Defendants' counsel about Mr. Sweetland's statements in the letter.

> Q. Mr. Sweetland, let me show you what's been marked as Deposition Exhibit Number 7. . . . My interest in that letter, though, is paragraph 1 where you make reference to John Doe Number 3.

> A. Yes.

> Q. Who is John Doe Number 3?

> A. That would just be a [way of identification] I would use for the person that I believe to be the person outside of Bank of America that was getting these credit reports.

> Q. Well in the lawsuit you have a John Doe 1, right?

> A. That's right.

> Q. And you have a John Doe Number 2, correct?

> A. That's correct.

> Q. And John Doe Number 2 you've alleged to be the person outside of the bank who received these credit reports or purchased or bought these credit reports, correct?

A.   That's right.

Q.   So why are we calling the John Doe in your April 24th, 2002, letter that's marked as Exhibit Number [7] John Doe Number 3?

A.   Well, my belief is, based upon my conversations with [my former client], that there's somebody else involved.

Q.   And when did you have those conversations with [your former client]?

A.   This would have been later in the case, probably p[a]st the initiation of discovery.

Q.   Give me a month time frame.

A.   If discovery began in December of 2001, this would have had to have been sometime in the first quarter of this year.

Q.   So sometime in January through March of 2002?

A.   That's correct.

Q.   You had a conversation with [your former client]?

A.   Well, one or more.

Q.   One or more. And that is when John Doe Number 3 came up?

A.   Well, again John Doe Number 3 is my term, not [my former client's]. That's somebody who just intellectually is categorizing people. It seemed to me to be convenient, if I've named John Doe Number 1 as the person inside the company, John Doe Number 2 as the person outside the company to whom these are given, I believe that there is a third individual that has some oversight or overarching role in this.

Q.   Well, specifically you described him in your letter as the kingpin of the network which obtained credit reports from Banc, with a C, of America Auto right?

A.   That's right.

Q.   And this information is from [your former client]?

A.   That's correct.

Q.   What is the name of John Doe Number 3?

A.   I do not know.

Q.   And did you ask [your former client] for the name?

A.   Yes, I did.

Q.   And?

A.   He did not give it to me.

Q.   Why not?

A.   I don't believe he wanted to.

Q.   Well, in your letter, in the second paragraph, you indicate, please be advised that I do not at present know the identity of this individual. I have made confidential arrangements, however, to have that information provided to me once any possibility of my own deposition or answers to interrogatories has passed. What confidential arrangements are you talking about?

A.   There were none. That was language put in there for the purposes of settlement bluster.

Q.   So this is a lie?

A.   That is correct. It is not true.

Q.   So you never made any arrangements to find out the identity of John Doe Number 3?

A.   No. I was attempting to find out the identity of John Doe Number 3, but while we were in settlement discussions, I wanted to make the representation, for the purposes of maximizing my clients' settlement position, that I could obtain an individual to provide to your in-house counsel.

Q.   And can you?

A.   No.

Q.   So at the time you made this statement, you were lying?

A.   That's correct.

Q.   Why are you unable to obtain the name of this person?

A.   Because [my former client] won't give it to me.

Q.   And why will he not give it to you?

A.   I don't know. You'd have to ask him.

Q.　Did you ask him why he wouldn't give it to you?

A.　I did. And he said, you don't want to know.

Q.　And what did you say then?

A.　Well, at some point I stopped asking. But I mean I certainly pressed him on it.

Sweetland Deposition at 71–76 (emphasis added).

After the deposition concluded, Defendants wrote to this Court, sent a copy of the transcript of Mr. Sweetland's deposition, and argued, inter alia, that Mr. Sweetland's self-acknowledged lie was evidence of his bad faith, warranting imposition of monetary sanctions against him for his failure to answer completely and non-evasively the interrogatories ordered by the Court. In response, Mr. Sweetland argued that Defendants could not rely on the mandatory sanctions of Rule 37(d), but, instead, any award of sanctions would fall within the discretionary sanctions of Rule 37(b). He further asserted that "[a] confidential settlement letter to defendants is not a proper substantive or procedural basis for any action by this Court" because the letter stated it was sent " 'under aegis of Fed.R.Evid. 408 and without prejudice or effect for any other purpose.' "

For reasons that will be explained below, I agree with Mr. Sweetland that his statements in the settlement letter sent to Defendants may not be considered by me in connection with the pending motion, as they have an insufficient causal nexus with the events that resulted in this Court ordering the interrogatories to, and deposition of, Mr. Sweetland. I do find, however, that sanctions are appropriate against him under Rule 37(b)(3) for failing to identify the source of the factual basis of Plaintiffs' claims and that this refusal caused Defendants to incur substantial costs and attorneys' fees, the reasonable portion of which should be awarded against Mr. Sweetland personally.

Moreover, I conclude that Mr. Sweetland woefully is misinformed about the scope of Evid. Rule 408 and the limited extent to which it is intended to shield from use statements offered in an effort to compromise disputed claims. Further, the statements made in the April 24, 2002, settlement letter and Mr. Sweetland's ready acknowledgment of their falsity during his deposition require me to refer this matter to this Court's disciplinary committee. In addition, from my review of the correspondence and pleadings authored by Mr. Sweetland in this case, it also is necessary to refer to the disciplinary committee the question of whether Mr. Sweetland answered with the required candor an inquiry by this Court's clerk's office regarding the location of his principal place of practice, which is relevant to whether he met the requirements of Local Rule 701.1 for admission to the bar of this Court.

DISCUSSION

A. The Imposition of Sanctions

Defendants seek an award of attorneys' fees because of costs and fees needlessly incurred in attempting to discover the factual basis of Plaintiffs' claims against them. They argue that Mr. Sweetland's admitted mendacity in the settlement letter he wrote is one factor to be considered by the Court in assessing whether to impose sanctions against Mr. Sweetland under Rule 37.

There are three primary ways that parties seek to recover attorneys' fees against an opposing party or counsel for abuse of the litigation process. The first way is Rule 11, which is not applicable in this case because it expressly does not apply to discovery disputes. Rule 11(d). The second way is the Court's inherent authority to prevent litigation abuse, which was discussed at considerable length by the United States Supreme Court in Chambers v. NASCO, 501 U.S. 32, 111 S.Ct. 2123, 115 L.Ed.2d 27 (1991). The third way is the rules of procedure relating to discovery, notably Rule 37, or a federal statute, such as 28 U.S.C. § 1927.

As discussed below, neither the court's inherent authority to impose sanctions nor Rule 37 is an appropriate tool in this case for addressing Mr. Sweetland's deceitful statements made in the settlement letter to the Defendants. As will be seen, however, this does not mean that the Court is without means to address Mr. Sweetland's mendacity. Moreover, it is entirely appropriate for this Court to impose sanctions, pursuant to Rule 37(b), concerning the myriad discovery abuses perpetrated by Mr. Sweetland, which were wholly independent of his conduct concerning the settlement letter

In Chambers, supra, 501 U.S. 32, 111 S.Ct. 2123, 115 L.Ed.2d 27, the Supreme Court ruled that there are three circumstances where a federal court may exercise its inherent authority to assess attorneys' fees: (a) under the "common fund" doctrine where courts historically have equity power to award such fees to a party whose litigation efforts benefit others directly; (b) as a sanction for willful disobedience of a court order; and (c) when a party or an attorney has acted in bad faith vexatiously, wantonly, or for an oppressive reason. Id. at 45–46, 111 S.Ct. 2123. The court made clear that the "American Rule," which restricts when attorneys' fees may be awarded to a litigant, limits the use of a court's inherent authority to impose sanctions to circumstances involving either bad faith conduct or willful disobedience of court orders. Id. at 47, 49, 111 S.Ct. 2123. The Court additionally noted that there are mechanisms, other than inherent authority, that may allow an award of attorneys' fees as a sanction, such as the rules of civil procedure or 28 U.S.C. § 1927, without requiring a finding of bad faith, and that a court may sanction using its inherent authority concurrently with rules of procedure or the federal statute. Id. at 49–50, 111 S.Ct. 2123. The Court cautioned, however, that "[b]ecause of their very potency, inherent powers must be exercised with restraint and discretion." Id. at 44, 111 S.Ct. 2123.

In U.S. v. Shaffer Equipment Company, 11 F.3d 450 (4th Cir.1993), the Fourth Circuit also has addressed when a district court may use its inherent authority to sanction an attorney in connection with deceitful conduct during the litigation process. Judge Niemeyer's comments in that case about an attorney's duty of candor during the litigation process are particularly instructive to this case. He said, relevantly:

> Our adversary system for the resolution of disputes rests on the unshakable foundation that truth is the object of the system's process which is designed for the purpose of dispensing justice. However, because no one has an exclusive insight into truth, the process depends on the adversarial presentation of evidence, precedent and custom, and argument to reasoned conclusions—all directed with unwavering effort to what, in good faith, is believed to be true on matters material to the disposition. Even the slightest accommodation of deceit or a lack of candor in any material respect quickly erodes the validity of the process. As soon as the process falters in that respect, the people are then justified in abandoning support for the system in favor of one where honesty is preeminent.

> While no one would want to disagree with these generalities about the obvious, it is important to reaffirm, on a general basis, the principle that lawyers, who serve as officers of the court, have the first line task of assuring the integrity of the process. Each lawyer undoubtedly has an important duty of confidentiality to his client and must surely advocate his client's position vigorously, but only if it is truth which the client seeks to advance. The system can provide no harbor for clever devices to divert the search, mislead opposing counsel or the court, or cover up what is necessary for justice in the end. Id. at 457–458.

The court added that while Rules 3.3 and 3.4 of the Rules of Professional Conduct impose a duty of candor to the court and opposing counsel throughout the litigation process,8 "neither these rules nor the entire Code of Professional

Responsibility displaces the broader general duty of candor and good faith required to protect the integrity of the entire judicial process." Id. at 458. The court concluded that "[t]he general duty of candor and truth thus takes its shape from the larger objective of preserving the integrity of the judicial system." Id.

As it presently is conducted, the judicial resolution of civil disputes certainly must include settlement negotiations involving pending litigation, as they are an integral part of this process. Far greater numbers of civil cases are brought each year than ever can be resolved through trial or motions practice, and the vast majority of such cases filed are disposed of through settlement. As the filing of civil cases outpaced the ability of courts to try them, alternative dispute resolution ("ADR") procedures almost universally have been adopted to provide either formal or informal procedures to settle cases. Indeed, in the federal system, ADR "[occurs] in all three types of courts—district, bankruptcy, and appellate—and [reflects] both a general societal trend toward greater use of ADR and a specific statutory authorization to use ADR." Guide to Judicial Management of Cases in ADR at 1 (Federal Judicial Center 2001). In fact, in 1998 Congress mandated that each district court adopt ADR procedures9 and, in this Court, so much value is placed in the efficacy of ADR to resolve cases promptly and inexpensively that the process is handled by judicial officers—the magistrate judges. Local Rule 607.

It does not require a rule of professional responsibility for a lawyer to know that, during the process of settlement negotiations, he or she may not lie to opposing counsel about a fact that is material to the resolution of the case. It is just as damaging to the integrity of our adversary system for an attorney knowingly to make a false statement of material fact to an opposing counsel during settlement negotiations, as it is to lie to a lawyer or the judge in court. It is one thing, however, to acknowledge the obvious importance of candor during the settlement process and quite another thing to invoke the court's inherent authority to sanction an attorney for intentionally deceitful conduct during settlement negotiations if that conduct is not sufficiently connected to a specific issue that must be ruled upon by the judge.

Like the Supreme Court, the Fourth Circuit has warned against the incautious use of a court's inherent authority, by stating in Shaffer Equipment, supra, that "[b]ecause the inherent power is not regulated by Congress or the people and is particularly subject to abuse, it must be exercised with the greatest restraint and caution, and then only to the extent necessary. . . ." 11 F.3d at 461–462 (citations omitted). Accordingly, a trial judge should restrain an understandable impulse immediately to address deceitful conduct by an attorney in connection with settlement negotiations and take a moment to reflect whether he or she should use the court's inherent authority to address it or refer it to a bar disciplinary committee.

Simply put, the question is whether a trial court, faced with credible allegations of serious ethical misconduct by an attorney in connection with a pending case, ought to undertake for itself the process of making factual determinations necessary fairly to resolve the issue, or instead refer the matter to an appropriate bar disciplinary committee. While each judge must make this call for himself or herself, the Court believes that, in this case, it is fairer to the parties, the attorneys, and the preservation of the integrity of our adversary system of dispute resolution to decline to exercise the inherent authority of the court and instead refer this matter to the Court's disciplinary committee pursuant to Local Rule 705.

Because this local rule creates detailed procedures to facilitate the fair resolution of allegations of ethical misconduct, and for the reasons that I will explain below, I specifically will refer to the disciplinary committee Mr. Sweetland's conduct during his settlement negotiations with Defendants' counsel. These negotiations insufficiently were connected with the narrow issue of discovery abuse that presently is pending to justify addressing them myself under the inherent authority of the Court.

Having decided to make a referral to the disciplinary committee, however, does not mean that Mr. Sweetland should not be required to pay to Defendants the costs and reasonable attorneys' fees relating to their effort to learn the factual basis for Plaintiffs' causes of action. Mr. Sweetland himself acknowledges that it is within the Court's discretion under Rule 37(b) to award such a sanction. And, based on a review of all the facts of record, I conclude that, in light of the unambiguous order of April 22, 2002, and Mr. Sweetland's subsequent refusal to answer completely and non-evasively the interrogatories that I ordered him to answer, Defendants were required to incur costs and attorneys' fees to compel and take his deposition.

Only after being deposed did Mr. Sweetland finally provide the information that he readily had available since at least as early as August 2000. Sweetland Deposition at 14. Given the succession of court orders requiring the disclosure of the facts underlying Plaintiffs' claims, the manifest importance of Defendants' need to know this information to conduct a defense, and the clarity of the Court's directive that it must be provided, I find that Mr. Sweetland's refusal to obey the April 22, 2002, order was not substantially justified and a sanction of costs and reasonable attorneys' fees against him personally, but not his clients, would not be unjust.

In this regard, I emphasize that, while the refusal to comply with the Court's April 22, 2002, order took the form of Mr. Sweetland's failure to provide complete and non-evasive interrogatory responses, he is sanctioned not in the capacity of a "witness," but in his capacity as Plaintiffs' counsel, which he has held since the inception of this lawsuit. The circumstances under which he found himself having to testify entirely were of his own making, as was explained during the April 22, 2002, hearing.

B.   The Referral to the Disciplinary Committee

1.   The April 24, 2002, Settlement Letter

Local Rule 704 adopts. the Rules of Professional Conduct "as they have been adopted by the Maryland Court of Appeals" to lawyers practicing before this Court. The Maryland Court of Appeals has adopted essentially verbatim the model rules prepared by the American Bar Association. Brown & Sturm v. Frederick Road, 137 Md.App. 150, 768 A.2d 62, 78 (2001). Rule 4.1 pertains to "truthfulness in statements to others" and requires, relevantly that "[i]n the course of representing a client a lawyer shall not knowingly (1) make a false statement of material fact or law to a third person." Rule 4.1(a). It is identical to the ABA Model Rule of the same number. Although there are few reported decisions in Maryland dealing with this Rule, it has been discussed extensively in the commentary to the ABA Model Rules, by legal treatises, and legal publications. An overview of these materials amply demonstrates why Mr. Sweetland's actions concerning the April 24, 2002, settlement letter must be referred to this Court's disciplinary committee.

The commentary to ABA Model Rule 4.1 makes the following points regarding its scope: (a) the rule addresses only false statements knowingly made, or information withheld when it should have been disclosed. The required state of mind, however, may be inferred from the surrounding circumstances and encompasses careless and recklessly negligent conduct; (b) an opposing counsel is a "third person" within the meaning of the rule, meaning that the duty of candor extends to an attorney representing a party adverse to the lawyer whose conduct is in question; (c) Rule 4.1(a) specifically applies to the process of negotiation.

In the April 24, 2002, settlement letter. . . Mr. Sweetland made the following statements that are relevant to the issue in dispute, which may be paraphrased as follows: (a) that if Defendants paid the demanded sum, or any agreed upon reduction thereof, Mr. Sweetland would provide to them the name and other identifying information regarding John Doe Number 3, described as the "kingpin of the network which obtained credit reports" from Defendants; (b) that Mr. Sweetland did not then know the identity of John Doe Number 3 because he had taken steps not to learn this until his deposition had passed but had made confidential arrangements to have that information provided to him once there was no longer any threat of his deposition; and (3) it was Mr. Sweetland's understanding that "it will be relatively easy to unravel the situation [regarding who 'penetrated' the security of Defendants] once I provide you with John Doe # 3's identity." In return for Mr. Sweetland's disclosures, Mr. Sweetland would recommend that each Plaintiff settle for $75,000.

During his deposition, Mr. Sweetland was asked what the confidential arrangements were that he had made to learn John Doe Number 3's identity, to which he answered, "There were none. That was language put there for the purposes of settlement bluster." Defendant's counsel pointedly asked, "So this is a lie?" Mr. Sweetland's succinctly stated "That is correct. It is not true." Next, he was asked, "So you never made any arrangements to find out the identity of John Doe Number 3?" Mr. Sweetland answered, "No. I was attempting to find out the identity of John Doe Number 3, but while we were in settlement discussions, I wanted to make the representation, for the purposes of maximizing my clients' settlement position, that I could obtain an individual to provide to your in-house counsel." Defendants' counsel persisted, "So at the time you made this statement, you were lying?" Mr. Sweetland answered, "That's correct."

It is clear, therefore, from Mr. Sweetland's own admission under oath that, at the time he wrote the letter, he knew he was not being truthful. With respect to whether his untruthful statements were material, there is little doubt that, from Defendants' perspective, they were. This entire lawsuit involves asserted liability against the Defendants because, allegedly, an employee, John Doe Number 1, sold information to a non-employee co-conspirator, John Doe Number 2, all, according to the settlement letter, at the instance of the "kingpin," John Doe Number 3. Throughout the case, Defendants have protested that they were not able to locate any employee that may have disclosed Plaintiffs' credit information. In response, Plaintiffs essentially have contended that the identities of the John Doe Defendants are irrelevant in determining whether Defendants are liable. Even assuming arguendo that Plaintiffs are correct, it still would be of paramount importance to the Defendants to learn the identity of John Doe Number 3 so they could take action to end his/her activities and cut off any potential future liability. Given that the only real term suggested by Mr. Sweetland for the more than $1.8 million that Defendants were being asked to pay was the identification of John Doe Number 3, it certainly is not unreasonable to conclude that the misrepresentation concerned facts material to the negotiations.

Mr. Sweetland views his comments as "settlement bluster," and may therefore believe that they did not address material statements of fact. However skeptically the Court might regard any such position, it is not my call to make. But what is clear is that there is more than a sufficient factual basis to compel the referral of this matter to the disciplinary committee of this Court. While the principal ethical rule discussed in this order was Rule 4.1, the cases and commentary make clear that other rules might potentially overlap with that rule when evaluating the conduct involved here. One such rule is 8.4(c) that states that it is professional misconduct for a lawyer to engage in conduct involving dishonesty, fraud, deceit or misrepresentation. Therefore, when the Disciplinary Committee takes up this matter, they will be free to explore whether violations of any rules they deem applicable occurred.

C. Calculation of Sanction Under Rule 37(b)

Defendants seek a Total of $5,361.00 in fees associated with the motion to compel Mr. Sweetland's deposition, $8,502.00 associated with the taking of his deposition, and costs of $992.25, for a grand total of $14,855.25. As explained below, the Court will award $7,657.00 as reasonable attorneys' fees and $992.25 in costs for a total of $8,649.25 to be paid personally by Mr. Sweetland within thirty days.

Defendants billed the following time for the following attorneys in connection with the motion to compel the deposition of Mr. Sweetland and the taking of the deposition itself ("the Motion"): (1) Ms. Ava Lias-Booker (admitted more than eight years—29.2 hours at $345/hr. or $10,074.00); (2) David E. Ralph (admitted more than five but less than eight years—14.0 hours at $220.00/hr or $3,080.00); (3) Jennifer B. Speargas (admitted less than five years, .6 hours at $175/hr. or $105.00); (4) John Ki (admitted less than five years, 1.3 hours at $175.hr. or $227.50); and (5) Paralegal Gina M. Trasatti (13 years experience, 3.5 hours at $120/hr. or $420.00).

Defendants provided a detailed chart itemizing these billings. The Court has reviewed it for reasonableness under Rule 37(b). The Court finds that it is not reasonable to have four attorney timekeepers billing on the motion and deposition, neither of which was especially difficult given the prior rulings of the

Court. Therefore, all of Ms. Speargas' and Mr. Ki's time will be eliminated. Further, the total hours billed by Ms. Lias-Booker—29.2—are excessive, and the fees sought for her time will be reduced by fifty percent to $5,037.00. Mr. Ralph's time also will be reduced by 4.0 hours to a total of $2,200.00. All of Ms. Trasatti's time is reasonable, totaling $420.00. The $992.25 in costs sought are reasonable. The total award therefore is $7,657.00 in fees and $992.25 in costs, for a grand total of $8,649.25. As explained, they are to be assessed against Mr. Sweetland personally.

Accordingly, the sanctions and actions referred to at pages one and two above are ordered.

SOLUTIONS: THE LAWYER SHOULD HAVE, WOULD HAVE, COULD HAVE. . .

There is a very simple rule at the heart of this case: Do not make misstatements of fact. Claiming to know something that you don't know is a misstatement. So is claiming that someone exists who is not real.

LEANING INTO PRACTICE

Scenario No. 1: The Case of the Lawyer Who Was Sued for Dealing from the Bottom of the Deck

Lawyer is in mediation on behalf of a defendant in a personal injury lawsuit. Lawyer tells opposing counsel that to "the best of his knowledge" there was only $200,000 in insurance coverage. But documents in his possession later showed a $1,000,000 policy. Plaintiff settles the case without knowing this fact. Once the larger policy is uncovered however, plaintiff sues the lawyer personally for fraud. Court holds that lawyer showed "reckless indifference to error" and that the euphemism of "to the best of my knowledge" was no defense.

Scenario No. 2: The Case of the Lawyer and the Client Who Passed Away

Lawyer represents person in a personal injury case. A tentative settlement is reached at a mediation that is to be finalized later. Unfortunately, the client passes away for reasons unrelated to the circumstances involving the lawsuit. Lawyer and opposing counsel go to court to finalize the settlement but Lawyer decides not to tell opposing counsel of the death until after the court approves the settlement. A court later determined this was a material misrepresentation by omission.

Scenario No. 3: The Case of the Bluffing Lawyer

Lois Lawyer represents Amir Client in a personal jury lawsuit. She and Amir agree to try and settle the case and Amir tells Lois to agree to no less than $10,000 but to try and get more. Lois calls up Clark Lawyer, counsel opposite, and tells him, "Clark I have a good case and you know it too! We want to settle but $50,000 is as low as we will go!" This is a standard negotiating technique and is not a violation of MR 4.1. But if Lois also makes a claim that she has certain evidence or witnesses that she does not have, that would be a material misrepresentation and MR 4.1 would be violated.

Section 3.   Limits on Zealous Representation

Model Rule 4.4: Respect for Rights of Third Persons

(a)   In representing a client, a lawyer shall not use means that have no substantial purpose other than to embarrass, delay, or burden a third person, or use methods of obtaining evidence that violate the legal rights of such a person.

(b)   A lawyer who receives a document or electronically stored information relating to the representation of the lawyer's client and knows or reasonably should know that the document or electronically stored information was inadvertently sent shall promptly notify the sender.

Deconstruction Exercise/Rule Rationale

The threshold issue here per the language of the Rule is whether the lawyer takes an action in the course of representing a client, just as with MR 4.1. The rule's coverage is expansive thanks to the use of the disjunctive "or." The key phrase is "substantial purpose" which entails the possibility that there is more than one reason for taking the contemplated action—one valid, the other invalid. This is called a "mixed motive" and is generally resolved by asking one question:" But for the desire to "embarrass, delay or burden" would the action be taken?" The answer to this question splits causation into determining the primary motive from the secondary motive. (We see the same analysis used in MR 3.2: Expediting Litigation and MR 7.6: Political Contributions to Obtain Government Legal Engagements or Appointments by Judges in which there can be more than one motive for the action taken or contemplated by the lawyer. A "but for" analysis is used in each to segregate the predominate reason.)

Subsection (b) deals with the inadvertent disclosure by a lawyer. The lawyer's duties are made clear, but the question remains—often determined by state law—on whether the attorney-client privilege is waived.

LEANING INTO PRACTICE

Scenario No. 1: The Lawyer and the Contentious Divorce

Orly Lawyer's client is going through a divorce that is proving to be very acrimonious. Joe client tells Orly: "I want you to depose her parents. They are elderly and she will settle in order to spare them the ordeal of being questioned under oath. "Orly comes to you and asks what she should do and what questions she should ask the client in determining her response to the client's directive.

Scenario No. 2: The Lawyer and Receipt of the Party Opposite's Strategy Memo

You are in practice and are going through your mail. You open a letter addressed to you, start to scan the letter and realize that it is a letter from counsel opposite to her client setting out her litigation/mediation strategy. It is multiple pages in length. You immediately turn the letter face down. What now? Yes, you call counsel opposite, but other issues remain. Do you read the rest of the letter? What questions do you ask yourself? Must you tell your client under MR 1.4?

X-Ray Questions (*Opinion 1794*)

In the following Opinion Letter, a lawyer directed a client who would be seeking a divorce to interview with other lawyers in their community regarding possible representation. Why? There was no intention of retaining those lawyers. Rather, the goal was to provide confidential information so that—if the spouse came to them for representation—the lawyer would be conflicted from representation. (This does occur especially in smaller communities with a limited supply of lawyers). Why is this practice an ethical violation? Is not everything fair, as the expression goes, in love and in war? Also, the lawyer did not directly engage in the misconduct but rather the client did. Should this make a difference?

Legal Ethics Opinion 1794 Confidentiality of Initial Consultation

Committee Opinion.
June 30, 2004.

You have presented a hypothetical situation in which a husband and wife are planning to divorce. They live in a small community with a limited number of attorneys. The husband wishes to prevent his wife from obtaining adequate counsel. Therefore, he visits each family law attorney in succession, shares his situation, but with no intent to hire them. He in fact already knows that he will retain Attorney A. The wife goes to one of the visited attorneys, Attorney B, seeking representation. When Attorney B writes the husband's attorney (A) establishing B's representation of the wife, Attorney A sends a letter back stating the wife's attorney (B) has a conflict of interest and must withdraw from the representation.

Prior to hiring her attorney, the wife first had gone to Attorney A for representation. Before their initial interview, Attorney A had the wife sign a disclaimer stating that:

> I understand that my initial interview with this attorney does not create an attorney/client relationship and that no such relationship is formed unless I actually retain this attorney.

He then listened to her story. After the interview, the attorney did a conflicts check, and announced he could not represent her as he already represented her husband. As part of their discussion, the wife had shared information regarding her finances and her personal life, including details that would relate to child custody issues. The wife tells her own attorney, Attorney B, of that appointment, and he writes Attorney A and asks him to withdraw from representing the husband.

While not present in this hypothetical, the committee notes that were an attorney to direct a new client to undertake this sort of strategic elimination of attorneys for the opposing party, that attorney would be in violation of Rule 3.4(j)'s (*Editor's Note: the Virginia equivalent of MR 4.4*) prohibition against taking any action on behalf of a client "when the lawyer knows or when it is obvious that such action would merely serve to harass or maliciously injure another." That such an attorney would not himself be attending the initial consultations does not remove the attorney from ethical impropriety; Rule 8.4(a) establishes that it is improper for an attorney to violate the rules through the actions of another.

Section 4. Common Law Negligence Claims

Model Rule 1.6(b)(1): Confidentiality of Information

(b)   A lawyer may reveal information relating to the representation of a client to the extent the lawyer reasonably believes necessary:

(1)   to prevent reasonably certain death or substantial bodily harm.

A lawyer has a duty not to reveal any information relating to the representation of a client. But there are exceptions. Note that this rule allows disclosure to prevent bodily harm—but it does not require it. It says the lawyer "may reveal information." However, in some special circumstances, a lawyer might have a common law duty beyond this rule to warn or disclose information to a third person of the potential risks or danger. Lawyers in these negligence claims are conflicted in which duty to obey: the duty of confidentiality or duty to warn foreseeable victims.

The strongest case for a lawyer's duty to breach confidentiality and warn a third person of danger is when the lawyer knows that a client has targeted foreseeable victims and is potentially dangerous to himself and others. But how far does this duty to warn extend?

Cases and Materials

X-Ray Questions (*Hawkins*)

Here a public defender was asked by the relative of a client not to seek a client's release from custody because of fear that he would, if allowed to be released, harm himself or others. What is the threshold question that the PD asked himself? Recall the lesson learned in *Baldwin*? What was it? Can you apply the above rule to these facts? The *Hawkins* court cites to a California case. As you read *Hawkins* ask yourself: what is the difference between this case and that case? Why does it matter?

Hawkins v. King County

Court of Appeals of Washington, Division One, 1979.
602 P.2d 361.

SWANSON A., JUDGE.

Michael Hawkins, acting through his guardian ad litem, and his mother Frances M. Hawkins, appeal from a summary judgment dismissing attorney Richard Sanders from an action sounding in tort. Appellants contend Sanders, court appointed defense attorney for Michael Hawkins, was negligent and committed malpractice by failing to divulge information regarding his client's mental state at a bail hearing. We find no error and affirm.

On July 1, 1975, Michael Hawkins was booked for possession of marijuana. Following his court appointment as Hawkins' defense counsel on July 3, 1975, Richard Sanders conferred with Hawkins for about 45 minutes, at which time Hawkins expressed the desire to be released from jail.

Also on July 3, 1975, Sanders talked with Palmer Smith, an attorney employed by Hawkins' mother Frances Hawkins, to assist in having Hawkins either hospitalized or civilly committed. Smith told Sanders then, and reiterated by letter, that Hawkins was mentally ill and dangerous. On July 8, 1975, Dr. Elwood Jones, a psychiatrist, telephoned and wrote Sanders and averred Hawkins was mentally ill and of danger to himself and others and should not be released from custody. Sanders represented that he intended to comply with his client's request for freedom.

On July 9, 1975, a district judge released Hawkins on a personal surety bond. At the bail hearing, Sanders did not volunteer any information regarding Hawkins' alleged illness or dangerousness, nor were any questions in that vein directed to him either by the judge or the prosecutor. Smith, Jones, and Mrs. Hawkins were informed of Hawkins' release, and all parties later met on two occasions in a counseling environment.

On July 17, 1975, about 8 days after his release, Michael Hawkins assaulted his mother and attempted suicide by jumping off a bridge, causing injuries resulting in the amputation of both legs. The Hawkinses commenced an action for damages against King County, the State of Washington, Community Psychiatric Clinic, Inc., and one of its employees on August 16, 1976, and amended the suit on November 30, 1977, to name Sanders a party defendant. Sanders filed a motion to dismiss for failure to state a claim. On June 16, 1978, the trial court granted Sanders' motion. Subsequently the trial court signed an amended order dated July 29, 1978, which described the earlier order of dismissal to be a summary judgment and permitted appellants Hawkins an interlocutory appeal.

On appeal, the Hawkinses essentially present two arguments: First, that by his failure at the bail hearing to disclose the information he possessed regarding Michael Hawkins' mental state, defense counsel Sanders subjected himself to liability for malpractice, as court rules and the Code of Professional Responsibility mandate such disclosure on ethical and legal grounds. Second, that by the same omission Sanders negligently violated a common-law duty to warn foreseeable victims of an individual he knew to be potentially dangerous to himself and others. *See Tarasoff v. Regents of Univ. of Cal.*, 17 Cal. 3d 425, 551 P.2d 334, 13 Cal. Rptr. 14 (1976).

Sanders asserts the Hawkinses have failed to demonstrate that he breached any duty owed to them and, as an attorney appointed by the court to represent an indigent defendant, that he was a quasi-judicial officer, immune from civil liability.

We defined the elements of a legal malpractice action in *Hansen v. Wightman*, 14 Wn. App. 78, 88, 538 P.2d 1238 (1975), as the existence of an attorney-client relationship, *the existence of a duty on the part of a lawyer,* failure to perform the duty, and the negligence of the lawyer must have been a proximate cause of damage to the client.

(Footnote and citations omitted. Italics ours.) The court, in *Cook, Flanagan & Berst v. Clausing,* 73 Wn.2d 393, 395, 438 P.2d 865 (1968), defined the standard of care for Washington lawyers:

[T]he correct standard to which the plaintiff is held in the performance of his professional services is that degree of care, skill, diligence and knowledge commonly possessed and exercised by a reasonable, careful and prudent lawyer in the practice of law in this jurisdiction.

We further note that the Code of Professional Responsibility sets standards of ethics for all members of the bar of this state. RCW 2.48.230, *In re Chantry,* 67 Wn.2d 190, 407 P.2d 160 (1965).

In considering appellants' argument that Hawkins' defense counsel breached an ethical and legal duty to disclose information to the court, we observe that a lawyer is ethically bound to advocate zealously his client's interests to the fullest extent permitted by law and the disciplinary rules. (CPR) DR 7–101(A)(1).

Appellants argue that the information Sanders received was particularly relevant to the issues the bail hearing judge is required to resolve on pretrial release pursuant to CrR 3.2. In support of this contention, appellants cite (CPR) DR 7–102(A)(3), which states:

(A) In his representation of a client, a lawyer shall not:

. . .

(3) Conceal or knowingly fail to disclose that which he is required by law to reveal.

Assuming without deciding that the information received by Sanders from Dr. Jones and Mrs. Hawkins' attorney did not constitute a "confidence or secret" which a lawyer generally may not reveal, neither CrR 3.2 nor JCrR 2.09 specifies who has the duty to provide facts for the court's consideration. The quoted rules state only that "the court shall, on the available information, consider the relevant facts . . ." JCrR 2.09(b); CrR 3.2(b). Further, the Hawkinses ignore an ethical standard of paramount importance: that an attorney must advocate zealously his client's interests to the fullest extent permissible by law and the disciplinary rules. (CPR) DR 7–101(A)(1).

While it can be argued that the draftsmen of JCrR 2.09 assumed defense counsel would participate in furnishing information for the court, there is no indication as to the length to which defense counsel should go in revealing information damaging to his client's stated interests. Manifestly, defense counsel has an ethical duty to disclose that which he is required by law to reveal. Appellants, however, have not cited any clear provision of the law which *requires* defense counsel to volunteer information damaging to his client's expressed desire to be released from custody.

We believe that the duty of counsel to be loyal to his client and to represent zealously his client's interests overrides the nebulous and unsupported theory that our rules and ethical code mandate disclosure of information which counsel considers detrimental to his client's stated interest. Because disclosure is not "required by law," appellants' theory of liability on the basis of ethical or court rule violations fails for lack of substance.

Turning then to the Hawkinses' theory of a common-law duty to warn or disclose, we note common-law support for the precept that attorneys must, upon learning that a client plans an assault or other violent crime, warn foreseeable victims. *See Tarasoff v. Regents of Univ. of Cal., supra; State ex rel. Sowers v. Olwell,* 64 Wn.2d 828, 394 P.2d 681, 16 A.L.R.3d 1021 (1964); *Dike v. Dike,* 75 Wn.2d 1, 448 P.2d 490 (1968). *Olwell* and *Dike* make clear our Supreme Court's willingness to limit the attorney's duty of confidentiality when the values protected by that duty are outweighed by other interests necessary to the administration of justice. The difficulty lies in framing a rule that will balance properly "the public interest and safety from violent attack" against the public interest in securing proper resolution of legal disputes without compromising a defendant's right to a loyal and zealous defense. We are persuaded by the position advanced by amicus "that the obligation to warn, when confidentiality would be compromised to the client's detriment, must be permissive at most, unless it appears beyond a reasonable doubt that the client has formed a firm intention to inflict serious personal injuries on an unknowing third person."

Because appellants rely to a great extent upon *Tarasoff* in arguing a common-law duty to disclose, we will demonstrate that the *Tarasoff* decision is inapposite even though the facts are equally atypical and tragic. Tatiana Tarasoff was killed by one Prosenjit Poddar. The victim's parents alleged that 2 months earlier Poddar confided his intention to kill Tatiana to a defendant, Dr. Moore, a psychologist employed by the University of California. After a brief detention of Poddar by the police at Moore's request, Poddar was released pursuant to order of Dr. Moore's superior. No one warned Tatiana of her peril. The plaintiffs claimed the defendant psychologists had a duty to warn foreseeable victims. Defendants denied owing any duty of reasonable care to Tatiana. The trial court sustained a demurrer to the complaint which was reversed on appeal. The Supreme Court of California concluded that the complaint could be amended to state a cause of action against the psychologists by asserting that they had or should have determined Poddar presented a serious danger to Tatiana, pursuant to the standards of their profession, but had failed to exercise reasonable care for her safety.

In *Tarasoff*, the defendant psychologists had first-hand knowledge of Poddar's homicidal intention and knew it to be directed towards Tatiana Tarasoff, who was wholly unaware of her danger. The knowledge of the defendants in *Tarasoff* was gained from statements made to them in the course of treatment and not from statements transmitted by others. Further, the California court in *Tarasoff* did not establish a new duty to warn, but only held that psychologists must exercise such reasonable skill, knowledge, and care possessed and exercised by members of their profession under similar circumstances.

In the instant case, Michael Hawkins' potential victims, his mother and sister, knew he might be dangerous and that he had been released from confinement, contrary to Tatiana Tarasoff's ignorance of any risk of harm. Thus, no duty befell Sanders to warn Frances Hawkins of a risk of which she was already fully cognizant. Further, it must not be overlooked that Sanders received no information that Hawkins planned to assault anyone, only that he was mentally ill and likely to be dangerous to himself and others. That Sanders received no information directly from Michael Hawkins is the final distinction between the two cases.

The common-law duty to volunteer information about a client to a court considering pretrial release must be limited to situations where information gained convinces counsel that his client intends to commit a crime or inflict injury upon unknowing third persons. Such a duty cannot be extended to the facts before us.

In view of our disposition of this case, we do not reach the question of respondent Sanders' claimed immunity from civil liability.

The decision of the Superior Court granting summary judgment dismissing the respondents as party defendants is affirmed.

SOLUTIONS: THE LAWYER SHOULD HAVE, WOULD HAVE, COULD HAVE. . .

Here the PD acted exactly as he should have acted. He identified the client as the person in custody and abided by his objective—to be released. Were the rule otherwise, then lawyers would be invested with too much discretion and the system prove unworkable.

WHAT'S NEXT?

We now turn to the fundamental duties that flow from the formation of the ACR: Obligations the lawyer owes to her client. Some of these rules are phrased in the absolute ("shall"), but with words being used as modifiers, to ensure that lawyers are held to realistic standards, not standards of perfection. Also note that some of these obligations survive the end of the ACR, while others exist so long as the relationship is ongoing. You will see how the formation of the ACR that you have studied and the spelling out the scope of the representation interlock with determining when the ACR is completed. We will also be introducing the concept of a lawyer's fiduciary duty to a client which rises above the contractual duty that we discussed in the ACR formation.

To assess your understanding of the material in this chapter, click here to take a quiz.

PART II

A Lawyer's Duties to the Client

CHAPTER 4

Lawyer Obligations During Representation and After

Coming Attractions

An ACR is formed. In the last chapter you studied the duties flowing to third persons from that formation. Now, we turn to the duties owing to the client. As the chart below reflects, there are duties during the ACR as well as after its conclusion. The duties of competence; diligence; communication; confidentiality and attorney-client privilege are present during the ACR. After the ACR is concluded, there continues to be a limited duty of diligence and a continuing and full-fledged duty of confidentiality and attorney-client privilege. As you might imagine, there are disputes over whether the ACR is ended. You will return, in making that determination, to the creation of the engagement letter you studied earlier in the casebook. Essentially the question to be asked is this: has the propose of the engagement been satisfied?

The following sections, stating with competence, illuminates how these important duties interact with the everyday legal practice of a lawyer.

Let's Chart It!

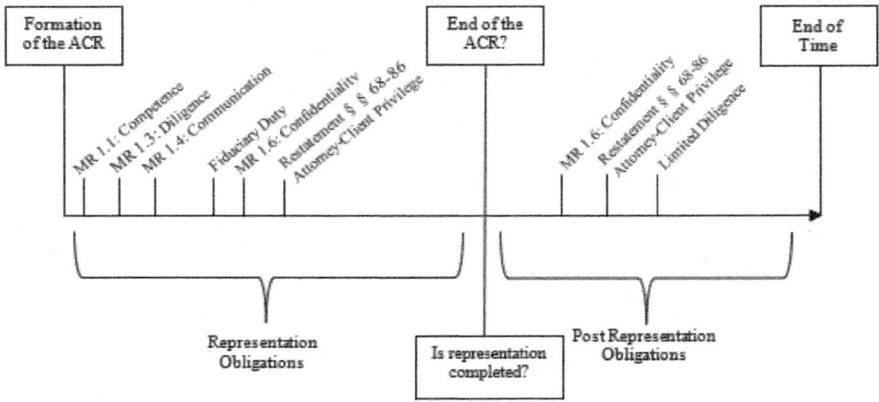

Section 1.   Competence

Model Rule 1.1: Competence

A lawyer shall provide competent representation to a client. Competent representation requires the legal knowledge, skill, thoroughness and preparation reasonably necessary for the representation.

Deconstruction Exercise/Rule Rationale

The Competence rule is straightforward (mostly), and it is mandatory. Note that the rule requires "reasonably necessary" skill/knowledge and not the highest level of skill/knowledge. And this is the first rule for a reason, isn't it? If a lawyer is not competent to handle a matter (or cannot make herself competent) then the lawyer should not go forward with the ACR. Textually, note how the required attributes of competence are grouped in the rule: there are personal dimensions that are a function of a lawyer's character (thoroughness and preparation) and then there are those that are a function of education and experience (knowledge and skill).

Finally, in assessing whether a lawyer violated MR 1.1, the Bar takes a snap-shot approach; namely, the Bar asks what did the lawyer know at the time that the lawyer made the now challenged decision or gave the now challenged counsel? The Bar does not second guess the lawyer's counsel or action with the wisdom of hindsight. Every lawyer makes mistakes; only some are a violation of MR 1.1. The rule does not place the burden on the lawyer to be the best. Rather the lawyer must be reasonably competent.

LEANING INTO PRACTICE

Scenario No. 1: The Case of the Dog Bite That Gets Complicated

Imagine you have just started your practice. A prospective client comes to you and explains that his son was bitten by the unleashed dog of the neighbor. The prospective client tells you that he told the neighbor that the dog is aggressive and needs to be on a leash if outside. The child received bite marks that were treated at the ER for $500. You have never handled a dog bite case before. Can you handle this one consistent with your MR 1.1 obligations? What if the bite becomes infected because of alleged negligent medical treatment? You have no background in medical malpractice litigation. What do you do now?

Scenario No. 2: The Case of MR 1.1 vs. MR 1.2

The client instructs you to draft specific portions of non-competition agreements for several of its employees. The client tells you, however, "I do not want you spending more than two or three hours on this project. If you can't get the job done in that time frame, I will find someone else who can." While the Model Rules permit a limited scope engagement, you reasonably believe the project will take ten to twelve hours to complete in a competent manner. Does the mandate of MR 1.1 trump the option of MR 1.2? Why? Remember, MR. 1.2 says that "a lawyer shall abide by a client's decisions concerning the objectives of representation." What if the client tells you that "I understand that you think that I am not giving you enough time to do the work. But I will sign whatever you want releasing you from malpractice liability for a bad job." Does this statement change your decision? Why or why not?

Scenario No. 3: The Case of the Troublesome Cousin

It is 1 a.m. You are working at your firm as a junior associate, pulling an all-nighter, when your cousin calls in a panic. "I have just been arrested for selling drugs, but I am innocent this time. I cannot spend another night in jail. Can you help me?" You are a corporate lawyer, and your knowledge of criminal law is limited to one law school class and bar review prep. Still, you are a lawyer with some basic knowledge of bail and the criminal justice system. Because your cousin cannot reach any other lawyer, you go to the jail, make an appearance on his behalf, and successfully bail him out. The managing partner of your firm tells you the next day (after you inform her why your billables took a slight dip the preceding day) "go ahead and represent her. We all have at least one relative like this!" What do you do now and why?

Cases and Materials

X-Ray Questions (*Orr*)

Orr was a well-known and respected lawyer in Nebraska. He was retained by a couple who came up with a great idea for a coffee shop and wanted to sell franchises. Having read franchise agreements for clients seeking to buy a franchise, Orr concluded that he was also competent to draft them as well. He failed to appreciate that there are complex federal and state statutes dealing with the *selling* of franchises. As you read this case, count the number of times that Orr was alerted to the crucial legal difference between selling and buying? Did he not understand his continuing duty of competence or did he not recognize it when deciding to take on the matter? Why did he fail to pay attention to the warning signs but rather charged forward? Did he wisely delegate the work to the junior lawyer in his firm? He finally withdrew from representation because he perceived a conflict between his firm and the client. What was the nature of the conflict? Google the business and see where it is today. Was the sanction imposed upon him by the state bar grievance committee commensurate with the harm done? Should it have been greater or is it the role of the grievance system to rehabilitate the lawyer and protect the public and that of the litigation system to punish the lawyer for malpractice and to make the client whole? Do you see the difference? So, would a violation of a Model Rule be *per se* malpractice or only evidence of malpractice? Why? This is a *per curiam* (unsigned) opinion. Two justices recused themselves? Why do you think? In this regard note that only 6,000 lawyers are licensed to practice in Nebraska.

State of Nebraska ex rel. Counsel for Discipline of the Nebraska Supreme Court v. Jeffrey L. Orr

Supreme Court of Nebraska, 2009.
759 N.W.2d 702.

PER CURIAM.

INTRODUCTION

Jeffrey L. Orr, respondent in this attorney disciplinary proceeding, was found to have violated his oath of office as an attorney and to have violated disciplinary rules requiring an attorney to competently represent a client. The only issue presented is the appropriate sanction to be imposed.

FACTS

The underlying conduct in this case involves Orr's representation of Steve Sickler and Cathy Mettenbrink in connection with the franchising of a coffee shop business. Sickler and Mettenbrink had opened their first coffee shop together, Barista's Daily Grind (Barista's), in Kearney, Nebraska, in December 2001. In September 2002, Sickler met with Orr and asked whether Orr could help Sickler and Mettenbrink franchise their business.

Orr was engaged in private practice in Kearney, and his experience with franchising was limited. Orr testified that he had read franchise agreements on behalf of clients who either were or were interested in becoming franchisees, but had never represented a franchisor. Orr's role in those cases had been to generally advise clients as to the rights of a franchisor and duties of a franchisee under the agreement. Orr's experience had required him to review franchise agreements and disclosure statements, but he had not reviewed state or federal law governing franchising.

In response to Sickler's inquiry, Orr stated that he had recently reviewed a franchisee's agreement and that he believed he could "handle" the franchising of Barista's. Orr told Sickler and Mettenbrink that he would begin working on a franchise agreement, and he completed the first draft in October 2002. Orr stated that he had recently reviewed a restaurant franchise agreement and then utilized that document when drafting the Barista's document. Although he had never before drafted a franchise agreement, Orr believed it was simply "a matter of contract drafting," which he believed he was competent to do. Orr contacted an attorney in Washington, D.C., for assistance with the trademark and copyright portions of franchising, and that attorney warned Orr that franchising was a specialized field.

In December 2002, Orr drafted a disclosure statement. Orr used the disclosure statement he had recently reviewed on behalf of the previously mentioned franchisee, as well as "FTC documents," to finish the statement in January 2003. Orr's understanding was that a disclosure statement was required by the Federal Trade Commission (FTC) in order to inform the franchisee of the more important terms and conditions of the franchise agreement.

From 2003 to 2006, Barista's sold 21 franchises. In July 2004, Sickler was contacted by a banker in Colorado, inquiring on behalf of a prospective franchisee. The banker requested the "UFOC" of Barista's, and, unaware of what a UFOC was, Sickler referred the banker to Orr. Orr determined that the then-current disclosure statement of Barista's was "compliant and valid" and could be used anywhere. Sickler testified that Orr told him that the UFOC was a requirement of federal law which Barista's was "probably going to have to get" if it was "going to be selling franchises out of state."

In August 2004, Orr revised the franchise agreement and disclosure statement at Sickler's request due to problems Barista's was having with a franchisee in Iowa. The Iowa franchisee had been provided with copies of the initial franchise agreement and disclosure statement. However, in February 2004, the Iowa franchisee's attorney sent a letter to Sickler suggesting that Barista's had not complied with federal disclosure requirements.

Sickler and Orr dispute at what point Orr was provided with a copy of that letter. But despite being aware that Barista's was working with prospective franchisees in Iowa and Colorado, Orr did not advise Sickler to seek input from local counsel in those states. And Sickler testified that the revised franchise agreement and disclosure statement were also provided to prospective franchisees in Kansas.

In October 2004, due to an unrelated dispute, Sickler and Mettenbrink sued the Colorado franchisees to terminate the franchises. A counterclaim was filed alleging deceptive and unfair trade practices, violation of FTC rules, and violation of Nebraska's Seller-Assisted Marketing Plan Act.

Orr's associate, Bradley Holbrook, became lead counsel for this litigation, although Orr remained primarily responsible for the representation of Barista's. Holbrook researched Nebraska law and discussed the case with Orr, including the fact that the Colorado franchisees were challenging the disclosure statement.

Disagreements were also ongoing with the Iowa franchisee, who eventually demanded rescission of the franchise agreement based on Barista's failure to comply with federal and Iowa disclosure laws. The Iowa franchisee's attorney demanded that Sickler return the franchise fee and pay attorney fees and other damages, and informed Sickler that he and Mettenbrink could be held personally liable under certain provisions of Iowa law. Sickler then informed Orr of the problem. Orr advised Sickler that the firm was going to contact an Omaha, Nebraska, attorney for a second opinion. Holbrook then contacted the Omaha attorney for a second opinion, which was provided in a June 2005 memorandum. It is not clear whether a copy of the memorandum was provided to Sickler and Mettenbrink, but they were ultimately informed of its conclusions and advised by Orr not to sell any more franchises without considerable changes to the disclosure statement.

A third version of the disclosure statement was created and used. Sickler stated he was told that the disclosure statement was now "compliant with every state," but Orr stated he also told Sickler that for out-of-state franchises, Sickler should get advice from local counsel. Orr stated that before the third revision of the disclosure statement, he had been under the impression that FTC requirements overrode state law. But he advised Sickler to obtain local counsel because he had become aware that state law could be more stringent than federal requirements.

The Iowa franchisee filed suit in Iowa and, according to Sickler, obtained personal judgments against Sickler and Mettenbrink. Barista's sold seven more franchises using the third disclosure statement, but was notified by the FTC in November 2005 that Barista's was under investigation. Holbrook contacted an attorney specializing in franchise law regarding the FTC investigation. The specializing attorney reviewed the franchise documents of Barista's and concluded those documents—including the third disclosure statement—did not comply with FTC rules. The attorney characterized the deficiencies as "major."

Recognizing that it now had a conflict of interest, Orr's law firm withdrew from representing Sickler and Mettenbrink. The attorney specializing in franchising law continued to represent Sickler and Mettenbrink, and Barista's, with respect to the FTC issues. The FTC civil penalty has been suspended indefinitely, and will not have to be paid so long as the disclosures of Barista's are truthful. By April 2006, however, the franchising of Barista's had "virtually been shut down." Orr's law firm has paid for the revision of the franchising documents, as well as the research and second opinion obtained regarding the original franchising document.

Formal charges were filed against Orr on August 24, 2007, alleging that Orr had violated several sections of the Nebraska Rules of Professional Conduct and several sections of the now-superseded Code of Professional Responsibility. This court appointed a referee, and after a hearing, the referee found that Orr had violated his oath of office as an attorney. The referee also found that Orr had violated Canon 1, DR 1–102(A)(1), and Canon 6, DR 6–101(A)(1) and (2), of the Code of Professional Responsibility, as well as §§ 1.1 and 8.4(a) of the Nebraska Rules of Professional Conduct (now codified at Neb. Ct. R. of Prof. Cond. §§ 3–501.1 and 3–508.4(a)). DR 1–102(A)(1) DR 1–102(A)(1) and § 3–508.4(a) prohibit an attorney from violating the relevant rules of conduct.

Section 3–501.1 provides that "[a] lawyer shall provide competent representation to a client. Competent representation requires the legal knowledge, skill, thoroughness, preparation and judgment reasonably necessary for the representation." Similarly, DR 6–101DR 6–101 provides that a lawyer shall not handle a legal matter "which the lawyer knows or should know that he or she is not competent to handle, without associating with a lawyer who is competent to handle it," or "without preparation adequate in the circumstances." The referee recommended that a public reprimand be issued.

Orr did not take exception to the referee's report. This court granted the Counsel for Discipline's motion for judgment on the pleadings, but ordered briefing and argument on the appropriate sanction to be imposed.

ANALYSIS

As an initial matter, we first note that because some of the conduct at issue occurred prior to September 1, 2005, it is governed by the now-superseded Code of Professional Responsibility; other conduct occurred on or after September 1, the effective date of the Nebraska Rules of Professional Conduct, and is therefore governed by those rules.

A proceeding to discipline an attorney is a trial de novo on the record. To sustain a charge in a disciplinary proceeding against an attorney, a charge must be supported by clear and convincing evidence. Violation of a disciplinary rule concerning the practice of law is a ground for discipline.

As noted, no exceptions were filed in response to the referee's report. When no exceptions to the referee's findings of fact are filed by either party in an attorney discipline proceeding, this court may, in its discretion, consider the referee's findings final and conclusive. We consider the finding of facts in the referee's report to be final and conclusive, and based on those findings, we conclude that the formal charges are supported by clear and convincing evidence. Specifically, we conclude that Orr violated his oath of office as an attorney, DR 1–102(A)(1) DR 1–102(A)(1) and DR 6–101(A)(1) and (2) DR 6–101(A)(1) and (2) of the Code of Professional Responsibility, and §§ 3–501.1 and 3–508.4(a) of the Nebraska Rules of Professional Conduct. Accordingly, we grant in part the Counsel for Discipline's motion for judgment on the pleadings.

The basic issues in a disciplinary proceeding against an attorney are whether discipline should be imposed and, if so, the type of discipline appropriate under the circumstances. Neb. Ct. R. § 3–304 states that the following may be considered as discipline for attorney misconduct:

(A) Misconduct shall be grounds for:

    (1) Disbarment by the Court; or

    (2) Suspension by the Court; or

    (3) Probation by the Court in lieu of or subsequent to suspension, on such terms as the Court may designate; or

    (4) Censure and reprimand by the Court[.]

(B) The Court may, in its discretion, impose one or more of the disciplinary sanctions set forth above.

Each attorney discipline case must be evaluated individually in light of its particular facts and circumstances. This court will consider the attorney's acts both underlying the alleged misconduct and throughout the proceeding. The determination of an appropriate penalty to be imposed also requires the consideration of any aggravating or mitigating factors.

We have previously stated that " 'the purpose of a disciplinary proceeding against an attorney is not so much to punish the attorney as it is to determine whether in the public interest an attorney should be permitted to practice.' " We also note that while Orr's conduct caused financial consequences to his clients, the Nebraska Rules of Professional Conduct "are designed to provide guidance to lawyers and to provide a structure for regulating conduct through disciplinary agencies. They are not designed to be a basis for civil liability." For those reasons, we accept the referee's recommendation of a public reprimand.

The referee explicitly found the existence of a number of mitigating factors, including the fact that Orr had practiced law for 40 years and has had no prior complaints or penalties. The referee noted that a number of clients, business and community leaders, and members of the bar sent letters of support and recommendation. Orr also has served the legal community and the community at large. And while the conduct occurred over a long period of time, only one client was involved, and Orr's misconduct was an isolated occurrence rather than part of a recurring pattern.

Although the Counsel for Discipline argued that the appropriate sanction in this case was a 60-day suspension, Orr failed to file exceptions to the referee's findings of fact. The referee found Orr negligently determined that he was competent and did not knowingly engage in the practice of law in which he was not competent. We have found no support in the case law for a suspension for incompetence without other misconduct, such as dishonesty. Furthermore, the ABA Standards for Imposing Lawyer Sanctions provide the appropriate sanction for an attorney's lack of competence under DR 6–101DR 6–101:

4.52 Suspension is generally appropriate when a lawyer engages in an area of practice in which the lawyer knows he or she is not competent, and causes injury or potential injury to a client.

4.53 Reprimand is generally appropriate when a lawyer:

(a)   demonstrates failure to understand relevant legal doctrines or procedures and causes injury or potential injury to a client; or

(b)   is negligent in determining whether he or she is competent to handle a legal matter and causes injury or potential injury to a client.

That is not to say we are unconcerned about Orr's conduct. We have said that "[i]t is inexcusable for an attorney to attempt any legal procedure without ascertaining the law governing that procedure." As a lawyer who has been practicing law for 40 years, Orr should have been aware that he was not competent to represent franchisors, and he was warned by another attorney that franchise law was a specialized area. At the very least, Orr should have done the research necessary to become competent in the area of franchise law. The fact that Orr did little or no research into state or federal franchising law until long after he first received notice that there was a problem with the franchising documents is inexcusable.

We take this opportunity to caution general practitioners against taking on cases in areas of law with which they have no experience, unless they are prepared to do the necessary research to become competent in such areas or associate with an attorney who is competent in such areas. General practitioners must be particularly careful when practicing in specialty areas. "If a general practitioner plunges into a field in which he or she is not competent, and as a consequence makes mistakes that demonstrate incompetence, the Code [of Professional Responsibility] demands that discipline be imposed . . . ."

Based upon our consideration of the record in this case, we conclude that Orr violated his oath of office as an attorney, DR 1–102(A)(1)DR 1–102(A)(1) and DR 6–101(A)(1) and (2)DR 6–101(A)(1) and (2) of the Code of Professional Responsibility, and §§ 3–501.1 and 3–508.4(a) of the Nebraska Rules of Professional Conduct. For the above reasons, we accept the recommendation of the referee and issue a public reprimand.

CONCLUSION

The motion of the Counsel for Discipline is sustained in part and in part overruled. We adopt the referee's findings of fact and find by clear and convincing evidence that Orr violated DR 1–102(A)(1)DR 1–102(A)(1) and DR 6–101(A)(1) and (2)DR 6–101(A)(1) and (2) of the Code of Professional Responsibility and §§ 3–501.1 and 3–508.4(a) of the Nebraska Rules of Professional Conduct, as well as his oath of office as an attorney. It is the judgment of this court that Orr should be, and hereby is, publicly reprimanded.

SOLUTIONS: THE LAWYER SHOULD HAVE, WOULD HAVE, COULD HAVE. . .

We speculate that Orr said something along these lines: "How hard could it be?" Well, as he discovered, pretty hard. A question that a lawyer should ask on a matter like this is: "Is there a regulatory scheme we need to be aware of?" The administrative state, as you have sensed from your other law school courses, is pervasive. Part of the art of ethical lawyering is knowing the right questions to ask. Had these questions been asked and answered, then Orr might have realized that his firm was not suited to handle the work. Or perhaps it could have taken on more of a general counsel role with the client. Orr could have, with informed consent of the client, associated with other lawyers who were more familiar with the franchise area, or perhaps his firm could have researched and studied the area to get up to speed (without charging the client or obtaining informed consent to do so). The lesson here is not necessarily to decline work that you are unfamiliar with but rather to make a sound decision by asking the right questions and to have a sober awareness of one's limitations, but still a reasonable view of one's talents and skills. Only you can be the judge. It is human nature to believe that we are smarter than we really are. But some humbleness—especially when clients entrust us with their dreams—is a virtue to cultivate.

Cases and Materials

X-Ray Questions (*Baldwin*)

As promised, we are revisiting *Baldwin*. It is an instructive case on multiple levels. To recap: Her career trajectory was derailed because it intersected with the horrific conduct of an assistant football coach, Jerry Sandusky, a 32-year veteran of the coaching staff of the Penn State football team. Let's recap: Sandusky was convicted of sexually molesting 10 boys, some at university facilities. Before his trial and conviction, there was a grand jury investigation into the potential responsibility of the university itself and also of three of its senior executives; namely whether they knew of the abuse (or suspected it) and failed to take appropriate action. A subpoena deuces tecum was served on the university and each of the three executives in their *individual* capacities As we have discussed, Baldwin decided that she could represent *both* the university and the executives. In scathing language, the state Supreme Court lambasted Baldwin for incompetence in her decision making. She had no criminal law experience; she failed to conduct research; she did not consider bringing in a more experienced criminal law attorney; she failed to advise the executives that each could assert their right against self-incrimination; she ignored the fundamental concept that the lawyer must clearly identify her client; and she had no idea that an executive could be investigated in both their individual capacity as well as their corporate capacity.

Take a moment and explain why it is important for the lawyer to identify who is the client in any situation but especially in this configuration. While this answer may seem self-evident, you will have a better understanding of the importance of doing so if you articulate the answer verbally or in writing.

As you read the case, also consider how she handled issues regarding electronic discovery. According to the Supreme Court, she essentially did nothing. What can account for her apparent inaction? She delegated the responsibility for complying with the subpoena and with electronic discovery. When, if ever, is delegation of a lawyer's responsibilities appropriate? What should she have done? Did she simply not know what she did not know? Why did no one in the office of the General Counsel, which was no doubt sizeable, tell here that separate lawyers were called for and that the university only was her client?

Finally, what did the Court consider her single most important failure? Can you see yourself making some of her mistakes? How would you seek to make sure that you do not? This case was a tragedy in the way it was handled because the result was not pre-ordained but could have been avoided.

Office of Disciplinary Counsel v. Cynthia A. Baldwin

Supreme Court of Pennsylvania, 2020.
225 A.3d 817.

JUSTICE DONOHUE.

In this matter, we consider the request of the Petitioner, the Office of Disciplinary Counsel ("ODC"), to impose discipline in the form of a public censure on Respondent, Cynthia A. Baldwin ("Respondent"), in connection with her representation of Pennsylvania State University ("Penn State") and three of its administrators during grand jury proceedings investigating matters relating to child abuse accusations against Gerald A. Sandusky ("Sandusky"), a former assistant football coach at Penn State. On November 21, 2017, the ODC filed a Petition for Discipline against the Respondent, charging her with violations of Rules 1.1, 1.6(a), 1.7(a) and 8.4(d) of the Pennsylvania Rules of Professional Conduct relating to her joint representation of Timothy Curley ("Curley"), Penn State's Athletic Director, Gary Schultz ("Schultz"), Penn State's former Senior Vice-President for Finance and Business, and Graham Spanier ("Spanier"), Penn State's president (collectively "Individual Clients") as well as Penn State (collectively with Individual Clients, the "Clients"). In its findings and recommendations, the Disciplinary Board of the Supreme Court of Pennsylvania ("Disciplinary Board") concluded that Respondent "failed to protect her clients' right to competent counsel and entitlement to unfettered loyalty, which serious misconduct contributed to criminal charges against her clients, and ultimately caused certain charges to be quashed, thereby prejudicing the administration of justice." Disciplinary Board's Report and Recommendations, 3/18/2019, at 48 (hereinafter, the "Disciplinary Board Report"). The Disciplinary Board recommended discipline in the form of a public censure by this Court. We impose discipline in the form of a public reprimand.

[. . . .]

II.   Factual and Procedural History

A.   Grand Jury Presentment

The facts underlying the ODC's Petition for Discipline against the Respondent are ultimately intertwined with Presentment No. 29, issued by the Thirty-Third Statewide Investigating Grand Jury on October 26, 2012 (hereinafter, the "Grand Jury Presentment"). We provide this summary of facts to provide context for our discussion and analysis of these disciplinary proceedings.

In 2009, the Office of Attorney General ("OAG") presented allegations of Sandusky's repeated sexual abuse of children to a statewide investigating grand jury. Of relevance here, the ensuing investigation uncovered two instances of abuse that took place on the Penn State campus, one in 1998 and a second in 2001.

The 1998 incident involved an eleven-year-old boy. Grand Jury Presentment at 6. Sandusky took the victim to the East Area Locker Room on Penn State's campus, where they wrestled and then used exercise machines. *Id.* Sandusky then insisted that they shower together. *Id.* Sandusky put his arms around the victim and squeezed him, making the boy very uncomfortable. *Id.* When Sandusky took the victim home, his mother asked why his hair was wet and became concerned upon learning of the joint shower. *Id.* The next morning, she filed a report with the University Police Department. *Id.* Centre County Children and Youth Services were also notified, but it referred the case to the Pennsylvania Department of Public Welfare, citing a conflict of interest due to its involvement with the Second Mile Foundation, a charity established by Sandusky in the 1970's that focused on assisting boys between the ages of eight and eighteen. *Id.* at 7.

Tom Harmon was the Chief of Police of the University Police Department in 1998.As his department's investigation proceeded, Chief Harmon kept Schultz, who oversaw the University Police Department as part of his administrative position at Penn State, updated on its progress. *Id.* at 8. Schultz, in turn, kept Curley and Spanier apprised of the investigation's progress, primarily through email messages. *Id.* at 9. On June 9, 1998, Schultz sent Curley an email, on which Spanier was copied, informing him that the Centre County District Attorney had decided not to pursue criminal charges against Sandusky. *Id.* at 10. The police report of the investigation was not filed in the usual location. Instead, it was assigned an administrative number, which made it difficult, if not impossible, to access the report without that number. *Id.* at 11.

The Grand Jury Presentment also reported that in 2001, Michael McQueary, then a graduate assistant for the football team, witnessed Sandusky with a young boy in a locker room shower on the University's main campus. *Id.* at 12. McQueary reported this incident to head football coach Joseph V. Paterno, *id.* at 13, who testified to the grand jury that McQueary described Sandusky as fondling or doing something of a sexual nature to a young boy in the shower. *Id.* Paterno further testified that in turn he relayed this information to Schultz and Curley. *Id.* at 14. Seven to ten days later, Schultz and Curley met with McQueary. *Id.* at 16. McQueary told the grand jury that he described to Schultz and Curley the sexual nature of what he had witnessed. *Id.*

Schultz then decided upon a plan that involved three parts. First, Curley would meet with Sandusky, tell him that they were aware of the 1998 incident, advise him to seek professional help, and prohibit him from ever again bringing boys into campus facilities. *Id.* at 15–16. Second, the chair of Second Mile would be notified. *Id.* And third, the matter would again be reported to the Pennsylvania Department of Public Welfare for investigation, as had been done in 1998. *Id.* Curley responded that he would prefer not to report the matter to the public welfare department so long as Sandusky was cooperative with their efforts. *Id.* at 16–17. Spanier was advised of the modified approach and agreed with the decision not to report the matter to an outside agency. *Id.* at 17–18. Curley then executed the revised two-part plan, conducting separate meetings with Sandusky and a Second Mile representative. *Id.* at 18–19.

B. Grand Jury Subpoenas to the Clients

On December 28, 2010, Respondent received a telephone call from the OAG regarding a grand jury investigation of multiple claims of child abuse against Sandusky. N.T. 5/23/18, at 366. The OAG asked Respondent to accept service of four subpoenas (which she later did), one for documents directed to Penn State and three for testimony from Curley, Schultz, and Paterno. *Id.* at 367. The subpoena duces tecum was directed to Penn State and requested "any and all records pertaining to Jerry Sandusky and incidents reported to have occurred on or about March 2002, and any other information concerning Jerry Sandusky and inappropriate contact with underage males both on and off University property. Response shall include any and all correspondence directed to or regarding Jerry Sandusky." Subpoena No. 1179, Attachment. The subpoenas to Curley, Schultz and Paterno were directed to them personally, without reference to Penn State or their employment titles. Subpoena No. 1176 (Curley); Subpoena No. 1178 (Schultz); Subpoena No. 1177 (Paterno). These three subpoenas indicated that the witnesses were to appear to testify before the grand jury on January 12, 2011, just nine days later. *Id.* Curley and Schultz were not served with a subpoena duces tecum.

Respondent first met with Curley in connection with his grand jury testimony in Spanier's office. N.T. 5/23/18, at 371. Respondent later testified that:

> I explained to them [Curley and Spanier] about the grand jury, how it was, that it wasn't like a regular courtroom, how many people were on, that there would be thirty-some people on it, and what they were doing, that it was an investigating grand jury because they really didn't know what a grand jury was, and I—I did explain that [Curley] could have a personal attorney to go with him to the grand jury, and that, you know, he shouldn't be nervous, just tell the truth, that's what all of this is about. . ."

Id. at 371. Respondent further testified that Spanier, in Curley's presence, instructed Respondent to go with Curley to the grand jury; that she told them she was general counsel and could not be Curley's personal attorney; that nothing Curley said would be confidential; and that Curley could retain a personal attorney. According to Respondent, Curley said that he did not know any lawyers. *Id.* at 372.

Respondent and Curley then met privately in Respondent's office. Respondent later indicated that they discussed what she had explained to him at the meeting in Spanier's office and reviewed his recollection of events involving Sandusky. *Id.* at 373–74. With respect to the 2001 incident, Respondent said that "basically he told me yes, he knew about this incident, and it had been described as horseplay." *Id.* Respondent's sole private conversation with Schultz before his grand jury testimony followed, and by Respondent's account, Schultz's recollections were in line with Curley's. *Id.* at 375. Respondent indicated that "[Schultz] told me the same thing that [Curley] told me, that it had been described as horseplay." *Id.* Respondent testified that neither Curley nor Schultz told her that a sex act had taken place between Sandusky and the boy in the shower, *id.* at 376, but the record does not reflect whether or not she specifically asked either of them whether one had occurred. During these meetings with Curley and Schultz, there was no discussion regarding the 1998 incident, as Respondent had no knowledge at that time that any such event had taken place. Both Curley and Schultz denied having any documents relating to Sandusky's activities. *Id.* at 377.

Based on these meetings, Respondent determined that their stories were consistent, as they "told me the same thing." *Id.* at 375. She further decided that the interests of Curley and Schultz were consistent with Penn State's interests. Accordingly, she made the judgment that she could represent them both before the investigating grand jury during their questioning. *Id.* at 378.

On the morning of January 12, 2011, Respondent accompanied Curley and Schultz to interviews with an OAG representative. Report and Recommendations of the Hearing Committee Report ("Hearing Committee Report"), Exhibit D (interview notes). Later that day, she then accompanied each of them to their appearances before the investigating grand jury. In his grand jury testimony, Curley testified that in 2001, Paterno contacted him (and Schultz) and requested an immediate meeting regarding an incident reported to him by McQueary. N.T. (grand jury), 1/12/2011 (Curley testifying), at 4–5. Paterno informed them that McQueary had seen Sandusky in the shower with a child and was "uncomfortable" with what he had observed. *Id.* at 5. According to Curley, when he and Schultz later met with McQueary, McQueary told them that Sandusky and the boy "were horsing around, that they were playful, and that it just did not feel appropriate." *Id.* at 7. Curley insisted that neither McQueary nor Paterno told them, in any form, that there was any sexual conduct involved, including anal intercourse. *Id.* Curley testified that he did not inform campus police of the incident because he did not think that what had been reported was a crime. *Id.* at 12.

Curley testified that he promptly advised Spanier regarding the incident. *Id.* at 8. He stated that he reported the incident to the executive director of the Second Mile Foundation and instructed Sandusky to refrain from bringing young people into the athletic facilities at Penn State. *Id.* at 10–11. Curley acknowledged that there was no follow up investigation into the 2001 report by McQueary. *Id.* at 13. He denied having any knowledge of the 1998 incident involving Sandusky. *Id.* at 13–14.

Also accompanied by Respondent, Schultz testified before the grand jury that he attended a meeting with Paterno and Curley regarding the 2001 incident.

Schultz indicated that Paterno had been informed by a graduate student of disturbing and inappropriate behavior by Sandusky in the shower. N.T. (grand jury), 1/12/2011 (Schultz testifying), at 5. Schultz also stated that he and Curley met with McQueary. *Id.* at 9–10. Unlike Curley, Schultz maintained that after talking to both Paterno and McQueary, he was of the view that what had occurred was sexual in nature. He told the grand jury:

Q.   Did you, nevertheless, form an impression about what type of conduct this might have been that occurred in the locker room?

A.   Well, I had the impression that it was inappropriate. Telling you what kind of thing I had in my mind without being clear, without him telling me, but you know. I had the feeling that there was perhaps some kind of wrestling around activity and maybe [Sandusky] might have grabbed the young boy's genitals or something of that sort is kind of the impression that I had.

Q.   Would you consider that to be inappropriate sexual conduct?

A.   Oh, absolutely. Well, I don't know the definition of sexual, but that's certainly inappropriate for somebody to do.

Q.   We can all agree that an adult male under no circumstances other than a doctor should be grabbing the genitals of a young boy?

A.   I agree completely with that.

Id. at 22–23.

Schultz testified that between himself, Curley and Spanier, it was agreed that Sandusky would be instructed to never again bring children into the football building. *Id.* at 11. Unlike Curley, Schultz further testified that it was his recollection that the three administrators agreed to request the same child protection agency that had investigated the 1998 incident be contacted regarding the 2001 events. *Id.*

The grand jury did not question Curley as to whether he was in possession of any documents relating to Sandusky. When asked if he had any such documents, Schultz responded as follows:

Q.   Do you believe that you may be in possession of any notes regarding the 2002 incident that you may have written memorializing what occurred?

A.   I have none of those in my possession. I believe that there were probably notes taken at the time. Given my retirement in 2009, if I even had them at that time, something that old would have probably been destroyed. I had quite a number of files that I considered confidential matters that go back years that didn't any longer seem pertinent. I wouldn't be surprised. In fact, I would guess if there were any notes, they were destroyed on or before 2009.

Id. at 16.

Schultz did not deny knowledge of the 1998 incident involving Sandusky, though he could not recall the specifics of what had occurred. He indicated that the matter was turned over to a Commonwealth-affiliated (rather than a local) child protection agency for investigation and that no charges were ever filed. *Id.* at 11. He testified that he kept Spanier advised as matters proceeded in 1998, as "it would have been a routine way of handling things, that I would have kept him informed [regarding the 1998 and 2001 incidents]." *Id.* at 17–18.

On March 22, 2011, OAG investigators interviewed Spanier, who was accompanied by Respondent. N.T. 5/23/18, at 386–87. On March 24, 2011, a subpoena was issued to Spanier for testimony before the grand jury on April 13, 2011. Subpoena No. 92 (Spanier). Respondent interviewed Spanier, found his testimony to be consistent with that of Curley and Schultz (even though their testimony was inconsistent with each others), and thus determined that she could accompany Spanier during his grand jury testimony. N.T., 5/23/18, at 387–88. Before the grand jury with respect to the 2001 incident, Spanier recalled that on one occasion Curley and Schultz sought his advice regarding a matter involving Sandusky "with a younger child . . . horsing around in the shower." N.T. (grand jury), 4/13/2011 (Spanier testifying), at 14. Spanier denied that Curley or Schultz told him that the horseplay could have been sexual in nature. *Id.* at 25–26. He indicated that he instructed them to inform Sandusky that he should not bring children under eighteen years of age into the locker room facilities and to contact the board chair of the Second Mile Foundation. *Id.* at 16–17. Spanier denied any knowledge of the 1998 incident. *Id.* at 34–35 ("I'm not aware of allegations against Mr. Sandusky in 1998. . . .").

On November 7, 2011, the Commonwealth charged Curley and Schultz with one count each of perjury and failure to report suspected child abuse. Hearing Committee Report, Exhibits Q, S. Respondent advised Curley and Schultz to retain private counsel and, at their request, made arrangements for them to do so. N.T., 5/23/2018, at 395. She also advised Spanier to hire private counsel. *Id.* at 396. Newly retained personal counsel for Curley and Schultz notified Respondent by letter that their clients each considered her to have been his personal attorney before the investigating grand jury and that they did not waive any claim of attorney-client privilege. *Id.*, Exhibits K(f), K(g), M. By letter dated June 22, 2012, Respondent, through counsel, denied the invocations of the attorney-client privilege by Curley and Schultz, insisting that as counsel for Penn State, she had acted solely in a corporate capacity with them before the grand jury and not in any individual capacity. *Id.*, Exhibit K(h).

In a letter dated December 19, 2011, counsel for the OAG advised Respondent that Penn State's continuing failure to provide documents in response to the subpoena duces tecum was concerning, and implicitly threatened the university with contempt of court "and any other appropriate measures applicable to obstruction against the institution and those individuals responsible for these decisions." N.T., 5/23/2018, at 402. Respondent was subsequently served with a subpoena to testify before the grand jury on October 26, 2012. Subpoena No. 883 (Baldwin). Four days prior to Respondent's grand jury testimony, the supervising judge of the grand jury held a conference to discuss privilege issues raised by private counsel for Schultz and Curley. Hearing Committee, Exhibit M. To resolve any conflicts, counsel for the OAG, Frank Fina ("Fina"), agreed not to ask Respondent any questions that implicated confidential communications. *Id.* at 11–12. Meanwhile, counsel for Penn State agreed to waive any attorney-client privileges, except to the extent that such privileges existed between Respondent and Curley and/or Schultz. Hearing Committee Report, Exhibits K(e), K(h).

During her grand jury testimony, Respondent stressed that she had made every effort to comply with the subpoena duces tecum, but that the three administrators had lied to her about the existence of multiple documents that reflected their detailed knowledge and participation in the 1998 and 2001 incidents.

> Q.   Did they [Schultz, Curley, and Spanier] ever in any way, shape, or form disclose to you when you were asking them for this material anything about 1998 or 2001 and the existence of e-mails from those events?
>
> A.   Never.
>
> Q.   We also know that Mr. Schultz had a file regarding Jerry Sandusky in his office; and that in that file were documents related to his retirement agreement.
>
> There were drafts and other documents related to his employment and his retirement and then there were handwritten notes and e-mails

pertaining to the 1998 crimes of Mr. Sandusky and the 2001 crimes of Mr. Sandusky.

Again, same question, did he ever reveal to you the existence of that Sandusky file or any of its contents?

A.   Never. He told me he didn't have anything.

N.T. (grand jury), 10/26/2012 (Respondent testifying), at 20. In other portions of her testimony, Respondent, in response to questions posed by counsel for the OAG, revealed the contents of numerous communications between herself and Curley, Schultz and Spanier. *See, e.g., id.* at 22.

On November 1, 2012, four days after Respondent testified before the investigating grand jury, several new charges were filed against Curley and Schultz, including endangering the welfare of children, obstruction of justice and conspiracy to commit obstruction of justice. Hearing Committee Report, Exhibits P, Q, R, S, T. On the same date, charges were filed against Spanier, including perjury, failure to report suspected child abuse, obstruction of justice, endangering the welfare of children and conspiracy to commit obstruction of justice. *Id.*, Exhibit U.

In 2014, Curley, Schultz and Spanier filed motions to preclude Respondent from testifying in the criminal trials in Dauphin County. Hearing Committee Report, Exhibit W. The trial court denied the motions, but the Superior Court reversed and quashed all of the perjury, obstruction of justice and related conspiracy charges. *Curley*, 131 A.3d at 1007; *Schultz*, 133 A.3d at 328; *Spanier*, 132 A.3d at 498. The Superior Court concluded that Respondent, during her grand jury testimony, had breached the attorney-client privilege. *Curley*, 131 A.3d at 1007; *Schultz*, 133 A.3d at 326; *Spanier*, 132 A.3d at 498. In its ruling, the Superior Court barred Respondent from testifying against Curley, Schultz or Spanier. *Curley*, 131 A.3d at 1007; *Schultz*, 133 A.3d at 328; *Spanier*, 132 A.3d at 498. The OAG did not appeal these rulings, but rather entered into plea bargains with Curley and Schultz, pursuant to which each pleaded guilty to one count of endangering the welfare of children. Spanier's case proceeded to trial, which resulted in a guilty verdict on one count of endangering the welfare of children. Curley and Schultz both testified for the Commonwealth.

C.   Disciplinary Proceedings

On November 24, 2014, the ODC initiated disciplinary proceedings by filing a Petition for Discipline against Respondent, charging her with violations of Rules 1.1, 1.6(a), 1.7(a) and 8.4(d) of our Rules of Professional Conduct. The

Hearing Committee conducted an evidentiary hearing and produced a thorough report that reviewed the evidence and made findings of fact and recommendations. The Hearing Committee determined that Respondent represented Curley, Schultz and Spanier in a personal capacity during their grand jury testimony. Hearing Committee Report at 39–42. The Hearing Committee, however, determined that Respondent did not violate Rule 1.7(a), as she had conducted a reasonable investigation into the interests of Penn State and the Individual Clients with respect to the grand jury investigation and had, based upon that investigation, reasonably concluded that the interests of Penn State and the individuals were consistent. *Id.* at 42–44. The Hearing Committee further concluded that Respondent did not violate Rule 1.1, as she had provided competent representation of Curley, Schultz and Spanier. *Id.* at 44–45. Further, Respondent did not violate RPC 1.6(a), as her testimony before the grand jury fell within exceptions to that rule and did not improperly reveal protected information about her representation of the individuals. *Id.* at 44–64. Because Respondent had not engaged in misconduct, the Hearing Committee determined that her actions were not prejudicial to the administration of justice, and therefore Respondent had not violated Rule 8.4(d). *Id.* at 65.

Both parties filed exceptions to the Hearing Committee's report. Respondent took issue with the Hearing Committee's determination that she represented Curley, Schultz and Spanier in their individual capacities, while the ODC filed exceptions to its rulings related to violations of Rules 1.1, 1.6(a), 1.7(a) and 8.4(d). On March 18, 2019, the Disciplinary Board issued a report reversing the determinations of the Hearing Committee. The Disciplinary Board agreed with the Hearing Committee that Respondent had represented the three administrators in their personal capacities before the grand jury but concluded that she failed to recognize the multiple conflicts of interest between her clients. Disciplinary Board Report at 28–30, 33–37. The Board further determined that Respondent did not exercise the legal knowledge, skill, thoroughness and preparation reasonably necessary for the representations of Curley, Schultz and Spanier before the grand jury. *Id.* at 30–33. She further failed to maintain the confidentiality of communications between herself and her clients. *Id.* at 37–42. Finally, the Disciplinary Board found that Respondent's conduct prejudiced the administration of justice. *Id.* at 42–43. The Disciplinary Board found that Respondent poses no danger to the public or the profession and that her character remains of the highest quality. The Disciplinary Board concluded that public censure, rather than a public reprimand, is the appropriate remedy in this case. *Id.* at 48.

Respondent poses two questions for this Court's consideration:

1.   Did the [ODC] establish by clear and convincing evidence that [Respondent] committed disciplinary violations of Rules 1.1, 1.6, 1.7 or 8.4 of the Rules of Professional Conduct?

2.   Was there any legitimate basis to impose any form of discipline upon [Respondent] in the absence of any aggravating factors, multiple mitigating factors and no prior disciplinary history?

Respondent's Brief at 2.

[. . . .]

B.   Competency Pa.R.P.C. 1.1

Pa.R.P.C. 1.1 requires counsel to render competent representation to clients. The Disciplinary Board, based upon its review of the evidentiary record, determined that Respondent "violated this rule, as she failed to exercise the legal knowledge, skill, thoroughness and preparation reasonably necessary for the representation of her clients before the grand jury, and further failed to properly advise and advocate on their behalf, to their detriment." Disciplinary Board Report at 30. For the reasons set forth herein, we agree with this conclusion.

By her own admission, Respondent had no criminal law experience and had never represented a client before a grand jury. N.T., 5/23/2018, at 430–31. She also did not testify that she consulted with counsel experienced in these areas in preparation for the grand jury testimony of Curley and Schultz or in responding to the subpoena duces tecum. *Id.* at 434. To the contrary, the record plainly reflects that Respondent did not exhibit any understanding of the magnitude of the challenge that she was facing. Respondent should have understood that by subpoenaing Curley and Schultz, the grand jury investigation was expanding beyond the conduct of Sandusky into the possible roles that individuals associated with Penn State may have had in facilitating or covering up his criminal acts, including in particular those that occurred on the Penn State campus. Their testimony potentially exposed Curley and Schultz (and later Spanier) to significant criminal liability, including prosecution for perjury, obstruction of justice, endangering the welfare of children, failure to report child abuse, and conspiracy. As representatives of Penn State, their testimony also potentially exposed the university to criminal liability as well as massive civil liability.

Despite the enormity of the situation confronting her, Respondent did very little in advance of her clients' appearances before the grand jury. She met separately with Curley and Schultz on one occasion each, at which time she provided a general review of the grand jury process, advised them of their right to counsel of their choosing, and told them to tell the truth. Nothing in the record, however, indicates that she spent any time with either Curley or Schultz reviewing the types of questions that they were likely to be asked by the grand jury or how best to respond to any such questions. Likewise, the record does not reflect that Respondent advised them of their rights to assert their rights against self-incrimination, or otherwise describe to them the nature and types of crimes to which they might be subjecting themselves if they did not assert this right. Instead, the substance of Respondent's self-described preparation of Curley and Schultz before their grand jury testimony was, in its totality, to "tell the truth." Despite having three additional months to prepare Spanier for his grand jury testimony, the record does not reflect that she did anything more in this regard than she had done for Curley and Schultz.

Respondent asserts that she did not prepare more diligently in advance of the grand jury appearances because Curley and Schultz lied to her, misrepresenting that they were free of all wrongdoing. Concurrent with the representations of Curley and Schultz, Respondent was representing Penn State with regard to its response to the subpoena duces tecum. While it is questionable whether an attorney can ever blindly rely on statements by a client regarding events that occurred years prior to anticipated testimony, it was below any reasonable standard of care to do so here where another client may have been in possession of relevant documents. The duty to investigate becomes all the more important when, as here, counsel undertakes the representation of multiple clients, one of which is a sophisticated institutional client with massive document retention capabilities.

Despite the urgent need, the record here reflects that Respondent conducted little or no independent investigation prior to accompanying Curley and Schultz into the grand jury room. She did not, for instance, interview any members of their staff to inquire regarding their knowledge of prior Sandusky investigations. She also did not have anyone search their offices for relevant documents. As of November 2011, eleven months after Schultz's grand jury testimony (in which he indicated that prior to his retirement he had kept notes regarding Sandusky matters, but thought they had "probably been destroyed"), a file containing said notes (with incriminating details regarding the 1998 and 2001 incidents) remained in his prior office. This file was later obtained by the OAG.

Most importantly, prior to producing the Individual Clients for testimony before the grand jury, Respondent failed entirely to coordinate a search of any of the electronically stored data, including emails, on Penn State's computers. As a result of her multiple representations, Respondent had both an obligation to advise Curley, Schultz and Spanier and an obligation to comply with the subpoena duces tecum served on Penn State in January 2011. According to the grand jury, Penn State, "had in place a well-defined historical practice and procedure for responding to subpoenas," and that "[s]ubpoenas that might encompass electronically stored data (such as emails and documents stored on a computer or network drive) would routinely be sent to the specialized unit called the "SOS." Grand Jury Presentment at 23. The SOS included "information technology professionals [who were] trained and dedicated to assembling responsive electronically stored data in response to litigation needs or other legal process." *Id.* Remarkably, however, the grand jury determined that this "well-defined historical practice and procedure" was not implemented by Respondent:

> None of the SOS professionals were ever shown subpoena 1179 before the arrests of Sandusky, Schultz and Curley [in November 2011]. Likewise, investigators contacted the information technology employees of Penn State, who were not members of the SOS unit but had access to the electronically stored data likely to be searched to fulfill the requirements of subpoena 1179. These information technology employees likewise stated that they were never requested to fulfill any requests for Sandusky related information.

Id. at 32.

During her grand jury testimony, Respondent insisted that she did involve Penn State's information technology professionals in her efforts to comply with the subpoena duces tecum.

> Q. Now, the subpoena duces tecum, Subpoena 1179, can you go through with the grand jury the efforts you made to enforce the subpoena and comply with it and what happened?

> A. Right. What we do is to send out a notice to everybody who is affected by that to say that you have to—you have to preserve everything and because we're going to have to turn over all of this information and so I did tell Tim Curley, Gary Schultz, [and] Graham Spanier that they would have to do that and turn over all of the information over.

Now, we have, of course, IT people, and we have other people who will help to get that information but that is what I told everybody, to try to get all of that information in and turn it over to the Office of Attorney General.

N.T. (grand jury), 10/26/2012 (Respondent testifying), at 16. In an interview with the Freeh group in February 2012, however, Respondent stated that "she did not investigate the Sandusky matter or look for Schultz, Paterno or Curley emails in the [Penn State] system that might relate to the Grand Jury's investigation." Freeh Report at 83 (citing interview with Respondent on February 29, 2012).

The significance of Respondent's failure to conduct a proper investigation prior to agreeing to represent Curley, Schultz and Spanier before the grand jury became abundantly clear when in November 2011 the Penn State Board of Directors intervened and ordered university personnel, including in particular its information technology professionals, to work directly with the OAG's office to obtain the emails and other documents sought by the subpoena duces tecum served back in January 2011.

> On November 8, 2011, the Board of Trustees of Penn State terminated Graham Spanier as the President of the University. The Board of Trustees also directed that University personnel were to cooperate with the law enforcement investigation of Jerry Sandusky and Penn State. Almost immediately following those two events, actual compliance with the Grand Jury subpoena (past and present) and cooperation with the investigation began to be realized. Law enforcement investigators, working in conjunction with [the] Penn State IT staff, were able to process massive amounts of electronically stored data and began a lengthy process of review and analysis. For the first four months of 2012, large amounts of evidence—much of which had been sought and subpoenaed more than a year prior—was uncovered and provided to investigators. This evidence included significant emails from 1998 reflecting knowledge of, and involvement with, the investigation of Sandusky with two young boys in May of 1998. In addition, significant emails were discovered, reflecting direct evidence of involvement by Graham Spanier, Gary Schultz, and Tim Curley in the failure of Penn State to report to child welfare or law enforcement authorities the crimes reported by Michael McQueary in February of 2001.

Grand Jury Presentment at 32.

As such, it is clear that information critical to Respondent's decision to represent simultaneously not only Penn State but also the three administrators was at all times contained within the university's computer servers and available for extraction upon request. Respondent did not conduct this investigation before agreeing to concurrently represent Penn State while personally representing Curley and Schultz (and later Spanier) in connection with their grand jury testimony. While we note that the subpoenas directed to Curley and Schultz provided only nine days between their service (on January 3, 2011) and the scheduled day for testimony (on January 12, 2011), an insufficient amount of time to conduct an investigation, it is also true that Respondent made no attempt to seek a delay. Respondent could have, but did not, request a continuance of their testimony from OAG counsel or file a motion for the same with the supervising judge. N.T., 5/23/2018, at 436. In the absence of adequate time to investigate and garner any documents in the possession of Penn State regarding the Sandusky matters that were generated, received or reviewed by Curley, Schultz and Spanier, Respondent could not conclude that the concurrent representation would be possible due to inadequate information upon which to make a conflict of interest analysis. Moreover, it was imperative for personal counsel for Curley, Schultz and Spanier to fully investigate the available evidence in order to give competent advice on invoking the privilege against self-incrimination in testimony before the grand jury. For these reasons, we conclude that Respondent failed to provide competent representation to clients in view of Rule 1.1.

SOLUTIONS: THE LAWYER SHOULD HAVE, WOULD HAVE, COULD HAVE. . .

Baldwin was plagued by an inability to ask herself this very fundamental question: "Who do I actually represent?" This failure was compounded by her failure to conduct any sort of meaningful investigation to determine the facts and circumstances of the emerging crisis; she was unable to intelligently determine whether there was an alignment of interests between the university and the executives. Telling the executives to obtain their own counsel early on would have been the wisest course, for the university, the executives and ultimately for her. What should she have done with respect to the electronic discovery sought by the government? In a bit you will read an Opinion Letter

> from the California Bar on electronic discovery. Reconsider your answer to this question after you read the Opinion Letter.

LEANING INTO PRACTICE

Scenario No. 1: The Case of the Lawyer Who Erred in His Judgment

Jose Lawyer is representing Nina Witness before a congressional committee. Jose reasonably believes that Nina has a legal right not to answer certain questions and so advises her. When Nina follows the advice, the committee chair cautions Nina that the failure to answer will result in a contempt situation and possible incarceration. Nina continues to refuse, is held in contempt and is convicted at a trial. Is Jose in violation of Model Rule 1.1? What information do you need to know to answer this question?

Scenario No. 2: The Case of the Inexperienced Lawyer and the Happy Client

Uchi Senior Partner wants Emmy New Associate to gain trial experience. Emmy is without any trial experience and the holder of a law license for 9 months. With the informed consent of the client, Uchi assigns Emmy to try the case by herself. The jury is taken with Emmy fresh and candid demeanor and finds for the client. The client is ecstatic at the result and so informs Uchi and Emmy. Is Uchi in violation of Model Rule 1.1? What about Emmy? Why or why not?

X-Ray Questions (*Opinion on E-Discovery*)

As we saw in *Baldwin*, electronic discovery is a feature in almost all litigation. GC Baldwin failed in her duty to exercise competence, in performing the discovery work herself, or in managing other lawyers or IT professionals in performing the work. The duty embodied in MR 1.1 is a non-delegable one. It is insufficient for purposes of MR 1.1 to merely send a transmittal letter or e-mails to a client or a vendor expert describing the task at hand and then absolving oneself of further responsibility. Is that not exactly what GC Baldwin did? As you read the opinion letter pay special attention to the section on delegation to others. Also consider competence in the area of electronic discovery and the continuing nature of the duty of competence whether through continuing education or through being constantly sensitive to whether the lawyer is in over her head (as with the morning following the late-night call from the cousin) or through realizing that the simple dog bite case is developing into a more complicated and specialized litigation. Finally, this Opinion Letter introduces you to the concept of spoliation that we will revisit later in the book. In short, a rule violation occurs when a lawyer fails to take steps to preserve documents, usually through what is called a Litigation Hold Letter.

So what appears like a simple documents request can develop—without an awareness of various ethical implications—into all sorts of knotty issues.

BEYOND THE CITE

THE STATE BAR OF CALIFORNIA STANDING COMMITTEE ON PROFESSIONAL RESPONSIBILITY AND CONDUCT FORMAL OPINION NO. 2015–193

ISSUES

What are an attorney's ethical duties in the handling of discovery of electronically stored information?

STATEMENT OF FACTS

Attorney defends Client in litigation brought by Client's Chief Competitor in a judicial district that mandates consideration of e-discovery2/ issues in its formal case management order, which is consistent with California Rules of Court, rule 3.728. Opposing Counsel demands e-discovery; Attorney refuses. They are unable to reach an agreement by the time of the initial case management conference. At that conference, an annoyed Judge informs both attorneys they have had ample prior notice that e-discovery would be addressed at the conference and tells them to return in two hours with a joint proposal.

In the ensuing meeting between the two lawyers, Opposing Counsel suggests a joint search of Client's network, using Opposing Counsel's chosen vendor, based upon a jointly agreed search term list. She offers a clawback agreement that would permit Client to claw back any inadvertently produced ESI that is protected by the attorney-client privilege and/or the work product doctrine ("Privileged ESI").

Attorney believes the clawback agreement will allow him to pull back anything he "inadvertently" produces. Attorney concludes that Opposing Counsel's proposal is acceptable and, after advising Client about the terms and obtaining Client's authority, agrees to Opposing Counsel's proposal. Judge thereafter approves the attorneys' joint agreement and incorporates it into a Case Management Order, including the provision for the clawback of

Privileged ESI. The Court sets a deadline three months later for the network search to occur.

Back in his office, Attorney prepares a list of keywords he thinks would be relevant to the case, and provides them to Opposing Counsel as Client's agreed upon search terms. Attorney reviews Opposing Counsel's additional proposed search terms, which on their face appear to be neutral and not advantageous to one party or the other, and agrees that they may be included.

Attorney has represented Client before, and knows Client is a large company with an information technology ("IT") department. Client's CEO tells Attorney there is no electronic information it has not already provided to Attorney in hard copy form. Attorney assumes that the IT department understands network searches better than he does and, relying on that assumption and the information provided by CEO, concludes it is unnecessary to do anything further beyond instructing Client to provide Vendor direct access to its network on the agreed upon search date. Attorney takes no further action to review the available data or to instruct Client or its IT staff about the search or discovery. As directed by Attorney, Client gives Vendor unsupervised direct access to its network to run the search using the search terms.

Subsequently, Attorney receives an electronic copy of the data retrieved by Vendor's search and, busy with other matters, saves it in an electronic file without review. He believes that the data will match the hard copy documents provided by Client that he already has reviewed, based on Client's CEO's representation that all information has already been provided to Attorney.

A few weeks later, Attorney receives a letter from Opposing Counsel accusing Client of destroying evidence and/or spoliation. Opposing Counsel threatens motions for monetary and evidentiary sanctions. After Attorney receives this letter, he unsuccessfully attempts to open his electronic copy of the data retrieved by Vendor's search. Attorney hires an e-discovery expert ("Expert"), who accesses the data, conducts a forensic search, and tells Attorney potentially responsive ESI has been routinely deleted from Client's computers as part of Client's normal document retention policy, resulting in gaps in the document production. Expert also advises Attorney that, due to the breadth of Vendor's execution of the jointly agreed search terms, both privileged information and irrelevant but highly proprietary information about Client's upcoming revolutionary product were provided to Chief Competitor in the data retrieval. Expert advises Attorney that an IT professional with litigation experience likely would have recognized the overbreadth of the search and prevented the retrieval of the proprietary information.

What ethical issues face Attorney relating to the e-discovery issues in this hypothetical?

DISCUSSION

I. <u>Duty of Competence</u>

A. Did Attorney Violate the Duty of Competence Arising From His Own Acts/Omissions?

While e-discovery may be relatively new to the legal profession, an attorney's core ethical duty of competence remains constant. Rule 3–110(A) provides: "A member shall not intentionally, recklessly, or repeatedly fail to perform legal services with competence." Under subdivision (B) of that rule, "competence" in legal services shall mean to apply the diligence, learning and skill, and mental, emotional, and physical ability reasonably necessary for the performance of such service. Read together, a mere failure to act competently does not trigger discipline under rule 3–110. Rather, it is the failure to do so in a manner that is intentional, reckless or repeated that would result in a disciplinable rule 3–110 violation. (See *In the Matter of Torres* (Review Dept. 2000) 4 Cal. State Bar Ct. Rptr. 138, 149 ("We have repeatedly held that negligent legal representation, even that amounting to legal malpractice, does not establish a [competence] rule 3–110(A) violation."); see also, *In the Matter of Gadda* (Review Dept. 2002) 4 Cal. State Bar Ct. Rptr. 416 (reckless and repeated acts); *In the Matter of Riordan* (Review Dept. 2007) 5 Cal. State Bar Ct. Rptr. 41 (reckless and repeated acts).)

Legal rules and procedures, when placed alongside ever-changing technology, produce professional challenges that attorneys must meet to remain competent. Maintaining learning and skill consistent with an attorney's duty of competence includes keeping "abreast of changes in the law and its practice, including the benefits and risks associated with relevant technology, . . ." ABA Model Rule 1.1, Comment [8]. Rule 3–110(C) provides: "If a member does not have sufficient learning and skill when the legal service is undertaken, the member may nonetheless perform such services competently by 1) associating with or, where appropriate, professionally consulting another lawyer reasonably believed to be competent, or 2) by acquiring sufficient learning and skill before performance is required." Another permissible choice would be to decline the representation. When e-discovery is at issue, association or consultation may be with a non-lawyer technical expert, if appropriate in the circumstances. Cal. State Bar Formal Opn. No. 2010–179.

Not every litigated case involves e-discovery. Yet, in today's technological world, almost every litigation matter *potentially* does. The chances are significant that a party or a witness has used email or other electronic communication, stores information digitally, and/or has other forms of ESI related to the dispute. The law governing e-discovery is still evolving. In 2009, the California Legislature passed California's Electronic Discovery Act adding or amending several California discovery statutes to make provisions for electronic discovery. See, e.g., Code of Civil Procedure section 2031.010, paragraph (a) (expressly providing for "copying, testing, or sampling" of "electronically stored information in the possession, custody, or control of any other party to the action.") However, there is little California case law interpreting the Electronic Discovery Act, and much of the development of e-discovery law continues to occur in the federal arena. Thus, to analyze a California attorney's current ethical obligations relating to e-discovery, we look to the federal jurisprudence for guidance, as well as applicable Model Rules, and apply those principles based upon California's ethical rules and existing discovery law.

We start with the premise that "competent" handling of e-discovery has many dimensions, depending upon the complexity of e-discovery in a particular case. The ethical duty of competence requires an attorney to assess at the outset of each case what electronic discovery issues might arise during the litigation, including the likelihood that e-discovery will or should be sought by either side. If e-discovery will probably be sought, the duty of competence requires an attorney to assess his or her own e-discovery skills and resources as part of the attorney's duty to provide the client with competent representation. If an attorney lacks such skills and/or resources, the attorney must try to acquire sufficient learning and skill, or associate or consult with someone with expertise to assist. Rule 3–110(C). Attorneys handling e-discovery should be able to perform (either by themselves or in association with competent co-counsel or expert consultants) the following:

- initially assess e-discovery needs and issues, if any;

- implement/cause to implement appropriate ESI preservation procedures;

- analyze and understand a client's ESI systems and storage;

- advise the client on available options for collection and preservations of ESI;

- identify custodians of potentially relevant ESI;

- engage in competent and meaningful meet and confer with opposing counsel concerning an e-discovery plan;

- perform data searches;

- collect responsive ESI in a manner that preserves the integrity of that ESI; and

- produce responsive non-privileged ESI in a recognized and appropriate manner.

See, e.g., *Pension Committee of the University of Montreal Pension Plan v. Banc of America Securities, LLC* (S.D.N.Y. 2010) 685 F.Supp.2d 456, 462–465 (defining gross negligence in the preservation of ESI), (abrogated on other grounds in *Chin v. Port Authority* (2nd Cir. 2012) 685 F.3d 135 (failure to institute litigation hold did not constitute gross negligence per se)).

In our hypothetical, Attorney had a general obligation to make an e-discovery evaluation early, prior to the initial case management conference. The fact that it was the standard practice of the judicial district in which the case was pending to address e-discovery issues in formal case management highlighted Attorney's obligation to conduct an early initial e-discovery evaluation.

Notwithstanding this obligation, Attorney made *no* assessment of the case's e-discovery needs or of his own capabilities. Attorney exacerbated the situation by not consulting with another attorney or an e-discovery expert prior to agreeing to an e-discovery plan at the initial case management conference. He then allowed that proposal to become a court order, again with no expert consultation, although he lacked sufficient expertise. Attorney participated in preparing joint e-discovery search terms without experience or expert consultation, and he did not fully understand the danger of overbreadth in the agreed upon search terms.

Even after Attorney stipulated to a court order directing a search of Client's network, Attorney took no action other than to instruct Client to allow Vendor to have access to Client's network. Attorney did not instruct or supervise Client regarding the direct network search or discovery, nor did he try to pre-test the agreed upon search terms or otherwise review the data before the network search, relying on his assumption that Client's IT department would know what to do, and on the parties' clawback agreement.

After the search, busy with other matters and under the impression the data matched the hard copy documents he had already seen, Attorney took no action to review the gathered data until after Opposing Counsel asserted spoliation and threatened sanctions. Attorney then unsuccessfully attempted to review the search results. It was only then, at the end of this long line of events, that Attorney finally consulted an e-discovery expert and learned of the e-discovery problems facing Client. By this point, the potential prejudice facing Client was significant, and much of the damage already had been done.

At the least, Attorney risked breaching his duty of competence when he failed at the outset of the case to perform a timely e-discovery evaluation. Once Opposing Counsel insisted on the exchange of e-discovery, it became certain that e-discovery would be implicated, and the risk of a breach of the duty of competence grew considerably; this should have prompted Attorney to take additional steps to obtain competence, as contemplated under rule 3–110(C), such as consulting an e-discovery expert.

Had the e-discovery expert been consulted at the beginning, or at the latest once Attorney realized e-discovery would be required, the expert could have taken various steps to protect Client's interest, including possibly helping to structure the search differently, or drafting search terms less likely to turn over privileged and/or irrelevant but highly proprietary material. An expert also could have assisted Attorney in his duty to counsel Client of the significant risks in allowing a third party unsupervised direct access to Client's system due to the high risks and how to mitigate those risks. An expert also could have supervised the data collection by Vendor.

Whether Attorney's acts/omissions in this single case amount to a disciplinable offense under the "intentionally, recklessly, or repeatedly" standard of rule 3–110 is beyond this opinion, yet such a finding could be implicated by these facts. See, e.g., *In the Matter of Respondent G.* (Review Dept. 1992) 2 Cal. State Bar Ct. Rptr. 175, 179 (respondent did not perform competently where he was reminded on repeated occasions of inheritance taxes owed and repeatedly failed to advise his clients of them); *In re Matter of Copren* (Review Dept. 2005) 4 Cal. State Bar Ct. Rptr. 861, 864 (respondent did not perform competently when he failed to take several acts in single bankruptcy matter); *In re Matter of Layton* (Review Dept. 1993) 2 Cal. State Bar

Ct. Rptr. 366, 377–378 (respondent did not perform competently where he "recklessly" exceeded time to administer estate, failed to diligently sell/distribute real property, untimely settled supplemental accounting and did not notify beneficiaries of intentions not to sell/lease property).

B. Did Attorney Violate the Duty of Competence by Failing to Supervise?

The duty of competence in rule 3–110 includes the duty to supervise the work of subordinate attorneys and non-attorney employees or agents. See Discussion to rule 3–110. This duty to supervise can extend to outside vendors or contractors, and even to the client itself. See California State Bar Formal Opn. No. 2004–165 (duty to supervise outside contract lawyers); San Diego County Bar Association Formal Opn. No. 2012–1 (duty to supervise clients relating to ESI, citing *Cardenas v. Dorel Juvenile Group, Inc.* (D. Kan. 2006) 2006 WL 1537394).

Rule 3–110(C) permits an attorney to meet the duty of competence through association with another lawyer or consultation with an expert. See California State Bar Formal Opn. No. 2010–179. Such expert may be an outside vendor, a subordinate attorney, or even the client, if they possess the necessary expertise. This consultation or association, however, does not absolve an attorney's obligation to supervise the work of the expert under rule 3–110, which is a non-delegable duty belonging to the attorney who is counsel in the litigation, and who remains the one primarily answerable to the court. An attorney must maintain overall responsibility for the work of the expert he or she chooses, even if that expert is the client or someone employed by the client. The attorney must do so by remaining regularly engaged in the expert's work, by educating everyone involved in the e-discovery workup about the legal issues in the case, the factual matters impacting discovery, including witnesses and key evidentiary issues, the obligations around discovery imposed by the law or by the court, and of any relevant risks associated with the e-discovery tasks at hand. The attorney should issue appropriate instructions and guidance and, ultimately, conduct appropriate tests until satisfied that the attorney is meeting his ethical obligations prior to releasing ESI.

Here, relying on his familiarity with Client's IT department, Attorney assumed the department understood network searches better than he did. He gave them no further instructions other than to allow Vendor access on the date of the network search. He provided them with no information regarding how discovery works in litigation, differences between a party affiliated vendor and a neutral vendor, what could constitute waiver under the law, what case-specific issues were involved, or the applicable search terms. Client allowed Vendor direct access to its entire network, without the presence of any Client representative to observe or monitor Vendor's actions. Vendor retrieved proprietary trade secret and privileged information, a result Expert advised Attorney could have been prevented had a trained IT individual been involved from the outset. In addition, Attorney failed to warn Client of the potential significant legal effect of not suspending its routine document deletion protocol under its document retention program.

Here, as with Attorney's own actions/inactions, whether Attorney's reliance on Client was reasonable and sufficient to satisfy the duty to supervise in this setting is a question for a trier of fact. Again, however, a potential finding of a competence violation is implicated by the fact pattern. See, e.g., *Palomo v. State Bar* (1984) 36 Cal.3d 785, 796 [205 Cal.Rptr. 834] (evidence demonstrated lawyer's pervasive carelessness in failing to give the office manager any supervision, or instruction on trust account requirements and procedures).

[. . .]

Editor's Note: Discussion on Duty of Confidentiality

CONCLUSION

Electronic document creation and/or storage, and electronic communications, have become commonplace in modern life, and discovery of ESI is now a frequent part of almost any litigated matter. Attorneys who handle litigation may not ignore the requirements and obligations of electronic discovery. Depending on the factual circumstances, a lack of technological knowledge in handling e-discovery may render an attorney ethically incompetent to handle certain litigation matters involving e-discovery, absent curative assistance under rule 3–110(C), even where the attorney may otherwise be highly experienced. It also may result in violations of the duty of confidentiality, notwithstanding a lack of bad faith conduct.

This opinion is issued by the Standing Committee on Professional Responsibility and Conduct of the State Bar of California. It is advisory only. It is not binding upon the courts, the State Bar of California, its Board of Trustees, any persons, or tribunals charged with regulatory responsibilities, or any member of the State Bar.

Section 2.　Diligence

Model Rule 1.3: Diligence

A lawyer shall act with reasonable diligence and promptness in representing a client.

Deconstruction Exercise/Rule Rationale

As with MR 1.1, a simple rule without exceptions. The duties of diligence and promptness are modified by a single word: "reasonable." And, as with competence, an obligation not of super-hero effort but of an effort called for under the circumstances. If competence rests on the "snapshot "principle, then diligence rests upon the principle that "no harm does not mean no foul." A winning brief, by way of example, does not excuse exhausting all extensions and pulling three all nighters in order to file the brief timely. And, further, diligence is extremely important vis-a-vis the caseload that a lawyer takes on; the two are twisted together like a pretzel. A lawyer cannot exercise reasonable diligence and exhibit promptness if the lawyer's caseload is excessive. This principle in turn is tethered to the lesson at the book's start that lawyers are not public utilities required to take on all who seek our services.

Scenario No. 1: The Case of the Overextended Lawyer

A lawyer takes on a large number of personal injury cases on the defendant's side. She usually just takes a short deposition of the plaintiff on the basic facts of the case—who, what when, where and how—and does not conduct formal discovery. 99% of the cases settle. One day, the lawyer has booked two depositions at the same time and asks her paralegal—who is awaiting bar results—to depose one of the plaintiffs using this bare bones model. The paralegal does; the client is very happy with the work done; and the case settles for a small amount. The lawyer is still in violation of MR 1.3 because "no harm does not mean no foul." The lawyer should either not take on so many cases or have a staff of lawyers sufficient to handle the intake. Next time, the result could be unmitigated disaster, not unbridled success. Would the answer be different if, the week following the deposition, the law clerk received news of bar passage?

Scenario No. 2: The Case of the Lawyer Who Ran out of Extension Requests

A lawyer has a brief due at the court of appeals. He has a very busy schedule and conflicts with other client matters intrudes on completing the brief. He has asked for and been granted the court's limit of three extensions and suddenly realizes that the brief is due in two days. So, he uses legal stimulants to stay up for two days straight and write the brief. It is an excellent brief and the client's objectives per MR 1.2 are achieved on appeal. Nonetheless he has violated MR 1.3 because he placed himself—and more importantly the client—in a possible untenable situation in which the client's objectives were endangered. And if he has adhered to MR 1.4 and communicated the situation to the client, he caused worry and anxiety to the client. Perhaps the lawyer will not be as fortunate the next time.

Cases and Materials

X-Ray Questions (*Rollins*)

We continue with a technology frame with this case and the following "Beyond the Cite." Here, the court set a summary judgment deadline in a personal injury case of an employee injured while performing his job duties. The defense lawyer met the deadline and submitted the summary judgment filings electronically to both the court and to the plaintiff's lawyer.

But the plaintiff's lawyer's email system routed the email to a junk folder. Seeing no response from the plaintiff, the trail judge granted the summary judgment. It was then that the plaintiff's lawyer realized the mix up. Why did he believe that a summary judgment had not been filed? Did he not think it odd and follow up on his instinct that something might be amiss? He could have called counsel opposite to ask. What lessons do you draw from his mistake? Not that this slip up, if an outlier to his generally good conduct, might be a technical violation of the rule and thus might not warrant punishment from the bar. But would he still be liable for a malpractice claim? What duty would he have breached? How would the client prove damages?

Kevin Rollins v. Home Depot USA, Incorporated

United States Court of Appeals, Fifth Circuit, 2021.
8 F.4th 393.

JAMES C. HO, CIRCUIT JUDGE:

This is a cautionary tale for every attorney who litigates in the era of e-filing. Kevin Rollins brought suit against his employer for personal injury. The employer filed a motion for summary judgment on the eve of the parties' agreed deadline for dispositive motions. But Rollins's counsel never saw the electronic notification of that motion. That's because, by all accounts, his computer's email system placed that notification in a folder that he does not regularly monitor. Nor did he check the docket after the deadline for dispositive motions had elapsed.

As a result, Rollins did not file an opposition to the summary judgment motion. So the district court subsequently entered judgment against Rollins.

Rollins seeks relief from that judgment under Federal Rule of Civil Procedure 59(e). But our precedents make clear that no such relief is available under circumstances such as this. Accordingly, the district court did not abuse its discretion in denying relief under Rule 59(e).

On appeal, Rollins additionally argues that a fact dispute precludes summary judgment. But he never presented that argument to the district court—not even in his Rule 59(e) motion. Accordingly, he forfeited the argument.

For these reasons, we affirm.

I.

Rollins was injured while moving a bathtub for his employer, Home Depot. He then sued Home Depot in state court. The case was subsequently removed to federal court.

Counsel for Rollins agreed to receive filings through the district court's electronic-filing system via the email address he provided, as attorneys typically do in federal courts across the country. The parties later agreed to a scheduling order requiring that all dispositive motions be filed by May 11, 2020.

On May 7, Home Depot filed its motion for summary judgment. Rollins's counsel contends—and Home Depot does not dispute—that the notification for that filing "was inadvertently filtered into a part of Rollins' counsel's firm email system listed as 'other,' instead of the main email box where all prior filings in the case were received." As a result, counsel did not see the electronic notification of Home Depot's motion. Nor did counsel learn of that motion when he contacted Home Depot's counsel a few days later to discuss the possibility of a settlement.

The scheduling order imposed a 14-day deadline to file and serve responses to any motions. After that deadline came and went without any response from Rollins, the district court reviewed the pleadings, granted Home Depot's motion for summary judgment, and entered final judgment on May 27.

But Rollins's counsel did not know any of this until June 3. That's when counsel reached out to Home Depot's counsel again to raise the possibility of settlement. In response, Home Depot's counsel informed him that the district court had already entered final judgment.

Rollins filed a motion under Federal Rule of Civil Procedure 59(e) to alter or amend the court's judgment against him. The district court denied the motion. Rollins now appeals.

II.

Rule 59(e) states, in full, that "[a] motion to alter or amend a judgment must be filed no later than 28 days after the entry of the judgment." FED. R. CIV. P. 59(e). This is "an extraordinary remedy that should be used sparingly." *Templet v. HydroChem Inc.*, 367 F.3d 473, 479 (5th Cir. 2004). "We review the denial of a Rule 59(e) motion only for abuse of discretion." *Simon v. United States*, 891 F.2d 1154, 1159 (5th Cir. 1990).

The text of Rule 59(e) does not specify the available grounds for obtaining such relief. But our court has explained that Rule 59(e) motions "are for the narrow purpose of correcting manifest errors of law or fact or presenting newly discovered evidence"—not for raising arguments "which could, and should, have been made before the judgment issued." *Faciane v. Sun Life Assurance Co. of Canada*, 931 F.3d 412, 423 (5th Cir. 2019) (quotation omitted). We have further noted that Rule 59(e) allows a party to alter or amend a judgment when there has been an intervening change in the controlling law. *See Schiller v. Physicians Res. Grp., Inc.*, 342 F.3d 563, 567–68 (5th Cir. 2003). None of those conditions are met here.

Rollins contends that the district court abused its discretion when it denied his Rule 59(e) motion, on the ground that the only reason his counsel did not know about Home Depot's motion for summary judgment was due to a glitch in his email system.

This argument is squarely foreclosed under our precedent. In *Trevino v. City of Fort Worth*, the plaintiffs' counsel failed to file a response to the defendant's motion to dismiss because, among other reasons, "defective antivirus software diverted court emails to a spam folder." 944 F.3d 567, 570 (5th Cir. 2019) (per curiam). After the district court granted the defendant's unopposed motion to dismiss, the plaintiffs sought relief under Rule 59(e). ID. We rejected the argument, explaining that "[f]ailure to file a response to a motion to dismiss is not a manifest error of law or fact" under Rule 59(e). *Id.* at 571. SEE ALSO *Templet*, 367 F.3d at 478–79 (concluding that the district court did not err in denying Rule 59(e) relief when plaintiffs failed to file a response to defendants' motion for summary judgment).

To be sure, we do not question the good faith of Rollins's counsel. But it is not "manifest error to deny relief when failure to file was within [Rollins's] counsel's 'reasonable control.'" *Trevino*, 944 F.3d at 571. Notice of Home Depot's motion for summary judgment was sent to the email address that Rollins's counsel provided. Rule 5(b)(2)(E) provides for service "by filing [the pleading] with the court's electronic-filing system" and explains that "service is complete upon filing or sending." FED. R. CIV. P. 5(b)(2)(E). That rule was satisfied here. Rollins's counsel was plainly in the best position to ensure that his own email was working properly—certainly more so than either the district court or Home Depot. Moreover, Rollins's counsel could have checked the docket after the agreed deadline for dispositive motions had already passed. *See Trevino*, 944 F.3d at 571 (stressing that "Plaintiffs had a duty of diligence to inquire about the status of their case."); *Two-Way Media LLC v. AT&T, Inc.*, 782 F.3d 1311, 1317 (Fed. Cir. 2015) (no abuse of discretion where district court found it "inexcusable for . . . counsel to fail to read all of the underlying orders they received, or—at minimum—to monitor the docket for any corrections or additional rulings"); *Fox v. Am. Airlines, Inc.*, 389 F.3d 1291, 1294 (D.C. Cir. 2004) (describing counsel's argument that the electronic-filing system was to blame as "an updated version of the classic 'my dog ate my homework' line").

In sum, the district court did not abuse its discretion in denying the Rule 59(e) motion.

SOLUTIONS: THE LAWYER SHOULD HAVE, WOULD HAVE, COULD HAVE. . .

Technology is a double-edged sword for lawyers. Technology can make the practice of law both easy and difficult. The lesson to learn in the *Rollins* case is to not depend on technology too much. Counsel for Rollins agreed to receive filings through the district court's electronic-filing system via the email address he provided. Later he stated that he never saw the electronic notification of that motion and that he does not regularly monitor the junk folder. Here, Rollin's counsel did not exercise due diligence by routinely checking all email folders or contacting counsel opposite.

X-Ray Questions (*Key Strategy Email Sent to Party Opposite*)

The following excerpt involves a new and relatively youthful partner at a large New York City law firm. He made the tech-based mistake of sending a highly confidential strategy memo to the opposite side. Specifically, it was *sent* to an official of a union seeking to organize a large client of the firm, namely the *New York Times*. That union official is not an attorney bound by the Model Rules. But what if the recipient was counsel opposite? And what if it was you as a lawyer receiving the memo? We know what MR 4.4(b) says to do—notify counsel opposite as soon as possible of its receipt—but would you read the memo? What if you had a long term and good working relationship with counsel opposite? Does that change your answer? Does your duty to zealously represented your client, with its corollary duty of undivided loyalty, mandate that you read the memo? If you were the one who made this mistake would you tell your client? (We will cover mistakes and so informing clients shortly under MR 1.4.) Finally, this event covers MR 1.1, not just MR 1.3. Note that the Model Rules include a requirement to be competent with technology in Comment 8 to MR 1.1: "(Lawyers must) maintain the requisite knowledge and skill . . . a lawyer should keep abreast of changes in the law and its practice, including the benefits and risks associated with relevant technology. . ." This requirement refers not only to the complicated but also to the mundane.

BEYOND THE CITE

By: Jody Serrano, *New York Times Lawyer Mistakenly Sends Private Email on Hot to Deal with the Union to. . . the Union*, August 13, 2021.

Anyone who's sent a private and important email, to multiple recipients knows it can be complicated. You have to check the order of the recipients, cc assistants that remind the higher-ups to read and respond to said message, and, most importantly, make sure you don't send the email to someone you're not supposed to. I bet one New York Times Lawyer is currently wishing the Earth would swallow him for forgetting that last one.

Last week, *Times* outside counsel Michael Lebowich, a partner at a law firm Proskauer Rose, made the mistake of emailing a memo titled "Tech Organizing Unit Scope Decision Option" to two representatives of the union for the outlet's technology and product employees, according to the Daily Beast. The memo detailed options *Times* could take to deal with the proposed union, the New York Times Tech Guild, and limits its impact. The Guild claims that 70% of the workers have pledged to vote in support of the union.

The *Times* has refused to voluntarily recognize the Guild, which represents about 600 workers, and has opted for holding an election carried out by the National Labor Relations Board. Both sides are also fighting over which employees are eligible to vote, which with the paper seeking to restrict the election to software engineers. Union representatives say this would slash the potential bargaining unit by more than a third. The Daily Beast states that Lebowich sent an e-mail to several of his coworkers at Proskauer Rose and to Andrew Gutterman, Times senior vice president and deputy general counsel. In addition, he cc'ed Rachel Sanders, an organizer for the New York chapter of the NewsGuild, a union for the news media that represents the Times' tech and product employees.

Lebowich lays out three options for the Times in the email. One option involved allowing for a larger union—i.e., allowing more employees to participate in the vote which—the law firm argued could possibly allow the paper to defeat the union proposal in an election. A second option called for permitting a medium-sized union. Meanwhile, authorizing a smaller union would probably mean the efforts would succeed, but would be limited in its scope and size.

The times decided to go with the most aggressive option The Daily Beast reported this would potentially create a union with less than 400 members.

Angela Guo, an organization member for the New York Times Tech Guild, told the outlets that the email showed the Times was not holding an election to ensure all voices were represented. Its goal was to make the union as weak as possible, she maintained.

"That is not a natural stance, that is not indicated of wanting a free and fair election in which everyone's voices are heard," Gou said. "This is just additional proof they are being disingenuous with their intentions."

A Times spokesperson told the Daily Beast that the email contained a "range of options the company has and considers for each choice," also acknowledging that it was sent to the union representative by accident.

"We have continued to assess our position, and today, as part of the NLRB process, we submitted a legal filing in response to the Guild's petition that outlines which groups we think should be organized together in the same unit, as well as who we think is and is not eligible for the unit," the Time spokesperson said. "Our view is that each of our functions has vastly different responsibilities, performs different work, and has separate supervision. This does not preclude employees from forming other units."

Section 3. Communication

One of the most common complaints from clients about their lawyers is the lawyer's failure to communicate effectively. And, it might be said, one of the most common complaints from lawyers about their clients is also lack of communication. On the lawyer's side, two core problems are likely to blame. A big part of the problem may simply be lawyers not being diligent, or being overwhelmed with high pressure work, leading client calls to be routinely delayed. Another problem is that lawyers often forget that even when decisions are entrusted to attorneys, consultation with clients is still required. On the client side, it is normal for people going through a legal process to be anxious about it, and to have unrealistic expectations about how long a legal process will take. This can lead to frequent calls from clients asking for updates during periods when a case is dormant.

How to avoid this problem? Some good law firms and legal aid providers try to overcome these problems by adopting strong office policies and practices. For instance, a firm can require that all client calls be returned within 48 hours. Some firms also systematically make contact every quarter with all clients with open matters, or at least every six months, even if nothing has changed in the case. Finally, it is often helpful to leave clear notes in client files indicating what message can be delivered to an anxious client if she calls, allowing the message to be delivered by a receptionist when the lawyer is not available. But since not everyone follows best practices, there is also a rule. Take note that the onus is upon the lawyer, not upon the client, to ensure efforts be made for effective communication. Again, a burden allocated to the lawyer as an undergirding principle of the rules. Note though that the burden is on the lawyer to reach out, not the client.

Model Rule 1.4: Communication

(a)   A lawyer shall:

(1)   Promptly inform the client of any decision or circumstance with respect to which the client's informed consent, as defined in Rule 1.0(e), is required by these Rules;

(2)   Reasonably consult with the client about the means by which the client's objectives are to be accomplished;

(3)   Keep the client reasonably informed about the status of the matter;

(4)   Promptly comply with reasonable requests for information; and

(5)   Consult with the client about any relevant limitation on the lawyer's conduct when the lawyer knows that the client expects assistance not permitted by the Rules of Professional Conduct or other law.

(b)   A lawyer shall explain a matter to the extent reasonably necessary to permit the client to make informed decisions regarding the representation.

Deconstruction Exercise/Rule Rationale

Notice the adverbs in (1) and (4): "promptly" and (2) "reasonably." How do they modify the communication duties? What other words could have been used? What message is being sent to lawyers and to clients? Notice as well in (5) the use of the verb "consult." Where have we seen this verb used previously in the Model Rules? Why is it being used here?

Instead of "promptly "the drafters could have used "immediately" or "as soon as possible." Yet they settled upon "promptly" meaning with "little or no delay "as a middle path to deliver a more nuanced message to lawyers. And "reasonably" resurfaces as a utility player of sorts making the lawyer's burden proportionate to the duty undertaken.

The duty of communication thus requires the lawyer to explain matters and give sufficient information so the client can intelligently make a decision about his or her case and set objectives as envisioned by MR 1.2. In some cases, a lawyer may withhold information from the client in circumstances where delaying the transmission of information is justified when the client would likely react imprudently to an immediate communication. Overall, the duty of communication is the glue that binds together the ACR.

Note, too, subsection (3) on reasonably keeping the client informed about the status of the matter. This provision seems innocuous enough. Does it deal with the lawyer telling the client of trial dates, or scheduling conflicts, or mediation dates? Yet there is an important "but" that follows. What if the lawyer commits malpractice? Does the language of the Rule cover that circumstance? As we will explore further in Section 4, a lawyer must inform a client of material mistakes and this duty naturally includes those mistakes that could result in a malpractice claim. The self-reporting obligation is embodied in the Restatement (Third) of the Law Governing Lawyers, Section 20 Cmt c: "If the lawyer's conduct of the matter gives the client a substantial malpractice claim against the lawyer, the lawyer must disclose that to the client." We will discuss this hard conversation later in this section.

A. Cross Cultural Communication

As stated at the start of this book in "Why Study Professional Responsibility?" we now live in a multiracial and multicultural country. The numbers from the Census do not have an agenda. You will practice law in this environment and experience Professional Responsibility in this context.

The concept of cross-cultural communication is often overlooked in law school. We are so focused on graduating law school and passing the bar exam, that we neglect the importance of understanding and appreciating the people we serve.

Lawyers are known to be great speakers and skilled at negotiating with opposing counsel. But some lawyers do not have cultural competency and understanding when interacting with clients. This lead to misunderstanding and miscommunication in the attorney-client relationship.

According to Canadian lawyer, Jatrine Bentsi-Enchill in her important article, *Client Communication: Measuring Your Cross-Cultural Competence*, Canadian Bar Journal. September 29, 2014:

> Effective cross-cultural communication is the ability to communicate with individuals from other cultures in a way that minimizes conflict, promotes greater understanding and maximized your ability to establish trust and rapport. . . . It requires lawyers to learn how to properly interpret nonverbal and verbal cues.

For lawyers, gaining an awareness of cultural differences can improve business development, staff retention, client service and most importantly, lawyer-client relationships.

To improve cross-cultural communication, keep in mind the following:

- *Accept and adapt to cultural differences.* Before meeting with your client, do some research on their culture. Be aware and accept the cultural differences. Be patient when speaking with your client. Most importantly, adapt to cultural differences, and your client will appreciate you. But at the same time, do not make assumptions. All cultural groups are internally diverse. Be curious, not judgmental.

- *Be open-minded.* Be flexible and opened-minded when communicating with clients. Avoid being judgmental because this will help client open up and explain their motivation in the matter. If you don't understand something, ask questions to clear any misunderstanding. Be mindful that there will be errors and mistakes. Understand that your client is an individual. Be ready to listen and learn.

- *Pay attention.* Focus on the client's story and allow her to talk. Be a good listener. Most attorneys have a problem with talking too much and not allowing their client to speak. And the lawyer's motivation is often admirable: to appear helpful, show concern, act empathetically. But these manifestations can be seen as not truly listening to the client's concerns. Pay attention to her body language and look for verbal and nonverbal cues. For example, in some countries, it is a sign of respect to nor give direct eye contact when speaking with someone. And, at the same time, such traditions have faded, or are more evident with some people than others.

- *Be patient.* Keep on practicing the skill of cross-cultural communication. Patience is key, it will take time and a lot of practice to get used to all this. When interacting with client, confirm and repeat the matter just so both parties can have a better understanding. Patience means being a good listener so you can understand your client. Often, clients feel unheard. Speak slowly and ask clients if they have any questions.

Let's further explore this area. What follows are two articles on being an effective cross-cultural communicator in your role as a lawyer. The book then discusses how you will experience prospective clients and clients who present such communication challenges and how to handle ethically these challenges when they arise.

X-Ray Questions

Do you accept the value of cross-cultural communication or do you believe that this is a fad or a politicly correct stance with little practical value? Reflect upon your life: Have you experienced these issues in your personal or professional life? The following article provides insight into how to work through these communication issues in your practice. Perhaps you are familiar with the famous stages of grief pioneered by Elizabeth Kubler-Ross What follows is a take on the stages of acceptance as to the value of cross-cultural communication. What are the stages? Have you seen them, either as the one trying to communicate or as the one being the object of the communication?

Which of the stages do you think you might have difficulty navigating and why? Do you agree with the definition of cross-culture competence?

BEYOND THE CITE

By: **Travis Adams,** *Cultural Competency: A Necessary Skill for the 21st Century Attorney,* 4 **WILLIAM MITCHELL LAW RAZA JOURNAL** 2 (2012– 2013).

I. INTRODUCTION

An effective lawyer must possess skills for cross-cultural engagement by developing cultural competency. Cultural competency, like other legal skills, requires a disciplined approach to viewing the world from different perspectives. When beginning law school, many first-year law students are challenged to let go of the belief that "there is one right answer" to legal problems. Law students are typically high achievers, accustomed to good grades, correct answers, and getting problems "right." After countless hours of studying and later being corrected in lecture halls by law professors, eventually most law students succumb to their training and stop seeing the law like an algebraic equation and instead consider legal problems from different perspectives. Legal professors facilitate this by playing "devil's advocate", asking students to argue the side they disagree with, and changing fact patterns on the spot in order to increase the complexity of a legal situation. Whether Torts, Property, Contracts, Criminal, Legal Writing or Constitutional Law, students are taught how to analyze and argue the law from different perspectives.

Arguing the law from different perspectives is an essential aspect of advocacy and part of our responsibility to zealously advocate for our clients. Effective advocacy involves more than a mastery of the law but also a deep understanding of the client and the facts surrounding the legal matter. In a tort case for negligence, a plaintiff's attorney will tell the story of a plaintiff who was careful, vulnerable, responsible, and victimized. Using the same facts, the defense will characterize the plaintiff as clumsy, reckless, greedy, and opportunistic. A skilled attorney can tell the most compelling story using the substantive law within the rules of evidence and procedure.

Advocacy requires an ability to see different perspectives because it is by nature a cross-cultural experience. Culture is the summation of an individual's ethnicity, race, gender, nationality, age, economic status, social status, language, sexual orientation, physical attributes, marital status, and a variety of other characteristics. The law is its own culture with values, attitudes, and norms of behavior. Any law student who has tried to communicate to friends and family "how class was today" understands this cross-cultural exercise. The world of proximate cause, appellate briefs, reasonableness standards, and motion hearings create a context for a law student that is unfamiliar to the outside world. For this reason, awareness, knowledge and skills involving how to navigate cultural difference are essential to the practice of law, even when the client and the attorney come from similar social locations and cultural groups. However, when an attorney and his or her client come from different cultural groups, effective advocacy utterly depends on cultural competency. As one scholar puts it, "to be effective in another culture, people must be interested in other cultures, be sensitive enough to notice cultural differences, and then also be willing to modify their behavior as an indication of respect for the people of other cultures."

This paper argues that cultural competency is an essential skillset for the 21st century attorney who seeks to deliver effective advocacy and serve justice. This paper begins by defining cultural competency and applies the definitions to the work of a lawyer. Arising from foundations of good anthropological and ethnographic practice, molded in professional standards of medicine, mental health, social work, and law, cultural competency demands self-awareness, immersion, repeated revision, open-mindedness, resistance to stereotyping, and attention to detail. This paper uses Milton Bennet's Intercultural Development Continuum (IDI) as a way to discuss and measure cultural competency. The IDI, an assessment tool used to survey individuals in order to measure their ability to engage in and recognize cultural differences, is a widely respected approach to cultural competency. While no tool is perfect or all encompassing, this paper's goal is to use a tool already accepted by a broad base of institutions in education, business, social services and other fields as a safe place to begin the conversation. By connecting the fields of cultural competency and lawyering, I argue that there is a growing need for training law students to be culturally competent.

Next, this paper will explore four central reasons for why cultural competency is essential to the 21st century attorney. First, we will look at the social and economic realities that continually make the legal world more multicultural and globalized than ever before. Second, this paper explores the tendency of individuals and groups to prefer homogenous spaces and favor that which is similar to them. Third, this paper will explore the prevalence of cultural competency in other disciplines to demonstrate how the legal world is falling behind in this area when compared to similar professions such as social work, education and medicine. Lastly, this paper will discuss the areas of the profession best served by cultural competent advocacy.

An analysis of cultural competency would not be complete without the recognition and serious consideration of the author's social location and context. Such cultural self-awareness is considered in social science to be the key to multicultural competence, especially for an attorney, because an attorney's awareness of his or her own culture allows for a more accurate understanding of cultural forces that affect him or her as a lawyer, his or her client, and the interaction of the two. I am a 26-year-old, white, heterosexual male from a middle class background. I am approaching my final year of law school and the majority of my legal training has occurred in the criminal and child protection realm. Only in the last five years have I been trained in cultural competency. I am grateful and indebted to have mentors and teachers who are culturally diverse to help me along in this journey. Without their mentorship, this paper, which marks an early checkpoint in a long journey of discovery, would not be possible.

II. WHAT IS CULTURAL COMPETENCY?

A wide range of academic and professional fields have studied cultural competency. As a result, the concept has generated different definitions and tools for measurement. Cultural competency tools use generalized benchmarks that signify an individual's competency development stage. Culture and personal development can seem like hard to pinpoint, lofty terms. The measurement tools discussed in this section will allow us to explore cultural competency and the law with a set of consistent terms and measurements.

Cultural competency is the ability to accurately understand and adapt behavior to cultural difference and commonality. A cultural competency tool, places individuals on a continuum that identifies their cultural competency ranging from a monocultural mindset on one end to an intercultural or global mindset on the other. The Development Model of Intercultural Sensitivity (DMIS) uses "stages" in order to explain patterns that emerge from systematic observations. The most important theoretical concept for cultural competency is that all experience is constructed. For instance, a middle aged lawyer walking down the street who witnesses a man rob another man at gunpoint will experience that event differently than a young child. Similarly, a European American person who happens to be in the vicinity of a Hmong New Year celebration may not have anything like the same experience a Hmong person has at the same event; assuming that the European American has no "Hmong" categories in her brain to construct that experience. As a result, the European American will likely create a meaning for the Hmong New Year event using one's own cultural experience.

It is important to keep in mind that cultural knowledge is not the same as cultural competence. An American Christian may have a broad knowledge of the religious practices of an Indian Hindi but will still experience and relate to every aspect of an Indian Hindi through the cultural lens of an American Christian. The brain typically fits every experience into a familiar category. The less developed a person's cultural competency level the fewer categories available to categorize and the more details of culture ignored or overgeneralized. It is much like a search function on a computer. Each time we have a new experience something in our brain goes back in time and searches through our life history. When our brain finds a file that is similar to the new experience it associates the new experience with the closest corresponding file. Then we react to the new experience accordingly.

We interact with other disciplines much the same way. Before a student enters law school he or she may read a legal case and the only "file" the student's brain uses is "law". However, after three years of law school the same student will read that same case law and create much more specific categories by which to file that case in her brain. What she once saw as just "law" will now be seen as "a Supreme Court case," "a Justice Stevens decision," "constitutional law," "First Amendment issue," "free speech," "time place manner restriction." When trained, the brain will categorize law, with greater particularity and appreciation for the distinct differences that exist within each legal situation. With respect to cultural differences, as one becomes more interculturally competent, nuances in communication style, gender roles, conflict style, perceptions of authority, ethics, and other aspects of culture become more evident. Sometimes it seems incredible "how deep the rabbit hole goes."

Like the person with very few cultural "categories," an ethnocentric mindset makes sense of cultural differences and commonalities based on one's own cultural values and practices. A person with this mindset would allow his or her stereotypes to make broad inferences about the situations he encounters and would have less complex perceptions and experiences of cultural difference and commonality. He or she may be able to recognize cultural differences such as food and clothing but may not notice deeper cultural differences such as conflict styles or relationship statuses.

On the other end of the spectrum, an ethnorelative mindset makes sense of cultural differences and commonalities based on one's own and other cultures' values and practices. This person does not make broad stereotypes but would notice cultural patterns in order to recognize cultural difference. A truly ethnorelative mindset allows one to express their alternative cultural experience in culturally appropriate feelings and behavior. These abilities make people much more likely to engage in, rather than to avoid, cultural difference.

In the legal setting, a person with a monocultural mindset would likely struggle interviewing a client who perceives time differently. For instance, a witness may not be accustomed to orienting a story based on hours, days, months, or years. If the lawyer comes from a culture where stories are told in a linear time-related manner, the monocultural mindset lawyer may perceive the client's failure to provide certain information as uncooperative, unintelligent, or untruthful. A person with an intercultural mindset would be quicker to recognize how a client's cultural difference may impact the client's storytelling. A cultural competent lawyer sees organizing and assessing facts as a cultural difference and not a deficit in character or intelligence.

(In learning to communicate cross culture) the first stage is Denial, one's own culture is experienced as the only real one and other cultures are ignored or vaguely identified. A Denial lawyer may avoid focusing on aspects of the client's story that feature cultural difference or perhaps completely avoid working in fields of law or geographic areas with culturally different people. The Denial lawyer may see culture in very simple categories such as "race" or "deserving or undeserving" of economic inequity. However, as the client's situation becomes more complex and dynamic, thus falling outside of the superficial categories created by the Denial lawyer, the lawyer may begin to ignore or avoid facts that fall outside of the client's experience. There is literally no field of law where ignoring cultural details would not impair an attorney's practice.

In the next stage, Defense, other cultures are recognized yet viewed negatively and the person's own culture is perceived as being the only one that is "normal." Recently, feminist and black liberation theorists have used the term "cultural imperialism" to describe this practice of normalizing one's own cultural expressions while viewing cultural differences in others as lacking and negative. In this way, a Defense prosecutor may have biases against people from a minority cultural group. These biases could cause the prosecutor not to trust people from this cultural group as much and seek more strenuous penalties for crimes than the prosecutor would seek for people of the prosecutor's own cultural group. Unfortunately, it is very common among prosecutors to take advantage of the fact that so many people in our society are in the Defense DMIS stage. In one gang-related criminal case in Minnesota involving an African American defendant, African-American defense witnesses, and an all white jury, the prosecution had accentuated its gang theory by arguing to the jury "[T]he people that are involved in this [defendant's] world are not people from your world . . . these are the defendant's people.

Defense orientations oftentimes occur much more subtly and less overtly prejudiced. Imagine a Defense attorney must represent her client in a business contract negotiation with another foreign business whose native culture features significantly different communication or negotiation habits from the attorney's cultural background. The foreign business representative does not exhibit behavior that the Defense attorney associates with politeness or friendliness even though this is exactly what the foreign business representative understands to be polite in his own cultural mindset. A Defense attorney would be at risk of labeling the foreign business representative as "uncivilized" or "less developed" rather than using a culturally different relational style. Even worse, the attorney could likely misinterpret the foreign business as unwilling to negotiate or untrustworthy in character. This could have a negative impact on the client.

Next, individuals in Minimization, tend to emphasize similarity and the cross-cultural applicability of economic, political, philosophical, or even behavioral traits. A person in Minimization may recognize superficial cultural realities such as food, language, or clothing but still utilizes one's own cultural patterns as central to an assumed universal reality. Using the business negotiation example from before, a Minimization lawyer may overestimate their appreciation for the home culture of the foreign business and be relatively tolerant. However, because the Minimization lawyer does not see her own culture clearly, if the negotiation goes poorly and conflict arises, the Minimization lawyer will still judge the other business's use of a different conflict resolution style as "lacking" or a poor choice. This is because the Minimization lawyer still sees the world through an ethnocentric lens and fails to see deeper cultural differences such as philosophy, ideology, and, in this case, conflict style. Lawyers involved in cross-cultural depositions, client interviews, or cross-examinations are likely to cause communicative misunderstandings if they view or treat people from different cultures as being "generally more similar to themselves than dissimilar."

Acceptance marks the DMIS stage where an individual takes a more globalized or ethnorelative perspective and one's own culture is experienced as just one of a number of equally complex worldviews. In her article on the "Five Habits of Culturally Competent Professionals" scholar Kimberly Barrett recommends taking time to review the major influences and processes in one's socialization—the role that family, friends, media, and the broader socio-historical, cultural environment have played in influencing one's views of groups other than one's own. Similarly, an *Acceptance* attorney working in a child protection setting for the first time and having his first client interview with a family would likely ask very different questions than an attorney in an ethnocentric DMIS stage would ask. The *Acceptance* attorney would be aware of how his own cultural context has informed his assumptions about a family unit. As a result, the attorney would assume less about the family norms and ask questions that demonstrate a broader and more complex understanding of how families can form themselves. The Acceptance attorney will have significant advantages in communication as well. Instead of viewing the whole world through the prism of American cultural archetypes, the Acceptance attorney will remember that more than one meaning may exist for verbal and nonverbal messages communicated between people from different cultures.

Unlike the *Denial* or *Defensive* attorney, the *Acceptance* attorney will be able to understand the difference between himself and the family he is interviewing while seeing them as equally human. However, this does not mean the *Acceptance* attorney must lose all sense of ethics because "everything is relative." Instead, by truly accepting the relativity of values within cultural context, and experiencing the world as organized by different values, the *Acceptance* attorney is able to maintain an ethical commitment in the face of cultural relativity. Cultural relativity does not mean ethical relativity, and an *Acceptance* attorney in the child protection scenario would be able to distinguish between how one's personal ethical commitment to protecting children and the cultural relativity of parenting styles.

A person in the last DMIS stage of cultural competency, *Adaptation*, can empathize with other cultures to the extent that he or she yields culturally appropriate perceptions and behaviors. Further, in *Adaptation*, a person retains his own cultural identity without assimilating to another culture. People in *Adaptation* have the acute ability to recognize patterns of cultural behavior, enabling allow them to define themselves broadly. Milton illustrated this when he described someone in *Adaptation* as having a, "German critical, Japanese indirect, Italian ironic, African American personal in addition to a primary European Male explicit style." To the extent that each behavior emerged from a real connection to the various cultures, they would all be authentically you. Another excellent example comes from Christine Zuni Cruz, a self-proclaimed "community lawyer" within Indigenous communities. She describes how she moves in and out of cultural behaviors as an attorney,

> "The three voices I speak in: native, lawyer, and clinician provide different perspectives. As native, I speak as a native person living within my native community; as lawyer, I speak from my experience in working within the community; as clinician, I speak combining the above voices, seeking to improve the lawyering done in the name of, on behalf of, for, and with native peoples and native nations. These voices inform my discussion of community and culture. The basis of my ideas stem from my experience of being part of a distinct native community, long served by lawyers and a profession external to the community. My perspective on community comes from my work within my own pueblo, and within other pueblos both as a lawyer and a judge. My perspective on culture is closely related to community, but it is also informed by the work I engaged in over several years to revise the New Mexico Children's code to provide greater cultural protection for native children and youth."

Cruz is aware of the different cultural contexts she moves in and out of and does not place a value judgment on one community over another based upon cultural behaviors. Further, Cruz has an appreciation for how her different cultural experiences have shaped her. The awareness of one's own cultural identity is essential for moving into the ethnorelative orientations of the DMIS.

The *Adaptation* attorney is best suited for the work of a lawyer because she can function as a "cultural chameleon": recognizing cultural differences and quickly picking up on acceptable and/or advantageous behaviors. The Adaptation attorney has the capacity to better communicate within the typical cross-cultural attorney-client relationship because she can put herself "in the client's shoes". Furthermore, the Adaptation attorney has a greater capacity to practice various legal disciplines and recognize the nuances in each field and cooperate with a variety of judges in each unique courtroom environment. He or she will more quickly observe and adapt to patterns of all kinds, something all lawyers seek to do. While all of these benefits exist within a relatively homogenous cultural world, the Adaptation attorney's greatest strengths and societal impact will be the result of the attorney's ability to work with a diverse range of clients and be able to perform zealous advocacy on their behalf.

Cultural competency is especially essential during depositions, a time where the *Adaptation* attorney's skills are put to the test. Nina Ivanichvili is CEO of www.LanguageAlliance.com, a firm specializing in legal translation and interpretation in over 80 languages. She designed a CLE called "A Lawyer's Guide to Cross-Cultural Depositions" in which she describes scenarios that test a lawyer's ability to recognize cultural difference. In one scenario, Ivanichvili describes an American attorney deposing a well-dressed, middle-aged, non-English-speaking woman in a civil lawsuit where the attorney is trying to establish the cost of the woman's clothing. The woman has had several jobs, is wearing decent clothing, and is middle aged. These attributes could lead the attorney to assume similarities between the woman and her American counterparts with regards to the woman's independence— financially or otherwise—from her husband. However, this woman is originally from a small, male-dominated village and does not know what her articles of clothing cost because her husband makes all the purchasing decisions in the family. The Adaptation attorney would be slower to make assumptions of cultural similarity. The Adaptation attorney would instead ask questions like, "Who handles the money in your household?" or "Who in your family purchases clothes?" Furthermore, the attorney would pick up on social cues and communication patterns such as responsiveness, silence, and social taboos in order to make the otherwise potentially timid deposed woman more comfortable and honest.

In the same way a law student receives training to recognize the difference between a tort law fact pattern and a contract law fact pattern, so too must a lawyer learn to identify cultural differences. The DMIS continuum assumes that contact with cultural difference generates pressure on an individual to change one's worldview. If an attorney worked at a firm where successful attorneys consistently used different approaches, it would become increasingly difficult for her to believe in only one system for drafting motions. Similarly, the more we understand how many different ways there are to live, the less ethnocentric our worldview becomes. Attorneys better serve their clients' interests by understanding culturally learned differences, recognizing commonalities between themselves and others, and acting on their insight in culturally and legally appropriate ways. impacts the legal profession.

X-Ray Questions

The following is a short excerpt from one of the first lawyers to explore competence in cross cultural communication in legal practice. It complements the foundation laid for you in the previous excerpt. Professor Bryant makes the important point that cross cultural competence is *not* replacing one stereotype with a more positive one; in other words, it is not embracing the idea that all Asians are studious or that all Hispanics/Latinos are family oriented or that all South Asians are hardworking entrepreneurs. She uses two examples—one involving credibility and the other the differences between individualistic and communitarian cultures, and reflects how those differences impact the practice of law. Do you agree with her views?

BEYOND THE CITE

By: Susan Bryant, *The Five Habits: Building Cross-Culture Competence in Lawyers,* 8 CUNY CLINICAL LAW REVIEW 33 (2001).

I. TEACHING SKILLS OF CROSS-CULTURAL LAWYERING As AN IMPORTANT PART OF TEACHING GOOD LAWYERING

For many years, companies choosing employees for overseas work and schools selecting students for overseas study gave personality tests to explore who would make good travelers, adjust more readily to cross-cultural encounters and respond appropriately in culturally sensitive ways. Generally, people who were flexible, less judgmental and more reflective were viewed as having the right personality to work in cross-cultural environments. This notion that success is dependent on personality has been replaced by the idea that cross-cultural competence is a skill that can be taught. As with learning of most skills, there are those who seem to have some natural talent and others who, as a result of experience, have developed special insights into cross-cultural work. However, everyone has the capacity to become more proficient at cross-cultural interaction and communication skills.

Almost all professions and businesses now recognize the importance of building cross-cultural skills. The United States is increasingly a multi-cultural country with a greater understanding that the "melting pot" did not happen. Materials have been developed and courses offered for training teachers, doctors, social workers, psychologists and psychiatrists about cross-cultural issues in their professions. As our world becomes more interactive, lawyers and clients inevitably will interact with those who are culturally different. Those whom we assume to be just like us may turn out not to be in some important ways while those whom we assume to be different may, in fact, not be so different.

As our profession becomes increasingly diverse, the tensions created by difference offer great potential for creative change. These same tensions, however, could result in negative judgments and misunderstanding. By teaching students how to recognize the influence of culture in their work and to understand, if not accept, the viewpoint of others, we provide students with skills that are necessary to communicate and work positively with future clients and colleagues.

To become good cross-cultural lawyers, students must first become aware of the significance of culture on themselves. Culture is like the air we breathe—it is largely invisible and yet we are dependent on it for our very being. Culture is the logic by which we give order to the world. Culture gives us our values, attitudes and norms of behavior. We are constantly attaching culturally-based meaning to what we see and hear, often without being aware that we are doing so. Through our invisible cultural lens, we judge people to be truthful, rude, intelligent or superstitious based on the attributions we make about the meaning of their behavior.

By teaching students cross-cultural lawyering skills and perspectives, we make the invisible more visible and thus help students understand the reactions that they and the legal system may have towards clients and that clients may have towards them. When two people (such as two student co-counsels or a student and a clinical teacher) working on the same case differ, we have the opportunity to explore why we are giving different meaning to the same behavior and words. By teaching the students about the influence of culture on their practice of law, we give them a framework for analyzing the changes that have resulted in their thinking and values as a result of their legal education. The law, as well as the legal system within which it operates, is a culture with strong professional norms that gives meaning to and reinforces behavior. How legal education influences the choices that students do or do not see is an important part of the cross-cultural analysis.

Cross-cultural lawyering occurs when lawyers and clients have different ethnic or cultural heritages and when they are socialized by different subsets within ethnic groups. By this definition, everyone is multi-cultural to some degree. Cultural groups and cultural norms can be based on ethnicity, race, gender, nationality, age, economic status, social status, language, sexual orientation, physical characteristics, marital status, role in family, birth order, immigration status, religion, accent, skin color or a variety of other characteristics.

In teaching about the importance of culture to lawyering, we want to avoid reinforcing stereotypes. By using a broad definition of culture, we hope to teach students that no single characteristic will completely define the lawyer's or client's' culture. For example, if we think about birth order alone as a cultural characteristic, we may not see any significance to this factor. Yet, if the client (or lawyer) comes from a society where "oldest son" has special meaning in terms of responsibility and privilege, identification of the ethnicity, gender or birth order alone will not be enough to alert the lawyer to the set of norms and expectations for how the "oldest son" is expected to behave. Instead, the lawyer needs to appreciate the significance of the combination of ethnicity, birth order, and gender to fully understand this aspect of the client's culture. A woman from the same culture may understand these responsibilities and privileges better than an outsider and yet, because her experiences are different, still may not fully understand.

A broad definition of culture recognizes that no two people can have exactly the same experiences and thus no two people will interpret or predict in precisely the same ways. Culture is enough of an abstraction that people can be part of the same culture, yet make different decisions in the particular. People can also reject norms and values from their culture. As we recognize these individual differences, we also know that sharing a common cultural heritage with a client tends to improve our predictions and interpretations and to reduce the likelihood of misunderstandings.

When lawyers and clients come from different cultures, several aspects of the attorney-client interaction may be implicated. The capacity to form trusting relationships, to evaluate credibility, to develop client-centered case strategies and solutions, to gather information and to attribute the intended meaning from behavior and expressions are all affected by cultural experiences. By using the framework of cross-cultural interaction, students can learn how to anticipate and name some of the difficulties they or their clients may be experiencing. By asking students as part of the cross-cultural analysis to identify ways in which they are similar to clients, we identify the strengths of connection. We also alert students who see themselves as "the same" as the client to be mindful of differences so that they do not substitute their own judgment for the client's as a result of over-identification or transference.

Lawyers and clients who do not share the same culture face special challenges in developing a trusting relationship in which genuine and accurate communication can occur. By teaching students concepts like "insider" and "outsider" status, we educate students as to why some lawyers and clients may experience great difficulties in building a relationship in which advice is accepted and information is exchanged freely. When the client's culture fosters a significant distrust of outsiders or of the lawyer's particular culture, the lawyer must work especially hard to earn trust in a culturally sensitive way. By teaching the concept of "insider" and "outsider" status, before students form a view of clients as "holding back," "lying," or "being unhelpful," we allow students to have a more nuanced hypothesis about what is occurring in these relationships.

Even in situations in which trust is established, students may experience cultural differences that significantly interfere with lawyers' and clients' capacities to understand one another's goals, behaviors and communications. Cultural differences often cause us to attribute different meaning to the same set of facts. One important goal of cross-cultural training is to help students make isomorphic attributions, i.e., to attribute to behavior and communication that which is intended by the actor or speaker. Students who are taught about the potential for misattribution can develop strategies for checking themselves and their interpretations.

Inaccurate attributions can cause lawyers to make significant errors in their representation of clients. Imagine a lawyer saying to a client, "If there is anything that you do not understand, please just ask me to explain" or "If I am not being clear, please just ask me any questions." The lawyer might assume that a client who does not then ask for clarification surely understands what the lawyer is saying. However, many cultural differences may explain a client's reluctance to either blame the lawyer for poor communication (the second question) or blame himself or herself for lack of understanding (the first question). Indeed, clients from some cultures might find one or the other of these results to be rude and, therefore, will feel reluctant to ask for clarification for fear of offending the lawyer or embarrassing himself.

Cultural differences may also cause lawyers and clients to misperceive body language and judge each other incorrectly. For an everyday example, take nodding while someone is speaking. In some cultures, this gesture indicates agreement with the speaker; in others, however, it simply indicates that the listener is hearing the speaker. Another common example involves eye contact. In some cultures, looking someone straight in the eye is a statement of open and honest communication while a diversion of eyes signals dishonesty. In other cultures, however, a diversion of eyes is a sign of respect. Students need to recognize these differences and plan for a representation strategy that takes them into account.

More generally, students need to be taught that concepts of credibility are very culturally determined. In examining the credibility of a story, lawyers and judges often ask whether the story makes "sense" as if "sense" were neutral. Consider, for example, a client who explains that the reason that she left her native country was that God appeared to her in a dream and told her it was time to leave. If the time of departure is critical to the credibility of her story, how will the fact-finder evaluate the client's credibility? Does the fact-finder come from a culture where dreams are valued, where an interventionist God is expected, or where major life decisions would be based on these expectations or values? Will the fact-finder, as a result of differences, find the story incredible or indicative of a disturbed thought process or, alternatively, as a result of similarities, find the client credible?

Categorization differences may cause lawyers and clients to view different information as relevant. Students who describe clients as "wandering all over the place" may be working with clients who categorize information differently than the students or the legal system. Lawyers and clients who have different time and space orientations may have difficulty understanding and believing each other. If a lawyer whose culture is oriented to hour, day, month, and year tries to get a time-line from a client whose culture is not oriented that way, she may incorrectly interpret the client's failure to provide the information as uncooperative, lacking intelligence, or, worse, lying. Clients who are unable to tell a linear time-related story may also experience the same reaction from judges and juries if the client's culture is unknown to the fact finders.

In other settings, the distinction between individual and collective cultures has been called the most important concept to grasp in cross-cultural encounters. Understanding this distinction and the differences that flow from it are also critically important for lawyers to understand. Teaching students to recognize some of the differences between individual and collective cultures will help them see how clients and lawyers define problems, identify solutions, and determine who are important players in a decision. For example, in analyzing the scenario described at the beginning of this article, students have very different interpretations as to why the brother might be there, based in part on whether the student sees the brother and sister as a unit or as separate individuals, one of whom has a legal problem. This assessment is very much related to the student's culture and family experience.

Students who explore differences in individual and collective cultures may come to appreciate different communication styles, values and views of the roles of the lawyer and client. In an individualistic culture, people are socialized to have individual goals and are praised for achieving these goals. They are encouraged to make their own plans and "do their own thing." Individualists need to assert themselves and do not find competition threatening. By contrast, in a collective culture, people are socialized to think in terms of the group, to work for the betterment of the group, and to integrate individual and group goals. Collectivists use group membership to predict behavior. Because collectivists are accepted for who they are and accordingly feel less need to talk, silence plays a more important role in their communication style.

Majority culture in the United States has been identified as the most individualistic culture in the world. Our legal culture reflects this commitment to individualism. For example, ethical rules of confidentiality and conflict of interests often require a lawyer to communicate with an individual client in private and may prohibit the lawyer from representing the group or taking group concerns into account. In addition, the Anglo-American legal system creates substantive laws that reflect a highly individualistic model of rights and responsibilities. Students trained under this system need to be alert to potential conflicts that may arise between a client's culture and the legal strategy designed for an adversarial, individualistic system. Students who understand this are better able to address the problems it creates for those clients who come from or embrace a more collective culture. Students who come from more collectivist cultures may themselves experience some of the cultural dissonance that such clients face.

Here is an example of how a result that appeared successful can nevertheless be unacceptable when viewed within the context of the client's collective culture. In this case, lawyers negotiated a plea to a misdemeanor assault with probation for a battered Chinese woman who had killed her husband and who faced a 25-year sentence if convicted of murder. The client, who had a strong self-defense claim, refused to plead to the misdemeanor charge because she did not want to humiliate herself, her ancestors, her children and their children by acknowledging responsibility for the killing. Her attorneys did not fully comprehend the concept of shame that the client would experience from such a plea until the client was able to explain that the possibility of 25 years in jail was far less offensive than the certain shame that would be experienced by her family (past, present and future) if she pled guilty. These negative reactions to what the lawyers initially viewed as an excellent result allowed the lawyers to examine the meaning of pleas, family, responsibility and consequences within a collective cultural context that was far different than their own.

In another case, lawyers had to change their strategy for presentation of evidence to make a claim that honored the cultural and religious norms of their client. In this case, lawyers arguing for political asylum for a female client wanted to present evidence of persecution by showing an injury to an area of her body that the client was committed, by religion and culture, to keeping private. Ultimately, the client developed a strategy of showing the injury to the INS lawyer who was also female. This strategy, challenging conventional legal advocacy and violating cultural norms of the adversarial system, allowed the client to present the case in a way that honored her values and norms.

Each of these cases presented stark cultural contrasts with clear connections to lawyering choices. In hindsight, it is easy to see the cultural contrasts and their effects on the clients' and lawyers' perceptions of what actions were appropriate and what accommodations were acceptable. In the heat of the moment, however, cases are more difficult, and the differences and similarities are more subtle and, at times, invisible. As clinical teachers, our job is to develop ways to make the invisible less so. The next section identifies some critical cross-cultural frameworks and vocabulary for giving our students a way of talking about differences and similarities, so that students will leave our programs better prepared to be lawyers in a multi-cultural world.

LEANING INTO PRACTICE

On October 6, 2021, the ABA issued Formal Opinion No. 500, "Language Access in the Client-Lawyer Relationship." The following are True/False questions based on the ABA's opinion. Answer the questions; and discuss the rationale for your answer with your professor and fellow students.

(1)   Emma Chen's native language is Chinese, but she has some limited fluency in English. She picks Abigail Lawyer to represent her in a lawsuit. Emma knows that Abigail only speaks English. Because Emma made the decision to select Abagail, she assumed the risk of poor communication effecting adversely on the representation.

True or False

(2)   Omar Lawyer speaks English as a native born American. Pedro Prospective Client (native Spanish speaker who speaks very limited English) meets with him to discuss possible representation. Omar, who studied Spanish for four years in high school, believes he can comminate, through a mixture of English and Spanish, with Pablo regarding the representation. Omar has met his ethical obligations under MR 1.4.

True or False

(3)   Linda Lawyer is in discussions with Kelli Smith on possible representation. Right now, Kelli is a prospective client whose native language is Polish. Kelli has some grasp of English. Linda sends Kelli a letter in English asking her to make a decision on the potential representation and, at the same time, emailing her husband, who is a native English speaker, asking him to tell Kelli to have the letter translated into Polish. She is complying with her ethical obligations provided no confidential information is given to the husband.

True or False

(4)   A bilingual family member of a client can never be an acceptable translator for a client with limited English-speaking ability.

True or False

(5)   A lawyer is hired by a Japanese national who speaks some English. The matter involves a complex negotiation between the Japanese national and a United States company on whether an agreement was reached on the terms of a contract. To assist in translation issues, the lawyer retains a native English speaker with a Ph.D. in the Japanese language but who has never lived in Japan. This retention is *per se* sufficient for purposes of MR 1.4.

True or False

(6)   John Lawyer meets with Mandela Smith who is from Nigeria. Mandela speaks a Nigerian dialect associated with the Ibo tribe and brings to the meeting with John a bilingual relative who is on a thirty-day visa to the United States. John determines that the expense of an interpreter would be a financial burden although he is arguably the most qualified lawyer for Mandela's matter. John's only option is to decline the representation.

True or False

(7)   Izzy Lawyer represented native Arabic speaker Malik who has limited English language skills. The ACR goes poorly, Malik terminates Izzy under MR 1.16, and files a Bar grievance against Izzy. Izzy defends by saying that he knew some Arabic and believed that Malik "understood more English than he was letting on." At the grievance hearing, Izzy offers testimony from Malik's supervisor at the restaurant kitchen where he works that corroborates Izzy's assessment of Malik's language skills. Izzy and the supervisor are both credible witnesses. There is no basis therefore to find a violation of MR 1.4.

True or False

Cases and Materials

X-Ray Questions (*Howe*)

In this case, a lawyer undertook, on a *pro bono* basis, the representation of a family who had lived unlawfully in the United States for over twenty years. The United States government sought to deport the family to Mexico. Only the daughter was bilingual, and the lawyer communicated to the parent through her. The representation went awry with missed deadlines because of miscommunication with the clients. This case ties together MR 1.1, MR 1.3, MR

1.4, and a new rule for you MR 8.5: Disciplinary Authority. How do these Rule interact in the case? How do the rules form an ecosystem? Do you think the lawyer was inept in his representation? Less than diligent? Was relying upon the daughter ever a viable alternative? Does relying upon the daughter satisfy the lawyer's duties under MR 1.4? Finally, do you think the discipline imposed was too harsh? After all, wasn't he just trying to help a family in need?

In re Disciplinary Action Against Howe

Supreme Court of North Dakota, 2014.
843 N.W.2d 325.

Opinion

PER CURIAM.

Attorney Henry H. Howe objected to a report of a hearing panel of the Disciplinary Board recommending that he be suspended from the practice of law for six months, that he pay costs and expenses of the proceedings and that he provide an accounting to his former clients of all costs and expenses incurred during the course of Howe's representation. We conclude clear and convincing evidence establishes Howe violated N.D.R. Prof. Conduct 1.1, competence; 1.3, diligence; and 1.4, communication. We order that Howe be suspended from the practice of law for six months and one day, that he pay $8,871.34 in costs of the disciplinary proceedings and that he provide his former clients an accounting of the costs and expenses associated with his representation.

I

Howe was admitted to practice law in North Dakota on July 27, 1973 and practices in Grand Forks as a member of the law firm Howe & Seaworth. Howe's disciplinary record includes suspensions ordered by this Court for 90 days in 1977 and 120 days in 2001, private reprimands from inquiry committees in 1988 and 1991 and admonitions from inquiry committees in 1995, 1998, 2001 and 2012. Howe is suspended by order of this Court for an unrelated matter, Supreme Court number 2014 ND 17, 842 N.W.2d 646.

This proceeding arises from Howe's representation of Elias Angel Camacho-Banda and Margarita Maya-Morales (collectively "Camachos"). The Camachos, undocumented Mexican nationals, have lived in the United States for over twenty years. The Camachos have four United States citizen children and one Mexican citizen child. Subsequent to a February 2007 traffic incident, authorities discovered the Camacho adults and one child did not have legal immigration status. The Camachos were placed in removal proceedings before the Executive Office for Immigration Review, Immigration Court, in Bloomington, Minnesota. The Camachos retained Howe to represent them in the removal proceedings.

During the immigration court's May 16, 2007 master calendar hearing, Howe conceded the Camachos were removable for staying in the United States past the time permitted and stated he would file their applications for cancellation of removal and adjustment of status. To prevail in canceling removal, the Camachos needed to establish removal would result in "exceptional and extremely unusual hardship to the alien's . . . child, who is a citizen of the United States" under 8 U.S.C. § 1229b(b)(1)(D). The immigration judge informed Howe he needed significant documentation of hardship, including documentation of one child's alleged learning disability. On May 16, 2007, Howe received an information sheet for gathering "biometrics," which explained the process for collecting fingerprints and personal information as required at immigration proceedings before final status decisions are made. Howe did not file the applications for cancellation of removal until November 21, 2008.

A merits hearing was held on December 1, 2008. Howe had not completed the biometrics process, including failing to obtain the Camachos' fingerprints. When asked why he did not complete the biometrics process, Howe blamed a calendaring error by his paralegal. Howe did not provide the hardship documentation requested by the judge, instead supplying only the children's school records. Further, the Camachos were the only witnesses called. The immigration judge chastised Howe for being unprepared, but allowed him thirty days to augment the Camachos' application for cancellation of removal. In addition to the clarification Howe already received on May 16, 2007 regarding supplemental materials the judge sought, the judge directed Howe to augment the file concerning the Camachos' son's learning disability, including letters from teachers and doctors and information regarding the special educational prospects in Mexico for a child with a learning disability.

The merits hearing was rescheduled for January 13, 2009. The Camachos were not present at the hearing because Howe failed to notify them of the rescheduled hearing. Howe blamed a change in office personnel. Howe later gave conflicting testimony to the hearing panel that he spoke to the Camachos about the date change, but that a miscommunication occurred because the Camachos' daughter who usually translated was not present. The judge agreed to reschedule the merits hearing from January 13, 2009 to October 21, 2009, warning Howe that if the Camachos again failed to appear, he would issue a removal order in their absence. The judge admonished Howe for failing to comply with formatting requirements for his filings.

Before the rescheduled merits hearing, Howe resubmitted duplicate documents, including country conditions and school records. Howe's submission was rejected for failing to comply with filing requirements. Howe attempted to fix the issues by resending his submission. The court noted that all the documents still were improperly submitted, but that it would nonetheless accept them. On April 23, 2010, Howe submitted additional articles about violence in Mexico, offered to demonstrate hardship. The Camachos' merits hearing was rescheduled to April 8, 2011. Howe obtained letters from the Camacho children's teachers, including a letter from the special education teacher and case manager for the child with the learning disability. Howe argues that while he possessed the letters, in his opinion the letters would not have helped meet the exceptional and extremely unusual hardship standard and possibly could have made things worse.

On April 8, 2011, Howe and the Camachos appeared at the rescheduled merits hearing, but because an interpreter was not available, the judge reserved the case for written submissions and closing arguments to be submitted within two weeks. Howe did not provide additional materials or submit written closing arguments. On November 15, 2011, the judge ordered the Camachos deported to Mexico. Howe was discharged, and the Camachos retained new counsel.

II

This Court decides disciplinary proceedings by making de novo review of the record compiled by the disciplinary board's hearing panel. *See Disciplinary Board v. Dyer*, 2012 ND 118, ¶ 8, 817 N.W.2d 351. This Court's procedure for reviewing disciplinary proceedings is:

> "Disciplinary counsel must prove each alleged violation by clear and convincing evidence, which means the trier of fact must be reasonably satisfied with the facts the evidence tends to prove and thus be led to a firm belief or conviction. We give the Disciplinary Board's findings, conclusions, and recommendations due weight, but we do not act as a mere rubber stamp. We consider each disciplinary matter on its own facts to decide which sanction, if any, is appropriate."

Disciplinary Board v. Hoffman, 2013 ND 137, ¶ 5, 834 N.W.2d 636 (quoting *Disciplinary Board v. Hann*, 2012 ND 160, ¶ 14, 819 N.W.2d 498).

III

Howe argues that because the Disciplinary Office of the Federal Immigration Court did not take disciplinary measures, this Court should defer to their nonaction and refrain from imposing disciplinary measures in North Dakota. Rule 8.5(a), N.D.R. Prof. Conduct, provides:

> "A lawyer admitted to practice in this jurisdiction is subject to disciplinary action in this jurisdiction even though the conduct of the lawyer giving rise to the discipline may have occurred outside of this jurisdiction and even when that conduct may subject or has subjected the lawyer to discipline by another jurisdiction."

This Court exercised jurisdiction over disciplinary matters arising from federal immigration proceedings involving North Dakota lawyers in the past. *Disciplinary Board v. Karlsen*, 2008 ND 235, 778 N.W.2d 522; *Disciplinary Board v. Vela*, 2005 ND 119, 699 N.W.2d 839; *Disciplinary Board v. Vela*, 2008 ND 42, 746 N.W.2d 1. Howe is a licensed North Dakota attorney. Under clear language in Rule 8.5(a), N.D.R. Prof. Conduct, and our judicial decisions, he is subject to discipline in this jurisdiction despite that the matter arose from a federal immigration proceeding and that disciplinary action was not taken by the federal immigration court. This Court has jurisdiction over this disciplinary case.

IV

Howe argues the hearing panel improperly accepted the immigration judge's comments as proof Howe failed to properly represent the Camachos. We decide disciplinary proceedings on a de novo review of the record and make our own determinations whether ethical violations have occurred. *Hann*, 2012 ND 160, ¶ 14, 819 N.W.2d 498.

A

Rule 1.1, N.D.R. Prof. Conduct, provides that "[a] lawyer shall provide competent representation to a client. Competent representation requires the legal knowledge, skill, thoroughness and preparation reasonably necessary for the representation." The knowledge and skill required in a particular case include consideration of the complexity of the matter and the lawyer's relevant training and experience. N.D.R. Prof. Conduct 1.1 cmt. 1. The comments also recognize that a lawyer may not need special training or experience to handle problems unfamiliar to the lawyer if the lawyer engages in adequate study. *Id.* at cmt. 2. Competence in a particular matter requires the "use of methods and procedures meeting the standards of competent practitioners" in a particular area, recognizing that some matters require more extensive treatment than others. N.D.R. Prof. Conduct 1.1 cmt. 6

To meet their burden for cancellation of removal, the Camachos were required to show exceptional and extremely unusual hardship to an American citizen family member. 8 U.S.C. § 1229b(b)(1)(D). Circumstances warranting a finding of exceptional and extremely unusual hardship include having a qualifying child with "compelling special needs in school." *In re Monreal-Aguinaga,* 23 I. & N. Dec. 56, 63 (BIA 2001). The immigration judge called Howe's attention to this burden during the December 1, 2008 hearing, requesting Howe to augment the application by providing letters from teachers and doctors and by providing information regarding education opportunities in Mexico for children with learning disabilities.

Howe provided the immigration judge with school assessments, noting the Camachos' son showed signs of dyslexia and adhered to a special education plan. But Howe did not provide documentation about special education availability in Mexico or affidavits from teachers or other professionals regarding the nature or severity of the boy's learning disability. Howe claims the updated information from the teachers would not have shown exceptional and extremely unusual circumstances because the school's education plan was so effective for the child. While Howe may be correct concerning the strategy behind withholding the affidavits, Howe failed to recognize that the country condition reports he submitted did not show details concerning the special education opportunities available in Mexico. The country condition reports and articles Howe submitted focused on pervasive violence in Mexico and on more general education statistics and issues, rather than whether special education opportunities were or were not available in Mexico. Howe also demonstrated a lack of preparation, including repeatedly failing to follow filing requirements, failing to file in a timely manner, failing to obtain supplementary information requested by the immigration judge and failing to provide a written submission or closing argument when given the opportunity.

The hearing panel did not blindly accept the immigration judge's comments as conclusive proof, and neither does this Court. Based on Howe's failure to comply with the immigration court's procedures and his failure to follow the roadmap laid out by the immigration judge on December 1, 2008, clear and convincing evidence establishes Howe did not act competently and violated Rule 1.1, N.D.R. Prof. Conduct.

B

Rule 1.3, N.D.R. Prof. Conduct, provides that "[a] lawyer shall act with reasonable diligence and promptness in representing a client." Reasonable diligence is defined as: "A fair degree of diligence expected from someone of ordinary prudence under circumstances like those at issue." *Black's Law Dictionary* 468 (7th ed.1999). Prompt is defined as: "quick to act or to do what is required[.]" *Webster's New World Dictionary* 1137 (2nd ed.1980). "Perhaps no professional shortcoming is more widely resented than procrastination." N.D.R. Prof. Conduct 1.3 cmt. 3.

Howe failed to diligently represent the Camachos in several ways. While Howe paid the biometrics fee and filed the biometrics forms, he did not obtain the Camachos' fingerprints and, therefore, did not complete the biometrics process before the merits hearing. The judge cannot make a decision regarding the Camachos' legal status in the United States until their updated criminal background information is obtained. 8 C.F.R. § 1003.47(g) ("In no case shall an immigration judge grant an application for immigration relief that is subject to the conduct of identity, law enforcement, or security investigations or examinations under this section until after [Department of Homeland Security ("DHS")] has reported to the immigration judge that the appropriate investigations or examinations have been completed and are current. . . ."). Even after the judge admonished Howe at the December 1, 2008 hearing to complete biometrics, Howe did not make an appointment for the Camachos to be fingerprinted before the January 13, 2009 merits hearing. Howe blamed a calendaring error to excuse his unpreparedness regarding the biometrics information, but he had more than a month to obtain the fingerprints, or at least make an appointment, before the January 13, 2009 hearing. Howe also failed to timely submit the applications for cancellation of removal. Howe stated on May 16, 2007 that he would file the Camachos' applications for cancellation of removal, yet he waited until November 21, 2008 to file the applications. The result was that the applications were filed just days before the merits hearing on December 1, 2008.

Howe also failed to communicate with his clients concerning important hearing dates, causing them to miss their January 13, 2009 merits hearing. Howe first blamed the communication failure on a change in office personnel. He later testified he spoke with the Camachos concerning the hearing date, but that a miscommunication occurred because the Camachos' daughter who usually translated was not present. Howe's arguments blaming his paralegal and changes in office personnel are to no avail because he is responsible for ensuring his nonlawyer staff's conduct comports with his professional obligations as an attorney under Rule 5.3(b), N.D.R. Prof. Conduct.

We conclude clear and convincing evidence establishes that Howe did not meet the diligence requirements for the Camachos' case and that he violated Rule 1.3, N.D.R. Prof. Conduct.

C

Disciplinary counsel alleged Howe failed to adequately communicate with his clients. Rule 1.4, N.D.R. Prof. Conduct, provides:

"(a) A lawyer shall:

(1)   promptly inform the client of any decision or circumstance with respect to which the client's consent is required by these Rules;

(2)   reasonably consult with the client about the means by which the client's objectives are to be accomplished;

(3)   make reasonable efforts to keep the client reasonably informed about the status of a matter;

(4)   promptly comply with the client's reasonable requests for information; and

(5)   consult with the client about any relevant information on the lawyer's conduct when the lawyer knows that the client expects assistance not permitted by these Rules or other law.

"(b) A lawyer shall explain a matter to the extent reasonably necessary to permit the client to make informed decisions regarding the representation."

Howe failed to communicate with the Camachos concerning key court dates and the fees and costs associated with representation. Howe offered two versions of how the missed hearing occurred. First, he said the Camachos missed their rescheduled merits hearing because he failed to notify them of the date due to a change in office personnel. Howe later argued that he tried to communicate the date, but confusion persisted because the Camachos' daughter was not there to translate. Reasonable efforts to ensure the client is informed of the status of the matter include assuring the Camachos understood their hearing was rescheduled despite their daughter not being available to translate. *Cf. Annotated Model Rules of Professional Conduct* R. 1.4 Annotation, at 60–61 (7th ed. 2011) ("[A] lawyer risks violating Rule 1.4 by communicating with a third party instead of directly with the client.") (citing *cf. Attorney Grievance Comm'n v. Lee*, 390 Md. 517,

890 A.2d 273 (2006) (lawyer who had difficulty communicating directly with imprisoned client, and who had previously communicated with client's mother, disciplined for failing to continue communication through mother)). Howe represented the Camachos pro bono, which may explain the lack of information given to the Camachos about Howe's time and effort on the matter; nevertheless, according to both Howe and the Camachos, the Camachos were never given statements of the costs and expenses incurred in the course of representation, despite paying Howe $4,050. This omission speaks to the greater lack of communication involved in Howe's representation under Rule 1.4, N.D.R. Prof. Conduct, rather than violating the fee rule, N.D.R. Prof. Conduct 1.5(a) and (b).

Based on Howe's failure to communicate dates, deadlines and financial arrangements, clear and convincing evidence establishes Howe did not adequately communicate with his clients, in violation of Rule 1.4, N.D.R. Prof. Conduct.

VI

In determining the appropriate discipline for Howe, the hearing panel considered aggravating factors under Standard 9.22 of the North Dakota Standards for Imposing Lawyer Sanctions, including prior disciplinary offenses, a pattern of misconduct, vulnerability of the victims and substantial experience in the practice of law. The hearing panel recommended a six-month suspension under Standard 4.42(b) because Howe engaged in a pattern of neglect and caused injury or potential injury to a client. The hearing panel also recommended Howe pay $8,871.34 in costs and expenses of the proceedings, as outlined in the Affidavit of Costs and Expenses, and that Howe provide a clear and precise accounting to the Camachos of costs and payments made during their attorney-client relationship.

We agree suspension is the appropriate sanction but, given Howe's conduct and history of discipline, conclude a six-month and one-day duration is appropriate, effective thirty days from this decision. Howe will need to show proof of rehabilitation under N.D.R. Lawyer Discipl. 4.5(A) before he may be reinstated to practice law. Howe is ordered to pay the costs of the disciplinary proceeding totaling $8,871.34 within thirty days of this decision. Howe must provide an accounting to the Camachos within thirty days of this decision.

VII

We conclude Howe violated N.D.R. Prof. Conduct 1.1, 1.3 and 1.4. We order Howe be suspended from the practice of law for six months and one day, effective thirty days from this opinion. We order that Howe pay $8,871.34 in costs and expenses of the proceedings within thirty days, payable to the Secretary of the Disciplinary Board, Judicial Wing, 1st Floor, 600 East Boulevard Avenue, Bismarck, ND 58505-0530. We order Howe to provide the Camachos with an accounting of the costs and expenses associated with Howe's representation within thirty days. Howe must comply with N.D.R. Lawyer Discipl. 6.3 regarding notice. Reinstatement is governed by N.D.R. Lawyer Discipl. 4.5.

SOLUTIONS: THE LAWYER SHOULD HAVE, WOULD HAVE, COULD HAVE. . .

Your obligations as lawyers exist irrespective of how much you are paid or whether you are paid at all. While aspirations, such as providing free legal services as urged by MR 6.1, are laudable, they are not a defense to Rule violations. Similarly, even when we are appointed, as in the *Stern* case, our adherence to the Rules is still paramount. There are no exceptions to the ACR here. Howe made some efforts, but they were half-hearted. Points for trying might factor into the sanction imposed but not upon whether there is a violation in the first place.

Cases and Materials

X-Ray Questions (*Green*)

In this case, a lawyer deposing the injured plaintiff made suggestions that his Chinese national origin and native culture could have contributed to his injuries. The trial court prohibited such questions from being asked. What was the source of its authority to make such an order? Why did the court take the action that it did? The court might have been able to rely upon MR 8.4(g), a fairly recent addition to the Rule that you will see in chapter 6, prohibiting a lawyer from engaging "in conduct that the lawyer knows or reasonably should know, is harassment or discrimination on the basis of race, sex, religion, national origin, disability, age, sexual orientation, gender identity, marital status or socioeconomic status in conduct rated to the practice of law." But is the issue that simple? Could there be times when a litigant's culture was relevant to his or her conduct? Is it ever fair under the Rules of Evidence to therefore permit such facts to come into evidence?

Romare J. Green v. Cosco Shipping Lines Co. Ltd., et al.

United States District Court, S.D. Georgia, Savannah Division, 2021.
2021 WL 5985123.

ORDER

CHRISTOPHER L. RAY, UNITED STATES MAGISTRATE JUDGE.

The Court previously directed the parties to each file a single motion detailing any outstanding discovery disputes. Doc. 45 at 1. They have complied. Defendants filed a Motion for Protective Order, doc. 54, to which Plaintiff responded, doc. 57, and Defendants replied, doc. 60. Plaintiff filed a "Motion Detailing Any Outstanding Discovery Disputes," doc. 55, which contains Plaintiff's Motion for Modification of the Court's Scheduling Order, *id.* at 3–8, and Plaintiff's Motion to Compel Depositions, *id.* at 8–12. Defendants have responded, doc. 56, Plaintiff replied, doc. 61, and Defendants sur-replied, doc. 63. All of these discovery motions are ripe for review.

I. BACKGROUND

As this Court has summarized before:

This case involves injuries Plaintiff suffered while working as a longshoreman on the M/V Cosco Shipping Camellia (the "Vessel") which Defendants own and operate. (Doc. 1, Attach. 1 at 3–5.) Plaintiff alleges that he was exiting the Vessel via a steep gangway when the handrail collapsed, causing him to fall off the gangway and land on the dock adjacent to the gangway. (*Id.* at 4.) Plaintiff alleges that he sustained serious injuries to his right shoulder as a result of the fall.

Doc. 51 at 1–2. During discovery, three issues arose which the parties are unable to resolve without the Court's involvement. The first issue centers on whether the Plaintiff is permitted to identify two additional experts, or if he is foreclosed from doing so by the expiration of his expert report disclosure deadline. *See* doc. 55 at 3–8. The second issue, raised in both Plaintiff's Motion to Compel and Defendants' Motion for Protective Order, is whether Defendants are obligated to produce for deposition five crewmembers identified by Plaintiff in his deposition notices. *See* doc. 54 at 8–15, doc. 55 at 8–12. And, the final issue, whether Defendants are entitled to an order directing Plaintiff's counsel to refrain from demeaning lines of questioning during any further depositions in this matter. *See* doc. 54 at 15–19.

II. ANALYSIS

[. . . .]

C. Plaintiff's Counsel's Deposition Conduct

The final issue before the Court is whether Defendants are entitled to an Order restricting Plaintiff's counsel's conduct during any further depositions in this matter. *See* doc. 54 at 15–17. Defendants seek six specific restrictions: 1) that Plaintiff's counsel be prevented from impugning Chinese culture or suggesting that it is to blame for any allegedly negligent or otherwise improper acts in this matter; 2) that Plaintiff's counsel be prevented from asking questions or making commentary suggesting that witnesses' alleged failure to do things the way Americans typically do them (as characterized by Plaintiff's counsel) constitutes improper or negligent behavior; 3) that Plaintiff's counsel be prevented from asking questions drawing distinctions between American and Chinese culture with the implication that Chinese culture or methods are inferior; 4) that Plaintiff's counsel be prevented from asking questions or giving narrative about what is fair to Plaintiff, or what a wonderful person or family man he is, or suggesting that deponents or Defendants do not care about Plaintiff; 5) that Plaintiff's counsel be prevented from asking witnesses about the god to which they swore prior to beginning the deposition in earnest or their religious beliefs; and 6) that future witnesses in this matter otherwise be shown respect. *Id.* at 15–16. Defendants do not seek sanctions against Plaintiff's counsel. *Id.* at 16.

Defendants' motion seeks these rather extraordinary protections because Plaintiff's counsel has demonstrated that he is unable or unwilling to show these common courtesies to witnesses in this case without the intervention of the Court. *See, e.g.*, doc. 54 at 3–6 (quoting from the deposition transcripts of Liu Jinlong, doc. 54-4, and Li Jinzhao, doc. 54-5). As the transcripts demonstrate, Plaintiff's counsel asked questions of the deponents that were demeaning to Chinese culture and to the deponents' own character and were generally harassing and threatening. *See id.* In response to objections from Defendants' counsel, Plaintiff's counsel appears to have doubled down, indicating that his lines of questioning were *intended* to demean Chinese culture, and that such an intent was justified, or at least would not subject him to censure, because of the current state of the American political landscape. *See* docs. 54-6, 54-7. In response to Defendants' request for a protective order, Plaintiff concedes that the questions were "admittedly tough," but argues that they were just part of the "vigorous cross-examination" that is "indispensable to revealing the truth." Doc. 57 at 15. Such characterization strains credulity.

The Federal Rules of Civil Procedure protect deponents from abusive questioning by permitting the deponent or a party to move to terminate or limit the deposition "on the ground that it is being conducted in bad faith or in a manner that unreasonably annoys, embarrasses, or oppressed the deponent or party." Fed. R. Civ. P. 30(d)(3)(A). The Rules also allow the Court to impose a sanction on "a person who impedes, delays, or frustrates the fair examination of the deponent." Fed. R. Civ. P. 30(d)(2). And the Local Rules of this Court mandate that witnesses be treated with fairness and consideration, and that they not be "shouted at, ridiculed, *or otherwise abused.*" S.D. Ga. L. Civ. R. 83.15 (emphasis added).

Plaintiff's counsel violated, at least, this Court's Local Rule when he asked questions of the deponents that were meant to demean their country of origin and their own moral character. He (again) crossed the line of appropriate cross-examination and "unquestionably frustrated the fair examination of [the deponents] with a barrage of arrogant, irrelevant, accusatory questions and caustic comments." *Horton v. Maersk Line, Ltd.*, 294 F.R.D. 690, 697 (S.D. Ga. 2013) (discussing conduct by Plaintiff's current counsel). Because he "violated ethical and professional norms" in deposing the witnesses, the Defendants "have standing to object to unprofessional deposition questioning of another." *Id.* at 697–98. Therefore, considering the Court has at least contemplated that additional limited depositions—albeit of expert witness—may be necessary in this case, the Court finds that Defendants are entitled to the relief that they seek, and their Motion for Protective Order is **GRANTED, in part**. Doc. 54, in part.

The Court imposes the following restrictions upon Plaintiff's counsel during any future depositions that may occur in this matter:

1)   Plaintiff's counsel shall not impugn Chinese culture or suggest that it is to blame for any allegedly negligent or otherwise improper acts in this matter;

2)   Plaintiff's counsel shall not ask questions drawing distinctions between American and Chinese cultures with the implication that Chinese culture is inferior;

3)   Plaintiff's counsel shall not ask questions or give narrative about what is fair to Plaintiff, or suggest that deponents or Defendants do not care about Plaintiff;

4)   Plaintiff's counsel shall not ask witnesses about the god to which they swear, or otherwise question them about religious beliefs; and

5)   Plaintiff's counsel shall show any future witnesses in this matter respect during their depositions.

III. CONCLUSION

Plaintiff's Motion for Modification of the Court's Scheduling Order is **GRANTED, in part** and **DENIED, in part**. Doc. 55. The parties are **DIRECTED** to confer and, within **FOURTEEN DAYS** from the date of this Order, submit a joint proposed Amended Scheduling Order containing any extended deadlines contemplated by this Order. Plaintiff's Motion to Compel is **DENIED**. Doc. 55, in part. Defendants' Motion for Protective Order is **GRANTED**. Doc. 54.

SO ORDERED this 16th day of December 2021.

SOLUTIONS: THE LAWYER SHOULD HAVE, WOULD HAVE, COULD HAVE. . .

The lawyer here should have established a predicate for the relevance of these questions. By way of example, what if Chinese culture frowned on reporting an unsafe working condition until the employer received all the facts needed to make the determination. This cultural mindset would go to show why he acted as he did. Maybe the lawyer could retain an expert in cultural communication who would testify on commination in Asian culture. In isolation, the questions are asked without a reasoned basis and therefore could be viewed as a form of harassment. But even if there might be some conceivable basis for arguing that culture induced negligent conduct, would you ever pursue that theory of a case? Why or why not?

B.   Model Rule 1.4(a)(3) and Informing Client of Malpractice

Behind every lawyer, there are endless deadlines and stress that they must handle. There is therefore the possibility for error. So, what should a lawyer do when she finds out there is a mistake? When should a lawyer inform the client of her mistake, and does it depend on what kind of mistake?

In this section, we will examine what is considered a "reportable" mistake or error and thus, the lawyer must inform the client of that mistake.

On April 17, 2018, the ABA's Standing Committee on Ethics and Professional Responsibility issued Formal Opinion 481, "A Lawyer's Duty to Inform a Current or Former Client on the Lawyer's Material Error." This Formal Opinion help lawyers and students recognize material errors that would reasonably be likely to harm or prejudice a current client. Clients should be told of such errors. However, if a material error is found after the termination of the ACR, then the lawyer has no obligation to inform the former client.

X-Ray Questions

Here is the test on whether to self-report possible malpractice as set out by the ABA. Why is the standard phrased in the disjunctive?

BEYOND THE CITE

One of the more perplexing challenges in experiencing professional responsibility is knowing when to disclose to a client that you made a material mistake. The *Bayview* case offers a clear example of when such disclosure is mandated. But not all scenarios are that clear. Knowing this, the ABA issued Formal Opinion 481. The committee concluded that the following rule provides sufficient parameters within which a lawyer can exercise the lawyer's judgment in deciding whether to disclose: An error is material if a disinterested lawyer would conclude that it is (a) reasonably likely to harm or prejudice a client or (b) of such a nature that it would reasonably cause a client to consider terminating the representation even in the absence of harm or prejudice."

Note two textual points. First, this formulation is rooted in MR 1.4: Communication and is not simply a free floating, untethered formulation. Comment 5 to the Rule provides a guiding principle that "the lawyer should fulfill reasonable client expectations for information consistent with the duty to act in the client's best interests, and the client's overall requirements as to the character of representation." The comments go on to state that a communication decision made by a lawyer—no matter how unpleasant the communication will be—must rely upon the bedrock principle that a lawyer may not withhold information from a client in order to serve the lawyer's own interest or convenience.

Second, we see yet again the extensive power of the small word, "or" which does some heavy lifting in the formulation. "Or" expands the reach of the formulation to encompass situations in which the lawyer may not be liable for malpractice, but which would cause the client to pause and consider whether this lawyer is the best for the representation at hand. And this goal is consistent with another fundamental principle; namely, that a client can terminate the ACR at any time and for any reason.

The opinion goes on to urge lawyers to conceptualize the decision on whether to disclose as being on a continuum, with each endpoint being a slam dunk decision. On the non-disclosure end of the spectrum are mistakes such as non-substantive typographical errors or missing a deadline that causes nothing more than delay. While on the other end of the spectrum are material errors that prejudice a client's rights or claims as we saw in *Bayview*.

What about former clients? Is there a duty to disclose a material mistake? The ABA Formal Opinion Letter performs a textual analysis on the language of MR 1.4. The result: no duty to disclose to a former client. Why? MR 1.4 speaks only of "the client" which is in the present tense. Had the drafters of the rule wanted to include "former clients" they knew how to do so but did not. By way of example, the drafters of the rules know how to distinguish between obligations with respect to current and former clients with respect to conflicts of interest (MR 1.7 (current clients) vs. MR 1.9 (former clients) but elected not to make the same distinctions here. The California State Bar issued an opinion in which it likewise concluded that former clients were not encompassed by the disclosure mandate. (California State Bar Committee on Professional Responsibility, Opinion 2009–178)

X-Ray Questions

Do you think a legal services organization such as the Legal Aid Clinic should be subject to the same ethical standards as a lawyer? If so, should the legal services organization inform the client of the error or omission? Do they have a duty to report the malpractice as well?

BEYOND THE CITE

New York State Bar Association Committee on Professional Ethics Opinion 743

Topic: Attorney's obligation to report to a client a significant error or omission that may give rise to a possible malpractice claim.

Digest: A legal services organization is subject to the same ethical standards as other law offices, and therefore must report to the client a significant error or omission that may give rise to a possible malpractice claim, and depending on the circumstances, it may be required to withdraw its representation of the client.

Code: DR 5–101(A); DR 6–102; DR 2–110(A)(2); EC 2–6; EC 2–8; EC 2–32; EC 5–1; EC 5–11; EC 7–7; and EC 7–8.

QUESTIONS

1.   Is a Legal Aid Society ("Society"), which provides legal services to low income clients, bound by the ethical standards which require attorneys to disclose significant errors and omissions to their clients?

2.   If so, may the Society continue as counsel if, after having made full disclosure of such an error, a client still wants the organization to continue its representation?

OPINION

As a general rule, whether an attorney has an obligation to disclose a mistake to a client will depend on the nature of the lawyer's possible error or omission, whether it is possible to correct it in the pending proceeding, the extent of the harm resulting from the possible error or omission, and the likelihood that the lawyer's conduct would be deemed unreasonable and therefore give rise to a colorable malpractice claim. Ordinarily, since lawyers have an obligation to keep their clients reasonably informed about the matter and to provide information that their clients need to make decisions relating to the representation, the Society's lawyer would have an obligation to disclose to the client the possibility that they have made a significant error or omission. See N.Y. State Op. 396 (1975); EC 7–7, EC 7–8.

DR 5–101(A) governs the question of whether the Society and its lawyers have a conflict of interest arising out of their personal interest in avoiding civil liability and, if so, whether the lawyers may nevertheless continue the representation with "the client's consent to the representation after full disclosure of the implications of the lawyer's interest." In general, under DR 5–101(A), the lawyers would have a conflict of interest if "the exercise of professional judgment on behalf of the client will be or reasonably may be affected by the lawyer's own" interest, and, in that event, the Society could continue the representation with the client's informed consent only if "a disinterested lawyer would believe that the representation of the client will not be adversely affected thereby."

This Committee's prior opinions provide guidance about how these principles generally apply when a lawyer has made a significant error or omission in the course of the representation, although their application will obviously vary depending on the facts of the particular case. For example, in N.Y. State 275 (1972), we addressed the situation of a lawyer who failed to file a claim within the statute of limitations period. We held that a lawyer had a professional duty to notify the client promptly that the lawyer had committed a serious and irremediable error, and of the possible claim the client may have against the lawyer for damages. Because the error could not be remedied and the representation was all but concluded, we further held that the lawyer should withdraw from the matter after having made the necessary full disclosure. In such a situation, not only was there an inherent conflict between the interest of the client and the lawyer's own interest, but, from an objective perspective, one could not be confident that the quality of the lawyer's work would be unaffected if the representation continued. We advised that, upon withdrawing, the lawyer should recommend that the client retain other counsel. See also DR 5–101(A); DR 6–102; EC 5–1; EC 2–6; and EC 5–11; N.Y. State 295 (1973) (reaffirming N.Y. State 275); N.Y. City 1995–2 (1995) (a lawyer failed to settle a judgment within time period prescribed by procedural rules).

Of course, not every possible error creates a possible claim for malpractice. Some errors can be corrected during the course of the representation. Others are not particularly harmful to the client's cause. In some cases, it may be questionable whether the lawyer acted erroneously at all. Therefore, when a lawyer makes a mistake in the representation of a client, the likelihood that the lawyer's representation will be affected adversely because of the lawyer's interest in avoiding civil liability will depend upon all the relevant facts.

Earlier opinions also make clear that the Society is subject to the same general standard as other law offices, even though its clients, who have limited financial resources, may find it more difficult to retain other counsel. See N.Y. City 1995–2 (1995) (holding that a legal services organization that may have committed malpractice should withdraw its representation and advise an indigent client to obtain legal advice from an attorney not employed by the organization); DR 5–101(A); EC–5–1; and EC 5–11. If the Society is required to withdraw from the representation because of the possibility that its lawyers' representation will be adversely affected by their own or the Society's interest, another legal services organization may be willing to undertake representation of the client or the client may be able to retain a private attorney on a contingency fee or on a pro bono basis. Unfortunately, it is also possible that the client may go unrepresented if another attorney is unavailable or unwilling to assume the matter. In any case, the Society cannot withdraw its representation until it "has taken steps to the extent reasonably practical to avoid foreseeable prejudice to the rights of the client," the specifics of which would depend on the circumstances of a particular case. See DR 2–110(A)(2); DR 6–102; EC 2–6; EC 2–8; and EC 2–32. However, if the matter is in litigation, the Society must seek permission from the Court before withdrawing. DR 2–110(A)(1).

CONCLUSION

The Society is bound by the same ethical standards as other law offices, and therefore has an obligation to report to the client that it has made a significant error or omission that may give rise to a possible malpractice claim. In such a situation, the Society will be required to withdraw as counsel if its continued representation would be adversely affected by its interest in avoiding civil liability.

LEANING INTO PRACTICE

As the New York Opinion says, not all errors are malpractice. Mistakes can often be corrected with no real injury to clients. But, of course, reasonable people might disagree about where to draw the line. Remember, when lawyers make mistakes there are really two issues. One is communication. The other is a conflict of interest. A lawyer cannot continue to represent someone who the lawyer knows may be able to sue for malpractice. And of course, on top of all this, there is human nature. No one likes admitting mistakes. This book is filled with extreme cases of lawyer misconduct. The question you should ask yourself is: What, if anything would you tell this client if you were this lawyer?

Scenario: The Case of the Pro Bono Asylum Case

Linda Lawyer takes on an asylum case pro bono, for a man who was a political dissident in a foreign country. She prepares his application with considerable thoroughness. She compiles evidence, and helps him write a strong declaration explaining his experiences. But she makes one, little mistake. She missed the instruction in the U.S. Government's application for asylum that requires two copies of the applications to be filed. The Department of Homeland Security sends it back to her, and she has to refile it. The result from this missing photocopy is just a one month delay in processing of the asylum application. In this particular case, it does not really hurt the client's chances. If you made a mistake like this, what, if anything, would you tell your client, if anything?

Section 4. Fiduciary Duty and Loyalty

A. Fiduciary Duty

Lawyers owe contractual duties to clients. These duties are either oral or written promises to perform a service-based task. By way of example, filing a timely answer to a lawsuit, or promising to thoroughly review records to determine if a lien has been filed on a client's property, or to file a divorce petition seeking child custody. The failure of the lawyer to perform these tasks leads to a contractual breach of contract and possibly a malpractice lawsuit against the lawyer if the disappointed client can establish negligence by the lawyer. But lawyers are professionals with a higher duty than, as Justice Cardozo once remarked, "the morals of the marketplace."

And that is a fiduciary duty—which you have likely learned about in your 1L classes or corporate law classes—which rises above a mere contractual obligation. It is a duty of loyalty described in one the following cases as a duty of "most abundant good faith" which "require[s] absolute and perfect candor, openness and honesty, and the absence of concealment or deception." This is consistent with the origin of the word "professional". In ancient Rome, advocates and physicians would go to the town square and speak to the assemblage. They would "profess" that their needs came ahead of the speaker's needs. Thus, the word 'professional."

If being "professional" sounds like a high standard, it's because it is a high standard. The rationale being that you, as a lawyer, are granted the *exclusive* privilege of practicing law. No one else can do so who is not licensed by the state. Indeed, it is a crime for a non-lawyer to practice law. In exchange for this exclusive right, lawyers bear an increased burden to act honorably towards their clients. A breach of that duty is a tort with tort like compensatory damages such as mental anguish as well as potential punitive damages.

Cases and Materials

X-Ray Questions (*Bayview*)

Here, a law firm failed to perfect its pleadings when retained by a loan company to foreclose upon a home loan. The firm's failure resulted in the debtor being able to escape loss of the collateral on the default. But the firm then engaged in peculiar conduct. It did not tell their client of the mistake. Why do you think so? What Model Rules were violated in their doing so? What factors elevated the facts of this case from mere negligence to breach of fiduciary duty? From a purely economic risk/reward analysis why does it make more sense to admit the negligence and suffer the consequences than hide the mistake and be sued for breach of fiduciary duty? What intangible damages could result from a breach of fiduciary duty lawsuit against the law firm?

Bayview Loan Servicing, LLC v. Law Firm of Richard M. Squire & Associates, LLC

United States District Court for the Eastern District of Pennsylvania, 2010.
2010 U.S. Dist. LEXIS 132108.

YOHN, J.

Plaintiffs, Bayview Loan Servicing, LLC ("Bayview") and its wholly-owned subsidiary IB Property Holdings, LLC ("IB"), bring this legal malpractice action against defendants, the law firm of Richard M. Squire & Associates, LLC (the "Squire Firm") and its employee M. Troy Freedman ("Freedman"). Plaintiffs claim that defendants represented them in a foreclosure action; that defendants failed to file a petition to fix the fair value of the relevant property within six months of the foreclosure sale, which is required by statute in order to pursue a deficiency judgment; and that as a result of defendants' failure plaintiffs lost any right to pursue the deficiency they were owed.

Defendants have filed a motion to dismiss for failure to state a claim under Fed. R. Civ. P. 12(b)(6). Defendants request that Counts I–II (breach of fiduciary duty), III (negligent supervision) and V (punitive damages) be dismissed with prejudice, and that Count IV (breach of contract) be dismissed with leave to amend. For the reasons explained below I will deny defendants' motion.

I.   Factual and Procedural Background

Bayview acquired the note and associated mortgage (collectively, the "Mortgage") at the center of this litigation from MetWest Commercial Lender, Inc. ("MetWest"). (Compl. ¶ 13.) The Mortgage represented a loan to an individual, Peter Pugliese, for an original principal amount of $262,500.00, and granted the holder of the Mortgage a lien on certain real property (the

"Property") to secure payment. (Compl. ¶¶ 10–11, 13.) Bayview assigned the Mortgage to IB. (Compl. ¶ 13.)

Peter Pugliese defaulted on the Mortgage in July 2007. (Compl. ¶ 17.) Plaintiffs then retained the Squire Firm to commence a foreclosure action against Peter Pugliese (the "Foreclosure Action"). (Compl. ¶ 18.) Plaintiff IB obtained an *in rem* judgment and judgment against Peter Pugliese in the amount of $287,992.56 in the Foreclosure Action on January 24, 2008. (Compl. ¶ 18; Opinion 2.) IB purchased the Property at a sheriff's sale on September 5, 2008. (Compl. ¶ 20.) IB subsequently sold the Property to a third party. (*Id.*)

On December 4, 2008, plaintiffs instructed defendants to seek a deficiency from Peter Pugliese in the amount of $374,998.01. (Compl. ¶¶ 21, 23.) Defendants, on behalf of plaintiffs, filed a lawsuit against Peter Pugliese for the deficiency on March 26, 2009, in the Berks County Court of Common Pleas (the "Deficiency Action"). (Compl. 25, 28.) However, defendants had failed to file a petition to fix fair value within six months of the sheriff's sale, as required under Pennsylvania law in order to pursue a deficiency, *see* 42 Pa. Cons. Stat. § 8103(a)–(d); the six-month period had expired on March 5, 2009. (Compl. ¶ 22.)

On April 27, 2009, Wendy Pugliese filed a petition in the Berks County Court of Common Pleas to mark the judgment against Peter Pugliese in the Foreclosure Action satisfied, released and discharged, based on plaintiffs' failure to file the required petition to fix fair value. (Opinion 3.) In response Freedman sent a letter to President Judge Schmehl, the presiding judge in that action, advising that Bayview had no objection to marking the judgment satisfied, released and discharged. (Compl. ¶ 26; Opinion 7–8.) Plaintiffs did not authorize this letter and were not informed of its existence at the time. (Compl. 26.) President Judge Schmehl granted Wendy Pugliese's petition and issued an order marking the judgment against Peter Pugliese in the Foreclosure Action satisfied on June 5, 2009. (Compl. ¶ 27.) Plaintiffs were not informed by defendants of this order. (*Id.*)

Despite the initial judgment against Peter Pugliese in the Foreclosure Action having been marked satisfied, a default judgment was entered against him in the Deficiency Action for $295,726.05 on July 13, 2009. (Compl. 28.) Sheriff's levies were served against Peter Pugliese for all his property and business on July 27, 2009. (Compl. ¶ 29.) Peter Pugliese then filed a petition to strike the default judgment, arguing that the original judgment had already been marked satisfied pursuant to President Judge Schmehl's order. (Compl. ¶ 30.) On October 4, 2009, Peter Pugliese's petition was granted and the Deficiency Action was dismissed. (Compl. ¶ 32.)

On October 14, 2009, plaintiffs moved to strike or open the order of June 5, 2009 marking the judgment against Peter Pugliese satisfied. (Opinion 3.) Judge Schmehl denied plaintiffs' motion on December 3, 2009, and on April 1, 2010 recommended that plaintiffs' appeal to the Pennsylvania Superior Court be denied. (Opinion 3–4, 8.)

Plaintiffs' filed this malpractice suit against the Squire Firm and Freedman on April 1, 2010. Defendants have now moved to dismiss for failure to state a claim.

II. Legal Standard

"To survive a motion to dismiss [pursuant to Rule 12(b)(6)], a complaint must contain sufficient factual matter, accepted as true, to 'state a claim to relief that is plausible on its face.' " *Ashcroft v. Iqbal*, 129 S. Ct. 1937, 1949, 173 L. Ed. 2d 868 (2009) (quoting *Bell Atl. Corp. v. Twombly*, 550 U.S. 544, 570, 127 S. Ct. 1955, 167 L. Ed. 2d 929 (2007)). Factual allegations "that are 'merely consistent with' a defendant's liability," or that permit the court to infer no more than "the mere possibility of misconduct" are not enough. *Id.* at 1949–50 (quoting *Twombly*, 550 U.S. at 557). Rather, the plaintiff must plead "factual content that allows the court to draw the reasonable inference that the defendant is liable for misconduct alleged." *Id.* at 1949. In evaluating a motion to dismiss, the court "must accept all of the complaint's well-pleaded facts as true, but may disregard any legal conclusions." *Fowler v. UPMC Shadyside*, 578 F.3d 203, 210–11 (3d Cir. 2009); see also *Iqbal*, 129 S. Ct. at 1949 ("Threadbare recitals of the elements of a cause of action, supported by mere conclusory statements, do not suffice.").

Plaintiffs incorrectly claim that a movant under Rule 12(b)(6) must demonstrate that the plaintiff "can prove no set of facts in support of his claim which would entitle him to relief." (Pl.'s Mem. in Opp'n to Defs.' Mot. to Dismiss ("Pls.' Resp.") 6.) As the Third Circuit recognized in *Fowler*, the "no set of facts" standard did not survive *Iqbal. Fowler*, 578 F.3d at 210 ("*Iqbal* . . . provides the final nail-in-the-coffin for the 'no set of facts' standard that applied to federal complaints before *Twombly*.").

III. Discussion

Defendants challenge plaintiffs' five counts on different grounds, and I will address each in turn. For the reasons set forth below I will deny defendants' motion in full.

A Counts I & II—Breach of Fiduciary Duty

Defendants argue that plaintiffs' breach of fiduciary duty claims against the Squire Firm (Count I) and Freedman (Count II) should be dismissed because a breach of fiduciary duty claim arises where a lawyer is disloyal to the client, and plaintiff has pleaded factual matter that supports at most a breach of defendants' duty of care. (Defs.' Mem. in Support of Mot. to Dismiss ("Defs.' Mot.")) Plaintiffs respond that they have pleaded both breach of fiduciary duty and negligent malpractice claims, presumably intending that each of Counts I and II encapsulate both theories of negligence and disloyalty. (Pls.' Resp. 3, 8.) No rule requires dismissal of a claim because multiple theories of liability are asserted in a single count, so I will examine the sufficiency of the well-pleaded facts in the complaint with respect to the elements of both types of claim.

i.   Negligence

Defendants do not directly challenge the sufficiency of the complaint with respect to a claim of negligence, likely because neither "negligence" nor "malpractice" are explicitly indicated by a heading. Regardless of the headings used, however, plaintiffs have stated a claim for negligence-based malpractice.

Under Pennsylvania law, a legal malpractice claim sounding in negligence requires the plaintiff to prove: (1) the employment of the attorney or other basis for a duty; (2) the failure of the attorney to exercise ordinary skill and knowledge; and (3) that such negligence was the proximate cause of damage to the plaintiff. *Kituskie v. Corbman*, 552 Pa. 275, 714 A.2d 1027, 1029 (Pa. 1998). The first element does not appear to be in dispute, and plaintiffs clearly have pleaded the second, but defendants assert that plaintiffs have failed to plead causation because they do not specifically allege that they would have succeeded in the underlying litigation in the absence of any breach of duty by defendants. (Defs.' Mot. 8–9.)

No doubt, to recover the lost deficiency that plaintiffs claim as damages they must show causation by proving that they would have recovered it in the underlying litigation but for defendants' negligence. *See Kituskie*, 714 A.2d at 1030 ("[A] legal malpractice action in Pennsylvania requires the plaintiff to prove that he had a viable cause of action against the party he wished to sue in the underlying case and that the attorney he hired was negligent in prosecuting or defending that underlying case."). At the pleading stage, however, I must ask whether plaintiffs have pleaded "factual content that allows the court to draw the reasonable inference that the defendant is liable for misconduct alleged." *Iqbal*, 129 S. Ct. at 1949. Plaintiffs have alleged that the Property was sold well below market value; Peter Pugliese owed plaintiffs "in excess of $377,499.00" as a deficiency; plaintiffs instructed defendants to pursue the resulting deficiency; defendants failed to file a petition to fix fair value, which is required in order to pursue a deficiency; and as a result of defendants' "careless, negligent and reckless conduct" plaintiffs suffered damages. (Compl. ¶ 20–21, 24, 36, 43.) Plaintiffs' allegations sufficiently plead the element of causation, and thus plaintiffs' have properly stated a claim for negligent malpractice.

ii.   *Disloyalty*

Defendants argue that a breach of fiduciary duty claim against an attorney requires allegations of disloyalty, not mere negligence, and that plaintiffs have therefore failed to state a claim for breach of fiduciary duty because the complaint does not assert that defendants' failure to file a petition to fix fair value was intentional, or caused by divided loyalty. (Defs.' Mot. 6–7.) Even assuming that defendants are correct that the plaintiffs' allegations do not suggest that the failure to file the petition to fix fair value was anything more than negligent, plaintiffs have stated a claim based on a theory of disloyalty because plaintiffs allege subsequent conduct by defendants that supports such a theory.

In Pennsylvania, "[a] cause of action may be maintained against an attorney for breach of his or her fiduciary duty to a client." *Gorski v. Smith*, 2002 PA Super 334, 812 A.2d 683, 711 (Pa. Super. Ct. 2002). "[T]he relationship between the attorney and his client is a fiduciary relationship." *Maritrans GP Inc. v. Pepper, Hamilton & Scheetz*, 529 Pa. 241, 602 A.2d 1277, 1287 (Pa. 1992). [S]uch duty demands undivided loyalty and prohibits the attorney from engaging in conflicts of interest, and breach of such duty is actionable." *Id.* at 1283. "[A]n attorney who undertakes representation of a client owes that client both a duty of competent representation and the highest duty of honesty, fidelity, and confidentiality." *Capital Care Corp. v. Hunt*, 2004 PA Super 64, 847 A.2d 75, 84 (Pa. Super. Ct. 2004).

In the context of Pennsylvania legal malpractice, "breach of fiduciary duty" has often been understood by courts to describe a claim for breach of an attorney's duty of loyalty, rather than an attorney's duty of care. *See, e.g., Meyers v. Sudfeld*, No. 05-cv-2970, 2006 U.S. Dist. LEXIS 6421, at 16 (E.D. Pa. 2006) (requiring "that the defendant negligently or intentionally failed to act in good faith and solely for the benefit of plaintiff" for a breach of fiduciary duty claim against an attorney). The precise legal standard in Pennsylvania for establishing a breach of fiduciary duty in this sense has not been as clearly articulated by the state's highest court as that for negligent malpractice, and district courts have turned to the Pennsylvania Suggested Standard Civil Jury Instructions to articulate the elements of such a claim. *See, e.g., McDermott v. Party City Corp.*, 11 F. Supp. 2d 612, 626 n.18 (E.D. Pa. 1998) (citing Pa. S.S.J.I. § 4.16 (1991)); *Meyers*, 2006 U.S. Dist. LEXIS 6421, at 16 (citing *McDermott*, 11 F. Supp. 2d at 626 n.18). A panel of the Third Circuit appears to have tacitly endorsed this approach. *See Dinger v. Allfirst Financial, Inc.*, 82 Fed. App'x 261, 265 (3d Cir. 2003) (quoting the breach of fiduciary duty standard used in *McDermott*, 11 F. Supp. 2d at 626 n.18) (non-precedential). In the absence of contrary authority, I will apply the same standard at this stage of the proceeding.

Thus, establishing a breach of fiduciary duty requires plaintiff to prove: "(1) that the defendant negligently or intentionally failed to act in good faith and solely for the benefit of plaintiff in all matters for which he or she was employed; (2) that the plaintiff suffered injury; and (3) that the agent's failure to act solely for the plaintiff's benefit . . . was a real factor in bring[ing] about plaintiff's injuries." *Meyers*, 2006 U.S. Dist. LEXIS 6421, at 16 (quoting *McDermott*, 11 F. Supp. 2d at 626 n.18); *see also* Pa. S.S.J.I. § 4.16.

Plaintiffs do not appear to assert that defendants failed to file the petition intentionally, or because of divided loyalty. However, plaintiffs assert that defendants attempted to hide their lapse by failing to inform plaintiffs that they had missed the deadline for filing a petition to fix fair value, informing President Judge Schmehl that they did not object to marking the judgment satisfied without consulting plaintiffs, failing to inform plaintiffs that the judgment was marked satisfied, and continuing to press the deficiency claim despite knowing it was unmeritorious. (Compl. 24–27; Pls.' Resp. 3.) These subsequent acts may constitute a failure "to act in good faith and solely for the benefit of plaintiff," *Meyers*, 2006 U.S. Dist. LEXIS 6421, at 16.

Of course, to recover on the theory that defendants' acts subsequent to their failure to file a petition to fix fair value were disloyal, plaintiffs will have to prove that such actions were "a real factor in bring[ing] about plaintiff[s'] injuries." *Id.* If there was no way to recover the deficiency once the original mistake was made, plaintiffs may be unable to recover the lost deficiency as damages under this theory of liability. At this stage, however, plaintiffs have sufficiently pleaded their claim.

B.   Count IV—Breach of Contract

Defendants assert that plaintiffs have failed to plead a contract-based malpractice claim because they do not properly allege harm resulting from defendants' failure to file a petition to fix fair value. (Def.'s Mot. 8.) More specifically, defendants assert that plaintiffs have failed to allege that they would have been successful in pursuing a deficiency against Peter Pugliese if defendants had properly filed a petition to fix fair value. (*Id.* at 9.) Defendants' argument is unavailing.

Although there is some degree of confusion in the relevant caselaw regarding the extent to which harm and causation are required elements of a contract-based malpractice claim, to the extent they are required plaintiff has met the burden of pleading them for the reasons discussed above with respect to plaintiffs' negligence claims.

[. . . .]

D. Count V—Punitive Damages

Defendants argue that plaintiffs' claim for punitive damages should be dismissed because the complaint alleges facts that, at most, support a finding of ordinary negligence. Plaintiffs have, however, alleged sufficient facts to support their request for punitive damages.

Under Pennsylvania law, "[p]unitive damages may be appropriately awarded only when the plaintiff has established that the defendant has acted in an outrageous fashion due to either 'the defendant's evil motive or his reckless indifference to the rights of others.' " *Phillips v. Cricket Lighters*, 584 Pa. 179, 883 A.2d 439, 445 (Pa. 2005) (quoting *Martin v. Johns-Manville Corp.*, 508 Pa. 154, 494 A.2d 1088, 1096 (Pa. 1985)). A punitive damages claim "must be supported by evidence sufficient to establish that (1) a defendant had a subjective appreciation of the risk of harm to which the plaintiff was exposed and that (2) he acted, or failed to act, as the case may be, in conscious disregard of that risk." *Hutchison v. Luddy*, 582 Pa. 114, 870 A.2d 766, 772 (Pa. 2005) (citing *Martin*, 494 A.2d at 1097–98).

Defendants rely on *McCartney v. Dunn & Conner, Inc.*, 386 Pa. Super. 563, 563 A.2d 525 (Pa. Super. Ct. 1989) to argue that plaintiffs have alleged facts that, at most, support a finding of ordinary negligence that does not support an award of punitive damages. However, *McCartney* was an appeal from a grant of summary judgment after discovery. Moreover, the allegations deemed insufficient in *McCartney* did not involve the kind of conscious wrongdoing plaintiffs allege in this case. Here, plaintiffs have not only alleged that defendants failed to make a necessary filing to prosecute their claim, but also that defendants subsequently engaged in a pattern of deliberate conduct that concealed and exacerbated that original mistake. (*See* Compl. ¶ 67 ("Plaintiffs . . . suffered injuries, damages and losses as a direct and proximate result of ... the Defendants' efforts to lie, hide and obscure [their] initial malpractice ....").) Even if the original mistake alone is insufficient, plaintiffs' allegations as a whole provide sufficient factual content to support a plausible claim for punitive damages.

IV. Conclusion

For the foregoing reasons I conclude that plaintiffs have properly pleaded each of their claims, and I will deny defendants' motion to dismiss.

SOLUTIONS: THE LAWYER SHOULD HAVE, WOULD HAVE, COULD HAVE...

When in doubt, resort to the truth. Some mistakes are not material and others can often be worked out. Here, the mistake was costly to the client. To cover it up was wrong because it kept the client in the dark and precluded it from dealing with the mistake in running its business. The failure to disclose put the lawyer's interest in saving face and avoiding a difficult conversation ahead of the client's need to know what was occurring. It is a violation of MR 1.4 in addition to being an arguable breach of fiduciary duty. Biting the bullet and disclosing is painful but certainly preferable for the client as well as the law firm. Failing to disclose only serves to compound the lawyer's ethical troubles and legal exposure for negligence/malpractice.

X-Ray Questions

Question 2 of this opinion deals with a conflict of interest that develops when the lawyer makes a mistake that can result in a malpractice claim. Why is there a conflict at that point between the lawyer and the client? Think back to *Orr* and the ultimate realization by Orr that he could no longer continue to represent the client. Why did he reach that conclusion. The Opinion also discusses telling the client to seek out other counsel to represent the client. While the word "malpractice" need not be used, the lawyer must tell the client that an error was made, and that other counsel should be consulted. Why? Is this requirement going too far with the lawyer essentially telling the client that a lawsuit against the lawyer should be considered? Moreover, because the client at a legal aid clinic is generally unsophisticated in legal matters, the lawyer must make "special efforts" in locating new counsel. How should a lawyer explain the situation to a new lawyer that will represent the client? How would you do so?

Formal Opinion 1995–2: Conflict of interest; waiver; duty to report malpractice

February 22, 1995

TOPIC: Conflict of interest; waiver; duty to report malpractice.

DIGEST: Where client has a possible malpractice claim against a legal services organization, the organization must withdraw from the representation, advise the client to get new counsel and assist the client in obtaining new counsel.

CODE: DRs 1–103(A), 2–110(A)(2), 5–102, 6–101(A)(3); ECs 2–7, 2–8, 5–9, 7–7, 7–8, 7–11.

QUESTIONS

(1)   Is an attorney who oversees legal work at a legal services organization and believes that the organization may have committed malpractice required to advise a client to seek legal advice from another attorney regarding a possible malpractice action against the organization?

(2)   Under these circumstances, may the legal services organization continue its representation of the client?

(3)   Is the legal services organization required to assist the client in finding new representation?

OPINION

The inquirer, who oversees the legal work at a legal services organization ("LSO"), has become aware of a situation that may have involved malpractice by LSO. Apparently, a favorable ruling was obtained in an action filed by LSO on behalf of a client. The court directed LSO to settle an order. LSO failed to settle the order within 60 days as required by 22 NYCRR § 202.48(b). More than two years later, when LSO attempted to cure the defect, the court advised both parties by letter that the judgment was rejected for lateness without prejudice to the client's right to make a motion to settle judgment beyond the 60-day period. LSO did not advise the client of that decision for five months, and the motion to settle the order late was not made until the following month. That motion was denied. In its opinion, the court stated that no explanation had been offered for the failure to bring that motion until six months after the court's notification. Shortly thereafter, LSO advised the client, who is indigent, that the motion had been denied. The inquirer is awaiting a recommendation from the LSO attorney handling the matter about whether that last decision should be appealed.

DR 6–101(A)(3) provides that a lawyer shall not "[n]eglect a legal matter entrusted to the lawyer." While it appears that neglect has taken place in the situation described, we express no opinion as to whether a violation of this disciplinary rule constitutes legal malpractice. Nor do we express an opinion as to whether the violation must be reported to an appropriate authority. See DR 1–103(A). We do, however, believe that it is incumbent upon LSO to take whatever action is necessary to minimize and, if possible, to reverse any prejudice this inaction has caused the client.

Where several options are available to a client, the attorney has a duty to inform the client of the possible courses of action and to give the client an honest evaluation of each. N.Y. State 425 (1975). Here, the client has different options. For example, the relief available to the client is likely to differ if the client brings a malpractice claim rather than an appeal. Moreover, it is conceivable that if the client were to have LSO prosecute the appeal, that fact might have a detrimental effect in a subsequent malpractice action. "[I]t is for the client and not the lawyer to decide what legal rights to assert or abandon," and that decision "must be an informed one, and not one imposed by the lawyer on [the] client by default or ignorance." Id.; see EC 7–7, EC 7–8.

Because of the clear-cut and irremediable potential malpractice claim, LSO has a conflict of interest. Therefore, we do not believe that LSO can properly advise this client about applicable rights and remedies, including the malpractice option, even if full disclosure of this conflict were made as required by DR 5–101(A) ("Except with the consent of the client after full disclosure, a lawyer shall not accept employment if the exercise of professional judgment on behalf of the client will be or reasonably may be affected by the lawyer's own financial, business, property or personal interests."). In addition, although the inquirer did not actually participate in the representation of the client, the inquirer is barred from giving advice to the client on this matter by virtue of being employed by LSO in an oversight capacity. In an opinion regarding a conflict in private practice, the New York State Bar Association has stated: "Even with full disclosure, client consent would be ineffective to cure the conflict if, for example, the lawyer had been personally involved in the acts of malpractice while associated with his former firm, or if the lawyer had been a partner in the firm at the time the acts were committed." N.Y. State 635 (1992). It is also possible that the inquirer might be a witness in a malpractice action against LSO. This presents another potential reason for withdrawal. DR 5–102; EC 5–9.

Because of this non-waivable conflict of interest, LSO may not represent the client on appeal and should withdraw from the representation. LSO's ethical obligations to the client are therefore governed by the rule regarding withdrawal from representation. Under DR 2–110(A)(2), LSO is required to take steps "to the extent reasonably practical to avoid foreseeable prejudice to the rights of the client." "Foreseeable prejudice" here includes the possibility that the client will never obtain the redress that a court had already determined was appropriate. A client's intelligence and experience should dictate, in part, what action the attorney takes to avoid prejudice to the rights of the client. EC 2–7.

We note that this client apparently has not taken steps to sue LSO, despite being twice informed of LSO's failures to take the steps required to further the case. This fact highlights the need for some attorney not employed by LSO to advise the client about possible options. While we do not believe the word "malpractice" must necessarily be used in directing the client to seek legal advice, the client must be advised of the need to receive such advice. Furthermore, because the client's present position appears to be wholly attributable to LSO's inaction, we believe LSO has a duty to make certain this client obtains other representation. Depending upon the client's intelligence and experience, LSO may provide assistance in locating new counsel. While the Code compels the conclusions reached in this opinion, we are mindful that most clients who require pro bono legal assistance will find it substantially difficult to obtain a lawyer on their own to pursue a malpractice claim or to follow through on the original matter. LSO should therefore make special efforts to assist such clients in locating new counsel. Selection of legal counsel is particularly difficult for persons of limited education or means. EC 2–7. Disinterested and informed advice and recommendations from other lawyers may be helpful. EC 2–8. It may be possible that another legal services organization or law clinic will be willing to undertake the representation or that a private attorney will do so on a contingent fee basis; otherwise, the client will have to obtain pro bono representation.

> **CONCLUSION**
>
> When a legal services organization may have committed malpractice to the detriment of its client, the organization should withdraw from the representation, advise the client to obtain legal advice from an attorney not employed by the organization, and assist the client in locating new counsel.

LEANING INTO PRACTICE

Answer the following statement with a "yes" or a "no"

A lawyer should disclosure the following mistakes.

➤ The lawyer fails to file a jury demand or pay a jury fee.

➤ Lawyer has a case in a jurisdiction with a split of authority on key issues in the case. Lawyer argues authority A; Court rejects that argument, uses authority Z, and client's case is therefore dismissed.

➤ Lawyer drafts an IOU for a client who is lending money; lawyer does not include an acceleration payment clause in the note should lendee miss a payment.

➤ Lawyer misspells name of key precedent in a brief but uses correct cite.

Cases and Materials

X-Ray Questions (*Perez*)

This case involves the sad circumstances of a truck driver who owned a trucking company. His truck collided with a school bus, killing 21 children. The lawyers retained to represent the company visited the driver in the hospital. They told him that they were his lawyers and took a statement from him on the circumstances of the accident. They later voluntarily gave that statement to the District Attorney who, using the statement, prosecuted the driver for manslaughter. The driver was acquitted. He then sued the lawyers claiming a breach of fiduciary duty.

How did the court analyze the issue of whether there was a claim of fiduciary duty? Of course, the first threshold question is this: was an ACR formed? If "no" there is one result and if "yes" then there is another. What should the lawyers have done had they wanted to represent both the company and the driver? Would joint representation even be possible? We have previously covered the terms of a joint representation agreement in our discussion of the *Baldwin* case. Go through the agreement and ask yourselves whether it would make sense to have one firm represent both. Why do you think the lawyers acted in the way that they did? Would knowing that they had recently left a large firm to set up their own shop inform your answer? Why? And keep in mind MR 1.6 which we will study later in this chapter. Without looking at MR 1.6 yet, ask yourself whether a lawyer is required, upon the demand of a D.A., to turn over documents such as the confidential statement from the driver who, believed he had formed an ACR with the lawyers. Why or why not? Is this case another example, as in *Baldwin* of a lawyer not fully understanding who he or she represents or was another factor at play here? If so, what was it?

Perez v. Kirk & Carrigan

Court of Appeals of Texas, Thirteenth District, Corpus Christi, 1991.
822 S.W.2d 261.

Ruben Perez appeals a summary judgment rendered against him on his causes of action against the law firm of Kirk & Carrigan, and against Dana Kirk and Steve Carrigan individually (henceforth all three will be collectively referred to as "Kirk & Carrigan"). We reverse the summary judgment and remand this case for trial.

The present suit arises from a school bus accident on September 21, 1989, in Alton, Texas. Ruben Perez was employed by Valley Coca-Cola Bottling Company as a truck driver. On the morning of the accident, Perez attempted to stop his truck at a stop sign along his route, but the truck's brakes failed to stop the truck, which collided with the school bus. The loaded bus was knocked into a pond and 21 children died. Perez suffered injuries from the collision and was taken to a local hospital to be treated.

The day after the accident, Kirk & Carrigan, lawyers who had been hired to represent Valley Coca-Cola Bottling Company, visited Perez in the hospital for the purpose of taking his statement. Perez claims that the lawyers told him that they were his lawyers too and that anything he told them would be kept confidential. With this understanding, Perez gave them a sworn statement concerning the accident. However, after taking Perez' statement, Kirk & Carrigan had no further contact with him. Instead, Kirk & Carrigan made arrangements for criminal defense attorney Joseph Connors to represent Perez. Connors was paid by National Union Fire Insurance Company which covered both Valley Coca-Cola and Perez for liability in connection with the accident.

Sometime after Connors began representing Perez, Kirk & Carrigan, without telling either Perez or Connors, turned Perez' statement over to the Hidalgo County District Attorney's Office. Kirk & Carrigan contend that Perez' statement was provided in a good faith attempt to fully comply with a request of the district attorney's office and under threat of subpoena if they did not voluntarily comply. Partly on the basis of this statement, the district attorney was able to obtain a grand jury indictment of Perez for involuntary manslaughter for his actions in connection with the accident.

Ruben Perez filed the present suit as a Plea in Intervention and Original Petition in a suit brought on behalf of the children injured in the accident against Valley Coca-Cola. Perez sued Kirk & Carrigan, along with Valley Coca-Cola, a number of other Coca-Cola entities, and National Union Fire Insurance Company. Perez asserted numerous causes of action against Kirk & Carrigan for breach of fiduciary duty, negligent and intentional infliction of emotional distress, violation of the Texas Deceptive Trade Practices-Consumer Protection Act, Tex. Bus. & Corp. Code Ann. § 17.41 et seq. (Vernon 1987), and conspiracy to violate article 21.21 of the Texas Insurance Code, Tex. Ins. Code Ann. art. 21.21 (Vernon Supp. 1991). Perez complained generally by his petition that Kirk & Carrigan had caused him to suffer public humiliation and emotional distress by turning over his supposedly confidential statement to the district attorney. In addition to the turnover of this statement, Perez alleged generally that Kirk & Carrigan, Valley Coca-Cola, and National Union engaged in an overall plan to shift the blame for the accident away from them and onto Perez, by concealing information tending to show that Valley Coca-Cola's faulty maintenance of the brakes on the truck was the real cause of the accident.

Kirk & Carrigan moved for summary judgment on all of the claims made against them by Perez, on the grounds that no attorney-client or other fiduciary relationship existed, that even if a fiduciary relationship did exist no damages resulted from the asserted breach, that all of Perez' claims basically allege groundless prosecution and therefore constitute an invalid claim for malicious prosecution, that Perez was not a consumer under the DTPA, and that Perez failed to state a cause of action for conspiracy to violate the Texas Insurance Code.

After hearing the motion for summary judgment, the trial court rendered judgment that Perez take nothing on his claims against Kirk & Carrigan. When the trial court then severed these claims from others within the suit, it became a final summary judgment, from which Perez presently appeals.

By his sole point of error, Perez complains simply that the trial court erred in granting Kirk & Carrigan's motion for summary judgment. The movant for summary judgment has the burden of showing that there is no genuine issue of material fact and that he is entitled to judgment as a matter of law. In deciding whether there is a disputed material fact issue precluding a summary judgment, evidence favorable to the non-movant will be taken as true, every reasonable inference must be indulged in the non-movant's favor, and any doubts must be resolved in his favor. *Nixon v. Mr. Property Management Co.*, 690 S.W.2d 546, 548–49 (Tex. 1985). The issue is whether the summary judgment proof establishes as a matter of law that there is no genuine issue of fact concerning one or more of the essential elements of the plaintiff's cause of action. *Sakowitz, Inc. v. Steck*, 669 S.W.2d 105, 107–08 (Tex. 1984); *Gibbs v. General Motors Corp.*, 450 S.W.2d 827, 828 (Tex. 1970)

Breach of Fiduciary Duty

With regard to Perez' cause of action for breach of the fiduciary duty of good faith and fair dealing, Kirk and Carrigan contend that no attorney-client relationship existed and no fiduciary duty arose, because Perez never sought legal advice from them.

An agreement to form an attorney-client relationship may be implied from the conduct of the parties. Moreover, the relationship does not depend upon the payment of a fee, but may exist as a result of rendering services gratuitously. *E.F. Hutton & Co. v. Brown*, 305 F.Supp. 371, 388 (S.D.Tex. 1969); *Kotzur v. Kelly*, 791 S.W.2d 254, 257 (Tex. App.—Corpus Christi 1990, no writ); *Prigmore v. Hardware Mut. Ins. Co. of Minnesota*, 225 S.W.2d 897, 899 (Tex. Civ. App.—Amarillo 1949, no writ).

In the present case, viewing the summary judgment evidence in the light most favorable to Perez, Kirk & Carrigan told him that, in addition to representing Valley Coca Cola, they were also Perez' lawyers and that they were going to help him. Perez did not challenge this assertion, and he cooperated with the lawyers in giving his statement to them, even though he did not offer, nor was he asked, to pay the lawyers' fees. We hold that this was sufficient to imply the creation of an attorney-client relationship at the time Perez gave his statement to Kirk & Carrigan.

The existence of this relationship encouraged Perez to trust Kirk & Carrigan and gave rise to a corresponding duty on the part of the attorneys not to violate this position of trust. Accordingly, the relation between attorney and client is highly fiduciary in nature, and their dealings with each other are subject to the same scrutiny as a transaction between trustee and beneficiary. *Archer v. Griffith*, 390 S.W.2d 735, 739 (Tex. 1964); *Gum v. Schaefer*, 683 S.W.2d 803, 805 n. 2 (Tex. App.—Corpus Christi 1984, no writ); *see also Willis v. Maverick*, 760 S.W.2d 642, 645 (Tex. 1988). Specifically, the relationship between attorney and client has been described as one of *uberrima fides*, which means, "most abundant good faith," requiring absolute and perfect candor, openness and honesty, and the absence of any concealment or deception. *Hefner v. State*, 735 S.W.2d 608, 624 (Tex. App.—Dallas 1987, pet. ref'd); *State v. Baker*, 539 S.W.2d 367, 374 (Tex. Civ. App.—Austin 1976, writ ref'd n.r.e.). In addition, because of the openness and candor within this relationship, certain communications between attorney and client are privileged from disclosure in either civil or criminal proceedings under the provisions of Tex. R. Civ. Evid. 503 and Tex. R. Crim. Evid. 503, respectively.

There is evidence that Kirk & Carrigan represented to Perez that his statement would be kept confidential. Later, however, without telling either Perez or his subsequently-retained criminal defense attorney, Kirk & Carrigan voluntarily disclosed Perez' statement to the district attorney. Perez asserts in the present suit that this course of conduct amounted, among other things, to a breach of fiduciary duty.

Kirk & Carrigan seek to avoid this claim of breach, on the ground that the attorney-client privilege did not apply to the present statement, because unnecessary third parties were present at the time it was given. *See* Tex. R. Civ. Evid. 503(a)(5); Tex. R. Crim. Evid. 503(a)(5). However, whether or not the Rule 503 attorney-client privilege extended to Perez' statement, Kirk & Carrigan initially obtained the statement from Perez on the understanding that it would be kept confidential. Thus, regardless of whether from an evidentiary standpoint the privilege attached, Kirk & Carrigan breached their fiduciary duty to Perez either by wrongfully disclosing a privileged statement or by wrongfully representing that an unprivileged statement would be kept confidential. Either characterization shows a clear lack of honesty toward, and a deception of, Perez by his own attorneys regarding the degree of confidentiality with which they intended to treat the statement.

This type of deceitful and fraudulent conduct within the attorney-client relationship has been treated as a tortious breach of duty in other contexts. *See* Burgin v. Godwin, 167 S.W.2d 614 (Tex. Civ. App.—Amarillo 1942, writ. ref'd w.o.m.); *Sherwood v. South*, 29 S.W.2d 805, 809 (Tex. Civ. App.—San Antonio 1930, writ ref'd) (if without consent the attorney uses confidential information from his client in order to advance the attorney's own personal interest and at the expense of the client's interest, he may be sued by his client for fraud).

In *Burgin*, for instance, the attorneys had a written agreement with their client for compensation, which the parties subsequently modified by an oral agreement. The attorneys later attempted to avoid the oral modification by asserting the statute of frauds. In holding that the attorneys were not entitled to the protections of the statute of frauds, the Amarillo Court of Appeals reasoned that the attorneys were under a duty to act with the most scrupulous fidelity and reveal to their client the exact status brought about by the contractual relationship and the need to reduce the oral modification to writing. *Burgin*, 167 S.W.2d at 619.

Similarly, in the present case, the attorneys were at least under a fiduciary duty not to misrepresent to Perez that his conversations with them were confidential. Kirk & Carrigan should not now be able to assert the lack of attorney-client privilege (as the attorneys in *Burgin* were not allowed to assert the statute of frauds) to excuse the harm caused by their own misrepresentation to Perez. We hold that it was error for the trial court to grant summary judgment on the ground that Kirk & Carrigan did not owe or breach a fiduciary duty to Perez.

In addition, however, even assuming a breach of fiduciary duty, Kirk & Carrigan also contend that summary judgment may be sustained on the ground that Perez could show no damages resulting from the breach. Kirk & Carrigan contend that their dissemination of Perez' statement could not have caused him any damages in the way of emotional distress, because the statement merely revealed Perez' own version of what happened. We do not agree. Mental anguish consists of the emotional response of the plaintiff caused by the tortfeasor's conduct. *Birchfield v. Texarkana Memorial Hospital*, 747 S.W.2d 361, 368 (Tex. 1987); *Automobile Insurance Co. v. Davila*, 805 S.W.2d 897, 907 (Tex. App.—Corpus Christi 1991, writ denied). It includes, among other things, the mental sensation of pain resulting from public humiliation. *Davila*, 805 S.W.2d at 907.

Regardless of the fact that Perez himself made the present statement, he did not necessarily intend it to be a public response as Kirk & Carrigan contend, but only a private and confidential discussion with his attorneys. Perez alleged that the publicity caused by his indictment, resulting from the revelation of the statement to the district attorney in breach of that confidentiality, caused him to suffer emotional distress and mental anguish. We hold that Perez has made a valid claim for such damages. *Cf. Billings v. Atkinson*, 489 S.W.2d 858 (Tex. 1973) (damages for mental suffering are appropriate for an invasion of privacy).

[. . . .]

In conclusion, for the reasons stated above, we sustain Perez' point of error. We REVERSE the summary judgment rendered against Perez and REMAND this case for trial.

SOLUTIONS: THE LAWYER SHOULD HAVE, WOULD HAVE, COULD HAVE. . .

The lawyers in this case formed an ACR—either express or implied—with Perez—and thus owed him the duties embodied in the Rules as well as fiduciary duty of loyalty. Another option would have been under MR 4.3 which sets out the rules for dealing with an unrepresented person. Thus, this rule provides that lawyers who know they are dealing with an unrepresented person mut make clear that they are not representing that person; that they are seeking to fulfill the objectives of their clients; and that they are not providing legal counsel to the person.

Cases and Materials

X-Ray Questions (*Clark Hill*)

This case deals with the People's Republic of China (PRC), political persecution, cyber hacking, and social media. It also provides an excellent analysis of the different types of claims that can be brought against a lawyer arising from a lawyer's representation of a client.

Here, a political dissident left the PRC and sought political asylum in the United States. He hired a law firm to assist him in accomplishing this goal. The client warned the firm that the PRC would likely seek to cyber-attack its computer system and extract documents relating to the representation. Supposedly, the firm assured him that it would take the necessary precautions. It may not have. In a great turn of phrase, the court writes that "Unfortunately for all parties, Plaintiff's warnings of a cyber-attack, apparently as unheeded as Cassandra's, proved prescient." Soon thereafter the firm withdrew from representation citing MR 1.16 that precludes representation if a lawyer will be both an advocate and a witness (here to testify on what the PCR allegedly did vis-a-vis its campaign of political persecution of the dissident and the hacking).

The dissident sued for breach of contract; breach of fiduciary duty; and legal malpractice. The court denied a Rule 12(b)(6) motion as to each. While the operative facts supporting the claims share some similarities, they are framed differently in order to support the respective claims. What was the promise that was breached to support the breach of contract? How did the plaintiff's lawyer then frame some of those facts to support the breach of fiduciary duty claim and to satisfy the heightened factual showing required to avoid dismissal of that claim? What duty was breached to—and how was it breached—to enable a claim of malpractice?

Guo Wengui v. Clark Hill, PLC, et al.

United States District Court, District of Columbia, 2020.
440 F.Supp.3d 30.

JAMES E. BOASBERG, UNITED STATES DISTRICT JUDGE.

This case features an asylum-application process gone awry, accompanied by alleged professional misconduct, foreign-government cyber hacking, and social-media propaganda campaigns. After Plaintiff Guo Wengui, a Chinese businessman and prominent political dissident, retained the services of the law firm Clark Hill, PLC to assist him with an asylum petition, someone—whom the parties presume to be associated with the Chinese government—hacked into the firm's computer servers. The hacker thereby gained access to Plaintiff's confidential information and then published that information on the Internet. Compounding Wengui's problems, the firm withdrew its representation in response to the attack. Plaintiff asserts that in making his information vulnerable to a targeted hacking and subsequently withdrawing from the matter, Defendants Clark Hill are liable for legal malpractice, breach of fiduciary duty, and breach of contract. Defendants now move to dismiss all claims.

To succeed on his tort claims, Wengui must "point to an act (or omission)" that "resulted in a loss" to him. See *Seed Co., Ltd. v. Westerman*, 840 F. Supp. 2d 116, 127 (D.D.C. 2012). Plaintiff has successfully pleaded that the alleged mishandling of his information and subsequent cyber attack resulted in damages. The withdrawal, however, may have added insult, but it did not add injury. In addition, he cannot establish that the withdrawal breached Defendants' contractual obligations to him. The Court therefore will dismiss all of Plaintiff's claims to the extent they rely on the theory that Defendants' withdrawal constituted a legally remediable wrong, but it will permit those claims to go forward that allege misrepresentations surrounding and mishandling of his confidential information. Finally, it dismisses the demand for punitive damages, as Plaintiff has not satisfied the high bar necessary for seeking such relief.

I. Background

A. Factual Background

As it must at this juncture, the Court draws the facts from the Complaint. See *Sparrow v. United Air Lines, Inc.*, 216 F.3d 1111, 1113 (D.C. Cir. 2000). Plaintiff is a "highly successful businessman" and "well-known Chinese dissident." ECF No. 1 (Complaint), ¶ 10. While living in China, he exposed "systemic corruption" and "widespread abuse of human rights" being perpetrated by the Communist Party of China (CCP), China's ruling political party. Id., ¶ 15. These activities naturally caught the attention of the CCP, which allegedly threatened his livelihood and that of his family in order to put an end to his subversive activities. Id., ¶¶ 18–19. Fearing further persecution, Plaintiff fled his native country in 2015, and he now resides in New York. Id., ¶ 10. Wengui's escape from China has not prevented further harassment. The Chinese government has, for example, sent emissaries to demonstrate against him outside of his home as part of a larger "malicious negative propaganda campaign" organized against him. Id., ¶¶ 23–24. In response to this cross-continental maltreatment, Plaintiff set about applying for political asylum in the United States.

The source of this dispute dates back to Plaintiff's negotiations with Defendant Thomas Ragland, an attorney and partner at Defendant Clark Hill, PLC—a firm comprising about 650 lawyers—regarding potential assistance with his asylum petition. Id., ¶¶ 11–12. Hoping to secure Plaintiff as a client, Ragland assured him that both he and the firm more broadly "were qualified, capable, and competent to represent plaintiff and to protect his interests fully and professionally." Id., ¶ 28. At a subsequent meeting in August 2016, Wengui conveyed to Ragland and other Clark Hill attorneys "his standing and visibility as a prominent Chinese political dissident" and "the risks associated with and attendant to plaintiff's position as a prominent visible critic of the Chinese regime." Id., ¶ 31. Plaintiff also "warned of the persistent and relentless cyber attacks that he and his associates had endured." Id.

In further meetings with the firm, Wengui continued to warn Defendants that they should "expect to be subjected to sophisticated cyber attacks." Id., ¶ 32. In taking on Plaintiff's case, Defendants accordingly agreed to "take special precautions to prevent improper disclosure of plaintiff's sensitive confidential information." Id., ¶ 33. These precautions would include distinct measures to impede or evade cyber attacks, by, for example, "not placing any of plaintiff's information on the firm's computer server," as doing so would make the information more vulnerable to hackings. Id. Relying on the firm's commitments regarding the protection of his confidential information, Plaintiff hired Defendants, executing a letter of retention and paying the firm a retainer fee of $10,000. Id., ¶ 36.

Unfortunately for all parties involved, Plaintiff's warnings of a cyber attack, apparently as unheeded as Cassandra's, proved prescient. On September 12, 2017, the firm's computer system was "hacked"—again, both parties assume that the hacking was orchestrated by the Chinese government—"apparently without great difficulty." Id., ¶ 41. The hacker obtained a substantial amount of Plaintiff's and his spouse's personal information, such as their passport identification numbers, as well as Plaintiff's application for political asylum. Id., ¶ 43. This information, including the contents of Wengui's asylum petition, was then published and disseminated on social media. Id., ¶ 44.

Following the attack, the parties' relationship quickly dissolved. On September 19, Clark Hill's General Counsel, Edward Hood, informed Plaintiff that the firm was terminating its involvement with his case. Id., ¶ 49. Hood explained that the attack might require Ragland, along with other members of the firm, to serve as witnesses at Plaintiff's asylum proceeding, as the hacking provided evidence of the political persecution from which Plaintiff sought asylum in the United States. Id. Hood posited that because the Rules of Professional Conduct bar attorneys from playing the dual role of witness and advocate, Defendants were required to withdraw from the matter. Id., ¶¶ 49–50. At the time of that withdrawal, Plaintiff had filed an asylum application and was awaiting a hearing. Id., ¶ 51.

B. Procedural History

On September 19, 2019, Wengui filed this action against Defendants in the Superior Court of the District of Columbia. Defendants then removed the case to this Court on diversity-jurisdiction grounds. See ECF No. 1 (Notice of Removal) at 1–2. Plaintiff's Complaint asserts four counts: (1) breach of fiduciary duty; (2) breach of contract; (3) legal malpractice; and (4) punitive damages. See Compl., ¶¶ 66–93. Defendants now move to dismiss all counts, maintaining that they fail to state plausible claims for relief.

II. Legal Standard

Federal Rule of Civil Procedure 12(b)(6) provides for the dismissal of an action where a complaint fails to "state a claim upon which relief can be granted." Although "detailed factual allegations" are not necessary to withstand a Rule 12(b)(6) motion, *Bell Atl. Corp. v. Twombly*, 550 U.S. 544, 555, 127 S.Ct.

1955, 167 L.Ed.2d 929 (2007), "a complaint must contain sufficient factual matter, accepted as true, to state a claim to relief that is plausible on its face." *Ashcroft v. Iqbal*, 556 U.S. 662, 678, 129 S.Ct. 1937, 173 L.Ed.2d 868 (2009) (internal quotation omitted).

In evaluating Defendants' Motion to Dismiss, the Court must "treat the complaint's factual allegations as true and must grant plaintiff the benefit of all inferences that can be derived from the facts alleged.' " *Sparrow*, 216 F.3d at 1113 (citation omitted) (quoting *Schuler v. United States*, 617 F.2d 605, 608 (D.C. Cir. 1979)) (citing *Leatherman v. Tarrant Cty. Narcotics Intelligence & Coordination Unit*, 507 U.S. 163, 164, 113 S.Ct. 1160, 122 L.Ed.2d 517 (1993)). The Court need not accept as true, however, "a legal conclusion couched as a factual allegation" nor an inference unsupported by the facts set forth in the Complaint. See *Trudeau v. FTC*, 456 F.3d 178, 193 (D.C. Cir. 2006) (quoting *Papasan v. Allain*, 478 U.S. 265, 286, 106 S.Ct. 2932, 92 L.Ed.2d 209 (1986)). Finally, even at the Rule 12(b)(6) stage, a court can review "documents attached as exhibits or incorporated by reference in the complaint" or "documents upon which the plaintiff's complaint necessarily relies." *Ward v. D.C. Dep't of Youth Rehab. Servs.*, 768 F. Supp. 2d 117, 119 (D.D.C. 2011) (internal quotation marks and citations omitted).

III. Analysis

In seeking dismissal here, Defendants argue that neither the cyber attack nor the withdrawal constitutes a ground for a viable claim of legal malpractice, breach of fiduciary duty, or breach of contract. In particular, they assert that their conduct surrounding these two events did not breach any duty owed to Plaintiff. They also argue that their actions, even if improper, did not cause him to suffer any actual damages. The Court will consider the two relevant events in turn, examining the separate counts in that context, albeit slightly out of sequence.

A.   Cyber Attack

As recounted above, the Complaint alleges that: Plaintiff warned Defendants of the risk of an impending cyber attack; Defendants misrepresented the manner in which they would protect Plaintiff's confidential information from such an attack; and Defendants then failed to protect this information, allowing it to be retrieved and then publicly disseminated by a third-party hacker. Defendants dispute that they made such representations and argue that, in any event, the cyber attack did not actually harm Plaintiff. The Court, however, rejects Defendants' premature attempt to litigate disputed facts at the pleading stage and will deny their Motion to Dismiss as it pertains to the cyber attack.

1.   *Breach of Fiduciary Duty*

Count I asserts that Defendants breached various fiduciary duties owed to Plaintiff, including the duty of good faith, the duty of loyalty, and the duty to protect Plaintiff's confidential records. See Compl., ¶ 68. To succeed on a claim of breach of fiduciary duty in the District of Columbia—the relevant jurisdiction here—Plaintiff must establish "(1) the existence of a fiduciary duty and (2) a violation of that duty that (3) proximately causes injury." Council on *Am.-Islamic Relations Action Network, Inc. v. Gaubatz*, 82 F. Supp. 3d 344, 353 (D.D.C. 2015) (citing *Shapiro, Lifschitz & Schram, P.C. v. Hazard*, 24 F. Supp. 2d 66, 75 (D.D.C. 1998)). It is axiomatic that the attorney-client relationship is fiduciary in nature. See *Thomas v. Nat'l Legal Prof'l Assocs.*, 594 F. Supp. 2d 31, 34 (D.D.C. 2009) ("[T]here is an ever present fiduciary responsibility that arches over every aspect of the lawyer-client relationship.") (quoting *Connelly v. Swick & Shapiro, P.C.*, 749 A.2d 1264, 1268 (D.C. 2000)). Defendants argue, however, that they did not breach any recognized fiduciary duties owed to Plaintiff and, in any event, did not cause any actual injury to him.

First, as to breach of duty, Wengui does not allege, contrary to Defendants' assertion, simply that "because there was a cyber incident, Defendants must have put up . . . 'unreasonable' security measures." ECF No. 12 (Def. MTD) at 12. It is true that some courts have gone so far as to hold that corporations maintain a duty to consumers to " 'protect against a criminal act of a third person,' which could include hacking into a private data system, 'if it is alleged that the entity had reason to anticipate the criminal act.' " *Attias v. CareFirst, Inc.*, 365 F. Supp. 3d 1, 21 (D.D.C. 2019) (quoting *In re Arby's Restaurant Group Inc., Litig.*, 2018 WL 2128441, at 5 (N.D. Ga. Mar. 5, 2018)). As a result, those courts have held that if a corporation fails to prevent a forseeable cyber attack, it thereby breaches fiduciary duties owed its customers. Id. This Court, however, need not go so far as to find that any corporation's failure to protect against any forseeable cyber attack, standing on its own, constitutes a breach of fiduciary duty.

A fiduciary relationship—like that between a lawyer and client—"is founded upon trust or confidence reposed by one person in the integrity and fidelity of another." *Democracy Partners v. Project Veritas Action Fund*, 285 F. Supp. 3d 109, 121 (D.D.C. 2018) (quoting *Bolton v. Crowley, Hoge, & Fein, P.C.*, 110 A.3d 575, 584 (D.C. 2015)). The duty of loyalty in this context "has been described as one of 'uberrima fides,' which means, most abundant good faith, requiring absolute and perfect candor, openness and honesty, and the absence of any concealment or deception." *Herbin v. Hoeffel*, 806 A.2d 186, 197 (D.C. 2002) (emphasis added) (quotation marks omitted); see also *Seed Co.*, 840 F. Supp. 2d at 126–27 (attorney breaches fiduciary duties when providing clients with "incorrect and misleading" advice); *Herbin*, 806 A.2d at 197 ("Disclosure of client confidences is contrary to the fundamental principle that the attorney owes a fiduciary duty to her client and must serve the client's interest with the utmost loyalty and devotion.") (quotation marks omitted).

Plaintiff has sufficiently pleaded that Defendants breached their duties of loyalty and good faith by misrepresenting the manner in which they would protect his confidential information in order to secure his business. Although they promised to take special precautions, they placed that information, including his asylum application, on their server and conveyed it via a firm email account—in direct contravention of his instructions—leaving Plaintiff vulnerable to the precise sort of machinations he had forewarned counsel about. See Compl., ¶¶ 2–3, 40–43. He further alleges that the firm breached the applicable duty of care in its treatment of his information by utilizing security measures that were "inadequate, unreasonable, and fell woefully far short of [D]efendants' promises, assurances, obligations, and commitments to provide adequate security measures." Id., ¶ 42. Discovery may reveal that Defendants never made any such misrepresentations to Plaintiff and were not negligent in their handling of his confidential information, but the well-pleaded allegations in the Complaint preclude granting Defendants' Motion to Dismiss.

Defendants argue in the alternative that even if they misled Plaintiff and were negligent in handling his confidential information, the cyber attack did not actually cause him any cognizable harm. Under D.C. law, not surprisingly, a breach of a fiduciary duty requires a showing of injury or damages. See *Headfirst Baseball LLC v. Elwood*, 239 F. Supp. 3d 7, 14 (D.D.C. 2017) (canvassing D.C. caselaw); see also *Becker v. Colonial Parking*, Inc., 409 F.2d 1130, 1136 (D.C. Cir. 1969) ("A simple breach of duty having no causal connection with the injury, we have admonished, cannot produce legal responsibility.") (quotation marks omitted). In arguing that Plaintiff has not made such a showing, Defendants rely on *Randolph v. ING Life Insurance & Annuity Company*, 973 A.2d 702 (D.C. 2009), where the District of Columbia Court of Appeals held that an "increased risk of future identity theft" does not qualify as an "actionable" injury "required to maintain a suit for common-law breach of fiduciary duty." Id. at 708.

Although this case, like Randolph, concerns a data breach, the similarities end there. In Randolph, an unknown burglar stole a laptop computer owned by the employee of an insurance company, which contained the plaintiffs' insurance information, including their names, addresses, and social-security numbers. Id. at 704. The DCCA reasoned that the plaintiffs had failed to plead "actual harm" because they had not alleged that the burglar stole the laptop in order to access their information or that their information had even been accessed since the laptop was stolen. Id. at 706–08. Instead, they simply alleged "the anticipation of future injury [identity theft] that has not materialized." Id. at 708; see also *In re Sci. Applications Int'l Corp. (SAIC) Backup Tape Data Theft Litig.*, 45 F. Supp. 3d 14, 19 (D.D.C. 2014) (dismissing case where plaintiffs' information, along with other items, was allegedly stolen from parked car because "mere loss of data— without evidence that it has been either viewed or misused—does not constitute an injury sufficient to confer standing").

Plaintiff, however, has gone well beyond pleading the anticipation of future injury and has instead alleged an actual injury resulting from Defendants' conduct. According to the Complaint, the Chinese government or someone associated with it hacked Defendants' server for the express purpose of stealing Plaintiff's information. The hacker then "published" the confidential material, including Plaintiff's application for political asylum and passport identification number, on social media. See Compl., ¶¶ 43–44. This chain of events occurred in the context of a broader propaganda campaign orchestrated by the CCP, one that included utilizing social-media platforms to spread information about Plaintiff and mobilizing demonstrators to protest his presence in the United States. Id., ¶¶ 22–24. Wengui therefore does not "speculate" as to potential uses of the stolen information; it has already been employed as part of the CCP's persecution and harassment of him. The Court therefore rejects Defendants' invitation to find that the cyber attack did not actually harm Plaintiff as a matter of law.

2.　*Legal Malpractice*

Count III alleges legal malpractice, asserting that Defendants breached their "common law" and "professional and ethical duties and obligations to plaintiff . . . by failing to use the required degree of professional care and skill in representing plaintiff," and in failing to maintain "reasonable security measures to secure their computer system from unauthorized access, as required and promised to plaintiff." Id., ¶¶ 82–85.

The elements of a legal-malpractice claim are similar to, but slightly distinct from, those for breach of fiduciary duty. See *Hickey v. Scott*, 738 F. Supp. 2d 55, 67 (D.D.C. 2010) (*quoting Shapiro, Lifschitz & Schram*, 24 F. Supp. 2d at 74). As Justice O'Conner has commented, "Lawyers are professionals, and as such they have greater obligations." *Zauderer v. Office of Disciplinary Counsel*, 471 U.S. 626, 676, 105 S.Ct. 2265, 85 L.Ed.2d 652 (1985) (O'Connor, J., concurring). To succeed on a legal-malpractice claim in the District of Columbia, "the plaintiff must show that (1) the defendant was employed as the plaintiff's attorney, (2) the defendant breached a reasonable duty, and (3) that breach resulted in, and was the proximate cause of, the plaintiff's loss or damages." *Beach TV Props., Inc. v. Solomon*, 306 F. Supp. 3d 70, 93 (D.D.C. 2018) (quoting *Martin v. Ross*, 6 A.3d 860, 862 (D.C. 2010)).

For the reasons recounted above, this count may also proceed as to the cyber attack because the Complaint identifies a breach of the duty of reasonable care owed by attorneys to their clients and actual damages. To be sure, attorneys cannot be held "liable for mistakes made in the honest exercise of professional judgment." *Biomet Inc. v. Finnegan Henderson LLP*, 967 A.2d 662, 665 (D.C. 2009). Honest mistakes, however, are a far cry from the conduct alleged here: misrepresentations made in order to secure a prospective client, the failure to follow promised procedures to adequately secure confidential information, and damages. See *Swann v. Waldman*, 465 A.2d 844, 846 (D.C. 1983) (finding plaintiff's allegations that attorney lied to him about attempting to obtain continuance and was negligent in failing to obtain expert witness sufficient to withstand motion for summary judgment on legal-malpractice claim).

3.   *Breach of Contract*

Plaintiff also brings a claim for breach of contract in Count II, alleging that the firm violated its contractual obligation to provide "competent representation" by undertaking a matter beyond its "professional or technical competence" and "neglecting to undertake reasonable security measures." Compl., ¶ 76. "To prevail on a claim of breach of contract, a party must establish (1) a valid contract between the parties; (2) an obligation or duty arising out of the contract; (3) a breach of that duty; and (4) damages caused by breach." *United States Conference of Mayors v. Great-W. Life & Annuity Ins. Co.*, 327 F. Supp. 3d 125, 129 (D.D.C. 2018), aff'd, 767 F. App'x 18 (D.C. Cir. 2019) (quoting *Tsintolas Realty Co. v. Mendez*, 984 A.2d 181, 187 (D.C. 2009)). Defendants concede that the parties entered into a valid contract (in this case, an engagement letter) that set forth their "respective obligations and expectations." See Def. MTD at 14. They dispute, however, that Plaintiff has alleged a breach of that contract.

Accepting the facts in the Complaint as true, Wengui has met his pleading burden—if just barely—of establishing that Defendants did not meet their contractual obligations. In particular, he alleges that they violated their obligations to provide "competent representation" and keep Plaintiff "reasonably informed about the status of the matter," Def. MSJ, Exh. A (Retainer Agreement) at 2, by misleading him as to the manner in which his information would be handled in the future, and then by failing to inform him when they eventually placed that information on their server. For the reasons stated in regard to the prior counts, this claim can proceed on the basis of failing to safeguard his information, which could amount to incompetent representation.

Going forward, however, Plaintiff may need to clarify this count because he appears to be exploring several different theories as to how Defendants breached the retainer agreement. First, he seems to be laying the groundwork for the introduction of extrinsic evidence. This evidence might demonstrate that Defendants orally amended the terms of the contract in making representations regarding higher-level protection of Plaintiff's personal information. See *Segal Wholesale, Inc. v. United Drug Serv.*, 933 A.2d 780, 784 (D.C. 2007) (extrinsic evidence "consistent with the terms of a partially integrated agreement is permissible"); see also *Stamenich v. Markovic*, 462 A.2d 452, 455 (D.C. 1983) (extrinsic evidence permissible to demonstrate "a contemporaneous agreement in addition to and not inconsistent with or a variation of the written agreement between the same parties, which was an essential inducement of the written contract" or where "fraud, mistake, or duress is alleged").

Alternatively, Plaintiff also appears to be seeking to demonstrate that Defendants violated a general obligation to provide competent representation in providing insufficient protection of client materials. See Compl., ¶ 76. Or, finally, he may be asserting that Defendants breached the "implied duty of good faith and fair dealing" that D.C. courts have found to be contained within all contracts, one that prohibits "evad[ing] the spirit of the contract" or "willfully render[ing] imperfect performance." *Murray v. Wells Fargo Home Mortg.*, 953 A.2d 308, 321 (D.C. 2008) (internal quotation marks omitted). Plaintiff will have to choose among these theories, and provide much more substantial support for them, should he decide to defend this count against further dispositive motions.

4. *Duplicative Nature of Claims*

Finally, the Court rejects Defendants' argument that the three claims chronicled above are necessarily "duplicative" of one other and thus that only one can proceed past the pleading stage. Under D.C. law, when a plaintiff's breach-of-fiduciary-duty claim rests on the same factual allegations and requests the same relief as his professional-malpractice claim, a court "as a matter of judicial economy, should dismiss" one of the claims as duplicative. See *N. Am. Catholic Educ. Programming Found., Inc. v. Womble, Carlyle, Sandridge & Rice, PLLC*, 887 F. Supp. 2d 78, 84 (D.D.C. 2012) (collecting cases). The same holds true for tort claims that arise out of the same factual circumstances as a breach-of-contract claim. See *Attias*, 365 F. Supp. 3d at 18 ("Under D.C. law, for a plaintiff to recover in tort for conduct that also constitutes a breach of contract, the tort must exist in its own right independent of the contract, and any duty upon which the tort is based must flow from considerations other than the contractual relationship.' ") (quoting *Choharis v. State Farm Fire & Cas. Co.*, 961 A.2d 1080, 1089 (D.C. 2008)).

Down the line, Plaintiff may indeed have to choose among his three common-law claims. At this early stage, however, it would be premature to dismiss any of the three as duplicative, given the fact-dependent nature of such an inquiry. While the counts all relate to the cyber attack generally, they may be predicated on distinct wrongs surrounding the attack. Defendants' conduct may have, for example, violated a Rule of Professional Responsibility—potentially creating liability for legal malpractice—which does not necessarily give rise to a breach of fiduciary duty. See, e.g., *Hickey*, 738 F. Supp. 2d at 67–68 (finding fee-related fiduciary-duty claim distinct from legal-malpractice claim concerning breach of Rule of Professional Responsibility in dispute over fees).

Finally, considerations of judicial economy do not weigh in favor of dismissal of any claims here. Allowing all three to proceed will not expand the scope of the case or potential avenues of discovery. At this juncture, therefore, the Court will decline Defendants' invitation to narrow Plaintiff's potential theories of relief. In sum, the Court will deny Defendants' Motion to Dismiss Counts I, II, and III to the extent that they rely on the theft of his personal information via cyber attack and Defendants' misrepresentations relating to protections from that attack.

B.   The Withdrawal

By contrast, Defendants' withdrawal from Plaintiff's asylum process—or, as Plaintiff labels the incident, their "firing" of him—does not provide grounds for a viable legal claim. As described above, Defendants terminated their representation of Wengui following the cyber attack. They explained in a letter to him that the attack had created "several ethical complications" related to their representation. See ECF No. 12–5 (Clark Hill Termination Letter) at 1. Defendants' "primary concern" was that "the cyberattack would require Mr. Ragland—and possibly other members of the Firm—to be a witness in [Plaintiff's] asylum proceeding" because they now had first-hand knowledge of China's prior persecution of Plaintiff, a factor relevant to that proceeding. Id.

In their Motion to Dismiss, Defendants argue that not only did their withdrawal not breach any duty owed to Wengui, but that it was in fact required by the Rules of Professional Conduct. See D.C. R. Prof. Conduct 1.16(a)(1) (D.C. Bar 2010) (attorney must withdraw from representing client if ongoing representation would violate Rule of Professional Conduct). Defendants again rely on Rule of Professional Conduct 3.7(a), which states that an attorney "shall not" act as an advocate for a client when she is "likely to be a necessary witness" in the proceeding. They also invoke Rule 1.7(b)(4), which requires withdrawal if the lawyer's ability to represent a client "reasonably may be adversely affected by the lawyer's responsibilities to or interests in a third party or the lawyer's own financial, business, property, or personal interests." Defendants explain that following the cyber attack, they had their "own interests in investigating and mitigating the incident—which conflicted with their representation of Plaintiff." Def. MTD at 8.

Regarding Rule 3.7(a), Plaintiff counters that Defendants' withdrawal was premature at best, given that Wengui "did not have an asylum interview, let alone any hearing" and "had not asked that Mr. Ragland be a witness." ECF No. 14 (Pl. Opp.) at 8. Additionally, Plaintiff argues that Rule 1.7(b)(4) raises "inherently factual issues" as to whether the cyber attack created a conflict of interest, issues that cannot be resolved at this stage. Id. at 21.

The Court need not settle these disputes because Wengui's fiduciary and malpractice claims run aground on a different shoal. Plaintiff has not sufficiently pled that Defendants' conduct, even if improper, damaged or prejudiced him. Both of these claims require a showing of damage or loss. See, e.g., *Seed Co.*, 840 F. Supp. 2d at 126 (plaintiff bringing malpractice claim "must point to an act (or omission) by the . . . [D]efendants that resulted in a loss" to him); *Randolph*, 973 A.2d at 708–09 (same regarding breach of fiduciary duty). As one court in this district described the applicable test when considering legal malpractice, the claim " 'does not accrue until the plaintiff-client has sustained some injury from the malpractice[,]' and the 'mere breach of a professional duty, causing only nominal damages, speculative harm, or the threat of future harm—not yet realized—does not suffice to create a cause of action for negligence.' " *Venable*

LLP v. Overseas Lease Grp., Inc., 2015 WL 4555372, at *2 (D.D.C. July 28, 2015) (quoting *Knight v. Furlow*, 553 A.2d 1232, 1235 (D.C. 1989)).

Plaintiff's claims predicated on the withdrawal do not plead damages that rise above the "speculative" or "nominal" level. Wengui does not dispute, for example, that at the time of Defendants' withdrawal, his asylum application had already been filed and he was awaiting an initial interview, which can take years to schedule. See Def. MTD at 20. He also does not claim to have experienced difficulties in finding a successor counsel with immigration-law expertise. As a result, Wengui has failed to factually substantiate his conclusory allegations that Defendants' withdrawal caused him "undue delay and complications," reputational harm, and prejudiced the outcome of his case. See Compl., ¶ 60; see also *Hinton v. Stein*, 278 F. Supp. 2d 27, 33 (D.D.C. 2003) (rejecting legal-malpractice claim where "[a]lthough there was a brief attorney-client relationship between the parties, defendant was justified in seeking to withdraw[,] . . . [h]er motion to withdraw was filed promptly[,] and there is no indication that plaintiff suffered any injury as a result of her withdrawal"). Put differently, the Complaint does not allege that Plaintiff "suffered any injury because of Defendant[s'] failure to represent him," and the Court will therefore dismiss his fiduciary-duty and malpractice claims to the extent that they rely on the withdrawal as the purported harm. Id.

Plaintiff's breach-of-contract claim based on the withdrawal is somewhat different, but also merits dismissal. A party may prevail on such a claim even if he "fails to prove actual damages," although he will be "entitled to no more than nominal damages." *Wright v. Howard Univ.*, 60 A.3d 749, 753 (D.C. 2013) (quoting *Bedell v. Inver Housing Inc.*, 506 A.2d 202, 205 (D.C. 1986)). With regard to the withdrawal, however, Plaintiff has failed to even gesture at provisions of the contract that Defendants breached in terminating their representation or at extrinsic evidence that might support such a claim. See Retainer Agreement at 2, 4 (attorney may terminate agreement for reasons permitted under Rules of Professional Conduct or if any conflict of interest arises).

C. Punitive Damages

The Court last tackles Count IV, which asserts a claim of punitive damages. Specifically, the Complaint alleges that Defendants violated Plaintiff's "rights" in an "intentional deliberate, [and] outrageous" manner. See Compl., ¶ 90. To begin, punitive damages are a form of relief, not a stand-alone cause of action. Although the count cannot survive independently, the Court considers whether such damages are available to Wengui at all. "To recover punitive damages," a plaintiff must establish that "the tortious act was committed with 'an evil motive, actual malice, deliberate violence or oppression' or in support of 'outrageous conduct in willful disregard of another's rights.' " *Embassy of Nigeria v. Ugwuonye*, 297 F.R.D. 4, 14 (D.D.C. 2013) (quoting *Robinson v. Sarisky*, 535 A.2d 901, 906 (D.C. 1988)). The imposition of punitive damages thus requires conduct that is "replete with malice." See *Dalo v. Kivitz*, 596 A.2d 35, 40 (D.C. 1991); see also *Hendry v. Pelland*, 73 F.3d 397, 400 (D.C. Cir. 1996) ("District of Columbia law allows punitive damages only if the attorney acted with fraud, ill will, recklessness, wantonness, oppressiveness, or willful disregard of the clients' rights.").

The Complaint does not plead such "outrageous" activity. Instead, if true, Wengui's allegations suggest that Defendants' failure to protect his information against hacking may mean that the firm acted "imprudently or incompetently, but they fall far short of showing the blatant wrongdoing necessary for a jury to infer that [Defendants] acted either with deliberate malice or conscious disregard of [their client's] rights." *Hendry*, 73 F.3d at 400; see also *Embassy of Nigeria*, 297 F.R.D. at 14 (rejecting punitive-damages claim where attorney stole client's tax refund and deposited it in firm's account). Plaintiff does not allege, for example, that Defendants intentionally left their server vulnerable to third-party hackings or stood to profit from such an event in any way. The Court therefore dismisses Count IV of the Complaint.

IV. Conclusion

For the foregoing reasons, the Court will grant in part and deny in part Defendants' Motion to Dismiss. A separate Order consistent with this Opinion will be issued this day.

SOLUTIONS: THE LAWYER SHOULD HAVE, WOULD HAVE, COULD HAVE. . .

What starts well ends well. You saw this at the start of the book when we covered the formation of the ACR and the agreement upon client goals and aims and its alignment with the services that the lawyer agrees to provide. Here there was a misalignment. Lawyers must ask a simple question: do we have the resources to meet client objectives and, if not, should we even agree to ACR formation? Or should we determine how to deepen our talent in order to satisfy expressed client needs? Here client and law firm

> miscommunication resulted in endangering the client/client's family and spawning multiple claims against the law firm. Talk it all out at the outset.

X-Ray Questions

While the requirements of fulfilling our fiduciary duties is admirable, is it realistic? We as lawyers seem to be required to go well beyond what any other business must. The author of the following article believes the profession needs to be more realistic about what is doable. Yet, we have an exclusive monopoly on practicing law. Is it so great a burden that—in exchange for this privilege—we are held to a standard of a fiduciary?

BEYOND THE CITE

By: Bruce A. Green, *The Lawyer as Lover: Are Courts Romanticizing the Lawyer-Client Relationship?* 32 TOURO L. REV. 139 (2016).

I. INTRODUCTION

Lawyers have a special relationship with their clients, in that lawyers are generally expected to devote themselves to their clients and their clients' causes no matter how morally undeserving those clients or causes happen to be (as long as lawyers do not help their clients break the law). Lawyers and judges largely take the attorney client relationship and its expectations for granted. Not so academics. For some years, moral philosophers and others have contemplated whether and how to justify a professional relationship that appears to sacrifice the greater public good for the individual client's benefit.'

Forty years ago, Professor Charles Fried of Harvard Law School took a swing at this question in an article called, The Lawyers Friend. Seeking to justify "the ideal of professional loyalty to one's client" that is intrinsic to "the traditional conception of the lawyer's role," Professor Fried argued that, like a friend or relative, a lawyer is morally entitled to give special priority to one person's interests by virtue of the special relationship. He characterized a lawyer as "his client's legal friend" or "limited-purpose friend," explaining that, "like a friend," a lawyer acts in another's "interests, not his own." Professor Fried acknowledged how friendships differ from lawyer-client relationships: "the ideal [friendship] is reciprocal" and not financially motivated. However, he regarded these differences as irrelevant to his argument that the lawyer's role justifies prioritizing the client's interests in order to "help to preserve and express the autonomy of his client vis-A-vis the legal system," even when the client is morally or socially unworthy.'

One may gain a different perspective on lawyers' fidelity to clients if, instead of analogizing lawyers to friends, one compares lawyer-client relationships to romantic ones—that is, if one envisions lawyers as lovers. Not lovers in a literal sense: initiating a sexual relationship with a client would be unethical and would get a lawyer into a heap of trouble.' To adapt Professor Fried's terminology, imagine the lawyer as a "legal" or "limited-purpose" lover, or as a lover in the legal system.

Unlike Fried's article, this essay is not a philosophical exploration of whether lawyers should be devoted to clients at public expense. Rather, drawing on particular cultural understandings, this essay is a normative exploration of whether lawyers can and should be devoted to clients not only at the expense of others' interests but also at the expense of their own self-interest. In particular, it asks whether lawyers can and should meet courts' expectations of loyalty, candor, and confidentiality.

The argument, here, is that just as pop singers might idealize attributes such as fidelity and candor in romantic relationships, courts sometimes romanticize analogous attributes such as loyalty and candor in lawyer-client relationships. Moreover, just as it is unrealistic to expect lovers consistently to achieve romantic ideals, it may be unrealistic to expect lawyers consistently to achieve analogous professional ideals. Although the analogy between lawyers and lovers will seem frivolous, it leads to a serious point: courts should adopt a less idealized rhetoric and express more realistic expectations of the lawyer-client relationship.

II. FROM THE BILLY JOEL CANON: THE ROMANTIC IDEAL

For insight into the romantic side of the "lawyer as lover" equation, one can look widely in popular culture, but it seems apt to look to the canon of Billy Joel, given the popularity of his music. Some of Billy Joel's songs are about loners—his Billy the Kid, for example, "always rode alone.' " However, many more of his lyrics are about people in relationships.

Some of these relationships might be described as professional ones— for example, his piano man's relationship to the audience.' But as one would expect of pop songs, a greater portion of Billy Joel's lyrics are about people in romantic relationships—not one-night-stands or hookups, but intimate relationships involving intense feeling and attraction. If the lyrics resonate with listeners, perhaps that is because they tell us something we already know about what lovers want and how lovers behave. What do lovers want from their counterparts?

What do they value in a relationship? What are the romantic ideals? Often sung in the first person—in the Billy Joel persona—the lyrics offer expected answers. The (presumably male) romantic partner wants candor, starting with honesty: "[h]onesty is . . . mostly what I need from you.' " The lover values companionship, constancy and commitment: "[s]he's got a way about her/ I don't know what it is/ But I know that I can't live without her." Romances are supposed to endure.

But what do lovers get? Billy Joel's lyrics suggest that the romantic ideals are ideals, not expectations and certainly not guarantees. They are not realistically attainable, at least not always. The Billy Joel canon acknowledges that romantic relationships fail—they "will not last forever," "and they may not even last a day." What begins "with a passionate start" usually ends in "cold remains," and the idea that the relationship will "go the distance" is entirely "a matter of trust." This is true in two senses. The success of a romantic relationship rests on mutual trust—lovers have to trust each other and be trustworthy. But even then, one has to trust in its survival—to take it as a matter of faith.

Even before romantic relationships are over, romantic ideals are hard to achieve. One cannot trust a romantic partner to keep one's deepest, darkest secrets: "we all fall in love/ But we disregard the danger/ Though we share so many secrets/ There are some we never tell." The romantic attributes are ideals that may not be fully attainable even by those who try hard. Lovers may value openness but do not entirely reveal themselves to each other: "Well we all have a face/ That we hide away forever/ . . . They're the faces of the stranger/ . . . Did you ever let your lover see/ The stranger in yourself?" Even when we try to be open, communication is too imperfect: "If I only had the words to tell you/ If you only had the time to understand/ Though I know it wouldn't change your feelings/ And I know you'll carry on the best you can." Lovers may want honesty, but: "Honesty is such a lonely word/ Everyone is so untrue/ Honesty is hardly ever heard." For Billy Joel's persona, it is often, perhaps always, impossible to achieve the ideal, to live up to the hopes and expectations of romantic relationships.

III. THE LAWYER-CLIENT RELATIONSHIP: WHY LAWYERS ARE LIKE LOVERS?

Are lawyers like lovers? One scholar has argued that law and love are incompatible. But at least with regard to the expectations that go with these different relationships, lawyers and lovers have something in common. The romantic ideals, such as commitment and candor, should seem familiar to lawyers, since these ideals find their counterparts in the legal profession's "core" fiduciary values of loyalty, confidentiality, and candor: they are hallmarks of the lawyer client relationship. Others have previously recognized this, observing, for example, that lawyers, like lovers, serve as confidants and are expected to be honest.

Although judges' descriptions of professional practice are not universally rosy, courts adopt a highly idealized rhetoric when they speak of lawyers' fiduciary duties under the common law of agency. This was true beginning at least as early as the mid-nineteenth century and continues to the present day. As Professor Wolfram has noted, 'contemporary judges describing lawyers' common-law duties to clients sometimes draw on Benjamin Cardozo's 1928 characterization of the fiduciary relationship between business partners and between co-venturers, whose fiduciary duties include "the duty of the finest loyalty. . . . Not honesty alone, but the punctilio of an honor the most sensitive . . . . Building on this and other early opinions, one judge wrote around a decade ago:

> The relationship existing between attorney and client is characterized as highly fiduciary, and requires proof of perfect fairness on the part of the attorney. Specifically, the relationship between attorney and client has been described as one of . . . most abundant good faith, requiring absolute and perfect candor, openness and honesty. . . .

Another contemporary judge has written: "The standards of the legal profession require undeviating fidelity of the lawyer to his client. No exceptions can be tolerated." What courts demand of lawyers "the finest loyalty," "the punctilio of the honor most sensitive," "absolute and perfect candor," and "undeviating fidelity": if one listens to pop music, aren't these exactly what one hopes to find in a lover?

In at least one respect, the romantic analogy seems more apt than Fried's fraternal one. While one presumably favors one's friends over strangers, the ideals of friendship do not preclude taking account of one's own interests and of others' interests when dealing with friends. Brougham famously said that "an advocate, in the discharge of his duty, knows but one person in all the world, and that person is his client." The ideals of unqualified self-sacrifice and single-minded devotion to another expressed by Brougham—and by the courts—seem more characteristic of romantic than fraternal relationships.

But there is an important difference between the expectations of lovers and lawyers: at least as far as Billy Joel's lyrics go, no one really expects lovers to live up to the romantic ideals in the absolute, at least not for long. He offers a vision of romance in which lovers are likely to betray, withhold and break up. The judicial conception of law practice, on the other hand, elevates the romantic ideals to legal commands. It is not enough for lawyers merely to aspire to loyalty or to hold it up as an ideal. Courts tell us we have a duty of loyalty—indeed, a duty of "undeviating fidelity"—and if we fall short we may be sanctioned, sued or even, at times, imprisoned." As for honesty, courts do not concede that it "is such a lonely word. . . hardly ever heard" from lawyers, but insist that lawyers behave as fiduciaries with "absolute and perfect candor, openness and honesty." Courts express the expectations of the lawyer-client relationship in absolute and idealized terms and then expect lawyers to live up to them.

Of course, courts' pronouncements may sometimes be dismissed as merely rhetorical flourishes, but not always. Courts sometimes give effect to a duty of loyalty that some would consider unexpectedly demanding. One example is the so-called "hot potato doctrine," which courts have developed in the context of ruling on motions to disqualify lawyers based on alleged conflicts of interest. In circumstances where it would ordinarily be permissible under the ethics rules for a lawyer to end an attorney-client relationship—e.g., where ending the relationship will not materially prejudice the client—some courts have held that it is impermissibly disloyal for the lawyer to drop the client for the purpose of representing that client's adversary. The explanation for the doctrine is that it is disloyal to end the relationship in order to be adverse to the client, even under circumstances where a lawyer would have been permitted to end the relationship for no reason at all, and even where the lawyer would have been allowed to represent the adversary if the prior representation had ended naturally. Given how easily one may exit a romantic relationship, notwithstanding prior professions of loyalty and fidelity, and the acrimony that often follows, it seems fair to say that more is expected of lawyers than of lovers, at least in this respect.

One might ask whether the courts, as well as lawyers who embrace the judicial rhetoric, are romanticizing professional values and virtues, expressing unrealistic expectations. For example, focusing on the duty of "absolute and perfect candor" espoused by some courts, Vincent Johnson has persuasively argued that "[i]f the phrase. . . is read literally and without qualification, it cannot possibly be an accurate statement of an attorney's obligations under all circumstances," and that in most situations, lawyers' disclosure obligations should be limited to what is reasonable. Leaving aside whether clients are morally worthy or unworthy, can lawyers realistically achieve the courts' stated expectations of undeviating fidelity and perfect candor?

IV. IMPEDIMENTS TO UNDEVIATING FIDELITY AND PERFECT CANDOR

Should lawyers be undeviatingly faithful to and perfectly candid with their clients, though lovers need not? Like lovers, lawyers are subject to pressures, distractions and self-interests that interfere with their ability to be loyal, forthcoming and trustworthy. Beneath the role of lawyer, as of the lover, we are only human. There is a growing professional literature, drawing on behavioral and social science teachings, exploring how common human failings undermine lawyers' ability to achieve professional ideals and expectations. Why should courts think lawyers are different and able to live up to high ideals when romantic partners cannot?

One way lawyers differ from lovers is that, in most cases, they do not have romantic affection toward their counterparts and may not have positive feelings at all. Lawyers may have passion for their work, and they may identify—or over-identify—with clients, but lawyers do not ordinarily love their clients. On the contrary, emotional and intellectual detachment from clients is considered a professional virtue necessary in order to give objective advice and assistance.' " Lovers may be expected to be blind to each other's' faults or even make a virtue of them: the Billy Joel persona promises his romantic partner to love her forever "just the way you are." But lawyers need not approve of their clients socially or morally. Some have considered whether lawyers should love their clients, not in the romantic sense, but in a religious, moral, spiritual, or fraternal sense. But, as Abbe Smith put it, in discussing lawyers' relationships with clients in a criminal defense practice:

> The worst aspect of the idealization of the lawyer client relationship
> . . . is the idea that lawyers have to love their clients. Defenders who
> claim to love all their clients are simply not being honest. Not all

clients are likeable. Not all clients are easy objects of empathy or compassion. Some can be downright loathsome.

Whatever one might think about the virtue of (chastely) loving one's clients, no one would seriously suggest that this is the norm.

Arguably, this distinction cuts in favor of greater expectations for lawyers than for lovers: emotional attachment and other complexities of romantic relationships create impediments for lovers not shared by lawyers to maintaining trust, loyalty, fidelity and confidentiality. On the other hand, romantic attraction and affection should make lovers more motivated than lawyers to achieve high expectations. If the popular conception of romance rightly recognizes that romantic partners cannot easily maintain undeviating fidelity and perfect candor toward loved ones, how can lawyers be expected to consistently achieve comparable ideals in relationships with clients whom they do not necessarily like?

Another obvious difference plainly cuts against higher demands on lawyers: whereas lovers conventionally pledge fidelity only to one another, most lawyers have multiple clients to whom they owe loyalty. Perhaps, as Brougham suggested, an advocate should think only about the one client being served at the moment, but that may not be easy. While lawyers should not neglect any given client's matter while trying to serve them all, it may be unrealistic to expect a lawyer at each moment to treat every client with "utmost care." Loyalty to clients may also be limited by competing obligations to third parties and to the courts." Even in the context of advocacy, courts themselves recognize that lawyers' duties to the client are tempered by competing obligations. Courts idealize lawyers' duties to the court, just as they idealize lawyers' duties to their clients. The conflicting obligations of lawyers suggests that it would be more difficult for lawyers to be undeviatingly loyal to their clients than for lovers to be undeviatingly loyal to their romantic partners.

There is one difference, however, that may unequivocally justify higher expectations for lawyers. Lawyers must qualify for a license, are trained and socialized, and are regulated by multiple authorities, the very point of which is to produce lawyers who behave better than people ordinarily do. One does not need a license to enter a romantic relationship. There is no such thing as unauthorized practice of love, and one need not possess any qualifications or receive training. Lawyers are taught to be fiduciaries and, if they lapse, they risk negative professional and financial consequences. Perhaps lawyers are therefore motivated to tread more carefully because the stakes are higher for lawyers who cheat on clients than for lovers who cheat on their romantic partners. This may explain why lawyers seem to have a better track record than lovers. But professional regulation has its limits, and even well-socialized lawyers may not find it easy or natural to resist pressures and incentives to fall short of the ideals of the lawyer-client relationship. Rather, professional regulation poses a dilemma for lawyers: being imperfect. Perhaps lawyers cannot be undeviatingly loyal and honest, and cannot entirely avoid letting secrets slip out, but they risk professional and financial harm if they slip up.

V. MAY LAWYERS TELL "PRETTY LIES"? THE LEGAL PROFESSION'S APPROACH

Do romantic partners really want or need what they say they want? Billy Joel sings, "I don't want some pretty face/ To tell me pretty lies/ All I want is someone to believe." But Billy Joel may not believe what he sings. He is not necessarily writing lyrics in his own voice. The Billy Joel persona may be lying to his fictional partner, perhaps as part of a seduction, or lying even to himself. And even if he truly wants absolute honesty, is that what he needs? Clancy Martin, a philosophy professor who recently authored a book titled "Love and Lies," argues that love and absolute honesty are incompatible: "[r]elationships last only if we don't always say exactly what we're thinking. We have to disguise our feelings, to feint, to smile sometimes when we want to shout. In short, we have to lie."

Likewise, with respect to lawyer-client relationships, one might ask from a normative perspective whether absolute loyalty, candor and confidentiality are desirable even assuming they are attainable. Concepts such as loyalty, candor and confidentiality have no fixed, intrinsic meaning. These concepts are constructed by courts and the legal profession. For the U.S. courts, the fiduciary duties can sound like almost sacred obligations, absolute and invariable. The profession tends to construct these duties in more realistic or relative terms; it has more forgiving and qualified expectations of lawyers, as reflected in the professional conduct rules, for which the bar has initial drafting responsibility, and in bar association ethics opinions interpreting the rules. In the profession's view, loyalty, candor and confidentiality are not absolute but should be qualified in light of others' interests or even in light of the client's best interests. Further, from the profession's perspective, these duties are not invariable, but are the default terms of a professional relationship, in that clients can generally negotiate for greater protection or bargain protections away to benefit the lawyer.

Professional conduct rules do not speak explicitly in terms of loyalty: they do not expressly obligate lawyers to be "loyal" to their clients or forbid "disloyalty." The rules restrict lawyers from engaging in representations involving conflicts of interest. The accompanying Comment roots this restriction in the concepts of "[l]oyalty and independent judgment," which are said to be "essential elements in the lawyer's relationship to a client." But the correlation between disloyalty and conflicts of interest is not necessarily exact. The core of disloyalty involves either acting against the client's interests with regard to the matter in which the client is represented or acting adversely to the client generally. Some courts speak of a "fiduciary duty to avoid conflicts of interest," but the equation between loyalty and the avoidance of conflicts seems questionable, at least if one has in mind how professional conduct rules define conflicts. The conflict of interest rules are prophylactic rules, and they are less about loyalty than about competence and confidentiality: the rules require lawyers to avoid situations where interests other than those of the client may lead lawyers to represent the client inadequately or misuse the client's confidences. This is made clear by provisions allowing a client to consent to the lawyer's representation, notwithstanding a conflict of interest, as long as the lawyer can provide "competent and diligent representation."

Insofar as the rules also address loyalty implicitly and in part, their concern may be with the client's perception rather than with the reality. In many situations, clients may give "informed consent" to a lawyer's conflict of interest under the rules, because the rules address risks of harm that may never occur." Further, the possibility of client consent is inconsistent with the concept to "*undeviating* fidelity" that courts attribute to the lawyer-client relationship.

In the course of interpreting professional conduct rules, bar association committees often refer to the "duty of loyalty," but typically look to the rules themselves to illuminate its scope, with the result that the legal profession sometimes approves of conduct that is harmful to a client and that some would intuitively consider disloyal. In other words, disloyalty is not necessarily forbidden under the professional conduct rules. For example, one might consider it "disloyal" for a lawyer to espouse personal views that are adverse to the client's interests or to seek to reform the law in ways that would prejudice the client, but the bar's position is that because the rules do not proscribe this conduct, clients are not always entitled to expect their lawyers to avoid prejudicing them outside the context of the lawyer's professional work." Likewise, one might consider it disloyal for a lawyer to represent a client's economic competitor, but the bar says that a lawyer ordinarily may do so, because this falls outside the restraint on "direct adversity." Even more contestably, the ABA has concluded that a lawyer may help one client write another client out of his will, regardless of how the lawyer's conduct is perceived by the client whose expectations are thwarted with the lawyer's aid. Perhaps the most compelling rejection of the judicial idea of "undeviating fidelity" is the professional conduct rule listing situations in which a lawyer may seek to end a lawyer-client relationship, including when "the client insists upon taking action . . . with which the lawyer has a fundamental disagreement," deliberately fails to pay the lawyer's fee, or "fails to cooperate in the representation."

As with "loyalty," the professional conduct rules do not speak explicitly of "candor" to clients. Nor do they, by their terms, establish an affirmative duty, as a matter of candor, to tell clients what they might want to know. The rules generally require truthfulness but not candor." One relevant professional rule, titled "Communication," requires lawyers to "reasonably consult with the client. . .keep the client reasonably informed . . . comply with reasonable requests for information . . . [and] . . . explain matters to the extent reasonably necessary." Even the accompanying explanation says nothing about candor per se, but observes that "[r]easonable communication between the lawyer and the client is necessary for the client effectively to participate in the representation." Another relevant professional conduct rule forbids dishonesty and deceit toward others, including clients, but it too is not a candor rule; it does not require lawyers to volunteer information that the client would want to know.

In interpreting professional conduct rules, bar association committees take a qualified approach to the idea of candor to the client. While judicial opinions sometimes say that lawyers must disclose everything they know of importance to the client, the professional duty to communicate is qualified. For example, an ethics opinion recognizes that the extent of the lawyer's disclosure obligation is limited by the duty to keep other clients' secrets, and that lawyers may continue a representation even when lawyers possess some relevant information they can never tell the client. The bar's critics have emphasized the influence of professional self-interest on professional self-regulation," and one might be tempted to credit professional self-interest for rules that are more forgiving and less demanding than judicial pronouncements on the lawyer-client relationship. But it is equally plausible that the bar has a clearer picture of the lawyer-client relationship and a better understanding of what is desirable and realistically achievable.

VI. DIFFERING VIEWS OF THE LAWYER-CLIENT RELATIONSHIP

At least in theory, it is possible to justify the occasional mismatch between common-law fiduciary duties and professional conduct rules that address the same aspects of the lawyer-client relationship. The courts' pronouncements are typically made in lawsuits involving lawyers' potential civil liability where the underlying question is how to allocate responsibility for financial harm to the client whose lawyer failed to achieve the ideal of loyalty, candor, or confidentiality. One might choose, in some situations, to allocate the cost to the lawyer even when the lawyer was not morally blameworthy for shortcomings. One might adopt a more forgiving standard to govern the same professional conduct for disciplinary purposes, because lawyers should not be punished unless their conduct is blameworthy.

There are at least two reasons why this explanation is unpersuasive or, at best, incomplete, however. First, opinions rarely acknowledge that fiduciary duties can differ from disciplinary duties because of the different procedural contexts in which these duties are elaborated and the different consequences of finding an impropriety. Second, the fairness of making a lawyer bear the cost of harmful conduct does not explain why courts order forfeiture of attorneys fees for breaches of the fiduciary duty of loyalty that cause no financial harm. Courts assume that clients are entitled to loyalty and that disloyalty is itself a wrong. Decisions on lawyers' fiduciary duties set a normative standard wholly apart from concerns about the allocation of risk or about financial harm.

The rhetoric about fiduciary duty does not inevitably lead to unrealistically high standards. Sometimes, despite their soaring rhetoric, courts look to the professional rules and understandings to give meaning to the fiduciary duties. Courts often look to the confidentiality and conflict-of-interest rules, in particular, to set the contours of the fiduciary duties of confidentiality and loyalty. It might be argued that, in some of these situations, the relevant rules are prophylactic rules that restrict conduct that should not be reached by agency law—for example, that failing to obtain the client's consent to an otherwise permissible conflict of interest under the professional conduct rule is not necessarily "disloyal" as a matter of agency law, and that the problem is one of inadequate disclosure. In these instances, one might argue, lawyers do not deserve to face civil liability on top of potential professional discipline. Even if this is the case, the lawyer is not being held to an unrealistically high standard as a matter of fiduciary duty, but is held to the preexisting disciplinary standard.

There is a risk, however, that in drafting professional conduct rules, the bar will defer to the courts' idealized view of the lawyer client relationship. That is a possible explanation for the development of Rule 1.7(a)(1) of the ABA Model Rules, which forbids a lawyer from representing a party adversely to a current client without the other client's consent. The rationale for the rule is that appearing adversely to one's client is disloyal. But, according to Professor Bussel, this principle was recognized only recently in the U.S. jurisprudence and is not recognized today in some common-law legal systems. The bar drafted professional conduct rules expressly forbidding a lawyer from appearing against a current client only after courts began to read this restriction into more vaguely worded conflict-of interest provisions.

There is also a risk that the courts' idealized view will influence their approach to professional discipline, notwithstanding the bar's contrary views. Consider, for example, a New York disciplinary action, *In re Holley*. The lawyer in question mistakenly accommodated a reporter's request for a copy of a document filed in a lawsuit in which the lawyer's firm represented a party. The lawyer was uninvolved in the lawsuit and unaware that the document was filed under seal. Disciplinary authorities brought a sanction proceeding based not on the lawyer's inadvertent violation of the court's sealing order but on his inadvertent disclosure of the client's confidential information.

At the time, the relevant confidentiality rule cut lawyers some slack. It did not protect all information relating to the representation, but allowed disclosure of non-privileged information when the disclosure would not harm or embarrass the client and was not of particular concern to the client. Moreover, the rule did not cover unwitting disclosures of confidential information, but only "knowing" disclosures.' " If the court document were publicly available, as the lawyer had assumed, there would have been no problem with sparing the reporter a trip to the courthouse by acceding to the reporter's request. So the implicit question in the case was whether lawyers must exercise utmost care to protect clients' confidences.

Both the lawyer-referee who heard the *Holley* case and four of the five members of the volunteer panel that subsequently reviewed the referee's recommendation concluded that the lawyer's mistaken conduct was not a sanctionable breach of duty. The state court rejected this view, however, and publicly sanctioned the lawyer. Declining to be bound by the terms of the confidentiality rule, the court held that the lawyer's "failure to take adequate precautions to safeguard confidential materials of a client, even if considered unintentional, was careless conduct that reflects adversely on his fitness to practice law."

Holley illustrates two problems with the courts' romanticization of the lawyer-client relationship. First, courts and others may take the soaring judicial rhetoric too seriously. Courts may treat lawyers with undue harshness, enforcing unrealistic or unfair expectations that fail to take account of lawyers' human fallibility, the pressures under which lawyers function and the competing interests that they legitimately serve. One can understand imposing civil liability on Holley for any harm he caused, on the assumption that he ought to have born the cost. But from both the rules' ex ante perspective and the ex post perspective of the lawyers who reviewed the evidence, his conduct was understandable and not deserving of moral opprobrium. Likewise, there is a risk that clients reading what courts write will develop unrealistic expectations of lawyers. In addition, lawyers may develop unrealistic expectations of themselves and therefore suffer the stress of trying to live up to an unrealistically high ideal.

Second, the inconsistent approaches to the lawyer-client relationship can cause confusion for courts, lawyers, and others. It may not always be clear to judges which standards to apply in a given situation—for example, whether to employ the professional rules as interpreted by the bar or whether to interpret fiduciary duties independently and more demandingly. It may also be unclear to lawyers where to look for guidance regarding the standards governing their conduct.

VII. CONCLUSION: FRIENDS, LOVERS AND LAWYERS

Lawyers have a special relationship with clients that gives rise to an expectation that they treat clients differently from strangers. Analogizing lawyers to friends or lovers may help explain this expectation, but there may be little need to explain. Lawyers' right and obligation to put clients' interests over those of the general public is probably not seriously contested.

At least for lawyers, the hard questions revolve around the extent and limits of the loyalty, candor and confidentiality duties. On these questions, it is not particularly illuminating to say that a lawyer is like a friend or lover. For one thing, the expectations of romance are almost certainly not universal: Billy Joel's lyrics express one vision, but not the only one. Even if there were a consensus on the duties of lovers, there is no reason why they should be the same for lawyers. Whatever the commonalities may be, lawyers are not lovers, but fiduciaries in an inherently asymmetric, nonexclusive, and ordinarily passionless relationship that is often short-lived by design.

On reflection, one might also question the utility of analogizing lawyers to other fiduciaries. Fiduciaries are not all identical. Lawyer-client relationships are not reciprocal, unlike the relationships among co-venturers and business partners. Lawyers are licensed and subject to judicial regulation that takes account of duties to others aside from clients. There is no reason why lawyers' fiduciary duties to clients should necessarily be identical to the duties of one business partner to another. Justice Cardozo's dictum, assuming it is not excessive even for co-venturers and business partners, may not fit equally for lawyers and other fiduciaries, of which there are many, including marital partners.

Labeling lawyers as "fiduciaries" and then invoking high flown language about fiduciary duties is not a reasonable way to decide how lawyers should behave. The practice of law is too complicated and contextual. Courts sometimes recognize this. Through the power to regulate the bar, courts adopt professional conduct rules that reflect more nuanced views of lawyers' obligations. The rules are ordinarily drafted by the bar, which might be expected to take account of the practical realities of the attorney-client relationship but might also be unduly concerned with lawyer-self-interest. This may or may not be the best way to determine lawyers' duties to clients for purposes of civil liability and discipline, but surely this is better than romanticizing the lawyer-client relationship in judicial prose. When it comes to ascertaining the scope of lawyers' fiduciary duties, courts should employ analyses, not just analogies.

B. Personal Conflicts/Loyalty

A variation on fiduciary duty is found in MR 1.7(a)(1)(2). This Rule deals with a lawyer's inability to give 100% effort and 100% loyalty to a client because the lawyer is being held back by a personal interest. Note that this rule is prophylactic in nature; in other words, actual harm to the client is not needed to establish a violation of the rule. Rather, the possibility of a conflict is what triggers the ethical obligations. Nor is there a need for there to be a showing of ill will or bad motive by the lawyer to sustain a bar grievance against the lawyer. The client bears no responsibility to raise the issues of a conflict in the lawyer's dealing with the client. Just as with Mrs. Togstad and the accidental formation of the ACR, it is the lawyer who is educated on the law and the ethical standards to which the lawyer must adhere, not the client. So, it is the lawyer who must alert the client to the possibility of a personal conflict just as it was Mr. Miller's duty to alert Mrs. Togstad on whether an ACR was or was not formed. This is true regardless of the education or legal sophistication of the client. The client can never know as much about the law and the legal system as a licensed lawyer.

Model Rule 1.7: Conflict of Interest: Current Clients

(a)   Except as provided in paragraph (b), a lawyer shall not represent a client if the representation involves a concurrent conflict of interest. A concurrent conflict of interest exists if:

(1)   the representation of one client will be directly adverse to another client; or

(2)   there is a significant risk that the representation of one or more clients will be materially limited by the lawyer's responsibilities to another client, a former client or a third person or by a personal interest of the lawyer.

(b)   Notwithstanding the existence of a concurrent conflict of interest under paragraph (a), a lawyer may represent a client if:

(1)   the lawyer reasonably believes that the lawyer will be able to provide competent and diligent representation to each affected client;

(2)   the representation is not prohibited by law;

(3)   the representation does not involve the assertion of a claim by one client against another client represented by the lawyer in the same litigation or other proceeding before a tribunal; and

(4)   each affected client gives informed consent, confirmed in writing.

Deconstruction Exercise/Rule Rationale

Note that this is a mandatory rule ("shall"). Look at (a)(2). Note that, unlike other conflicts that involve more than one client, this conflict type involves just the lawyer and their professional or personal interests. To be clear, not every theoretical tension is an impermissible conflict. Always check modifiers; here, "risk" is modified by "significant." So, the risk of impaired representation must—relative to other types of risk—involve more than a mere passing chance or minor possibility. The rule accommodates the reality that human life is complicated; no one is entirely free of competing interests in their lives.

What does (a)(1) deal with? While (2) which encompasses a lawyer's personal life, this subsection encompasses the representation of a client. But what does "directly adverse" mean The Merriam-Webster Dictionary defines adverse as "opposed to one's interests" Who would, in the legal context, be opposed to a client's interests? Certainly, the party opposite in a lawsuit. But that is a given. And this rule talks about another "client" of the lawyer being adverse to an existing client. So, it forbids representing two clients at the same time when they are co-defendants in a personal injury lawsuit and each blames the other as being the cause of the accident. We will explore this in depth in Chapter 5. But the language of the rule is expansive with adverse interest the scenario diagrammed below.

Let's Chart It!

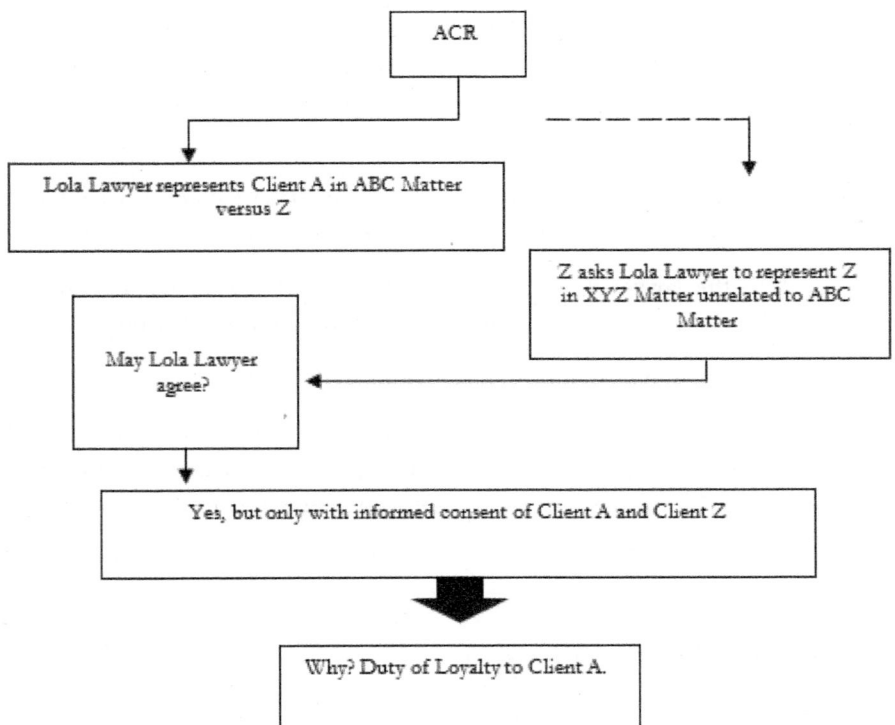

LEANING INTO PRACTICE

Scenario No. 1: The Case of the NFL Quarterback, the Rapacious Owner, and the Temptation for the Lawyer

Emmy Lawyer represents the quarterback of an NFL football team. She is negotiating his new contract. The owner of the team decides he will negotiate directly with Emmy. The owner is an entrepreneurial sort and is very impressed with Emmy's negotiation skills. He tells her, "I like your style. I like it a lot. What if I hire you to help us go after these deadbeats who leased my luxury suites at the stadium and are not paying?" Can Emmy say "yes" under MR 1.7(A)(1)? Why or why not?

Scenario No. 2: The Cases of the Lawyer and Intimacy

(In answering (2) and (3) consider the language in the Rule about personal interests.)

Juan Lawyer is representing a plaintiff in a breach of contract lawsuit. An answer has just been filed and he notices that his current spouse had filed an answer representing the defendant. Should Juan and/or the spouse recuse themselves from representing the parties in the lawsuit? Consider the language in the Rule about "personal." Answer "yes" or "no" and explain your answer.

Would you change your answer if—instead of a currently married couple—we change the facts to:

(a)   Previous spouse

(b)   Engaged to be married

(c)   Close friends but not romantically involved

Scenario No. 3: The Lawyer and a Friend with Benefits

Lola Lawyer is an assistant district attorney. She is in a "friend with benefits" relationship with the public defender, Nicole Lawyer. They each end up on opposing sides of a case. They agree to refrain from any sexual activity while the case is ongoing and thus conclude that they need not tell their respective employers, the DA's Office and the Public Defender's Office, and the defendant. Is this an appropriate course of action? Why? What if we have the same litigation configuration but they have broken up as of 1 month ago? 6 months ago? 12 months ago? Same answer?

X-Ray Questions

New lawyers often understand the theory that as professionals they will need to sacrifice for the profession and for the client. But the concrete reality is often not explained to them prior to starting practice. Here are three sacrifices lawyers make that others in the workforce do not. Do any come as a surprise to you? Do you believe these sacrifices are unfair? Can you see how the sacrifices are crucial to the effective functioning of our profession?

BEYOND THE CITE

By: Michael Maslanka, *Three Sacrifices for Practicing Law*, Texas Lawyer Online, November 21, 2021.

Private Benjamin is a 1980 comedy with Goldie Hawn (for a new generation, she's the mother of Kate Hudson) in the title role of Judy Benjamin, a good natured, affluent, newly widowed young woman who-on a flyer-joins the Army after speaking to a quota driven recruiter. Rough and tumble boot camp is definitely not what she was promised. So, taking a reasonable tone, she tells Captain Lewis, her drill instructor:

"I think they sent me to the wrong place. See, I did join the Army, but I joined a different Army. I joined the one with the condos and the private rooms. . . .To be truthful with you, I can't sleep in a room with twenty strangers . . . and I mean look at this place. The Army couldn't afford drapes. I'll be up at the crack of dawn here!" https://youtu.be/rbH_RrOAAfA. (A colleague's favorite scene is when Benjamin is marching in the rain letting loose with, "I want to go to lunch!")

I think about the initial travails of Judy Benjamin when teaching Professional Responsibility (PR) and in speaking with relatively new lawyers (and even more senior ones). "Wait, you're telling me that my oath stops me from conduct that I consider perfectly reasonable and my business and no one else's!?!" In short, this is not the Army I signed up for. And my answer is: "Well, yes I am." It's the wisdom of St. Luke 12: 48 (KJV): "For unto whomsoever much is given, of him shall much be required." Here are three of the sacrifices that the profession requires of us in exchange for the privilege of practicing law.

Sacrifice No. 1: "You can't have sex with whomever you please!"

Let's start with what we know. If you are related to counsel opposite, then you can proceed with representation of your client but only if your client gives informed consent; that is, the pros, alternatives and cons (P.A.C.) representation are explained fully and the client agrees to representation in the circumstances. But what is still elusive to us? What about lawyers who are counsel opposite but involved in an intimate sexual relationship with one another?

On July 29, 2020, the ABA chimed in by issuing Formal Opinion No. 494. Their answer "(both) lawyers must disclose the relationship to their respective clients and the lawyers each must reasonably believe that they can deliver competent and diligent representation and each client gives informed consent (P.A.C.) in writing to the representation." How hard can it be to figure out there is, at a minimum, a potential conflict because of pillow talk/sexual discord/emotions running amok?

Apparently, pretty hard! A California appeals court reversed a conviction because the defense lawyer decided not to tell his client that he was sexually involved with the prosecutor; the New York Bar Association wasted valuable resources in declaring that "a dating relationship. . .is inconsistent with the independence of professional judgment required (by the rules)"; and the New Jersey Supreme Court held that fees will be forfeited when there is no disclosure of the relationship and informed consent is not obtained. Despite all of this pre-existing precedent, the ABA was required to state the obvious.

If the need for a simple sacrifice here and in Sacrifices Nos. 2 and 3 is so self-evident, why then do many lawyers, law professors, and judges profess shock and amazement over acknowledging a fundamental conflict? Perhaps it is because lawyers believe that they are entitled. Or that, as the dominant zeitgeist (after all, we as lawyers are part of a culture) tells us, there are no absolute values, only personal ones. A third explanation comes from an amazing and action oriented new book published a few months ago, Beyond the Rules: Behavioral Legal Ethics and Professional Responsibility (West Academic Publishing 2021) from Professors Catherine Gage O'Grady and Tigran W. Eldred who tell us that lawyers (like non-lawyers) engage in "motivated reasoning." What's that? Each of us generate emotionally based rationales in order to justify the unjustified and the unwarranted results we desire. Their point: understand this cognitive dynamic and self-correct.

Sacrifice No. 2: "You can't always say whatever you want, whenever you want, to whomever you want!"

Clients tell us their confidences. We must refrain from, without client consent, either disclosing or using same. A basic rule until following it becomes inconvenient for the lawyer and then, well, the lawyer wraps himself in the sanctity of the First Amendment. In 2011, the California Supreme Court spiked a lawyer's political expression when he used a former client's confidential information against it in a political campaign. The lawyer represented a real estate developer. He was hired because of his knowledge of the workings of the Beverly Hills City Council where the deal was pending. The lawyer won approval of this client's controversial project. Two years later brought a change of heart to the lawyer, with him campaigning in a referendum to revoke approval. The Supreme Court reversed the dismissal of the developer's breach of fiduciary duty claim and held-simply and correctly—(relying on the Restatement of the Law Governing Lawyers), "The requirement that a lawyer not misuse a client's confidential information. . .applies to discussion of public issues." And note that the developer needed only show, in order to prevail, that the lawyer was exposed to confidential information, during the attorney client relationship not that he used it in campaigning. Bottom line from the Court: "The First Amendment [does not] protect such duplicity," Oasis West Realty LLC v. Goldman et al.

Sacrifice No. 3: "You forfeit capitalism!"

Yes, that's right! "Is nothing sacred?" some lawyers will bemoan. Look though at Texas Rule of 5.06 that prohibits a lawyer from cutting this deal, "Yes, I will settle my case against your client, and I will agree to never sue your client again if you make it worth my while by paying me not to sue." Violation! But are not such lawyers just leveraging their positions to make money? And what's wrong with that? Plenty. As lawyers the good we can do for the public often comes ahead of the good we can do for ourselves. . . (In fact, the word "professional" derives from the Latin "professus" which comes from ancient advocates telling the assemblage in the town square that their needs came first.) This type of side deal deprives the public of the most skilled lawyers to serve their needs.

Look at a case from the Oregon Supreme Court that resulted in a yearlong suspension for two plaintiffs lawyers. They tried to cha-cha around the Oregon version of the Texas rule. How? As part of the settlement of a lawsuit, the lawyers for the plaintiffs (distributors of machine parts) proposed that they would provide legal "consulting" services to the defendant, the manufacturer. Their argument as to why no violation: we are not directly foreclosing our ability to represent future plaintiffs-"oh no, we are merely indirectly doing so because we would be conflicted out in light of the consulting gig. Not our fault!" As I suggest to my PR students, "if you can't walk through the front door, then you can't crawl through the back window."

The lawyers in each of these sacrifice scenarios came to the crossroads. They picked the wrong path, which brings us back to Judy Benjamin. Now understanding that there is only one type of Army, and she is in it, she is marching in a pounding rain on the parade grounds. She is told to report to the rec room. To her surprise, her loving but patronizing parents are there to take her home. They explain that all of their friends think she is recovering from a mental breakdown.; that they will now keep their loving eyes on her so she does not go astray; that she need no longer stay with a "bunch of" unmentionables. Judy's face clouds over, and you can tell she is thinking hard, digging deep inside herself, coming to a decision. Captain Lewis says "sign right here and you can leave." Judy stands up, dripping wet, balancing the weight of her weapon and her gear and says, "I think I'll stay." She *smartly salutes* Captain Lewis and then her parents. In that moment, she transforms from Judy Benjamin to Private Benjamin. She is better for it. As Ryan Holiday writes, "A person isn't brave, generally. We are brave, specifically. . .and that is enough." When tempted-as we will be-to reject the true and honest path, take a moment to think of Private Benjamin: proud soldier and, role model. Pass the popcorn!

Section 5.   Personal Conflicts/Temptations

Model Rule 1.8: Current Clients; Specific Rules

(a)   A lawyer shall not enter into a business transaction with a client or knowingly acquire an ownership, possessory, security or other pecuniary interest adverse to a client unless:

> (1)   the transaction and terms on which the lawyer acquires the interest are fair and reasonable to the client and are fully disclosed and transmitted in writing in a manner that can be reasonably understood by the client;

(2) the client is advised in writing of the desirability of seeking and is given a reasonable opportunity to seek the advice of independent legal counsel on the transaction; and

(3) the client gives informed consent, in a writing signed by the client, to the essential terms of the transaction and the lawyer's role in the transaction, including whether the lawyer is representing the client in the transaction.

(b) A lawyer shall not use information relating to representation of a client to the disadvantage of the client unless the client gives informed consent, except as permitted or required by these Rules.

(c) A lawyer shall not solicit any substantial gift from a client, including a testamentary gift, or prepare on behalf of a client an instrument giving the lawyer or a person related to the lawyer any substantial gift unless the lawyer or other recipient of the gift is related to the client. For purposes of this paragraph, related persons include a spouse, child, grandchild, parent, grandparent or other relative or individual with whom the lawyer or the client maintains a close, familial relationship.

(d) Prior to the conclusion of representation of a client, a lawyer shall not make or negotiate an agreement giving the lawyer literary or media rights to a portrayal or account based in substantial part on information relating to the representation.

(e) A lawyer shall not provide financial assistance to a client in connection with pending or contemplated litigation, except that:

(1) a lawyer may advance court costs and expenses of litigation, the repayment of which may be contingent on the outcome of the matter;

(2) a lawyer representing an indigent client may pay court costs and expenses of litigation on behalf of the client; and

(3) a lawyer representing an indigent client pro bono, a lawyer representing an indigent client pro bono through a nonprofit legal services or public interest organization and a lawyer representing an indigent client pro bono through a law school clinical or pro bono program may provide modest gifts to the client for food, rent, transportation, medicine and other basic living expenses. The lawyer:

(i) may not promise, assure or imply the availability of such gifts prior to retention or as an inducement to continue the client-lawyer relationship after retention;

(ii)   may not seek or accept reimbursement from the client, a relative of the client or anyone affiliated with the client; and

(iii)   may not publicize or advertise a willingness to provide such gifts to prospective clients.

Financial assistance under this Rule may be provided even if the representation is eligible for fees under a fee-shifting statute.

(f)   A lawyer shall not accept compensation for representing a client from one other than the client unless:

(1)   the client gives informed consent;

(2)   there is no interference with the lawyer's independence of professional judgment or with the client-lawyer relationship; and

(3)   information relating to representation of a client is protected as required by Rule 1.6.

. . . .

(j)   A lawyer shall not have sexual relations with a client unless a consensual sexual relationship existed between them when the client-lawyer relationship commenced.

Deconstruction Exercise/Rule Rationale

MR 1.7 tells you that a lawyer owes undivided loyalty to a client. MR 1.9 tells you that your knowledge of a client's affairs cannot be used against a client, either to your advantage or to the advantage of a new client. MR 1.8 which you will now study tells you that you cannot prioritize your needs over the needs of a client.

Note that this is yet another illustration of the client centric nature of the Rules. And, each section of MR 1.8 is prophylactic in purpose and in design; that is, they are meant to keep a lawyer out of an ethical pickle in the first instance. They are, for the most part, absolute rules admitting of no or few exceptions. At its core, MR 1.8 recognizes the importance that a lawyer plays in a client's legal life—trusted advisor, wise counselor, dependable ally. The holistic role that MR 2.1 envisions. But because lawyers are also just human beings, with the frailty of human beings subject to temptation that MR 1.8 exists.

➤   MR 1.8(a): Going Into Business with a Client

The rule applies to "business transactions." Other phrases could have been used: "contractual relationships" or "business dealings" but they were not. The drafters were aiming here, as in the other rules, for broad coverage. Moreover, there are three concrete hurdles—(a)(1), (a)(2), and (a)(3)—that must be surmounted for the lawyer not to be in violations of the rule (including telling the client to retain an independent lawyer to review the fairness of the transaction between the client and the lawyer). Miss one of the three? Rule violation. The rule seeks to prevent intentional exploitation of the client or client acquiescence in their lawyer's counsel and advice.

> MR 1.8(b): Use of Confidential Client Information

This rule should be read in conjunction with MR 1.6 which requires that a lawyer not disclose information learned during the course of representing a client. Here, that a lawyer cannot use such information for their own benefit absent the informed consent of the client. As we saw in chapter 2, the client owns the monetary proceeds from a settlement as well as any unearned portion of a fee. Similarly, here, the client owns the confidential information which cannot be used by the lawyer.

> MR 1.8(c): Soliciting a Gift

Here we re-visit the issue discussed in Chapter 1 in *Brooke*. Lawyers occupy, as we wrote, a special place vis-a-vis the client. Thus, the potential for overreaching is always present. Note the use of the active verb "solicit" meaning that the lawyer asks the client for a gift. And "solicit "is a broad enough concept to include making a mere "suggestion" to give a gift. And because "gift" is modified by "substantial," the rule does not concern itself with gifts given in a social context such as a holiday or in appreciation for services performed. The rule expresses the overall orientation of the Model Rules as a whole to take a common sense, practical approach to ethical concerns.

> MR 1.8(d): Exclusion of Media Rights Relating to the Representation

Clients own their life stories. It belongs to them. A lawyer cannot own an interest in the underlying matter being litigated. By way of example, if the matter being litigated is over ownership of a patent, the lawyer cannot accept part ownership in lieu of a fee if the client prevails in the litigation. The lawyer stops solely being a lawyer and now effectively becomes a part owner of the patent. The question then becomes whether the client's objectives come first or the lawyer's desire to be part owner of a patent, even subconsciously, is given priority by the lawyer. Same with literary rights when the client's life story or a part thereof is the subject natter of the litigation. The lawyer's temptation is to make the life story more interesting and thus increase its value. Note how the structure of the rule forbids not merely making an agreement to obtain ownership but also merely negotiating with the client to do so.

> ➤ MR 1.8(e): Financial Assistance to a Client

This rule was amended recently to allow a lawyer to provide "modest" assistance for living expenses to a client in connection with existing or pending litigation provided that the lawyer is representing the client on a pro bono basis. Even then there are three prohibitions on lawyer conduct in this circumstance, including in (c), on publicizing or advertising to the public a willingness to do so. The rules do not want to allow inducing of ACR formation on a basis other than the meshing of the right lawyer for the client. Otherwise, the rule prohibits providing any financial assistance to the client. (Not all states follow this part of the Model Rules Texas, for instance has long permitted financial assistance for personal matters in connection with litigation. Again, the rule's purpose is to avoid lawyers putting themselves into situations when into a situation in which they will be tempted to place their needs ahead of the client's needs.

Model Rule 1.8(a)

(a)   A lawyer shall not enter into a business transaction with a client or knowingly acquire an ownership, possessory, security or other pecuniary interest adverse to a client unless:

(1)   the transaction and terms on which the lawyer acquires the interest are fair and reasonable to the client and are fully disclosed and transmitted in writing in a manner that can be reasonably understood by the client;

(2)   the client is advised in writing of the desirability of seeking and is given a reasonable opportunity to seek the advice of independent legal counsel on the transaction; and

(3)   the client gives informed consent, in a writing signed by the client, to the essential terms of the transaction and the lawyer's role in the transaction, including whether the lawyer is representing the client in the transaction.

Cases and Materials

X-Ray Questions (*Liggett*)

Here a lawyer represented a home builder. Pursuant to a standard contract, the builder undertook to build a house for the lawyer which was unrelated to the lawyer's representation of the home builder. But, there was a problem. One of the clauses was rewritten by the lawyer. A disagreement arose over this contract terms and the contractor filed suit against the lawyer. The contractor prevailed at the Indiana Supreme Court. How did the lawyer fail to adhere to MR 1.8(a)? Why did the court reject the argument that the agreement was merely a form agreement that is exempted under MR 1.8(a)? How did the court allocate the burden of proof to the parties? Why? The builder is presumably a sophisticated businessperson. In that light, is this burden of proof in litigation a fair one? Why does the client get the benefit of the doubt?

Ronald D. Liggett, d/b/a Liggett Construction Company v. Dean A. Young and Elisabeth Young

Supreme Court of Indiana, 2007.
877 N.E.2d 178.

DICKSON, JUSTICE.

The plaintiff, Ronald Liggett, d/b/a Liggett Construction Company, brings this appeal to challenge a trial court summary judgment ruling in a contract dispute arising from Liggett's construction of a private residence for his attorney, defendant Dean Young, and Young's wife, Elisabeth. To address whether the parties' attorney-client relationship affects the resolution of this dispute, we granted transfer, and now reverse the trial court.

In 2001, when sued by a supplier of bricks and materials used in the construction of the Youngs' home, Liggett initiated a third-party complaint against the Youngs. The Youngs' answer included a counterclaim against Liggett seeking damages for allegedly negligent and untimely performance of the work under the building contract. After further counterclaims and motions for summary judgment were presented, the trial court granted partial summary judgment in favor of the Youngs as to all of Liggett's claims against them. Expressly finding no just reason for delay, the trial court entered final judgment in favor of the Youngs and against Liggett as to all of Liggett's claims against the Youngs. Liggett appealed, and the Court of Appeals affirmed. *Liggett v. Young,* 851 N.E.2d 968 (Ind.Ct.App.2006).

Among Liggett's issues on appeal, we find one to be dispositive: "Whether the trial judge erred in finding no genuine issue of material fact with respect to the enforceability of a contract drafted and entered into between an attorney and his builder/client." Appellant's Br. at 1.

Before addressing this issue, however, we note the somewhat unconventional procedural posture of this case in the trial court. The motion for partial summary judgment filed by the Youngs was supported only by Dean Young's affidavit referring to the parties' building contract, asserting full payment, and attaching the contract as an exhibit. Opposing the Youngs' motion, Liggett's affidavit asserted the existence of unpaid additional labor and materials from change orders; attached exhibits consisting of plans and specifications related to the construction; and asserted that at the time of the contract, Dean Young was serving as Liggett's attorney and had assured Liggett that "that there would be no problems" as a result of Young's "dual status" as Liggett's attorney and party to the contract. Appellant's App'x at 59. Finding it undisputed that "the Youngs have paid the full price called for under the contract," the trial court granted the Youngs' motion for partial summary judgment. The court did not address Liggett's assertions regarding the fact or implications of Dean Young's "dual status" as both a contracting party with and lawyer for Liggett. Following the appointment of a special judge, the appearance of new counsel for Liggett, and a series of further pleadings, Liggett filed a motion for summary judgment. Finding that it was "in effect" a motion to reconsider the previous ruling on the Youngs' motion for partial summary judgment, Appellant's App'x at 12, the trial court undertook such reconsideration and addressed the new arguments presented by Liggett, but declared itself to be "constrained to review the record and evidence as same existed" on the date of the initial order granting partial summary judgment, and did not consider any new designated evidence submitted to support or oppose Liggett's motion for summary judgment. With a detailed explanatory order, the trial court denied Liggett's summary judgment and affirmed the previous order granting the Youngs' motion seeking partial summary judgment as to Liggett's claims against the Youngs.

1.   Professional Conduct Rule 1.8

Liggett's appeal contends in part that the Youngs failed to carry their burden on summary judgment to prove that the construction contract was not void by reason of Indiana Professional Conduct Rule 1.8, which restricts an attorney's ability to engage in transactions with the attorney's client. Liggett urges that Dean Young violated this rule by drafting the construction contract for the project, and that attorney/client transactions are presumptively invalid as the product of undue influence. In response, the Youngs contend (a) that Liggett's designation of evidence on summary judgment, claiming an entitlement to receive the contract price plus an additional amount, is inconsistent with his claim that the contract should be found void, and (b) that the construction contract was a standard commercial transaction to which Rule 1.8 does not apply.

Summary judgment is appropriate only when the designated evidence shows there is no genuine issue of material fact and the moving party is entitled to judgment as a matter of law. Indiana Trial Rule 56(C); *Biddle v. BAA Indianapolis, LLC*, 860 N.E.2d 570, 575 (Ind.2007); *Gunkel v. Renovations, Inc.*, 822 N.E.2d 150, 152 (Ind.2005); *Worman Enterprises, Inc. v. Boone County Solid Waste Mgmt. Dist.*, 805 N.E.2d 369, 373 (Ind.2004). We construe all facts and reasonable inferences in favor of the non-moving party. *Gunkel*, 822 N.E.2d at 152. Furthermore, we carefully review summary judgment decisions to ensure a party is not improperly denied its day in court. *Id.; Reeder v. Harper*, 788 N.E.2d 1236, 1240 (Ind.2003); *St. Vincent Hosp. and Health Care Ctr., Inc. v. Steele*, 766 N.E.2d 699, 702 (Ind.2002).

At all relevant times (from the contract date of July 2, 1999, through the date the Youngs filed their complaint, April 2, 2001), Rule 1.8(a) of the Indiana Rules of Professional Conduct provided as follows:

(a) A lawyer shall not enter into a business transaction with a client or knowingly acquire an ownership, possessory, security or other pecuniary interest adverse to a client unless:

(1) the transaction and terms on which the lawyer acquires the interest are fair and reasonable to the client and are fully disclosed and transmitted in writing to the client in a manner which can be reasonably understood by the client;

the client is given a reasonable opportunity to seek the advice of independent counsel in the transaction; and the client consents in writing thereto.

The Comment to Rule 1.8, as relevant to subsection (a), emphasized the general principle that "all transactions between client and lawyer should be fair and reasonable to the client," and added that, "[i]n such transactions a review by independent counsel on behalf of the client is often advisable." Ind. Prof. Cond. R. 1.8 cmt. (1999). But the Comment also noted an exception:

Paragraph (a) does not, however, apply to standard commercial transactions between the lawyer and the client for products or services that the client generally markets to others, for example, banking or brokerage services, medical services, products manufactured or distributed by the client, and utilities services. In such transactions, the lawyer has no advantage in dealing with the client, and the restrictions in paragraph (a) are unnecessary and impracticable.

Id. The parties disagree regarding whether their transaction falls within this "standard commercial transaction" exception. The Youngs argue that they fall within the exception because the transaction involves a product and/or service that Liggett, a building contractor, generally markets to others. Liggett contends that it does not apply because the dispute centers on the interpretation of the construction contract drafted by his lawyer, Dean Young.

Regardless of whether this transaction does not qualify as a standard commercial transaction and thus subjects Dean Young to the requirements of Rule 1.8(a), the Rules of Professional Conduct have limited application outside of the attorney disciplinary process. On the dates relevant to this case, the Preamble to the Indiana Rules of Professional Conduct stated in part:

> Violation of a Rule should not give rise to a cause of action nor should it create any presumption that a legal duty has been breached. The Rules are designed to provide guidance to lawyers and to provide a structure for regulating conduct through disciplinary agencies. They are not designed to be a basis for civil liability, but reference to these rules as evidence of the applicable standard of care is not prohibited. Furthermore, the purpose of the Rules can be subverted when they are invoked by opposing parties as procedural weapons. The fact that a rule is a just basis for a lawyer's self-assessment, or for sanctioning a lawyer under the administration of a disciplinary authority, does not imply that an antagonist in a collateral proceeding or transaction has standing to seek enforcement of the Rule.

Ind. R. Prof. Cond. Preamble (1999–2004).

Prior decisions are inconsistent regarding whether this language in the pre-2005 Preamble should be applied to preclude resort to Rule 1.8(a) in resolving the issue of civil liability. Two opinions have indicated that violation of the Rules of Professional Conduct *may* serve as a basis for civil liability. *See Trotter v. Nelson,* 684 N.E.2d 1150, 1153 (Ind.1997) ("The Rules at issue . . . are explicit judicial declarations of Indiana public policy and, akin to contravening a statute, agreements in violation of these rules are unenforceable."); *Picadilly, Inc., v. Raikos,* 582 N.E.2d 338, 342 (Ind.1991) ("An attorney who breaches any of these duties may face both disciplinary action and a legal malpractice claim."). But neither of these cases address the above-quoted Preamble language. On the other hand, in *Sanders v. Townsend,* 582 N.E.2d 355 (Ind.1991), this Court explicitly declared that this language in the Preamble "make[s] it clear that [the Rules of Professional Conduct] do not purport to create or describe any civil liability . . ." *Id.* at 359.

In *Sanders*, the clients sued their lawyer, asserting that the lawyer breached fiduciary duties by coercing them into an inadequate settlement. This Court affirmed summary judgment for the lawyer, noting that the client's contention was that the lawyer "breached his fiduciary duties to them . . . in violation of the Indiana Code of Professional Responsibility . . ." *Id.* at 358–59. We held "that to subject attorneys to suit for constructive fraud based on a violation of the fiduciary duties that are regulated under the Rules of Professional Conduct . . . would create unreasonable, unwarranted, and cumulative exposure to civil liability." *Id.* at 359. We infer from the reference to "cumulative exposure to civil liability" that *Sanders* stands for the proposition that, while civil liability in damages may not be predicated on a claimed violation of a specific professional conduct rule relating to fiduciary duties, a client nevertheless may seek damages if the attorney's conduct constitutes a breach of fiduciary duty at common law.

We conclude that this holding from *Sanders* prevails over any statements to the contrary in *Picadilly* and *Trotter* because of the language of the Preamble and its express consideration in *Sanders* and because there exists an independent common law basis, apart from violation of Rule 1.8, on which a client may seek recourse in damages.

2. Common Law Attorney-Client Fiduciary Duty

Claims involving separate attorney-client transactions have long been governed by principles of Indiana law that guide the resolution of this appeal.

> Indiana case law recognizes that transactions entered into during the existence of a fiduciary relationship are presumptively invalid as the product of undue influence. Transactions between an attorney and client are presumed to be fraudulent, so that the attorney has the burden of proving the fairness and honesty thereof.

Matter of Smith, 572 N.E.2d 1280, 1285 (Ind.1991). *See also Sweeney v. Vierbuchen*, 224 Ind. 341, 348, 66 N.E.2d 764, 766–767 (1946); *Olds v. Hitzemann*, 220 Ind. 300, 305, 42 N.E.2d 35, 37–38 (1942); *Lucas v. Frazee*, 471 N.E.2d 1163, 1166–67 (Ind.Ct.App.1984); *Briggs v. Clinton County Bank & Trust Co.*, 452 N.E.2d 989, 999 (Ind.Ct.App.1983); *Blasche v. Himelick*, 140 Ind.App. 255, 259–260, 210 N.E.2d 378, 381 (1965); *Castle v. Kroeger*, 111 Ind.App. 43, 53–54, 39 N.E.2d 459, 463–464 (1942).

This statement of general principle does not endeavor to specifically address standard commercial transactions between a lawyer and a client in which the lawyer does not render legal services. But, parallel to the "standard commercial transaction" exception noted in the Comment to Professional Conduct Rule 1.8, such transactions are likewise generally considered as not subject to the common law prohibition against attorney-client transactions. *See* Section 126 of the Restatement (Third) of The Law Governing Lawyers, particularly comment (c).

During the trial court's consideration of the Youngs' motion for partial summary judgment, and Liggett's later summary judgment motion that was treated as a motion to reconsider the Youngs' motion, the designated matters considered by the court did not expressly assert that Dean Young had prepared the contract in question. The parties' construction contract, however, was in the form of a pre-printed "Building, Construction and No-Lien Agreement" approved by the Indiana State Bar Association, the header of which declared: "the selection of a form of instrument, filling in blank spaces, striking out provisions and insertion of special clauses, constitutes the practice of law and should be done by a lawyer." Appellant's App'x at 32, 51. And Liggett's affidavit in opposition to the Youngs' motion for partial summary judgment specifically asserts that Dean Young drafted Paragraph 12 of the construction contract, Appellant's App'x at 59, which assertion the Youngs do not dispute. Liggett's affidavit also asserted that at the time the contract was entered, Dean Young was serving "as Liggett's personal attorney." Appellant's App'x at 59. The Youngs did not respond to that assertion in the summary judgment proceeding, and acknowledge that at the time of the contract's execution, Dean Young "was acting as the attorney for Liggett on an unrelated matter." Appellees' Br. at 2.

The designated matter considered by the trial court does not include any evidence showing that Dean Young's transaction with his client Ronald Liggett was fair and honest, or was a standard commercial transaction that should be exempted from the common law presumption of invalidity due to undue influence. Nor do the Youngs designate any materials to overcome the presumption. And while Liggett's initial opposition to the Youngs' partial summary judgment motion did not expressly assert any claim of presumed invalidity, unfairness, or dishonesty, his supporting affidavit did assert Dean Young's dual status as both Liggett's attorney and party to the contract. In Liggett's subsequent motion for summary judgment (which the court treated as a motion for reconsideration), he expressly raised issues of "illegality and constructive fraud." Appellant's App'x at 97. Noting both Dean Young's dual status and that Young was responsible for drafting the contract, Liggett asserted that Rule 1.8(a) applies to render the contract void as an illegal contract, *id.* at 108–110, or as a constructive fraud, *id.* at 110–111.

While excluding the further evidentiary materials supporting and opposing Liggett's motion for summary judgment, the trial court did acknowledge that "Liggett contends that the written contract should be declared void based upon the fact that Young was serving as Liggett's attorney on unrelated matters." Addressing this claim, the trial court found that (a) in responding to the Youngs' summary judgment motion, Liggett had not expressly asserted that the contract was void but had affirmed the validity of the contract and claimed that he had completed his contractual obligations; and that (b) even "if Liggett had made a timely challenge to the validity of the written contract, such an argument would fail." After quoting the "standard commercial transactions" exclusion described in the Comment to Rule 1.8., App'x at 16–17, the trial court concluded:

> 26. The evidence before the Court establishes that Liggett was a building contractor. With respect to the subject matter of this case, the Youngs were the clients and Liggett was the professional. Consequently, Rule 1.8 of the Indiana rules of Professional Conduct does not apply.

Appellant's App'x at 16–17.

As a preliminary matter, we observe that Liggett did not, by asserting completion of his obligations under the contract, forego his claim that the construction contract was void due to Dean Young's dual status in the transaction. A party may plead inconsistent, alternative claims or theories. Ind. Trial Rule 8(E)(2); *Reeder v. Harper,* 788 N.E.2d 1236, 1243 n. 5 (Ind.2003); *Cahoon v. Cummings,* 734 N.E.2d 535, 542 (Ind.2000); *Foster v. Evergreen Healthcare, Inc.,* 716 N.E.2d 19, 28 (Ind.Ct.App.1999). Of greater significance, however, is that Liggett's claims against the Youngs are for materials and labor not included in the original base construction contract but result instead from additional items that Liggett claims were performed at the Youngs' request. These claims derive from custom language drafted by Young and inserted subparagraph (b) in paragraph "12. ADDITIONAL COVENANTS" of the preprinted contract. This sub-paragraph 12(b) states: "(b) Subject to changes which from time to time may be made following construction [sic] between Builders and Owners, and, where necessary, following consultation with Owners' construction/ mortgage lenders." Appellant's App'x at 34.

With respect to Liggett's contentions regarding the dual status of Dean Young as both a party to the contract with Liggett and as Liggett's attorney at the time, we conclude that the designated evidence on the Youngs' motion for partial summary judgment did not affirmatively establish the absence of a genuine issue of material fact as to whether, in light of Dean Young's fiduciary relationship as Liggett's attorney, the building contract transaction was fair and honest so as to overcome the common law presumption that the contract was fraudulent. Nor was there designated matter showing that the transaction, the centerpiece of which was a contract allegedly prepared and modified by attorney Dean Young, should as a matter of law be treated as a standard commercial transaction to which the common law presumption did not apply. Under such circumstances, the Youngs are not entitled to partial summary judgment foreclosing Liggett's claims against them.

Having previously granted transfer, thereby automatically vacating the opinion of the Court of Appeals, Ind. Appellate Rule 58(A), we now reverse both (a) the trial court's final judgment in favor of the Youngs and against Liggett as to all of Liggett's claims against the Youngs and (b) the grant of the Youngs' motion for partial summary judgment as to Liggett's claims. This cause is remanded to the trial court for resolution of the remaining claims of each party in a manner consistent with this opinion.

SHEPARD, C.J., and SULLIVAN and RUCKER, JJ., concur.

BOEHM, J., concurs in result with separate opinion.

SOLUTIONS: THE LAWYER SHOULD HAVE, WOULD HAVE, COULD HAVE. . .

Lawyers are skilled professionals. Their clients entrust them with important matters. This trust and reliance spills over into any personal business engaged in by the lawyer and the client. Had the lawyer here understood that principle then he would've likely refrained from rewriting a provision of the contract. He could have hired a lawyer to negotiate the change, but he elected to do it himself. Again, the lawyer who knows the rule and the reason for the rule will always have an advantage the practice of law over the lawyer who only knows the rule.

Cases and Materials

X-Ray Questions (*Holmes*)

This case deals with a fee agreement between a lawyer and a client that generated tremendous return for the lawyer with very little work by the lawyer. Note that MR 1.8(a) uses the phrase "business transactions." Why such a broad phrase? The drafters could have used "contractual relationship" or "business dealings "but they did not. Why? We see here how a fee agreement is a "business transaction." The court repeats the mantra that attorney-client relationships are not ordinary business contracts. What does the court mean by this? Ask yourself, how would this dispute have been resolved under normal contract law? Also, we see here how what you learned about fees in Chapter 2 appears in this rule, once again illustrating how the Rules operate as an ecosystem, not a linear study one rule after the other? What ethical rule on fees did you learn in Chapter 2? Does Holmes run afoul of here?

Holmes v. Loveless

Court of Appeals of Washington, Division 1., 2004.
122 Wash.App. 470.

Opinion

The fee a lawyer collects for legal services must be reasonable. Attorney fee agreements are subject to continued review for reasonableness over the course of the agreement. We conclude that the trial court erred in enforcing a contingent fee agreement under which a law firm received five percent of the cash distributions from a joint venture in exchange for rendering legal services at a discount. That discount was valued at $8 000 off regular rates; the cash distributions over 30 years have exceeded $380,000. Further enforcement of this agreement cannot be justified on any principled basis. We reverse.

FACTS

Joseph D. Holmes, Jr. and John F. Kruger are retired attorneys and former partners in the Seattle law firm that is now known as Karr Tuttle Campbell. In 1970, Holmes and his law firm began providing legal services to C.E. Loveless, a real estate developer. In 1972, Loveless and Barclay Tollefson, another real estate developer, started a joint venture called "Loveless/Tollefson Properties" to develop The Nugget Mall, a shopping center in Juneau, Alaska.

In a fee agreement dated January 15, 1972, Holmes' law firm agreed to provide legal services to the Loveless/Tollefson joint venture at a discounted rate until June 30, 1974. The discounted rate was intended to cover the law firm's overhead expenses. Thereafter, legal fees would be charged at the full rate. In exchange, Karr Tuttle would receive five percent of any cash distributions produced by the joint venture. The agreement contained a conflict of interest provision advising Loveless and Tollefson that their individual interests could be different and that, due to the law firm's prior representation of Loveless, Tollefson should have the agreement reviewed by other counsel. Loveless had entered into several other similar agreements with Karr Tuttle, each pertaining to different joint ventures with different business partners. Loveless initially proposed that Karr Tuttle obtain a seven percent ownership interest in the joint venture, but Karr Tuttle declined this offer and countered with the five percent cash distribution idea. Tollefson had not been a party to such an agreement before the Loveless/Tollefson Properties joint venture was formed. The agreement contained no provision allowing the joint venture to unilaterally terminate the agreement.

The joint venture began making distributions in the early 1980's. Gradually, the shopping center became more successful and it underwent several phases of expansion. In 1986, Loveless and Tollefson raised concerns about the effect of the expansions on the method of calculating cash distributions. When they raised their concerns, Holmes asked another Karr Tuttle partner to assist with the negotiations as a more neutral facilitator. The parties resolved the dispute by entering into a written addendum to the 1972 agreement in which the parties agreed that the joint venture would pay Loveless and Tollefson certain development fees and leasing commissions before the cash distributions were calculated.

The law firm subsequently assigned its interest in the agreement to Holmes and Kruger. By 2001, the joint venture had distributed approximately $380,000 to the law firm and its assignees. At that time, the joint venture notified Holmes that the agreement was no longer enforceable and it terminated payments. Shortly thereafter, it made a large distribution to Loveless and Tollefson. Holmes and Kruger (hereinafter collectively referred to as "Holmes") filed a lawsuit to enforce the agreement and recoup their share of the distribution. On cross-motions for summary judgment, the trial court ruled in Holmes' favor.

ANALYSIS

Appellate review of a trial court's order granting summary judgment is de novo. *Ski Acres, Inc. v. Kittitas County,* 118 Wash.2d 852, 854, 827 P.2d 1000 (1992). Summary judgment is proper if the pleadings, affidavits, depositions, or admissions on file show that there is no genuine issue as to any material fact and that the moving party is entitled to judgment as a matter of law. *Meissner v. Simpson Timber Co.,* 69 Wash.2d 949, 951, 421 P.2d 674 (1966).

A fee agreement that violates the Rules of Professional Conduct (RPC) is against public policy and unenforceable. *Simburg, Ketter, Sheppard & Purdy, L.L.P. v. Olshan,* 97 Wash.App. 901, 909, 988 P.2d 467 (1999). Deciding whether "an attorneys conduct violates the relevant Rules of Professional Conduct is a question of law." *Eriks v. Denver,* 118 Wash.2d 451, 457–58, 824 P.2d 1207 (1992). Professional misconduct may also be a basis for denying or disgorging fees. *Eriks,* 118 Wash.2d at 462, 824 P.2d 1207.

The joint venture's challenge to the fee agreement is premised upon two ethical rules: one governing attorney-client business transactions and another prohibiting excessive fees. Before September 1,1985, the Code of Professional Responsibility (CPR) governed attorney conduct in Washington. Since September 1, 1985, the RPC has regulated lawyer conduct. Thus, both the CPR, which was in effect when the 1972 agreement was made, and the RPC, effective now and when the 1986 addendum was made, are involved in this dispute.

As an initial matter, we conclude that it is appropriate to review the 1972 agreement and the 1986 addendum under the provisions governing business transactions, as well as the provisions for fee agreements. Holmes asserts that the 1972 agreement is not a "business transaction," but this conclusion is not supported by the evidence. Although the law firm declined to obtain an ownership interest in the joint venture, its compensation was directly linked to the joint venture's profits. This is sufficient evidence to conclude that the fee agreement falls within the scope of the business transaction rule.

RPC 1.8 provides:

A lawyer who is representing a client in a matter:

(a) Shall not enter into a business transaction with a client or knowingly acquire an ownership, possessory, security or other pecuniary interest adverse to a client unless:

(1) The transaction and terms on which the lawyer acquires the interest are fair and reasonable to the client and are fully disclosed and

transmitted in writing to the client in a manner which can be reasonably understood by the client;

(2) The client is given a reasonable opportunity to seek the advice of independent counsel in the transaction; and

(3) The client consents thereto.

RPC 1.5(a) provides:

(a) A lawyer's fee shall be reasonable. The factors to be considered in determining the reasonableness of a fee include the following:

(1) The time and labor required, the novelty and difficulty of the questions involved, the skill requisite to perform the legal service properly and the terms of the fee agreement between the lawyer and client;

(2) The likelihood, if apparent to the client, that the acceptance of the particular employment will preclude other employment by the lawyer;

(3) The fee customarily charged in the locality for similar legal services;

(4) The amount involved in the matter on which legal services are rendered and the results obtained;

(5) The time limitations imposed by the client or by the circumstances;

(6) The nature and length of the professional relationship with the client;

(7) The experience, reputation, and ability of the lawyer or lawyers performing the services; and

(8) Whether the fee agreement or confirming writing demonstrates that the client had received a reasonable and fair disclosure of material elements of the fee agreement and of the lawyer's billing practices.

To some degree, the excessive fee and business transaction provisions overlap when attorneys and clients use business transactions as compensation for legal services. When the fee generated by a business transaction is not fair and reasonable, the business transaction is not fair and reasonable. This is demonstrated in this court's decision in *Cotton v. Kronenberg*, 111 Wash.App. 258, 44 P.3d 878 (2002), *review denied*, 148 Wash.2d 1011, 62 P.3d 890 (2003), which analyzed a fee agreement involving the exchange of real property for legal services under RPC 1.8. In *Cotton,* the attorney agreed to defend a client from criminal charges in exchange for a nonrefundable transfer of real property and a mobile home. This court concluded that the attorney violated the business transaction provision, RPC 1.8, when he was disqualified from the case, but refused to refund the value of the property received. Focusing on the "fair and reasonable" language of RPC 1.8(a)(1), this court held that the attorney's failure to fulfill his obligation to his client, as well as the disparity between the $42,000 value of the real estate and the $10,000 to $30,000 estimate for legal fees based upon hourly rates, rendered the agreement unenforceable. *Cotton,* 111 Wash.App. at 270–71, 44 P.3d 878.

The *Cotton* court also noted that the time frame for evaluating the reasonableness of a fee is not restricted to the time of entry into the agreement. It explained:

> As Professor Hazard explains in his work on ethics, a fee agreement that may seem fair to a client at the time that the agreement is signed must be reevaluated under the applicable rules when subsequent events alter the circumstances of the relationship. For example, if a client offers an attorney an interest in a fledgling company in exchange for legal representation, and the value of that share in the company unexpectedly increases greatly, the value of the fee may become unreasonably large in proportion to the work performed.

Cotton, 111 Wash.App. at 271–72, 44 P.3d 878. *Cotton* did not address the excessive fee prohibition of RPC 1.5(a), but the above-cited quotation provides persuasive support for the joint venture's argument that an attorney's ethical obligation to avoid charging an excessive fee is continuous throughout the life of the agreement. *In re Swartz,* 141 Ariz. 266, 686 P.2d 1236 (1984), cited by the joint venture, shares this view. It held that an attorney's ethical duties require self-monitoring to ensure that there is no violation of DR 2–106, the CPR provision governing fee agreements:

> [A] fee agreement between lawyer and client is not an ordinary business contract. The profession has both an obligation of public service and duties to clients which transcend ordinary business relationship and prohibit the lawyer from taking advantage of the client. Thus, in fixing and collecting fees the profession must remember that it is "a branch of the administration of justice and not a mere money getting trade." ABA Canons of Professional Ethics, Canon 12. We hold, therefore, that if at the conclusion of a lawyer's services it appears that a fee, which seemed reasonable when agreed

upon, has become excessive, the attorney may not stand upon the contract; he must reduce the fee. What is reasonable and within permissible limits will be determined by the circumstances, including the factors list in DR 2–106.

Swartz, 686 P.2d at 1243. We follow these cases by holding that it is appropriate to hold attorneys to a standard of continued adherence to the rules prohibiting excessive fees. The terms of the 1972 agreement and the 1986 addendum must be evaluated with this in mind.

Holmes argues that *Cotton* is distinguishable for two reasons. Analyzing *Cotton* as an excessive fee case, Holmes states that the agreement in *Cotton* was not contingent, whereas the 1972 agreement was contingent upon the success of the joint venture. Second, the attorney in *Cotton* never fulfilled his end of the bargain because he was forced to withdraw. In contrast, Karr Tuttle provided discounted legal services for two and one-half years as provided in the 1972 agreement.

These factors are certainly appropriate to consider when evaluating the reasonableness of the fee collected from the joint venture, but they do not resolve the question presented, which is whether the 1972 agreement is subject to further enforcement. Although the joint venture does not contend that it is entitled to a refund of fees, it argues continued enforcement of the agreement is not fair and reasonable, even after the contingent nature and successful completion of the work are considered. Holmes argues that the fees are fair and reasonable, relying upon *Bauermeister v. McReynolds,* 253 Neb. 554, 571 N.W.2d 79 (1997), a Nebraska Supreme Court decision upholding a contingent fee agreement similar to the one here.

In *Bauermeister,* a joint venture to develop a landfill lacked the funds to pay for legal services, so it offered its lawyer, McReynolds, a royalty to be paid if the landfill proposal succeeded. McReynolds rejected the joint venture's initial royalty fee offer as excessive but agreed to provide services for a royalty fee based upon landfill gate receipts that was one-third of the one originally offered. *Bauermeister,* 571 N.W.2d at 90. Several years after the landfill opened, one of the parties to the joint venture sought rescission of the agreement and claimed the fees were excessive. By that time, McReynolds had received $900,000 and was expected to receive up to $4 million.

The Nebraska Supreme Court analyzed the parties' agreement and a subsequent assignment under the CPR provisions for business transactions with a client, DR 5–104(A), and for excessive fees, DR 2–106. It concluded that the fee agreement was not a prohibited transaction under DR 5–104(A) because the attorney's and the client's interests did not differ and the client consented to the agreement after full disclosure. *Bauermeister*, 571 N.W.2d at 91. The objecting party claimed that it was not fully advised of the conflicts of interest when its individual attorney at the time of the joint venture's formation subsequently joined the firm that advised the joint venture. The court rejected this argument because all parties clearly understood that the firm represented the joint venture, not the individuals behind it, and the joint venture consented to the royalty provision upon full disclosure.

The court also analyzed the fee for excessiveness under DR 2–106. The trial court decided that the fee was excessive, but the Nebraska Supreme Court disagreed and cited numerous DR 2–106 factors in support of its conclusion. Those factors were: the slim likelihood of successfully opening the landfill; the large investment of work performed on a contingent basis (worth $250,000) that precluded the attorney from working for two large clients paying hourly fees; the joint venture's inability to afford other counsel; the attorney's special skills in working with local government officials; and the $1.4 million in financial benefits enjoyed by the client. *Bauermeister*, 571 N.W.2d at 91–92.

The 1972 fee agreement is similar to *Bauermeister* in some respects. Neither agreement was a classic contingent fee. Instead, compensation was tied to the success of a business venture. Although neither law firm possessed an outright ownership interest, both were entitled to a portion of the profits. In both cases, the attorneys negotiated down from the client's original proposed profit-sharing formula. Furthermore, in *Bauermeister*, the attorney opined that the likelihood of success was small. Here, while it is uncertain what the parties' expectations were for the joint venture's success, it is not disputed that Loveless and the law firm entered into numerous similar agreements on other joint ventures for which there was no significant revenue generated. Thus, it is reasonable to conclude that the likelihood of success was not great.

But several key differences are apparent. From the outset, the financial burden on Karr Tuttle was minimal compared to the one on the firm in *Bauermeister*. Rather than defer all compensation until the joint venture began profitable operations, Karr Tuttle received some hourly compensation. In addition, this reduced rate was offered for only two and one-half years, after which the full rate was paid. Even after accounting for inflation, the $8,000 out-of-pocket cost to Karr Tuttle was much less than the $250,000 investment made by the firm in *Bauermeister*. Additionally, unlike the firm in *Bauermeister*, there is no evidence that the agreement precluded Karr Tuttle from working for other fee-paying clients.

These differences are significant in evaluating whether continued enforcement is reasonable. Holmes may have provided services valuable to the joint venture, but he assumed very little risk in the agreement. Other employment was not precluded, and the discount was provided only for a limited time. His firm still covered its overhead expenses. In comparison with *Bauermeister,* the return to Holmes has been enormously favorable, and he has not demonstrated any special circumstances, such as particular expertise or unusual demands on his time, that would justify continued enforcement of the agreement. While the five percent provision may have been reasonable at the outset given the small percentage it represented of the development's total revenue, at this point over 30 years later, the amount of fee reduction does not justify further enforcement of the agreement. After analyzing the RPC 1.5(a) factors, we agree with the joint venture's contention that the time has been reached when making additional distributions under the agreement would result in an excessive fee.

Another substantial factor that we consider is the lack of a termination date for cash distributions, especially compared with the limited discount period. The joint venture received a discounted rate for only two and one-half years, but this agreement could potentially generate distributions to the attorneys and their estates indefinitely. The agreement contains a termination provision that may be exercised at the attorneys' discretion, but the joint venture is not afforded that option. We do not mean to suggest that such a provision would be necessary for the validity of the agreement; however, with the circumstances presented here, the lack of a such a provision has led to an excessive fee situation.

In addition to arguing that the attorney fee will become excessive if the agreement is enforced, the joint venture argues that the 1972 agreement was a prohibited business transaction. The first reason is Holmes' failure to advise the parties to obtain independent review of the agreement. This argument touches on the validity of the agreement from its inception. Although the joint venture does not seek a refund of distributions already paid, even if it had sought this remedy, we would reject this contention. The record does not show that the law firm violated the ethical rules pertaining to entering into business transactions with clients.

Because the agreement was signed in 1972, DR 5–104(A) is the relevant provision. DR 5–104(A) does not require that a lawyer advise a client in all situations to consult independent counsel before entering into a business transaction with the lawyer. *See Pollock v. Marshall,* 391 Mass. 543, 462 N.E.2d 312, 321 (Mass.1984). Here, Loveless and Tollefson were both experienced real estate developers. Loveless instigated the agreement, believing that it would be beneficial to the joint venture to defer payment of legal fees until it became profitable. As in *Bauermeister,* there is no evidence that the law firm and the joint venture had differing interests at the time the 1972 agreement was signed. It is clear that the joint venture was the client and that the joint venture consented to the agreement upon full disclosure. Furthermore, the agreement contained a conflict of interest provision specifically advising Loveless and Tollefson of the possibility that their individual interests could conflict. Under these circumstances, we find no violation of DR 5–104(A).

In 1986, when the addendum was signed, RPC 1.8(a) was in effect. RPC 1.8(a) requires lawyers to ensure that clients with whom they transact business have a reasonable opportunity to consult outside counsel. In hindsight, the use of a Karr Tuttle partner to mediate the dispute may not have been advisable, but the record shows that both Tollefson and Loveless considered retaining outside counsel, but decided not to. This is conclusive evidence that they had a reasonable opportunity to consult with counsel.

Tollefson and Loveless also argue that the agreement was unfair because they did not fully understand how the agreement worked, but the evidence does not support this contention. Both appear to have sufficiently understood its provisions to perform the 1972 agreement over several years and to demand certain modifications of it in 1986. Consequently, while there is evidence that Loveless and Tollefson did not like the agreement after the joint venture became profitable, the contention that they did not understand it is not supported by the evidence.

Lastly, Holmes argues that the joint venture waived its right to repudiate the 1972 agreement by entering into the 1986 addendum, but as noted above by the Arizona Supreme Court in *Swartz,* agreements between attorneys and clients are different from ordinary business contracts. No agreement in violation of the RPC is enforceable. Because fee agreements are subject to continuous review, entering into a negotiated resolution of a fee dispute does not preclude subsequent judicial review where additional fees are generated in the interim.

In sum, we conclude that the 1972 agreement and 1986 addendum are no longer enforceable because the fee would not be reasonable. We reverse and remand for entry of judgment in favor of Loveless, Tollefson, and the joint venture.

> ### SOLUTIONS: THE LAWYER SHOULD HAVE, WOULD HAVE, COULD HAVE. . .
>
> The lawyers here enjoyed good fortune but at a high price to the clients. They put their needs ahead of the client needs. Had they asked themselves one question and answered it honestly then this litigation could have been avoided. The question? If the shoe was on the other foot—that is, our riles reversed—would we consider that we were being treated fairly? The Golden Rule is, when you think about it, an ethical rule as well.

Model Rule 1.8(b)

(b)   A lawyer shall not use information relating to representation of a client to the disadvantage of the client unless the client gives informed consent, except as permitted or required by these Rules.

LEANING INTO PRACTICE

Scenario: The Case of the Lawyer and the Nonpublic Information

Lupe Lawyer represents a real estate developer and her company in a variety employment law matters bit not in real estate. At lunch, while discussing a discrimination complaint against the developer's company, the developer tells her that she believes that a shopping mall will be built at the intersection of Vine and Maple. This information is not yet public. The client tells Lupe that she is planning to buy three parcels of land near the proposed development and build parking garages. Lupe goes to her wife, tells her about the plan, and instructs her to buy these three parcels through a shell company. When the client goes through with the purchase then Lupe's shell company can then sell the parcels at an inflated price. The wife does so. Is Lupe in violation of this rule? Does it matter that Lupe does not do real estate work for the client? Why? Or that Lupe is not making the purchases directly? Why?

Model Rule 1.8(c)

(c)   A lawyer shall not solicit any substantial gift from a client, including a testamentary gift, or prepare on behalf of a client an instrument giving the lawyer or a person related to the lawyer any substantial gift unless the lawyer or other recipient of the gift is related to the client. For purposes of this paragraph, related persons include a spouse, child, grandchild, parent, grandparent or other relative or individual with whom the lawyer or the client maintains a close, familial relationship.

LEANING INTO PRACTICE

Scenario: The Case of the Lawyer and Moma's Ring

Lola Lawyer represents a country and western singer. While the singer is not yet famous, she has potential. Lola prepares contracts with musical venues and a recording label. One day Lola tells her client "I really admire your ring. It is so beautiful.' The singer responds by telling her it is vary valuable and that her mother gave it to her as she was dying. After: "Moma Gave Me A Gift" wins a Grammy, Lola gets a box hand delivered to her office with the ring inside and a note "You are the best lawyer. I could not have done it without you." Lola puts on the ring and keeps it. Has Lola violated the rule? Explain your answer.

Model Rule 1.8(d)

(d)   Prior to the conclusion of representation of a client, a lawyer shall not make or negotiate an agreement giving the lawyer literary or media rights to a portrayal or account based in substantial part on information relating to the representation.

LEANING INTO PRACTICE

Scenario: The Case of the Lawyer and the Trial for Murder

KiKi Lawyer is representing a woman accused of murdering her late husband—the mayor of a large city—because he was allegedly involved sexually with another woman. The client has run out of money and offers KiKi this deal "I will give the rights to the story of my childhood to you as payment for your legal fees." The childhood has nothing to do with the murder or the defense of same. KiKi accepts the deal. Is KiKi in violation of the Rule? Why would it be a violation? What would the rationale be for making it a violation?

Model Rule 1.8(e)

(e)   A lawyer shall not provide financial assistance to a client in connection with pending or contemplated litigation, except that:

(1)   a lawyer may advance court costs and expenses of litigation, the repayment of which may be contingent on the outcome of the matter;

(2)   a lawyer representing an indigent client may pay court costs and expenses of litigation on behalf of the client; and

(3)   a lawyer representing an indigent client pro bono, a lawyer representing an indigent client pro bono through a nonprofit legal services or public interest organization and a lawyer representing an

indigent client pro bono through a law school clinical or pro bono program may provide modest gifts to the client for food, rent, transportation, medicine and other basic living expenses. The lawyer:

> (i)   may not promise, assure or imply the availability of such gifts prior to retention or as an inducement to continue the client-lawyer relationship after retention;

> (ii)   may not seek or accept reimbursement from the client, a relative of the client or anyone affiliated with the client; and

> (iii) may not publicize or advertise a willingness to provide such gifts to prospective clients.

Financial assistance under this Rule may be provided even if the representation is eligible for fees under a fee-shifting statute.

LEANING INTO PRACTICE

Scenario: The Case of the Lawyer and the Engagement Ring

John Lawyer represents Izzi Client in a personal injury lawsuit in which John's fee is on a contingency basis. Izzi is given a loan of $2,000 to help pay Izzy's rent so that Izzy is not evicted. John also has a personal life and is dating Heidi. After two years of dating Heidi gives him an ultimatum: "I want an engagement ring now or we are done as a couple." John reads that a typical ring costs $10,000, which John does not have, but which he thinks he can borrow. Would John be tempted to settle Izzi's case for less than it is worth to help Izzi pay back the loan? Or to settle the lawsuit suit more quickly than normal, before all discovery is completed, so as to expedite the loan repayment? If John does settle the case now would there be a basis for a bar grievance against him? Why?

Note that we will revisit MR 1.8 when we discuss transactions between the lawyer and the client. These scenarios will help the foundation for our more extended discussion in Chapter 8 on transactional ethics.

Section 6.   Confidential Information

Model Rule 1.6: Confidentiality of Information

(a)   A lawyer shall not reveal information relating to the representation of a client unless the client gives informed consent, the disclosure is impliedly authorized in order to carry out the representation or the disclosure is permitted by paragraph (b).

(b)   A lawyer may reveal information relating to the representation of a client to the extent the lawyer reasonably believes necessary:

(1)   to prevent reasonably certain death or substantial bodily harm;

(2)   to prevent the client from committing a crime or fraud that is reasonably certain to result in substantial injury to the financial interests or property of another and in furtherance of which the client has used or is using the lawyer's services;

(3)   to prevent, mitigate or rectify substantial injury to the financial interests or property of another that is reasonably certain to result or has resulted from the client's commission of a crime or fraud in furtherance of which the client has used the lawyer's services;

(4)   to secure legal advice about the lawyer's compliance with these Rules;

(5)   to establish a claim or defense on behalf of the lawyer in a controversy between the lawyer and the client, to establish a defense to a criminal charge or civil claim against the lawyer based upon conduct in which the client was involved, or to respond to allegations in any proceeding concerning the lawyer's representation of the client;

(6)   to comply with other law or a court order; or

(7)   to detect and resolve conflicts of interest arising from the lawyer's change of employment or from changes in the composition or ownership of a firm, but only if the revealed information would not compromise the attorney-client privilege or otherwise prejudice the client.

(c)   A lawyer shall make reasonable efforts to prevent the inadvertent or unauthorized disclosure of, or unauthorized access to, information relating to the representation of a client.

Let's Chart It!

Is there an attorney-client relationship? If yes, proceed to the inside of the box? This diagram represents how MR 1.6 operates. If there is an ACR formed, then there is entry into the box. Once inside the box then there are buckets representing exceptions to the broad rule embodied in MR 1.6(a) So, then, ask yourself, what does the "?" represent? That's right: if the facts presented do not fit within one of the exception buckets, then the matter must be attained as confidential by the lawyer. MR 1.6 protects the client from their own lawyer, who is all too human and can crater to the temptation of discussing the interesting aspects of their professional lives to those outside of the ACR.

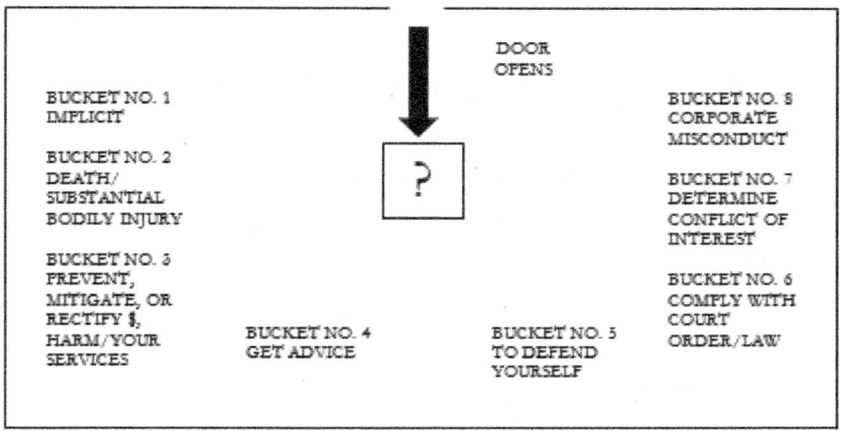

Model Rule 1.6(a)

A lawyer shall not reveal information relating to the representation of a client unless the client gives informed consent, the disclosure is impliedly authorized in order to carry out the representation or the disclosure is permitted by paragraph (b).

Deconstruction Exercise/Rule Rationale

MR 1.6 requires that lawyers maintain the confidences of clients that are "related to" the representation. *Anything* from *any source* learned in the course of the representation must be kept confidential. This is a broad rule, protecting much more than just the statements of the client. The first exception is embedded in this section; namely, "impliedly." The import of this word is to empower a lawyer to carry out the typical lawyer functions arising from formation of the ACR such as relating the facts to other firm lawyers or to counsel opposite to seek a settlement (if that is a client goal).

LEANING INTO PRACTICE

Scenario No. 1: The Case of the Lawyer and the Assassin

Esmeralda Lawyer practices criminal defense law in New York City. She represents Gabby Client, a professional hit woman for the mafia, who is under indictment for the murder of a prominent public official. Gabby tells Esmeralda, "By the way, as long as we are talking, I wanted you to know that I did actually murder two people in Guam several years ago. I got away with that. The FBI is still looking for the bodies!" Even though those murders are unrelated to do with the alleged murder in New York City, the information is protected by MR 1.6 because it was learned by Esmeralda during the course of representing Gabby. Can you explain why?

Scenario No. 2 The Case of the Lawyer and the Referral

Sam Lawyer meets with a prospective client who needs help registering securities. Sam does not perform legal work involving securities regulation, and thus is not competent by experience or by self-education given the complexity of the area. So, he exercises the option of refusal/referral and gets the client's OK to refer the matter to Joe Lawyer who is competent. While Joe learned the information about the matter from Sam, and not the client, the information is still entitled to MR 1.6 protection. Can you explain why?

Cases and Materials

X-Ray Questions (*Matter of Anonymous*)

We see in this case that the lawyer revealed confidences about the representation to the client's friends out of a well-intentioned motive; to help a despondent client. The court essentially rejects the lawyer's motive as a defense. Why? Do you agree? Should the rule be amended to empower a lawyer's discretion to reveal confidential information if—in the lawyer's independent judgment—the revelation would be of assistance to the client? The lawyer here realizes that she was only disclosing matters of public record and therefore the information was not truly confidential because any person can check the court filings. Why did the court reject this argument? Finally, consider the formation of the ACR in this opinion. How did the court reason out that an ACR was finally formed? Recall the lesson learned at the start of the book.

In the Matter of Anonymous, Respondent

Supreme Court of Indiana, 2010.
932 N.E.2d 671.

Attorney Discipline Action Hearing Officer Lynn Murray

PER CURIAM.

This matter is before the Court on the report of the hearing officer appointed by this Court to hear evidence on the Indiana Supreme Court Disciplinary Commission's "Verified Complaint for Disciplinary Action." The

Respondent's admission to this state's bar subjects her to this Court's disciplinary jurisdiction. *See* IND. CONST. art. 7, § 4.

We find that Respondent engaged in attorney misconduct by improperly revealing information relating to the representation of a former client. For this misconduct, we find that Respondent should receive a private reprimand.

Background

Respondent represented an organization that employed "AB." Respondent became acquainted with AB though this connection. In December 2007, AB and her husband were involved in an altercation to which the police were called, during which, AB's husband asserted, she threatened to harm him. In January 2008, AB phoned Respondent and told her about her husband's allegation and that she and her husband had separated. In a second phone call that month, AB asked Respondent for a referral to a family law attorney. Respondent gave AB the name of an attorney in Respondent's firm. Respondent then called this attorney to inform her of the referral and to give her AB's phone number. The attorney called AB that same day and arranged a meeting the following day, when AB retained the attorney. AB told the attorney about the December 2007 incident and directed her to file a divorce petition. Respondent was aware that AB had retained the attorney from her firm and had filed for divorce. AB and her husband soon reconciled, however, and, at AB's request, the divorce petition was dismissed and the firm's representation of AB ended.

In March or April 2008, Respondent was socializing with two friends, one of whom was also a friend of AB's. Unaware of AB's reconciliation with her husband, Respondent told her two friends about AB's filing for divorce and about her husband's accusation. Respondent encouraged AB's friend to contact AB because the friend expressed concern for her. When AB's friend called AB and told her what Respondent had told him, AB became upset about the revelation of the information and filed a grievance against Respondent.

The Commission charged Respondent with violating Professional Conduct Rule 1.9(c)(2), which prohibits revelation of information relating to the representation of a former client except as the Professional Conduct Rules permit or require. The hearing officer concluded that Respondent violated the rule as charged. The hearing officer found no facts in aggravation and the following facts in mitigation: (1) Respondent has no disciplinary history; and (2) Respondent was cooperative with the Commission.

Neither party filed a petition for review of the hearing officer's report. When neither party challenges the findings of the hearing officer, the Court accepts and adopts those findings but reserves final judgment as to misconduct and discipline. *See Matter of Levy,* 726 N.E.2d 1257, 1258 (Ind.2000).

Discussion

Rules addressing revelation of confidential information. The Rules of Professional Conduct ("Rules") contain several interrelated rules protecting the confidentiality of information relating to legal representations and consultations. Respondent is accused of violating Professional Conduct Rule 1.9(c), which sets forth the following duties owing to *former* clients:

A lawyer who has formerly represented a client in a matter or **whose present or former firm has formerly represented a client in a matter shall not thereafter:**

> (1) use information relating to the representation to the disadvantage of the former client except as these Rules would permit or require with respect to a client, or when the information has become generally known; or

> (2) **reveal information relating to the representation** except as these Rules would permit or require with respect to a client.

(Emphasis added.)

Professional Conduct Rule 1.6(a), which covers duties to *current* clients, states: "A lawyer shall not reveal information relating to representation of a client unless the client gives informed consent, the disclosure is impliedly authorized in order to carry out the representation or the disclosure is permitted by paragraph (b)." Paragraph (b) allows disclosure under conditions not applicable to the current case, such as to prevent commission of a crime or to comply with a court order.

Professional Conduct Rule 1.18, which covers duties to *prospective* clients, states:

> (a) A person who discusses with a lawyer **the possibility of forming a client-lawyer relationship** with respect to a matter is a prospective client.

> (b) Even when no client-lawyer relationship ensues, **a lawyer who has had discussions with a prospective client shall not use or reveal information learned in the consultation,** except as Rule 1.9 would permit with respect to information of a former client.

(Emphasis added.)

Respondent's revelation of the information at issue was a violation of Rule 1.9(c)(2). Respondent argued to the hearing officer that AB initially gave her the information at issue for the purpose of seeking *personal* rather than professional advice and only later phoned her again to ask for an attorney referral. Thus, she argued, the information was not confidential when AB first disclosed it to her, subsequent events did not change its nature, and she violated no ethical obligation in later revealing it.

The first January 2008 phone conversation did not include discussion of the possibility of forming an attorney-client relationship. If AB's communication with Respondent had ended with that phone call, revelation of the information at issue would not have been a violation of Respondent's ethical duties. "A person who communicates information unilaterally to a lawyer, without any reasonable expectation that the lawyer is willing to discuss the possibility of forming a client-lawyer relationship, is not a 'prospective client' within the meaning of paragraph (a)." Ind. Prof. Cond. R. 1.18 cmt. [2].

The information at issue, however, was disclosed to Respondent not long before the second call in which AB asked for an attorney referral and Respondent recommended an attorney from her firm. At that point, if not before, AB became a prospective client under Rule 1.18. The formation of an attorney-client relationship with Respondent's firm followed immediately thereafter, and the information at issue was highly relevant to the representation. Respondent then revealed the information with knowledge that her firm had been retained to represent AB in the matter. Under these circumstances, we conclude that once AB became a prospective client, the information became subject to the confidentiality protections of the Rules.

Respondent presented evidence that AB disclosed the information at issue to others, including some of AB's co-workers. Respondent argued to the hearing officer that AB's disclosure of the information to others indicated that AB's disclosure to Respondent in the first phone conversation was personal rather than professional in nature and not intended to be confidential. However, the fact that a client may choose to confide to others information relating to a representation does not waive or negate the confidentiality protections of the Rules, which we have found apply to the information at issue.

Respondent also argued to the hearing officer that revelation of the information at issue was not barred because it could be discovered by searching various public records and the internet. True, the filing of a divorce petition is a matter of public record, but Respondent revealed highly sensitive details of accusations AB's husband made against her to the police. There is no evidence that this information was contained in any public record. Moreover, the Rules contain no exception allowing revelation of information relating to a representation even if a diligent researcher could unearth it through public sources.

Although we find it unnecessary in this case to explore the outer boundaries of the Rules concerning client confidences, the protection provided is broad.

> The attorney-client privilege and work-product doctrine apply in judicial and other proceedings in which a lawyer may be called as a witness or otherwise required to produce evidence concerning a client. The rule of client-lawyer confidentiality applies in situations other than those where evidence is sought from the lawyer through compulsion of law. The confidentiality rule, for example, applies not only to matters communicated in confidence by the client but also to **all information relating to the representation, whatever its source.**"

Ind. Prof. Cond. R. 1.6 cmt. [3] (emphasis added). An attorney has a duty to prospective, current, and former clients to scrupulously avoid revelation of such information, even if, as may have been the case here, the attorney is motivated by personal concern for the client.

Conclusion

The Court concludes Respondent violated Professional Conduct Rule 1.9(c)(2) by improperly revealing information relating to the representation of a former client. For Respondent's professional misconduct, the Court imposes a private reprimand.

The costs of this proceeding are assessed against Respondent. The hearing officer appointed in this case is discharged.

The Clerk of this Court is directed to give notice of this opinion to the hearing officer, to the parties or their respective attorneys, and to all other entities entitled to notice under Admission and Discipline Rule 23(3)(d). The Clerk is further directed to post this opinion to the Court's website, and Thomson Reuters is directed to publish a copy of this opinion in the bound volumes of this Court's decisions.

All Justices concur.

SOLUTIONS: THE LAWYER SHOULD HAVE, WOULD HAVE, COULD HAVE. . .

While the lawyer's motive was pure (to help the client with any emotional issues), we have seen that lawyer's motives—no matter how well intentioned—are not a defense to a grievance that a Rule was violated. Yes, a defense of "I meant well" might impact the severity of a sanction but that goes to mitigation and not to responsibility.

A. Exceptions for Physical and Financial Harm

Model Rule 1.6(b)(1–3)

(b) A lawyer may reveal information relating to the representation of a client to the extent the lawyer reasonably believes necessary:

(1) to prevent reasonably certain death or substantial bodily harm;

(2) to prevent the client from committing a crime or fraud that is reasonably certain to result in substantial injury to the financial interests or property of another and in furtherance of which the client has used or is using the lawyer's services;

(3) to prevent, mitigate or rectify substantial injury to the financial interests or property of another that is reasonably certain to result or has resulted from the client's commission of a crime or fraud in furtherance of which the client has used the lawyer's services;

Deconstruction Exercise/Rule Rationale

Some rules can work without exceptions; others cannot. MR 1.6 falls into the second category. MR 1.6(a) is an absolute rule with exceptions. As you read the exception, pay special attention to the modifiers used: "reasonably" before "belief;" "certain" before "death;" "substantial" before "harm." Why were these words used? Think of them as "speed bumps" to disclosure of confidential information. In other words, the rule prioritizes maintaining confidentiality and these modifiers act to slow down a lawyer who is considering disclosing confidential client information.

These exceptions above were added in 2003. One revision that did not make the cut was insertion of "imminent" before "death or substantial bodily harm." This proved too far a bridge to cross for the drafters because it would foreclose disclosure in a situation in which there would be substantial bodily harm or death but not immediately. By way of example, a company knowingly permits toxic substances from its factories into a city's water supply. While the harm will be serious, it may take several months or years to manifest.

It's worth noting that the Model Rule says lawyers "may" disclose information to prevent death or substantial bodily harm. Some states have parted ways with the ABA on this and have *mandated* disclosure. For example, Nevada's version of 1.6 has an extra that provision says: "A lawyer shall reveal information relating to the representation of a client to the extent "the lawyer reasonably believes necessary" to prevent a criminal act that the lawyer believes is likely to result in reasonably certain death or substantial bodily harm." Do you think the ABA is right to allow lawyers to have discretion over whether to reveal information in this situation? And yes, we see yet again the concept of: "to the extent" with its focus on a nuanced judgment to be made by the lawyer.

Finally, an exception to confidentiality exists if financial harm will result to another. Yet again, the structure of the rule contains numerous "speed bumps" to slow down any release of confidential indignation. The most critical of these is the answer to this threshold question: Were the services of the lawyer actually used in perpetrating a fraud or crime? If not—no matter how egregious or outrageous the conduct—the lawyer cannot reveal the confidence. And even if the lawyer's services were used, the lawyer must maintain silence *unless* these services caused the crime or fraud and that same resulted in "substantial injury" to the financial interests or property of another. The rule structure illuminates the utmost importance that the rules place upon maintaining a client's confidences and secrets. Lawyers represent clients and seek their best interests and are officers of the court and seek to preserve the integrity of the legal system but are not, except in narrow and cabined circumstances, public guardians.

Cases and Materials

X-Ray Questions (*McClure*)

This case deals with the horrific murder of a mother and her two children. Attorney Mecca was appointed to represent the man accused of murdering the mother. The children were, however, missing at the time. The defendant played down with Mecca whether he knew the whereabouts of the children. After they were missing for nine days, Mecca concluded from what his client had told him that he knew where the children were and told the police how to find their bodies. The defendant was convicted of murdering the children and the mother. He appealed, arguing that Mecca breached confidentiality in making the disclosure to law enforcement and he thus received ineffective assistance of counsel under the Sixth Amendment. Apply MR 1.6(b)(1)'s language to these facts before reading the case. What should be the result? What single fact should the answer turn on? Did Mecca violate MR 1.6? The majority at the appeals court did not buy his argument and reverse the conviction. We do not provide their opinion. But after reading the dissent, can you sense their motivation? Perhaps you've heard the phrase "hard cases make for bad law." Is that the case here?

McClure v. Thompson

United States Court of Appeals, Ninth Circuit, 2003.
323 F.3d 1233.

FERGUSON, CIRCUIT JUDGE, dissenting:

I respectfully dissent. The majority erred when it held that the disclosure of the location of two of McClure's victims' bodies by his defense attorney did not constitute deficient performance under *Strickland v. Washington,* 466 U.S. 668, 104 S.Ct. 2052, 80 L.Ed.2d 674 (1984). McClure's attorney, Christopher Mecca, breached one of the most sacred obligations of the attorney-client relationship, the duty of confidentiality, and in turn violated McClure's Sixth Amendment right to counsel. Based on an utterly unreasonable interpretation of the events surrounding the disclosure at issue in this case, the majority finds that Mecca met an exception to the duty of confidentiality. As a result, the majority holds that it was reasonable for Mecca to believe that two missing children were alive but dying, when he disclosed their location to authorities, without McClure's consent, without asking McClure directly whether he had killed them, and without conducting any investigation to find out.

While purportedly applying the *Strickland* standard, "reasonableness under prevailing professional norms," *id.* at 688, 104 S.Ct. 2052, the majority conducts a wholly subjective analysis of Mecca's behavior, not even attempting to define "reasonableness" or provide an objective standard by which Mecca's behavior may be judged.

By applying a subjective analysis, the majority creates an unguided test which effectively undermines the basic tenet of the duty of confidentiality embodied in the Sixth Amendment right to counsel. In essence, the majority's rule allows a defense attorney to disclose client confidences in an alleged effort to prevent a future crime, even if:

(a) the attorney has made merely a nominal attempt to resolve his own doubts about whether disclosure is necessary and has never directly questioned his client to confirm or allay his suspicions;

(b) the lawyer has virtually no evidence that the potential victims are in immediate danger;

(c) the evidence demonstrates that the attorney knew that the impending crime in question was likely concluded and was aware that her disclosure would fall so far below professional standards that it would likely result in disbarment.

While defining "reasonableness" may be an elusive task, I refuse to subscribe to the majority's opinion, which provides no limitations or guidance to practitioners. Instead, I look to existing case law and our profession's ethical rules to guide my analysis in this case. Even accepting the facts as determined by the lower courts, an objective analysis of Mecca's behavior reveals that it falls below not only professional ethical standards, but also constitutional standards for effective assistance of counsel under *Strickland* and its progeny. While *Strickland* and Model Rule 1.6 supply the standard under which Mecca's conduct should be judged, there nevertheless remains the difficult task of defining what behavior is "reasonable." Under either the "firm factual basis test" or even the majority's broad inquiry, Mecca's behavior fell well short of reasonably effective assistance of counsel.

I

The notion that lawyers are obligated to safeguard a client's secrets and confidences is well established. An attorney's duty of confidentiality emanates from the profession's ethical rules, the evidentiary attorney-client and work product privileges, and the Sixth Amendment. One of the oldest and most sacrosanct duties of an attorney, the duty of confidentiality in the United States dates back to 1908 and the first incantation of the ethical rules for lawyers, the American Bar Association's Canons of Professional Ethics. Canon 6 provided that lawyers had an "obligation to represent the client with undivided fidelity and not to divulge his secrets or confidences." While the duty of confidentiality has evolved as our profession has evolved, the underlying principle remains steadfast: an attorney should not reveal his client's confidences without first obtaining their informed consent.

The duty to guard a client's confidences is, of course, not absolute, and the ethical rules recognize as much. Because an attorney's duty of confidentiality must be balanced against the public's interest in safety and justice, Model Rule

1.6 carves out two exceptions. Both exceptions allow an attorney to disclose a client's confidences "to the extent [he or she] reasonably believes necessary," either "to prevent the client from committing a criminal act that the lawyer believes is likely to result in imminent death or substantial bodily harm," or "to establish a claim or defense on behalf of the lawyer" in particular controversies. The majority erroneously finds that the first exception applies in this case, thereby justifying Mecca's disclosure of the location of the bodies of two of McClure's victims, Michael and Tanya Jones.

The Supreme Court has made clear that an attorney's duty of confidentiality intersects with the Sixth Amendment right to counsel. "[The Sixth Amendment] obviously involves the right to keep the confidences of the client from the ear of the Government which these days seeks to learn more and more of the affairs of men." *Russo v. Byrne,* 409 U.S. 1219, 1221, 93 S.Ct. 21, 34 L.Ed.2d 30 (1972). As such, an attorney's unwarranted breach of the duty of confidentiality is not only an ethical violation, but also implicates the Sixth Amendment right to effective assistance of counsel.

II

Identifying the relevant rules and governing standard is merely the first part of the analysis. As the majority correctly notes, the next logical step is determining what constitutes an objectively reasonable belief under the first exception to Model Rule 1.6 and for purposes of *Strickland.* In a somewhat distinct but related context, Justice O'Connor has commented that the word unreasonable "is no doubt difficult to define. That said, it is a common term in the legal world and, accordingly, federal judges are familiar with its meaning." *Williams v. Taylor,* 529 U.S. 362, 410, 120 S.Ct. 1495, 146 L.Ed.2d 389 (2000) (interpreting AEDPA's requirement that a state court adjudication be "contrary to, or involve an unreasonable application of clearly established law."). Thus, the majority's failure to give meaning to the standard in this case is not excused by the inherent difficulty attached to the task.

As a general matter, Mecca's behavior should be judged against that of a "reasonable attorney." In other words, what would a reasonable attorney in Mecca's position have done, if anything, with the information that McClure gave him? Framed in accordance with *Strickland* and Model Rule 1.6, was Mecca's belief that the children were alive reasonable and was disclosure reasonable under the circumstances?

A.   A "firm factual basis" is the proper standard for judging an attorney's disclosure of client confidences under the ethical rules.

The majority embarks upon an erroneous path at the outset by rejecting McClure's contention that Mecca was required to have a "firm factual basis" before disclosing the location of the children's bodies to the authorities. Maj. Op. at 1245–46. As McClure notes, both case law and current ethical standards have long required that an attorney have a substantial basis for her belief that a client plans to engage in criminal conduct, before disclosing to the authorities. *See, e.g., United States v. Omene,* 143 F.3d at 1171 (stating that the court was "concerned that Omene's counsel did not lay out a firm factual basis for his position."); *United States v. Scott,* 909 F.2d 488, 493 (11th Cir.1990) (advising defendant that "he could be precluded from testifying, without confirmation that[he] intended to commit perjury . . . forced [him] to choose between two constitutionally protected rights."); *United States v. Long,* 857 F.2d 436, 445–46 (8th Cir.1988) (holding that "it is absolutely essential that a lawyer have a firm factual basis before adopting a belief of impending [criminal conduct]" by his client); *Jackson v. United States,* 928 F.2d 245, 248 (8th Cir.1991) (finding that the evidentiary hearing "provided a reasonable factual basis for believing that Jackson would lie if he took the stand.").

While the standard is primarily applied in alleged perjury cases, therefore implicating a different set of ethical rules, the underlying principles remain the same. By rejecting the "firm factual basis" standard, the majority creates the contradictory notion that the ethical rules and pertinent case law mandate a lower standard for breaching the duty of confidentiality in a manner that implicates a client in a murder, versus perjury. Nevertheless, the majority applies a totally unguided "objective reasonableness in light of the surrounding circumstances" standard. Maj. Op. at 1245.

While I am familiar with *Strickland's* mandate that we give deference to a defense attorney's choices and judgment, I do not believe *Strickland* permits the total abdication of meaningful review that the majority's analysis reflects. Our case law and ethical rules suggest a number of factors that should enter into the reasonableness calculus. First, how much information did the attorney possess suggesting that a crime was going to be committed before he disclosed? Relatedly, how much investigation did the attorney conduct to inform herself of the circumstances and resolve any doubts she may have had? Third, how convinced was the attorney that their client was going to commit a crime (for example, did he believe beyond a reasonable doubt?)?

Applying the above analysis to the case at hand, it is obvious that Mecca's chosen course of action fell short of what is required of effective counsel. Indeed, even under the majority's open ended test, a review of the *undisputed* facts reveals that Mecca failed to engage in even a minimal level of investigation before disclosing the location of the children, rendering his belief that the children were alive both illogical and unreasonable.

B.   Mecca's behavior was unreasonable because he did not possess sufficient information to make his belief that the children were alive reasonable and it was unreasonable for him to rely on the little information he had.

The unreasonableness of Mecca's belief that the children were alive becomes clear by reviewing what occurred in the days leading up to the disclosure. Mecca was hired by McClure's family on Saturday, April 28, 1984. By Sunday, although McClure initially proclaimed his innocence, Mecca began to think that McClure "was involved in[Carol] Jones's murder and the disappearance of her children." This was because by this time McClure had sought Mecca's assistance in destroying evidence which McClure said might contain blood, as well as due to a meeting between Mecca, McClure and McClure's family during which it was revealed that McClure's family believed he may have been involved in the crime. By Monday evening, Mecca "became convinced that petitioner had killed Carol Jones and began to question whether petitioner had killed the children[,]" due in no small part to the manner in which McClure was beginning to reveal certain information, such as his sexual fantasies about young girls and his drug use. Despite his doubts, on Tuesday, Mecca never directly inquired whether McClure had killed the children, although they specifically discussed the children that day.

Curiously, Mecca based much of his belief that the children were alive on a comment that McClure made to him on Monday, that "Satan killed Carol," but "Jesus saved the kids." Specifically, Mecca wrote in his notes that these statements hit him so abruptly, he immediately assumed that it meant the children were alive. Maj. Op. at 1237. In the face of mounting evidence pointing to the fact that the children were most likely dead, this assumption was utterly unreasonable. As Mecca himself admits, it was a hope against all hope. By Tuesday, the date of the disclosure, a reasonable attorney would have understood the complete unlikelihood that McClure spared the children, particularly after viewing the map to the bodies that McClure drew for him.

While the above is sufficient to render Mecca's belief that the children were alive unreasonable, the way in which McClure conveyed to Mecca the location of the bodies, as well as the content of the map itself, would not lead a reasonable attorney to believe the children were alive. McClure had exhibited odd behavior throughout the days preceding the disclosure, placing numerous desperate calls to Mecca from the jail and asking Mecca to dispose of crime scene evidence. When McClure finally told Mecca where the children were, he did so obscurely: in the course of discussing "places he had been with the family[,]" McClure drew a rough map, never directly telling Mecca what he would find there. The map showed two locations, which were more than sixty miles apart from one another, in a deserted and wooded area. Receiving such information after the children had been missing for eight days, although surely disturbing, is insufficient to lead a reasonable attorney to believe the children were alive and that disclosure of that information was warranted, much less necessary.

The majority focuses on the fact that the District Court found that "McClure knew the true facts and he deliberately withheld them, leading Mecca to believe the children were alive[,]" noting that McClure "controlled the flow of information." Maj. Op. at 1247. However, this does not change the fact that Mecca had very little information on which to base his belief and the little he had overwhelmingly and sadly pointed to the children's demise.

C.   Mecca's conduct was unreasonable because, in the face of almost no information supporting his belief, Mecca conducted no investigation to verify his belief that the children were still alive.

Faced with almost no information to support his wishful thinking, Mecca compounded his error by conducting virtually no investigation about the children. The majority cites the District Court's findings that Mecca " 'attempted to discern whether the children were alive' and 'that Mecca investigated to the best of his ability under extremely difficult circumstances.' " *Id.* at 1247. However, neither the District Court nor the majority ever identify what steps Mecca took to inform himself of the condition of the children. This is because Mecca did not conduct any investigation whatsoever. The fact of the matter is that by the time Mecca disclosed the location of the children's bodies, enough had transpired between himself, McClure's family, and McClure that a reasonable attorney would not have reasonably believed the children would be found alive.

Mecca never directly asked McClure whether he had killed the children. Why Mecca did not do so is unexplainable. It could not have hurt McClure's case had he answered in the affirmative; that information would certainly have been covered by the attorney-client privilege. The closest Mecca came to asking McClure was when Mecca advised him that they were obligated to disclose the location of the children if there was any possibility that they were alive, to prevent a possible assault from becoming murder. McClure did not respond. To infer that they were alive from McClure's silence is illogical. In fact, a reasonable person would most likely have inferred that there was no possibility that the children were alive, because McClure had just been informed that he was required to disclose if there was.

Besides directly inquiring with McClure, Mecca could have also conducted some investigation outside of the jail cell. Mecca could have armed himself with the map and driven to the locations on the map to determine once and for all if the children were alive. Moreover, both Mecca and McClure testified that they discussed the option of Mecca doing so; why Mecca chose not to and instead went to the authorities is beyond reason. Indeed, if he truly believed the children were alive in the woods, at risk of exposure and starvation, it is inexplicable that he would not have immediately gone to assist them. While locating the bodies himself would undeniably have been a great burden, criminal defense attorneys should be prepared to meet the myriad challenges of their vocation-investigating and uncovering disturbing evidence related to their representation is but one; confronting moral and ethical dilemmas competently is another.

> D.   Mecca's conduct was unreasonable because Mecca had no more
> than a bare suspicion, based entirely on his own wishful thinking, that
> the children were alive.

Mecca purportedly believed the children were alive; however, his words and actions at the time of the disclosure indicate that his belief was pallid. Since Mecca testified in hindsight about his belief that the children were alive, the majority emphasizes the lower courts' credibility determination in favor of Mecca. Even accepting that veracity of Mecca's belief, examining the strength of that belief betrays the government's assertions that it was reasonable. It is true that Model Rule 1.6 does not indicate what is required beyond a "reasonable belief[,]" but surely an inkling alone cannot suffice to support a reasonable belief.

The majority omits a number of undisputed facts about the events leading up to Mecca's disclosure that show Mecca was not as certain about the children's vitality at the time of the disclosure as he is today. First, Mecca repeatedly used the word "bodies" when referring to the children in his notes taken shortly after the disclosure. For example, Mecca wrote: " 'McClure related to me . . . one place where a body might be' and then 'described [where] the other body would be located.' " Maj. Op. at 1236. Additionally, Mecca recorded the following after the prosecutor had refused to negotiate a plea for McClure: " 'The only option I had, as far as I was concerned, was to disclose the whereabouts of the body [sic].' " *Id.* at 1237. Mecca also wrote, " 'I arranged to have the information released anonymously to the Sheriff's Department with directions to the bodies.' " *Id.* at 1237. Although Mecca attempted to explain his choice of words by explaining that he made the notes after the bodies were located, this answer is unsatisfying.

Examining Mecca's mental state around the time of the disclosure is also illuminating. After his conversation with McClure on Monday, Mecca testified, " '[t]he conclusion I came to was that, without telling me, he told me he had killed three people.' " *Id.* at 1238. When discussing McClure's comment that " 'Satan killed Carol, but Jesus saved the kids[,]' " Mecca stated that he " 'kind of felt that [McClure] was talking about a sexual thing, but, in any event, [he] wasn't sure.' " *Id.* at 1237. In addition, Mecca stated the following regarding the Jesus/Satan comment: " 'I allowed myself to believe that these kids might somehow be alive.' " *Id.* at 1239. Mecca's own words suggest the absurdity of this belief-he *allowed* himself to believe it because it was so incredulous. Finally, Mecca practically admitted that his belief was weak in discussing the possibility that the children were alive. He testified that he " 'felt it was a possibility. I wouldn't say a strong possibility.' " *Id.*

Finally, Mecca attempted to negotiate a deal with the prosecution in exchange for the information about the children's bodies. If Mecca strongly believed the children were alive but dying, and his concern for their welfare was as great as he claims, why would he continue to jeopardize their lives by first trying to strike a deal for his client?

While it is true that the events leading up to Mecca's disclosure unfolded rapidly and were no doubt incredibly stressful, it is not unfair to expect a reasonable criminal defense attorney to be capable of competently dealing with these types of situations. It was not such a brief period of time that Mecca's lack of investigation and rash disclosure can be justified. In short, Mecca had agreed to represent an individual who was accused of killing a woman whose children were missing. Over the course of a few days, McClure revealed himself to be a mentally disturbed individual who fantasized about sex with young girls and enlisted his attorney's help in destroying evidence related to the murders. Perhaps Mecca is correct that there was no way to be 100% certain at the time whether the children were alive or dead, and perhaps we should not question whether he truly personally believed that the children were alive. But as a criminal defense attorney, Mecca had a responsibility to inform himself, investigate, and support his belief by facts before taking the extreme step of disclosing McClure's confidential information to the police. When an attorney falls below this standard, courts should not be afraid to name the problem: deficient performance under the Sixth Amendment guarantee of effective assistance of counsel.

In the end, it is clear that not only did Mecca lack a "firm factual basis" for his belief that the children were alive, he had virtually no basis whatsoever, nor did he make a reasonable effort to gain one-at best, Mecca's "investigation" can be characterized as paltry. The danger of the majority's decision is that it risks making Mecca's conduct the standard for attorneys who may find themselves in a similar predicament in the future.

III

I too sympathize with Mecca for being concerned with the welfare of the children, as do the majority, the District Court and the state court. It would scarcely be wrong to criticize him for, as the District Court stated, being "a human being." However, because at the time of the disclosure Mecca was playing a critical and unique role as McClure's defense attorney, I cannot sanction his behavior. It seems that the time has come for Mecca to take responsibility for the choice he made to breach his client's confidence and for a court, *this court*, to recognize that whether or not Mecca did the "right" thing does not diminish the fact that his doing so constituted an abdication of his professional duties and rendered his performance as McClure's defense attorney deficient under the Sixth Amendment. Mecca's concern for the children is certainly understandable and laudable, however, it does not negate the infirmity of McClure's conviction. Therefore, I must dissent.

SOLUTIONS: THE LAWYER SHOULD HAVE, WOULD HAVE, COULD HAVE. . .

The question boils down to whether the lawyer possesses a reasonable belief that the disclosure of the client's confidence will prevent substantial bodily harm or death. A reasonable belief is a contextual decision made on concrete facts and likely probabilities, not speculation, guess work, or hope. The dissent in this case has some cogent points. While it is only natural to hope the children were still alive, the length of time they were missing made that not just unlikely but close to impossible. Finally, Mecca's own delay in reporting the confidence to the police undercut his argument that he came to a reasonable belief that the children were alive. After all, if time is of the essence, why wait?

B. Other Exceptions to Confidentiality

Model Rule 1.6(b)(4–7)

(b)   A lawyer may reveal information relating to the representation of a client *to the extent* the lawyer reasonably believes necessary:

> (4)   to secure legal advice about the lawyer's compliance with these Rules;
>
> (5)   To establish a claim or defense on behalf of the lawyer in a controversy between the lawyer and the client, to establish a defense to a criminal charge or civil claim against the lawyer based upon conduct in which the client was involved, or to respond to allegations in any proceeding concerning the lawyer's representation of the client;
>
> (6)   to comply with other law or a court order; or
>
> (7)   to detect and resolve conflicts of interest arising from the lawyer's change of employment or from changes in the composition or ownership of a firm, but only if the revealed information would not compromise the attorney-client privilege or otherwise prejudice the client.

Deconstruction Exercise/Rule Rationale

You might think of these as the exceptions for practical necessity. Lawyers sometimes need advice about the practice of law. But they could not get it if they could not talk about their cases to own lawyers or other lawyers to assist on resolving the different ethical dilemmas. It also is be unfair to let a client complain or sue about a lawyer's conduct, but then prevent the lawyer from talking about the case in her own defense. By way of example, a lawyer warns a client in an email that the client's planned course of conduct would fail, and it does. If the lawyer is sued for malpractice, the lawyer must be allowed to place into evidence that portion of the email containing the warning. Also, some revelation of confidential information is necessary to screen for conflicts of interest. These rules illustrate why confidentiality could never be an entirely absolute rule.

There are three "speed bumps" baked into these rules. They are in the precatory language to the rules: "may" and "to the extent" and "reasonably necessary."

➢ "May"

Again, the lawyer uses judgment in deciding whether to reveal confidences. It is impossible to contemplate every possible scenario and thus develop hard and fast rules.

➢ "To the extent"

This is classic lawyer language because it reflects a nuanced understanding of an issue. And here it is a "speed bump" because it restrains the amount and type of confidential information that can be disclosed. Stated differently, it means just enough and no more than necessary.

➢ "Reasonably believes necessary"

This phrase, in conjunction with the previous phrase, places the burden squarely on the lawyer to put a brake on over disclosure.

C. Corporate Misconduct Exception to Confidentiality

Model Rule 1.13: Organization as Client

(a) A lawyer employed or retained by an organization represents the organization acting through its duly authorized constituents.

(b) If a lawyer for an organization knows that an officer, employee or other person associated with the organization is engaged in action, intends to act or refuses to act in a matter related to the representation that is a violation of a legal obligation to the organization, or a violation of law that reasonably might be imputed to the organization, and that is likely to result in substantial injury to the organization, then the lawyer shall proceed as is reasonably necessary in the best interest of the organization. Unless the lawyer reasonably believes that it is not necessary in the best interest of the organization to do so, the lawyer shall refer the matter to higher authority in the organization, including, if warranted by the circumstances to the highest authority that can act on behalf of the organization as determined by applicable law.

(c) Except as provided in paragraph (d), if

(1) despite the lawyer's efforts in accordance with paragraph (b) the highest authority that can act on behalf of the organization insists upon or fails to address in a timely and appropriate manner an action, or a refusal to act, that is clearly a violation of law, and

(2) the lawyer reasonably believes that the violation is reasonably certain to result in substantial injury to the organization, then the lawyer may reveal information relating to the representation whether or not Rule 1.6 permits such disclosure, but only if and to the extent the lawyer reasonably believes necessary to prevent substantial injury to the organization.

(d) Paragraph (c) shall not apply with respect to information relating to a lawyer's representation of an organization to investigate an alleged violation of law, or to defend the organization or an officer, employee or other constituent associated with the organization against a claim arising out of an alleged violation of law.

(e) A lawyer who reasonably believes that he or she has been discharged because of the lawyer's actions taken pursuant to paragraphs (b) or (c), or who withdraws under circumstances that require or permit the lawyer to take action under either of those paragraphs, shall proceed as the lawyer reasonably believes necessary to assure that the organization's highest authority is informed of the lawyer's discharge or withdrawal.

(f) In dealing with an organization's directors, officers, employees, members, shareholders or other constituents, a lawyer shall explain the identity of the client when the lawyer knows or reasonably should know that the organization's interests are adverse to those of the constituents with whom the lawyer is dealing.

(g) A lawyer representing an organization may also represent any of its directors, officers, employees, members, shareholders or other constituents, subject to the provisions of Rule 1.7. If the organization's consent to the dual representation is required by Rule 1.7, the consent shall be given by an appropriate official of the organization other than the individual who is to be represented, or by the shareholders.

Let's Chart It!

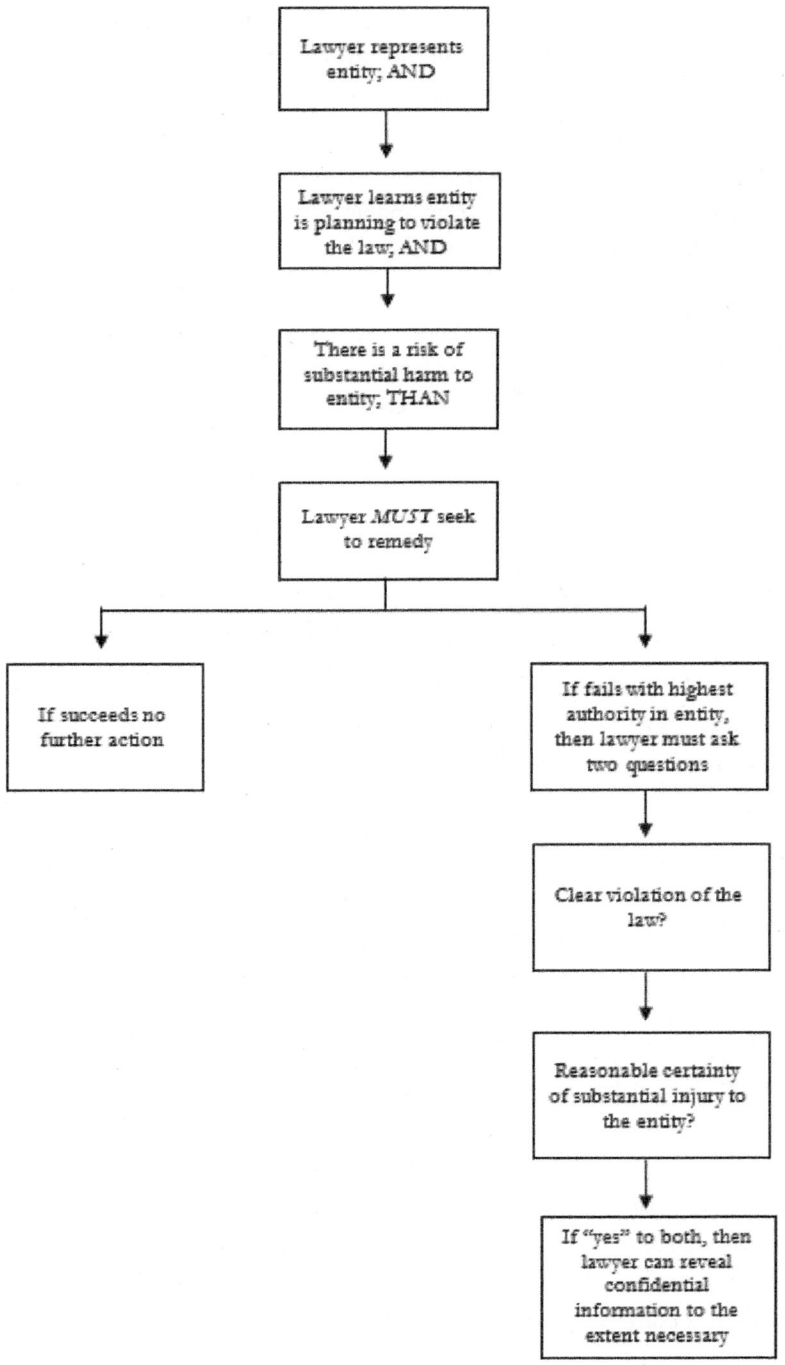

Deconstruction Exercise/Rule Rationale

This rule was substantially revised in 2003 in light of the Enron scandal and similar marks on the legal profession. It remains somewhat confusing in as much as it seeks to serve two different values, each in tension with the other. On one end of the spectrum, there is the need to not reveal the confidences of a client, while on the other end of the spectrum is the need to protect the client from making decisions or refraining from making decisions that will likely result in substantial harm to the organization. The challenge is that because an organization involves many people, addressing misconduct by its officers may require revealing damaging information to other people. The rule tries to solve this challenge by reminding lawyers to know the identity of their client. Do you represent an organization, or an officer of the organization in an individual capacity? In good times, representing the CEO and the company might seems like one and the same. But in bad times, they are very different. Entitles are functionally people and have a legal existence entitled to be protected. In short, the entity is the client although it acts through its constituents. But since lawyers talk and interact with the constituents—the flesh and blood people who run the organization—it is easy to become confused about who the client is.

A few key textual points. The caption of the rule does not limit itself to corporations but rather uses a sweeping term, "organizations." Thus, unions, trade associations, general and limited partnerships, and government agencies are all governed by the rule. But there is another part that limits its scope. A lawyer's duty to protect the organizational client goes no further than "matter(s) related to the (lawyer's) representation." Thus, a lawyer retained for tax advice need not protect the organization on an environmental issue. If the rule were otherwise, the rule would be too unwieldy to enforce and a lawyer without expertise in an area would be required to sort out whether an action planned on or one avoided would pose "substantial" risk to the organization.

What does a lawyer who represents an organization need to be on the lookout for on the road to possible releasing of confidential information of an organizational client? First, note that the rule applies to officers and employees of an organization and also the expansive and seemingly unlimited "or other person associated" with an organization. Note also that the rule covers violations of law or "legal obligations" of the organization. This means that a violation of a contract might trigger a lawyer's obligations, as well as violations of criminal and regulatory law.

If such a person is violating legal obligations, and it "is likely to result in substantial injury to the organization," the lawyer must use judgment in deciding how best to protect the client—that is, the organization not the person who is engaging in the offending conduct. That may mean that the lawyer suddenly must defend an organization against its own leadership. The lawyer should first try to convince or persuade the problematic person to change. A lawyer can do so by asking that a decision to act or to refrain from acting be reconsidered, or suggesting that perhaps a second opinion other than the lawyer's be secured on the legal wisdom of acting/not acting. Note how MR 2.1 and a lawyer's role as an "advisor," not merely a technician, comes into play at this juncture.

If the lawyer is unable to change the course of action leading to substantial risk to the entity/organization, then the lawyer "shall" raise the issue with the highest authority in the organization. That likely means taking the issue to the organization's governing board. This is where the clash with confidentiality is most visible. Since boards involve larger numbers of people, informing the board of an explosive piece of information creates a significant risk that the information will spread.

What if the highest authority "insists" on continuing the course of problematic action or resists taking appropriate action? "Insists" implies that the lawyer made several efforts to persuade the higher-level constituents but did not succeed. If the lawyer still *"reasonably believes"* that the legal violation is *"reasonably certain"* to result in substantial harm to the organization, "then the lawyer shall proceed as is *"reasonably necessary"* in the best interest of the organization." Here the rule becomes quite open-ended, probably because there are so many different kinds of organizations and so many different kinds of problems. The Rule allows revealing information in this situation that would otherwise be protected by MR 1.6, but it does not say to whom or how. To law enforcement? To shareholders or members? A lawyer's guideposts here are to act with reasonableness, and to not reveal more than is needed. Remember, the Rule itself carefully prescribes an escalation of steps that prevent more drastic measures from being necessary.

And finally, what if the bad-acting executive fires the lawyer because the lawyer tries to stop the bad acts? Well, there is a rule for that scenario. The lawyer "shall" inform the organization's highest authority of the discharge and the reason for it—even after being discharged.

Section 7. Attorney-Client Privilege (ACP) v. Confidential Information

The Attorney-Client Privilege (ACP) is a rule of evidence derived from the common law. Its requirements are found in the Restatement 68 et seq., not in the Rules. It is a cousin of other privilege rules, like spousal privilege, clerical privilege, and other rules protecting confidences shared with medical personnel and therapists. Like all privilege rules, it favors secrecy at the expense of the truth. It precludes other counsel or the tribunal from discovering important evidence. Why have it then? Our rules are designed to incentivize a person to tell the truth—the entire truth—to a lawyer. Our system of justice places a premium on this type of consultation. But as you saw in other contexts, there is a tradeoff. Here, to invoke the ACP the client and the lawyer must *strictly* adhere to the predicate elements necessary to invoke the ACP and must not waive the privilege. The following Q and A will assist in understanding how the ACP operates in practice and how it is experienced my lawyers.

Q: What is the difference between MR 1.6 and the ACP?

A: MR 1.6 is intended to protect the client from the client's lawyer divulging the client's confidential information. It covers all of the information that a lawyer learns about the client, not only what the client says. By contrast, the ACP is intended to protect attorney and client *communications* from the prying eyes of counsel opposite or a governmental entity. It only protects the communication between clients and lawyers, and thus is more narrow.

Q: What triggers the ability to invoke successfully the ACP as a shield against disclosure?

A: Merely speaking with a lawyer does not trigger the ACP for any topic discussed. If it did, then the privilege would swallow whole the law of evidence. Rather, the ACP is *only* triggered when the purpose of the person initiating the conversation is to seek legal assistance. No specific words or catch phrases need to be used, however. As we saw in other areas, this intent can be inferred from the circumstances.

Q: Is the ACP lost or waived if a third party is present when the lawyer and the client or the prospective client consult with one another?

A: Here is the question to ask: why is the third person present? If the person is needed to interpret from one language to another, no waiver of the privilege. If the person is present to help translate topics on which has the lawyer is unfamiliar—such as accounting principles or medical terminology—there is no waiver. If the person is present in order to facilitate the client's communication with the lawyer, for example if the client is disabled or is incompetent and needs the third party's assistance, there is no waiver. In other words, if the third person is needed to assist the lawyer in providing legal advice or in preparing a case, then the purpose of the privilege is still being served.

Scenario No. 1: The Case of the Girlfriend Who Is Also a Lawyer

A man is arrested for murdering a co-worker in her apartment. From the police station, he telephones his girlfriend, who is also a criminal defense lawyer. He tells her that he was scared; that he previously visited the apartment on a work-related matter and thus his fingerprints are likely in the apartment; and asks her, "What if we got a little frisky? What if my sperm is found in the apartment?" She does not provide any specific advice and tries to console him.

Privileged or not privileged?

Scenario No. 2: CC'ing the Lawyer

A manager is sending an email to another manager on the performance issues of a minority employee. The email deals with genuine concerns that the sender of the email has regarding the employee. The sender CC's the company's lawyer.

Privileged or not privileged?

Scenario No. 3: Business Advice v. Legal Advice

Roberta Ortega is the C.E.O. of a company. She is considering buying a competitor in order to increase market share and because it is now selling at a discounted price. Ortega sets out her rationale in a memo and cc's other C-level executives as well as the lawyer for the company. The email concerns mostly the business wisdom of making the purchase. None of those cc'd are asked any questions.

Privileged or not privileged?

Scenario No. 4: The Case of Body Language in an ACP Communication

Ollie Client comes to speak to Pauli Lawyer who is defending him on a charge of robbery. Pauli says "the police report says that the robber has a tattoo of an owl in a tree of his ankle. Do you have one?" Ollie says nothing but pulls up his pant leg and shows just such a tattoo.

Privileged or not privileged?

Section 8.   Waiver of ACP

There are various ways to waive the ACP. No one right is absolute and the ACP is no exception.

> ➤   At a deposition or at trial, a witness is asked the topics that he and his lawyer went over in preparation to testify—not what was said between lawyer and client but only the topics discussed. The witness answers. This answer "opens the door" to the content of the conversations unlike answering on whether there was a meeting on its length. *Nguyen v Excel Corporation*, 197 F. 3d 200 (5th Cir. 1999)

> ➤   A lawyer meets with his client at a restaurant. They discuss the client's case and are overheard at the next table. The lawyer takes no precautions to ensure privacy. The discussion is overheard by a friend of the litigant opposite who then testifies at the trail on what she heard.

> (The key is remembering that if you say something is important and confidential, then you treat it as important and confidential.)

> ➤   The client seeks out legal advice on a proposed course of action, The advice is that the course of action complies with the law. Later a claim is brought against the client who seeks to use the consultation as an affirmative defense, arguing that it acted in good faith before embarking on its planned conduct. The statute under which it is being sued allows for such a defense. The client cannot resist discovery into the lawyer's advice because that would be unfair; the client would be using the fact of advice as both a sword and a shield. *In re Seagate Technology, LLC*, 497 F. 3d 1360 (Fed. Cir. 2007)

Cases and Materials

X-Ray Questions (*Purcell*)

This case focuses on the interception between MR 1.6 and the ACP and waiver under the crime fraud exception. You know about the first two; here is the third leg of the stool. The ACP is lost if the client seeks to use the lawyer's services in order to commit a crime or fraud. Why? The ACP cannot be misused by the client to do wrong yet be shielded from *how* the wrong was committed by the ACP——namely use of the ACR.

Here a recently terminated maintenance employee of an apartment building went to a lawyer to discuss his termination. During the course of the meeting, he threatened to set fire the building on fire. Faced with a decision, the lawyer used his discretion under MR 1.6, reported the threat to law enforcement, and the client was arrested in the act.

So far, so good. But the D.A., in prosecuting the client for arson, sought the lawyer's testimony. The lawyer resisted based on the ACP; the D.A. argued waiver under the crime fraud exception. Based only on what you now know, who wins? Why? Do you see the interrelationship between the concepts? What is it?

Purcell v. District Attorney for Suffolk Dist.

Supreme Judicial Court of Massachusetts, Suffolk, 1997.
676 N.E.2d 436.

Opinion

WILKINS, CHIEF JUSTICE.

On June 21, 1994, Joseph Tyree, who had received a court order to vacate his apartment in the Allston section of Boston, consulted the plaintiff, Jeffrey W. Purcell, an attorney employed by Greater Boston Legal Services, which provides representation to low-income individuals in civil matters. Tyree had recently been discharged as a maintenance man at the apartment building in which his apartment was located. On the day that Tyree consulted Purcell, Purcell decided, after extensive deliberation, that he should advise appropriate authorities that Tyree might engage in conduct harmful to others. He told a Boston police lieutenant that Tyree had made threats to burn the apartment building.

The next day, constables, accompanied by Boston police officers, went to evict Tyree. At the apartment building, they found incendiary materials, containers of gasoline, and several bottles with wicks attached. Smoke detectors had been disconnected, and gasoline had been poured on a hallway floor. Tyree was arrested and later indicted for attempted arson of a building.

In August, 1995, the district attorney for the Suffolk district subpoenaed Purcell to testify concerning the conversation Purcell had had with Tyree on June 21, 1994. A Superior Court judge granted Purcell's motion to quash the subpoena. The trial ended in a mistrial because the jury was unable to reach a verdict.

The Commonwealth decided to try Tyree again and once more sought Purcell's testimony. Another Superior Court judge concluded that Tyree's statements to Purcell were not protected by the attorney-client privilege, denied Purcell's motion to quash an anticipated subpoena, and ordered Purcell to testify. Purcell then commenced this action, pursuant to G.L. c. 211, § 3 (1994 ed.), in the single justice session of this court. The parties entered into a stipulation of facts, and a single justice reserved and reported the case to the full court.

There is no question before this court, directly or indirectly, concerning the ethical propriety of Purcell's disclosure to the police that Tyree might engage in conduct that would be harmful to others. As bar counsel agreed in a memorandum submitted to the single justice, this court's disciplinary rules regulating the practice of law authorized Purcell to reveal to the police "[t]he intention of his client to commit a crime and the information necessary to prevent the crime." S.J.C. Rule 3:07, Canon 4, DR 4–101(C)(3), as appearing in 382 Mass. 778 (1981). The fact that the disciplinary code permitted Purcell to make the disclosure tells us nothing about the admissibility of the information that Purcell disclosed. See *Kleinfeld v. State,* 568 So.2d 937, 939–940 (Fla.Dist.Ct.App.1990).

The district attorney does not press the fact that Purcell may not be entitled to relief under G.L. c. 211, § 3, because he could resist testifying, be held in contempt, and then appeal. A single justice has reported this case, implicitly indicating that a discretionary exercise of authority under G.L. c. 211, § 3, in Purcell's favor would be appropriate if his legal position is sound.

The attorney-client privilege is founded on the necessity that a client be free to reveal information to an attorney, without fear of its disclosure, in order to obtain informed legal advice. *Matter of a John Doe Grand Jury Investigation,* 408 Mass. 480, 481–482, 562 N.E.2d 69 (1990). It is a principle of long standing. See *Foster v. Hall,* 29 Mass. 89, 12 Pick. 89, 93 (1831). The debate here is whether Tyree is entitled to the protection of the attorney-client privilege in the circumstances.

The district attorney announces the issue in his brief to be whether a crime-fraud exception to the testimonial privilege applies in this case. He asserts that, even if Tyree's communication with Purcell was made as part of his consultation concerning the eviction proceeding, Tyree's communication concerning his contemplated criminal conduct is not protected by the privilege. We shall first consider the case on the assumption that Tyree's statements to Purcell are protected by the attorney-client privilege unless the crime-fraud exception applies.

"It is the purpose of the crime-fraud exception to the attorney-client privilege to assure that the 'seal of secrecy,' . . . between lawyer and client does not extend to communications 'made for the purpose of getting advice for the commission of a fraud' or crime" (citation omitted). *United States v. Zolin,* 491 U.S. 554, 563, 109 S.Ct. 2619, 2626, 105 L.Ed.2d 469 (1989), quoting *O'Rourke v. Darbishire,* [1920] App. Cas. 581, 604 (P.C.). There is no public interest in the preservation of the secrecy of that kind of communication. See *United States v. Zolin, supra* at 562–563, 109 S.Ct. at 2625–2626; *Matter of John Doe Grand Jury Investigation, supra* at 486, 562 N.E.2d 69.

Our cases have not defined a crime-fraud exception to the attorney-client privilege with any precision. In *Matter of John Doe Grand Jury Investigation, supra* at 486, 562 N.E.2d 69, the court stated that there was "no legitimate interest of a client and no public interest would be served by a rule that would preserve the secrecy of" a conversation between attorney and client in a conference related to the possible future defrauding of an insurance company. We cited *Commonwealth v. Dyer,* 243 Mass. 472, 138 N.E. 296, cert. denied, 262 U.S. 751, 43 S.Ct. 700, 67 L.Ed. 1214 (1923), in which we said that "[t]here is no privilege between attorney and client where the conferences concern the proposed commission of a crime by the client." *Id.* at 505–506, 138 N.E. 296. The cases cited in our *Dyer* opinion and the facts of that case—the attorney was alleged to be part of the conspiracy—demonstrate that the exception asserted concerned conferences in which the attorney's advice was sought in furtherance of a crime or to obtain advice or assistance with respect to criminal activity.

We, therefore, accept the general principle of a crime-fraud exception. The Proposed Massachusetts Rules of Evidence adequately define the crime-fraud exception to the lawyer-client privilege set forth in rule 502(d)(1) as follows: "If the services of the lawyer were sought or obtained to enable or aid anyone to commit or plan to commit what the client knew or reasonably should have known to be a crime or fraud." We need not at this time consider seemingly minor variations of the exception expressed in various sources. See Restatement (Third) of the Law Governing Lawyers § 132, and authorities cited in Reporter's Note at 465–466 (Proposed Final Draft No. 1 1996). The applicability of the exception, like the existence of the privilege, is a question of fact for the judge.

The district attorney rightly grants that he, as the opponent of the application of the testimonial privilege, has the burden of showing that the exception applies. See M.A. Larkin, Federal Testimonial Privileges § 2:07, at 2–150 (1995); P.R. Rice, Attorney-Client Privilege in the United States § 8:3, at 571–572 (1993); S.N. Stone & R.K. Taylor, Testimonial Privileges § 1.65, at 1–173—1–174 (2d ed.1995). In its *Zolin* opinion, the Supreme Court did not have to decide what level of showing the opponent of the privilege must make to establish that the exception applies. See *United States v. Zolin, supra* at 563–564 n. 7, 109 S.Ct. at 2626–2627 n. 7. We conclude that facts supporting the applicability of the crime-fraud exception must be proved by a preponderance of the evidence. However, on a showing of a factual basis adequate to support a reasonable belief that an in camera review of the evidence may establish that the exception applies, the judge has discretion to conduct such an in camera review. *United States v. Zolin, supra* at 572, 109 S.Ct. at 2630–2631. Once the judge sees the confidential information, the burden of proof normally will be unimportant.

In this case, in deciding whether to conduct a discretionary in camera review of the substance of the conversation concerning arson between Tyree and Purcell, the judge would have evidence tending to show that Tyree discussed a future crime with Purcell and that thereafter Tyree actively prepared to commit that crime. Without this evidence, the crime of arson would appear to have no apparent connection with Tyree's eviction proceeding and Purcell's representation of Tyree. With this evidence, however, a request that a judge inquire in camera into the circumstances of Tyree's apparent threat to burn the apartment building would not be a call for a "fishing expedition," and a judge might be justified in conducting such an inquiry. The evidence in this case, however, was not sufficient to warrant the judge's finding that Tyree consulted Purcell for the purpose of obtaining advice in furtherance of a crime. Therefore, the order denying the motion to quash because the crime-fraud exception applied cannot be upheld.

There is a consideration in this case that does not appear in other cases that we have seen concerning the attorney-client privilege. The testimony that the prosecution seeks from Purcell is available only because Purcell reflectively made a disclosure, relying on this court's disciplinary rule which permitted him to do so. Purcell was under no ethical duty to disclose Tyree's intention to commit a crime. He did so to protect the lives and property of others, a purpose that underlies a lawyer's discretionary right stated in the disciplinary rule. The limited facts in the record strongly suggest that Purcell's disclosures to the police served the beneficial public purpose on which the disciplinary rule was based.

We must be cautious in permitting the use of client communications that a lawyer has revealed only because of a threat to others. Lawyers will be reluctant to come forward if they know that the information that they disclose may lead to adverse consequences to their clients. A practice of the use of such disclosures might prompt a lawyer to warn a client in advance that the disclosure of certain information may not be held confidential, thereby chilling free discourse between lawyer and client and reducing the prospect that the lawyer will learn of a serious threat to the well-being of others. To best promote the purposes of the attorney-client privilege, the crime-fraud exception should apply only if the communication seeks assistance in or furtherance of future criminal conduct. When the opponent of the privilege argues that the communication itself may show that the exception applies and seeks its disclosure in camera, the judge, in the exercise of discretion on the question whether to have an in camera proceeding, should consider if the public interest is served by disclosure, even in camera, of a communication whose existence is known only because the lawyer acted against his client's interests under the authority of a disciplinary rule. The facts of each situation must be considered.

It might seem that this opinion is in a posture to conclude by stating that the order denying the motion to quash any subpoena to testify is vacated and the matter is to be remanded for further proceedings concerning the application of the crime-fraud exception. However, the district attorney's brief appears to abandon its earlier concession that all communications between Tyree and Purcell should be treated as protected by the attorney-client privilege unless the crime-fraud exception applies. The question whether the attorney-client privilege is involved at all will be open on remand. We, therefore, discuss the issue.

The attorney-client privilege applies only when the client's communication was for the purpose of facilitating the rendition of legal services. See Rule 502(b) of the Proposed Massachusetts Rules of Evidence; Restatement (Third) of the Law Governing Lawyers § 118 (Proposed Final Draft No. 1 1996) (communication "for the purpose of obtaining or providing legal assistance"); 8 J. Wigmore, Evidence § 2292, at 554 (McNaughton rev. ed.1961) (communication relating to seeking legal advice). See also *In re Richard Roe, Inc.*, 68 F.3d 38, 40 (2d Cir.1995) ("the crime-fraud exception does not apply simply because privileged communications would provide an adversary with evidence of a crime or fraud"); *United States v. United Shoe Mach. Corp.*, 89 F.Supp. 357, 358

(D.Mass.1950) (communication "for the purpose of securing primarily either [i] an opinion on law or [ii] legal services or [iii] assistance in some legal proceeding"); *People v. Clark*, 50 Cal.3d 583, 622, 268 Cal.Rptr. 399, 789 P.2d 127, cert. denied, 498 U.S. 973, 111 S.Ct. 442, 112 L.Ed.2d 425 (1990) (crime-fraud exception "permits disclosure only of communications made to *enable* or *aid* anyone to commit or plan to commit a crime or fraud"). The burden of proving that the attorney-client privilege applies to a communication rests on the party asserting the privilege. *United States v. Harrelson*, 754 F.2d 1153, 1167 (5th Cir.), cert. denied, 474 U.S. 908, 106 S.Ct. 277, 88 L.Ed.2d 241, and cert. denied, 474 U.S. 1034, 106 S.Ct. 599, 88 L.Ed.2d 578 (1985); M.A. Larkin, Federal Testimonial Privileges § 2.05[2], at 2–98 (1995); P.R. Rice, Attorney-Client Privilege in the United States § 11:9, at 971 (1993); S.N. Stone & R.K. Taylor, Testimonial Privileges § 1.61, at 1–161 (2d ed.1995). The motion judge did not pass on the question whether the attorney-client privilege applied to the communication at all but rather went directly to the issue of the crime-fraud exception, although not using that phrase.

A statement of an intention to commit a crime made in the course of seeking legal advice is protected by the privilege, unless the crime-fraud exception applies. That exception applies only if the client or prospective client seeks advice or assistance in furtherance of criminal conduct. It is agreed that Tyree consulted Purcell concerning his impending eviction. Purcell is a member of the bar, and Tyree either was or sought to become Purcell's client. The serious question concerning the application of the privilege is whether Tyree informed Purcell of the fact of his intention to commit arson for the purpose of receiving legal advice or assistance in furtherance of criminal conduct. Purcell's presentation of the circumstances in which Tyree's statements were made is likely to be the only evidence presented.

This is not a case in which our traditional view that testimonial privileges should be construed strictly should be applied. See *Three Juveniles v. Commonwealth*, 390 Mass. 357, 359–360, 455 N.E.2d 1203 (1983), cert. denied sub nom. *Keefe v. Massachusetts*, 465 U.S. 1068, 104 S.Ct. 1421, 79 L.Ed.2d 746 (1984); *Commonwealth v. O'Brien*, 377 Mass. 772, 775, 388 N.E.2d 658 (1979). A strict construction of the privilege that would leave a gap between the circumstances in which the crime-fraud exception applies and the circumstances in which a communication is protected by the attorney-client privilege would make no sense. The attorney-client privilege "is founded upon the necessity, in the interest and administration of justice, of the aid of persons having knowledge of the law and skilled in its practice, which assistance can only be safely and readily availed of when free from the consequences or the apprehension of disclosure." *Matter of a John Doe Grand Jury Investigation,* 408 Mass. 480, 481–482, 562 N.E.2d 69 (1990), quoting *Hunt v. Blackburn,* 128 U.S. 464, 470, 9 S.Ct. 125, 127, 32 L.Ed. 488 (1888). Unless the crime-fraud exception applies, the attorney-client privilege should apply to communications concerning possible future, as well as past, criminal conduct, because an informed lawyer may be able to dissuade the client from improper future conduct and, if not, under the ethical rules may elect in the public interest to make a limited disclosure of the client's threatened conduct.

A judgment should be entered in the county court ordering that the order denying the motion to quash any subpoena issued to Purcell to testify at Tyree's trial is vacated and that the matter is remanded for further proceedings consistent with this opinion.

So ordered.

SOLUTIONS: THE LAWYER SHOULD HAVE, WOULD HAVE, COULD HAVE. . .

Lawyers are often unfamiliar with the crime fraud exception to the ACP. This exception is set out in Restatement 81 of The Law Governing Lawyers. The court in this case discusses the exception. The key is that the client *uses* the lawyer's services to commit a crime. Here is Section 82:

The attorney-client privilege does not apply to a communication occurring when a client:

(a) consults a lawyer for the purpose, later accomplished, of obtaining assistance to engage in a crime or fraud or aiding a third person to do so, or

(b) regardless of the client's purpose at the time of consultation, uses the lawyer's advice or other services to engage in or assist a crime or fraud.

Neither prong existed in his case and thus no waiver of the ACP. Note that waiver is only triggered if the crime/fraud is "later accomplished "by the client. Why this language? Imagine this scenario: the client comes to a lawyer intending to use the legal knowledge or skills given by the lawyer in order to engage in fraud. The lawyer talks the client out of the proposed conduct. Should the ACP be waived? No. A bad intention that is not acted upon should not be punished by stripping away the ACP. Note too (b). If the client comes to the lawyer with no wrongful intentions, but then decides to use the advice/information to engage in wrongful acts, then the ACP is stripped away. The bottom line: the ACP is lost if it is misused.

Cases and Materials

X-Ray Questions (*In re Copper*)

While this case involves high stakes business litigation, its lessons are applicable to all litigation. A company was involved in a lawsuit with public relations ramifications. Accordingly, a PR firm was retained to assist the law firm in managing this aspect of the litigation. The party opposite sought discovery of the communications between the PR firm and the law firm. After all, it reasoned, the PR firm was not a client, and the privilege is called the *Attorney-Client Privilege* for a reason. How did the trial court deal with this argument? What was the essence of its rationale?

The case also introduces you to another privilege, the work product doctrine, that is embodied in the Federal Rules of Civil Procedure. There are two versions. One expansive and the other narrow: (a) documents are protected from disclosure that are created in anticipation of litigation versus (b) documents created to assist in the actual litigation. Which option does the trial court pick? Why?

In re Copper Market Antitrust Litigation

United States District Court, S.D. New York., 2001.
200 F.R.D. 213.

OPINION

SWAIN, DISTRICT JUDGE.

Plaintiffs Viacom Inc. and Emerson Electric Co. ("Plaintiffs") move to compel the production of documents listed on the privilege log (the "Privilege Log") produced by non-party Robinson Lerer & Montgomery ("RLM") in response to a subpoena issued from this Court on March 9, 2000. For the reasons set forth below, Plaintiffs' motion is denied.

FACTUAL BACKGROUND

This motion arises out of multi-district litigation pending in the Western District of Wisconsin. On or about September 27, 1999, Plaintiffs brought an action against Sumitomo Corporation ("Sumitomo"), Sumitomo Corporation of

America, Global Minerals and Metals Corporation and Credit Lyonnais Rouse, Ltd., alleging that the defendants conspired to manipulate global copper prices. By the subpoena dated March 9, 2000, Plaintiffs requested that RLM produce documents relating to RLM's public relations consulting work for Sumitomo. Because the March 9, 2000, subpoena issued from this Court, the Court has jurisdiction to determine Plaintiffs' motion. Fed.R.Civ.P. 45(c)(2)(B). Although the parties differ as to the legal significance of their respective factual proffers, none of the facts proffered is disputed in any material respect. The relevant factual background is as follows.

The signal event giving rise to the underlying antitrust litigation occurred during a deposition conducted in April 1996 by the Commodities Futures Trading Commission ("CFTC"), when Yasuo Hamanaka ("Hamanaka"), then head of Sumitomo's Non-Ferrous Metals Division, disclosed that he had executed an unauthorized power of attorney relating to hundreds of millions of dollars in copper trading. Anticipating a CFTC investigation and other litigation Sumitomo retained RLM, a "crisis management" public relations firm, on or about May 23, 1996, to handle public relations matters arising from the copper trading scandal. Declaration of Yasutomo Katsuno, dated August 30, 2000, ¶ 2 (hereinafter "Katsuno Decl."); Affidavit of Elizabeth Sigler Mather, sworn to August 31, 2000, ¶ 7 (hereinafter "Mather Aff."). Both the investigation and civil litigation ensued promptly.

Sumitomo hired RLM because it had no prior experience in dealing with issues relating to publicity arising from high profile litigation and because Sumitomo lacked experience in dealing with the Western media. Only two of the three executives in Sumitomo's Corporate Communications Department had English language facility and those individuals' English language skills were not sufficiently sophisticated for media relations. Katsuno Decl., ¶¶ 4–5; Mather Aff., ¶¶ 11–15. Working largely out of Sumitomo's Tokyo headquarters with Sumitomo's Corporate Communications Department, RLM acted as Sumitomo's agent and its spokesperson when dealing with the Western press on issues relating to the copper trading scandal. Katsuno Decl., ¶¶ 8–9. The chief object of RLM's engagement was damage control, *i.e.*, the management of press statements in the context of anticipated litigation "to ensure that they do not themselves further damage the client." Mather Aff., ¶ 2. "RLM's primary goal in representing Sumitomo was to help the Company make the statements it needed to make, but to do so within the necessary legal framework—all with the realization, indeed the expectation, that each such statement might subsequently be used by Sumitomo's adversaries in litigation." Mather Aff., ¶ 23. In the course of providing its services to Sumitomo, RLM conferred frequently with Sumitomo's outside counsel, Paul, Weiss, Rifkind, Wharton & Garrison ("Paul Weiss") (Mather Aff., ¶ 24) and Sumitomo's in-house counsel. Katsuno Decl., ¶ 10.

RLM dealt with the western press on Sumitomo's behalf, while Sumitomo's internal Corporate Communications Department dealt with the Japanese press. Katsuno Decl., ¶ 8. RLM's public relations duties included preparing statements for public release and internal documents designed to inform Sumitomo employees about what could and could not be said about the scandal. Affidavit of Roberta Kaplan, sworn to August 30, 2000, ¶¶ 6–8 (hereinafter the "Kaplan Aff."). RLM's duties also included drafting, in collaboration with Sumitomo's counsel, public relations documents, press releases, talking points, and Questions and Answers ("Q and As") to be used as a framework for press inquiries. The press releases were intended for different audiences, including regulators and other parties with whom Sumitomo anticipated litigation. Mather Aff., ¶ 30. RLM prepared many drafts of the documents, incorporating legal advice from Paul Weiss and Sumitomo in-house counsel. Mather Aff., ¶ 28. All documents prepared by RLM relating to legal issues arising from the CFTC investigation or the Hamanaka scandal were vetted with Sumitomo's in-house counsel and/or outside counsel. Mather Aff., ¶ 26. RLM had the authority to make decisions on behalf of Sumitomo concerning its public relations strategy. Katsuno Decl., ¶¶ 3–6, 8–10; Mather Aff., ¶¶ 11–21.

RLM was the functional equivalent of an in-house public relations department with respect to Western media relations, having authority to make decisions and statements on Sumitomo's behalf, and seeking and receiving legal advice from Sumitomo's counsel with respect to the performance of its duties. Mather Aff., ¶ 21; Katsuno Aff., ¶¶ 9–10.

On March 9, 2000, Plaintiffs served a subpoena requesting that RLM produce all documents relating to RLM's public relations consulting work for Sumitomo in connection with the copper trading scandal. Kaplan Aff., ¶ 10. RLM produced approximately 15,000 pages of documents in response. Kaplan Aff., ¶ 12. Most of the documents were produced in April 2000, approximately six weeks after the subpoena was issued. Kaplan Aff., ¶ 12. In preparing for the production, the attorney in charge at Paul Weiss gave instructions to the persons reviewing the documents as to what documents should be produced, what documents should be withheld, and what material should be redacted. Kaplan Aff., ¶ 18. On June 27, 2000, RLM delivered the Privilege Log along with the final portion of its production. Kaplan Aff., ¶ 23. On June 23–24 2000, prior to the final production, Paul Weiss undertook a re-review of the documents. Kaplan Aff., ¶ 20. As a result of that review, Paul Weiss discovered that 17 documents it contends are privileged and/or work-product had been produced in error. The attorney in charge of the production reviewed the 17 documents the next business day and, the following day, simultaneously with RLM's final production, Paul Weiss informed Plaintiffs' counsel that in preparing the Privilege Log it had discovered that certain documents (hereinafter the "Disputed Documents") had been inadvertently produced. Kaplan Aff., ¶¶ 20–22.

RLM has asserted both attorney-client privilege and work-product immunity with respect to the 583 communications listed on the Privilege Log. Plaintiffs argue that the documents listed in the Privilege Log are not protected by the attorney-client privilege or work-product immunity. Plaintiffs contend that the attorney-client privilege is inapplicable because RLM, a third party, was involved in the communications as to which the privilege is asserted. Similarly, Plaintiffs argue that the work-product doctrine is inapplicable because of RLM's third-party status, because its public relations work for Sumitomo was not exclusively litigation-related, and because the work was not done at the request of Sumitomo's attorneys. They further assert that any privilege that may be applicable to the documents listed on the Privilege Log has been waived by disclosure of the information to RLM, a third party, and/or by the production of the Disputed Documents.

DISCUSSION

ATTORNEY-CLIENT PRIVILEGE

Where, as here, subject matter jurisdiction is based on a federal question, privilege issues are governed by federal common law. *See von Bulow v. von Bulow*, 811 F.2d 136, 141 (2d Cir.1987), *cert. denied*, 481 U.S. 1015, 107 S.Ct. 1891, 95 L.Ed.2d 498 (1987). Proposed Rule of Evidence 503, also known as Supreme Court Standard 503, establishes a benchmark for determining the scope of the attorney-client privilege under federal common law:

> A client has a privilege to refuse to disclose and to prevent any other person from disclosing confidential communications made for the purpose of facilitating the rendition of professional legal services to the client, (1) between himself or his representative and his lawyer or his lawyer's representative, or (2) between his lawyer and his lawyer's representative, or (3) by him or his lawyer to a lawyer representing another in a matter of common interest, or (4) between

representatives of the client or between the client and a representative of the client, or (5) between lawyers representing the client.

Supreme Court Standard 503(b). Under Supreme Court Standard 503, confidential communications made for the purpose of obtaining legal advice between a client's representative and the client's attorney, between representatives of a client, or between attorneys for a client should be protected from disclosure under the attorney-client privilege.

Consistent with Supreme Court Standard 503, courts have held that the attorney-client privilege protects communications between lawyers and agents of a client where such communications are for the purpose of rendering legal advice. *Upjohn Co. v. United States*, 449 U.S. 383, 101 S.Ct. 677, 66 L.Ed.2d 584 (1981); *United States v. Schwimmer*, 892 F.2d 237, 243 (2d Cir.1989), *cert. denied*, 502 U.S. 810, 112 S.Ct. 55, 116 L.Ed.2d 31 (1991) (attorney-client privilege protects communications made to agents assisting client); *CSC Recovery Corp. v. Daido Steel Co., Ltd.*, No. 94 Civ. 9214, 1997 WL 661122 at *3 (S.D.N.Y. Oct. 22, 1997) (attorney-client privilege protects communications between clients and attorneys and agents of both); *H.W. Carter & Sons, Inc. v. William Carter Co.*, No. 95 Civ. 1274, 1995 WL 301351 at *3 (S.D.N.Y. May 16, 1995) (communications by public relations consultants who assisted attorneys in rendering legal advice protected by the attorney-client privilege).

In *Upjohn Co. v. United States*, the Supreme Court reviewed the principles underlying the scope of the attorney-client privilege in the corporate context with respect to communications between a client's representative or agent and a client's attorney. The Court focused on the purpose of the attorney-client privilege: "The privilege recognizes that sound legal advice or advocacy serves public ends and that such advice or advocacy depends upon the lawyer being fully informed by the client. . . . 'The lawyer-client privilege rests on the need for the advocate and counselor to know all that relates to the client's reasons for seeking representation if the professional mission is to be carried out.' " *Upjohn*, 449 U.S. at 389, 101 S.Ct. 677 (quoting *Trammel v. United States*, 445 U.S. 40, 51, 100 S.Ct. 906, 63 L.Ed.2d 186 (1980)). The Supreme Court's analysis in *Upjohn* looked to which of the corporate client's agents possess the relevant information the attorney needs to render sound legal advice. *See Upjohn*, 449 U.S. at 391–392, 101 S.Ct. 677 (restricting relevant communications to those made by the control group of a corporation frustrates the purpose of the privilege because it discourages communication by the corporation's noncontrol group agents who possess the information needed by the attorney). *See also United States v. Kovel*, 296 F.2d 918, 922 (2d Cir.1961) ("[w]hat is vital to the privilege is that the communication be made in confidence for the purpose of obtaining legal advice from the lawyer.'").

The *Upjohn* Court based its holding that the communications at issue were privileged on determinations that the communications had been made to Upjohn's counsel by its employees acting at the direction of their corporate superiors; that the information was needed to supply a basis for legal advice concerning potential litigation relating to the subject matter of the communications; that the communications concerned matters within the scope of the employees' corporate duties; and that the employees were aware that the communications were for the purpose of rendering legal advice for the corporation. *See Upjohn*, 449 U.S. at 394, 101 S.Ct. 677. The Supreme Court held that, "consistent with the underlying purposes of the attorney-client privilege, these communications must be protected against compelled disclosure." *Upjohn*, 449 U.S. at 395, 101 S.Ct. 677. The Supreme Court's functional approach in *Upjohn* thus looked to whether the communications at issue were by the Upjohn agents who possessed relevant information that would enable Upjohn's attorney to render sound legal advice.

In *In re Bieter Co.*, 16 F.3d 929 (8th Cir.1994), the Eighth Circuit applied these principles to a claim of attorney-client privilege with respect to communications with a consultant who had been retained by a real estate development company, finding that the consultant's confidential communications to the company's attorneys were protected by the attorney-client privilege. The court held that in determining whether a corporation's communications were protected by the attorney-client privilege, there was no reason to distinguish between persons on the corporation's payroll and the consultant. *In re Bieter*, 16 F.3d at 937.

In *Bieter*, a real estate partnership had hired a consultant to assist in a real estate development. The venture failed and the real estate partnership commenced litigation. Because the consultant was involved in the subject matter of the litigation arising from the failed real estate venture, the court in *Bieter* determined that the consultant was "precisely the sort of person with whom a lawyer would wish to confer confidentially in order to understand [the real estate firm's] reasons for seeking representation." *Id.*, at 938. In sum, the Eighth Circuit asked whether the consultant's relationship to the company was of the kind that justified application of the attorney-client privilege and found that, because the consultant was involved in the activities which were the subject matter of the ensuing litigation and because the consultant possessed the information required by the attorney for informed advice, the consultant's confidential communications to counsel were protected. *Id.*

The Court finds persuasive the reasoning of the *Bieter* court. *Upjohn* teaches that the attorney-client privilege "exists to protect not only the giving of professional advice to those who can act on it but also the giving of information to the lawyer to enable him to give sound and informed advice." *Upjohn*, 449 U.S. at 390, 101 S.Ct. 677. The Supreme Court in *Upjohn* looked to whether the corporation's agents possessed the information needed by the corporation's attorneys in order to render informed legal advice. *See Upjohn*, 449 U.S. at 391, 101 S.Ct. 677. In applying the principles set forth by the Supreme Court in *Upjohn*, there is no reason to distinguish between a person on the corporation's payroll and a consultant hired by the corporation if each acts for the corporation and possesses the information needed by attorneys in rendering legal advice. *See In re Grand Jury Subpoenas Dated January 20, 1998*, 995 F.Supp. 332, 340 (E.D.N.Y.1998) (citing *Bieter* for the principle that the court's concern is with "identifying those representatives who can fairly be equated with the 'client' for purposes of the privilege"). These principles, although articulated in the context of corporate employee relationships, inform this Court's analysis of RLM's ability to assert the attorney-client privilege with respect to its communications with Sumitomo's inside and outside counsel, and Sumitomo's disclosure of privileged information to RLM. Moreover, although the immediate context of the *Bieter* court's decision was factual communications with a consultant who had in effect functioned as a principal with respect to the events underlying the litigation the principles to be gleaned from the decision are not so limited.

RLM was, essentially, incorporated into Sumitomo's staff to perform a corporate function that was necessary in the context of the government investigation, actual and anticipated private litigation, and heavy press scrutiny obtaining at the time. Sumitomo retained RLM to deal with public relations problems following the exposure of the copper trading scandal. Sumitomo's internal resources were insufficient to cover the task. RLM's public relations duties included preparing statements for public release and internal documents designed to inform Sumitomo employees about what could and could not be said about the scandal. Kaplan Aff., ¶¶ 6–8. RLM possessed authority to make decisions on behalf of Sumitomo concerning its public relations strategy. Katsuno Decl., ¶¶ 3–6, 8–10; Mather Aff., ¶¶ 11–21. The legal ramifications and potential adverse use of such communications were material factors in the development of the communications. In formulating communications on

Sumitomo's behalf, RLM sought advice from Sumitomo's counsel and was privy to advice concerning the scandal and attendant litigation.

In addition, RLM's communications concerned matters within the scope of RLM's duties for Sumitomo, and RLM employees were aware that the communications were for the purpose of obtaining legal advice from Paul Weiss and/or Sumitomo's in house attorneys. Under the principles set out in *Upjohn*, RLM's independent contractor status provides no basis for excluding RLM's communications with Sumitomo's counsel from the protection of the attorney-client privilege. *Cf. McCaugherty v. Siffermann*, 132 F.R.D. 234, 239 (N.D.Cal.1990) (under *Upjohn*, there is no principled basis for distinguishing consultant's communications with attorneys and corporate employee's communications with attorneys when each acted in the scope of their employment).

The Court therefore finds that, for purposes of the attorney-client privilege, RLM can fairly be equated with the Sumitomo for purposes of analyzing the availability of the attorney-client privilege to protect communications to which RLM was a party concerning its scandal-related duties. Accordingly, confidential communications between RLM and Sumitomo's counsel, or between RLM and Sumitomo, or among RLM, Sumitomo's in-house counsel and Paul Weiss that were made for the purpose of facilitating the rendition of legal services to Sumitomo can be protected from disclosure by the attorney-client privilege.

The Court finds unpersuasive Plaintiffs' argument that third-party consultants come within the scope of the privilege only when acting as conduits or facilitators of attorney-client communications. The case law cited by Plaintiffs arises in a factual context that is readily distinguishable from this case. *See, e.g., United States v. Kovel*, 296 F.2d 918 (privilege applies to communications of a third-party made at the request of an attorney or the client where the purpose of the communication was to put in usable form information obtained from the client); *cf. Occidental Chemical Corp. v. OHM Remediation Services, Corp.*, 175 F.R.D. 431, 436–37 (W.D.N.Y.1997) (no privilege attaching to communications from consultant who was not hired to assist in the rendition of legal services). For example, in *United States v. Ackert*, 169 F.3d 136 (2d Cir.1999), a recent case following the reasoning in *Kovel* and relied upon by Plaintiffs, the court determined that communications between an investment banker and an attorney made for the purpose of providing information to the attorney so that he could better advise his client were not privileged. In so finding, the court held that the communications with the third-party investment banker did not serve to facilitate or translate communications with the attorney's client. Moreover, in

Ackert, the investment banker was neither the attorney's client nor an agent of the client.

By contrast, in this case, RLM is the functional equivalent of a Sumitomo employee. Accordingly, the analysis set forth in *Kovel* and its progeny concerning whether the privilege applies to communications made to third parties for the purpose of facilitating attorney-client communications is inapposite.

WORK-PRODUCT IMMUNITY

Plaintiffs contend that communications to and from RLM are not protected by work-product immunity because RLM was hired by Sumitomo as a public relations consultant and was not hired to assist Paul Weiss in providing legal advice. Plaintiffs argue that the materials that RLM claims are protected by work-product immunity were generated in the ordinary course of RLM's public relations services provided in connection with the copper trading scandal. In addition, Plaintiffs argue that communications between Paul Weiss and Sumitomo which were disclosed to RLM are not protected by work-product immunity because any such immunity was waived upon disclosure to RLM. Under the circumstances of this case, Plaintiffs' contentions concerning the applicability of work-product immunity to the items listed on the Privilege Log are misplaced.

Analysis of work-product immunity begins with Federal Rule of Civil Procedure 26(b)(3). Rule 26(b)(3) provides in relevant part:

> a party may obtain discovery of documents . . . otherwise discoverable . . . and prepared in anticipation of litigation or for trial by or for another party or by or for that other party's representative (including the other party's attorney, consultant, surety, indemnitor, insurer, or agent) only upon a showing that the party seeking discovery has substantial need of the materials in the preparation of the party's case and that the party is unable without undue hardship to obtain the substantial equivalent of the materials by other means. In ordering discovery of such materials when the required showing has been made, the court shall protect against disclosure of mental impressions, conclusions, opinions, or legal theories of an attorney or other representative of a party concerning the litigation.

Fed.R.Civ.P. 26(b)(3).

A document is prepared "in anticipation of litigation" within the meaning of the Rule if, "in light of the nature of the document and the factual situation in the particular case, the document can be fairly said to have been prepared or obtained because of the prospect of litigation." *United States v. Adlman*, 134 F.3d 1194, 1202 (2d Cir.1998) (rejecting the formulation that work-product immunity protects only documents primarily to assist in litigation and adopting the broader test set forth in 8 Charles Alan Wright, Arthur R. Miller & Richard L. Marcus, *Federal Practice & Procedure* § 2024, at 343 (2d ed.1994)). Documents prepared in the ordinary course of business, or that would have been created whether or not litigation was anticipated, are not protected by work-product immunity. *Id.* It is firmly established, however, that a document that assists in a business decision is protected by work-product immunity if the document was created because of the prospect of litigation. *Id.* In addition, contrary to Plaintiffs' assertions, documents prepared in anticipation of litigation need not be created at the request of an attorney. *Bank of New York v. Meridien BIAO Bank Tanzania*, No. 95 Civ. 4856, 1996 WL 490710, at *2 (S.D.N.Y. Aug. 27, 1996). Once it is established that a document was prepared in anticipation of litigation, work-product immunity protects "documents prepared by or for a representative of a party, including his or her agent." *Occidental Chemical Corp. v. OHM Remediation Services Corp.*, 175 F.R.D. at 434.

RLM asserts, and Plaintiffs do not dispute, that RLM has not withheld purely business-related documents and other types of non-privileged communications with Sumitomo's attorneys. The Privilege Log, together with the affidavits submitted by RLM and the supplements thereto, make clear that the materials listed on the Privilege Log were prepared in collaboration with Sumitomo's counsel, including Paul Weiss, in the context of the litigation ensuing from the copper trading scandal. Kaplan Aff., at ¶¶ 7–8; Mather Aff., ¶¶ 24–30. The uncontroverted affidavits submitted by RLM in opposition to the instant motion make clear that RLM's services were provided initially because of the prospect of the CFTC's investigation and then because of the actual litigation which ensued thereafter.

RLM specializes in litigation-related crisis management. Mather Aff., ¶ 3. The firm was hired shortly after Hamanaka's confession, when it was apparent that the CFTC might commence an enforcement action against Sumitomo. Mather Aff., ¶ 7. Elizabeth Mather, RLM's principal representative for the Sumitomo engagement, states that "[f]rom the outset, RLM knew its representation was litigation-related." Mather Aff., ¶ 8. Further, it is clear that Sumitomo retained RLM to make sure that its public statements would not result in further exposure in the litigation which grew out of the copper trading scandal. Mather Aff., ¶¶ 23–24, 29–30; Katsuno Decl., ¶ 10. In light of these uncontroverted facts, the Court finds that the materials listed on the Privilege Log were prepared by RLM or delivered to RLM in anticipation of litigation and that such documents are protected by work-product immunity. For the same reasons, listed documents prepared by Sumitomo or its counsel also are protected by work-product immunity.

INADVERTENT PRODUCTION/WAIVER

Plaintiffs contend that the Disputed Documents should be produced because RLM waived any claim to privilege by producing them. However, "inadvertent production will not waive the privilege unless the conduct of the producing party or its counsel evinced such extreme carelessness as to suggest that it was not concerned with the protection of the asserted privilege." *Lloyds Bank PLC v. Republic of Ecuador,* No. 96 Civ. 1789, 1997 WL 96591 at *3 (S.D.N.Y. Mar. 5, 1997), *quoting Desai v. American International Underwriters,* No. 91 Civ. 7735, 1992 WL 110731 at *1 (S.D.N.Y. May 12, 1992).

Lois Sportswear, U.S.A., Inc. v. Levi Strauss & Co., 104 F.R.D. 103, 105 (S.D.N.Y.1985), *aff'd,* 799 F.2d 867 (2d Cir.1986), identifies the following factors for consideration in determining whether inadvertent production constitutes waiver of a claim of privilege: (1) the reasonableness of the precautions taken to prevent inadvertent disclosure, (2) the time taken to rectify the error, (3) the scope of the production, (4) the extent of the disclosure, and (5) overriding issues of fairness.

The Reasonableness of Precautions

The mere fact of disclosure does not establish that a party's precautions undertaken to protect the privileged evidence were unreasonable. *See Prescient Partners, L.P. v. Fieldcrest Cannon, Inc.,* No. 96 Civ. 7590, 1997 WL 736726, at * 5 (S.D.N.Y. Nov. 26, 1997); *Bank Brussels Lambert v. Credit Lyonnais (Suisse) S.A.,* 160 F.R.D. 437, 443 (S.D.N.Y.1995). Rather, a court must examine whether "the procedure[s] followed in maintaining the confidentiality of the document[s] [were] . . . so lax, careless, inadequate or indifferent to consequences as to constitute a waiver." *Martin v. Valley National Bank of Arizona,* No. 89 Civ. 8361, 1992 WL 196798, at *3 (S.D.N.Y. Aug. 6, 1992) (citations omitted). Inadvertent production will not waive the privilege unless the conduct of the producing party or its counsel evinced such extreme carelessness as to suggest that they were not concerned with the protection of the privilege. *See Lloyds Bank PLC,* 1997 WL 96591, at *3 (citations omitted).

Here, the Paul Weiss attorney overseeing the production gave specific instructions to the document production team concerning which documents were to be produced, which documents were to be withheld and which documents were to be redacted. Kaplan Aff., ¶ 18; Supplemental Affidavit of Roberta Kaplan, sworn to October 16, 2000, ¶ 5. In addition, the production team performed an additional, final, review of the documents prior to completion of the production. Kaplan Aff., ¶ 20. The Court finds that Paul Weiss took reasonable precautions to prevent inadvertent disclosure. These procedures were not so lax, careless, inadequate or indifferent to consequences as to render inadvertent production of the Disputed Documents a waiver.

Time Taken to Rectify the Error

The relevant correction period begins when the party realizes that an error has been made. *Lloyds Bank PLC,* 1997 WL 96591 at *5. Here, Paul Weiss discovered the error while checking the production on June 23, 2000 and June 24, 2000. Kaplan Aff., ¶ 20. The attorney in charge reviewed the 17 documents at issue on June 26, 2000 and notified opposing counsel of the inadvertent production on June 27, 2000. Kaplan Aff., ¶ 22. The Court finds that there was no material delay by Paul Weiss in asserting the privilege once the error was realized.

The Scope of the Production and the Extent of the Inadvertent Disclosure

Approximately 15,000 pages of documents were produced by RLM. Of this amount, RLM claimed privilege with respect to 583 documents; of that number 17 documents were produced inadvertently. The Court finds that the number of documents inadvertently produced in RLM's production was relatively small in comparison with the total production and is well within margin of error that courts have found acceptable. *See, e.g., Baker's Aid v. Hussmann Foodservice Co.,* No. 87 Civ. 0937, 1988 WL 138254, at *5 (E.D.N.Y. Dec. 19, 1988) (noting that "[c]ourts have routinely found that where a large number of documents are involved, there is more likely to be an inadvertent disclosure than a knowing waiver"); *Lois Sportswear,* 104 F.R.D. at 105 (where twenty-two documents out of 16,000 pages reviewed, and out of 3,000 pages requested, were claimed to be privileged, the Court held that disclosure did not constitute a waiver); *Data Systems of New Jersey, Inc. v. Philips Business Data Systems, Inc.,* No. 78 Civ. 6015, slip op. (S.D.N.Y. Jan. 8, 1981) (where one document was privileged among the several thousand produced, the Court held that the privilege was not waived); *Desai,* 1992 WL 110731 (where seventeen documents were privileged out of a "large production", the court held that privilege was not waived).

Fairness

Overall issues of fairness weigh in favor of RLM. Plaintiffs have not demonstrated that they would be prejudiced by maintaining the privilege of the Disputed Documents. Depriving a party of information in an otherwise privileged document is not prejudicial. *See Prescient Partners,* 1997 WL 736726, at *7. However, finding waiver would be prejudicial to RLM because the documents involve attorney-client communications about case strategy. *Id.*

Based on the foregoing, the Court finds that production of the Disputed Documents was inadvertent and that it did not result in waiver of the privilege and work-product protection claimed by RLM in the Privilege Log with respect to the Disputed Documents or other documents identified in the Privilege Log.

RLM'S PRIVILEGE LOG

Plaintiffs contend RLM has not set forth sufficient information in the Privilege Log to support work-product immunity. "The standard for testing the adequacy of the privilege log is whether, as to each document, it sets forth specific facts that, if credited, would suffice to establish each element of the privilege or immunity claimed. The focus is on the specific descriptive portion of the log, and not on the conclusory invocations of the privilege or work-product rule . . . ." *Golden Trade v. Lee Apparel Company, et al.,* Nos. 09 Civ. 6291, 90 Civ. 6292, 1992 WL 367070 at *5 (S.D.N.Y. Nov. 20, 1992). Rule 45(d)(2) of the Federal Rules of Civil Procedure provides that:

> When information subject to a subpoena is withheld on a claim that it is privileged or subject to protection as trial preparation materials, the claim shall be made expressly and shall be supported by a description of the nature of the documents, communications or things not produced that is sufficient to enable the demanding party to contest the claim.

Fed.R.Civ.P. 45(d)(2). Local Civil Rule 26.2(a)(2)(A) of this Court requires provision of certain specified types of information with regard to documents withheld upon claim of privilege including, where not apparent, the relationship of the author, addressees and recipients to each other.

It is the proponent's burden to establish the factual basis for a claim that the attorney-client privilege or work-product immunity protects a document from disclosure. *CSC Recovery Corp.,* 1997 WL 661122, at * 2. Courts have discretion in determining whether a claim of privilege has been sufficiently supported. *Id.* (courts may rely upon privilege logs and supporting affidavits in assessing whether a claim of privilege has been adequately supported).

The Privilege Log contains information concerning the date, type of document, author, addressees, a short description of each document and the privilege or immunity asserted with respect to each. Submissions by the parties in connection with this motion have made clear the relationship of authors and addressees to each other with respect to documents for which work-product immunity is claimed. Affidavits submitted in opposition to Plaintiffs' motion to compel make clear the context in which the documents identified on the Privilege Log were generated. As explained above, the affidavits establish that RLM was the functional equivalent of Sumitomo's employee for purposes of confidential communications made to Sumitomo's attorneys seeking legal advice.

Moreover, the affidavits submitted by RLM establish that work-product of RLM and Sumitomo's attorneys was created in anticipation of litigation. Accordingly, the Court finds that the Privilege Log facially meets the requirements set forth in the Local Rules.

OBJECTIONS CONCERNING PARTICULAR DOCUMENTS

Plaintiffs contend that RLM's privilege and work-product claims fail as to the Disputed Documents because RLM's participation in communications and/or preparation of certain of the documents precludes the work-product and attorney-client privilege claims. Plaintiffs also argue that RLM has failed to establish the basis of privilege claims with respect to documents heavily redacted or produced in blank and should therefore be required to produce those documents. Plaintiffs' argument concerning the significance of RLM's participation in communications is, as explained above, ineffective to defeat the work-product and attorney-client privilege claims.

With respect to their arguments concerning specific Disputed Documents, Plaintiffs submitted the Affidavit of Reginald R. Smith, sworn to July 28, 2000, (the "Smith Affidavit"), which contains Exhibit R, a chart identifying by letter designation the specific items in the Disputed Documents that Plaintiffs contend should be not be protected. Because the document designations in Exhibit R and the document designations in the Privilege Log differ, the Court, by order dated March 9, 2001, directed RLM to provide an affidavit correlating the entries listed in Exhibit R to the Smith Affidavit to corresponding entries in the Privilege Log in order to assist the Court's determination of Plaintiffs' motion. RLM provided such correlation in the Supplemental Affidavit of

Roberta Kaplan, sworn to March 21, 2001 (the "Supplemental Kaplan Affidavit"). In addition to providing the correlation table, the Supplemental Kaplan Affidavit includes redacted copies of the Disputed Documents as they were kept in RLM's files, indicating portions of the documents that would have been withheld had they not inadvertently been produced. Plaintiffs submitted a letter response to the Supplemental Kaplan Affidavit dated April 2, 2001, asking the Court to conduct an *in camera* review of the documents listed on the Privilege Log. RLM further responded by letter dated April 10, 2001, arguing that the Court should deny Plaintiffs' request.

The Court has reviewed thoroughly the Privilege Log, the Smith Affidavit, the Supplemental Kaplan Affidavit and the correspondence related thereto. If the Privilege Log was insufficient, the additional information provided to the Court clearly establishes the sufficiency of RLM's claims for purposes of Rule 45(d). Accordingly, for the reasons set forth below, the Court finds that the information provided by RLM in the Privilege Log and its factual submissions in response to this motion is sufficient to warrant denial of Plaintiffs' motion to compel. In light of the foregoing, no *in camera* review of the documents listed in the Privilege Log is necessary.

Rule 45(d)(1) of the Federal Rules of Civil Procedure provides that: "[a] person responding to a subpoena to produce documents shall produce them as they are kept in the usual course of business or shall organize and label them to correspond with the categories in the demand." Fed.R.Civ.P. 45(d)(1). In the Supplemental Kaplan Affidavit, RLM explains that it produced documents to Plaintiffs as they were maintained in the usual course of business. Thus, for example, memoranda with attachments and cover sheets were produced together and logged as one document for purposes of the Privilege Log. The descriptions contained in the Privilege Log pertain to the portions of the documents that were redacted or not produced pursuant RLM's privilege claims. Supplemental Kaplan Affidavit, ¶ 3. The Court finds that such procedures comply with Rule 45(d)(1) of the Federal Rules of Civil Procedure.

The Court will refer to Plaintiffs' designations in Exhibit R to the Smith Affidavit in its discussion of Plaintiffs' arguments concerning specific documents.

Documents D, M, W, GG, are blank pages that were apparently redacted completely. Plaintiffs contend that RLM has shown no valid basis for the claim of protection for these documents. Document D corresponds to Privilege Log No. 516 and is identified in the Privilege Log as a two-page document consisting of a memorandum from a Paul Weiss attorney to Masatoshi Inada (subsequently identified by RLM as a member of Sumitomo's legal department). The Court finds that RLM has identified sufficiently the basis of the privilege claim pertaining to Document D. Document M, together with Documents L, N, O, and P, corresponds to Privilege Log No. 569, which is described as an eight page memorandum. RLM represents that portions of the memorandum contain summaries of legal advice from Sumitomo counsel. Supplemental Kaplan Affidavit, ¶¶ 21–22. Document M also is identified sufficiently to support RLM's claim of privilege. *See National Education Training Group, Inc. v. Skillsoft Corp.*, No. M8–85, 1999 WL 378337, at *3 (S.D.N.Y. June 10, 1999) (distribution of legal advice within corporation is privileged). Document W, together with Documents V and X, corresponds to Privilege Log No. 571, which describes the privileged material in the document as pertaining to summaries of legal advice. Supplemental Kaplan Affidavit, ¶¶ 25–26. Document W is described sufficiently for purposes of RLM's privilege claims. Document GG, together with documents EE, FF, and HH, corresponds to Privilege Log No. 583, which describes the entry as a thirteen-page document. The Supplemental Kaplan Affidavit further describes the document as consisting of a cover memo containing legal advice and including translations selected by Sumitomo counsel. Supplemental Kaplan Affidavit, ¶¶ 35–36. RLM has identified sufficiently the basis of the privilege claim pertaining to this document. *Cf. Plant Genetic Systems, N.V. v. Northrup King Co.*, 174 F.R.D. 330, 331 (D.Del.1997) (selection of documents in anticipation of litigation is protected as work-product).

Document R is a fax cover sheet. According to the Supplemental Kaplan Affidavit, it is part of an eight-page document consisting of a cover memorandum with two attachments. Supplemental Kaplan Affidavit, ¶ 23. The Privilege Log lists the document as number 570. Document R is the fax cover sheet to the first attachment. The Privilege Log indicates that the document is a memorandum concerning advice of Sumitomo counsel. The Supplemental Kaplan Affidavit further identifies the first attachment (containing document R) as a six-page client memorandum. *Id.* Accordingly, RLM has identified sufficiently Document R for purposes of its privilege claim. *Cf. IBJ Whitehall Bank & Trust Co. v. Cory & Associates, Inc.*, No. 97 Civ. 5827, 1999 WL 617842, at *7 (N.D.Ill. Aug. 12, 1999) (fax cover sheet indicating that the attached document is drafted by attorneys is privileged). Document AA is also a fax cover sheet which is a constituent of a nineteen-page document identified as number 576 on the Privilege Log. The Privilege Log identifies the privileged material in the document as translations and the Supplemental Kaplan Affidavit describes the fax cover sheet as containing work product because it describes and identifies Paul Weiss' selection of articles to be translated. Supplemental Kaplan

Affidavit, ¶ 32. Accordingly, Document AA is identified sufficiently for purposes of RLM's privilege claims.

As indicated above, Documents EE, FF and HH correspond to Privilege Log No. 583. Supplemental Kaplan Affidavit, ¶¶ 35–36. As explained above and in light of the proffers set forth in the affidavits submitted by RLM in support of its privilege claims, representing that RLM's work-product was prepared in connection with the litigation arising from the copper trading scandal, the Court finds sufficient basis for RLM's privilege claims with respect to these documents.

Documents A (corresponding to Privilege Log No. 481), B (corresponding to Privilege Log No. 484), C (corresponding to Privilege Log No. 515), G (corresponding to Privilege Log No. 545), H, I and J (corresponding to Privilege Log No. 547), K (corresponding to Privilege Log No. 554), L (corresponding to Privilege Log No. 569), Q (corresponding to Privilege Log No. 570), V and X (corresponding to Privilege Log No. 571) and, BB (corresponding to Privilege Log No. 577) are described in the Privilege Log as internal RLM memoranda or memoranda between RLM and Sumitomo dealing with or summarizing advice from Sumitomo's counsel. The Privilege Log, together with RLM's supporting affidavits, identifies these documents sufficiently to identify the basis of RLM's privilege and/or work-product claims. *See National Education Training Group, Inc. v. Skillsoft Corp.*, 1999 WL 378337, at *3; *Abbott Laboratories v. Airco, Inc., et al.*, No. 82 C 3292, 1985 WL 3596, at *4 (N.D.Ill. Nov. 4, 1985) (memoranda of information or advice directed to or received from an attorney, prepared by an agent of the client or attorney, as a record of that advice or request, are protected by the attorney-client privilege).

Document F corresponds to Privilege Log No. 528 and is an RLM internal memorandum copied to Sumitomo counsel. The Supplemental Kaplan Affidavit describes the document as containing summaries of legal advice. Supplemental Kaplan Affidavit, ¶ 15. Document F is described sufficiently for purposes of RLM's privilege claims.

Document N corresponds to Privilege Log No. 569 and is one page of an eight-page document which is described in the Privilege Log as summarizing advice from Sumitomo counsel. According to the Supplemental Kaplan Affidavit, the entire document was produced, but three lines of the memorandum denominated Document N should have been redacted for privilege as summaries of legal advice. Supplemental Kaplan Affidavit, ¶ 22. The Court finds that RLM has sufficiently described the privilege claim pertaining to Privilege Log No. 569. Document P is also part of Privilege Log No. 569.

According to the Supplemental Kaplan Affidavit, Document P is a memorandum for which no privilege is claimed except for three lines which summarize legal advice. *Id.* Document P thus is identified sufficiently for purposes of RLM's privilege claims. Document O is also part of Privilege Log No. 569 and consists of draft Q and As which the Supplemental Kaplan Affidavit describes as containing legal advice. *Id.*

Documents U and S correspond to Privilege Log No. 570, which is an eight-page memorandum with attachments. Privilege Log No. 570 identifies the basis for the privilege claim as advice from counsel. According to the Supplemental Kaplan Affidavit, portions of the document should have been redacted or withheld as privileged. Supplemental Kaplan Affidavit, ¶ 24. Document T also corresponds to Privilege Log No. 570. RLM's description of the documents constituting Privilege Log No. 570, including the description contained in the Supplemental Kaplan Affidavit, identifies sufficiently the basis of the claim of protection for Documents U, S and T.

Document Y corresponds to Privilege Log No. 572 which is described in the Privilege Log as a memorandum to Sumitomo counsel. The Supplemental Kaplan Affidavit describes most of the document as containing non-privileged material except for certain portions which should have been redacted because the portions contain legal advice from counsel. Supplemental Kaplan Affidavit, ¶ 28. The Court finds that Document Y is identified sufficiently for purposes of RLM's privilege claims.

Documents CC and DD correspond to Privilege Log No. 577, which identifies the privileged material in the document as pertaining to a legal advice. Supplemental Kaplan Affidavit, ¶ 34. Documents CC and DD are identified sufficiently for purposes of RLM's privilege claims.

Document Z corresponds to Privilege Log No. 574, which describes the privileged material in the document as a draft letter from Paul Weiss concerning the resignation of Akiyama (Sumitomo's former president). Supplemental Kaplan Affidavit, ¶¶ 29–30. The Court finds that Document Z is identified sufficiently for purposes of RLM's privilege claims.

Document E corresponds to Privilege Log No. 527, which describes the document as memoranda summarizing advice from Sumitomo counsel. The Supplemental Kaplan Affidavit describes Privilege Log No. 527 as a six-page document consisting of five memoranda and an undated timeline. Supplemental Kaplan Affidavit, ¶ 12. The Supplemental Kaplan Affidavit indicates that the memoranda, which were produced to Plaintiffs, are not privileged, but that one paragraph of the timeline contains privileged information concerning legal advice which should have been redacted. Supplemental Kaplan Affidavit, ¶ 13. Plaintiffs contend that the timeline contains no date, author or recipient. The information provided by the Supplement Kaplan Affidavit satisfies that Court, however, that the timeline was produced together with the four preceding memoranda. The Privilege Log entry for Document E is sufficient for purposes of the preserving a claim of privilege.

CONCLUSION

For the reasons set forth herein Plaintiffs' motion is denied. RLM shall Court, on ten days' notice to Plaintiffs' counsel, a proposed order consistent with this opinion.

SOLUTIONS: THE LAWYER SHOULD HAVE, WOULD HAVE, COULD HAVE. . .

Lawyers can use the services of non-lawyers to assist them in providing legal advice and, in doing so, not waive the ACP. Yet lawyers sometimes see this general concept as a green light to have people attend meetings who are not needed to assist—whether a friend for general emotional support or a witness supporting the client's claim. Because the ACP is a privilege operating to restrict the search for truth, courts will strictly guard the exceptions allowing for the presence of a third party. The litigant in this case carefully thought our beforehand the reasons for the presence of the PR agency beforehand. When challenged, they were ready.

Cases and Materials

X-Ray Questions (*EEOC v. BDO USA, L.L.P.*)

This case focuses on an important part of the implementation of the ACP: privilege logs. What mistake did the trial court make in applying the concept of the ACP? Recall that we have discussed that the ACP is a narrow privilege designed to be used in very narrow and specific circumstances. How did the trial court manage to apply this very basic principle? Whose burden of proof is it to establish privilege so as to shield a document from production? As with the preceding case, what lessons have you learned from the case in putting assembling a solid privilege log.

EEOC v. BDO USA, L.L.P.

United States Court of Appeals, Fifth Circuit, 2017.
876 F.3d 690.

Opinion

CARL E. STEWART, CHIEF JUDGE:

IT IS ORDERED that our prior panel opinion, *EEOC v. BDO USA, L.L.P.* 856 F.3d 356 (5th Cir. 2017), is WITHDRAWN, and the following opinion is SUBSTITUTED therefor.

During the course of an employment discrimination investigation, the Equal Employment Opportunity Commission ("EEOC") brought a subpoena enforcement action against BDO USA, L.L.P. ("BDO") in federal district court. The EEOC sought production of information relating to the investigation and asserted that BDO's privilege log failed to establish that the attorney-client privilege protected the company's withheld documents. The district court held that the log was sufficient and also granted BDO's request for a protective order. For the reasons that follow, we VACATE and REMAND.

I.   BACKGROUND

BDO, a financial and consulting services firm, hired Hang Bower as a Human Resources ("HR") Manager in 2007. Bower, an Asian-American female, was eventually promoted to Chief Human Resources Officer, the company's highest-ranking HR position. While at BDO, Bower was responsible for investigating discrimination complaints and communicated with both in-house and outside counsel. Bower resigned from her employment with BDO on January 15, 2014.

On July 9, 2014, Bower filed a charge with the EEOC, alleging that BDO violated Title VII and the Equal Pay Act by subjecting her and other female employees to gender discrimination, retaliation, and a hostile work environment. Bower claimed, *inter alia*, that: (1) as a result of her efforts to assure compliance with company policies, BDO removed her from leadership meetings, decreased her job responsibilities, reprimanded her, and ordered her to stop investigating certain employees; (2) in retaliation for her "expressed determination" to investigate male managers and a male partner, she was stripped of her investigatory authority and removed from the Chief Compliance Officer position; (3) top corporate management shielded a male manager accused of discrimination and blocked an appropriate investigation; (4) BDO fired or constructively discharged female employees who complained about mistreatment; and (5) BDO discriminated against non-white employees. On August 18, 2014, BDO filed a position statement in response to Bower's charge, providing additional information, denying the allegations, and arguing that the charge should be dismissed for lack of probable cause.

Between October 2014 and June 2015, the EEOC issued three Requests for Information ("RFIs") to BDO, seeking details related to the individual and class-wide claims in Bower's charge. In December 2014, BDO filed another position statement that outlined BDO's investigation policy and rejected Bower's allegations that the company blocked her attempts to investigate discrimination claims. BDO, however, objected to providing other information it believed was "far beyond the scope of Bower's individual charge." BDO also alleged that the EEOC was eliciting—and Bower was revealing—attorney-client privileged communications between Bower and BDO's in-house and outside counsel. In June 2015, BDO stated that it could not provide any additional information until the matter was "transferred to a new investigator who ha[d] not been tainted by reviewing, or eliciting, privileged information."

On July 14, 2015, the EEOC issued a subpoena to BDO, seeking documents and information relating to the investigation. In response, BDO provided some, but not all, of the requested information and created a privilege log cataloging withheld documents as to which it asserted attorney-client privilege. The 278 entries in the log's final version referenced "confidential" emails, memoranda, and other documents, and included communications between (1) Bower and in-house and outside counsel, (2) other BDO employees and in-house and outside counsel, (3) non-attorney employees with counsel courtesy copied, and (4) non-attorney employees regarding legal advice (but not involving any attorneys).

On December 10, 2015, the EEOC filed a subpoena enforcement action in federal district court. According to the EEOC, BDO's refusal to comply with the subpoena had "delayed and hampered the investigation," and the privilege log BDO submitted contained various deficiencies: certain entries "lack[ed] sufficient detail and specificity," were "simply incomplete," and/or appeared to reference communications that were not exchanged with or copied to an attorney, or that appeared only to courtesy copy counsel. On February 4, 2016, BDO filed its response, which included a request for a protective order enjoining the EEOC from questioning Bower and BDO employees regarding their conversations with BDO's counsel, and requiring the EEOC to return or destroy evidence of witness interviews and other documents that memorialized the privileged conversations.

On February 9, 2016, the magistrate judge presided over the show cause hearing. She rejected the EEOC's contention that communications BDO claimed were privileged were not protected and stated that the EEOC had not "made a sufficient showing" that the privilege log reflected "an improperly claimed privilege." Ultimately, the magistrate judge denied the EEOC's request to enforce the subpoena and for an in camera review of the documents, explaining: "I am not going to look through 278 documents. I decline to do that. The privilege log seems adequate." The magistrate judge also granted BDO the protective relief it requested, stating that it was "not Ms. Bower's job to decide what's attorney-client [privilege]" and that "anything that comes out of [BDO's] lawyer's mouth is legal advice."

The EEOC filed objections to the magistrate judge's order in the district court, arguing that the decision was based "on incorrect interpretations of the facts and the applicable law." The EEOC appended to its objections Bower's declaration, which stated, *inter alia*, that many of the communications she exchanged with BDO's counsel were for the purpose of seeking or imparting business, not legal, advice regarding officer investigations and how to carry out her HR duties. Similarly, Bower maintained that emails exchanged between her and other non-attorneys pertaining to these investigations were made for the primary purpose of conveying business directives or factual information. Bower further claimed that, in order to protect communications from disclosure in future legal proceedings, BDO required her to forward to or courtesy copy in-house counsel on virtually all communications pertaining to employee investigations and to include in HR-related emails a false designation that the communication was prepared "at the request of legal counsel."

BDO filed an opposition to the EEOC's objections, arguing that they should be overruled and that the district court did not have discretion to consider Bower's declaration. On March 21, 2016, the district court summarily affirmed the magistrate judge's order. The EEOC timely appealed, seeking that (1) the question of whether the attorney-client privilege is available to the withheld documents on BDO's privilege log be remanded to the district court and (2) the protective order be reversed and remanded.

II. DISCUSSION

A. Privilege Log

We begin with the question of whether the district court erred when it accepted BDO's claim of attorney-client privilege based on the privilege log.

1.   Legal Standards

"The application of the attorney-client privilege is a 'question of fact, to be determined in the light of the purpose of the privilege and guided by judicial precedents.' " *In re Auclair*, 961 F.2d 65, 68 (5th Cir. 1992) (quoting *Hodges, Grant & Kaufmann v. United States*, 768 F.2d 719, 721 (5th Cir. 1985)); *see also Upjohn Co. v. United States*, 449 U.S. 383, 396, 101 S.Ct. 677, 66 L.Ed.2d 584 (1981). "The clearly erroneous standard of review applies to the district court's factual findings." *King v. Univ. Healthcare Sys., L.C.*, 645 F.3d 713, 721 (5th Cir. 2011) (quoting *United States v. Neal*, 27 F.3d 1035, 1048 (5th Cir. 1994)). We review de novo the district court's application of the controlling legal standards. *See id.*; *In re Avantel, S.A.*, 343 F.3d 311, 318 (5th Cir. 2003).

"The attorney-client privilege limits the normally broad disclosure requirements of Federal Rule of Civil Procedure 26 . . . ." *SmithKline Beecham Corp. v. Apotex Corp.*, 232 F.R.D. 467, 472 (E.D. Pa. 2005). For a communication to be protected under the privilege, the proponent "must prove: (1) that he made a *confidential* communication; (2) to a lawyer or his subordinate; (3) for the primary purpose of securing either a legal opinion or legal services, or assistance in some legal proceeding." *United States v. Robinson*, 121 F.3d 971, 974 (5th Cir. 1997). Determining the applicability of the privilege is a "highly fact-specific" inquiry, and the party asserting the privilege bears the burden of proof. *Stoffels v. SBC Commc'ns, Inc.*, 263 F.R.D. 406, 411 (W.D. Tex. 2009) (citing *United States v. Kelly*, 569 F.2d 928, 938 (5th Cir. 1978)); *see also Hodges*, 768 F.2d at 721. "Once the privilege has been established, the burden shifts to the other party to prove any applicable exceptions." *Perkins v. Gregg Cty.*, 891 F.Supp. 361, 363 (E.D. Tex. 1995) (citation omitted). Ambiguities as to whether the elements of a privilege claim have been met are construed against the proponent. *See Scholtisek v. Eldre Corp.*, 441 F.Supp.2d 459, 462–63 (W.D.N.Y. 2006) (listing cases).

Because the attorney-client privilege "has the effect of withholding relevant information from the fact-finder," it is interpreted narrowly so as to "appl[y] only where necessary to achieve its purpose." *Robinson*, 121 F.3d at 974 (quoting *Fisher v. United States*, 425 U.S. 391, 403, 96 S.Ct. 1569, 48 L.Ed.2d 39 (1976)). In keeping with this well-settled principle and the broad investigatory and subpoena authority given to agencies, courts have indicated that the privilege should be granted cautiously where administrative investigations are involved. *See F.T.C. v. TRW, Inc.*, 628 F.2d 207, 211 (D.C. Cir. 1980) (citing *Okla. Press Publ. Co. v. Walling*, 327 U.S. 186, 213, 66 S.Ct. 494, 90 L.Ed. 614 (1946)); *see also Cavallaro v. United States*, 284 F.3d 236, 245–46 (1st Cir. 2002) ("We note, but do not rely on, the doctrine of construing the privilege narrowly, which has particular force in the context of IRS investigations given the 'congressional policy choice *in favor of disclosure* of all information relevant to a legitimate IRS inquiry.' ") (quoting *United States v. Arthur Young & Co.*, 465 U.S. 805, 816, 104 S.Ct. 1495, 79 L.Ed.2d 826 (1984)) (emphasis in original).

2.   Analysis

The EEOC argues that the district court erred when it concluded that all communications between a corporation's employees and its counsel are per se privileged and inverted the burden of proof, requiring that the EEOC prove that BDO improperly asserted the attorney-client privilege as to its withheld documents. *See Hodges*, 768 F.2d at 721. Although the magistrate judge did not explicitly address the burden of proof issue, she did, for example, state to the EEOC: "You haven't made a sufficient showing that that's an improperly claimed privilege when Counsel is . . . copied on a lot of these—on all these documents."

These pronouncements plainly run afoul of well-settled attorney-client privilege principles. There is no presumption that a company's communications with counsel are privileged. *See TVT Records v. Island Def Jam Music Grp.*, 214 F.R.D. 143, 148 (S.D.N.Y. 2003); *see also NLRB v. Interbake Foods, LLC*, 637 F.3d 492, 502 (4th Cir. 2011) ("[I]t is true . . . that the attorney-client privilege does not apply simply because documents were sent to an attorney"). Indeed, more is required. To begin, "[i]t is vital to a claim of [attorney-client] privilege that the communication have been made and maintained in confidence." *Robinson*, 121 F.3d at 976 (quoting *United States v. Pipkins*, 528 F.2d 559, 563 (5th Cir. 1976)). "[A] confidential communication between client and counsel is privileged only if it is generated for the purpose of obtaining or providing legal assistance . . . ." *In re Cty. of Erie*, 473 F.3d 413, 419 (2d Cir. 2007). Additionally, "communications by a corporation with its attorney, who at the time is acting solely in his capacity as a business advisor, [are not] privileged," *Great Plains Mut. Ins. Co. v. Mut. Reinsurance Bureau*, 150 F.R.D. 193, 197 (D. Kan. 1993), nor are documents sent from one corporate officer to another merely because a copy is also sent to counsel, *Freeport-McMoran Sulphur, LLC v. Mike Mullen Energy Equip. Res., Inc.*, No. 03-1496, 2004 WL 1299042, at *25 (E.D. La. June 4, 2004).

For these reasons, courts have stated that simply describing a lawyer's advice as "legal," without more, is conclusory and insufficient to carry out the proponent's burden of establishing attorney-client privilege. *See United States v. Chen*, 99 F.3d 1495, 1502 (9th Cir. 1996) ("Calling the lawyer's advice 'legal' or 'business' advice does not help in reaching a conclusion; it *is* the conclusion.").

In *Exxon Mobil Corp. v. Hill*, this circuit explained that where there is a mixed discussion of business and legal advice, courts should consider the "context . . . key," ultimately seeking to glean the "manifest purpose" of the communication. 751 F.3d 379, 382 (5th Cir. 2014).

Given the "broad" and "considerable discretion" district courts have in discovery matters, we will not analyze the privilege logs in the first instance. *See Winfun v. Daimler Chrysler Corp.*, 255 Fed.Appx. 772, 774 (5th Cir. 2007) (quoting *Sierra Club, Lone Star Chapter v. Cedar Point Oil Co., Inc.*, 73 F.3d 546, 569 (5th Cir. 1996)). Nevertheless, the error below counsels us to reiterate that although Rule 26 "does not attempt to define for each case what information must be provided," 1993 Advisory Comm. Notes to Fed. R. Civ. P. 26 ¶ 33, a privilege log's description of each document and its contents must provide sufficient information to permit courts and other parties to "test[ ] the merits of" the privilege claim. *United States v. El Paso Co.*, 682 F.2d 530, 541 (5th Cir. 1982); *Interbake Foods, LLC*, 637 F.3d at 502 ("When a party relies on a privilege log to assert these privileges, the log must 'as to each document . . . set[ ] forth specific facts that, if credited, would suffice to establish each element of the privilege or immunity that is claimed.' ") (quoting *Bowne, Inc. v. AmBase Corp.*, 150 F.R.D. 465, 474 (S.D.N.Y. 1993)). Continual failure to adhere to Rule 26's prescription may result in waiver of the privilege where a court finds that the failure results from unjustified delay, inexcusable conduct, or bad faith. *See United States v. Philip Morris Inc.*, 347 F.3d 951, 954 (D.C. Cir. 2003).

3.   Conclusion

Based on the foregoing, by adopting the magistrate judge's recommendation, the district court erred when inverting the burden of proof, requiring that the EEOC prove that BDO improperly asserted the attorney-client privilege as to its withheld documents, and concluding that all communications between a corporation's employees and its counsel are *per se* privileged. Accordingly, we vacate the district court's judgment and remand for a determination applying the correct attorney-client privilege principles and legal standards.

B.   Protective Order

We turn next to the question of whether the district court applied the correct legal standard when it granted BDO's request for a protective order.

1. Legal Standard

"[T]his court reviews discovery orders for abuse of discretion . . . ." *Crosswhite v. Lexington Ins. Co.*, 321 Fed.Appx. 365, 367 (5th Cir. 2009); *see also Sanders v. Shell Oil Co.*, 678 F.2d 614, 618 (5th Cir. 1982) (reviewing protective order under abuse of discretion standard); *McLeod, Alexander, Powel & Apffel, P.C. v. Quarles*, 894 F.2d 1482, 1485 (5th Cir. 1990) (analyzing the district court's adoption of the magistrate's judge's denial of a protective order for abuse of discretion). However, whether the district court used the correct legal standard in determining whether to issue a protective order is reviewed de novo. *See In re Avantel, S.A.*, 343 F.3d 311, 318 (5th Cir. 2003) (a court "review[s] the application of the controlling law de novo" in an attorney-client privilege case).

A "court may, for good cause, issue an order to protect a party or person from annoyance, embarrassment, oppression, or undue burden or expense." Fed. R. Civ. P. 26(c)(1). The movant bears the burden of showing that a protective order is necessary, "which contemplates a particular and specific demonstration of fact as distinguished from stereotyped and conclusory statements." *In re Terra Int'l*, 134 F.3d 302, 306 (5th Cir. 1998) (quoting *United States v. Garrett*, 571 F.2d 1323, 1326 n.3 (5th Cir. 1978)). "A trial court enjoys wide discretion in determining the scope and effect of discovery," and it is therefore "unusual to find an abuse of discretion in discovery matters." *Sanders*, 678 F.2d at 618.

2. Analysis

After considering the parties' arguments, the magistrate judge concluded that the EEOC had communicated with witnesses and obtained information about their discussions with BDO attorneys. Based on these findings, she ordered the EEOC to: (1) refrain from communicating with Bower or other BDO employees about conversations with BDO's counsel; (2) disclose employees' names, dates of disclosure, and the substance of their conversations with BDO's counsel; (3) produce notes of each of these conversations, redacting the EEOC's work product; (4) return to BDO any documents containing privileged communications; and (5) destroy any notes or documents that were created as a result of reviewing the documents. The EEOC argues that the magistrate judge's decision to grant the protective order was grounded in the same legal error as the order denying the EEOC's application for subpoena enforcement—an "overly broad" legal standard that "wrongly swe[pt] under the umbrella of non-disclosure all communications involving an attorney."

We agree that the trial court appears to have applied an incorrect legal standard. During the show cause hearing, the magistrate judge on several occasions articulated an overly broad definition of attorney-client privilege. For example, during a colloquy with the EEOC regarding the protective order, the magistrate judge stated, "Frankly, anything that comes out of that lawyer's mouth is legal advice," explained that her position was that "anything that's communicated from or to [c]ounsel is privileged and [Bower] cannot discuss that in any manner," and said to counsel, "I'm telling you that if it's communications from or to an attorney, it's privileged." The magistrate judge also approved BDO's contention that "the default position should be that if the conversation is with an attorney, a lawyer who has an ethical responsibility, should not invade that privilege" and rejected the EEOC's assertion that "it's not legal advice when [Bower is] being told to do things that are not ethical, that are not within the bounds of her position." These statements support the EEOC's claim that the magistrate judge granted and determined the scope of the protective order based on an erroneous interpretation of the law.

We do not, however, hold that a protective order is unwarranted, and we leave the decision whether to grant such an order to the trial court.

3. Conclusion

Because the magistrate judge's incorrect application of the legal standard may have affected both her analysis of the allegedly disclosed communications and the breadth of the protections she imposed in her order, we remand so that BDO's request for protection may be considered under the proper legal standard for determining privilege.

III. CONCLUSION

For the foregoing reasons, we VACATE the district court's judgment and REMAND for a determination consistent with this opinion.

SOLUTIONS: THE LAWYER SHOULD HAVE, WOULD HAVE, COULD HAVE. . .

Trial court judges can also be confused on the scope of the ACP. The judge in this case certainly was. And whether the ACP applies can be a difficult call (as we will study later) when a lawyer—fulfilling their MR 2.1 role as both legal technicians and general, holistic business counselors—mixes legal advice with business advice. For now, understand the fundamental principles of the ACP and do not be hesitant to challenge a court that misunderstands them.

X-Ray Questions

Do you think it can be challenging to draw the line between saying just enough in a privilege log to be able to invoke the privilege and saying not enough and becoming entangled in a discovery dispute?

BEYOND THE CITE

New lawyers are often assigned to prepare a privilege log. Here are some thoughts based on a Continuing Legal Education presentation by the Nebraska firm of BairdHolm.

Pitfall No. 1: Log? What's a log?

The failure to provide a log can result in waiver of a privilege. By way of example, say that there is a memo from a lawyer to a manager at a company. The memo provides legal advice on whether to terminate an employee. The memo is therefore covered by the ACP. If a request for documents is broad enough to encompass such a memo then the memo must be noted on a log. Note that many courts, especially in the federal system, have what are called Local Rules that describe what must be listed in a log and the format for same. Always check.

Pitfall No. 2: Lack of factual specificity as to what is being withheld

Always ask the purpose of a rule. Here it is so that relevant information is not withheld from a party opposite. But it is also to provide enough factual detail on the log so that—here we go again with an even playing field—the party opposite can make its own determination of whether the document should be withheld because of a privilege. How should the documents be listed? If possible, a separate itemization. *In Re Universal Serv. Fund Tel. Billing Practices Litigation*, 232 F.R.D. 669, 674 (D. Kan. 2005).

Now, some courts will—if the production involves voluminous documents—allow the withheld items to be described by categories. *S.E.C. v. Nacchio*, 2007 WL 219966 (D. Colo. 2007) states: "in appropriate circumstances the court may permit the holder of withheld documents to provide summaries of the documents by category or otherwise limit the extent of (its) disclosure. This would certainly be the case if (a) a document-by-document listing would be unduly burdensome and (b) the additional log would be of no material benefit to the discovering party in assessing whether the privilege claim is well-grounded."

Pitfall No. 3: **Lack of legal specificity in the reason for withholding**

The same rationale as above applies. Broad conclusions such as "letter re-claim" or "report in anticipation of litigation" are arguably insufficient to provide enough information to the party opposite.

Pitfall No. 4: **The party opposite will get it when they get it**

Communicate with counsel opposite on document production and the log. This is epically true when ESI (electronically store information) is involved. (Recall our earlier discussion on electronic evidence and a lawyer's duty of competence. Moreover, do not tender a witness without producing some sort of log. Why? The party opposite can argue that it was prejudiced in examining a witness because it lacked a document and ask to re-depose the witness. Provide the log, if at all possible, with your answers to discovery.

Section 9. End of the Attorney-Client Relationship

There are duties an attorney has to a prospective client. And there are duties that continue after an ACR has ended. The duties and obligations surviving are the duty to maintain confidences, the obligation to preserve the attorney client privilege, confidentiality, and possibly limited diligence. But what does it mean to end the ACR? How is it accomplished? Which Model Rules are implicated? As we will see, the end of the relationship is, in many ways, the mirror image of its formation.

> ➤ The relationship could be ended when its objectives (which are set by the client) have been achieved or attempts to achieve them have run their course. And how is this determined? Ideally, by what the original engagement letter or retainer agreement states. This is why, as we draw a full circle, it is crucial to explain in the engagement letter—clearly and transparently—what the lawyer will be doing for the client and what the lawyer will *not* be doing for the client. If not, then there will be confusion on whether the lawyer's duties and responsibilities have come to a close. For example, if the initial round of litigation fails, is the attorney obligated to pursue an appeal? That and similar issues should be spelled out in advance.

> Examples of triggers demonstrating the end of the ACR would include the sending of the final invoice or the signing of a disengagement letter stating that the representation is completed and the ACR ended absent a new engagement latter.

> The client has an unrestricted right to terminate the representation, for whatever reason and at whatever time. We will see this below in MR 1.16.

> When overt acts by the client are inconsistent with the continuation of the ACR; that is an implied cessation of the ACR just as there can be an implied creation of the ACR. By way of example, one court found that a person was a former client because he refused to pay the lawyer's bills and then retained new counsel for the matter at hand. *Artromick Int'l v. Drustar, Inc.*, 134 F.R.D. 226 (S.D. Ohio 1991) A person may become a former client when a firm represented him only in discrete natters and the client retained a new firm to handle such matters. *Waterbury Garment Corp. v. Strata Prods., Inc.*, 554 F. Supp. 63 (S.D.N.Y 1982).

> But note that some representation is episodic in nature and the circumstances can lead to a conclusion that an ACR was not ended. By way of example, some clients expect continuous representation though their legal needs arise infrequently and at indeterminate times. *See, e.g., Parallel Iron, LLC v. Adobe Sys. Inc.*, 2013 WL 789207 (D. Del. 2013). (Concluding that Adobe was a current client when a law firm had done intermittent patent work between 2006 and 2012 and had not made clear to Adobe that its representation was terminated). Again, the burden of clarity falls upon the lawyer, just as in *Togstad.*

Model Rule 1.16: Declining or Terminating Representation

(a)   Except as stated in paragraph (c), a lawyer shall not represent a client or, where representation has commenced, shall withdraw from the representation of a client if:

(1)   the representation will result in violation of the rules of professional conduct or other law;

(2)   the lawyer's physical or mental condition materially impairs the lawyer's ability to represent the client; or

(3)　the lawyer is discharged.

(b)　Except as stated in paragraph (c), a lawyer may withdraw from representing a client if:

(1)　withdrawal can be accomplished without material adverse effect on the interests of the client;

(2)　the client persists in a course of action involving the lawyer's services that the lawyer reasonably believes is criminal or fraudulent;

(3)　the client has used the lawyer's services to perpetrate a crime or fraud;

(4)　the client insists upon taking action that the lawyer considers repugnant or with which the lawyer has a fundamental disagreement;

(5)　the client fails substantially to fulfill an obligation to the lawyer regarding the lawyer's services and has been given reasonable warning that the lawyer will withdraw unless the obligation is fulfilled;

(6)　the representation will result in an unreasonable financial burden on the lawyer or has been rendered unreasonably difficult by the client; or

(7)　other good cause for withdrawal exists.

(c)　A lawyer must comply with applicable law requiring notice to or permission of a tribunal when terminating a representation. When ordered to do so by a tribunal, a lawyer shall continue representation notwithstanding good cause for terminating the representation.

(d)　Upon termination of representation, a lawyer shall take steps to the extent reasonably practicable to protect a client's interests, such as giving reasonable notice to the client, allowing time for employment of other counsel, surrendering papers and property to which the client is entitled and refunding any advance payment of fee or expense that has not been earned or incurred. The lawyer may retain papers relating to the client to the extent permitted by other law.

Deconstruction Exercise/Rule Rationale

Note initially that MR 1.16 is divided into a mandatory section and a permissive section. In the first, the lawyer must act as prescribed; in the second, the lawyer is required to use judgment and discretion. One mandatory area is when the clients ask the lawyer to act or refrain from acting in a way that would violate the rules of professional conduct. Recall that we examined a possible retention agreement between a lawyer and a client earlier that contemplates this possibility and allows the lawyer to withdraw. But understand that the lawyer must first remind the client of this provision; explain the nature of the ethical issue; and seek to convince the client to withdraw the request to act or not to act. Otherwise, the lawyer could too easily use an ethical issue as a convenient pretext to end the ACR that has turned out to be more difficult than anticipated. (And this client dilemma can be avoided by following Walt Bachmann's advice regarding L.A.S. (Lawyer Avoidance Syndrome).

As you consider the permissive side of the rule, ask yourself whether the lawyer needs a good reason to fire a client. The mandatory part of the rule states explicitly that a lawyer must withdraw if the client decides—even without cause or a good reason—to end the ACR. Actually, the lawyer may end the ACR for any reason at all but *only* provided that there is no material prejudice to the client as a result of the withdrawal (or, if the matter is in litigation, with the permission of the court). This is subsection (a). Now let's look at the language of subsection (4). Why is the word "repugnant" used? What other words could have been selected? Why the word "insists"? Finally, let's study subsections (5) and (6) which use the concept of reasonableness when it comes to a lawyer making a living as a lawyer. Just as a lawyer is not a public utility and is not required to take on all prospective clients, so too a lawyer is not obligated to loan out money to all who ask. Yet as a professional our rights in this second regard are prescribed by a reasonableness standard.

Cases and Materials

X-Ray Questions (*Revise Clothing*)

As you read this case, focus your attention on the engagement letter between the firm and the client. The firm argued that the reason that its services were sought was accomplished; thus, the client was not a current client, and it was free to sue the now former client provided that the new representation did not run afoul of MR 1.9. The court agreed. Why did the court so rule? What was in the engagement letter, and it's conduct showed that the firm's representation was at an end? What else did the firm do to conclusively establish that the ACR was over? Had the firm not done so, what would be the result?

Revise Clothing, Inc. v. Joe's Jeans Subsidiary, Inc.

United States District Court, S.D. New York, 2010.
687 F.Supp.2d 381.

JAMES C. FRANCIS IV, UNITED STATES MAGISTRATE JUDGE.

A motion to disqualify counsel in this action presents two critical issues of professional responsibility. First, when does an attorney-client relationship terminate? Second, once the relationship has ended, under what circumstances may counsel take on representation adverse to the former client?

This is a trademark infringement case concerning back pocket stitching on denim jeans. Defendants and third-party plaintiffs Joe's Jeans Subsidiary, Inc. and Joe's Jeans, Inc. (collectively, "Joe's Jeans") contend that jeans manufactured by plaintiff Revise Clothing Inc. ("Revise") and sold at retail by third-party defendants Target Corporation and Target Brands, Inc. (collectively, "Target") infringe Joe's Jeans' trademark back pocket design. Revise initiated this action, seeking a declaratory judgment that it has not infringed.

Revise now moves for an order disqualifying the law firm of Pryor Cashman LLP ("Pryor Cashman") as counsel for Joe's Jeans. According to Revise, Pryor Cashman has a conflict of interest because it currently represents Revise. Furthermore, Revise argues that even if that engagement has concluded, Pryor Cashman obtained confidential information during the course of that representation that now places Revise at a disadvantage if Pryor Cashman is allowed to continue to represent Joe's Jeans. While Pryor Cashman concedes that it previously represented Revise, it contends that the prior engagement has long since terminated. The firm also maintains that because the two matters are unrelated, any confidential information it received earlier from Revise could not be used to the detriment of Revise in the instant litigation.

Joe's Jeans has also moved to strike the affidavit of Mohammed Sadiqulla, the Chief Financial Officer of Revise, which Revise submitted in support of its disqualification motion. In the alternative, Joe's Jeans asks that the Court consider its surreply.

In addition to submitting affidavits and legal memoranda, the parties presented evidence at a hearing on November 20 and December 7, 2009.

For the reasons set forth below, Joe's Jeans' motion to strike Mr. Sadiqulla's affidavit is denied, but its alternative application that the Court consider its surreply is granted. The motion by Revise to disqualify Pryor Cashman as counsel for Joe's Jeans is denied.

Background

In October 2007, Gordon Troy, an attorney who had represented Revise in intellectual property matters, contacted Brad Rose, a partner at Pryor Cashman, requesting that Pryor Cashman represent Revise in connection with a dispute it was having with Jean City USA and Wet Jeans, Inc. (collectively, "Wet Jeans") (Declaration of Brad D. Rose dated Oct. 2, 2009 ("Rose Decl."), ¶ 3; Tr. at 148). Mr. Troy and Mr. Rose had met in 2003 and subsequently enjoyed a professional relationship. (Rose Decl., ¶ 2). Mr. Troy advised Mr. Rose that Wet Jeans was selling jeans that bore a mark substantially similar to Revise's VANILLA STAR trademark. (Rose Decl., ¶ 3; Tr. at 148). Although Mr. Troy had sent Wet Jeans a cease and desist letter, Wet Jeans continued its allegedly infringing activity. (Rose Decl., ¶ 3).

On November 7, 2007, Mr. Sadiqulla contacted Mr. Rose and asked to discuss the case. (Rose Decl., ¶ 4 & Exh. A). The next day, Mr. Sadiqulla, together with the Chief Executive Officer of Revise, Sandeep Behl, met with Mr. Rose and Nicole Kaplan, another Pryor Cashman attorney. (Rose Decl., ¶ 4). Mr. Sadiqulla maintains that the meeting lasted two hours (Tr. at 113), while Mr. Rose and Ms. Kaplan contend that it took an hour or less, as reflected in Mr. Rose's time records. (Tr. at 216–17; Def. Exh. 4). More importantly, Mr. Sadiqulla asserts that he revealed a wide range of confidential information during the meeting:

> When we first met Nicole and Brad, basically they wanted to feel what the size of the company was, whether it was worth it for them to go forward, whether we had the capacity to—to pay the legal bills.
>
> And once we went along we gave them all the information, basically our sources where we were selling, whether it was private label or branded business, and we had given them—we thought of giving them the name of the stores we were doing business with that litigation was of no use, so we had to disclose who we were selling and who they were trying to sell—they in the sense of Wet Jeans was trying to sell, and at what price points we were selling and what price points they were trying to sell. (Tr. at 89). According to Mr. Sadiqulla, he disclosed the customers to which Revise sells either its own brands or private label merchandise. (Tr. at 90). Further, he revealed the

volume of sales, the overhead structure, and the profit margin for his business. (Tr. at 91–92, 97).

Mr. Rose, by contrast, did not recall having any specific conversation regarding Revise's finances (Tr. at 27–28), and he contends that the discussion focused entirely on the trademarks at issue. (Tr. at 29). Similarly, according to Ms. Kaplan,

> Revise came to the firm and explained about the problem they were having with Wet Jeans, Jeans City. They showed us the correspondence that had gone back and forth between Gordon [Troy] and counsel for Jeans City, or Wet Jeans. They showed us their trademark registration for the Vanilla Star brand trademark and they brought with them a green army jacket as a sample of the Vanilla Star merchandise.

(Tr. at 217–18). Ms. Kaplan asserted that the Revise representatives did not discuss any trademarks other than VANILLA STAR; they did not discuss the design of their jeans, the back pocket stitching, their private label work, their manufacturing process, sales to Target, or any of their customers. (Tr. at 218–19). Indeed, she explained that although Mr. Sadiqulla and Mr. Behl mentioned that they had received returns of Wet Jeans merchandise, they did not at that time identify the customers who had made the erroneous returns. (Tr. at 219).

Following that meeting, Mr. Rose prepared a retainer agreement that he forwarded to Revise. (Rose Decl., ¶ 6). The agreement provided that Pryor Cashman would represent Revise "in connection with the trademark infringement claims to be asserted against Wet Jeans, Inc." (Pl. Exh. 3 at 1). The agreement further stated that Pryor Cashman could terminate the attorney-client relationship if it did so "in a manner which complies with applicable law, court rules and the New York Code of Professional Responsibility." (Pl. Exh. 3 at 2).

On November 14, 2007, Ms. Kaplan placed a telephone call to Mr. Troy to discuss the Wet Jeans matter further. (Tr. at 149, 219; Def. Exh. 4, entry for Nov. 14, 2007). According to Mr. Troy, he revealed extensive confidential information about Revise to Ms. Kaplan during this conversation. He characterized the discussion as follows:

> We talked about the size of the company, that, you know, the—that, you know—you know, how many, you know, different seasons they have, what is the range of their products, who do they sell to—I mean, real, you know, details about their business to understand who this client is, because even though they're in the jeans business doesn't

mean they're the same as the next jean manufacturer. They're all different.

Revise basically sells to—as Mr. Sadiq explained, they—that is—they sell to Federated Department Stores. They sell to these big, massive chains, whether it be, you know. Target, Walmart, Federated. There's—I don't know, there's this—Kohl's, I think, is the name of one. There's another—there's a big one in the south that is a major customer of Revise—and explained the distribution of these products.

We talked about the fact they they've got an office in California. The reason why they have an office for—in California is that all their—you know, their product at that point was being manufactured in the Orient, whether it be China, Vietnam, India, and it was being shipped into L.A. because it's more efficient to ship to L.A. and then distribute from L.A. I mean, we talked about all the infrastructure business aspects of how Revise worked.

(Tr. at 174–76). Ms. Kaplan, by contrast, insists that the conversation related exclusively to Wet Jeans and to the history of the communications between Mr. Troy and Wet Jeans' counsel. (Tr. at 219–20). She denies discussing any of the topics that Mr. Troy testified to, including Revise's distribution networks, its office locations, or the details of its infrastructure. (Tr. at 220–21). Following the telephone conversation, Mr. Troy sent Ms. Kaplan an e-mail, attaching the relevant Wet Jeans correspondence and identifying the attorneys with whom he had communicated about the matter. (Pl. Exh. 7).

Pryor Cashman prepared a complaint against Wet Jeans and filed it in late November 2007. (Rose Decl., ¶¶ 8–9). However, it did not serve the complaint at that time, and instead mailed a copy to Wet Jeans' counsel along with a cease and desist letter. (Rose Decl., ¶ 9). By December, the parties were in negotiations, and the case was resolved with a settlement agreement executed in May 2008. (Rose Decl., ¶¶ 10, 12). Pursuant to that agreement, Wet Jeans agreed to certify the date on which it had sold off all allegedly infringing merchandise, and it further agreed not to sell apparel with any mark similar to Revise's VANILLA STAR trademark. (Pl. Exh. 5, ¶¶ 1, 2). The agreement further provided for notice and an opportunity to cure in the event that either side breached any of the terms. (Pl. Exh. 5, ¶ 9). Where notice to Revise was required under the agreement, it was to be delivered to Mr. Rose at Pryor Cashman. (Pl. Exh. 5, ¶ 12).

At the same time that Pryor Cashman was involved in the Wet Jeans litigation, it also performed limited trademark investigations—known as "knockout searches"—on behalf of Revise. Revise was interested in marketing apparel with the slogans "Smart Girls Rock" and "Live the Dream," and asked Pryor Cashman to determine whether these terms were already subject to trademark protection. (Tr. at 223). Accordingly, in December 2008, counsel performed computerized searches of trademark office databases using different permutations of the requested terms. (Tr. at 47–49, 222–23). For these services, Pryor Cashman billed for 1.5 hours of Ms. Kaplan's time and 0.25 hours of Mr. Rose's time. (Tr. at 222–23; Def. Exh. 4, entries for 12/12/07).

After the Wet Jeans litigation concluded, Pryor Cashman archived its files related to the matter. (Rose Decl., ¶ 13). However, the firm continued to send Revise e-mail "blasts" offering services related to trademark law. (Tr. at 51, 98–99).

In the spring of 2009, Joe's Jeans discovered that Target was selling jeans under the "Xhileration" label that contained stitching on the back pocket in the form of an inverted arc. (Complaint, Exh. 2). Joe's Jeans believed that this infringed its registered trademark for back pocket stitching, and its counsel at that time, Jordan A. LaVine of the Philadelphia firm of Flaster Greenberg, therefore sent a cease and desist letter to Target on March 5, 2009. (Complaint, Exh. 2). Target forwarded this letter to its supplier, Revise, and on March 20, 2009, Mr. Troy replied on behalf of Revise, disputing the assertions made by Joe's Jeans. (Complaint, Exh. 3). When the parties were unable to resolve their differences, Revise filed the instant action against Joe's Jeans on April 21, 2009.

Also in April, Joe's Jeans engaged Pryor Cashman as its counsel. (Tr. at 6). Aware that the firm had previously represented Revise, Mr. Rose contacted Ms. Kaplan and confirmed that the earlier matter had been completed, (Tr. at 8). On May 11, Mr. Rose contacted Mr. Troy in an effort to resolve the dispute between Joe's Jeans and Revise. (Tr. at 14–15). According to Mr. Troy, Mr. Rose volunteered that because of Pryor Cashman's representation of Revise, he would not represent Joe's Jeans further if the parties were unable to reach an accommodation. (Tr. at 161–62). Mr. Rose denies making any such statement. (Tr. at 16). The next day, Mr. Troy sent a follow-up e-mail addressing a number of issues that the two had discussed and stating that "[m]y client consents to allow you to represent Joe's Jeans for the limited purposes of settlement." (E-mail of Gordon E.R. Troy dated May 12, 2009, attached to Pl. Exh. 1). When a quick resolution was not achieved and Pryor Cashman continued to represent

Joe's Jeans as the litigation moved forward, Revise filed the instant disqualification motion.

Initially, Revise supported its motion with a declaration executed by Mr. Troy. (Declaration of Gordon E.R. Troy dated Sept. 15, 2009). Joe's Jeans responded in part by challenging Mr. Troy's declaration as conclusory and inadmissible, as it appeared to be based on information beyond his personal knowledge. (Memorandum of Law in Opposition to Motion of Revise Clothing, Inc. to Disqualify Counsel at 2, 17–18). Revise then proffered Mr. Sadiqulla's affidavit as part of its reply papers. Joe's Jeans, in turn, moved to strike that affidavit or, in the alternative, for consideration of its surreply.

Discussion

A.   *Motion to Strike*

A court has discretion to consider documents filed in violation of procedural rules. *See Ruggiero v. Warner-Lambert Co.,* 424 F.3d 249, 252 (2d Cir.2005); *Coyle v. Crown Enterprises, Inc.,* No. 05-CV-891F, 2009 WL 763401, at *8 (W.D.N.Y. March 19, 2009); *Aurora Loan Services, Inc. v. Posner, Posner & Associates, P.C.,* 513 F.Supp.2d 18, 20 (S.D.N.Y.2007). It is plainly improper to submit on reply evidentiary information that was available to the moving party at the time that it filed its motion and that is necessary in order for that party to meet its burden. *See Tolliver v. McCants,* No. 05 Civ. 10840, 2009 WL 1473445, at *3 (S.D.N.Y. May 26, 2009); *Aurora Loan Services,* 513 F.Supp.2d at 20; *Seneca Insurance Co. v. Wilcock,* No. 01 Civ. 7620, 2005 WL 2898460, at *8 (S.D.N.Y. Nov. 3, 2005). Nevertheless, Joe's Jeans has suffered no prejudice because it has submitted a surreply and also had the opportunity to present evidence at the evidentiary hearing. Therefore, I will consider Joe's Jeans' surreply and will not strike Mr. Sadiqulla's affidavit. *See Toure v. Central Parking Systems of New York,* No. 05 Civ. 5237, 2007 WL 2872455, at *2 (S.D.N.Y. Sept. 28, 2007) (allowing new argument in reply where non-moving party submitted surreply); *Lee v. Coughlin,* 26 F.Supp.2d 615, 617 n. 2 (S.D.N.Y.1998).

B.   *Disqualification Motion*

1.   *General Principles*

In considering a motion to disqualify counsel, a court must "balance 'a client's right freely to choose his counsel' against 'the need to maintain the highest standards of the profession.' " *Hempstead Video, Inc. v. Incorporated Village of Valley Stream,* 409 F.3d 127, 132 (2d Cir.2005) (quoting *Government of India v. Cook Industries, Inc.,* 569 F.2d 737, 739 (2d Cir.1978)). Thus, although any doubt should be resolved in favor of disqualification, *Hull v. Celanese Corp.*, 513 F.2d 568, 571 (2d Cir.1975); *Merck Eprova AG v. ProThera, Inc.*, 670 F.Supp.2d 201, 207–08 (S.D.N.Y.2009); *Bowens v. Atlantic Maintenance Corp.*, 546 F.Supp.2d 55, 86 (E.D.N.Y.2008); *Blue Planet Software, Inc. v. Games International, LLC*, 331 F.Supp.2d 273, 275 (S.D.N.Y.2004), motions to disqualify counsel are disfavored and subject to a high standard of proof, in part because they can be used tactically as leverage in litigation. *See Evans v. Artek Systems Corp.*, 715 F.2d 788, 791–92 (2d Cir.1983) (noting "high standard of proof" for disqualification motions because they are "often interposed for tactical reasons"); *see also Merck*, 670 F.Supp.2d at 207; *Leslie Dick Worldwide, Ltd. v. Soros*, No. 08 Civ. 7900, 2009 WL 2190207, at *6 (S.D.N.Y. July 22, 2009); *Medical Diagnostic Imaging, PLLC v. CareCore National, LLC*, 542 F.Supp.2d 296, 306–07 (S.D.N.Y.2008); *Scantek Medical, Inc. v. Sabella*, 693 F.Supp.2d 235, 238, No. 08 Civ. 453, 2008 WL 5210562, at *2 (S.D.N.Y. Dec. 12, 2008). Indeed, any motion to disqualify can cause delay, added expense, and interference with the attorney-client relationship. *Scantek Medical*, 393 F.Supp.2d at 238, 2008 WL 5210562, at *2; *Ello v. Singh*, No. 05 Civ. 9625, 2006 WL 2270871, at *2 (S.D.N.Y. Aug. 7, 2006) (citing cases).

In deciding disqualification motions, courts look to the American Bar Association Model Rules of Professional Conduct and to state disciplinary rules including, in this forum, the New York Rules of Professional Conduct. *Leslie Dick Worldwide*, 2009 WL 2190207, at *5 & n. 14. However, because the authority to disqualify an attorney is a function of the court's inherent supervisory power, *see Hempstead Video*, 409 F.3d at 132; *Merck*, 670 F.Supp.2d at 207–08; *Medical Diagnostic Imaging*, 542 F.Supp.2d at 305; *Skidmore v. Warburg Dillon Read LLC*, No. 99 Civ. 10525, 2001 WL 504876, at *2 (S.D.N.Y. May 11, 2001), these rules provide guidance only and are not conclusive. *See Hempstead Video*, 409 F.3d at 132; *Merck*, 670 F.Supp.2d at 207–08; *Medical Diagnostic Imaging*, 542 F.Supp.2d at 305–06; *Blue Planet Software*, 331 F.Supp.2d at 275; *Skidmore*, 2001 WL 504876, at *2. Thus, disqualification may be justified even in the absence of a clear ethical breach "where necessary to preserve the integrity of the adversary process. . . ." *Board of Education of the City of New York v. Nyquist*, 590 F.2d 1241, 1246 (2d Cir.1979). But, by the same token, "not every violation of a disciplinary rule will necessarily lead to disqualification." *Hempstead Video*, 409 F.3d at 132. Indeed, "[m]ere appearance of impropriety will not alone serve as a sufficient basis for granting a disqualification motion. Rather, the motion will be granted only if the facts present a real risk that the trial will be tainted." *United States Football League v. National Football League*, 605 F.Supp. 1448, 1452 (S.D.N.Y.1985) (footnote omitted); *accord Hickman v. Burlington Bio-Medical Corp.*, 371 F.Supp.2d 225, 229

(E.D.N.Y.2005); *Guerrilla Girls, Inc. v. Kaz,* No. 03 Civ. 4619, 2004 WL 2238510, at *2 (S.D.N.Y. Oct. 4, 2004).

"The standard for disqualification varies depending on whether the representation is concurrent or successive." *Hempstead Video,* 409 F.3d at 133. It is " 'prima facie improper' for an attorney to simultaneously represent a client and another party with interests directly adverse to that client." *Id.* (quoting *Cinema 5, Ltd. v. Cinerama, Inc.,* 528 F.2d 1384, 1387 (2d Cir.1976)). In such cases, a "per se" standard applies and the attorney must be disqualified unless he can demonstrate " 'at the very least, that there will be no actual or *apparent* conflict in loyalties or diminution in the vigor of his representation.' " *Id.* (quoting *Cinema 5,* 528 F.2d at 1387). This standard is based on the ethical principle that an attorney must exercise independent judgment on behalf of a client. This obligation is embodied in Rule 1.7 of the New York Rules of Professional Conduct, which states in pertinent part that a lawyer shall not represent a client if a reasonable lawyer would conclude that either:

> (1)   the representation will involve the lawyer in representing differing interests; or

> (2)   there is a significant risk that the lawyer's professional judgment on behalf of a client will be adversely affected by the lawyer's own financial, business, property or other personal interests.

Rule 1.7(a).

A different standard applies where an attorney is in a position adverse to a former client. In a case of successive representation, an attorney may be disqualified where:

> (1)   the moving party is a former client of the adverse party's counsel;

> (2)   there, is a substantial relationship between the subject matter of the counsel's prior representation of the moving party and the issues in the present lawsuit; and

> (3)   the attorney whose disqualification is sought had access to, or was likely to have had access to, relevant privileged information in the course of his prior representation of the client.

Hempstead Video, 409 F.3d at 133 (citing *Evans,* 715 F.2d at 791); *see also Blue Planet Software,* 331 F.Supp.2d at 275–76. This standard is grounded in the ethical requirement that an attorney protect client confidences. This duty is articulated in Rule 1.6, which states in part that "[a] lawyer shall not knowingly reveal confidential information . . . or use such information to the disadvantage of a client or for the advantage of the lawyer or a third person[.]" Rule 1.6(a).

2. *Termination of the Attorney-Client Relationship*

Revise argues that the standard for concurrent representation governs the pending motion because, at the time that Pryor Cashman was engaged by Joe's Jeans in this case, it was still representing Revise. Revise offers three theories as support for this contention. First, it maintains that it reasonably expected Pryor Cashman to provide all litigation-related services going forward. (Tr. at 98, 117, 254–55). Second, Revise argues that Pryor Cashman continued to be responsible for representing it in the Wet Jeans matter in particular. (Pl. Reply at 6; Troy Decl., ¶¶ 5–6; Tr. at 255–57; Affidavit of Mohammed Sadiqulla dated Oct. 9, 2009 ("Sadiqulla Off."), ¶ 13). And, third, it contends that Pryor Cashman failed to explicitly sever the attorney-client relationship. (Pl. Reply at 6; Troy Decl., ¶ 6; Tr. at 254). None of these theories withstands scrutiny.

a. *Scope of the Engagement*

When an attorney-client relationship ends depends largely on the purpose for which it was created:

> In what is perhaps the most typical situation, an attorney-client relationship created between a lawyer and a lay party is terminated, simply enough, by the accomplishment of the purpose for which it was formed in the first place. This rule is really a corollary of the principles that an attorney-client relationship arises only as to the particular matter or transaction on which the lawyer has expressly or implicitly bound himself to work, and that, unless the lawyer is on a general retainer covering the entire period involved, the relationship does not extend to business or affairs of the lay party as to which the lawyer was not initially contracted.

48 Am. Jur. Proof of Facts 2d § 18 (footnotes omitted). Thus, the first step here is to ascertain the nature of the retainer that created the relationship between Revise and Pryor Cashman. "General retainers are used to secure the services of a specific attorney for any contingency that may arise in the future. A special retainer has reference to a particular case or service[.]" Richard A. Lord, 23 Williston on Contracts § 62:2 (4th ed.) (footnotes omitted).

Revise argues that the Pryor Cashman retainer in this case "extended to the representation beyond the Wet Jeans case." (Tr. at 254). If, by this, Revise means to suggest that the language of the retainer contemplated work on other matters, Revise is mistaken. The retainer specifically refers to Pryor Cashman's representation of Revise "in connection with the trademark infringement claims to be asserted against Wet Jeans, Inc." (Pl. Exh. 3 at 1). There is certainly no language implying that Pryor Cashman was to perform any other particular services for Revise or that it was to serve as counsel in unspecified matters that might arise in the future.

The limited nature of Pryor Cashman's engagement is consistent with the origin of the relationship. Mr. Troy was Revise's long-time counsel. Rather than handling the Wet Jeans matter himself, he referred it to Pryor Cashman because, as he testified, "at that particular junction, I was involved in another piece of litigation where—with co-counsel that I just did not have the time to deal with the immediacy of the situation. . . ." (Tr. at 145). Mr. Troy's explanation conforms with Mr. Sadiqulla's understanding, at least as expressed in his affidavit, that "Mr. Troy did not have the time to represent Revise in an infringement case that needed to be filed right away." (Sadiqulla Aff., ¶ 2). In other words, Pryor Cashman's representation of Revise in the Wet Jeans case was expected to be a one-time arrangement, and Mr. Troy would continue to represent Revise in the future.

Nevertheless, Mr. Sadiqulla now asserts that he expected Pryor Cashman to represent Revise in all future litigation matters. (Tr. at 117). Any such expectation would have been wholly unreasonable. The retainer was narrowly drawn to refer only to the Wet Jeans matter. Had Mr. Sadiqulla expressed any desire to have Pryor Cashman represent Revise in future litigation, Mr. Rose would surely have acted in Pryor Cashman's interest by drafting a more comprehensive agreement.

Nor does Pryor Cashman's transmission of e-mail blasts indicate that the firm continued to represent Revise. In *Applied Technology Ltd. v. Watermaster of America, Inc.*, No. 07 Civ. 6620, 2009 WL 804127 (S.D.N.Y. March 26, 2009), a party seeking disqualification argued that its receipt of a law firm newsletter demonstrated that it was a current client of the firm. *Id.* at *6. The court rejected this contention, stating that "a mass-mailed newsletter, which may also have been sent to former or prospective clients as a way to generate business, does not support such a conclusion." *Id.* The same rationale applies here. Finally, Mr. Sadiqulla's suggestion that Pryor Cashman would represent Revise in future litigation matters is belied by his own conduct. When Revise was first threatened with litigation by Joe's Jeans, Mr. Sadiqulla sought assistance from Mr. Troy, not from Pryor Cashman, even though it was not until later that Pryor Cashman began representing Joe's Jeans. (Tr. at 117–18).

To be sure, Pryor Cashman did some work for Revise that was not related to the Wet Jeans litigation: it conducted preliminary trademark searches for two slogans that Revise was considering using. However, this work consumed all of one and three-quarters hours of attorney time. Such *de minimis* legal work, performed as a courtesy for an existing client, is not sufficient to transform a limited engagement into a general retainer.

b.   *Termination of the Wet Jeans Matter*

Of course, the fact that the retainer is a narrow one is of little significance if the very matter for which Pryor Cashman was retained by Revise was still ongoing when the firm began to represent Joe's Jeans. Revise contends that this was in fact the case here because, even after a settlement was reached in the Wet Jeans matter, there remained the possibility that Wet Jeans would breach the agreement, necessitating further litigation. (Pl. Reply at 6).

Counsel may have an ongoing attorney-client relationship with a party even after litigation has concluded when, for example, the resolution of a lawsuit obligates the parties to perform acts in the future. *See Irwin v. Mascott*, 196 Fed.Appx. 455 (9th Cir.2006) (denying motion my counsel to withdraw where client subject to injunction and contempt). But there was no such obligation here. While Wet Jeans was required by the settlement agreement to sell off its inventory of allegedly infringing product, it had already done so (Tr. at 225), and it provided an affidavit attesting to its compliance. (Pl. Exh. 5, ¶ 2; Tr. at 233). Of course, Wet Jeans also had a continuing duty not to infringe. But the inclusion of a prohibitory injunction in a judgment or a settlement agreement does not give rise to an attorney-client relationship that continues in perpetuity.

Nor does the analysis change merely because the settlement agreement in this case identified Pryor Cashman as the entity to be notified in the event of a default. Just as the fact that an attorney is counsel for a party does not make that attorney the party's agent for service of process, *see United States v. Ziegler Bolt and Parts Co.*, 111 F.3d 878, 881 (Fed.Cir.1997); *Kruska v. Perverted Justice Foundation, Inc.*, No. CV-08-0054, 2009 WL 4041941, at *2 (D.Ariz. Nov. 16, 2009), so too, the fact that an attorney agrees to act as agent for service of process does not create an attorney-client relationship or extend one that has otherwise terminated. When parties, for matters of convenience, designate counsel as their agents for service, they have not bestowed on counsel the panoply of duties and obligations that arise in a full attorney-client relationship.

c.   *The Need for Formal Termination*

Finally, Revise argues that its attorney-client relationship with Pryor Cashman persisted because Pryor Cashman never formally terminated it. Revise, however, has identified no rule of professional responsibility that requires a law firm to announce the conclusion of its engagement. Indeed, any such requirement would conflict with the principle cited above that the relationship is terminated upon the accomplishment of the purpose for which it was created.

Nevertheless, Revise maintains that the retainer agreement in this case imposed a special duty on Pryor Cashman to memorialize the conclusion of the attorney-client relationship. Revise relies on the provision in the retainer that states:

> The attorney-client relationship is one of mutual trust and confidence, and you are, of course, free to terminate our relationship at any time. We will also be free to terminate the relationship at any time, and should that unlikely event occur, we will do so in a manner which complies with applicable law, court rules, and the New York Code of Professional Responsibility.

(Pl. Exh. 3 at 2, ¶ 4). But this language adds nothing to the analysis. First, this provision appears to refer to the means by which counsel may withdraw during the course of an ongoing matter which may, for example, require leave of court. As such, it is irrelevant to the issue of when a matter is concluded. Second, even if it did relate to termination of the attorney-client relationship at the completion of an engagement, this provision simply requires compliance with "applicable law, court rules, and the New York Code of Professional Responsibility," none of which obligate counsel to send its client a letter announcing the termination.

Pryor Cashman unquestionably represented Revise. However, that representation—for the specific purpose of handling the Wet Jeans litigation— ended by the time that the firm began to represent Joe's Jeans. Therefore, the conflict standards for successive representation rather than those for concurrent representation apply to the instant disqualification motion.

3.   *Successive Representation*

As discussed above, a conflict may lead to disqualification where: (1) counsel for the adverse party previously represented the moving party, (2) the subject matter of the prior representation is substantially related to the present lawsuit, and (3) counsel had, or was likely to have had, access to relevant confidential information during the course of the prior representation. *Hempstead Video,* 409 F.3d at 133; *Evans,* 715 F.2d at 791. In this case, there is no dispute that the first requirement has been met because Pryor Cashman previously represented Revise. It is hotly contested, however, whether the second and third criteria have been satisfied.

a.   *Substantial Relationship*

The second prong is established "only upon a showing that the relationship between issues in the prior and present cases is 'patently clear.' Put more specifically, disqualification has been granted or approved recently only when the issues involved have been 'identical' or 'essentially the same.' " *Government of India,* 569 F.2d at 739–40 (citations and footnote omitted); *accord Leslie Dick Worldwide,* 2009 WL 2190207, at *9; *Bennett Silvershein Associates v. Furman,* 776 F.Supp. 800, 803 (S.D.N.Y.1991). "It is the congruence of *factual* matters, rather than areas of law, that establishes a substantial relationship between representations for disqualification purposes." *United States Football League,* 605 F.Supp. at 1460 n. 26; *accord Leslie Dick Worldwide,* 2009 WL 2190207, at *9; *Blue Planet Software,* 331 F.Supp.2d at 277; *Mitchell v. Metropolitan Life Insurance Co.,* No. 01 Civ. 2112, 2002 WL 441194, at *8 (S.D.N.Y. March 21, 2002) ("[T]he relevant inquiry is not limited to whether there are common legal claims or theories . . ., but extends to whether there are common factual issues that are material to the adjudication of the prior and current representations."). Accordingly, "[t]his standard is easily applied to cases where both the prior and present representation involve litigation: 'if the facts giving rise to an issue which is material in both the former and the present litigations are as a practical matter the same, then there is a "substantial relationship" between the representations for purposes of a disqualification motion.' " *Guerrilla Girls,* 2004 WL 2238510, at *3 (quoting *United States Football League,* 605 F.Supp. at 1459).

Once it is established that a substantial relationship exists between the prior and current matters, it is presumed that counsel who participated in both had access during the first litigation to confidential information that would be relevant in the second. This presumption, however, is rebuttable. *See Government of India,* 569 F.2d at 741 (Mansfield, J., concurring); *Silver Chrysler Plymouth, Inc. v. Chrysler Motors Corp.,* 518 F.2d 751, 753–54 (2d Cir.1975); *Leslie Dick Worldwide,* 2009 WL 2190207, at *12 (collecting cases); *Wieme v. Eastman Kodak Co.,* No. 02-CV-6021, 2004 WL 2271402, at *2 (W.D.N.Y. Sept. 7, 2004).

Here, there is no substantial relationship between the Wet Jeans litigation and the current case. Although both matters concern apparel that may be subject to trademark protection, the similarity ends there. The Wet Jeans case dealt with the use of a mark that was allegedly deceptively similar to Revise's VANILLA STAR principal register trademark. That mark, which consists exclusively of words, was issued to Revise for use in a wide variety of clothing, including shirts, pants, jackets, and jeans. (Trademark Reg. No. 2,762,901, attached as Exh. A to Complaint in *Revise Clothing, Inc. v. Wet Jeans,* attached as Exh. B to Rose Decl.). Indeed, the sample that Revise provided to Pryor Cashman in connection with the Wet Jeans case was a jacket, not a pair of jeans. This case, by contrast, concerns a supplemental register trademark for the design for back pocket stitching on jeans, pants, and denims. (Trademark Reg. No. 3,506,808, attached as Exh. 1 to Complaint). The prior case had nothing to do with stitching design, while the current case has nothing to do with any mark consisting of words.

Revise makes much of the argument that the line of clothing that was ultimately sold under Target's Xhileration private label originated as a Vanilla Star design. In his affidavit, Mr. Sadiqulla stated that "[t]he product over which Joe's Jeans has sued Revise is essentially the VANILLA STAR product line that we sued Wet Jeans over, and the only difference is that Revise has privately labeled it for Target." (Sadiqulla Aff., ¶ 9). Subsequently, he explained that after the VANILLA STAR jeans had been sold in Target stores, Target expressed interest in buying a similar line from Revise for sale under a private label. (Tr. at 93–94). However, Mr. Sadiqulla admitted that, on one hand, the Xhileration jeans never display a VANILLA STAR mark and, on the other hand, the VANILLA STAR jeans do not have back pocket stitching similar to the Xhileration design. (Tr. at 121–23). Thus, even if the Xhileration jeans at issue in this litigation evolved in some way from the VANILLA STAR line, the elements that are critical to the legal issues in this case are distinct from those that were important in the Wet Jeans case.

Nonetheless, Revise contends that in the course of representation in the Wet Jeans matter, Pryor Cashman had access to its strategic thinking. (Tr. at 262; Letter of Gordon E.R. Troy dated Aug. 12, 2009 ("Troy 8/12/09 Letter"), attached as Tab 4 to Troy Decl., at 3). However, "[w]here the only allegation of similarity is the attorney's alleged insight into the former client's general litigation thinking, similarity is not established." *Scantek,* 693 F.Supp.2d at 239, 2008 WL 5210562, at *3 (citations and quotation marks omitted); *accord Hickman,* 371 F.Supp.2d at 230; *Matthews v. LeBoeuf, Lamb, Greene & MacRae,* 902 F.Supp. 26, 31 (S.D.N.Y.1995). Indeed, "if insight into a former client's general 'litigation thinking' were to constitute 'relevant privileged information,' then disqualification would be mandated in virtually every instance of successive representation." *Vestron, Inc. v. National Geographic Society,* 750 F.Supp. 586, 595 (S.D.N.Y.1990).

Revise also argues that Pryor Cashman was necessarily privy to its general business and marketing strategies and infrastructure. (Tr. at 89, 175–76, 261–63; Troy 8/12/09 Letter at 3). "Where an attorney's representation of a client is general in nature, he may be disqualified from representing an adverse party in later litigation, but only if the later litigation puts at issue the client's entire background." *Scantek*, 693 F.Supp.2d at 239, 2008 WL 5210562, at *3 (citations omitted). That was not the case here for two reasons. First, Pryor Cashman's representation of Revise was not "general in nature;" it was limited to the Wet Jeans case and to two minimal trademark searches. Second, the current litigation, which involves only allegations of infringement of one design element on denim jeans, does not place in issue Revise's "entire background." Thus, background information that a diligent lawyer might obtain about the client upon accepting an engagement does not disqualify that lawyer from subsequently representing an adverse party unless that information is central to the claims in the later matter. *Compare Applied Technology*, 2009 WL 804127, at *7 (facts regarding former client's business structure not "necessary" to counterclaims in later litigation) *with United States Football League*, 605 F.Supp. at 1460 ("attorney's knowledge of the business plans, economic organization, prospective market position and other such background information" found relevant to subsequent antitrust litigation where moving party's market behavior was an essential issue). Here, information about Revise's business infrastructure is extraneous to the narrow trademark claims in this lawsuit.

Revise places great reliance on *Miroglio, s.p.a. v. Morgan Fabrics Corp.*, 340 F.Supp.2d 510 (S.D.N.Y.2004), a case in which counsel who had represented one party in three prior copyright matters was disqualified from representing an adverse party in a subsequent action alleging infringement of a design for fabric. *Id.* at 511. There, however, counsel learned very specific information about the first client that could have been used against it in the later case:

> The three copyright issues on which [the lawyer] recently represented [the former client] related specifically to fabric designs. . . . In order to competently represent [the former client] on these issues, a reasonable attorney would be expected to acquire a minimum base of knowledge about how [the former client] goes about creating designs. The degree of originality required before a fabric design becomes copyrightable and the extent of copying of a fabric design that constitutes infringement were questions within the scope of the prior representation and are issues that are likely to arise in this litigation.

Id. at 513. In *Miroglio,* then, the prior and current representations were closely related because both involved copyrights for fabric design. That is a far cry from this case, where the previous litigation concerned a trademark name that Revise owns and the current litigation involves Joe's Jeans' trademark for a stitching design.

Revise, therefore, has failed to demonstrate that Pryor Cashman's prior representation of it is substantially related to the instant case. Consequently, there is no presumption that the firm obtained relevant confidential information in the course of the earlier litigation.

    b.   *Access to Confidential Information*

The presumption is a substitute for proof: it "arises in order to forestall a direct inquiry into whether confidential information was in fact transmitted by the client." *United States Football League,* 605 F.Supp. at 1461. Accordingly,

> in order to grant a disqualification motion, a court should not require proof that an attorney actually had access to or received privileged information while representing the client in a prior case. Such a requirement would put the former client to the Hobson's choice of either having to disclose the privileged information in order to disqualify his former attorney or having to refrain from the disqualification motion altogether.

Government of India, 569 F.2d at 740 (citations omitted). However, a moving party that is unable to demonstrate a substantial relationship between prior and current matters should not be foreclosed from showing that its former attorney actually received confidential information that may now be used against it. *See Hickman,* 371 F.Supp.2d at 231 ("The failure to prove a substantial relationship between the earlier and present litigation destroys any presumption of relevant shared confidences and Defendants' papers point to no particular instance of any such confidence."); *Matthews,* 902 F.Supp. at 31 (noting invitation to moving party to submit affidavits specifying confidential information allegedly disclosed). Revise was given such an opportunity here. Moreover, the transcript of the evidentiary hearing was filed under seal so that the parties "could reveal to me *in camera* the full scope of the attorney-client relationship between" Pryor Cashman and Revise. *United States Football League,* 605 F.Supp. at 1462 (utilizing confidentiality order and sealing to permit disclosure of communications to rebut inference that confidential information was revealed in prior representation).

I am not persuaded that Revise actually disclosed relevant confidential information to Pryor Cashman. Revise maintains that Pryor Cashman has implicitly admitted that it received privileged information because it redacted certain documents from the prior representation before submitting them in connection with the instant motion. (Tr. at 40–45, 94–95; Pl. Exh. 2). But this proves nothing. It goes without saying that Pryor Cashman exchanged privileged communications with Revise during the time that it represented Revise in the Wet Jeans matter, including documents discussing legal strategies in that case. But those communications, which obviously are confidential, are not relevant to this litigation and therefore do not give Pryor Cashman an advantage that it could now use against its former client.

Nor do I credit the evidence proffered by Revise that it disclosed detailed business information to Pryor Cashman, were that information to be relevant in this case. Even when assured that the record would be maintained under seal, Mr. Sadiqulla was vague about the specific information allegedly conveyed. He referred to discussing the volume of Revise's business, but did not identify it in any detail. (Tr. at 91). He said he gave Pryor Cashman his company's sales figures, but he did not specify those figures. (Tr. at 91). He testified that he discussed Revise's overhead structure, but he did not say what he told Pryor Cashman about the number of Revise employees or the budget for overhead. (Tr. at 91–92). And, when Mr. Sadiqulla stated that he revealed his company's profit margin to counsel, he admitted that it was only the profit margin on the VANILLA STAR line of merchandise at issue in the Wet Jeans litigation. (Tr. at 92). Furthermore, the details that Mr. Sadiqulla states that he provided to Pryor Cashman are incongruent with what he suggests was a primary purpose of the discussion in the first place: to convince the law firm that Revise had the capacity to pay its legal bills. (Tr. at 89). Finally, if Mr. Sadiqulla had provided Pryor Cashman with confidential information that could be used against Revise, it would have made little sense for Revise to agree that Pryor Cashman could represent Joe's Jeans for purposes even of negotiating a settlement.

Mr. Troy's testimony is similarly open to doubt. Although he testified at the hearing that he had a telephone discussion with Ms. Kaplan on November 14, 2007 that went into the details of Revise's business (Tr. at 174–77), he failed to mention this at all in the declaration he submitted in support of the motion to disqualify. There, he stated only that "[o]n or about November 14, 2007, I turned over all of my pre-litigation files concerning the Wet Jeans matter to Pryor Cashman, and subsequently had no further communication or involvement with Pryor Cashman or Revise concerning the Wet Jeans Matter."

(Troy Decl., ¶ 2). This narrower description of the November 14 discussion is consistent with Ms. Kaplan's testimony, in which she stated that she and Mr. Troy discussed only the history of the communications in the Wet Jeans case. (Tr. at 219–21). It is also more consistent with the e-mail that Mr. Troy himself sent to Ms. Kaplan following their conversation. In that e-mail, he referred only to his communications with the attorneys for Wet Jeans. (Pl. Exh. 7).

Thus, with neither the benefit of a presumption that Pryor Cashman had access to confidential information nor proof that such information was actually communicated, Revise's motion for disqualification must be rejected. *Conclusion*

For the reasons discussed above, the motion by Joe's Jeans to strike the reply affidavit of Mr. Sadiqulla is denied, but its alternative application that I consider its surreply is granted. Revise's motion to disqualify the firm of Pryor Cashman as counsel for Joe's Jeans is denied.

SO ORDERED.

SOLUTIONS: THE LAWYER SHOULD HAVE, WOULD HAVE, COULD HAVE. . .

Lawyers can take a valuable lesson from this case; namely, the best way to make clear that an ACR is completed is (a) set out clearly the scope of the representation in the original engagement letter and (b) send a notice to the client explaining that the ACR is completed. Subsequent marketing activities with the client—such as inviting the client to a seminar or sending a newsletter is not inconsistent with the end of the ACR.

Scenario No. 1: The Case of the Withdrawing Lawyer v. the Unmovable Judge and the Winner Is . . .

Joe Lawyer represents Patty Client in a lawsuit pending in state court. Patty makes numerous demands on Joe that are unreasonable and arguably in violation of some of the Model Rules. Joe Lawyer asks the court for permission to withdraw from representation and argues that no material prejudice will befall the client because discovery is in its initial stages and no trial date has been set. The trial judge denies the motion. Joe has no recourse because courts have the inherent power to control their dockets.

Scenario No. 2: The Case of the Hopeful Lawyer

Jill Wong is a lawyer at Wong & Wong, Attorneys and Counselors at Law. Jill recently completed a patent registration for Esteban Garcia, a client who is a brilliant scientist. Jill sent him a letter saying that she was closing the file, wishing him well, and asking that she and her firm be considered for future work from him. A grateful Esteban writes back "I certainly will. You are the first I will consider! I promise!" From time-to-time Jill sends him an update on patent law matters that she and her firm send to certain clients. Additionally, she writes comments on developments he should generally be aware of. Is there a continuous ACR? No. The matter was completed, and Jill's conduct objectively makes that clear; an aspiration of future business, without *more*, does not create an ACR.

Section 10. Model Rule 1.3: Diligence Post ACR

MR 1.3 on diligence interacts with MR 1.16. Note that the language of MR 1.3 itself is very brief: "(a) lawyer shall act with reasonable diligence and promptness in representing a client." Comment (4) to the rule states that unless the relationship is terminated as provided in MR 1.16, a lawyer should carry through to conclusion all matters undertaken for a client." This may seem like a simply applied test but not always as we will discuss in the first case below, *Barnes v. Turner*. Moreover, are there circumstances in which the lawyer has represented the client over several years in varying matters but has not performed any legal work recently? ACR or no ACR? The comment points out that a client may assume that the lawyer is serving on a continuing basis. The only exception is if the lawyer gives notice that the ACR has ended. It is not up to the client to ask as to whether it is over, but rather up to the lawyer to inform the client. Just as with Mrs. Togstad who had no affirmative duty to check back with Mr. Miller; as with formation of the ACR, so too with dissolution.

Model Rule 1.3: Diligence

A lawyer shall act with reasonable diligence and promptness in representing a client.

Comment to MR 1.3:

[1]   A lawyer should pursue a matter on behalf of a client despite opposition, obstruction or personal inconvenience to the lawyer, and take whatever lawful and ethical measures are required to vindicate a client's cause or endeavor. A lawyer must also act with commitment and dedication to the interests of the client and with zeal in advocacy

upon the client's behalf. A lawyer is not bound, however, to press for every advantage that might be realized for a client. For example, a lawyer may have authority to exercise professional discretion in determining the means by which a matter should be pursued. See Rule 1.2. The lawyer's duty to act with reasonable diligence does not require the use of offensive tactics or preclude the treating of all persons involved in the legal process with courtesy and respect.

[2]   A lawyer's workload must be controlled so that each matter can be handled competently.

[3]   Perhaps no professional shortcoming is more widely resented than procrastination. A client's interests often can be adversely affected by the passage of time or the change of conditions; in extreme instances, as when a lawyer overlooks a statute of limitations, the client's legal position may be destroyed. Even when the client's interests are not affected in substance, however, unreasonable delay can cause a client needless anxiety and undermine confidence in the lawyer's trustworthiness. A lawyer's duty to act with reasonable promptness, however, does not preclude the lawyer from agreeing to a reasonable request for a postponement that will not prejudice the lawyer's client.

[4]   Unless the relationship is terminated as provided in Rule 1.16, a lawyer should carry through to conclusion all matters undertaken for a client. If a lawyer's employment is limited to a specific matter, the relationship terminates when the matter has been resolved. If a lawyer has served a client over a substantial period in a variety of matters, the client sometimes may assume that the lawyer will continue to serve on a continuing basis unless the lawyer gives notice of withdrawal. Doubt about whether a client-lawyer relationship still exists should be clarified by the lawyer, preferably in writing, so that the client will not mistakenly suppose the lawyer is looking after the client's affairs when the lawyer has ceased to do so. For example, if a lawyer has handled a judicial or administrative proceeding that produced a result adverse to the client and the lawyer and the client have not agreed that the lawyer will handle the matter on appeal, the lawyer must consult with the client about the possibility of appeal before relinquishing responsibility for the matter. See Rule 1.4(a)(2). Whether the lawyer is obligated to prosecute the appeal for the client depends on the scope

of the representation the lawyer has agreed to provide to the client. See Rule 1.2.

[5] To prevent neglect of client matters in the event of a sole practitioner's death or disability, the duty of diligence may require that each sole practitioner prepare a plan, in conformity with applicable rules, that designates another competent lawyer to review client files, notify each client of the lawyer's death or disability, and determine whether there is a need for immediate protective action. Cf. Rule 28 of the American Bar Association Model Rules for Lawyer Disciplinary Enforcement (providing for court appointment of a lawyer to inventory files and take other protective action in absence of a plan providing for another lawyer to protect the interests of the clients of a deceased or disabled lawyer).

Cases and Materials

X-Ray Questions (*Barnes*)

In this transactional case, a lawyer represented a client who sold a business. The purchase price was paid out over time and was secured with an IOU and a blanket lien on the buyer's assets. The lien had to be renewed every five years or it lapsed. The lawyer failed to renew the lien; the buyer went belly up; and the seller therefore had no security interest in the remaining balance owed on the purchase price. A malpractice lawsuit followed alleging that the lawyer was negligent in failing to renew the lien.

As you read this case, recall 1L Torts. To sue in negligence, which is the essence of a malpractice case, there must first be a duty and that duty must be breached, causing damages. How does the court reason out that there was a beached duty to the client? Why did the lawyer fail to act? Perhaps it was a lack of competence or one of diligence? Is this not the mirror image of *Togstad*, with this lawyer walking around every day with a ticking time bomb of an ongoing ACR without a clue that he has one ticking away? What can a lawyer do to avoid this predicament?

Barnes, et al. v. Turner

Supreme Court of Georgia, 2004.
278 Ga. 788.

FLETCHER, CHIEF JUSTICE.

The issue in this legal malpractice case is what duty attorney David Turner, Jr. owed his client, William Barnes, Jr., with respect to maintaining Barnes's security interest that lapsed. The Court of Appeals held that Turner's only duty was to inform Barnes that his security interest required renewal in five years. Because under that view the statute of limitations expired before Barnes filed his malpractice action, the Court of Appeals affirmed the trial court's decision to grant Turner's motion to dismiss. We conclude, however, that if Turner failed to inform Barnes of the renewal requirement, Turner undertook a duty to renew the security interest himself. The statute of limitations has not expired for an alleged breach of that duty, and therefore we reverse.

On October 1, 1996, Barnes sold his company, William Barnes' Quality Auto Parts, Inc., to James and Rhonda Lipp for $220,000. The Lipps paid $40,000 at the closing and executed a ten-year promissory note in favor of Barnes for the $180,000 balance. The note was secured by a blanket lien on the Lipps's assets. On October 30, 1996, Turner perfected Barnes's security interest by filing UCC financing statements. Viewing the facts in the light most favorable to Barnes (as the non-moving party), Turner did not, however, inform Barnes that under OCGA § 11–9–515, financing statements are only effective for five years, although their renewal for another five years is expressly provided for in that statute. The renewal is affected by filing continuation statements no earlier than six months before the end of the initial period. No renewal statements were filed, and on October 30, 2001, the original statements lapsed.

Unknown to Barnes, the Lipps had pledged the same collateral to F&M Bank and Trust Company and to Mid-State Automotive Distributors on December 28, 1998, and January 29, 2001, respectively. Both of these companies filed UCC financing statements, which put them in a senior position to Barnes when his financing statements lapsed. Barnes is still owed more than $142,792.09 under the promissory note, and James Lipp is now in Chapter 7 bankruptcy.

Barnes sued Turner for malpractice on October 18, 2002. The trial court granted Turner's motion to dismiss. Finding that the only possible incident of malpractice was Turner's failure to inform Barnes of the renewal requirement in

October 1996, the Court of Appeals held that the four-year statute of limitations had run and affirmed the trial court. We granted Barnes's petition for certiorari.

Barnes contends that the Court of Appeals erred in simply looking to Turner's actions in October 1996 as constituting the malpractice. If Turner had renewed the financing statements in 2001, Barnes argues, there would have been no lapse in his security interest and thus no malpractice. Barnes contends that Turner's duty was to safeguard his security interest, which Turner could have satisfied by *either* informing Barnes of the renewal requirement or renewing the financing statements in 2001. Under this view, Turner breached his duty in 2001, when he failed to do both, and thus the statute of limitations on Barnes's action has not expired. For the following reasons, we agree.

A motion to dismiss should only be granted if "the allegations of the complaint, when construed in the light most favorable to the plaintiff with all doubts resolved in the plaintiff's favor, disclose with certainty that the plaintiff would not be entitled to relief under any state of provable facts." Accordingly, the grant of Turner's motion to dismiss was only proper if Barnes's duty ended in 1996.

Turner contends that he was not retained to file renewal statements. While Georgia's appellate courts have not previously addressed this issue, decisions from other states make clear that an attorney in Turner's position must at least file original UCC financing statements, even absent specific direction from the client. We agree. An attorney has the duty to act with ordinary care, skill, and diligence in representing his client. In sale of business transactions where the purchase price is to be paid overtime and collateralized, it is paramount that the seller's attorney prepare and file UCC financing statements to perfect his client's security interest. We further hold, for the reasons given below, that if the financing statements require renewal before full payment is made to the seller, then the attorney has some duty regarding this renewal. Otherwise, the unpaid portion of the purchase price becomes unsecured and the seller did not receive the protection he bargained for.

Safeguarding a security interest is not some unexpected duty imposed upon the unwitting lawyer; it goes to the very heart of why Turner was retained: to sell Barnes's business in exchange for payment. We do not, as the dissent contends, demand that the lawyer "ascertain the full extent of the client's 'objectives' "; only that the lawyer take reasonable, legal steps to fulfill the client's *main, known* objective—to be paid for the business he sold.

The dissent views only the sale of the business as important since this is what happens at the closing; but why does a client sell his business if not to receive payment? When the dissent argues that Turner's duty was simply to "close" the transaction, it fails to recognize that closing this particular transaction meant taking the reasonable steps that competent attorneys would take to legally secure their clients' right to receive payment for the businesses they have sold. Where payment is to be made in less than five years, Georgia law does not require renewal of the initial financing statements and thus the lawyer's duty is only to file the initial statements. But where payment is to take longer than five years, the lawyer—being trusted by his client to know how to safeguard his security interest under Georgia law—has some duty regarding renewal of the financing statements. The question is the nature of that duty.

Under the dissent's view, a client has to specifically ask his lawyer to renew the financing statements for this to be among the lawyer's duties. But how can the client be expected to know of this legal requirement? He hires the lawyer because the lawyer knows the law. The client cannot be expected to explicitly ask the lawyer to engage in every task necessary to fulfill the client's objectives.

The Court of Appeals held that a failure to inform by Turner was the sole possible grounds for malpractice. But this is too narrow a definition of Turner's duty. The duty was not necessarily to inform Barnes of the renewal requirement; often transactional attorneys do no such thing and simply renew the financing statements themselves. These attorneys have not breached a duty. Turner's duty was to safeguard Barnes's security interest. There were two means of doing so: by informing Barnes of the renewal requirement, or by renewing the financing statements himself in 2001. Either one would have been sufficient to comply with Turner's duty, and any breach of that duty occurred only upon Turner's failure to do both.

Further, if Turner's only duty arose in 1996, then Barnes had to bring suit before the financing statements could even be renewed to comply with the four-year statute of limitations. Barnes contends that any such action would have been dismissed as unripe because he was still a secured party at the time. He is correct. The dissent's view deprives Barnes and any clients in his position of any remedy for malpractice. The dissent's view precludes Barnes from ever maintaining a malpractice suit against Turner, who failed to take a simple, necessary action that will likely leave Barnes without his business and without over 78% of the purchase price he is still owed for that business.

The dissent's hyberbole about the effect of this opinion mischaracterizes our holding, which is based on a unique set of facts: a collateralized, payment-over-time arrangement in exchange for a sale of business where the payment period exceeds the five-year life span afforded to initial financing statements under OCGA § 11–9–515. The lawyer, being retained to protect his client's interests in connection with the sale of his business, is the only party who knows the legal requirements for maintaining the effectiveness of the security interest. He can either share this knowledge with his client—a very simple step—or renew the financing statements before they expire—an equally simple step. The dissent's concern over the expansion of attorney duties is unwarranted.

The dissent also argues that imposing a duty to renew on Turner is an adoption of the "continuous representation rule," which Georgia courts have rejected except in personal injury cases. Under this rule, a continuing relationship or continuing wrong can toll the statute of limitations. In the case cited by the dissent, *Hunter, Maclean, Exley & Dunn, P.C. v. Frame*, the alleged malpractice was only that material financial information was omitted from the closing documents; there was not, as in the present case, some further action beyond the closing at issue, and thus *Hunter, Maclean* is inapposite to our situation. The continuous representation rule is not implicated in this case. We are *not* holding that a failure to inform by Turner in 1996 was a continuing wrong that tolled the statute of limitations until 2001. To the contrary, we are holding that a failure to inform in 1996 means that Turner undertook a duty to renew in 2001, and the statute of limitations began running from the date of alleged breach of *that* duty.

In light of the foregoing considerations, we reverse the Court of Appeals's decision that affirmed the trial court's grant of Turner's motion to dismiss. Barnes's malpractice action was filed within four years of the failure to renew the financing statements in 2001, and thus may proceed.

Judgment reversed.

SOLUTIONS: THE LAWYER SHOULD HAVE, WOULD HAVE, COULD HAVE...

This case could have been avoided with more open communication between the lawyer and the client. Go back to MR 1.4(a)(2) and the duty to "reasonably consult with the client about the means by which the client's objectives are to be accomplished." This encompasses the client receiving the full purchase price, not just as to the means legally (a secured IOU) by which this goal will be accomplished but also the mechanism by which it will be accomplished. (Renewal of the lien). Additionally, while the practice of law is

> an art, it is also a science. Thus, consider drafting checklists for transactions (as well as litigation matters) so that all key tasks are accounted for.

Becoming a Professional: Part 1

At this juncture in the book, we wanted to pause and ask you to engage in the following exercise: read and consider these common challenges confronted by a new lawyer; pick out the three that you believe will pose the greatest challenges for you; explain why this is the case and what you will do to meet the challenges.

BEYOND THE CITE

By: James R. Howie & Melissa Miller: *Ten Mistakes You Don't Want to Make in You First Five Years of Law Practice* (As edited).

The novelty and stress that come along with the first five years of a new lawyer's practice can provide a perfect breeding ground for simple mistakes. Bad habits and practices can grow to haunt you as you continue to develop as a lawyer. As most lawyers know, reputation is everything—among judges and masters, opposing counsel, and potential new clients and co-workers. The following are some common mistakes made by lawyers in their first five years of practice, along with some tips on how, and why, to avoid them.

Some things are obvious so we will not spend much time on them. Actively avoid lying. Fight hard but fight fair. Don't promise what you cannot, or won't, deliver. Enjoy your life outside the law, and if you don't have a life, get one!

1.   *Not Knowing When to Ask for Help*

A failure to communicate limits and availability regarding workload can lead to missed deadlines and a failure to meet expectations of colleagues and clients. This can, in turn, create a reputation of poor work ethic and unreliability different tasks.

2.   *Being Afraid to Admit a Mistake*

Everyone makes mistakes. It is your ability to handle those mistakes that determines your ability to be a good lawyer. Most mistakes can be fixed, but many can become bigger problems if left too long out of embarrassment or fear. Attempts to hide a mistake can potentially negate your malpractice coverage.

3. *Relying Too Heavily on Your Firm*

Your firm is there to provide an overarching support system. But lawyers have a law license not a firm.

4. *Inappropriate Behavior Outside of Work*

We have all heard the urban legends about new lawyers doing crazy and inappropriate things at functions in and outside of work. They make interesting stories and most of us do not think of ourselves as being capable of such things. But it is possible we will lapse is it not?

5. *Gossip*

The legal world is a small one and you never know when you will meet someone in a different context later on in your career. Assistants can become lawyers and lawyers can move firms. Gossip is toxic and can burn bridges fast.

6. *Unwillingness to Accept Criticism*

This frequent mistake is related to not knowing when to ask for help. All of us as new lawyers yearn to prove ourselves as lawyers and receiving criticism can seem harsh and discouraging. A failure to accept useful criticism can make you appear unwilling to learn to be better. That being said, not every senior lawyer, or client for that matter, knows how to best hand out criticisms.

7. *Ignoring Business Development*

Business development is for partners—False. Business development is for any lawyer who wants to make partner—True.

Yes, the partners bring in the most business and files. However, the skills that partners use to bring in business and files do not spontaneously develop the day you become a partner. Sustaining relationships with alumni, networking, following-up and "putting yourself out there," are important skills to learn and practice right from the beginning. It can take years to build a solid client or referral base. Being a good lawyer is not worth very much if you do not have any clients to work for.

8.   *Not Reading the Law*

The law is ever evolving. And, it evolves fast. Graduating from law school is not the end of your education, but rather the start of your education.

9.   *Inaccurate Docketing of Time*

All the good work that you do is only half of the equation. You must accurately record your time and send out resulting bill/invoice in order for you to be paid.

10.   *Procrastinating*

All-nighters cramming for exams may work for some in law school, but this never works well in practice. The longer you leave something, the more panic-inducing it can become. In a career that carries inherent stress along with it, minimizing that stress is key to longevity, and affects personal as well as professional success.

As discussed above, it is important to communicate with your colleagues, your client and your staff about prioritizing tasks and files. In doing so, it is helpful to abide by the chart on the right to sort the stacks of paper on your desk (or the growing inbox in your email or electronic mailbox):

Many lawyers practice in the first quadrant. This leads to high stress and burn out. It is preferable to always be dealing with the second quadrant— important, but not urgent. This is not reality, but is at least something to strive towards. It is at least helpful to prioritize, which makes the to-do list a little more manageable. The biggest waste of time is spending too much effort in the third quadrant. These unimportant items end up on our short list, but could have been dealt with either by delegating, setting up time slots in advance to deal with emails, phone calls, etc., or failing to prioritize tasks at an earlier stage.

11.   *"I was only trying to help"*

Many of you became lawyers because you have a deep seated and sincere desire to help other people. But the inability to say "no" can lead a lawyer into the inadvertent formation of an ACR or even proving incorrect or guidance to a person. While the sentiment is admirable it is also very hazardous.

Conclusion

> The first five years of practice mold who you are as a lawyer. It is, therefore, important to ensure that you develop good habits that carry you forward into the future. The first step in developing these good habits could be realizing which of the above mistakes you may be making, and taking steps to avoid those errors. Your clients and colleagues will thank you, and your future will be much better for it.

Becoming a Professional: Part 2

Nancy Lawyer represents Lola Client. Lola was moderately injured (sore back, some days off at work) resulting from a rear end collision caused by Pete. Nancy writes a demand letter to Pete's insurance company suggesting pre-suit mediation. Emmy Lawyer has been appointed by the insurance company to represent Pete. The mediation is agreed upon. Emmy comes into possession though of a doctor's report about Lola that Nancy is unaware of. This is what it says:

> One thing that bothers me about Lola's health is that while she is an otherwise healthy 24-year-old, she has an aneurysm which is a dilation of the aorta. I do not know if this came out of the accident. I cannot make firm predictions on how it will develop, but it might rupture with further dilation and could cause death. As I said, it is hard to make predictions, but death would be in the realm of possibility.

The insurance company and Pete tell Emmy to reveal the report. Recall this is a pre-suit mediation and so no compulsory pre-trial disclosures have not kicked in, and to settle it on the cheap. The adjuster at the insurance company tells Emmy: "That Nancy has the reputation as an ambulance chaser, and she will make a big deal out of this aneurysm! What a drama queen!" Emmy comes to you under MR 1.6(b)(4) for ethical advice. Is there anything more you want to know? What advice do you give her?

WHAT'S NEXT?

Litigation is divided into various stages for the practicing lawyer: early considerations; discovery; trial. You will deal with specific ethical issues in each stage. You will be pulled in conflicting directions. By way of example, your ethical duty of zealous representation to your client will be in tension with your ethical duty to preserve the integrity of the legal system. There is also an overarching duty to ensure that the litigants—your client and the party opposite—compete on an even playing field so that the ensuing fight is a fair one.

> To assess your understanding of the material in this chapter, click here to take a quiz.

PART III

The Lawyer Before Trial

CHAPTER 5

Claim Commencement/
Early Considerations

Coming Attractions

An ACR is formed. The lawyer has learned the client's problem, helped the client decide goals, and develops a strategy to achieve them. But while the lawyer must advocate with zeal for the client, the lawyer must simultaneously protect the integrity of the legal system in which the matter is being litigated. There is an undeniable tension between these two obligations. That is the focus of this chapter.

We start where all litigation considerations start: Deciding whether a claim should be filed, or a defense asserted, in the first place. We will examine how to determine when a claim or assertion is frivolous and should not be made. And we will look as well at determining when a Motion to Disqualify counsel opposite should be made. This decision, as we discussed earlier in the *Skybell* case, is generally made at the outset of a lawsuit.

As you read the cases and materials, imagine yourself as the lawyer making these early decisions. How would you decide what to do? Can you feel the tension between competing obligations? Ask yourself: why are these decisions difficult?

Section 1.   Frivolous Claims

Model Rule 3.1: Meritorious Claims and Contentions

A lawyer shall not bring or defend a proceeding, or assert or controvert an issue therein, unless there is a basis in law and fact for doing so that is not frivolous, which includes a good faith argument for an extension, modification or reversal of existing law. A lawyer for the defendant in a criminal proceeding, or the respondent in a proceeding that could result in incarceration, may nevertheless so defend the proceeding as to require that every element of the case be established.

Model Rule 2.1: Advisor

In representing a client, a lawyer shall exercise independent professional judgment and render candid advice. In rendering advice, a lawyer may refer not only to law but to other considerations such as moral, economic, social and political factors, that may be relevant to the client's situation.

Model Rule 1.2(d): Scope of Representation and Allocation of Authority Between Client and Lawyer

A lawyer . . .(may) counsel or assist a client to make a good faith effort to determine the validity, scope, meaning or application of the law.

Deconstruction Exercise/Rule Rationale

These three rules need be understood in tandem. Lawyers are not mere legal technicians as MR 2.1 makes clear—we are counselors and advisors as well. In performing this role, we do not simply carry out our client's instructions, especially if unfounded or baseless. We render "candid" advice and use our independent judgment in doing so. The drafters could have modified "advice" with "professional" or "legal" or "adequate", but they chose the word "candid." Why? It sends the message that lawyers must give advice that is frank, straightforward, and direct. Sometimes the client needs to be told that a claim is frivolous and cannot be asserted. Euphemistic phrasing or indirect communication will not always adequately deliver the message. But the question remains: what constitutes a frivolous claim or defense? Clients are entitled to assert a claim or a defense if there is some arguable basis to do so. Comment 2 to MR 3.1 sheds light on the analysis:

> The filing of an action or defense or similar action taken for a client is not frivolous merely because the facts have not first been fully substantiated or because the lawyer expects to develop vital evidence only by discovery. What is required of lawyers, however, is that they inform themselves about the facts of their clients' cases and the applicable law and determine that they can make good faith arguments in support of their clients' positions. Such action is not frivolous even though the lawyer believes that the client's position ultimately will not prevail. The action is frivolous, however, if the lawyer is unable either to make a good faith argument on the merits of the action taken or to support the action taken by a good faith argument for an extension, modification or reversal of existing law.

Finally, the purpose of MR 1.2(d) is to allow a lawyer to counsel a client to disobey a law in order to provide standing in order to challenge its legality. This provision provides a safe-harbor in which a lawyer can ethically assert such a claim.

LEANING INTO PRACTICE

Scenario No. 1: The Case of the Client Who Won't Let Go

Kelli Client seeks to retain a lawyer to challenge the validity of the 16th Amendment to the United States Constitution, which empowers Congress to set a federal income tax. This matter has been litigated many times since the amendment become operative in 1913; all challenges have failed. No new legal analysis has been developed to analyze the issue of constitutionality. Should a lawyer assert an argument that Kelli need not pay her federal income taxes because the amendment is unconstitutional?

Scenario No. 2: The Case of the Morally Odious Ruling

You are a lawyer in 1900. *Plessy* is the law of the land. A prospective client seeks to file a lawsuit that would racially integrate a school district. Assuming MR 3.1 is applicable, can you ethically take on the case and file the lawsuit? What if there was no Rule? Same answer?

Do you recall from your Con Law class the basis upon which the Court relied in overturning *Plessy* in the *Brown* decision? How does your knowledge from 1L Civ Pro on 12(b)(6) motions factor into your answer.

Cases and Materials

X-Ray Questions (*Neely*)

The lawyers here lost their client's case on summary judgment. The lawyers were then sanctioned by the West Virginia Bar because one of the factual paragraphs in their original complaint ended up being unsupported by any evidence. The state's Supreme Court thought there was no violation. Why? As you read the case, think about the undeniable tension between discouraging claims without a factual or legal basis and the value of allowing a case to begin without all the facts being necessarily known. Is it ever practical to require that a litigant have 100% certainty on all aspects of their case or defense from the start? What would be the effect of such a rule? Do you see that an assertion can be made in good faith and that many of the supporting facts will be developed in discovery? How does your knowledge from your first-year civil procedure class on rule 12(b)(6) factor into your answer?

Lawyer Disciplinary Board v. Richard F. Neely and Roger D. Hunter

Supreme Court of Appeals of West Virginia, 1998.
207 W.Va. 21.

PER CURIAM:

This disciplinary proceeding was instituted by the complainant, Office of Disciplinary Counsel [hereinafter "ODC"] of the West Virginia State Bar against Roger D. Hunter and Richard F. Neely, members of the Bar. Mr. Hunter and Mr. Neely were charged with violating Rule 3.1 of the West Virginia Rules of Professional Conduct. Mr. Neely was also charged with violating Rule 4.4.

However, the Lawyer Disciplinary Board [hereinafter "Board"] found that the ODC only proved that Mr. Hunter and Mr. Neely violated Rule 3.1. The Board recommends admonishment. Based upon our review of the recommendation, all matters of record, and the briefs and argument of counsel, we disagree with the Board's recommendation, and we find that the complaint against Mr. Hunter and Mr. Neely should be dismissed.

I

The proceeding against Mr. Hunter and Mr. Neely involved their representation of Linda and Quewanncoii Stephens. Mr. and Mrs. Stephens have a son, Quinton, who is autistic. In September 1990, when Quinton was approximately nine months old, he was enrolled in the Fort Hill Child Development Center [hereinafter Center].

On December 2, 1994, Mrs. Stephens received a phone call from a staff member at the Center asking her to pick up Quinton because the day care employee who was responsible for his supervision was not at work, and Quinton was disrupting the other children during nap time. When Mrs. Stephens arrived at the Center, she found Quinton alone in the director's office strapped to a posture correcting chair, which she had provided, with his hands and face covered with partly-dried fecal material. According to Mrs. Stephens, the room was dark and the blinds were drawn. The employee who had been watching Quinton claimed that she left him alone for about ninety seconds to get a change of diaper for him. Mrs. Stephens immediately removed Quinton from the Center, and shortly thereafter, she and her husband consulted with Mr. Hunter, who was then practicing law with the law firm of Bowles, Rice, McDavid, Graff and Love.

After meeting with the Stephenses, Mr. Hunter wrote a letter to Jean Hawks, the Center's director and owner, and asked that she have her liability carrier contact him promptly. Mr. Hunter also sent letters of complaint to the state Child Protective Services and the federal Office of Civil Rights. Child Protective Services investigated the matter and concluded that Quinton had not been maltreated because he had been watched by an employee of the Center during the forty-five minutes it took Mrs. Stephens to arrive at the Center. The employee had only left Quinton alone for ninety seconds when she went to get a diaper.

Subsequently, Mr. Hunter left the law firm of Bowles, Rice, McDavid, Graff and Love and became a partner of Neely & Hunter. Mr. Hunter took the Stephens' case with him, and Mr. Neely took the lead in preparing the pleadings and handling of the case. On June 12, 1995, Mr. Neely filed a civil action in the name of Linda, Quewanncoii, and Quinton Stephens against the Center and Ms. Hawks.

The complaint alleged that Mr. and Mrs. Stephens and Quinton had suffered intentional infliction of emotional distress based upon the outrageous conduct of the defendants and that Quinton had suffered damages from an intentional battery on December 2, 1994. The complaint further alleged that as a result of interviews with persons associated with the Center, the plaintiffs believed that the December 2, 1994 incident was "but one of many instances in which an autistic child, known to have special needs, in direct contravention of the expressed direction of his parents and of his health care providers, knowingly and willfully and intentionally was strapped to a chair in a dark room for many hours and left alone as a result of his mental and physical handicap." The damages clause asked for $1,500,000.00 in compensatory damages and $1,500,000.00 in punitive damages.

Thereafter, Mr. Hunter submitted answers to interrogatories on behalf of the plaintiffs listing the names of several individuals who served as the basis for the allegation that Quinton had in many instances been left alone in a dark room for many hours. However, none of the individuals testified to such incidents during discovery.

On December 11, 1995, the defendants moved for summary judgment. The court dismissed Mr. and Mrs. Stephens causes of action for intentional infliction of emotional distress. The court also dismissed Quinton's claim for intentional infliction of emotional distress for the "many instances" in which he was allegedly strapped in a chair in a dark room for many hours. This claim was dismissed because the only evidence plaintiffs produced during discovery was the testimony of Mary Ellen Davis, Quinton's special education teacher, that one day she found Quinton in the chair in his classroom when all the other children were up and about in the same room. Finally, the claim for punitive damages was dismissed for being duplicative of the claim for damages from intentional infliction of emotional distress. Only Quinton's claim for intentional infliction of emotional distress was permitted to go forward.

Subsequently, the plaintiffs requested a voluntary dismissal of the remaining claim in order to appeal the summary judgment order. The defendants then filed a motion for sanctions under Rule 11 of the West Virginia Rules of Civil Procedure. Thereafter, the parties reached an agreement whereby the plaintiffs agreed to dismiss the appeal and all claims with prejudice in return for the defendants dismissing the Rule 11 motion and agreeing not to seek attorney sanctions against either Mr. Hunter or Mr. Neely.

On March 17, 1997, the Investigative Panel of the Board filed a Statement of Charges in this matter. Mr. Neely was charged with violating Rule 4.4 of the West Virginia Rules of Professional Conduct based on the settlement demand letters he sent to the Center's insurance company. Mr. Neely and Mr. Hunter were both charged with violating Rule 3.1 in that the complaint filed by Mr. Neely asserted emotional distress counts on behalf of Linda and Quewanncoii Stephens, a count of intentional battery on behalf of Quinton Stephens, and a count of emotional distress based on many alleged instances where Quinton had been left alone in a dark room for many hours.

On October 10, 1997, the Hearing Panel Subcommittee issued a report which dismissed the Rule 4.4 charge and by majority vote, found a violation of Rule 3.1 by both Mr. Hunter and Mr. Neely. The Board recommended admonishment.

Thereafter, pursuant to Rules 3.11 and 3.13 of the West Virginia Rules of Lawyer Disciplinary Procedure, Mr. Hunter and Mr. Neely filed a notice of objection to the Hearing Panel Subcommittee Report with this Court.

II

In this proceeding, the Board found a violation of Rule 3.1 based solely on the allegations set forth in paragraph VII of the complaint. The Board concluded that a reasonable attorney should have known that the allegations set forth in paragraph VII were unwarranted and that Mr. Hunter and Mr. Neely knew they were without basis. In reaching this decision, the Board recognized that the entire lawsuit was not baseless or frivolous because Quinton Stephens' intentional tort claim survived the motion for summary judgment. In effect, the

Board seeks to admonish Mr. Hunter and Mr. Neely for factual assertions set forth in a single paragraph of a complaint that later proved to be false.

This case illustrates the difficulties in determining what is a frivolous lawsuit. In COMMITTEE ON LEGAL ETHICS OF THE WEST VIRGINIA STATE BAR V. DOUGLAS, 179 W.Va. 490, 370 S.E.2d 325 (1988), this Court set forth a test to determine whether a lawyer had advanced a frivolous claim. However, the Code of Professional Responsibility was in effect at that time. DR 7–102(A)(2) provided that a lawyer shall not "[k]nowingly advance a claim or defense that is unwarranted under existing law, except that he may advance such claim or defense if it can be supported by good faith argument for an extension, modification, or reversal of existing law." Recognizing that DR 7–102(A)(2) was aimed at frivolousness, this Court set forth a twofold inquiry under the rule. The test first required an objective determination of whether the claim or defense was " 'unwarranted' under the law." A more subjective determination of whether the lawyer asserted the claim or defense with knowledge that it was unwarranted completed the inquiry. DOUGLAS, 179 W.Va. at 500–01, 370 S.E.2d at 335–36 (citations omitted).

With the adoption of the Rules of Professional Conduct, and more specifically Rule 3.1, an objective standard was established to determine the propriety of pleadings and other court papers. Hazard and Hodes, THE LAW OF *Lawyering*, A HANDBOOK ON THE MODEL RULES OF PROFESSIONAL CONDUCT § 3.1:301 (2d ed. 1994 Supp.). Nonetheless, the term "frivolous," now a part of the rule, remains undefined. However, the Comment to the rule is instructive regarding what conduct is permissible and what constitutes frivolousness. The Comment provides, in pertinent part:

> The filing of an action or defense or similar action taken for a client is not frivolous merely because the facts have not first been fully substantiated or because the lawyer expects to develop vital evidence only by discovery. Such action is not frivolous even though the lawyer believes that the client's position ultimately will not prevail. The action is frivolous, however, if the client desires to have the action taken primarily for the purpose of harassing or maliciously injuring a person or if the lawyer is unable either to make a good faith argument on the merits of the action taken or to support the action taken by a good faith argument for an extension, modification or reversal of existing law.

It is obvious that the drafters of the rules acknowledged that when lawyers prepare and file pleadings in civil actions, they routinely make factual allegations in support of their theories of liability and assert defenses in response thereto, some of which ultimately prove to be unsubstantiated. The Comment suggests that these practices do not warrant discipline under Rule 3.1. In fact, federal courts have been reluctant to impose sanctions for such practices under Rule 11.SEE KAMEN V. AMERICAN TELEPHONE & TELEGRAPH CO., 791 F.2d 1006, (2d Cir.1986) (counsel's reliance on his client's assertion that defendant received funding from the United States government making it subject to suit under the Rehabilitation Act of 1973 constituted a reasonable pre-filing inquiry precluding sanctions); KRAEMER V. GRANT COUNTY, 892 F.2d 686 (7th Cir.1990) (sanctions unwarranted where attorney did everything possible to gather information including hiring a private investigator and instituted suit only after hostile attitude of potential defendants made it necessary to use the discovery process to gather additional information).

While we remain concerned about the increasing number of cases that clog our court dockets, we recognize that there are instances where an attorney has exhausted all avenues of pre-suit investigation and needs the tools of discovery to complete factual development of the case. An action or claim is not frivolous if after a reasonable investigation, all the facts have not been first substantiated. A complaint may be filed if evidence is expected to be developed by discovery. A lawyer may not normally be sanctioned for alleging facts in a complaint that are later determined to be untrue.

As previously discussed, the specific allegations in paragraph VII of the Stephens' complaint were not ultimately supported by the facts developed during discovery. Nonetheless, the record indicates that Mr. Hunter and Mr. Neely conducted a reasonable investigation of the case. Because of his autism, Quinton was unable to provide any information about his care at the Center. However, Mrs. Stephens provided the details of what happened on December 2, 1994. In addition, she related at least three other incidents which suggested that the Center may not have been rendering adequate supervision of Quinton. Mrs. Stephens also told Mr. Neely about conversations she had with some of the employees at the Center which caused her to believe that Quinton's posture correcting chair had been used for discipline or management purposes against her specific directions. The record indicates that Mr. Hunter and Mr. Neely received no cooperation from the defendants during their investigation. In the end, they were left with the choice of advising the Stephenses to give up or file the complaint and proceed with discovery. Given these circumstances, we find that Mr. Hunter and Mr. Neely did not violate Rule 3.1.

Accordingly, based on all of the above, the complaint filed against Mr. Hunter and Mr. Neely is dismissed.

Charges dismissed.

SOLUTIONS: THE LAWYER SHOULD HAVE, WOULD HAVE, COULD HAVE. . .

In comparing *Baldwin* and this case, there was due diligence shown by the lawyer in the latter but not in the former. How so? Understand that the Bar, when investigating a complaint against you, will take a "snap-shot" of your conduct, knowledge, and mindset *at the time* that you filed the complaint or interposed your defense. So, ask yourself before you file anything with a court: if this is how my defense will be determined to a grievance then what will my defense consist of? This thought process is called prospective hindsight and is a useful tool in ethical decision making. The technique requires you to imagine a future event in which you are in ethical trouble; and to then imagine, in hindsight, how you should have handled the matter in order to avoid the imagined predicament.

A. Federal Rule of Civil Procedure 11

This rule is one of the mainstays empowering a federal court to impose sanctions upon a lawyer for asserting a frivolous claim or defense.

Fed. R. Civ. Pro. 11(b)

By presenting to the court a pleading, written motion, or other paper—whether by signing, filing, submitting, or later advocating it—an attorney or unrepresented party certifies that to the best of the person's knowledge, information, and belief, formed after an inquiry reasonable under the circumstances:

(1) it is not being presented for any *improper purpose*, such as to harass, cause unnecessary delay, or needlessly increase the cost of litigation;

(2) the claims, defenses, and other legal contentions are warranted by existing law or by a *nonfrivolous* argument for extending, modifying, or reversing existing law or for establishing new law;

(3)　the factual contentions have evidentiary support or, if specifically so identified, *will likely have* evidentiary support after a reasonable opportunity for further investigation or discovery; and

(4)　the denials of factual contentions are warranted on the evidence or, if specifically, so identified, are *reasonably* based on belief or a lack of information.

Fed. R. Civ. Pro. 11(c)

(1)　If, after notice and a reasonable opportunity to respond, the court determines that Rule 11(b) has been violated, the court may impose an appropriate sanction on any attorney, law firm, or party that violated the rule or is responsible for the violation. Absent exceptional circumstances, a law firm must be held jointly responsible for a violation committed by its partner, associate, or employee.

(2)　A motion for sanctions must be made separately from any other motion and must describe the specific conduct that allegedly violates Rule 11(b). The motion must be served under Rule 5, but it must not be filed or be presented to the court if the challenged paper, claim, defense, contention, or denial is withdrawn or appropriately corrected within 21 days after service or within another time the court sets. If warranted, the court may award to the prevailing party the reasonable expenses, including attorney's fees, incurred for the motion.

(3)　On its own, the court may order an attorney, law firm, or party to show cause why conduct specifically described in the order has not violated Rule 11(b).

(4)　A sanction imposed under this rule must be limited to what suffices to deter repetition of the conduct or comparable conduct by others similarly situated. The sanction may include nonmonetary directives; an order to pay a penalty into court; or, if imposed on motion and warranted for effective deterrence, an order directing payment to the movant of part or all of the reasonable attorney's fees and other expenses directly resulting from the violation.

(5)　The court must not impose a monetary sanction:

(A)　against a represented party for violating Rule 11(b)(2); or

(B)　on its own, unless it issued the show-cause order under Rule 11(c)(3) before voluntary dismissal or settlement of the claims made by or against the party that is, or whose attorneys are, to be sanctioned.

(6)   An order imposing a sanction must describe the sanctioned conduct and explain the basis for the sanction.

Deconstruction Exercise/Rule Rationale

Just as with the Model Rules, Rule 11 uses expansive language, especially by baking in the disjunctive "or" in the first two lines. The drafters also expanded the rule's reach to cover "other paper," which is anything that is filed by a lawyer. This is coupled with the language of "later advocating" in order to cover those who did not file the document but who later argue in favor of its contents. Note (3) and how Rule 11 correlates with MR 3.1 when it states that there is no violation if factual assertions made will "likely" (i.e., more probable than not) have support after further investigation or discovery. Finally, consider the 21-day safe harbor provision which allows an alleged wayward litigant to see the light and withdraw the alleged offending paper. Why does the Rule allow this escape hatch? In a word, efficiency. If counsel opposite can convince the lawyer that the argument asserted is without a basis, then time does not need to be wasted and fees incurred in drafting motions to dismiss nor scarce judicial resources expenses in ruling on same.

An important feature of Rule 11 is that in a civil suit it governs the defendant's conduct, not only the plaintiff. A defendant's counsel may not deny factual allegations without a factual basis for the denial. This is a prime example of an ethical rule that demands lawyers prioritize the efficient working of the judicial system over the interests of their clients. For a defendant, it would always be advantageous to make the plaintiff work hard and prove every claim. But the rule mandates that lawyers work to narrow disputes and not force the other party to litigate over assertions the defendant cannot really contest.

But there are caveats. First, this rule applies only to truly factual allegations. Many allegations seem factual, but in fact call for a measure of interpretation. Consider the following two allegations:

A: The defendant's driver's license was expired at the time of the accident.

B: The defendant was driving at an excessive speed.

Allegation A, absent some other factors, seems like something that is simply true or untrue, without being subject to interpretation. As a result, if the defendant's lawyer knows that her client had a suspended license, she cannot deny this allegation. But allegation B is different. Even if the defendant knows she was driving well over the speed limit, "excessive" is still a matter of interpretation. Thus, the rule might not require the defendant to admit this allegation.

Cases and Materials

X-Ray Questions (*Mattel*)

This case should never have been filed. A hefty price tag came with the decision by the lawyer to assert the claim. Why were sanctions imposed under Rule 11? What is it that the defense lawyers did to set up the plaintiff's lawyer to take the fall for having to pay their fees? As you read through the case, sketch out a timeline of events that proved crucial in the court's decision. Also, in reading the case ask yourself why did the appeals court decline to impose additional sanctions?

Harry R. Christian v. Mattel, Inc., et al.

United States Court of Appeals, Ninth Circuit, 2002.
286 F.3d 1118.

McKEOWN, CIRCUIT JUDGE.

It is difficult to imagine that the Barbie doll, so perfect in her sculpture and presentation, and so comfortable in every setting, from "California girl" to "Chief Executive Officer Barbie," could spawn such acrimonious litigation and such egregious conduct on the part of her challenger. In her wildest dreams, Barbie could not have imagined herself in the middle of Rule 11 proceedings. But the intersection of copyrights on Barbie sculptures and the scope of Rule 11 is precisely what defines this case.

James Hicks appeals from a district court order requiring him, pursuant to Federal Rule of Civil Procedure 11, to pay Mattel, Inc. $501,565 in attorneys' fees that it incurred in defending against what the district court determined to be a frivolous action. Hicks brought suit on behalf of Harry Christian, claiming that Mattel's Barbie dolls infringed Christian's Claudene doll sculpture copyright. In its sanctions orders, the district court found that Hicks should have discovered prior to commencing the civil action that Mattel's dolls could not have infringed Christian's copyright because, among other things, the Mattel dolls had been created well prior to the Claudene doll and the Mattel dolls had clearly visible copyright notices on their heads. After determining that Hicks had behaved "boorishly" during discovery and had a lengthy rap sheet of prior litigation misconduct, the district court imposed sanctions.

We hold that the district court did not abuse its discretion in determining that the complaint filed by Hicks was frivolous under Rule 11. In parsing the language of the district court's sanctions orders, however, we cannot determine with any degree of certainty whether the district court grounded its Rule 11 decision on Hicks' misconduct that occurred outside the pleadings, such as in oral argument, at a meeting of counsel, and at a key deposition. This is an important distinction because Rule 11 sanctions are limited to misconduct regarding signed pleadings, motions, and other filings. Fed.R.Civ.P. 11. Consequently, we vacate the district court's orders and remand for further proceedings consistent with this opinion. In so doing, we do not condone Hicks' conduct or suggest that the district court did not have a firm basis for awarding sanctions. Indeed, the district court undertook a careful and exhaustive examination of the facts and the legal underpinnings of the copyright challenge. Rather, the remand is to assure that any Rule 11 sanctions are grounded in conduct covered by Rule 11 and to ensure adequate findings for the sizeable fee award.

BACKGROUND

As context for examining the district court's determination that the underlying copyright action was frivolous, we begin by discussing the long history of litigation between Mattel and Hicks' past and current clients: Harry Christian; Christian's daughter, Claudene; and the Collegiate Doll Company ("CDC"), Claudene's proprietorship.

I.   PRIOR LITIGATION BETWEEN MATTEL AND CDC

Mattel is a toy company that is perhaps best recognized as the manufacturer of the world-famous Barbie doll. Since Barbie's creation in 1959, Mattel has outfitted her in fashions and accessories that have evolved over time. In perhaps the most classic embodiment, Barbie is depicted as a slender-figured doll with long blonde hair and blue eyes. Mattel has sought to protect its intellectual property by registering various Barbie-related copyrights, including copyrights protecting the doll's head sculpture. Mattel has vigorously litigated against putative infringers.

In 1990, Claudene Christian, then an undergraduate student at the University of Southern California ("USC"), decided to create and market a collegiate cheerleader doll. The doll, which the parties refer to throughout their papers as "Claudene," had blonde hair and blue eyes and was outfitted to resemble a USC cheerleader.

Mattel soon learned about the Claudene doll. After concluding that it infringed certain Barbie copyrights, Mattel brought an administrative action before the United States Customs Service in 1996 in which it alleged that the Claudene doll, manufactured abroad, had pirated the head sculpture of the "Teen Talk" and "SuperStar" Barbies. The Customs Service ruled in CDC's favor and subsequently released a shipment of Claudene dolls. Undaunted, Mattel commenced a federal court action in 1997 in which it once again alleged that CDC infringed various of Mattel's copyrights. At the time, Claudene Christian was president of CDC and Harry Christian was listed as co-founder of the company and chief financial officer. CDC retained Hicks as its counsel. After the court dismissed CDC's multiple counterclaims, the case was settled. Mattel released CDC from any copyright infringement liability in exchange for, among other things, a stipulation that Mattel was free to challenge CDC's alleged copyright of the Claudene doll should CDC "or any successor in interest" challenge Mattel's right to market its Barbie dolls.

II. THE PRESENT ACTION

Seizing on a loophole in the parties' settlement agreement, within weeks of the agreement, Harry Christian, who was not a signatory to the agreement, retained Hicks as his counsel and filed a federal court action against Mattel. In the complaint, which Hicks signed, Christian alleged that Mattel obtained a copy of the copyrighted Claudene doll in 1996, the year of its creation,2 and then infringed its overall appearance, including its face paint, by developing a new Barbie line called "Cool Blue" that was substantially similar to Claudene. Christian sought damages in the amount of $2.4 billion and various forms of injunctive relief. In an apparent effort to demonstrate that the action was not a sham, Claudene Christian and CDC were also named as defendants. Subsequently, Hicks alleged in a letter to Mattel's counsel that an additional doll called "Virginia Tech University Barbie" also infringed the Claudene doll copyright. Hicks, however, never amended the complaint to plead allegations about Virginia Tech Barbie.

Two months after the complaint was filed, Mattel moved for summary judgment. In support of its motion, Mattel proffered evidence that the Cool Blue Barbie doll contained a 1991 copyright notice on the back of its head, indicating that it predated Claudene's head sculpture copyright by approximately six years. Mattel therefore argued that Cool Blue Barbie could not as a matter of law infringe Claudene's head sculpture copyright. Mattel similarly contended that the copyright on the Virginia Tech Barbie's head sculpture also significantly predated the purported copyright on the Claudene head sculpture. Virginia Tech

Barbie and other Barbie dolls contained a head sculpture that was copyrighted in 1976 and originally appeared on SuperStar Barbie.

At a follow-up counsel meeting required by a local rule, Mattel's counsel attempted to convince Hicks that his complaint was frivolous. During the videotaped meeting, they presented Hicks with copies of various Barbie dolls that not only had been created prior to 1996 (the date of Claudene's creation), but also had copyright designations on their heads that pre-dated Claudene's creation. Additionally, Mattel's counsel noted that the face paint on some of the earlier-created Barbie dolls was virtually identical to that used on Claudene. Hicks declined Mattel's invitation to inspect the dolls and, later during the meeting, hurled them in disgust from a conference table.

Having been unsuccessful in convincing Hicks to dismiss Christian's action voluntarily, Mattel served Hicks with a motion for Rule 11 sanctions. In its motion papers, Mattel argued, among other things, that Hicks had signed and filed a frivolous complaint based on a legally meritless theory that Mattel's prior-created head sculptures infringed Claudene's 1997 copyright. Hicks declined to withdraw the complaint during the 21-day safe harbor period provided by Rule 11, and Mattel filed its motion.

Seemingly unfazed by Mattel's Rule 11 motion, Hicks proceeded with the litigation and filed a motion pursuant to Federal Rule of Civil Procedure 56(f) to obtain additional discovery. In particular, he sought information regarding the face painting on certain Barbie dolls and the face paint/head sculpture combinations used by Mattel after 1996. The district court summarily denied the motion. It later noted, in the context of its summary judgment order, that "it is unclear what [Christian] is requesting when he seeks access to post-1996 Barbies."

Hicks then began filing additional papers that were characterized by frequency and volume. Following official completion of the summary judgment briefing schedule, Hicks filed what was styled as a "supplemental opposition." In those papers, Christian asserted for the first time that the head sculpture of Mattel's CEO Barbie (which was created in 1998) infringed Christian's copyright in the Claudene doll. He did not, however, move for leave to amend the complaint.

Hicks later filed additional papers alleging that several additional Barbie dolls infringed the Claudene sculpture. As with CEO Barbie, no motion for leave to amend the complaint was filed. Then, following oral argument, Hicks filed a copy of a supplemental registration of Claudene that the United States

Copyright Office had issued five days prior to the argument. The supplemental registration clarified that the nature of the original Claudene copyright "was intended to be the sculpture and the painted face" and that the nature of authorship covered both two-dimensional artwork and three-dimensional sculpture.

III. THE DISTRICT COURT'S ORDERS

The district court granted Mattel's motions for summary judgment and Rule 11 sanctions. The court ruled that Mattel did not infringe the 1997 Claudene copyright because it could not possibly have accessed the Claudene doll at the time it created the head sculptures of the Cool Blue (copyrighted in 1991) and Virginia Tech (copyrighted in 1976) Barbies. The court also rejected Christian's theory that the Mattel dolls had infringed the totality of Claudene's appearance, including its face paint, because the copyright is "limited in scope and extends only to 3-dimensional sculptures and not 2-Dimensional artwork. . . ." Alternatively, the court found that Mattel had been using lighter-colored face paint "on dolls produced before the Claudene doll was created in 1996, such as Colonial Barbie (1994) and Pioneer Barbie (1995)," and therefore could not have infringed the later-created Claudene doll even if the Claudene copyright protected two-dimensional artwork. Finally, the court found that Mattel, as owner of various Barbie head sculpture copyrights, had "the exclusive right to prepare derivative works of its own copyrighted works. See 17 U.S.C. § 106(2). Thus, Mattel has the right to paint and re-paint its own copyrighted sculptures."

In adjudicating the summary judgment motion, the district court did not consider any of Christian's supplemental summary judgment filings. It noted that the papers not only "exceeded the permissible page limits," but also "failed to adhere to Local Rule 3.4.1," which established various type font requirements.

As for Mattel's Rule 11 motion, the district court found that Hicks had "filed a meritless claim against defendant Mattel. A reasonable investigation by Mr. Hicks would have revealed that there was no factual foundation for [Christian's] copyright claim." Indeed, the district court noted that Hicks needed to do little more than examine "the back of the heads of the Barbie dolls he claims were infringing," because such a perfunctory inquiry would have revealed "the pre-1996 copyright notices on the Cool Blue and [Virginia Tech] Barbie doll heads."

Additionally, the district court made other findings regarding Hicks' misconduct in litigating against Mattel, all of which demonstrated that his conduct fell "below the standards of attorneys practicing in the Central District of California." The district court singled out the following conduct:

- Sanctions imposed by the district court against Hicks in a related action against Mattel for failing, among other things, to file a memorandum of law in support of papers styled as a motion to dismiss and failing to appear at oral argument;

- Hicks' behavior during the Early Meeting of Counsel, in which he "toss[ed] Barbie dolls off a table";

- Hicks' interruption of Christian's deposition after Christian made a "damaging admission . . . that a pre-1996 Barbie doll allegedly infringed the later created Claudene doll head. . . ." When asked whether the prior-created Pioneer Barbie doll infringed Claudene, Christian stated, "I think so . . . [b]ecause it's got the look. . . ." At that juncture, Hicks requested an immediate recess, during which he lambasted his client in plain view of Mattel's attorneys and the video camera.

- Hicks' misrepresentations during oral argument on Mattel's summary judgment motion about the number of dolls alleged in the complaint to be infringing and whether he had ever reviewed a particular Barbie catalogue (when a videotape presented to the district court by Mattel demonstrated that Hicks had reviewed it during a deposition);

- Hicks' misstatement of law in a summary judgment opposition brief about the circuit's holdings regarding joint authorship of copyrightable works.

After Mattel submitted a general description of the fees that it incurred in defending against Christian's action, the court requested Mattel to submit a more specific itemization and description of work performed by its attorneys. Mattel complied.

The district court awarded Mattel $501,565 in attorneys' fees. At the outset of its order, the court summarized the findings in its earlier order, namely that it had "predicated its [Rule 11] decision" on Hicks' filing a frivolous complaint and "further found" that he had " 'behaved boorishly, misrepresented the facts and misstated the law.' " In discussing Rule 11's purpose of deterring such conduct, the district court made further findings about Hicks' behavior during prior proceedings—some of which were completely unrelated to this case. The prior litigation referenced by the district court included the following:

- The district court's earlier award of attorneys' fees to Mattel in a related action, and certain behavior by Hicks during the earlier-settled copyright infringement action that Mattel had filed against CDC;

- Hicks' failure to comply with a briefing schedule established by the First Circuit in an unrelated action in 1996; and

- Hicks' filing of conclusory opposition papers in an unrelated action in the Southern District of New York in response to a summary judgment motion in 1986.

The district court next considered various arguments that Hicks had advanced in opposition to Mattel's fee application. Hicks first contended, without much elaboration, that a fee award would have a "ruinous" effect on his finances and ability to practice law. The district court held, however, that "repeated reprimands and sanctions" imposed in prior litigations "clearly have not had the desired deterrent effect on his behavior," and it concluded that Hicks would not be punished sufficiently if the court were to impose mere "non-monetary sanctions." Hicks also argued (somewhat ironically) that Mattel's fees request was excessive in light of how simplistic it should have been to defend against Christian's action. The district court disagreed, reasoning that like the court in *Brandt v. Schal Assocs., Inc.*, 960 F.2d 640, 648 (7th Cir.1992), the judiciary has " 'little sympathy for the litigant who fires a big gun, and when the adversary returns fire, complains because he was firing blanks.' "

Having rejected Hicks' reasons for eschewing a fees award, the district court made the following observations and findings:

The court has considered whether an award of monetary sanctions less than the fees actually incurred would represent an appropriate sanction. The court has concluded that it would not. There is no dispute that Mr. Hicks was directly responsible for filing and pursuing this frivolous suit. Nor is there any dispute that the fees sought were actually incurred and paid. Moreover, the court is satisfied from the documentation provided by Mattel's counsel that the fees incurred were reasonable. While recognizing the significant burden this award imposes, the court has concluded that in light of Mr. Hicks' failure to respond to lesser sanctions and his continuing disregard for the most basic rules governing an attorney's professional conduct, the costs of his unacceptable behavior should fall squarely on him. Finally, while the court may reimburse an adverse party for expenses incurred in disposing of frivolous litigation, it can never compensate the judicial system for the time spent to dispose of an action that should never have been brought. The court can only hope that a sanction of this size will, at last, put a stop to Mr. Hicks' continuing pattern of abuse.

Emphasis added.

* * * * * *

The court is satisfied that the other attorneys' fees Mattel has claimed are both reasonable and proximately caused by Mr. Hicks' pursuit of this frivolous action. [T]he Court grants Mattel its attorneys' fees in the amount of $501,565.00.

Original emphasis.

DISCUSSION

I.   STANDARDS OF REVIEW

The standard of review is particularly important here with reference to the district court's summary judgment determination in favor of Mattel. That order has not been appealed and Christian is not a party to this appeal. Hicks argues that we should review the summary judgment order to determine whether there was a genuine issue of material fact as to whether Mattel infringed Claudene. While such a determination could be instructive in determining whether a complaint was frivolous when filed (because a plaintiff who survives a summary judgment motion would necessarily have demonstrated that there are triable, potentially meritorious issues), we review the district court's factual findings and legal conclusions under a far more deferential standard than the traditional de novo review of a summary judgment order. We review the district court's decision to impose Rule 11 sanctions—and, if they are warranted, the reasonableness of the actual amount imposed—for abuse of discretion. *Cooter & Gell v. Hartmarx Corp.*, 496 U.S. 384, 401, 405, 110 S.Ct. 2447, 110 L.Ed.2d 359 (1990). In conducting our review of the district court's factual findings in support of the sanctions, we "would be justified in concluding that [the court] had abused its discretion in making [the findings] only if [they] were clearly erroneous." *Id.* at 386, 110 S.Ct. 2447. The district court's legal findings must be affirmed unless they result from a "materially incorrect view of the relevant law." *Id.* at 402, 110 S.Ct. 2447.

II.   IMPOSITION OF RULE 11 SANCTIONS

The district court found that Hicks "filed a meritless claim against defendant Mattel. A reasonable investigation by Mr. Hicks would have revealed that there was no factual foundation for plaintiff's copyright claim." Hicks challenges these findings, arguing that the issues were "more complex" than the district court recognized. Before considering this operative issue, we first consider Rule 11 principles that guide our review.

A.   GENERAL RULE 11 PRINCIPLES

Filing a complaint in federal court is no trifling undertaking. An attorney's signature on a complaint is tantamount to a warranty that the complaint is well grounded in fact and "existing law" (or proposes a good faith extension of the existing law) and that it is not filed for an improper purpose.

Rule 11 provides in pertinent part:

(a)   Signature. Every pleading, written motion, and other paper shall be signed by at least one attorney of record in the attorney's individual name. . . .

(b)   Representations to Court. By presenting to the court (whether by signing, filing, submitting, or later advocating) a pleading, written motion, or other paper, an attorney or unrepresented party is certifying to the best of the person's knowledge, information, and belief, formed after an inquiry reasonable under the circumstances . . .

> (2)   the claims, defenses, and other legal contentions therein are warranted by existing law or by a nonfrivolous argument for the extension, modification, or reversal of existing law or the establishment of new law;

> (3)   the allegations and other factual contentions have evidentiary support or, if specifically so identified, are likely to have evidentiary support after a reasonable opportunity for further investigation or discovery[.]

Fed.R.Civ.P. 11.

The attorney has a duty prior to filing a complaint not only to conduct a reasonable factual investigation, but also to perform adequate legal research that confirms whether the theoretical underpinnings of the complaint are "warranted by existing law or a good faith argument for an extension, modification or reversal of existing law." *Golden Eagle Distrib. Corp. v. Burroughs Corp.*, 801 F.2d 1531, 1537 (9th Cir.1986). One of the fundamental purposes of Rule 11 is to "reduce frivolous claims, defenses or motions and to deter costly meritless maneuvers, . . . [thereby] avoid[ing] delay and unnecessary expense in litigation." *Id.* at 1536 (internal quotation marks and citations omitted). Nonetheless, a finding of significant delay or expense is not required under Rule 11. Where, as here, the complaint is the primary focus of Rule 11 proceedings, a district court must conduct a two-prong inquiry to determine (1) whether the complaint is legally or factually "baseless" from an objective perspective, and (2) if the attorney has conducted "a reasonable and competent inquiry" before signing and filing it. *Buster v. Greisen*, 104 F.3d 1186, 1190 (9th Cir.1997).

B. THE DISTRICT COURT'S FINDINGS REGARDING THE MERITLESS CLAIM

1. DID HICKS HAVE AN ADEQUATE LEGAL OR FACTUAL BASIS FOR FILING THE COMPLAINT?

Hicks filed a single claim of copyright infringement against Mattel. The complaint charges that the Cool Blue Barbie infringed the copyright in the Claudene doll head. In addition, in a subsequent letter to Mattel's counsel, he claimed that Virginia Tech Barbie also infringed Claudene. Hicks cannot seriously dispute the district court's conclusions that, assuming the applicability of the doctrine of prior creation, Christian's complaint was legally and factually frivolous. Indeed, as a matter of copyright law, it is well established that a prior-created work cannot infringe a later-created one. See *Grubb v. KMS Patriots, L.P.*, 88 F.3d 1, 5 (1st Cir.1996) (noting that "prior creation renders any conclusion of access or inference of copying illogical.").

Copyright infringement requires proof that a plaintiff owns a valid copyright in the work and that the defendant copied the work. *Feist Pub'n, Inc. v. Rural Tel. Serv. Co., Inc.*, 499 U.S. 340, 361, 111 S.Ct. 1282, 113 L.Ed.2d 358 (1991). Proof of copying often revolves around whether the defendant had sufficient access to copy the work. Access is only a theoretical issue in this case, however. By simple logic, it is impossible to copy something that does not exist. Thus, if Mattel created its doll sculptures before CDC created Claudene in 1994, it is factually and legally impossible for Mattel to be an infringer.

The record of creation is telling and conclusive. The Cool Blue Barbie doll uses the Neptune's Daughter doll head which was created in 1991, some six years before the Claudene doll. The Virginia Tech Barbie doll uses the SuperStar sculpture which Mattel created in 1976. The SuperStar doll was the subject of the just-completed federal court litigation, and Hicks should have been well aware of the prior creation, not to mention that the copyright notice (including date of creation) appears prominently on the back of the dolls' heads.

Recognizing the futility of attacking prior creation, Hicks argues that the paint on the Claudene doll's face features a light makeup that is distinctive and that the two Barbie dolls thus infringe Claudene's overall appearance and presentation. This argument fails because, among other things, Mattel used the light face paint on the Pioneer Barbie, which was created two years before the Claudene doll, thus defeating once again any claim of copying. It also bears noting that Mattel has been repainting various doll heads for decades. Under Hicks' theory, CDC's use of an infringing doll head coupled with "new" face paint would result in liability for Mattel's repainting of its prior-created Barbie doll sculptures. Neither common sense nor copyright law countenance such a result, even if the Claudene doll were deemed a derivative work. See *Entm't Research Group, Inc. v. Genesis Creative Group, Inc.,* 122 F.3d 1211, 1220 (9th Cir.1997) (holding that owners of copyrighted works have broad latitude to copyright derivatives thereof if they have "adequate originality").

In the face of facts and law clearly against his client, Hicks sought to resurrect the copyright claim by deluging the district court with supplemental filings, including entirely new claims regarding a different assortment of Barbie dolls and non-Barbie dolls. The dolls included, for example, the CEO doll, which used the 1991 Neptune's Daughter head with a modified mouth.

The district court did not consider any of Hicks' supplemental filings, noting that Hicks failed to comply with local rules regarding page limitations and typefaces. Given the chameleon nature of the claims and Hicks' flip-flop from the sculpture-plus-painting theory back to the sculpture-only theory, the district court was justified in putting an end to Hicks' serial filings. The district court has considerable latitude in managing the parties' motion practice and enforcing local rules that place parameters on briefing. We cannot say that the court abused its discretion by declining to consider Hicks' multitudinous efforts to circumvent the court's local rules and to expand the scope of an already frivolous suit. At some point, enough is enough. See *Ashton-Tate Corp. v. Ross,* 916 F.2d 516, 520 (9th Cir.1990) (noting that "the process of evaluating a summary judgment motion would be flouted if requests for more time, discovery, or the introduction of supplemental affidavits had to be considered even if requested well after the deadline set for the introduction of all information needed to make a ruling has passed.").

Consequently, in the face of undisputed evidence concerning the prior-creation of the Barbie dolls, the district court did not abuse its discretion by ruling that the complaint was frivolous.

2. DID HICKS CONDUCT AN ADEQUATE FACTUAL INVESTIGATION?

The district court concluded that Hicks "filed a case without factual foundation." Hicks, having argued unsuccessfully that his failure to perform even minimal due diligence was irrelevant as a matter of copyright law, does not contest that he would have been able to discover the copyright information simply by examining the doll heads. Instead, he argues that the district court did not understand certain "complex" issues. Simply saying so does not make it so. The district court well understood the legal and factual background of the case. It was Hicks' absence of investigation, not the district court's absence of analysis, that brought about his downfall.

The district court did not abuse its discretion in concluding that Hicks' failure to investigate fell below the requisite standard established by Rule 11.

III. THE DISTRICT COURT'S ADDITIONAL FINDINGS REGARDING MISCONDUCT

Hicks argues that even if the district court were justified in sanctioning him under Rule 11 based on Christian's complaint and the follow-on motions, its conclusion was tainted because it impermissibly considered other misconduct that cannot be sanctioned under Rule 11, such as discovery abuses, misstatements made during oral argument, and conduct in other litigation.

Hicks' argument has merit. While Rule 11 permits the district court to sanction an attorney for conduct regarding "pleading[s], written motion[s], and other paper[s]" that have been signed and filed in a given case, Fed.R.Civ.P. 11(a), it does not authorize sanctions for, among other things, discovery abuses or misstatements made to the court during an oral presentation. See *Bus. Guides, Inc. v. Chromatic Communications Enter.*, 892 F.2d 802, 813 (9th Cir.1989) (holding that misstatements made during oral argument cannot constitute sanctionable offenses under Rule 11); *In re Yagman*, 796 F.2d at 1187 (holding that discovery abuses cannot be sanctioned under Rule 11); see also Fed.R.Civ.P. 11, advisory committee notes, 1993 Amendments, Subdivisions (b) and (c) ("The rule applies only to assertions contained in papers filed with or submitted to the court. It does not cover matters arising for the first time during oral presentations to the court, when counsel may make statements that would not be made if there had been more time for study and reflection.").

In its January 5, 2000, order, the district court cited multiple bases for its Rule 11 findings:

Mr. Hicks has filed a case without factual foundation. Moreover, while this court cannot evaluate Mr. Hicks' conduct in the litigation before Judge Matz, his conduct in this case and the related one pending before this court has fallen below the standards expected of attorneys practicing in the Central District of California. In the related case, this court has already ordered Mr. Hicks to personally pay plaintiff's attorney's fees incurred as a result of his culpable conduct. Order of July 13, 1999, in CV99–4667. In connection with the instant motion and the discovery preceding it, he has behaved boorishly, misrepresented the facts, and misstated the law. Accordingly, the court grants defendant's motion for Rule 11 sanctions against Mr. Hicks.

Original emphasis.

In connection with the conclusion on boorish behavior, the court cited Hicks' conduct ("tossing Barbie dolls off a table") at a meeting of counsel and his interruption of a deposition following a damaging admission by his client. The charge of misrepresentation of facts was based on a statement made at oral argument that he had never seen a particular catalogue while a videotape of exhibit inspections showed him "leisurely thumbing through the catalogue." Hicks' conflicting representations in pleadings as to the identity of allegedly infringing Barbie dolls was an additional example of misrepresentation noted by the court. Finally, the court determined that Hicks made misrepresentations in his briefs concerning the law of joint authorship in the copyright context.

The district court's subsequent June 12, 2000, order contained a somewhat oblique description of why it had decided to sanction Hicks and reiterated the multiple broad categories that justified sanctions:

The court predicated its decision to impose sanctions on the finding that the claims Mr. Hicks brought against Mattel were 'meritless' and 'without factual foundation.' It further found that Mr. Hicks 'has behaved boorishly, misrepresented the facts, and misstated the law.'

Further, in determining that monetary sanctions were appropriate, the district court considered Hicks' "failure to respond to lesser sanctions" imposed in earlier actions and his "continuing disregard for the most basic rules governing an attorneys' professional conduct."

The orders clearly demonstrate that the district court decided, at least in part, to sanction Hicks because he signed and filed a factually and legally meritless complaint and for misrepresentations in subsequent briefing. But the orders, coupled with the supporting examples, also strongly suggest that the court considered extra-pleadings conduct as a basis for Rule 11 sanctions. Although the court also referenced conduct in related litigation, it is unlikely that the court based its order on such conduct because Hicks had already been sanctioned for violating local rules in the context of the related litigation and the court noted that fact.

The laundry list of Hicks' outlandish conduct is a long one and raises serious questions as to his respect for the judicial process. Nonetheless, Rule 11 sanctions are limited to "paper[s]" signed in violation of the rule. Conduct in depositions, discovery meetings of counsel, oral representations at hearings, and behavior in prior proceedings do not fall within the ambit of Rule 11. Because we do not know for certain whether the district court granted Mattel's Rule 11 motion as a result of an impermissible intertwining of its conclusion about the complaint's frivolity and Hicks' extrinsic misconduct, we must vacate the district court's Rule 11 orders.

We decline Mattel's suggestion that the district court's sanctions orders could be supported in their entirety under the court's inherent authority. To impose sanctions under its inherent authority, the district court must "make an explicit finding [which it did not do here] that counsel's conduct constituted or was tantamount to bad faith." *Primus Auto. Fin. Serv., Inc. v. Batarse*, 115 F.3d 644, 648 (9th Cir.1997) (internal quotation marks omitted). We acknowledge that the district court has a broad array of sanctions options at its disposal: Rule 11, 28 U.S.C. § 1927,11 and the court's inherent authority. Each of these sanctions alternatives has its own particular requirements, and it is important that the grounds be separately articulated to assure that the conduct at issue falls within the scope of the sanctions remedy. See, e.g., *B.K.B. v. Maui Police Dep't.*, 276 F.3d 1091, 1107 (9th Cir.2002) (holding that misconduct committed "in an unreasonable and vexatious manner" that "multiplies the proceedings" violates § 1927); *Fink v. Gomez*, 239 F.3d 989, 991–992 (9th Cir.2001) (holding that sanctions may be imposed under the court's inherent authority for "bad faith" actions by counsel, "which includes a broad range of willful improper conduct"). On remand, the district court will have an opportunity to delineate the factual and legal basis for its sanctions orders.

IV. THE DISTRICT COURT'S DECISION TO AWARD ATTORNEYS' FEES

Hicks raises various challenges to the quantum of attorneys' fees. Because we are vacating the district court's Rule 11 orders on other legal grounds, we express no opinion at this stage about the particular reasonableness of any of the fees the district court elected to award Mattel. We do, however, encourage the district court on remand to ensure that the time spent by Mattel's attorneys was reasonably and appropriately spent in relation to both the patent frivolousness of Christian's complaint and the services directly caused by the sanctionable conduct. See Fed.R.Civ.P. 11, advisory committee notes, 1993 Amendments, Subdivisions (b) and (c) (noting that attorneys' fees may only be awarded under Rule 11 for those "services directly and unavoidably caused" by the sanctionable conduct).

CONCLUSION

We vacate the district court's Rule 11 orders and remand for further proceedings consistent with this opinion.

VACATED and REMANDED.

**SOLUTIONS: THE LAWYER SHOULD HAVE,
WOULD HAVE, COULD HAVE. . .**

The plaintiff could have avoided being sanctioned if he performed his due diligence and created a simple timeline of events before filing the Complaint. If he had, he would have seen graphically that the central claim of the suit was factually impossible. But he failed to determine—or simply decided to ignore—the basic facts of the case. Sanctions like these are generally imposed in situations in which the lawyer is given more than sufficient warning that the lawyer's conduct is wanting and needs to be corrected. Was that not the situation with Orr? While his warnings came via other lawyers, and the warnings in this case came via a statutory imperative, the lesson is the same: pay attention.

X-Ray Questions (*There's a Time and a Place for Everything*)

This short article drives home the point that lawyers need to read a rule carefully to make sure that they ate using the right litigation tool for the task at hand. While Rule 11 is powerful, it is not without limits, as the lawyers in this article discovered.

BEYOND THE CITE

By: **Michael Stefanilo Jr.**, *Rule 11 Sanctions Are Not Fit for Every Occasion: There's a Time and a Place for Everything*, April 30, 2020.

The rules of civil procedure afford litigators numerous weapons to employ when confronted with diverse difficulties during the litigation process, including issues related to the conduct of opposing counsel. Yet, the threat of Rule 11 sanctions is often both overstated and misapplied by attorneys, particularly when cited in the context of discovery disputes. Critically, counsel should make certain to proceed with caution when actually filing a motion for sanctions under Rule 11, and be sure to adhere to all of the formalities of the rule's proscriptive text. A proper submission to the court requires familiarity with both the substantive and procedural limitations and prerequisites of Rule 11(c)(2), and should be invoked sparingly.

In March 2020, the Southern District of New York took occasion to issue a reminder of the appropriate setting for Rule 11 sanctions and the manner in which to seek them. In Gym Door Repairs, Inc. v. Young Equip. Sales, Inc., No. 15-CV-4244 (JGK) (S.D.N.Y. Mar. 12, 2020), the court opined that the backdrop for the plaintiffs' motion for sanctions against the defendants was improper, adopting a magistrate's report and recommendation that the plaintiffs' motion be denied. The court summarized:

> More particularly, [the plaintiffs'] Rule 11 motion (1) was directed to a discovery dispute rather than to a proper subject of Rule 11; (2) failed to provide the requisite 21 day safe harbor notice required under Rule 11; and (3) improperly combined their Rule 11 motion with a motion under Rule 37, rather than making their Rule 11 motion separate from any other motion as Rule 11 requires.

Id. at *1. In Gym Door, the plaintiffs learned through a third-party Freedom of Information Law (in New York, referred to as "FOIL") request that a small number of documents sought during discovery had not been produced by the defendants. This fact was unearthed after summary judgment had been entered in favor of the defense. As a result, the plaintiffs moved for Rule 11 sanctions against the offending parties.

As a threshold matter, the court confirmed that the additional records would not have impacted its decision to enter judgment against the plaintiffs at the Rule 56 stage. Regardless, the court held, the motion ran afoul of the strictures of Rule 11. First, the plaintiffs sought sanctions over a discovery dispute, which the court found was improper. Rule 11(c) limits the subject matter of a motion for sanctions to violations of the assurances enumerated in Rule 11(b). This includes only the improper presentation to the court of "a pleading, written motion, or other paper" through "signing, filing, submitting, or later advocating it" when one of four circumstances are not true "after an inquiry reasonable under the circumstances":

> it is not being presented for any improper purpose, such as to harass, cause unnecessary delay, or needlessly increase the cost of litigation;

> the claims, defenses, and other legal contentions are warranted by existing law or by a nonfrivolous argument for extending, modifying, or reversing existing law or for establishing new law; the factual contentions have evidentiary support or, if specifically so identified, will likely have evidentiary support after a reasonable opportunity for further investigation or discovery; and the denials of factual contentions are warranted on the evidence or, if specifically so identified, are reasonably based on belief or a lack of information.

Fed. R. Civ. P. 11(b). In Gym Door, none of the aforementioned conditions applied to the conduct of the defendants, even if the records had been improperly withheld.

Second, the court took issue with the plaintiffs' failure to "provide the requisite 21-day safe harbor notice required under Rule 11 . . ." Gym Door, supra, at *1. Rule 11(b)(2) prohibits a motion for sanctions to be filed with the court unless notice has been given to the offending party and a 21-day period is afforded for correction of the violation. Fed.R. Civ. P. 11(b)(2).

Finally, "a motion for sanctions must be made separately from any other motion and must describe the specific conduct that allegedly violates Rule 11(b)." Id. In Gym Door, the plaintiffs sought sanctions in conjunction with a motion filed under Rule 37. The court strictly interpreted the text of Rule 11 as prohibiting the combination of Rule 11 relief with that afforded by Rule 37. Gym Door, supra, at *1.

The lesson to be learned from Gym Door is straightforward but instructive: Attorneys should take extra precaution when seeking sanctions under Rule 11. The rules of civility would seem to suggest that motions for sanctions under Rule 11 not only be filed sparingly but, when appropriate, should (1) be submitted to the court in accordance with the procedural prerequisites of the rule's text and (2) result from violations of the substantive assurances that the rule governs.

Section 2.   Conflicts: Early Consideration

A.   Concurrent Representation and Disqualification

Model Rule 1.7(b)

(b)   Notwithstanding the existence of a concurrent conflict of interest under paragraph (a), a lawyer may represent a client if:

(1)   the lawyer reasonably believes that the lawyer will be able to provide competent and diligent representation to each affected client;

(2)   the representation is not prohibited by law;

(3)   the representation does not involve the assertion of a claim by one client against another client represented by the lawyer in the same litigation or other proceeding before a tribunal; and

(4)   each affected client gives informed consent, confirmed in writing.

Deconstruction Exercise/Rule Rationale

Concurrent representation occurs when a lawyer represents two parties on the same side of the "v." There are situations where this is permissible, but it is complicated. A lawyer could never be on both sides of the "v." however. Think back to our discussion in the *Baldwin* case in which the lawyer represented both executives of the university and the university. Lawyers may be tempted to believe that two clients are not as adverse to each other as they really are. Subsection (1) is an objective standard, not a subjective one; the question is whether a disinterested lawyer, looking at the circumstances of representation, would conclude that there is a *possibility* of divided lawyer loyalties between the clients. This issue arises in the formation of the ACR and, as we will see in the following case, early on in the course of litigation.

Cases and Materials

X-Ray Questions (*Murray*)

This is an employment discrimination case in which four white police offers claim they were discriminated against because of their race. They had each been denied the promotion to the position of Chief of Police and each asserted that he was the most qualified for the position. The ethical rub came because there was only one promotion slot open and each plaintiff claimed that he, not the others, was the most qualified person for the position. Yet one lawyer undertook the representation of all four. What is the conflict? How would that concurrent representation play out, on a practical level, in litigation and in trial? Is it a conflict that can be cured by informed consent of each plaintiff? Are some conflicts simply unconsentable? What consequences will flow from the granting of a DQ motion?

Patrick B. Murray, et al. v. Village of Hazel Crest, et al.

United States District Court, Eastern Division, 2006.
2006 WL 3589969.

HART, J.

Before this court are four related cases that have been assigned to the same judge for purposes of coordinated discovery and pretrial proceedings and, if appropriate, a single trial. The cases, however, have not been consolidated; they remain separately pending cases. Each case is brought by a different plaintiff: Patrick Murray (06 C 1372), Michael Garofalo (06 C 3674), David Nelson (06 C 3675), and Mark Peers (06 C 3735). Each plaintiff was formerly employed as a sergeant in the Police Department of defendant Village of Hazel Crest. Also named as defendants are Robert Donaldson, mayor/village president of Hazel Crest; Gary Jones, police chief of Hazel Crest since April 22, 2005; and Robert Palmer, village manager of Hazel Crest. Each plaintiff applied for the position of deputy chief of police and alleges that he suffered discrimination because of race when an allegedly less-qualified African-American patrol officer was promoted to that position effective July 12, 2005. There is only one deputy chief position at the police department. Each plaintiff also alleges that he was constructively discharged as a result of his treatment, Murray and Nelson on December 1, 2005, Garofalo in June 2006, and Peers in March 2006. Each plaintiff alleges in his complaint that his damages include the loss of income that he would have earned had he been promoted to Deputy Chief and each seeks injunctive relief in the form of a promotion. Each plaintiff also alleges lost wages from being forced to resign and damages for emotional injury. Each plaintiff also seeks reinstatement.

Each plaintiff is represented by attorneys Patricia Rummer and Richard Lowell. Defendant Village of Hazel Crest has moved to disqualify counsel from representing any of the plaintiffs on the ground that conflicts of interest exist among the plaintiffs because each plaintiff contends that he should have been the one promoted to deputy chief of police. Counsel contend this is not a conflict and that each client desires to be represented by them.

Local Rule 83.51.7 provides:

(a)   A lawyer shall not represent a client if the representation of that client will be directly adverse to another client, unless:

  (1)   the lawyer reasonably believes the representation will not adversely affect the relationship with the other client; and

  (2)   each client consents after disclosure.

(b)   A lawyer shall not represent a client if the representation of that client may be materially limited by the lawyer's responsibilities to another client or to a third person, or by the lawyer's own interests, unless:

  (1)   the lawyer reasonably believes the representation will not be adversely affected; and

  (2)   the client consents after disclosure.

(c)   When representation of multiple clients in a single matter is undertaken, the disclosure shall include explanation of the implications of the common representation and the advantages and risks involved.

Local Rule 83.51.9 provides in part:

(a)   A lawyer who has formerly represented a client in a matter shall not thereafter represent another person in the same or a substantially related matter in which the person's interests are materially adverse to the interests of the former client unless the former client consents after disclosure.

. . .

(c)   A lawyer who has formerly represented a client in a matter or whose present or former law firm has formerly represented a client in a matter shall not thereafter:

  (1)   use information relating to the representation to the disadvantage of the former client except as LR83.51.6 or

LR83.53.3 would permit or require with respect to a client, or
when the information has become generally known; or

(2) reveal information relating to the representation except as
LR83.51.6 or LR83.53.3 would permit or require with respect to
a client.

Although defendants cite to both section (a) and section (b) of Rule
83.51.7, it is sections (b) and (c) that apply to representation of multiple plaintiffs
in the same case. See N.D. Ill. Loc. R. 83.51.7 Committee Comment, "Conflicts
in Litigation." Material limits on the attorney's ability to represent the clients
may arise from "incompatibility in positions in relation to an opposing party."
Id.

It is a defense to plaintiffs' Title VII failure to promote damages claims, as
well as their claims for promotion and reinstatement, that a particular plaintiff
would not have been promoted even if there had been no discrimination. 42
U.S.C. § 2000e–5(g)(2). This can be shown by proof that an applicant other than
the particular plaintiff would have been selected even if there had been no
discrimination. See *Bishop v. Gainer*, 272 F.3d 1009, 1016 (7th Cir.2001), cert.
denied, 535 U.S. 1055, 122 S.Ct. 1912, 152 L.Ed.2d 822 (2002); *Beland v.
Veneman*, 2004 WL 3253703 *3–4 (D.D.C. Dec.21, 2004). The defense that
another person would have instead been selected would also apply to any § 1983
discrimination claim that plaintiffs may ultimately be pursuing. See *Bishop*, 272
F.3d at 1016. To the extent one plaintiff proves that he was the one that would
have been promoted if not for discrimination, he provides a defense against the
claims of the other three defendants. Thus, the attorney gathering or presenting
evidence as to the qualifications of one plaintiff (which is absolutely necessary
in order to pursue that plaintiff's interests) is in direct conflict with the interests
of the other three plaintiffs who each want to show he is the most qualified or
otherwise most likely to have been promoted.

Plaintiffs contend none of them need show that he would have actually
been promoted because each can proceed on a "lost-chance theory." See *Bishop*,
272 F.3d at 1016–17. Under that theory, damages are calculated based on the
probability that the applicant would have been promoted. See id. If there are
multiple applicants for the position, a successful plaintiff's back pay and front
pay is calculated based on the probability that he or she would have been
promoted absent discrimination. Where there was more than one plaintiff
seeking the same position, each could recover lost pay based on each plaintiff's
probability of obtaining the promotion absent discrimination. For example, if
there were five applicants for a position, four plaintiffs and a third person who

was selected because of his or her race, and each one (including the one actually selected) was equally qualified to perform the work and equal as to other selection criteria as well, then each plaintiff had a 20% chance of being selected and would be entitled to 20% of the additional income he or she would have received if selected. Under the lost-chance theory, and assuming no option of nonselection for the position, the probabilities that each applicant would have been selected must total 100%. Awarding damages based on probabilities that total in excess of 100% would improperly result in an award of duplicative damages. See *Bishop*, 272 F.3d at 1016. Since the individual probabilities for all applicants must total 100%, any successful proof that a particular applicant had a greater probability of being selected means that the probable hiring of other applicants must decrease. Thus, even under the lost-chance theory, the plaintiffs in the present cases would be in direct competition with each other regarding lost wages. Assuming liability can be proven, any successful showing of greater capability by one plaintiff has a direct negative impact on the other plaintiffs. The corollary is that showing one of the plaintiffs is less capable has a positive impact on the other plaintiffs. Even though plaintiffs also claim some damages that are not based directly on lost wages from not being promoted, they are still in direct and irreconcilable conflict regarding back pay and front pay whether proceeding on a lost-chance theory or simply seeking to prove that each was the only one that would have been promoted.

In their surreply, counsel contends for the first time that each plaintiff seeks only his 25% share and not to prove he was more likely to have been promoted than the others. The facts alleged, however, do not support that it would be impossible to differentiate among the plaintiffs so that a 25% apportionment after proof of discriminatory intent is the only likely result. Counsel imply that plaintiffs are willing to forego the possibility of greater damages in the interest of the cost-saving of sharing counsel. There is, however, no indication that plaintiffs have been fully advised of the possibilities and consented after full disclosure. There is also no indication each plaintiff has been advised of the strengths or weaknesses of his individual claim. Given their representation of all four plaintiffs, as well as their own self-interest in continuing to represent all four, counsel have an actual conflict simply trying to give such advice. Additionally, counsel's speculative result of requiring defendants to take away the promotion and hold a new competition for the position is unlikely.

Finding the existence of a direct conflict of interest does not end the matter since it is possible that the conflict is waivable. Plaintiffs' attorneys point to the affidavits they have provided and contend they have satisfied the requirements of Local Rule 83.51.7. Even ignoring the conclusory nature of the affidavits, they do not show that Rule 83.51.7 is satisfied. The affidavit from each of plaintiffs' attorneys contains the following identical paragraphs:

I have carefully examined the applicable law and the facts to determine whether any conflict exists with respect to representing all four of the plaintiffs. I have determined as a result that there is no conflict with respect to my representation of the four individuals with respect to their claims in these cases.

Each of the four plaintiffs has expressly stated that he desires to be represented by the same counsel.

Despite the assertions by counsel that they have examined the law and facts and have determined that no conflict exists, the above discussion of the law shows that plaintiffs necessarily are in conflict regarding their pursuit of lost income, a form of relief that all have requested. The fact that all of them have stated that they desire to be represented by the same counsel does not satisfy the requirement of waiver because such consent must occur "after disclosure." N.D. Ill. Loc. R. 83.51.7(b)(2). See also *id.* 83.51.7(c). The affidavits are silent as to any disclosures that were made. However, before requiring that counsel make full disclosures to their clients and determine if they are willing to continue to consent to representation, it should first be determined whether such a waiver is possible. As stated in the "Disclosure and Consent" section of the Committee Comment to Local Rule 83.51.7, "when a disinterested lawyer would conclude that the client should not agree to the representation under the circumstances, the lawyer involved cannot properly ask for such agreement or provide representation on the basis of the client's consent."

Here, the four plaintiffs have a common interest in showing that defendants selected the winning candidate because of his race and in showing the lack of qualifications of the candidate that was selected. There are also likely to be some economies in being represented by the same attorneys. However, plaintiffs are in direct conflict with each other regarding showing who is the most likely to have been selected for the promotion. Each plaintiff has an interest in showing that he is highly qualified as well as an interest in showing that other plaintiffs lacked qualifications. The issues in conflict will have a substantial impact on any damages that are recovered. This is a situation where a disinterested attorney would determine that each plaintiff should have his own attorney. Plaintiffs' attorneys would not be able to vigorously pursue damages on behalf of one plaintiff without coming into direct conflict with the interests of the other plaintiffs. Counsel will be disqualified from representing multiple plaintiffs in this case.

Defendants contend that present counsel should not have the option of remaining in the case by representing only one plaintiff, that they should be disqualified from representing any plaintiff in this case. Local Rule 83.51.9 applies to that issue. See N.D. Ill. Loc. R. 83.51.7, Committee Comment, "Loyalty to a Client." If consent is obtained from the other three plaintiffs, it is possible that the attorneys could continue to represent one of the clients, or that each of the current attorneys (who apparently are independent practitioners) could each represent one plaintiff. See N.D. Ill. Loc. R. 83.51.9(a). Whether such representation would be appropriate may depend on whether plaintiffs have already revealed confidential information to the attorneys that would give unfair advantage to one of the other plaintiffs. If counsel desires to continue to represent one of the plaintiffs, counsel must carefully consider whether such representation would be appropriate and must obtain the consent of the other plaintiffs, including after each of the other plaintiffs has retained his new counsel.

Discovery in this case will be stayed until January 24, 2007. The new discovery closing date will be May 15, 2007. Plaintiffs shall retain new counsel by no later than January 5, 2007. New counsel shall promptly move for leave to substitute their appearances for former counsel. If, on the advice of new counsel, any plaintiff desires to amend his existing complaint, that plaintiff must file an amended complaint by no later than January 8, 2007. If current counsel remains in any case, counsel shall file a pleading in that case so stating. In the three cases other than Murray, defendants' counsel shall promptly meet with new counsel to discuss whether any agreement can be reached similar to the July 19, 2006 order entered in the Murray case. Defendants shall answer or otherwise plead in those cases by no later than January 22, 2007. The next status hearing for these cases will be held on January 10, 2007 at 11:00 a.m.

IT IS THEREFORE ORDERED that defendants' motion to disqualify counsel [31] (filed in 06 C 1372) is granted in part and denied in part. The present attorneys for plaintiffs are disqualified from representing more than one plaintiff in these four cases and may only represent one of the plaintiffs by obtaining the counseled consent of the three other plaintiffs. Discovery in the four cases is stayed until January 24, 2007 and all discovery is to be completed by no later than May 15, 2007. Defendants in 06 C 3674, 06 C 3675, and 06 C 3735 shall answer or otherwise plead by no later than January 22, 2007. A status hearing for all four cases will be held on January 10, 2007 at 11:00 a.m.

SOLUTIONS: THE LAWYER SHOULD HAVE, WOULD HAVE, COULD HAVE. . .

The lawyer was disqualified from representing the four plaintiffs. Why? Because he could not reasonably believe that each of the four was the *most* qualified for the position. The lawyer could have avoided this outcome by selecting only one of the four to represent from the outset and sticking with that selection. The option became impossible, however, once all four became former clients about whom the lawyer likely learned confidential information. The lawyer could not reasonably think that each of the four was the most qualified for the one slot; that should have been clear from the start. Finally, the lawyer could not also arguably continue to represent even one of the plaintiffs. Why? Because he likely has possessed detailed knowledge as to each of their cases, and thus, under MR 1.9, cannot represent one against another.

Cases and Materials

X-Ray Questions (*In re Dresser*)

The following case involves a somewhat different concurrent representation scenario at the commencement of litigation. A lawyer represented a client (Dresser Industries) in two lawsuits related to the oil and gas industry. But then the lawyer was offered his dream gig of representing multiple plaintiffs in a lawsuit involving the drill bits used for oil and gas exploration. But Dresser was a defendant in the drill bit suit. The two cases are unrelated to the drill bits litigation. So, what's the harm to Dresser if the lawyer takes on the drill bits litigation while he continues to represent Dresser. Why would Dresser need to give informed consent? After all, the drill bit litigation and the two lawsuits were 100% unrelated. What is the harm to Dresser? Are there some special rights that are accorded an initial client by virtue of the fact that its ACR preceded a subsequent client? What would they be?

In re Dresser Industries, Inc.

United States Court of Appeals, Fifth Circuit., 1992.
972 F.2d 540.

Opinion

E. GRADY JOLLY, CIRCUIT JUDGE:

In this petition for a writ of mandamus, we determine whether a law firm may sue its own client, which it concurrently represents in other matters. In a word, no; and most certainly not here, where the motivation appears only to be the law firm's self-interest. We therefore grant the writ, directing the district judge to disqualify counsel.

I

The material facts are undisputed. This petition arises from a consolidated class action antitrust suit brought against manufacturers of oil well drill bits. *Red Eagle Resources et al. v. Baker Hughes, et al.,* No. H-91-0627, 1992 WL 170614 (S.D.Tex.) (*"Drill Bits"*).

Dresser Industries, Inc., ("Dresser") is now a defendant in *Drill Bits,* charged—by its own lawyers—with conspiring to fix the prices of drill bits and with fraudulently concealing its conduct. Stephen D. Susman, with his firm, Susman Godfrey, is lead counsel for the plaintiff's committee. As lead counsel, Susman signed the amended complaint that levied these charges against Dresser, his firm's own client.

Susman Godfrey concurrently represents Dresser in two pending lawsuits. *CPS International, Inc. v. Dresser Industries, Inc.,* No. H-85-653 (S.D.Tex.) (*"CPS"*), is the third suit brought by CPS International, a company that claims Dresser forced it out of the compressor market in Saudi Arabia. CPS International initially sued Dresser for antitrust violations and tortious interference with a contract. The antitrust claim has been dismissed, but the tort claim is scheduled for trial. Susman Godfrey has represented Dresser throughout these actions, which commenced in 1985. During its defense of Dresser, Susman Godfrey lawyers have had relatively unfettered access to data concerning Dresser's management, organization, finances, and accounting practices. Susman Godfrey's lawyers have engaged in privileged communications with Dresser's in-house counsel and officers in choosing antitrust defenses and other litigation strategies. Susman Godfrey has also, since 1990, represented Dresser in *Cullen Center, Inc., et al. v. W.R. Gray Co., et al.,* a case involving asbestos in a Dresser building, which is now set for trial in Texas state court.

On October 24 and November 24, 1991, Susman Godfrey lawyers wrote Dresser informing it that Stephen Susman chaired the plaintiffs' committee in *Drill Bits,* that Dresser might be made a *Drill Bits* defendant, and that, if Dresser replaced Susman Godfrey, the firm would assist in the transition to new counsel. Dresser chose not to dismiss Susman Godfrey in *CPS* and *Cullen Center.*

Dresser was joined as a defendant in *Drill Bits* on December 2, 1991. Dresser moved to disqualify Susman as plaintiffs' counsel on December 13. Both Dresser and Susman Godfrey submitted affidavits and depositions to the district court, which, after a hearing, issued a detailed opinion denying the motion.

The district court noted that Southern District local rule 4B provides that the code of professional responsibility for lawyers practicing in that district is the Code of Responsibility of the State Bar of Texas. Although the court further noted that other district courts look to other codes in deciding motions to disqualify, nevertheless, it concluded that "Dresser's motion to disqualify Susman Godfrey is governed wholly by the Texas Disciplinary Rules of Professional Conduct." The court then focused on Texas Disciplinary Rule 1.06, which provides:

> (b) . . . [E]xcept to the extent permitted in paragraph (c), a lawyer shall not represent a person if the representation of that person:

> (1) involves a substantially related matter in which that person's interests are materially and directly adverse to the interests of another client of the lawyer or the lawyer's firm; or

> (2) reasonably appears to be or become adversely limited by the lawyer's or law firm's responsibilities to another client or to a third person or by the lawyer's or law firm's own interests.

> (c) A lawyer may represent a client in the circumstances described in (b) if:

> (1) the lawyer reasonably believes the representation of each client will not be materially affected; and

> (2) each affected or potentially affected client consents to such representation after full disclosure. . . .

The district court described the *Drill Bits* complaint as a civil antitrust case, thus somewhat softening Dresser's description of it as an action for fraud or criminal conduct. The court held, "as a matter of law, that there exists no relationship, legal or factual, between the *Cullen Center* case and the *Drill Bits* litigation," and that no similarity between *Drill Bits* and the *CPS* suits was material. The court concluded that "Godfrey's representation of the plaintiffs in the *Drill Bits* litigation does not reasonably appear to be or become adversely limited by Susman Godfrey's responsibilities to Dresser in the *CPS* and *Cullen Center* cases," and accordingly denied the motion to disqualify. Finally, the court denied permissive interlocutory appeal under 28 U.S.C. § 1292(b).

IV

We turn, then, to the current national standards of legal ethics to first consider whether this dual representation amounts to impropriety. Neither the ABA Model Rules of Professional Conduct nor the Code of Professional Responsibility allows an attorney to bring a suit against a client without its consent. This position is also taken by the American Law Institute in its drafts of the *Restatement of the Law Governing Lawyers*.

Unquestionably, the national standards of attorney conduct forbid a lawyer from bringing a suit against a current client without the consent of both clients. Susman's conduct violates all of these standards—unless excused or justified under exceptional circumstances not present here.

Exceptional circumstances may sometimes mean that what is ordinarily a clear impropriety will not, always and inevitably, determine a conflicts case. Within the framework we announced in *Woods*, Susman, for example, might have been able to continue his dual representation if he could have shown some social interest to be served by his representation that would outweigh the public perception of his impropriety. Susman, however, can present no such reason. There is no suggestion that other lawyers could not ably perform his offices for the plaintiffs, nor is there any basis for a suggestion of any societal or professional interest to be served. This fact suggests a rule of thumb for use in future motions for disqualification based on concurrent representation: However a lawyer's motives may be clothed, if the sole reason for suing his own client is the lawyer's self-interest, disqualification should be granted.

V

We find, therefore, that Dresser's right to the grant of its motion to disqualify counsel is clear and indisputable. We further find that the district court clearly and indisputably abused its discretion in failing to grant the motion. We have thus granted the petition and have issued the writ of mandamus, directing the United States District Court for the Southern District of Texas to enter an order disqualifying Stephen D. Susman and Susman Godfrey from continuing as counsel to the plaintiffs in *Red Eagle Resources et al. v. Baker Hughes, et al.*, No. H-91-0627, 1992 WL 170614.

WRIT GRANTED.

SOLUTIONS: THE LAWYER SHOULD HAVE, WOULD HAVE, COULD HAVE. . .

This case involves what is labeled the "hot potato" doctrine; that is, the lawyer—to resolve a conflict—unilaterally decides to drop the original client. And the conflict is one of loyalty. While the two matters are unrelated, Dresser will wonder: will our lawyer sell us out in the drill bits litigation in order to gain favor with the more attractive clients that he represents there? This is why the lawyer can only undertake representation of the prospective client with the informed consent of Dresser. Dresser can make that decision, but the lawyer cannot make the decision for Dresser. In short, as the goes, "Dance with The One That Brought You."

https://www.youtube.com/watch?v=wcBplbfXgSY.

LEANING INTO PRACTICE

Scenario No. 1: The Case of the Negligent Doctor or the Inattentive Nurse?

Omar Doctor and Judy Nurse are each sued for professional negligence by the estate of a deceased patient. Miguel Lawyer makes an appearance in the lawsuit for both and files a denial for each as their lawsuit answers. As Miguel gets into the case, he realizes that the Doctor will blame the Nurse ("He gave me the wrong medicine") and the nurse will blame the Doctor. ("I gave her what I thought he wrote down, but she has such bad handwriting that I misread the instruction.") Is there a conflict in this representation? Can it be resolved by the informed consent of the doctor and the nurse for the lawyer to represent her? Is this conflict one that is *never* consentable?

Scenario No. 2: The Case of the Opera Star and the New Opera House

Rossina Client is a famous opera star. Bella Lawyer is representing her in negotiations with the Opera Company over the percentage that she will receive from merchandise the opera house sells. The manager of the Opera Company tells Bella that he likes the way she negotiates and wants to hire her to buy a piece of land upon which the Opera Company will build its new opera house.

The two representations are unrelated. Can Bella take on the Opera Company as a client? Can she do so without the approval of Rossina? Is there a conflict in this scenario? If so, is it consentable by Rossina and the Opera Company? Why? What would make it different than Scenario No. 1? Assume the role of Bella and write out how you would explain informed consent in this situation to Rossina?

B. Former Clients and Disqualification

The duty of loyalty that attorneys owe to clients is strongest with current clients. But even after the end of an ACR a conflict can occur. With former clients, the primary concern is less about loyalty and more about protecting confidentiality. Here is the scenario: Lawyer represents Client A and concludes the representation; later Prospective Client Z comes to Lawyer and wants to sue now former Client A. Can Lawyer take on representation of Client Z? It is best if a lawyer recognizes the potential conflict before agreeing to represent the new Client. Part of routine conflict checks should be a search of former clients of the firm. But sometimes firms fail to recognize a potential conflict early, or do not properly assess the risks.

The following chart outlines the dynamics of MR 1.9 which resolves this ethical dilemma.

Let's Chart It!

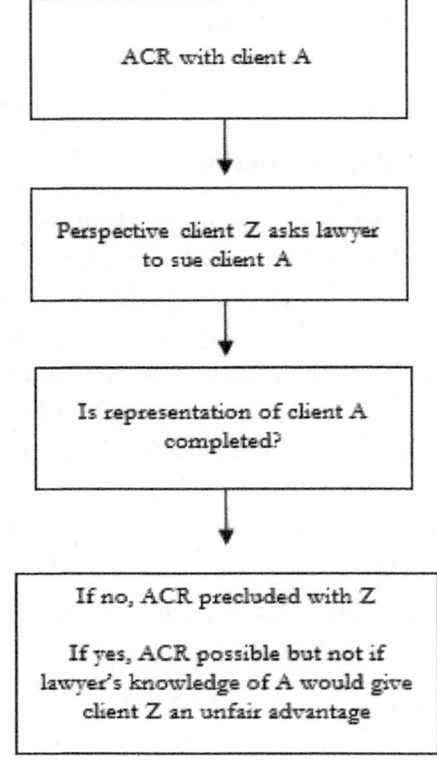

Model Rule 1.9: Duties to Former Clients

(a) A lawyer who has formerly represented a client in a matter shall not thereafter represent another person in the same or a substantially related matter in which that person's interests are materially adverse to the interests of the former client unless the former client gives informed consent, confirmed in writing.

(b) A lawyer shall not knowingly represent a person in the same or a substantially related matter in which a firm with which the lawyer formerly was associated had previously represented a client

(1) whose interests are materially adverse to that person; and

(2) about whom the lawyer had acquired information protected by Rules 1.6 and 1.9(c) that is material to the matter; unless the former client gives informed consent, confirmed in writing.

(c)   A lawyer who has formerly represented a client in a matter or whose present or former firm has formerly represented a client in a matter shall not thereafter:

> (1) use information relating to the representation to the disadvantage of the former client except as these Rules would permit or require with respect to a client, or when the information has become generally known; or

> (2) reveal information relating to the representation except as these Rules would permit or require with respect to a client.

Deconstruction Exercise/Rule Rationale

MR 1.7 (current clients) is about loyalty; MR 1.9 (former clients) is about knowledge. The essence of the rule is whether the new client will gain an unfair advantage in the litigation because of the former representation. As we will explore in depth in the next chapter, the rules seek to impose an even playing field upon litigants. Insider knowledge alters the even playing field. Ask yourself: what other options did the drafters have with respect to former clients? The drafters could have imposed an absolute bar upon a lawyer ever representing a person now adverse to a former client, but they didn't. A stricter rule would impair the public's ability to hire lawyers of their choice. A rule permitting a disqualification motion to sort out the conflict issue with an option for informed consent ultimately proved the best option for the public at large and for our system of justice. The next case illustrates the dynamics of this rule.

Cases and Materials

X-Ray Questions (*Ockrassa*)

Conflicts under MR 1.9 arise in both civil law and criminal law contexts. Here a former assistant public defender (PD) represented a client convicted of two DUIs. The person was later accused of a third DUI and faced a severe punishment because of the multiple offenses. The defendant therefore sought to challenge the validity of the two prior convictions. The issue? The former PD was *now* the assistant DA assigned to prosecute his former clint. The assistant DA insisted there was no conflict. Indeed, his two managing lawyers agreed. The court disagreed. Why? Hint: MR 1.7 is about loyalty, but MR 1.9 is about knowledge. A 90-day suspension was imposed. Does this seem harsh? What is the core conflict issue? In addition, focus on two elements of this case. First, the reporting of a fellow lawyer for a Rule's violation (MR 8.3: Reporting Professional Misconduct). Who is doing the reporting in this case? Why?

Consider how the Rule operates both in theory and in practice. Second, the two supervisors agreed with the conclusion reached by Ockrassa. The court rejected this as a defense. Why? After all, the supervisors were (presumably) more experienced and wiser than Ockrassa. Why was it not a defense for the lawyer here to say, "but my supervisors told me it was ethical for me to act as the prosecutor?"

In re Steven R. Ockrassa a Member of the State Bar of Arizona

Supreme Court of Arizona, 1990.
799 P.2d 1350.

CORCORAN, JUSTICE.

The State Bar filed a complaint on January 12, 1988, alleging that respondent violated the ethical rules regarding conflicts of interest. The Hearing Committee (Committee) filed its report on September 13, 1988, finding that respondent violated Ethical Rule 1.9, Rules of Professional Conduct, contained in Rule 42, Rules of the Supreme Court. The Committee recommended an informal reprimand.

The Disciplinary Commission (Commission) heard oral argument on the matter on November 12, 1988. Its report, issued on December 6, 1988, recommended that respondent be suspended from the practice of law for 90 days. Respondent timely appealed. We have jurisdiction pursuant to Ariz. Const. art. 6, § 5(3), and rule 53(e), Arizona Rules of the Supreme Court.

Facts

Respondent was a contract public defender for the City of Kingman in 1982 and 1983. During that time, he was appointed to represent Carl Jay Otto in three criminal cases alleging violations of A.R.S. § 28–692(A), which prohibits driving under the influence of intoxicating liquors (DUI). Mr. Otto was convicted in all three cases. Two of the convictions were obtained as a result of plea agreements, the other following a jury trial. Respondent's representation of Mr. Otto terminated on February 28, 1983.

In 1986, respondent was employed as a deputy county attorney pursuant to a contract with the Mohave County Attorney's office. In that capacity, respondent represented the state in two criminal actions against the same Mr. Otto, who was charged with DUI as a third offense within the preceding 60 months. *See* A.R.S. § 28–692.01. These felony actions were filed in Mohave

County Superior Court as CR-8444 and CR-8552. Defendant Otto filed a notice of disclosure that he would assert the invalidity and insufficiency of the prior convictions and a conflict of interest on the part of respondent. He also filed a motion in limine in CR-8444 to suppress any allegation of prior conviction. Respondent had represented Mr. Otto in both prior convictions alleged by the state.

The deputy public defender who represented Mr. Otto in CR-8444 and CR-8552 requested that respondent withdraw as prosecutor, citing a conflict of interest based on respondent's prior defense representation of Mr. Otto. The deputy public defender expressed his concerns in a letter to respondent, who declined to withdraw. Subsequently, when the alleged conflict of interest was raised in the criminal prosecution involving Mr. Otto, the trial judge advised the deputy public defender that he had an ethical obligation to report perceived violations of the Rules of Professional Conduct to the State Bar. *See* ER 8.3(a); *In re Himmel,* 125 Ill.2d 531, 127 Ill.Dec. 708, 533 N.E.2d 790 (1988). Shortly thereafter, Mr. Otto pleaded guilty to the criminal charges in CR-8444 and CR-8552. At no time did Mr. Otto consent to respondent's representation of the state.

Kenneth D. Everett, the Mohave County Public Defender, informed the State Bar of respondent's conduct. In response to the Bar's letter of inquiry, respondent denied that a conflict of interest existed because the prior representation had been concluded, was remote in time, and had no prejudicial effect on the outcome of the case. He noted that, before prosecuting Mr. Otto, he discussed the matter with his superiors, the Mohave County Attorney and his chief criminal deputy. Neither believed that the situation presented an ethical problem.

After a finding of probable cause, the State Bar filed a formal complaint against respondent. The complaint alleged in Count 1 that the foregoing facts established a violation of ER 1.9. The complaint also alleged as Count 2 that respondent previously had been sanctioned for violations of the Rules of Professional Conduct. Respondent filed an answer, the parties agreed on a stipulated statement of facts, and the matter was set for hearing before the Committee. A hearing was held on June 30, 1988.

In its report, filed on September 13, 1988, the Committee concluded that the allegations of Count 1 had been established by clear and convincing evidence and constituted a violation of ER 1.9. The Committee found that respondent was previously censured on July 12, 1984, for a conflict of interest violation and for failing to reveal the conflict to his client or to act to eliminate the conflict for many months. The Committee also found that respondent was informally reprimanded on September 5, 1984, for conflict of interest and revealing client confidences, and on December 6, 1985, for failing to appear at a scheduled deposition, inconveniencing his client, and failing to adequately prepare his client for a scheduled deposition. The Committee noted that "Respondent has engaged in a course of conduct evidencing a lack of appreciation of conflicts of interest." Based on these findings, the Committee recommended that respondent be informally reprimanded.

Respondent filed a notice of appeal from the Committee report and the Commission heard the matter on November 12, 1988. The Commission adopted the Committee's findings of fact and conclusions of law, but recommended a 90-day suspension. The Commission recommended the increased sanction based on its finding that "Respondent repeatedly ignored his duty to withdraw in this case upon clear evidence and after demand. His prior sanctions indicate an unacceptable pattern of conduct." Respondent appealed to this court from the Commission's recommendation.

Discussion

This court sits as the ultimate "trier of both fact and law in the exercise of our supervisory responsibility over the State Bar." *In re Neville,* 147 Ariz. 106, 108, 708 P.2d 1297, 1299 (1985). However, we give serious consideration to the findings and recommendations of the Committee and Commission. *In re Petrie,* 154 Ariz. 295, 297, 742 P.2d 796, 798 (1987). Charges of professional misconduct must be established by clear and convincing evidence. *In re Kersting,* 151 Ariz. 171, 172, 726 P.2d 587, 588 (1986).

ER 1.9 provides:

A lawyer who has formerly represented a client in a matter shall not thereafter:

(a) represent another person in the same or a substantially related matter in which that person's interests are materially adverse to the interests of the former client unless the former client consents after consultation; or

(b) use information relating to the representation to the disadvantage of the former client except as ER 1.6 would permit with respect to a client or when the information has become generally known.

Undoubtedly, respondent's interests as prosecutor were materially adverse to those of his former client, Mr. Otto. However, respondent argues that his 1986 DUI prosecution of Mr. Otto is not substantially related to the earlier DUI charges in which he served as defense counsel. We find respondent's argument meritless. Mr. Otto was charged with DUI as a third offense within 60 months. The validity of his prior convictions was directly in issue. Mr. Otto had disclosed his intention of asserting invalidity and insufficiency of the prior convictions as a defense.

Respondent claims that this factor is not determinative because the prior DUI convictions are not considered elements of the offense; rather, they serve to enhance punishment. *See State ex rel. Collins v. Udall,* 149 Ariz. 199, 200, 717 P.2d 878, 879 (1986). We do not believe that, in the context of multiple DUI offenses, a "substantial relationship" is established only if the prior conviction is an element of the subsequent offense. One of the aims of ER 1.9 is to protect the client. *See* ER 1.9 comment. Respondent's conduct in prosecuting Mr. Otto created a substantial danger that confidential information revealed in the course of the attorney/client relationship would be used against Mr. Otto by respondent, his former attorney. Although respondent claims that he does not remember the content of any such confidential communications by Mr. Otto, the protection of the rule should not be so lightly cast aside.

> [T]he [substantial relationship] test itself is premised, at least in part, on the presumption that a lawyer who now wants to represent an interest adverse to a former client has received confidences of that former client, which he should not be allowed to use now against the former client. The majority of courts that have considered the issue have held that the presumption that a lawyer received such confidences may not be rebutted.

Lawyers' Manual on Professional Conduct 51:201 (ABA/BNA 1990).

We need not decide whether the presumption is irrebuttable in this case because respondent presented evidence insufficient to raise that issue. Our State Bar Committee on the Rules of Professional Conduct, in an informal ethics opinion, recognized the presumption of receipt of client confidences in interpreting the former Code of Professional Responsibility. The committee noted that "if the attorney switches sides in the same case or a substantially related case, it is presumed that the former client communicated confidential information to the attorney." Opinion No. 81–29, at 4 (Sept. 17, 1981). The opinion concluded that "[a]n attorney who previously represented a client in defense of a criminal case cannot later prosecute his or her former client in another criminal case." Opinion 81–29, at 3. Although the opinion did not apply the current Rules of Professional Conduct, the Committee on the Rules of Professional Conduct has continued to examine subsequent representation cases carefully. *See* Opinion No. 89–04 (May 3, 1989) (former county attorney is ethically prohibited from representing defendants whom he prosecuted personally); Opinion No. 85–6 (Oct. 18, 1985) (former public defender who becomes a prosecutor cannot participate in the prosecution of co-conspirators of his former client where the charges are based on the same transaction).

ER 1.9 also aims to avoid a public perception of "switching sides." The comment to the rule provides:

> [A] lawyer who recurrently handled a type of problem for a former client is not precluded from later representing another client in a wholly distinct problem of that type even though the subsequent representation involves a position adverse to the prior client. Similar considerations can apply to the reassignment of military lawyers between defense and prosecution functions within the same military jurisdiction. The underlying question is whether the lawyer was so involved in the matter that the subsequent representation can be justly regarded as a changing of sides in the matter in question.

Thus, matters will tend to be substantially related when such a danger exists. Respondent did not "switch sides" in the middle of a single criminal proceeding against Mr. Otto. However, the nature of the DUI offense, with its exponential punishment for multiple offenses, makes respondent's conduct more akin to "switching sides" than had the subsequent prosecution involved, for example, forgery. We decline to view the subsequent DUI charge as a "wholly distinct problem of the same type," primarily because of the danger that respondent received confidential communications during the prior representation.

Respondent attempts to minimize the gravity of his conduct by placing blame "higher up the ladder." The fact that respondent's superiors did not believe that respondent's prosecution of Mr. Otto presented an ethical problem does not weigh heavily in respondent's favor. Even minimal research would have disclosed that this court and the State Bar Committee on the Rules of Professional Responsibility have consistently found ethical violations in similar circumstances. In *State v. Latigue*, this court disqualified the entire Maricopa County Attorney's Office from prosecuting a matter due to the Chief Deputy County Attorney's prior representation of the defendant in the same matter. 108 Ariz. 521, 502 P.2d 1340 (1972). *Latigue* is distinguishable because it was decided under the former Code of Professional Responsibility and involved a motion for disqualification based on an attorney "switching sides" during a single criminal proceeding. Additionally, we note that the current Rules of Professional Conduct contain significant changes affecting vicarious disqualification. We believe that *Latigue* and the existing informal ethics opinions contain sufficiently applicable language to alert respondent to the potential ethical problems his conduct created, regardless of the opinions of his superiors.

We find, by clear and convincing evidence, that respondent's conduct in prosecuting Mr. Otto constituted a violation of ER 1.9(a). We now turn to the appropriate sanction to be imposed.

Sanction

In determining the appropriate sanction for a violation of the Rules of Professional Conduct, we consider the American Bar Association's *Standards for Imposing Lawyer Sanctions. In re Morris,* 164 Ariz. 391, 393, 793 P.2d 544, 546 (1990). In imposing sanctions, we consider (a) the duty violated; (b) the lawyer's mental state; (c) the actual or potential injury caused by the lawyer's misconduct; and (d) the existence of aggravating or mitigating factors. *Standard* 3.0; *see Morris,* 164 Ariz. at 395, 793 P.2d at 548. The purposes of lawyer discipline are to protect the public and to deter future ethical violations. *In re Tarletz,* 163 Ariz. 548, 554, 789 P.2d 1049, 1055 (1990).

Standard 4.3, governing failure to avoid conflicts of interest, provides that "[s]uspension is generally appropriate when a lawyer knows of a conflict of interest and does not fully disclose to a client the possible effect of that conflict, and causes injury or potential injury to a client." *Standard* 4.32. The commentary notes that "suspension is appropriate when a lawyer knows or *should know* that the interests of a client are materially adverse to the interests of a former client in a substantially related matter, and causes injury or potential injury to the former or the subsequent client." *Standard* 4.32 commentary (emphasis added). *Standard* 4.33, which also is arguably applicable, provides that "[r]eprimand is generally appropriate when a lawyer is negligent in determining whether the representation of a client may be materially affected by the lawyer's own interests, or whether the representation will adversely affect another client, and causes injury or potential injury to a client." The commentary to that standard notes that "[c]ourts also impose reprimands in cases of subsequent representation."

In choosing between an informal reprimand and suspension, we consider respondent's prior disciplinary violations as aggravating circumstances, rather than as separate counts of the complaint. Rule 54(k)(4), Rules of the Supreme Court; *see In re Wines*, 135 Ariz. 203, 206, 660 P.2d 454, 457 (1983). *Standard* 8.2 recommends suspension when "a lawyer has been reprimanded for the same or similar misconduct and engages in further acts of misconduct that cause injury or potential injury to a client, the public, the legal system, or the profession." Because respondent has demonstrated an insensitivity to conflicts of interest evidenced by a pattern of misconduct, we find that suspension is the appropriate sanction. We adopt the Commission's recommendation that respondent be suspended for a period of 90 days.

We must tailor the discipline in each situation to the individual facts of the case to achieve the purposes of discipline. *Wines*, 135 Ariz. at 207, 660 P.2d at 458. Although *Standard* 2.3 recommends that suspensions be equal to or greater than 6 months, we believe that a 90-day suspension is appropriate in this case. Respondent is a public lawyer who is unlikely to receive any income during the period of his suspension, unlike lawyers in private practice who may continue to receive fees from work performed before the suspension.

Disposition

Respondent is suspended from the practice of law for a period of 90 days and ordered to pay the State Bar $1,595.27 in costs and expenses.

FELDMAN, V.C.J., and CAMERON and MOELLER, JJ., concur.

SOLUTIONS: THE LAWYER SHOULD HAVE, WOULD HAVE, COULD HAVE. . .

The violation of MR 1.9 is clear. Recall that a conflict is not *necessarily* about a lawyer committing an act that hurts a client but rather about lawyers placing themselves in a position in which there is a heightened risk of this happening. Perhaps the lawyer here forged ahead because neither he—nor his supervisors—understood this critical distinction. (Perhaps he thundered "I will not have my integrity questioned!"). Moreover, the violation here is so clear that the green light from the supervisors did not matter; there was no debatable question.

Finally, this case alerts you to a new rule, MR 5.2: Responsibilities of A Subordinate Lawyer. We will revisit the Rule in a later chapter. For now, understand that a subordinate lawyer is not only bound by the Rules but must adhere to them despite contrary instructions from a supervisory lawyer. The only exception is if the supervisory lawyer's resolution of an arguable ethical dilemma is reasonable. Here, the opinions of the supervisory lawyers did not matter because the Rule violation was clear and there was no valid contrary argument that could be raised.

C. Imputed Conflicts: When Lawyers Change Firms

Once, a lawyer went to work for one or possibly two firms in their career; now lawyers will work with several firms in their careers and maybe one or two government entities. This reality makes it critical to remember that individual conflicts result in disqualification (DQ) of that lawyer moving firms and the new firm unless a "screen" is established. In short: if a firm's new lawyer has a conflict, then the whole firm has the same conflict unless the new lawyer is screened out from the lawyer's new colleagues.

The practical conflicts question then is this: Lawyer Frank works at ABC firm; that firm represents Big Company; Frank leaves to go to XYZ firm that represents Small Company. XYZ firm represents Small Company that is locked in fierce litigation with, you guessed it, Big Company. Is Frank's new firm now disqualified from continuing the representation? No, provided that Frank has no knowledge of the litigation from working at ABC firm. If he does have such knowledge, then Frank must be screened out from any interactions at XYZ firm on the litigation to ensure that his knowledge does not—directly or indirectly— seep into his new firm and give it an unfair advantage. Essentially, the new lawyer's knowledge, if any, of the lawsuit must be insulated from the rest of the new firm. This is where the mechanics of MR 1.10 come into play.

The Rules also deal with what is sometimes characterized as "the revolving door" that is, the situation in when lawyer serves as a government lawyer and then enters private practice. The imputation rule is MR 1.11. While it too has a screening requirement, it differs from MR 1.10 in that it focuses on how deeply involved is the lawyer in the Why? Government hierarchy might mean that the lawyer's knowledge is of a very general and merely ministerial nature. If so, DQ is not required.

Model Rule 1.10: Imputation of Conflicts of Interest: General Rules

(a)   While lawyers are associated in a firm, none of them shall knowingly represent a client when any one of them practicing alone would be prohibited from doing so by Rules 1.7 or 1.9, unless

(1)   the prohibition is based on a personal interest of the disqualified lawyer and does not present a significant risk of materially limiting the representation of the client by the remaining lawyers in the firm; or

(2)   the prohibition is based upon Rule 1.9(a) or (b) and arises out of the disqualified lawyer's association with a prior firm, and

    (i)   the disqualified lawyer is *timely* screened from any participation in the matter and is apportioned no part of the fee therefrom;

    (ii)   written notice is promptly given to any affected former client to enable the former client to ascertain compliance with the provisions of this Rule, which shall include a description of the screening procedures employed; a statement of the firm's and of the screened lawyer's compliance with these Rules; a statement that review may be available before a tribunal; and an agreement by the firm to respond promptly to any written inquiries or objections by the former client about the screening procedures; and

    (iii)   certifications of compliance with these Rules and with the screening procedures are provided to the former client by the screened lawyer and by a partner of the firm, at *reasonable intervals* upon the former client's written request and upon termination of the screening procedures.

(b)   When a lawyer has terminated an association with a firm, the firm is not prohibited from thereafter representing a person with interests materially adverse to those of a client represented by the formerly associated lawyer and not currently represented by the firm, unless:

    (1)   the matter is the same or substantially related to that in which the formerly associated lawyer represented the client; and

    (2)   any lawyer remaining in the firm has information protected by Rules 1.6 and 1.9(c) that is material to the matter.

(c)   A disqualification prescribed by this rule may be waived by the affected client under the conditions stated in Rule 1.7.

(d)   The disqualification of lawyers associated in a firm with former or current government lawyers is governed by Rule 1.11.

Deconstruction Exercise/Rule Rationale

As you read this Rule, pay special attention to the language in (a)(2). What is the common theme? The key is to establish the screen promptly, once the firm learns that the new lawyer has knowledge of the litigation because of prior employment. Note the use of "timely" and "promptly." Why is a prompt screen important? Because a bell cannot be unrung. Once knowledge comes over to the new firm it can spread like a contagion. The rule is focused on the possibility of information spreading, and not the actual spreading. Vigilance is key as you will see in the two cases we selected for this section of the book.

Let's Chart It!

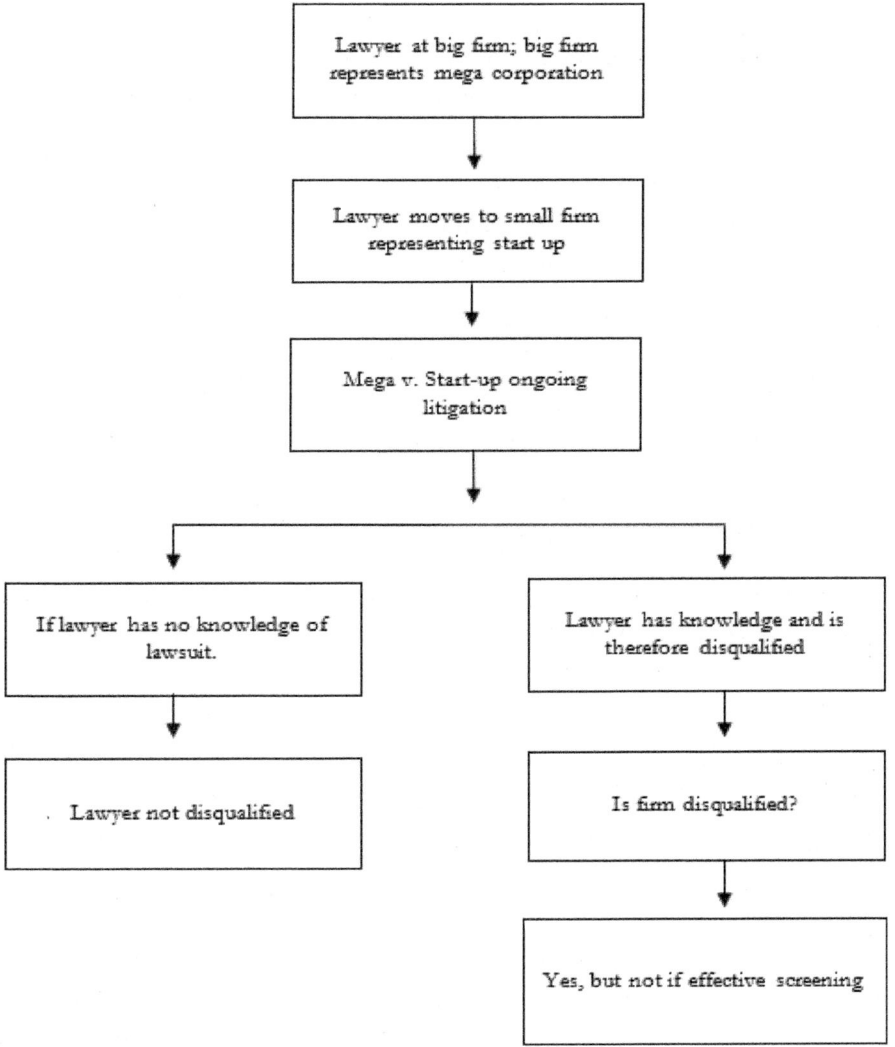

Model Rule 1.11(a)–(b): Special Conflicts of Interest for Former & Current Government Officers & Employers

(a)   Except as law may otherwise expressly permit, a lawyer who has formerly served as a public officer or employee of the government:

    (1)   is subject to Rule 1.9(c); and

    (2)   shall not otherwise represent a client in connection with a matter in which the lawyer participated personally and substantially as a public officer or employee, unless the appropriate government agency gives its informed consent, confirmed in writing, to the representation.

(b)   When a lawyer is disqualified from representation under paragraph (a), no lawyer in a firm with which that lawyer is associated may knowingly undertake or continue representation in such a matter unless:

    (1)   the disqualified lawyer is timely screened from any participation in the matter and is apportioned no part of the fee therefrom; and

    (2)   written notice is promptly given to the appropriate government agency to enable it to ascertain compliance with the provisions of this rule.

Deconstruction Exercise/Rule Rationale

For MR 1.1, the operative words are "personally and substantially." If the lawyer is "personally" involved only, then the knowledge acquired might not be of import and thus no screen necessary; similarly, if involvement is only of a "substantial" nature, there is no indication of the degree of intimacy with that knowledge (even if of import) and thus no screen necessary. It takes both personal and substantial participation to trigger a screening obligation.

Cases and Materials

X-Ray Questions (*Papyrus*)

This is a classic imputation case. A lawyer switches firms and the prior firm seeks not only his DQ from a lawsuit in which the law firms represent opposing litigants but also the DQ of his new firm. What was the basis for its motion? Why do you think it was so fixated on getting the other firm DQ'd from the litigation? Who benefits? What are the overall concerns of the court on whether to grant the DQ motion? Can you bring in your earlier lessons on how a client is entitled to the lawyer of choice and the importance of that value? What tipped the scales in favor of the court denying the DQ motion?

Papyrus Technology Corp. v. New York Stock Exchange, Inc.

United States District Court, S.D. New York, 2004.
325 F.Supp.2d 270.

OPINION & ORDER

CASEY, DISTRICT JUDGE.

This case arises from the allegations of Papyrus Technology Corp. ("Papyrus") that the New York Stock Exchange, Inc. ("NYSE") committed patent infringement and breach of contract. Specifically, Papyrus alleges that the NYSE violated its four patents for a wireless device that enables brokers to make and receive inquiries, receive and execute orders, and provide instructions for orders. Papyrus further alleges that the NYSE breached its contractual obligations by not paying to use the proprietary technology. The NYSE counterclaims for a declaratory judgment that the NYSE has not violated the four patents.

The issues presently before the Court, however, have little to do with patent infringement and the work of the stock exchange. Instead, the present dispute implicates the work of attorneys, the ethics of the profession, and a litigant's right to choose its counsel. The NYSE moves to disqualify Mr. Tedd Van Buskirk and the law firm of Frommer Lawrence & Haug ("Frommer") from serving as Papyrus's counsel. The NYSE claims that while an associate at Milbank, Tweed, Hadley & McCloy ("Milbank"), which represents NYSE, Van Buskirk had access to and received NYSE confidences or secrets material to this case. As a result, the NYSE argues that Van Buskirk and Frommer may not represent Papyrus. For the reasons set forth below, NYSE's motion is **GRANTED IN PART AND DENIED IN PART**.

BACKGROUND

From May 1988 through June 2001, Van Buskirk was an associate in Milbank's twelve-member intellectual property group. (Declaration of Tedd W. Van Buskirk, dated March 9, 2004 [3/9/04 Van Buskirk Decl.] ¶ 2; Declaration of Christopher E. Chalsen [Chalsen Decl.] ¶¶ 5–6.) While he worked for Milbank, the NYSE retained the firm to provide advice on the Papyrus patents, which are the subject of this dispute. (*Id.* ¶ 9.) It is undisputed that Van Buskirk never worked on the NYSE-Papyrus matter while at Milbank. (*Id.*; 3/9/04 Van Buskirk Decl. ¶¶ 3, 7; Declaration of Tedd W. Van Buskirk, dated April 8, 2003 [sic] [4/8/04 Van Buskirk Decl.] ¶ 11.)

Nonetheless, the NYSE contends that Van Buskirk received NYSE confidences or secrets related to the patents on several instances. First, the NYSE avers that Van Buskirk attended weekly meetings of the intellectual property group, at which confidential client matters were discussed. (Chalsen Decl. ¶¶ 8, 11.) Papyrus responds that the discussions at these meetings concerned developments in intellectual property law, for which Van Buskirk received continuing legal education credit. (4/8/04 Van Buskirk Decl. ¶¶ 17–18.) Second, the NYSE proffers that Van Buskirk actually received NYSE confidences or secrets when he received three emails concerning the NYSE-Papyrus matter. (Email, Ex. A to Chalsen Decl.; Emails, Ex. A to Declaration of Chris L. Holm [Holm Decl.].) Each was sent on August 24, 2000, by Milbank partners; two were addressed to the entire Milbank intellectual practice group while the third was sent solely between Milbank partners (therefore, it appears that Van Buskirk never received the third email). (Email, Ex. A to Chalsen Decl.; Emails, Ex. A to Holm Decl.; 4/8/04 Van Buskirk Decl. ¶¶ 4–9.) To the extent that he did receive confidential information on the NYSE-Papyrus matter, Van Buskirk no longer recalls its substance. (3/9/04 Van Buskirk Decl. ¶ 3; 4/8/04 Van Buskirk Decl. ¶¶ 4, 6, 10, 12, 18.)

In addition to alleging that Van Buskirk actually received NYSE confidences or secrets, the NYSE contends that he had access to such information. For example, the NYSE points to the fact that Milbank's files relating to the NYSE-Papyrus matter were stored near Van Buskirk's office. (Chalsen Decl. ¶¶ 12–13.) The NYSE further posits that Van Buskirk (like all Milbank intellectual property attorneys) had access to a centralized electronic document management system and that he could have accessed electronic versions of documents. (*Id.* ¶ 14.) Papyrus counters that Van Buskirk never had reason to review either the paper or electronic documents and never did so. (4/8/04 Van Buskirk Decl. ¶¶ 13–15.) Moreover, Papyrus argues that Milbank's electronic document management system tracks when a person has accessed an electronic document and records the person's name and time of access, but that the NYSE has not furnished evidence to demonstrate Van Buskirk reviewed these files. (*Id.* ¶ 16.)

Van Buskirk transferred from Milbank to Frommer in June 2001. (Chalsen Decl. ¶ 5; 3/9/04 Van Buskirk Decl. ¶ 2.) Since then, Papyrus approached Frommer about suing the NYSE for patent infringement after its long-time attorneys at Darby & Darby withdrew on conflict grounds. (Declaration of Edgar H. Haug [Haug Decl.] ¶ 2; Patterson Decl. ¶¶ 3, 10–13; Chalsen Decl. ¶ 18.) Around November 2003, Papyrus retained the fifty-member Frommer law firm to represent it in this action. (Haug Decl. ¶¶ 2, 16.)

Immediately after Papyrus approached Frommer, it conducted a conflict check by, among other things, circulating a memo to all attorneys. (*Id.* ¶ 2.) In response to the memo, Van Buskirk informed a Frommer partner that he previously worked at Milbank where he had been aware of a dispute between Papyrus and the NYSE. (3/9/04 Van Buskirk Decl. ¶ 6; Haug Decl. ¶ 3.) However, Van Buskirk stated that he had neither worked on the NYSE-Papyrus matter nor on any other NYSE matter. (3/9/04 Van Buskirk Decl. ¶ 6; Haug Decl. ¶ 3.) Van Buskirk further advised the partner that he did not recall learning any privileged or confidential NYSE information while at Milbank. (3/9/04 Van Buskirk Decl. ¶ 6; Haug Decl. ¶ 3.) Because Van Buskirk had previously worked at Milbank and had a general knowledge of the NYSE-Papyrus matter, he was not assigned to work on the case. (3/9/04 Van Buskirk Decl. ¶ 6; Haug Decl. ¶ 4.)

On March 1, 2004, for the first time, NYSE's counsel raised Van Buskirk's previous employment as a reason for disqualification of both Van Buskirk and Frommer. (*Id.* ¶ 9; Amundson Decl. ¶ 2.) On March 5, 2004, when Milbank provided Frommer a redacted copy of an email message that listed Van Buskirk as an addressee, Frommer immediately implemented a formal screen to ensure that Van Buskirk was not involved with or had access to information regarding the NYSE-Papyrus matter. (Haug Decl. ¶ 10; Amundson Decl. ¶ 4.) Frommer instituted the following screening mechanisms: (1) all Frommer employees were directed to refrain from discussing the Papyrus litigation with Van Buskirk; (2) all Frommer employees were instructed that Van Buskirk should not see any written materials related to the NYSE-Papyrus matter; and (3) Van Buskirk was ordered to refrain from communicating with anyone about or reviewing any written materials related to the NYSE-Papyrus matter. (Haug Decl. ¶ 11.) All Frommer employees have agreed in writing to abide by these restrictions. (*Id.* ¶ 12.) Finally, Frommer has sealed the firm's document management system (typically accessible by any firm employee) so that only the team working on the case may access electronic documents. (*Id.* ¶ 13.) While at Frommer, Van Buskirk has performed no work on the NYSE-Papyrus matter. (3/9/04 Van Buskirk Decl. ¶ 5; 4/8/04 Van Buskirk Decl. ¶ 19.)

DISCUSSION

There are two instances when an attorney may be subject to possible disqualification: (1) when the challenged attorney is concurrently representing adverse interests so that the attorney's vigor in pursuing one of them may be questioned; and (2) when the attorney has successively represented adverse interests, raising the possibility that confidences or secrets derived from the former representation may be used in the current representation to the former client's detriment. *See United States Football League,* 605 F.Supp. at 1452. This motion implicates the latter.

Disqualification motions premised on an attorney's prior representation of a now adverse client are committed to the discretion of the district court. *See Cheng,* 631 F.2d at 1055. In addition, such motions are generally viewed with disfavor in this Circuit. *See Evans,* at 791–92; *Song v. Dreamtouch, Inc.,* No. 01 Civ. 0386, 2001 WL 487413, at *4 (S.D.N.Y. May 8, 2001); *Interpetrol Bermuda, Ltd. v. Rosenwasser,* No. 86 Civ. 5631, 1988 WL 140801, at *1 (S.D.N.Y. Dec.20, 1988). For this reason, the Second Circuit has directed that courts faced with disqualification motions take a "restrained approach that focuses primarily on preserving the integrity of the trial process." *Armstrong v. McAlpin,* 625 F.2d 433, 444 (2d Cir.1980), *vacated on other grounds and remanded,* 449 U.S. 1106, 101 S.Ct. 911, 66 L.Ed.2d 835 (1981); *see also United States Football League,* 605 F.Supp. at 1463 n. 31 ("Courts are not policemen of the legal profession; that is a matter for the disciplinary arm of the bar. Disqualification is granted to protect the integrity of the proceedings, not to monitor the ethics of attorneys' conduct."); *cf. Wheat v. United States,* 486 U.S. 153, 160, 108 S.Ct. 1692, 100 L.Ed.2d 140 (1988) (stating that in criminal trials "federal courts have an independent interest in ensuring [trials] are conducted within the ethical standards of the profession and that legal proceedings appear fair to all who observe them."). Moreover, a district court must consider the factual record underlying such a motion in detail to determine whether the party seeking disqualification has sustained the high standard of proof necessary to disqualify opposing counsel. *See Evans,* 715 F.2d at 791; *Gov't of India,* 569 F.2d at 739; *UCAR,* 2002 WL 31519616, at *2; *Fields-D'Arpino,* 39 F.Supp.2d at 415.

The NYSE contends that under the New York State Bar Association's Disciplinary Rules Van Buskirk must be disqualified from representing Papyrus and that his disqualification ought to be imputed to the entire Frommer firm. Although New York's Disciplinary Rules are not binding on federal courts—as they were intended for use in disciplinary proceedings rather than in attorney disqualification motions—the Court refers to these rules, and to the Committee on Professional Ethics's opinions interpreting them, for guidance. *See, e.g., Cheng,* 631 F.2d at 1055–56; *Stratavest,* 903 F.Supp. at 666; *United States Football League,* 605 F.Supp. at 1463 n. 31. Moreover, this Court requires that attorneys adhere to New York's Disciplinary Rules. *See* S.D.N.Y. Local Civil R. 1.3, 1.5.

I.   Van Buskirk's Disqualification under Disciplinary Rule 5–108

Disciplinary Rule 5–108(A) warns that:

[A] lawyer who has represented a client in a matter shall not, without the consent of the former client after full disclosure:

1.   Thereafter represent another person in the same or a substantially related matter in which that person's interests are materially adverse to the interests of the former client.

2.   Use any confidences or secrets of the former client except as permitted by DR 4–101. . . .

New York courts have explained that a disqualifying conflict exists on the basis of a former representation when: (1) an attorney-client relationship previously existed between the moving party and the opposing counsel; (2) the matters involved in the current and former representations are the same or substantially related; and (3) the interests of the present client and the former client are materially adverse. *See Tekni-Plex, Inc. v. Meyner & Landis,* 89 N.Y.2d 123, 651 N.Y.S.2d 954, 674 N.E.2d 663, 667 (1996). There is no material dispute that Milbank represented the NYSE during Van Buskirk's tenure as an associate, that Frommer represents Papyrus on essentially the same matter, or that the NYSE and Papyrus hold adverse interests. The disputed issue is whether an attorney-client relationship existed between the NYSE and Van Buskirk.

Papyrus argues that disqualification is unnecessary because there existed no attorney-client relationship between the NYSE and Van Buskirk. For purposes of D.R. 5–108(A), a lawyer need not have an express attorney-client relationship with the former client. *See Glueck v. Jonathan Logan, Inc.,* 653 F.2d 746, 748–49 (2d Cir.1981) (stating that "the issue is not whether [the attorney's] relationship to [the former client] is in all respects that of attorney and client, but whether there exists sufficient aspects of an attorney-client relationship for purposes of triggering inquiry into the potential conflict involved"); *Marshall v. State of New York Div. of State Police,* 952 F.Supp. 103, 108 (N.D.N.Y.1997) (concluding that in attorney disqualification motions whether the attorney's "relationship with the [former client] rose to the level of 'attorney-client' is not the ultimate issue.").

Rather, a lawyer has "represented a client" if the lawyer has obtained or had access to confidences or secrets of the former client. *See* N.Y. State Bar Ass'n Comm. on Prof'l Ethics, Op. 723 (1999) [Ethics Op. 723]. While at Milbank, Van Buskirk received emails and had access to files regarding the NYSE-Papyrus matter. Therefore, under D.R. 5–108(A), he represented the NYSE.

Disciplinary Rule 5–108(A) is "premised on the irrebuttable presumption that a lawyer who formerly represented a client will have obtained secrets and confidences of the client." *Id.* Moreover, there exists a presumption that Van Buskirk had access to NYSE confidences or secrets relevant to this case because Milbank represented the NYSE while Van Buskirk worked there. *See Decora,* 899 F.Supp. at 135–36; *United States Football League,* 605 F.Supp. at 1461. The Court is therefore not required to inquire whether confidential information was in fact transmitted to Van Buskirk. "Such an inquiry would be improper; it would put the movant to the choice of either revealing its confidences in order to prevail on the motion or else refraining from moving to disqualify." *Id.* The redacted email correspondence adequately demonstrates that Van Buskirk was actually exposed to NYSE confidences or secrets. Therefore, Van Buskirk represented the NYSE under D.R. 5–108(A) and must be disqualified from representing Papyrus.

II.   Frommer's Disqualification under Disciplinary Rule 5–105(D)

The Court next turns to the remaining and presumably essential issue of the case: whether Frommer must be disqualified due to Van Buskirk's association with it. Under D.R. 5–105(D), the taint of a disqualified attorney may be imputed to the attorney's entire firm. The imputation rule is premised on the presumption that if confidences or secrets were disclosed to one member of a firm, each individual attorney in the firm has or may (intentionally or inadvertently) become privy to those confidences. Unlike the inquiry under D.R. 5–108(A), this presumption may be rebutted. *See United States Football League,* 605 F.Supp. at 1461 n. 28; *Kassis v. Teacher's Ins. & Annuity Ass'n,* 93 N.Y.2d 611, 695 N.Y.S.2d 515, 717 N.E.2d 674, 677 (N.Y.1999). In order to rebut this presumption, Frommer has manufactured a screen to fence Van Buskirk from the case. The NYSE contends that the screen was belatedly constructed and that as erected it fails to adequately enclose Van Buskirk.

Neither the New York Code of Professional Responsibility nor the American Bar Association's Code of Professional Responsibility recognize the use of screening devices except in cases involving former government lawyers or judges. *See Mitchell v. Metro. Life Ins. Co.*, No. 01 Civ. 2112, 2002 WL 441194, at *9 (S.D.N.Y. Mar.21, 2002). However, courts have recognized that under appropriate circumstances a screen may rebut the presumption of shared confidences. *See, e.g., Lambert v. Chase Manhattan Bank, N.A.*, Nos. 93 Civ. 1317, 5298, 6876, 8270, 1996 WL 66130 (S.D.N.Y. Feb.15, 1996); *In re Del-Val Fin. Corp. Sec. Litig.*, 158 F.R.D. 270 (S.D.N.Y.1994); *Cummin v. Cummin*, 264 A.D.2d 637, 695 N.Y.S.2d 346, 347 (App.Div.1999). A per se rule of disqualification based on imputed confidences would be, as the New York State Court of Appeals has remarked, "unnecessarily preclusive because it disqualifies all members of a law firm indiscriminately, whether or not they share knowledge of a former client's confidences and secrets." *Solow v. W.R. Grace & Co.*, 83 N.Y.2d 303, 610 N.Y.S.2d 128, 632 N.E.2d 437, 440 (1994); *see also Kassis*, 695 N.Y.S.2d 515, 717 N.E.2d at 677 (holding that the disciplinary rule of imputation does not establish mandatory disqualification and stating that "because disqualification of a law firm may have significant adverse consequences to the client and others, 'it is particularly important that the Code of Professional Responsibility not be mechanically applied when disqualification is raised in litigation.' ") (quoting *S & S Hotel Ventures v. 777 S.H. Corp.*, 69 N.Y.2d 437, 515 N.Y.S.2d 735, 508 N.E.2d 647, 651 (1987)).

The touchstones of the imputation inquiry are the significance of the prohibited lawyer's involvement in and knowledge of the former client's confidences or secrets. *See, e.g., Cheng*, 631 F.2d at 1054, 1057–58; *Crudele*, 2001 WL 1033539, at *3–6; *United States Football League*, 605 F.Supp. at 1451–52. Several factors may guide a court in undertaking this inquiry.

As a threshold matter, a court must examine the degree to which the tainted attorney represented the former client. For example, when an associate has played an "appreciable role" in representing an adversary in the same matter, a screen will, as a matter of law, fail to rebut the presumption of shared confidences or secrets. *See Kassis*, 695 N.Y.S.2d 515, 717 N.E.2d at 678. In *Kassis*, the court held that because a tainted attorney "appeared as sole counsel" for the adversary and was "sufficiently knowledgeable and steeped in the files of [the] case," the existence of a screen was inconsequential. *Id.* This is not the case when a tainted attorney performs only minimal work for an adversary. In *Del-Val*, for instance, the law firm Proskauer Rose Goetz & Mendelson ("Proskauer") was the subject of a disqualification motion. The court disqualified a Proskauer partner based on his previous representation, but declined to disqualify the entire firm. *See Del-Val*, 158 F.R.D. at 274–75. The court determined that the presumption of shared confidences was rebuttable in part because the tainted attorney's involvement in the representation had been peripheral. *Id.* at 274. Likewise, in *Lambert,* the court determined that the Milbank firm could rebut the presumption of shared confidences. The court premised its conclusion on the fact that, although a Milbank associate had performed eight-hundred hours of work for an adverse client while at another firm, the work consisted largely of document review and participation in depositions. *Id.* at *1. Given the nature of this work, the court concluded that "[w]hile [it] understands that [the associate] will have been privy to relevant confidences, including some strategy considerations, he was, plainly, not a strategy-maker." *Id.* Here, it is undisputed that Van Buskirk was not a strategy-maker; in fact, he performed no work on the NYSE-Papyrus matter while at Milbank. Given that Van Buskirk's previous involvement in the case was minuscule, Frommer may rebut the presumption of shared confidences or secrets.

Although no bright line rule exists, another pertinent consideration as to whether the presumption has been rebutted is the relative recency of Van Buskirk's employment with Milbank. For example, in *Lambert,* the court noted that the associate had been separated from his prior firm for more than a year. *Id.; see also Wieme v. Eastman Kodak Co.,* Nos. 02 Civ. 6021L, 6212, 2003 WL 23163157, at *5 (W.D.N.Y. Sept. 22, 2003) (noting that, although not dispositive, the passage of time is a relevant factor in a disqualification inquiry). Here, almost thirty months had passed between the time Van Buskirk worked at Milbank and when Papyrus retained Frommer. Such a gap in time weighs in Papyrus's favor.

Moreover, a party may attempt to rebut the presumption of shared knowledge through affidavits setting-forth the tainted attorney's recollection of any confidential information and whether the attorney shared such information with co-workers. *See Del-Val,* 158 F.R.D. at 274 (weighing disqualified attorney's affidavit stating that he did not speak to anyone at firm regarding previous representation of former client and that he no longer recalled the confidential information he received). Papyrus has submitted affidavits by Van Buskirk to rebut the presumption of shared knowledge. In these affidavits, Van Buskirk states that he does not recall any confidential information gleaned from his time at Milbank. Moreover, he states that he did not speak to anyone at Frommer regarding the substance of the case. Each of the Frommer attorneys who worked on the NYSE-Papyrus matter before a formal screen was instituted likewise affirm. These affidavits also weigh against imputing Van Buskirk's disqualification to Frommer.

Another reason why Van Buskirk's conflict should not be imputed to Frommer is that Van Buskirk's actual receipt of NYSE confidences or secrets was limited. The record chiefly consists of two emails Van Buskirk received some four years ago. The emails were correspondence between Milbank partners and were merely copied to the entire Milbank intellectual property group. Thus, Van Buskirk received the emails even though he was not working on the case. The passage of time since Van Buskirk received these emails and their wide distribution suggest that their contents (even if Van Buskirk recalled them) are unlikely to be highly significant to the current issues in this case. *See* Restatement (Third) of the Law Governing Lawyers § 124(2)(a) (establishing as a factor for not imputing a former client conflict to affiliated lawyers the situation when "confidential client information communicated to the personally prohibited lawyer is unlikely to be significant in the subsequent matter"). The limited record establishing Van Buskirk's actual receipt of NYSE confidences or secrets weighs against disqualifying Frommer.

Likewise, proof that Van Buskirk had access to NYSE confidences or secrets while at Milbank is scant. The NYSE posits that Van Buskirk had access to a centralized electronic document management system and that he could have accessed electronic versions of documents. The record contains uncontroverted evidence that the Milbank document system included a feature that could track each occasion when a person accessed an electronic document and record the person's name and time of access. However, NYSE has furnished no evidence to demonstrate that Van Buskirk ever accessed the electronic files. Thus, NYSE's evidence largely consists of the fact that documents relevant to this case were kept in a cabinet near Van Buskirk's office; but, Van Buskirk states that he never had reason to look at these files. As a young associate at a large New York law firm, it appears unlikely that Van Buskirk would have combed the files of an unassigned case. His statements in this regard are therefore credible. This factor also weighs against imputation.

The above factors are not alone sufficient to rebut the presumption of shared confidences. However, Frommer has also screened Van Buskirk from the case. Thus, the presumption is further rebutted by Frommer's screen.

The screen requires all of Frommer's employees to refrain from discussing the Papyrus litigation with Van Buskirk and from showing him written materials related to it. *See, e.g., Del-Val,* 158 F.R.D. at 273 (discussing similar screen that rebutted the presumption of shared confidences). Moreover, Frommer has ordered Van Buskirk to refrain from communicating with anyone about or reviewing any written materials related to the case. *Id.* Frommer has sealed the firm's document management system so that only members of the team working on the case may access electronic documents. *Id.* Finally, all Frommer employees have agreed in writing to abide by these restrictions. This screen evidences Van Buskirk's and Frommer's understanding of their ethical obligations in this matter. More importantly, it adequately isolates Van Buskirk from the case, thereby immunizing Frommer from his taint.

The Court next must determine whether the screen was timely erected. In November 2003, Papyrus approached Frommer about representing it in a lawsuit against the NYSE. Frommer conducted an intra-firm conflicts check, and learned that Van Buskirk, although he did no work on the matter and could not recall receiving confidential information about it, was aware that Milbank had represented the NYSE. For this reason, the lead partner on the case and Van Buskirk agreed that he would not work on it.

Approximately three months later, in a March 1, 2004, letter, Milbank raised the conflict issue with Frommer. Milbank alleged that Van Buskirk had received NYSE confidential and privileged information when he received an August 24, 2000, email. A Frommer partner immediately discussed the Milbank letter with Van Buskirk, who stated that he did not recall receiving any such email. On March 4, 2004, Frommer requested details about the email Van Buskirk allegedly received. On March 5, 2004, Milbank responded by furnishing a redacted email message sent by a Milbank partner to the entire intellectual property group, which included Van Buskirk. The very same day Frommer received the redacted email, it instituted a formal screen. Thus, when Frommer received actual notice that NYSE confidences or secrets may have been disclosed to Van Buskirk, it immediately established appropriate screening mechanisms. The Court concludes that Frommer timely screened Van Buskirk.

Given these facts, the Court concludes that there is no real danger that Papyrus may have gained or will gain an unfair advantage over the NYSE if Frommer represents it and that it would be highly unjust to disqualify each member of the Frommer firm. *See id.* at 275. For the foregoing reasons, Frommer has rebutted the presumption of shared confidences or secrets.

CONCLUSION

Significant competing interests are inherent in a motion to disqualify an attorney. The Court must balance the general policy favoring a party's right to choose its counsel while ensuring that a litigant will not obtain an unfair advantage over an adversary at trial. Having weighed these interests, the Court concludes that Van Buskirk must be disqualified; however, the Court harbors no doubt that, in light of the facts presented here, Frommer's screening measures are timely and effective. Van Buskirk may not represent Papyrus, but his disqualification is not imputed to Frommer.

SOLUTIONS: THE LAWYER SHOULD HAVE, WOULD HAVE, COULD HAVE...

The firm moving to disqualify the new firm was essentially engaging in an expensive litigation gambit. But the payoff could be major: Stripping the opposing party of its attorneys of choice. That can be a major litigation advantage. But the challenged firm had acted quickly and in doing so protected its client.

Cases and Materials

X-Ray Questions (*Martin*)

The previous case shows a successful screen. We selected the *Martin* case because it shows the opposite. The defense lawyer in a discrimination lawsuit joins the firm of counsel opposite in the middle of the litigation. The lawyer who joined the opposing firm is DQ'd from representing the plaintiff. Why? What analysis did the court conduct in order to reach its decision? The more interesting question, however, is whether the entire plaintiff's firm is also DQ'd. Why did the court say, "yes?" What should the lawyer in charge of the plaintiff's firm have done that he did not do? How were the three plaintiffs harmed because the lawyer did not establish an effective screen? What do you think the plaintiffs did *after* the DQ motion was granted?

Martin v. AtlantiCare

United States District Court, D. New Jersey, 2011.
2011 WL 5080255.

OPINION

JOEL SCHNEIDER, UNITED STATES MAGISTRATE JUDGE.

After Lisa Grosskruetz, Esquire, did substantial substantive defense work on this case while employed by defendants' law firm, Morgan, Lewis and Bockius, LLP ("Morgan"), she left Morgan and went to work for plaintiffs' law firm, Costello & Mains, P.C. The question before the Court is whether Costello & Mains should be disqualified because it employed a side-switching attorney.

Under the circumstances presented herein the answer is an emphatic yes. Accordingly, defendants' Motion to Disqualify Plaintiffs' Counsel is GRANTED.

Discussion

Fact Background

Plaintiffs Shelly Martin ("Martin"), Karla Mayfield and Donna Davis filed this lawsuit on October 28, 2010 in the Superior Court of New Jersey. The case was removed to federal court on December 28, 2010. All plaintiffs allege, *inter alia,* that defendants discriminated and retaliated against them because of their race and ethnicity. Plaintiff Martin also alleges that her employer, ARMC, violated the New Jersey Wage and Hour Law and the Fair Labor Standards Act by not paying her for work in excess of forty hours per week. Martin brings this claim on behalf of herself and as a "collective action" on behalf of similarly situated workers.

Plaintiffs are represented by Costello & Mains ("CM"). The managing partner of the firm is Kevin Costello ("Costello" or "KC"). Defendants are represented by Morgan. As noted, the side-switching attorney at issue is Lisa Grosskruetz ("LG"). At the inception of the case, defendants' defense was coordinated by a three-attorney team at Morgan. The supervising partner-in-charge was Richard Rosenblatt, Esquire ("RR"). The other attorneys on the original defense team were LG and Prashanth Jayachandran, Esquire, ("PJ"). LG started working for Morgan on November 22, 2010 after having litigated employment matters in New Jersey for 23 years. PJ has been admitted to practice for 12 years and has extensive experience representing employers in wage and hour class and collective actions.

According to her time records LG started working on this case for Morgan on November 24, 2010. LG left Morgan on March 4, 2011. During the approximately 4½ months she was employed at Morgan LG worked 108.2 hours on the case. During the same time period RR worked only 13.1 hours on the case and PJ worked 49.6 hours. *See* PJ Declaration ¶ 3. This motion to disqualify arises from the fact that after LG left Morgan on March 4, 2011, she started working for CM on March 7, 2011. *See* LG Declaration ¶ 1. LG subsequently left CM on April 15, 2011 and is no longer working for the firm. Defendants were not notified of LG's side-switching before LG started working at CM. Defendants first learned that their former defense counsel was employed at their adversary's law firm when PJ noticed LG's name on CM's letterhead.

The parties do not dispute that LG is disqualified from representing plaintiffs pursuant to New Jersey Rule of Professional Conduct ("RPC") 1.9. Defendants argue that since LG is disqualified from representing plaintiffs, the disqualification should be imputed to CM pursuant to RPC 1.10. Defendants argue LG had "primary responsibility" for the defense of this matter while she was employed at Morgan and therefore she cannot be adequately screened. Defendants also argue that even if LG did not have primary responsibility CM still must be disqualified because LG was not adequately screened. In addition, defendants argue disqualification is appropriate because they did not receive timely written notice of LG's side-switching. Plaintiffs dispute that LG had primary responsibility for defendants' defense while she worked at Morgan. Plaintiffs also argue LG was adequately screened and that defendants received timely notice of LG's side-switching.

Motions to Disqualify

In the District of New Jersey, issues regarding professional ethics are governed by L. Civ. R. 103. 1(a). This Rule provides that the Rules of Professional Conduct of the American Bar Association as revised by the New Jersey Supreme Court shall govern the conduct of members of the bar admitted to practice in the District. *See* L. Civ. R. 103.1(a); *Carlyle Towers Condo. Ass'n, Inc. v. Crossland Sav., FSB*, 944 F.Supp. 341, 344–45 (D.N.J.1996). When deciding a motion to disqualify counsel the movant bears the burden of proof that disqualification is appropriate. *City of Atlantic City v. Trupos ("Trupos")*, 201 N.J. 447, 462–63, 992 A.2d 762 (2010); *Maldonado v. New Jersey, ex rel. Admin. Off. Of Cts.-Prob. Div.*, 225 F.R.D. 120, 136–37 (D.N.J.2004). The movant's burden is a heavy one since "[m]otions to disqualify are viewed with 'disfavor' and disqualification is considered a 'drastic measure which courts should hesitate to impose except when absolutely necessary.'" *Alexander v. Primerica Holdings, Inc.*, 822 F.Supp. 1099, 1114 (D.N.J.1993) (quoting *Schiessle v. Stephens*, 117 F.2d 417, 420 (7th Cir.1983) (internal quotation marks and citation omitted)). Nevertheless, "a motion for disqualification calls for [courts] to balance competing interests, weighing the need to maintain the highest standards of the profession against a client's right freely to choose his counsel." *Trupos*, 201 N.J. at 462, 992 A.2d 762 (citing *Dewey v. R.J. Reynolds Tobacco Co.*, 109 N.J. 201, 218, 536 A.2d 243 (1988). In weighing this balance the Court is mindful that "there is no right to demand to be represented by an attorney [or law firm] disqualified because of an ethical requirement." *Id.*

When determining whether to disqualify counsel the Court must closely and carefully scrutinize the facts to prevent unjust results. *Montgomery Acad. v.*

Kohn, 50 F.Supp.2d 344, 349 (D.N.J.1999). In *Steel v. Gen. Motors Corp.,* 912 F.Supp. 724, 733 (D.N.J.1995) (citation omitted), the court noted that its balancing "involves a 'painstaking analysis of the facts and precise application of precedent.' " *Id.* In addition, "[t]he decision whether to disqualify a law firm by imputation is best undertaken on a case-by-case basis, weighing the facts as they exist at the time the motion to disqualify is made. New Jersey courts have consistently eschewed per se rules of disqualification, stressing the 'fact-sensitive nature' of a decision to disqualify counsel." *Cardona v. Gen. Motors Corp.,* 942 F.Supp. 968, 976 (D.N.J.1996).

Since disqualification issues are intensely fact-specific, it is essential to approach such issues with a sense of practicality as well as a precise understanding of the underlying facts. *Murphy v. Simmons,* Civ. No. 06–1535(WHW), 2008 WL 65174, at *5 (D.N.J. Jan.3, 2008) (citation and quotation omitted). Accordingly, the Court scrutinized the parties' detailed submissions and is deciding defendants' motion based on the extensive written record and oral argument. The record includes the Declarations of Rosenblatt, Jayachandran, and Donna Michael-Ziereis, Esquire (defendants' Associate General Counsel). The record also includes the Certifications of Grosskreutz, Costello and Deborah L. Mains, Esquire. In addition, the Court reviewed *in camera* Morgan's bills from November 22, 2010 to February 28, 2011, which include each timekeeper's contemporaneous descriptions of his or her work. The Court also reviewed *in camera* a representative sample of LG's privileged e-mails while she worked at Morgan.

In order to decide defendants' motion it was not necessary to hold a formal evidentiary hearing or to hear LG's live testimony. New Jersey case law is quite clear that a motion to disqualify should ordinarily be decided on the basis of affidavits and documentary evidence except where "the court cannot with confidence decide the issue on the basis of the information contained in those papers . . . ." *Dewey,* 109 N.J. 201, 222, 536 A.2d 243 (1988). In *Dewey* the Court also noted that "a hearing should be held only when it is indispensable to resolution of the [disqualification] issue." *Id.* This is necessary to protect against the revelation of client confidences which the RPC's are designed to protect. *Id.* at 222–23, 536 A.2d 243. Given the detailed record, the Court determined that live testimony was not necessary.

RPC 1.9 and 1.10(c)

RPC 1.10(c) provides the framework for deciding defendants' motion. This RPC reads:

(c) When a lawyer becomes associated with a firm, no lawyer associated in the firm shall knowingly represent a person in a matter in which that lawyer is disqualified under RPC 1.9 unless,

(1) the matter does not involve a proceeding in which the personally disqualified lawyer had primary responsibility;

(2) the personally disqualified lawyer is timely screened from any participation in the matter and is apportioned no part of the fee therefrom; and

(3) written notice is promptly given to any affected former client to enable it to ascertain compliance with the provisions of this Rule.

As RPC 1.10(c) dictates, the Court must first determine whether LG is disqualified under RPC 1.9, which governs duties to former clients. RPC 1.9 provides:

(a) A lawyer who has represented a client in a matter shall not thereafter represent another client in the same or a substantially related matter in which that client's interests are materially adverse to the interests of the former client unless the former client gives informed consent confirmed in writing.

(b) A lawyer shall not knowingly represent a person in the same or a substantially related matter in which a firm with which the lawyer formerly was associated had previously represented a client,

(1) whose interests are materially adverse to that person; and

(2) about whom the lawyer, while at the former firm, had personally acquired information protected by RPC 1.6 and RPC 1.9(c) that is material to the matter unless the former client gives informed consent, confirmed in writing.

As has previously been discussed, LG joined CM immediately after leaving Morgan where she worked on the defense of the present case. Although plaintiffs minimize LG's role while at Morgan, they acknowledge that LG is disqualified from working on the case pursuant to RPC 1.9(a) and (b).

Having determined that LG is disqualified from representing plaintiffs pursuant to RPC 1.9, the pertinent issue becomes whether LG's disqualification is imputed to CM. To make this determination the Court must assess the three elements of RPC 1.10(c). First, whether LG had primary responsibility for the case while she worked at Morgan. Second, whether LG was adequately screened upon joining CM. Third, whether timely notice was provided to defendants of LG's side switching. The Court must conduct a "painstaking analysis of the facts" as to each of these elements. *See Dewey,* 109 N.J. at 205, 536 A.2d 243 (citation and quotation omitted).

"Primary Responsibility"

The focus of the parties' arguments centers on whether LG had primary responsibility for the defense of the litigation while she was employed at Morgan. Primary responsibility is defined in the "terminology" section of the RPC's as "actual participation in the management and direction of the matter at the policy-making level or responsibility at the operational level as manifested by the continuous day-to-day responsibility for litigation or transaction decisions." RPC 1.0(h). Since "surmise alone" cannot support disqualification, *Trupos,* 201 N.J. at 469, 992 A.2d 762, the evidence will be closely analyzed to determine if LG had primary responsibility.

If the Court determines that LG had "primary responsibility" while at Morgan its inquiry is complete and defendants' motion must be granted. Pursuant to RPC 1.10(c)(1), an attorney with primary responsibility cannot be screened at her new firm. *See In re Gabapentin Patent Litigation ("Gabapentin"),* 407 F.Supp.2d 607, 611 (D.N.J.2005) (screening of individual attorneys from involvement in a case at the firm was insufficient alone to overcome the imputed disqualification, where the individuals had primary responsibility in the same matter while acting as counsel for the opposing party).

The 2004 amendments to the RPC's, which added a screening option to RPC 1.10, "constitute[d] a major change in New Jersey's approach to the question of imputed disqualification in the context of representation adverse to a former client." Kevin H. Michels, *New Jersey Attorney Ethics: The Law of New Jersey Lawyering,* § 24:3–1 at 583 (2010) (hereinafter "Michels"). Pursuant to the present version of RPC 1.10:

> an attorney who worked on the matter while at the prior firm, but who did not have "primary responsibility," can be screened from the matter after switching to the new firm. . . . If the attorney had primary responsibility for the matter before switching firms, however, screening would not cure the imputed conflict. *Id.*

If LG did not have primary responsibility, the Court must then analyze RPC 1.10(c)(2)and (3). If LG was adequately screened and is not apportioned a fee from the case, and if adequate written notice was given to her affected former client, e.g., AtlantiCare, then defendants' motion should be denied. *See* Michels, *supra* ("The attorney's limited, peripheral involvement with the adverse party before switching firms would not prevent the new firm from continuing in the matter if the attorney were properly screened").

Plaintiffs and LG minimize LG's role while at Morgan. LG alleges she "was assigned to perform certain limited tasks with regard to this matter." LG Certification ¶ 1 ("LG Cert."). Plaintiffs argue, "the work Ms. Grosskreutz performed while an associate at Morgan Lewis concerned nothing more than review of mostly irrelevant and/or discoverable documents and interviews of witnesses that elicited discoverable information." Brief in Opposition ("Opp.Brief") at 8. *See also* Supplemental Brief in Opposition ("Supp.Brief") at 9.

Defendants present a drastically different view of LG's role. Defendants argue, "Ms. Grosskreutz was an integral part of the defense team and she was 'intimately involved in defendants' legal strategy.' " Memorandum of Law in Support of Defendants' Motion ("Memo. of Law") at 1. Defendants further argue, "Ms. Grosskreutz' hours were spent receiving and analyzing privileged and confidential information, being privy to defendants' litigation strategy, and assisting in tactical development of Defendants' defense." *Id.* at 10. In addition, defendants argue, "Ms. Grosskreutz was an important member of the defense team. She had primary responsibility because (1) she worked more than any other lawyers on this matter combined during the initial investigating and pleadings phase and (2) she was privy to confidential work product material during her representation of Defendants." Reply Memorandum of Law in Support of Defendants' Motion to Disqualify ("Reply Memo.") at 4.

Plaintiff's characterization of LG's role at Morgan as "limited" does not comport with the evidence. This is illustrated by the fact that from November 2010 to March 2011 LG worked 108.2 hours on the case, almost twice as many hours as the combined total of the other two members of the Morgan defense team. Further, LG's Certification supports defendants' argument that she played an integral role while at Morgan. LG acknowledges that she prepared all or part of defendants' removal papers and motion to dismiss, reviewed client documents for relevancy, consulted with defendants' in-house counsel, prepared witness outlines, interviewed defendants' witnesses, prepared witness summaries, and spoke with plaintiffs' counsel. LG's contemporaneous time billing entries also contradict her allegation that she only performed "limited tasks." LG Cert. ¶ 1. According to her billing entries LG researched relevant legal issues, prepared legal papers, analyzed plaintiffs' complaints, reviewed background investigation materials about plaintiffs provided by the client, exchanged e-mails with the client, reviewed client documents, prepared representation letters, analyzed plaintiffs' discovery directed to defendants, reviewed and analyzed plaintiffs' personnel files with regard to the defense of their discrimination claims, prepared witness outlines, interviewed witnesses, prepared witness summaries, communicated with her clients about plaintiffs, and identified relevant and responsive documents. These are hardly "limited" roles. LG's descriptions evidence that she played a substantial and substantive role in AtlantiCare's defense.

Defendants' Declarations provide further evidence of LG's integral defense role. RR provided Morgan's strategic leadership. RR Declaration ¶ 5. RR alleges that LG was "intimately involved in every facet of the defense" (*id.* ¶ 6) and that she "took an active operational role in almost all aspects of [Morgan's] defense of this matter" (*id.* ¶ 7). RR also states that the Morgan team would "make collaborative decisions as to how to address issues arising in the case" (*id.* ¶ 6). In addition, RR stated that LG would make recommendations for how to proceed with AtlantiCare's defense (*id.*) and he would brief LG on his communications with the client (*id.* ¶ 9). RR's staffing plan was for LG and PJ "to share primary responsibility for the day-to-day operational management of the case with [his] oversight and direction as needed." *Id.* ¶ 4. RR expected that eventually LG "would assume virtually the sole day-to-day lead operational role" by the time PJ became fully involved in another case pending in Boston. *Id.* RR explained that given LG's experience "the staffing plan was to have [LG] handle the bulk of the day-to-day case handling." *Id.*

AtlantiCare's in-house counsel corroborates Morgan's Declarations. She swore:

> Lisa Grosskreutz, a former Morgan Lewis associate, was actively representing AtlantiCare and the individual defendants in this case during her tenure at Morgan Lewis. We sent volumes of documents and materials to Morgan Lewis related to the case, which Ms. Grosskreutz reviewed. Ms. Grosskreutz also interviewed several witnesses. She communicated with me regarding her witness interviews and her review of documents related to this case. I also spoke with Ms. Grosskreutz regarding our legal strategy and our internal efforts to collect relevant documents. In addition, Ms. Grosskreutz is aware of AtlantiCare's investigation into matters raised by the Complaint.

Declaration of Donna Michael-Ziereis, Esquire ¶ 3.

LG's e-mails also evidence her integral defense role. The e-mails demonstrate that the Morgan defense team and AtlantiCare regularly communicated about the status of the case and defense strategies. The e-mails also demonstrate that LG was privy to information protected by the attorney-client privilege and work-product doctrine. In addition, the e-mails show that LG provided her strategic input on different employment related issues.

The foregoing evidence demonstrates to the Court that LG's actions fit squarely within the meaning of the term "primary responsibility" as the term is defined in the RPC's. In order to have primary responsibility it was not necessary for LG to be the supervising attorney on the file or the partner in charge of the file. This is evident by the fact that the applicable definition merely requires "participation" in the "management and direction of the matter at the policy-making level." LG plainly "participated" in the management of the case as she took the "laboring oar" in AtlantiCare's defense and she regularly consulted with the Morgan defense team about defense strategy. Further, as PJ was "out of pocket" in February 2011, and RR's role at the time was minimal, LG was essentially responsible for AtlantiCare's entire defense before she left Morgan. LG also had "responsibility at the operational level" as manifested by the "continuous day-to-day responsibility for litigation or transaction decisions." This is evidenced by LG's regular and continuous work on the file from when she started at Morgan to when she left. Given the breadth of her work and the number of hours she worked on the case, it cannot be reasonably challenged that LG had operational and decisional responsibilities.

The Court finds that LG had "primary responsibility" even though she was not the "supervising attorney" on the file and even though she shared defense responsibility with her colleagues.

The term "primary responsibility" has not been extensively addressed in the case law. Nonetheless, the decision in *United States of America v. Pelle*, No. CRIM. 05–407(JBS), 2007 WL 674723 (D.N.J. Feb. 28, 2007), discusses the issue in detail. In *Pelle*, the defendant sought to substitute new counsel, United Defense Group ("UDG") of Studio City, CA, to represent him over the objections of the United States. Before they joined UDG, two UDG attorneys, Lorilee and Angelyn Gates, represented "CW", a confidential witness who was expected to testify against Pelle at trial. This representation occurred while Lorilee and Angelyn were employed by CW's law firm, Criminal Defense Associates ("CDA") of Woodland, CA. The issue presented was whether the conflict that prevented Lorilee and Angelyn from representing Pelle was imputed to the UDG law firm pursuant to RPC 1.10(c).

The evidence in *Pelle* demonstrated that after CW was arrested, Lorilee traveled to New Jersey for CW's detention hearing and spoke with CW for 30 minutes to prepare for the hearing. At the hearing CW was released on conditions of bail. Thereafter, CW and Lorilee had no contact. While at CDA, Angelyn made telephone calls to gather preliminary information. She was not sure if she spoke with CW. Neither Lorilee or Angelyn worked on Pelle's defense after they left UDG to work at CDG. After Lorilee and Angelyn left UDG to work for CDG, CW pleaded guilty to a conspiracy pursuant to 18 U.S.C. § 2423(e) and named Pelle as his co-conspirator. CW was expected to testify as a material witness for the government in the case against Pelle. Pelle's proposed new trial counsel at UDG averred that he never spoke with Lorilee and Angelyn about the Pelle case or their representation of CW. UDG argued that despite employing CW's former attorneys, they could represent Pelle if the attorneys were screened from any participation in Pelle's defense. The United States objected to the representation.

As an initial matter, the court ruled that Lorilee and Angelyn should be disqualified from representing Pelle. *Id.* at *4. The Court then examined whether the disqualification was imputed to CDG pursuant to RPC 1.10. In this regard the Court focused on whether Lorilee and Angelyn had "primary responsibility" for defending CW. The court defined the term as follows:

> The term "primary responsibility" in RPC 1.10(c) is not self-defining. It includes the attorney who has sole responsibility or principal responsibility, and it would not connote an attorney whose contact with the client's file was incidental or technical. The purpose of the ethical requirement animates its meaning. The undoubted purpose is to assure that the conflict of an attorney who had substantial access to the former client's confidences and legal strategies will be imputed to the attorney's new firm, which may not represent an adverse interest in the same or similar matter.

Id. at *5. In deciding that Lorilee and Angelyn had "primary responsibility" the court focused on the fact that Lorilee interviewed CW, Lorilee and Angelyn obtained confidential information, and they developed strategy to represent CW at his detention hearing. *Id.* at *6. The court also noted CW's defense was a "team approach" which was divided by function. *See also Gabapentin*, 407 F.2d at 609 (noting that the side-switching attorneys had primary responsibility since they "were fully engaged in and primarily responsible for the pretrial representation of [their former client], and in the course thereof, were privy to confidential attorney work-product and privileged information. . . .")

LG's role in AtlantiCare's defense is much more extensive than the roles Lorilee and Angelyn played in the *Pelle* case. Here, LG not only interviewed AtlantiCare's witnesses and communicated with its in-house counsel, but she also prepared motion papers, analyzed relevant documents, prepared discovery responses and helped develop AtlantiCare's defense strategy. LG was an integral member of AtlantiCare's defense team.

When it decided that the disqualified attorneys had "primary responsibility," the court in *Pelle* was persuaded by the fact that the attorneys actually obtained confidential information regarding the former client (CW) in the same matter. The court noted that "a heightened precaution" was necessary in cases where "the disqualified attorney actually obtained confidential information regarding the former client in the same or similar matter." *Id.* at 5. The court also observed that "[t]he substantial roles performed by Angelyn Gates and Lorilee Gates, including their exposure to confidential information and strategies of defending CW, amount to primary responsibility within the intent of RPC 1.10(c)(1)." *Id.* at *6.

Here, the Court finds that LG obtained AtlantiCare's confidential and privileged information. This is supported by the Declarations of Rosenblatt, Jayachandran and Michael-Ziereis, and is documented in the e-mails the Court reviewed. LG was an "integral" member of Morgan's defense team. It therefore cannot be credibly disputed that LG had immediate and easy access to AtlantiCare's privileged and confidential information. Based on the evidence presented, plaintiffs' argument that "Ms. Grosskreutz [did] not receive any confidential information while employed at Morgan Lewis" (Supp. Brief at 10) is incredulous.

The Court finds LG had primary responsibility for AtlantiCare's defense for the same reasons expressed in *Pelle:*

> The Court . . . cannot overlook the cumulative weight of the collective responsibilities of the two attorneys Gates in representing CW, and the fact that actual confidential and tactical information was imputed to them during their time as his attorneys at Criminal Defense Associates.

Id. at *6. Similarly, LG's responsibilities at Morgan were extensive and substantive, and she gained confidential and privileged information. The Court finds that LG had a "direct," "substantial" and "meaningful" role in AtlantiCare's defense. *See id.* at *4, *6. LG, therefore, had primary responsibility for AtlantiCare's defense within the meaning of RPC 1.10(c).

Plaintiffs' arguments in opposition to defendants' motion are unavailing. Defendants argue the Court should accept LG's characterization of her work as limited because defendants' Declarations are biased. This argument is specious. The Court has no reason to question the accuracy of defendants' Declarations. Further, defendants' Declarations are consistent with LG's e-mails and time entries. Indeed, as noted herein, LG's averments, and not those of the defendants, are questionable.

The Court does not agree with plaintiffs' conclusion that LG played a minimal and unimportant defense role. LG's document reviews, witness interviews, etc. were significant and integrally related to the defense of the case. This work is not, as plaintiffs argue, "mechanical." Document review, preparing briefs and interviewing witnesses are all integral to an effective litigation defense. Moreover, the Court agrees with defendants that:

> However much Costello & Mains wish to mistakenly downplay [LG's] role, the fact remains that she interviewed multiple witnesses and prepared memoranda memorializing those meetings in detail. She prepared pleadings. She participated with co-counsel in developing strategy. These are not some minor tasks that a junior lawyer had been asked to perform in passing because of a shortage of resources.

Reply Memo. at 7.

The Court discounts plaintiffs' argument that even if CM received information from LG regarding the case, the information would have been discoverable and not subject to any privilege. *See* Opp. Brief at 10 ("LG herself has certified that many of the documents she reviewed were not relevant to this litigation, and, further, that none of the documents she reviewed would have been subject to any claim of privilege."). This argument has been rejected in various decisions. "Other courts have rejected the notion that the potential disclosure of confidential information in discovery could somehow ameliorate a conflict under Rule 1.9." *H20 Plus, LLC v. Arch Pers. Care Prods., L.P.*, Civ. No. 10–3089(WJM), 2010 WL 4869096, at *11 (D.N.J. Nov.23, 2010), *aff'd*, 2011 WL 1078584 (D.N.J. March 21, 2011)). As the court in *H20 Plus* noted:

> [A] discovery disclosure based standard governing disqualification is illogical and impractical. A simple example demonstrates the difficulties with such a standard. Say a lawyer adverse to a former client files a motion and prevails and the suit never reaches discovery. In theory, a lawyer could have confidential information from a client and use it to craft a motion to dismiss a subsequent complaint. If that

motion were to be granted, the lawyer, operating under a conflict, would have successfully avoided disqualification only because the lawyer was particularly adept at using confidential information to his/her benefit before discovery ever commenced .... Tying disqualification to future discovery is simply unworkable. It also does not comport with the policies that RPC 1.9 is premised upon.

2010 WL 4869096, at *12. The Court harbors the same concerns here. While some of the information LG had access to may be disclosed in discovery, it is also likely that other materials are privileged and not subject to production. The outcome of defendants' disqualification motion should not be dependent on a document by document analysis of what is and is not discoverable, otherwise:

> A former client seeking to keep a lawyer from side-switching would essentially be required to disclose privileged communications simply to maintain a level playing field and meet its burden of persuasion on a motion to disqualify. Every disqualification motion would have the potential to turn into a subdispute over complex privilege issues relating to documents and communications-all before the case even started. Such a standard would be manifestly unworkable and improper.

Id. The Court also agrees with defendants' argument that, "[f]ailure to disqualify Plaintiffs' counsel under these circumstances would undermine the confidence that clients have in their outside counsel." Memo. of Law at 11.

Screening

As noted, since LG had "primary responsibility" at Morgan, her conflict is imputed to CM pursuant to RPC 1.10(c) and defendants' motion to disqualify must be granted. However, even if LG did not have primary responsibility, defendants' motion would still be granted because plaintiffs cannot satisfy the screening requirement in RPC 1.10(c)(2).

Pursuant to the 2004 amendments to the RPC's, screening may cure an imputed conflict in an instance where the disqualified attorney did not have primary responsibility. RPC 1.10(c)(2) does not give detailed guidance on what needs to be done except to say that the disqualified lawyer must be screened from any participation in the matter and the screening must be timely. However, RPC 1.10(f) provides some guidance:

Any law firm that enters a screening arrangement, as provided by this Rule, shall establish appropriate written procedures to insure that: (1) all attorneys and other personnel in the law firm screen the personally disqualified attorney from any participation in the matter, (2) the screened attorney acknowledges the obligation to remain screened and takes action to insure the same, and (3) the screened attorney is apportioned no part of the fee therefrom.

In addition, RPC 1.10(1) (Terminology) states:

"Screened" denotes the isolation of a lawyer from any participation in the matter through the timely adoption and enforcement by a law firm of a written procedure pursuant to RPC 1.10(f) which is reasonably adequate under the circumstances to protect information that the isolated lawyer is obligated to protect under these Rules or other law.

Kevin Costello provided the only evidence as to LG's screening. His Certification states that upon LG's hiring "she was immediately screened from any contact or communication regarding the present matter." Costello Certification ¶ 3. The details of the screening were not included in the Certification. However, Costello represented at oral argument that LG was told before she started working for him that she was "not going to work on AtlantiCare." September 15, 2011 Transcript 28:9–11. Costello represented that the first day LG came to work he told everyone in his office that LG "can't touch this file," "she can't see this file," she "can't go to that file drawer herself," and she can't "click on AtlantiCare" on the "case management system." *Id.* Tr. 28:9 to 29:6. Costello also claims he had a reminder meeting with everyone in his office. *Id.* 29:6–19. Costello acknowledges that his firm did not have a written screening policy.

RPC 1.10(f) and 1.0(e) indicate in clear and unmistakable terms that to be adequate a screening procedure must be in writing. CM never established a written procedure and for this reason alone its screening was inadequate. CM argues its screening was adequate because the RPC's do not provide a time frame for when a written screening procedure must be deployed. September 15, 2011 Tr. 30:8–10. Therefore, CM argues, even though it did not have a written screening procedure when LG started at CM, nor at any time during the 6–7 weeks she worked there, CM's screening was adequate. This argument defies all notions of common sense. If the purpose of a screening procedure is to protect information the isolated lawyer is required to protect, written procedures should be in place before a disqualified lawyer starts work. At a minimum, the procedures should be in place when the employment starts, not after the disqualified lawyer leaves the firm. It makes no sense for the RPC's to require a written screening procedure but to find that the written procedure can be adopted after the disqualified lawyer leaves the firm. *"[T]imely* screening arrangements are essential to the avoidance of firm disqualification." *LaSalle Nat'l Bank v. County of Lake,* 703 F.2d 252, 259 n. 3 (7th Cir.1983) (emphasis in original).

In addition, even if CM's screening procedure was put in writing, the procedure CM used was inadequate. Although there is no definitive New Jersey guidance on the elements of an effective screen, the Court has no hesitation in finding CM's procedure inadequate. There is no indication that the AtlantiCare file was physically separated from CM's other files. In addition, the file was not specially secured or "kept under lock and key," LG and CM's employees did not acknowledge in writing CM's procedures, and LG was not "locked out" of the AtlantiCare file on CM's computer system. These are the sorts of procedures that are put in place in instances where courts have found screens to be adequate. *See Opalinski v. Robert Half Int'l Inc.,* C.A. No. 10–2069(SDW)(MCA) 2011 WL 1042762 (D.N.J. March 18, 2011); *see also LaSalle Nat'l Bank,* 703 F.2d at 259; *Holcombe v. Quest Diagnostics,* 675 F.Supp.2d 515, 519 (E.D.Pa.2009); *State Bar of Nevada Standing Committee on Ethics and Professional Responsibility,* Formal Opinion No. 39 (April 24, 2008).

RPC 1.10(b)

LG left CM on April 15, 2011, which is the same day defendants filed the present motion. Plaintiffs argue that because LG left CM, the present motion should be governed by RPC 1.10(b). Pursuant to this subsection of the Rule:

> When a lawyer has terminated an association with a firm, the firm is not prohibited from thereafter representing a person with interests materially adverse to those of a client represented by the formerly associated lawyer and not currently represented by the firm, unless: (1) the matter is the same or substantially related to that in which the formerly associated lawyer represented the client; and (2) any lawyer remaining in the firm has information protected by RPC 1.6 and RPC 1.9(c) that is material to the matter.

Defendants argue that severing a relationship with a disqualified attorney does not cure imputed disqualification. *See* Reply Memo. at 10 (citing *Lawler v. Isaac,* 249 N.J.Super. 11, 592 A.2d 1 (App.Div.1991)). Defendants also argue that "even if RPC 1.10(b) were to somehow control now that [LG] is no longer associated with [CM], both elements of the rule can easily be established so that [LG's] conflict must still be imputed to [CM]." *Id.* at 11, 592 A.2d 1.

This issue was addressed in *Pravak v. The Meyer Eye Grp., PLC*, No. 07-2433-JPM-dkv, 2008 WL 4372914 (W.D.Tenn. Sept.19, 2008). In *Pravak*, the court found that a disqualified attorney could not "cure" imputed disqualification by terminating his employment with the firm. The decision noted:

> [I]f a lawyer was allowed to 'cure' an imputed disqualification by simply leaving his current firm, that lawyer would be able to undertake representation of a client adverse to a partner's former client, appropriate confidential information about the former client to aid his current client, and detriment of the former current firm and opening This is not the type of use that information to the client by simply leaving his an office across the street. This is not the type of conduct considered acceptable under the TRPC.

Id. at *8. This Court agrees, and finds further support for this conclusion in *Cardona*, 942 F.Supp. at 976, wherein the court found that a rule permitting the cleansing of an imputed conflict by the mere dismissal of a side-switching attorney "would not provide any disincentive to a law firm that contemplates hiring an attorney who has formerly represented an adverse party." *Accord Lawler v. Isaac*, 249 N.J.Super. 11, 17, 592 A.2d 1 (App.Div.1991) ("The firm must be disqualified even if the associate disclosed none of his previously acquired knowledge and even though he is no longer employed by [the firm.]").

For the reasons discussed, therefore, the Court finds that RPC 1.10(b) is not applicable to the conflict imputation issue before it.

Conclusion

In sum, the Court finds that Costello and Mains must be disqualified because LG's conflict is imputed to the entire firm. Since LG had "primary responsibility" for AtlantiCare's defense while she worked at Morgan, screening cannot prevent the conflict imputation. In addition, even if LG did not have primary responsibility, disqualification is appropriate because CM did not employ an adequate screening procedure.

Accordingly, for all the foregoing reasons, defendants' "Motion to Disqualify Plaintiffs' Counsel Costello & Mains, P.C." [Doc. No. 18] is GRANTED. An appropriate Order will be entered.

> ## SOLUTIONS: THE LAWYER SHOULD HAVE, WOULD HAVE, COULD HAVE. . .
>
> The rule is very client centric. The failure to screen is a serious ethical violation. It can also be an expensive one for the law firm that fails to do one; after all, someone must pay for a new law firm to get up to speed.
>
> It is worth observing that screens are not necessarily easy. They require prompt identification of the conflict, and rigorous internal organization systems to keep the tainted lawyer effectively separate. Not all firms are capable of doing this, and not all want to. Some firms simply decline representation that would require a screen. If so, there are—as we saw in this case—consequences.

Becoming a Professional

X-Ray Questions

Consider the ethics of the lawyer in the following opinion letter. If a DQ is a litigation tactic, so too is what the lawyer did. But what is it contrary to the rules and as importantly, the objectives that the rules are designed to meet. Here, what are those objectives? What was the effect of the lawyer's conduct that would make it sanctionable? Remember that the lawyer who knows the rule and the reason for the rule will always—in a legal firefight—have an advantage over a lawyer who only knows the rule. (True in PR and true in whatever area in which you decide to practice).

As you read the opinion letter take special note of the language on a lawyer telling a client to meet with other lawyers as a ruse to create a conflict. This tactic does not immunize the lawyer from an ethical violation; if one cannot walk thought the front door, one cannot crawl through the back window. This, a lawyer is forbidden from using a client to create a conflict and then hiding behind the argument of "But I did not do anything."

Finally, this clip from "The Sopranos" deftly illustrates the issue here.

https://youtu.be/0JaxdFDfaHc

Legal Ethics Opinions

LEGAL ETHICS OPINION 1794

CONFIDENTIALITY OF INITIAL CONSULTATION

You have presented a hypothetical situation in which a husband and wife are planning to divorce. They live in a small community with a limited number of attorneys. The husband wishes to prevent his wife from obtaining adequate counsel. Therefore, he visits each family law attorney in succession, shares his situation, but with no intent to hire them. He in fact already knows that he will retain Attorney A. The wife goes to one of the visited attorneys, Attorney B, seeking representation. When Attorney B writes the husband's attorney (A) establishing B's representation of the wife, Attorney A sends a letter back stating the wife's attorney (B) has a conflict of interest and must withdraw from the representation.

Prior to hiring her attorney, the wife first had gone to Attorney A for representation. Before their initial interview, Attorney A had the wife sign a disclaimer stating that:

> I understand that my initial interview with this attorney does not create an attorney/client relationship and that no such relationship is formed unless I actually retain this attorney.

He then listened to her story. After the interview, the attorney did a conflicts check, and announced he could not represent her as he already represented her husband. As part of their discussion, the wife had shared information regarding her finances and her personal life, including details that would relate to child custody issues. The wife tells her own attorney, Attorney B, of that appointment, and he writes Attorney A and asks him to withdraw from representing the husband.

Under the facts presented you have asked the committee to opine as to whether either attorney needs to withdraw from this matter.

Rule 1.6(a) establishes the basic duty of client confidentiality:

> A lawyer shall not reveal information protected by the attorney-client privilege under applicable law or other information gained in the professional relationship that the client has requested be held inviolate or the disclosure of which would be embarrassing or

would be likely to be detrimental to the client unless the client consents after consultation, except for disclosures that are impliedly authorized in order to carry out the representation, and except as stated in paragraphs (b) and (c).

The committee notes that the exceptions outlined in paragraphs (b) and (c) are not at issue in the present hypothetical.

At first blush, Rule 1.6 may seem to apply only to those instances where the potential client actually hires the attorney. The committee opines that such a literal reading of Rule 1.6 is too narrow. This committee has on more than one occasion stressed the importance of an attorney's duty of confidentiality as a "bedrock principle of legal ethics." See, LEOs ##1643, 1702, 1749, and 1787. As such, the principle should be interpreted broadly to assure that the public feels safe in providing personal information to attorneys to obtain legal services. The "Scope" section of the Rules of Professional Conduct specifically references application of Rule 1.6's confidentiality duty to the context of initial consultations. That section states, in pertinent part:

> Most of the duties flowing from the client-lawyer relationship attach only after the client has requested the lawyer to render legal services and the lawyer has agreed to do so. But there are some duties, such as that of confidentiality under Rule 1.6, that may attach when the lawyer agrees to consider whether a client-lawyer relationship shall be established.

This committee has consistently applied Rule 1.6 to initial consultations in prior opinions. The court in *Gay v. Luihn Food Systems, Inc.*, 54 Va. Cir. 468 (Isle of Wight County 2001) agreed with that line of opinions and outlined them as follows:

> A long line of Legal Ethics Opinions issued by . . . the Virginia State Bar likewise recognizes that a prospective client's "initial consultation with an attorney creates an expectation of confidentiality which must be protected by the attorney even where no attorney-client relationship arises in other respects." Va. Legal Ethics Op. 1546, LE Op. 1546 (Aug. 12, 1993); *see also* Va. Legal Ethics Ops. 1697, LE Op. 1697 (June 24, 1997); 1642, LE Op. 1642 (June 9, 1995); 1638, LE Op. 1638 (April 19, 1995); 1633, LE Op. 1633 (June 9, 1995); 1613, LE Op. 1613 (Jan. 13, 1995); 1453, LE Op. 1453 (March 24, 1992); 1189, LE Op. 1189 (Nov. 17, 1988);

1039, LE Op. 1039 (Feb. 17, 1988); 949, LE Op. 949 (July 8, 1987); 629, LE Op. 629 (Nov. 13, 1984); 452, LE Op. 452 (Apr. 12, 1982); 318, LE Op. 318 (June 6, 1979). An attorney, therefore, has a "duty to keep confidential those consultations that occur outside formal attorney-client relationships which nonetheless create an expectation of confidentiality." Va. Legal Ethics Op. 1642, LE Op. 1642 (June 9, 1995).

Gay v. Luihn Food Systems, Inc., 5 Cir. CL00121, 54 Va. Cir. 468 (2001).

As stated in Comment 2 to Rule 1.6, the ethical obligation to hold inviolate confidential information of the client "encourages people to seek early legal assistance." To enable that result, people must be comfortable that the information imparted to an attorney while seeking legal assistance will not be used against them.

In the present scenario, Attorney A agreed to an interview with the wife as she was seeking legal representation in that divorce. As part of that interview, she disclosed to the attorney information regarding her finances and her personal life, in particular information that would be relevant to the child custody issue that is part of this divorce. As Attorney A received confidential information that is pertinent to his representation of the husband against the wife, this attorney may not represent the husband unless the wife consents to his use of the information in this case.

This committee is not dissuaded from that conclusion by the use of a disclaimer by Attorney A. The disclaimer he provided to the wife for signature disclaimed only that no attorney/client relationship had been formed; it did not on its face address confidentiality. As outlined earlier in this opinion, an attorney/client relationship is not required for the duty of confidentiality to be triggered; that duty arises also during a person's initial consultation with a lawyer in seeking possible representation if facts are such that no attorney/client relationship is formed. Accordingly, the disclaimer of an attorney/client relationship by this attorney is ineffective to permit him the unconsented use of information imparted by the wife. As stated above, he can only use this information, and in turn, represent the husband, only if the wife consents to that use, after consultation.

The committee notes that the conclusion that this disclaimer failed to eliminate the attorney's duty of confidentiality is limited to this particular disclaimer. While general disclaimers regarding the attorney/client relationship may not be effective, there may be others that would be. To be effective, the disclaimer must clearly demonstrate that the prospective client has given informed consent to the attorney's use of confidential information protected under Rule 1.6. Nonetheless, in the present scenario, as the particular disclaimer used failed to address the confidentiality of information provided and as important information was communicated by the wife to Attorney A, A's duty to keep that information confidential prevents A from properly representing the husband, absent the wife's consent. Attorney A must withdraw from the representation unless that consent from the wife is obtained.

Your request also inquires whether Attorney B has a conflict of interest arising from his earlier appointment with the husband. The potential for a conflict of interest for Attorney B is distinguishable from that for Attorney A. The basis for the conclusions drawn in the discussion of Attorney A's conflict is that the potential client (in that discussion, the wife) has a reasonable expectation of confidentiality. The committee maintains that when most members of the public contact a lawyer to discuss obtaining legal services from that lawyer, those members of the public assume the details of the conversation will remain private. However, the husband did not meet with Attorney B for the legitimate purpose of obtaining legal representation; he in fact had already decided he would retain Attorney A. His primary purpose in meeting with Attorney B was to preclude him from representing the wife. The husband's purpose does not create the sort of "reasonable expectation of confidentiality" Rule 1.6 exists to protect. Accordingly, no duty of confidentiality is created for Attorney B out of the visit with this husband who misrepresented his purpose for the appointment. The committee opines that as Attorney B has no duty to maintain the confidentiality of information received from the husband, no conflict of interest was triggered by that initial consultation. Attorney B is not required to withdraw.

While not present in this hypothetical, the committee notes that were an attorney to direct a new client to undertake this sort of strategic elimination of attorneys for the opposing party, that attorney would be in violation of Rule 3.4(j)'s prohibition against taking any action on behalf of a client "when the lawyer knows or when it is obvious that such action would merely serve to harass or maliciously injure another." That such an attorney would not himself be attending the initial consultations does not remove the attorney from ethical impropriety; Rule 8.4(a) establishes that it is improper for an attorney to violate the rules through the actions of another.

Committee Opinion

June 30, 2004

WHAT'S NEXT?

Now that we have examined a lawyer's obligations at the outset of litigation, we need to start looking at the conduct of litigation. Litigation is the most challenging part of our adversary legal system when it comes to our ethical obligations. On the one hand we are mandated to be zealous advocates for our clients but on the other hand we are required to adhere to our obligations as officers of the court.

> To assess your understanding of the material in this chapter,
> click here to take a quiz.

CHAPTER 6

Pretrial Issues: Discovery, Settlement/Mediation, Special Considerations

Coming Attractions

In this chapter we explore the concept—simple to state, harder to apply—of the "even playing field" once litigation is underway. This concept goes to the heart of the American legal system which—while based on an adversary model—nonetheless mandates that certain principles of fair play be adhered to.

Therefore, there are very specific commandments to obey. You cannot manufacture evidence. You cannot unlawfully impede access to evidence. We cannot block access to a witness. You cannot seek to do an end run around a lawyer and appeal directly to their client.

The evidence that each side assembles fairly then funnels into an early event in the litigation process; namely, seeking to settle a matter, either before suit is filed or after some discovery is conducted. Here, too, though, fair play is key. Lawyers must negotiate using the truth We will therefore revisit MR 4.1 and representations in settlement. And we will introduce you to a new concept; namely, overly vigorous advocacy as a disallowed tool of negotiation.

As you have seen in other areas of professional responsibility, there are rules that are unique to those who practice in the area of criminal law. As with these other rules, these are informed by certain Constitutional rights. These rules pertain both to a government's obligation to engage in certain pre-trial disclosures as well as its duty to ensure that an accused receives a fair trial. In this sense, those who possess the power of the state must act, as a comment to a Model Rule vividly describes it, a "minister of justice."

Finally, the underlying tension in this chapter is between two competing values: in one corner, loyalty to clients and zealousness in their representation and—in the other corner—fealty to our legal system and zealousness for its care.

Section 1. Manufacturing Evidence/Impeding Access to Evidence

You might be saying to yourself, "I would never falsify evidence!" or "I would not even think about impeding access to evidence," but we all are tempted. Corners can be cut. Little ones, then bigger ones. Consider this as you read the following two cases.

A. Fairness to Opposing Party and Counsel

Model Rule 3.4(a)(b): Fairness to Opposing Party and Counsel

A lawyer shall not:

> (a) unlawfully obstructs another party's access to evidence or unlawfully alter, destroy or conceal a document or other material having potential evidentiary value. A lawyer shall not counsel or assist another person to do any such act.

> (b) falsify evidence, counsel or assist a witness to testify falsely, or offer an inducement to a witness that is prohibited by law

Deconstruction Exercise/Rule Rationale

Note that "obstruct" is modified by "unlawfully." Why? Well, a lawyer might interpose a valid objection to a party opposite's obtaining evidence or having access to it. Consider the attorney-client privilege. Absent "obstruct," the invocation of the ACP would violate the Rule. Recall the earlier analogy that if lawyer cannot walk through the front door, then the lawyer cannot crawl through the back window. MR 3.4 must therefore be read in tandem with MR 8.4(a): Misconduct which includes "knowingly" assisting or inducing another to violate the Rules or to violate the Rules through the acts of another.

Two final deconstruction points. First, note again the use of the disjunctive "or" which expands the reach of the rule to numerous contexts. Second and importantly, consider how "evidentiary" is modified by "potential." Why? Because to write the rule otherwise would result in the lawyer being the one to decide whether evidence was or was not relevant and permit a lawyer to create roadblocks to its access.

Cases and Materials

X-Ray Questions (*Statzer*)

While engaged in a legal dispute with her former legal assistant, a lawyer deposed the assistant. At the deposition, the lawyer displayed, on the conference room table, for all to see, audio cassette tapes. The cassettes were either blank or full of irrelevant information, but the lawyer's conduct at the deposition suggested that the tapes were recordings of conversations between the lawyer and the assistant. Ultimately, the lawyer's ruse was discovered. The result? Six-month probated suspension from practicing law and an opinion that is forever recorded in the case reports.

This case introduces you to a new concept: A "tribunal." (MR 1.0(m)). Under the Rules, a tribunal is a person or entity sitting in an adjudicative capacity, such as a court or an arbitrator. Ancillary proceedings (such as a deposition) are therefore likewise governed by the Rules. Thus, the lawyer's conduct was governed by MR 3.4. The lawyer argued that her tactic worked and that she was only seeking the truth. Thus, no Rule violation. The Court rejected this rationale. Why? Does the reason she gives for her conduct have any merit? Isn't it the job of a lawyer to achieve certain articulated goals? Do you consider what Statzer did to be cheating? How does the Ohio Supreme Court think of it? Why?

Cincinnati Bar Association v. Statzer

Supreme Court of Ohio, 2003.
101 Ohio St.3d 14.

O'CONNOR, J.

{¶ 1}   Respondent, Joni Elizabeth Statzer of Cleves, Ohio, Attorney Registration No. 0067179, was admitted to the Ohio bar in 1996.

On June 17, 2002, relator, Cincinnati Bar Association, charged respondent with violations of the Code of Professional Responsibility in a two-count complaint. Relator later amended its complaint to include a third count of misconduct.

{¶ 2}   A panel appointed by the Board of Commissioners on Grievances and Discipline heard the cause on May 14, 2003, and made findings of fact, conclusions of law, and a recommendation. The panel dismissed the first and second counts of the complaint, finding no clear and convincing evidence that respondent had violated any Disciplinary Rules. See Gov.Bar R. V(6)(H); Ohio State Bar Assn. v. Reid (1999), 85 Ohio St.3d 327, 708 N.E.2d 193, paragraph two of the syllabus. The first count alleged that, to avoid discipline, respondent had induced her former legal assistant to execute a false affidavit claiming that her law office had prepared a client's file for retrieval. The second count alleged that respondent knew but did not report to relator that a former associate had induced the same legal assistant to provide false testimony to absolve the associate of blame for having missed a hearing. The panel determined that the testimony of the legal assistant, a central witness on these counts, lacked credibility. The panel also found that respondent's counsel had sufficiently reported to relator that respondent had knowledge of claimed misconduct involving the former associate.

{¶ 3}   With respect to the third count, the record shows that respondent deposed her former legal assistant on November 20, 2002, in anticipation of the panel hearing, at the office of one of relator's attorneys. During the proceeding, which was attended by respondent's and relator's legal counsel, respondent conspicuously placed nine audio cassette tapes in front of her former legal assistant. By suggestively labeling the tapes and referring to them during questioning, respondent implied that she had recorded conversations with the legal assistant that could impeach and personally embarrass the legal assistant. Respondent also intermittently cautioned the legal assistant to answer truthfully or risk perjuring herself.

{¶ 4}   Respondent's suggestive display of the cassettes was intended to mislead the legal assistant. The tapes were actually blank or held information unrelated to the legal assistant, and consequently, respondent did not offer the tapes as evidence during or after the deposition. The panel found that respondent had thereby violated DR 1–102(A)(4), which prohibits a lawyer from engaging in conduct involving fraud, deceit, dishonesty, or misrepresentation, and DR 7–106(C)(1), which prohibits a lawyer appearing in a professional capacity before a tribunal from alluding to any matter that will not be supported by admissible evidence.

{¶ 5}   In recommending a sanction for this misconduct, the panel reviewed the mitigating and aggravating considerations listed in Section 10 of the Rules and Regulations Governing Procedure on Complaints and Hearings Before the Board of Commissioners on Grievances and Discipline of the Supreme Court. The panel determined that in attempting to mislead the legal assistant, respondent "engaged in a deceptive practice during the disciplinary process." The panel found no other aggravating factors and identified no mitigating factors.

{¶ 6}   Having found that respondent violated DR 1–102(A)(4), the panel concluded that she should receive an actual suspension of her law license, the sanction ordinarily required for this infraction. See Cincinnati Bar Assn. v. Florez, 98 Ohio St.3d 448, 2003-Ohio-1730, 786 N.E.2d 875, and Disciplinary Counsel v. Fowerbaugh (1995), 74 Ohio St.3d 187, 658 N.E.2d 237. But, see, Cleveland Bar Assn. v. Cox, 98 Ohio St.3d 420, 2003-Ohio-1553, 786 N.E.2d 454, ¶ 18; Toledo Bar Assn. v. Kramer (2000), 89 Ohio St.3d 321, 323, 731 N.E.2d 643 (A lesser sanction may be appropriate for an attorney's violation of DR 1–102[A][4] where the misconduct is an isolated incident in an otherwise unblemished legal career). The panel also found respondent's misconduct similar to that committed in Columbus Bar Assn. v. King (1998), 84 Ohio St.3d 174, 702 N.E.2d 862, wherein two attorneys were disciplined for surreptitiously taping a telephone call in which one of them had solicited arguably slanderous remarks about his client from an opposing party and then added the slander allegation to the pending claim. In King, we suspended one attorney from the practice of law for one year, suspended the other attorney for six months, and conditionally stayed both suspensions. Here, the panel recommended suspending respondent's license for one year and staying six months of that sanction on the condition that she engage in no further misconduct. Pursuant to Gov.Bar R. V(6)(L), the board adopted the panel's findings and recommendation.

{¶ 7}   Relator urges us to find that respondent lied during the investigation leading to Count I about whether she had actually returned the client's case file that was the subject of the prior grievance against her. In response to relator's inquiry, respondent assured the investigator in writing that the client's file had been copied and made available to the client, and she included with her response the legal assistant's affidavit, later recanted, to this effect. Relator argues that this representation is contradicted by other documents in which respondent stated that she would not release the file until the client paid her legal fees, by the client's new attorneys, who testified that respondent did not comply with their requests for the file, and by her former client, who testified that she never received the file. Relator insists that these contradictions discredit respondent's story, notwithstanding the legal assistant's unreliable account of what may or may not have happened after the client discharged respondent.

{¶ 8}   Upon review, we acknowledge that these inconsistencies exist; however, they do not warrant disregarding the panel's findings as adopted by the board. The panel observed the witnesses firsthand and thus possessed an enviable vantage point in assessing the credibility and weight of their testimony. For this reason, we ordinarily defer to a panel's credibility determinations in our independent review of professional discipline cases unless the record weighs heavily against those findings. Cleveland Bar Assn. v. Cleary (2001), 93 Ohio St.3d 191, 198, 754 N.E.2d 235.

{¶ 9}   Here, the panel questioned respondent at length and unanimously dismissed Count I after finding insufficient evidence to conclude that she had acted dishonestly.

Supplanting the panel's judgment on this issue would require proof of the variety in Findlay/Hancock Cty. Bar Assn. v. Filkins (2000), 90 Ohio St.3d 1, 734 N.E.2d 764, in which we rejected recommended findings of misconduct because the panel had relied largely on the uncorroborated testimony of a witness who had admittedly lied often, including once under oath. The inconsistencies asserted by relator simply do not compare. Relator's first objection, therefore, is overruled, and we adopt the recommendation to dismiss Count I.

{¶ 10}   Additionally, relator objects to the panel's unanimous decision to dismiss Count II. Relator argues that respondent had a duty to report under DR 1–103(A) (a lawyer possessing unprivileged knowledge of misconduct as defined by DR 1–102 shall report such knowledge to an appropriate authority) that her legal assistant told respondent that she had testified falsely at the direction of respondent's former associate. We disagree, again out of deference to the panel. The panel found that the allegations in Count II depended "in large part" on the legal assistant's "frail credibility." We take from this that the panel considered the legal assistant's claim so inherently unreliable that, in retrospect, it did not invoke the reporting requirement in DR 1–103(A), regardless of whether the claim ultimately turned out to be true. Moreover, the panel found that respondent's counsel did report to relator other allegations of misconduct against the associate that were based on respondent's personal experience. Accordingly, relator's second objection is also overruled, and Count II is dismissed.

{¶ 11}   In her objections to the panel's findings as adopted by the board relative to Count III, respondent asserts that while DR 7–106(C)(1) prohibits an attorney's reference to matters that will not be supported by admissible evidence when appearing "before a tribunal," it does not apply to the deposition respondent conducted at the office of relator's attorney. Respondent also contends that her conduct during the deposition of the legal assistant did not constitute a violation of DR 1–102(A)(4). We reject both arguments.

{¶ 12}   "Tribunal" is defined in the Code of Professional Responsibility as "all courts and all other adjudicatory bodies," but we have not construed this term as narrowly as respondent urges us to do today. In Disciplinary Counsel v. Levin (1988), 35 Ohio St.3d 4, 517 N.E.2d 892, an attorney became verbally abusive during a * *1122 deposition. We found that in making his insulting and profane remarks, the attorney had acted before a tribunal in violation of DR 7–106(C)(2) (asking any question before a tribunal that the attorney has no reason to believe is relevant to the case and that is intended to degrade a witness or other person), 7–106(C)(5) (failing to comply with known local customs of courtesy or practice while appearing before a tribunal), 7–106(C)(6) (engaging in undignified or discourteous conduct degrading to a tribunal), and 7–106(C)(7) (intentionally or habitually violating an established rule of procedure or evidence). Id. at 7, 517 N.E.2d 892.

{¶ 13}   We continue to adhere to this view. Although depositions are conventionally conducted without direct judicial supervision, such proceedings are nevertheless always subject to judicial intervention and oversight under Civ.R. 30(D) (court may terminate or limit the scope of a deposition upon a showing of bad faith or harassment on the part of a deponent or party) and, thus, are within the boundaries of the judicial setting. And because there is ordinarily no presiding authority, "it is even more incumbent upon attorneys to conduct themselves in a professional and civil manner during a deposition." Matter of Golden (1998), 329 S.C. 335, 343, 496 S.E.2d 619.

{¶ 14}   Depositions may be used to investigate an adversary's case or to preserve testimony for impeachment or for the record. Civ.R. 32(A). Any deposition that is to be used as evidence must generally be filed in court. Id. It therefore follows that these proceedings are to be conducted as if before a tribunal, including in accordance with DR 7–106(C)(1). In fact, depositions taken in Gov.Bar R. V proceedings must be filed with the board pursuant to Civ.R. 32. Section 3(B) of the Rules and Regulations Governing Procedure on Complaints and Hearings Before the Board of Commissioners on Grievances and Discipline.

{¶ 15}   Respondent, however, urges us to distinguish trial conduct from "discovery depositions," arguing that the latter require greater freedom of inquiry into matters that may be relevant but inadmissible. See Civ.R. 26(B)(1) (inadmissible *19 evidence reasonably calculated to lead to the discovery of admissible evidence is also discoverable). This was particularly the case, respondent insists, in the deposition of the legal assistant. She argues that wide latitude was imperative during that proceeding to draw honest testimony from a theretofore untrustworthy witness and that use of the audio cassette tapes was merely a tactic intended to achieve this legitimate end.

{¶ 16}   We recognize that the discovery process, particularly the pursuit of information through deposition, cannot be overly restricted if it is to remain effective. We must draw the line, however, when an attorney engages in subterfuge that intimidates a witness. While respondent's primary purpose during the legal assistant's deposition may have been to elicit the truth, her tactic also tricked the legal assistant into thinking that the revelation of embarrassing confidences was at stake.

{¶ 17}   Throughout these proceedings, respondent has asserted that her "bluff" worked. Regardless, the success of her tactic is not at issue, and respondent can not, with any degree of certainty, assert that her witness would not have testified truthfully in the absence of her subterfuge. Further, while such deception may induce truthful testimony, it is just as likely to elicit lies if a witness believes that lies will offer security from the false threat. Respondent's deceitful tactic intimidated her witness by creating the false impression that respondent possessed compromising personal information that she could offer as evidence. For these reasons, we agree that respondent violated DR 1–102(A)(4) and 7–106(C)(1).

{¶ 18}   As a sanction for respondent's misconduct, relator advocates respondent's indefinite suspension from the practice of law based on arguments that respondent committed misconduct in connection with Counts I and II, in addition to Count III. Respondent, on the other hand, argues that the complaint should be dismissed. In the alternative, she asserts that the panel and board ignored mitigating evidence and, therefore, the sanction recommended by the board—a one-year suspension with six months conditionally stayed—is too severe. Respondent proposes that a public reprimand would be more appropriate.

{¶ 19}   We find that either proposed sanction, as well as the board's recommendation, would be incommensurate with respondent's misconduct. An indefinite suspension would be too harsh in light of our dismissal of Counts I and II, while no more than a public reprimand would unduly minimize the severity of respondent's conduct.

{¶ 20}   As to the board's recommendation, we find that there are mitigating factors for which the board did not account. Specifically, the panel and board did not mention that there is no evidence of respondent's having been professionally disciplined before now, the grievances lodged against her notwithstanding. Moreover, respondent has a professional history of dutiful service to clients, including the client whose case file she supposedly has not returned. In fact, another of respondent's associates testified that respondent had worked tirelessly on this client's behalf for years while representing her in a contentious divorce and related allegations of abuse. Finally, respondent cooperated in these proceedings.

{¶ 21}   On the basis of these mitigating factors, we temper our disposition in accordance with the rule that a stayed suspension is sometimes warranted by mitigating concerns, notwithstanding a violation of DR 1–102(A)(4). See Disciplinary Counsel v. Markijohn, 99 Ohio St.3d 489, 2003-Ohio-4129, 794 N.E.2d 24 (attorney who falsely reported contributions to his law firm's retirement plan violated DR 1–102[A][4], but his good character, lack of any disciplinary record, and personal difficulties were sufficiently mitigating to stay the ordered six-month suspension), and Disciplinary Counsel v. Wrenn, 99 Ohio St.3d 222, 2003-Ohio-3288, 790 N.E.2d 1195 (assistant prosecutor who did not disclose potentially exculpatory DNA results violated DR 1–102[A][4] and three other Disciplinary Rules, but his background and acknowledged poor judgment were sufficiently mitigating to stay the ordered six-month suspension).

{¶ 22}   Consistent with this authority, we order that respondent be suspended from the practice of law in Ohio for six months, and we stay this sanction on the condition that she engage in no further misconduct. If respondent violates this condition, the stay will be lifted, and respondent will serve the entire period of actual suspension. Costs are taxed to respondent.

Judgment accordingly.

SOLUTIONS: THE LAWYER SHOULD HAVE, WOULD HAVE, COULD HAVE. . .

There is no substitute for diligent preparation. To wit: training in witness examination; knowing a case fully and completely; and being conversant in the law. There legal skills are not tricky or subterfuge. They create optimal results for the client.

LEANING INTO PRACTICE

Scenario: The Case of the Lawyer and the Empty Folder

Pablo Lawyer is cross examining a witness at a trial. Pablo correctly believes that the witness is engaged in criminal activity but the documents that would prove this true have not yet arrived. But the trial is going on now; the witness is on the stand; and Pablo wants to cross examine on the criminal activity so as to weaken the witness's credibility. The following Q and A transpires:

Pablo: You've engaged in criminal activity have you not?

Witness: No, I have not. I am an innocent man and a good man.

Pablo then pulls up a file folder from his briefcase with blank sheets of paper in it. There are no markings on the file's cover. The witness, as Pablo intended, sees the file and observes Pablo thumbing through the papers (but does not know they are blank).

Pablo: (Holding the file); Are you really sure you did not engage in any criminal activity? Records do exist you know!

Witness: Ok fine I have a criminal record. You obviously have the documents on me.

Is Pablo in violation of the Model Rules? Is this case the same as the cassette deposition or is it different? How so? What if Pablo was operating on a hunch that the witness had a criminal record and there are no documents on their way? Same answer, different answer? What if he does not suggest there are documents but just guesses at possible criminal activity because the witness is such a shady character? Rule or no rule violation?

Cases and Materials

X-Ray Questions (*In re Ryder*)

This case is a variation of *Statzer.* There the lawyer was creating the appearance of evidence that did not exist; by contrast, in the following case the lawyer is concealing and hiding evidence that did exist. An experienced criminal defense lawyer, he took possession of money that be believed his client stole from a bank, as well as a shotgun he believed was used in the bank robbery. He then, in order to be able to argue that the items did not belong to the client, received a power of attorney from his client, used it to move the cash and the gun from his client's safety deposit box to one controlled solely by the lawyer. But the FBI figured out the transfer and seized the items from the lawyer's box.

Note the issue of whether Ryder" knew" the items were part of the bank robbery. What is the definition of "knowledge "in MR 1.0(f)? Can you see the difference between explicit knowledge and implicit knowledge? (The case was decided before the Model Rules were promulgated but the concepts are identical and were embodied in the Rules). What is the difference between the two forms?

Ryder claimed—and the court assumed—that he was intending to give the gun used and the money taken to the police and FBI without divulging the identity of his client. Doing so would be consistent with his ethical duties. But he waited to do so, however. Why did the waiting matter to his detriment in the court's view? In hindsight what should Ryder have done? If he selected a different course of action, he very likely would have avoided the 18-month suspension from federal court practice. Why?

In re Ryder

United States District Court E.D. Virginia, 1967.
263 F. Supp. 360.

Opinion

MEMORANDUM

PER CURIAM.

This proceeding was instituted to determine whether Richard R. Ryder should be removed from the roll of attorneys qualified to practice before this court. Ryder was admitted to this bar in 1953. He formerly served five years as an Assistant United States Attorney. He has an active trial practice, including both civil and criminal cases.

In proceedings of this kind the charges must be sustained by clear and convincing proof, the misconduct must be fraudulent, intentional, and the result of improper motives. See In re Fisher, 179 F.2d 361 (7th Cir. 1950), cert. denied sub nom. Kerner v. Fisher, 340 U.S. 825, 71 S.Ct. 59, 95 L.Ed. 606 (1950). We conclude that these strict requirements have been satisfied. Ryder took possession of stolen money and a sawed-off shotgun, knowing that the money had been stolen and that the gun had been used in an armed robbery. He intended to retain this property pending his client's trial unless the government discovered it. He intended by his possession to destroy the chain of evidence that linked the contraband to his client and to prevent its use to establish his client's guilt.

On August 24, 1966 a man armed with a sawed-off shotgun robbed the Varina Branch of the Bank of Virginia of $7,583. Included in the currency taken were $10 bills known as 'bait money,' the serial numbers of which had been recorded.

On August 26, 1966 Charles Richard Cook rented safety deposit box 14 at a branch of the Richmond National Bank. Later in the day Cook was interviewed at his home by agents of the Federal Bureau of Investigation, who obtained $348 from him. Cook telephoned Ryder, who had represented him in civil litigation. Ryder came to the house and advised the agents that he represented Cook. He said that if Cook were not to be placed under arrest, he intended to take him to his office for an interview. The agents left. Cook insisted to Ryder that he had not robbed the bank. He told Ryder that he had won the money, which the agents had taken from him, in a crap game. At this time Ryder believed Cook.

Later that afternoon Ryder telephoned one of the agents and asked whether any of the bills obtained from Cook had been identified as a part of the money taken in the bank robbery. The agent told him that some bills had been identified. Ryder made inquiries about the number of bills taken and their denominations. The agent declined to give him specific information but indicated that several of the bills were recorded as bait money.

The next morning, Saturday, August 27, 1966, Ryder conferred with Cook again. He urged Cook to tell the truth, and Cook answered that a man, whose name he would not divulge, offered him $500 on the day of the robbery to put a package in a bank lockbox. Ryder did not believe this story. Ryder told Cook that if the government could trace the money in the box to him, it would be almost conclusive evidence of his guilt. He knew that Cook was under surveillance and he suspected that Cook might try to dispose of the money.

That afternoon Ryder telephoned a former officer of the Richmond Bar Association to discuss his course of action. He had known this attorney for many years and respected his judgment. The lawyer was at home and had no library available to him when Ryder telephoned. In their casual conversation Ryder told what he knew about the case, omitting names. He explained that he thought he would take the money from Cook's safety deposit box and place it in a box in his own name. This, he believed, would prevent Cook from attempting to dispose of the money. The lawyers thought that eventually F.B.I. agents would locate the money and that since it was in Ryder's possession, he could claim a privilege and thus effectively exclude it from evidence. This would prevent the government from linking Ryder's client with the bait money and would also destroy any presumption of guilt that might exist arising out of the client's exclusive possession of the evidence.

Ryder testified:

'I had sense enough to know, one, at that time that apparently the F.B.I. did have the serial numbers on the bills. I had sense enough to know, from many, many years of experience in this court and in working with the F.B.I. and, in fact, in directing the F.B.I. on some occasions, to know that eventually the bank—that the F.B.I. would find that money if I left that money in the bank. There was no doubt in my mind that eventually they would find it. The only thing I could think of to do was to get the money out of Mr. Cook's possession. * * * The idea was that I assumed that if anybody tried to go into a safety deposit box in my name, the bank officials would notify me and that I would get an opportunity to come in this court and argue a question of whether or not they could use that money as evidence.'

The lawyers discussed and rejected alternatives, including having a third party get the money. At the conclusion of the conversation Ryder was advised, 'Don't do it surreptitiously and to be sure that you let your client know that it is going back to the rightful owners.'

On Monday morning Ryder asked Cook to come by his office. He prepared a power of attorney, which Cook signed:

'KNOW YOU ALL MEN BY THESE PRESENTS, that I, CHARLES RICHARD COOK do hereby make, constitute and appoint, R. R. RYDER as my Attorney at Law and in fact and do authorize my said Attorney to enter a safety deposit box rented by me at the Richmond National Bank and Trust Company, 2604 Hull Street, Richmond, Virginia, said box requiring Mosler Key Number 30 to open the same and I further authorize the said Attorney to remove the contents of the said box and so dispose of the said contents as he sees fit and I direct the officials of the said bank to cooperate with my said attorney towards the accomplishment of this my stated purpose.'

Ryder did not follow the advice he had received on Saturday. He did not let his client know the money was going back to the rightful owners. He testified about his omission:

'I prepared it myself and told Mr. Cook to sign it. In the power of attorney, I did not specifically say that Mr. Cook authorized me to deliver that money to the appropriate authorities at any time because for a number of reasons. One, in representing a man under these circumstances, you've got to keep the man's confidence, but I also put in that power of attorney that Mr. Cook authorized me to dispose of that money as I saw fit, and the reason for that being that I was going to turn the money over to the proper authorities at whatever time I deemed that it wouldn't hurt Mr. Cook.'

Ryder took the power of attorney which Cook had signed to the Richmond National Bank. He rented box 13 in his name with his office address, presented the power of attorney, entered Cook's box, took both boxes into a booth, where he found a bag of money and a sawed-off shotgun in Cook's box. The box also contained miscellaneous items which are not pertinent to this proceeding. He transferred the contents of Cook's box to his own and returned the boxes to the vault. He left the bank, and neither he nor Cook returned.

Ryder testified that he had some slight hesitation about the propriety of what he was doing. Within a half-hour after he left the bank, he talked to a retired judge and distinguished professor of law. He told this person that he wanted to discuss something in confidence. Ryder then stated that he represented a man suspected of bank robbery. The judge recalled the main part of the conversation:

'* * * And that he had received from this client, under a power of attorney, a sum (of) money which he, Mr. Ryder, suspected was proceeds of the robbery, although he didn't know it, but he had a suspicion that it was; that he had placed this money in a safety deposit vault at a bank; that he had received it with the intention of returning it to the rightful owner after the case against his client had been finally disposed of one way or the other; that he considered that he had received it under the privilege of attorney and client and that he wanted responsible people in the community to know of that fact and that he was telling me in confidence of that as one of these people that he wanted to know of it. 'Q. Did he say anything to you about a sawed-off shotgun? 'A. I don't recall. If Mr. Ryder says he did, I would not deny it, but I do not recall it, because the— my main attention in what he was saying was certainly drawn to the fact that the money was involved, but I just cannot answer the question emphatically, but if Mr. Ryder says he told me, why, I certainly wouldn't deny it.'

Ryder testified that he told about the shotgun. The judge also testified that Ryder certainly would not have been under the impression that he—the judge— thought that he was guilty of unethical conduct.

The same day Ryder also talked with other prominent persons in Richmond—a judge of a court of record and an attorney for the Commonwealth. Again, he stated that what he intended to say was confidential. He related the circumstances and was advised that a lawyer could not receive the property and if he had received it he could not retain possession of it.

On September 7, 1966 Cook was indicted for robbing the Varina Branch of the Bank of Virginia. A bench warrant was issued and the next day Ryder represented Cook at a bond hearing. Cook was identified as the robber by employees of the bank. He was released on bond. Cook was arraigned on a plea of not guilty on September 9, 1966.

On September 12, 1966 F.B.I. agents procured search warrants for Cook's and Ryder's safety deposit boxes in the Richmond National Bank. They found Cook's box empty. In Ryder's box they discovered $5,920 of the $7,583 taken in the bank robbery and the sawed-off shotgun used in the robbery.

On September 23, 1966 Ryder filed a motion to suppress the money obtained from Cook by the agents on August 26, 1966. The motion did not involve items taken from Ryder's safety deposit box. The motion came on to be heard October 6, 1966. Ryder called Cook as a witness for examination on matters limited to the motion to suppress. The court called to Ryder's attention papers pertaining to the search of the safety deposit boxes. Ryder moved for a continuance, stating that he intended to file a motion with respect to the seizure of the contents of the lockbox.

On October 14, 1966 the three judges of this court removed Ryder as an attorney for Cook; suspended him from practice before the court until further order; referred the matter to the United States Attorney, who was requested to file charges within five days; set the matter for hearing November 11, 1966; and granted Ryder leave to move for vacation or modification of its order pending hearing.

The United States Attorney charged Ryder with violations of Canons 15 and 32 of the Canons of Professional Ethics of the Virginia State Bar. Ryder did not move for vacation or modification of the order, and the case was heard as scheduled by the court en banc. After the transcript was prepared and the case briefed, the court heard the argument of counsel on December 27, 1966.

At the outset, we reject the suggestion that Ryder did not know the money which he transferred from Cook's box to his was stolen. We find that on August 29 when Ryder opened Cook's box and saw a bag of money and a sawed-off shotgun, he then knew Cook was involved in the bank robbery and that the money was stolen. Ryder knew that the man who this. Ryder knew that the man who had robbed the bank used a sawed-off shotgun. He disbelieved Cook's story about the source of the money in the lockbox. He knew that some of the bills in Cook's possession were bait money.

Judge Learned Hand observed in United States v. Werner, 160 F.2d 438, 441 (2d Cir. 1947):

'The defendants ask us to distinguish between 'knowing' that goods are stolen and merely being put upon an inquiry which would have led to discovery; but they have misconceived the distinction which the decisions have made. The receivers of stolen goods almost never 'know' that they have been stolen, in the sense that they could testify to it in a court room.'

Judge Hand then went on to say (160 F.2d 442):

'But that the jury must find that the receiver did more than infer the theft from the circumstances has never been demanded, so far as we know; and to demand more would emasculate the statute * * *.'

In Melson v. United States, 207 F.2d 558, 559 (4th Cir. 1953), the court said:

'It is well settled that knowledge that goods have been stolen may be inferred from circumstances that would convince a man of ordinary intelligence that this is the fact.'

We also find that Ryder was not motivated solely by certain expectation the government would discover the contents of his lockbox. He believed discovery was probable. In this event he intended to argue to the court that the contents of his box could not be revealed, and even if the contents were identified, his possession made the stolen money and the shotgun inadmissible against his client. He also recognized that discovery was not inevitable. His intention in this event, we find, was to assist Cook by keeping the stolen money and the shotgun concealed in his lockbox until after the trial. His conversations, and the secrecy he enjoined, immediately after he put the money and the gun in his box, show that he realized the government might not find the property.

We accept his statement that he intended eventually to return the money to its rightful owner, but we pause to say that no attorney should ever place himself in such a position. Matters involving the possible termination of an attorney-client relationship, or possible subsequent proceedings in the event of an acquittal, are too delicate to permit such a practice.

We reject the argument that Ryder's conduct was no more than the exercise of the attorney-client privilege. The fact that Cook had not been arrested or indicted at the time Ryder took possession of the gun and money is immaterial. Cook was Ryder's client and was entitled to the protection of the lawyer-client privilege. Continental Oil Co. v. United States, 330 F.2d 347 (9th Cir, 1964).

Regardless of Cook's status, however, Ryder's conduct was not encompassed by the attorney-client privilege. A frequently quoted definition of the privilege is found in United States v. United Shoe Mach. Corp., 89 F.Supp. 357, 358 (D.Mass.1950):

'The privilege applies only if (1) the asserted holder of the privilege is or sought to become a client; (2) the person to whom the communication was made (a) is a member of the bar of a court, or his subordinate and (b) in connection with this communication is acting as a lawyer; (3) the communication relates to a fact of which the attorney was informed (a) by his client (b) without the presence of strangers (c) for the purpose of securing primarily either (i) an opinion on law or (ii) legal services or (iii) assistance in some legal proceeding, and not (d) for the purpose of committing a crime or tort; and (4) the privilege has been (a) claimed and (b) not waived by the client.'

The essentials of the privilege have been stated in 8 Wigmore, Evidence § 2292 (McNaughton Rev.1961):

'(1) Where legal advice of any kind is sought (2) from a professional legal adviser in his capacity as such, (3) the communications relating to that purpose, (4) made in confidence (5) by the client, (6) are at his instance permanently protected (7) from disclosure by himself or by the legal adviser, (8) except the protection be waived.'

It was Ryder, not his client, who took the initiative in transferring the incriminating possession of the stolen money and the shotgun from Cook. Ryder's conduct went far beyond the receipt and retention of a confidential communication from his client. Counsel for Ryder conceded, at the time of argument, that the acts of Ryder were not within the attorney-client privilege.

Ryder's reliance upon United States v. Judson, 322 F.2d 460 (9th Cir. 1963) and Schwimmer v. United States, 232 F.2d 855 (8th Cir. 1956), cert. denied 352 U.S. 833, 77 S.Ct. 48, 1 L.Ed.2d 52 (1956), is unfounded. In both of these cases subpoenas duces tecum were served upon lawyers requiring them to produce papers deposited with them by their clients. Judson turns upon the application of the Fifth Amendment. The court said at 322 F.2d 466:

'Clearly, if the taxpayer in this case * * * had been subpoenaed and directed to produce the documents in question, he could have properly refused. The government concedes this. But instead of closeting himself with his myriad tax data drawn up around him, the taxpayer retained counsel. quite predictably, in the course of the ensuing attorney-client relationship the pertinent records were turned over to the attorney. The government would have us hold that the taxpayer walked into his attorney's office unquestionably shielded with the Amendment's protection, and walked out with something less.

'The thrust of the Fifth Amendment is that 'prosecutors are forced the search for independent evidence instead of relying upon proof extracted from individuals by force of law.' United States v. White, supra, 322 U.S. (694,) at 698 (64 S.Ct. 1248, 88 L.Ed. 1542).'

Schwimmer (232 F.2d 855) concerned papers which had been contained in a lawyer's files. The lawyer had discontinued his practice and had stored the papers with a manufacturing company. The court recognized that the lawyer had standing to quash a subpoena duces tecum. The case turned upon the Fourth Amendment. The court recognized that production of one's private books and papers by subpoena duces tecum for use against him in a criminal proceeding is prohibited by the Amendment. The fact that the papers were in the constructive possession of the attorney did not remove them from its protection. The court also recognized that the attorney had sufficient interest in the papers to be permitted to take a part in the proceedings to determine their admissibility.

Not all papers in a lawyer's file are immune. The rule is summarized in McMormick, Evidence, § 93 at p. 188 (1954):

'If a document would be subject to an order for production if it were in the hands of a client, it would be equally subject if it is in the hands of an attorney.'

The basic difficulty with Ryder's reliance upon Judson and Schwimmer is that this proceeding is not concerned with the concealment of Cook's papers or other articles of an evidentiary nature. Neither Cook nor his attorney could be compelled to produce merely evidentiary articles nor could such articles be seized in a legal search. Cf. Hayden v. Warden, 363 F.2d 647 (4th Cir. 1966), cert. granted, 385 U.S. 926, 87 S.Ct. 290, 17 L.Ed.2d 210 (1966) (No. 480, 1966 Term). In Harris v. United States, 331 U.S. 145, 154, 67 S.Ct. 1098, 1103, 91 L.Ed. 1399 (1947), Mr. Chief Justice Vinson said:

'This Court has frequently recognized the distinction between merely evidentiary materials, on the one hand, which may not be seized either under the authority of a search warrant or during the course of a search incident to arrest, and on the other hand, those objects which may validly be seized including the instrumentalities and means by which a crime is committed, the fruits of crime such as stolen property, weapons by which escape of the person arrested might be effected, and property the possession of which is a crime.'

Ryder, an experienced criminal attorney, recognized and acted upon the fact that the gun and money were subject to seizure while in the possession of Cook.

In Clark v. United States, 289 U.S. 1, 15, 53 S.Ct. 465, 469, 77 L.Ed. 993 (1933), Mr. Justice Cardozo expressed a dictum, which is apt to the aid Ryder gave Cook:

'We turn to the precedents in the search for an analogy, and the search is not in vain. There is a privilege protecting communications between attorney and client. The privilege takes flight if the relation is abused. A client who consults an attorney for advice that will serve him in the commission of a fraud will have no help from the law. He must let the truth be told.'

Securities & Exchange Comm. v. Harrison, 80 F.Supp. 226, 230 (D.D.C.1948), aff'd, 87 U.S.App.D.C. 232, 184 F.2d 691 (1950), judgment order vacated as moot, 340 U.S. 908, 71 S.Ct. 290, 95 L.Ed. 656 (1951), describes the privilege and its limitations:

'That privilege has long been recognized as a very proper and necessary one to insure full and complete revelation by a person to an attorney to the end that the client may be properly advised, represented, and, in appropriate cases, defended by that attorney. To subject such revelations to exposure by the testimonial process would inevitably lead to concealments which would impair proper representation and thus interfere with proper administration of justice. While it relates to the rights of an individual, it is nonetheless recognized, as so many of our fundamental rights are, as essentially in the public interest. This privilege has, however, never been intended to be, and should not be, a cloak or shield for the perpetration of a crime or fraudulent wrong doing. One who consults an attorney to secure aid or assistance in the perpetration of a future crime or fraudulent wrong doing is not consulting that attorney for the legitimate purposes which are protected by the privilege. If, therefore, it be shown by evidence other than the disclosure of the communications between client and attorney that aid or assistance is being sought for the perpetration of crime or fraudulent wrongdoing, there is no immunity to the testimonial process respecting such communications.'

In Clark v. State, 159 Tex.Cr.R. 187, 261 S.W.2d 339 (1953), cert. denied, reh. denied sub nom. Clark v. Texas, 346 U.S. 855, 905, 74 S.Ct. 69, 98 L.Ed. 369 (1953), a lawyer's advice to get rid of a gun used to commit a murder was admissible in evidence. The court observed the conversation was not within the realm of legitimate professional conduct and employment. Cf. Comment, Fruits of the Attorney-Client Privilege: Incriminating Evidence and Conflicting Duties, 3 Duquesne U.L.Rev. 239, 247 (1965), which criticizes Clark. In argument, it was generally conceded that Ryder could have been required to testify in the prosecution of Cook as to the transfer of the contents of the lockbox.

'The primary duty of a lawyer engaged in public prosecution is not to convict, but to see that justice is done. The suppression of facts or the secreting of witnesses capable of establishing the innocence of the accused is highly reprehensible.

'15. How Far a Lawyer May Go in Supporting a Client's Cause. Nothing operates more certainly to create or to foster popular prejudice against lawyers as a class and to deprive the profession of that full measure of public esteem and confidence which belongs to the proper discharge of its duties than does the false claim, often set up by the unscrupulous in defense of questionable transactions, that it is the duty of the lawyer to do whatever may enable him to succeed in winning his client's cause.

'It is improper for a lawyer to assert in argument his personal belief in his client's innocence or in the justice of the cause.

'The lawyer owes 'entire devotion to the interest of the client, warm zeal in the maintenance and defense of his rights and the exertion of his utmost learning and ability,' to the end that nothing be taken or be withheld from him, save by the rules of law, legally applied. No fear of judicial disfavor or public unpopularity should restrain him from the full discharge of his duty. In the judicial forum the client is entitled to the benefit of any and every remedy and defense that is authorized by the law of the land, and he may expect his lawyer to assert every such remedy or defense. But it is steadfastly to be borne in mind that the great trust of the lawyer is to be performed within and not without the bounds of the law. The office of attorney does not permit, much less does it demand of him for any client, violation of law or any manner of fraud or chicane. He must obey his own conscience and not that of his client.

'32. The Lawyer's Duty In Its Last Analysis. No client, corporate or individual, however powerful, nor any cause, civil or political, however important, is entitled to receive, nor should any lawyer render any service or advice involving disloyalty to the law whose ministers we are, or disrespect of the judicial office, which we are bound to uphold, or corruption of any person or persons exercising a public office or private trust, or deception or betrayal of the public. When rendering any such improper service or advice, the lawyer invites and merits stern and just condemnation. Correspondingly, he advances the honor of his profession and the best interests of his client when he renders service or gives advice tending to impress upon the client and his undertaking exact compliance with the strictest principles of moral law. He must also observe and advise his client to observe the statute law, though until a statute shall have been construed and interpreted by competent adjudication, he is free and is entitled to advise as to its validity and as to what he conscientiously believes to be its just meaning and extent. But above all a lawyer will find his highest honor in a deserved reputation for fidelity to private trust and to public duty, as an honest man and as a patriotic and loyal citizen.

'37. Confidence of a Client. It is the duty of a lawyer to preserve his client's confidences. This duty outlast the lawyer's employment, and extends as well to his employees; and neither of them should accept employment which involves or may involve the disclosure or use of these confidences, either for the private advantage of the lawyer or his employees or to the disadvantage to the client, without his knowledge and consent, and even though there are other available sources of such information. A lawyer should not continue employment when he discovers that this obligation prevents the performance of his full duty to his former or to his new client.

If a lawyer is accused by his client, he is not precluded from disclosing the truth in respect to the accusation. The announced intention of a client to commit a crime is not included within the confidences which he is bound to respect. He may properly make such disclosures as may be necessary to prevent the act or protect those against whom it is threatened.'

The money in Cook's box belonged to the Bank of Virginia. The law did not authorize Cook to conceal this money or withhold it from the bank. His larceny was a continuing offense. Cook had no title or property interest in the money that he lawfully could pass to Ryder. The Act of Assembly authorizing the promulgation of the Canons of Ethics in Virginia forbids inconsistency with § 18.1–107 Code of Virginia, 1950, which provides:

'If any person buy or receive from another person, or aid in concealing, any stolen goods or other thing, knowing the same to have been stolen, he shall be deemed guilty of larceny thereof, and may be proceeded against, although the principal offender be not convicted.'

No canon of ethics or law permitted Ryder to conceal from the Bank of Virginia its money to gain his client's acquittal.

Cook's possession of the sawed-off shotgun was illegal. 26 U.S.C. § 5851. Ryder could not lawfully receive the gun from Cook to assist Cook to avoid conviction of robbery. Cook had never mentioned the shotgun to Ryder. When Ryder discovered it in Cook's box, he took possession of it to hinder the government in the prosecution of its case, and he intended not to reveal in pending trial unless the government discovered it and a court compelled its production. No statute or canon of ethics authorized Ryder to take possession of the gun for this purpose.

SOLUTIONS: THE LAWYER SHOULD HAVE, WOULD HAVE, COULD HAVE. . .

While Ryder's intentions and motivations may have been admirable, it is not his call to determine the timing of the disclosure of the cash and the weapon. The rule contains no such exception in it. Thus, good faith by the lawyer plays no role in deciding whether the rule was violated. The rule is the rule. Follow it.

Cases and Materials

X-Ray Questions (*Meredith*)

This case is a variation of the facts in the preceding case. A defendant in a criminal matter retained a lawyer to defend him. The lawyer's investigator discovered, in a dumpster behind the client's apartment building, the wallet of the alleged victim who was robbed. The investigator looked there because of what the defendant told his lawyer. The wallet was turned over to the police but only after it was removed from its location. The issue: does the ACP protect the conversation between the defense lawyer and the investigator on looking into the dumpster. What competing values does the court identify in making its decision? How does the court reconcile these values in its holding? Do you agree with its decision?

Two final rule points. What if a lawyer comes to know of the perjury *after* the trial concludes. The tension between the values of fairness and certainty arises yet again. If the matter has been resolved through final appeals and judgment, the lawyer has no obligations. At some point, a litigation matter must conclude.

Second, a lawyer will sometimes engage in ex parte conduct with a court, usually when the lawyer seeks injunctive relief on behalf of the client. As with the duty to inform the court of directly adverse authority, so too here with the lawyer bring responsible for alerting the court as to facts that would be made in opposition to the relief sought. Again, so that a correct decision is made.

People v. Meredith

Supreme Court of California, 1981.
29 Cal.3d 682.

Opinion

TOBRINER, JUSTICE.

Defendants Frank Earl Scott and Michael Meredith appeal from convictions for the first degree murder and first degree robbery of David Wade. Meredith's conviction rests on eyewitness testimony that he shot and killed Wade. Scott's conviction, however, depends on the theory that Scott conspired with Meredith and a third defendant, Jacqueline Otis, to bring about the killing and robbery. To support the theory of conspiracy the prosecution sought to show the place where the victim's wallet was found, and, in the course of the case this piece of evidence became crucial. The admissibility of that evidence comprises the principal issue on this appeal.

At trial the prosecution called Steven Frick, who testified that he observed the victim's partially burnt wallet in a trash can behind Scott's residence. Scott's trial counsel then adduced that Frick served as a defense investigator. Scott himself had told his former counsel that he had taken the victim's wallet, divided the money with Meredith, attempted to burn the wallet, and finally put it in the trash can. At counsel's request, Frick then retrieved the wallet from the trash can. Counsel examined the wallet and then turned it over to the police.

The defense acknowledges that the wallet itself was properly admitted into evidence. The prosecution in turn acknowledges that the attorney-client privilege protected the conversations between Scott, his former counsel, and counsel's investigator. Indeed the prosecution did not attempt to introduce those conversations at trial. The issue before us, consequently, focuses upon a narrow point: whether under the circumstances of this case Frick's observation of the location of the wallet, the product of a privileged communication, finds protection under the attorney-client privilege.

This issue, one of first impression in California, presents the court with competing policy considerations. On the one hand, to deny protection to observations arising from confidential communications might chill free and open communication between attorney and client and might also inhibit counsel's investigation of his client's case. On the other hand, we cannot extend the attorney-client privilege so far that it renders evidence immune from discovery and admission merely because the defense seizes it first.

Balancing these considerations, we conclude that an observation by defense counsel or his investigator, which is the product of a privileged communication, may not be admitted unless the defense by altering or removing physical evidence has precluded the prosecution from making that same observation. In the present case the defense investigator, by removing the wallet, frustrated any possibility that the police might later discover it in the trash can. The conduct of the defense thus precluded the prosecution from ascertaining the crucial fact of the location of the wallet. Under these circumstances, the prosecution was entitled to present evidence to show the location of the wallet in the trash can; the trial court did not err in admitting the investigator's testimony.

The other contentions presented by Scott, and all contentions raised by codefendant Meredith, were fully addressed in the Court of Appeal opinion. We affirm the convictions, as modified, for the reasons stated in that opinion.

We first summarize the evidence other than that relating to the discovery and location of the victim's wallet. Our summary is based upon the testimony of Jacqueline Otis and Laurie Ann Sam, the key prosecution witnesses, upon the statement given the police by defendant Scott, and upon Scott's trial testimony.

On the night of April 3, 1976, Wade (the victim) and Jacqueline Otis, a friend of the defendants, entered a club known as Rich Jimmy's. Defendant Scott remained outside by a shoeshine stand. A few minutes later codefendant Meredith arrived outside the club. He told Scott he planned to rob Wade, and asked Scott to go into the club, find Jacqueline Otis, and ask her to get Wade to go out to Wade's car parked outside the club.

In the meantime, Wade and Otis had left the club and walked to a liquor store to get some beer. Returning from the store, they left the beer in a bag by Wade's car and reentered the club. Scott then entered the club also and, according to the testimony of Laurie Ann Sam (a friend of Scott's who was already in the club), Scott asked Otis to get Wade to go back out to his car so Meredith could "knock him in the head."

When Wade and Otis did go out to the car, Meredith attacked Wade from behind. After a brief struggle, two shots were fired; Wade fell, and Meredith, witnessed by Scott and Sam, ran from the scene.

Scott went over to the body and, assuming Wade was dead, picked up the bag containing the beer and hid it behind a fence. Scott later returned, retrieved the bag, and took it home where Otis and Meredith joined him.

We now recount the evidence relating to Wade's wallet, basing our account primarily on the testimony of James Schenk, Scott's first appointed attorney. Schenk visited Scott in jail more than a month after the crime occurred and solicited information about the murder, stressing that he had to be fully acquainted with the facts to avoid being "sandbagged" by the prosecution during the trial. In response, Scott gave Schenk the same information that he had related earlier to the police. In addition, however, Scott told Schenk something Scott had not revealed to the police: that he had seen a wallet, as well as the paper bag, on the ground near Wade. Scott said that he picked up the wallet, put it in the paper bag, and placed both behind a parking lot fence. He also said that he later retrieved the bag, took it home, found $100 in the wallet and divided it with Meredith, and then tried to burn the wallet in his kitchen sink. He took the partially burned wallet, Scott told Schenk, placed it in a plastic bag, and threw it in a burn barrel behind his house.

Schenk, without further consulting Scott, retained Investigator Stephen Frick and sent Frick to find the wallet. Frick found it in the location described by Scott and brought it to Schenk. After examining the wallet and determining that it contained credit cards with Wade's name, Schenk turned the wallet and its contents over to Detective Payne, investigating officer in the case. Schenk told Payne only that, to the best of his knowledge, the wallet had belonged to Wade.

The prosecution subpoenaed Attorney Schenk and Investigator Frick to testify at the preliminary hearing. When questioned at that hearing, Schenk said that he received the wallet from Frick but refused to answer further questions on the ground that he learned about the wallet through a privileged communication. Eventually, however, the magistrate threatened Schenk with contempt if he did not respond "yes" or "no" when asked whether his contact with his client led to disclosure of the wallet's location. Schenk then replied "yes," and revealed on further questioning that this contact was the sole source of his information as to the wallet's location.

At the preliminary hearing Frick, the investigator who found the wallet, was then questioned by the district attorney. Over objections by counsel, Frick testified that he found the wallet in a garbage can behind Scott's residence.

Prior to trial, a third attorney, Hamilton Hintz, was appointed for Scott. Hintz unsuccessfully sought an in limine ruling that the wallet of the murder victim was inadmissible and that the attorney-client privilege precluded the admission of testimony concerning the wallet by Schenk or Frick.

At trial Frick, called by the prosecution, identified the wallet and testified that he found it in a garbage can behind Scott's residence. On cross-examination by Hintz, Scott's counsel, Frick further testified that he was an investigator hired by Scott's first attorney, Schenk, and that he had searched the garbage can at Schenk's request. Hintz later called Schenk as a witness: Schenk testified that he told Frick to search for the wallet immediately after Schenk finished talking to Scott. Schenk also stated that Frick brought him the wallet on the following day; after examining its contents Schenk delivered the wallet to the police. Scott then took the stand and testified to the information about the wallet that he had disclosed to Schenk.

The jury found both Scott and Meredith guilty of first degree murder and first degree robbery. It further found that Meredith, but not Scott, was armed with a deadly weapon. Both defendants appeal from their convictions.

Defendant Scott concedes, and we agree, that the wallet itself was admissible in evidence. Scott maintains, however, that Evidence Code section 954 bars the testimony of the investigator concerning the location of the wallet. We consider, first, whether the California attorney-client privilege codified in that section extends to observations which are the product of privileged communications. We then discuss whether that privileged status is lost when defense conduct may have frustrated prosecution discovery.

Section 954 provides, "(T)he client . . . has a privilege to refuse to disclose, and to prevent another from disclosing, a confidential communication between client and lawyer . . . ." Under that section one who seeks to assert the privilege must establish that a confidential communication occurred during the course of the attorney-client relationship. 8 Wigmore, Evidence (McNaughton rev. ed. 1961) s 2292; Witkin, Cal. Evidence (2d ed. 1966) s 794.)

Scott's statements to Schenk regarding the location of the wallet clearly fulfilled the statutory requirements. Moreover, the privilege did not dissolve when Schenk disclosed the substance of that communication to his investigator, Frick. Under Evidence Code section 912, subdivision (d), a disclosure which is "reasonably necessary" to accomplish the purpose for which the attorney has been consulted does not constitute a waiver of the privilege. If Frick was to perform the investigative services for which Schenk had retained him, it was "reasonably necessary," that Schenk transmit to Frick the information regarding the wallet. Thus, Schenk's disclosure to Frick did not waive the statutory privilege.

The statutes codifying the attorney-client privilege do not, however, indicate whether that privilege protects facts viewed and observed as a direct result of confidential communication. To resolve that issue, we turn first to the policies which underlie the attorney-client privilege, and then to the cases which apply those policies to observations arising from a protected communication.

The fundamental purpose of the attorney-client privilege is, of course, to encourage full and open communication between client and attorney. "Adequate legal representation in the ascertainment and enforcement of rights or the prosecution or defense of litigation compels a full disclosure of the facts by the client to his attorney. . . . Given the privilege, a client may make such a disclosure without fear that his attorney may be forced to reveal the information confided to him." (City & County of S. F. v. Superior Court, supra, 37 Cal.2d at p. 235, 231 P.2d 26. See also People v. Canfield (1974) 12 Cal.3d 699, 705, 117 Cal.Rptr. 81, 527 P.2d 633; People v. Atkinson (1870) 40 Cal. 284, 285.)

In the criminal context, as we have recently observed, these policies assume particular significance: " 'As a practical matter, if the client knows that damaging information could more readily be obtained from the attorney following disclosure than from himself in the absence of disclosure, the client would be reluctant to confide in his lawyer and it would be difficult to obtain fully informed legal advice.' . . . Thus, if an accused is to derive the full benefits of his right to counsel, he must have the assurance of confidentiality and privacy of communication with his attorney." (Barber v. Municipal Court (1979) 24 Cal.3d 742, 751, 157 Cal.Rptr. 658, 598 P.2d 878, citing Fisher v. United States (1976) 425 U.S. 391, 403, 96 S.Ct. 1569, 1577, 48 L.Ed.2d 39.)

Judicial decisions have recognized that the implementation of these important policies may require that the privilege extend not only to the initial communication between client and attorney but also to any information which the attorney or his investigator may subsequently acquire as a direct result of that communication. In a venerable decision involving facts analogous to those in the instant case, the Supreme Court of West Virginia held that the trial court erred in admitting an attorney's testimony as to the location of a pistol which he had discovered as the result of a privileged communication from his client. That the attorney had observed the pistol, the court pointed out, did not nullify the privilege: "All that the said attorney knew about this pistol, or where it was to be found, he knew only from the communications which had been made to him by his client confidentially and professionally, as counsel in this case. And it ought therefore, to have been entirely excluded from the jury. It may be, that in this particular case this evidence tended to the promotion of right and justice, but as was well said in Pearce v. Pearce, 11 Jar. 52, in page 55, and 2 De Gex & Smale 25–27: 'Truth like all other good things may be loved unwisely, may be pursued too keenly, may cost too much.' " (State of West Virginia v. Douglass (1882) 20 W.Va. 770, 783.)

This unbearable cost, the Douglass court concluded, could not be entirely avoided by attempting to admit testimony regarding observations or discoveries made as the result of a privileged communication, while excluding the communication itself. Such a procedure, Douglass held, "was practically as mischievous in all its tendencies and consequences, as if it has required (the attorney) to state everything, which his client had confidentially told him about this pistol. It would be a slight safeguard indeed, to confidential communications made to counsel, if he was thus compelled substantially, to give them to a jury, although he was required not to state them in the words of his client." (Id., at p. 783.)

More recent decisions reach similar conclusions. In State v. Olwell (1964) 64 Wash.2d 828, 394 P.2d 681, the court reviewed contempt charges against an attorney who refused to produce a knife he obtained from his client. The court first observed that "(t)o be protected as a privileged communication . . . the securing of the knife . . . must have been the direct result of information given to Mr. Olwell by his client." (P. 683.) (Emphasis added.) The court concluded that defense counsel, after examining the physical evidence, should deliver it to the prosecution, but should not reveal the source of the evidence; "(b)y thus allowing the prosecution to recover such evidence, the public interest is served, and by refusing the prosecution an opportunity to disclose the source of the evidence, the client's privilege is preserved and a balance reached between these conflicting interests." (P. 685.) (See also Anderson v. State (D.C.App.Fla.1974) 297 So.2d 871.)

Finally, we note the decisions of the New York courts in People v. Belge (Sup.Ct.1975) 83 Misc.2d 186, 372 N.Y.S.2d 798, affirmed in People v. Belge (App.Div.1975) 50 A.D.2d 1088, 376 N.Y.S.2d 771. Defendant, charged with one murder, revealed to counsel that he had committed three others. Counsel, following defendant's directions, located one of the bodies. Counsel did not reveal the location of the body until trial, 10 months later, when he exposed the other murders to support an insanity defense.

Counsel was then indicted for violating two sections of the New York Public Health Law for failing to report the existence of the body to proper authorities in order that they could give it a decent burial. The trial court dismissed the indictment; the appellate division affirmed, holding that the attorney-client privilege shielded counsel from prosecution for actions which would otherwise violate the Public Health Law.

The foregoing decisions demonstrate that the attorney-client privilege is not strictly limited to communications, but extends to protect observations made as a consequence of protected communications. We turn therefore to the question whether that privilege encompasses a case in which the defense, by removing or altering evidence, interferes with the prosecution's opportunity to discover that evidence.

In some of the cases extending the privilege to observations arising from protected communications the defense counsel had obtained the evidence from his client or in some other fashion removed it from its original location (State v. Olwell, supra, 394 P.2d 681; Anderson v. State, supra, 297 So.2d 871); in others the attorney did not remove or alter the evidence (People v. Belge, supra, 372 N.Y.S.2d 798; State v. Sullivan, supra, 373 P.2d 474). None of the decisions, however, confronts directly the question whether such removal or alteration should affect the defendant's right to assert the attorney-client privilege as a bar to testimony concerning the original location or condition of the evidence.

When defense counsel alters or removes physical evidence, he necessarily deprives the prosecution of the opportunity to observe that evidence in its original condition or location. As the amicus Appellate Committee of the California District Attorneys Association points out, to bar admission of testimony concerning the original condition and location of the evidence in such a case permits the defense in effect to "destroy" critical information; it is as if, he explains, the wallet in this case bore a tag bearing the words "located in the trash can by Scott's residence," and the defense, by taking the wallet, destroyed this tag. To extend the attorney-client privilege to a case in which the defense removed evidence might encourage defense counsel to race the police to seize critical evidence. (See In re Ryder (E.D.Va.1967) 263 F.Supp. 360, 369; Comment, The Right of a Criminal Defense Attorney to Withhold Physical Evidence Received From His Client (1970) 38 U.Chi.L.Rev. 211, 227–228.)

We therefore conclude that courts must craft an exception to the protection extended by the attorney-client privilege in cases in which counsel has removed or altered evidence. Indeed, at oral argument defense counsel acknowledged that such an exception might be necessary in a case in which the police would have inevitably discovered the evidence in its original location if counsel had not removed it. Counsel argued, however, that the attorney-client privilege should protect observations of evidence, despite subsequent defense removal, unless the prosecution could prove that the police probably would have eventually discovered the evidence in the original site.

We have seriously considered counsel's proposal, but have concluded that a test based upon the probability of eventual discovery is unworkably speculative. Evidence turns up not only because the police deliberately search for it, but also because it comes to the attention of policemen or bystanders engaged in other business. In the present case, for example, the wallet might have been found by the trash collector. Moreover, one physical evidence (the wallet) is turned over to the police, they will obviously stop looking for it; to ask where, how long, and how carefully they would have looked is obviously to compel speculation as to theoretical future conduct of the police.

We therefore conclude that whenever defense counsel removes or alters evidence, the statutory privilege does not bar revelation of the original location or condition of the evidence in question. We thus view the defense decision to remove evidence as a tactical choice. If defense counsel leaves the evidence where he discovers it, his observations derived from privileged communications are insulated from revelation. If, however, counsel chooses to remove evidence to examine or test it, the original location and condition of that evidence loses the protection of the privilege. Applying this analysis to the present case, we hold that the trial court did not err in admitting the investigator's testimony concerning the location of the wallet.

Defendants' other contentions attacking the trial and verdict were fully addressed by the Court of Appeal. We agree with that court's resolution of the issues there presented, and therefore reject defendant's contentions as without merit. (See People v. James (1977) 19 Cal.3d 99, 118, 137 Cal.Rptr. 447, 561 P.2d 1135.)

We further agree with the Court of Appeal that the judgment against defendants should be modified, and adopt as our own that portion of the Court of Appeal opinion. It reads as follows:

"When a defendant commits multiple violations incident to a single objective, conviction is proper for each violation but the defendant may not be punished for more than one. (People v. Miller (1977) 18 Cal.3d 873, 885, 135 Cal.Rptr. 654, 558 P.2d 552.) The evidence reveals a single course of conduct with one objective, and thus defendants may be punished only for the most serious offense, first degree murder. Conviction for the robbery is appropriate, but the execution of sentence for the robbery must be stayed pending the service of sentence for the murder, such stay to become permanent upon the completion of the murder sentence. (Id., at p. 886, 135 Cal.Rptr. 654, 558 P.2d 552.)

"Finally, the judgment must be modified in respect to the finding that Meredith used a firearm in the commission of the offense. (P) The information charged that Meredith was armed with a deadly weapon, to wit, a pistol. The court instructed the jury on being armed with a deadly weapon. The verdict returned by the jury was that Meredith was armed with a deadly weapon, to wit, a pistol. The abstract of judgment states that Meredith used a firearm in the commission of the offense. This finding must be stricken. The allegation and finding that a defendant was armed with a deadly weapon will not support a finding that the defendant used a firearm. (People v. Najera (1972) 8 Cal.3d 504, 509–510, 105 Cal.Rptr. 345, 503 P.2d 1353.) The judgment may not be modified to include the finding of being armed with a deadly weapon, since being armed with a deadly weapon is an essential element of the offense of first degree robbery. (People v. Hartsell (1973) 34 Cal.App.3d 8, 12, 109 Cal.Rptr. 627.) Nor may the judgment be modified to make the special finding of being armed with a deadly weapon during the murder, for the terms of Penal Code section 12022 cannot be applied to a conviction where the sentence is life imprisonment. (People v. Walker (1976) 18 Cal.3d 232, 243, 133 Cal.Rptr. 520, 555 P.2d 306.) Penal Code section 3024 is inapplicable to a life sentence, since the minimum date for parole for a life sentence exceeds the minimum sentence under Penal Code section 3024. (See Pen.Code, s 3046.)"

The superior court is directed to modify its judgment to stay the service of sentence on the robbery convictions, such stay to become permanent upon completion of service of the sentences for murder, and to strike from the abstract of judgment of Meredith the finding of use of a firearm. The superior court is further directed to forward a certified copy of the amended abstract of judgment to the Director of Corrections. The judgment, as so modified, is affirmed.

SOLUTIONS: THE LAWYER SHOULD HAVE, WOULD HAVE, COULD HAVE. . .

When a lawyer comes into possession of evidence—in a criminal or a civil case—the lawyer must go Full Stop and ask: is this of "potential" evidentiary value per the language of the Rule? If so, the lawyer must then ask: What are my obligations to provide access to the evidence? As applied, the Rule has a powerful bias toward evidence being discoverable and towards

> disclosing. We will further explore this concept shortly in the context of a
> DA's disclosure duties.

Section 2. Preserving Evidence/Facilitating Access to Evidence

Cases and Materials

X-Ray Questions (*Surowiec*)

This case is the flip side of manufacturing and/or withholding evidence. Here, a company received a demand letter from a lawyer threatening a lawsuit and outlining the rationale for suit. What was the rationale? Was the company on sufficient notice of the basis of the putative claim? Did the in-house lawyer from the company take any steps to preserve documents related to the claim? Can you fathom the basis for his decision? (Recall from your earlier readings that the work product rule would have shielded from disclosure any memos or communication regarding the demand letter). What was the harshest penalty that the court could have imposed for the blasé mindset of the in-house lawyer? Why was that penalty not imposed? Consider how you would exploit the penalty at a trial or in a mediation if you were representing the plaintiffs. What would you do?

Surowiec v. Capital Title Agency, Inc.

United States District Court, D. Arizona, 2011.
790 F.Supp.2d 997.

ORDER

DAVID G. CAMPBELL, DISTRICT JUDGE.

In November 2006, Plaintiff James Surowiec purchased a condominium unit located in Scottsdale, Arizona from developer Shamrock Glen, LLC. Scott Romley, an employee with Capital Title Agency, Inc. ("Capital"), served as escrow agent for the transaction. Plaintiff alleges, among other things, that Romley failed to disclose before closing that the property would remain encumbered by deeds of trusts held by certain investors in the Shamrock Glen development. Plaintiff claims that those junior liens and related foreclosure actions brought by the investors have prevented him from selling the condominium, resulting in financial loss.

Plaintiff filed suit against Romley and Capital in November 2009. Doc. 1. The amended complaint asserts claims for breach of contract, breach of fiduciary duty, fraud, negligent misrepresentation, negligence, and breach of the implied covenant of good faith and fair dealing. Doc. 27. Plaintiff seeks compensatory and punitive damages. *Id.*

The parties have filed motions for summary judgment. Docs. 79, 92. Plaintiff has filed two motions for sanctions. Docs. 82, 97. The motions are fully briefed. For reasons that follow, the Court will grant in part Defendants' summary judgment motion, deny Plaintiff's summary judgment motion, and grant in part the motions for sanctions.

I.   Summary Judgment Standard.

A party seeking summary judgment "bears the initial responsibility of informing the district court of the basis for its motion, and identifying those portions of [the record] which it believes demonstrate the absence of a genuine issue of material fact." *Celotex Corp. v. Catrett*, 477 U.S. 317, 323, 106 S.Ct. 2548, 91 L.Ed.2d 265 (1986). Summary judgment is appropriate if the evidence, viewed in the light most favorable to the nonmoving party, shows "that there is no genuine issue as to any material fact and that the movant is entitled to judgment as a matter of law." Fed.R.Civ.P. 56(a). Only disputes over facts that might affect the outcome of the suit will preclude the entry of summary judgment, and the disputed evidence must be "such that a reasonable jury could return a verdict for the nonmoving party." *Anderson v. Liberty Lobby, Inc.*, 477 U.S. 242, 248, 106 S.Ct. 2505, 91 L.Ed.2d 202 (1986).

II.   Defendants' Summary Judgment Motion.

Defendants move for summary judgment on the ground that Plaintiff cannot establish the amount of compensatory damages with reasonable certainty. Doc. 79 at 1. Defendants further argue that summary judgment is appropriate on the claim for punitive damages because there is no evidence that Defendants acted with an evil mind or malice toward Plaintiff. *Id.* The Court will address each argument in turn.

A.   Compensatory Damages.

It is well established "that 'certainty in amount' of damages is not essential to recovery when the *fact* of damage is proven." *Gilmore v. Cohen*, 95 Ariz. 34, 386 P.2d 81, 82 (1963) (citations omitted; emphasis in original). This rule is "simply a recognition that doubts as to the extent of injury should be resolved in favor of the innocent plaintiff and against the wrongdoer." *Id.* The plaintiff in every case, however, "should supply some reasonable basis for computing the amount of damage and must do so with such precision as, from the nature of his claim and the available evidence, is possible." *Id.*

Because Defendants do not seek summary judgment as to liability, the Court will assume the allegations of wrongdoing on their part can be proven at trial. Construing the evidence in the light most favorable to Plaintiff, a jury reasonably could conclude that Plaintiff has suffered more than $100,000 in compensatory damages as a result of Defendants' misconduct.

Plaintiff purchased his condominium unit as a short-term investment. Doc. 100 ¶ 33. He paid $137,000 for the unit in November 2006. *Id.* ¶ 40. He expected to receive a marketable title free and clear of all liens (*id.* ¶ 13), and would not have bought the property if he had known that it remained encumbered with liens (Doc. 113–2 at 56–57). In May 2007, after discovering that the property was encumbered by numerous liens and likely subject to future litigation, Plaintiff was advised by title and real estate experts that the title problems had to be resolved before the property could be sold. Doc. 100 ¶ 36. While Plaintiff waited for some resolution through the fall of 2007, similar unencumbered units in the Shamrock Glen development sold for more than $130,000. *Id.* ¶ 41. As of June 2010, Plaintiff's unit remained subject to liens and was appraised at $31,000. *Id.* ¶¶ 39, 44. Accepting this evidence as true, a jury could find with reasonable certainty that Plaintiff has suffered more than $100,000 in damages taking into account the $137,000 purchase price, the $130,000 selling price for units in the fall of 2007, the property's current value of $31,000, and the fact that Defendants' actions prevented Plaintiff from selling the property when its value was higher.

Plaintiff's damages are speculative, Defendants contend, because he has made no serious effort to sell the property. Doc. 79 at 6. But Plaintiff's real estate expert, Roger Williams, has opined that the liens on the property rendered it virtually unmarketable, making any attempt to sell an exercise in futility. Doc. 100 ¶ 42. Defendants assert that Mr. Williams contradicted his own opinion by admitting during his deposition that there are buyers who purchase property with title defects. Doc. 112 ¶ 42. This purported inconsistency goes to the weight of Mr. William's opinion, not its admissibility. "Credibility determinations, the weighing of evidence, and the drawing of inferences from the facts are jury functions, not those of a judge [.]" *Anderson,* 477 U.S. at 255, 106 S.Ct. 2505.

Defendants further assert that because Plaintiff still holds title to the property, he will reap the benefits from the expected real estate market rebound.

Doc. 79 at 7. Defendants, of course, are free to make this argument to the jury, but a potential future boom in the real estate market does not render uncertain the damages currently suffered by Plaintiff.

Defendants argue for the first time in their reply brief that Plaintiff cannot establish that their actions caused the loss in market value, as opposed to the steep decline in the Arizona real estate market. Doc. 111 at 3–5. The Court will not consider this argument. "It is well established in this circuit that courts will not consider new arguments raised for the first time in a reply brief." *Bach v. Forever Living Prods. U.S., Inc.*, 473 F.Supp.2d 1110, 1122 n. 6 (W.D.Wash.2007) (citing *Lentini v. Cal. Ctr. For the Arts*, 370 F.3d 837 n. 6 (9th Cir.2004)); *see Gadda v. State Bar of Cal.*, 511 F.3d 933, 937 n. 2 (9th Cir.2007).

Moreover, while Plaintiff makes clear that the liens were not a positive selling point and certainly did not increase the property's value (Doc. 99 at 18 n. 4), he does not dispute that the decrease in value is due in part to the general downturn in the real estate market. Plaintiff claims that he was unable to sell the property as the downturn worsened because it was encumbered by liens Defendants failed to extinguish at closing. A plaintiff "is not required to prove causation to a certainty; 'the jury must be permitted to make causal judgments from its ordinary experience without demanding impossible proof about what would have occurred if the defendant behaved [properly].' " *Harris v. State ex rel. Dep't of Transp.*, No. 1 CA-CV 10-0019, 2010 WL 5313761, at *4 (Ariz.Ct.App. Dec. 21, 2010) (citation omitted). Whether Defendants' alleged misconduct caused damages is for the jury to decide.

Defendants' reliance on *Soilworks v. Midwest Industrial Supply, Inc.*, 575 F.Supp.2d 1118 (D.Ariz.2008), is misplaced. The lost profit damages sought in that case fell far short of the "reasonable certainty" standard because the plaintiff presented no documents or other information in support of its damages claim. *Id.* at 1128. Plaintiff, by contrast, has presented evidence from which damages in excess of $100,000 reasonably may be found.

The Court will deny Defendants' summary judgment motion with respect to compensatory damages.

B. Punitive Damages.

Punitive damages are those damages awarded "in excess of full compensation to the victim in order to punish the wrongdoer and deter others from emulating his conduct." *Linthicum v. Nationwide Life Ins. Co.*, 150 Ariz. 326, 723 P.2d 675, 679 (1986). "Punishment is an appropriate objective in a civil case only if the defendant's conduct or motive 'involves some element of outrage similar to that usually found in a crime.' " *Gurule v. Ill. Mut. Life & Cas. Co.*, 152 Ariz. 600, 734 P.2d 85, 86 (1987) (quoting *Rawlings v. Apodaca*, 151 Ariz. 149, 726 P.2d 565, 578 (1986)). Where the defendant did not act with an "evil mind," compensatory damages usually provide sufficient deterrence. *Id.*

Plaintiff claims that the requisite evil mind may be inferred from Romley's active participation in an ongoing fraud. Doc. 99 at 14. But to recover punitive damages, "something more is required over and above the 'mere commission of a tort.' " *Linthicum*, 723 P.2d at 679 (quoting *Rawlings*, 726 P.2d at 578). This "something more" must be established by clear and convincing evidence. *Id.* at 681.

When ruling on summary judgment, the Court must also consider the burden of proof to be satisfied at trial—in this case, clear and convincing evidence of an evil mind. As the Supreme Court has explained, "in ruling on a motion for summary judgment, the judge must view the evidence presented through the prism of the substantive evidentiary burden." *Anderson v. Liberty Lobby*, 477 U.S. 242, 254, 106 S.Ct. 2505, 91 L.Ed.2d 202 (1986). No triable issue of fact exists if the plaintiff presents insufficient evidence for a jury to find an evil mind by clear and convincing evidence. *See id.* at 254–55, 106 S.Ct. 2505.

The Arizona Supreme Court has made clear that "punitive damages are not recoverable in every fraud case, even though fraud is an intentional tort." *Rawlings*, 726 P.2d at 578 n. 8; *see Dawson v. Withycombe*, 216 Ariz. 84, 163 P.3d 1034, 1062 & n. 27 (Ariz.Ct.App.2007). Even when construed in his favor, Plaintiff's evidence does not show "aggravated and outrageous" conduct on the part of Defendants sufficient to support an award of punitive damages. *Linthicum*, 723 P.2d at 680. Plaintiff admits that the title commitment and HUD-1 settlement statement he received prior to closing disclosed the existence of the junior lienholders and indicated that they were to be paid nothing out of escrow while the seller, Shamrock Glen, was to be paid more than $10,000. Docs. 80, 100 ¶¶ 6–11. While Romley otherwise may have mishandled the escrow, particularly given his knowledge that investors expected to paid (Doc. 100 ¶ 21), his misconduct constitutes fraud or breach fiduciary duty, not "aggravated, wanton, reckless or malicious intentional wrongdoing [.]" *Dawson*, 163 P.3d at 1062. Plaintiff has failed to present sufficient evidence for a reasonable jury to find an evil mind by clear and convincing evidence.

Because there is no triable issue as to an award of punitive damages against Romley, Capital may not be held vicariously liable for such damages. *See id.* Defendants' motion for summary judgment will be granted with respect to punitive damages.

III. Plaintiff's Summary Judgment Motion.

Plaintiff seeks summary judgment on his claim for breach of fiduciary duty. Doc. 92. "The escrow relationship gives rise to two specific fiduciary duties to the principals: to comply strictly with the terms of the escrow agreement and to disclose facts that a reasonable escrow agent would perceive as evidence of fraud being committed on a party to the escrow." *Maxfield v. Martin,* 217 Ariz. 312, 173 P.3d 476, 478 (Ariz.Ct.App.2007); *see Maganas v. Northroup,* 135 Ariz. 573, 663 P.2d 565, 569 (1983). Defendants breached their fiduciary duties, Plaintiff claims, by failing to disclose that the junior lienholders would not be paid out of escrow, that escrow funds were being diverted to the seller, that the seller intended to provide equity gifts to certain buyers, and that blank pre-signed releases would be recorded in lieu of unit-specific releases provided directly by the junior lienholders. Doc. 92 at 8.

Whether an escrow agent has breached a fiduciary duty generally "is a question for the trier of fact." *Mur-Ray Mgmt. Corp. v. Founders Title Co.,* 169 Ariz. 417, 819 P.2d 1003, 1009 (Ariz.Ct.App.1991). Defendants have presented evidence that they timely disclosed to Plaintiff that the junior lienholders would be paid no money out of escrow (Doc. 110 ¶ 49) and that the seller was to be paid $10,191.57 from escrow proceeds (*id.* ¶ 48). Defendants also have presented evidence that the junior lienholders executed valid releases for each unit without placing any restrictions on their use (*id.* ¶ 56), and that it was not until after Plaintiff closed escrow on his unit that they learned a certain investor objected to the use of the pre-signed releases in future transactions (*id.* ¶¶ 58–64). The equity gifts were made by the seller after Plaintiff closed escrow. *Id.* Plaintiff has presented no evidence showing that, prior to his closing, Defendants had knowledge of the seller's intention to make those gifts. The Court concludes that whether Defendants have breached a fiduciary duty by failing to follow the terms of the escrow agreement or failing to disclose known fraud, *see Maganas,* 663 P.2d at 568, is a question of fact for the jury. *See Mur-Ray Mgmt.,* 819 P.2d at 1009.

Moreover, in an action asserting a claim for breach of fiduciary duty, "like all tort actions, a plaintiff must allege and prove the existence of a duty owed, a breach of that duty, and damages causally related to such breach." *Smethers v. Campion,* 210 Ariz. 167, 108 P.3d 946, 949 (Ariz.Ct.App.2005). Plaintiff argues that a breach of fiduciary duty is established as a matter of undisputed fact, but he makes no attempt in his summary judgment motion to prove the essential elements of causation and damages. *See Smethers,* 108 P.3d at 949 ("The elements of breach and causation, and the measure of damages, if any, are generally questions for the trier of fact."). Plaintiff's motion for summary judgment on the claim for breach of fiduciary duty (count two) will be denied.

IV. Spoliation of Evidence.

"The failure to preserve electronic or other records, once the duty to do so has been triggered, raises the issue of spoliation of evidence and its consequences." *Thompson v. U.S. Dep't of Housing & Urban Dev.*, 219 F.R.D. 93, 100 (D.Md.2003). Spoliation is the destruction or material alteration of evidence, or the failure to otherwise preserve evidence, for another's use in litigation. *See Ashton v. Knight Transp., Inc.*, 772 F.Supp.2d 772, 799–800, 2011 WL 734282, at *25 (N.D.Tex. Feb. 22, 2011). Plaintiff seeks various sanctions against Defendants for spoliation of emails and other electronic records concerning, among other things, Romley's involvement with title and escrow problems in the sale of Shamrock Glen properties. Doc. 82.

"A party seeking sanctions for spoliation of evidence must prove the following elements: (1) the party having control over the evidence had an obligation to preserve it when it was destroyed or altered; (2) the destruction or loss was accompanied by a 'culpable state of mind;' and (3) the evidence that was destroyed or altered was 'relevant' to the claims or defenses of the party that sought the discovery of the spoliated evidence [.]" *Goodman v. Praxair Servs., Inc.*, 632 F.Supp.2d 494, 509 (D.Md.2009) (quoting *Thompson*, 219 F.R.D. at 101); *see Victor Stanley, Inc. v. Creative Pipe, Inc. ("Victor Stanley II")*, 269 F.R.D. 497, 520–21 (D.Md.2010); *In re Napster, Inc. Copyright Litig.*, 462 F.Supp.2d 1060, 1070–78 (N.D.Cal.2006); *Zubulake v. UBS Warburg LLC ("Zubulake IV")*, 220 F.R.D. 212, 216 (S.D.N.Y.2003). The Court will address each element separately.

A. Duty to Preserve—the Trigger Date.

It is well established that the "duty to preserve arises when a party knows or should know that certain evidence is relevant to pending or future litigation." *Ashton*, 772 F.Supp.2d at 800, 2011 WL 734282, at *26. Stated differently, the duty to preserve is triggered "not only during litigation, but also extends to the period before litigation when a party should reasonably know that evidence may be relevant to anticipated litigation." *Morford v. Wal-Mart Stores, Inc.*, No. 2:09-cv-02251-RLH-PAL, 2011 WL 635220, at *3 (D.Nev. Feb. 11, 2011); *see Zubulake IV*, 220 F.R.D. at 216; *Napster*, 462 F.Supp.2d at 1067–68.

Capital was on notice of reasonably foreseeable litigation concerning title and escrow deficiencies in the sale of Shamrock Glen properties, as well as Romley's direct involvement in those deficiencies, no later than April 28, 2007, when an attorney for Shamrock Glen sent a letter to Capital's in-house counsel,

Lawrence Phelps. Doc. 82–3. The letter explained that in response to inquiries from homeowners about outstanding liens on their properties, Shamrock Glen investigated the matter and was surprised to learn that while there had been more than twenty units sold, Capital had recorded only four releases from the investors. *Id.* at 2. The threat of future litigation was clear: the letter informed Phelps that some investors "have sought independent legal advice and are anticipated to claim approximately two million dollars in damages," warned that Capital "faces significant potential exposure" in the matter, requested that Phelps provide Shamrock Glen with a copy of Capital's title insurance policy for the property, and advised that it may be prudent for him to provide the insurer with "written notification of these *anticipated claims.*" *Id.* at 3 (emphasis added).

The likelihood of litigation was underscored by other related events. Romley sought legal advice with respect to his involvement in Shamrock Glen in December of 2006 or January of 2007, and apparently sought it from Phelps. Doc. 98, Ex. 10, at 93–94. Phelps testified that by February 1, 2007, he knew litigation was "certainly possible." Doc. 82, Ex. 1 at 137. On April 30, 2007, an email sent to Romley and copied to Phelps asserted, in bold and underscored language, that "[t]his matter must get cleared up immediately or I can assure you that litigation is imminent." Doc. 98, Ex. 12.

Capital addresses only the April 28 letter, and relegates even this discussion to a footnote in its response brief. Noting that the letter does not mention Plaintiff by name, Capital asserts that the letter triggered no duty to preserve evidence relating to any potential claim *by Plaintiff.* Doc. 95 at 3 n. 4. But the duty to preserve evidence "is a duty owed to the *court,* not to the party's potential adversary[.]" *Ashton,* 772 F.Supp.2d at 800, 2011 WL 734282, at *26 (citing *Victor Stanley II,* 269 F.R.D. at 525–26) (emphasis in original). Moreover, the threat of litigation from homeowners such as Plaintiff is readily apparent from the face of the letter because it discusses the liens encumbering their properties (Doc. 82–3 at 2) and explicitly states that Capital faces "significant potential exposure" for its "failures to the various investors, *homeowners,* and Shamrock Glen" (*id.* at 3) (emphasis added).

Where a "letter openly threatens litigation, then the recipient is on notice that litigation is reasonably foreseeable and the duty to preserve evidence relevant to that dispute is triggered." *Goodman,* 632 F.Supp.2d at 511. "The preservation obligation runs first to counsel, who has 'a duty to advise his client of the type of information potentially relevant to the lawsuit and of the necessity of preventing its destruction.'" *See Richard Green (Fine Paintings) v. McClendon,* 262 F.R.D. 284, 290 (S.D.N.Y.2009) (citations omitted).

When Mr. Phelps, as in-house counsel for Capital, received the April 28, 2007 letter, he was "obligated to suspend [Capital's] document retention/destruction policy and implement a 'litigation hold' to ensure the preservation of relevant documents." *Goodman,* 632 F.Supp.2d at 511 (quoting *Thompson,* 219 F.R.D. at 100). He did not. Mr. Phelps testified that he issued no litigation hold and did not otherwise takes steps to suspend Capital's routine destruction of emails more than 30 days old. Nor did he seek to preserve the emails then existing on Mr. Romley's computer.

Capital's reliance on *Napster* is misplaced. *Napster* stands for the unremarkable proposition that no duty to preserve arises absent a reasonable expectation of being "named as a defendant in any pending or future litigation." 462 F.Supp.2d at 1068. Once a party knows that litigation is reasonably anticipated, the party owes a duty to the judicial system to ensure preservation of relevant evidence. *See Ashton,* 772 F.Supp.2d at 800–01, 2011 WL 734282, at *26; *Goodman,* 632 F.Supp.2d at 511.

B.   Culpability.

"Courts have not been uniform in defining the level of culpability—be it negligence, gross negligence, willfulness, or bad faith—that is required before sanctions are appropriate[.]" *Ashton,* 772 F.Supp.2d at 800, 2011 WL 734282, at *26. Nor is there consensus as to how the level of culpability is to be determined, or what prejudice, if any, may be presumed from culpable conduct. At least one court has concluded that, once the duty to preserve is triggered, the failure to issue a written litigation hold constitutes gross negligence per se and prejudice may be presumed "because that failure is likely to result in the destruction of relevant information." *Pension Committee of Univ. of Montreal Pension Plan v. Banc of America Sec. ("Pension Committee"),* 685 F.Supp.2d 456, 465 (S.D.N.Y.2010). Other courts have found the failure to implement a litigation hold to be an important factor in determining culpability, but not per se evidence of culpable conduct giving rise to a presumption of relevance and prejudice. *See, e.g., Haynes v. Dart,* No. 08 C 4834, 2010 WL 140387, at *4 (N.D.Ill. Jan. 11, 2010); *Sampson v. City of Cambridge,* 251 F.R.D. 172, 181–82 (D.Md.2008); *see also Victor Stanley II,* 269 F.R.D. at 524, 529–31 (discussing how courts differ in the fault they assign where a party fails to implement a litigation hold).

The Court disagrees with *Pension Committee*'s holding that a failure to issue a litigation hold constitutes gross negligence per se. Per se rules are too inflexible for this factually complex area of the law where a wide variety of circumstances may lead to spoliation accusations. An allegedly spoliating party's culpability must be determined case-by-case.

In this case, Capital has provided no reasonable explanation for its failure to preserve. It does not claim that the April 28 letter was overlooked or misunderstood, that preservation was not feasible, or that it undertook some preservation efforts and innocently failed to take others. Capital instead minimizes the April 28 letter, arguing that it did not provide notice of a potential lawsuit from the plaintiff. As noted above, however, the duty of preservation is not owed to specific potential plaintiffs, but to the judicial system. The Court finds that the April 28 letter and the other events that occurred before and shortly after the letter clearly placed Capital on notice that litigation was likely. The anticipated litigation was known to Capital's lawyer, Mr. Phelps, as was Romley's role at the center of the problem. Capital's complete failure to suspend its ongoing destruction of emails and to capture the evidence on Mr. Romley's computer was more than negligent. The Court finds it constituted gross negligence.

C.   Scope of the Duty to Preserve—Relevant Evidence.

Some courts have concluded that the scope of the duty to preserve is coextensive with disclosure obligations and available discovery under Rule 26 of the Federal Rules of Civil Procedure. *See, e.g., Zubulake IV*, 220 F.R.D. at 217–18; *Young v. Facebook, Inc.*, No. 5:10-cv-03579-JF/PVT, 2010 WL 3564847, at *1 (N.D.Cal. Sept. 13, 2010) (parties have a duty to preserve evidence "that they know is relevant or reasonably could lead to the discovery of admissible evidence"). The Court need not determine the outer contours of the duty in this case. Whatever those outer boundaries, they clearly encompassed ongoing emails to and from Romley and information on Romley's computer. *See Zubulake IV*, 220 F.R.D. at 218 (duty to preserve certainly extends to "key players"); *Goodman*, 632 F.Supp.2d at 512.

In *Rimkus Consulting Group, Inc. v. Cammarata,* 688 F.Supp.2d 598 (S.D.Tex.2010), the court declined to follow the approach taken in *Pension Committee* of presuming relevance and prejudice when the spoliating party is grossly negligent, noting that requiring "a showing that the lost information is relevant and prejudicial is an important check on spoliation allegations and sanctions motions." 688 F.Supp.2d at 616–17. *Rimkus* also made clear, however, that when "the evidence in the case as a whole would allow a reasonable fact finder to conclude that the missing evidence would have helped the requesting party support its claims or defenses, that may be a sufficient showing of both relevance and prejudice to make [sanctions] appropriate." *Id.* at 617. The Court has no doubt that this standard is satisfied here.

The Court is familiar with the facts and evidence in this case, having held several discovery conference calls with the parties (Docs. 29, 42, 46, 74) and having considered the summary judgment evidence (Docs. 80, 93, 100, 110) and evidence presented in connection with the motion for sanctions (*see* Docs. 82, 95, 98). That evidence, when considered as a whole and in light of Plaintiff's claims, permits the reasonable inference that Capital's failure to put a litigation hold in place resulted in the loss of relevant evidence. As of April 2007, Capital routinely deleted electronic records pursuant to its 30-day retention policy. Although Capital asserts that it began preserving all emails as a matter of course in October of 2007, its failure to stop email destruction in April of 2007 resulted in the loss of emails between March and September of 2007, not to mention older emails on Romley's computer. The year 2007 was a period of intense communication and negotiation concerning the Shamrock Glen problem, and the Court has no doubt that preserving emails exchanged in March through September of that year would have provided valuable information to Plaintiff. Similarly, acting in April of 2007 to preserve the older emails then on Romley's computer surely would have preserved valuable evidence for Plaintiff. One example is the February 1, 2007 email that managed to survive and provided very helpful evidence to Plaintiff. Doc. 95–2 at 2. Plaintiff has shown relevance and prejudice.

D.   Appropriate Sanction.

Because spoliation is considered an abuse of the judicial process, *see Ashton,* 772 F.Supp.2d at 800, 2011 WL 734282, at *26, courts may impose sanctions "as part of their inherent power to 'manage their own affairs so as to achieve the orderly and expeditious disposition of cases.' " *Morford,* 2011 WL 635220, at *3 (quoting *Napster,* 462 F.Supp.2d at 1066); *see Victor Stanley II,* 269 F.R.D. at 534. Courts in this Circuit have suggested that a "finding of fault or simple negligence is a sufficient basis on which a [c]ourt can impose sanctions against a party that has destroyed documents." *Melendres v. Arpaio,* No. CV-07-2513-PHX-GMS, 2010 WL 582189, at *5 (D.Ariz. Feb. 12, 2010) (citing *Unigard Sec. Ins. Co. v. Lakewood Eng'g & Mfr'g Corp.,* 982 F.2d 363, 369 n. 2 (9th Cir.1992)). The Court need not determine whether sanctions may be imposed for mere negligence given the finding of gross negligence on the part of Capital. "Sanctions that a federal court may impose for spoliation include assessing attorney's fees and costs, giving the jury an adverse inference instruction, precluding evidence, or imposing the harsh, case-dispositive sanctions of dismissal or judgment." *Victor Stanley II,* 269 F.R.D. at 533; *see Morford,* 2011 WL 635220, at *3. While the court has discretion to impose spoliation sanctions, *see Leon v. IDX Systems Corp.,* 464

F.3d 951, 957–58 (9th Cir.2006), it "must determine which sanction best (1) deters parties from future spoliation, (2) places the risk of an erroneous judgment on the spoliating party, and (3) restores the innocent party to their rightful litigation position." *Ashton*, 772 F.Supp.2d at 804, 2011 WL 734282, at *30 (citing *Victor Stanley II*, 269 F.R.D. at 533–34).

Plaintiff primarily seeks the entry of a default judgment against Defendants. Doc. 8–14. Plaintiff alternatively seeks a sanction of preclusion (*id.* at 14–15), but does not identify what evidence should be precluded. *See Leon*, 464 F.3d at 960 (preclusion sanction for spoliation would be futile). This Circuit has established a five-part test to determine whether a terminating sanction is just: " '(1) the public's interest in expeditious resolution of litigation; (2) the court's need to manage its dockets; (3) the risk of prejudice to the party seeking sanctions; (4) the public policy favoring disposition of cases on their merits; and (5) the availability of less drastic sanctions.' " *Valley Eng'rs Inc. v. Elec. Eng'g Co.*, 158 F.3d 1051, 1057 (9th Cir.1998) (citation omitted); *see Leon*, 464 F.3d at 958 (citing *Anheuser-Busch, Inc. v. Natural Beverage Distribs.*, 69 F.3d 337, 348 (9th Cir.1995)).

The first two factors favor a default judgment. Because the Court and the public have a strong interest in judicial efficiency and the prompt resolution of litigation, Capital's failure to preserve evidence, and the resulting delay caused by multiple discovery disputes and the instant motion for sanctions, weigh in favor of default judgment. *See Leon*, 464 F.3d at 958 n. 5. The fourth factor, as always, weighs against a terminating sanction. The fifth factor also weighs against a case-dispositive sanction as the lesser sanction of an adverse inference instruction is available. The third factor—prejudice—" 'looks to whether the spoliating party's actions impaired the non-spoliating party's ability to go to trial or threatened to interfere with the rightful decision of the case.' " *Leon*, 464 F.3d at 959 (citation and brackets omitted). While it is apparent that Plaintiff has been prejudiced by the spoliation of emails and other communications concerning Romley's involvement with the Shamrock Glen development, the Court cannot conclude that the spoliation will force Plaintiff to rely on " 'incomplete and spotty' " evidence at trial. *Leon*, 464 F.3d at 959 (quoting *Anheuser-Busch*, 69 F.3d at 354). Applying the five-factor test, the Court finds entry of default judgment to be unwarranted. *See Goodman*, 632 F.Supp.2d at 519 (finding terminating sanction inappropriate where the spoliating party did not act in bad faith); *Napster*, 462 F.Supp.2d at 1078 (the court should "impose the 'least onerous sanction' given the extent of the offending party's fault and the prejudice to the opposing party").

Alternatively, Plaintiff seeks an adverse inference jury instruction. Doc. 82 at 15. "When a party is prejudiced, but not irreparably, from the loss of evidence that was destroyed with a high degree of culpability, a harsh but less extreme sanction than dismissal or default is to permit the fact finder to presume that the destroyed evidence was prejudicial." *Rimkus,* 688 F.Supp.2d at 618. The Court finds an adverse inference instruction to be warranted in this case. The parties shall submit proposed adverse inference instructions with the other jury instructions to be filed before trial.

Plaintiff's motion for sanctions for spoliation of evidence will be denied with respect to the requests for default judgment or preclusion, but granted as to the request for an adverse inference instruction.

V.   Plaintiff's Motion for Sanctions Under Rule 37 and Inherent Powers.

Plaintiff seeks sanctions for alleged discovery abuses on the part of Capital under Rule 37 and the Court's inherent powers. Doc. 97. According to Plaintiff, Capital has acted in bad faith by misrepresenting that document searches were ongoing and electronic data was lost during data migration, by using only literal search terms and thereby ensuring that no documents would be found, and by identifying no specific responsive document in a "last minute data dump." *Id.* at 2. Plaintiff seeks severe sanctions, including an *in camera* examination of Mr. Phelps' conduct for disciplinary purposes, an order striking Defendants' expert witness report and testimony, and an order declaring that all privilege claims have been waived. *Id.* at 15–16. Plaintiff also seeks monetary sanctions, including attorneys' fees and costs. *Id.* at 16. The Court finds that monetary sanctions are warranted.

"Because of their very potency, inherent powers must be exercised with restraint and discretion." *Chambers v. NASCO, Inc.,* 501 U.S. 32, 44, 111 S.Ct. 2123, 115 L.Ed.2d 27 (1991). The imposition of sanctions under a federal court's inherent powers is warranted where a party has acted in bad faith, that is, "vexatiously, wantonly, or for oppressive reasons." *Id.* at 45–46, 111 S.Ct. 2123 (citations omitted). Rule 37 sanctions are appropriate only where the discovery violation is "due to willfulness, bad faith, or fault of the party." *Fair Housing of Marin v. Combs,* 285 F.3d 899, 905 (9th Cir.2002) (citations omitted).

The Court is familiar with the alleged discovery abuses. *See* Docs. 29, 42, 46, 74, 96. Based on that knowledge, and having considered the facts and arguments presented in the parties' briefs (Docs. 97, 103, 108), the Court finds that Capital acted willfully in connection with its response (or lack thereof) to Plaintiff's initial request for production of documents served in February 2010, specifically, requests 3, 4, and 5. Doc. 97–1 at 2–6. Those requests sought all emails from Romley regarding the failure to follow title commitment instructions and all communications of Romley, from the date Capital began serving as the title agency for Shamrock Glen until the date of Romley's termination, including written correspondence and emails directed to the investor lienholders or otherwise pertaining to the Shamrock Glen development. *Id.* at 3. Capital responded in March 2010 by asserting boilerplate objections and producing no documents. *Id.* at 10–11.

Plaintiff's requests specifically sought communications of Romley pertaining to the Shamrock Glen development, but the search parameters designed by Mr. Phelps included only Plaintiff's name and escrow number— "James M. Surowiec" and "20060669." *Id.* at 31–32. Those terms were not calculated to capture communications to or from Romley as sought in the document request. Not surprisingly, they produced "zero results." *Id.* at 32.

The Court ordered a new search in August 2010 (Doc. 42), which resulted in the production of more than 4,000 documents (*see* Doc. 97–3 at 54, Ex. 20). This substantial production was made only three days before the close of discovery (*see* Docs. 14, 40), and required a second-round of depositions of Defendant Romley, Mr. Phelps, and Mr. Brightly (*see* Doc. 73).

"Selection of the appropriate search and information retrieval technique requires careful advance planning by persons qualified to design effective search methodology," and the "implementation and methodology selected should be tested for quality assurance[.]" *Victor Stanley, Inc. v. Creative Pipe, Inc.*, 250 F.R.D. 251, 262 (D.Md.2008). Capital's unreasonably narrow search for documents using only Plaintiff's name and escrow number, and its assertion of unfounded boilerplate objections to document requests 3, 4, and 5, are inexcusable. Given that thousands of responsive documents were discovered once a proper search was performed, and in light of the late production of those documents, the Court concludes that Capital acted willfully in failing timely and adequately to respond to the document requests.

District courts are given "particularly wide latitude" to issue Rule 37 sanctions. *Yeti by Molly, Ltd. v. Deckers Outdoor Corp.*, 259 F.3d 1101, 1106 (9th Cir.2001). Similarly, pursuant the inherent power to control their dockets, district courts have discretion to impose a variety of sanctions for discovery abuses. *Oliva v. Sullivan*, 958 F.2d 272, 273 (9th Cir.1992). The Court concludes that Capital's conduct warrants an award of monetary sanctions, but no harsher sanction.

Plaintiff requests an award of attorneys' fees and costs incurred as a result of Capital's misconduct. Doc. 97 at 16. Under Rule 37(d)(3), an offending party may be ordered to pay the other party's "reasonable expenses" caused by the discovery abuse. With respect to pro se litigants, including those that are licensed attorneys, the general rule is that attorneys' fees are not a payable "expense" under Rule 37 "as there is no direct financial cost or charge associated with the expenditure of one's own time." *Pickholtz v. Rainbow Techs., Inc.,* 284 F.3d 1365, 1375 (Fed.Cir.2002); *see Fosselman v. Gibbs,* No. CV 06-00375 PJH (NJV), 2010 WL 1446661, at *1 (N.D.Cal. Apr. 7, 2010); *see also Kay v. Ehrler,* 499 U.S. 432, 438, 111 S.Ct. 1435, 113 L.Ed.2d 486 (1991) (licensed attorney proceeding pro se not entitled to an award attorneys' fees). The "reasonable expenses" awardable under Rule 37 do include, however, "actual costs incurred as a result of misconduct [.]" *Fosselman,* 2010 WL 1446661, at *1.

"Fees to pro se litigants are awardable under the court's inherent power." *Jacobs v. Scribner,* No. 1:06-cv-01280-AWI-GSA-PC, 2011 WL 98585, at *1 (E.D.Cal. Jan. 12, 2011). A rule to the contrary "would place a pro se litigant at the mercy of an opponent who might engage in otherwise sanctionable conduct." *Pickholtz,* 284 F.3d at 1375.

As a sanction for Capital's discovery abuses, the Court, pursuant to Rule 37 and its inherent powers, will require Capital to (1) reimburse the actual expenses Plaintiff incurred as a result of the misconduct, including the expense for the second-round of depositions, and (2) pay reasonable attorneys' fees to compensate Plaintiff for the time he spent challenging the misconduct, preparing for and taking the additional depositions, and bringing the instant motion.

The parties are directed to confer in good faith to resolve any disputes concerning the amount of reasonable expenses and fees. *See* LRCiv 54.2(d)(1). If the parties are unable to agree, Plaintiff may file a motion pursuant to Local Rule 54.2. Any such motion shall be filed, with a supporting memorandum, on or before **May 20, 2011,** with the response and reply briefs due in accordance with the time periods provided in Local Rule 54.2(b)(3) and (4).

IT IS ORDERED:

1.   Defendants' motion for summary judgment (Doc. 79) is **granted in part** and **denied in part.** The motion is granted with respect to punitive damages and denied as to compensatory damages.

2.   Plaintiff's motion for summary judgment (Doc. 92) is **denied.**

3.   Plaintiff's motion for sanctions for spoliation of evidence (Docs. 82, 97) is **granted in part** and **denied in part** as set forth in this order.

4.   Plaintiff's motion for sanctions pursuant to Rule 37 and the Court's inherent powers (Doc. 97) is **granted in part** and **denied in part** as set forth in this order.

5.   Plaintiff's motion to strike reply brief (Doc. 114) is **denied.**

6.   The Court will set a final pretrial conference by separate order

7.   By separate order the Court will also require the parties, during the month of June, to hold a settlement conference with Ninth Circuit mediators in Phoenix.

SOLUTIONS: THE LAWYER SHOULD HAVE, WOULD HAVE, COULD HAVE. . .

The type of letter sent here is called a "demand letter." When a client receives a demand letter: first, the company's insurance broker and insurance company should be notified; second a litigation hold letter must be put into place. On the first, the failure to timely notify can result in loss of insurance coverage for the lawsuit if filed; on the second, the company is subject to a spoliation argument, as you saw in this case. This is why the use of a litigation hold letter is crucial and why we provide sample next. Finally, recall that the hold letter itself is discoverable in any subsequent lawsuit. Consequently, care must be taken as to what is said and how it is said because the drafter will be second guessed by counsel opposite.

A.   Litigation Hold Letters/Hold Notices

X-Ray Questions (*Sample Litigation Hold Letter/Notice*)

Documents must be preserved once a lawsuit is reasonably believed to be on the horizon. A Litigation Hold letter does just that. But its usefulness is lost in two instances. First, when it is written to paper the file, not educate the recipient. So, the following example is broken down into questions and answers, where the purpose is to induce the recipient to read the memo and take appropriate action. Second, when the memo is sent to a person accused of the discrimination or harassment without additional precautions being taken.

Finally, this is a suggested template. Do not follow any template without question Are the any improvements you would make to the template? What are they? Explain your thinking.

BEYOND THE CITE

IMPORTANT LITIGATION HOLD NOTICE

TO:

FROM:

DATE:

    RE: Preservation & Retention of Documents

WHY ARE YOU RECEIVING THIS MEMO?

COMPANY. ("the Company") recently received notice of a claim by Plaintiff. Generally, Plaintiff alleges that

_____.

While the Company is confident Plaintiff's allegations are without merit and intends to defend itself vigorously, it is important that we continue to retain all documents and data that may assist us in our defense of this matter or may be needed to satisfy our discovery obligations under the court rules. Failure to do so may subject the Company to serious legal sanctions.

WHAT ARE YOU REQUIRED TO DO BECAUSE OF THIS MEMO?

This memorandum, therefore, is to notify you of your legal obligation to retain and preserve records, including paper documents and electronic data, which may be relevant to this matter and to describe the steps you must take to do so. This memorandum applies to documents that currently exist as well as those created in the future.

Furthermore, effective immediately, and until cancelled in writing, all records management and/or destruction policies related to the categories of documents described in this notice are suspended and all such categories of documents must be retained and not destroyed.

WHAT DOCUMENTS AND INFORMATION MUST YOU PRESERVE?

To assist you in determining what may be relevant to this matter, the following is a non-exclusive list of documents and information which must be preserved:

- Plaintiff's personnel file and payroll records.

- Any and all e-mail messages and other documents regarding Plaintiff's employment, performance, workplace conduct, or the termination of her employment.

- Any all e-mail messages and other documents regarding Plaintiff allegations that _____.

- Any and all e-mail messages, documents, and other items related to Plaintiff.

- All documents evidencing communications to/from Plaintiff, including correspondence via her personal e-mail account, notes, and memoranda.

Please note that your legal obligation to retain and preserve documents regarding the categories described above applies to documents of every kind, regardless of whether the documents exist in paper or electronic form. For example, responsive documents may include e-mail messages, voicemail messages, text messages, instant messages, correspondence, memoranda, handwritten notes, word processing files (e.g., MS Word, WordPerfect), spreadsheets, and PowerPoint presentations. This Litigation Hold likewise applies regardless of where responsive information is located, including, but not limited to, documents and information located on the Company's network servers, back-up tapes, computer hard-drives, DVDs, CD-ROMs, floppy disks, USB flash/thumb drives, laptop computers, handheld or pocket PC's (e.g., Palm Pilots) and/or smartphone devices (Blackberry, iPhone, etc.).

In addition, electronic documents located on an assistant's computer and/or client-related networks must be preserved as well as documents or information stored or located in a place other than the Company's facilities— such as your home, on removable media, on a non-Company computer, etc. If you are uncertain as to whether to retain a document, please err on the side of preservation at this time.

HOW DO YOU PRESERVE DOCUMENTS AND INFORMATION?

How to Preserve Paper Documents:

For all paper documents and files subject to this memorandum that are currently being maintained in filing cabinets or the like, and that will continue to be used from time to time in the ordinary course of business, please affix to the file cabinet or container the following note: *"Contents subject to Litigation Hold. Make and use copies only. Do not remove originals except to copy and return."*

For all other paper documents subject to this memorandum that can feasibly be segregated from routinely used business files, please segregate and store in separate boxes or files and affix a note with your name, the date, and the following note: *"Contents subject to Litigation Hold. Make and use copies only. Do not remove originals except to copy and return."*

How to Preserve Electronic Documents, Including E-mails:

For all electronic documents or data subject to this memorandum, you must refrain from taking any action which may delete, destroy, alter or modify such documents or data. This may include copying or moving the electronic documents or data to different locations or storage media. If you are in possession of a portable electronic storage device which contains documents or data subject to this memorandum, you must preserve and retain the portable electronic storage device. If you believe that electronic documents or data must be moved in order to ensure that they are properly preserved and retained, please notify the undersigned immediately so appropriate arrangements can be made.

As it relates to e-mail messages, you must retain and not delete any and all e-mail messages regarding or relating to the categories described above. This directive includes e-mail messages (including attachments) located in "In box," "Drafts," "Sent," "Archive," and "Trash/Deleted Items" folders, as well as any other similarly categorized folders, including responsive messages which may be created in the future. Upon receipt of this notice, you must also begin saving all responsive "Sent" e-mail messages, even if your practice is not to save "Sent" e-mail messages.

CONCLUSION

In summary, you should take all steps necessary, including instructing other employees under your supervision, to save all documents in your possession, custody or control that relate in any way to the subjects described above. While we know this may impose a burden on you, it is critical that you comply with this request until we have a better idea of the exact issues that may be involved in this matter.

Please forward this memorandum to all persons reporting to you who may also have documents covered by this notice and provide a list of those persons to me.

These individuals may include the following:

- Anyone who supervised Plaintiff;

- Anyone who had input into any employment decisions involving Plaintiff (including, among other things, the decisions to)

- Any coworkers who might be witnesses to Plaintiff's performance, her workplace conduct, or her allegations against the Company.

If you have any questions or concerns about the requirements set forth above, please let me know. Lastly, please sign the acknowledgment below and return it to me immediately.

ACKNOWLEDGMENT

I have reviewed the memorandum concerning document retention practices relating to the Plaintiff's matter. I agree to follow the instructions in that memorandum.

Signature: _____

Name (printed): _____

Date: _____

Section 3. Access to Witnesses/Parties

So far, we have been dealing with objects; now we shift our focus to dealing with people. Model Rule 4.2, 4.3, and 3.4(f)(1)(2) are grouped together because they each deal with how a lawyer can ethically deal with witnesses or unrepresented parties who will be witnesses on their own behalf. However, the rationales vary between rules.

Model Rule 4.2: Communication with Person Represented by Counsel

In representing a client, a lawyer shall not communicate about the subject of the representation with a person the lawyer knows to be represented by another lawyer in the matter, unless the lawyer has the consent of the other lawyer or is authorized to do so by law or a court order.

Model Rule 4.3: Dealing with Unrepresented Person

In dealing on behalf of a client with a person who is not represented by counsel, a lawyer shall not state or imply that the lawyer is disinterested. When the lawyer knows or reasonably should know that the unrepresented person misunderstands the lawyer's role in the matter, the lawyer shall make reasonable efforts to correct the misunderstanding. The lawyer shall not give legal advice to an unrepresented person, other than the advice to secure counsel, if the lawyer knows or reasonably should know that the interests of such a person are or have a reasonable possibility of being in conflict with the interests of the client.

Model Rule 3.4(f)(1)(2): Fairness to Opposing Party and Counsel (Witnesses)

A lawyer shall not:

(f) request a person other than a client to refrain from voluntarily giving relevant information to another party unless:

(1) the person is a relative or an employee or other agent of a client; and

(2) the lawyer reasonably believes that the person's interests will not be adversely affected by refraining from giving such information.

Deconstruction Exercise/Rule Rationale

Model Rule 4.2 is a cornerstone of our adversary system in which lawyers counsel with clients and speak on their behalf. Without this rule, a lawyer could simply circumvent the person's lawyer in finding out the story, making settlement pitches, convincing them of what is not necessarily in their best interests. Our adversary system would, essentially, cease to function. The rule, like others, ensures an even playing field. One wrinkle: is the employee of an entity covered by this rule? This is a hot topic. If a rank-and-file employee, no. As a general rule if it is a manager, the rule applies; if a former manager, no application unless the manager was a decisionmaker in a matter that is the subject of ongoing litigation

Model Rule 4.3 presumes the same even playing field function albeit in the context of an unrepresented person. Because lawyers are trained and skilled advocates, an unpresented person is at a disadvantage in dealing with them.

Thus, the lawyer must make clear that the lawyer is representing a person or entity that has its own agenda and that the lawyer is not representing the unrepresented person.

Model Rule 3.4(f)(1)(2) empowers lawyers—in very limited circumstances—to counsel a witness not to voluntarily assist in providing information to another "party." Note the use of the conjunctive "and" which narrows the scope of the rule. A lawyer cannot impede the access of a party opposite or a counsel opposite from accessing a witness and eliciting information from them. Note the word "voluntarily." Of course, a party can depose a witness through regular process, but this rule empowers a party to avoid the cost and expense of doing so.

LEANING INTO PRACTICE

Scenario No. 1: The Case of the Lawyer Opposite and the Talkative Client

Rosa Lawyer is scheduled to depose Party Opposite on Tuesday at 1 pm in Rosa's offices, but the party opposite gets her days mixed up and shows up on Monday at 1 pm without her lawyer. Rosa is told that party opposite is in the waiting room. She goes out and offers her some coffee and says that she will validate her parking ticket. Party opposite tells her, "I would like to talk about the case. My lawyer says you and your client are not interested in settlement." But in reality, this is a falsehood. Rosa says, "no, we are." A 15-minute disscusion ensues about the case and settlement. Is Rosa in violation of the Rule?

Scenario No 2: The Case of the Dissatisfied Client

Tom Client is unsure about the quality of representation he is receiving from Wanda Lawyer in a lawsuit to which Tom is a party. So, Tom goes to speak to Anwar Lawyer—who is not involved in Tom's litigation—to obtain an opinion on the quality of Tom's representation. Anwar asks a number of questions about the representation and Tom answers candidly. Anwar sends a bill to Tom for the consultation. Is Anwar in violation of the Rule? Why or why not?

Scenario No. 3: The Case of the Vacationing Witness

Betty Lawyer is representing a party in a lawsuit against XYZ Company. She is preparing for trial in two weeks. She is therefore interviewing an employee who tells her facts that are helpful for each side. The witness tells her that she has preplanned/prepaid a vacation trip in two weeks from when the trial is scheduled and asks Betty whether she should go. Betty honestly explains that the case is very unlikely to be tried and says she should go on vacation. Is Betty in violation of the Rule?

Section 4. Settlement Discussions: Permissible v. Impermissible

Settlement negotiation can occur anywhere on a litigation timeline, but most often after the conclusion of discovery and the filing of dispositive motions not yet decided. Yes, there are instances when they are conducted after a lawsuit is threatened but not yet filed. But wherever they fall on the timeline, the ethical duties owed by lawyers are the same.

A. Impermissible Lawyer Representations

When lawyers are negotiators, another set of ethical considerations become very important. Like any negotiators, lawyers will seek leverage for their clients. That is their job. But there are limits. The first limitation on what lawyers can do to get leverage is honesty.

Model Rule 4.1 (Revisited)

In the course of representing a client a lawyer shall not knowingly . . . make a false statement of material fact or law to a third person.

Deconstruction Exercise/Rule Rationale

This rule runs counter to the public perception of attorneys. But in fact, when a lawyer, who is acting as a lawyer, asserts a fact, people are supposed to be able to rely on it.

In fact, honesty and integrity are essential to legal practice. It is no joke. Much of our justice system is really an honor system. When lawyers tell each other—and courts—something, it is important that they be able to rely on it. This can include some weighty matters. If a lawyer tells his or her opposing counsel before discovery that, "We have video evidence that your client ran a red light, and we hope you consider this when your look at our settlement offer," the other side should be able to rely on the fact that this video actually exists. Lawyers are not allowed to bluff about such things. And in business negotiations, with money on the line, dishonesty could be criminal. If a lawyer asserts, "My client only has the debts she has disclosed," when the lawyer knows that is not true, the lawyer could face prosecution, civil liability, and bar sanctions.

Honesty also includes small matters, like when an attorney asks for an extension of time. Judges and opposing counsel should not need to ask for verification when a lawyer explains personal or professional circumstances motivating a request. One of the authors of this casebook was in a car accident the morning of a day when a major appellate brief is due, and needed to get medical treatment. The opposing counsel helped file a request for an extension, never asked for any verification. Such a gesture, and the trust behind it, makes the practice of law much more bearable.

Like everything else in law (and life), the issue of honesty and legal practice. First of all, no matter what the rules say, it would be horribly naïve to pretend that lawyers never lie. Lawyers are human. But if bar sanctions are not enough incentive, reciprocity should be. Trust is earned, legal communities are small, and when lawyers learn that one of their colleagues cannot be trusted, it is likely to make life much harder for that attorney.

The second complexity may relate the substantive reason by lawyers may be perceived as untrustworthy. It is one thing to lie about a verifiable, objective fact. To do that violates Rule 4.1. But it is another thing to advocate for a client by making claims that are inherently subjective. Puffery, as it is sometimes called, is different from false statements of fact. One is allowed, and one is not. But this also means that when lawyers listen to each other, we should be able to detect when an objective fact is being asserted, and when the other attorney may just be offering empty words." Here is what we mean:

Allowed	Not Allowed
"Look, this is a strong case and I'd love to take it to a jury." *(When in reality the lawyer and client are nervous about trial and would like to find a way to settle the matter.")*	"You should know that we have four witnesses lined up who saw the key event." *(When in fact there is only one witness.)* What would be a permissible way to say this, that would not violate the rule?

Another problematic way for lawyers to seek leverage in negotiation is to use the threat of potential litigation. As a general, default rule, speech related to litigation is protected by the First Amendment. And, since attorneys can make subjective statements in advocacy, there is nothing wrong with a lawyer saying (essentially) "we will file suit, we are confident we will win, and so you should negotiate an agreement with us instead." But there are limits, as the following celebrity case illustrates.

Cases and Materials

X-Ray Questions (*Mauro*)

Michael Flatley, of Lord of the Dance fame, was accused of rape by a woman after what he claims was a consensual sexual relationship. The woman's lawyer wrote a demand letter that is extensively quoted in the opinion. What did the woman's lawyer do or say that crossed the line between permissible and lawful advocacy and impermissible and unlawful extortion? How could her lawyer have framed the communications to *Flatley* so as not to cross the line?

Flatley v. Mauro

Supreme Court of California, 2006.
139 P.3d 2.

J. MORENO.

Plaintiff Michael Flatley, a well-known entertainer, sued defendant D. Dean Mauro, an attorney, for civil extortion, intentional infliction of emotional distress and wrongful interference with economic advantage. Flatley's action was based on a demand letter Mauro sent to Flatley on behalf of Tyna Marie Robertson, a woman who claimed that Flatley had raped her, and on subsequent telephone calls Mauro made to Flatley's attorneys, demanding a seven-figure payment to settle Robertson's claims. Mauro filed a motion to strike Flatley's complaint under the anti-SLAPP statute. (Code Civ. Proc., § 425.16.) He argued that the letter was a prelitigation settlement offer and therefore Flatley's complaint arose from Mauro's exercise of his constitutionally protected right of petition. The trial court denied the motion. The Court of Appeal held that, because Mauro's letter and subsequent telephone calls constituted criminal extortion as a matter of law, and extortionate speech is not constitutionally protected, the anti-SLAPP statute did not apply. Therefore, it affirmed denial of Mauro's motion to strike. We granted Mauro's petition for review.

We conclude that, consistent with the legislative intent underlying the anti-SLAPP statute as revealed by the statutory language, and consistent with our existing anti-SLAPP jurisprudence, a defendant whose assertedly protected speech or petitioning activity was illegal as a matter of law, and therefore unprotected by constitutional guarantees of free speech and petition, cannot use the anti-SLAPP statute to strike the plaintiff's complaint. Applying this principle in the specific circumstances of the case before us, we agree with the Court of Appeal's conclusion. Mauro's communications constituted criminal extortion as a matter of law and, as such, were unprotected by constitutional guarantees of free speech or petition. Therefore, the anti-SLAPP statute does not apply. Accordingly, we affirm the decision of the Court of Appeal.

I.   FACTS AND PROCEDURAL HISTORY

Michael Flatley is a performer and dance impresario who owns "the stock of corporations that present live performances by Irish dance troupes throughout the world." On March 4, 2003, Tyna Marie Robertson sued Flatley in Illinois for battery and intentional infliction of emotional distress based on allegations that Flatley had raped her in his hotel suite in Las Vegas on the night of October 19–20, 2002. Robertson was represented by D. Dean Mauro, an Illinois attorney. Robertson and Mauro then appeared on television, where Robertson described the alleged rape "in extremely lurid detail."

On March 6, 2003, Flatley filed his complaint in the present action in California against Mauro, Robertson and Doe defendants. In a second amended complaint, Flatley alleged five causes of action for civil extortion, defamation, fraud, intentional infliction of emotional distress, and wrongful interference with prospective economic advantage. The civil extortion, intentional infliction of emotional distress and wrongful interference causes of action were alleged against all defendants; the defamation and fraud causes of action were alleged against Robertson alone.

Mauro answered with a general denial and asserted various affirmative defenses including that Flatley's claims were barred by section 425.16, the anti-SLAPP statute. On August 1, 2003, Mauro filed a motion to strike Flatley's complaint under that statute.

Flatley's opposition to the motion argued that Mauro's communications constituted criminal extortion and were therefore not protected by the anti-SLAPP statute. He argued further that he could demonstrate a probability of prevailing on the merits. In support of his opposition, Flatley filed several declarations, including his own and those of his personal secretary, Thomas Trautmann, and his attorneys, John Brandon, Bertram Fields, and Richard Cestero.

The declarations submitted by Flatley set forth the following scenario:

Flatley met Robertson in Las Vegas sometime before October 2002. Robertson was very friendly and Flatley gave her the telephone number of his personal secretary, Thomas Trautmann (Trautmann) in the event she wanted to reach Flatley.

In October 2002, Robertson called Trautmann to arrange a rendezvous with Flatley. On October 19, 2002, Robertson arrived at Flatley's two-bedroom suite in the Venetian Hotel in Las Vegas. She was told that one room was for Flatley and the other was for Trautmann. Robertson put her belongings in Flatley's bedroom. She did not request alternate accommodations or protest the accommodations offered.

That evening, Flatley and Robertson had dinner together. Upon returning to Flatley's hotel room, Robertson excused herself to the bathroom. Flatley disrobed and got into bed. Robertson reappeared, nude, and entered Flatley's bed, where she remained for the night. According to Flatley, everything that transpired between him and Robertson that night was consensual. At no time did Trautmann, who was in the next room with the door open, hear any cry or complaint of any kind.

The next morning, Robertson entered the common area of the suite, and kissed Flatley in Trautmann's presence. Her demeanor was relaxed and happy. She ate breakfast with Flatley, speaking affectionately to him and cordially to Trautmann. Upon leaving, she kissed Flatley again and said she hoped to see him again.

On January 2, 2003, Mauro sent a letter addressed to Flatley that was received by Flatley's attorney, John Brandon. The letter emphasized certain text, using various font sizes, boldface type, capital letters, underlining, and italics.5In small print, it stated: "This communication is governed by all applicable common law decisions of the State of Illinois and Rule 408 of the U.S. Federal Rules of Evidence. All information contained herein is for settlement purposes only." The subject line stated in all-capital, boldface, underlined type: **"LAWSUIT AGAINST MICHAEL FLATLEY, INDIVIDUALLY, AND UNICORN ENTERTAINMENT, INC., AND THE VENETION** [SIC] **RESORT-HOTEL-CASINO VENTURE GROUP[.]"** Mauro identified his client as "Jane Doe" and referred to a report on file with the Las Vegas Police Department. The next line stated "Date of Rape/Sex Assault: **October 19–20, 2002."**

The letter was addressed: "DEAR FLATLEY, ET. AL. [SIC] [¶] Please be advised that we represent a women [SIC] with whom you engaged in forcible sexual assault on or about October 19–20, 2003 [SIC: 2002]. Please consider this our **FIRST,** and **ONLY,** attempt to amicably resolve this claim against all Defendants named in the Complaint at Law enclosed herein."

On the second page, a large caption announced "**NOTICE OF CLAIM & ATTORNEY'S LIEN**". The letter continued: "Please consider this as Notice of our Attorneys' [SIC] Liens. We hereby make a claim and lien in the amount of 40% of the Total Recovery of all funds obtained through trial or settlement, plus all costs of suit, and attorney fees leveled against you." After urging Flatley to contact his insurance carrier, the letter states "Tell them to contact me directly." It warns that Flatley's failure to do so will result in the filing of a lawsuit and that "all judgment proceeds" will be sought "**DIRECTLY FROM YOUR PERSONAL ASSETS.**" The letter then states: **"YOU ARE GRANTED UNTIL JANUARY 30, 2002,** [SIC: 2003] **TO RESOLVE THIS MATTER.** The amounts claimed in the lawsuit are **NATURALLY NEGOTIABLE PRIOR TO SUIT.**" The letter warns, however, that if Flatley fails to meet the January 30 deadline "all offers to compromise, settle and amicably resolve this case will be **AUTOMATICALLY** WITHDRAWN." The letter then goes on to "advise[ ]" Flatley that Mauro has retained "several forensic expert witnesses" whose opinions "shall be disclosed in detail in the public filed court documents in this litigation." Mauro also advises Flatley that he has "worked at Lloyd's of London, and [is] familiar with International Law. These causes of action allow for PUNITIVE DAMAGES. Punitive Damages are non-dischargeable in bankruptcy, and are recognized under British Law. We can therefore execute and collect any award against **MICHAEL FLATLEY** PERSONALLY in the U.S., or the U.K." Next, Mauro refers to his expert **"Economist Frank Maguire"** who will testify "as to the amount of punitive damages which the law recognizes to justify 'sending a message' or what constitutes a 'deterrent.' "

The first paragraph of the third page of Mauro's letter refers Flatley to a "settlement of **$100,000,000.00**" awarded as punitive damages in an unidentified case. The second full paragraph then states that an investigation into Flatley's assets for purposes of determining an appropriate award of punitive damages, will require "an in-depth investigation" and that any information would then "**BECOME A MATTER OF PUBLIC RECORD, AS IT MUST BE FILED WITH THE COURT,** as it will be part of the bases of several of our expert's [SIC] testimony." The third paragraph states in its entirety: "**Any and all information, including Immigration, Social Security Issuances and Use, and IRS and various State Tax Levies and information will be exposed.** We are positive the media worldwide will enjoy what they find." After a paragraph describing the potential testimony of two other experts, John Lombardi and David K. Hirshey, apparently with respect to the failure of the Las Vegas hotel in which the alleged rape occurred to "provide requisite safeguards for our client," the fifth paragraph again warns that "**all pertinent information and documentation, if in violation of any U.S. Federal, Immigration, I.R.S., S.S. Admin., U.S. State, Local, Commonwealth U.K., or International Laws, shall immediately [be] turned over to any and all appropriate authorities.**" The final paragraph warns that once the lawsuit is filed additional causes of action "shall arise" including "Defamatory comments, Civil Conspiracy, Reckless Supervision" which are "just the beginning" and that "ample evidence" exists "to prove each and every element for all these additional causes of action. Again, these actions allow for **Punitive Damages.**"

At the top of the final page of the letter is the caption: "**FIRST & FINAL TIME-LIMIT SETTLEMENT DEMAND.**" Beneath it a paragraph warns that there shall be "**NO CONTINUANCES NOR ANY DELAYS.** If we do not hear from you, then we shall know you are not interested in amicably resolving this claim and we shall immediately file suit." At the bottom of the page, beneath Mauro's signature, a final paragraph warns Flatley that, along with the filing of suit, press releases will be disseminated to various media sources, including but not limited to "**Fox News Chicago, Fox News Indiana, Fox News Wisconsin, and the U.S. National Fox News Network; WGN National U.S. Television; All Local Las Vegas Television, radio stations and newspapers; The Chicago Tribune, The Chicago Southern Economist, The News Sun, The Beacon News, The Daily Herald, The New York Times, The Washington Post; ALL National U.S. Television**

**Networks of NBC, ABC and CBS; as well as INTERNET POSTINGS
WORLDWIDE, including the BRITISH BROADCASTING
COMPANY, and the Germany National News Network Stations."**

Attached to the letter were 51 pages of material, including a draft of
Robertson's complaint against Flatley, Robertson's medical records pertaining
to treatment for the alleged rape, certificates of achievement awarded to Mauro,
newspaper articles chronicling Mauro's multimillion-dollar cases and
settlements, and the curricula vitae of Mauro's experts.

Among the attachments was a letter Robertson wrote to the Las Vegas
Police Department on November 17, 2002. The letter refers to a telephone call
she had made to the police department on November 14 in which she reported
the rape. She asked that the letter, which described the rape, be added to the
earlier report because she "did not get an adequate opportunity to explain." She
added, however, that she had no "interest in seeing the Initial Incident
Complaint form," because she was "a private person, and this is not something
about which I can openly or freely explain to people." She also wrote that she
could not at that time go into "more specific, or graphic details" because she
was not "in any condition to relive this."

The record does not show that Robertson provided any additional
information to the police, or that the police took any action regarding her
allegation. According to Flatley's and Trautmann's declarations, no one in the
Las Vegas Police Department contacted either Flatley or his representatives
about the allegation and Flatley remained unaware of the allegation until
Brandon received Mauro's letter.

Upon receipt of Mauro's letter, Brandon immediately called Mauro. Mauro
gave Brandon a deadline of January 30, 2003, "to offer sufficient payment." On
January 9, 2003, Mauro telephoned Brandon to complain that he had not heard
from Flatley or Flatley's representatives. Brandon explained that he was not
handling the matter but offered to pass along any message. Mauro told him that
he would not extend the January 30, 2003 deadline. He added: "I know the tour
dates; I am not kidding about this; it will be publicized every place he [Flatley]
goes for the rest of his life." He added that dissemination of the story "would
be immediate to any place where he [Flatley] and the troupes are performing
everywhere in the world."

On January 10, 2003, Mauro again called Brandon, who was in a meeting,
and left a message with Brandon's secretary. The message read: "Dean Mauro
needs a call back in one-half hour, otherwise they are going public." When

Brandon returned Mauro's call, Mauro "complained that people were investigating the matter before contacting him and were doing so in an intimidating manner. He said that if he did not receive a call by 8 p.m. Central Standard Time . . ., he would 'go public and the January 30 deadline is gone.' " He said, "I already have the news media lined up" and would "hit him [Flatley] at every single place he tours." Brandon read this back to Mauro to confirm its accuracy. When Brandon asked Mauro why he was concerned about Flatley's attorneys investigating Robertson's claim before making an offer, Mauro stated that this "case is like an insurance claim where the adjuster would call the lawyer to acknowledge the attorney's lien." Brandon asked Mauro if acknowledging the lien was a problem. Mauro said "never mind about that, just pass on the message." Brandon conveyed the message to Bertram Fields, the attorney handling the matter for Flatley.

Fields called Mauro later that day. Mauro told Fields he knew how to "play hardball" and that if Flatley did not pay an acceptable amount, he and Robertson would "go public." Mauro said he would ensure that the story would follow Flatley wherever he or his troupes performed and would "ruin" him. Fields asked Mauro how much he was demanding and Mauro replied "it would take seven figures."

Fields reported Mauro's conduct to the FBI and arranged for Flatley to give the FBI a voluntary interview without the presence of counsel. Hoping to allow the FBI more time to investigate, Fields wrote Mauro asking him to extend the deadline. Mauro extended the deadline by one day in a letter that complained that Fields had failed to return Mauro's numerous messages. "You have my personal cell phone number, on 24 hours daily, and we still have received no substantive conversation of any kind for nearly a month."

Flatley did not pay Robertson and Mauro.

Mauro's reply to Flatley's opposition to the motion to strike argued that his January 2, 2002 letter was a prelitigation settlement offer in furtherance of his constitutional right of petition and, therefore, protected by section 425.16, subdivision (e)(1) and (4). He argued further that Flatley had failed to demonstrate a probability of prevailing on any of his causes of action.

On September 22, 2003, the trial court denied Mauro's motion to strike. It found that Mauro had not satisfied his initial burden to show that his communication was protected by section 425.16. Mauro appealed (§ 904.1, subd. (a)(13)), and the Court of Appeal affirmed, holding that, as a matter of law, Mauro's communications constituted criminal extortion and therefore were not protected under section 425.16. The Court of Appeal did not address whether Flatley had demonstrated a probability of prevailing on the merits. We granted Mauro's petition for review.

II. DISCUSSION

A. The Anti-SLAPP Statute Does Not Apply to Speech and Petitioning Activity That is Illegal as a Matter of Law and, Therefore, Not Constitutionally Protected.

1. GENERAL PRINCIPLES REGARDING *Section 425.16*

The anti-SLAPP statute, section 425.16, allows a court to strike any cause of action that arises from the defendant's exercise of his or her constitutionally protected rights of free speech or petition for redress of grievances. (§ 425.16, subd. (b)(1).) . . . s noted, the purpose of section 425.16 is to prevent the chilling of "the valid exercise of the constitutional rights of freedom of speech and petition for the redress of grievances" by "the abuse of the judicial process." (§ 426.16, subd. (a).) As a necessary corollary to this statement, because not all speech or petition activity is constitutionally protected, not all speech or petition activity is protected by section 425.16. (See, e.g., LAM V. NGO (2001) 91 Cal.App.4th 832, 851, 111 Cal.Rptr.2d 582 [violence and other criminal acts are not protected by the First Amendment even if committed out of political motives at a political demonstration; nor would Doe defendants who engaged in such activity be protected by the anti-SLAPP statute].) The "scope of [section 425.16] is not without limits, as demonstrated in . . . cases finding lawsuits were not within its protection. [Citations.]" (PAUL V. FRIEDMAN (2002) 95 Cal.App.4th 853, 864, 117 Cal.Rptr.2d 82.) The case most often cited in support of this proposition is PAUL FOR COUNCIL V. HANYECZ (2001) 85 Cal.App.4th 1356, 102 Cal.Rptr.2d 864 disapproved on other grounds in EQUILON ENTERPRISES V. CONSUMER CAUSE, INC. (2002) 29 Cal.4th 53, 68, footnote 5, 124 Cal.Rptr.2d 507, 52 P.3d 685. . . .

3. THE LITIGATION PRIVILEGE AND *Section 425.16*

Mauro argues: "All litigation-related speech, lawful or not, is in furtherance of petition or free speech rights." Thus, he argues, even assuming his letter was extortion, it is nonetheless protected by Code of Civil Procedure section 425.16 because it falls within subdivision (e)(1) and (2). In advancing this argument, he invokes the litigation privilege set forth in Civil Code section 47, subdivision (b). He argues, first, that section 425.16 protects litigation communication to the same degree that such communication is protected by the litigation privilege and then reasons from this premise that section 425.16 must also protect unlawful litigation-related communication because the litigation privilege does. He claims PAUL is inapplicable to this case because it did not involve litigation-related communications protected by section 425.16, subdivision (e)(1) or (2) but, rather, noncommunicative conduct protected by subdivision (e)(4). We disagree.

"The principal purpose of [Civil Code] section [47, subdivision (b)] is to afford litigants and witnesses [citation] the utmost freedom of access to the courts without fear of being harassed subsequently by derivative tort actions." (SILBERG V. ANDERSON (1990) 50 Cal.3d 205, 213, 266 Cal.Rptr. 638, 786 P.2d 365.)Additionally, the privilege promotes effective judicial proceedings by encouraging " 'open channels of communication and the presentation of evidence' " without the external threat of liability (IBID.), and "by encouraging attorneys to zealously protect their clients' interests." (ID. at p. 214, 266 Cal.Rptr. 638, 786 P.2d 365.) "Finally, in immunizing participants from liability for torts arising from communications made during judicial proceedings, the law places upon litigants the burden of exposing during trial the bias of witnesses and the falsity of evidence, thereby enhancing the finality of judgments and avoiding an unending roundelay of litigation, an evil far worse than an occasional unfair result." (IBID.)

To accomplish these objectives, the privilege is "an 'absolute' privilege, and it bars all tort causes of action except a claim of malicious prosecution." (HAGBERG V. CALIFORNIA FEDERAL BANK (2004) 32 Cal.4th 350, 360, 7 Cal.Rptr.3d 803, 81 P.3d 244.) The litigation privilege has been applied in "numerous cases" involving "fraudulent communication or perjured testimony." (SILBERG V. ANDERSON, SUPRA, 50 Cal.3d at p. 218, 266 Cal.Rptr. 638, 786 P.2d 365; see, e.g., HOME INS. CO. V. ZURICH INS. CO. (2002) 96 Cal.App.4th 17, 20, 22–26, 116 Cal.Rptr.2d 583 [attorney's misrepresentation of available insurance policy limits to induce the settlement of a lawsuit]; DOCTORS' CO. INS. SERVICES V. SUPERIOR COURT (1990) 225 Cal.App.3d 1284, 1300, 275 Cal.Rptr. 674 [subornation of perjury]; CARDEN V. GETZOFF (1987) 190 Cal.App.3d 907, 915, 235 Cal.Rptr. 698 [perjury]; STEINER V. EIKERLING (1986) 181 Cal.App.3d 639, 642–643, 226 Cal.Rptr. 694 [preparation of a forged will and presentation of it for probate]; O'NEIL V. CUNNINGHAM(1981) 118 Cal.App.3d 466, 472–477, 173 Cal.Rptr. 422 [attorney's letter sent in the course of judicial proceedings allegedly defaming his client].) The privilege has also been held to apply to "statements made prior to the filing of a lawsuit." (HAGBERG V. CALIFORNIA FEDERAL BANK, SUPRA, 32 Cal.4th at p. 361, 7 Cal.Rptr.3d 803, 81 P.3d

244.) Seizing upon these principles, Mauro maintains that section 425.16 similarly protects any prelitigation-related communications even if that communication constitutes extortion. Assuming without deciding that the litigation privilege may apply to such threats, we conclude that they are nonetheless not protected under the anti-SLAPP statute because the litigation privilege and the anti-SLAPP statute are substantively different statutes that serve quite different purposes, and it is not consistent with the language or the purpose of the anti-SLAPP statute to protect such threats.

There is, of course, a relationship between the litigation privilege and the anti-SLAPP statute. Past decisions of this court and the Court of Appeal have looked to the litigation privilege as an aid in construing the scope of subdivision (e)(1) and (2) with respect to the first step of the two-step anti-SLAPP inquiry—that is, by examining the scope of the litigation privilege to determine whether a given communication falls within the ambit of subdivisions (e)(1) and (2).

For example, in BRIGGS V. EDEN COUNCIL FOR HOPE & OPPORTUNITY, SUPRA, 19 Cal.4th 1106, 81 Cal.Rptr.2d 471, 969 P.2d 564, we declined to read into section 425.16, subdivision (e)(1) and (2), which protect statements made before, or in connection with, an issue pending before an official proceeding, a further requirement that the statements concern an issue of public significance. In so holding, we observed that imposing a " 'public issue' requirement" as a condition to protecting litigation-related communications under the anti-SLAPP statute would produce an "anomalous result." (BRIGGS V. EDEN COUNCIL FOR HOPE & OPPORTUNITY, SUPRA, 19 Cal.4th at p. 1121, 81 Cal.Rptr.2d 471, 969 P.2d 564.) Litigation-related communications that did not involve a public issue would not be protected under the anti-SLAPP statute but would nonetheless be privileged under the litigation privilege, and protected by state and federal constitutional guarantees of the right of petition. (IBID.) Thus, in BRIGGS, we bolstered our interpretation of the scope of the protection afforded to litigation-related communications under the anti-SLAPP statute by looking at whether our result was consistent with the scope of the protection afforded to such communications by the litigation privilege. Nowhere in BRIGGS, however, did we suggest, much less hold, that the scope of those protections are identical in every respect.

The litigation privilege is also relevant to the second step in the anti-SLAPP analysis in that it may present a substantive defense a plaintiff must overcome to demonstrate a probability of prevailing. (See, e.g., KASHIAN V. HARRIMAN (2002) 98 Cal.App.4th 892, 926–927, 120 Cal.Rptr.2d 576 [Where plaintiff's defamation action was barred by Civil Code section 47, subdivision (b), plaintiff cannot demonstrate a probability of prevailing under the anti-SLAPP statute]; DOVE AUDIO, INC. V. ROSENFELD, MEYER & SUSMAN (1996) 47 Cal.App.4th 777, 783–785, 54 Cal.Rptr.2d 830[Defendant's prelitigation communication was privileged and trial court therefore did not err in granting motion to strike under the anti-SLAPP statute].)

Notwithstanding this relationship between the litigation privilege and the anti-SLAPP statute, as we have observed, the two statutes are not substantively the same. In JARROW FORMULAS, INC. V. LAMARCHE, SUPRA, 31 Cal.4th 728, 3 Cal.Rptr.3d 636, 74 P.3d 737, we declined to create a categorical exemption from section 425.16 for malicious prosecution actions even though such claims are exempt from the litigation privilege. We rejected the plaintiff's "attempted analogy between the litigation privilege and the anti-SLAPP statute" as "inapt," explaining "the litigation privilege is an entirely different type of statute than section 425.16. The former enshrines a substantive rule of law that grants absolute immunity from tort liability for communications made in relation to judicial proceedings [citation]; the latter is a procedural device for screening out meritless claims [citation]." (JARROW FORMULAS, INC., at p. 737, 3 Cal.Rptr.3d 636, 74 P.3d 737.)

Nor do the two statutes serve the same purposes. The litigation privilege embodied in Civil Code section 47, subdivision (b) serves broad goals of guaranteeing access to the judicial process, promoting the zealous representation by counsel of their clients, and reinforcing the traditional function of the trial as the engine for the determination of truth. Applying the litigation privilege to some forms of unlawful litigation-related activity may advance those broad goals notwithstanding the "occasional unfair result" in an individual case. (SILBERG V. ANDERSON, SUPRA, 50 Cal.3d at p. 214, 266 Cal.Rptr. 638, 786 P.2d 365; DOCTORS' CO. INS. SERVICES V. SUPERIOR COURT, SUPRA, 225 Cal.App.3d at p. 1300, 275 Cal.Rptr. 674 [the litigation privilege applies to subornation of perjury because "it is in the nature of a statutory privilege that it must deny a civil recovery for immediate wrongs—sometimes even serious and troubling ones—in order to accomplish what the Legislature perceives as a greater good"].)

Section 425.16 is not concerned with securing for litigants freedom of access to the judicial process. The purpose of section 425.16 is to protect the valid exercise of constitutional rights of free speech and petition from the abuse of the judicial process (§ 425.16, subd. (a)), by allowing a defendant to bring a motion to strike any action that arises from any activity by the defendant in furtherance of those rights. (§ 425.16, subd. (b)(1).) By necessary implication, the statute does not protect activity that, because it is illegal, is not in furtherance of constitutionally protected speech or petition rights. (WILCOX V. SUPERIOR COURT, SUPRA, 27 Cal.App.4th at p. 819, 33 Cal.Rptr.2d 446 ["If the defendant's act is not constitutionally protected how can doing the act be 'in furtherance' of the defendant's constitutional rights?"].) Thus, the rationale for applying the litigation privilege to some forms of illegal conduct— like perjury—because the occasional bad result is justified by the larger goal of access to the judicial process is simply not transferable to the anti-SLAPP statute because the latter statute does not promote the same goals as the former. Moreover, by its very terms, section 425.16 does not apply to activity that is not in furtherance of the constitutional rights of free speech or petition and this would necessarily include illegal activity that falls outside protected speech and petition rights. (See, WILCOX, at p. 820, 33 Cal.Rptr.2d 446 [the anti-SLAPP statute would not apply to a defendant's act of burning down a developer's office as a political protest].)

Conversely, Civil Code section 47 states a statutory privilege, not a constitutional protection. As we recognized in OREN ROYAL OAKS VENTURE V. GREENBERG, BERNHARD, WEISS & KARMA (1986) 42 Cal.3d 1157, 232 Cal.Rptr. 567, 728 P.2d 1202, that statutory privilege is specific and limited in nature. In OREN, we concluded that while Civil Code section 47 prohibited an action based on a party's statements made during settlement negotiations, it did not preclude the use of those statements as evidence of the party's intent to establish an abuse of process claim. (OREN, SUPRA, 42 Cal.3d at pp. 1167–1168, 232 Cal.Rptr. 567, 728 P.2d 1202.) We stated: " 'The privileges of Civil Code section 47, UNLIKE EVIDENTIARY PRIVILEGES WHICH FUNCTION BY THE EXCLUSION OF EVIDENCE [citation], operate as limitations upon liability.' (Italics added.) Indeed, on brief reflection, it is quite clear that section [47, subdivision (b)] has never been thought to bar the EVIDENTIARY use of every 'statement or publication' made in the course of a judicial proceeding. . . ." (OREN, at p. 1168, 232 Cal.Rptr. 567, 728 P.2d 1202.)

By parity of reasoning, Civil Code section 47 does not operate as a limitation on the scope of the anti-SLAPP statute. The fact that Civil Code section 47 may limit the liability of a party that sends to an opposing party a letter proposing settlement of proposed litigation does not mean that the settlement letter is also a protected communication for purposes of section 425.16.12 Therefore, we reject Mauro's contention that, because some forms of illegal litigation-related activity may be privileged under the litigation privilege, that activity is necessarily protected under the anti-SLAPP statute.

B. Mauro's Assertedly Protected Conduct Was Criminal Extortion as a Matter of Law and Was Undeserving of the Protection of the Anti-SLAPP Statute.

1. STANDARD OF REVIEW

"Review of an order granting or denying a motion to strike under section 425.16 is de novo. (SYLMAR AIR CONDITIONING V. PUEBLO CONTRACTING SERVICES, INC. (2004) 122 Cal.App.4th 1049, 1056, 18 Cal.Rptr.3d 882.) We consider 'the pleadings, and supporting and opposing affidavits upon which the liability or defense is based.' (§ 425.16, subd. (b)(2).) However, we neither 'weigh credibility [nor] compare the weight of the evidence. Rather, . . . [we] accept as true the evidence favorable to the plaintiff [citation] and evaluate the defendant's evidence only to determine if it has defeated that submitted by the plaintiff as a matter of law.' (HMS CAPITAL, INC. V. LAWYERS TITLE CO. (2004) 118 Cal.App.4th 204, 212, 12 Cal.Rptr.3d 786.)" (SOUKUP V. HAFIF, SUPRA, 39 Cal.4th at p. 269, fn. 3, 46 Cal.Rptr.3d at p. 645, 139 P.3d at p. 36, fn. 3.)

2. EXTORTION

"Extortion is the obtaining of property from another, with his consent . . . induced by a wrongful use of force or fear. . . ." (Pen.Code, § 518.) Fear, for purposes of extortion "may be induced by a threat, either: [¶] . . . [¶] 2. To accuse the individual threatened . . . of any crime; or, [¶] 3. To expose, or impute to him . . . any deformity, disgrace or crime[.]" (Pen.Code, § 519.) "Every person who, with intent to extort any money or other property from another, sends or delivers to any person any letter or other writing, whether subscribed or not, expressing or implying, or adapted to imply, any threat such as is specified in Section 519, is punishable in the same manner as if such money or property were actually obtained by means of such threat." (Pen.Code, § 523.)

Extortion has been characterized as a paradoxical crime in that it criminalizes the making of threats that, in and of themselves, may not be illegal. "[I]n many blackmail cases the threat is to do something in itself perfectly legal, but that threat nevertheless becomes illegal when coupled with a demand for money." (PHILIPPINE EXPORT & FOREIGN LOAN GUARANTEE CORP. V. CHUIDIAN (1990) 218 Cal.App.3d 1058, 1079, 267 Cal.Rptr. 457.)13 The extortion statutes "all adopted at the same time and relating to the same subject matter, clearly indicate that the legislature in denouncing the wrongful use of fear as a means of obtaining property from another had in mind threats to do the acts specified in section 519, the making of which for the purpose stated is declared to be a wrongful use of fear induced thereby." (PEOPLE V. BEGGS (1918) 178 Cal. 79, 83, 172 P. 152.) "It is the means employed [to obtain the property of another] which the law denounces, and though the purpose may be to collect a just indebtedness arising from and created by the criminal act for which the threat is to prosecute the wrongdoer, it is nevertheless within the statutory inhibition. The law does not contemplate the use of criminal process as a means of collecting a debt." (ID. at p. 84, 172 P. 152; PEOPLE V. TUFUNGA (1999) 21 Cal.4th 935, 955, 987 P.2d 168 [In BEGGS "we explained that because of the strong public policy militating against self-help by force or fear, courts will not recognize a good faith defense to the satisfaction of a debt when accomplished by the use of force or fear"]; LINDENBAUM V. STATE BAR (1945) 26 Cal.2d 565, 573, 160 P.2d 9 [For purposes of extortion "[i]t is immaterial that the money which petitioner sought to obtain through threats may have been justly due him"]; GOMEZ V. GARCIA (9th Cir.1996) 81 F.3d 95, 97 ["The law of California was established in 1918 that belief that the victim owes a debt is not a defense to the crime of extortion"].)

Moreover, threats to do the acts that constitute extortion under Penal Code section 519 are extortionate whether or not the victim committed the crime or indiscretion upon which the threat is based and whether or not the person making the threat could have reported the victim to the authorities or arrested the victim. (PEOPLE V. SANDERS (1922) 188 Cal. 744, 756, 207 P. 380; PEOPLE V. GOLDSTEIN (1948) 84 Cal.App.2d 581, 587, 191 P.2d 102; PEOPLE V. HESSLINK (1985) 167 Cal.App.3d 781, 787, 213 Cal.Rptr. 465.) Furthermore, the crime with which the extortionist threatens his or her victim need not be a specific crime. "[T]he accusations need only be such as to put the intended victim of the extortion in fear of being accused of some crime. The more vague and general the terms of the accusation the better it would subserve the purpose of the accuser in magnifying the fears of his victim, and the better also it would serve to protect him in the event of the failure to accomplish his extortion and of a prosecution for his attempted crime." (PEOPLE V. SANDERS, SUPRA, at pp. 749–750, 207 P. 380; PEOPLE V. MASSENGALE (1968) 261 Cal.App.2d 758, 764–765, 68 Cal.Rptr. 415.)

Attorneys are not exempt from these principles in their professional conduct. Indeed, the Rules of Professional Conduct specifically prohibit attorneys from "threaten[ing] to present criminal, administration, or disciplinary charges to obtain an advantage in a civil dispute." (Cal. Rules of Prof. Conduct, rule 5–100(A).)14

In LIBARIAN V. STATE BAR (1952) 38 Cal.2d 328, 239 P.2d 865, we upheld disciplinary action against Librarian who, after losing at trial, sent a letter to opposing counsel, accusing his opponent's client of perjury and threatening to use the perjury charge as the basis of a new trial motion and a criminal complaint unless opposing counsel's client paid Librarian's client. "Although no action was taken either by Librarian or Siegel to prosecute Nadel, the record clearly shows conduct which is in violation of Librarian's oath and duties as an attorney. The threats contained in the letter indicate an attempt to commit extortion. The sending of a threatening letter with intent to extort money is 'punishable in the same manner as if such money . . . were actually obtained' (Pen.Code, § 523) and the crime of extortion involves moral turpitude." (ID. at pp. 329–330, 239 P.2d 865; BARTON V. STATE BAR (1935) 2 Cal.2d 294, 297, 40 P.2d 502 [The conduct of an attorney who threatened an oil company with reporting adulteration of its gasoline to the prosecutor unless it paid his clients was not only grounds for disbarment but "constituted an attempt to extort money as said crime is defined in sections 518, 519 and 524 of the Penal Code"]; STATE V. HARRINGTON (1969) 128 Vt. 242, 260 A.2d 692, 699 [attorney's suggestion in letter demanding $175,000 settlement in divorce case that he might advise his client to report husband to Internal Revenue Service and United States Custom Service constituted "veiled threats [that] exceeded the limits of respondent's representation of his client in the divorce action" and supported attorney's extortion conviction].) As these cases illustrate, a threat that constitutes criminal extortion is not cleansed of its illegality merely because it is laundered by transmission through the offices of an attorney. Bearing these principles in mind, we turn to the instant case.

3.   APPLICATION

Extortion is not a constitutionally protected form of speech. (R.A.V. V. CITY OF ST. PAUL (1992) 505 U.S. 377, 420, 112 S.Ct. 2538, 120 L.Ed.2d 305 (conc. opn. of Stevens, J.) ["Although the First Amendment broadly protects 'speech,' it does not protect the right to . . . 'extort' "]; UNITED STATES V. QUINN (5th Cir.1975) 514 F.2d 1250, 1268 ["It may categorically be stated that extortionate speech has no more constitutional protection than that uttered by a robber while ordering his victim to hand over the money, which is no protection at all"].) The purpose of the anti-SLAPP statute, of course, is to protect "the valid exercise of the constitutional rights of speech and petition for the redress of grievances." (§ 425.16, subd. (a).) Flatley argues that the letter Mauro sent on behalf of Robertson, and his subsequent telephone calls to Flatley's attorneys, constituted extortion as a matter of law and, therefore, the trial court correctly dismissed Mauro's motion to strike Flatley's action as a SLAPP. (PAUL, SUPRA, 85 Cal.App.4th at pp. 1366–1367, 102 Cal.Rptr.2d 864.) Mauro maintains that his activity on behalf of Robertson amounted to no more than the kind of permissible settlement negotiations that are attendant upon any legal dispute or, at minimum, that a question of fact exists regarding the legality of his conduct precluding a finding that it was illegal as a matter of law. We review the question de novo. (SOUKUP V. HAFIF, SUPRA, 39 Cal.4th at p. 269, fn. 3, 46 Cal.Rptr.3d at p. 645, 139 P.3d at p. 36, fn. 3.)

Preliminarily, we note that, in the proceedings below, Mauro did not deny that he sent the letter nor did he contest the version of the telephone calls set forth in Brandon's and Field's declarations in opposition to the motion to strike. We may therefore view this evidence as uncontroverted. (See STATE V. HARRINGTON, SUPRA, 260 A.2d at p. 699 ["The acts which he performed and the words that he wrote are established by direct and documentary evidence that is not contradicted."].)

At the core of Mauro's letter are threats to publicly accuse Flatley of rape and to report and publicly accuse him of other unspecified violations of various laws unless he "settled" by paying a sum of money to Robertson of which Mauro would receive 40 percent. In his follow-up phone calls, Mauro named the price of his and Robertson's silence as "seven figures" or, at minimum, $1 million. The key passage in Mauro's letter is at page 3 where Flatley is warned that, unless he settles, "an in-depth investigation" will be conducted into his personal assets to determine punitive damages and this information will then "**BECOME A MATTER OF PUBLIC RECORD, AS IT MUST BE FILED WITH THE COURT. . . . [¶] Any and all information, including Immigration, Social Security Issuances and Use, and IRS and various State Tax Levies and information will be exposed.** We are positive the media worldwide will enjoy what they find." This warning is repeated in the fifth paragraph: "**[A]ll pertinent information and documentation, if in violation of any U.S. Federal, Immigration, I.R.S., S.S. Admin., U.S. State, Local, Commonwealth U.K., or International Laws, shall immediately [be] turned over to any and all appropriate authorities.**" Finally, Flatley is warned that once the lawsuit is filed additional causes of action "shall arise" including "Defamatory comments, Civil Conspiracy, Reckless Supervision" which are "just the beginning" and that "ample evidence" exists "to prove each and every element for all these additional causes of action. Again, these actions allow for **Punitive Damages.**"

At the top of the final page of the letter is the caption: **"FIRST & FINAL TIME-LIMIT SETTLEMENT DEMAND.**" Beneath it a paragraph warns that there shall be "**NO CONTINUANCES NOR ANY DELAYS.**" At the bottom of the page, beneath Mauro's signature, a final paragraph warns Flatley that, along with the filing of suit, press releases will be disseminated to numerous media sources and placed on the Internet.

In his first telephone conversation with Brandon, Mauro gave Flatley a deadline of the end of the month "to offer sufficient payment," apparently without any further discussion of the particulars of Robertson's claim. In his call to Brandon, one week after he sent the letter, Mauro complained that he had not yet heard from Flatley and told Brandon he would not extend the deadline and "I know the tour dates; I am not kidding about this it will be publicized every place he [Mr. Flatley] goes for the rest of his life," and that dissemination of the story "would be immediate to any place where he and the troupes are performing everywhere in the world." The very next day, January 10, Mauro called Brandon again and, after leaving a message threatening to "go[ ] public" if Brandon did not return his call within a half-hour, Mauro "complained that people were investigating the matter before contacting him and were doing so in an intimidating manner. He said that, if he did not receive a call by 8:00 p.m. Central Standard Time that night from a representative of Mr. Flatley with authority, he would 'go public and the January 30 deadline is gone.' He said, 'I already have the news media lined up' and would 'hit him [Mr. Flatley] at every single place he tours.' "

Later that day, when Fields spoke to Mauro, Mauro told him "he knew how to play 'hardball' and that, if Mr. Flatley did not pay an acceptable amount, they would 'go public,' would see that their story would follow him wherever he or his groups performed and would 'ruin' him." In response to Fields' query about how much money Mauro wanted to avoid this, Mauro said "it would take 'seven figures.' " He repeated that the deadline to respond was January 30.

Evaluating Mauro's conduct, we conclude that the letter and subsequent phone calls constitute criminal extortion as a matter of law. These communications threatened to "accuse" Flatley of, or "impute to him," "crime[s]" and "disgrace" (Pen.Code, § 519, subds.2, 3) unless Flatley paid Mauro a minimum of $1 million of which Mauro was to receive 40 percent. That the threats were half-couched in legalese does not disguise their essential character as extortion. (LIBARIAN V. STATE BAR, SUPRA 38 Cal.2d at pp.

329–330, 239 P.2d 865; STATE V. HARRINGTON, SUPRA, 260 A.2d at p.
699.)

Mauro's letter accuses Flatley of rape and also imputes to him other,
unspecified violations of various criminal offenses involving immigration and
tax law as well as violations of the Social Security Act. With respect to these
latter threats, Mauro's letter goes on to threaten that "[w]e are positive the media
worldwide will enjoy what they find." Thus, contrary to Mauro's claim that he
did nothing more than suggest that, if evidence of other criminal conduct
became public knowledge it would receive media attention, the letter implies
that Mauro is already in possession of information regarding such criminal
activity and is prepared to disclose this information to the "worldwide" media.
Whether Flatley in fact committed any violations of these various laws is
irrelevant. (PEOPLE V. GOLDSTEIN, SUPRA, 84 Cal.App.2d at p. 587, 191
P.2d 102 [For purposes of extortion, "[a] false accusation of crime is often as
harmful as one that is true"].) Moreover, the threat to disclose criminal activity
entirely unrelated to any alleged injury suffered by Mauro's client "exceeded the
limits of respondent's representation of his client" and is itself evidence of
extortion. (STATE V. HARRINGTON, SUPRA, 260 A.2d at p. 699 [attorney's
veiled threat to have his client in a divorce action inform on her husband to the
Internal Revenue Service and Bureau of Immigration and Naturalization
supports attorney's conviction of extortion].) That Mauro did not specify these
other criminal offenses is of no import—"the accusations need only be such as
to put the intended victim of the extortion in fear of being accused of some
crime." (PEOPLE V. SANDERS, SUPRA, 188 Cal. at p. 749, 207 P. 380.)
Indeed, the very vagueness of the accusation serves the dual purpose of
"magnifying the fear of his victim" and "protect[ing]" the extortionist "in the
event of the failure to accomplish his extortion and . . . prosecution." (PEOPLE
V. MASSENGALE, SUPRA, 261 Cal.App.2d at p. 765, 68 Cal.Rptr. 415.)

Mauro also threatened to accuse Flatley of raping Robertson unless he paid
for her silence. Mauro argues that this threat cannot be the basis of a finding of
extortion because Robertson had already reported the rape to the Las Vegas
police department by the time the letter was sent. In the circumstances of this
case, we reject his argument for the following reasons. We begin by examining
the pleadings. (§ 425.16, subd. (b)(2).) Flatley's complaint alleged that the
purpose of Robertson's telephone call to the Las Vegas Police Department was
not to file an actual crime report but simply to "create a 'sham' record of a police
report that would make her threats more ominous. . . . [S]he wanted to prevent
the police from taking any action that might make the matter public, since any

public report of police action would necessarily spoil Robertson's scheme to extort a payment from [Flatley] to avoid such publicity."

These allegations are supported by the declarations of Mauro and Trautmann that they were never contacted by the police in connection with the alleged rape before Mauro sent his letter to Flatley's lawyers, and the absence of any evidence that the police ever took any action on the complaint. Moreover, Robertson's letter to the Las Vegas Police Department and Mauro's statements to the media after he filed Robertson's lawsuit—that she did not return to Las Vegas to pursue her complaint because she was too traumatized—support the conclusion that whatever complaint Robertson made to the Las Vegas police was insufficient to trigger a police investigation. Mauro's declaration did not deny that he was aware that the Las Vegas police had not launched an investigation into Robertson's allegations when he sent the letter to Flatley. Yet, the letter was careful to include the number of a police report made to the Las Vegas Police Department as if to hold a police investigation over Flatley's head. Thus, as Flatley alleges, the incomplete police report appears to have existed only to make the threat of disclosure more ominous and the need to "settle" with Robertson and Mauro all the more urgent. Under these circumstances, the fact that Robertson may have made some report to the police did not render her threat to publicly accuse Flatley of rape unless he paid her and Mauro any less extortionate. (PEOPLE V. UMANA (2006) 138 Cal.App.4th 625, 640, 41 Cal.Rptr.3d 573 ["Although section 519, subdivision 2, speaks in terms of ACCUSING the victim of a crime, there is no reasonable basis for drawing a distinction between the initial accusation of a crime and continued pursuit of a criminal charge"].)

Moreover, in addition to the threats to accuse Flatley publicly of rape and violations of other laws, Mauro also alleged that he had in his possession "ample evidence" to support claims against Flatley for defamation and civil conspiracy and that these were "just the beginning." At minimum, these were threats that Flatley would be exposed to various kinds of opprobrium and he would be disgraced thereby unless he met Mauro's demands. (Pen.Code, § 519, subd. 3 [threat "to impute" "disgrace" sufficient to establish extortion].)

Lastly, any doubt as to extortionate character of the letter is dispelled by the accounts from Brandon and Fields of Mauro's telephone calls to them within a week of having sent the letter. In his very first conversation with Brandon, Mauro did not discuss the particulars of the claim or express an interest in negotiations but simply stated a deadline for Flatley "to offer sufficient payment." In a follow-up phone call, he objected to Flatley's investigation of

Robertson's allegation and threatened to withdraw the January 30 deadline, thus further demonstrating that it was never his intention to engage in settlement negotiations. Instead, the insistent theme of his conversations with Flatley's lawyers is the immediate and extensive threat of exposure if Flatley failed to make a sufficient offer of money. This culminates in Mauro's threat to "go public" and "ruin" Flatley if the January 30 deadline was not met. We conclude that Mauro's conduct constituted criminal extortion as a matter of law in violation of Penal Code sections 518, 519 and 523.

Accordingly, because the activity forming the basis of Mauro's motion to strike Flatley's action was extortion as a matter of law and, therefore, not constitutionally protected activity for purposes of section 425.16, we further conclude that the trial court did not err when it denied Mauro's motion to strike.

III. DISPOSITION

The judgment of the Court of Appeal is affirmed.

SOLUTIONS: THE LAWYER SHOULD HAVE, WOULD HAVE, COULD HAVE. . .

Part of the lawyer's mistake was not investigating the case as well as he should have, and then failing to change course even when dispositive evidence against his client came to light. But of course, there are often no witnesses to this type of incident. Even still, the lawyer seemed to stress the threat of smearing Flatley in public as much or more than the threat of legal action. A lawyer is on stronger ground if speaking solely about litigation, not about besmirching someone's reputation.

Cases and Materials

X-Ray Questions (*Malin*)

The following case involves some salacious allegations, just as the *Flatley* case did. And in this case, the client engaged in some serious violations of privacy against another person. But in this case the court did not think the lawyer crossed any line. Can you identify what made the difference between the two cases? How did the lawyer properly frame the allegations in this case as opposed to the previous case?

Malin v. Singer

California Court of Appeal, 2013.
217 Cal.App.4th 1283.

SUZUKAWA, J.

Defendants appealed from an order denying their special motion to strike plaintiff's complaint under Code of Civil Procedure section 425.16, the anti-SLAPP statute. The trial court denied the motion under the first step of the statutory analysis on the ground that the claims did not arise from protected speech or petitioning activities. We affirm in part and reverse in part.

FACTS AND PROCEDURAL BACKGROUND

Plaintiff Michael Malin and Lonnie Moore own The Dolce Group, a consortium of restaurants and nightclubs that includes the Geisha House restaurant. Malin, Moore, and defendant Shereene Arazm are general partners of Geisha House, LLC (company).

In 2011, Arazm consulted her attorney, defendant Martin D. Singer, regarding Malin and Moore's alleged misappropriation of company assets. On Arazm's behalf, Singer sent Malin a demand letter and draft of Arazm's proposed complaint. The demand letter contained what Malin contends was an extortionate threat to disclose certain personal information if he did not pay to settle Arazm's claims. In the disputed portion of the letter, Singer stated that Malin had misused company resources to arrange sexual liaisons with older men, including "Judge [first and last name omitted], a/k/a 'Dad' (see enclosed photo)." (We have omitted the judge's name because the demand letter was filed under seal to protect the judge's privacy.) In order to place the allegedly extortionate threat in its proper context, we have quoted the letter below and italicized the disputed language:

"I am litigation counsel to Shereene Arazm. I am writing to you with respect to your outrageous, malicious, wrongful and tortious conduct. As a result of your embezzlement, conversion and breach of fiduciary duty, you have misappropriated more than a million dollars from my client. As a result thereof, my client intends to file the enclosed lawsuit against you, Lonnie Moore, and various business entities that you and Mr. Moore control. As alleged in the Complaint, you, Mr. Moore and several of your co-conspirators have been embezzling and stealing money from Ms. Arazm and Geisha House, LLC for years. As set forth in detail in the Complaint, you and Mr. Moore have devised various schemes to embezzle money from the restaurants and clubs which you own and/or manage, including, but not limited to Geisha House and WonderLand. You and Mr. Moore have created a special account or 'ledger,' which allows you to keep tabs on how the stolen funds are divided among you, Mr. Moore and your various co-conspirators. My client intends, as part of the lawsuit, to seek a full-fledged forensic accounting of the books and records for Geisha House, LLC, 2HYPE Productions, Inc., LTM Consulting, Inc., and Malin & Moore Enterprises, LLC, in addition to your personal accounts.

"In addition, as set forth in the Complaint, we have information that you and Mr. Moore have engaged in insurance scams designed to defraud not only the insurers of your establishments, but also the insurers of WonderLand. You have also taken steps to hide your assets from creditors as well as from the taxing authorities. We are aware that you have converted my client's monies and deposited them in accounts in the Cook Islands. We have also confirmed that you have planned to illegally transfer your shares in Geisha House Los Angeles to Sylvain Bitton in a further attempt to hide from creditors and avoid tax liability.

"BECAUSE MR. MOORE HAS ALSO RECEIVED A COPY OF THE ENCLOSED LAWSUIT, I HAVE DELIBERATELY LEFT BLANK SPACES IN PORTIONS OF THE COMPLAINT DEALING WITH YOUR USING COMPANY RESOURCES TO ARRANGE SEXUAL LIAISONS WITH OLDER MEN SUCH AS 'UNCLE JERRY,' JUDGE [NAME REDACTED], A/K/A 'DAD' (SEE ENCLOSED PHOTO), AND MANY OTHERS. WHEN THE COMPLAINT IS FILED WITH THE LOS ANGELES SUPERIOR COURT, THERE WILL BE NO BLANKS IN THE PLEADING.

"My client will file the Complaint against you and your other joint conspirators unless this matter is resolved to my client's satisfaction within five (5) business days from your receipt of this Complaint. . . ." (Italics added.)

As indicated above, Singer included with the letter a photograph of the judge and a copy of the draft complaint. The draft complaint did not identify any alleged sexual partners, but contained several blank spaces and redactions that, according to the letter, would be filled in before the complaint was filed. The draft complaint stated in relevant part: "[O]ver the past several months, _____ has arranged through email and through Internet websites such as craigslist.org to have multiple sexual encounters with [redacted] which include _____. Based on information and belief, _____ used company resources to facilitate these rendezvous and to communicate with various   [redacted]   including   _____,   _____,   and _____."

After he received the demand letter, Malin sued Singer and Arazm for civil extortion, violation of civil rights, and intentional and negligent infliction of emotional distress. (MALIN V. SINGER (Super.Ct.L.A.County, No. BC466547).) In turn, Arazm sued Malin for conversion, breach of contract, breach of fiduciary duty, accounting, and civil conspiracy. (ARAZM V. CARRI (Super.Ct.L.A.County, No. BC466696).) Both actions were assigned to the same trial court as related cases.

I. Malin's Complaint Against Arazm and Singer

In his complaint's preliminary fact allegations, Malin alleged that at Arazm and Singer's behest, unknown individuals had retrieved his private communications and e-mails through illegal computer hacking and wiretapping activities. Malin's complaint alleged causes of action for: (1) civil extortion based on the demand letter (Pen.Code, §§ 519, 523) (first cause of action); (2) violation of civil rights based on the illegal wiretapping and computer hacking activities (Pen.Code, § 502, subd. (c)(1), (2); 18 U.S.C. § 2510 et seq.) (second cause of action); and (3) intentional and negligent infliction of emotional distress (third and fourth causes of action).

II. Arazm and Singer's Special Motion to Strike Malin's Complaint

Arazm and Singer moved to strike Malin's complaint as a SLAPP suit arising from the exercise of Arazm's constitutionally protected rights of speech or petition. The moving parties argued that because all of Malin's causes of action were based on protected statements made in contemplation of litigation, his complaint was subject to dismissal under the anti-SLAPP statute.

Arazm and Singer contended that Malin's claims were based on their protected: (1) statements made before a judicial proceeding (§ 425.16, subd. (e)(1)); (2) statements made in connection with an issue under consideration or review in a judicial proceeding (§ 425.16, subd. (e)(2)); and (3) "conduct in furtherance of the exercise of the constitutional right of petition or the constitutional right of free speech in connection with a public issue or an issue of public interest" (§ 425.16, subd. (e)(4)).

Arazm and Singer denied any involvement in the computer hacking and wiretapping activities alleged in Malin's complaint. Alternatively, they argued that even if the "allegations of computer hacking and wiretapping were true (they are not), it is evident from the context of Malin's allegations that he is complaining about pre-litigation information-gathering . . ., which are clearly protected activities."

Finally, Arazm and Singer argued that Malin was incapable of establishing a probability of success on the merits under the second prong of section 425.16. They claimed that because all of their alleged activities were covered by the litigation privilege (Civ.Code, § 47, subd. (b)), it was impossible for Malin to prevail on his claims.

In opposition, Malin argued that FLATLEY V. MAURO (2006) 39 Cal.4th 299, 46 Cal.Rptr.3d 606, 139 P.3d 2 (FLATLEY) was "effectively IDENTICAL" to this case. Malin urged the court to apply the FLATLEY exception and deny the motion to strike the extortion claim because Singer's demand letter constituted criminal extortion as a matter of law. Malin also urged the court to follow GERBOSI V. GAIMS, WEIL, WEST & EPSTEIN, LLP (2011) 193 Cal.App.4th 435, 122 Cal.Rptr.3d 73 (GERBOSI), and deny the motion to strike the claims arising from the alleged wiretapping and computer hacking activities because Arazm and Singer's liability for those alleged criminal activities was "a question of fact for the jury subject to discovery."

In reply, Singer and Arazm sought to distinguish FLATLEY. They argued "the FLATLEY exception only applies if 'either the defendant concedes, or the evidence conclusively establishes, that the assertedly protected speech or petition activity was illegal as a matter of law.' ([39 Cal.4th] at p. 320, 46 Cal.Rptr.3d 606, 139 P.3d 2.)" The FLATLEY exception does not apply here, they argued, because they "have not conceded, and Malin has not conclusively shown, that the Letter was illegal as a matter of law."

III. Order of Denial

The trial court denied the anti-SLAPP motion under the first step of the section 425.16 analysis based on FLATLEY and GERBOSI. It concluded that because the activities targeted by Malin's complaint—wiretapping, computer hacking, and extortion—were illegal as a matter of law, the complaint was not subject to early dismissal under the anti-SLAPP statute. The court stated in relevant part:

"1. Defendants' Special Motion to Dismiss the Complaint on file herein as an unmeritorious SLAPP lawsuit is DENIED pursuant to FLATLEY V. MAURO (2006) 39 Cal.4th 299, 46 Cal.Rptr.3d 606, 139 P.3d 2 and GERBOSI V. GAIMS, WEIL, WEST & EPSTEIN (2011) 193 Cal.App.4th 435, 122 Cal.Rptr.3d 73. On the cause of action alleging wiretapping and computer hacking, under GERBOSI V. GAIMS, allegations of this type of activity that is illegal as a matter of law are not covered by Code of Civil Procedure § 425.16. Because the other causes of action in Plaintiff's Complaint are based on the same activity alleged in [these] two causes of action, the Court similarly finds that those causes of action are not covered by § 425.16.

"2.　In so ruling, the Court makes the following findings:

"(a)　The allegations of sexual misconduct contained in the demand letter in this case are very tangential to the causes of action in Defendants' complaint, which have to do with a business dispute and alleged misuse of company resources.

"(b)　The letter is best read as extortion as a matter of law. It threatens to reveal the names of sexual partners, including a retired superior court judge, and enclosed a photo of one of the alleged sexual partners. This is well beyond a typical demand letter saying that a party is going to file a complaint if some sort of settlement or accommodation is not reached. Rather, it accuses or imputes to the Plaintiff some disgrace or crime or threatens to expose some secret affecting him for purposes of obtaining money. The letter states that the blanks in the draft Complaint will be filled in when the Complaint is filed.

"3.　Because the letter and the wiretapping/computer hacking activities alleged in Plaintiff's Complaint are illegal as a matter of law, there is no need to reach the second prong of the analysis under the anti-SLAPP statute. All causes of action arise out of the extortion or wire tapping/computer hacking allegations."

Arazm and Singer timely appealed from the order denying their special motion to strike. (§§ 425.16, subd. (i), 904.1, subd. (a)(13).)

DISCUSSION

Section 425.16 provides an expedited procedure for dismissing lawsuits that are filed primarily to inhibit the valid exercise of the constitutionally protected rights of speech or petition. (§ 425.16, subd. (a); DIGERATI HOLDINGS, LLC V. YOUNG MONEY ENTERTAINMENT, LLC (2011) 194 Cal.App.4th 873, 883, 123 Cal.Rptr.3d 736 (DIGERATI).) "The purpose of the anti-SLAPP statute is to encourage participation in matters of public significance and prevent meritless litigation designed to chill the exercise of First Amendment rights. (§ 425.16, subd. (a).) The Legislature has declared that the statute must be 'construed broadly' to that end. (IBID.)" (DIGERATI, SUPRA, at p. 883, 123 Cal.Rptr.3d 736.)

A special motion to strike a complaint under section 425.16 involves two steps. First, the moving party has the initial burden of making a threshold showing that the challenged cause of action is one arising from a protected activity. (§ 425.16, subd. (b)(1).) In order to meet this burden, the moving party must show that the act underlying the challenged cause of action fits one of the categories described in section 425.16, subdivision (e). CABRAL V. MARTINS (2009) 177 Cal.App.4th 471, 478, 99 Cal.Rptr.3d 394.) Under section 425.16, subdivision (e)(1), a protected activity includes any written or oral statement or writing made before a legislative, executive, or judicial proceeding, or any other official proceeding authorized by law.

Once the moving party has made the threshold showing, the burden shifts to the opposing party. Under step two of the statutory analysis, the opposing party must demonstrate a probability of prevailing on the claim. (§ 425.16, subd. (b)(1).) A cause of action is subject to dismissal under the statute only if both steps of the anti-SLAPP analysis are met.

I.   Standard of Review

In an appeal from an order granting or denying a motion to strike under section 425.16, the standard of review is de novo. (SOUKUP V. LAW OFFICES OF HERBERT HAFIF (2006) 39 Cal.4th 260, 269, fn. 3, 46 Cal.Rptr.3d 638, 139 P.3d 30 (SOUKUP).) In considering the pleadings and supporting and opposing declarations, we do not make credibility determinations or compare the weight of the evidence. Instead, we accept the opposing party's evidence as true and evaluate the moving party's evidence only to determine if it has defeated the opposing party's evidence as a matter of law. (IBID.)

In the following parts, we conclude in part II that Malin's first cause of action for civil extortion is subject to dismissal under the anti-SLAPP statute. We conclude in part III. that Malin's second cause of action for violation of civil rights and third and fourth causes of action for intentional and negligent infliction of emotional distress are not subject to dismissal under the anti-SLAPP statute because they did not arise from protected activities. Finally, we conclude in part IV. that Arazm and Singer's right to costs and attorney fees as partially prevailing defendants under section 425.16 must be determined, in the first instance, by the trial court on remand.

II. Malin's Extortion Claim, Which Is Based on a Demand Letter That Does Not Constitute Criminal Extortion as a Matter of Law, Is Subject to Dismissal Under the Anti-SLAPP Statute

Malin's extortion claim is based on a demand letter that was written by an attorney on behalf of his client in anticipation of litigation. Ordinarily, a demand letter sent in anticipation of litigation is a legitimate speech or petitioning activity that is protected under section 425.16. (See BRIGGS V. EDEN COUNCIL FOR HOPE & OPPORTUNITY (1999) 19 Cal.4th 1106, 1115, 81 Cal.Rptr.2d 471, 969 P.2d 564 [" 'communications preparatory to or in anticipation of the bringing of an action or other official proceeding' " are protected by section 425.16] (BRIGGS).) But in FLATLEY, the Supreme Court articulated an exception for a demand letter that was so extreme that it was found to constitute criminal extortion as a matter of law. (FLATLEY, SUPRA, 39 Cal.4th 299, 46 Cal.Rptr.3d 606, 139 P.3d 2; MENDOZA V. HAMZEH (2013) 215 Cal.App.4th 799, 155 Cal.Rptr.3d 832 (MENDOZA).) We refer to the exception to the general rule stated in BRIGGS—that a demand letter sent in anticipation of litigation is a legitimate speech or petitioning activity that is protected under section 425.16—as the FLATLEY exception.

Arazm and Singer contend the trial court erroneously denied their special motion to strike the extortion claim by applying the FLATLEY exception to Singer's demand letter, which, unlike the letter in FLATLEY, does not constitute criminal extortion as a matter of law. We agree. Under the first step of the statutory analysis, we conclude that because Singer's demand letter does not constitute criminal extortion as a matter of law, the FLATLEY exception does not apply and, under the general rule articulated in BRIGGS, Singer's demand letter is a protected speech or petitioning activity under the anti-SLAPP statute. Under the second step of the statutory analysis, we conclude Singer's demand letter is protected by the litigation privilege (Civ.Code, § 47, subd. (b)), which precludes Malin from prevailing on his claim for extortion.

A. THE CRIME OF EXTORTION GENERALLY

The crime of extortion is defined as " 'the obtaining of property from another, with his consent . . . induced by a wrongful use of force or fear. . . .' (Pen.Code, § 518.) Fear, for purposes of extortion 'may be induced by a threat, either: [¶] . . . [¶] 2. To accuse the individual threatened . . . of any crime; or, [¶] 3. To expose, or impute to him . . . any deformity, disgrace or crime.' (Pen.Code, § 519.) 'Every person who, with intent to extort any money or other property from another, sends or delivers to any person any letter or other writing, whether subscribed or not, expressing or implying, or adapted to imply, any threat such as is specified in Section 519, is punishable in the same manner as if such money or property were actually obtained by means of such threat.' (Pen.Code, § 523.)" (FLATLEY, SUPRA, 39 Cal.4th at p. 326, 46 Cal.Rptr.3d 606, 139 P.3d 2.)

As the Supreme Court recognized in FLATLEY, extortion "has been characterized as a paradoxical crime in that it criminalizes the making of threats that, in and of themselves, may not be illegal. '[I]n many blackmail cases the threat is to do something in itself perfectly legal, but that threat nevertheless becomes illegal when coupled with a demand for money.' (PHILIPPINE EXPORT & FOREIGN LOAN GUARANTEE CORP. V. CHUIDIAN (1990) 218 Cal.App.3d 1058, 1079, 267 Cal.Rptr. 457.)" (FLATLEY, SUPRA, 39 Cal.4th at p. 326, 46 Cal.Rptr.3d 606, 139 P.3d 2, fn. omitted.) Criminal extortion laws prohibit the wrongful use of threats to obtain the property of another, regardless whether a debt is actually owed. " '[The] belief that the victim owes a debt is not a defense to the crime of extortion.' " (ID. at p. 327, 46 Cal.Rptr.3d 606, 139 P.3d 2.)

When a demand for money is accompanied by a threat to report a crime, the demand may constitute criminal extortion, even if the threat is vaguely worded. "[T]he crime with which the extortionist threatens his or her victim need not be a specific crime. '[T]he accusations need only be such as to put the intended victim of the extortion in fear of being accused of some crime. The more vague and general the terms of the accusation the better it would subserve the purpose of the accuser in magnifying the fears of his victim, and the better also it would serve to protect him in the event of the failure to accomplish his extortion and of a prosecution for his attempted crime.' [Citations.]" (FLATLEY, SUPRA, 39 Cal.4th at p. 327, 46 Cal.Rptr.3d 606, 139 P.3d 2.)

Attorneys are subject to "these principles in their professional conduct. Indeed, the Rules of Professional Conduct specifically prohibit attorneys from 'threaten[ing] to present criminal, administration, or disciplinary charges to obtain an advantage in a civil dispute.' ([Cal.] Rules of Prof. Conduct, rule 5–100(A).)" (FLATLEY, SUPRA, 39 Cal.4th at p. 327, 46 Cal.Rptr.3d 606, 139 P.3d 2, fn. omitted.)

B. FLATLEY

In FLATLEY, an attorney, defendant D. Dean Mauro, represented a client, defendant Tyna Marie Robertson, who allegedly was raped by plaintiff Michael Flatley. Flatley, a well-known "performer and dance impresario," owned stock in companies that provided live dance performances throughout the world. (FLATLEY, SUPRA, 39 Cal.4th at p. 305, 46 Cal.Rptr.3d 606, 139 P.3d 2.)

Mauro and Robertson made television appearances in which Robertson "described the alleged rape 'in extremely lurid detail.' " (FLATLEY, SUPRA, 39 Cal.4th at p. 306, 46 Cal.Rptr.3d 606, 139 P.3d 2, fn. omitted.) After sending a demand letter on Robertson's behalf, Mauro telephoned Flatley's attorney to warn that he would " 'go public' " with the rape allegations, which would be " 'publicized every place he [Mr. Flatley] goes for the rest of his life' . . . ." (ID. at p. 330, 46 Cal.Rptr.3d 606, 139 P.3d 2.) In subsequent phone calls, Mauro continued to threaten to " 'go public' " with a story that " 'would follow [Flatley] wherever he or his groups performed and would "ruin" him.' In response to Fields's [(Flatley's attorney)] query about how much money Mauro wanted to avoid this, Mauro said 'it would take "seven figures." ' He repeated that the deadline to respond was January 30." (IBID.)

Flatley sued Robertson and Mauro for "civil extortion, defamation, fraud, intentional infliction of emotional distress, and wrongful interference with prospective economic advantage." (FLATLEY, SUPRA, 39 Cal.4th at p. 306, 46 Cal.Rptr.3d 606, 139 P.3d 2.) Mauro filed a special motion to strike Flatley's complaint under section 425.16, which was denied. The order of denial was affirmed by the Court of Appeal and the California Supreme Court.

In concluding that Mauro was not entitled to relief under the anti-SLAPP statute, the Supreme Court noted that "[e]xtortion is not a constitutionally protected form of speech. [Citations.]" (FLATLEY, SUPRA, 39 Cal.4th at p. 328, 46 Cal.Rptr.3d 606, 139 P.3d 2.) The court found that because Flatley's complaint was based on illegal activities, it was not subject to dismissal under the anti-SLAPP statute: "[W]here a defendant brings a motion to strike under section 425.16 based on a claim that the plaintiff's action arises from activity by the defendant in furtherance of the defendant's exercise of protected speech or petition rights, but either the defendant concedes, or the evidence conclusively establishes, that the assertedly protected speech or petition activity was illegal as a matter of law, the defendant is precluded from using the anti-SLAPP statute to strike the plaintiff's action." (ID. at p. 320, 46 Cal.Rptr.3d 606, 139 P.3d 2.)

In analyzing whether Mauro's demand letter fit the "extortion as a matter of law" exception, the Supreme Court stated: "At the core of Mauro's letter are threats to publicly accuse Flatley of rape and to report and publicly accuse him of other unspecified violations of various laws unless he 'settled' by paying a sum of money to Robertson of which Mauro would receive 40 percent. In his follow-up phone calls, Mauro named the price of his and Robertson's silence as 'seven figures' or, at [a] minimum, $1 million. The key passage in Mauro's letter is at page 3 where Flatley is warned that, unless he settles, 'an in-depth investigation' will be conducted into his personal assets to determine punitive damages and this information will then **'BECOME A MATTER OF PUBLIC RECORD, AS IT MUST BE FILED WITH THE COURT. . . . [¶] Any and all information, including Immigration, Social Security Issuances and Use, and IRS and various State Tax Levies and information will be exposed.** We are positive the media worldwide will enjoy what they find.' This warning is repeated in the fifth paragraph: '**[A]ll pertinent information and documentation, if in violation of any U.S. Federal[ ] Immigration, I.R.S., S.S. Admin., U.S. State, Local, Commonwealth U.K., or International Laws, shall immediately [be] turned over to any and all appropriate authorities.**' " (FLATLEY, SUPRA, 39 Cal.4th at p. 329, 46 Cal.Rptr.3d 606, 139 P.3d 2.)

The Supreme Court further stated that in "[e]valuating Mauro's conduct, we conclude that the letter and subsequent phone calls constitute criminal extortion as a matter of law. These communications threatened to 'accuse' Flatley of, or 'impute to him,' 'crime[s]' and 'disgrace' (Pen.Code, § 519, subds.2, 3) unless Flatley paid Mauro a minimum of $1 million of which Mauro was to receive 40 percent. That the threats were half-couched in legalese does not disguise their essential character as extortion. [Citations.] [¶] Mauro's letter accuses Flatley of rape and also imputes to him other, unspecified violations of various criminal offenses involving immigration and tax law as well as violations of the Social Security Act. With respect to these latter threats, Mauro's letter goes on to threaten that '[w]e are positive the media worldwide will enjoy what they find.' Thus, contrary to Mauro's claim that he did nothing more than suggest that, if evidence of other criminal conduct became public knowledge it would receive media attention, the letter implies that Mauro is already in possession of information regarding such criminal activity and is prepared to disclose this information to the 'worldwide' media. Whether Flatley in fact committed any violations of these various laws is irrelevant. [Citation.] Moreover, the threat to disclose criminal activity entirely unrelated to any alleged injury suffered by Mauro's client 'exceeded the limits of respondent's representation of his client' and is itself evidence of extortion. [Citation.]" (FLATLEY, SUPRA, 39 Cal.4th at pp. 330–331, 46 Cal.Rptr.3d 606, 139 P.3d 2.)

The Supreme Court concluded that Mauro's demand letter "constituted criminal extortion as a matter of law . . . based on the specific and extreme circumstances of this case." (FLATLEY, SUPRA, 39 Cal.4th at p. 332, fn. 16, 46 Cal.Rptr.3d 606, 139 P.3d 2.) In reaching this conclusion, the court explained it was not implying "that rude, aggressive, or even belligerent prelitigation negotiations, whether verbal or written, that may include threats to file a lawsuit, report criminal behavior to authorities or publicize allegations of wrongdoing, necessarily constitute extortion. (PHILIPPINE EXPORT & FOREIGN LOAN GUARANTEE CORP. V. CHUIDIAN, SUPRA, 218 Cal.App.3d at p. 1079, 267 Cal.Rptr. 457 ['a person, generally speaking, has a perfect right to prosecute a lawsuit in good faith, or to provide information to [the] newspapers'].)" (FLATLEY, SUPRA, at p. 332, fn. 16, 46 Cal.Rptr.3d 606, 139 P.3d 2.) The court cautioned that its discussion of what constitutes "extortion as a matter of law" was "limited to the specific facts of this case." (ID. at p. 333, fn. 16, 46 Cal.Rptr.3d 606, 139 P.3d 2.) It further "emphasize[d] that the question of whether the defendant's underlying conduct was illegal as a matter of law is preliminary, and unrelated to the second prong question of whether the plaintiff has demonstrated a probability of prevailing, and the showing required to establish conduct illegal as a matter of law—either through defendant's concession or by uncontroverted and conclusive evidence—is not the same showing as the plaintiff's second prong showing of probability of prevailing." (FLATLEY, SUPRA, 39 Cal.4th at p. 320, 46 Cal.Rptr.3d 606, 139 P.3d 2.)

C. MENDOZA

In MENDOZA, SUPRA, 215 Cal.App.4th 799, 155 Cal.Rptr.3d 832, Division One of this district applied the FLATLEY exception to a demand letter written by an attorney, Reed Hamzeh, on behalf of a client, Guy Chow, who was involved in an employment dispute with Miguel Mendoza. Hamzeh's demand letter stated that Chow's company had suffered losses in excess of $75,000 as a result of Mendoza's fraud, conversion, and breach of contract. The letter warned that if Mendoza did not reimburse the company's losses, a lawsuit would be filed and Mendoza would be reported to state and local prosecutors, the Internal Revenue Service, the Better Business Bureau, and other customers and vendors.

After receiving the demand letter, Mendoza sued Hamzeh for civil extortion, intentional infliction of emotional distress, and unfair business practices. Mendoza alleged that the threat in Hamzeh's demand letter to report him to state and local prosecutors and the Internal Revenue Service constituted criminal extortion.

Hamzeh moved to strike Mendoza's complaint under the anti-SLAPP statute. In opposition, Mendoza argued to deny the motion under the FLATLEY exception, which he claimed was controlling authority. The motion was denied.

In affirming the trial court's ruling, the appellate court stated: "The anti-SLAPP statute does not apply to the threats at issue in Hamzeh's demand letter. Hamzeh threatened to report Mendoza 'to the California Attorney General, the Los Angeles District Attorney, the Internal Revenue Service regarding tax fraud, [and] the Better Business Bureau,' and to disclose the alleged wrongdoing to Mendoza's customers and vendors if Mendoza did not pay 'damages exceeding $75,000.' Regardless of whether Mendoza committed any crime or wrongdoing or owed Chow money, Hamzeh's threat to report criminal conduct to enforcement agencies and to Mendoza's customers and vendors, COUPLED WITH A DEMAND FOR MONEY, constitutes 'criminal extortion as a matter of law,' as articulated in *Flatley*. (FLATLEY, SUPRA, 39 Cal.4th at p. 330, 46 Cal.Rptr.3d 606, 139 P.3d 2.)" (MENDOZA, SUPRA, 215 Cal.App.4th at p. 806, 155 Cal.Rptr.3d 832, fn. omitted.)

D. SINGER'S DEMAND LETTER DOES NOT CONSTITUTE EXTORTION AS A MATTER OF LAW

In contrast with the demand letters in FLATLEY and MENDOZA, Singer's demand letter did not expressly threaten to disclose Malin's alleged wrongdoings to a prosecuting agency or the public at large. Malin argues that Singer's demand letter nonetheless constituted actionable extortion because it "contained, at the very least, an EXTORTION DEMAND that threatened to not only embarrass [Malin] and force him to 'settle' with the Appellants on whatever terms they deemed 'reasonable,' but also to EXPOSE and EMBARRASS various innocent third parties who had NO CONNECTION WHATSOEVER to the dispute between Ara[zm] and [Malin]. [¶] No matter how the Appellants attempt to gloss this paragraph and the other threats set forth in the July 25, 2011 letter, they clearly constituted an overt threat by the Defendants to either: **'accuse the individual threatened. . .of any crime; or,. . .[t]o expose, or impute to him . . .any deformity, disgrace or crime; or . . .[t]o expose any secret affecting him or them' for purposes of obtaining money.** (Pen.Code § 519(2), (3) and (4).) This is the very definition of criminal extortion. [Citations.]"

There are two problems with Malin's argument. First, the "secret" that would allegedly expose him and others to disgrace was inextricably tied to

Arazm's pending complaint. The demand letter accused Malin of embezzling money and simply informed him that Arazm knew how he had spent those funds. There is no doubt the demand letter could have appropriately noted that the filing of the complaint would disclose Malin had spent stolen monies on a car or a villa, if that had been the case. The fact that the funds were allegedly used for a more provocative purpose does not make the threatened disclosure of that purpose during litigation extortion. We cannot conclude that the exposure of Malin's alleged activities would subject him to any more disgrace than the claim that he was an embezzler.

Second, to the extent that Malin contends the threatened disclosure of secrets affecting a third party, his alleged sexual partner, necessarily constitutes extortion, he is mistaken. Penal Code section 519, subdivision 1 defines extortion as a threat "[t]o do an unlawful injury to the person or property of the individual threatened or of a third person. . . ." The third person referred to in subdivision 1 need not have a special relationship to the individual threatened. In contrast, the remainder of Penal Code section 519 criminalizes the threats: "2. To accuse the individual threatened, or any relative of his, or member of his family, of any crime; or, [¶] 3. To expose, or to impute to him or them any deformity, disgrace or crime; or, [¶] 4. To expose[ ] any secret affecting him or them." When read in context, it is clear that the third party referred to in Penal Code section 519, subdivisions 3 and 4 must be a relative of the individual threatened or a member of his or her family. Malin's complaint does not allege that Singer's demand letter threatened to expose a secret of a third party with whom he had a special relationship as defined by the extortion statute. Thus, the threatened disclosure of a secret affecting a third party, who is neither a relative nor a family member, does not constitute extortion. (See PEOPLE V. UMANA (2006) 138 Cal.App.4th 625, 639, 41 Cal.Rptr.3d 573 [only threats that fall within one of the four categories of § 519 will support a charge of extortion].)

We conclude that Singer's demand letter does not fall under the narrow exception articulated in FLATLEY for a letter so extreme in its demands that it constituted criminal extortion as a matter of law. We see a critical distinction between Singer's demand letter, which made no overt threat to report Malin to prosecuting agencies or the Internal Revenue Service, and the letters in FLATLEY and MENDOZA, which contained those express threats and others that had no reasonable connection to the underlying dispute.

Because the demand letter in this case is readily distinguishable from the demand letters in FLATLEY and MENDOZA, this case falls under the general rule stated in BRIGGS: " '[J]ust as communications preparatory to or in anticipation of the bringing of an action or other official proceeding are within the protection of the litigation privilege of Civil Code section 47, subdivision (b). . . [,] such statements are equally entitled to the benefits of section 425.16.' " (Briggs, supra, 19 Cal.4th at p. 1115, 81 Cal.Rptr.2d 471, 969 P.2d 564 citation omitted.)

Applying the general rule enunciated in BRIGGS, we conclude that Malin's extortion claim is based on a speech or petitioning activity that falls within the ambit of the anti-SLAPP statute. The special motion to strike must therefore be decided under the second step of the statutory analysis. Although the trial court did not conduct a second step analysis, we nevertheless "can address that question as it is subject to independent review. [Citation.]" (ROBERTS V. LOS ANGELES COUNTY BAR ASSN. (2003) 105 Cal.App.4th 604, 615–616, 129 Cal.Rptr.2d 546.)

E. THE LITIGATION PRIVILEGE BARS MALIN'S CLAIM FOR EXTORTION

Under the second step of the section 425.16 analysis, Malin must demonstrate a probability of prevailing on his claim for extortion. For the reasons that follow, we conclude he has failed to meet this burden because his claim for extortion is barred by the litigation privilege under Civil Code section 47, subdivision (b). (See DIGERATI, SUPRA, 194 Cal.App.4th at p. 888, 123 Cal.Rptr.3d 736 ["A plaintiff cannot establish a probability of prevailing if the litigation privilege precludes the defendant's liability on the claim."].)

1. THE LITIGATION PRIVILEGE GENERALLY

The litigation privilege applies "to any communication (1) made in judicial or quasi-judicial proceedings; (2) by litigants or other participants authorized by law; (3) to achieve the objects of the litigation; and (4) that have some connection or logical relation to the action." (SILBERG V. ANDERSON (1990) 50 Cal.3d 205, 212, 266 Cal.Rptr. 638, 786 P.2d 365.) " 'The privilege "is not limited to statements made during a trial or other proceedings, but may extend to steps taken prior thereto, or afterwards." [Citation.]' (ACTION APARTMENT [ASSN., INC. V. CITY OF SANTA MONICA (2007)] 41 Cal.4th 1232,] 1241, 63 Cal.Rptr.3d 398, 163 P.3d 89.) The litigation privilege is interpreted broadly in order to further its principal purpose of affording litigants and witnesses the utmost freedom of access to the courts without fear of harassment in derivative tort actions. (IBID.) The privilege is absolute and applies regardless of malice. [Fn. omitted.] (ACTION APARTMENT, at p. 1241, 63 Cal.Rptr.3d 398, 163 P.3d 89.)" (DIGERATI, SUPRA, 194 Cal.App.4th at p. 889, 123 Cal.Rptr.3d

736.) However, the privilege does not apply to malicious prosecution actions. (ID. at p. 889, 123 Cal.Rptr.3d 736, fn. 8.)

"A prelitigation communication is privileged only if it 'relates to litigation that is contemplated in good faith and under serious consideration' (ACTION APARTMENT, SUPRA, 41 Cal.4th at p. 1251, 63 Cal.Rptr.3d 398, 163 P.3d 89). . . . The requirement of good faith contemplation and serious consideration provides some assurance that the communication has some " "connection or logical relation" " to a contemplated action and is made " "to achieve the objects" " of the litigation. (IBID.) 'Whether a prelitigation communication relates to litigation that is contemplated in good faith and under serious consideration is an issue of fact.' (*Ibid.*; accord, FELDMAN V. 1100 PARK LANE ASSOCIATES (2008) 160 Cal.App.4th 1467, 1487, 74 Cal.Rptr.3d 1.)" (DIGERATI, SUPRA, 194 Cal.App.4th at p. 889, 123 Cal.Rptr.3d 736.)

2. ANALYSIS

Singer and Arazm contend the April 10, 2012 order in the related action, in which the same trial court denied Malin's motion to strike the sexual misconduct allegations from Arazm's complaint, demonstrates the relevance of the demand letter's sexual misconduct allegations to Arazm's conversion claim. We agree. In denying Malin's motion to strike, the trial court stated in the April 10, 2012 order that embezzlement was "one of the main allegations of [Arazm's] conversion claim. As regards the allegations of Mr. Malin's sexual activity, [Arazm] alleges that Mr. Malin engaged in these activities using company money and property, tying these allegations into Mr. Malin's alleged misuse of company resources. The motion to strike these allegations is DENIED."

Malin argues, however, that the April 10, 2012 order is "IRRELEVANT, because the standards relating to a determination of issues on a demurrer and motion to strike are substantively different from that utilized in determining a § 425.16 motion to dismiss." We are not persuaded by Malin's argument. On the contrary, the April 10 order is relevant to our determination that the litigation privilege applies to Singer's demand letter, given the similarity of the sexual misconduct allegations in both the letter and subsequent complaint. Malin has cited no evidence in support of his position that the demand letter's sexual misconduct allegations were not related to Arazm's proposed lawsuit or that the lawsuit was not contemplated in good faith and under serious consideration when the letter was sent.

In order for a prelitigation communication such as Singer's demand letter to be privileged under Civil Code section 47, subdivision (b), it must "relate[ ] to litigation that is contemplated in good faith and under serious consideration." (ACTION APARTMENT, SUPRA, 41 Cal.4th at p. 1251, 63 Cal.Rptr.3d 398, 163 P.3d 89.) The April 10 order demonstrates that the sexual misconduct allegations, which the court refused to strike from Arazm's complaint, were related to the demand letter that preceded the complaint.

We conclude Singer's demand letter was logically connected to litigation that was contemplated in good faith and under serious consideration when the letter was sent. The demand letter is therefore protected by the litigation privilege. Because a plaintiff cannot establish a probability of prevailing where the litigation privilege precludes liability (DIGERATI, SUPRA, 194 Cal.App.4th at p. 888, 123 Cal.Rptr.3d 736), the requirements for striking the extortion claim under section 425.16 have been met.

III. The Wiretapping and Computer Hacking Allegations Are Not Subject to Dismissal Under the Anti-SLAPP Statute

The trial court refused to dismiss Malin's claims arising from illegal wiretapping activities based on GERBOSI, SUPRA, 193 Cal.App.4th 435, 122 Cal.Rptr.3d 73, which held that such claims are not subject to dismissal under the anti-SLAPP statute. We conclude the trial court's ruling was correct as to the claims for violation of civil rights and intentional and negligent infliction of emotional distress, which are based on the illegal wiretapping and computer hacking allegations.

Arazm and Singer contend the trial court erred by relying on GERBOSI, SUPRA, 193 Cal.App.4th 435, 122 Cal.Rptr.3d 73, to conclude that the alleged computer hacking and wiretapping were not protected by the anti-SLAPP statute because they constitute illegal activities. They argue that because they do not concede they engaged in such activities, "the PLAINTIFF has the burden to establish that the conduct was illegal as a matter of law." As we will explain, Arazm and Singer misperceive their burden in an anti-SLAPP case.

Our Supreme Court stated in SOUKUP, SUPRA, 39 Cal.4th 260, 286–287, 46 Cal.Rptr.3d 638, 139 P.3d 30: "[O]nce the defendant has made the required threshold showing that the challenged action arises from assertedly protected activity, the plaintiff may counter by demonstrating that the underlying action was illegal as a matter of law because either the defendant concedes the illegality of the assertedly protected activity or the illegality is conclusively established by the evidence presented in connection with the motion to strike." Here, as in GERBOSI, Arazm and Singer have not demonstrated that the challenged action arises from protected activity.

In GERBOSI, an attorney (Gaims) allegedly hired an investigator to conduct illegal wiretapping activities and was sued by Finn for claims arising from those and other activities. Gaims moved to strike all of the claims under the anti-SLAPP statute. In affirming the denial of the motion as to the wiretapping claims, the court stated that Gaims's "status as a member of the bar does not automatically confer the protections of the anti-SLAPP statute as to all of Finn's claims. To the extent Finn alleges criminal conduct, there is no protected activity as defined by the anti-SLAPP statute. [Citation.] As a result, Finn's first cause of action for invasion of privacy, third cause of action for eavesdropping, and fourth cause of action for violation of the [unfair competition law] (which is predicated on violations of the Pen.Code) are outside the protective umbrella of an anti-SLAPP special motion to strike procedure. Each is based on alleged criminal activity." (GERBOSI, SUPRA, 193 Cal.App.4th at p. 445, 122 Cal.Rptr.3d 73.)

Arazm and Singer seize on GERBOSI's reference to "alleged criminal activity" and insist the appellate court's conclusion that mere allegations of criminal conduct are enough to apply the narrow exception to the anti-SLAPP statute established by FLATLEY is at odds with established case law. They misconstrue the GERBOSI court's reasoning.

As noted, Arazm and Singer had the burden to show "the challenged cause of action arises from protected activity." (RUSHEEN V. COHEN (2006) 37 Cal.4th 1048, 1056, 39 Cal.Rptr.3d 516, 128 P.3d 713.) "In the anti-SLAPP context, the critical point is whether the plaintiff's cause of action itself was BASED ON an act in furtherance of the defendant's right of petition or free speech. [Citations.] 'A defendant meets this burden by demonstrating that the act underlying the plaintiff's cause [of action] fits one of the categories spelled out in section 425.16, subdivision (e). . . .' " (CITY OF COTATI V. CASHMAN (2002) 29 Cal.4th 69, 78, 124 Cal.Rptr.2d 519, 52 P.3d 695.) "If the defendant does not demonstrate this initial prong, the court should deny the anti-SLAPP motion and need not address the second step." (HYLTON V. FRANK E. ROGOZIENSKI, INC. (2009) 177 Cal.App.4th 1264, 1271, 99 Cal.Rptr.3d 805.)

Arazm and Singer fail to meet their threshold burden of showing that Malin's civil rights claim is based on an act that constitutes protected activity within the meaning of the statute. In an attempt to do so, they urge the gravamen of Malin's cause of action arises from acts in furtherance of their right to conduct prelitigation investigation. They are incorrect. The ACTS underlying Malin's civil rights and related emotional distress causes of action are computer hacking and wiretapping. Those acts do not fit one of the categories of protected conduct defined by the Legislature in section 425.16, subdivision (e), and Arazm and Singer do not contend otherwise. As a result, they are not entitled to relief under the anti-SLAPP statute.

The following illustration in GERBOSI aptly demonstrates this point: "[I]f Finn filed a personal injury complaint alleging that Gaims physically assaulted her in an attempt to dissuade her from testifying against Pfeifer in his wrongful termination lawsuit, could Gaims invoke the anti-SLAPP statute to strike the complaint by denying Finn's assault allegations? We are certain that the answer is no. The bottom line is this: section 425.16 was not enacted to protect an attorney who allegedly hired an 'investigator' like Anthony Pellicano to wiretap telephones so as to get an unfair advantage in a client's legal matters. [¶] Because Finn's causes of action alleging that Gaims engaged in wiretapping activity do not fall within the protective ambit of the anti-SLAPP statute, we need not determine whether Finn showed a probability of prevailing on those causes of action. Again, the record suggests that Gaims may well have winning defenses to Finn's causes of action alleging criminal activity, but those defenses must be established by a procedural tool other than the anti-SLAPP motion procedure." (GERBOSI, SUPRA,193 Cal.App.4th at pp. 446–447, 122 Cal.Rptr.3d 73.)

Even if we were to accept Arazm and Singer's assertion that they are innocent of the criminal computer hacking and wiretapping allegations, their claim is "more suited to the second step of an anti-SLAPP motion. A showing that a defendant did not do an alleged activity is not a showing that the alleged activity is a protected activity." (GERBOSI, SUPRA, 193 Cal.App.4th at p. 446, 122 Cal.Rptr.3d 73.) For the same reason, the contention in the reply brief that Singer's associate, defendant Brettler, is entitled to a dismissal under the anti-SLAPP statute because Malin presented no evidence showing he was engaged in any improper conduct is misplaced.

IV. Attorney Fees and Costs

Arazm and Singer contend that as partially prevailing defendants in an anti-SLAPP motion, they are entitled to costs and attorney fees under section 425.16, subdivision (c). As the issue of fees and costs has not been fully briefed, we remand with directions to the trial court to consider the issue in light of the following guidelines.

"The special motion to strike—or so-called anti-SLAPP motion—is subject to statutory fee shifting as follows. 'In any action subject to [the special motion to strike], a prevailing defendant . . . shall be entitled to recover his or her attorney's fees and costs. If the court finds that a special motion to strike is frivolous or is solely intended to cause unnecessary delay, the court shall award costs and reasonable attorney's fees to a plaintiff prevailing on the motion, pursuant to [Code of Civil Procedure] [s]ection 128.5.' (Code Civ. Proc., § 425.16, subd. (c).)

"Thus, under Code of Civil Procedure section 425.16, subdivision (c), any SLAPP defendant who brings a successful motion to strike is entitled to mandatory attorney fees. The fee-shifting provision was apparently intended to discourage such strategic lawsuits against public participation by imposing the litigation costs on the party seeking to 'chill the valid exercise of the constitutional rights of freedom of speech and petition for the redress of grievances.' (ID., subd. (a).) The fee-shifting provision also encourages private representation in SLAPP cases, including situations when a SLAPP defendant is unable to afford fees or the lack of potential monetary damages precludes a standard contingency fee arrangement. As will appear, by its terms, Code of Civil Procedure section 425.16 permits the use of the so-called lodestar adjustment method under our long-standing precedents, beginning with SERRANO V. PRIEST (1977) 20 Cal.3d 25, 141 Cal.Rptr. 315, 569 P.2d 1303." (KETCHUM V. MOSES (2001) 24 Cal.4th 1122, 1131, 104 Cal.Rptr.2d 377, 17 P.3d 735 (KETCHUM.)

In this case, because Arazm and Singer only partially prevailed on their special motion to strike under section 425.16, there are numerous factors to be considered in determining their right to fees and costs. Those factors were discussed at length in MANN V. QUALITY OLD TIME SERVICE, INC. (2006) 139 Cal.App.4th 328, 344–345, 42 Cal.Rptr.3d 607:

"An award of attorney fees to a partially prevailing defendant under section 425.16, subdivision (c) thus involves competing public policies: (1) the public policy to discourage meritless SLAPP claims by compelling a SLAPP plaintiff to bear a defendant's litigation costs incurred to eliminate the claim from the lawsuit; and (2) the public policy to provide a plaintiff who has facially valid claims to exercise his or her constitutional petition rights by filing a complaint and litigating those claims in court. (§§ 425.16, 425.17; see KETCHUM, SUPRA, 24 Cal.4th at p. 1131, 104 Cal.Rptr.2d 377, 17 P.3d 735.) In balancing these policies, we conclude a defendant should not be entitled to obtain AS A MATTER OF RIGHT his or her entire attorney fees incurred on successful and unsuccessful claims merely because the attorney work on those claims was overlapping. Instead, the court should first determine the lodestar amount for the hours expended on the successful claims, and, if the work on the successful and unsuccessful causes of action was overlapping, the court should then consider the defendant's relative success on the motion in achieving his or her objective, and reduce the amount if appropriate.

"This analysis includes factors such as the extent to which the defendant's litigation posture was advanced by the motion, whether the same factual allegations remain to be litigated, whether discovery and motion practice have been narrowed, and the extent to which future litigation expenses and strategy were impacted by the motion. The fees awarded to a defendant who was only partially successful on an anti-SLAPP motion should be commensurate with the extent to which the motion changed the nature and character of the lawsuit in a practical way. The court should also consider any other applicable relevant factors, such as the experience and abilities of the attorney and the novelty and difficulty of the issues, to adjust the lodestar amount as appropriate. (See KETCHUM, SUPRA, 24 Cal.4th at p. 1132, 104 Cal.Rptr.2d 377, 17 P.3d 735.)"

DISPOSITION

The order denying the special motion to strike Malin's complaint is reversed in part as to the first cause of action for extortion, and affirmed in part as to the second cause of action for invasion of privacy and the third and fourth causes of action for intentional and negligent infliction of emotional distress. The matter is remanded with directions to the superior court to grant the special motion to strike the first cause of action for extortion. In accordance with the views expressed herein, the trial court is to determine Arazm's and Singer's rights, as partially prevailing defendants, to fees and costs incurred in the motion below. If the trial court awards Arazm and Singer the fees and costs incurred in the motion below, their right to attorney fees incurred on appeal is to be determined by the trial court. Costs on appeal, with the exception of attorney fees to be determined by the trial court, are to be borne by the parties.

SOLUTIONS: THE LAWYER SHOULD HAVE, WOULD HAVE, COULD HAVE. . .

It is not the nature of the allegations made that drives the determination of whether a claim is a legitimate effort at settlement or criminal extortion. Rather, it is the nature of how the settlement issue is raised and framed. As we saw in both cases, words matter, and they matter a lot. Jere. The lawyer was precise in explaining that the possibly embarrassing facts would

> inevitably be revealed and did not use these facts as a separate cudgel to bring about a settlement.

Section 5. The Lawyer at Mediation

Many cases are ordered by a court to mediation or the parties, prior to or during the lawsuit, voluntarily go to mediation. The courts will order mediation early in the litigation process as a way of managing their dockets. The more cases that are settled, the less cases that need to be tried. In either event, the lawyer is confronted with ethical issues as we see in the following case.

Cases and Materials

X-Ray Questions (*In re Potts*)

This case illustrates yet again that the Rules are a complex ecosystem rather than a simplistic organism. One set of facts generate a discussion of several of the Rules. Potts, a lawyer knew that his clients, at a mediation, did not want to inform the party opposite of a very valuable asset so that it could not be subject to division in any settlement. What was his first mistake leading to his violation of several rules and a public reprimand? How did MR 1.2 and MR 1.16, both of which we have studied, play into the calculus of his violations? What did he do that resulted in his violation of MR 3.3 and his duty y of candor to the tribunal? In an ironic twist, how was his violation discovered? What lesson do you derive from the answer to this question?

(Note that Montana, unlike the Model Rules, has a different version of MR 16's disclosure allowances).

In re Potts

Supreme Court of Montana, 2007.
158 P.3d 418.

OPINION AND ORDER

¶ 1 The Commission on Practice of the Supreme Court of the State of Montana (the Commission) entered its Findings of Fact, Conclusions of Law, and Recommendations on January 5, 2006, regarding a complaint filed against Steven T. Potts (Potts), an attorney licensed to practice law in the State of Montana. The Commission concluded that Potts violated Rules 1.2(d) and 3.3(a)(2) of the Montana Rules of Professional Conduct (M.R.P.C.) during his representation of heirs in a will contest. We adopt the Commission's Findings of Fact and Conclusions of Law. We order Potts to appear before this Court for public censure.

¶ 2   Potts presents the following issues for review:

¶ 3 1.   Whether Rule 1.6, M.R.P.C., required Potts to maintain his clients' confidences to the exclusion of being candid with opposing counsel and candid with the tribunal.

¶ 4 2.   Whether Potts violated Rule 1.2(d), M.R.P.C.

¶ 5 3.   Whether Potts violated Rule 3.3(a)(2), M.R.P.C.

¶ 6 4.   Whether the Commission improperly excluded Potts's proposed expert witness testimony.

¶ 7 5.   Whether the Commission improperly excluded a portion of Potts's testimony as inadmissible hearsay.

¶ 8 6.   Whether the Commission's proposed sanctions are appropriate.

FACTUAL AND PROCEDURAL BACKGROUND

¶ 9   This disciplinary action arises from Potts's representation in a will contest involving the estate of Ernestine Stukey (Ernestine). Ernestine died March 8, 2001. Ernestine was survived by her daughter, Evon Leistiko (Evon), her six grandchildren, including Tyson Leistiko (Tyson), and her niece, Charlene Howard (Charlene).

¶ 10 Ernestine executed a will on January 14, 1998, disinheriting Evon and bequeathing most of her estate to Charlene. The will designated Charlene and Ernestine's friend, Verna Kessner (Verna), as co-personal representatives of her estate.

¶ 11 Ernestine's mental health deteriorated over the next two years, and she was involuntarily committed to the Montana State Hospital at Warm Springs. Evon petitioned the Third Judicial District, Deer Lodge County, to become Ernestine's conservator. The district court appointed Evon as conservator. The law firm of Church, Harris, Johnson & Williams, P.C. (Ernestine's attorneys) represented Ernestine's interests throughout the conservatorship proceedings.

¶ 12 Evon filed an initial inventory (initial inventory) with the district court in the conservatorship proceedings, reporting Ernestine's net worth as $1,254,795. The initial inventory included several accounts with a total worth of approximately $270,000, that Evon held in joint tenancy ownership with Ernestine or in which Evon was named as a beneficiary to the accounts (joint tenancy accounts). Ernestine established these joint tenancy accounts with Evon in 1967 and 1991.

¶ 13 As Ernestine's conservator and guardian, Evon petitioned the court to distribute gift money totaling $160,000 from Ernestine's estate to family members. The district court denied the petition on January 24, 2001, and authorized Ernestine's attorneys to investigate Evon's conduct as conservator. Ernestine's attorneys petitioned the court to remove Evon as conservator as a result of the investigation. Ernestine's attorneys later filed an action seeking recovery of monetary damages for Evon's alleged breach of fiduciary duty and self dealing related to the conservatorship proceedings. Ernestine's attorneys alleged that Evon had misappropriated $10,000 of Ernestine's money and engaged in other mismanagement of Ernestine's funds while Ernestine was incapacitated.

¶ 14 Without notifying the district court or Ernestine's attorneys, Evon moved Ernestine to an assisted living facility in the state of Washington. Ernestine purportedly executed a second will (second will) with assistance of Washington counsel on February 12, 2001, while staying in the Alzheimer's Unit of the facility. The second will appointed Evon as personal representative and bequeathed the bulk of the estate to Evon and Evon's family.

¶ 15 Ernestine died on March 8, 2001. A will contest ensued. Ernestine's attorneys filed a petition in the Eighth Judicial District, Cascade County, on March 13, 2001, to probate Ernestine's 1998 will. Evon filed a competing petition to probate Ernestine's second will in Chelan County, Washington, on March 23, 2001.

¶ 16 Evon also filed a second inventory (second inventory) with her petition to probate Ernestine's second will in Chelan County, Washington. This second inventory reported $1,253,000 as the gross value of Ernestine's estate. Evon's report of the estate's total value in the second inventory comported with the total estate value in the initial inventory that she had filed in the conservatorship proceeding in the Third Judicial District, Deer Lodge County. It also matched the total estate value that she reported in the final inventory (final inventory) to the Third Judicial District, filed May 10, 2001, in the conservatorship proceedings. All three inventories filed by Evon listed all of Ernestine's assets and included the joint tenancy accounts. None of the three inventories distinguished between probate assets and nonprobate assets, such as the joint tenancy accounts.

¶ 17 Evon retained Potts to represent her and the six grandchildren, including Tyson, in the will contest in the Eighth Judicial District, Cascade County. Evon's attorney in the conservatorship proceeding provided Potts with Evon's legal file. These files included the hearing transcript regarding the unauthorized gifts, the accountings, the inventories, and the wills.

¶ 18 Attorney Ward E. Taleff (Taleff) represented Charlene. Attorney Sue Ann Love (Love) represented the University of Wisconsin, a beneficiary under Ernestine's 1998 will. Attorney Greg Hatley (Hatley) represented a church holding a charitable interest in Ernestine's estate under the 1998 will. Attorneys from Church, Harris, Johnson & Williams, P.C., represented Ernestine's estate.

¶ 19 The parties agreed to mediate all disputes concerning the will contest and Evon's alleged misconduct in the conservatorship proceedings. Ernestine's attorneys filed a confidential settlement brochure that indicated the parties assumed a total estate value of $1.2 million, as Evon had reported in the three inventories, as the basis for settlement.

¶ 20 Potts attended the settlement conference on November 12 and 13, 2001, with his clients, Evon and Tyson. At that time, Evon already had claimed a fraction of the joint tenancy accounts and was working to obtain the rest of the $270,000. Evon never disclosed this fact at the mediation, even though the other parties apparently assumed that they were negotiating based on the $1.2 million total estate value that included the joint tenancy accounts. Potts also remained silent as to whether the settlement included the joint tenancy accounts.

¶ 21 The parties reached an agreement during the second day of the mediation. They drafted a memorandum of understanding (memorandum) before departing the mediation to memorialize the terms of their settlement. The memorandum purported to resolve both the will contest and conservatorship dispute. It called for portions of Ernestine's estate to go to specific beneficiaries and for fifty percent of the remainder to go to Charlene and for fifty percent of the remainder to go to Evon and Ernestine's grandchildren. The memorandum referred to the division of "the Estate," but failed to assign a particular dollar value to the total settlement. The memorandum also made no mention of the three separate inventories that Evon had filed in the conservatorship and probate proceedings as representing the value of "the Estate." The memorandum further stated that the parties would stipulate to the dismissal of the conservatorship action filed against Evon and the Washington probate proceeding. Glenn Tremper (Tremper), one of the attorneys representing Ernestine's estate from Church, Harris, Johnson &

Williams, P.C., signed the memorandum along with attorneys Taleff, Love, and Potts. Evon, Tyson, Charlene, and Verna also signed the memorandum.

¶ 22 In the week following the settlement conference, Tremper suspected that Evon was attempting to secure the joint tenancy accounts. Tremper telephoned Potts to discuss the matter on November 20, 2001. Tremper wrote a letter to Potts on the same day as the telephone conversation, asking Potts to confirm that the parties had reached the settlement in the mediation "based upon the good faith assumption that Ernestine's estate includes the assets identified by Evon as belonging to Ernestine in her proposed Final Accounting before Judge Mizner," in the conservatorship proceeding. The final accounting of the conservatorship proceeding before Judge Mizner included the joint tenancy accounts and valued the total estate at $1.2 million. Tremper's letter requested that Potts let him know "immediately" if his clients had a different understanding of the settlement.

¶ 23 Potts showed Tremper's letter to his client, Tyson. Potts testified that he advised Tyson that any questions concerning what assets were included in the estate "will get cleared up," but that he would prefer to resolve any such dispute "sooner rather than later." Tyson instructed Potts not to respond because he wanted to deal only with a personal representative to be appointed later by the court. Potts did not answer the letter. Tremper construed Potts's silence as confirmation that the parties had based the settlement on the $1.2 million total estate value that Evon had reported to the courts in the initial, second, and final inventories.

¶ 24 One week later, Potts drafted and circulated a stipulation that purported to resolve "all" disputes regarding the division of Ernestine's "estate" as stated in the memorandum. The stipulation called for the appointment of attorney R. William Walsh (Walsh) to serve as personal representative of Ernestine's estate. The stipulation also dismissed the probate proceedings in Chelan County, Washington, and dismissed the conservatorship action against Evon in the Third Judicial District, Deer Lodge County. Potts, Taleff, Hatley, and Love signed the stipulation filed in the Eighth Judicial District, Cascade County on November 28, 2001. Attorney Dan Shannon of Church, Harris, Johnson & Williams, P.C., signed the stipulation on behalf of Tremper in representation of Verna and Charlene.

¶ 25 A battle soon erupted over the meaning and effect of the stipulation and the memorandum. Walsh filed a petition in the Eighth Judicial District on September 3, 2002, asking for the court's direction on distribution of the joint tenancy accounts. Charlene argued in response that Evon was not entitled to claim the joint tenancy accounts outside the settlement agreement. The district court held a hearing on February 3, 2003, and determined that Evon had no right to the joint tenancy accounts because the parties had relied on the $1.2 million total estate value, as she had reported in the final inventory in the conservatorship proceeding, as the basis of the settlement. We affirmed the district court's determination that, although the memorandum was ambiguous, the parties intended the $1.2 million total estate value, including the joint tenancy accounts, to be included in the memorandum and the settlement. *In Re Estate of Stukey*, 2004 MT 279, ¶¶ 75–76, 323 Mont. 241, ¶¶ 75–76, 100 P.3d 114, ¶¶ 75–76. *(Stukey I)*. We later affirmed the personal representative's request to distribute the estate according to the formula set forth in *Stukey I. See In Re Estate of Stukey*, 2005 MT 349N, 330 Mont. 401, 126 P.3d 507. *(Stukey II)*.

¶ 26 The Office of Disciplinary Counsel of the State of Montana (ODC) received a complaint regarding Potts's conduct surrounding the settlement. ODC investigated and filed a formal complaint against Potts on August 19, 2004, alleging that Potts committed two counts of professional misconduct. The first count alleges that Potts engaged in or assisted in client fraud, a violation of Rule 1.2(d), M.R.P.C., by following his client's instructions not to disclose material information to opposing counsel. The second count charges that Potts breached the duty of candor to the tribunal, a violation of Rule 3.3(a)(2), M.R.P.C., by failing to disclose material information to the district court presiding over the contested will action.

¶ 27 The Commission heard the matter on July 27 and 28, 2005. Tremper testified before the Commission that "the estate" encompassed the $1.2 million total value of Ernestine's estate, as Evon had reported to the courts in the initial, second, and final inventories. Tremper admitted that he knew Evon had asserted an interest in at least some of the joint tenancy accounts. He testified that he believed, based on discussions at the mediation, however, that the settlement included the joint tenancy accounts to satisfy both the will contest and the claim for damages related to Evon's alleged mishandling of funds while Ernestine had been incapacitated. Tremper also testified that Potts assured him in their telephone conversation shortly after the mediation that the settlement encompassed the $1.2 million total value of the estate. Potts denied having made the statement.

¶ 28 Potts testified that he believed the settlement conference included only probate assets and not the joint tenancy accounts that Evon held with Ernestine. He further testified that he was "confused" by Evon's conduct regarding the joint tenancy accounts. Evon contradicted Potts, however, in testimony given at a February 3, 2003, hearing in the Eighth Judicial District to determine the basis of the settlement as stated in the memorandum. Evon testified that her lawyer knew, before the November mediation, that she had planned to obtain the joint tenancy accounts. The Commission admitted Evon's previous testimony at the disciplinary hearing. Potts does not contest here the Commission's decision to admit Evon's previous testimony on this point. Potts also admitted that Tyson had told him as early as four months before the mediation that Evon planned to obtain jointly held property regardless of the outcome of any settlement.

¶ 29 The Commission determined that the parties to the mediation had negotiated the settlement based on the $1.2 million total value of the estate as Evon had reported to the courts in three separate inventories and two petitions. The Commission found that Potts's clients, Evon and Tyson, had informed him well in advance of the mediation that Evon had intended to take the joint tenancy accounts outside of any settlement agreement. The Commission further found that Potts failed to answer Tremper's specific inquiry as to whether the joint tenancy accounts were included in the settlement. Potts instead had drafted and circulated the stipulation declaring that all disputes had been settled. The Commission found that Potts had failed to inform the district court and the other parties that the value of the settlement remained at issue.

¶ 30 The Commission concluded that, based on these findings, clear and convincing evidence supported the conclusion that Potts knew that his clients were using his services to perpetuate fraud in violation of Rules 1.2(d) and 3.3(a)(2), M.R.P.C., as the rules existed in 2001. The Commission concluded that Potts's clients had negotiated a settlement based on Ernestine's $1.2 million estate and then improperly had taken money outside the settlement agreement. The Commission concluded that Potts had an ethical obligation to inform his clients that he would not actively or passively assist in their fraudulent conduct. As a result, the Commission determined that clear and convincing evidence supported the finding that Potts had failed to fulfill this ethical obligation, a violation of Rule 1.2(d), M.R.P.C. The Commission also determined that the duty of candor toward the tribunal under Rule 3.3(a)(2), M.R.P.C., superseded Potts's duty of confidentiality under Rule 1.6, M.R.P.C. Finally, the Commission determined that Potts violated his duty of candor toward the tribunal when he failed to disclose material facts to the district court. The Commission recommended that Potts be censured publicly, be suspended from the practice of law for a period of thirty days, and be required to pay the costs of the disciplinary proceedings. Potts objects.

STANDARD OF REVIEW

¶ 31 This Court "possesses original and exclusive jurisdiction and responsibility under Article VII, Section 2(3) of the 1972 Montana Constitution and the provisions of Chapter 61, Title 37, Montana Code Annotated, in addition to its inherent jurisdiction, in all matters involving admission of persons to practice law in the State of Montana, and the conduct and disciplining of such persons." *See* Introduction, Montana Rules for Lawyer Disciplinary Enforcement (MRLDE). We created the Commission in 1965 to act under the aegis of this Court for the purpose of receiving, investigating, and reporting on allegations of misconduct of lawyers in the State of Montana. *Matter of Goldman*, 179 Mont. 526, 529, 588 P.2d 964, 966 (1978).

¶ 32 As a result, our review of the Commission's decisions differs from the scope of review applicable in an appeal of a decision by an agency-selected hearings examiner, wherein such factual findings are difficult to overturn. *Goldstein v. Commission on Practice*, 2000 MT 8, ¶ 30, 297 Mont. 493, ¶ 30, 995 P.2d 923, ¶ 30. Instead, we review *de novo* the Commission's findings of fact, conclusions of law, and recommendations. *Goldstein*, ¶ 30. Our duty includes weighing the evidence upon which the Commission's findings rest. *Goldman*, 179 Mont. at 545, 588 P.2d at 974. Even in light of our duty to weigh the evidence, we remain reluctant to reverse the decision of the Commission when its findings rest on testimonial evidence. We recognize that the Commission stands in a better position to evaluate conflicting statements after observing the character of the witnesses and their statements. *Goldman*, 179 Mont. at 545, 588 P.2d at 975.

DISCUSSION

¶ 33 *Whether Rule 1.6, M.R.P.C., required Potts to maintain his clients' confidences to the exclusion of being candid with opposing counsel and candid with the tribunal.*

¶ 34 Potts argues that Rule 1.6, M.R.P.C., prevented him from disclosing his clients' allegedly fraudulent conduct to anyone, including the court. Rule 1.6, M.R.P.C., prohibits a lawyer from revealing "information relating to representation of a client unless the client consents after consultation. . . ." Potts contends that his clients never consented to revealing such information. Potts further points out that Rule 1.6, M.R.P.C., sets out a few exceptions to the duty of confidentiality, but provides no exception for reporting or disclosing client fraud. Potts contends that the Commission erred by failing to consider the duty of confidentiality under Rule 1.6, M.R.P.C., in its analysis of Rule 1.2(d),

M.R.P.C., in which the Commission concluded that Potts had assisted in client fraud.

¶ 35 Rule 3.3(a)(2) sets forth the duty of candor toward the tribunal and prohibits a lawyer from failing "to disclose a material fact to a tribunal when disclosure is necessary to avoid assisting a criminal or fraudulent act by the client." Once Potts made representations to the court in the signed stipulation, the duty of candor to the tribunal as stated in Rule 3.3(a)(2), M.R.P.C., trumped any duty of confidentiality that he owed to his clients. *See* State Bar of Montana Advisory Ethics Opinion 87–0326. Regardless of the duty of confidentiality as stated in Rule 1.6, M.R.P.C., Potts had an affirmative duty to be truthful in his statements to the court as mandated by Rule 3.3(a)(2), M.R.P.C.

¶ 36 Alternatively, Rule 1.6, M.R.P.C., may have absolved Potts from disclosing any information relating to the representation of his clients even if they had engaged in fraudulent conduct. Under Rule 1.6(b)(1), M.R.P.C., a lawyer may disclose information relating to client representation only if the client consents to a disclosure or to prevent a client from committing a criminal act that the lawyer believes is likely to result in imminent death or substantial bodily harm. The rule provides no exception for disclosing fraudulent conduct of a client to prevent, rectify, or mitigate fraud. Potts could not have disclosed his clients' confidences under Rule 1.6, M.R.P.C.

¶ 37 Rule 1.6, M.R.P.C., does not stand alone, however, and thus our analysis does not end here. Rule 1.2(d), M.R.P.C., prohibits the lawyer from counseling or assisting a client to engage in conduct that the lawyer knows is criminal or fraudulent. Under certain circumstances, a lawyer's nondisclosure of a material fact can be taken too far even in light of the duty of confidentiality. Nondisclosure of client information "can amount to a misrepresentation in some circumstances and can also have the effect of assisting a criminal or fraudulent act by a client, thus implicating the lawyer in the client's wrongdoing." ABA Center for Professional Responsibility, *A Legislative History of the Model Rules of Professional Conduct* 215 (1999). Under Rule 4.1, M.R.P.C., such nondisclosures can be revealed only to "a third person when disclosure is necessary to avoid assisting a criminal or fraudulent act by a client, *unless* disclosure is prohibited by Rule 1.6." (Emphasis added).

¶ 38 Here, Rule 1.6, M.R.P.C., prevented Potts from disclosing his clients' information because his clients had not consented to a disclosure and his clients' conduct was not likely to result in imminent death or substantial bodily harm so as to warrant disclosure outside of their consent. Potts cannot use the duty of confidentiality, however, to shield himself from other potential misconduct.

Potts, while maintaining his duty of confidentiality, also must comply with the other rules of professional conduct, including Rule 1.2(d), M.R.P.C., the rule that prohibits a lawyer from assisting a client in fraud.

¶ 39 Rule 1.16, M.R.P.C., requires a lawyer to withdraw from representing a client if such representation will result in violation of the rules of professional conduct. Potts should have withdrawn from representation as soon as his clients' demands for nondisclosure of information propelled his services into the realm of assisting in his clients' fraudulent behavior. We concede that Rule 1.6, M.R.P.C., prevented Potts from disclosing the information against his clients' wishes. We will not endorse legitimate nondisclosure under Rule 1.6, M.R.P.C., however, as an excuse for noncompliance with Rule 1.2(d), M.R.P.C. The Commission, therefore, did not err by failing to consider the duty of confidentiality in its analysis of whether Potts violated Rule 1.2(d), and assisted in his clients' fraudulent conduct.

¶ 40 *Whether Potts violated Rule 1.2(d), M.R.P.C.*

¶ 41 Rule 1.2(d), M.R.P.C., prohibits a lawyer from counseling "a client to engage, or assist a client, in conduct that the lawyer knows is criminal or fraudulent. . . ." Potts argues first that his clients did not commit any underlying fraud so he cannot be accused of having assisted in fraudulent conduct. Second, Potts contends that the memorandum was ambiguous, as determined by our decision in *Stukey I,* ¶ 75, and thus cannot serve as a basis for determining fraud. Potts next suggests that he did not know at the time of the events that his clients' conduct was fraudulent. Finally, Potts asserts that his failure to apprise the other parties of relevant information falls outside the definition of fraud.

¶ 42 Potts argues that the Commission's finding that his clients engaged in fraud rests on the erroneous conclusion that the joint tenancy accounts were included in Ernestine's estate. Potts contends that his clients, Evon and Tyson, never engaged in fraudulent conduct because the joint tenancy accounts passed as a matter of law to Evon upon Ernestine's death and as a result could not have been included as a part of the settlement basis.

¶ 43 The 2001 M.R.P.C. fails to provide a specific definition of "fraud" or "fraudulent." The allegedly fraudulent conduct in this case surrounds Evon's representations of the basis of the settlement value. Settlement agreements are contracts and subject to the provisions of contract law. *Dambrowski v. Champion Intern. Corp.,* 2003 MT 233, ¶ 9, 317 Mont. 218, ¶ 9, 76 P.3d 1080, ¶ 9. Under contract principles, a party's conduct rises to the level of actual fraud when he acts with the intent to deceive another to induce him to enter into the contract. *See* § 28–2–405, MCA.

¶ 44 A party commits actual fraud by making a "suggestion as a fact that which is not true by one who does not believe it to be true." Section 28–2–405, MCA. Actual fraud also occurs when a party suppresses "that which is true by one having knowledge or belief of the fact," or by making a promise without any intention of performing it, or through "any other act fitted to deceive." Section 28–2–405, MCA. Conduct constituting constructive fraud consists of "any breach of duty, which, without an actually fraudulent intent, gains an advantage to the person in fault or anyone claiming under him by misleading another to his prejudice. . . ." Section 28–2–406, MCA.

¶ 45 Potts's clients refused to waive confidential mediation communications, thus we do not have the privilege of reviewing Potts's version of what happened in mediation. We are convinced by testimony of others and evidence presented at the disciplinary hearing before the Commission that Potts's clients, Evon and Tyson, engaged in fraudulent conduct during their procurement of the settlement agreement.

¶ 46 The evidence shows that Evon represented in three inventories to the courts that $1.2 million constituted the total value of Ernestine's estate. These inventories made no distinction between probate and nonprobate assets, such as the joint tenancy accounts. By the time the parties met for mediation, Evon had taken a fraction of the joint tenancy accounts from the $1.2 million estate and was working to secure the rest.

¶ 47 By all accounts in the record, Evon never disclosed to the other parties at the mediation her intent to take part of the $1.2 million estate. Evon suggested as fact, or at the very least by her silence perpetuated, the untrue statement that the settlement basis constituted the full $1.2 million value of the estate. Evon knew, however, at the time of the mediation that the $1.2 million value did not represent an accurate settlement basis because she already had taken a fraction of that money and had intended to secure several hundred thousand dollars in the days after the mediation. Evon's misrepresentation of the value of the estate fraudulently induced the other parties to enter into the settlement agreement. The settlement agreement benefited Evon in that it included a stipulation to dismiss the conservatorship action against her and the potential liability associated with it.

¶ 48 Tyson also engaged in fraud by suppressing the truth that the settlement value could not have included the full $1.2 million. Potts testified that

Tyson informed him months before the mediation that Evon had intended to take the joint tenancy accounts from the estate. After mediation, Tremper informed Potts and his clients, including Tyson, that Evon's final inventory comprised the basis of the settlement. Tremper requested that Potts notify him immediately if there had been a different understanding of the settlement. Tyson instructed Potts not to respond. Tyson's suppression of this relevant fact caused Tremper to believe that the settlement basis included the joint tenancy accounts.

¶ 49 We now turn to Potts's argument that we deemed the memorandum to be ambiguous in *Stukey I,* ¶ 75, thus it cannot serve as a basis for finding fraud. We concluded that the term "remainder," as stated in the memorandum, was ambiguous and capable of two meanings in that it may or may not have included the joint tenancy accounts in the estate value. *Stukey I,* ¶ 75. We also determined, however, that the "bulk of the evidence" showed that the negotiating parties had relied on Evon's final inventory, making no distinction between probate and nonprobate assets, for the basis of the settlement value. *Stukey I,* ¶ 76.

¶ 50 We recognize that the memorandum emerged after two long days of negotiations and the weariness of the parties likely contributed to its somewhat skeletal outline. Nonetheless the parties allowed material ambiguities to remain in the memorandum. The memorandum refers to the division of "the Estate," but makes no mention of the particular dollar value of "the Estate." Tremper testified that he believed that "the Estate" and the settlement basis included both probate and nonprobate assets to satisfy the will contest and damages sought for Evon's alleged breach of fiduciary duties in relation to the conservatorship proceedings. The memorandum hints at Tremper's belief by dismissing both the will contest and conservatorship dispute, but fails to state the inclusion of the joint tenancy accounts. These significant ambiguities lead us to agree with Potts that the memorandum cannot provide the sole basis for finding that Potts violated Rules 1.2(d) and 3.3(a)(2), M.R.P.C.

¶ 51 The memorandum constitutes only a first step, however, as most of Potts's alleged misconduct occurred after the parties had executed the memorandum. Tremper first brought the memorandum's ambiguity to light in his telephone conversation with Potts. Tremper immediately followed up with a letter to Potts on November 20, 2001, asking for confirmation that the settlement amount included the $1.2 million total value relied on by the parties.

¶ 52 Potts's client, Tyson, could have been forthcoming with the truth— that Evon already had claimed part of the funds from the joint tenancy accounts and soon would grab the rest. Instead, Tyson, with the help of Potts's services as a lawyer, encouraged the ambiguity by failing to respond to Tremper's inquiry. Potts maintains he had no duty to correct opposing counsel's error. We disagree.

¶ 53 Rule 4.1, M.R.P.C., prohibits Potts from knowingly making a false statement of fact to a third party. Comment 1, Rule 4. 1, ABA Model R. Prof. Conduct, provides that a lawyer, while having no affirmative duty to inform an opposing party of relevant facts, must be truthful when dealing with others on a client's behalf. Comment 1 also warns that "a misrepresentation can occur if the lawyer incorporates or affirms a statement of another person that the lawyer knows is false . . . or by omissions that are the equivalent of affirmative false statements." Statements of price estimates or value during negotiations are not considered material facts requiring disclosure unless nondisclosure would otherwise constitute fraud. *See* Comment 2, Rule 4.1, ABA Model R. Prof. Conduct.

¶ 54 In light of the guidance provided by the comments to the ABA Model Rules, we find the holding in *State ex rel. Neb. State Bar v. Addison*, 226 Neb. 585, 412 N.W.2d 855 (1987), persuasive in this matter. In *Addison*, the Nebraska Supreme Court determined that a lawyer engaged or assisted in fraud and knowingly made a false statement of fact when he negotiated a release of a hospital's lien based on the hospital's mistaken belief that two insurance policies were in place instead of three. *Addison*, 412 N.W.2d at 856. The *Addison* court suspended the lawyer from practice for the period of six months based on the referee's findings that the lawyer's omission in failing to correct the hospital's false impression constituted a violation of the tenets of professional conduct. *Addison*, 412 N.W.2d at 856.

¶ 55 Similarly, Potts knew that the parties held different understandings as to the settlement basis and he failed to correct the mistake. Tremper's letter raised the question of whether $1.2 million represented the total value of the estate. The letter specifically requested Potts to respond if his clients had a different understanding as to the basis of the settlement. Tyson instructed Potts not to respond even though Tyson had told Potts months before that Evon intended to take the joint tenancy accounts outside of any settlement. Potts's testimony that he advised Tyson that the problem would have to be "cleared up" at some point shows that he knew the settlement basis was at issue. Potts's omission constituted a misrepresentation that assisted in his clients' fraudulent purpose of taking the joint tenancy accounts outside of the settlement agreement, a violation of Rule 1.2(d), M.R.P.C. Potts could have avoided this situation by withdrawing from representation under Rule 1. 16, M.R.P.C.

¶ 56 Potts next argues that he did not know at the time of the events in question that his clients' conduct was fraudulent, and, therefore, he cannot be accused of violating Rule 1.2(d), M.R.P.C. Evon testified at a February 3, 2003, hearing that her lawyer knew before the mediation that she would claim the joint tenancy accounts outside of any settlement agreement. The Commission admitted Evon's testimony on this point at the disciplinary proceedings, and Potts does not raise the issue on appeal.

¶ 57 Neither Potts nor his clients, Evon and Tyson, disclosed Evon's plans concerning the joint tenancy accounts at the November mediation. They offered no correction to the parties who had negotiated the settlement based on the $1.2 million total estate value that Evon had reported to the court in her final inventory in the conservatorship proceedings. Evon already had claimed a small portion of the money from the joint tenancy accounts by that time and was working on obtaining the remainder of the $270,000 in the week following the settlement. The evidence supports the Commission's finding that Potts knew of Evon's fraudulent conduct in misrepresenting to the other parties and the court her intent to secure the joint tenancy accounts outside the settlement.

¶ 58 Finally, Potts argues that his conduct did not constitute fraud under the definition provided in the April 1, 2004, amendments to the M.R.P.C. We note first that the ODC never accused Potts of fraud. The ODC accused Potts of assisting his clients in engaging in fraudulent conduct. Second, we note that the M.R.P.C., as they existed in 2001, at the time of the conduct in question, provided no definition of fraud or fraudulent conduct. As stated in ¶¶ 47–48, we conclude, however, that Potts's clients, Evon and Tyson, knowingly misrepresented the truth in order to prompt the other parties to the settlement to act to their detriment. In particular, Tyson directed Potts not to respond to Tremper's letter that had asked for confirmation on the settlement amount. Potts did more than acquiesce to his client's demands of silence in the face of Tremper's inquiries. Potts assisted in his clients' fraud by drafting, circulating, and filing with the court a stipulation, stating that all disputes had been settled, when he knew that the other parties had relied on Evon's misrepresentation of the settlement basis in reaching the agreement. We agree with the Commission's conclusion that Potts violated Rule 1.2(d), M.R.P.C.

¶ 59 *Whether Potts violated Rule 3.3(a)(2), M.R.P.C.*

¶ 60 Potts argues that he could not have violated Rule 3.3(a)(2), M.R.P.C., because his clients were not engaging in continuing fraudulent acts and Potts was not assisting in such fraudulent acts. Potts further argues that he did not know at the time that his clients' conduct was fraudulent.

¶ 61 Rule 3.3(a)(2), M.R.P.C., sets forth the duty of candor toward the tribunal and prohibits a lawyer from knowingly failing "to disclose a material fact to a tribunal when disclosure is necessary to avoid assisting a criminal or fraudulent act by the client." As stated in ¶¶ 47–48, Potts's clients engaged in fraudulent conduct that intended to deceive the other parties as to the scope of the settlement. Potts assisted in their deception.

¶ 62 Potts also violated the duty of candor toward the tribunal when he failed to disclose to the court the material fact that, contrary to what the parties believed, Evon planned on taking the joint tenancy accounts. Tremper's letter notified Potts that the settlement basis was at issue. Potts acknowledged the fact that the value of the settlement would have to be cleared up "sooner or later." At his client's request, Potts said nothing to Tremper about the potential misunderstanding. Knowing that this ambiguity existed in the memorandum, Potts nevertheless proceeded to misrepresent in the signed stipulation to the court that "all" disputes had been settled, when in fact they were just beginning to brew under the surface. The stipulation caused the parties to forge ahead with the settlement, even though Potts and his clients knew that no agreement had been reached on the settlement amount.

¶ 63 Tremper's letter put Potts on notice that the parties were relying on Evon's $1.2 million final inventory as the value of the settlement when they signed the stipulation drafted by Potts and filed it with the district court. Potts did not report to the district court in the stipulation that Evon had taken some, and planned to take the rest, of the joint tenancy accounts outside the $1.2 million settlement. Potts had a duty of truthfulness in filing or representing any matter to the court. Potts's failure to do so violated Rule 3.3(a)(2), M.R.P.C.

¶ 64 *Whether the Commission improperly excluded Potts's proposed expert witness testimony.*

¶ 65 Potts argues that he should have been allowed to present expert witness testimony at his disciplinary hearing on the interplay between the duty of confidentiality and the duty of candor as stated in the M.R.P.C. The Montana Rules of Evidence apply to formal disciplinary proceedings before the Commission. Rule 12(C)(2), MRLDE. Under Rule 702, M.R. Evid., a party may offer expert testimony to assist the trier of fact in understanding the evidence or determining a fact in issue. Expert opinions that state a legal conclusion or apply the law to the facts are inadmissible. *Perdue v. Gagnon Farms, Inc.*, 2003 MT 47, ¶ 28, 314 Mont. 303, ¶ 28, 65 P.3d 570, ¶ 28. Potts disclosed to the Commission that the expert witness would opine that Potts did not violate the Rules of

Professional Conduct. The Commission properly excluded Potts's expert testimony as improperly offering an opinion on a legal question. *Perdue*, ¶ 28.

¶ 66 *Whether the Commission improperly excluded a portion of Potts's testimony as inadmissible hearsay.*

¶ 67 Potts argues that the Commission improperly excluded as hearsay his testimony regarding what Tremper had told him concerning the joint tenancy accounts. Potts testified that Tremper stated, three days before the parties signed the stipulation, that Tremper was "going after" the joint tenancy accounts if the case did not settle immediately. The Commission struck this statement from Potts's testimony on grounds that it constituted inadmissible hearsay. Potts argues that the statement does not qualify as hearsay because he did not offer the comment to prove the truth of the matter asserted—that Tremper would go after the joint tenancy accounts. He contends that he offered the statement instead to show Tremper's knowledge that the joint tenancy accounts existed and that the parties intended to exclude the accounts from the settlement.

¶ 68 Hearsay is "a statement, other than the one made by the declarant while testifying at the trial or hearing, offered in evidence to prove the truth of the matter asserted." Rule 801(c), M.R. Evid. Hearsay is inadmissible unless the Montana Rules of Evidence provide an exception. Rule 802, M.R. Evid. A statement offered to show the effect on the witness, but not for the truth of the matter asserted, falls outside of the definition of hearsay. *Vincelette v. Metropolitan Life Ins., Co.,* 1998 MT 259, ¶ 19, 291 Mont. 261, ¶ 19, 968 P.2d 275, ¶ 19.

¶ 69 Potts appears to have offered the statement to demonstrate Tremper's alleged knowledge that the parties had intended to exclude the joint tenancy accounts from the settlement, and not for the truth of the matter asserted that Tremper would go after the joint tenancy accounts. Potts offered Tremper's statement to explain its effect on him, showing why he believed the joint tenancy accounts were separate from the settlement. For that reason, we conclude that the statement falls outside the definition of hearsay and that the Commission should have allowed it in evidence at Potts's disciplinary hearing. *Vincelette*, ¶ 19

¶ 70 We also conclude, however, that improperly excluding the statement does not warrant reversal of the Commission's decision. An error must cause substantial prejudice to warrant reversal. *See In re A.J.E.,* 2006 MT 41, ¶ 28, 331 Mont. 198, ¶ 28, 130 P.3d 612, ¶ 28. The Commission's error in excluding the statement did not substantially prejudice Potts.

¶ 71 Tremper admitted on direct examination that he knew the joint tenancy accounts existed, but he believed them to be included in the settlement to satisfy Evon's alleged self dealing in the conservatorship proceedings. Tremper stated this belief in a letter to Potts dated November 20, 2001, that the Commission admitted into evidence at Potts's disciplinary hearing. Potts admitted that he did not respond to the letter. The nonresponse reasonably caused Tremper to believe that the parties intended to include the joint tenancy accounts in the settlement.

¶ 72 Tremper's knowledge of the joint tenancy accounts before the settlement conference does not change the fact that Potts later made a false representation to the court in the stipulation. The stipulation wrongfully reported to the court that the parties had resolved all of the disputes surrounding the will contest and conservatorship. Tremper's letter informed Potts as to Tremper's belief that the settlement included the joint tenancy accounts. Potts ignored Tremper's inquiry. He proceeded to represent falsely in the stipulation to the court that the parties had resolved all the disputes surrounding the will contest and conservatorship.

¶ 73 *Whether the Commission's proposed sanctions are appropriate.*

¶ 74 Potts urges the Court to consider the mitigating factors as stated in the 1991 American Bar Association Standards for Imposing Lawyer Sanctions when determining the appropriateness of his discipline. Under ABA § 9.32, mitigating factors include: 1) the absence of prior discipline; 2) absence of a dishonest or selfish motive; 3) full and free disclosure and cooperative attitude toward the proceedings; and 4) character and reputation.

¶ 75 Potts contends that he has satisfied all the mitigating factors, including maintaining good character and reputation as an attorney since becoming a member of the State Bar of Montana in 1986. He argues that this factor renders a public censure unwarranted. The Commission responds that Potts's transgression includes aggravating factors, such as dishonesty, that warrant the imposition of a 30-day suspension from the practice of law or even harsher discipline.

¶ 76 We consider the following factors in determining the appropriate discipline for lawyer misconduct: 1) the duty violated; 2) the lawyer's mental state; 3) the actual or potential injury caused by the lawyer's misconduct; and 4) the existence of aggravating or mitigating factors. Rule 9(B), MRLDE. We conclude that public censure is appropriate in light of Potts's misconduct in this matter and other mitigating circumstances.

¶ 77 The evidence clearly demonstrates that Potts assisted his clients in their fraudulent conduct by misrepresenting the scope of the settlement to the other parties, a violation of Rule 1.2(d), M.R.P.C. The evidence also supports the conclusion that Potts misrepresented to the district court that all disputes had been settled when in fact he knew that the settlement agreement lacked the requisite meeting of the minds to be enforceable, a violation of Rule 3.3(a)(2), M.R.P.C. Potts's misconduct resulted in considerable injury to the parties, requiring one district court proceeding and two appeals to this Court to determine the meaning and scope of the memorandum and stipulation.

¶ 78 The first sentence of the preamble to the M.R.P.C. (2005) states that a lawyer must "pursue the truth." The duties of candor toward the tribunal under Rule 3.3(a), M.R.P.C., and the prohibition against assisting in a client's fraudulent conduct under Rule 1.2(d), M.R.P.C., guide the lawyer in this quest for truth. In breaching this fundamental tenet, Potts shunned his most basic responsibility owed to the profession.

¶ 79 This level of misconduct ordinarily would draw punishment in the form of suspension from the practice of law or disbarment. Mitigating factors warrant a lighter penalty in this case. First, the evidence shows that the parties entered into a vague settlement agreement that failed to define the basis and scope of the agreement. Potts certainly took advantage of this rushed agreement for his clients' benefit and against the duty of truthfulness incumbent upon a lawyer. Potts should not carry all the blame, however, for the extra litigation resulting from the vague agreement. Though we do not condone Potts's conduct in this matter, we recognize that the other parties could have resolved the question of the basis and scope of the settlement by specifically assigning a dollar amount to the estate value in the memorandum. Next, Potts benefits from the fact that the district court limited the actual damage caused by his misconduct. The district court determined that Potts's clients, Evon, had no right to the joint tenancy accounts in light of the parties' reliance on the $1.2 million total estate value. As a result, the actual damages occasioned by Potts's misconduct take the form of increased litigation costs rather than the hundreds of thousands of dollars of which the parties to the settlement agreement would have been deprived. Finally, the absence of any prior discipline against Potts and his character and good reputation to this point militate in his favor.

¶ 80 In light of these mitigating factors, especially Potts's history of compliance with the rules of professional conduct and his character and good reputation to this point, we determine that the Commission's recommendation to suspend Potts from practice is unwarranted. We conclude that a public censure will apprise Potts sufficiently of the gravity of his misconduct under the given circumstances. Moreover, a public censure will alert the public that the

Court will not tolerate such misconduct from a lawyer. We also order Potts to pay the costs of the disciplinary proceedings before the Commission.

ORDER

THEREFORE IT IS ORDERED:

¶ 81 1.   Steven T. Potts is ordered to appear before the Supreme Court of the State of Montana on May 2, 2007, at 1:30 p.m., for the administration of a public censure;

¶ 82 2.   Steven T. Potts shall pay, or make arrangements to pay, the costs of the proceedings before the Commission. Pursuant to Rule 9(A)(8), MRLDE, Disciplinary Counsel is directed to assemble and serve upon Steven T. Potts an itemized list of the costs and expenses incurred in this matter. Steven T. Potts shall then have 10 days thereafter to file written objections and, if he desires, to request a hearing before an Adjudicatory Panel;

¶ 83 3.   It is further ordered that Potts's Motion to Strike Portions of ODC's Brief, filed with this Court on August 10, 2006, is denied;

¶ 84 4.   The Clerk of this Court is directed to mail copies of this Order to Steven T. Potts by certified mail, return receipt requested, and by ordinary mail to Steven T. Potts's attorney, the Chairman and the Secretary of the Commission on Practice, the Clerk of the Federal District Court for the District of Montana, the Clerk of the Circuit Court of Appeals of the Ninth Circuit, the Office of Disciplinary Counsel, the Executive Director of the State Bar of Montana, and by electronic transmission to all Clerks of the District Courts of the State of Montana and to all District Judges.

/s/Brian Morris

/s/John Warner

/s/Jeffrey M. Sherlock

District Court Judge Jeffrey M. Sherlock sitting for Justice W. William Leaphart

/s/Kurt Krueger

District Court Judge Kurt Krueger sitting for Justice James C. Nelson

---

SOLUTIONS: THE LAWYER SHOULD HAVE, WOULD HAVE, COULD HAVE. . .

Be honest. Be transparent. Be candid. Know that the client is not always right. Know that your judgment is valuable. Know that it is your law license to keep or to lose.

A public reprimand in some jurisdictions is no walk in the park. The lawyer is required to physically go to the state Supreme Court to be admonished by the justices. Click this link to watch how it played out for one Florida lawyer who was later disbarred.

https://www.youtube.com/watch?v=rscvOFekUV4

A. Cross Cultural Issues in Negotiations

X-Ray Questions

As we have discussed, communication is essential for lawyers. This is true not only in client counseling but in the resolution process as well. The following article gives insight into culture and resolution. The ability to skillfully use cultural competence comes into play at mediations because knowledge of the law and our court system intersects with how litigants view negotiations and resolutions through their cultural prism.

Do you consider yourself to come from a high context or a low context culture? From one that values the specific expression or the ambiguous evasion? How have these concepts played out in your life? Do you see how they would play out in the conflict resolution process?

Section 6.   Criminal Law and Pre-Trial Considerations

Now we shift gears to the area of criminal law and the ethical questions driven by Constitutional law principals. While MR 3.6 applies to both civil and criminal matters, its focus is in the criminal law area.

Model Rule 3.6: Trial Publicity & Criminal Matters

(a)   A lawyer who is participating or has participated in the investigation or litigation of a matter shall not make an extrajudicial statement that the lawyer knows or reasonably should know will be disseminated by means of public communication and will have a substantial likelihood of materially prejudicing an adjudicative proceeding in the matter.

(b)   Notwithstanding paragraph (a), a lawyer may state:

(1)   the claim, offense or defense involved and, except when prohibited by law, the identity of the persons involved;

(2)   information contained in a public record;

(3)   that an investigation of a matter is in progress;

(4)   the scheduling or result of any step in litigation;

(5)   a request for assistance in obtaining evidence and information necessary thereto;

(6)   a warning of danger concerning the behavior of a person involved, when there is reason to believe that there exists the likelihood of substantial harm to an individual or to the public interest; and

(7)   in a criminal case, in addition to subparagraphs (1) through (6):

i.   the identity, residence, occupation and family status of the accused;

ii.   if the accused has not been apprehended, information necessary to aid in apprehension of that person;

iii.   the fact, time and place of arrest; and

iv.   the identity of investigating and arresting officers or agencies and the length of the investigation.

(c)   Notwithstanding paragraph (a), a lawyer may make a statement that a reasonable lawyer would believe is required to protect a client from the substantial undue prejudicial effect of recent publicity not initiated by the lawyer or the lawyer's client. A statement made pursuant to this paragraph shall be limited to such information as is necessary to mitigate the recent adverse publicity.

(d)   No lawyer associated in a firm or government agency with a lawyer subject to paragraph (a) shall make a statement prohibited by paragraph (a).

Deconstruction Exercise/Rule Rationale

The key issue is set out in the first line to the Comments "It is difficult to strike a balance between protecting the right to a fair trial and safeguarding the right to free expression." This theme threads its way through the Rules and resurfaces in the conflict between lawyer advertising with the right to free expression of lawyers colliding with the need to protect the consumer (i.e. prospective clients).

For now, let's unpack subsection (a). Coverage? "Or" does its usual job of expanding coverage; here not only to lawyers who are currently engaged in the investigation or litigation of a matter (civil or criminal) but to those who were previously so engaged.

What is prohibited? Statements made by the lawyer or at the lawyer's behest outside the judicial process, involving a proceeding that will determine the legal rights and consequences, that the lawyer knows or should know will be spread out into the public sphere by means of "public communication." The drafters could have used a narrower term than "public communication"—such as "media"—but that would imply television and newspapers when the vectors of public communication are much broader. But the lawyer is only sanctioned if the communication will (not perhaps or likely) have a "substantial likelihood" (less than "certainty" but several notches above "possibility") and then only of "materially prejudicing" the adjudicative proceeding. It is the last phrasing which truly strikes the balance between these tights.

Cases and Materials

X-Ray Questions (*Gentile*)

The following case involves the conflict between the right of free expression versus the legal system's interest in litigating cases through the proper judicial process, not through the press. Here are the facts. Dominic Gentile was a criminal defense lawyer in Las Vegas. He represented a person accused of theft. Based upon his investigation, he concluded that two police officers were more likely the culprits. Because trial of his client was not imminent, and because he wanted to stem speculation on guilt that was focused on his client, he held a press conference and laid out his theory. The Nevada Bar Association was less than pleased and the matter found its way to the Supreme Court of the United States. The case changed the types of extrajudicial judicial statements that lawyers could make. How does the Court frame the conflict? What policy considerations are implicated? How does the Court balance these competing values? The rule as it now exists has a safe harbor provision explicitly identifying appropriate public statements.

Gentile v. State Bar of Nevada

Supreme Court of the United States, 1991.
501 U.S. 1030.

Opinion

JUSTICE KENNEDY announced the judgment of the Court and delivered the opinion of the Court with respect to Parts III and VI, and an opinion with respect to Parts I, II, IV, and V in which JUSTICE MARSHALL, JUSTICE BLACKMUN, and JUSTICE STEVENS join.

Hours after his client was indicted on criminal charges, petitioner Gentile, who is a member of the Bar of the State of Nevada, held a press conference. He made a prepared statement, which we set forth in Appendix A to this opinion, and then he responded to questions. We refer to most of those questions and responses in the course of our opinion.

Some six months later, the criminal case was tried to a jury and the client was acquitted on all counts. The State Bar of Nevada then filed a complaint against petitioner, alleging a violation of Nevada Supreme Court Rule 177, a rule governing pretrial publicity almost identical to ABA Model Rule of Professional Conduct 3.6. We set forth the full text of Rule 177 in Appendix B. Rule 177(1) prohibits an attorney from making "an extrajudicial statement that a reasonable person would expect to be disseminated by means of public communication if the lawyer knows or reasonably should know that it will have a substantial likelihood of materially prejudicing an adjudicative proceeding." Rule 177(2) lists a number of statements that are "ordinarily . . . likely" to result in material prejudice. Rule 177(3) provides a safe harbor for the attorney, listing a number of statements that can be made without fear of discipline notwithstanding the other parts of the Rule.

Following a hearing, the Southern Nevada Disciplinary Board of the State Bar found that Gentile had made the statements in question and concluded that he violated Rule 177. The board recommended a private reprimand. Petitioner appealed to the Nevada Supreme Court, waiving the confidentiality of the disciplinary proceeding, and the Nevada court affirmed the decision of the board.

Nevada's application of Rule 177 in this case violates the First Amendment. Petitioner spoke at a time and in a manner that neither in law nor in fact created any threat of real prejudice to his client's right to a fair trial or to the State's interest in the enforcement of its criminal laws. Furthermore, the Rule's safe harbor provision, Rule 177(3), appears to permit the speech in question, and Nevada's decision to discipline petitioner in spite of that provision raises concerns of vagueness and selective enforcement.

I

The matter before us does not call into question the constitutionality of other States' prohibitions upon an attorney's speech that will have a "substantial likelihood of materially prejudicing an adjudicative proceeding," but is limited to Nevada's interpretation of that standard. On the other hand, one central point must dominate the analysis: this case involves classic political speech. The State Bar of Nevada reprimanded petitioner for his assertion, supported by a brief sketch of his client's defense, that the State sought the indictment and conviction of an innocent man as a "scapegoat" and had not "been honest enough to indict the people who did it; the police department, crooked cops." See *infra*, Appendix A. At issue here is the constitutionality of a ban on political speech critical of the government and its officials.

A

Unlike other First Amendment cases this Term in which speech is not the direct target of the regulation or statute in question, see, *e.g.*, *Barnes v. Glen Theatre, Inc.*, 501 U.S. 560, 111 S.Ct. 2456, 115 L.Ed.2d 504 (1991) (ban on nude barroom dancing); *Leathers v. Medlock*, 499 U.S. 439, 111 S.Ct. 1438, 113 L.Ed.2d 494 (1991) (sales tax on cable and satellite television), this case involves punishment of pure speech in the political forum. Petitioner engaged not in solicitation of clients or advertising for his practice, as in our precedents from which some of our colleagues would discern a standard of diminished First Amendment protection. His words were directed at public officials and their conduct in office.

There is no question that speech critical of the exercise of the State's power lies at the very center of the First Amendment. Nevada seeks to punish the dissemination of information relating to alleged governmental misconduct, which only last Term we described as "speech which has traditionally been recognized as lying at the core of the First Amendment." *Butterworth v. Smith*, 494 U.S. 624, 632, 110 S.Ct. 1376, 1381, 108 L.Ed.2d 572 (1990).

The judicial system, and in particular our criminal justice courts, play a vital part in a democratic state, and the public has a legitimate interest in their operations. See, *e.g.*, *Landmark Communications, Inc. v. Virginia*, 435 U.S. 829, 838–839, 98 S.Ct. 1535, 1541–1542, 56 L.Ed.2d 1 (1978). "[I]t would be difficult to single out any aspect of government of higher concern and importance to the people than the manner in which criminal trials are conducted." *Richmond Newspapers, Inc. v. Virginia,* 448 U.S. 555, 575, 100 S.Ct. 2814, 2826, 65 L.Ed.2d 973 (1980). Public vigilance serves us well, for "[t]he knowledge that every criminal trial is subject to contemporaneous review in the forum of public opinion is an effective restraint on possible abuse of judicial power. . . . Without publicity, all other checks are insufficient: in comparison of publicity, all other checks are of small account." *In re Oliver,* 333 U.S. 257, 270–271, 68 S.Ct. 499, 506–507, 92 L.Ed. 682 (1948). As we said in *Bridges v. California,* 314 U.S. 252, 62 S.Ct. 190, 86 L.Ed. 192 (1941), limits upon public comment about pending cases are

"likely to fall not only at a crucial time but upon the most important topics of discussion. . . .

"No suggestion can be found in the Constitution that the freedom there guaranteed for speech and the press bears an inverse ratio to the timeliness and importance of the ideas seeking expression." *Id.,* at 268–269, 62 S.Ct., at 196–197.

In *Sheppard v. Maxwell,* 384 U.S. 333, 350, 86 S.Ct. 1507, 1515, 16 L.Ed.2d 600 (1966), we reminded that "[t]he press . . . guards against the miscarriage of justice by subjecting the police, prosecutors, and judicial processes to extensive public scrutiny and criticism."

Public awareness and criticism have even greater importance where, as here, they concern allegations of police corruption, see *Nebraska Press Assn. v. Stuart,* 427 U.S. 539, 606, 96 S.Ct. 2791, 2825, 49 L.Ed.2d 683 (1976) (Brennan, J., concurring in judgment) ("[C]ommentary on the fact that there is strong evidence implicating a government official in criminal activity goes to the very core of matters of public concern"), or where, as is also the present circumstance, the criticism questions the judgment of an elected public prosecutor. Our system grants prosecutors vast discretion at all stages of the criminal process, see *Morrison v. Olson,* 487 U.S. 654, 727–728, 108 S.Ct. 2597, 2637–2638, 101 L.Ed.2d 569 (1988) (SCALIA, J., dissenting). The public has an interest in its responsible exercise.

B

We are not called upon to determine the constitutionality of the ABA Model Rule of Professional Conduct 3.6 (1981), but only Rule 177as it has been interpreted and applied by the State of Nevada. Model Rule 3.6's requirement of substantial likelihood of material prejudice is not necessarily flawed.

Interpreted in a proper and narrow manner, for instance, to prevent an attorney of record from releasing information of grave prejudice on the eve of jury selection, the phrase substantial likelihood of material prejudice might punish only speech that creates a danger of imminent and substantial harm. A rule governing speech, even speech entitled to full constitutional protection, need not use the words "clear and present danger" in order to pass constitutional muster.

> "Mr. Justice Holmes' test was never intended 'to express a technical legal doctrine or to convey a formula for adjudicating cases.' *Pennekamp v. Florida*, 328 U.S. 331, 353 [66 S.Ct. 1029, 1040, 90 L.Ed. 1295] (1946) (Frankfurter, J., concurring). Properly applied, the test requires a court to make its own inquiry into the imminence and magnitude of the danger said to flow from the particular utterance and then to balance the character of the evil, as well as its likelihood, against the need for free and unfettered expression. The possibility that other measures will serve the State's interests should also be weighed." *Landmark Communications, Inc. v. Virginia, supra*, 435 U.S., at 842–843, 98 S.Ct., at 1543–1544.

The drafters of Model Rule 3.6 apparently thought the substantial likelihood of material prejudice formulation approximated the clear and present danger test. See ABA Annotated Model Rules of Professional Conduct 243 (1984) ("formulation in Model Rule 3.6 incorporates a standard approximating clear and present danger by focusing on the likelihood of injury and its substantiality"; citing *Landmark Communications, supra*, at 844, 98 S.Ct., at 1544; *Wood v. Georgia*, 370 U.S. 375, 82 S.Ct. 1364, 8 L.Ed.2d 569 (1962); and *Bridges v. California, supra*, 314 U.S., at 273, 62 S.Ct., at 198, for guidance in determining whether statement "poses a sufficiently serious and imminent threat to the fair administration of justice"); G. Hazard & W. Hodes, The Law of Lawyering: A Handbook on the Model Rules of Professional Conduct 397 (1985) ("To use traditional terminology, the danger of prejudice to a proceeding must be both clear (material) and present (substantially likely)"); *In re Hinds*, 90 N.J. 604, 622, 449 A.2d 483, 493 (1982) (substantial likelihood of material prejudice standard is a linguistic equivalent of clear and present danger).

The difference between the requirement of serious and imminent threat found in the disciplinary rules of some States and the more common formulation of substantial likelihood of material prejudice could prove mere semantics. Each standard requires an assessment of proximity and degree of harm. Each may be capable of valid application. Under those principles, nothing inherent in Nevada's formulation fails First Amendment review; but as this case demonstrates, Rule 177 has not been interpreted in conformance with those principles by the Nevada Supreme Court.

II

Even if one were to accept respondent's argument that lawyers participating in judicial proceedings may be subjected, consistent with the First Amendment, to speech restrictions that could not be imposed on the press or general public, the judgment should not be upheld. The record does not support the conclusion that petitioner knew or reasonably should have known his remarks created a substantial likelihood of material prejudice, if the Rule's terms are given any meaningful content.

We have held that "in cases raising First Amendment issues . . . an appellate court has an obligation to 'make an independent examination of the whole record' in order to make sure that 'the judgment does not constitute a forbidden intrusion on the field of free expression.' " *Bose Corp. v. Consumers Union of United States, Inc.,* 466 U.S. 485, 499, 104 S.Ct. 1949, 1958, 80 L.Ed.2d 502 (1984) (quoting *New York Times Co. v. Sullivan,* 376 U.S. 254, 284–286, 84 S.Ct. 710, 728–729, 11 L.Ed.2d 686 (1964)).

Neither the disciplinary board nor the reviewing court explains any sense in which petitioner's statements had a substantial likelihood of causing material prejudice. The only evidence against Gentile was the videotape of his statements and his own testimony at the disciplinary hearing. The Bar's whole case rests on the fact of the statements, the time they were made, and petitioner's own justifications. Full deference to these factual findings does not justify abdication of our responsibility to determine whether petitioner's statements can be punished consistent with First Amendment standards.

Rather, this Court is

"compelled to examine for [itself] the statements in issue and the circumstances under which they were made to see whether or not they do carry a threat of clear and present danger to the impartiality and good order of the courts or whether they are of a character which the principles of the First Amendment, as adopted by the Due Process Clause of the Fourteenth Amendment, protect." *Pennekamp v. Florida,* 328 U.S. 331, 335, 66 S.Ct. 1029, 1031, 90 L.Ed. 1295 (1946).

" 'Whenever the fundamental rights of free speech . . . are alleged to have been invaded, it must remain open to a defendant to present the issue whether there actually did exist at the time a clear danger; whether the danger, if any, was imminent; and whether the evil apprehended was one so substantial as to justify the stringent restriction interposed by the legislature.' " *Landmark Communications, Inc. v. Virginia,* 435 U.S., at 844, 98 S.Ct., at 1544 (quoting *Whitney v. California,* 274 U.S. 357, 378–379, 47 S.Ct. 641, 649–650, 71 L.Ed. 1095 (1927) (Brandeis, J., concurring)).

Whether one applies the standard set out in *Landmark Communications* or the lower standard our colleagues find permissible, an examination of the record reveals no basis for the Nevada court's conclusion that the speech presented a substantial likelihood of material prejudice.

Our decision earlier this Term in *Mu'Min v. Virginia,* 500 U.S. 415, 111 S.Ct. 1899, 114 L.Ed.2d 493 (1991), provides a pointed contrast to respondent's contention in this case. There, the community had been subjected to a barrage of publicity prior to Mu'Min's trial for capital murder. News stories appeared over a course of several months and included, in addition to details of the crime itself, numerous items of prejudicial information inadmissible at trial. Eight of the twelve individuals seated on Mu'Min's jury admitted some exposure to pretrial publicity. We held that the publicity did not rise even to a level requiring questioning of individual jurors about the content of publicity. In light of that holding, the Nevada court's conclusion that petitioner's abbreviated, general comments six months before trial created a "substantial likelihood of materially prejudicing" the proceeding is, to say the least, most unconvincing.

A.

Pre-Indictment Publicity. On January 31, 1987, undercover police officers with the Las Vegas Metropolitan Police Department (Metro) reported large amounts of cocaine (four kilograms) and travelers' checks (almost $300,000) missing from a safety deposit vault at Western Vault Corporation. The drugs and money had been used as part of an undercover operation conducted by Metro's Intelligence Bureau. Petitioner's client, Grady Sanders, owned Western Vault. John Moran, the Las Vegas sheriff, reported the theft at a press conference on February 2, 1987, naming the police and Western Vault employees as suspects.

Although two police officers, Detective Steve Scholl and Sargeant Ed Schaub, enjoyed free access to the deposit box throughout the period of the theft, and no log reported comings and goings at the vault, a series of press reports over the following year indicated that investigators did not consider these officers responsible. Instead, investigators focused upon Western Vault and its owner. Newspaper reports quoted the sheriff and other high police officials as saying that they had not lost confidence in the "elite" Intelligence Bureau. From the beginning, Sheriff Moran had "complete faith and trust" in his officers. App. 85.

The media reported that, following announcement of the cocaine theft, others with deposit boxes at Western Vault had come forward to claim missing items. One man claimed the theft of his life savings of $90,000. *Id.,* at 89. Western Vault suffered heavy losses as customers terminated their box rentals, and the company soon went out of business. The police opened other boxes in search of the missing items, and it was reported they seized $264,900 in United States currency from a box listed as unrented.

Initial press reports stated that Sanders and Western Vault were being cooperative; but as time went on, the press noted that the police investigation had failed to identify the culprit and through a process of elimination was beginning to point toward Sanders. Reports quoted the affidavit of a detective that the theft was part of an effort to discredit the undercover operation and that business records suggested the existence of a business relation between Sanders and the targets of a Metro undercover probe. *Id.,* at 85.

The deputy police chief announced the two detectives with access to the vault had been "cleared" as possible suspects. According to an unnamed "source close to the investigation," the police shifted from the idea that the thief had planned to discredit the undercover operation to the theory that the thief had unwittingly stolen from the police. The stories noted that Sanders "could not be reached for comment." *Id.,* at 93.

The story took a more sensational turn with reports that the two police suspects had been cleared by police investigators after passing lie detector tests. The tests were administered by one Ray Slaughter. But later, the Federal Bureau of Investigation (FBI) arrested Slaughter for distributing cocaine to an FBI informant, Belinda Antal. It was also reported that the $264,900 seized from the unrented safety deposit box at Western Vault had been stored there in a suitcase owned by one Tammy Sue Markham. Markham was "facing a number of federal drug-related charges" in Tucson, Arizona. Markham reported items missing from three boxes she rented at Western Vault, as did one Beatrice Connick, who, according to press reports, was a Colombian national living in San Diego and "not facing any drug related charges." (As it turned out, petitioner impeached Connick's credibility at trial with the existence of a money laundering conviction.) Connick also was reported to have taken and passed a lie detector test to substantiate her charges. *Id.,* at 94–97. Finally, press reports indicated that

Sanders had refused to take a police polygraph examination. *Id.,* at 41. The press suggested that the FBI suspected Metro officers were responsible for the theft, and reported that the theft had severely damaged relations between the FBI and Metro.

B.

The Press Conference. Petitioner is a Las Vegas criminal defense attorney, an author of articles about criminal law and procedure, and a former associate dean of the National College for Criminal Defense Lawyers and Public Defenders. *Id.,* at 36–38. Through leaks from the police department, he had some advance notice of the date an indictment would be returned and the nature of the charges against Sanders. Petitioner had monitored the publicity surrounding the case, and, prior to the indictment, was personally aware of at least 17 articles in the major local newspapers, the Las Vegas Sun and Las Vegas Review-Journal, and numerous local television news stories which reported on the Western Vault theft and ensuing investigation. *Id.,* at 38–39; see Respondent's Exhibit A, before Disciplinary Board. Petitioner determined, for the first time in his career, that he would call a formal press conference. He did not blunder into a press conference, but acted with considerable deliberation.

1.

Petitioner's Motivation. As petitioner explained to the disciplinary board, his primary motivation was the concern that, unless some of the weaknesses in the State's case were made public, a potential jury venire would be poisoned by repetition in the press of information being released by the police and prosecutors, in particular the repeated press reports about polygraph tests and the fact that the two police officers were no longer suspects. App. 40–42. Respondent distorts Rule 177when it suggests this explanation admits a purpose to prejudice the venire and so proves a violation of the Rule. Rule 177 only prohibits the dissemination of information that one knows or reasonably should know has a "substantial likelihood of materially prejudicing an adjudicative proceeding." Petitioner did not indicate he thought he could sway the pool of potential jurors to form an opinion in advance of the trial, nor did he seek to discuss evidence that would be inadmissible at trial. He sought only to counter publicity already deemed prejudicial. The Southern Nevada Disciplinary Board so found. It said petitioner attempted

> "(i) to counter public opinion which he perceived as adverse to Mr. Sanders, (ii) . . . to refute certain matters regarding his client which had appeared in the media, (iii) to fight back against the perceived efforts

of the prosecution to poison the prospective juror pool, and (iv) to publicly present Sanders' side of the case." App. 3–4.

Far from an admission that he sought to "materially prejudic[e] an adjudicative proceeding," petitioner sought only to stop a wave of publicity he perceived as prejudicing potential jurors against his client and injuring his client's reputation in the community.

Petitioner gave a second reason for holding the press conference, which demonstrates the additional value of his speech. Petitioner acted in part because the investigation had taken a serious toll on his client. Sanders was "not a man in good health," having suffered multiple open-heart surgeries prior to these events. *Id.*, at 41. And prior to indictment, the mere suspicion of wrongdoing had caused the closure of Western Vault and the loss of Sanders' ground lease on an Atlantic City, New Jersey, property. *Ibid.*

An attorney's duties do not begin inside the courtroom door. He or she cannot ignore the practical implications of a legal proceeding for the client. Just as an attorney may recommend a plea bargain or civil settlement to avoid the adverse consequences of a possible loss after trial, so too an attorney may take reasonable steps to defend a client's reputation and reduce the adverse consequences of indictment, especially in the face of a prosecution deemed unjust or commenced with improper motives. A defense attorney may pursue lawful strategies to obtain dismissal of an indictment or reduction of charges, including an attempt to demonstrate in the court of public opinion that the client does not deserve to be tried.

2.

Petitioner's Investigation of Rule 177. Rule 177 is phrased in terms of what an attorney "knows or reasonably should know." On the evening before the press conference, petitioner and two colleagues spent several hours researching the extent of an attorney's obligations under Rule 177. He decided, as we have held, see *Patton v. Yount*, 467 U.S. 1025, 104 S.Ct. 2885, 81 L.Ed.2d 847 (1984), that the timing of a statement was crucial in the assessment of possible prejudice and the Rule's application, accord, *Stroble v. California*, 343 U.S. 181, 191–194, 72 S.Ct. 599, 604–606, 96 L.Ed. 872 (1952). App. 44.

Upon return of the indictment, the court set a trial date for August 1988, some six months in the future. Petitioner knew, at the time of his statement, that a jury would not be empaneled for six months at the earliest, if ever. He recalled reported cases finding no prejudice resulting from juror exposure to "far worse" information two and four months before trial, and concluded that his proposed statement was not substantially likely to result in material prejudice. *Ibid.*

A statement which reaches the attention of the venire on the eve of *voir dire* might require a continuance or cause difficulties in securing an impartial jury, and at the very least could complicate the jury selection process. See ABA Annotated Model Rules of Professional Conduct 243 (1984) (timing of statement a significant factor in determining seriousness and imminence of threat). As turned out to be the case here, exposure to the same statement six months prior to trial would not result in prejudice, the content fading from memory long before the trial date.

In 1988, Clark County, Nevada, had population in excess of 600,000 persons. Given the size of the community from which any potential jury venire would be drawn and the length of time before trial, only the most damaging of information could give rise to any likelihood of prejudice. The innocuous content of petitioner's statements reinforces my conclusion.

3.

The Content of Petitioner's Statements. Petitioner was disciplined for statements to the effect that (1) the evidence demonstrated his client's innocence, (2) the likely thief was a police detective, Steve Scholl, and (3) the other victims were not credible, as most were drug dealers or convicted money launderers, all but one of whom had only accused Sanders in response to police pressure, in the process of "trying to work themselves out of something." Appendix A, *infra,* at 2736. App. 2–3 (Findings and Recommendation of the State Bar of Nevada, Southern Nevada Disciplinary Board). He also strongly implied that Steve Scholl could be observed in a videotape suffering from symptoms of cocaine use. Of course, only a small fraction of petitioner's remarks were disseminated to the public, in two newspaper stories and two television news broadcasts.

The stories mentioned not only Gentile's press conference but also a prosecution response and police press conference. See App. 127–129, 131–132; Respondent's Exhibit A, before Disciplinary Board. The chief deputy district attorney was quoted as saying that this was a legitimate indictment, and that prosecutors cannot bring an indictment to court unless they can prove the charges in it beyond a reasonable doubt. App. 128–129. Deputy Police Chief Sullivan stated for the police department: " 'We in Metro are very satisfied our officers (Scholl and Sgt. Ed Schaub) had nothing to do with this theft or any other. They are both above reproach. Both are veteran police officers who are dedicated to honest law enforcement.' " *Id.,* at 129. In the context of general public awareness, these police and prosecution statements were no more likely to result in prejudice than were petitioner's statements, but given the repetitive publicity from the police investigation, it is difficult to come to any conclusion but that the balance remained in favor of the prosecution.

Much of the information provided by petitioner had been published in one form or another, obviating any potential for prejudice. See ABA Annotated Model Rules of Professional Conduct 243 (1984) (extent to which information already circulated significant factor in determining likelihood of prejudice). The remainder, and details petitioner refused to provide, were available to any journalist willing to do a little bit of investigative work.

Petitioner's statements lack any of the more obvious bases for a finding of prejudice. Unlike the police, he refused to comment on polygraph tests except to confirm earlier reports that Sanders had not submitted to the police polygraph; he mentioned no confessions and no evidence from searches or test results; he refused to elaborate upon his charge that the other so-called victims were not credible, except to explain his general theory that they were pressured to testify in an attempt to avoid drug-related legal trouble, and that some of them may have asserted claims in an attempt to collect insurance money.

C.

Events Following the Press Conference. Petitioner's judgment that no likelihood of material prejudice would result from his comments was vindicated by events at trial. While it is true that Rule 177's standard for controlling pretrial publicity must be judged at the time a statement is made, *ex post* evidence can have probative value in some cases. Here, where the Rule purports to demand, and the Constitution requires, consideration of the character of the harm and its heightened likelihood of occurrence, the record is altogether devoid of facts one would expect to follow upon any statement that created a real likelihood of material prejudice to a criminal jury trial.

The trial took place on schedule in August 1988, with no request by either party for a venue change or continuance. The jury was empaneled with no apparent difficulty. The trial judge questioned the jury venire about publicity. Although many had vague recollections of reports that cocaine stored at Western Vault had been stolen from a police undercover operation, and, as petitioner had feared, one remembered that the police had been cleared of suspicion, not a single juror indicated any recollection of petitioner or his press conference. App. 48–49; Respondent's Exhibit B, before Disciplinary Board.

At trial, all material information disseminated during petitioner's press conference was admitted in evidence before the jury, including information questioning the motives and credibility of supposed victims who testified against Sanders, and Detective Scholl's ingestion of drugs in the course of undercover operations (in order, he testified, to gain the confidence of suspects). App. 47. The jury acquitted petitioner's client, and, as petitioner explained before the disciplinary board,

> "when the trial was over with and the man was acquitted the next week the foreman of the jury phoned me and said to me that if they would have had a verdict form before them with respect to the guilt of Steve Scholl they would have found the man proven guilty beyond a reasonable doubt." *Id.,* at 47–48.

There is no support for the conclusion that petitioner's statements created a likelihood of material prejudice, or indeed of any harm of sufficient magnitude or imminence to support a punishment for speech.

III

As interpreted by the Nevada Supreme Court, the Rule is void for vagueness, in any event, for its safe harbor provision, Rule 177(3), misled petitioner into thinking that he could give his press conference without fear of discipline. Rule 177(3)(a) provides that a lawyer "may state without elaboration . . . the general nature of the . . . defense." Statements under this provision are protected "[n]otwithstanding subsection 1 and 2(a-f)." By necessary operation of the word "notwithstanding," the Rule contemplates that a lawyer describing the "general nature of the . . . defense" "without elaboration" need fear no discipline, even if he comments on "[t]he character, credibility, reputation or criminal record of a . . . witness," and even if he "knows or reasonably should know that [the statement] will have a substantial likelihood of materially prejudicing an adjudicative proceeding."

Given this grammatical structure, and absent any clarifying interpretation by the state court, the Rule fails to provide " 'fair notice to those to whom [it] is directed.' " *Grayned v. City of Rockford,* 408 U.S. 104, 112, 92 S.Ct. 2294, 2301, 33 L.Ed.2d 222 (1972). A lawyer seeking to avail himself of Rule 177(3)'s protection must guess at its contours. The right to explain the "general" nature of the defense without "elaboration" provides insufficient guidance because "general" and "elaboration" are both classic terms of degree. In the context before us, these terms have no settled usage or tradition of interpretation in law. The lawyer has no principle for determining when his remarks pass from the safe harbor of the general to the forbidden sea of the elaborated.

Petitioner testified he thought his statements were protected by Rule 177(3), App. 59. A review of the press conference supports that claim. He gave only a brief opening statement, see Appendix A, *infra*, p. 2736–2737, and on numerous occasions declined to answer reporters' questions seeking more detailed comments. One illustrative exchange shows petitioner's attempt to obey the rule:

> "QUESTION FROM THE FLOOR: Dominick, you mention you question the credibility of some of the witnesses, some of the people named as victims in the government indictment.
>
> "Can we go through it and *elaborate* on their backgrounds, interests—
>
> "MR. GENTILE: *I can't because ethics prohibit me from doing so.*
>
> "Last night before I decided I was going to make a statement, I took a good close look at the rules of professional responsibility. There are things that I can say and there are things that I can't. Okay?
>
> "I can't name which of the people have the drug backgrounds. I'm sure you guys can find that by doing just a little bit of investigative work." App. to Pet. for Cert. 11a (emphasis added).

Nevertheless, the disciplinary board said only that petitioner's comments "went beyond the scope of the statements permitted by SCR 177(3)," App. 5, and the Nevada Supreme Court's rejection of petitioner's defense based on Rule 177(3)Rule 177(3) was just as terse, App. to Pet. for Cert. 4a. The fact that Gentile was found in violation of the Rules after studying them and making a conscious effort at compliance demonstrates that Rule 177Rule 177 creates a trap for the wary as well as the unwary.

The prohibition against vague regulations of speech is based in part on the need to eliminate the impermissible risk of discriminatory enforcement, *Kolender v. Lawson*, 461 U.S. 352, 357–358, 361, 103 S.Ct. 1855, 1858–1859, 1860, 75 L.Ed.2d 903 (1983); *Smith v. Goguen*, 415 U.S. 566, 572–573, 94 S.Ct. 1242, 1246–1247, 39 L.Ed.2d 605 (1974), for history shows that speech is suppressed when either the speaker or the message is critical of those who enforce the law. The question is not whether discriminatory enforcement occurred here, and we assume it did not, but whether the Rule is so imprecise that discriminatory enforcement is a real possibility. The inquiry is of particular relevance when one of the classes most affected by the regulation is the criminal defense bar, which has the professional mission to challenge actions of the State. Petitioner, for instance, succeeded in preventing the conviction of his client, and the speech in issue involved criticism of the government.

IV

The analysis to this point resolves the case, and in the usual order of things the discussion should end here. Five Members of the Court, however, endorse an extended discussion which concludes that Nevada may interpret its requirement of substantial likelihood of material prejudice under a standard more deferential than is the usual rule where speech is concerned. It appears necessary, therefore, to set forth my objections to that conclusion and to the reasoning which underlies it.

Respondent argues that speech by an attorney is subject to greater regulation than speech by others, and restrictions on an attorney's speech should be assessed under a balancing test that weighs the State's interest in the regulation of a specialized profession against the lawyer's First Amendment interest in the kind of speech that was at issue. The cases cited by our colleagues to support this balancing, *Bates v. State Bar of Arizona*, 433 U.S. 350, 97 S.Ct. 2691, 53 L.Ed.2d 810 (1977); *Peel v. Attorney Registration and Disciplinary Comm'n of Ill.*, 496 U.S. 91, 110 S.Ct. 2281, 110 L.Ed.2d 83 (1990); *Ohralik v. Ohio State Bar Assn.*, 436 U.S. 447, 98 S.Ct. 1912, 56 L.Ed.2d 444 (1978); and *Seattle Times Co. v. Rhinehart*, 467 U.S. 20, 104 S.Ct. 2199, 81 L.Ed.2d 17 (1984), involved either commercial speech by attorneys or restrictions upon release of information that the attorney could gain only by use of the court's discovery process. Neither of those categories, nor the underlying interests which justified their creation, were implicated here. Petitioner was disciplined because he proclaimed to the community what he thought to be a misuse of the prosecutorial and police powers. Wide-open balancing of interests is not appropriate in this context.

A

Respondent would justify a substantial limitation on speech by attorneys because "lawyers have special access to information, including confidential statements from clients and information obtained through pretrial discovery or plea negotiations," and so lawyers' statements "are likely to be received as especially authoritative." Brief for Respondent 22. Rule 177Rule 177, however, does not reflect concern for the attorney's special access to client confidences, material gained through discovery, or other proprietary or confidential information. We have upheld restrictions upon the release of information gained "only by virtue of the trial court's discovery processes." *Seattle Times Co. v.*

Rhinehart, supra, 467 U.S., at 32, 104 S.Ct., at 2207. And *Seattle Times* would prohibit release of discovery information by the attorney as well as the client. Similar rules require an attorney to maintain client confidences. See, *e.g.*, ABA Model Rule of Professional Conduct 1.6 (1981).

This case involves no speech subject to a restriction under the rationale of *Seattle Times*. Much of the information in petitioner's remarks was included by explicit reference or fair inference in earlier press reports. Petitioner could not have learned what he revealed at the press conference through the discovery process or other special access afforded to attorneys, for he spoke to the press on the day of indictment, at the outset of his formal participation in the criminal proceeding. We have before us no complaint from the prosecutors, police, or presiding judge that petitioner misused information to which he had special access. And there is no claim that petitioner revealed client confidences, which may be waived in any event. Rule 177Rule 177, on its face and as applied here, is neither limited to nor even directed at preventing release of information received through court proceedings or special access afforded attorneys. Cf. *Butterworth v. Smith*, 494 U.S., at 632–634, 110 S.Ct., at 1381–1382. It goes far beyond this.

B

Respondent relies upon *obiter dicta* from *In re Sawyer*, 360 U.S. 622, 79 S.Ct. 1376, 3 L.Ed.2d 1473 (1959), *Sheppard v. Maxwell*, 384 U.S. 333 (1966), and *Nebraska Press Assn. v. Stuart*, 427 U.S. 539, 96 S.Ct. 2791, 49 L.Ed.2d 683 (1976), for the proposition that an attorney's speech about ongoing proceedings must be subject to pervasive regulation in order to ensure the impartial adjudication of criminal proceedings. *In re Sawyer* involved general comments about Smith Act prosecutions rather than the particular proceeding in which the attorney was involved, conduct which we held not sanctionable under the applicable ABA Canon of Professional Ethics, quite apart from any resort to First Amendment principles. *Nebraska Press Assn.* considered a challenge to a court order barring the press from reporting matters most prejudicial to the defendant's Sixth Amendment trial right, not information released by defense counsel. In *Sheppard v. Maxwell*, we overturned a conviction after a trial that can only be described as a circus, with the courtroom taken over by the press and jurors turned into media stars. The prejudice to Dr. Sheppard's fair trial right can be traced in principal part to police and prosecutorial irresponsibility and the trial court's failure to control the proceedings and the courthouse environment. Each case suggests restrictions upon information release, but none confronted their permitted scope.

At the very least, our cases recognize that disciplinary rules governing the legal profession cannot punish activity protected by the First Amendment, and that First Amendment protection survives even when the attorney violates a disciplinary rule he swore to obey when admitted to the practice of law. See, *e.g.*, *In re Primus*, 436 U.S. 412, 98 S.Ct. 1893, 56 L.Ed.2d 417 (1978); *Bates v. State Bar of Arizona, supra.* We have not in recent years accepted our colleagues' apparent theory that the practice of law brings with it comprehensive restrictions, or that we will defer to professional bodies when those restrictions impinge upon First Amendment freedoms. And none of the justifications put forward by respondent suffice to sanction abandonment of our normal First Amendment principles in the case of speech by an attorney regarding pending cases.

V

Even if respondent is correct, and as in *Seattle Times* we must balance "whether the 'practice in question [furthers] an important or substantial governmental interest unrelated to the suppression of expression' and whether 'the limitation of First Amendment freedoms [is] no greater than is necessary or essential to the protection of the particular governmental interest involved,' " *Seattle Times, supra*, 467 U.S., at 32, 104 S.Ct., at 2207 (quoting *Procunier v. Martinez*, 416 U.S. 396, 413, 94 S.Ct. 1800, 1811, 40 L.Ed.2d 224 (1974)), the Rule as interpreted by Nevada fails the searching inquiry required by those precedents.

A

Only the occasional case presents a danger of prejudice from pretrial publicity. Empirical research suggests that in the few instances when jurors have been exposed to extensive and prejudicial publicity, they are able to disregard it and base their verdict upon the evidence presented in court. See generally Simon, Does the Court's Decision in *Nebraska Press Association* Fit the Research Evidence on the Impact on Jurors of News Coverage?, 29 Stan.L.Rev. 515 (1977); Drechsel, An Alternative View of Media-Judiciary Relations: What the Non-Legal Evidence Suggests About the Fair Trial-Free Press Issue, 18 Hofstra L.Rev. 1 (1989). *Voir dire* can play an important role in reminding jurors to set aside out-of-court information and to decide the case upon the evidence presented at trial. All of these factors weigh in favor of affording an attorney's speech about ongoing proceedings our traditional First Amendment protections. Our colleagues' historical survey notwithstanding, respondent has not demonstrated any sufficient state interest in restricting the speech of attorneys to justify a lower standard of First Amendment scrutiny.

Still less justification exists for a lower standard of scrutiny here, as this speech involved not the prosecutor or police, but a criminal defense attorney. Respondent and its *amici* present not a single example where a defense attorney has managed by public statements to prejudice the prosecution of the State's case. Even discounting the obvious reason for a lack of appellate decisions on the topic—the difficulty of appealing a verdict of acquittal—the absence of anecdotal or survey evidence in a much-studied area of the law is remarkable.

The various bar association and advisory commission reports which resulted in promulgation of ABA Model Rule of Professional Conduct 3.6 (1981), and other regulations of attorney speech, and sources they cite, present no convincing case for restrictions upon the speech of defense attorneys. See Swift, Model Rule 3.6: An Unconstitutional Regulation of Defense Attorney Trial Publicity, 64 B.U.L.Rev. 1003, 1031–1049 (1984) (summarizing studies and concluding there is no empirical or anecdotal evidence of a need for restrictions on defense publicity); see also Drechsel, *supra,* at 35 ("[D]ata showing the heavy reliance of journalists on law enforcement sources and prosecutors confirms the appropriateness of focusing attention on those sources when attempting to control pre-trial publicity"). The police, the prosecution, other government officials, and the community at large hold innumerable avenues for the dissemination of information adverse to a criminal defendant, many of which are not within the scope of Rule 177 or any other regulation. By contrast, a defendant cannot speak without fear of incriminating himself and prejudicing his defense, and most criminal defendants have insufficient means to retain a public relations team apart from defense counsel for the sole purpose of countering prosecution statements. These factors underscore my conclusion that blanket rules restricting speech of defense attorneys should not be accepted without careful First Amendment scrutiny.

B

Respondent uses the "officer of the court" label to imply that attorney contact with the press somehow is inimical to the attorney's proper role. Rule 177posits no such inconsistency between an attorney's role and discussions with the press. It permits all comment to the press absent "a substantial likelihood of materially prejudicing an adjudicative proceeding." Respondent does not articulate the principle that contact with the press cannot be reconciled with the attorney's role or explain how this might be so.

Because attorneys participate in the criminal justice system and are trained in its complexities, they hold unique qualifications as a source of information about pending cases. "Since lawyers are considered credible in regard to pending litigation in which they are engaged and are in one of the most knowledgeable positions, they are a crucial source of information and opinion." *Chicago Council of Lawyers v. Bauer,* 522 F.2d 242, 250 (CA7 1975). To the extent the press and public rely upon attorneys for information because attorneys are well informed, this may prove the value to the public of speech by members of the bar. If the dangers of their speech arise from its persuasiveness, from their ability to explain judicial proceedings, or from the likelihood the speech will be believed, these are not the sort of dangers that can validate restrictions. The First Amendment does not permit suppression of speech because of its power to command assent.

One may concede the proposition that an attorney's speech about pending cases may present dangers that could not arise from statements by a nonparticipant, and that an attorney's duty to cooperate in the judicial process may prevent him or her from taking actions with an intent to frustrate that process. The role of attorneys in the criminal justice system subjects them to fiduciary obligations to the court and the parties. An attorney's position may result in some added ability to obstruct the proceedings through well-timed statements to the press, though one can debate the extent of an attorney's ability to do so without violating other established duties. A court can require an attorney's cooperation to an extent not possible of nonparticipants. A proper weighing of dangers might consider the harm that occurs when speech about ongoing proceedings forces the court to take burdensome steps such as sequestration, continuance, or change of venue.

If as a regular matter speech by an attorney about pending cases raised real dangers of this kind, then a substantial governmental interest might support additional regulation of speech. But this case involves the sanction of speech so innocuous, and an application of Rule 177(3)'s safe harbor provision so begrudging, that it is difficult to determine the force these arguments would carry in a different setting. The instant case is a poor vehicle for defining with precision the outer limits under the Constitution of a court's ability to regulate an attorney's statements about ongoing adjudicative proceedings. At the very least, however, we can say that the Rule which punished petitioner's statements represents a limitation of First Amendment freedoms greater than is necessary or essential to the protection of the particular governmental interest, and does not protect against a danger of the necessary gravity, imminence, or likelihood.

The vigorous advocacy we demand of the legal profession is accepted because it takes place under the neutral, dispassionate control of the judicial system. Though cost and delays undermine it in all too many cases, the American judicial trial remains one of the purest, most rational forums for the lawful determination of disputes. A profession which takes just pride in these traditions may consider them disserved if lawyers use their skills and insight to make untested allegations in the press instead of in the courtroom. But constraints of professional responsibility and societal disapproval will act as sufficient safeguards in most cases. And in some circumstances press comment is necessary to protect the rights of the client and prevent abuse of the courts. It cannot be said that petitioner's conduct demonstrated any real or specific threat to the legal process, and his statements have the full protection of the First Amendment.

VI

The judgment of the Supreme Court of Nevada is

Reversed.

SOLUTIONS: THE LAWYER SHOULD HAVE, WOULD HAVE, COULD HAVE. . .

Strict adherence to MR 3.6 offers lawyers a guide. Most rules invest the lawyer with discretion and expect the lawyer to exercise good judgment. Here, the Rule states explicitly what you can do and what you cannot do when talking to the press about a case:

[A] lawyer may state:

(1)   the claim, offense or defense involved and, except when prohibited by law, the identity of the persons involved;

(2)   information contained in a public record;

(3)   that an investigation of a matter is in progress;

(4)   the scheduling or result of any step in litigation;

(5)   a request for assistance in obtaining evidence and information necessary thereto;

(6)   a warning of danger concerning the behavior of a person involved, when there is reason to believe that there exists the likelihood of substantial harm to an individual or to the public interest; and

(7)   in a criminal case, in addition to subparagraphs (1) through (6):

(i)   the identity, residence, occupation and family status of the accused;

(ii) if the accused has not been apprehended, information necessary to aid in apprehension of that person;

(iii) the fact, time and place of arrest; and

(iv) the identity of investigating and arresting officers or agencies and the length of the investigation.

Cases and Materials

X-Ray Questions (*Salvador Perricone*)

This case deals with the intersection of the lessons from *Gentile* and the fairly recent development of social media. As an Assistant United States Attorney in New Orleans, Perricone posted comments on his online blog—under an alias—regarding pending federal criminal matters in Louisiana. He claimed that he did so to deal with the stress of the job and not to harm any person or to impair their Constitutional rights. How did the Louisiana Supreme Court look at this argument when deciding to impose a sanction upon him? The Court disagreed with the recommendation of the Bar that he only be suspended and decided to impose the ultimate penalty of disbarment. Why? What was the deciding factor, in the Court's view, that elevated the punishment? How did the Court use the language of *Gentile* to support its decision?

In re: Salvador R. Perricone

Supreme Court of Louisiana., 2018.
263 So.3d 309.

PER CURIAM.

This disciplinary matter arises from formal charges filed by the Office of Disciplinary Counsel ("ODC") against respondent, Salvador R. Perricone, an attorney licensed to practice law in Louisiana.

UNDERLYING FACTS

The underlying facts of this case are largely undisputed. By way of background, respondent commenced employment as an Assistant United States Attorney ("AUSA") with the United States Attorney's Office for the Eastern District of Louisiana ("USAO") in 1991. At all times relevant to these proceedings, respondent was a Senior Litigation Counsel and the USAO's training officer.

During the times pertinent to these proceedings, a New Orleans newspaper, *The Times-Picayune*, maintained an Internet website identified as nola.com. The website typically permitted readers to post comments to news stories using pseudonyms and/or anonymous identities.

Beginning in or around November 2007 and continuing through March 14, 2012, respondent was a frequent poster of comments on a myriad of subjects on nola.com, including comments on cases which he and/or his colleagues at the USAO were assigned to prosecute. Of the more than 2,600 comments respondent posted, between one hundred and two hundred—less than one percent—related to matters being prosecuted in the USAO. None of the comments identified respondent by name or as an employee of the USAO. Rather, respondent posted on nola.com using at least five online identities: "campstblue," "legacyusa," "dramatis personae," "Henry L. Mencken1951," and "fed up."

ATTORNEY DISCIPLINARY PROCEEDING

Count I

In 2009, the FBI and the USAO commenced an investigation into allegations of corruption against various Jefferson Parish officials. In particular, investigations included allegations involving improper health insurance contracts between government entities and/or contractors and an insurance company owned by Tim Whitmer, the Jefferson Parish Chief Administrative Officer. Among the insurance contracts under investigation was one with River Birch, Inc., a privately held landfill company owned by Fred Heebe, whose company had been awarded a $160 million landfill contract with Jefferson Parish.

In February 2011, a federal grand jury indicted Henry Mouton, a former member of the Louisiana Wildlife and Fisheries Commission. The indictment charged that "co-conspirator A" paid Mr. Mouton more than $400,000 to use his influence with the Commission to force the closure of the Old Gentilly Landfill, which competed with River Birch. In June 2011, Mr. Mouton pleaded guilty to conspiracy.

An additional investigation alleged embezzlement by Dominick Fazzio, the chief financial officer for River Birch, and his brother-in-law, Mark Titus. Mr. Titus pleaded guilty and cooperated in the subsequent indictment of Mr. Fazzio for fraud and money laundering. Respondent was not on the prosecution team in that case, which was assigned to United States District Judge Ginger Berrigan in the Eastern District, but he did enroll for the limited purpose of disqualifying attorney Stephen London as Mr. Fazzio's trial counsel.

During the pendency of these investigations and prosecutions, respondent began commenting on nola.com using the pseudonym "Henry L. Mencken1951":

> If Heebe had one firing synapse, he would go speak to Letten's posse and purge himself of this sordid episode and let them go after the council and public officials. Why prolong this pain. . .perhaps Queen Jennifer has something to say about that.
>
> -December 18, 2011, 10:21 a.m.
>
> Heebe comes from a long line of corruptors.
>
> -September 3, 2011, 10:55 a.m.
>
> Heebe's goose is cooked.
>
> -September 4, 2011, 10:45 a.m.

As regards a nola.com story announcing the indictment of Mr. Mouton, respondent commented using his pseudonym "legacyusa," writing:

> I read the indictment. . .there is no legitimate reason for this type of behavior in such a short period of time and for a limited purpose. GUILTY!!!
>
> -February 26, 2011, 9:16 a.m.

As regards a nola.com article on the indictment of Mr. Fazzio, respondent posted a comment using his pseudonym "dramatis personae" and wrote:

> Well, Mr. Fazzio, I hope you have room in your scrap book for your conviction and mug shot. London didn't too well with Archie Kaufman. You're next.
>
> -August 5, 2011, 3:09 p.m.

Following Judge Berrigan's decision to disqualify Mr. Fazzio's attorney due to a conflict, Mr. Fazzio hired Arthur "Buddy" Lemann as his new attorney, as reported on nola.com. Respondent commented using "Henry L. Mencken1951," writing:

> Looks like Fazzio got a lemon. That book you refer to Mr. Rioux is about all of his losses. The guy is a clown and Fazzio is going down.

-January 13, 2012, 10:36 p.m.

In another post following Judge Berrigan's disqualification order, respondent commented as "Henry L. Mencken1951" and wrote:

It's the right decision. Judges don't take this action lightly. There must be something going on we don't know about or the TP is too stupid (more likely) to understand. Please get to the bottom of this, PLEASE!!!

-January 5, 2012, 7:36 p.m.

Radio personality Garland Robinette was featured in an article in *The Times-Picayune* which reported that Mr. Heebe provided him a $250,000 interest-free loan allegedly in exchange for Mr. Robinette's on-air opposition to reopening the Old Gentilly Landfill rather than honoring the $160 million River Birch contract. Mr. Robinette had been notified that he was the subject of an investigation by the FBI and the USAO. Using "Henry L. Mencken1951," respondent wrote on nola.com:

Looks like he got another 250K to keep his mouth shut.

What a show!! WWL radio is dead!!!

-September 6, 2011, 10:13 a.m.

TRANSLATION: Heebe's attorney won't let me talk, lest I implicate his client. Additionally, I am New Orleans Royalty and I don't have to explain anything to anyone.

-September 7, 2011, 7:59 a.m.

Count II

Respondent prosecuted Mose Jefferson, the brother of Congressman William Jefferson, in a case in which he was indicted for bribing former Orleans Parish School Board president Ellenese Brooks-Simms. During the trial, respondent posted comments on nola.com about Mose Jefferson and his attorney, Mike Fawer, under the pseudonym "campstblue":

Fawer has screwed his client!!!! He revealed exactly what Mose needed on the board to get what Mose wanted.

Good job Mike!!!! You're just as arrogant as Ellenese . . . and the jury knows it.

-August 15, 2009, 9:19 p.m.

They got the corrupted, now they have to get the corruptor.

-August 16, 2009, 7:41 p.m.

In a second indictment not personally prosecuted by respondent, Mose Jefferson, his sister Betty Jefferson, and Renee Gill Pratt were charged with sending funds to a Jefferson-controlled non-profit. William Jefferson was then pending trial on corruption charges in Virginia. Using the name "legacyusa," respondent posted:

> The sad part of all this is that Bill is preventing his siblings from pleading guilty and cooperating, thus exposing them to more prison time. Additionally, local defense attorneys are just milking these cases for their own ego gratification and financial enrichment. Something is sick about our system.

-May 22, 2009, 9:40 p.m.

Count III

On September 4, 2005, six days after Hurricane Katrina struck New Orleans, a group of New Orleans police officers shot at unarmed civilians crossing the Danziger Bridge. Two persons were killed and four others were wounded. In July 2010, six officers were indicted in federal court for their roles in either the shooting or the ensuing alleged cover-up of the shooting. United States District Judge Kurt Engelhardt presided over the trial which commenced on June 22, 2011 and ended on August 5, 2011, when the jury returned guilty verdicts against all defendants. On April 4, 2012, Judge Engelhardt sentenced the defendants to terms of incarceration ranging from 6 to 65 years.

While respondent was not part of the prosecution team, he nevertheless posted comments on nola.com prior to and during the trial, including as the jury was deliberating. Posting as "dramatis personae," respondent stated:

> I agree with [nola.com poster] Cauane. The same hurricane that hit Orleans Parish, hit Jefferson, St. Bernard, Plaquemine, and St. Tammany. Yet, the only police force to use deadly force throughout the city was the venerable NOPD. Perhaps we would be safer if the NOPD would leave next hurricanes and let the National Guard assume all law enforcement duties. GUILTY AS CHARGED.

-August 3, 2011, 7:06 a.m.

Even prior to the trial, in response to an article regarding a rumored plea by a police officer co-defendant, respondent, posting as "legacyusa," warned:

Despite defense attorney's protestations to the contrary, It would be prudent for those involve to consider the track record of the US Attorney's Office. Letten's people are not to be trifled with.

-February 23, 2010, 6:17 p.m.

As regards police officer co-defendant Archie Kaufman, respondent wrote:

The cover up is always worse than the crime. Archie, your time is up.

-February 23, 2010, 10:44 p.m.

Following the publication of an article about a cooperating defendant and government witness, respondent as "legacyusa" wrote:

The Feds never forget. . . .this officer is doing the right thing. . . .wish the others would, then IT would be over.

-May 20, 2010, 10:41 p.m.

During the trial, respondent as "legacyusa" posted:

NONE of these guys should had have ever been given a badge. We should research how they got on the police department, who trained them, who supervised them and why were they ever been promoted. You put crap in B you get crap out!!!

-June 22, 2011, 8:19 a.m.

Also during the trial, respondent as "dramatis personae" denigrated the testimony given by one of the defendants:

Where is Madison's gun? Come on officer, tell us. You shot because you wanted to be part of something, you thought, was bigger than you. You let your ego control your emotions. You wanted to be viewed as a big man among the other officers. That's the creed of the NOPD and I hope the jury ignores your lame explanation and renders justice for Mr. Madison. To do less, is to sanction any cop who decides it is in his best interest to put a load of buckshot in the back of a disabled american in broad daylight.

-July 28, 2011, 8:16 a.m.

While the jury deliberated, respondent as "dramatis personae" stated:

I don't think the jury will leave the dead and wounded on the bridge.

-August 4, 2011, 5:53 p.m.

When respondent's online commenting was discovered and reported to Judge Engelhardt, an investigation ensued. Following the investigation, Judge Engelhardt reversed the convictions of the Danziger Bridge defendants and granted their motions for new trial, citing "grotesque prosecutorial misconduct," including respondent's online commenting as well as other instances of prosecutorial misconduct by the USAO, by members of the Department of Justice, and by federal law enforcement. In finding defendants were denied due process, Judge Engelhardt stated:

> [I]t is difficult to conceive, much less accept, that this time-honored constitutional procedure successfully withstood an attack of the ferocity seen here, a campaign extending back to the commencement of the DOJ's active investigation of this case in 2008, and continuing through the acceptance of related plea agreements, the indictment, and the trial itself. To conclude that such misconduct was only a little unfair, but not enough to be harmful, turns the fundamental principle of due process on its head.

Judge Engelhardt clearly found the conduct of Perricone to be intentional. Judge Engelhardt found Perricone "viewed posting of highly-opinionated comments as a 'public service.'" The district court also found that the fact that the government's actions, including Perricone's actions, were conducted anonymously made "it all the more egregious, and forces the Court, the defendants, and the public into an indecent game of 'catch-me-if-you-can.'"

The Department of Justice appealed Judge Engelhardt's decision, and on August 18, 2015, the United States Fifth Circuit Court of Appeals affirmed the order and remanded the case for a new trial. In so doing, the court noted that the government acknowledged "significant, repeated misconduct by Perricone," and explained:

> The government concedes Perricone "intentionally committed professional misconduct" violating (a) federal regulations restricting extrajudicial statements by DOJ personnel relating to civil and criminal proceedings, (b) DOJ policies and (c) court and state bar rules of professional conduct. The government acknowledges that besides his postings in this case, Perricone posted "thousands" of anonymous comments on various topics over the course of several years.

Following this ruling, Judge Engelhardt accepted a plea deal brokered by defense lawyers and the Department of Justice, which called for the Danziger

Bridge defendants to plead guilty to significantly lesser offenses in exchange for substantially reduced prison sentences ranging from 3 to 12 years.

DISCIPLINARY PROCEEDINGS

In April 2017, the ODC filed formal charges against respondent. The ODC alleged that because respondent's client (the Department of Justice and the USAO) forbid extrajudicial statements by an AUSA such as those set forth in the formal charges, respondent placed his own interests above those of his client, in violation of Rule 1.7(a)(2) of the Rules of Professional Conduct Rule 1.7(a)(2) of the Rules of Professional Conduct. The ODC further alleged that respondent made extrajudicial statements about the guilt or innocence of defendants and/or others under investigation or prosecution that had a substantial likelihood of materially prejudicing an adjudicative proceeding, in violation of Rule 3.6, and of heightening public condemnation of the accused, in violation of Rule 3.8(f); that respondent's conduct was prejudicial to the administration of justice, in violation of Rule 8.4(d); and that respondent violated or attempted to violate the Rules of Professional Conduct, or did so through another, in violation of Rule 8.4(a).

Respondent answered the formal charges and admitted the factual allegations therein, including all of the quoted posts on nola.com. He stated that he made the anonymous online comments to relieve stress, not for the purpose of influencing the outcome of a defendant's trial. He further stated that his anonymous comments did not identify him as an AUSA, and as such, he did not intend, nor did he reasonably expect, that his conduct would influence the outcome of a trial, prejudice the fairness of any subsequent legal proceeding, or otherwise prejudice the administration of justice. Accordingly, respondent denied violating the Rules of Professional Conduct.

Hearing Committee Report

Prior to a hearing in the matter, respondent and the ODC filed into the record a stipulation that respondent violated Rules 3.6, 3.8(f), 8.4(a), 8.4(d) of the Rules of Professional Conduct. Respondent reserved his right to present evidence of his mental intent as regards those violations, and all other factors under Supreme Court Rule XIX, § 10(C).

A hearing in mitigation was conducted. Respondent presented the testimony of various character witnesses. Additionally, respondent called Dr. Ron Cambias, his treating psychologist since May 2016. Dr. Cambias testified that respondent suffered from complex post-traumatic stress disorder ("PTSD") triggered by numerous situations in which respondent, who was formerly employed as a police officer and FBI agent, had witnessed the gruesome deaths of others and had, himself, been threatened with physical harm, including gunfire. Dr. Cambias opined that respondent's online postings were the result of his PTSD.

At the conclusion of the hearing, the committee rendered its report. The committee explained that respondent testified he thought his blogging activities would help him to deal with the stress of his work as an AUSA, although he acknowledged that it actually exacerbated his stress and anxiety. The committee also discussed the expert testimony of Dr. Cambias. After reviewing this evidence, the committee found credible respondent's testimony that he was under a great deal of stress at work, especially in the period following Hurricane Katrina, when public corruption being investigated by the USAO was rampant. However, the committee noted it was "skeptical" of Dr. Cambias' diagnosis of PTSD and its causative role in respondent's blogging but recognized no countervailing opinion testimony was offered.

The committee accepted respondent's stipulations that his actions violated Rules 3.6, 3.8(f), 8.4(a), and 8.4(d). The committee found that respondent also violated Rule 1.7(a)(2) by placing his own interests, *i.e.*, his need to "vent" about the criminal cases being prosecuted by the USAO, above the interests of that office, his client, in having those cases proceed unimpeded.

The committee determined that respondent violated duties owed to his client, the public, the legal system, and the profession, and found he acted knowingly. The mistrial granted in the Danziger Bridge case was certainly an actual, serious injury, as was the harm done by respondent to the post-Katrina recovery in New Orleans. Considering the ABA's *Standards for Imposing Lawyer Sanctions*, the committee determined the applicable baseline sanction is suspension.

In aggravation, the committee found the following factors: a selfish (but not dishonest) motive, a pattern of misconduct, multiple offenses, and substantial experience in the practice of law (admitted 1979). In mitigation, the committee recognized that at the time of respondent's misconduct, there were no regulations, rules, or guidelines regarding anonymous Internet postings. Other mitigating factors are the absence of a prior disciplinary record, absence of a dishonest motive, personal or emotional problems, full and free disclosure and a cooperative attitude toward the disciplinary proceedings, character and reputation, imposition of other penalties or sanctions, and remorse.

Considering all of these factors, especially the absence of any guidelines or other authority in the 2007–2012 time period during which respondent's anonymous, online postings occurred, and the longstanding harm respondent's actions caused to the USAO, a majority of the committee recommended respondent be suspended from the practice of law for two years, with one year deferred. One member of the committee would have recommended that the entire suspension be deferred.

Disciplinary Board Recommendation

After reviewing this matter, the disciplinary board determined that the hearing committee's factual findings are not manifestly erroneous, and that the committee correctly found respondent violated the Rules of Professional Conduct, both as stipulated (Rules 3.6, 3.8(f), 8.4(a), and 8.4(d)) and as additionally found by the committee (Rule 1.7(a)(2)).

The board determined that respondent violated duties owed to his client (the USAO), the public, the legal system, and the profession. He acted knowingly and intentionally. For example, although his online comments materially prejudiced the Danziger Bridge case, respondent did not intend that particular outcome. Thus, his conduct with regard to Rule 3.6 was knowing. However, his conduct with regard to Rule 3.8(f) was intentional, as there is clear evidence that respondent intended to heighten public condemnation of various individuals being investigated or prosecuted by the USAO. As recounted in the formal charges, respondent's comments speculated on the guilt of various individuals subject to prosecution or investigation and cast these individuals in a very negative light. Respondent claims he did this only to relieve the stress he was under caused by his undiagnosed PTSD. However, respondent also testified that he engaged in "arguments" with other online commenters that were not related to matters being investigated or prosecuted by the USAO, such as LSU football. The board did not find it credible that while respondent was attempting to influence other commenters regarding benign topics like LSU football, he was not attempting to influence others with his comments about the guilt of various individuals subject to investigation or prosecution. Rather, the board found that respondent intended to heighten public condemnation of the individuals referenced in the formal charges with his online comments.

The board found the actual harm and potential for harm caused by respondent's misconduct is significant. Among other things, it found respondent's misconduct was a significant factor B although not the sole factor B that led Judge Engelhardt to grant a new trial in the Danziger Bridge case. It also noted respondent's online commenting received significant media attention. These actions harmed the perception of the legal profession and tarnished the reputation of the USAO. The publicity that respondent's conduct received diminished the public's faith in the legal system. Additionally, his actions caused delay and additional expenses in several pending proceedings.

In aggravation, the board found the following factors: a selfish motive, a pattern of misconduct, multiple offenses, and substantial experience in the practice of law. In mitigation, the board found the absence of a prior disciplinary record, absence of a dishonest motive, personal or emotional problems, full and free disclosure and a cooperative attitude toward the disciplinary proceedings, character and reputation, imposition of other penalties or sanctions, and remorse.

However, the board specifically rejected respondent's argument that the hearing committee should have recognized the mitigating factor of mental disability due to his PTSD diagnosis. Citing ABA Standard 9.32(i) and *In re: Stoller*, 04-2758 (La. 5/24/05), 902 So.2d 981, the board found respondent failed to prove his PTSD caused the misconduct. It pointed out Dr. Cambias testified that someone with PTSD can operate at a high level and that respondent knew right from wrong. Thus, there does not appear to be clear and convincing evidence supporting the causation element. Based on the foregoing, the board concluded that the committee's determination that mental disability is not a mitigating factor appears to be reasonable and not erroneous.

Turning to the issue of an appropriate sanction, the board noted that there is no disciplinary case law in Louisiana discussing inappropriate extrajudicial statements by a prosecutor. However, the board took guidance from *In re: McCool*, 15-0284 (La. 6/30/15), 172 So.3d 1058, in which an attorney was disbarred for launching a lengthy social media campaign to affect the outcome of a case she was handling. The board found that the extensive scope of respondent's misconduct and the significant actual and potential harm it caused justifies a sanction on par with that imposed in *McCool*.

Based on this reasoning, the board recommended respondent be disbarred. The board also recommended that respondent be assessed with the costs and expenses of the proceeding.

One board member dissented as to the sanction, finding that disbarment is not warranted and that a two- to three-year suspension is appropriate for respondent's misconduct.

Respondent filed an objection to the disciplinary board's recommendation. Accordingly, the case was docketed for oral argument pursuant to Supreme Court Rule XIX, § 11(G)(1)(b).

DISCUSSION

The underlying facts of this matter are not in dispute. It suffices to say that beginning in November 2007 and continuing through mid-March 2012, respondent, under various pseudonyms, frequently posted comments on an online site. Although these comments concerned a myriad of subjects, some pertained to cases which he and/or his colleagues at the USAO were assigned to prosecute. When discovered, respondent's actions caused serious, actual harm in the River Birch and Danziger Bridge cases and, most profoundly, to the reputation of the USAO. There was a potential for harm in the Jefferson and Gill-Pratt cases.

Respondent stipulated that his conduct violated Rules 3.6, 3.8(f), 8.4(a), and 8.4(d) of the Rules of Professional Conduct. He did not admit to the violation of Rule 1.7(a)(2) alleged in the formal charges, but that rule violation was found by both the hearing committee and the disciplinary board, and respondent did not lodge an objection in this court to said finding. Accordingly, like the underlying facts, the rule violations in this matter are not in dispute.

We now turn to a determination of the appropriate sanction for respondent's actions. In determining a sanction, we are mindful that disciplinary proceedings are designed to maintain high standards of conduct, protect the public, preserve the integrity of the profession, and deter future misconduct. *Louisiana State Bar Ass'n v. Reis*, 513 So.2d 1173 (La. 1987). The discipline to be imposed depends upon the facts of each case and the seriousness of the offenses involved considered in light of any aggravating and mitigating circumstances. *Louisiana State Bar Ass'n v. Whittington*, 459 So.2d 520 (La. 1984).

Here, respondent violated duties owed to his client, the public, the legal system, and the profession. Respondent acted knowingly in that he knew his online postings were forbidden; however, he did not make the posts with the specific intent to harm the outcome of the various criminal proceedings. Respondent acted intentionally in that he intended his posts would have the effect of heightening public condemnation of the individuals referenced in the formal charges.

Standard 5.22 of the ABA's *Standards for Imposing Lawyer Sanctions* provides that suspension is generally appropriate when a lawyer in an official or governmental position knowingly fails to follow proper procedures or rules, and causes injury or potential injury to a party or to the integrity of the legal process. Considering this standard, the applicable baseline sanction in this matter is suspension.

In aggravation, the following factors apply: a selfish motive, a pattern of misconduct, multiple offenses, and substantial experience in the practice of law. In mitigation, the following factors apply: absence of a prior disciplinary record, absence of a dishonest motive, personal or emotional problems, full and free disclosure and a cooperative attitude toward the disciplinary proceedings, character and reputation, imposition of other penalties or sanctions, and remorse.

Respondent's arguments in this court center almost entirely on whether we should recognize the mitigating factor of mental disability due to his diagnosis of complex PTSD. In *In re: Stoller*, 04-2758 (La. 5/24/05), 902 So.2d 981, we cited four criteria which must be met for respondents to properly assert chemical dependency or mental disability as a mitigating factor: (1) there is medical evidence that the respondent is affected by a chemical dependency or mental disability; (2) the chemical dependency or mental disability caused the misconduct; (3) the respondent's recovery from the chemical dependency or mental disability is demonstrated by a meaningful and sustained period of successful rehabilitation; and (4) the recovery arrested the misconduct and recurrence of that misconduct is unlikely. The ABA commentary indicates that in considering issues of chemical dependency or mental disability offered as mitigating factors in disciplinary proceedings, the "greatest weight" should be assigned when the disability is the sole cause of the offense.

As noted by the board, the focus of the inquiry in the instant case is on the second factor—namely, whether respondent's PTSD caused the misconduct at issue. Based on our review of the record, we find no clear and convincing support for the conclusion that respondent's mental condition had any causative effect on his misconduct. Respondent's psychologist testified that someone with PTSD can operate at a high level and that respondent knew right from wrong. This testimony is corroborated by respondent's own admission that even before his conduct was discovered, he knew he should not be engaged in posting extrajudicial comments. When asked why he engaged in commenting in a prohibited way, respondent candidly admitted that he was angry over public corruption and he vented this anger in the caustic criticism leveled against all who, in his judgment, warranted accountability, even though he knew this was improper.

Respondent's own testimony reveals he was aware that he should not post these comments, yet he decided to do so anyway. Clearly, any mental disability from which respondent suffered did not prevent him from knowing his actions were wrong. Under these circumstances, we find absolutely no support for the conclusion that respondent has proven his mental condition caused the misconduct. Accordingly, we decline to consider his mental disability in mitigation.

In formulating an appropriate sanction, we acknowledge the situation presented in this case is *res novo* in our jurisprudence, and our prior case law provides little useful guidance. However, we begin from the well-settled proposition that public officials (and prosecutors in particular) are held to a higher standard than ordinary attorneys. *In re: Griffing*, 17-0874 (La. 10/18/17), 236 So.3d 1213. Respondent was clearly in an important position of public trust. His actions betrayed that trust and caused actual harm to pending prosecutions. Once discovered, his conduct tarnished the reputation of the USAO and brought the entire legal profession into disrepute.

In this age of social media, it is important for all attorneys to bear in mind that "[t]he vigorous advocacy we demand of the legal profession is accepted because it takes place under the neutral, dispassionate control of the judicial system." *Gentile v. State Bar of Nevada*, 501 U.S. 1030, 1058, 111 S.Ct. 2720, 115 L.Ed.2d 888 (1991). As the Court in *Gentile* wisely explained, "[a] profession which takes just pride in these traditions may consider them disserved if lawyers use their skills and insight to make untested allegations in the press instead of in the courtroom." *Id.*

Respondent's conscious decision to vent his anger by posting caustic, extrajudicial comments about pending cases strikes at the heart of the neutral dispassionate control which is the foundation of our system. Our decision today must send a strong message to respondent and to all the members of the bar that a lawyer's ethical obligations are not diminished by the mask of anonymity provided by the Internet.

In summary, considering respondent's position of public trust as a prosecutor, his knowing and intentional decision to post these comments despite his acknowledgment that it was improper to do so, and the serious harm respondent's conduct has caused both to individual litigants and to the legal profession as a whole, we must conclude he has failed to comply with the high ethical standards we require of lawyers who are granted the privilege to practice law in this state. The only appropriate sanction under these facts is disbarment.

DECREE

Upon review of the findings and recommendations of the hearing committee and disciplinary board, and considering the record, the briefs, and oral argument, it is ordered that Salvador R. Perricone, Louisiana Bar Roll number 10515, be and he hereby is disbarred. His name shall be stricken from the roll of attorneys, and his license to practice law in the State of Louisiana shall be revoked. All costs and expenses in the matter are assessed against respondent in accordance with Supreme Court Rule XIX, § 10.1, with legal interest to commence thirty days from the date of finality of this court's judgment until paid.

CRICHTON, J., additionally concurs and assigns reasons.

I agree with the per curiam in all respects, and in particular, that respondent has failed to prove by clear and convincing evidence that Post Traumatic Stress Disorder was the cause for his misconduct. I write separately to note that this case highlights the difference between disbarment and permanent disbarment in attorney disciplinary proceedings. Respondent took a voluntary absence from the practice of law during the pendency of these proceedings (approximately five years), in lieu of receiving an interim suspension. However, as the per curiam discusses in footnote 10, absent a formal interim suspension, La. Supreme Court Rule XIX does not provide authority for respondent to receive credit for self-imposed absence from the profession. Had respondent agreed to interim suspension at the outset and received disbarment upon conclusion of formal disciplinary proceedings, respondent would be legally entitled to file a petition for reinstatement much sooner than under the present circumstances. In other words, the sanction of disbarment imposed at this point in respondent's profession, at the age of 67, is arguably akin to permanent disbarment and essentially a legal profession death sentence. Whether respondent would ever be readmitted—even conditionally readmitted—is a question for another day, but the sanction of disbarment now precludes any consideration of it for five years from the date of this opinion.

> ### SOLUTIONS: THE LAWYER SHOULD HAVE, WOULD HAVE, COULD HAVE. . .
>
> As lawyers you will deal with stress. There are resources that will assist a lawyer confronting such issues. These are confidential services. But the lawyer self-help method here of letting it "all hang out" on social media is not a viable option.

LEANING INTO PRACTICE

Scenario: The Case of the TV Reporter, the DA, and the "Off-the-Record" Interview

Gianna DA has just come out of a court hearing in which she represented her office in the prosecution of a high-profile white-collar defendant. There are a number of TV reports on the courthouse steps and Gianna gives a standard response to their various questions consistent with MR 3.6. Kelli Reporter though stays after the other reporters leave and asks Gianna: "What's the real story? Just between us. Off the record." Gianna says: "Ok, here is the deal. This defendant has been a crook for a long time, and we have evidence that we can't use that she has stolen millions." Gianna goes on in this vein for twenty minutes. Unknown to her, Kelli has a tape recorded in her backpack; records it all. Has Gianna violated the Rule?

Section 7. Civil Settlement/Criminal Plea Bargaining/ Cultural Issues

Resolution of a civil or a criminal matter often occurs early in the litigation process. Here are two legal issues to be aware of, one in the civil context and the other in the criminal.

A. Settlement of Multiple Parties: Current Clients: Specific Rules

Model Rule 1.8(g)

(g) A lawyer who represents two or more clients shall not participate in making an aggregate settlement of the claims of or against the clients, or in a criminal case an aggregated agreement as to guilty or nolo contendere pleas, unless each client gives informed consent, in a writing signed by the client. The lawyer's disclosure shall include the existence and nature of all the claims or pleas involved and of the participation of each person in the settlement.

Deconstruction Exercise/Rule Rationale

The key here is transparency. For the multiple clients represented by the lawyer and as Comment 16 to the Rule points out, other Rules are implicated as well:

> "Differences in willingness to make or accept an offer of settlement are among the risks of common representation of multiple clients by a single lawyer. Under Rule 1.7, this is one of the risks that should be discussed before undertaking the representation, as part of the process of obtaining the clients' informed consent. In addition, Rule 1.2(a) protects each client's right to have the final say in deciding whether to accept or reject an offer of settlement and in deciding whether to enter a guilty or nolo contendere plea in a criminal case. The rule stated in this paragraph is a corollary of both these Rules and provides that, before any settlement offer or plea bargain is made or accepted on behalf of multiple clients, the lawyer must inform each of them about all the material terms of the settlement, including what the other clients will receive or pay if the settlement or plea offer is accepted. See also Rule 1.0(e) (definition of informed consent). Lawyers representing a class of plaintiffs or defendants, or those proceeding derivatively, may not have a full client-lawyer relationship with each member of the class; nevertheless, such lawyers must comply with applicable rules regulating notification of class members and other procedural requirements designed to ensure adequate protection of the entire class."

Transparency is the key.

B. Trial Disclosure in a Criminal Case

Model Rule 3.8: Special Responsibilities of a Prosecutor

The prosecutor in a criminal case shall:

> (a) refrain from prosecuting a charge that the prosecutor knows is not supported by probable cause;
>
> (b) make reasonable efforts to assure that the accused has been advised of the right to, and the procedure for obtaining, counsel and has been given reasonable opportunity to obtain counsel

(c)   not seek to obtain from an unrepresented accused a waiver of important pretrial rights, such as the right to a preliminary hearing;

(d)   make timely disclosure to the defense of all evidence or information known to the prosecutor that tends to negate the guilt of the accused or mitigates the offense, and, in connection with sentencing, disclose to the defense and to the tribunal all unprivileged mitigating information known to the prosecutor, except when the prosecutor is relieved of this responsibility by a protective order of the tribunal;

(e)   not subpoena a lawyer in a grand jury or other criminal proceeding to present evidence about a past or present client unless the prosecutor reasonably believes:

(1)   the information sought is not protected from disclosure by any applicable privilege;

(2)   the evidence sought is essential to the successful completion of an ongoing investigation or prosecution; and

(3)   there is no other feasible alternative to obtain the information;

(f)   except for statements that are necessary to inform the public of the nature and extent of the prosecutor's action and that serve a legitimate law enforcement purpose, refrain from making extrajudicial comments that have a substantial likelihood of heightening public condemnation of the accused and exercise reasonable care to prevent investigators, law enforcement personnel, employees or other persons assisting or associated with the prosecutor in a criminal case from making an extrajudicial statement that the prosecutor would be prohibited from making under Rule 3.6 or this Rule.

(g)   When a prosecutor knows of new, credible and material evidence creating a reasonable likelihood that a convicted defendant did not commit an offense of which the defendant was convicted, the prosecutor shall:

(1)   promptly disclose that evidence to an appropriate court or authority, and

(2)   if the conviction was obtained in the prosecutor's jurisdiction,

(i) promptly disclose that evidence to the defendant unless a court authorizes delay, and

(ii) undertake further investigation, or make reasonable efforts to cause an investigation, to determine whether the defendant was convicted of an offense that the defendant did not commit.

(h) When a prosecutor knows of clear and convincing evidence establishing that a defendant in the prosecutor's jurisdiction was convicted of an offense that the defendant did not commit, the prosecutor shall seek to remedy the conviction.

Deconstruction Exercise/Rule Rationale

The first part of the rule sets the tone for the entire rule; namely, the job of a prosecutor is to use the enormous power of the state to convict the guilty, not prosecute the innocent. Look at (d). What is the key word? The one upon which the entire Rule hinges? It is "tends." The prosecutor's job is to seek justice, not to weigh whether the evidence is probative. When in doubt, the defendant gets the benefit of that doubt. Subsection (g) posits a tension between two competing values: on the one hand the value of ensuring that the guilty are punished but, on the other hand, the value of the conclusiveness of legal proceedings. This second value finds voice in the use of the conjunctive "and," not the use of the disjunctive "or." Thus: the prosecutor's duty to remedy a possible wrongful conviction is only triggered when evidence comes to light that is "new and credible and material," *and* couple this with the burden in (h) of this clear and convincing evidence. From this you see that the rule's bias is towards conclusiveness of judgments, not on the goal of justice.

C. Disclosure in Plea Bargaining

In criminal law practice efforts are made prior to a trial to resolve the matter. This is the plea-bargaining phase. It is well established (but as we will see shortly not always followed) practice as mandated by the United Sates Supreme Court for the prosecutor to disclose exculpatory evidence to the criminal defendant prior to trial. But the ethical issue that is dividing courts is whether this duty extends to the pre-plea stage of the process. A Petition for Certiorari recently filed highlights this important issue.

Cases and Materials

X-Ray Questions (*Williamson County*)

This cert petition sets out an area of contention; namely does the ethical duty of disclosure apply prior to engaging in plea bargaining with the defendant? MR 3.8 in its current form is informed by the United Sates Supreme Court decision in *Brady* that is discussed in the petition. What are the arguments for a good faith extension, per MR 3.1, of *Brady* to the plea-bargaining process? What is the argument? How do the appeals court currently deal with the question?

Troy Mansfield, Petitioner v. Williamson County, Respondent

Supreme Court of the United States, 2022.
2022 WL 3928308.

PETITION FOR A WRIT OF CERTIORARI

This petition seeks resolution of a critical issue that has divided courts around the country: whether the due process right to exculpatory evidence recognized in *Brady* applies to pretrial plea negotiations.

The court of appeals' decision below further entrenches a well-defined split of authority. Five circuit courts and five state courts of last resort have all held that *Brady* applies to exculpatory evidence at the plea-bargaining stage. Four circuit courts, however, have declined to recognize a constitutional entitlement to exculpatory *Brady* material at the plea-bargaining stage. One of those, the Fifth Circuit, has now gone so far as to hold that there is no right to *Brady* material even when prosecutors are fully aware of exculpatory evidence establishing a defendant's innocence and affirmatively lie to conceal that evidence during plea negotiations. Pet.App.8a.

Bound by precedent to reach this conclusion, Judges Higginbotham and Costa each wrote separately to criticize this minority position and call on this Court to resolve the split. Concurring in his own decision below, Judge Higginbotham explained that because 97% of federal convictions arise from guilty pleas, his circuit's limit on *Brady* is a "signal flaw in the jurisprudence of plea bargaining." Pet.App.11a–12a. At a minimum, Judge Higginbotham asked for a definitive resolution of "the acknowledged circuit split" because "the want of certitude shadows the federal criminal dockets across the country." Pet.App.12a–13a.

Judge Costa also argued that the Fifth Circuit is on the wrong side of the circuit split. In his view, requiring disclosure of exculpatory evidence before a plea is "consistent with *Brady*" and its lineage and "retains *Brady's* vitality" in a "system of pleas rather than trials." Pet.App.14a–15a. He emphasized that resolution is needed because it is "not tenable" to deny defendants in some jurisdictions the right to exculpatory evidence before they are deprived of their liberty while affording that right in others. Pet.App.15a.

The Court should accept the judges' invitation, grant a writ of certiorari, and finally bring uniformity to this important constitutional question.

OPINIONS BELOW

The Fifth Circuit's decision (Pet.App.1a–15a) is reported at 30 F.4th 276. The magistrate judge's ruling granting Williamson County's motion for summary judgment (Pet.App.16a–35a) is not reported but is available at 2020 WL 13146202.

JURISDICTION

On March 31, 2022, the Fifth Circuit affirmed and entered judgment. Pet.App.36a, 38a. Mansfield did not seek rehearing given recent en banc precedent. *See Alvarez v. City of Brownsville*, 904 F.3d 382, 392 (5th Cir. 2018) (en banc). On June 10, 2022, he timely applied for an extension of time to file this petition. No. 21A827. Justice Alito granted the application, extending the time to file until August 26, 2022. *Id.*; S. Ct. R. 13.5; *see* 28 U.S.C. § 2101(c).

The district court had jurisdiction under 28 U.S.C. §§ 1331 and 1343. The Fifth Circuit had jurisdiction under 28 U.S.C. § 1291. This Court has jurisdiction under 28 U.S.C. § 1254(1).

CONSTITUTIONAL PROVISIONS AND STATUTES INVOLVED

This case implicates the Due Process Clause of the Fourteenth Amendment, which prevents States from "depriv[ing] any person of life, liberty, or property, without due process of law." U.S. Const. amend. XIV, § 1.

INTRODUCTION

Williamson County prosecutors hid exculpatory evidence in their own file and lied to conceal it-all in accordance with an official policy of the DA's office designed to coerce defendants to plead guilty. Faced with a risk of spending the rest of his life in prison, Mansfield accepted an unusually lenient plea offer all but guaranteed to induce him to plead guilty to a heinous crime he did not commit: indecency with a child. Pet.App.49a–50a. Mansfield served 120 days, but the crushing stigma of his false label as a convicted child sex offender plagued him and his family for much longer. *See* Pet.App.57a–59a. When, after 23 years, the truth emerged, a Texas judge vacated the judgment, finding that Mansfield's "due process rights were violated in a manner that rendered his plea involuntary." Pet.App.69a.

Texas's court of last resort for criminal appeals has long recognized that a defendant's right to exculpatory evidence "extends to guilty pleas as well as to contested cases." *Ex parte Lewis,* 587 S.W.2d 697, 700 (Tex. Crim. App. 1979). But the federal jurisdiction where Texas lies, the Fifth Circuit, does not. *See* Pet.App.8a–9a; *Alvarez,* 904 F.3d at 392. Three other circuits-the First, Second, and Fourth-agree with the Fifth that the due process right guaranteed in *Brady* does not apply until trial. But five others-the Sixth, Seventh, Eighth, Ninth, and Tenth (plus four state high courts besides Texas)-have recognized that *Brady* applies to plea bargaining as well.

This split creates significant uncertainty given that nearly 49 out of 50 federal criminal cases prosecuted to conclusion end in pleas rather than trials. The split has also given rise to absurd geographic disparities. For example, as in this case, the amount of process a defendant is due-and possibly the outcome of his case-varies depending on whether he is charged by state or federal authorities in Texas, or whether he is charged with the same federal crime on the other side of the Red River in neighboring Oklahoma.

Even as they affirmed the dismissal of Mansfield's *Brady* claim on the ground that Fifth Circuit precedent foreclosed applying *Brady* to plea-bargaining, Judges Higginbotham and Costa wrote concurrences calling on this Court to "definitively resolve the acknowledged circuit split" by "bring[ing] exculpatory evidence within the reach of *Brady.*" Pet.App.12a. For Judge Costa, the importance of the question presented "is not debatable" because "affording defendants in many jurisdictions" but not others "a constitutional right to exculpatory evidence" during plea bargaining "is not tenable"-especially, in Judge Higginbotham's words, in a "system in which almost everyone pleads guilty." Pet.App.14a–15a.

"The split on this issue begs for resolution." Pet.App.15a (Costa, J.). The Court should do so here.

STATEMENT OF THE CASE

In *Brady v. Maryland*, this Court held that "suppression by the prosecution of evidence favorable to an accused upon request violates due process where the evidence is material either to guilt or to punishment." 373 U.S. 83, 87 (1963). Based on the requirements of the Due Process Clause, the rule announced in *Brady* is rooted in the basic principle that a "contrivance by a state to procure the conviction and imprisonment of a defendant" through falsity and deception is "inconsistent with the rudimentary demands of justice." *Mooney v. Holohan*, 294 U.S. 103, 112 (1935) (per curiam); *see also United States v. Bagley*, 473 U.S. 667, 675 (1985) (purpose of *Brady* rule is "to ensure that a miscarriage of justice does not occur").

Here, prosecutors had evidence that they knew demonstrated Mansfield's innocence. Yet they concealed the undisputedly-exculpatory evidence to coerce a guilty plea from an innocent defendant. Mansfield seeks redress under § 1983, but has thus far been denied justice.

A.   Prosecutors hide exculpatory evidence from Mansfield and coerce him into pleading guilty.

In 1992, Mansfield was indicted in Williamson County for "one of the most heinous crimes-sexual misconduct with a child." Pet.App.13a (Costa, J.); *see also* Pet.App.16a–17a. Right away, a prosecutor saw problems with the case, noting in the case file that the "[c]hild's version to me differs from [the] version to police (greatly differs)." Pet.App.42a.

Months later, an interview with the alleged victim and her mother only increased these doubts. After "[s]pen[ding] 2 hours [with] this witness," the prosecutor noted that it "will be nigh impossible to sponsor her in court." *Id.* "She told me she does not remember what happened! . . . At one point, told me nothing happened, then says little boy"-another 4-year-old child—"might have done it." *Id.* Given this information, and the victim's mother's desire that she "not have to go through it," the prosecutor concluded that she "cannot testify." *Id.*

Just a day earlier, the District Attorney's office had been ordered by the state criminal court to disclose any exculpatory evidence to Mansfield. Pet.App.40a–41a. But they did not. Pet.App.44a. In violation of the order, they withheld the information they had learned during the interview. Pet.App.44a; Pet.App.94a (deposition of ADA John Prezas on behalf of Williamson County DA's office).

As trial approached, the prosecutors knew they had no complaining witness and were in a bind. The Williamson County DA's office "didn't lose cases," and the prosecutors who worked there internalized the maxim that "you don't try a case you can lose." Pet.App.82a (deposition of current Williamson County DA Shawn Dick). At the same time, dismissing indictments was all but forbidden. Pet.App.89a (Dick).

The prosecutors' solution was to make Mansfield an offer he couldn't refuse. Although the charges he faced carried a possible sentence of life imprisonment, Mansfield was offered a plea bargain of only 120 days in county jail, which could be completed on weekend work release. Pet.App. 46a–47a, 62a. This was an "unusually light" punishment recommendation given the crime alleged. Pet.App.3a.

The terms of the plea deal thus presented Mansfield with a "Hobson's choice." *Id.* He could plead guilty to a crime he did not commit and serve (relatively little) time and register as a sex offender. Pet.App.57a–58a, 61a–62a. Or he could face trial in Williamson County-where, that year, prosecutors neither dropped any felony charges nor lost any trials.

To further ensure that Mansfield would take the deal, prosecutors lied about the strength of their evidence. *See* Pet.App.93a (Prezas), 101a–03a (deposition of Mansfield's former defense attorney Stephen Cihal). Contrary to what they had observed during the interview, they told Mansfield the alleged victim was a "strong witness," a "good witness," and still "very adamant that Mr. Mansfield did this to her." Pet.App.97a, 101a (Cihal). They also said-again in contrast to the interview-that the victim's "mother wanted Mr. Mansfield prosecuted." Pet.App.97a. And they claimed to be ready to adduce at trial other (nonexistent) inculpatory evidence, such as a videotaped statement, physical evidence, and an expert witness, that would "put [Mansfield] under the jail." Pet.App.105a (Cihal), 109a (deposition of Troy Mansfield).

Prosecutors threatened to withdraw the offer if Mansfield did not accept before the September 1993 trial setting. Pet.App.104a (Cihal). This was another apparent lie, as the prosecutor had previously suggested that, since they couldn't put the victim on the stand, this case "be disposed of w/out trial." Pet.App.42a. But Mansfield did not know this-even though he was entitled to-and he took the deal. Pet.App.46a–47a.

B.   Williamson County's "closed file" policy institutionalizes the constitutional violation.

This conduct was standard procedure for the Williamson County DA's office. For decades, then-District Attorney Ken Anderson (who later gained notoriety as "the only prosecutor-past or present-who has ever spent time in jail for misconduct that led to a wrongful conviction" in the high-profile *Morton* murder case) had enforced a so-called "closed file" policy. The policy prevented defendants from reviewing material in the prosecution's files-including inculpatory evidence, *Brady* evidence, or evidence a court ordered disclosed-before trial. Pet.App.4a; Pet.App.88a–90a (Dick). And when prosecutors did disclose *Brady* evidence, they would orally (and selectively) paraphrase it rather than show it to defense counsel. Pet.App.74a, 80a (deposition of former DA Ken Anderson).

The purposes of the closed-file policy were both philosophical and tactical. For Anderson, the presumption of innocence "sound[ed] great in the abstract," but in reality "overbalanced the system in the other direction," allowing guilty defendants to "walk[ ]." Pet.App.78a (Anderson). As he explained to a Court of Inquiry, Anderson simply "d[id] not believe in the release of [exculpatory *Brady*] evidence if it may result in freeing an individual that he believes is guilty." In accordance with the policy, he directed prosecutors to withhold *Brady* evidence from defendants and "see what you can get" them to plead guilty to. Pet.App.88a–89a (Dick). Anderson also encouraged prosecutors to delay as long as possible before providing any exculpatory evidence, "[b]ecause the more time [defense attorneys] have to work with it, the more time they would have to massage what they were going to say." Pet.App.79a (Anderson).

Current District Attorney Shawn Dick also explained that Anderson's "closed file" policy was designed to force defendants-even those who, like Mansfield, were innocent-to weigh the possibility of relative freedom if they pled guilty against the risk of years in prison if convicted at trial. Pet.App.86a–87a.

C.   Mansfield learns what happened, and his conviction is vacated.

Meanwhile, for more than two decades, Mansfield—all the while having to endure the uniquely pernicious label of child sex offender-had no idea that he had been a victim of decisions made under this policy. *See* Pet.App.49a–56a. It was not until after revelations about Anderson's "unethical" policies and practices came to light in the unrelated *Morton* case that new counsel for Mansfield requested access to his case file and discovered the exculpatory evidence that had been hidden from him. Pet.App.63a–65a; Pet.App.92a (Prezas); *see* Pet.App.4a.

Relying on the prosecutor's notes, Mansfield applied for a writ of habeas corpus in Texas state court. Pet.App.63a–67a. He argued that "the State violated his due process rights by failing to disclose exculpatory evidence"-the State did not disagree-and that his plea "was involuntary because had the State disclosed the information contained in the prosecutor's notes, he would not have accepted the plea bargain." Pet.App.64a–65a, 67a.

In a 2016 order, the court agreed with the parties that the victim's statements in the interview notes "constitute the type of information that *Brady v. Maryland[ ]* and its progeny requires the State to disclose," and it concluded that failing to disclose them "violated ADMansfield's due process rights." Pet.App.67a. It also found that, because "the undisclosed information regarding the alleged victim [had] a 'direct nexus' to [Mansfield]'s plea," the prosecutors' failure to turn it over "render[ed] [his] plea involuntary." Pet.App.69a. The court granted Mansfield's application on both grounds. Pet.App.70a.

By this time, Anderson was long gone. *See* Brandi Grissom, *Judge Ken Anderson Resigns Amid Ethics Lawsuit,* Tex. Tribune (Sept. 3, 2013, 3:00 PM), bit.ly/3R9bNtH (Anderson appointed to bench in 2002 but resigned following ethics investigation over *Morton* case). The current Williamson County District Attorney's Office declined to re-prosecute Mansfield and agreed that, but for the prosecutors' improper conduct in 1993, the case should have been dismissed. Pet.App. 85a–86a (Dick).

D.   Mansfield's *Brady* claim is foreclosed by controlling circuit precedent.

Two years later, Mansfield sued Williamson County in the Western District of Texas under 42 U.S.C. § 1983. The complaint alleged that county prosecutors had, pursuant to the closed-file policy, coerced Mansfield's plea in violation of his due process rights in two different ways: (i) "[f]ailing to disclose exculpatory evidence" under *Brady,* and (ii) affirmatively lying about evidence against him. Pet.App.19a–20a, 28a–29a.

During discovery, Mansfield elicited admissions from Williamson County's designees that:

- prosecutors' failure to disclose the exculpatory interview notes "was a *Brady* violation" (Pet. App.91a);

- prosecutors violated the criminal court's order to disclose exculpatory evidence (Pet.App.94a);

- Mansfield's plea was "not voluntary," and therefore "legally invalid," "because he did not have the information that he needed for it to be a voluntary plea" (Pet.App.93a);

- Mansfield's due process rights were violated (Pet.App.91a); *accord* Pet.App.88aa (Dick, in his personal capacity); and

- Mansfield suffered an "unfair and inappropriate outcome" (Pet.App.9 la).

And yet, despite this and other evidence, the magistrate judge (to whose jurisdiction the parties had consented, Pet.App.38a) granted the County's motion for summary judgment. Pet.App.16a.

The magistrate judge considered both theories on which Mansfield had alleged a due process violation—(1) prosecutors' failure to turn over exculpatory evidence as required by *Brady*, and (2) their lies about the strength of their case- and rejected them. Pet.App. 22a–34a. As to the *Brady* claim-the only one Mansfield challenges here-the magistrate judge held that the Fifth Circuit's en banc decision in *Alvarez v. City of Brownsville* foreclosed applying *Brady* to plea negotiations, so there was no constitutional violation. Pet.App.22a–29a (citing 904 F.3d 382 (5th Cir. 2018)); Pet.App.33a–34a. The magistrate judge rejected Mansfield's alternative "lying" theory as well and entered summary judgment for Williamson County. Pet.App.34a–35a.

A Fifth Circuit panel affirmed in a published opinion. Pet.App.2a. Writing for the panel, Judge Higginbotham affirmed the dismissal of the lying theory on causation grounds. He then turned to Mansfield's separate argument that prosecutors violated *Brady* by withholding exculpatory evidence. Pet.App.8a. Bound by *Alvarez* and earlier circuit precedent holding that "there is no constitutional right to exculpatory evidence during plea bargaining," the panel concluded that Mansfield's *Brady* claim was "foreclosed." Pet.App.8a. The panel "note[d] the severity of [Mansfield's] allegations," but held that they could not support a § 1983 claim. Pet.App.9a.

Judges Higginbotham concurred in his own opinion, and Judge Costa added a special concurrence. Pet. App. 10a–15a. Both judges underscored the importance of applying *Brady* to pretrial plea negotiations and the need for this Court's intervention.

REASONS FOR GRANTING THE PETITION

This case presents a clear circuit split on an important and recurring question: whether *Brady* requires prosecutors to disclose exculpatory evidence before a guilty plea.

In their respective concurrences, Judges Higginbotham and Costa both called for this Court to resolve this "acknowledged circuit split." Pet.App.12a (Higginbotham, J., concurring); *accord* Pet.App.15a (Costa, J., concurring) (split "begs for resolution"). Five federal courts of appeals (for the Sixth, Seventh, Eighth, Ninth, and Tenth Circuits) and five state high courts (in Texas, Utah, South Carolina, Nevada, and West Virginia) have recognized that due process demands such disclosure. Four others have held that it does not-including the Fifth Circuit, which, in reaffirming its position here, went to a startling extreme: not only may the government suppress evidence of factual innocence, it may lie to conceal the evidence and coerce a plea. *See* S. Ct. R. 10(a)–(b).

As this split has deepened, the incidence of resolution-by-plea has increased to alarming levels. By 2011, the rate at which federal criminal cases prosecuted to conclusion were resolved by guilty plea "had risen to 97 percent." Michael Nasser Petegorsky, *Plea Bargaining in the Dark: The Duty to Disclose Exculpatory Brady Evidence During Plea Bargaining,* 81 Fordham L. Rev. 3599, 3611 (2013). As Judge Higginbotham—and many other judges and scholars, including now-Third Circuit Judge Bibas—recognized, "we cannot look away from uncertainties within the processing of ninety-seven percent of the federal criminal docket." Pet.App.11a–12a (citing Stephanos Bibas, *Designing Plea Bargaining from the Ground Up: Accuracy and Fairness Without Trials as Backstops,* 57 Wm. & Mary L. Rev. 1055 (2016); Stephanos Bibas, *Regulating the Plea-Bargaining Market: From Caveat Emptor to Consumer Protection,* 99 Calif. L. Rev. 1117 (2011); Stephanos Bibas, *Plea Bargaining Outside the Shadow of Trial,* 117 Harv. L. Rev. 2464 (2004)).

The need for certainty is especially pressing in the Fifth Circuit, where more than one in four federal criminal cases originates. The geographic and jurisdictional disparities this split creates are untenable. If Mansfield, for example, had lived in neighboring Oklahoma rather than Texas and had been subject to Tenth Circuit law (which requires disclosure) instead of Fifth Circuit law (which does not), the outcome of his case would have been entirely different. And if Mansfield had pled guilty in federal court in Texas, his conviction would not have been overturned despite discovering that the prosecutors withheld evidence of his innocence. Or-as is the case here-even though a Texas state court applying its controlling precedent found that the prosecution violated Mansfield's federal due process rights, the federal court in Texas was foreclosed from doing so under Fifth Circuit law for exactly the same conduct. Such arbitrariness is inconsistent with the concept of justice and needs to be reconciled. After four decades of uncertainty, this case presents an opportunity for this Court to put the issue to rest and resolve the circuit split on this important question.

I.   Fourteen circuits and state high courts have split on whether *Brady* applies pre-plea.

A total of 14 circuits and state high courts have split over whether *Brady* applies during plea bargaining as well as trial. Five circuits and five state high courts have held or otherwise recognized that it does. *See, e.g., Smith v. Baldwin*, 510 F.3d 1127, 1148 (9th Cir. 2007); *United States v. Ohiri*, 133 F. App'x 555, 562 (10th Cir. 2005); *McCann v. Mangialardi*, 337 F.3d 782, 788 (7th Cir. 2003); *White v. United States*, 858 F.2d 416, 423 (8th Cir. 1988); *Campbell v. Marshall*, 769 F.2d 314, 324 (6th Cir. 1985); *Buffey v. Ballard*, 782 S.E.2d 204, 218 (W. Va. 2015); *State v. Huebler*, 275 P.3d 91, 96–97 (Nev. 2012); *Hyman v. State*, 723 S.E.2d 375, 380 (S.C. 2012); *Medel v. State*, 184 P.3d 1226, 1235 (Utah 2008); *Lewis*, 587 S.W.2d at 700–01.

Other circuit courts have rejected or expressed serious doubts that a defendant has a right to *Brady* material before pleading guilty. *See, e.g., United States v. Mathur*, 624 F.3d 498, 506–07 (1st Cir. 2010); *Friedman v. Rehal*, 618 F.3d 142, 154 (2d Cir. 2010); *United States v. Moussaoui*, 591 F.3d 263, 285 (4th Cir. 2010). The Fifth Circuit has long shared that view. *See, e.g., Alvarez, 904 F.3d at 392; United States v. Conroy*, 567 F.3d 174, 178 (5th Cir. 2009); *Matthew v. Johnson*, 201 F.3d 353, 361–62 (5th Cir. 2000). Indeed, it has declined to require disclosure of *Brady* material during plea bargaining even when prosecutors affirmatively lie to conceal exculpatory evidence. *See* Pet.App.7a–8a.

A.   The Fifth Circuit splits from 10 other circuits and state courts that applied *Brady* to plea bargaining.

It was not always this way. For more than two decades after *Brady* was decided, no federal appellate court or state high court had occasion to consider how the right recognized there applied outside the context of trial. When the issue began to recur in the 1980s, three circuits (and, earlier, a state court of last resort) held that the government must disclose exculpatory information pre-plea, and another circuit had recognized that possibility. It was not until 2000 that the Fifth Circuit broke this streak.

1.   The issue first arose in a federal appellate decision in 1985 in the Sixth Circuit, when the court considered whether the prosecution's "prior withholding of [ ] *Brady* information"-a gun found in the murder victim's pocket-"so taint [ed] the plea-taking as to render the guilty plea involuntary or unintelligent." *Campbell v. Marshall,* 769 F.2d 314, 315 (6th Cir. 1985). Because "knowledge of the gun's presence was important" but not "controlling in the decision whether to plead," the court found no due process violation. *Id.* at 324. Still, *Campbell* marked the first time a federal appellate court recognized the possibility that a *Brady* violation, which renders "unavailable" information that would "aid in [a defendant's] evaluation of the possibilities of success on trial," might rise to the level of a constitutional violation. *Id.*

Three years later, the Eighth Circuit adopted this position in *White v. United States,* 858 F.2d 416 (8th Cir. 1988). The court echoed the Sixth Circuit's reasoning that the prosecution's suppression of exculpatory evidence that would otherwise be available "to aid [the defendant] in evaluating the chance for success at trial" is an available (if not guaranteed) path by which to challenge a guilty plea as unknowing or involuntary. *Id.* at 422. The Eighth Circuit concluded that, while the plea at issue did not meet that standard, nothing "preclude[d] a collateral attack upon a guilty plea based on a claimed *Brady* violation." *Id.; accord Nguyen v. United States,* 114 F.3d 699, 705 (8th Cir. 1997) (citing *White,* 858 F.2d at 422).

The Tenth Circuit reached the same conclusion in *United States v. Wright,* 43 F.3d 491 (10th Cir. 1994). As in *Campbell,* the evidence at issue in *Wright* turned out not to be material, and there was no *Brady* violation. *Id.* at 497. But this did not prevent the Court from repeating *Brady's* admonishment that because a guilty plea represents "the defendant's consent that judgment of conviction may be entered without a trial," waiver of the trial right must be a voluntary and "knowing, intelligent act[ ] done with sufficient awareness of the relevant circumstances and likely consequences." *Brady,* 397 U.S. at 495. Given the "importance to the integrity of our criminal justice system that guilty pleas be knowing and intelligent," the court held that, "under certain limited circumstances, the prosecution's violation of *Brady* can render a defendant's plea involuntary." *Wright,* 43 F.3d at 496 (citing, inter alia, *White,* 858 F.2d at 422).

The Ninth Circuit held even more squarely that "a defendant challenging the voluntariness of a guilty plea may assert a *Brady* claim." *Sanchez v. United States,* 50 F.3d 1448, 1453 (9th Cir. 1995). Although there again happened to be no *Brady* violation-the prosecutors were not aware of the connection between the exculpatory evidence and the defendants' case, and it was not material anyway-the court acknowledged the possibility that a violation could occur during plea bargaining. *See id.* Because "a defendant's decision whether or not to plead guilty is often heavily influenced by his appraisal of the prosecution's case," a waiver of the trial right cannot be " 'intelligent and voluntary' if entered without knowledge of material information withheld by the prosecution." *Id.* (quotation marks omitted). If *Brady* could not be invoked "after a guilty plea," "prosecutors may be tempted to deliberately withhold exculpatory information as part of an attempt to elicit guilty pleas." *Id.*

The Second Circuit focused on this alternate rationale-preventing prosecutorial mischief-in *United States v. Avellino*, 136 F.3d 249 (2d Cir. 1998). Again, the court recognized that "[t]he government's *[Brady]* obligation . . . is pertinent not only to an accused's preparation for trial but also to his determination of whether or not to plead guilty"—not only because "[t]he defendant is entitled to make that decision with full awareness of favorable material evidence," but because the plea "resulted from impermissible conduct by state agents." *Id.* at 255 (quoting *Brady*, 397 U.S. at 757); *see also Miller v. Angliker*, 848 F.2d 1312, 1320 (2d Cir. 1988) (*Brady* can apply pre-guilty plea).

Soon after, the South Carolina Supreme Court adopted the Second Circuit's rationale in becoming the first state high court to hold that a defendant "may challenge the voluntary nature of his guilty plea . . . by asserting an alleged *Brady* violation." *Gibson v. State*, 514 S.E.2d 320, 523–24 (S.C. 1999) (citing *Avellino*, 136 F.3d at 255). Technically speaking, however, it was not the first state *court of last resort* to reach this conclusion; the Texas Court of Criminal Appeals-that state's court of last resort for criminal cases-had long recognized that *Brady's* protection against "the nondisclosure of favorable information . . . extends to guilty pleas as well as to contested cases." *Ex parte Lewis*, 587 S.W.2d 697, 700 (Tex. Crim. App. 1979).

2.   In *Matthew v. Johnson*, however, the Fifth Circuit split from these courts, expressly rejecting the application of *Brady* to plea bargaining. 201 F.3d 353, 364 (5th Cir. 2000). Rejecting some cases discussed above and overreading others, it reasoned that "a *Brady* violation is defined in terms of the potential effects of undisclosed information on a judge's or jury's assessment of guilt," and therefore cannot apply to "an individual waiving his right to trial." *Id.* at 362 (declining to adopt Second Circuit's rule in *Miller* and pointing out that there had been no *Brady* violations in *Campbell* and *White); accord Conroy*, 567 F.3d at 178.

Becoming a Professional: Part 1

Given how hard it is to define clear standards defining litigation abuse, much is left to individual attorneys to decide how they want to practice law. To be clear, there are enforceable rules. Lawyers can and will be sanctioned for litigation abuse. But the ambiguity of the rules, and the fear of deterring legitimate use of the courts, means that discipline cases will tend to be extreme. Our legal system requires testing, which means that good lawyers will often file cases that fail. Almost every famous court precedent that changed the law started with a lawyer advancing an argument that could have been called baseless when it was first filed. One recalls James Comey's admonishment to his attorneys at the U.S. Attorney's Office for the Southern District of New York that if they never file cases that they might lose, they are part of the "chickenshit club."

So, where would you draw the line between aggressive advocacy and abuse? Consider the following very common scenario, which occurs frequently in immigration law:

In American immigration law, it is common for an immigrant to be deportable, and yet also eligible for a visa to stay legally in the United States. This seemingly contradictory situation occurs because many visas have quotas and because U.S. Citizenship and Immigration Services is horribly backlogged in processing applications, leading to multi-year waits. A lawyer defending an undocumented immigrant against deportation—known as removal—may thus conclude that the best course of action is to delay the removal proceedings.

The question is: How to delay? Sometimes there is a straightforward answer because individual Immigration Judges or prevailing policy allow continuances in this situation. If that is the prevailing rule, an attorney can simply tell the court exactly what is happening, and get the time needed for her client. But in the ever shifting world of immigration policy, this straightforward and ethically unproblematic approach is not always possible. During some periods in recent history, the Immigration Courts have not permitted such continuances. And some individual Immigrant Judges are more reluctant to grant them.

An immigration lawyer and her client still have some options to consider. They could file an application for asylum (based on fear of persecution abroad) or cancellation of removal (based on extreme hardship to an immigrant's family members). Such applications typically require a trial-like "individual hearing" in Immigration Court. The Immigration Courts are so backlogged that the hearing might not be scheduled for many years, which means that even if the application is ultimately denied the client might have gained the time needed for her visa to come through. The question an immigration lawyer must ask is: How strong must such an application be to ethically go through with it? Taking just the asylum option, consider the following possibilities:

a) What if the client tells her lawyer she has absolutely no fear of anyone harming her in her country, which means that there is likely no way to file an asylum application without fabricating information?

b) What if the client is genuinely worried about her safety in her country because there is an extremely high crime rate, but asylum law does not grant relief for people fearing general crime?

c) What if the client fears a kind of persecution that current law rejects as a basis for asylum, but many immigrant advocates are pressing politically and in court to change the law?

Becoming a Professional: Part 2

X-Ray Questions

Michael Morton was wrongfully convicted of the brutal murder of his wife. The crime was committed in a small Texas town. The DA at the time withers exculpatory evidence. The DA, who later became a judge, was sent to prison for his failure. Texas then enacted the following statute to prevent this from occurring again. What are the key elements? Why won't an honor system work? Research whether your state has a similar statute. If so, compare it to the Texas law. What is similar and what is different?

BEYOND THE CITE
S.B. No. 1611 AN ACT Relating to discovery in a criminal case. BE IT ENACTED BY THE LEGISLATURE OF THE STATE OF TEXAS: SECTION 1. This act shall be known as the Michael Morton Act. SECTION 2. Article 39.14, Code of Criminal Procedure, is amended by amending Subsection (a) and adding Subsection (c) through (n) to read as follows:

(a)   Subject to the restrictions provided by Section 264.408, Family Code, and Article 39.15 of this code, as soon as practicable after receiving a timely request from the defendant the state shall produce and permit the inspection and the electronic duplication, copying, and photographing, by or on behalf of the defendant, of any offense reports, any designated documents, papers, written or recorded statements of the defendant or a witness, including witness statements of law enforcement officers but not including, the work product of counsel in the case and their investigators and their notes or report, or any designated books, accounts, letters, photographs, or objects or other tangible things not otherwise privileged that constitute or contain evidence material to any matter involved in the action and that are in the possession, custody, or control of the state or any person under contract with the state The state may provide to the defendant electronic duplicates of any documents or other information described by this article. rights granted to the defendant under this article do not extend to written communications between the state and an agent, representative, or employee of the state. This article does not authorize [the removal of the documents, items, or information from the possession of the state], and any inspection shall be in the presence of a representative of the state.

. . . .

(c)   If only a portion of the applicable document, item, or information is subject to discovery under this article, the state is not required to produce or permit the inspection of the remaining portion that is not subject to discovery and may withhold or redact that portion. The state shall inform the defendant that a portion of the document, item, or information has been withheld or redacted. On request of the defendant, the court shall conduct a hearing to determine whether withholding or redaction is justified under this article or other law.

(d)   In the case of a pro se defendant, if the court orders the state to produce and permit the inspection of a document, item, or information under this subsection, the state shall permit the pro se defendant to inspect and review the document, item, or information but is not required to allow electronic duplication as described by Subsection (a).

(e)   Except as provided by Subsection (f), the defendant, the attorney representing the defendant, or an investigator, expert, consulting legal counsel, or other agent of the attorney representing the defendant may not disclose to a third party any documents, evidence, materials, or witness statements received from the state under this article unless:

> (1)   a court orders the disclosure upon a showing of good cause after notice and hearing after considering the security and privacy interests of any victim or witness; or

> (2)   the documents, evidence, materials, or witness statements have already been publicly disclosed.

(f)   The attorney representing the defendant, or an investigator, expert, consulting legal counsel, or agent for the attorney representing the defendant, may allow a defendant, witness, or prospective witness to view the information provided under this article, but may not allow that person to have copies of the information provided, other than a copy of the witness's own statement. Before allowing that person to view a document or the witness statement of another under this subsection, the person possessing the information shall redact the address, telephone number, driver's license number, social security number, date of birth, and any bank account or other identifying numbers contained in the document or witness statement. For purposes of this section, the defendant may not be the agent for the attorney representing the defendant.

(g)   Nothing in this section shall be interpreted to limit an attorney's ability to communicate regarding his or her case within the Texas Disciplinary Rules of Professional Conduct, except for the communication of information identifying any victim or witness, including name, except as provided in Subsections (e) and (f), address, telephone number, driver's license number, social security number, date of birth, and bank account information or any information that by reference would make it possible to identify a victim or a witness. Nothing in this subsection shall prohibit the disclosure of identifying information to an administrative, law enforcement, regulatory, or licensing agency for the purposes of making a good faith complaint.

(h)   Notwithstanding any other provision of this article, the state shall disclose to the defendant any exculpatory, impeachment, or mitigating document, item, or information in the possession, custody, or control of the state that tends to negate the guilt of the defendant or would tend to reduce the punishment for the offense charged.

(i)   The state shall electronically record or otherwise document any document, item, or other information provided to the defendant under this article.

(j)   Before accepting a plea of guilty or nolo contendere, or before trial, each party shall acknowledge in writing or on the record in open court the disclosure, receipt, and list of all documents, items, and information provided to the defendant under this article.

(k)   If at any time before, during, or after trial the state discovers any additional document, item, or information required the disclosed under Subsection (h), the state shall promptly disclose the existence of the document, item, or information to the defendant or the court.

(l)   A court may order the defendant to pay costs related to discovery under this article, provided that costs may not exceed the charges prescribed by Subchapter F, Chapter 552, Government Code.

(m)   To the extent of any conflict, this article prevails over Chapter 552, Government Code. (n) This article does not prohibit the parties from agreeing to discovery and documentation requirements equal to or greater than those required under this article.

SECTION 3. The change in law made by this Act applies to the prosecution of an offense committed on or after the effective date of this Act. The prosecution of an offense committed before the effective date of this Act is covered by the law in effect when the offense was committed, and the former law is continued in effect for this purpose. For purposes of this section, an offense is committed before the effective date of this Act if any element of the offense occurs before the effective date.

SECTION 4. This Act takes effect January 1, 2014.

WHAT'S NEXT?

Now we move to the next step in litigation; namely the trial itself. There are multiple ethical rules that are triggered by circumstances arising at trial—from lawyer tricks masquerading as legitimate strategy to a client who wants to engage in perjury to Constitutional Law issues on the right to testify in one's defense. The underlying ethical frame though is how to go about creating an "even playing field" in trial so that the client *and* the system each receive their due.

To assess your understanding of the material in this chapter, click here to take a quiz.

The Lawyer at Trial

CHAPTER 7

Ethical Issues at Trial

Coming Attractions

The tension between competing ethical values is most pronounced at a trial. While lawyers seek, for their client's sake (and often their own) to reframe a loss as a win, it is hard to avoid the binary mindset of either "I won, or I lost." The duty to zealously represent the client seeking to win collides head-on with the duty to zealously preserve the integrity of the legal system. This friction is inescapable. How do the Rules resolve the tension? They seek to structure a fair fight on the record (defined as what the court allows into evidence and how that evidence is admitted). The specific goal is for clients—win, lose, draw—to walk away from the dispute believing that it was a fair fight and for observers to reach the same conclusion. The goal is for the public to feel confident having their disputes resolved by this system.

Section 1.   Even Playing Field at Trial

A.   Unethical Trial Tactics

Model Rule 3.4(e): Fairness to Opposing Party and Counsel

A lawyer shall not:

> (e)   in trial, allude to any matter that the lawyer does not reasonably believe is relevant or that will not be supported by admissible evidence, assert personal knowledge of facts in issue except when testifying as a witness, or state a personal opinion as to the justness of a cause, the credibility of a witness, the culpability of a civil litigant or the guilt or innocence of an accused.

Deconstruction Exercise/Rule Rationale

Note the use of "allude" in the first line. Why this word and not another? The drafters could have used "state" or "declare" or "refer" could they have not? They selected allude because they wanted the most ambiguous word possible in order to cover as much conduct as possible. In short, a precise word to communicate a vague concept. But what is the object of "allude"? The drafters provide a laundry list of tactics that create an unbalanced playing field. At their core the items on the list—while certainly effective tactics—are unethical because they allow the record to be cluttered with statements that cannot be contradicted nor disputed.

Cases and Materials

X-Ray Questions (*Gilster*)

This case is an illustration of how a lawyer snatched defeat from the jaws of victory. It is a sexual harassment case. The verdict was large. So, what was the problem? In her final argument—in rebuttal, the last words spoken by lawyers at a trial—she felt compelled to interject that she (the lawyer) was herself the victim of sexual harassment while in college; that she did not complain about it; and look at how brave her client was in comparison to her. Why did the lawyer make this argument? Did she have an improper motive or was it because she was in the midst of a heated trial? Should her motive come into play in deciding the outcome of this appeal? In your study of the Rules thus far, has a lawyer's motives ever been a viable defense? What did she say that created an uneven playing field?

Gilster v. Primebank

United States Court of Appeals, Eighth Circuit, 2014.
747 F.3d 1007.

Opinion

LOKEN, CIRCUIT JUDGE.

Primebank and Joseph Strub ("Defendants") appeal a $900,000 jury verdict in favor of Plaintiff Mindy Gilster on her claims of unlawful sexual harassment and retaliation under Title VII of the Civil Rights Act of 1964, 42 U.S.C. §§ 2000e *et seq.*, and the Iowa Civil Rights Act, Iowa Code § 216.6. Defendants argue they are entitled to a new trial because the district court erred in overruling their objection to improper rebuttal closing argument by Gilster's counsel, and then abused its discretion in denying Defendants' post-trial motion because this argument, while improper, was not sufficiently prejudicial to warrant a new trial. Concluding this is one of those relatively rare cases where Defendants have made a sufficient showing of prejudice caused by "plainly unwarranted and clearly injurious" closing argument, we reverse and remand for a new trial. *See Morrissey v. Welsh Co.,* 821 F.2d 1294, 1303 (8th Cir.1987) (standard of review).

I.

We briefly summarize evidence from the six-day jury trial that bears on the prejudicial closing argument issue presented on appeal. Joseph Strub as Market President of Primebank's branch in Sioux City, Iowa, hired Gilster as Credit Administrator in December 2007. Gilster filed an internal sexual harassment complaint in July 2009, alleging continuing sexual harassment by Strub. Gilster testified that the harassment started "around the summer of 2008." She finally overcame her reluctance to make a formal complaint when Gilster inquired about a possible bonus and Strub replied, in front of the entire small staff, that Gilster should "take out your teeth, come into my office, and shut the door." According to Gilster, Strub also made comments about her legs when she wore skirts; placed his arm around her shoulders and said that they "should hook up"; approached her from behind while she was fixing breakfast in the employee break room, placed his hands on the counter alongside hers, and pressed his pelvis against her backside; and massaged her shoulders "intimately" when she was seated at her desk.

Primebank investigated Gilster's complaint. Strub admitted making the "take out your teeth" comment; he denied her other allegations of continuing sexual harassment. Primebank "found that there was substance" to Gilster's complaint and disciplined Strub by issuing a formal reprimand, requiring him to attend sexual harassment training at a local community college, instructing him to stop harassing Gilster, and warning him not to retaliate.

Though Gilster reported no further instances of overt sexual harassment by Strub directed to her, she began complaining of retaliation by Strub in late July 2009, complaints that continued and intensified until Primebank fired her in February 2011. According to Gilster, Strub began avoiding her after she complained and changed his voicemail message to direct callers to contact a less experienced employee rather than Gilster. Primebank investigated the retaliation complaints. Strub explained that he was "quiet" for a few days after Gilster's initial complaint, but the office was quickly back to normal. He changed his voicemail message when he went on vacation because Gilster was just returning, and the other employee had been dealing with new clients while Gilster was away. The Primebank officers to whom Gilster complained considered this a legitimate business reason that was "not retaliatory." Gilster testified that Strub never put her back on his voicemail message.

Gilster subsequently complained that Strub denied her a promised promotion to a salaried position in December 2009. Primebank officers investigated the complaint and concluded that the position Gilster wanted did not exist and her current position could not be an exempt salaried position. When Primebank took no action on this complaint, Gilster hired counsel and filed a complaint of sexual harassment and retaliation with the Iowa Civil Rights Commission. Primebank responded by interviewing Gilster's co-workers, making them aware that Gilster had complained of harassment by Strub. Several employees complained to Primebank about Gilster beginning in late 2009, complaints that her former co-workers characterized at trial as reflecting a downturn in Gilster's work performance rather than retaliation. Gilster testified that the co-worker interviews made her work environment more "difficult" and "hostile." Co-workers testified that a change in Gilster's attitude led to a tense environment in the office.

Gilster filed this lawsuit in September 2010. Primebank's human resources officer was directed to encourage Gilster's co-workers to report any performance problems. In December 2010, Gilster received a worse performance review than in periods before she complained of Strub's harassment. Gilster "felt that there was a big target on [her] back." On February 3, 2011, staff discovered that Gilster's emails from her office computer were being monitored. Gilster reacted in a way Primebank management considered disruptive. On February 7, she filed a second discrimination complaint with the Iowa Human Rights Commission. Three days later, Primebank fired Gilster. She filed a Second Amended Complaint. The case proceeded to trial.

At trial, the parties disputed the extent and nature of Strub's initial harassment, whether Strub or any other Primebank employee retaliated against Gilster, and whether Primebank's reasons for termination were pretextual. Witness credibility was crucial, as the parties introduced sharply conflicting testimony regarding who was to blame for what obviously became an exceedingly unpleasant workplace in the months leading up to Gilster's termination. Primebank witnesses offered two nonretaliatory reasons for Gilster's termination; vigorous cross-examination by her attorneys made it plausible for the jury to infer that these reasons were pretextual.

There was also conflicting evidence regarding the extent and the cause of Gilster's emotional distress. Gilster, her husband, and a nurse practitioner, Elizabeth Pratt, provided detailed evidence of emotional distress. But Gilster initially told Nurse Pratt in August 2008 that her anxiety and depression began in December 2007, before she alleged that Strub began sexually harassing her. Gilster saw Nurse Pratt again in November 2008, but she did not complain of workplace harassment until July 2009, just after filing her internal complaint.

Gilster testified that she suffered enhanced injury from Strub's harassment because she had been sexually abused as a child, but she never discussed this history with Nurse Pratt. Gilster, her husband, and Nurse Pratt provided testimony supporting a claim of future emotional distress that Gilster allegedly suffered after she was fired, including depression, anxiety, excessive alcohol consumption, and self-mutilation. But Gilster only saw a counselor once, and Nurse Pratt had not seen Gilster since August 2010.

The jury found both Primebank and Strub liable for unlawful sexual harassment and retaliation. The verdict awarded Gilster over $900,000. The district court reduced the verdict to eliminate obvious duplications and excesses and denied Defendants' post-trial motion for new trial. This appeal followed.

II.

The issue on appeal is whether counsel for Gilster during rebuttal closing argument made improper remarks that were so "plainly unwarranted and clearly injurious" that they warrant a new trial. *Morrissey*, 821 F.2d at 1303. We review the district court's denial of a new trial for abuse of discretion. *Billingsley v. City of Omaha*, 277 F.3d 990, 997 (8th Cir.2002).

In our view, counsel's rebuttal argument included numerous comments that clearly violated the following provisions in Rule 32:3.4 of the Iowa Rules of Professional Conduct, titled Fairness to Opposing Party and Counsel:

> A lawyer shall not . . . in trial, allude to any matter . . . that will not be
> supported by admissible evidence, assert personal knowledge of facts
> in issue except when testifying as a witness, or state a personal opinion
> as to the justness of a cause, the credibility of a witness, [or] the
> culpability of a civil litigant. . . .

Thus, the critical question is whether the comments were sufficiently prejudicial to require the new trial the district court denied. In considering this issue, our focus is on counsel's final remarks, which appear on pages 1470–71 of the trial transcript:

> Mindy told you when she made her complaint back in 2009 she
> feared . . . retaliation and that making her complaints and what effect
> it would have on her career.

> Mindy Gilster had the strength to make that complaint back on
> July 2, 2009. I sure didn't. Back in 2006 I was sexually harassed by a
> professor at Drake, but I was on my way out. I was a third-year law
> student, and I had been a student bar association president for the last

year, and I was well respected and liked by my peers. I had a great
relationship with the dean of the law school because of my role as
president. But I refused to be that—

> [DEFENSE COUNSEL]: Excuse me, counsel. Your Honor, I
> do not think this is appropriate for argument.
>
> THE COURT: Overruled.
>
> MS. TIMMER: And I refused to stand up for myself. It takes
> great strength and fearlessness to make a complaint against your
> supervisor.
>
> Given my calling as a civil rights lawyer, I am constantly amazed
> by the strength and courage that my clients have when facing their
> employers and supervisors, the people who hold all the power. It is
> my sincere hope that one day my daughter, my friends, my sisters will
> live in a community where they will not be silenced by fear. And you
> can ensure this happens with your verdict.
>
> I am fortunate that in the course of my life and in my work I've
> had the opportunity to represent these women who are so strong to
> make these complaints. I'm fortunate in my life that for the last two
> years I've had the honor of representing Miss Mindy Gilster and that
> I got to try this case.
>
> But the power and responsibility that I've held on Mindy's case
> for the last two years is now over, and I am particularly fortunate that
> I can give the power and responsibility for correcting injustices like
> those we have seen in this courtroom to somebody else. I give it to
> you.

In denying Defendants' post-trial motion, the district court concluded that
it should have sustained the above objection because it was improper for counsel
to "testify as an expert witness" about her other clients' courage, citing *United
States v. Segal,* 649 F.2d 599, 604 (8th Cir.1981). However, the court concluded,
Defendants did not "make a concrete showing of prejudice" from this improper
argument because counsel's "analogy to her own life" did not "vouch[ ] for the
credibility of Gilster's claims" but merely "emphasized evidence already in the
record"; "Gilster's success did not hinge only on her credibility"; the size of the
verdict was not evidence that "counsel's remarks prejudiced the jury"; and,
"[p]erhaps most important of all," the court's instructions at the start and end
of the trial told the jury that "statements, arguments, questions, and comments
by the lawyers are not evidence." We disagree.

In determining whether Defendants made the requisite showing of prejudice, the entire trial must be our context. *See Silbergleit v. First Interstate Bank of Fargo, N.A.*, 37 F.3d 394, 398 (8th Cir.1994). In *Whittenburg v. Werner Enterprises, Inc.*, 561 F.3d 1122, 1131–32 (10th Cir.2009), the Tenth Circuit identified "three separate factors, long used to mark the boundaries between when a new trial is and is not required." We conclude that each of those factors is present here.

First, the remarks in question "were not 'minor aberrations' made in passing." *Id.* at 1131. Counsel made a deliberate strategic choice to make emotionally-charged comments at the end of rebuttal closing argument, when they would have the greatest emotional impact on the jury, and when opposing counsel would have no opportunity to respond. Referring to an experience in her own life was "plainly calculated to arouse [the jury's] sympathy." *Id.* at 1129. Counsel then ended the argument by "giving" to the jury "the power and responsibility for correcting injustices." This was no different than a prosecutor urging the jury at the end of a criminal case "to be the conscience of the community," an improper argument that, in a close case, may warrant a new trial. *United States v. Johnson*, 968 F.2d 768, 771–72 (8th Cir.1992). Moreover, counsel's recounting of her personal experience—facts that were not in evidence—was aimed at enhancing her client's credibility by telling the jury that counsel, too, had endured similar misconduct. "[T]he cardinal rule of closing argument [is] that counsel must confine comments to evidence in the record and to reasonable inferences from that evidence." *Whittenburg*, 561 F.3d at 1128–29; *see People v. Hayes*, 183 Ill.App.3d 752, 132 Ill.Dec. 45, 539 N.E.2d 355, 358–60 (1989) (reversing sexual assault conviction and remanding for a new trial because prosecutor vouched for the victim's credibility by describing a personal experience).

Indeed, improper vouching permeated counsel's rebuttal argument. Earlier, counsel had argued:

> And I assure you Mindy Gilster did not make up the fact that her uncle sexually abused her at age 12. It was not a fact she brought in here to arouse sympathy or ask for more money. It's just the facts, folks.

> * * *

> All I can tell you is from my conversations with Mindy is that she doesn't recall saying [anxiety and depression] started [when Nurse Pratt's records reflected].

On appeal, Gilster concedes that it was improper vouching when counsel assured the jury that her client testified truthfully about past sexual abuse and about when her depression and anxiety began. Yet the district court brushed this vouching aside, reiterating that "Gilster's case did not turn solely on her own credibility." Counsel also repeatedly referred to the experiences of other clients, again arguing evidence not in the trial record, which the district court acknowledged was improper:

> There are plenty of my former clients who I was able to ensure were back in the workplace and everything has been fine and they still work there.

* * *

> Some of us deal with things in different ways. There's no doubt. I have clients who go to church more, who talk to their pastor or their priest, who go out with their friends or family members, who confide in—who do actually go see counselors. I have clients who turn to alcohol, a glass of wine before bed.

The second factor identified by the court in *Whittenburg* is that "the district court declined to take any specific curative action." 561 F.3d at 1131. Here, as in *Whittenburg*, the district court overruled defense counsel's timely objection to the improper argument, which told the jury they could appropriately consider the argument in the deliberations they were about to begin. True, the district court's general instructions included a reminder that counsel's arguments are not evidence, but this did not dissuade the court in *Whittenburg* from remanding for a new trial:

> The district court's decision to overrule the objection to counsel's argument and deem it appropriate was never undone and remained the most specific and timely guidance from the court to the jury with respect to the propriety of counsel's closing remarks. *Id.* at 1132.

We agree. Indeed, in *Morrissey*, we concluded that the district court committed "*reversible error*" when it failed to sustain defendant's objection to an argument that was "an emotional appeal to the jury to punish the company." 821 F.2d at 1304; *see N.Y. Central R.R. v. Johnson*, 279 U.S. 310, 318, 49 S.Ct. 300, 73 L.Ed. 706 (1929) ("The failure of the trial judge to sustain petitioner's objection or otherwise to make certain that the jury would disregard the appeal, could only have left them with the impression that they might properly be influenced by it in rendering their verdict, and thus its prejudicial effect was enhanced.").

The third factor identified by the court in *Whittenburg* is also present in this case—"the size of the damage award, while not beyond the bounds of rationality, suggest[s] that counsel's comment had a prejudicial effect." 561 F.3d at 1132. As we have explained, both the cause and the extent of Gilster's emotional damages were vigorously contested. Gilster's testimony was the only evidence that she suffered sexual abuse as a child that increased her emotional injury from Strub's harassment. Gilster and Nurse Pratt differed as to why Gilster sought treatment for depression and anxiety in the summer of 2008. And no evidence other than Nurse Pratt's equivocal opinion supported Gilster's testimony that she would suffer emotionally for the rest of her life as a result of Defendants' actions. Counsel's vouching and sympathy-arousing personal experience were directly aimed at enhancing these damages. Given the jury's decision to award Gilster $40,000 for past emotional distress, $200,000 for future emotional distress, and $600,000 punitive damages, we cannot say that this improper argument "did not accomplish the purpose which it was clearly intended to accomplish, namely, the enhancement of damages." *Id.* at 1132–33, quoting *Chicago & N.W. Ry. v. Kelly,* 84 F.2d 569, 576 (8th Cir.1936); *accord Morrissey,* 821 F.2d at 1303 ("We cannot say on the record before us that there is no correlation between the large sum awarded ... and the obviously prejudicial argument made by plaintiff['s] counsel.").

In *Stollings v. Ryobi Technologies, Inc.,* the Seventh Circuit noted that "the weight of the evidence" is another relevant factor in determining "whether the improper argument deprived a party of a fair trial." 725 F.3d 753, 760 (7th Cir.2013). Though not determinative, we agree this is a relevant factor. Again, it points toward the need for a new trial in this case. After the jury returned its verdict, the district court commented, "it was kind of a tough case. It could go either way." And unlike the district court, we conclude that Gilster's credibility, which counsel's improper argument was intended to enhance, was a key issue as to liability, as well as damages. Only Gilster described Strub's alleged harassment other than the "take out your teeth" comment, because her former female co-workers testified they did not observe such conduct or experience it themselves. Gilster's testimony describing retaliatory actions by Strub and other Primebank officers, and her opinion that the reasons given for her termination were false, were contradicted by her co-workers, as well as by her supervisors and by the Primebank decisionmakers. The hard-fought trial warranted hard-hitting, but not improper, closing argument.

Having carefully reviewed the entire trial record, we are left with the firm conviction that the timing and emotional nature of counsel's improper and repeated personal vouching for her client, using direct references to facts not in evidence, combined with the critical importance of Gilster's credibility to issues of both liability and damages, made the improper comments unfairly prejudicial and require that we remand for a new trial. This is not an action we take lightly, for it means that Gilster is deprived of a favorable jury verdict, and that all the witnesses may need to endure again what was surely a stressful, unpleasant trial. However, as we said many years ago in an opinion that has been frequently cited by other courts, "when a lawyer departs from the path of legitimate argument, [s]he does so at [her] own peril and that of [her] client." *Kelly*, 84 F.2d at 573.

The judgment of the district court including the award of attorneys' fees is reversed and the case is remanded for further proceedings not inconsistent with this opinion.

SOLUTIONS: THE LAWYER SHOULD HAVE, WOULD HAVE, COULD HAVE. . .

Yes, a trial is a challenging event in a lawyer's professional life, whether it is your first or your hundredth trial. But we are the professionals, not the clients. Thus, we must ensure that we always act in their best interest and not allow the pressure to cloud our judgment. The rule applies to our egos as well; a professional puts the needs of the client ahead of their needs. Always remember that you as the lawyer are the least important person in the courtroom.

Cases and Materials

X-Ray Questions (*Thoreen*)

A criminal defense lawyer swapped out, at counsel table during trial, his client for a look alike. When the defendant was "identified" by a witness, the stratagem was revealed by the lawyer. His tactic was a way to demonstrate his client's innocence. It did not work out that way. While this advocacy was certainly zealous, it was unethical. How did the court reason its way to that conclusion? In answering this question, ask this equally important question: what was the court's rationale for its decision? What competing values were at stake and how did the court reconcile those values? One reason we included this case was because the lawyer was subject to criminal penalties. How so? The opinion tosses around the phase "obstruction of justice." You are used to hearing that language from news reports on criminal behavior but why is it being used in this context? Is what he did really so bad?

U.S. v. Thoreen

United States Court of Appeals, Ninth Circuit, 1981.
653 F.2d 1332.

EUGENE A. WRIGHT, CIRCUIT JUDGE:

I.   INTRODUCTION

The issue before us is whether an attorney may be found in criminal contempt for pursuing a course of aggressive advocacy while representing his client in a criminal proceeding such that, without the court's permission or knowledge, he substitutes someone for his client at counsel table with the intent to cause a misidentification, resulting in the misleading of the court, counsel, and witnesses; a delay while the government reopened its case to identify the defendant; and violation of a court order and custom.

We affirm the district court's finding of criminal contempt. The conclusion that this appeal was untimely is reversed.

II.   FACTS

By February 1980, Thoreen, an attorney, had practiced law for almost five years. He was a member of the bars of the State of Washington and of the Western District of Washington. He had made numerous court appearances and participated in one trial and several pretrial appearances before Judge Jack E. Tanner of the Western District of Washington.

In February 1980, he represented Sibbett, a commercial fisher, during Sibbett's non-jury trial before Judge Tanner for criminal contempt for three violations of a preliminary injunction against salmon fishing. In preparing for trial, Thoreen hoped that the government agent who had cited Sibbett could not identify him. He decided to test the witness's identification.

He placed next to him at counsel table Clark Mason, who resembled Sibbett and had Mason dressed in outdoor clothing denims, heavy shoes, a plaid shirt, and a jacket-vest.

Sibbett wore a business suit, large round glasses, and sat behind the rail in a row normally reserved for the press.

Thoreen neither asked the court's permission for, nor notified it or government counsel of, the substitution.

On Thoreen's motion at the start of the trial, the court ordered all witnesses excluded from the courtroom. Mason remained at counsel table.

Throughout the trial, Thoreen made and allowed to go uncorrected numerous misrepresentations. He gestured to Mason as though he was his client and gave Mason a yellow legal pad on which to take notes. The two conferred. Thoreen did not correct the court when it expressly referred to Mason as the defendant and caused the record to show identification of Mason as Sibbett.

Because of the conduct, two government witnesses misidentified Mason as Sibbett. Following the government's case, Thoreen called Mason as a witness and disclosed the substitution. The court then called a recess.

When the trial resumed, the government reopened and recalled the government agent who had cited Sibbett for two of the violations. He identified Sibbett, who was convicted of all three violations.

On February 20, 1980, Thoreen was ordered to appear on February 27 and show cause why he should not be held in criminal contempt. At the hearing, Judge Tanner found him in criminal contempt.

The order was lodged with the court on March 28. The signed order was filed and entered on the civil docket on March 31. In a letter of April 2, the court clerk said he mailed a copy to Thoreen and to his attorney. Thoreen's copy went to an incorrect address. The order of August 12, however, finds that the clerk did not send a copy to Thoreen's attorney until April 7.

Eleven days later, on April 11, Thoreen filed a notice of appeal.

On July 9, this court entered an order remanding to the district court to rule whether that court's order was entered properly and, if not, whether Thoreen's delay in filing was due to excusable neglect. The district court found (1) the order was entered properly, (2) the clerk mailed a copy to Thoreen's attorney on April 7, (3) Thoreen filed his notice of appeal one day after the ten-day limit for filing criminal appeals expired, and (4) his delay was not due to excusable neglect because he had notice of the court's ruling from the show cause hearing on February 27.

The action has been docketed consistently as a civil matter as was the underlying contempt action against Sibbett.

III. DISCUSSION

A. JURISDICTION

Federal Rule of Appellate Procedure 4(a) provides that appeals as of right from civil cases shall be filed within 30 days from entry of judgment. Federal Rules of Appellate Procedure 4(b) says that a criminal appeal must be filed within ten days after entry. A judgment "is entered within the meaning of (4(b)) when it is entered in the criminal docket." *Id.*

Thoreen argues that he filed timely because the case was docketed consistently as a civil matter and the order has never been entered on a criminal docket. The government argues the court lacks jurisdiction because the contempt proceeding was criminal and Thoreen failed to file within the ten-day period.

We agree with the government that the contempt proceeding was criminal, but hold that Thoreen's appeal was timely because the clerk did not enter the judgment on the criminal docket. The ten-day period had not begun to run. See United States v. Ronne, 414 F.2d 1340, 1342 n.1 (9th Cir.1969). A notice of appeal filed after the court's announcement of its order, but before its entry is timely because it is "treated as filed after such entry and on the day thereof." 9 Wright's Federal Practice, P 204.20 at 4–133 (1980).

Alternatively, the appeal is timely under Rule 4(a) because it was filed within 30 days of the entry of the judgment on the civil docket.

B.   CONTEMPT

Judge Tanner found Thoreen in criminal contempt for the substitution because it was imposed on the court and counsel without permission or prior knowledge; the claimed identification issue did not exist; it disrupted the trial; it deceived the court and frustrated its responsibility to administer justice; and it violated a court custom. He found Mason's presence in the courtroom after giving the order excluding witnesses another ground for contempt because Thoreen planned that Mason would testify when the misidentification occurred. Judge Tanner held also that Thoreen's conduct conflicted with DR 1–102(A)(4), DR 7–102(A)(6) and DR 7–106(C)(5) of the Washington Code of Professional Responsibility.

Thoreen's principal defense is that his conduct was a good faith tactic in aid of cross-examination and falls within the protected realm of zealous advocacy. He argues that as defense counsel he has no obligation to ascertain or present the truth and may seek to confuse witnesses with misleading questions, gestures, or appearances. See United States v. Wade, 388 U.S. 218, 257–58, 87 S.Ct. 1926, 1947–48, 18 L.Ed.2d 1149 (1967) (Justice White, dissenting and concurring in part).

He argues also that (1) in the absence of a court rule controlling who may sit at counsel table, his failure to give notice of the substitution is not misbehavior within 18 U.S.C. s 401(1) (1976); (2) he did not intend to deceive; and (3) the exclusion order was not directed at Mason.

1.   Zealous Advocacy

While we agree that defense counsel should represent his client vigorously, regardless of counsel's view of guilt or innocence, Wade, supra; Washington Code of Professional Responsibility (CPR), Canon 7, we conclude that Thoreen's conduct falls outside this protected behavior.

Vigorous advocacy by defense counsel may properly entail impeaching or confusing a witness, even if counsel thinks the witness is truthful, and refraining from presenting evidence even if he knows the truth. Wade, supra. When we review this conduct and find that the line between vigorous advocacy and actual obstruction is close, our doubts should be resolved in favor of the former. Commonwealth of Pennsylvania v. Local 542 International Union of Operating Engineers, 552 F.2d 498, 509 (3rd Cir.), cert. denied sub nom., Freedman v. Higginbotham, 434 U.S. 822, 98 S.Ct. 67, 54 L.Ed.2d 79 (1977).

The latitude allowed an attorney is not unlimited. He must represent his client within the bounds of the law. Wade, supra; CPR Canon 7. As an officer of the court, he must "preserve and promote the efficient operation of our system of justice." Chapman v. Pacific Tel. & Tel., 613 F.2d 193, 197 (9th Cir.1979).

Thoreen's view of appropriate cross-examination, which encompasses his substitution, crossed over the line from zealous advocacy to actual obstruction because, as we discuss later, it impeded the court's search for truth, resulted in delays, and violated a court custom and rule. Moreover, this conduct harms rather than enhances an attorney's effectiveness as an advocate.

It is fundamental that in relations with the court, defense counsel must be scrupulously candid and truthful in representations of any matter before the court. This is not only a basic ethical requirement, but it is essential if the lawyer is to be effective in the role of advocate, for if the lawyer's reputation for veracity is suspect, he or she will lack the confidence of the court when it is needed most to serve the client.

American Bar Association Standards for Criminal Justice, The Defense Function 4.9 (1980) (footnote omitted) (herein The Defense Function).

2.   Criminal Contempt

18 U.S.C. s 401 (1976) provides

A court of the United States shall have power to punish by fine or imprisonment, at its discretion, such contempt of its authority, and none other, as

(1)   Misbehavior of any person in its presence or so near thereto as to obstruct the administration of justice;

(3)   Disobedience or resistance to its lawful writ, process, order, rule, decree, or command.

(emphasis added).

Contumacious misbehavior punishable under section 401(1) must be willful, In re Gustafson, 650 F.2d 1017 at 1019–1021 (9th Cir., 1981) (en banc), and must " 'actually obstruct' " the district judge in the performance of his judicial duties. Id.

One may be found in contempt for disobeying an order pursuant to section 401(3) "only if the order is clear and definite, and the contemnor has knowledge of it." United States v. Baker, 641 F.2d 1311, 1315 (9th Cir.1981).

a.   Contumacious Misbehavior and Obstruction of Justice

Because Thoreen's conduct was in the court's presence, our inquiry turns to whether it constituted contumacious misbehavior that obstructed the administration of justice.

Misbehavior punishable under section 401(1) has been defined as "conduct inappropriate to the particular role of the actor, be he judge, juror, party, witness, counsel or spectator." United States v. Seale, 461 F.2d 345, 366 (7th Cir.1972). See also, Gordon v. United States, 592 F.2d 1215, 1218 (1st Cir.), cert. denied, 441 U.S. 912, 99 S.Ct. 2011, 60 L.Ed.2d 384 (1979). Requiring adherence to these roles ensures "that a judicial proceeding (will be) confined to a rational search for truth in the context of defined legal issues." Seale, supra, 461 F.2d at 366–67.

Contumacious misbehavior by an attorney includes disobeying a court's rulings or instructions, Gustafson, supra, and deceiving the court. Examples of contumacious deceptive behavior are misrepresenting oneself as a practicing attorney, Bowles v. United States, 50 F.2d 848, 851 (4th Cir.), cert. denied 284 U.S. 648, 52 S.Ct. 29, 76 L.Ed. 550 (1931); an attorney's swearing to and filing of admittedly false affidavits and supplemental complaint, plus the pursuit of meritless litigation, Letts v. Icarian Development Co., S.A., No. 74 C 2252 (N.D.Ill., September 15, 1980); and an attorney's presentation of false evidence, United States v. Ford, 9 F.2d 990, 991 (D.Mont.1925).

Making misrepresentations to the court is also inappropriate and unprofessional behavior under ethical standards that guide attorneys' conduct. These guidelines, in effect in Washington and elsewhere, decree explicitly that an attorney's participation in the presentation or preservation of false evidence is unprofessional and subjects him to discipline. See CPR DR 7–102(A)(4), (5), (6); EC 7–6, 7–26; The Defense Function 4.93.

Substituting a person for the defendant in a criminal case without a court's knowledge has been noted as an example of unethical behavior by the ABA Committee on Professional Ethics. See Informal Opinion No. 914, 2/24/66 (decided under the former ABA Code of Professional Responsibility).

Ethical standards establish the outermost limits of appropriate and sanctioned attorney conduct. While we acknowledge that a court's power to discipline or disbar an attorney " 'proceeds upon very different grounds' from those which support a court's power to punish for contempt," Cammer v. United States, 350 U.S. 399, 408 n.7, 76 S.Ct. 456, 460 n.7, 100 L.Ed. 474 (1956) (quoting Ex Parte Robinson, 86 U.S. 505, 19 Wall. 505, 512, 22 L.Ed. 205), we consider and apply ethical benchmarks when determining whether an attorney's conduct is inappropriate to his role and thus constitutes contumacious misbehavior.

Counsel's conduct must cause an actual obstruction of justice before criminal contempt lies. In re Michael, 326 U.S. 224, 228, 66 S.Ct. 78, 80, 90 L.Ed. 30 (1945); Gustafson, supra. The standard is whether the obstruction or disruption is material. In re Kirk, 641 F.2d 684, 687 (9th Cir.1981); Seale, supra, 461 F.2d at 369.

The seriousness of the misbehavior has some bearing on whether the conduct is materially obstructive. Seale, supra. Mere disrespect, insult, or an affront to a court's sense of dignity are insufficient. Brown v. United States, 356 U.S. 148, 153, 78 S.Ct. 622, 625, 2 L.Ed.2d 589 (1958); Gordon, supra, 592 F.2d at 1217; United States v. Trudell, 563 F.2d 889, 892 (8th Cir.1977); Seale, supra.

There is a point where "mere words are so offensive and so unnecessary that their very utterance creates a delay which is an obstruction of justice." Gordon, supra. See Seale, supra, 461 F.2d at 370. A pro se litigant's vituperative outburst, for example, constitutes an obstruction because it causes a delay in the time involved in the litigant's delivery of his outburst and in the time necessary to get the court proceedings back on track. Gordon, supra.

Conduct lacking vituperation, violence, or physical force may be found obstructive. In re Chaplain, 621 F.2d 1272, 1277 (4th Cir.), cert. denied, 449 U.S. 834 101 S.Ct. 106, 66 L.Ed.2d 40 (1980); Commonwealth of Pennsylvania, supra. Flouting a court's commands in a polite, respectful, and subdued manner has been found to be "the essence of obstructing the administration of justice." Id. See also, United States v. Abascal, 509 F.2d 752, 754 (9th Cir.), cert. denied, 422 U.S. 1027, 95 S.Ct. 2621, 45 L.Ed.2d 684 (1975).

Making misrepresentations to the fact finder is inherently obstructive because it frustrates the rational search for truth. It may also delay the proceedings. In In re Dellinger, 502 F.2d 813, 816 (7th Cir.1974), cert. denied, 420 U.S. 990, 95 S.Ct. 1425, 43 L.Ed.2d 671 (1975), for example, the Seventh Circuit held that an attorney obstructed justice by putting inadmissible evidence before the jury, hampering its ability to decide the case according to the legal principles provided them. A witness's sham denial of knowledge similarly obstructs justice by closing off avenues of inquiry and stifling a jury's ability to ascertain the truth. United States v. Griffin, 589 F.2d 200, 205 (5th Cir.), cert. denied, 444 U.S. 825, 100 S.Ct. 48, 62 L.Ed.2d 32 (1979).

The record supports Judge Tanner's conclusion that Thoreen's substitution was misbehavior that obstructed justice. It was inappropriate because it was done without consent, and violated a court custom to allow only counsel, parties, and others having the court's permission to sit forward of the rail. This conduct is deemed unprofessional and may subject an attorney to disciplinary measures in Washington. CPR DR 7–106(C)(5).

Thoreen's argument that he may not be held in contempt for violating the custom and practice because he lacked notice of it is unpersuasive. Generally, "an absence of any warning that borderline conduct is regarded as contumacious could be fatal to a contempt citation." Seale, supra, 461 F.2d at 366. See also, Baker, supra, 641 F.2d at 1315. Nevertheless, a contemnor need not have specific warning or be aware that his acts may subject him to criminal sanctions as opposed to other penalties. Seale, supra. Certain conduct is inherently inappropriate and self-noticing. Gordon, supra, 592 F.2d at 1218 n.3.

In federal and state courts of general jurisdiction, only attorneys and parties customarily sit at counsel table. Others do so only with the court's permission.

Thoreen's years in practice included trial and pretrial experience in Judge Tanner's court and presumably in other courts. Viewing the evidence in the light most favorable to the government, we cannot accept Thoreen's contention that he was unaware of this widespread custom.

His violation of the order to exclude witnesses by keeping Mason at counsel table is both a second example of misbehavior and independent grounds for contempt under s 401(3). He argues, however, that he did not violate the order because it was not directed at Mason because (1) Mason would not change his testimony after hearing other testimony and (2) it was unclear that Mason would be a witness.

This argument belies the facts. The order, made at Thoreen's request, did not distinguish between witnesses who might alter their testimony and those who might not. He acknowledges that he intended from the outset to call Mason as a witness after the anticipated misidentification occurred. By failing to have Mason leave, he made an unfortunate error in judgment. See, e. g., United States v. Baer, 575 F.2d 1295, 1301 (10th Cir.1978) (an attorney's attempt to disprove that he was the person charged with two traffic violations (1) when he knew he was the person charged and (2) by relying on the failure to place "Jr." following his name, is inexcusable, tragic gamesmanship); In re Serra, 484 F.2d 947, 948 (9th Cir.1973) (contemptuous for an attorney to frustrate a court discovery order to produce medical reports by instructing the medical witness to make no written reports).

Thoreen's argument that the substitution did not obstruct justice because he corrected it before the court ruled on it, see, e. g., United States v. Turk, 10 F.Supp. 957, 959 (E.D.N.Y.1934) (a correction of perjurious testimony before the court issued its decision purged contempt), ignores the evidence of obstruction and disruption that occurred despite his revelation. The deception delayed proceedings in the time taken for witnesses' misidentification of the defendant and the time required to recall one witness to identify Sibbett correctly. Of greater importance is that it impeded the court's ability to ascertain the truth.

Nor is reliance on a misrepresentation necessary to a finding that deceptive or misleading conduct obstructed justice. Delay or hindering the court's ability to ascertain the truth is sufficient.

b.　Intent

To be held in criminal contempt, the contemnor must have the requisite intent.

"(A)n attorney possesses the requisite intent only if he knows or reasonably should be aware in view of all the circumstances, especially the heat of the controversy, that he is exceeding the outermost limits of his proper role and hindering rather than facilitating the search for truth." (citation omitted).

In re Kirk, supra, 641 F.2d at 687.

Proof of an evil motive or of an actual intent to obstruct justice is unnecessary. Commonwealth of Pennsylvania, supra, 552 F.2d at 510; Seale, supra, 461 F.2d at 398. Intent must be proved beyond a reasonable doubt. Baker, supra, 641 F.2d at 1317; In re Kirk, supra.

Intent may be inferred from facts and circumstances. Baker, supra. An attorney's intent may be inferred if his "conduct discloses a reckless disregard for his professional duty." In re Farquhar, 492 F.2d 561, 564 (D.C.Cir.1973) (citation omitted).

Good faith is a defense to a finding of intent, Baker supra, but it does not immunize all conduct undertaken by an attorney on behalf of a client. Seale, supra. It requires only that a court allow an attorney great latitude in his pursuit of vigorous advocacy. *Id.*

Thoreen admits he planned and intended the substitution, but defends by asserting that (1) it was a good faith effort to prove misidentification and attack the credibility of the government witnesses; (2) he never intended to misrepresent any facts to the court or to obstruct justice; and (3) he believed the court knew Sibbett's identity from the pretrial hearing.

The record shows that Sibbett's identification was not an issue, contradicting the need to attack credibility. The testimony about Sibbett's violations was thorough, credible, and not in conflict.

Thoreen's alleged belief that the court would remember Sibbett from a pretrial proceeding is unrealistic because that hearing took place several months earlier and Sibbett was but one of many persons cited for violating the salmon fishing injunction.

His alleged lack of intent to deceive the court or to obstruct justice is irrelevant. Section 401(1) does not require specific intent. It suffices that he should have been aware that his conduct exceeded reasonable limits and hindered the search for truth.

CONCLUSION

Thoreen's error in judgment was unfortunate. The court's ire and this criminal contempt conviction could have been avoided easily and the admirable goal of representing his client zealously preserved if only he had given the court and opposing counsel prior notice and sought the court's consent.

Nonetheless, viewing the evidence in the light most favorable to the government, we find that there is sufficient evidence to find beyond a reasonable doubt that Thoreen violated 18 U.S.C. s 401(1) and (3). Baker, supra. The district court's findings were not clearly erroneous. *Id.*

We AFFIRM the contempt conviction.

We REVERSE the finding that this appeal was untimely.

SOLUTIONS: THE LAWYER SHOULD HAVE, WOULD HAVE, COULD HAVE. . .

Diligent work in developing the facts, understanding the law, and improving trial advocacy skills are the only ethical ways to serve the client at trial. While dramatically appealing, stunts distort the even playing field. This clip from the television show "Better Call Saul" dramatizes how a maneuver, like the one in this case, is effectuated.

https://www.youtube.com/watch?v=YCcq2BkxiaE

Section 2. The Lawyer's Representations to the Tribunal

Ethical issues arise because a lawyer is responsible for the lawyer's own statements and representations and assertions to a tribunal (recall that MR 1.0, terminology, defines a "tribunal" as any adjudicative body that makes binding legal determinations, including forums such a binding arbitration) as well as the testimony given by clients and witnesses.

Model Rule 3.3: Candor Towards the Tribunal

(a)   A lawyer shall not knowingly:

    (1) make a false statement of fact or law to a tribunal or fail to correct a false statement of material fact or law previously made to the tribunal by the lawyer;

(2)   fail to disclose to the tribunal legal authority in the controlling jurisdiction known to the lawyer to be directly adverse to the position of the client and not disclosed by opposing counsel; or

(3)   offer evidence that the lawyer knows to be false. If a lawyer, the lawyer's client, or a witness called by the lawyer, has offered material evidence and the lawyer comes to know of its falsity, the lawyer shall take reasonable remedial measures, including, if necessary, disclosure to the tribunal. A lawyer may refuse to offer evidence, other than the testimony of a defendant in a criminal matter, that the lawyer reasonably believes is false.

(b)   A lawyer who represents a client in an adjudicative proceeding and who knows that a person intends to engage, is engaging or has engaged in criminal or fraudulent conduct related to the proceeding shall take reasonable remedial measures, including, if necessary, disclosure to the tribunal.

(c)   The duties stated in paragraphs (a) and (b) continue to the conclusion of the proceeding, and apply even if compliance requires disclosure of information otherwise protected by Rule 1.6.

(d)   In an ex parte proceeding, a lawyer shall inform the tribunal of all material facts known to the lawyer that will enable the tribunal to make an informed decision, whether or not the facts are adverse.

Deconstruction Exercise/Rule Rationale

Why use the word "candor?" Do not "candor" and "truthfulness" have identical meanings? A dictionary definition of "candor" is this: "the quality of being open and honest in expression; frankness." So, "candor" implies a broader and a more transcendent one for the lawyer. By way of example, (a)(1) is written to place a greater burden on the lawyer. Read it carefully. A lawyer is forbidden from making a false representation (fact or law) to a tribunal *regardless* of its materiality. This obligation is complimentary to the ones in MR 4.1 and MR 8.4(c). By contrast, the rule's burden is lighter as to falsity of fact or law made earlier in the proceeding but not of a material nature. Why? A trade-off between the time-consuming aspiration of perfection and the need for efficiency in litigating a matter.

We see the importance of efficiency in (a)(2) on the lawyer's legal assertions when there is controlling authority in the jurisdiction in which the matter is being litigated. But does not this duty conflict with a lawyer's duty of zealous representation? After all, if the lawyer for the party opposite is not well informed on the law, why should the well informed lawyer's client be punished? Because the appeals court is likely to catch the failure to cite controlling authority and remand the case to the trial court translating to a waste of judicial resources. While zealous representation of the client is an important value, there are equally important values that must be recognized.

A. The Lawyer's Factual Assertions to the Tribunal

Model Rule 3.3(a)(1): Candor Toward the Tribunal

(a)   A lawyer shall not knowingly:

(1)   make a false statement of fact or law to a tribunal or fail to correct a false statement of material fact or law previously made to the tribunal by the lawyer;

LEANING INTO PRACTICE

Scenario No. 1: The Case of the Dark and Stormy Sky: Version #1

Uchi Lawyer is giving her opening statement in a personal injury case. Her paralegal tells her that on the day of the accident the sky was dark and stormy. In actuality, it was sky blue. The paralegal was mistaken and Uchi does not know otherwise. Has Uchi violated the Rule?

Scenario No. 2: The Case of the Dark and Stormy Sky: Version #2

Same as #1 but during trial, Uchi discovers that the statement is false. Uchi decides that she does not want to correct it. Has she violated the Rule?

Scenario No. 3: The Case of the Dark and Stormy Sky: Version #3

Whether the sky was dark and stormy is immaterial to the liability issues in the lawsuit. In fact, the sky was clear blue. Uchi knows that the sky was clear blue but, because she likes the sound of a "dark and stormy sky" she elects to keep it in her opening statement. Has she violated the Rule?

B. The Lawyer's Legal Assertions to the Tribunal

Model Rule 3.3(a)(2)

A lawyer shall not knowingly:

(2)   fail to disclose to the tribunal legal authority in the controlling jurisdiction known to the lawyer to be directly adverse to the position of the client and not disclosed by opposing counsel;

Cases and Materials

X-Ray Questions (*Williams*)

The issue here was whether an appeals court possessed jurisdiction. A lawyer failed to cite authority establishing that it did not. When called on it, the lawyer engaged in a rhetorical technique called "sophistry" which is defined as offering arguments that are superficially plausible but generally fallacious. Can you identify the argument that fits this definition? Can you explain in your own words the rationale behind the rule and why the court was upset at him?

People v. Williams

California Court of Appeal, 2022.
290 Cal.Rptr.3d 582.

Opinion

THE COURT.

We conclude we have no jurisdiction to entertain defendant Keith Williams's (defendant's) appeal. We publish our opinion to emphasize an attorney's duty of candor to this court.

I.   BACKGROUND

A.   Trial Court Proceedings

The facts of defendant's crime are not important for our purposes. A trial jury found him guilty of robbery and burglary. In 1996, the trial court sentenced him to 35 years to life in prison, with the bulk of that sentence attributable to the "Three Strikes" law.

Decades later, in early 2021, defendant filed in the trial court what he styled as a "Petition for Modification of Sentence (Pursuant to P.C. 1170(d)(1).).)." Defendant asked the court to modify his 1996 judgment based on "charging and sentencing policies" adopted by Los Angeles County District Attorney George Gascón. In a memorandum of points and authorities accompanying his petition, defendant quoted Penal Code section 1170, subdivision (d)(1) and argued his 1996 sentence could be modified or recalled because "the district attorney's office considers that only 15 years of the 25 years [he] already served is more than enough" and the court could consider, under the same statutory provision, his good conduct in prison.

The trial court denied defendant's section 1170, subdivision (d)(1) petition for modification of sentence without appointing counsel for defendant. A minute order memorializing the court's ruling explains the petition was "denied as untimely" (coming, as it did, well after the 120-day period and without the requisite accompanying recommendation).

B.   *Proceedings on Appeal*

Defendant, in propria persona, noticed an appeal from the trial court's ruling. That set in motion the key events for our purposes.

Upon receipt of the notice of appeal, the clerk of this court forwarded it to the California Appellate Project (CAP) for a recommendation on appointment of counsel. The case was later assigned to this Division of the Court of Appeal for decision, and CAP was appointed to represent defendant in this appeal.

After CAP's Executive Director assumed responsibility for serving as counsel for defendant in this appeal, counsel filed a brief in this court captioned "APPELLANT'S OPENING BRIEF (*PEOPLE V. SERRANO* (2012) 211 Cal.App.4th 496, 149 Cal.Rptr.3d 706 [(*Serrano*)])."

The short statement of the case in the brief included, pursuant to the provisions of the Rules of Court that require it (Cal. Rules of Court, rules 8.204(a)(2)(B), 8.360(a)), a one-sentence statement purporting to explain why the order appealed from is appealable. This is that sentence: "Appellant filed a Notice of Appeal from the ruling as an order after judgment affecting substantial rights. ([ ] Pen. Code, § 1237, subd. (b).)" The remainder of the brief requested this court to follow the procedures described in *Serrano*.

Submitted with the opening brief itself was a sworn declaration of counsel stating it was made "IN SUPPORT OF REQUEST THAT THIS COURT FOLLOW THE PROCEDURES SET FORTH IN *PEOPLE v. SERRANO* [Citation]." Counsel declared he informed defendant of the "right to file a supplemental brief" and further stated he did not move to withdraw as counsel "at this time" but "remain[ed] available to brief any issues that the Court requests." As is customary when such a brief is filed, the Attorney General did not file a respondent's brief or otherwise appear in this proceeding.

Upon receipt of the opening brief and assignment of the cause to a panel for decision, this court sought to discharge its duty to assure itself that it had jurisdiction to decide the appeal. (See, e.g., *Jennings v. Marralle* (1994) 8 Cal.4th 121, 126, 32 Cal.Rptr.2d 275, 876 P.2d 1074.) Naturally, that first involved reviewing the statement of appealability included in the opening brief that we have already quoted ("Appellant filed a Notice of Appeal from the ruling as an order after judgment affecting substantial rights") and counsel's request that we process the appeal in accordance with the procedures outlined in *Serrano*. Independent research by the court, however, uncovered published authority—never cited in the opening brief—holding that a reviewing court has no jurisdiction to entertain an appeal of a section 1170, subdivision (d)(1) ruling of the type here because it is a nonappealable order. (See, e.g., *People v. Chlad* (1992) 6 Cal.App.4th 1719, 1725–1726, 8 Cal.Rptr.2d 610 ["[S]ince we have concluded the trial court no longer had jurisdiction to recall Chlad's sentence when it issued the order denying his motion, denial of the motion could not have affected Chlad's substantial rights. (See *People v. Roe* (1983) 148 Cal.App.3d 112, 118, 195 Cal.Rptr. 802 [ ] [judgment entered by the court after losing its jurisdiction under § 1170, subd. (d), has no effect and cannot be appealed]. [¶] The trial court's . . . order denying Chlad's motion to modify sentence is not an appealable order"])] (*Chlad*).)

After reviewing authority that supports finding the order in question to be a nonappealable order, this court directed counsel to submit a letter brief addressing: "(1) whether, consistent with the holding in [*Chlad*], the appeal is taken from a nonappealable order, and (2) whether the absence of a citation to *Chlad* (or other authority to the same effect) in the opening brief constitutes a violation of the Rules of Professional Conduct." By citation, this court specifically directed counsel's attention to the rule that states a lawyer shall not "fail to disclose to the tribunal[ ] legal authority in the controlling jurisdiction known[ ] to the lawyer to be directly adverse to the position of the client and not disclosed by opposing counsel . . . ." (Rules Prof. Conduct, rule 3.3(a)(2) (Rule 3.3(a)(2)).)

Counsel submitted a short letter in response to this court's direction. It is remarkable both for what it says, and what it does not.

Beginning with what the letter does not say, there is no contention that *Chlad* is distinguishable, nor any argument that *Chlad* should not be followed. There is no assertion in the letter that *Chlad* (or authority to the same effect) was unknown to counsel at the time he filed the opening brief. There is no assertion that the absence of a citation to such authority in the opening brief was attributable to mistake, inadvertence, or administrative error.

Turning to what the letter does say, counsel asserts he appropriately did not cite authority indicating we have no jurisdiction to entertain this appeal. In counsel's words: "While Rule 3.3 requires attorneys to disclose controlling legal authority adverse to a position which he is arguing, counsel did not here advocate any legal position in his brief. At no point did counsel argue or state that the appeal was proper. Counsel only stated the basis of *his client's belief* that the appeal was proper, as required by this Court." (Emphasis ours.) The letter further asserts that including "[a] statement in the brief that the ruling appealed from is not appealable or a statement citing case law holding that a given ruling is not appealable would be equivalent to stating that the appeal is frivolous," which counsel believes (chiefly relying on *People v. Wende* (1979) 25 Cal.3d 436, 158 Cal.Rptr. 839, 600 P.2d 1071 (*Wende*)) he cannot do consistent with his duties as a defense attorney who does not seek to withdraw from representation of a client.

After receiving the letter brief, we set the matter for oral argument. Counsel waived his appearance.

II. DISCUSSION

The summary of the pertinent background facts we have already provided well foreshadows the reasons for our bottom-line disposition of this appeal. We shall accordingly spend the bulk of our discussion reviewing a lawyer's duty of candor to the court.

A. A Defense Attorney Has an Obligation to Disclose Known Authority Holding This Court Has No Jurisdiction to Decide an Appeal When the People Do Not Cite Such Authority

Application of Rule 3.3(a)(2) is, on the face of the rule itself, rather straightforward under these circumstances. It prohibits an attorney from (1) failing to disclose to (2) a tribunal (3) legal authority in this State that is (4) known to the lawyer to be directly adverse to the position of the client and (5) not disclosed by opposing counsel. Each of these elements is satisfied on the record here. There is an undisputed failure to disclose *Chlad* and like authority to this court. That authority is directly adverse to defendant's position, at least insofar as he maintains he should be able to prosecute this appeal. And there is no assertion from counsel that *Chlad* and similar authority was unknown to him (or unknown to be adverse to his prosecution of this appeal) at the time counsel filed the opening brief.

Counsel, however, offers two arguments seemingly directed at establishing he did not fail to comply with his duty of candor to this court. He argues, first, that he personally made no affirmative representation that the order appealed from is an appealable order such that this court has jurisdiction. And counsel contends, second, that he need not make this court aware of applicable authority under the circumstances because disclosing authority that the appeal is taken from a nonappealable order is tantamount to a concession that the appeal is frivolous, which he cannot concede without withdrawing from the representation. Both points are unpersuasive.

Take first counsel's contention that he personally made no affirmative representation in the opening brief that the order appealed from is an appealable order. Even taken on its own terms, the contention is irrelevant: Rule 3.3(a)(2) prohibits a lawyer from knowingly failing to disclose adverse authority, not just from making affirmative representations that are inconsistent with such authority. But the argument should not be taken on its own terms. Counsel is responsible for the content of briefs he files in this court (see, e.g., *In re Rozzo* (2009) 172 Cal.App.4th 40, 64, fn. 11, 91 Cal.Rptr.3d 85), and asserting a legal basis for taking the appeal that reads as a representation by counsel but is perhaps phrased in a sufficiently ambiguous manner to later permit attribution solely to a client does not properly evade that responsibility. Furthermore, counsel's assertion that he did not advocate any legal position in his opening brief and "at no point . . . state[d] that the lower court's ruling was legally appealable" is incorrect. The brief itself "requests this Court to follow the procedures set forth in *People v. Serrano*" and counsel's accompanying declaration is expressly submitted in support of the request that this court follow the *Serrano* procedure. We have already summarized that procedure in the margin (a defendant is invited to personally file a supplemental brief with any contentions he or she wishes to raise and, at least in the eyes of *Cole* and other courts, a reviewing court must address any such contentions in a written opinion). That procedure should not be followed in an appeal where a court determines it has no jurisdiction to proceed. In other words, by the very act of prosecuting the appeal and requesting *Serrano* procedures to be followed, counsel represented to this court that we had the jurisdiction that permits following those procedures.

Consider next counsel's argument that his duty to refrain from arguing against his client trumps the duty of candor he owes to this court. This is a false choice; the two duties are readily reconciled because the duty of candor is one of disclosure, not acquiescence. That is to say, adverse on-point authority must be cited, but a lawyer is free to marshal arguments to persuade a court to reach a contrary conclusion. In more concrete terms, counsel here had an obligation to cite *Chlad* or similar authority in his opening brief's statement of appealability, but he was free to argue that the case authority is somehow distinguishable on its facts or unpersuasively reasoned such that this court should not follow it. That, of course, is not what counsel did, and failing to cite applicable authority is all the more unfortunate when done in an appeal where, as here, an attorney knows the adverse party will not be making an appearance.

Counsel protests, though, that his chosen course of action is compelled by *Wende, supra*, 25 Cal.3d 436, 158 Cal.Rptr. 839, 600 P.2d 1071; *People v. Feggans* (1967) 67 Cal.2d 444, 62 Cal.Rptr. 419, 432 P.2d 21 (*Feggans*); and *Serrano, supra*, 211 Cal.App.4th 496, 149 Cal.Rptr.3d 706. Again, the claim is incorrect even when taken on its own terms.

In *Feggans*, our Supreme Court explained that United States Supreme Court precedent requires a defense attorney to "prepare a brief to assist the court in understanding the facts and the legal issues in the case. The brief must set forth a statement of the facts with citations to the transcript, discuss the legal issues with citations of appropriate authority, and argue all issues that are arguable. Moreover, counsel serves both the court and his client by advocating changes in the law if argument can be made supporting change. If counsel concludes that there are no arguable issues and the appeal is frivolous, he may limit his brief to a statement of the facts and applicable law and may ask to withdraw from the case, but he must not argue the case against his client." (*Feggans, supra*, 67 Cal.2d at 447, 62 Cal.Rptr. 419, 432 P.2d 21.) Subsequently in *Wende*, our Supreme Court clarified that it is not "necessary" for a defense attorney to seek leave to withdraw as counsel when he or she concludes no arguable issues can be raised on appeal. (*Wende, supra*, 25 Cal.3d at 442, 158 Cal.Rptr. 839, 600 P.2d 1071 ["So long as counsel has not disabled himself from effectively representing his client by describing the case as frivolous, no reason appears why he should be required to request to withdraw. Indeed, there may be practical benefits to the court and the client from counsel's remaining on the case, as has been noted by some commentators and courts"].) Both *Feggans* and *Wende* (in citing *Feggans*) accordingly require an attorney who believes there are no arguable issues to nonetheless provide the reviewing court with a statement of "applicable law"; counsel concedes as much in his letter brief. The requirement to inform the court of applicable law applies to a brief's statement of appealability just as it does to any other statement of the law. Much like a defense attorney cannot knowingly refrain from citing applicable law to give the incorrect impression that only force, and not fear, can be an appropriate predicate for a robbery conviction, counsel cannot knowingly fail to cite applicable law that discusses what qualifies as an appealable order to give the incorrect impression that this court has jurisdiction when it does not.

We hasten to add, however, that we do not accept the premise of counsel's argument in the first place. The *Wende* line of cases is of limited relevance because the question here is not whether any issue raised on appeal would be frivolous; the question is whether this court has jurisdiction to entertain the appeal regardless of its substantive merit. We reiterate that attorneys have significant latitude to make arguments that an order is appealable and jurisdiction appropriate—and such arguments can be made even in the face of significant published authority holding to the contrary. (Cf. *Feggans, supra*, 67 Cal.2d at 447, 62 Cal.Rptr. 419, 432 P.2d 21 ["counsel serves both the court and his client by advocating changes in the law if argument can be made supporting change"].) But in the infrequent circumstance where appointed counsel determines that there is in fact no argument that he or she can responsibly make in service of the proposition that this court has jurisdiction to hear and decide an appeal, it is appropriate for counsel in that circumstance to withdraw from the representation. What cannot be done is to prosecute an appeal that counsel knows a reviewing court has no jurisdiction to decide while refraining from citing known, applicable law that would reveal the jurisdictional flaw.

We shall address one additional question, albeit not one raised in counsel's letter brief: if appointed counsel files a *Serrano* brief that most often leads to dismissal of an appeal, why does it matter whether that dismissal occurs because the court finds the appeal to be abandoned or because jurisdiction is lacking? There are two responses. First, following the *Serrano* procedure, with its solicitation for supplemental briefing from the defendant, invariably and unnecessarily delays dismissal of nonappealable cases. Second, unnecessary delay is compounded, and other problems arise, in those circumstances where the defendant *does* file a supplemental brief. When that occurs, the defendant expends wasted time and effort in preparing a brief, this court expends wasted time and effort in reviewing that brief, and—if the appealability problem is not discovered by the court on its own—courts customarily expend wasted time and effort preparing a written opinion that addresses the defendant's contentions in a case where it has no jurisdiction to do so.

B.   *Defendant's Appeal Must Be Dismissed for Lack of Jurisdiction*

Fortunately, this court's own research in this case has mitigated some of the aforementioned problems. The trial court here denied defendant's section 1170, subdivision (d) petition because it was untimely and unaccompanied by a statutorily authorized recommendation for resentencing. We follow precedent holding the trial court's denial is a nonappealable order. (See, e.g., *Chlad, supra*, 6 Cal.App.4th at 1725–1726, 8 Cal.Rptr.2d 610 [order denying a section 1170, subdivision (d) motion to recall sentence is not an appealable order because the trial court no longer had jurisdiction to recall the defendant's sentence when it issued the order denying his motion; a defendant has no standing to bring an untimely section 1170, subdivision (d) motion]; see also *People v. Torres* (2020) 44 Cal.App.5th 1081, 1084, 258 Cal.Rptr.3d 307 ["If the trial court does not have jurisdiction to rule on a motion to vacate or modify a sentence, an order denying such a motion is nonappealable, and any appeal from such an order must be dismissed"] (*Torres*); *People v. Turrin* (2009) 176 Cal.App.4th 1200, 1208, 98 Cal.Rptr.3d 471; *People v. Roe, supra*, 148 Cal.App.3d at 117, 195 Cal.Rptr. 802.) Indeed, we were given no reason not to follow this authority when we invited counsel to so argue (nor by defendant when the clerk, upon receiving the opening brief claiming the matter should proceed according to *Serrano* procedures, invited defendant to submit a supplemental brief). Being taken from a nonappealable order, we are obligated to dismiss the appeal for lack of jurisdiction. (*People v. Durham* (1969) 70 Cal.2d 171, 176, fn. 1, 74 Cal.Rptr. 262, 449 P.2d 198; *Torres, supra*, at 1084, 258 Cal.Rptr.3d 307.)

C.   *Conclusion*

An order akin to the order here denying section 1170, subdivision (d)(1) relief is not an appealable order. An order denying a habeas corpus petition is not an appealable order. (*In re Clark* (1993) 5 Cal.4th 750, 767, fn. 7, 21 Cal.Rptr.2d 509, 855 P.2d 729.) An attorney who prosecutes an appeal while failing to cite known authority that this court has no jurisdiction to entertain it violates the attorney's duty of candor (where the authority is not otherwise brought to the attention of the court by another party to the appeal). Any such future violation, in the view of this court, may warrant disciplinary review by the State Bar or other corrective action.

DISPOSITION

The appeal is dismissed.

SOLUTIONS: THE LAWYER SHOULD HAVE, WOULD HAVE, COULD HAVE. . .

Note that the rule still allows a lawyer to seek to distinguish the facts of their case from the precedent or to make a good faith argument, as we saw in MR 1.2, for a rejection or modification of existing law. Doing so is the art of lawyering.

Section 3. Client/Witness Representations to the Court

A. The Client's Right to Testify in a Criminal Proceeding

Model Rule 3.3(a)(3)(b)

(a)   A lawyer shall not knowingly:

(3)   offer evidence that the lawyer knows to be false. If a lawyer, the lawyer's client, or a witness called by the lawyer, has offered material evidence and the lawyer comes to know of its falsity, the lawyer shall take reasonable remedial measures, including, if necessary, disclosure to the tribunal. A lawyer may refuse to offer evidence, other than the testimony of a defendant in a criminal matter, that the lawyer reasonably believes is false.

(b)   A lawyer who represents a client in an adjudicative proceeding and who knows that a person intends to engage, is engaging or has engaged in criminal or fraudulent conduct related to the proceeding shall take reasonable remedial measures, including, if necessary, disclosure to the tribunal.

Cases and Materials

X-Ray Questions (*Midgett*)

The trial lawyer is the gatekeeper of the truth at a trial. MR 3.3(b), (c), and (d) set out the partners of this duty. In a criminal trial, a defendant has a Constitutional right to testify, and a lawyer is prohibited from depriving a client of that right and cannot refuse to allow the defendant to testify. But as the Supreme Court held in *Nix v. Whiteside*, 475 US 157 (1986), a defendant does not have a right to perjury. In *Nix*, a public defender represented a man accused of murder. At their initial meetings, the accused admitted that he shot the man and did not raise self-defense. Subsequently, the accused changed his story to one of self-defense because, as he told the PD, if he did not then he was facing the death penalty. And this is how he wanted to testify. The Court sided with the PD who refused to allow him to do so. The practical issue is how does a lawyer "know" if the client is wanting to offer perjury or is simply telling what sounds like an unbelievable story. The *Midgett* case applies *Nix*. How did the appeals court do so? Why did it reach the result that it did? Is it that hard to judge a client's credibility or is that simply a skill that lawyers develop as they become more experienced? Had this been a civil case would the lawyer's options, per the rule, be different? How so?

U.S. v. Midgett

United States Court of Appeals, Fourth Circuit., 2003.
342 F.3d 321.

OPINION

TRAXLER, CIRCUIT JUDGE:

In November 2000, Paul Dameron Midgett was convicted of damaging a vehicle by means of fire and injuring another thereby in violation of 18 U.S.C.A. § 844(i) (West 2000), bank robbery in violation of 18 U.S.C.A. § 2113(a) (West 2000), and threatening a bank teller with gasoline in the course of a bank robbery in violation of 18 U.S.C.A. § 2113(d) (West 2000). He received life sentences on all three convictions under the federal "three strikes" law. *See* 18 U.S.C.A. § 3559(c) (West 2000). Because the court erred in forcing Midgett to choose between his right to a lawyer and his right to testify on his own behalf, we vacate and remand for a new trial.

I.

In October 1999, J.W. Shaw, Jr., was eating lunch in his van at a worksite in Mecklenburg County, North Carolina, when a man approached him with a cup of gasoline, threw it in his face, and demanded his money. After Shaw gave the man his billfold, the assailant ignited the gasoline with a lighter, inflicting burns to Shaw's face, neck, ears, and hands. In November 1999, Paul Midgett and Theresa Russell were charged with this crime (Count One), as well as with using a similar technique later the same day to rob a bank in Union County, North Carolina (Counts Two and Three). Russell eventually agreed to cooperate with the government; Midgett decided to go to trial.

From the outset, Midgett and his lawyer appear to have been at odds. Before trial began, Midgett's lawyer moved to withdraw because of disagreements with his client as to how to proceed. Among other matters, Midgett complained about his lawyer's degree of preparation and his unwillingness to pursue certain issues to Midgett's satisfaction—including a "third person" defense Midgett sought to offer in relation to the Count One crime. Midgett steadfastly maintained to his lawyer that a friend of Russell was driving around with the two of them at the time they encountered Shaw. According to Midgett, it was Russell's friend, and not Midgett, who had committed the assault on Shaw, while Midgett lay in a drug-induced sleep in the back of the vehicle. Midgett was prepared to offer this testimony himself, but his lawyer did not want Midgett to take the stand because he did not believe Midgett's version of events.

Notified of problems emerging between client and attorney prior to trial, the court conducted a hearing and determined that there was no reason justifying withdrawal, Midgett's counsel having demonstrated due diligence in planning and preparing for trial. For the first of several times, the court offered Midgett the choice of proceeding on his own or continuing with his lawyer. Midgett remarked that "there's no way I could do it myself," J.A. 55, and so his lawyer remained. The next day, before the jury was impaneled, the court asked Midgett whether he intended to testify, to which Midgett replied, "We haven't made a decision yet and I really—to be honest, my lawyer really doesn't want me, but I kind of wanted to, but we haven't made a decision yet." J.A. 69. Trial began and several government witnesses testified, from whom defense counsel was able on cross-examination to bring out certain facts helpful to Midgett. For example, Midgett's lawyer elicited that Shaw had not been able to identify Midgett in a photographic lineup and that another witness to the attack on Shaw had described the culprit to investigators as a tall individual (Midgett being relatively short).

Later that day, after a private conference with Midgett, his lawyer announced to the court that he "must pursuant to the rules of professional conduct move to withdraw." J.A. 138. The judge and Midgett's counsel then left the courtroom for what appears to have been an off-the-record discussion which neither Midgett nor the government attorney attended. When they returned, the court addressed Midgett:

> [Y]our attorney explains to me that you are requesting him to offer evidence and present a defense which he does not intend to offer and considers improper to make . . . and has so advised you, but you nevertheless insist that you are going to offer the defense, whatever it is, if he doesn't. . . . I have told him that I will give you the option of proceeding without an attorney from this point or continuing in his representation. . . . So you better talk with [him] and let me know if you want him to continue to represent you or if you want him to step aside and we'll continue the trial.

J.A. 139, 140. Midgett ultimately responded that "I'll continue with [him] being my attorney, but I don't want it, I do it under protest. I do not agree with it at all." J.A. 141–42. The court instructed Midgett's counsel to describe in an affidavit filed under oath and under seal with the court his reasons for declining to offer the defense proposed by Midgett. The government then continued its case, during which defense counsel subjected Midgett's co-defendant Theresa Russell to cross examination as to the favorable plea agreement she expected in exchange for her testimony against Midgett.

The following day, after the government rested its case and Midgett's motion for acquittal was denied, the court asked whether the defense had evidence to present. Again, Midgett's lawyer raised the issue of his conflict with his client. Defense counsel stated that he had repeatedly recommended to Midgett that testifying was not in his best interests. At the court's prompting, Midgett's lawyer further asserted that

> I indicated to you in chambers that I felt I needed to withdraw because I was duty bound to make that motion, and you directed me to tell you why, and at that point I indicated that it is my belief that Mr. Midgett is going to offer information when he testifies that is not in any way truthful or in existence that I can determine from any source. . . . [A]nd based on what has been represented to me and I understand is about to happen if and when he takes the stand, I am duty bound to move to withdraw at this point. I can say that the issue relates to whether or not a third person was at the scene at the time of the destruction incident when Mr. Shaw was burned, a third person actually did the act. And I have investigated that, I have asked for an identity from this supposed person. I have asked the co-defendant directly whether this person exists. . . . There's nothing whatsoever that I can find to corroborate any such representation.

J.A. 297–98. Rather than permitting his lawyer to withdraw, the court offered Midgett the choice of either acceding to defense counsel's refusal to put him on the stand or representing himself without further assistance of counsel. Midgett repeated that he did not "feel . . . qualified to [represent himself] . . . I'm saying I want to [take the stand], but I can't." J.A. 300. In response, Midgett's lawyer told the court:

> I don't think he's being denied his right to testify. He's got a choice here today what he wants to do. He knows the parameters. I have asked him a number of times to give me the name or a way to find this person, and he can't do it and no one else corroborates it.

J.A. 301. The court agreed, stating that "if the defendant chooses to take the witness stand, I will permit [him] to withdraw." J.A. 302. Midgett responded:

"I say again, Your Honor, I want to take the witness stand, but I can't because I can't do it without counsel." J.A. 302. The court finally told Midgett that

> if there is any problem with your taking the stand and not being able to take the stand because of your wanting to bring before the jury an issue that doesn't exist and for which you have absolutely no evidence to offer other than your own testimony, . . . the court is of the opinion that any resulting problem is a problem of your own making, and the trial will not be further delayed. . . . The time has come that we're going to finish the case, and you and the appellate courts may take it from there.

J.A. 303. Midgett declined to testify and his lawyer offered no other evidence. In his closing statement, defense counsel referred to various weaknesses and inconsistencies in the statements of certain witnesses, including Theresa Russell's motive to give testimony favorable to the government and Shaw's inability to identify Midgett in the photographic lineup. The jury took little time to convict Midgett on all three counts.

After trial the court granted defense counsel's motion to withdraw, stating that:

> It was clear throughout the course of the trial that [Midgett] repeatedly conferred with counsel and was satisfied with counsel's performance except as it related to . . . [the] defense that a third party was responsible for the crime charged in Count One, when counsel's thorough investigation and the overwhelming evidence indicated the guilt of the Defendant and no one else.

J.A. 372. New counsel was appointed and immediately filed a motion for new trial, which was denied; several further motions for new trial were subsequently filed and denied in turn. This appeal by new counsel followed.

Midgett raises several issues on appeal. In particular, he claims that the district court erred in conditioning his right to counsel on his waiver of his right to testify. It is to this issue that we now turn.

II.

The question of what a lawyer should do when confronted by potentially perjurious testimony has long caused consternation in the legal profession, producing heated debate and little consensus. On the one hand are the series of constitutional rights to which a defendant is entitled and for which the defendant's lawyer is called to provide zealous advocacy; on the other hand are the lawyer's obligations to the court to seek the furtherance of justice. Similarly, the court itself is obliged to ensure that the constitutional rights of the defendant are protected, while also seeing that proceedings are conducted fairly and truthfully. Midgett argues that these obligations were not adequately met when his lawyer, disbelieving Midgett's proffered testimony, sought to withdraw from representing him and approached the court to discuss the lack of corroborative evidence in support of Midgett's case. Likewise, Midgett argues that the court should not have confronted him with a choice between exercising his right to take the stand and his right to be represented by counsel. Under these circumstances, we agree.

The Sixth Amendment guarantees a criminal defendant the right to the assistance of counsel at trial. *See, e.g., Gideon v. Wainwright,* 372 U.S. 335, 83 S.Ct. 792, 9 L.Ed.2d 799 (1963). It is also clear that a criminal defendant has a constitutional right to testify on his own behalf at trial. *See Rock v. Arkansas,* 483 U.S. 44, 107 S.Ct. 2704, 97 L.Ed.2d 37 (1987). Although the right to testify is not explicitly set forth in the Constitution, we find its origins in the due process clause of the Fourteenth Amendment, the compulsory process clause of the Sixth Amendment, and as a "necessary corollary to the Fifth Amendment's guarantee against compelled testimony." *Id.* at 52, 107 S.Ct. 2704. Notwithstanding its constitutional stature, however, the defendant's right to testify is "not unlimited." *United States v. Teague,* 953 F.2d 1525, 1530 (11th Cir.1992) (en banc). In particular, "the right to testify clearly does not include the right to commit perjury." *Id.* This limitation was explicitly recognized in *Nix v. Whiteside,* 475 U.S. 157, 106 S.Ct. 988, 89 L.Ed.2d 123 (1986), the case upon which the government relies in answer to Midgett's argument on appeal.

In *Nix,* the defendant expressly indicated to his lawyer that he intended to perjure himself at trial by offering testimony that he had seen a gun in the hand of his victim, when he had previously told his lawyer that he had not seen a gun, but only feared that the victim had one. The defendant made clear to his lawyer that he had not seen a weapon, but thought that testifying to having seen one was necessary to persuade the jury of his innocence. On pain of withdrawal, his lawyer would not allow him to testify to his having seen the gun. Although the defendant alleged that his lawyer's refusal to allow him to testify as he proposed constituted ineffective assistance of counsel under the Sixth Amendment, the Supreme Court disagreed, concluding that the "right to counsel includes no right to have a lawyer who will cooperate with planned perjury." *Nix,* 475 U.S. at 173, 106 S.Ct. 988. Under *Nix,* then, the defendant's right to counsel and his right to testify on his own behalf are circumscribed in instances where the defendant has made manifest his intention to commit perjury. Unlike *Nix,* however, where the defendant actually admitted to his lawyer that he planned to perjure himself, Midgett never told his lawyer or otherwise indicated to him that his intended testimony was perjurious. Rather, Midgett consistently maintained that his third-person defense was true and that he believed his co-defendant could corroborate his story.

The question, then, is whether the information known to defense counsel was sufficient to show that Midgett's testimony would be perjurious so as to bring this case within the rule set forth in *Nix.* We conclude that it was not. We recognize that Midgett's "mystery man did it" defense lacked other corroboration. Among other things, Midgett's co-defendant actually testified that no one else was in the van during the arson/robbery, and, although he had been unable to do so in an earlier photographic lineup, Shaw did identify Midgett in court as his assailant. Midgett also sent a letter to Shaw that might have been interpreted by the jury as a feeble apology for what had happened to the victim—though the letter is altogether too vague and indirect to be described as an acknowledgment of guilt.

Notwithstanding these obstacles to his case, Midgett had apparently been consistent in his interviews with his lawyer that a third person committed the Count One crime and that he did not. Defense counsel's responsibility to his client was not dependent on whether he personally believed Midgett, nor did it depend on the amount of proof supporting or contradicting Midgett's anticipated testimony regarding how the incident happened. In this situation, Midgett never indicated to his attorney that his testimony would be perjurious. Thus, his lawyer had a duty to assist Midgett in putting his testimony before the jury, which would necessarily include his help in Midgett's direct examination. *Nix,* 475 U.S. at 189, 106 S.Ct. 988 (Blackmun, J., concurring) ("Except in the rarest of cases, attorneys who adopt the role of the judge or jury to determine the facts pose a danger of depriving their clients of the zealous and loyal advocacy required by the Sixth Amendment." (internal quotation marks, citations, and punctuation omitted)).

Defense counsel's mere belief, albeit a strong one supported by other evidence, was not a sufficient basis to refuse Midgett's need for assistance in presenting his own testimony. *See United States ex rel. Wilcox v. Johnson,* 555 F.2d 115, 122 (3d Cir.1977) ("While defense counsel in a criminal case assumes a dual role as a zealous advocate and as an officer of the court, neither role would countenance disclosure to the Court of counsel's private conjectures about the guilt or innocence of his client. It is the role of the judge or jury to determine the facts, not that of the attorney." (internal quotation marks omitted)). This assessment is consistent with Rule 3.3(a)(3) of the Model Rules of Professional Conduct, which requires that a lawyer "not knowingly offer evidence that the lawyer *knows* to be false," but also states that "[a] lawyer may refuse to offer evidence, *other than the testimony of a defendant in a criminal matter,* that the lawyer *reasonably believes* is false." (emphasis added). Far-fetched as Midgett's story might have sounded to a jury, it was not his lawyer's place in these circumstances to decide that Midgett was lying and to declare this opinion to the court. *Cf. United States v. Shaffer Equip. Co.,* 11 F.3d 450, 459 (4th Cir.1993) (observing that "a mere suspicion of perjury by a client does not carry with it the obligation to reveal that suspicion to the court under [West Virginia's] Rule 3.3"); *Hoke v. Netherland,* 92 F.3d 1350, 1360 (4th Cir.1996) (noting that mere beliefs on the part of a lawyer, even if "directly contradictory in substance" to the testimony of a witness, are different from knowledge of falsity and do not suffice to establish subornation of perjury (internal citations omitted)).

As this discussion makes clear, we believe Midgett's trial lawyer failed to carry out his duty to zealously defend his client. The issue on appeal, however, is not whether counsel was ineffective so as to warrant a new trial, but whether the district court erred by forcing Midgett to choose between testifying or retaining counsel. We believe that, in the circumstances of this case, the court did err in this regard, given that the court effectively mirrored defense counsel's error by deciding that Midgett's testimony would be perjurious. To be sure, the court had an obligation not to permit *known* perjury from being placed before the jury, *see Nix,* 475 U.S. at 162, 106 S.Ct. 988. In this case, however, the court merely believed the defendant's potential testimony would be dramatically outweighed by other evidence, a situation that did not warrant the extreme sanction imposed by the court.

The record reveals that, during the colloquy after the close of the government's case, the court defended the choice it imposed on Midgett by declaring that "your wanting to bring before the jury an issue that doesn't exist and *for which you have absolutely no evidence to offer other than your own testimony* . . . [amounts to] a problem of your own making." J.A. 303 (emphasis added). Thus, the court based its ultimatum on an inappropriate weighing of the evidence. Specifically, the court treated as irrefutable proof of an intent to commit perjury the fact that Midgett did not produce corroborating witnesses and sought merely to offer his own testimony. The defendant was told to waive either his right to counsel or his right to testify because neither his counsel nor the court was satisfied that his testimony would be truthful. In so doing, the court leveled an ultimatum upon Midgett which, of necessity, deprived him of his constitutional right to testify on his own behalf. *See Johnson,* 555 F.2d at 120–21 ("A defendant in a criminal proceeding is entitled to certain rights. . . . He is entitled to all of them; he cannot be forced to barter one for another. When the exercise of one right is made contingent upon the forbearance of another, both rights are corrupted."). Forcing this "Hobson's choice" upon the defendant constituted error that calls for a new trial.

III.

We conclude that, in the circumstances of this case, the court impermissibly forced the defendant to choose between two constitutionally protected rights: the right to testify on his own behalf and the right to counsel. Because all three convictions were affected by this error, each is vacated and the case remanded for a new trial.

VACATED AND REMANDED

SOLUTIONS: THE LAWYER SHOULD HAVE, WOULD HAVE, COULD HAVE. . .

Midgett's testimony was always consistent was it not? This is unlike what we saw in *Nix v. Whiteside* where the testimony changed completely. That complete shift creates a strong inference that the client was about to lie. Finally recall this: the lawyer has the trump card. The lawyer can, as the Comment to the Rule states, "remonstrate" with the client. "Remonstrate" is several levels above counseling. It means "make a forcefully reproachful protest." And if the client does not acquiesce then the lawyer can compromise the client's confidences and inform the tribunal of the plan for perjury. Work with your professor on how you would interact with Nix and Whiteside and explore options to address the issues.

LEANING INTO PRACTICE

Scenario No. 1: The Case of the Confused Victim and the Truthful Witnesses

Orly Lawyer represents a defendant accused of brutally mugging a man. The man was so disoriented by the attack that he told the police that was attacked at 8 pm. This found its way into the police report. In fact, he was attacked at 6 pm. The client has a truthful alibi for 6 pm; he was at the movies with two friends who will so testify. These witnesses knew nothing on whether their friends committed the crime. The client will not be testifying. Can the lawyer offer the testimony of the two friends? The client will not be testifying.

Scenario No. 2: The Case of the Lying Client

Lawrence Client is charged with vehicular manslaughter. He testifies at his trial that he was not driving. Emmy Lawyer believes that he is telling the truth. The jury acquits him. That night over several martinis, Lawrence tells Emmy: "I can't believe the jury bought my story. Hell, I was behind the wheel all the time. I guess my pretty face and my smooth tongue got me out of trouble yet again!" Emmy comes to you as a fellow lawyer and asks what she should do now? What's your response?

Section 4. The Lawyer's Role in Preparing a Witness to Testify

The preparation of a witness to testify—whether in a civil or a criminal matter—is a key function of a trial lawyer. It is a challenging task, both strategically and ethically. The lawyer must meld the roles of advocate with officer of the court.

Cases and Materials

X-Ray Questions (*Resolution Trust Corporation*)

Witness preparation is an art. It requires fidelity to the truth yet, at the same time, the perspective of an advocate. How to fuse the two? As a jury consultant once told one of your authors, "you cannot change the facts, but you can change the story." As you read this case, keep this counsel in mind. The lawyers, as is typical, came into the witness meeting with a pre-conceived, albeit not unreasonable, belief as to the facts and the narrative that thy wanted to advance. The witness had another. How did they reconcile the competing versions? What was their home base, so to speak, in ensuring that they were zealous representatives for their client but officers of the court? Note that the trial judge conducted a hearing in which the witness testified. What was her key testimony relied on by the appeals court? What analogy was used by the appeals court in arriving at the decision to reverse?

Resolution Trust Corp. v. Bright

United States Court of Appeals, Fifth Circuit, 1993.
6 F.3d 336.

Opinion

KAZEN, DISTRICT JUDGE:

This appeal arises out of a lawsuit filed in May 1992 by the Resolution Trust Corporation ("RTC") against H.R. "Bum" Bright and James B. "Boots" Reeder, based on their alleged misconduct in connection with activities at Bright Banc Savings Association, Dallas ("Bright Banc"). Approximately two months after the suit was filed, appellees moved for a protective order and sanctions against the RTC for the manner in which its attorneys, Peter F. Lovato III and Thomas D. Graber, interviewed a former Bright Banc employee. After four days of hearings on the motion for sanctions, the district court issued an oral order on October 19, 1992, finding that the attorneys, appellants herein, impermissibly attempted to persuade the witness to sign an affidavit containing statements which the witness had not previously told appellants. The order disbarred the attorneys from practicing before the district judge and disqualified the attorneys' law firm, Hopkins & Sutter, from further representing RTC in the underlying case. In a December 28, 1992 written order, the court assessed attorneys' fees against the law firm for costs incurred by appellees in prosecuting the sanctions motion. Appellants timely appealed the district court's decision. We reverse.

A.   *Factual Background*

On May 14, 1992, the RTC filed suit in federal district court charging appellees Bright and Reeder, as shareholders, directors and officers of Bright Banc, with fraud, negligence, and breach of fiduciary and other duties owed to the bank's shareholders. As part of their pre-filing investigation of the case, attorneys Lovato and Graber conducted several interviews—all voluntary—with Barbara Erhart, formerly the Senior Vice President of Finance Support at Bright Banc. Erhart had worked closely with defendant Reeder and had contact with defendant Bright on "critical matters."

The primary focus of the Erhart interviews was the method Bright Banc used to calculate the amount of non-cash assets it had converted to cash for a December 1986 report on the bank's financial health to the Federal Home Loan Bank Board ("FHLBB"). The RTC attorneys, including Lovato and Graber, questioned Erhart extensively about who made and authorized the computations used in the report. At the conclusion of the third interview,

Lovato and Graber asked Erhart to return to their office the next day—April 9, 1992—to review and sign an affidavit summarizing what she had told them in the course of the prior interviews.

When Erhart arrived at the office of Hopkins & Sutter on April 9th, she was not immediately given the affidavit. Instead, the attorneys questioned her again about the cash conversion calculations. As Lovato and Graber spoke to Erhart, they made some last-minute changes to the draft. The changes were incorporated into a revised draft which Graber then presented to Erhart. He warned her that it "contained a couple of things [they hadn't] discussed with [her]," but which the attorneys nevertheless believed to be true. Erhart was instructed to read the affidavit "very carefully."

Erhart made several changes to the draft affidavit. Some related only to semantical differences, while others reflected Erhart's disagreement with substantive claims in the affidavit. Lovato and Graber questioned Erhart extensively about the changes she made. During this questioning, the attorneys asked Erhart whether she could reword some of her changes to emphasize that Bright and Reeder were more directly involved in the decision to use the controversial cash conversion computations. Erhart declined because she did not have personal knowledge of the statements the attorneys wanted her to include in her affidavit. With respect to some of the statements in the affidavit, the attorneys were not content to accept Erhart's initial refusal to revise her changes. In an effort to have Erhart see things their way, Lovato and Graber described their understanding of how certain events transpired at Bright Banc, presented Erhart with independent evidence to support this interpretation of events, and aggressively challenged some of Erhart's assumptions about Bright and Reeder. After making their case for further revisions, Lovato and Graber asked Erhart whether she believed them and whether she was now convinced that their version of certain events was correct. Erhart, unconvinced, declined to alter the initial changes she had made to the draft affidavit.

When it was clear to the attorneys that Erhart would not sign a statement agreeing with the attorneys' version of some of the disputed events at Bright Banc, they incorporated Erhart's handwritten changes into a new draft affidavit. Erhart read this draft and made a few changes which were then included in a third draft. Erhart read and approved this version of the affidavit, signed it and left the offices of Hopkins & Sutter.

Approximately one month later, Erhart told appellees' attorneys that she had given a statement to appellant-attorneys regarding some of the transactions at issue in the underlying law suit. Appellees' counsel then arranged for Erhart to give them an *ex parte* statement on June 12, 1992 about her meetings with Lovato and Graber. This statement was transcribed by the court reporter but never signed by Erhart. However, she later adopted portions of it during testimony before Judge Kendall on August 9, 1992.

In that testimony, Erhart stated, among other things, that she did not think Lovato and Graber were asking her to say something she did not believe but rather were trying to determine if she could see the case the way they did. She denied being harassed or intimidated and expressed the view that "they were doing their job, just like everybody else." The district court essentially disregarded this testimony, finding it contrary to Erhart's earlier *ex parte* statement given to appellees' attorneys, and concluding that the change must have been the result of "obvious job pressure." Erhart's earlier statement clearly has a different tone from her subsequent court testimony. For example, she earlier described Lovato as having been particularly aggressive in attempts to persuade her to agree with appellants' version of certain events, "almost like browbeating me." Nevertheless, even in her *ex parte* statement, Erhart indicated that Lovato and Graber were not trying to have her change facts but rather to agree with a different "interpretation" or "slant" from the facts.

B.   *The Motion For Sanctions*

On July 15, 1992, Bright and Reeder moved for sanctions and a protective order against the RTC based on Lovato and Graber's conduct during the Erhart interviews. The motion alleged that the manner in which the RTC's attorneys interviewed Erhart violated Texas Disciplinary Rules of Professional Conduct 3.04, 4.01(a) and 4.04(a) and probably violated 18 U.S.C. §§ 1503, 1512. Appellees also called upon the court to exercise its "inherent powers" to sanction the RTC for intimidating Erhart. The motion asked the court to prevent the RTC from using any notes or statements obtained through the Erhart interviews, to order the RTC not to make any further contact with Erhart, and to award attorneys fees to Bright and Reeder for their efforts in bringing and prosecuting the motion for sanctions.

On July 20, 1992, the district court ordered that both sides refrain from contacting Erhart while the sanctions motion was pending. Hearings on the sanctions motion were held over the course of several days from August to October 1992.

C. The District Court's Decision

The district court issued an oral ruling on the motion for sanctions on October 19, 1992. This ruling was further clarified in separate written orders issued on October 23 and December 28, 1992.

The court found that Lovato and Graber "knowingly attempted to get a key witness . . . to commit to a sworn statement that they knew contained assertions of fact she had not made or told them previously in matters highly relevant to the plaintiff's civil claim." It found that the attorneys were "going to try to talk her into" those statements. The Court was particularly troubled because the draft affidavit given to Erhart added matters only in areas "that established or buttressed the [RTC's] claims." The court characterized the attorneys' actions concerning the draft affidavit as "tampering with" or attempting to "manufacture" evidence to "cause, or aid in, Defendants' downfall."

Based on its inherent power to regulate the conduct of attorneys, Judge Kendall disbarred Lovato and Graber from practicing before him. He assessed $110,000 in attorneys fees against Hopkins & Sutter for expenses incurred by Bright and Reeder in the prosecution of the sanctions motion. Pursuant to its authority under Local Rule 13.2 (N.D.Tex.), the court removed Hopkins & Sutter from further representing the RTC in the underlying action. Finally, it ordered the firm not to charge the RTC for defending against the sanction motion. No sanctions were assessed against the RTC. Lovato, Graber and Hopkins & Sutter timely appealed.

D. Disbarment of Lovato and Graber

The district court disbarred attorneys Lovato and Graber from practicing before it pursuant to the court's inherent powers to discipline attorneys. It is beyond dispute that a federal court may suspend or dismiss an attorney as an exercise of the court's inherent powers. *In re Snyder,* 472 U.S. 634, 643–644, 105 S.Ct. 2874, 2880, 86 L.Ed.2d 504 (1985); *Matter of Thalheim,* 853 F.2d 383, 389 (5th Cir.1988). However, before sanctioning any attorney under its inherent powers, the court must make a specific finding that the attorney acted in "bad faith." *Thalheim,* 853 F.2d at 389. The United States Supreme Court has held that a court's imposition of sanctions under its inherent powers is reviewable under the abuse-of-discretion standard. *Chambers v. NASCO, Inc.,* 501 U.S. 32, ___, 111 S.Ct. 2123, 2138, 115 L.Ed.2d 27 (1991). A court abuses its discretion when its ruling is based on an erroneous view of the law or on a clearly erroneous assessment of the evidence. *Cooter & Gell v. Hartmarx Corp.,* 496 U.S. 384, 405,

110 S.Ct. 2447, 2461, 110 L.Ed.2d 359 (1990). In the specific context of a disqualification motion, this circuit reviews fact findings for "clear error" while "carefully examining" the district court's application of relevant ethical standards. *In re American Airlines, Inc.*, 972 F.2d 605, 609 (5th Cir.1992), *cert. denied* 507 U.S. 912, 113 S.Ct. 1262, 122 L.Ed.2d 659 (1993).

Because disbarment is a quasi-criminal proceeding, any disciplinary rules used to impose this sanction on attorneys must be strictly construed, resolving ambiguities in favor of the person charged. *Thalheim*, 853 F.2d at 388. The Texas Disciplinary Rules of Professional Conduct do not expressly apply to sanctions in federal courts, but a federal court may nevertheless hold attorneys accountable to the state code of professional conduct. *See In re Snyder*, 472 U.S. at 645 n. 6, 105 S.Ct. at 2881 n. 6; *In re Finkelstein*, 901 F.2d 1560, 1564 (11th Cir.1990).

The district court failed to make specific findings of how appellants violated the Disciplinary Rules. In its oral findings, the court concluded that Lovato and Graber engaged in "inappropriate conduct, conduct that probably violates the DRs, unethical conduct, as well as a probable violation of the obstruction of justice statutes." We shall assume that the district court's comments referred to the Disciplinary Rules invoked by Appellees in their motion for sanctions.

The sanctionable conduct found by the district court was the attorneys' inclusion of statements in draft affidavits that had not been previously discussed with Erhart, combined with the attorneys' attempts to persuade Erhart to agree with their understanding of how certain events transpired at the bank. Placing statements in a draft affidavit that have not been previously discussed with a witness does not automatically constitute bad-faith conduct. *See U.S. v. Brand*, 775 F.2d 1460, 1469 (11th Cir.1985) (giving witness affidavit with statements not previously discussed not obstruction of justice). It is one thing to ask a witness to swear to facts which are knowingly false. It is another thing, in an arms-length interview with a witness, for an attorney to attempt to persuade her, even aggressively, that her initial version of a certain fact situation is not complete or accurate. Disciplinary Rules 3.04(b) and 4.01(a) concern the former circumstance, not the latter. The district court never found that appellants asked Erhart to make statements which they knew to be false. Indeed, the district court pretermitted any consideration of the truth of the draft affidavits. Appellees nevertheless argue that because appellant attorneys attempted to persuade Erhart to adopt certain statements which she had not expressly made and which she refused to adopt, the attorneys thereby were either making or urging the making of "false" statements in violation of DRs 3.04(b) and 4.01(a). We disagree. The district court characterized the attorneys' behavior as "manufacturing" evidence, but there is no indication that the attorneys did not have a factual basis for the additional statements included in the draft affidavit. *See Koller v. Richardson-Merrell,* 737 F.2d 1038, 1058–59 (D.C.Cir.1984), *vacated on other grounds* 472 U.S. 424, 105 S.Ct. 2757, 86 L.Ed.2d 340 (1985). On the contrary, appellants have attempted to demonstrate in a detailed chart that the contested portions of the affidavit were based either on their notes of interviews with Erhart or on evidence from other sources (e.g., internal bank memorandum).We recognize that the Texas Disciplinary Rules are not the sole authority governing a motion to disqualify in federal court; rather, such a motion must be determined by standards developed under federal law. *In re Dresser Industries, Inc.,* 972 F.2d 540, 543 (5th Cir.1992). Our source for professional standards has been the canons of ethics developed by the American Bar Association. *Id.* The district court opinion, however, makes no reference to any national canons which would add to the analysis here, nor do appellees. A court obviously would be justified in disbarring an attorney for attempting to induce a witness to testify falsely under oath, *see Thalheim,* 853 F.2d at 390 (citing *U.S. v. Friedland,* 502 F.Supp. 611, 619 (D.N.J.1980), *aff'd.* 672 F.2d 905 (3d Cir.1981)), but this record does not support the conclusion that Lovato and Graber engaged in such behavior. While the attorneys were persistent and aggressive in presenting their theory of the case to Erhart, they nevertheless made sure that Erhart signed the affidavit only if she agreed with its contents. The attorneys never attempted to hide from Erhart the fact that some statements were included in draft affidavits that had not been discussed with her previously. Instead, they brought the statements to her attention and warned her to read them carefully. Additionally, Lovato and Graber never claimed to be neutral parties. Erhart knew that these attorneys were advocates for a particular position, and she was also in communication with attorneys who were advocating the contrary position. Were Erhart giving testimony at a deposition or at trial, the attorneys for either side would not be required to accept her initial testimony at face value but would be able to confront her with other information to challenge her testimony or attempt to persuade her to change it.

Appellees also alleged that RTC attorneys violated Disciplinary Rule 4.04(a), which prohibits an attorney from burdening a third party without a valid "substantial purpose" or violating a third party's legal rights. The district court findings do not reveal that Lovato and Graber committed either wrong. The attorneys' sometimes laborious interviews with Erhart were conducted with the goal of eliciting an accurate and favorable affidavit from a key witness in the underlying case. Additionally, the district court made no findings that the interviews violated Erhart's legal rights, nor does the record contain any evidence to support such a finding.

E. Sanctions Against The Law Firm

The district court ordered the firm of Hopkins & Sutter to pay $100,000 in attorneys' fees to appellees for their prosecution of the sanction motion and also restrained the firm from charging the RTC for defending against the motion. The court assessed attorneys' fees under its inherent power to do so against counsel who have conducted themselves "in bad faith." *Chambers*, 501 U.S. at ___, 111 S.Ct. at 2133. It found that Lovato and Graber acted in bad faith because they tampered with or attempted to manufacture evidence and concluded that "a law firm may not escape the consequences of misconduct committed by one of its attorneys." The Supreme Court in *Chambers* described three exceptions to the so-called "American Rule," which prohibits fee-shifting in most cases. The exception pertinent to the instant case is that a court may assess attorney's fees when a party acts "in bad faith, vexatiously, wantonly, or for oppressive reasons." 501 U.S. at ___, 111 S.Ct. at 2133. The Supreme Court compared this exception to the requirement under Rule 11, Fed.R.Civ.P., providing that the signer of a paper warrants that it is not interposed for any improper purpose, such as to harass or to cause unnecessary delay or needless increase in the cost of litigation. *Id.* at n. 10. We understand the district court's finding of "bad faith" to be grounded exclusively on the proposition that attorneys Lovato and Graber wrongfully tried to tamper with or manufacture evidence. Because we have already found that the record does not support that conclusion, the assessment of attorney's fees cannot be sustained.

The trial court did not elaborate, either orally or in writing, on its order restraining Hopkins & Sutter from charging the RTC for time spent defending the motion for sanctions. Neither side has specifically addressed that sanction on appeal. Nevertheless, in view of the conclusions we have heretofore announced, there would likewise be no justification for this sanction.

F. Conclusion

We conclude that the district court abused its discretion when it issued its sanctions ruling against appellants. We REVERSE and REMAND for proceedings not inconsistent with this opinion.

SOLUTIONS: THE LAWYER SHOULD HAVE, WOULD HAVE, COULD HAVE. . .

The lawyers in this case went back again and again to the home base of "we only want the truth." Too often, lawyers, in their zeal to prepare the testimony of a witness, seek to put their theory of the case front and center and not the story of the witness. Trouble can then ensue. A way to prepare with your own witness and with your client as a witness is to use a white board or a flip chart; ask the witness what she or he wants the jury and the jury to know; write these down. Then talk with the witness about how to best get those points across. This way is ethical because while it is the story of the witness, it is also one shaped by the lawyer/advocate.

LEANING INTO PRACTICE

BEYOND THE CITE

The clip from the movie "Anatomy of a Murder" shows the actor Jimmy Stewart advising his client, an Army officer accused of murder. Stewart is giving what criminal defense lawyers call "The Talk" in which the lawyer walks a fine line between determining the facts of the matter but not learning the actual truth in the event the client is actually guilty of the charges. If the latter, the lawyer's tactical options become limited. Is Stewart crossing the line between fairly explaining the legal system and unfairly telling the client exactly what to say and how to say it?

https://youtu.be/JTnF14D8_-I

https://youtu.be/MEtgDNVcdK8

Did the lawyer in either clip go too far in preparing the witness? How so? In Boston Legal, the lawyer kept going back to the home base of "if true?" Is that sufficient to permit *any* advice given on how to testify? With the Jimmy Stewart clip, notice not only the words that were said but the looks from Stewart and the pauses between what he says. Can looks and pauses also be a way to communicate? One way for criminal defense lawyers to handle prep issues is not to ask the client what the client believes the facts are from the client's viewpoint but rather what the client suspects the other side might say transpired. This way, the lawyer can honestly say the client never told him that he committed the crime. Perhaps the only way is to prohibit outright lying "I know you told me that the person you shot did not have a weapon and you did not believe that he did, but you must testify that you honestly believed that he did."

A final point. Note in the Boston Legal clip that the co-counsel tells the lead lawyer "Now, I have a duty to report you." What's that all about? MR 8.3: Reporting Professional Misconduct provides in pertinent part as follows: "A lawyer who knows that another lawyer has committed a violation of the Rules of Professional Conduct that raises a substantial question as to that lawyer's honesty, trustworthiness or fitness as a lawyer in other respects, shall inform the appropriate professional authority." Deconstruct the rule, considering its rationale, and answer this question: does she have such a duty here?

Section 5. The Lawyer's Conduct at Trial

A. The Lawyer's Role in Maintaining Decorum of the Tribunal

Model Rule 3.5: Impartiality & Decorum of the Tribunal

A lawyer shall not:

(a)   seek to influence a judge, juror, prospective juror or other official by means prohibited by law;

(b)   communicate ex parte with such a person during the proceeding unless authorized to do so by law or court order;

(c)   communicate with a juror or prospective juror after discharge of the jury if:

(1)   the communication is prohibited by law or court order

(2)   the juror has made known to the lawyer a desire not to communicate; or

(3)   the communication involves misrepresentation, coercion, duress or harassment; or

(d)   engage in conduct intended to disrupt a tribunal.

Deconstruction Exercise/Rule Rationale

The rule focuses on "the record." You will hear this phrase throughout your legal career and is an essential feature of your course in evidence. The record is the testimony and exhibits from a trial. It is what a judge or a jury uses to reach an adjudication of a lawsuit and what the appeals court uses to determine whether there is reversible error. Subsections (a), and (b) designed to protect the integrity of the record as the source of decision making untainted by other influences. (We saw this in the first case to this chapter when the lawyer essentially inserted "personal testimony" into the record.) Here, the rule deals not with actual improper influence but rather with efforts to "seek to influence" a decision maker, judge or juror, in an inappropriate fashion. Note that the effort does not, per the language of the rule, need to be successful. Rather, the operative verb is "seek," not "accomplish."

Subsection (d) is tied to the concept in the title of "decorum." While this may seem like an old fashioned, Victorian era word, it is directly on point to what is expected of a lawyer in a trial. The effective functioning of a trial in its search for justice breaks down when lawyers behave badly, when the virtue of "zealous representation" is misused, and when a lawyer believes in victory at all costs, even damage to the judicial system which provides the basis of our careers. MR 3.5(d) acts as a guard rail to such conduct.

Cases and Materials

X-Ray Questions (*Cadorna*)

Here we have another instance of a lawyer found in criminal contempt of the court. The facts are more fully developed in the second case which involves this lawyer's conduct and the Colorado Supreme Court's punishment of him. The jury apparently liked this lawyer and found for his client. The court granted the defendant a new trial because the conduct so polluted the proceedings.

Cadorna v. *The City and County of Denver*

United States District Court, D. Colorado, 2006.
562 F.Supp.2d 1302.

ORDER OF CONTEMPT

BLACKBURN, DISTRICT JUDGE.

This order is entered pursuant to Fed.R.Crim.P. 42(b) to certify, confirm, reiterate, expatiate, and supplement the findings of fact, conclusions of law, and order of contempt (with sanctions) entered summarily by the court during trial (outside the presence of the jury) on Wednesday, June 28, 2006, against Mark E. Brennan, attorney for plaintiff, as punishment for the criminal contempt committed by him in the presence of the court.

During the course of the eight-day trial conducted in this case, the court had admonished, warned, and instructed Mr. Brennan on various occasions not to interrupt the court. Notwithstanding those earlier admonitions, warnings, and instructions, on the seventh day of trial held on Wednesday, June 28, 2006, at approximately 11:25 a.m., Mr. Brennan again interrupted the court. During a conference at the bench, the court was pronouncing its ruling on plaintiff's oral request that a defense may-call witness remain available for possible rebuttal testimony by plaintiff, when Mr. Brennan repeatedly interrupted the court after the court had instructed him yet again not to do so. Accordingly, the court terminated the bench conference, removed the jury from the courtroom, and certified the following on the record:

> During the court's colloquy with counsel and the plaintiff at its bench in consideration and potential resolution of plaintiff's request that the defendant make available for potential rebuttal testimony Tracy Howard, a defendant may-call witness, in the course of its ruling, Mr. Brennan continually and without cause interrupted the court in its remarks. If this had been the first such rude, contemptuous interruption, the court would have simply ignored it as I have during this trial on so many previous occasions, but enough is enough. Once again I find that the conduct of counsel on this occasion in rudely interrupting the court despite its previous instructions and requirements to the contrary to be contemptuous. It is offensive to the dignity of this court. It has effected yet another delay in these trial proceedings, again to the detriment of the court, the parties, counsel, and importantly this trier of fact. Therefore, I find that Mr. Brennan has committed a direct contempt of court, the sanction for which shall be the imposition of a fine of $500, and I warn Mr. Brennan that for each subsequent violation, that fine shall be doubled.

In responding to this act of contempt, which was committed in the presence of the court, the court exercised its authority under 18 U.S.C. § 401 and Fed.R.Crim.P. 42(b) to summarily punish criminal contempt committed in the presence of the court. The contemptuous conduct implicated 18 U.S.C. § 401(1) and (3).

THEREFORE, IT IS ORDERED as follows:

1.   That Mark E. Brennan, attorney for plaintiff, is found guilty of contempt of court; and

2.   That as a punitive sanction to vindicate the dignity of the court, Mark E. Brennan shall pay to the Clerk of the Court the sum of Five Hundred Dollars ($500.00) by July 19, 2006.

Done in chambers July 12, 2006, pursuant to Fed.R.Crim.P. 42(b), to certify, confirm, reiterate, expatiate, and supplement the findings of fact, conclusions of law, and order of contempt entered summarily by the court during trial on June 28, 2006.

Cases and Materials

X-Ray Questions (*Brennan*)

Why was a suspension imposed upon Brennan? What was the nature his conduct that rose above mere disagreement with the court and into a rule violation? Consider how you would deal with his conduct if you were counsel opposite. What would you do, if anything? Is there some point where he crossed a line of propriety or is this just an example or numerous wrongful acts piling up?

Also, this case introduces you to ABA Standard 3.0 that sets out criteria for the imposition of discipline for a violation of the Rules. In applying the standard, how did the court deal with the lawyer's argument that his actions were purely client centered and thus not deserving of punishment? Are a lawyer's motivations—in what you have studied this far—ever an effective affirmative defense to a charge of a rule violation? Should the invocation of the rubric of "zealous representation" operate as a magic wand excusing lawyer conduct? Why or why not?

The People of the State of Colorado, Complainant v. Mark Edward Brennan, Respondent

Supreme Court of Colorado, 2009.
240 P.3d 887.

DECISION AND ORDER IMPOSING SANCTIONS PURSUANT TO C.R.C.P. 251.19(b)

I.   *DISCIPLINARY ISSUE ADDRESSED*

A lawyer shall not engage in conduct intended to disrupt a tribunal or conduct prejudicial to the administration of justice. Respondent repeatedly ignored admonitions from a judge to follow trial protocol and openly expressed disdain for his rulings thereby disrupting and impeding the proceedings. He also verbally abused court staff and opposing counsel. If Respondent engaged in this conduct with the intent to disrupt the tribunal, what is the appropriate sanction?

II. *SUMMARY*

Respondent engaged in a pattern of progressively egregious misconduct during an eight-day jury trial. His conduct was not the product of human frailty in the course of a contentious trial. To the contrary, Respondent purposely challenged a federal district court judge, because he believed the judge held a bias in favor of his opponent. Ultimately, the judge found Respondent in contempt of court for his insolent behavior and disrespect for the authority of the tribunal. Yet, even after the judge entered the contempt order, Respondent persisted in his impertinent behavior.

After carefully reviewing the entire trial record and the testimony of the witnesses, including Respondent, the Hearing Board finds by clear and convincing evidence the following:

- Respondent knew the import of, yet willfully disregarded, Judge Robert Blackburn's repeated admonitions to refrain from his improper behavior. Respondent therefore intentionally disrupted the tribunal thereby violating Colo. RPC 3.5(c) (a lawyer shall not engage in conduct intended to disrupt a tribunal).

- Respondent refused to obey unambiguous orders of the judge directed to him multiple times and engaged in obstreperous behavior in and outside the presence of the jury thereby violating Colo. RPC 8.4(d) (it is professional misconduct for a lawyer to engage in conduct that is prejudicial to the administration of justice).

SANCTION IMPOSED: ATTORNEY SUSPENDED FROM THE PRACTICE OF LAW FOR A PERIOD OF ONE YEAR AND ONE DAY.

III. *PROCEDURAL HISTORY*

The People filed a "Complaint" alleging two separate ethical violations against Respondent: Colo. RPC, 3.5(c) (a lawyer shall not engage in conduct intended to disrupt a tribunal); and Colo. RPC 8.4(d) (a lawyer should not engage in conduct prejudicial to the administration of justice) on May 29, 2008. On November 12, 2008, Respondent filed an "Answer" after the PDJ had granted various extensions of time and denied Respondent's multiple motions to dismiss.

The Hearing Board commenced the hearing pursuant to C.R.C.P. 251.18 on July 14, 2009 and concluded it on July 16, 2009. The parties urged the Hearing Board to review the entire trial transcript from which these disciplinary claims arose. The PDJ also admitted the People's exhibits 1, 2, 12, and 13, as well as Respondent's exhibits A, B, C, D (1 and 2), and E. The PDJ also adopted the separate Trial Management Orders submitted by the parties.

IV. *FINDINGS OF FACT AND RULE VIOLATIONS*

Jurisdiction

Respondent has taken and subscribed the oath of admission and the Colorado Supreme Court admitted him to the Bar on October 30, 1984. He is registered upon the official records under Attorney Registration No. 14012. Therefore, he is subject to the jurisdiction of the Colorado Supreme Court and the Hearing Board in these disciplinary proceedings pursuant to C.R.C.P. 251.1(b). Respondent's registered business address is P.O. Box 2556, Centennial, CO 80161.

Background

William Cadorna hired Respondent following his dismissal from the Denver Fire Department ("DFD") in 2003. The DFD fired Mr. Cadorna after his immediate supervisor initiated an investigation accusing Mr. Cadorna of stealing a cookbook from a Safeway store while on duty. At the DFD's behest, Mr. Cadorna was later charged with misdemeanor theft in Denver Municipal Court. When a jury could not reach a verdict, the Denver City Attorney's Office dismissed the theft case.

At the time of his dismissal, Mr. Cadorna was approximately fifty years old and had worked for the DFD for twenty-seven years. After Mr. Cadorna's discharge, Respondent challenged the dismissal before the Civil Service Commission. The judge in the Civil Service proceedings upheld the dismissal. While the judge found there had *not* been good cause to believe Mr. Cadorna committed theft while on duty, the judge nevertheless found that state law would not permit Mr. Cadorna to be reinstated. Despite the judge's decision, Mr. Cadorna applied for and received a medical disability retirement from the City and County of Denver ("the City").

After Mr. Cadorna exhausted all of his remedies in the administrative proceedings before the Civil Service Commission including the appeals process, Respondent filed an age discrimination suit on behalf of Mr. Cadorna against the City in the federal district court: *William R. Cadorna v. City and County of Denver,*

04-CV-1067-REB-CBS. Respondent sought damages for violating the Age Discrimination in Employment Act and denial of substantive due process. He also sought to be reinstated as a firefighter. Furthermore, Respondent argued the refusal to reinstate Mr. Cadorna based upon a state statute that used age as a criterion violated the Age Discrimination in Employment Act.

In the Civil Service Commission's decision and later in the appellate proceedings, the DFD and the City took the position there had been good cause to terminate Mr. Cadorna even though the Civil Service judge found there was insufficient evidence to justify his dismissals based upon the DFD's claim that he had committed theft. Further, the City claimed Mr. Cadorna had applied for retirement *before* his dismissal and therefore had voluntarily decided to leave the fire department before the DFD terminated him. Thus, the City argued Mr. Cadorna had not been fired because of his age; he had voluntarily resigned before the City took any action against him.

In the proceedings before the Civil Service Commission as well as those in federal court, Respondent vigorously argued Mr. Cadorna should have been reinstated because he had been terminated as a result of DFD's shoddy investigation. Respondent argued the Safeway manager, who signed a criminal complaint charging Mr. Cadorna with theft, did so without knowing the facts and at the behest of Mr. Cadorna's supervisor who had a long-standing grudge against Mr. Cadorna.

The same Safeway manager who signed the theft complaint against Mr. Cadorna testified for the City in the criminal court, but failed to disclose evidence that Respondent claimed was exculpatory: a cookbook bearing Mr. Cadorna's name and what appeared to be his badge number on the inside cover was found in the store after Mr. Cadorna claimed to have misplaced it there. Respondent's position was that a clerk gave Mr. Cadorna permission to take a cookbook after Mr. Cadorna told the clerk he had misplaced his cookbook in the Safeway store while on duty and shopping for groceries for the firehouse. The City's position was Mr. Cadorna, at a minimum, obtained the cookbook without permission from someone in authority at the store and did so by improperly using his position as a firefighter to pressure the clerk into letting Mr. Cadorna take a new cookbook without paying for it.

Preliminary Proceedings in Judge Blackburn's Court

Before the trial began in federal court, Judge Robert E. Blackburn ("the Court") issued two separate orders pursuant to D.C.COLO.LCivR 43.1 and REB Civ. Practice Standard IV.A.1 detailing trial procedures in his court. These orders included protocol for handling objections. Objections had to be made succinctly and supported by the applicable law. Lawyers were not allowed to "speechify" their objections or responses in front of the jury, and stipulations needed to be prepared before trial commenced.

In addition, the lawyers were required to "review the Trial Checklist with the courtroom deputy clerk." The clerk in turn advised the parties that the Court did not permit them to be speaking while the Court issued the oath to a witness. Furthermore, the parties were not to address witnesses by their first names.

Before the trial commenced, Respondent filed a motion to disqualify Judge Blackburn. Judge Blackburn denied the motion. Before denying the motion, Judge Blackburn admonished Respondent for the content and tone of an email Respondent had sent to his clerk in preliminary proceedings.

Early Stages of Trial in Federal District Court

During the first two days of trial, Judge Blackburn admonished Respondent and the City Attorneys on occasion for not following the protocol outlined in his pre-trial order. Respondent responded cordially and professionally to these early admonitions, which generally related to Respondent's habit of asking questions before the judge had an opportunity to rule on the pending objections. In this context, Judge Blackburn admonished *both* parties by stating:

> We are done. Again the trial practice order—and counsel read it, both of you please. I have had you ask me questions over the last couple of days about the contents of that order that are absolutely plain, and one of the things that are plain is the protocol for marshalling objections, Mr. Brennan, and that's objection, response, reply, and then the ruling, and that's where we are.

The Hearing Board finds Respondent's initial breaches of the Court's protocol insufficient to establish by clear and convincing evidence that he intended to disrupt the tribunal or knowingly engaged in conduct prejudicial to the administration of justice. However, Respondent was then on notice Judge Blackburn would not tolerate further breaches of courtroom protocol.

Nevertheless, knowing that Judge Blackburn repeatedly admonished him for not following the Court's protocol, Respondent continued to do so and openly challenged the admonitions. When Judge Blackburn *sua sponte* admonished Respondent for reading from a document not yet admitted into evidence, Respondent, in the presence of the jury, protested the admonition stating:

I wonder if the jury should be hearing this kind of remonstration all the time which I think has a tendency to prejudice them against me. Because you are in essence passing judgment upon my competence as an attorney in their presence.

Judge Blackburn then removed the jury and stated to Respondent:

Mr. Brennan, I find those final remarks deliberately made in the presence of the jury to be highly disrespectful of the court, in violation of Rule 103(c), and an effort on your part, apparently, to pad the record with injected prejudice.

The only way the Court can stop inappropriate behavior when it sees it is to do so on the record, and I did so, and that's *a fortiori*, sir, when this is not the first or second but the multiple time in which you insist in disregarding the admonishment of this Court, which is proper and appropriate, not to suggest to the jury evidence which has not yet been admitted. And I will expect you to conform your conduct accordingly.

Respondent replied to the Court's admonition by arguing the City "shape-shift[ed] into a new version of the facts every time the one that it formerly adopted is shot down." Judge Blackburn then reprimanded the parties for not preparing stipulations in a timely fashion and "exhorted" them to stipulate to exhibits upon which there was no controversy. The City then advised the Court that they had tried to confer with Respondent on the exhibits before the trial commenced but Respondent had refused to do so. Respondent responded, "That's absolute nonsense." Judge Blackburn firmly stated to both Respondent and the City, "That's enough."

The Hearing Board finds at this point in the trial Respondent knew or should have known Judge Blackburn was understandably growing impatient with his failure to abide by the Court's rules of protocol and interfering with a properly conducted trial.

Nevertheless, Respondent continued to disregard Judge Blackburn's orders. Up to this point Judge Blackburn was understandably troubled Respondent continued to "speechify" objections, interrupt the Court, and make editorial comments about the evidence. The Hearing Board finds after Judge Blackburn issued multiple warnings to stop disobeying the Court's direct orders, Respondent, at this point, *knowingly* and *intentionally* failed to abide by the Court's continued admonitions.

Judge Blackburn Warns Respondent that He will be Held in Contempt

Towards the end of the third day of trial, Judge Blackburn felt compelled to halt the proceedings after Respondent made an editorial comment about a witness's appearance. The Court took a fifteen minute recess and admonished Respondent as follows:

Mr. Brennan, enough is enough. You are going to have to find it within your power to resist what apparently is the almost irresistible to comment editorially as you conduct examination during the trial of this case.

And no longer will you be able, regardless of how well intended your remarks are, to compliment a witness as he or she testifies.

Both of those practices are unacceptable and inappropriate in the trial of this action. Please exert your best efforts now, under pain and penalty of contempt of court, to conform your conduct to the simple requirements of this court. Thank you.

When Respondent resumed the questioning of the witness, he again made another editorial comment about a witness's testimony. Giving Respondent the benefit of the doubt, the Hearing Board cannot discern this second editorial comment alone was intended to disrupt the tribunal. However, thereafter, we note Respondent's attitude toward Judge Blackburn and his authority became increasingly disrespectful and contemptuous. We therefore find from this point forward, Respondent was not only aware of his conduct and its consequences, but he began to intentionally focus his animus toward the tribunal and its authority.

Respondent Continues to Disregard the Judge Blackburn's Admonitions

When Respondent continued to disregard Judge Blackburn's numerous admonitions to stop talking while the Court was speaking, editorializing about evidence in front of the jury, and interrupting witnesses before they could complete their answers, Judge Blackburn terminated Respondent's cross-examination of a witness as a sanction. During an exchange *outside the jury's presence*, Judge Blackburn stated the following to Respondent:

After being repeatedly admonished, warned by the court with the threat of sanction, including but not limited to termination of cross-examination, Mr. Brennan again violated this court's reasonable requirement, recognized by all courts, that he not editorialize during the propounding of a question or in connection with an answer.

And yet, again he, in addressing this witness improperly, "There is a straight answer." That personal comment on the evidence by an attorney in any court, including Federal Court, remains improper and inappropriate, the sanction for which is plaintiff's cross examination is now terminated.

Thereafter, Judge Blackburn reminded Respondent his conduct was "the quintessence of contempt of court." In this exchange, Respondent continued to argue with Judge Blackburn and refused to clear the podium when ordered to do so. At this point, the court reporter became concerned that the presence of a United States Marshal might be required in order for Respondent to acknowledge Judge Blackburn's direct order. Further, the court reporter reasonably felt physically threatened by Respondent's behavior. The Hearing Board notes Respondent is a big man, at least six feet tall, with a stocky build and voice that booms, especially when he is angry or agitated as when the Court terminated his cross-examination.

Judge Blackburn Admonishes Respondent for Making Facial Expressions

On the fourth day of trial, after Judge Blackburn sustained the City's objection on an evidentiary matter, the Court again admonished Respondent for making facial expressions in the jury's presence in response to the ruling. Judge Blackburn excused the jury, and admonished Respondent as follows:

Mr. Brennan, frankly I can do without the facial expressions and the communications that are made when this court makes a ruling that is adverse to you.

Also during the fourth day of trial, in the hallway just outside the courtroom, Respondent called one of the City's attorneys a "fucking weasel" after the attorney reminded Respondent that he should not coach his client during a recess. Respondent admits he made this statement. Further, on another occasion out of the jury's presence, Respondent called a second attorney representing the City a "pinche cabron" and "hijo de puta." Again, Respondent admitted using these derogatory and pejorative phrases in addressing Mr. Lujan, one of the attorneys defending the City against Mr. Cadorna's claims.

Court Holds Respondent in Contempt

On the final day of the trial, outside the presence of the jury during a bench conference, Judge Blackburn asked Respondent to make an offer of proof before calling a rebuttal witness. In his offer, Respondent stated he was calling the witness to cross-examine an official at the policy-making level on the subject of age discrimination. Respondent stated that the Court had precluded him from doing so and thereby deprived Mr. Cadorna an opportunity to present crucial evidence on that subject. Respondent went on to tell Judge Blackburn, "If you want to take up any of my conduct in this trial, that's fine. Just so it doesn't affect this trial to the detriment of my client."

Judge Blackburn responded by stating, "I have no personal or professional contempt for you." Respondent then stated, "I have sensed otherwise, your Honor, with all due respect." Judge Blackburn again reminded Respondent that he had been admonished numerous times, but nevertheless continued to repeatedly insist on having the last word, even when the Court attempted to rule and move forward. Judge Blackburn characterized Respondent's conduct in this exchange as an attempt to "bully" the Court. The Hearing Board agrees with Judge Blackburn's characterization.

Again during this exchange, Judge Blackburn admonished Respondent to stop talking while the Court was speaking. And again, Respondent refused to abide by the Court's order stating, "I am not trying to bully you, sir." Judge Blackburn then excused the jury and fined Respondent $500.00 for what the Court described as "contemptuous" behavior. Respondent sarcastically responded, "May I inquire while we are waiting when you want that paid, your Honor?"

In light of the numerous admonitions Judge Blackburn issued to Respondent before this last exchange, the Hearing Board has no doubt Respondent intended to disrupt the proceedings. The Hearing Board finds Respondent's words and actions demonstrate clear and convincing evidence of his disrespect and contempt for the Court's authority. Respondent's repeated failure to abide by Judge Blackburn's authority also proves by clear and convincing evidence that he intended to disrupt the tribunal.

While the Hearing Board finds the written record alone supports our findings on Respondent's intent to disrupt the proceedings, we also note the court reporter's testimony, supported by her contemporaneous notes made during the trial concerning Respondent's conduct, corroborates our findings. Never before in her years of reporting had she ever found it necessary to take notes on an attorney's conduct during a trial. Respondent's words and actions were so physically and verbally threatening that this veteran court reporter felt she might have to summon a United States Marshal to maintain order.

The court reporter testified to Respondent's rude behavior, his facial expressions following Judge Blackburn's rulings, and to the inappropriate comment he made to her during a recess suggesting Judge Blackburn was doing everything he could to help the City win the case. The Hearing Board finds this testimony to be credible because she witnessed and recorded the entire trial making specific notes about Respondent's behavior, including Respondent's conduct outside the presence of the jury.

Respondent's Testimony

Respondent characterized his trial demeanor as simply "bad manners." He claims he never intended to show disrespect toward the Court or disrupt the proceedings. We do not believe this statement. Respondent stated he no longer wishes to be an attorney because "the profession is corrupt." Specifically, Respondent believes the City, the DFD, and Judge Blackburn conspired to deprive his client of his Constitutional rights. While the Hearing Board finds Respondent fervently believed the forgoing to be true, we also find this belief does not excuse his misconduct.

In determining Respondent's credibility or lack thereof as the trier of fact, the Hearing Board considers Respondent's *demeanor and manner* during these disciplinary proceedings. Respondent was bombastic, sarcastic, and contemptuous of the disciplinary process. Respondent was thirty minutes late for the first day of the disciplinary hearing and offered that he had been delayed at a train crossing. During the disciplinary hearing he made highly improper statements, including accusing Judge Blackburn's clerk's father of being a member of the Ku Klux Klan. Later, he asked the same witness, who hailed from the South, "who got the shotgun and who got the pickup when you got your divorce." At one point, he called the Hearing Board a "kangaroo court."

The PDJ twice held Respondent in contempt of court for his insolent and disrespectful behavior during the disciplinary hearing. After witnessing first-hand Respondent's demeanor in these proceedings, the Hearing Board gives no weight to his claim that he meant no disrespect to the judge, opposing counsel, and witnesses. However, we only considered Respondent's conduct in these proceedings for the *limited* purpose of accessing his credibility and not as proof that he violated Colo. RPC 3.5(c) and Colo. RPC 8.4(d) as charged in the People's complaint.

Based upon the foregoing findings and conclusions, the Hearing Board finds by clear and convincing evidence that Respondent violated Colo. RPC, 3.5(c), a lawyer shall not engage in conduct intended to disrupt a tribunal and

Colo. RPC 8.4(d), a lawyer should not engage in conduct prejudicial to the administration of justice.

V. *SANCTIONS*

The American Bar Association *Standards for Imposing Lawyer Sanctions* (1991 & Supp.1992) ("ABA *Standards*") and Colorado Supreme Court case law are the guiding authorities for selecting and imposing sanctions for lawyer misconduct. In imposing a sanction after a finding of lawyer misconduct, the Hearing Board must first consider the duty breached, the mental state of the lawyer, the injury or potential injury caused, and the aggravating and mitigating evidence pursuant to ABA *Standard* 3.0.

ABA Standard 3.0 Considerations—Duty, Mental State, and Injury

We begin with the proposition that members of the legal profession must adhere to the highest ethical standards regardless of the lawyers perceived motive for deviating from these standards. The Hearing Board finds that Respondent violated his duty to the legal system. Respondent specifically violated his duty to the legal system by disrupting the Court and thereby interfering with the legal process. Lawyers are officers of the court with the duty to abide by legal rules of substance and procedure affecting the administration of justice. Respondent failed to comply with this duty.

The Hearing Board next finds Respondent *knowingly* and *intentionally* engaged in the established misconduct. He was aware of the nature or attendant circumstances of his conduct, despite his claims that he was simply acting zealously on behalf of his client and he did not intend to disrupt the tribunal. We reject this argument because our review of the record is to the contrary and Respondent has no credibility on this point. The facts amply demonstrate Respondent's repeated refusal to abide by Judge Blackburn's rulings and we find this conduct demonstrates his knowing and intentional conduct.

Finally, the Hearing Board finds Respondent caused injury and potential injury to the legal system, and the profession. Respondent's intentional disregard and disdain for the Court's authority is inimical to our system of justice. The fact that one of the jurors the People interviewed wondered whether the City had "gotten to the judge" is evidence of injury he has caused.

ABA Standard 3.0 Considerations—Aggravating Factors

Aggravating circumstances are any considerations or factors that may justify an increase in the degree of discipline to be imposed. The Hearing Board considered evidence of the following aggravating circumstances in deciding the appropriate sanction:

Pattern of Misconduct and Multiple Offenses—9.22(c) and (d)

The pattern of misconduct is set forth in our findings above. Suffice it to say Respondent's misconduct pervaded the proceedings. Although Respondent acted respectfully in the early stages of the trial, his conduct became increasingly obstreperous as the trial proceeded. Generally, the Hearing Board finds his conduct in the trial to have been boorish and insolent to a degree that he impeded the proceedings. Respondent amply demonstrated he uses bullying tactics when he does not get his way.

However, we note that Respondent's pattern of misconduct was within a single trial. There was no evidence of a pattern outside the trial. Therefore, we do not find clear and convincing evidence of a pattern of misconduct. Nor do we find clear and convincing evidence of multiple offenses. While the People brought two separate claims under the Colorado Rules of Professional Conduct, the gravamen of Respondent's misconduct was his disrespect for Judge Blackburn and the judicial process. Therefore, we do not find this sufficient to find multiple offenses.

Substantial Experience in the Practice of Law—9.22(i)

Respondent has held his law license for nearly twenty-five years. He should have recognized that his conduct was highly improper based upon his experience in the legal profession. Even a novice lawyer would recognize how improper and disrespectful it is to directly challenge a judge's authority in the manner Respondent challenged Judge Blackburn's authority.

ABA Standard 3.0 Considerations—Mitigating Factors

Mitigating factors are any considerations or factors that may justify a reduction in the degree of discipline to be imposed.

Absence of Prior Discipline 9.32(a)

Respondent has no prior discipline in nearly twenty-five years of practice. The Hearing Boards finds this to be a substantial mitigating factor.

Imposition of Other Penalties 9.32(k)

Judge Blackburn found Respondent in contempt of court and fined him $500.00 for his obstreperous conduct. While this sanction is a penalty Respondent has suffered as a result of his misconduct, the Hearing Board does not grant inordinate weight to it because this monetary sanction does not fully address the ethical issues or conduct we address herein.

Analysis Under ABA Standards and Colorado Case Law

The Hearing Board considers the following standards most appropriate given our finding that Respondent intended to disrupt a tribunal and engaged in conduct that is prejudicial to the administration of justice. ABA *Standard* 6.21 provides:

> Disbarment is generally appropriate when a lawyer knowingly violates a court order or rule with the intent to obtain a benefit for the lawyer or another, and causes serious injury of potentially serious injury to a party, or causes serious or *potentially serious* interference with a legal proceeding (emphasis added).

ABA *Standard* 6.22 provides:

> Suspension is appropriate when a lawyer knowingly violates a court order or rule, and there is injury or potential injury to a client or a party, or potential *interference* with a legal proceeding (emphasis added).

Although the Hearing Board has found that Respondent knowingly and repeatedly violated court orders and did so intending to disrupt the tribunal by insolently challenging its authority, we do not find that disbarment is the appropriate sanction. Instead, the Hearing Board finds that ABA *Standard* 6.22 is the most appropriate standard to apply in this case. We make this finding, in part, because of Judge Blackburn's diligence in reasonably moving the trial forward in spite of Respondent's recalcitrance.

Although there were delays, we cannot find clear and convincing evidence they were serious or potentially serious given Judge Blackburn's ability to move the trial forward and the absence of the need for a mistrial. We also make this finding because the jury was intelligent, conscientious, and sophisticated. Most important, they followed Judge Blackburn's instructions in reaching a verdict. They did so, in part, because Judge Blackburn maintained control of the courtroom. We therefore find the evidence presented shows Respondent's misconduct interfered, rather than substantially interfered, with the trial. Thus, ABA *Standard* 6.22 is most applicable.

It is fundamental to our system of justice that lawyers maintain the respect due the tribunal, witnesses, and fellow lawyers. The gravamen of Respondent's misconduct concerns his insolent behavior and disrespect toward the tribunal. In addition, he engaged in bullying tactics and inappropriate statements to opposing counsel and court staff. Colorado case law dealing with these subjects holds that even an isolated occurrence of such misconduct warrants discipline. *See People v. Dalton*, 840 P.2d 351, 352 (Colo.1992) *citing Losavio v. District Court*, 182 Colo. 180, 512 P.2d 266, 268 (1973).

The Colorado Supreme Court has approved a public censure for a lawyer who posed questions to witnesses concerning evidence the court had ruled inadmissible and commented on the same when the evidence showed the conduct was an aberration from the lawyer's normal conduct. *People v. Janiszewski*, 901 P.2d 476, 477 (Colo.1995). However, as we find above, Respondent acted intentionally in disobeying the Court's orders and such actions were not an aberration in the context of a single trial. Respondent's conduct throughout the eight-day trial grew increasingly belligerent as we noted above.

If a single inappropriate comment had been directed to opposing counsel, witnesses or parties during a highly contested trial, a public censure would generally be appropriate. *People v. Sharpe*, 781 P.2d 659, 660 (Colo.1989) (where a deputy district attorney called a witness a "chili eating bastard").

Nevertheless, a single act of disobedience to a direct order of the court may be sufficiently egregious to warrant a suspension. In *In re Roose*, 69 P.3d 43, 46 (Colo.2003), the Colorado Supreme Court imposed a suspension of a year and a day when the evidence clearly showed a lawyer walked out of court despite the court's admonition she remain and continue representing her client in a scheduled hearing. In *Roose*, the court found the Hearing Board's recommended sanction of disbarment too harsh because the evidence showed respondent acted knowingly, not intentionally. The Supreme Court found that suspension rather than disbarment the most appropriate sanction stating:

> In the absence of a finding of intent to obtain a benefit by disobeying the district court's order or to deceive the court of appeals, the appropriate sanction for both knowingly submitting materially false statements and knowingly violating a court order, as long as those acts caused at least some injury to a party or adverse effect on the legal proceeding, is suspension. *See* ABA *Standards* 6.12 and 6.22; *See also In the Matter of Attorney C*, 47 P.3d 1167, 1173 (Colo.2002).

The Hearing Board finds *Roose* helpful in its analysis. However, Respondent engaged in much more harmful and culpable conduct than *Roose* when he repeatedly disobeyed and undermined Judge Blackburn's authority throughout an eight-day trial. *Roose* walked out of court and that was the extent of her misconduct before the court. Respondent, on the other hand, continued to disrupt the proceedings in what we find to be a pattern of challenging the Court. Although Respondent perceived such action was necessary to deal with a corrupt system of justice, we find that no excuse or mitigation for his misconduct.

"Unless order is maintained in the courtroom and disruption prevented, reason cannot prevail and constitutional rights to liberty, freedom and equality under law cannot be protected. The dignity, decorum and courtesy [that] have traditionally characterized the courts of civilized nations are not empty formalities. They are essential to an atmosphere in which justice can be done." *Code of Trial Conduct* § 17 (American College of Trial Lawyers 1983). *Matter of Vincenti*, 92 N.J. 591, 458 A.2d 1268, 1275 (1983). Like the Respondent in *Vincenti*, Respondent engaged in a pattern of sarcastic and disrespectful behavior toward the Court, witnesses, and opposing counsel.

Based upon this authority, the Hearing Board finds a suspension of a minimum of a year and a day is consistent with Colorado case law and the ABA Standards.

VI. *CONCLUSION*

Trial attorneys must not lose their perspective and engage in misconduct even though such behavior occurs in the heat of a hard fought trial. If they engage in a single act of misconduct, the sanction rarely warrants a lengthy suspension. This is especially so if the lawyer thereafter abides by the court's admonition to stop engaging in the offending conduct. However, Respondent's misconduct and bullying tactics pervaded the trial. At the core of Respondent's misconduct is his flawed but firmly held belief that he was justified in conducting himself as he did. Indeed, Respondent argues that he should receive a commendation for taking on Mr. Cadorna's case and fighting a corrupt system of justice.

There is a point at which zealously representing a client does harm to our judicial system, especially when the lawyer disregards the legitimate orders of the tribunal as Respondent did here. The Hearing Board believes this case demonstrates what can happen when an attorney abandons respect for the tribunal under the guise of zealous representation.

Yet, we find that Respondent's lack of a prior discipline in nearly twenty-five years of practice an indication that rehabilitation may be possible. The Hearing Board therefore concludes that a suspension of one year and one day is the appropriate sanction.

VII. *ORDER*

The Hearing Board therefore ORDERS:

1.   MARK E. BRENNAN, Attorney Registration No. 14012 is hereby SUSPENDED from the practice of law for a period of ONE YEAR AND ONE DAY. The suspension SHALL become effective thirty-one (31) days from the date of this order in the absence of a stay pending appeal pursuant to C.R.C.P. 251.27(h).

2.   Respondent, as a condition precedent to any petition for reinstatement pursuant to C.R.C.P. 251.29(c), SHALL submit to an Independent Medical Examination ("IME") by a qualified doctor agreeable to the People. Respondent, not the People, shall be responsible for the cost of the IME. Once a qualified expert is chosen, it is Respondent's duty to advise the PDJ so that an appropriate order may be drafted and presented to the doctor as to what issues to address in a report to the PDJ. The doctor shall have access to all records in the People's possession, as well as this opinion, before meeting with Respondent for the scheduled IME.

3.   Respondent SHALL pay the costs of these proceedings. The People shall submit a "Statement of Costs" within fifteen (15) days from the date of this order. Respondent shall have ten (10) days thereafter to submit a response.

SOLUTIONS: THE LAWYER SHOULD HAVE, WOULD HAVE, COULD HAVE. . .

It is difficult to deal with a person who acts in an apparently dysfunctional manner. Follow trial protocol and do not be verbally abusive to any person working in the tribunal. A few thoughts are given in the following BTC.

X-Ray Questions

Lawyers who act in a manner inconsistent with profession pose a challenge for those whose actions is consistent. The following article offers some counsel on dealing with this ethical dilemma. Always remember that you have 0% control of how others act but 100% control of your response to them.

BEYOND THE CITE

By: Michael P. Maslanka, *Dealing with Dysfunctional Counsel*, Texas Lawyer, January 7, 2008.

General counsel manage lawyers, either in-house or out. Those lawyers must deal with dysfunctional opposing counsel, who often profit from their nuttiness and are just as often unrepentant about it. It takes a toll, making the GCs' lawyers less efficient and more miserable. What's to be done?

GCs need to use their positions as bully pulpits to urge judges to be judges. They get paid to make decisions. So, decide. It is frustrating to go to court for relief and have a busy judge say, "You and Mr. Dysfunction go into my conference room, and don't come back until you work it out." (A note to lawyers: Don't run to the court every time your hair gets mussed up in litigation. Only go when it is really important.) When judges judge, they can at least start to corral the dysfunctional among us.

But, no matter what a GC urges, judges cannot fundamentally change a dysfunctional lawyer. No reprimand will change his conduct. No amount of ethics training will bring her wisdom. No amount of yelling will mend what is broken inside him.

Instead, as my mom used to say, "Talk to them in a language they can understand."

Look at U.S. District Judge Robert Blackburn, a 19-year veteran of the federal bench in Denver. He presided over an age discrimination case, Cadorna v. City and County of Denver, in which the plaintiff's lawyer insulted a witness on the stand, ignored objections and rolled his eyes upon receiving an adverse ruling from the judge. There was more, but that's the gist of it. A big verdict was returned. What was the judge to do? In September 2007 he tossed out the verdict and granted the city's motion for a new trial, lamenting in his order that the plaintiff's lawyer perversely made it seem as if it were the judge trying to stop the truth from getting to the jury. Listen to his frustration in his order granting a new trial: "Short of . . . incarcerating counsel for contempt, I exhausted [all] traditional means" and "I have seen nothing comparable . . . [as the] disrespectful cockalorum, grandstanding, bombast, bullying, and hyperbole [as exhibited] by plaintiff's counsel." In keeping with mom's advice, he decided that the conduct deprived the employer of a fair trial and gave the employer a new one.

Be creative. Let's say a lawyer engages in unprofessional conduct. The employer loses the trial. The dysfunctional lawyer seeks all of her attorney's fees, which can be huge. Argue that fees are awarded, at least in part, on a lawyer's "professional competence." Conduct unbecoming a member of the bar is a far cry from competence. Or, ask for a reduction of fees or, as some cases permit, no attorney's fees whatsoever.

FLOAT AND STING

Is there anything a GC can do, aside from undertaking legally based efforts? Yes, but know this: The dysfunctional enjoy causing an uproar. They relish generating anxiety and embrace controversy. So GCs, in coaching their lawyers, need to look to what at first looks like an offbeat pairing Muhammad Ali and Buddha.

First, Ali. Recall the rumble in the jungle where a fearsome looking George Foreman was fighting Ali, who was on the comeback trail. Ali did the rope-a-dope, letting Foreman punch himself out. Same in the law: Sooner or later the sheer effort of being difficult exhausts Mr. Dysfunctional. The trick is not to respond, which just feeds the dysfunction.

Now, Buddha. A man, upon hearing of Buddha's equanimity, set out to anger him. So, he verbally abused him every day, in every way. Nothing worked, and the man exclaimed to Buddha, "How can you be so peaceful when I've been so offensive?" Buddha replied, "You've offered me the gift of anger and if someone offers you a gift you do not accept, it still belongs to the giver." Buddha then smiled and walked off.

General counsel are affected by the dysfunctional lawyer, even if by only one degree of separation. While dysfunction can be managed, it can't be cured. That's a hard truth.

But, here's a saving grace. GCs, by encouraging their lawyers to acknowledge professionalism by other lawyers, inoculate the system from dysfunction's spread. Focus your energy on what you can change, not what you can't.

Cases and Materials

X-Ray Questions (*American Eagle Airlines*)

This case involved an allegation that the plaintiff was the victim of race discrimination. He prevailed in a jury trial. His lawyers sought recovery of their fees per the civil rights statutes. But because if their conduct at trial, the judge reduced them substantially. As you can see from the opinion, he did do with surgical precision. What specific conduct by the lawyers did the judge take into account in making the reduction? Do you think the reduction influenced the lawyers in their future conduct? Build the defense lawyers have done anything else during the trial to stop the conduct? Did the conduct of the plaintiff's lawyers move their case forward s d help them prevail? Why or why not?

Lee v. American Eagle Airlines, Inc.

United States District Court, S.D. Florida, Miami Division, 2000.
93 F.Supp.2d 1322.

ORDER ON ATTORNEY'S FEES AND COSTS

MIDDLEBROOKS, DISTRICT JUDGE.

This Cause came before the Court upon Plaintiff's Amended Verified Motion for Attorney's Fees and Costs, filed November 4, 1999 (DE# 310). The Court has reviewed the pertinent portions of the file and is otherwise fully informed in the premises.

I.   Introduction

"Let's kick some ass," Marvin Kurzban said loudly to his client, Anthony Lee, and his co-counsel, Ira Kurzban. I had taken the bench, and Court was in session. Opposing counsel and their client representatives were seated across the aisle. The jury was waiting to be called into the courtroom. Mr. Kurzban's comment was suited more to a locker room than a courtroom of the United States, and the conduct of Plaintiff's counsel that followed disrupted the adversary system and interfered with the resolution of a civil dispute.

The trial of this case lasted approximately fourteen days. The jury found that American Eagle Airlines had subjected Mr. Lee to a racially hostile work environment in violation of Title VII of the Civil Rights Act of 1964, 42 U.S.C. § 2000e, *et seq.*, and 42 U.S.C. § 1981. As compensation, the jury awarded Mr. Lee $300,000. In addition, the jury awarded Mr. Lee $650,000 in punitive damages. The jury denied Mr. Lee's other claim, also premised on Title VII and § 1981, finding that Mr. Lee had not been terminated because of his race. This motion seeking attorney's fees and costs pursuant to 42 U.S.C. § 1988 followed.

As the prevailing party in a Title VII action, the Plaintiff now seeks $1,611,910.50 in attorney's fees. This request presents the question of whether unprofessional and disruptive conduct of counsel which prolongs the proceedings and creates animosity which interferes with the resolution of a cause can be considered in determining an award of attorney's fees.

In their post-trial motions, counsel for the parties filed opposing affidavits concerning additional misconduct that was not directly observed by the Court. Since these affidavits presented vastly different versions of events, an evidentiary hearing was held; counsel and other witnesses testified.

These issues have been distasteful and time consuming. There is a great temptation to simply move on and ignore the issue. It is unpleasant to hear lawyers accusing each other of lies and misrepresentations. Unprofessionalism on the part of lawyers is a distraction and takes time away from other pending cases; it also embroils the Court in charges and counter charges. However, the functioning of our adversary system depends upon being able to rely upon what a lawyer says. So, confronted by affidavits of counsel that were directly contradictory, I decided to hear testimony and make credibility findings. These findings are based upon direct observations by the Court, the transcript of the trial, and the evidentiary hearing.

In addition, we contacted the Florida Bar to determine whether counsel had been the subject of complaints regarding unprofessional conduct. The Florida Bar forwarded a record of a previous complaint by a state court judge concerning the conduct of Marvin Kurzban. In response to that complaint, and immediately before the trial in this cause, the Florida Bar had directed Mr. Kurzban to attend an ethics class and pay a fine.

II.   Findings of Fact Pertaining to Misconduct by Counsel

Discovery in this case was rancorous from the beginning. As is often the case, counsel for both sides contributed to the lack of civility. The tone of depositions was harsh, witnesses were treated with discourtesy, and discovery disputes were abundant. The transcripts of the depositions in this case are weighted down with bitter exchanges between the lawyers. (*See, e.g.,* Dep. of Raphael Perez, at 120–121, 161–164; Dep. of German Agosto at 22–28.)

Testimony at the evidentiary hearing reflected that this uncivil conduct also continued during conversations between counsel. The testimony of a young lawyer formerly with the Defendant's counsel's law firm was particularly poignant. This lawyer testified that during telephone conversations with Ira Kurzban, she was hung up on, told that she had only been assigned to work on the case because she was African-American, and wrongly accused of misrepresentations. She testified that her experience with opposing counsel in this case was a factor in her decision to leave her litigation practice.

This testimony was not only powerful and credible, but it also reflects the corrosive impact this type of unprofessional behavior can have upon the bar itself. A litigation practice is stressful and often exhausting. Unprofessional litigation tactics affect everyone exposed to such behavior and the ripple effect of incivility is spread throughout the bar.

The trial began. Testimony at the evidentiary hearing reveals that Mr. Kurzban's "Let's kick some ass" comment was not an aberration. A client representative of the Defendant, a lawyer for American Airlines, testified that she and others were subjected to a barrage of comments out of the hearing of the Court and jury which she likened to trash talk at a sporting event. Local counsel for the Defendant was called a "Second Rate Loser" by Marvin Kurzban. She testified that each day as court began, Marvin Kurzban would say, "Let the pounding begin." In front of defense counsel's client, Mr. Kurzban would ask, "How are you going to feel when I take all of your client's money?" When walking out of the courtroom, Marvin Kurzban would exclaim, "Yuppies out of the way."

Other than Mr. Kurzban's opening comment, I was unaware of this conduct towards opposing counsel and their client's representatives, although counsel for the Defendants alluded to it during the trial. (Tr. 477). However, I observed continuing misconduct during the trial itself.

Early in the trial, an episode occurred when defense counsel brought to the Court's attention that after an instruction to a witness not to discuss his testimony during a break in his testimony for lunch, Ira and Marvin Kurzban had approached the witness and had a discussion—with an open deposition transcript in hand. Marvin Kurzban responded, "That's a lie." The Kurzbans then explained that they had the transcript open because they were looking at it, but that they were not talking with the witness about it. Their explanation was that they were talking about where they were going for lunch. I accepted the explanation, but with the observation that it was an exercise of poor judgment. (Tr. 324–325).

Shortly afterward, Marvin Kurzban objected to a question, and I overruled his objection. He continued to argue his point, then he visibly expressed his dismay with the ruling. I asked counsel to approach for a sidebar conference, wherein I advised him that for the third time he had made visible displays of disagreement with rulings by nodding his head or looking upward at the ceiling. I told him to stop that conduct and to cease making speaking objections. (Tr. 351–352).

Subsequently, I warned both counsel again; once before the jury (Tr. 571–572), and again at the close of the mornings testimony. (Tr. 578–583). Ira Kurzban responded that he was way beyond acrimony with opposing counsel.

After this warning, defense counsel followed the Court's admonition and refused to respond to provocations from opposing counsel. Later than day, Marvin Kurzban interrupted an appropriate cross-examination and requested a sidebar to accuse counsel of intentionally delaying the examination so that he could not reach a witness. (Tr. 678).

Despite repeated warnings, Plaintiff's counsel continued to address comments to opposing counsel rather than to the Court (Tr. 263; 292; 487; 871) and interject inappropriate comments before the jury. (Tr. 913; 1073; 1693–1694; 1729; 1753–54; 2002; 2240).

The belligerence of Plaintiff's counsel, particularly Marvin Kurzban, spread like a contagion through the courtroom. On September 22, 1999, I returned to the bench after a luncheon break. Marvin Kurzban wanted to raise a matter prior to the jury's return.

Mr. Kurzban stated:

I am concerned about the record, Your Honor. I went over to the . . . Mr. Reporter there, when we took the first break, and asked him about the ability to get a page typed. And instead I ended up having names called at me and a confrontation. I only bring it to the Court's attention because I am concerned about the record being clear. I feel this Court Reporter for whatever reason . . . I don't know the gentlemen, never met him before—is either unstable based on his reaction and not competent to be reporting or has some bias.

(Tr. 1161).

At the next recess, I asked the Court Reporter what had happened. He indicated that at the break, which was a brief break for him inasmuch as we had a calendar call scheduled during that luncheon break, Marvin Kurzban asked him for a portion of transcript. The reporter responded that he could not produce those pages over the break (because he had to report the calendar call). Marvin Kurzban responded, "What are you here for, just to look pretty?" The Court Reporter responded with an epithet, at which point Marvin Kurzban remarked, "We're not talking about your family." Then Mr. Kurzban said, "I guess money talks," suggesting that since the Defendant was ordering daily copy, the reporter was biased in their favor. At that point, the Court Security Officer intervened.

I required the Court Reporter to apologize for his behavior. Because of the accusation of bias, I arranged for other Court Reporters to cover the remainder of the trial.

I learned that accusations of bias followed any disagreement with positions espoused by Plaintiff's counsel: "There's no question that he's entitled to it, so it's no—if I understand what Your Honor's saying, you don't want it to go in front of the jury for whatever reason." (Tr. 313). "Your Honor, I know you're angry at me, but I hope you're not taking it out on my client." (Tr. 1337). "In fact, I think that the Court has exhibited extreme bias in this case and your rulings on objections." (Tr.1984). "Well, Your Honor, I respectfully disagree with you, that's for a court of appeals ultimately to decide, but to put a motive on it I think it exhibits a substantial amount of bias on behalf of Your Honor." (Tr.1985). "And I concur with what my brother has said. There's been clear animous by this Court to this side." (Tr.1989). "I've practiced 26 years and I've tried over 50 cases, and I've won multimillion dollar verdicts on more than a dozen cases. I don't need for this Court to allow a witness to have his wife introduced. I can't think of any reason or purpose, other than prejudice, that this Court would allow such an act to occur." (Tr. 2104).

Disturbing behavior by both Marvin Kurzban and Ira Kurzban occurred repeatedly during the trial. When confronted about their conduct, they would deny that which I had just observed and then lash out in a personal attack. For instance, after I overruled an objection made by Ira Kurzban, Marvin Kurzban laughed. (Tr. 2149). Other examples of their conduct following rulings include Marvin Kurzban tossing a pen; Ira Kurzban exclaiming, "This is outrageous"; the rolling of eyes; exasperated looks at the ceiling; and flailing of arms. I warned counsel about this behavior. (Tr. 1829).

After the episode of Marvin Kurzban laughing at my ruling, I asked counsel to approach the bench. Marvin Kurzban responded: "I didn't laugh. What I started doing was writing a note, saying to my brother . . . I didn't realize I was saying it out loud—we're not trying his case. That's what the objection was, because he's telling about his problems." Ira Kurzban then interjected: "I'd like to add, Your Honor, there's a continuing pattern of conduct we believe shows enormous bias and has turned this trial into a circus-like atmosphere." (Tr. 2149).

Ira Kurzban then listed a litany of complaints about rulings which he stated should result in a mistrial. (When offered a mistrial, the Plaintiff declined.) (Tr. 2141–2152). Defense counsel and the Court Security officer also heard a laugh. (Tr. 2153, 2210).

Shortly thereafter, during a discussion between the Court, Marvin Kurzban, and defense counsel about the admissibility of an exhibit a witness had allegedly drawn during a videotaped deposition but which was not on the Plaintiff's exhibit list, Ira Kurzban walked to the video machine and begin playing the videotape of the deposition in front of the jury. I directed that the machine be turned off and we took a fifteen minute break. (Tr. 2202).

After the break, defense counsel raised the issue and requested some sanction. I asked Ira Kurzban for an explanation. He responded:

> Mr. Kurzban: Yes, Your Honor. First, Mr. Connor asked me not to tamper with the tape now, because you were going to come out and rule. I assume he didn't have any ex parte communication with you. I'm a little perturbed about the fact that somehow he knew you were coming out to make a ruling, which I was totally unaware.

> The Court: I think he knew that I was coming back after a 15 minute break. There has been absolutely no contact between me and Mr. Connor or any other lawyer in this case between the time I left the bench 15 minutes ago and when I returned now. Now, is there some reason why you would make that accusation?

> Ira Kurzban: Yes, Your Honor.

> The Court: All right. What was it?

> Ira Kurzban: Mr. Connor said the Judge is going to come out here, he's going to impose some sanction. That's what Mr. Connor said, Your Honor, you are not here.

> I'm simply saying that's what Mr. Connor did. I'm not accusing you of anything. We can have the marshal testify that I should not touch the tape because you were going to impose sanctions.

> The Deputy: No, no.

> The Court: The marshal is nodding no. Mr. Marshal?

> The Deputy: No mention of sanctions was ever made.

(Tr. 2205).

Mr. Kurzban then stated that he had put the tape into the machine so that it would be ready if needed and that the tape began playing accidentally. I accepted his explanation but stated:

> [I]f I can't rely on lawyers being able to respect each other and be respected and accept what other people say in the courtroom, this

system can't work. It's as important to me as whether or not you have a law degree. . . . I'm beginning to really have a problem with what you are telling me is happening, based on what I'm seeing and what others in the courtroom are seeing. So you all really need to think about that.

(Tr. 2210).

During a cross-examination concerning how much time the witness spent on various shifts, Marvin Kurzban held a file towards the witness and asked:

Marvin Kurzban: I have your personnel file (indicating). How many times did you have to work between 1992 and 1994, sir? Do you think it was more than a handful of times?

(Tr. 1868–1869).

After an objection, and out of the presence of the jury, I asked Mr. Kurzban for the witness's personnel file. (Tr. 1876). He responded:

Marvin Kuzban: Actually, we do have Mr. Blades's personnel file, when it was produced among all the other personnel files in Miami of the people. I don't know if that box is here or I left it in the office. I think the personnel files that we were given by counsel is in the office.

The Court: So it wasn't in the folder that you picked up and carried to the stand?

Marvin Kurzban: No it wasn't, Your Honor.

The Court: You said, "Mr. Blades, we have your personnel file here!"

* * * * * *

The Court: You believe it is permissible to pick up a file from your desk, carry it to the witness stand and tell the witness "Mr. Blades, we have your personnel file," and then begin questioning him? You believe that's appropriate court examination?

Marvin Kurzban: I do, on hostile witnesses; on cross-examination, I believe that I'm entitled to have that witness believe I'm going to question him on something whether or not I have that in my hand or not. Yes, I do.

* * * * * *

The Court: I believe, frankly, that it is inappropriate to make a deliberate misrepresentation to a witness or to ask, implying in your questioning something that is not true.

Marvin Kurzban: Neither was I implying something that wasn't true, nor was I making a misrepresentation. The question was about how many times he worked, Your Honor. The question wasn't: In your personnel file it says something. I didn't make any such misrepresentation.

(Tr 1877–1878).

Mr. Kurzban insisted that he had the personnel file back at his office. He was asked to produce it and he responded that he would the following day. The file was never produced.

At the end of the trial, defense counsel Connor approached Ira Kurzban and offered his hand in congratulations. Mr. Kurzban refused to shake his hand. The trial ended much like it had begun.

At the evidentiary hearing, Plaintiff's counsel were unrepentant, attacking opposing counsel and accepting no responsibility for their own actions. They argued that the perceived misconduct was only a matter of style and the exercise of first amendment rights. In keeping with that "style," Marvin Kurzban ended the hearing with the proclamation that he had called his opponent a loser, but not a second-rate loser because, "I don't rate losers." Mr. Kurzban's testimony reflects that he has no clue about what it means to be a lawyer.

III. Analysis

Courts presiding over civil rights actions may, in their discretion, award the prevailing party a "reasonable attorney's fee (including expert fees)" as part of its costs. *See* 42 U.S.C. § 1988; 42 U.S.C. § 2000e–5(k). Although the presiding court has discretion, a prevailing plaintiff is to be awarded attorney's fees "in all but special circumstances." *Christiansburg Garment Co. v. EEOC,* 434 U.S. 412, 417, 98 S.Ct. 694, 54 L.Ed.2d 648 (1978); *see also New York Gaslight Club, Inc. v. Carey,* 447 U.S. 54, 63, 100 S.Ct. 2024, 64 L.Ed.2d 723 (1980); *Dowdell v. City of Apopka, Florida,* 698 F.2d 1181, 1190–91 (11th Cir.1983). This presumption in favor of awarding attorney's fees is a reflection of Congress' clear intent to "cast the Title VII plaintiff in the role of 'a private attorney general,' vindicating a policy of the highest priority." *Christiansburg Garment,* 434 U.S. at 417, 98 S.Ct. 694. By awarding prevailing plaintiffs their attorney's fees, the section "make[s] it easier for a plaintiff of limited means to bring a meritorious suit." *Id.* at 420, 98 S.Ct. 694 (quoting 110 Cong.Rec. 12724 (1964) (remarks of Sen. Humphrey)).

Courts determining attorney's fee awards begin by determining the "lodestar": the product of the number of hours reasonably expended on the litigation and a reasonable hourly rate for the attorney's services. *See Hensley v. Eckerhart,* 461 U.S. 424, 433, 103 S.Ct. 1933, 76 L.Ed.2d 40 (1983); *American Civil Liberties Union of Georgia v. Barnes,* 168 F.3d 423, 427 (11th Cir.1999) *Loranger v. Stierheim,* 10 F.3d 776, 781 (11th Cir.1994). This lodestar may then be adjusted for the results obtained. *See Eckerhart,* 461 U.S. at 435–3, 103 S.Ct. 19337; *Barnes,* 168 F.3d at 427; *Loranger,* 10 F.3d at 781; *Norman v. Hous. Auth.* 836 F.2d 1292, 1302 (11th Cir.1988).

1.   The reasonable hourly rate

"A reasonable hourly rate is the prevailing market rate in the relevant legal community for similar services by lawyers of reasonably comparable skills, experience, and reputation." *Loranger,* 10 F.3d at 781 (quoting *Norman,* 836 F.2d at 1299) (citing *Blum v. Stenson,* 465 U.S. 886, 895–96 n. 11, 104 S.Ct. 1541 (1984)). The party seeking attorney's fees, in this case Mr. Lee, bears the burden of producing "satisfactory evidence that the requested rate is in line with prevailing market rates." *Id.* To be satisfactory, evidence must consist of "more than the affidavit of the attorney performing the work." *Id.*

Prior to adoption of the lodestar formula, the so-called *"Johnson* factors" governed fee awards. *See Johnson v. Georgia Highway Express, Inc.,* 488 F.2d 714, 717–19 (5th Cir.1974). Although the lodestar formula has since displaced the *"Johnson* factors," the Eleventh Circuit has permitted district courts to consider the factors in establishing a reasonable hourly rate. *See Loranger,* 10 F.3d at 781 n. 6. Among those factors is the experience, reputation, and ability of the attorneys and the skill requisite to perform the legal service properly. *See Johnson,* 488 F.2d at 717–19. As explained more fully in the findings of misconduct, contained in Section II, *supra,* the conduct of Ira Kurzban and Marvin Kurzban both during and prior to trial was very troubling. In my estimation, the manner in which a lawyer interacts with opposing counsel and conducts himself before the Court is as indicative of the lawyer's ability and skill as is mastery of the rules of evidence. Upon review of the trial transcripts and the evidence presented during the evidentiary hearing on attorney conduct and based on observations at trial, I find that the conduct of Ira Kurzban and Marvin Kurzban in the litigation of this case fell far below acceptable standards, especially in light of the $300 hourly rate the attorneys claim. Accordingly, I find "special circumstances" justifying a departure from counsels' requested rates: Ira Kurzban shall be awarded $150 per hour for his pretrial work and $0 for his trial work; Marvin Kurzban's rate for this action is $0. *Cf. Chaney v. New Orleans Pub. Facility Management, Inc.*, 1998 WL 87617 (E.D.La. Feb.20, 1998) (denying prevailing party attorneys' fees in Title VII action, finding performance of plaintiff's attorneys did not merit attorneys' fees).

For further support of the above rate reductions, we rely upon our "inherent power" to sanction attorney misconduct. "It is well-established that '[c]ertain implied powers must necessarily result to our Courts of justice from the nature of their institution,' powers 'which cannot be dispensed with in a Court, because they are necessary to the exercise of all others.' For this reason, 'Courts of justice are universally acknowledged to be vested, by their very creation, with power to impose silence, respect, and decorum, in their presence, and submission to their lawful mandates.' These powers are 'governed not by rule or statute but by the control necessarily vested in courts to manage their own affairs so as to achieve the orderly and expeditious disposition of cases.' " *Chambers v. NASCO, Inc.*, 501 U.S. 32, 43, 111 S.Ct. 2123, 115 L.Ed.2d 27 (1991) (internal citations omitted).

Among these powers is the contempt sanction, "which a judge must have and exercise in protecting the due and orderly administration of justice and in maintaining the authority and dignity of the court. . . ." *Id.* (quoting *Cooke v. United States*, 267 U.S. 517, 539, 45 S.Ct. 390, 69 L.Ed. 767 (1925)). "The inherent power of a court to manage its affairs necessarily includes the authority to impose reasonable and appropriate sanctions upon errant lawyers practicing before it," *Kleiner v. First Nat'l Bank of Atlanta*, 751 F.2d 1193, 1209 (11th Cir.1985) (quoting *Flaksa v. Little River Marine Constr. Co.*, 389 F.2d 885, 888 (5th Cir.1968)).

A finding that counsels' conduct "constituted or was tantamount to bad faith" must precede any sanction levied pursuant to a court's inherent powers. *See Roadway Express*, 447 U.S. at 767, 100 S.Ct. 2455; *DLC Management Corp. v. Town of Hyde Park*, 163 F.3d 124, 136 (2d Cir.1998). The Court of Appeals for the Second Circuit requires that bad faith be shown by (1) "clear evidence" or (2) "harassment or delay or . . . other improper purposes." *DLC Management* (quoting *United States v. International Brotherhood of Teamsters*, 948 F.2d 1338, 1345 (2d Cir.1991)). Where imposed for the purpose of deterring misconduct rather than remedying some prejudice, as here, the District of Columbia Circuit has held that sanctions must be supported by "clear and convincing evidence" of "flagrant or egregious misconduct." *Bonds v. District of Columbia*, 93 F.3d 801, 809

(D.C.Cir.1996); *Shepherd v. American Broad. Cos.*, 62 F.3d 1469, 1478 (D.C.Cir.1995). Before imposing a severe sanction based on principles of deterrence, a district court must consider whether a lesser sanction is more proportionate to the misconduct. *See id.*

In this case, we are imposing a lesser sanction. We did not dismiss this case, but rather permitted it to go the jury. Moreover, although counsel were warned during the trial that further disruptive conduct would be a basis for criminal contempt, that sanction was not employed. We have also elected not to deny Plaintiff's fee request altogether, though we are reducing it significantly. *Cf. Kleiner*, 751 F.2d at 1209 ("Since misconduct by a party courts the risk of outright dismissal, lesser sanctions undoubtedly attend the court's inherent power to discipline intentional attorney misconduct. . . ."). Additionally, our sanction is supported by "clear and convincing" evidence of "flagrant or egregious" misconduct demonstrating counsels' "bad faith." In assessing attorney misconduct, the Court had the benefit of an exhaustive evidentiary hearing concerning attorney misconduct and trial transcripts replete with examples of unprofessional behavior. Most significantly, much of the misconduct in this matter occurred before the Court. Plaintiff's counsels' continued misbehavior in the face of repeated verbal reprimands and warnings that the Court intended to revisit counsels' misconduct at a later date demonstrated counsels' "bad faith."

There is precedent for denying a party attorney's fees to which it was otherwise statutorily entitled as a sanction for attorney misconduct. In *Litton Sys., Inc. v. American Tel. and Tel. Co.*, 700 F.2d 785 (2d Cir.1983), the Second Circuit Court of Appeals affirmed the district court's denial of attorney's fees to a prevailing plaintiff in an antitrust suit. The plaintiff was entitled to its costs and fees under, among other provisions, the Clayton Act, 15 U.S.C. § 15. *See Litton*, 700 F.2d at 826–27. Though the *Litton* court based its decision on its power to sanction disobedience of court orders under Federal Rule of Civil Procedure 37(b), it noted that "[g]iven the court's express findings of bad faith, it could also have imposed sanctions on [the plaintiff] as an exercise of its inherent powers." *Id.* at 827.

In addition, the Court reduces the rates sought by Plaintiff for associate work. Magistrate Judge Barry L. Garber recently found, by order dated May 5, 1999, that $125 was a reasonable hourly rate for associates in *Faragher v. City of Boca Raton*. In *Gupta v. Florida Bd. of Regents*, Magistrate Judge Stephen T. Brown, in a recommendation dated August 17, 1999, noted that the parties agreed to an hourly rate of $125 for associates. Accordingly, the Court finds that $125 is the prevailing hourly rate in the Southern District for associate work. Thus, the work of Brian Torres, Raquel Libman, Jed Kurzban, and Florence Zolin shall be billed at a rate of $125 per hour. Peter Hoffer, who has eight years of civil rights litigation experience, shall be billed at $175.

2. The number of hours reasonably expended

Defendant argues that not all of the 3,269.54 hours claimed by Plaintiff were "reasonably expended." Specifically, Defendant contends that Plaintiff claims hours from another case, which are not compensable in this matter, and that Plaintiff did not exercise proper billing judgment.

i. Hours spent on another case

Defendant points out that although Plaintiff initiated the action before this Court on March 21, 1997, Plaintiff has submitted time records with dates as early as August 1994. Dft's Resp. at 5. Defendant surmises that many of these entries are for work done on other cases and thus are not compensable. *Id.; See* Tab 2 attached to Steinberg aff. for list of these entries. Plaintiff replies that the Kurzban firm had begun representing Mr. Lee in 1994, before the firm's formal retention by Mr. Lee and commencement of this action, and that the work underlying these entries was the basis for Plaintiff's hostile environment claim. Pltf's Reply at 8; Supp. aff. of Ira Kurzban at ¶ 2. Initially, Ira Kurzban represents that he advised Mr. Lee and other black mechanics at American Eagle who complained of racism at American Eagle, then Flagship Airlines. Supp. aff. of Ira Kurzban at ¶ 2. Thereafter, Mr. Kurzban assisted Plaintiff in his negotiations with American Eagle and in his claims before the Equal Employment Opportunity Commission (EEOC). *Id.*

Kurzban, Kurzban et al. may collect fees for legal services it provided Mr. Lee prior to commencement of this action or its formal retention by Mr. Lee. *See New York Gaslight Club, Inc. v. Carey*, 447 U.S. 54, 100 S.Ct. 2024, 64 L.Ed.2d 723 (1980) (awarding fees for work done by prevailing Title VII plaintiff in state administrative and judicial proceedings); *see also Dowdell v. City of Apopka, Florida*, 698 F.2d 1181, 1188 (11th Cir.1983) (awarding fees for time spent prior to formal commencement of the lawyer-client relationship). Defendant does not seem to contest this, but rather asks the Court to strike those hours it claims were clearly not spent on matters related to this case. Dft's Resp. at 6 n. 3.

We begin by striking those entries, dated prior to the commencement of this action, that appear to relate to motions practice and other matters in a pending lawsuit or which do not seem sufficiently related to this action. These entries add up to 137.15 hours. *See* Appendix A attached to this Order. In addition, the Court reduces by 50% the remaining hours claimed between

August 10, 1994 and January 2, 1997. *See Loranger,* 10 F.3d at 783 (permitting across-the-board percentage cuts in the number of hours claimed where a fee application is voluminous). We find Plaintiff's documentation to be inadequate for purposes of demonstrating that these hours were reasonably expended in the litigation of this matter. *See Hensley,* 461 U.S. at 433, 103 S.Ct. 1933. While the information gathered at this stage was likely helpful in the eventual litigation of Mr. Lee's claims, the information was being gathered for other purposes. Accordingly, the Court is not convinced that all the time claimed, or even most of it, was reasonably expended in the pursuit of Mr. Lee's claims.

ii   Billing judgment

Fee applicants must exercise "billing judgment." *Barnes,* 168 F.3d at 428 (quoting *Hensley,* 461 U.S. at 434, 103 S.Ct. 1933). That means that they must exclude from their fee applications "excessive, redundant, or otherwise unnecessary [hours]," which are hours "that would be reasonable to bill to a client and therefore to one's adversary irrespective of the skill, reputation or experience of counsel." *Id.* (internal citations omitted). Defendant maintains that further reductions are warranted based on Plaintiff's counsels' time and record keeping practices. Vague entries, according to Defendant, preclude the Court from determining that hours were reasonably expended, and cannot be cured by Plaintiff's counsel's *post hoc,* hand-written notes. Defendant also contests counsels' repetitious charges, claims for hours spent by attorneys "getting up to speed," and excessive time spent on certain activities.

While wary of counsels' after-the-fact, clarifying notes, the Court does not ignore the added detail and takes counsel at their word that the additions are supported by reference to red books, pertinent files, and their own memories. Pltf's Reply at 15. The Court is more concerned about the excessive number of hours billed in this case in light of its nature. This case involved racial harassment endured by a single plaintiff at a single site of employment. Although this matter was hotly contested, due in large part to overzealousness on both sides, the $1,611,910.50 in fees sought by Plaintiff's counsel based on 3,269.54 hours is clearly excessive. This view is supported by a review of recent awards in employment discrimination cases in the Southern District, which the Court may consider under *Johnson. See* note 3 *supra.* This case was not so much more lengthy or complex than these cases to justify such a grossly disproportionate award. Indeed, in *Commella v. City of Hollywood,* Case No. 94-6468-CIV-HURLEY, Judge Hurley, following a eight-day trial, awarded $191,524.75 in attorneys' fees. The award followed a jury verdict in favor of the plaintiff on her sexually hostile work environment and retaliation claims.

To account for the excessive number of hours claimed in this case, we reduce Plaintiff's counsels' hours by 40% across-the-board. *See Loranger*, 10 F.3d at 783 (permitting across-the-board percentage cuts in the number of hours claimed where a fee application is voluminous). In addition, the Court reduces by one-third Ira Kurzban's non-contemporaneous October 8, 1998 entry, allotting 30 hours to the reading of "all new 11th Circuit cases on employment discrimination related to case" over the past six months.

3.   The lodestar figure

    i.   Reasonable hours

For the period August 10, 1994 to January 2, 1997, after deleting hours unrelated to this litigation, the Court recognizes 106.4 hours. We then reduce that figure by 50%, as explained above, for Plaintiff's failure to establish that those hours were spent on matters sufficiently related to this litigation, leaving 53.2 hours. All but one of these hours was billed to Brian Torres or Raquel Libman; the other hour was billed to Ira Kurzban. For the period January 2, 1997 to September 14, 1999, the date the trial began, we recognize the following hours: 1,879.85 hours for Ira Kurzban; 682.24 hours for Raquel Libman; 669.2 hours for Peter Hoffer; 28.6 hours for Jed Kurzban; and 12 hours for Florence Zolin. Finally, for the trial period, we credit 81.7 hours to Jed Kurzban.

Next the Court cuts counsels' hours by 40% across-the-board for the period January 2, 1997 through trial, having found, upon review of counsels' billing records and other employment discrimination cases in the District, counsels' claimed hours to be excessive:

- Ira Kurzban: 1,879.85 x .6 = 1,127.91 hours
- Raquel Libman: 682.24 x .6 = 409.34 hours
- Peter Hoffer: 669.2 x .6 = 401.52 hours
- Jed Kurzban: (28.6 + 81.7) x .6 = 66.18 hours
- Florence Zolin: 12 x .6 = 7.2 hours

ii   Multiplied by the reasonable hourly rates

Associates:	534.92 x $125 = $66,865
Peter Hoffer:	401.52 x $175 = $70,266
Ira Kurzban:	1,128.91 x $150 = $169,336.50
Final lodestar:	**$306,467.50**

4. The results obtained

As noted above, the lodestar may then be adjusted for the results obtained. *See Hensley,* 461 U.S. at 435–37, 103 S.Ct. 1933; *Barnes,* 168 F.3d at 427; *Loranger,* 10 F.3d at 781; *Norman v. Hous. Auth.* 836 F.2d 1292, 1302 (11th Cir.1988). This factor is particularly important where, as here, Plaintiff is deemed "prevailing" even though he succeeded on only one of his claims for relief. *See Hensley,* 461 U.S. at 434, 103 S.Ct. 1933.

The Court finds that as in many civil rights cases, Plaintiff's claims involve a common core of facts and related legal theories. *Id.* at 435, 103 S.Ct. 1933. Accordingly, the Court does not treat Plaintiff's suit as a series of discreet claims, readily separated for purposes of apportioning hours between prevailing and non-prevailing claims. *Id.* Rather, the Court focuses on the overall results achieved by Plaintiff in relation to the hours reasonably expended by Plaintiff's counsel on the litigation. *Id.* Having done this, the Court finds that Plaintiff achieved only limited success, rendering the product of the hours reasonably expended on the litigation as a whole and the reasonable hourly rates an excessive fee recovery. *Id.* at 436, 103 S.Ct. 1933. While Plaintiff's recovery on his hostile environment claim was significant, he was unable to convince the jury that he had been discharged based on his race. Moreover, the Court dismissed on summary judgment Plaintiff's claims for intentional and negligent infliction of emotional distress, as well as his state civil rights claims. (DE# 197). At trial, the Court granted Defendant's Motion for Judgment as a Matter of Law on Plaintiff's claims of negligent training, retention, and supervision. (DE # 288). Even though Plaintiff's claims were "interrelated, nonfrivolous, and raised in good faith," we may reduce the lodestar to account for his limited success. *Id.*

For guidance in reducing the lodestar, we turn to *Bohen v. City of E. Chicago,* 666 F.Supp. 154 (N.D.Ind.1987), a case involving similar facts: plaintiff prevailed on her sexual harassment claim, but failed on her discriminatory discharge claim. *Bohen,* 666 F.Supp. at 155. Judge Easterbrook, sitting by designation, reduced the plaintiff's fees to account for her limited success, but did so only by 10% across-the-board. *Id.* at 156. He noted that the same witnesses dealt with both aspects of the case and that since the claimed harassment was extensive, it would have been necessary to examine the plaintiff's whole period of employment even without the discharge claim. *Id.* Noting that at least some time was spent solely on the discharge claim, though he could not say precisely how much, Judge Easterbrook concluded that the plaintiff's counsel would have spent about 90% of the time it did had there been no discharge claim. *Id.* The same reasoning applies here. However, the Court awards Plaintiff 80% of the lodestar, estimating that 20% of Plaintiff's counsels' time was devoted exclusively to the discharge claim. Specifically, the Court finds that significant time was spent by Plaintiff examining Defendant's alleged early release program, which was only tangentially related to the hostile environment claim.

Final lodestar figure adjusted for results obtained: $306,467.50 \times .8 = $ **$245,174**

IV. Costs

The Court recognizes that the traditional limits on what costs may be taxed, *see* 28 U.S.C. § 1920, do not apply to requests submitted under § 1988 and that the Eleventh Circuit traditionally takes a liberal approach when reimbursing attorney expenses. *See Dowdell v. City of Apopka*, 698 F.2d 1181, 1192 (11th Cir.1983); *Mallory v. Harkness*, 923 F.Supp. 1546, 1557 (S.D.Fla.1996). However, Plaintiff still bears the burden of submitting a request for expenses that would enable the Court to determine what expenses were incurred and whether Plaintiff is entitled to them. *See Loranger*, 10 F.3d at 784. Plaintiff's entries for photocopy, telephone, and fax charges are wholly devoid of explanation. The Court has no way of knowing whether the rates paid for the photocopies were reasonable or even whether these expenses were related to this action. Therefore, the Court will not tax these costs or others that lack description. Moreover, the Court finds that the costs incurred prior to commencement of the action are not taxable. *See Dowdell*, 698 F.2d at 1192 ("We hold that, with the exception of routine office overhead normally absorbed by the practicing attorney, all reasonable expenses incurred in case preparation, *during the course of litigation, or as an aspect of settlement* of the case may be taxed as costs under section 1988.") (emphasis added).

Having deleted expenses associated with the above-described entries, we tax **$67,150.63** as costs.

V. Conclusion

As I considered this issue, I reflected upon a letter recently received from a trial lawyer following a discussion on civility and professionalism with the Miami Chapter of the American Board of Trial Advocates. This lawyer stated:

It seems to me that the courts are basically facing this issue as one of education. Hence, we have seminars, guidelines and articles from both that state and federal bench explaining what lawyers should do to be civil and professional to each other. However, I do not think that problem is that lawyers do not know how to act in a civil manner. Rather, I think some lawyers will simply do that with which they can get away.

Special masters, grievance committees and educational seminars are not as effective as a sanction for uncivil behavior.

I know our federal court is quite busy and that the time it takes to consider uncivil behavior may have to be taken from some other pending case. However, I would submit that eliminating uncivil behavior not only helps that case, but every other case in which that lawyer is involved. Moreover, as the word spreads as to the price to be paid for unprofessionalism, other lawyers and other cases will be implicated.

I believe that this reduction in attorney fees is an appropriate response to the conduct by Plaintiff's counsel in this case, but I am not convinced it will deter future misconduct. I frankly considered denying fees altogether but while I have reviewed many of the depositions, I did not observe everything that happened during the pretrial phase of the case. The reduction in attorneys' fees based upon misconduct of counsel is therefore approximately $358,423.20.

For the foregoing reasons, it is hereby ORDERED AND ADJUDGED that Plaintiff's Amended Verified Motion for Attorney's Fees and Costs (DE# 310) is **GRANTED.** Based on the foregoing we award Plaintiff **$312,324.63** in fees and costs.

Furthermore, because of the misconduct of counsel which occurred in this case, a copy of this order shall be sent to the Florida Bar and the Peer Review Committee for the Southern District of Florida for any action deemed appropriate.

SOLUTIONS: THE LAWYER SHOULD HAVE,
WOULD HAVE, COULD HAVE. . .

We selected this case because it touches upon a fact pattern that was not a violation in 2000, but is now; namely, MR 8.4(g). Misconduct involving (a) "discrimination or harassment" (b) "on the basis of race, sex, religion, national origin, ethnicity, disability, age, sexual orientation, gender identity, marital status, or socioeconomic status "and that (c) occurs in "conduct related to the practice of law." It is (c) that is ambiguous, but the ambiguity is clarified in Comments 3 and 4 and is intended to be very expansive encompassing both managing a law firm and the actual practice of law. Thus, comments perhaps designed to gain a mental advantage over counsel opposite—such as the comment to the Black lawyers—would run afoul of this rule.

Section 6.   The Lawyer as Witness

Model Rule 3.7: The Lawyer as Witness

(a)   A lawyer shall not act as advocate at a trial in which the lawyer is likely to be a necessary witness unless:

(1)   the testimony relates to an uncontested issue;

(2)   the testimony relates to the nature and value of legal services rendered in the case; or

(3)   disqualification of the lawyer would work substantial hardship on the client.

(b)   A lawyer may act as advocate in a trial in which another lawyer in the lawyer's firm is likely to be called as a witness unless precluded from doing so by Rule 1.7 or Rule 1.9.

Deconstruction Exercise/Rule Rationale

This is an absolute rule with some exceptions. It is designed to throw a penalty flag whenever a lawyer seeks to serve in the role of lawyer representing a client *and* a factual witness. The rule is different from the case that kicked off this chapter. Why? There, the lawyer was a witness while in the role of an advocate. Here, by contrast, the rule prohibits a lawyer from essentially taking the witness stand and offering substantive testimony. The rule's language is prospective in nature, requiring the lawyer to anticipate whether it is "likely" (more than 50% probability) to be a "necessary" witness. What other words could have been used other than "necessary?" Why do you think this word was selected over others? If the prongs of "likely" and "necessary" are satisfied, then the lawyer should not become involved in the litigation as a lawyer/advocate. The rule is designed to avoid the natural confusion of a jury as to whether the lawyer is speaking as a fact witness as to what occurred, and evaluate the statements in that light, or as an advocate, and review the arguments from that perspective. A lawyer who will likely be both a witness and advocate will be subject to a DQ motion.

Cases and Materials

X-Ray Questions

At times, case circumstances will ensnare a lawyer into being a witness in a case that the lawyer is handling. This is known as the lawyer/advocate rule. Because having a lawyer as both a client's advocate and often key witness gives an unfair advantage, the rule prohibits the lawyer from performing the dual roles. But the state versions of the Model Rules are sometimes different, as we see in California. How does the Model Rule differ in operation from the state rule? Are the goals sought to be accomplished the same or different?

BEYOND THE CITE

By: David C. Carr, California Legal Ethics: *Rule 3.7: One of These Things Is Not Like the Others.*

Lopez v. Lopez, Second App. Dist., Div. 4, case no. B315959, filed 7/20/22.

The Second Appellate District has reversed a trial court ruling disqualifying a lawyer from representing his wife in litigation where the lawyer was likely to be called as a witness. This case provides one of those 'teaching moments' on a topic that is the subject of some confusion among lawyers, and, apparently, some judges: the differences between the California Rules of Professional Conduct and the American Bar Association (ABA) Model Rules of Professional Conduct.

Some of the confusion may be the result of the way professional responsibility has been taught by law schools. I will offer myself up as an example. I went to an ABA-accredited law school in Los Angeles, longer ago than I care to remember. So long ago that we actually studied the 1969 ABA Code of Professional Responsibility, with its confusing hodgepodge of Canons, "ECs" (ethical considerations) and "DRs" (disciplinary rules.) We also learned a little of the then recently adopted ABA Model Rules. But our instruction never acknowledged, let only elucidated, the then-existing 1975 California Rules of Professional Conduct, the actual discipline rules that would be binding on the majority of us who would go on to practice in California. The California rules were not tested on the version of the Multi-state Professional Responsibility Examination (MPRE) that I took and passed in 1986. I did not even realize that California had its one distinctly different set of disciplinary rules until March 27, 1989, the day I began work at the State Bar of California.

Legal ethics education has improved since those days. My impression is that even law schools that aspire to be "national" make some effort to acquaint students with the California rules. I know from my own teaching experience is that it is difficult to teach two very different sets of professional responsibility rules. The adoption of California's own version of the Model Rules in 2018 has made it easier, although California's rules have many differences with the Model Rules, including our version of the lawyer witness rule, Rule 3.7, which tripped up the trial judge in the Lopez case. Unlike the Model Rule 3.7, our Rule allows the lawyer to serve as a witness with the informed consent of the client, as did former California Rule 5–220 (the 1975 California rules did not address this issue.) But that exception is not absolute; Comment 3 states that a judge may still disqualify a lawyer who will be a witness if necessary to protect the trier of fact from being misled or the opposing party from being prejudiced.

This is a useful reminder that disqualification is a judicial remedy that is broader than the rules of professional conduct and may be invoked in the exercise of a trial judge's discretion to prevent unfairness. And, in the trial judge's defense, it is clear that they are situations where the ABA Model Rules can be utilized as guidance on California questions, even after the adoption of our new rules in 2018. Pre-2018 case law held that "the ABA Model Rules of Professional Conduct may be considered as a collateral source, particularly in areas where there is no direct authority in California and there is no conflict with the public policy of California." State Comp. Ins. Fund v. WPS, Inc. (1999) 70 Cal. App. 4th 644, 656. California Rule 1.0 states that the Rules of Professional Conduct "are intended to regulate professional conduct of lawyers through discipline"; Comment 4 to that Rule states that "ethics opinions and rules and standards promulgated by other jurisdictions and bar associations may also be considered" in addressing ethical issues not related to discipline.

So maybe that trial judge wasn't so dumb after all. Confusion about the proper role of the California Rules of Professional Conduct still exists as well as geographical reach. Are they just discipline rules, black-letter law like criminal statutes or do they serve a prophylactic role in guiding lawyer conduct. Of course, the answer is both, despite the long-standing California shibboleth about them being only discipline rules. This confusion was what the wacky 1969 ABA Code of Professional Responsibility was trying to address through its three-part structure of Canons, ECs and DRs. Maybe the 1969 Code wasn't so dumb either.

Cases and Materials

X-Ray Questions (*Lopez*)

This recent case illustrates how a California trial court incorrectly applied the ABA rules to an advocate/witness issue that manifested itself in a motion to disqualify counsel on that basis. Can you explain how the trial court misapplied the ABA rule? What should it have done? Note too, the return of concept of "informed consent." Is it always a cure all for an ethical dilemma or merely one factor to consider?

Lopez v. Lopez

Court of Appeal, Second District, Division 4, California, 2022.
81 Cal.App.5th 412.

INTRODUCTION

In this opinion, we hold the trial court failed to apply the proper legal standards, and thereby abused its discretion, in disqualifying attorney Daniel Boone from representing appellant Cynthia Lopez under the advocate-witness rule. We publish to further clarify the standards applicable to a disqualification motion under the advocate-witness rule, having previously done so in affirming an attorney's disqualification in *Doe v. Yim* (2020) 55 Cal.App.5th 573, 269 Cal.Rptr.3d 613 (*Yim*).

In 2015, appellant, then proceeding pro se, brought this action against respondent Kenneth Lopez, her brother, alleging he had falsely accused her of committing crimes against him and their elderly parents. In January and February 2016, respondent emailed Boone (appellant's husband since June 2015, her former coworker at his law firm, and later her counsel in this action), warning that if appellant did not settle the action, respondent would file a cross-complaint the next day, which he did. The court subsequently dismissed respondent's cross-complaint. In May 2017, appellant retained Boone to represent her pro bono or at a discounted rate, having been advised by Boone that he would likely need to testify at trial, and having executed informed written consent to Boone's representation notwithstanding his expected dual role as advocate and witness. Appellant then filed a first amended complaint, adding allegations concerning respondent's emails to Boone, and a claim of malicious prosecution based on respondent's filing of his dismissed cross-complaint. Boone continued representing appellant in this action for over four years.

In August 2021, two months before trial, respondent moved to disqualify Boone as appellant's counsel under California's advocate-witness rule, viz., rule 3.7 of the Rules of Professional Conduct (Rule 3.7). Appellant opposed the motion, principally relying on Rule 3.7's exception for cases in which the attorney has obtained the client's informed written consent to the attorney's dual role. Appellant also argued respondent's disqualification motion was untimely and tactically motivated. Although neither party specified the precise subject matter of Boone's expected testimony, appellant represented his testimony would concern his receipt of respondent's January and February 2016 emails, and the emails' undisputed contents.

In September 2021, the court held a hearing, issuing in advance a tentative ruling disqualifying Boone from all phases of the litigation. Appellant observed that the tentative ruling failed to apply Rule 3.7 and its informed-consent exception, instead applying rule 3.7 of the ABA Model Rules of Professional Conduct (the ABA Rule), which was not binding and lacked any informed-consent exception. Appellant also argued the tentative ruling was overbroad in disqualifying Boone from all phases of the litigation because, inter alia, Rule 3.7 is limited on its face to trial. The same day, the court adopted its tentative ruling, finding respondent's motion timely and not tactically motivated, and applying the ABA Rule to disqualify Boone from all phases of the litigation. The court did not cite Rule 3.7, address the rule's informed-consent exception, or find that Boone's disqualification was necessary "to protect the trier of fact from being misled or the opposing party from being prejudiced." (Rules Prof. Conduct, rule 3.7(a), com. 3.) Nor did the court address Rule 3.7's limitation to advocacy "in a trial." (*Id.*, rule 3.7(a).)

On appeal from the disqualification order, appellant contends the court abused its discretion by (1) failing to apply the proper legal standards in disqualifying Boone under the advocate-witness rule; and (2) erroneously finding that respondent's disqualification motion was timely and not tactically motivated.

Agreeing with appellant's first contention, we need not reach her second. We conclude the court abused its discretion in disqualifying Boone from all phases of the litigation because it failed to apply the proper legal standards, viz., Rule 3.7's informed-consent exception and limitation to trial. Accordingly, we reverse the disqualification order.

PROCEEDINGS BELOW

A. *Early Litigation and Prior Appeal*

In November 2015, appellant, proceeding pro se, initiated this action against respondent, her brother, asserting claims of defamation and infliction of emotional distress. (*Lopez v. Lopez* (June 10, 2019, No. B287383) 2019 WL 2417376, at *1, 2019 Cal.App.Unpub. LEXIS 3976, at *2 (*Lopez I*).) Appellant alleged that in 2014 and early 2015, respondent falsely accused her of committing bank fraud and identity theft against him and their elderly parents. (*Ibid.*) In January 2016, respondent filed a cross-complaint. (*Ibid.*) In January 2017, appellant retained attorney Justin Romig to represent her in this action. In February 2017, the trial court (Judge Richard Rico) dismissed respondent's cross-complaint. (*Ibid.*)

In May 2017, appellant filed a substitution-of-attorney form replacing her former counsel with Boone, her husband since June 2015 and her former coworker at Boone's law firm. In June 2017, appellant filed a first amended complaint, reasserting her original claims for defamation and emotional distress and adding new claims for malicious prosecution (based on respondent's filing of his dismissed cross-complaint), abuse of process, and " '[i]njunctive [r]elief.' " (*Lopez I, supra*, 2019 WL 2417376, at *1, 2019 Cal.App.Unpub. LEXIS 3976, at *2–*3.) The first amended complaint newly alleged that in January 2016, respondent defamed appellant by email to her former coworkers.

In September 2017, respondent filed a special motion to strike the first amended complaint under Code of Civil Procedure section 425.16 (anti-SLAPP motion). (*Lopez I, supra*, 2019 WL 2417376, at *1–2, 2019 Cal.App.Unpub. LEXIS 3976, at *4.) In opposition to the anti-SLAPP motion, appellant submitted, inter alia, a declaration from Boone. (*Id.* at *2, 2019 Cal.App.Unpub. LEXIS 3976, at *5.) Boone declared that on January 27, 2016 (the day before respondent filed his cross-complaint), respondent emailed Boone at Boone's law firm (appellant's former workplace), encouraging Boone to advise appellant to settle the matter, and indicating respondent would otherwise report the matter to various government agencies and file a cross-complaint. On February 15, 2016, respondent again emailed Boone, stating in relevant part: "[M]ore evidence came to light about your wife that is very damning. Since you are married you will ultimately be responsible for any judgment's [*sic*] against your wife." Boone declared that respondent's emails were immediately and permanently accessible not only to Boone but also to all other firm employees.

In November 2017, the court denied respondent's anti-SLAPP motion. (*Lopez I, supra*, 2019 WL 2417376, at *2, 2019 Cal.App.Unpub. LEXIS 3976, at *6.) Respondent filed an appeal, to which appellant responded, still represented by Boone. (*Id.* at *1, 2019 Cal.App.Unpub. LEXIS 3976, at *1.) In July 2019, we reversed the anti-SLAPP order with respect to one claim immaterial to this appeal, but otherwise affirmed the denial of respondent's anti-SLAPP motion, allowing the majority of appellant's claims to proceed. (*Id.* at *1, *7, 2019 Cal.App.Unpub. LEXIS 3976, at *1–*2, *20.)

B. Association and Illness of Co-Counsel

From August 2019 to May 2021, Boone continued to represent appellant in moving to recover fees and costs incurred in opposing respondent's anti-SLAPP motion, litigating discovery motions, and engaging in discovery. In May 2021, three months before trial was set to begin, appellant filed an association-of-attorney form signed by attorney Michael Trauben, designating Trauben's law firm as Boone's co-counsel.

In July 2021, appellant filed an ex parte application for a trial continuance, based principally on Trauben's expected unavailability due to a medical emergency that had hospitalized him and would require surgery in mid-August. In support of the continuance request, Boone declared, inter alia, that Trauben's association as "co-counsel and trial counsel" had been necessary because Boone was "expected to be a witness at trial." At a hearing on the request, respondent did not oppose a short continuance, but questioned why Boone could not "do the trial" alone; respondent did not acknowledge or object to Boone's expressed intent to testify at trial.

The court continued the hearing to August 12, 2021. On that date, the court found appellant had failed to produce sufficient information concerning Trauben's health to establish good cause for a continuance, but nevertheless continued the trial to October 18, 2021, to account for developments in the COVID-19 pandemic. At the conclusion of the August 12 hearing, the court held an informal discovery conference (IDC) in chambers, which was not reported. During the IDC, Boone again stated he intended to testify at trial.

C. Disqualification Motion

On August 23, 2021, respondent filed a motion to disqualify Boone as appellant's counsel under the advocate-witness rule, viz., Rule 3.7. Respondent acknowledged he did not know the subject matter of Boone's expected testimony, but asserted, "[I]t hardly takes an evidentiary foundation to believe that whatever [Boone] testifies to will involve contested issues." Without attempting to identify any contested issue to which Boone's testimony might be relevant, respondent argued that allowing Boone to continue representing appellant would prejudice respondent and the integrity of the judicial process, because the jury might be confused as to whether Boone's statements at trial were evidence or argument. Respondent's motion papers mentioned that Boone was appellant's husband, but did not seek to disqualify Boone on this ground.

The next day, the court held a hearing on respondent's ex parte application to shorten the time for hearing the disqualification motion. The court repeatedly stated it was "shocked" to have learned Boone was married to his client. Respondent emphasized that his motion was based on the advocate-witness rule. Through an associate from Trauben's firm, appellant represented that Boone's expected testimony would concern only "minor uncontested issues" related to "his receipt of a few emails from defendant, and undisputed contents therein." Respondent did not dispute this representation, but argued that Boone's testimony would be "predisposed" toward appellant in light of their marriage. The court set the motion for hearing on September 16, 2021.

D. Opposition and Reply

On September 9, 2021, appellant filed a written opposition to respondent's disqualification motion, supported by declarations from appellant and Boone. Appellant declared that in April 2017 (three months after she had retained attorney Romig), having found she could no longer afford Romig's services, she asked Boone to represent her pro bono or at a discounted rate. According to both declarations, Boone advised appellant he would likely need to testify at trial, explained potential problems associated with his expected dual role as advocate and witness, and recommended that she obtain independent advice on the matter. In May 2017, after obtaining independent advice from other attorneys, appellant executed informed written consent to Boone's dual role. Throughout his representation, Boone provided his services pro bono or, in the case of "extensive motion practice and oral argument," at a discounted hourly rate of $150.

In her opposition brief, appellant argued that under Rule 3.7's informed-consent exception, Boone's disqualification was precluded as a matter of law, or at least unwarranted in light of the balance of interests at stake. Appellant argued she would be prejudiced by Boone's disqualification notwithstanding the association of Boone's co-counsel, because his co-counsel could not prepare for trial as successfully or cost-effectively without assistance from Boone, whom appellant knew to be capable and who provided his services to her pro bono or at a discounted rate. In contrast, she argued, respondent had failed to show that allowing Boone to continue representing her would cause any prejudice to respondent or to the integrity of the judicial process. Appellant further argued the disqualification motion was untimely and tactically motivated, as respondent had been put on notice during the anti-SLAPP litigation that Boone would likely testify at trial "about [respondent]'s email showing malice," but respondent had raised no objection to Boone's dual role until Boone's co-counsel suffered a medical emergency on the eve of trial. Finally, appellant observed that respondent had failed to identify any prohibition against an attorney representing the attorney's spouse, as no such prohibition existed.

In reply, respondent asserted he was "not arguing that Mr. Boone should not represent Plaintiff," but instead was seeking to "disqualify Mr. Boone as counsel because he has chosen to testify on his wife's behalf so that [respondent] can get a fair trial . . . ." Respondent implied appellant's informed written consent was defective because it was executed before the adoption of Rule 3.7, and argued that in any event, her consent did not preclude disqualification to avoid prejudice to respondent and to the integrity of the judicial process.

E. Hearing and Ruling

On September 16, 2021, the court held a hearing on respondent's disqualification motion, confirming at the outset that counsel had read its tentative ruling disqualifying Boone. Appellant observed that the tentative ruling failed to apply Rule 3.7, instead applying the ABA Rule, which was not binding and lacked any informed-consent exception. Appellant also requested clarification of the scope of the tentative ruling, observing that Rule 3.7 was limited on its face to trial, and arguing that respondent's reply brief sought disqualification only at trial (which respondent denied). Otherwise, appellant generally repeated the arguments in her written opposition. Respondent submitted on the tentative ruling, but additionally asserted that his motion papers sought Boone's disqualification "for all purposes," including representation "behind the scenes." The court indicated it would verify whether respondent's motion papers had sought such broad disqualification and, if so, disqualify Boone from all phases of the litigation, including the preparation of trial material such as a witness list or motion in limine.

Later that day, the court issued an order disqualifying Boone as appellant's counsel from all phases of the litigation under the ABA Rule. The court did not cite Rule 3.7 or its informed-consent exception. Although the court noted appellant had relied on her informed written consent, the court did not otherwise discuss her consent.

In disqualifying Boone under the ABA Rule, the court acknowledged "it [wa]s unclear what precise testimony Mr. Boone intend[ed] to provide." Without addressing appellant's representations that Boone's testimony would concern respondent's January and February 2016 emails to Boone, the court further stated, "[I]t appears that Mr. Boone intends to provide substantive testimony concerning the underlying family dispute on behalf of Plaintiff, who is his wife." The court reasoned: "Mr. Boone would not just be expected to present objective testimony for a client who he is also advocating for, but would [also] be expected to present objective testimony for his wife in a highly contested family matter while also advocating for her as her attorney. This dual role clearly impairs his credibility as a witness and diminishes his effectiveness as an advocate. [¶] . . . [¶] Because Plaintiff already associated with co-counsel in May 2021, the Court is persuaded that no prejudice will result to Plaintiff as a result of this disqualification." The court did not find that Boone's dual role posed a risk of misleading the jury or prejudicing respondent. Nor did the court address appellant's argument that Boone's co-counsel could not prepare for trial as successfully or cost-effectively without Boone's assistance.

The court rejected appellant's arguments that: (1) the disqualification motion was untimely and tactically motivated; and (2) respondent's reply brief had limited the scope of the requested disqualification to trial. The court did not address the ABA Rule's language limiting its prohibition to advocacy at trial (or the corresponding language in Rule 3.7).

DISCUSSION

Appellant contends the trial court abused its discretion in disqualifying Boone from representing her in all phases of the litigation under the advocate-witness rule. As explained below, we agree.

A. *Principles*

1. **Attorney Disqualification**

"A trial court's authority to disqualify an attorney derives from its inherent power, codified at Code of Civil Procedure section 128, subdivision (a)(5), to control the conduct of its ministerial officers and of all other persons connected with its proceedings in furtherance of justice. [Citation.] Disqualification may be ordered as a prophylactic measure against a prospective ethical violation likely to have a substantial continuing effect on future proceedings." (*Yim, supra,* 55

Cal.App.5th at 581, 269 Cal.Rptr.3d 613; but see *In re Jasmine S.* (2007) 153 Cal.App.4th 835, 843, 63 Cal.Rptr.3d 593 [" 'an appearance of impropriety by itself does not support a lawyer's disqualification' "].)

" ' "Generally, a trial court's decision on a disqualification motion is reviewed for abuse of discretion.' " [Citation.] Under this standard, the trial court's legal conclusions are reviewed de novo, but its factual findings are reviewed only for the existence of substantial evidence supporting them, and its " 'application of the law to the facts is reversible only if arbitrary and capricious." ' " (*Yim, supra,* 55 Cal.App.5th at 581, 269 Cal.Rptr.3d 613.) "However, the trial court's discretion is limited by the applicable legal principles." (*People ex rel. Dept. of Corporations v. SpeeDee Oil Change Systems, Inc.* (1999) 20 Cal.4th 1135, 1144, 86 Cal.Rptr.2d 816, 980 P.2d 371 (*SpeeDee Oil*); accord, *In re Charlisse C.* (2008) 45 Cal.4th 145, 150, 84 Cal.Rptr.3d 597, 194 P.3d 330 ["we conclude the trial court applied the wrong legal standard in ordering [public law office]'s disqualification and therefore abused its discretion"].) "In any event, a disqualification motion involves concerns that justify careful review of the trial court's exercise of discretion." (*SpeeDee Oil, supra,* 20 Cal.4th at 1144, 86 Cal.Rptr.2d 816, 980 P.2d 371.)

2. The Advocate-Witness Rule

Rule 3.7 provides: "A lawyer shall not act as an advocate in a trial in which the lawyer is likely to be a witness unless: [¶] (1) the lawyer's testimony relates to an uncontested issue or matter; [¶] (2) the lawyer's testimony relates to the nature and value of legal services rendered in the case; or [¶] (3) the lawyer has obtained informed written consent from the client." (Rules Prof. Conduct, rule 3.7(a), fn. omitted.) A comment to the rule clarifies that the informed-consent exception is not absolute: "Notwithstanding a client's informed written consent, courts retain discretion to take action, up to and including disqualification of a lawyer who seeks to both testify and serve as an advocate, to protect the trier of fact from being misled or the opposing party from being prejudiced." (*Id.,* com. 3, asterisk omitted, citing *Lyle v. Superior Court* (1981) 122 Cal.App.3d 470, 175 Cal.Rptr. 918 (*Lyle*).) "In other words, a court retains discretion to disqualify a likely advocate-witness as counsel, notwithstanding client consent, where there is 'a convincing demonstration of detriment to the opponent or injury to the integrity of the judicial process.' " (*Yim, supra,* 55 Cal.App.5th at 582, 269 Cal.Rptr.3d 613, quoting *Lyle, supra,* at 482, 175 Cal.Rptr. 918.)

Rule 3.7 is limited on its face to trial. (Rules Prof. Conduct, rule 3.7(a) [absent specified exception, "A lawyer shall not act as an advocate *in a trial* in which the lawyer is likely to be a witness" (italics added)]; see also ABA Model Rules Prof. Conduct, rule 3.7(a) [absent specified exception, "A lawyer shall not act as advocate *at a trial* in which the lawyer is likely to be a necessary witness" (italics added)].) In *Yim*, however, "to effectuate the rule's purpose of avoiding factfinder confusion," we interpreted the rule's use of the term "trial" to encompass a "pretrial evidentiary hearing at which counsel is likely to testify." (*Yim, supra*, 55 Cal.App.5th at 583, 269 Cal.Rptr.3d 613.) Further, finding no California authority on point, but agreeing with most courts that had considered the issue, we " 'recognize[d] that an attorney who intends to testify at trial may not participate in "any pretrial activities which carry the risk of revealing the attorney's dual role to the jury." [Citation.] In particular, a testifying attorney should not take or defend depositions.' " (*Ibid.*) We did not consider whether the advocate-witness rule could be further extended to other pretrial activities. (See *id.* at 586, 269 Cal.Rptr.3d 613.)

"In exercising its discretion to disqualify counsel under the advocate-witness rule, a court must consider: (1) " "whether counsel's testimony is, in fact, genuinely needed" "; (2) 'the possibility [opposing] counsel is using the motion to disqualify for purely tactical reasons'; and (3) 'the combined effects of the strong interest parties have in representation by counsel of their choice, and in avoiding the duplicate expense and time-consuming effort involved in replacing counsel already familiar with the case.' [Citation.] '[T]rial judges must indicate on the record they have considered the appropriate factors . . . .' " (*Yim supra*, 55 Cal.App.5th at 583, 269 Cal.Rptr.3d 613; see also *id.* at 585–586, 269 Cal.Rptr.3d 613; cf. *SpeeDee Oil, supra*, 20 Cal.4th at 1144–1145, 86 Cal.Rptr.2d 816, 980 P.2d 371 [careful review of disqualification orders is mandated by concerns that may include "a client's right to chosen counsel" and "the financial burden on a client to replace disqualified counsel"].)

B. Analysis

We conclude the trial court failed to apply the proper legal standards, and thereby abused its discretion, in disqualifying Boone from representing appellant in all phases of the litigation under the advocate-witness rule. First, the court failed to apply Rule 3.7's informed-consent exception. Indeed, the court failed even to cite Rule 3.7, instead applying the ABA Rule, which is not binding and lacks any informed-consent exception. Although the court noted appellant had relied on her informed written consent, it did not otherwise discuss her consent or its relevance. Nor did the court find that Boone's disqualification was necessary, notwithstanding appellant's informed written consent, in order to "protect the trier of fact from being misled or the opposing party from being prejudiced." (Rules Prof. Conduct, rule 3.7, com. 3.) The court found only that Boone's dual role would impair *his* credibility as a witness (for appellant) and diminish *his* effectiveness as an advocate (for appellant). It made no finding of prejudice to respondent, much less of potential confusion. (See *Smith, Smith & Kring v. Superior Court (Oliver)* (1997) 60 Cal.App.4th 573, 578, 70 Cal.Rptr.2d 507 ["Where a lawyer representing a party in trial is also a witness during the trial, his or her effectiveness, both as a lawyer and as a witness, may be impaired in the eyes of the fact finder. Such disadvantage enures to the detriment of the party being represented by the lawyer serving such a dual function"].)

Even had the court found a risk that Boone's dual role would mislead the jury, such a finding would have been speculative on the limited factual record before the court. Although the court stated it "appear[ed]" Boone would provide "substantive testimony concerning the underlying family dispute," the court did not expressly reject appellant's contrary representations that Boone's testimony would concern only his receipt of respondent's January and February 2016 emails, and the emails' undisputed contents. Respondent had neither challenged these representations nor attempted, through discovery or a request for an offer of proof, to discern the substance of Boone's expected testimony. Without further information, the court could not reasonably have found a " 'convincing demonstration of detriment to the opponent or injury to the integrity of the judicial process.' " (*Yim, supra,* 55 Cal.App.5th at 582, 269 Cal.Rptr.3d 613, quoting *Lyle, supra,* at 482, 175 Cal.Rptr. 918.) In disregarding appellant's informed written consent without finding any such detriment, the court failed to acknowledge her consent's significance under Rule 3.7, and thereby abused its discretion. (See *Smith, Smith & Kring v. Superior Court (Oliver), supra,* 60 Cal.App.4th at 579–582, 70 Cal.Rptr.2d 507 [trial court abused its discretion in disqualifying counsel under advocate-witness rule, where record did not indicate court "recognized the importance" of client's written consent to counsel's dual role, which should have been given " 'great weight' "].)

The court further abused its discretion in failing to apply Rule 3.7's limitation to advocacy "in a trial." (Rules Prof. Conduct, rule 3.7(a).) The court disqualified Boone from all phases of the litigation, without acknowledging this limitation (or the corresponding limitation in the ABA Rule), and without finding, as we did in *Yim,* that an extension of the rule to specified pretrial activities would effectuate the rule's purpose of avoiding factfinder confusion. (See *Yim, supra,* 55 Cal.App.5th at 577, 583, 585, 269 Cal.Rptr.3d 613.) Indeed, as explained above, the court made no finding of a risk of factfinder confusion, which would have been speculative, in any event, on the limited factual record before the court. Nevertheless, the court extended the advocate-witness rule to *all* pretrial activities, including behind-the-scenes activities unlikely to pose any risk of factfinder confusion, such as preparing a witness list or motion in limine. Because Boone's categorical disqualification from all pretrial activities was not supported by Rule 3.7's text, or by reasoned findings concerning the rule's purpose, we conclude it constituted an abuse of discretion.

Respondent's reliance on *Yim* is misplaced. As noted, *Yim* does not support Boone's categorical disqualification from all pretrial activities. Even with respect to Boone's disqualification at trial, *Yim* is distinguishable. There, a mother represented her daughter in suing the mother's ex-husband, alleging he had exploited the marriage to sexually abuse the daughter when she was a minor. (*Yim, supra*, 55 Cal.App.5th at 576–577, 269 Cal.Rptr.3d 613.) Less than two months after the suit was filed, the ex-husband promptly moved to disqualify the mother under the advocate-witness rule. (*Id.* at 577–578, 269 Cal.Rptr.3d 613.) The trial court applied the rule in disqualifying the mother at trial, expressly accepting evidence that the mother had obtained her daughter's informed written consent, but "explaining why it nevertheless deemed the informed-consent exception inapplicable due to the risk of prejudice to [the ex-husband] and to the integrity of the judicial process." (*Id.* at 585, 269 Cal.Rptr.3d 613; see also *id.* at 579–580, 269 Cal.Rptr.3d 613.) In affirming, we concluded the record showed the mother was almost certain to be a key witness concerning her ex-husband's alleged sexual abuse of her daughter and her daughter's resulting damages. (*Id.* at 584, 269 Cal.Rptr.3d 613.) We further concluded the mother's dual role posed a risk of misleading the jury into mistaking her arguments as evidence based on her extensive personal knowledge of her ex-husband, which could prejudice him. (*Id.* at 584–585, 269 Cal.Rptr.3d 613.) Finally, we concluded that by explaining why it rejected the daughter's reliance on the informed-consent exception, the court demonstrated it had properly considered the daughter's interest in remaining represented by her counsel of choice, particularly because she had not asserted that this interest was "heightened by any purported burden" in retaining new counsel or in paying for duplication of her mother's efforts, which had not progressed beyond the "early stages" of the litigation. (*Id.* at 585, 269 Cal.Rptr.3d 613.)

The record before us here is materially different. Rather than explain why it rejected appellant's reliance on Rule 3.7's informed-consent exception, the trial court applied a different, non-binding rule, which lacked any such exception. It did so despite its acknowledged uncertainty regarding the subject matter of Boone's expected testimony, without finding that Boone was likely either to be a key witness or to make any argument the jury could perceive to be based on his personal knowledge of respondent (if any). Finally, the court failed to demonstrate that it had properly considered appellant's heightened interest in remaining represented by Boone, who had gained mastery over the case by litigating it for over four years, and who was providing his services pro bono or at a discounted rate. (See *Liberty National Enterprises, L.P. v. Chicago Title Ins. Co.* (2011) 194 Cal.App.4th 839, 848, 123 Cal.Rptr.3d 498 [client would have suffered "extreme" prejudice from disqualification of counsel who had "gained mastery" over case by litigating it for two years]; *Lyle, supra,* 122 Cal.App.3d at 482, 175 Cal.Rptr. 918 [client was entitled to trial court's consideration of asserted financial hardship in replacing counsel who was providing services pro bono].) Specifically, the court suggested Boone and his recently retained co-counsel were interchangeable, without addressing appellant's argument that she would be prejudiced by Boone's disqualification because his co-counsel could not prepare for trial as successfully or cost-effectively without his assistance. In so doing, the court failed to apply the proper legal standards in disqualifying Boone at trial, requiring reversal of the disqualification order.

DISPOSITION

The order disqualifying Boone as appellant's counsel is reversed. Appellant is awarded her costs on appeal.

SOLUTIONS: THE LAWYER SHOULD HAVE, WOULD HAVE, COULD HAVE. . .

Always rely on facts, not opinions or arguments. Here, there were no facts that the lawyer would be, in any sense of the word, "advocating" for the client. Thus, there would be no danger of confusion on the part of the jury.

Scenario: The Case of the Client Request and the Helpful Lawyer

Monty Lawyer represents a small company in an employment matter. The company wants to terminate an employee. Monty walks them through the process, the reasons to give the employee in the termination meeting, and the follow up separation paperwork. Monty prepares a script for the client to read. The client tells Monty, "Look we are a small company and do not have HR staff. Would you meet with the employee? It would be so much easier if you did this for us in person with the employee than if we did it in person. As you know, we don't have an HR department." Monty agrees, meets with the employee, and reads from the script he wrote. The termination goes off without hitch. Later, the employee sues for wrongful termination, Monty is retained to defend the lawsuit and a DQ motion is filed by the employee's lawyer. Should the motion be granted? Why? Would the result be the same or different depending on the rule that was used?

Becoming a Professional

Both of the following excerpts focus on the use of cultural competence in representing a client at trial. Indeed, the second excerpt notes that a valuable discipline to draw upon is being an effective lawyer is anthropology. Lawyers will continue to rely upon additional disciplines—not just their legal training—in serving their clients. What disciplines other than the law do you think would be helpful in becoming an effective lawyer? How so? Have you had any experiences in that regard that you can reflect upon and share?

BEYOND THE CITE

By: Travis Adams, "*Cultural Competency: A Necessary Skill for the 21st Century Attorney*," Law Raza: Vol 4: Iss. 1, Article 2, 2012.

> **D. *Ethnocentrism limits the attorney's ability to tell her client's story***

The telling of stories holds an important role, not just in capital punishment mitigation, but also in the legal system as a whole. The courts are a place where many of the activities making up social life within that society simultaneously are represented, contested, and inverted. When working cross culturally, a lawyer's cultural competency will be tested when the facts may be undisputed, but the meaning of the facts offer a completely different explanation for "what happened". Two federal cases provide excellent examples of the necessity of cultural competency when it comes to telling the story of the "other".

First, in Mashpee Tribe v. Town of Mashpee, lawyers were faced with a decision on how to tell the plaintiff's story. In this case, the Mashpee Tribe filed a land claim suit against United States government to recover tribal lands alienated from them in violation of the Indian Non Intercourse Act of 1790. This Act prohibited the transfer of Indian tribal land to non-Indians without approval of the federal government. However, in order to have standing to sue the Mashpee had to first establish that they were a federally recognized Tribe. While this seemed like a rather straightforward legal issue, the challenges the court faced in its efforts to define "Indian Tribe" were complex. The Mashpee's strategies in sustaining themselves as a people played against them in the court of law. These strategies included: fighting wars against the Europeans, using controlled and selective methods of assimilation into white culture, mixing with other races, and selling their land. Confusingly, the Mashpee were ruled to not be a Tribe in 1790, ruled to be a tribe in 1834 and 1842, but again were ruled not a tribe in 1869 and 1870. After forty days of testimony from tribal members, historians and social scientists, the Mashpee's case was dismissed because the tribe was ruled to not have maintained a "tribal identity" throughout its history.

The challenge of establishing federal tribal recognition for the Mashpee was insurmountable for two reasons. First, the Mashpee were forced to fit the story of their tribe into a language that did not give meaning to their history and social practices. Telling their legal story required using Eurocentric tools of the English language, the rules of evidence, and legal precedent. Requiring a particular way of telling a story not only strips away meaning but also causes certain culturally significant events to appear unintelligible to the culturally incompetent. The Mashpee lacked the technical language to effectively communicate their tribal identity within the Western Eurocentric understanding of the community.

Second, as stated before, the facts of this case were not disputed, but their meaning was viewed entirely different. The Mashpee viewed their story as one of cultural survival and support that they were in fact a tribe. However, to the court those same facts proved that the Mashpee no longer existed as a "separate" cultural group and as such, the Mashpee were divested from their land. Regardless of whose fault it was, in the end the Mashpee lost their case because their narrative did not fit into the dominant narrative's ethnocentric legal definition of a "tribe."

In the second case, City of Richmond v. J.A. Croson Co., the Supreme Court struck down a Richmond ordinance that set aside thirty percent of the subcontracting work on city construction jobs for minority firms because the ordinance denied white contractors "equal protection of the laws". Legal scholar Thomas Ross describes this case as an excellent example of how judges, like all advocates, rely on storytelling to communicate one's worldview. Justice Scalia's concurring opinion and justice Marshall's dissent each describe a different story, picking and choosing which facts to tell the reader, in order to communicate their ideology on affirmative action. Scalia tells a story from his cultural location, using symmetry as the standard for justice. In his Eurocentric view, equal protection is the same law whether drawn for whites or blacks and that principal endures any argument of a historical reality.

Marshall's dissent, tells the story of racism. He tells the story of Richmond endorsing state-sponsored racism for centuries and now it finds itself in a place in need of a remedy. Marshall's opinion is deeply specific and contextual to Richmond's history and political climate. However, Marshall's critique of the other Justice's opinions and their lack of empathy to the experience of racism is the most powerful aspect of his opinion. Marshall writes:

> The majority's view that remedial measures undertaken by municipalities with black leadership must face a stiffer test of Equal Protection Clause scrutiny than remedial measures undertaken by municipalities with white leadership implies lack of political maturity on the part of this Nation's elected minority officials that is totally unwarranted. Such insulting judgments have no place in constitutional jurisprudence.

Two Court Justices wrote entirely different opinions. One was founded on the perceived universal principal of "fairness as symmetry." The other was deeply contextual and deeply personal. Both of the opinions reflect the cultural background of the Justices. While Justice Scalia masks cultural subjectivity through claims of objective principle, Justice Marshall quite plainly speaks about the history of racism and admonishes his fellow jurists for lacking any sense of that same perspective. Seeing the most brilliant legal minds end up in such entirely different places during one opinion demonstrates the power and significance of culture. *The City of Richmond v. J.A. Croson Co.*, should serve as a reminder that while the law may seek to be neutral, our lives and worldviews are not. The culturally competent attorney is one who recognizes how our own cultural context influences one's storytelling and makes objectivity impossible.

WHAT'S NEXT?

The next chapter deals with ethical issues involved in transactional law. The foundation you have learned is the same, but its foundation is different.

To assess your understanding of the material in this chapter, click here to take a quiz.

PART V

The Lawyer as Transactional Advocate

CHAPTER 8

Transactional Ethics

Coming Attractions

Some of you will practice in the litigation/trial work, others will practice in the transactional law sphere, and some will have a mixture of practices. This chapter is devoted to transactional law, which involves unique ethical challenges. The transactional practice of law involves many different skill sets, with lawyers playing many different roles. Sometimes it means lawyers negotiate business deals for their clients, usually leading to the drafting and signing of some kind of contract. Sometimes this type of practice involves lawyers in hardnosed negotiation to get the best deal. In other cases, clients may already have an informal handshake agreement on the basic framework of an agreement, and they may task their attorneys with putting it in writing. Other forms of transactional lawyering involve writing documents where there is no obvious or immediate party on the other side. Writing a will or helping a client prepare and application to a government agency are obvious examples.

Section 1.   General Rules that Set the Framework for Transactional Practice

Competence and Diligence

Competence and diligence should not need restating—but yet they are frequently forgotten. The duties to be competent and diligent in legal work do not have exceptions for transactional lawyering. Even when there are no deadlines from a court, and even when a client cannot win or lose immediately in court, lawyers must do perform their job well, and on time. Now, a different take on familiar rules.

Model Rule 1.1

A lawyer shall provide competent representation to a client. Competent representation requires the legal knowledge, skill, thoroughness and preparation reasonably necessary for the representation.

Model Rule 1.3

A lawyer shall act with reasonable diligence and promptness in representing a client.

Deconstruction Exercise/Rule Rationale

A lawyer who does not get the work done for a client breaches her obligations under the rule. Same for a lawyer who prepares a document without taking into account relevant legal pitfalls. Bar sanctions and civil liability under malpractice may follow.

But there's more.

Objectives, Means and Candid Advice

Model Rule 1.2

A lawyer shall abide by a client's decisions concerning the objectives of representation and . . . shall consult with the client as to the means by which they are to be pursued.

Model Rule 2.1

In representing a client, a lawyer shall exercise independent professional judgment and render candid advice. In rendering advice, a lawyer may refer not only to law but to other considerations such as moral, economic, social and political factors, that may be relevant to the client's situation.

Deconstruction Exercise/Rule Rationale

We have covered the rule distinguishing objectives and means already, but it is important to look again at its implications in transaction practice, especially for defining what it means to be competent and diligent. When the end product of a lawyer's work will be the production of a document, it is tempting for an attorney to become too passive. If a client thinks he or she already knows what she wants done, the client may think that the lawyer's job is merely to be a scrivener—to simply write down what the client says, and to present things as the client framed them.

When a contract later proves faulty or an application prepared by a lawyer later is rejected, it is not uncommon for lawyers to defend themselves through some version of "that's what my client told me to write." In part, this may be simple laziness. If this were the duty of care, then lawyers could just ask clients for information in the proper format, and consider their work done. It also may be the result of pressure from clients. Clients may think they know what they want, and they may not like lawyers who raise uncomfortable questions about things that might go wrong, or suggest that the client's preferred approach might not be the best one.

That is why it is important to distinguish a client's objective from the means of achieving those objectives. Lawyers need to always remember what their clients are trying to achieve. They want a deal finalized, and to be profitable. Or, they want an application filed with an agency, and to be approved. But responsibility for the means of achieving that belongs to the lawyer. That is why lawyers cannot be just scriveners and scribes for our clients. Our clients may think they have an idea in mind about how to present their cases. But it is the lawyer's job to find the best ethical means, and to consult with our clients about how we recommend pursuing their goals, and do so ethically.

Here, it is important to remember lawyers' dual roles as advisors and advocates. Just as a lawyer at trial shapes a narrative and theory of the case to put the facts forward in a light most favorable to the client, a lawyer preparing an application for a government benefit would want to present the facts in a way calculated to improve the chances of the application being granted. The rule requiring lawyers to exercise independent judgment and to render candid advice is another reminder that lawyers cannot simply without questioning write down what their clients say. Lawyers must guide their clients through minefields they might not even see. ABA Comment to Rule 2.1 states:

> In general, a lawyer is not expected to give advice until asked by the client. However, when a lawyer knows that a client proposes a course of action that is likely to result in substantial adverse legal consequences to the client, the lawyer's duty to the client under Rule 1.4 [Communication] may require that the lawyer offer advice if the client's course of action is related to the representation. . . . A lawyer ordinarily has no duty to initiate investigation of a client's affairs or to give advice that the client has indicated is unwanted, but *a lawyer may initiate advice to a client when doing so appears to be in the client's interest.*

Remember, Rule 1.4 requires lawyers to "explain a matter to the extent reasonably necessary to permit the client to make informed decisions regarding the representation." All of this means that lawyers always remain potentially responsible for ill-advised means to achieve a client's goals. A lawyer cannot hide behind a client's ill-informed preferences when a transaction goes badly in a way that should have been foreseeable.

BEYOND THE CITE

Q & A: Michael Kagan and Lori Johnson

Q: First of all, transactional drafting is a lot of what lawyers do, but it does not seem to get as much attention in discussions of legal ethics. Why do you think that is?

A: I think there are a variety of reasons for this, the most formative of which is the Anglo-American distinction between barristers and solicitors. Our legal system was somewhat modeled on the English common law system, where barristers specialize in courtroom advocacy and litigation, while solicitors advise clients on necessary course of legal action and draft related documents. Solicitors do not often appear in front of the court, and their role was viewed as somewhat more informal. This carried over into our jurisprudence, as you can see even the earliest iterations of our professional conduct rules focused mostly on the formalized, court-focused role of the litigator.

The rules primarily seek to place boundaries on the zeal with which litigators advocate for their clients during disputes. Transactional lawyers have been viewed as engaging in a more cooperative, counseling role, which might not be viewed as requiring the same level of ethical control to ensure fairness. However, I view the work of transactional lawyers as inherently a form of advocacy. Even in a friendly transaction, the lawyer is working to achieve the best possible outcome for their client, and as such may be tempted to cross ethical boundaries. The Model Rules of Professional Conduct should provide more robust guidance for these transactional lawyers, especially because they practice outside of the watchful eyes of the court system.

Q: What led you to think that plain language might have ethical pitfalls? You were going against the grain when you pointed that out. [Some have argued that contract drafters should avoid jargon that clients may not understand in favor of "plain language." Prof. Johnson advises caution about that.]

A: Stylistic changes in drafting are, of course, beneficial to the initial users of any contract. The "plain language" movement suggests that simplifying contractual language makes documents more concise and readable to lay people who are often tasked with performance of the obligations. However, in a situation where contractual obligations are not fulfilled, litigation is often filed to enforce the contract's terms. In those instances, the final arbiter of contractual meaning is often the judge adjudicating the dispute. Judges are constricted by precedent, and precedent often suggests that in absence of specific legal language, certain contractual obligations cannot be enforced. For example, the phrase "time is of the essence" is not necessarily understandable by a layperson. However, without that language, in most jurisdictions a court would rule that failure to timely perform is not a material breach. If the parties intend timely performance to be required, they are best served by the lawyer including this time-tested, consistently-interpreted language.

Q: Do you think plain language still has a place? What advice would you give lawyers on when to use the plain language approach?

A: Plain language most certainly has a place in transactional drafting. Much of the legalese and jargon used in traditional contracts is not in the same category as legally operative terms like "time is of the essence." For example, beginning the recitals of a contract with the term "whereas" adds no meaning, and serves only to make the document seem less accessible to the lay reader. Simply numbering the recitals is a much cleaner, more readable approach. However, drafters of contracts must make conscious decisions when removing such language to ensure that its removal will not have unforeseen legal ramifications. This decision-making process requires attention to detail, and often even some legal research.

Q: As you point out, legal jargon offers precision and that can protect client interests. But the downside of jargon is that clients may not understand what they are being asked to sign. What can a lawyer do to overcome this?

A: Client counseling is a critical component of transactional lawyering. It is our job as attorneys and advocates for our clients to ensure that they are fully cognizant of their obligations under a contract. An ethical lawyer must closely review contracts with their clients and explain legally operative terms that may be unfamiliar.

Q: How should lawyers think about the rule that clients set the objectives of representation, but lawyers also cannot be mere scriveners. There is tension there, right? How can that be navigated?

A: Again, this is a situation where client counseling is critically important. I like to refer to Model Rule of Professional Conduct 2.1, which permits lawyers to advise their clients regarding additional considerations, including "moral, economic, social, and political factors." Our goal should be to ethically engage with our client to achieve their goals. This approach sometimes requires tempering client expectations or adjusting their vision. A transactional lawyer should always serve as an advisor, as well as an advocate and drafter.

X-Ray Questions

Let's follow-up on Professor Johnson's insights.

➤ She has thought quite extensively about the implications of the duties of competence and diligence in contractual drafting. Her concern about legal ethics has led her to push back against the plain language movement. The plain language movement is a school of thought that lawyers should write documents in a style that regular people can understand—meaning avoiding legalese. Prof. Johnson has a different take. She argues that in contract writing, legalese serves a useful purpose. It invokes terminology honed over many years by lawyers and courts to impact precise meanings that protect client's interests. Since the contractual terminology is a means of achieving a client's objectives, Professor Johnson argues that precision should not be sacrificed in an effort to achieve greater accessibility. But one may counter that plain language documents empower clients, while legalese empowers lawyers. Is this a problem? Does Professor Johnson strike the right balance? If not, where should the balance be struck?

➤ Do you agree with her view that zealous advocacy manifests itself differently in the lawyer' role as a transactional advocate as opposed to a straight up litigator/trial lawyer? If so, how so?

➤ True or False? Explain your answer: "The ideal role of the transactional attorney is to draft a document that will provide the greatest benefit to a specific client while attempting to fairly reflect the terms of the deal agreed upon by the parties."

➤ What is an "impermissible" clause, as she characterizes it? Is inserting one in an agreement subject to a possible MR 1.2 violation? Is it not the job of the counsel opposite to counsel their client on what terms to agree to and not the job for the lawyer to do the other side's lawyering for it? Is there a parallel between her thoughts on this topic and what you have already studied in the non-transactional area?

➤ She lists several common causes often seen in agreements. What are the ethical implications of using them?

BEYOND THE CITE

By: Lori D. Johnson, *The Ethics of Non-Traditional Contract Drafting*, 84 U. Cin. L. Rev. 595 (2016).

I.   Introduction

"My biggest problem with modernity may lie in the growing separation of the ethical and the legal." ~ Nassim Nicholas Taleb

The modern transactional attorney's daily practice consists of structuring, counseling, advising, negotiating and drafting the terms of clients' contracts, down to the smallest detail. In essence, using language to bring to life the often complex and delicate arrangements between parties entering into business relationships. The words of a contract can carry millions of dollars worth of importance, can provide the client with rights, or strip them away, depending on how an opposing party or court interprets them. Therefore, every time a transactional lawyer makes a language choice, they are engaging a form of client advocacy, attempting to prepare a contract that sits at the intersection of applicable law, client interests, and the business deal.

Why then, do the American Bar Association (ABA) Model Rules of Professional Conduct (Model Rules) provide such scarce guidance to transactional practitioners engaged in contract drafting choices? The modern transactional attorney is buffeted with choices on how best to structure the language of a client's contract. The lawyer, the law firm, and even the client may have tested forms, and today's drafter may also be trained in the benefits of the plain-language approach to drafting. The way in which the Model Rules apply to transactional attorneys must evolve to provide guidance to attorneys grappling with these competing voices.

This Article seeks to clarify the role of the modern transactional attorney, and show that heightened ethical responsibilities exist when seeking to rephrase traditional, tested contract language into modern prose. Specifically, the competence and diligence duties imposed by the Model Rules require particularly careful research, consideration, and cost-consciousness to be assured that the new construction will efficiently and effectively achieve the client's goals. Further, enhanced communication with the client is required to determine the client's risk tolerance in connection with proposed untested language.

* * *

II. The Plain Language Movement's Impact on Drafting

As the number of law students leaving law school with a foundation in contract drafting instruction increases, so too does the tension between the traditional drafting style employed by some seasoned practitioners, and the influence of the relatively recent call by certain commentators for a broader use of plain language in contract drafting. The dawn of the modern plain language movement has coincided with the increase in legal drafting instruction in law schools, and the game-changing attitudes of some modern drafting scholars concerning modernizing language choices have become more instructive to young lawyers.

The plain language movement began with David Mellinkoff's *The Language of the Law* in 1963 and expanded in Richard Wydick's widely cited *Plain English for Lawyers* in 1979. These works formed the basis of a movement spanning more than fifty years and encompassing hundreds of books in the U.S. and abroad touting its many benefits. While the earliest applications of the movement focused on "consumer contracts" and other public documents, more recently, some scholars of drafting style have argued that its benefits extend to the context of sophisticated contracts.

Specifically, Bryan Garner, in his widely influential book *Legal Writing in Plain English*, suggests applying the plain language movement to contracts to make their language accessible to "ordinary readers." Further, Kenneth Adams, author of the ABA's *Manual of Style for Contract Drafting*, suggests that drafters should "turn[ ] traditional contract prose into a specialized version of standard English." These scholars go beyond the call for the removal of pure "lawyerisms" and suggest revisions to some of the most deeply-rooted language used by contract drafters.

However, going beyond the removal of "pure gobbledygook" and meaningless jargon (such as "aforementioned" and "hereinafter") to suggest a broader re-writing of traditional contract language extends beyond the initial policies of the plain language movement. It is correct that removing most archaic lawyerisms reduces ambiguity and increases readability of contracts. However, earlier proponents of clear drafting style understood that contracts embody a "[c]ommunication based on the language habits" of a particular speech community, and therefore require some "adherence to the existing conventions of language."

Particularly, Reed Dickerson suggested that adherence to traditional language is compelling in the context of transactional drafting because contracts constitute a communication whose "ultimate audience" goes beyond the parties, including "the courts and other agencies that may be called upon to enforce them." While Garner is correct to note that "only a small fraction of 1%" of all contracts are ever litigated, this statistic fails to recognize that the specter of litigation influences the behavior of drafters and parties to contracts in a pre-litigious setting. The certainty of a consistent judicial application in a particular jurisdiction can have significant impact on the choice of terms and parties' behavior in structuring a transaction.

Dickerson's theory concerning the consideration of the judicial reader is reflected by modern drafting scholars who have recognized that best practice in drafting "requires the drafter to think about the contract from the perspective of all persons that may later be called upon to interpret it," including "the parties" as well as "judges, arbitrators, or other decision makers who may be called upon to resolve a dispute by construing the agreement in light of the language, context, and pertinent legal rules."

By suggesting untested constructions in place of traditional terms, Adams and Garner propose the use of experimental constructions in place of language consistently interpreted by decision makers. This choice carries risk avoided when using tested terms. Specifically, the concept of "learning externalities" proposed by Mitu Gulati and Robert Scott suggests that "standard, widely used" terms are known, understood, and less likely to be "erroneous[ly] interpret[ed] by a court." This theory suggests that higher risk of misinterpretation and decreased efficiency may result by the use of alternative, untested language.

Further, modern critics of the plain language movement have noted that terms of art, and even the broader subset of "technical language" of the law remain incomprehensible to a lay audience, despite any rephrasing, because understanding such language requires "specialized knowledge of the legal context" in which the terms operate. Further, any "translation of such expressions" is "insufficient to make them fully intelligible, because their incomprehensibility lies in the fact that they refer to a legal rule, practice, concept, or doctrine" lying outside their plain linguistic meaning.

Nevertheless, one policy suggested in support of removing tested constructions is a resistance to "the idea that if a court offers its interpretation of confusing contract language, we're forevermore committed to using that confusing contract language to convey that meaning." Yet, not all tested terms are confusing, and in some instances, a court's preferred construction of a term may be in the client's best interest. In such circumstance, the ethics of advocacy dictate that a transactional attorney should use the tested term. These ethical obligations must be further explored to understand the ethical duties of the contract drafter in making language choices.

III. Ethical Implications of Drafting

To better understand the weaknesses of the current ethical guidelines as applied to the modern transactional attorney engaged in complex language choices, one must examine: (A) the history of regulation of transactional attorneys in the U.S. legal profession; (B) the absence of neutrality in modern drafting practice; (C) the evolving role of transactional attorneys as advocates in the U.S. legal system; and (D) the existing Model Rules that ethics scholars have argued apply to the behavior of transactional attorneys.

A. History of Professional Regulation of Transactional Attorneys

Little scholarship or commentary exists concerning the ethical duties of attorneys engaged in drafting contracts. The paucity of regulation and discussion of the behavior of transactional attorneys can be traced to the fact that the predecessors to the current Model Rules, including: (i) the ABA Canons of Professional Ethics (the Canons); and (ii) the ABA Code of Professional Responsibility (the Code), focused primarily on the behavior of litigating attorneys.

The Canons, published in 1908, "dealt almost exclusively with the dilemmas" of the litigator, and the Code, published in 1969, offered little improvement. Even the "aspirational" Ethical Considerations of the Code, meant to "suggest proper ethical behavior" served as "basically a guide to the litigating attorney" working in the adversarial context.

Scholars active at the time of the drafting of the Code recognized an ongoing "historical bias" toward regulating the role of the litigator more stringently than the role of the transactional attorney. Even as early as 1976, ethics scholars noted this bias was "inappropriate" due to the evolving role of the mid-century transactional attorney as a counselor and advisor in preventive functions.

Nonetheless, the current Model Rules, originally drafted in 1983, a version of which have been adopted in 49 states and the District of Columbia, are similarly premised on an adversarial, litigation-based system. Modern drafting scholars have acknowledged that "with limited exceptions" there are no Model Rules directly on point concerning professional behavior by transactional attorneys.

The few Model Rules acknowledged as applying to the role of the transactional attorney provide limitations on making misrepresentations and assisting clients in undertaking fraudulent behavior. Beyond these fraud-based proscriptions, the Model Rules provide little guidance to transactional attorneys in their daily tasks of translating clients' cooperative business deals into workable and enforceable documents. Such work often goes on behind closed doors, rather than in the open forum of the courtroom, making discipline more difficult. However, the informal nature of transactional practice should provide a strong incentive for a more readily applicable set of behavioral standards.

Consistent with the goal of attempting to regulate the behavior of attorneys during the drafting process, Gregory Duhl authored a recent and comprehensive examination of the ethics of contract drafting. Duhl's analysis supports a thesis that the goal of ethical obligations imposed on drafters should be consistent with contract law and its purpose of promoting trust between contracting parties. However, this obligation exists in tension with the reality that in the sophisticated commercial context, each side to the transaction typically retains their own counsel, who draft and negotiate contract terms on their specific client's behalf.

Complicating the issue of regulating ethics during the drafting process is the private nature of such non-litigation practice. Most often, errors and ethical lapses in drafting are only discovered and raised by a party seeking to "avoid an unfavorable contract" after its execution. Additionally, the role of the drafter is often "unconstrained by" the types of "formal procedures" applicable to trial attorneys, making it "more difficult to state comprehensively the ethical considerations" of transactional practice.

This article proposes that ethical guidelines for contract drafters arise from a broader set of Model Rules than those most often identified by ethics and drafting scholars. Further, the applicable Model Rules should, whether through interpretive opinions by the ABA, revisions to the comments to the Model Rules, or otherwise, be designed as clear and enforceable at the time of the initial drafting and negotiation of a contract. Such an understanding and potential revision of the Model Rules encourages ethical behavior throughout the contract drafting process, particularly in light of the aforementioned calls for changes in contract language.

B. Role of the Modern Transactional Attorney: Not a Mere Scrivener

To understand legal ethics as applied to the modern practice of sophisticated contract drafting, those regulating the profession must come to understand the multifaceted role of today's sophisticated transactional attorney. While litigators and clients may view the art of drafting as mere "wordsmithing," and scholars of ethics tend to treat transactional attorneys as advisors rather than advocates, neither of these views provides a complete understanding of current sophisticated transactional practice. Therefore, Duhl's notion of the promotion of trust as a basis for ethical obligations in transactional practice faces challenges grounded in misunderstandings of the modern transactional attorney's role.

Yet, Duhl's concept of trust creation has its merits. First, the aspirational goal of promoting trust between parties might serve as an appropriate basis for drafting ethics where opposing parties have been categorically unrepresented. An example is attorney preparation of form or adhesion contracts applying to consumers or individuals who will sign with little or no chance to review or negotiate the terms. In such circumstances, ethics scholars have warned that drafters should attempt to do away with the sense of "adversarial tradition" and draft fairly to promote trust. However, this is not the usual scenario in complex transactional practice in the U.S., where each party typically retains its own counsel and terms are heavily negotiated between parties.

Additionally, Duhl's ideal of trust in drafting ethics could also apply in a legal system where the drafter of the contract acts as a neutral scrivener. For example, civil law countries employ notaries to draft transactional documents to reflect the "subjective will of *all parties*." These neutral scriveners also counsel all parties in connection with the terms and consequences of the documents. In this role, civil law notaries act objectively to promote trust in ways not undertaken (and not permitted) by U.S. transactional attorneys. In a notarial system, the ideal of trust promotion could also help to shape ethical guidelines.

However, in the drafting and negotiation of sophisticated contracts in the U.S., each side of the deal typically retains their own attorney, responsible for negotiating, reviewing, and drafting contract terms on their behalf. While it is possible in some circumstances for a U.S. attorney to be retained as a neutral scrivener of a document, this is an unusual scenario wherein the drafter must take extreme care to clearly define her role as representative of neither party individually. Doing so is fraught with potential conflicts of interest under the Model Rules, and therefore most often avoided by the prudent attorney.

Even in a friendly, cooperative transaction, there exists the possibility that the structure of an agreement or inclusion of a particular term will benefit one side or another. Proceeding with dual representation in the face of this specter of conflict is prohibited under Model Rule 1.7, which provides that "a lawyer shall not represent a client if . . . there is a significant risk that the representation of one or more clients will be materially limited by the lawyer's responsibilities to another client."

Scholars of transactional law and ethics have recognized that the directly adverse conflicts prohibited under Model Rule 1.7 "can . . . arise in transactional matters." The revisions to the Model Rules in 2000 even expanded the commentary to Model Rule 1.7 to clarify that the rules "equate the representation of buyers or sellers in buy-sale transactions with the representation of plaintiffs or defendants in lawsuits."

As such, the Model Rules implicitly recognize "the same amount of adversity," between attorneys representing opposing parties in buy-sell type transactions and those engaged in litigation. While it has been noted that the Model Rules themselves "do not provide a clear answer about whether business advisors should be guided by zealous advocacy," the practice of transactional lawyering clearly positions attorneys to advance client goals, which constitutes some level of advocacy. Thus, the suggested modes of viewing drafters as neutral, trust-promoting advisors are insufficient, and the related attempts to provided ethical guidelines on this basis fall short.

C.   *Boundaries on the Transactional Attorney as Advocate*

One weakness of the existing scholarship on drafting ethics is rooted in the traditional paradigm of the litigator as "advocate," and the transactional attorney as "advisor." As demonstrated, there exists more overlap between these two realms than traditionally understood. At the root of this tension lies the "incomplete and often confusing messages found in professional conduct rules about the business advisor's role." The role of the transactional attorney must be re-examined and reframed in order to determine the most advantageous set of ethical guidelines for the modern transactional attorney.

Modern scholars of drafting recognize that today's transactional attorneys do not merely draft contracts, but also negotiate disputes, analyze precedent, evaluate business issues, and "add value to the deal" by "advance [ing] client objectives." Even traditional ethics scholars who promoted the old-fashioned framing of the transactional attorney's role as a pure advisor were forced to recognize that the attorney's task in structuring a transaction "is to guide the client . . . to act in such a manner that the result will be *beneficial*."

This shift in perception is reflected in modern scholarship concerning the best practices of transactional attorneys, which recognizes that client expectations are the "foremost" concern of the good drafter. The question becomes how a transactional attorney should ideally strive to achieve this benefit for the client when the Model Rules fail to provide the same "comprehensive, consistent guidance" provided to litigators.

It is clear that the traditional construct of the "zealous advocate" often championed by the litigator does not provide a good fit for the role of the modern transactional attorney. Advocacy that is too zealous can lure the transactional attorney into acting more as the client's "instrument" in entering into potentially ill-advised, though technically legal, transactions. Overzealous advocacy on behalf of a transactional client can begin to hedge toward fraud, one of the main problems currently recognized by ethics scholars and regulated by the Model Rules in the transactional setting. This issue is further discussed in Part III.D. of this Article.

The ideal role of the transactional attorney is to draft a document that will provide the greatest benefit to a specific client while attempting to fairly reflect the terms of the deal agreed upon by the parties. In this way, a transactional attorney can still "add value to the deal" from a client's perspective while avoiding "crossing the line" into re-cutting the deal or committing fraud. The value the attorney adds for the client can include persuading opposing parties to act in favorable ways during the term of the contract as well as setting the client up for success in advance of a potential dispute.

As such, the "best approach" to contract drafting is "one that is deal-preserving and with the judge in mind." This recognition of client benefit is not wholly inconsistent with the idea of contract drafting as a fair and cooperative enterprise. Contract drafting experts have noted that a "contract can be both pro-client and pro-relationship at the same time." A contract that withstands the interpretation of a court and aligns party interests "will ultimately be in [the] client's best interest."

When viewing a contract as a document that exists to persuade parties to act in favorable ways and gives rise to favorable interpretations, it becomes clear that drafting terms in a contract on behalf of a client constitutes a form of advocacy. Scholars of rhetoric and advocacy have noted that agreement with a proposed conclusion "rests upon the ability of one proponent to persuade another, or to persuade an authoritative decision maker, to read a document or to understand a situation in a certain way." This mode of persuasion is most certainly undertaken by a sophisticated drafter preparing a contract on behalf of a client.

Thus, contract drafters' attempts to control the actions of opposing parties and interpretations of a judge constitute advocacy. As such, these actions become part of the adversarial system that the Model Rules attempt to regulate. However, the Model Rules, as currently interpreted and enforced, do not provide guidance to transactional attorneys engaged in the role of advocate. Many checks placed on the advocacy of attorneys under the Model Rules are inherent in "the watching" function of the courts. Yet, "no one is watching" when a transactional attorney is at work.

Recognizing contract drafting as the work of two or more advocates, it is simply insufficient to rely on the limited guidance of the Model Rules currently identified in scholarship as applying to transactional practitioners and hope that "attorneys . . . police each other." There are only a handful of Model Rules and related comments commonly identified to constrain drafters' conduct. These limitations primarily are focused on the commission of fraud. A deeper discussion of the Model Rules, as currently interpreted, and identification of opportunities within the existing Model Rules to shape the behavior of contract drafters as advocates must be undertaken.

D. Enforcement Against Transactional Attorneys Under the Current Model Rules

In his recent examination of the ethics of contract drafting, Gregory Duhl argued that the most evident violations of the Model Rules by contract drafters occur where the drafter engages in fraudulent or "fraudulent-type" behavior. These behaviors are regulated under Model Rules 1.2(d), 4.1(a) and

(b) and 8.4. Yet, these rules "place only limited restrictions on a lawyer's conduct in drafting contracts."

Specifically, Rule 1.2(d) states that "[a] lawyer shall not counsel a client to engage, or assist a client, in conduct that the lawyer knows is criminal or fraudulent." Rule 4.1 states that

> [i]n the course of representing a client a lawyer shall not knowingly . . . fail to disclose a material fact when disclosure is necessary to avoid assisting a criminal or fraudulent act by a client." Finally, Rule 8.4 says "[i]t is professional misconduct for a lawyer to . . . engage in conduct involving dishonesty, fraud, deceit or misrepresentation.

Based on these rules, Duhl hypothesizes three types of fraudulent or near-fraudulent drafting that could result in ethical violations: (a) knowingly drafting false representations and warranties; (b) committing fraud, conscious ambiguity, or transcription error; and (c) knowingly drafting invalid or "iffy" provisions.

These violations envision a spectrum of behavior in the realm of fraud and deception, but not including reckless or negligent behavior. Drafting expert Tina Stark agrees that whether a drafter's behavior "cross[es] the line" into the realm of the unethical is judged on a spectrum. Stark notes the emphasis on fraud in the current Model Rules, and posits a theory of "intersectionality" where client behavior falls on a spectrum ranging from legal and not fraudulent, to criminal and fraudulent. A lawyer's actions in assisting the client move in tandem from ethical to unethical in relation to the client's place on the spectrum, with some gray area at the midpoint of the scale.

Yet, according to Duhl, the Model Rules do provide some concrete guidance as to where certain types of drafter behavior will fall on such an ethical scale. Specifically, Model Rule 1.0 defines the term "fraud" for purposes of discipline to require "a purpose to deceive." Duhl suggests that some form of scienter by the attorney must be present for the fraud-based Model Rules he identifies (1.2(d), 4.1(a), (b), 8.4) to be violated. Additionally, no reliance or injury need occur, as the Model Rules themselves do not require such. According to Duhl, the inquiry into violation of the Model Rules on the basis of fraud turns on the existence of intent to deceive by the attorney, rather than the outcome or injury.

Duhl notes that one of the clearest behaviors that could land an attorney in disciplinary hot water is knowingly incorporating misrepresentations of material facts, such as misstatements of company financial information, into a contract. If the contract is executed, the attorney has assisted a fraud in violation of Rule 1.2(d), and even if the contract stalls, the inclusion by the attorney of the terms in a draft contract could constitute an indirect "representation that the statements are true" in violation of Rules 4.1(a) and 8.4.

Duhl notes additional drafting behaviors on the clearly-fraudulent end of the spectrum, including attorneys' failure disclose scrivener's errors made by opposing parties, and concealment or failure to point out alterations to a document. Duhl's examination of the "more subtle form[s]" of potential drafting fraud are of more interest and paint a closer picture to the question at hand, dealing with the use of innovative and untested plain language in contract drafting.

In his analysis of drafting behavior that runs afoul of the Model Rules as currently interpreted, Duhl notes two types of behavior that fall into the gray area between clearly fraudulent and clearly permissible. The first being the use of "conscious ambiguity," which Duhl defines as an attorney's knowing use of "a clause in an agreement with two contradictory meanings" or to which "the parties attach different meanings." Duhl notes that such behavior "at its extreme" could be considered " 'dishonest' and violate Rule 8.4."

Next, Duhl delves into the biggest gray area, the inclusion of "iffy" or potentially "invalid" terms. The types of terms Duhl highlights include "impermissible" clauses that "mislead parties"—especially consumers—as to their rights. He determines that the inclusion of such clauses could rise to the level of fraud in violation of Model Rule 1.2(d), but only where the clause is known to be invalid and likely to mislead—rather than merely "iffy."

While "iffy" or unenforceable clauses pose a slightly different consideration from the re-drafting of traditional clauses into modern language, the ethical implications are similar. In the case of an untested construction of a traditional term, a lawyer is less sure of the potential judicial interpretation of a clause. Therefore, using such a clause brings more potential risk than the use of a tested clause. It follows that Duhl's recognition of the heightened burden of knowledge about the clause's potential enforceability applies in both circumstances.

By analogizing the drafting of "iffy" clauses to the redrafting of tested terms into untested modern language, it becomes clear that the Model Rules require a measure of research-based knowledge as to the meaning and enforceability of untested contract terms before they are included in a contract. This Article continues by positing that this knowledge requirement invokes the drafting attorney's ethical obligations of competence, allocation of authority, diligence, and communication.

IV. Applying the Model Rules to Modern Drafting Style

Due to the focus on fraudulent drafting, ethics scholars overlook the potential applicability of other core ethical rules to the practice of transactional drafting. Specifically, Model Rules 1.1, 1.2, 1.3, and 1.4, concerning competence, allocation of authority, diligence, and communication respectively, are not frequently or deeply discussed in connection with the ethical duties of attorneys drafting contracts. However, each of the aforementioned rules applies when one views transactional attorneys as advocates engaged in persuasive word choices advancing client interests. The Model Rules themselves recognize that all attorneys, even transactional attorneys, carry the role of advocate, by requiring all attorneys to "act with competence, commitment and dedication to the interest of the client . . . upon the client's behalf."

The Model Rules discussed below put in place important safeguards on lawyers' behavior as advocates, and certainly apply to attorneys making non-traditional language choices in contracts. These advocacy-oriented rules require the lawyer to be fully informed of the relevant precedent, to undertake the work necessary to be assured that unique phrasing of clauses does not disadvantage the client, and to keep the client informed of and involved in the decisions the lawyer makes concerning word choices.

The potential impact of each of these Model Rules on the behavior of attorneys using non-traditional terms will be discussed. The analysis will begin with the competence and diligence rules, and then analyze the allocation of authority and communication rules in tandem.

A. Model Rule 1.1—Competence

The competence duty under the Model Rules requires that "[a] lawyer shall provide competent representation to a client," which entails "the legal knowledge, skill, thoroughness, and preparation reasonably necessary for the representation." Broadly speaking, this duty imposes upon attorneys "an ethical obligation to write well." Simply being "exposed to contract drafting" either in law school or in practice does not prepare an attorney to competently draft.

Expertise in drafting, as in any legal discipline, can be obtained through "necessary study," as provided in the comments to Model Rule 1.1. However, competence in drafting requires not only a "thorough grounding in contract law" but also a more nuanced understanding of how the law "is to be applied on behalf of the client." A core competency in contract drafting requires adequate satisfaction of the "client's wishes by the provisions of the document." In this way, the competence duty necessitates client advocacy, in conjunction with the requirement that the document be appropriately drafted and enforceable.

Further, the transactional attorney, like any other lawyer, "should be careful in performing legal work." Specifically, it long has been noted that the duties of an attorney structuring a transaction require "an examination of legal and extra-legal indicators, the most well-recognized of which is how a court will respond to a given factual situation." The drafter must consider whether "a court will rule unfavorably if certain facts occur." To make these determinations, a transactional lawyer must attain a strong "background in the legal rules governing contract interpretation" as well as "a routine for keeping current on relevant statutory mandates and case law."

This level of competence requires knowledge of the typical interpretation of tested terms and recognition that non-traditional word choices may give rise to unpredictable applications by a court in a variety of factual scenarios. Therefore, in fulfilling her ethical obligations, the drafter must recognize her duty as an advocate of the client and consider whether the use of a non-traditional term helps or harms the client if the contract falls into dispute.

In a rare, early discussion of the competence duty as it relates to the role of the transactional attorney, an article by ethics scholars Louis M. Brown and Harold A. Brown noted that competence is best served in the transactional context by considering the "damage which could be done to the [transactional] client by incompetence." Therefore, competence in the transactional context requires not merely knowledge of the applicable law, but also applying a lawyer's legal knowledge to the particular needs of a particular client.

The transactional lawyer's "aspirations of competence" should include attaining "the knowledge and skill to grasp the client's goals, to reframe them if necessary, to initiate the discussion of alternative courses of conduct and, along with the client, to be creative regarding the uses of the law." This early framing of the duty by the Brown article implicitly requires that the transactional attorney use the law in the way most beneficial to achieving such client goals.

A more recent article provides another framework for applying the competence rule to transactional attorneys. Christina Kunz posits that transactional attorneys drafting contracts have a heightened competence duty when it comes to potentially invalid clauses. She notes that Comment 2 to Model Rule 1.1 mentions "some important legal skills, such as the analysis of precedent . . . and legal drafting, [that] are required in all legal problems." Such problems include drafting contract terms and require the analysis of precedent concerning the potential interpretation the term. Kunz focuses on substantively "iffy" clauses, but the uncertainty of judicial interpretation associated with untested variations of traditional terms is analogical.

This duty to research and inform is particularly high where, as Kunz notes, the particular clause has been "criticized" in another jurisdiction. In such a case, Kunz suggests that "[t]he lawyer should seriously consider urging the client to consider practicalities," such as effects on the "parties' relationship, performance on both sides, public perceptions, other contracts with the same language and other concurrent negotiations."

The same considerations ring true for a lawyer's decision to rephrase a clause with a settled meaning into terms that have a less predictable method of interpretation in the courts. The lawyer must consider and advise the client of potential risks concerning the way other parties will view the clause, whether other contracts exist which use the more modern language in lieu of the traditional phrases, whether those contracts have been litigated, and the view of the jurisdiction in which the contract will be enforced.

Further, the duty to be informed about the view of the jurisdiction in which the contract will be enforced is critically important to drafting a contract that provides benefit to the client, a recognized goal of the transactional attorney. Since contracts are essentially authorless documents, it has been recognized in literary scholarship that contracts "enlist the attendant authority of the law." Thus, courts' interpretations of the meaning of contract language become a critically important mode by which a drafter can set boundaries around meaning, and therefore control potential outcomes for a client.

It is settled that liability for legal malpractice may not arise in circumstances where the law is unsettled as to whether to include certain terms in a document. However, this does not negate the fact that "[l]egal uncertainty can manifest in the preparation of documents if the precise language and content have not been judicially construed." This uncertainty affects the decision whether the competent lawyer should rephrase a tested term into a modern, untested variation.

While attorneys are not "required to predict infallibly how a court will interpret documents that they have drafted," the competence duty requires "the legal knowledge, skill, thoroughness, and preparation reasonably necessary for the representation." This baseline level of knowledge includes knowledge about the preferred phrasing of terms, or at the very least, current, applicable judicial interpretations of terms selected.

The requirement of deeply researching and understanding the impact of rephrasing terms as an element of competency is heightened in the context of contract drafting, because "each word or provision in a contract may be subjected to greater scrutiny and challenge by opposing counsel whereas the meanings of words or phrases in a brief or pleading are rarely the primary target or focus of even the most zealous advocate."

And yet, even in litigation documents, such as complaints, where word choices are of less import, the competent attorney is exhorted to rely on "legal precedent" and perform "sufficient research and analysis" to be assured that the document adequately advances a client's claim. It has been considered a failure of competence to advance "novel claims and new interpretations of law" in a complaint insufficiently supported by precedent. Similarly, the competent transactional lawyer should not use untested terms in a contract without a deep, thoroughly researched consideration of the consequences on enforceability, parties' behaviors, and potential judicial interpretations.

B. Model Rule 1.3—Diligence

The diligence duty under the Model Rules requires that "[a] lawyer . . . act with reasonable diligence and promptness in representing a client," including "tak[ing] whatever lawful and ethical measures are required to vindicate a client's cause." In fulfilling this duty, the lawyer must act "with commitment and dedication to the interests of the client and with zeal in advocacy upon the client's behalf," yet the "lawyer is not bound . . . to press for every advantage that may be realized for a client."

Further, because the diligence duty requires "promptness," the "modifying [of] a previously drafted contract," which would likely include tested terms of art, "require[s] significantly less time than drafting a contract from scratch." Such widely-available contracts and terms not only aid the attorney in meeting the promptness requirement, but may also assist in furthering the interests of the client, as traditionally-composed contracts are often "generally accepted within the industry" in which the client operates.

Of course, the competence duty requires that such standard forms be fully understood, researched, and reviewed, so as not be used "blindly." As noted, "[g]ood drafting takes care, practice, sound judgment, and a lot of effort." Nonetheless, the " 'precedent-based drafting approach' . . . makes sense" in many circumstances, particularly where clients are fee-sensitive, operate in a highly standardized industry, or the lawyer has developed the forms based on research and practice experience.

As has been noted by drafting scholars, "the lawyer owes a duty to the client to keep . . . legal fees on a diet," a goal which can be achieved through drafting a contract which "rais[es] few issues." The higher risk and added research burdens arising under the competence duty when using untested language would undoubtedly increase fees. Therefore, particularly with regard to fee-sensitive clients, use of non-traditional language and the attendant increase in related research fees may constitute an unethical disservice.

In all cases, the lawyer has a duty to communicate with the client at the outset of the relationship concerning the client's expectations regarding fees, as well as the client's tolerance for increased costs based on non-traditional language changes. Discussion of these issues comprises the basis of the allocation of authority between the attorney and client, as well as the communication duty of the attorney, which will be discussed below.

C. Model Rules 1.2 and 1.4—Allocation of Authority & Communication

Model Rule 1.2 provides that "a lawyer shall abide by a client's decisions concerning the objectives of the representation and, as required by Rule 1.4, shall consult with the client as to the means by which they are to be pursued." The comments to Model Rule 1.2 make clear that decisions concerning "the purpose" of the representation are allocated to the client, while the decisions of the lawyer are entitled to deference concerning the "means to be used to accomplish [client] objectives, particularly with respect to technical, legal and tactical matters."

This allocation of authority regarding the "means" of the representation, however, is subject to communication with the client, as emphasized in the text of and comments to Model Rule 1.2(a). Specifically, Comment 1 to Model Rule 1.2 invokes the communication requirement under Model Rule 1.4(a)(2) concerning the means utilized by the lawyer to achieve the client's objective. To properly follow this rule, a lawyer must "reasonably consult with the client about the means by which the client's objectives are to be accomplished." The duties under Model Rules 1.2 and 1.4 are therefore inextricably linked when dealing with choices made by a transactional attorney in drafting documents on a client's behalf.

Specifically, it has been recognized by scholars of drafting ethics that "[i]n drafting documents on behalf of a client, the lawyer clearly has an obligation to explain the contents of those documents to the client so that the client understands the legal ramifications of executing the documents." Further, even where the "underlying conduct of the attorney is appropriate" there exists a requirement to advise the client about the consequences of a proposed construction of a contract.

Thus, the research and recognition of potential uncertainty associated with the use of untested terms required under the competence duty trigger an enhanced duty to inform the client under Model Rule 1.4(a)(2). This requirement enhances the historical view of the heightened requirements of Model Rule 1.4 in the transactional setting. In the context of a transactional representation, the client is the lawyer's *"raison d'etre"* and therefore the "amount of communication" required to ensure the lawyer is fulfilling the client's goal "may be much greater" than in litigation practice.

Christina Kunz in her article on drafting ethics under the UCC notes that "[i]n many situations, a candid dialogue between lawyer and client will resolve the ethical tension" associated with the selection of "iffy" clauses. She notes the need for balance between the rights of opposing parties and the requirement for zealous representation as motivating the lawyer's decisions regarding how to draft clauses in these circumstances.

Thus, in deciding whether to incorporate a non-traditional construction of a tested term, a transactional attorney has the duty to consult and communicate with the client regarding the potential outcomes and uncertainty associated with such choice. This duty has not been clearly delineated with regard to the transactional practitioner. However, as the interpretation of an untested term certainly could impact the outcome and enforcement of a contract by a judge, this decision inherently is connected to the "objectives" or outcomes of the representation.

Model Rule 1.2 allocates decisions concerning the outcome of representation to the client. Model Rule 1.2 requires careful explanation by the attorney before such rephrasing occurs. Additionally, the lawyer should defer to the client concerning associated potential increases in fees. Practically speaking, the Model Rules require the attorney to explain and confirm with the client the decision to cast aside traditional terms of art in a contract that has well-documented, consistent judicial interpretations. This is particularly true where tested interpretations effectively achieve the client's objective at a lower cost.

Further, a failure of the attorney to gain an understanding of the nature of the client's "business objectives" could also lead to an inability to meet the requirements of Model Rule 1.2. This is especially true where the client operates in a particular industry. Typically, industries will operate and communicate using specialized "customs and jargon," the understanding of which may be essential to achieving the client's goals.

In such cases, redrafting of tested terms, even where helpful to clarity or brevity, may undercut the client's position vis-à-vis contracting parties in a heavily regulated industry. Model Rules 1.2 and 1.4, properly viewed, require consultation with the client concerning the potential impact on client objectives in these circumstances. As a result, revision of traditional terms into alternative language may lead to frustration of client goals, potentially resulting in ethical violations.

This discussion ebbs into the practical considerations of how a transactional attorney can meet their ethical duties when faced with the call for a broader use of plain language. In order to better understand the problems posed by language choices, and the ethical implications of the behavior of drafters in making these choices, one must turn to case studies of attorneys in practice.

V.   Case Studies: Drafters & Language Choice

In order to demonstrate the problem faced by drafters when seeking to modernize traditional language, one must analyze specific suggestions made by plain language drafting commentators and apply the holdings of recent case law dealing with such language choices. The below examples constitute only a handful of recent instances of courts' interpretations of traditional contract language to the detriment of contract parties. Further, in order to illustrate the duty to communicate the impact of these changes to clients, one also must review malpractice decisions concerning languages choices.

A.   The Problem of Shall vs. Will

One of the most pioneering recent suggestions for the modernization of contract language comes from Bryan Garner, who instructs drafters to "[d]elete every *shall.*" Garner correctly notes that shall very often is misused by drafters. The term shall is "supposed to mean 'has a duty to,'" but it often is distorted by drafters who pair it with "neither" or "nothing," to alter its meaning.

Despite the efforts of other drafting experts to reform and standardize the use of shall (by instructing drafters to limit their use of the term only to statements of obligation), Garner is still safe to surmise that based on its rampant misuse, the term "*shall* is a mess." Garner notes that a shall-less style in transactional drafting is preferable and suggests the use of the term "will" to indicate obligation.

While Garner and the other critics of shall have a valid point, that the misuse of the term is endemic, the ethical drafter must consider in each circumstance whether the *appropriate* use of the term might be more likely to achieve a client's goals. In order to fulfill the duties of competence and diligence, a lawyer must be informed as to whether controlling law in the jurisdiction in which the contract will be enforced has criticized the use of "will" as an alternative.

For example, a recent case out of the Supreme Court of Texas refused to find an obligation where the term "will" was used. In the *Lubbock* opinion, the court interpreted the terms of a lease between the Lubbock County Water Control and Improvement District (the Water District) and Church & Akin, L.L.C. (the Company).

The Water District had leased property to the Company, on which the Company operated a marina, gasoline station, and convenience store. The lease provided, in pertinent part, that "[t]he marina *will* issue catering tickets that *will* be redeemed at the gate for admittance to the lake. These tickets *will* be redeemed by the marina at the price of $1.00 each. They *will* only be available to persons coming into the marina."

Counsel for the Company argued this provision obligated the Company to regulate access to the marina, thus providing a service to the Water District for purposes of obtaining a waiver of the Water District's sovereign immunity. The court disagreed, based in part on a finding that the language did not "constitute an agreement by [the Company] to provide a service" to the Water District. Specifically, the court noted that the provision created no "implied duty" on the part of the Company to issue the tickets. Rather, the court found that the provision stood for the proposition that the Company "intended to" issue the tickets.

The court's majority opinion was met with a vigorous dissent, agreeing with the Company's position that the disputed term created an obligation sufficient to fall under the statutory waiver of immunity applied to contracts for provision of services to a government entity. The dissent argued that "[i]n this context, 'will,' although it has many possible meanings depending on context, here indicates a mandatory requirement."

Nonetheless, this opinion creates a strong uncertainty as to whether Garner's preferred method of obligating parties to act is enforceable in a Texas court. Based on the ethical duties discussed in Part IV, it is clear that a competent, diligent attorney practicing in Texas would do well to research this issue, and if the attorney intended to use the term "will," as suggested by Garner, advise the client of the associated risks of enforcement.

B. The Problem of Claims "Arising Out of or Relating to" a Contract

The phrase "arising out of or relating to" is a consistently used component of many contracts' dispute resolution provisions. Traditionally, contract drafters who desire a broad arbitration provision provide that mandatory arbitration applies to disputes "arising out of or relating to" the particular contract, and those who desire a more narrow construction use the phrase "arising under" the contract. The addition of the phrase "relating to" is typically interpreted to broaden the arbitration provision to apply not only to contract disputes, but also to other disputes such as tort claims between the parties to the contract.

Plain-language drafting proponent Kenneth Adams expresses concerns related to the use of the traditional language as the method to set the scope of the coverage of dispute resolution provisions. Specifically, Adams notes that:

> It would indeed be a good idea to state precisely the types of claims
> that are to be submitted to arbitration. But instead of precision,

arising out of or relating to uses two vague standards that offer little predictability as to what falls within the scope of the provision. In particular, invoking the broader *relating to* standard could result in a party's being unpleasantly surprised by the consequences of something unexpectedly falling within the scope of the provision.

As an alternative, Adams suggests focusing on "the transaction contemplated by the contract." For example, with regard to a confidentiality provision, Adams suggests using the phrase "*any disputes arising out of this agreement or the Recipient's handling, disclosure, or use of any Confidential Information.*" According to Adams, this approach would permit parties to bring a "broad but predictable set of claims within the scope of a provision."

However, Adams' approach fails to take into account the consistently broad judicial interpretations of arbitration clauses, however phrased, particularly in the federal courts. In fact, the issue of unpredictable judicial interpretation is not necessarily solved by the use of a more transaction-focused arbitration provision. In a recent case, the Court of Appeals of Georgia ordered arbitration based on a broad interpretation of a very specific, transaction-oriented clause.

In *Kormanik*, Chris and Mary Kormanik sued DBGS, LLC d/b/a DirectBuy of Greenville (DirectBuy) for negligent misrepresentation based on shoddy work by a contractor recommended to them by DirectBuy. The Kormanik's membership agreement with DirectBuy provided:

> [DirectBuy] staff and . . . [o]wners stand ready to help you resolve *any problem you may encounter with your Membership or with any order you place through DirectBuy,* but if we are not able to achieve a satisfactory resolution for you, you and we agree to avoid the needless delays, expenses, and uncertainties of court proceedings by submitting all such unresolved disputes exclusively to private, expedited, and confidential arbitration.

DirectBuy sought to arbitrate the Kormaniks' claim regarding the recommended contractor pursuant to the foregoing provision, but the trial court denied DirectBuy's motion to compel arbitration "on the ground that the Kormaniks' claim for negligent misrepresentation concerning the contractor recommendation did not involve their DirectBuy membership or . . . a problem with their order." However, the Court of Appeals of Georgia reversed, noting Georgia's "clear public policy in favor of arbitration."

The use of the phrase "any problem you may encounter with your Membership or with any order" comes closer to Adams' suggestion that arbitration provisions focus on the "transaction contemplated by the contract" (in this case, the Kormaniks' membership in a company selling home furnishings and fixtures). However, the court in *Kormanik* imposed a far broader reading of the provision than either party could have predicted, compelling arbitration on a claim relating to an outside contractor recommendation.

The court took guidance from the broad interpretation of arbitration clauses in federal cases, noting that Georgia's arbitration code "closely tracks" federal arbitration law. The court found that "[a]s a matter of federal law, any doubts concerning the scope of arbitrable issues should be resolved in favor of arbitration." The court looked to the "factual allegations in the complaint" rather than the "legal causes of action" to determine that the negligent misrepresentation claim fell under the seemingly narrow arbitration clause.

Thus, the parties to the contract in *Kormanik*, should they have desired to keep their arbitration clause more narrow, would have been better served by including the traditional narrowing phrase "arising under" (which was absent from the arbitration clause in question). Instead, the use of non-traditional, transaction-focused language, led to an unpredictable judicial result.

The court's broad interpretation of the language in *Kormanik* demonstrates the potentially unpredictable results of an arbitration clause, even one that follows Adams' advice to focus on the transaction rather than traditional scope-defining terms. The *Kormanik* case makes clear that even a very detailed, non-traditional construction can still lead to an unpredictable result based on the policies of the jurisdiction in which the language is interpreted.

Based on this precedent and the associated risk of broad interpretation, the competent and diligent drafter should research precedent of the jurisdiction in which the contract is likely to be enforced to determine how broadly an arbitration agreement will be construed and advise the client with regard to the risks associated with any proposed construction of the term. Even a seemingly narrow construction of a clause term might lead to more unpredictable results than a traditional term, depending on judicial interpretation.

C. Malpractice and Informing the Client

The foregoing cases provide examples of outcomes of non-traditional drafting resulting in injury to a client's position. These cases highlight the need for competence and diligence in researching and understanding the laws of the jurisdiction in which a drafter works in order to make informed language choices. However, neither case discusses the duties of the drafter during the contract formation phase in communicating with clients concerning potential language changes.

Cases concerning violations of Model Rule 1.4 dealing with communication in the transactional context are scarce. Therefore, one must turn to legal malpractice cases to find examples of the level of communication required between lawyer and client when considering language changes in contracts during the negotiation and drafting phases. Malpractice cases have imposed a requirement for attorneys to explain operative language choices to clients, even sophisticated clients, if those language changes can have potential consequences of interpretation.

In a relevant case before the Supreme Court of New York, Appellate Division, the law firm of Mandel, Resnik & Kaiser (Mandel) was retained to represent E.I. Electronics, Inc. (EIE) in a transaction whereby EIE "was to be acquired, in whole or in part," by General Electric (GE). The court laid out the stages of the proposed transaction:

> The acquisition was structured in three stages: (1) an initial purchase [by GE] of a 35% interest [in EIE], (2) a call option exercisable by GE enabling it to purchase an additional 14% interest and (3) a put option exercisable by [EIE] requiring GE to purchase the remaining interest in [EIE].

An original version of the agreement drafted by the Mandel firm provided that EIE's put option (forcing GE to buy the remaining shares in EIE), was exercisable at any time after GE's call option period expired. The final, signed version, however, included a change made by the Mandel firm, in response to negotiations with GE's attorneys, that made the exercise of the put option conditional on the call option having been exercised. In essence, the final version, as drafted by the Mandel firm, made EIE's ability to exercise the lucrative put option contingent upon GE's exercising its call option first.

Erran Kagan, the principal of EIE, a sophisticated businessman and licensed attorney, later disputed the changes to the agreement and refused to pay Mandel's attorney's fees. Mandel sued EIE for unpaid fees, and EIE counterclaimed for legal malpractice. In the counterclaim, EIE alleged that the Mandel firm, in negotiating and drafting the terms of the put option, permitted changes to the provision not sufficiently explained to Erran Kagan. EIE and Kagan claimed that the effect of the changes robbed them of their ability to exercise their desired put option.

In denying the Mandel firm's motion for summary judgment on the malpractice claim and remanding for further fact-finding, the court's primary concern was that the Mandel firm had "failed to apprise [Kagan] concerning the effect of the amendment to its put option." Mandel made "no assertion that the change was discussed with Erran Kagan or that its significance was explained." The court downplayed the importance of Kagan's sophistication, noting that a question of fact remained regarding the "extent of the reliance" by Kagan on Mandel's advice, and the extent to which Kagan "understood the word 'closing' " as included in the document.

While the *Mandel* decision was a malpractice case rather than an ethics opinion, the court's analysis is instructive with regard to the competence, diligence, allocation of authority, and communication duties of an attorney under the Model Rules as discussed in Part IV of this Article. One of the required elements of a malpractice action in New York, where the *Mandel* case was litigated, requires the plaintiff to prove that the defendant attorney "failed to exercise the degree of care, skill, and diligence commonly possessed and exercised by an ordinary member of the legal community."

This malpractice standard closely tracks the requirement in Model Rule 1.1 that requires a competent attorney to use "the legal knowledge, skill, thoroughness and preparation reasonably necessary for the representation." Further, in certain jurisdictions, violations of Model Rule 1.1 can serve as evidence of malpractice liability, supporting the close link between the standards asserted under the Model Rule and the common law of attorney malpractice.

Thus, the *Mandel* case stands for the proposition that the competent lawyer must fully explain the significance of operative language changes to a client, even in the context of sophisticated transactional practice. Comparable to the language change in the put option drafted in the *Mandel* case, one might envision a situation where changing a traditional term to more modern language might similarly impact the interpretation and enforcement of a contract, such as occurred in the *Lubbock* case.

> *Mandel* makes clear that in order to fulfill the duty of care, a reasonableness duty analogical to the competence duty in the Model Rules, enhanced communication with the client is required before changes are made to legally significant terms of the contract. This duty applies to transactional attorneys working to obtain maximum benefit for their clients. Therefore, ways in which the Model Rules and enforcement of ethical standards can be enhanced to make this duty clear and evenly enforced amongst transactional practitioners must be considered.

Section 2.   Specific Rules for Special Transactions: Revisiting Model Rule 1.8

There are a few specific provisions of the Model Rules that address specific aspects of transactional practice. In discussing these rules, we will revisit MR 1.8.

A.   Crime & Fraud

Remember that under Rule 1.6, one of the exceptions to confidentiality is if "to prevent the client from committing a crime or fraud that is reasonably certain to result in substantial injury to the financial interests or property of another and in furtherance of which the client has used or is using the lawyer's services." There is a complimentary provision, in Rule 4.1, stating that a lawyer "shall not knowingly [] fail to disclose a material fact to a third person when disclosure is necessary to avoid assisting a criminal or fraudulent act by a client."

The trigger for this exception is that the lawyer's services were somehow used to further the crime or fraud. The most likely way this would happen is if a lawyer prepared some type of document—perhaps a contract, perhaps an opinion letter—which turned out to be entangled with a fraudulent enterprise.

B.   Self-Dealing in Transactional Law

The most extensive collection of provision in the Model Rule specifically addressing transactional practice is found in Rule 1.8, which is a miscellaneous listing of specific rules restricting particular threats to a healthy lawyer-client relationship. Most of these specific rules have a common thread: Lawyers must avoid self-dealing when preparing documents and transactions for clients. That could happen if a lawyer writes him or herself into a will, or suddenly becomes an investor in the client's business. There are many ways lawyers might engage in self-dealing, and each one leads to its own set of prohibitions and safeguards. The following chart summarizes rules:

Let's Chart It!

Type of Self-Dealing	Exceptions
Soliciting gifts from clients	Only allowed if the lawyer is a family member of the client
Writing a will that gives a gift to the lawyer or a close relation of the lawyer	Only allowed if the lawyer is a family member of the client
Acquiring literary or media rights to a client's story	Only allowed after the conclusion of the representation.
Prospectively limiting the lawyer's liability in malpractice	Only allowed if the client has independent counsel.
Settling a malpractice claim against the lawyer with an unrepresented client	Only allowed if the client is advised in writing of the desirability of obtaining independent legal advice.
Entering a business transaction with the client or acquiring an ownership interest in the client's business	Only allowed if: • The terms "are fair and reasonable to the client and are fully disclosed and transmitted in writing in a manner that can be reasonably understood" • The client is advised in writing of the desirability of obtaining independent legal advice, AND • The client gives detailed and explicit informed consent.

While the kind of self-dealing described in these rules will often seem unseemly, it may arise with good intentions. For example, a lawyer may be so enthusiastic about a client's business venture that the lawyer wants to become an investor in it. That does not inherently indicate any malicious intent. But it still presents problems. For one, the client's advisor now wants in on the deal, making it harder for the client to negotiate effectively. That is why the rule requires not just informed, written consent, but also "fair and reasonable" terms. In other words, this is not a time for cutthroat negotiations; the bar and possibly a court may be able to second guess the fairness of the deal struck. A lawyer who tries to do this would be well advised to give the client an especially good deal. And also: The ABA Comment makes clear that these safeguards apply to any business transactions with a client, even if it is not the subject of the negotiation. The Comment gives the example of "a lawyer drafting a will for a client learns that the client needs money for unrelated expenses and offers to make a loan to the client."

Even when allowed, there is good reason for lawyers to just say "no" to these sorts of arrangements. Remember that a lawyer is always required to deliver competent services and exercise independent judgement. Rule 1.7 generally prohibits representation if there is a significant risk that the representation [] will be materially limited by . . . a personal interest of the lawyer." When a lawyer becomes more personally entangled with a client's affairs, his or her ability to exercise independent judgement becomes more threatened. It will be harder to give sober advice on business law if the lawyer is also an investor in the business. For that reason, a lawyer who wants to be an investor would be well advised to refer the client to another attorney for the legal work. It will be harder to advise a client on options for writing a will if the lawyer is a possible beneficiary, or if the will might lead to conflict in a family of which the lawyer is part. For these reasons, even though the rules allow preparing a will for a family member, a lawyer would be well advised to refer their family to someone else.

Model Rule 1.8(j)

A lawyer shall not have sexual relations with a client unless a consensual sexual relationship existed between them when the client-lawyer relationship commenced.

This rule applies to all lawyers although there is an interesting twist with lawyers who deal with an entity such as a corporation. The rule is simple: no sex with clients unless the sexual relationship predated the formation of the ACR. But what if the client is an organization? For purposes of the rule, the client is the constituent of the organization that directs or supervises lawyers concerning the organization's legal affairs. Note that under this definition the person that so directs need not be a lawyer. It could include, by way of example, the CFO.

The Model Rule makes an exception not found in the equivalent rules from the American Medical Association or American Psychological Association. The Model Rules allow lawyers to offer legal services to a person with whom he or she already has an intimate relationship. In allowing this exception, the ABA is arguably being consistent. As we have already seen, the Model Rules also allow lawyers to write a will for a family member, even if they lawyer will be a beneficiary. The ABA thus seems to approve of the possibility of lawyers doing legal favors for family and intimate relations. Yet, there is good reason to question if the ABA is making the right choice here. Perhaps with a pre-existing relationship there is somewhat less concern about exploitation. But the concerns about lawyers being unable to exercise objective and independent judgement or of being reluctant to deliver candid advice seem just as pertinent.

Some states are not been willing to go even as far as the Model Rules. Here are some examples.

- California did not adopt an explicit rule against sexual relations until 2018. The California Rule is similar to the Model Rule, but it adds a provision that no disciplinary action should be taken unless the State Bar "has attempted to obtain the client's statement regarding, and has considered, whether the client would be unduly burdened by further investigation or a charge." This extra provision was based on a similar provision in Minnesota. It was added to address concerns that third parties might use knowledge of a sexual relationship to punish the lawyer when the client did not want any invasion of the couple's privacy, and presumably did not feel a need for official action.

- Nevada's Supreme Court adopted the Model Rule, but added an additional exception: "This paragraph does not apply when the client is an organization." This may reflect a view that exploitation is less likely with an organizational client.

- New York only prohibits sexual relations with clients in domestic relations (i.e. divorce) matters, where a lawyer makes sex a quid-pro-quo requirement for legal services, or otherwise employs coercion or intimidation. In other words, New York allows consensual sex with clients except in domestic relations cases.

- Texas' Disciplinary Rules of Professional Conduct do not explicitly restrict sexual relationships with clients at all. In 2011, Texas lawyers voted down to adopt a provision similar to the

Model Rules' approach. And it was not close; 72 percent voted no. Consider: Do you think there is any legitimate reason for lawyers to oppose a rule restricting sexual relations with clients?

It is worth asking and debating why the legal profession has been so much more reluctant than other professions to draw a clear line against sex with clients. A Comment to the New York rules illustrates the ambivalence:

> [S]exual relations between lawyers and their clients are dangerous and inadvisable. Out of respect for the desires of consenting adults, however, paragraph (j) does not flatly prohibit client-lawyer sexual relations in matters other than domestic relations matters. Even when sexual relations between a lawyer and client are permitted under paragraph (j), however, they may lead to incompetent representation in violation of Rule 1.1.

This comment should be a warning. Even if state bars and supreme courts have not always been willing to formally ban or discipline sexual relationships with client, there a many good reasons to avoid them. And even in the absence of an explicit rule, lawyers can never offer representation if they cannot live up the requirements for competence, independence, objective judgment, and candid advice. Intimate emotional entanglements make this much harder, if not impossible.

Section 3. Ethical Drafting of Deal Documents

X-Ray Questions

Let's follow-up on Professor Johnson's insights.

The following discusses how certain of the Model Rules interact with transactional work. From your earlier reading, can you explain how the dynamics of transactional practice differ from the dynamics of litigation/trial practice? Take a moment to set out the differences. Let's now drill down to some ethical questions you will encounter in a transactional practice. What ethical considerations are there in to deciding whether to "cut and paste" agreement provisions from earlier used documents? If a partner used some of these provisions in her work, is it permissible to simply incorporate them into your draft? If so, what are those circumstances? Why is it important to fully understand the client's business model in order to conform to the Rules? Finally, are there additional communication duties with respect to clients that are inherent in practicing transactional law? What are they and why do they exist?

BEYOND THE CITE

By: Lori D. Johnson, *The Ethics of Non-Traditional Contract Drafting*, 84 U. CIN. L. REV. 595 (2016).

[. . .]

IV. APPLYING THE MODEL RULES TO MODERN DRAFTING STYLE

Due to the focus on fraudulent drafting, ethics scholars overlook the potential applicability of other core ethical rules to the practice of transactional drafting. Specifically, Model Rules 1.1, 1.2, 1.3, and 1.4, concerning competence, allocation of authority, diligence, and communication respectively, are not frequently or deeply discussed in connection with the ethical duties of attorneys drafting contracts. However, each of the aforementioned rules applies when one views transactional attorneys as advocates engaged in persuasive word choices advancing client interests. The Model Rules themselves recognize that all attorneys, even transactional attorneys, carry the role of advocate, by requiring all attorneys to "act with competence, commitment and dedication to the interest of the client . . . upon the client's behalf."

The Model Rules discussed below put in place important safeguards on lawyers' behavior as advocates, and certainly apply to attorneys making non-traditional language choices in contracts. These advocacy oriented rules require the lawyer to be fully informed of the relevant precedent, to undertake the work necessary to be assured that unique phrasing of clauses does not disadvantage the client, and to keep the client informed of and involved in the decisions the lawyer makes concerning word choices.

The potential impact of each of these Model Rules on the behavior of attorneys using non-traditional terms will be discussed. The analysis will begin with the competence and diligence rules, and then analyze the allocation of authority and communication rules in tandem.

A. Model Rule 1.1—Competence

The competence duty under the Model Rules requires that "[a] lawyer shall provide competent representation to a client," which entails "the legal knowledge, skill, thoroughness, and preparation reasonably necessary for the representation." Broadly speaking, this duty imposes upon attorneys "an ethical obligation to write well." Simply being "exposed to contract drafting" either in law school or in practice does not prepare an attorney to competently draft.

Expertise in drafting, as in any legal discipline, can be obtained through "necessary study," as provided in the comments to Model Rule 1.1. However, competence in drafting requires not only a "thorough grounding in contract law" but also a more nuanced understanding of how the law "is to be applied on behalf of the client." A core competency in contract drafting requires adequate satisfaction of the "client's wishes by the provisions of the document." In this way, the competence duty necessitates client advocacy, in conjunction with the requirement that the document be appropriately drafted and enforceable.

Further, the transactional attorney, like any other lawyer, "should be careful in performing legal work." Specifically, it long has been noted that the duties of an attorney structuring a transaction require "an examination of legal and extra-legal indicators, the most well recognized of which is how a court will respond to a given factual situation." The drafter must consider whether "a court will rule unfavorably if certain facts occur." To make these determinations, a transactional lawyer must attain a strong "background in the legal rules governing contract interpretation" as well as "a routine for keeping current on relevant statutory mandates and case law.' "

This level of competence requires knowledge of the typical interpretation of tested terms and recognition that non-traditional word choices may give rise to unpredictable applications by a court in a variety of factual scenarios. Therefore, in fulfilling her ethical obligations, the drafter must recognize her duty as an advocate of the client and consider whether the use of a non-traditional term helps or harms the client if the contract falls into dispute.

In a rare, early discussion of the competence duty as it relates to the role of the transactional attorney, an article by ethics scholars Louis M. Brown and Harold A. Brown noted that competence is best served in the transactional context by considering the "damage which could be done to the [transactional] client by incompetence." Therefore, competence in the transactional context requires not merely knowledge of the applicable law, but also applying a lawyer's legal knowledge to the particular needs of a particular client.' "

The transactional lawyer's "aspirations of competence" should include attaining "the knowledge and skill to grasp the client's goals, to reframe them if necessary, to initiate the discussion of alternative courses of conduct and, along with the client, to be creative regarding the uses of the law." This early framing of the duty by the Brown article implicitly requires that the transactional attorney use the law in the way most beneficial to achieving such client goals.

A more recent article provides another framework for applying the competence rule to transactional attorneys. Christina Kunz posits that transactional attorneys drafting contracts have a heightened competence duty when it comes to potentially invalid clauses. She notes that Comment 2 to Model Rule 1.1 mentions "some important legal skills, such as the analysis of precedent . . . and legal drafting, [that] are required in all legal problems." Such problems include drafting contract terms and require the analysis of precedent concerning the potential interpretation the term. Kunz focuses on substantively "iffy" clauses, but the uncertainty of judicial interpretation associated with untested variations of traditional terms is analogical.

This duty to research and inform is particularly high where, as Kunz notes, the particular clause has been "criticized" in another jurisdiction. In such a case, Kunz suggests that "[t]he lawyer should seriously consider urging the client to consider practicalities," such as effects on the "parties' relationship, performance on both sides, public perceptions, other contracts with the same language and other concurrent negotiations."

The same considerations ring true for a lawyer's decision to rephrase a clause with a settled meaning into terms that have a less predictable method of interpretation in the courts. The lawyer must consider and advise the client of potential risks concerning the way other parties will view the clause, whether other contracts exist which use the more modem language in lieu of the traditional phrases, whether those contracts have been litigated, and the view of the jurisdiction in which the contract will be enforced.

Further, the duty to be informed about the view of the jurisdiction in which the contract will be enforced is critically important to drafting a contract that provides benefit to the client, a recognized goal of the transactional attorney. Since contracts are essentially authorless documents, it has been recognized in literary scholarship that contracts "enlist the attendant authority of the law." Thus, courts' interpretations of the meaning of contract language become a critically important mode by which a drafter can set boundaries around meaning, and therefore control potential outcomes for a client.

It is settled that liability for legal malpractice may not arise in circumstances where the law is unsettled as to whether to include certain terms in a document. However, this does not negate the fact that "[l]egal uncertainty can manifest in the preparation of documents if the precise language and content have not been judicially construed." This uncertainty affects the decision whether the competent lawyer should rephrase a tested term into a modern, untested variation.

While attorneys are not "required to predict infallibly how a court will interpret documents that they have drafted," the competence duty requires "the legal knowledge, skill, thoroughness, and preparation reasonably necessary for the representation." This baseline level of knowledge includes knowledge about the preferred phrasing of terms, or at the very least, current, applicable judicial interpretations of terms selected.

The requirement of deeply researching and understanding the impact of rephrasing terms as an element of competency is heightened in the context of contract drafting, because "each word or provision in a contract may be subjected to greater scrutiny and challenge by opposing counsel whereas the meanings of words or phrases in a brief or pleading are rarely the primary target or focus of even the most zealous advocate."

And yet, even in litigation documents, such as complaints, where word choices are of less import, the competent attorney is exhorted to rely on "legal precedent" and perform "sufficient research and analysis" to be assured that the document adequately advances a client's claim. It has been considered a failure of competence to advance "novel claims and new interpretations of law" in a complaint insufficiently supported by precedent. Similarly, the competent transactional lawyer should not use untested terms in a contract without a deep, thoroughly researched consideration of the consequences on enforceability, parties' behaviors, and potential judicial interpretations.

B.   *Model Rule 1.3—Diligence*

The diligence duty under the Model Rules requires that "[a] lawyer. act with reasonable diligence and promptness in representing a client," including "tak[ing] whatever lawful and ethical measures are required to vindicate a client's cause." In fulfilling this duty, the lawyer must act "with commitment and dedication to the interests of the client and with zeal in advocacy upon the client's behalf," yet the "lawyer is not bound . . . to press for every advantage that may be realized for a client.

Further, because the diligence duty requires "promptness,' " the "modifying [of] a previously drafted contract," which would likely include tested terms of art, "require[s] significantly less time than drafting a contract from scratch." Such widely-available contracts and terms not only aid the attorney in meeting the promptness requirement, but may also assist in furthering the interests of the client, as traditionally-composed contracts are often "generally accepted within the industry" in which the client operates.

Of course, the competence duty requires that such standard forms be fully understood, researched, and reviewed, so as not be used "blindly." As noted, "[g]ood drafting takes care, practice, sound judgment, and a lot of effort." Nonetheless, the " 'precedent-based drafting approach'. . . makes sense" in many circumstances, particularly where clients are fee-sensitive, operate in a highly standardized industry, or the lawyer has developed the forms based on research and practice experience.

As has been noted by drafting scholars, "the lawyer owes a duty to the client to keep . . . legal fees on a diet," a goal which can be achieved through drafting a contract which "rais[es] few issues. The higher risk and added research burdens arising under the competence duty when using untested language would undoubtedly increase fees. Therefore, particularly with regard to fee-sensitive clients, use of nontraditional language and the attendant increase in related research fees may constitute an unethical disservice.

In all cases, the lawyer has a duty to communicate with the client at the outset of the relationship concerning the client's expectations regarding fees, as well as the client's tolerance for increased costs based on non-traditional language changes. Discussion of these issues comprises the basis of the allocation of authority between the attorney and client, as well as the communication duty of the attorney, which will be discussed below.

C.   *Model Rules 1.2 and 1.4—Allocation of Authority & Communication*

Model Rule 1.2 provides that "a lawyer shall abide by a client's decisions concerning the objectives of the representation and, as required by Rule 1.4, shall consult with the client as to the means by which they are to be pursued." 38 The comments to Model Rule 1.2 make clear that decisions concerning "the purpose" of the representation are allocated to the client, while the decisions of the lawyer are entitled to deference concerning the "means to be used to accomplish [client] objectives, particularly with respect to technical, legal and tactical matters.' "

This allocation of authority regarding the "means" of the representation, however, is subject to communication with the client, as emphasized in the text of and comments to Model Rule 1.2(a). Specifically, Comment 1 to Model Rule 1.2 invokes the communication requirement under Model Rule 1.4(a)(2) concerning the means utilized by the lawyer to achieve the client's objective. To properly follow this rule, a lawyer must "reasonably consult with the client about the means by which the client's objectives are to be accomplished." The duties under Model Rules 1.2 and 1.4 are therefore inextricably linked when dealing with choices made by a transactional attorney in drafting documents on a client's behalf.

Specifically, it has been recognized by scholars of drafting ethics that "[i]n drafting documents on behalf of a client, the lawyer clearly has an obligation to explain the contents of those documents to the client so that the client understands the legal ramifications of executing the documents." Further, even where the "underlying conduct of the attorney is appropriate" there exists a requirement to advise the client about the consequences of a proposed construction of a contract.

Thus, the research and recognition of potential uncertainty associated with the use of untested terms required under the competence duty trigger an enhanced duty to inform the client under Model Rule 1.4(a)(2). This requirement enhances the historical view of the heightened requirements of Model Rule 1.4 in the transactional setting. In the context of a transactional representation, the client is the lawyer's "raison d'etre" and therefore the "amount of communication" required to ensure the lawyer is fulfilling the client's goal "may be much greater" than in litigation practice.

Christina Kunz in her article on drafting ethics under the UCC notes that "[i]n many situations, a candid dialogue between lawyer and client will resolve the ethical tension" associated with the selection of "iffy" clauses. 147 She notes the need for balance between the rights of opposing parties and the requirement for zealous representation as motivating the lawyer's decisions regarding how to draft clauses in these circumstances.

Thus, in deciding whether to incorporate a non-traditional construction of a tested term, a transactional attorney has the duty to consult and communicate with the client regarding the potential outcomes and uncertainty associated with such choice. This duty has not been clearly delineated with regard to the transactional practitioner. However, as the interpretation of an untested term certainly could impact the outcome and enforcement of a contract by a judge, this decision inherently is connected to the "objectives" or outcomes of the representation.

Model Rule 1.2 allocates decisions concerning the outcome of representation to the client. Model Rule 1.2 requires careful explanation by the attorney before such rephrasing occurs. Additionally, the lawyer should defer to the client concerning associated potential increases in fees. Practically speaking, the Model Rules require the attorney to explain and confirm with the client the decision to cast aside traditional terms of art in a contract that has well-documented, consistent judicial interpretations. This is particularly true where tested interpretations effectively achieve the client's objective at a lower cost.

Further, a failure of the attorney to gain an understanding of the nature of the client's "business objectives" could also lead to an inability to meet the requirements of Model Rule 1.2.151 This is especially true where the client operates in a particular industry. Typically, industries will operate and communicate using specialized "customs and jargon," the understanding of which may be essential to achieving the client's goals.

In such cases, redrafting of tested terms, even where helpful to clarity or brevity, may undercut the client's position vis-A-vis contracting parties in a heavily regulated industry. Model Rules 1.2 and 1.4, properly viewed, require consultation with the client concerning the potential impact on client objectives in these circumstances. As a result, revision of traditional terms into alternative language may lead to frustration of client goals, potentially resulting in ethical violations.

This discussion ebbs into the practical considerations of how a transactional attorney can meet their ethical duties when faced with the call for a broader use of plain language. In order to better understand the problems posed by language choices, and the ethical implications of the behavior of drafters in making these choices, one must turn to case studies of attorneys in practice.

[. . .]

Section 4. The Lawyer's Ethical Duty to Inquire into a Deal's Legality

On April 29, 2020, the American Bar Association issued Formal Opinion 491 captioned "Obligations Under Rule 1.2(d) to Avoid Counseling or Assisting in a Crime or Fraud in Non-Litigation Settings" for transactional lawyers to refer to in meeting their ethical obligations. The opinion states that the transactional lawyer must refer to MR 1.1 (Competence); MR 1.3 (Diligence); MR 1.13 (Organization as client); MR 1.16 (Confidentiality); and MR 8.4 (Misconduct). Note that the opinion states at the outset that it does not address the application of these rules in the representation of a client or a prospective client who requests legal services in connection with litigation. Why is that, do you think? Think back to earlier in our course of study and the dividing line between a client who is contemplating doing an act that is legally wrong or ethically dubious and one that has, in fact, carried out such act. In the first instance there is the lawyer's duty to counsel and advise to avoid such actions; by contrast, in the second scenario, the act is completed and thus the lawyer's duty is to zealously represent the client within the bounds of the rules of professional responsibility.

The Opinion cuts to the quick: Ascertaining whether a client seeks to use a lawyer's services for prohibited conduct can be delicate. Clients are generally entitled to be believed rather than doubted. . .a lawyer who has knowledge of facts that creates high probability that a client seeking the lawyer's services in a transaction to further criminal or fraudulent activity has a duty to inquire further to avoid assisting that activity under Rule 1.2(d). Failure to make a reasonable inquiry is willful blindness punishable under the actual knowledge standard of (MR 1.0(f))." Where else have we discussed the concept, as Ben Franklin put it, that "half the truth is often the greatest lie"?

BEYOND THE CITE

AMERICAN BAR ASSOCIATION

STANDING COMMITTEE ON ETHICS AND PROFESSIONAL RESPONSIBILITY

FORMAL OPINION 491

APRIL 29, 2020

Obligations Under Rule 1.2(d) to Avoid Counseling or Assisting in a Crime or Fraud in Non-Litigation Settings

Model Rule 1.2(d) prohibits a lawyer from advising or assisting a client in conduct the lawyer "knows" is criminal or fraudulent. That knowledge may be inferred from the circumstances, including a lawyer's willful blindness to or conscious avoidance of facts. Accordingly, where facts known to the lawyer establish a high probability that a client seeks to use the lawyer's services for criminal or fraudulent activity, the lawyer has a duty to inquire further to avoid advising or assisting such activity. Even if information learned in the course of a preliminary interview or during a representation is insufficient to establish "knowledge" under Rule 1.2(d), other rules may require the lawyer to inquire further in order to help the client avoid crime or fraud, to avoid professional misconduct, and to advance the client's legitimate interests. These include the duties of competence, diligence, communication, and honesty under Rules 1.1, 1.3, 1.4, 1.13, 1.16, and 8.4. If the client or prospective client refuses to provide information necessary to assess the legality of the proposed transaction, the lawyer must ordinarily decline the representation or withdraw under Rule 1.16. A lawyer's reasonable evaluation after inquiry and based on information reasonably available at the time does not violate the rules. This opinion does not address the application of these rules in the representation of a client or prospective client who requests legal services in connection with litigation.

[. . . .]

X-Ray Questions (*Formal Opinion 2018–4*)

The following opinion letter is from the New York State Bar. The scenario deals with a lawyer who is retained to sell a business at a price higher than its worth; that the proceeds have been directed by the client to go to a bank in a country with laws favoring bank secrecy; and that the client has two passports both from countries in which there are bank secrecy laws. The lawyer suspects that the client is engaged in money laundering or tax evasion.

How does the opinion letter involve MR 1.1 on competence? But is not the duty of competence limited to whether the lawyer can perform the tasks asked of by the client? Does a lawyer have an implicit duty—even if unasked for by the client—to offer an opinion on whether a transaction could be unlawful? if the lawyer does not make inquiries could it be that she could unwittingly stumble into a violation of MR 1.2(d)? Would that be a violation of 1.2(d) or is MR 1.2(d) limited—by the very way it is written—to a conscious decision by a lawyer to assist a client in a criminal or fraudulent act? How does the opinion letter deal with this question? What does the opinion letter say about the interplay of MR 1.16(c)(2) on lawyer withdrawal from representation and MR 1.4(a)(5) on client communication? Think back to the advice at the start of the book on whether to represent someone. Do you see how it plays into this question?

BEYOND THE CITE

ASSOCIATION OF THE BAR OF THE CITY OF NEW YORK COMMITTEE ON PROFESSIONAL ETHICS

Formal Opinion 2018–4: Duties When an Attorney is Asked to Assist in a Suspicious Transaction

Digest

The New York Rules of Professional Conduct (the "Rules") prohibit a lawyer from knowingly assisting a client's crime or fraud but do not explicitly address a lawyer's duty when the lawyer merely has doubts about the lawfulness of the client's conduct; nor do the Rules explicitly require a lawyer to investigate in such circumstances in order to ascertain whether the legal services would in fact assist a crime or fraud before assisting the client. Nevertheless, when a lawyer is asked to assist in a transaction that the lawyer suspects may involve a crime or fraud, a duty of inquiry in some circumstances is implicit in the Rules. First, in order to render competent representation as required by Rule 1.1, a lawyer has a duty to the client in some circumstances to undertake an inquiry into suspicious transactions to render reasonable and candid advice to the client about whether to undertake the proposed conduct and the consequences of doing so. Second, notwithstanding the absence of an explicit requirement, a duty to inquire into suspicious transactions under some circumstances is implicit in the duty to avoid knowingly assisting wrongful conduct. The lawyer's inquiry must be consistent with the confidentiality duty of Rule 1.6, which governs disclosures the lawyer may make to third parties during the inquiry, as well as with the duty to keep the client informed during the representation. If the lawyer concludes that the client will engage or is engaging in a crime or fraud, the lawyer must not assist, or further assist, the wrongdoing. The lawyer may undertake remedial measures to the extent permitted by the exceptions to the confidentiality rule.

RULES: 1.1, 1.2, 1.6, 1.16, 2.1, 8.4

Question

When an individual client asks a lawyer to provide legal assistance in a transaction, and the lawyer suspects that the legal services may assist the client's crime or fraud, to what extent must the lawyer investigate to allay or confirm the suspicions, and what other conduct must the lawyer undertake under the Rules?

OPINION:

I. Introduction

In the context of the following scenario, this opinion addresses lawyers' obligations under the Rules when the lawyer is retained to assist an individual client in a transaction that appears to the lawyer to be suspicious.

> A lawyer represents a client in the sale of a business in New York. The client advises the lawyer that the proceeds of the transaction will be used to purchase a different business. The client directs that after the first transaction closes, all payments be sent to a bank in a well-known secrecy jurisdiction. The client then asks the lawyer to proceed with the purchase. In preparing the documents and doing general due diligence, the lawyer realizes that the proposed purchase price is much more than the business is worth. The lawyer also learns inadvertently that the client has two passports, each from a secrecy jurisdiction different than the one in which the bank is located. The lawyer suspects, but does not know, that the transaction will involve a fraud or crime, such as money laundering or tax evasion, on the part of the client.

As set forth below, a number of Rules and considerations bear on whether a transactional lawyer has a duty to investigate the client's conduct in this scenario and whether there are other steps that must be taken. These include the lawyer's duties of competence [Rule 1.1], of confidentiality [Rule 1.6], and to refrain from assisting a client in conduct that the lawyer knows is illegal or fraudulent [Rule 1.2(d)].

II. A Transactional Lawyer May Have a Duty to Inquire When Serious Questions are Raised Regarding Whether the Lawyer is Assisting the Client in a Crime or Fraud

a. *The duty of competence may require the lawyer to conduct due diligence into the client's potentially fraudulent conduct*

Rule 1.1(a) requires a lawyer to provide "competent representation to a client." In many contexts, the very purpose of the representation is to provide advice about the lawfulness of a client's proposed course of conduct or to assist the client in structuring a proposed transaction in a manner that conforms to the law. Rule 1.2(d) authorizes a lawyer to "discuss the legal consequences of any proposed course of conduct with a client," and in such cases, Rule 1.1 presupposes that the lawyer will provide competent advice about whether the proposed conduct would be unlawful or about how to achieve the client's objectives within the law.

Regardless of the client's objectives, competent representation presupposes that the lawyer is rendering assistance in carrying out a client's lawful objectives. Committing a crime or engaging in other illegal or fraudulent conduct is not a lawful objective. Rule 1.2(d) forbids a lawyer from assisting the client in conduct that the lawyer knows to be illegal or fraudulent. But even if the lawyer does not have the requisite knowledge under Rule 1.2(d), furthering a client's illegal or fraudulent transaction—thereby subjecting a client to criminal or civil liability—may run afoul of the Rules if the lawyer did not act competently under Rule 1.1(a). In general, assisting in a suspicious transaction is not competent where a reasonable lawyer prompted by serious doubts would have refrained from providing assistance or would have investigated to allay suspicions before rendering or continuing to render legal assistance.

Further, Rules 1.4 and 2.1 require lawyers to render reasonable, candid advice. Unless the lawyer inquires in response to serious suspicions, the lawyer will not be in a position to advise the client about the attendant risks of civil or criminal liability. Thus, the duty of competence not only protects the client, but also in some situations requires the lawyer to take the steps necessary, including additional inquiry, to ensure that she is providing competent advice.

What constitutes a suspicion sufficient to trigger inquiry will depend on the circumstances. In many representations, there is no reason for the lawyer to doubt the lawfulness of the client's proposed actions. On the other hand, there may be representations where the circumstances raise suspicions or questions. For example, in the hypothetical above, the lawyer may have a duty to inquire of the client as to the reasons for a purchase of a business at a higher-than-market price and for running the funds through a bank in a secrecy jurisdiction to determine whether the transaction is being used to launder money, to avoid legitimate taxes, or for some other criminal or fraudulent purpose. Depending upon the answer, the lawyer may conclude that the transaction is legitimate, that she needs to make further inquiry, or that she must not provide further assistance in the transaction.

These conclusions are consistent with Comment [5] to Rule 1.1 which notes that "[c]ompetent handling of a particular matter includes inquiry into an analysis of the factual and legal elements of the problem," and with other authorities. See, e.g., N.Y. City 2015–3 (2015) (a lawyer who believes he is the victim of a scam by a purported prospective client has a duty of competence to investigate further before proceeding with the matter); ABA Informal Op. 1470 (1981) ("Opinion 1470") ("[A] lawyer should not undertake representation in disregard of facts suggesting that the representation might aid the client in perpetrating a fraud or otherwise committing a crime."); cf. N.Y. City 2018–2 (2018) ("The duty of competence under Rule 1.1 establishes additional duties in the post-conviction context, including, in some cases, a duty to investigate new potentially exculpatory evidence regardless of whether Rule 3.8(c) is triggered.").

b.   *A lawyer who fails to investigate potentially fraudulent conduct may also violate Rule 1.2(d), depending on the circumstances*

Rule 1.2(d) prohibits a lawyer from assisting a client in conduct that the lawyer knows to be criminal or fraudulent. "Knowledge" under the Rules is defined as "actual knowledge of the fact in question . . . [which] may be inferred from the circumstances." Rule 1.0(k). However, consistent with the criminal law standard of "conscious avoidance," a lawyer may be deemed to have knowledge that the client is engaged in a criminal or fraudulent transaction if the lawyer is aware of serious questions about the legality of the transaction and renders assistance without considering readily available facts that would have confirmed the wrongfulness of the transaction. See N.Y. City 2018–2 (2018) ("Conscious avoidance of the fact in question may also constitute knowledge under the Rules, as under criminal law") (citing N.Y. City 99–02 (1999) ("Lawyers have an obligation not to shut their eyes to what was plainly to be seen . . . A lawyer cannot escape responsibility by avoiding inquiry.")).

Opinion 1470 similarly recognized that when lawyers are aware that the client's proposed course of conduct is likely to be illegal, they "cannot escape responsibility by avoiding inquiry" but "must be satisfied, on the facts before [them] and readily available to [them], that [they] can perform the requested services without abetting fraudulent or criminal conduct and without relying on past client crime or fraud to achieve results the client now wants"; if lawyers are not satisfied that the client's conduct is lawful, they have "a duty of further inquiry" before rendering assistance. Thus, while Rule 1.2(d) does not require lawyers to inquire when there is no ground for suspicion, they cannot ignore "red flags." Cf. Rebecca Roiphe, The Ethics of Willful Ignorance, 24 Geo. J. Legal Ethics 187 (2011), citing In re Blatt, 63 324 A.2d 15, 17–19 (N.J. 1974) (holding that "a lawyer committed misconduct by helping a client effect a purchase after failing to investigate its suspicious nature"); In re Dobson, 427 S.E.2d 166, 166–68 (S.C. 1993) (sanctioning "an attorney for helping his client while remaining deliberately ignorant of his client's criminal conduct" and holding that the court would "not countenance the conscious avoidance of one's ethical duties as an attorney").

III. Limits on the Lawyer's Duty to Inquire

Ordinarily, a lawyer will begin an inquiry by seeking information from the client before turning to other sources. After concluding a reasonable inquiry, the lawyer may ordinarily credit the client when there are doubts. Whether a particular inquiry is adequate will vary with the circumstances.

To the extent that the lawyer must seek information from others, the Rules may impose conditions or limits. In general, the duty under Rule 1.4 to keep the client reasonably informed will require the lawyer to explain why there are doubts about the legality of the transaction and what steps the lawyer proposes to take to allay or confirm suspicions. If suspicions are sufficiently serious to give rise to a duty of inquiry under Rule 1.2(d), then the lawyer would render further assistance at her peril. A lawyer's fear that a client may seek to cover up his actions does not eliminate the duty of communication. Rule 1.4(a)(5). If the lawyer does suspect a cover-up and cannot persuade the client to be forthcoming, she may choose to terminate the representation. Rule 1.16(c)(2). Similarly, if the client will not authorize such an inquiry, the lawyer may have no realistic choice other than to cease assisting in the particular transaction, because to continue the representation may put her in jeopardy of violating Rule 1.2(d). And, needless to say, a client's refusal to authorize and assist in an inquiry into the lawfulness of the client's proposed conduct will ordinarily constitute an additional, and very significant, "red flag."

If the client green-lights an inquiry but refuses to pay for the time required to conduct it, the lawyer must decide whether to conduct the inquiry at her own expense or terminate the representation. The lawyer may discontinue the representation based on concerns as to the legality of the transaction. See Rule 1.2(f) (permitting a lawyer to refuse to participate in conduct that the lawyer believes to be unlawful, even if there is support for an argument that the conduct is legal); Rule 1.2, Cmt. [15].

Further, any inquiry must be undertaken consistently with the confidentiality duty under Rule 1.6. Ordinarily, without client consent, the lawyer cannot conduct the inquiry in a manner that discloses client confidences to third parties. See NYCBA Formal Op. 2015–3.

IV. Remedial Obligations

If a lawyer gains knowledge during the course of representation that a client is engaged in unlawful conduct (or plans to be), the lawyer has a range of options. The lawyer's remedial steps should be dictated by such factors as the lawyer's knowledge of the facts at hand, the seriousness of the client's misconduct, and the extent of the lawyer's involvement in the client's misconduct. When the lawyer has actual knowledge of prospective wrongdoing, the lawyer may not assist in the wrongdoing and, further, must counsel the client against the illegal course of conduct under Rule 1.4(a)(5). This counseling obligation derives from the duty of competence under Rule 1.1. Despite the challenges involved in "persuading a client to take necessary preventive or corrective action" under Rule 1.4, such communications are appropriate not only to assist the client but to mitigate any risks the attorney is assuming by continuing to represent the client. Rule 1.2(d), Cmt. [10].

In our hypothetical situation, if the lawyer determines that the client may be engaged in tax fraud or tax evasion, the lawyer may choose to counsel the client to pay the appropriate taxes or take other corrective action. There may also be circumstances in which corrective action is not possible and the lawyer may have no alternative but to resign.[6] Rule 1.16(b)(1).

If it becomes clear during a lawyer's representation that the client has failed to take necessary corrective action, and the lawyer's continued representation would assist client conduct that is illegal or fraudulent, Rule 1.16(b)(1) mandates that the lawyer withdraw from representation. Comment [10] to Rule 1.2(d) states that the lawyer's obligations are "to avoid assisting the client" and to "remonstrate with the client" when the representation will result in violation of the Rules or other law. Withdrawal alone may be insufficient in some circumstances, for example, where the lawyer believes there is continued third-party reliance on an inaccurate opinion or representation. In that case, the lawyer may engage in "noisy withdrawal," which permits the attorney to give notice of the fact of withdrawal and to disaffirm any opinion, document, affirmation or the like. Rule 1.2(d), Cmt [10]; see Rule 1.6(b)(3); Rule 4.1, Cmt. [3]. The lawyer must also decide whether and how to prevent any serious harm that will result from the client's conduct, including whether to reveal the client's confidential information to accomplish that end. In general, the potentially applicable exceptions to the ordinary confidentiality duty provide that the lawyer may disclose confidences to prevent criminal conduct or for other specified purposes, but not that the lawyer must do so. See Rule 1.6(b)(1), (2) & (3).

Throughout the process described above, the prudent lawyer would be well advised to keep a record of the decision making process and the basis for the steps she has (or has not) taken.

V. Conclusion

When asked to represent a client in a transaction that a lawyer believes to be suspicious, the lawyer has an implicit duty under some circumstances to inquire into the client's conduct. If the lawyer believes that her client is entering into a transaction that is illegal or fraudulent, the lawyer ordinarily must attempt to inquire in order to provide competent representation to the client under Rule 1.1. Further, under Rule 1.2(d), which forbids knowingly assisting a client's illegal or fraudulent conduct, a lawyer has the requisite knowledge if the lawyer is aware of serious questions about the legality of the transaction and renders assistance without considering readily available facts that would have confirmed the wrongfulness of the transaction. Implicit in the rule, therefore, is the obligation to take reasonably available measures to ascertain whether the client's transaction is illegal or fraudulent. The lawyer's inquiry must be consistent with the confidentiality duty of Rule 1.6, which governs disclosures the lawyer may make to third parties during the inquiry, as well as with the duty to keep the client informed during the representation. If the lawyer concludes that the client's conduct is illegal or fraudulent, the lawyer must not further assist the wrongdoing and may undertake remedial measures to the extent permitted by the exceptions to the confidentiality rule.

LEANING INTO PRACTICE

Domingo is a wealthy 88-year-old widower whose only child is deceased but who has a granddaughter, Reyna and a grandson, Noel. For five years, Domingo has used Attorney Jose to draw up and implement an estate plan, including a trust, a will, a health-care power of attorney and a financial power of attorney. Jose has also helped Domingo transfer real estate into the trust, sell real estate, and make gifts.

Domingo's financial power of attorney provided that it would not be effective except upon Domingo's incapacity, as certified in writing by a physician. The trust had a similar mechanism whereby Domingo was trustee, but upon his incapacity as certified, successors would assume the administration of the trust. The power of attorney provided that Reyna and Bank were to serve jointly once Domingo could not; the trust provided that Reyna, another individual and Bank would serve as successor co-trustees in the same event. Domingo told Jose that while he loved Reyna and appreciated her care and attention, he did not want her to serve alone as attorney-in-fact or as successor trustee because of Reyna's financial problems and because he did not care for her husband, Omar. Domingo had loaned Reyna considerable sums over the years, which Reyna had not repaid, including money Reyna was supposed to use to re-shingle her roof, which Omar had squandered on concert tickets in Puerto Rico. Reyna had also made demands upon Jose to make Domingo follow through on a promise Domingo made that he would make a gift to Reyna of a life estate in a certain "Ranchito" he owned which Reyna wanted to develop. Further, on several occasions Reyna had brought Domingo to Jose's office to change Domingo's will and trust to leave Reyna her shares under the will and the trust outright and not for life, but on each occasion, Domingo told Jose he was still thinking about it and did not want to make the changes.

Domingo's health deteriorated, and because of chronic pain Domingo went into a depression, no longer wanted to get out of bed or get dressed, and was not bathing or eating regularly. Jose became concerned and arranged for a physician visit and a home health aide, though Reyna complained that Jose was "interfering." Domingo was also not paying quarterly estimated tax payments, and utility bills went unpaid.

Reyna came to Jose's office and demanded that she be made sole attorney-in-fact. Jose explained that a physician needed to certify that Domingo would no longer handle his own affairs, which would trigger the power of attorney with co-attorneys-in-fact and trigger the need for successor co-trustees, and Jose said he would begin that process.

Reyna, unsatisfied with Jose's approach, then consulted Attorney Melissa, telling Melissa that Domingo wanted a new power of attorney making Reyna sole attorney-in-fact. (It is not clear whether Reyna told Melissa that Jose had been approached on the matter of a new power of attorney and that Jose declined to draw up a new power of attorney; for purposes of this Opinion, the author will assume she did not.) Melissa prepared the new power of attorney. Melissa sent a paralegal who was a notary to Domingo to secure Domingo's signature, but Melissa never saw or consulted with Domingo, and considered Reyna to be Melissa's client. The paralegal brought a letter from Melissa to

Domingo and read it to him; the letter stated Reyna was Domingo's client. and that if Domingo had any questions or reservations about the power of attorney, Domingo should contact his own attorney. In the presence of the paralegal and the home health aide, Grandfather indicated he understood the document and wanted to sign it, and he did.

Jose did contact Domingo's physician, who certified in writing that Domingo was incapacitated. The letter from the physician was dated one week before Domingo executed the new power of attorney which Melissa prepared.

Reyna as purported sole attorney-in-fact is now beginning to take action. She has fired Jose as Domingo's attorney and hired Melissa to be Domingo's new attorney to do a new estate plan for Domingo, and she is demanding that Jose turn over all files relating to Domingo and the trust. When Jose received a letter from Domingo instructing Jose to turn over his documents to Reyna, Jose went to visit Domingo to seek clarification. Domingo told Jose he remembers signing the letter and the power of attorney because Reyna wanted him to, but that he didn't understand them.

Issues:

Melissa wants to know whether his client Reyna as attorney-in-fact and successor trustee is entitled to Domingo's files and the trust records from Jones (and whether Jose is committing an ethical violation by refusing to provide the information), and Jose wants to know whether he can resist the demand for the files and otherwise take steps to protect Domingo's interests. Certain other ethics issues which neither Smith nor Jones have raised are implicated by the facts and merit discussion. A statement of the issues is as follows:

(1) Who is Melissa's client in the preparation of the power of attorney, Reyna or Domingo?

(2) Is Domingo a continuing client of Jose as to estate-planning and incapacity-planning matters? If so, was Melissa obligated to contact Jose as Domingo's attorney and not to contact Domingo directly? If not, has Melissa provided advice to an unrepresented person.

(3) May Jose take protective actions regarding Domingo?

(4) Did Melissa properly supervise his paralegal in delegating any obligation to ascertain Domingo's capacity and freedom from undue influence?

Section 5. The ACP in Deal Making

Cases and Materials

X-Ray Questions (*In re Grand Jury*)

The ACP dynamics in deal making are different than in litigation. How so? There is a mixture of legal advice and general business advice per MR 2. 1 as we mentioned earlier in the discussion of privilege logs. How does this court propose to segregate the two? How does it compare the test it articulates from other tests? What is the difference between "*a* primary purpose" and "*the* primary purpose?" Can there be that great a difference with use of one article as opposed to the other? On October 3, 2022, The United States Supreme Court granted the cert petition filed in this case.

In re Grand Jury

United States Court of Appeals, 2022.
23 F.4th 1088.

AMENDED OPINION

LEE, CIRCUIT JUDGE:

Given our increasingly complex regulatory landscape, attorneys often wear dual hats, serving as both a lawyer and a trusted business advisor. Our court, however, has yet to articulate a consistent standard for determining when the attorney-client privilege applies to dual-purpose communications that implicate both legal and business concerns.

In this case, the grand jury issued subpoenas related to a criminal investigation. The district court held Appellants—whom we identify as "Company" and "Law Firm"—in contempt after they failed to comply with the subpoenas. The district court ruled that certain dual-purpose communications were not privileged because the "primary purpose" of the documents was to obtain tax advice, not legal advice. Appellants argue that the district court erred in relying on the "primary purpose" test and should have instead relied on a broader "because of" test. We affirm and conclude that the primary-purpose test governs in assessing attorney-client privilege for dual-purpose communications.

BACKGROUND

Company and Law Firm were each served with grand jury subpoenas requesting documents and communications related to a criminal investigation. The target of the criminal investigation is the owner of Company as well as a client of Law Firm. In response to the grand jury subpoenas, Company and Law Firm each produced some documents but withheld others, citing attorney-client privilege and the work-product doctrine.

The government moved to compel production of the withheld documents, which the district court granted in part. In those orders, the district court explained that these documents were either not protected by any privilege or were discoverable under the crime-fraud exception. Company and Law Firm disagreed with the district court's privilege rulings, so they continued to withhold the disputed documents. The government followed up with motions to hold Company and Law Firm in contempt, both of which the district court again granted. These appeals followed, and we have jurisdiction under 28 U.S.C. § 1291.

STANDARD OF REVIEW

Whether the attorney-client privilege applies to specific documents represents "a mixed question of law and fact which this court reviews independently and without deference to the district court." *United States v. Richey*, 632 F.3d 559, 563 (9th Cir. 2011) (cleaned up). The district court's legal rulings about the scope of the privilege are reviewed de novo. *Id.* So is the district court's choice of the applicable legal standard. *Fjelstad v. Am. Honda Motor Co.*, 762 F.2d 1334, 1337 (9th Cir. 1985). We review the district court's factual findings for clear error. *Richey*, 632 F.3d at 563.

ANALYSIS

I.   District Courts in Our Circuit Have Applied Both the "Primary Purpose" and "Because Of" Tests for Attorney-Client Privilege Claims for Dual-Purpose Communications.

"The attorney-client privilege protects confidential communications between attorneys and clients, which are made for the purpose of giving legal advice." *United States v. Sanmina Corp.*, 968 F.3d 1107, 1116 (9th Cir. 2020). Generally, communications related to an attorney's preparation of tax returns are not covered by attorney-client privilege. *Olender v. United States*, 210 F.2d 795, 806 (9th Cir. 1954). So, for example, "a client may communicate the figures from his W-2 Form to an attorney while litigation is in progress, but this information certainly is not privileged." *United States v. Abrahams*, 905 F.2d 1276, 1283–84 (9th Cir. 1990), *overruled on other grounds by United States v. Jose*, 131 F.3d 1325 (9th Cir. 1997). On the other hand, if a client seeks a lawyer's legal advice to figure out what to claim on a tax return, then that advice may be privileged. *Abrahams*, 905 F.2d at 1284.

But some communications might have more than one purpose, especially "in the tax law context, where an attorney's advice may integrally involve both legal and non-legal analyses." *Sanmina*, 968 F.3d at 1118. *Sanmina*, for example, involved communications about the propriety of a particular tax deduction, which could have both a non-legal purpose (tax compliance considerations) as well as potentially a legal purpose (seeking advice on what to do if the IRS challenged the deduction). *Id.* at 1117–18.

When dual-purpose communications are involved, there are two potential tests that courts have adopted: the "primary purpose" test and the "because of" test. Under the "primary purpose" test, courts look at whether the primary purpose of the communication is to give or receive legal advice, as opposed to business or tax advice. *See In re County of Erie*, 473 F.3d 413, 420 (2d Cir. 2007) ("We consider whether the predominant purpose of the communication is to render or solicit legal advice."). The natural implication of this inquiry is that a dual-purpose communication can only have a single "primary" purpose.

On the other hand, the "because of" test—which typically applies in the work-product context—"does not consider whether litigation was a primary or secondary motive behind the creation of a document." *In re Grand Jury Subpoena (Mark Torf/Torf Env't Mgmt.)*, 357 F.3d 900, 908 (9th Cir. 2004). It instead "considers the totality of the circumstances and affords protection when it can fairly be said that the document was created because of anticipated litigation, and would not have been created in substantially similar form but for the prospect of that litigation." *Id.* (cleaned up). It is a broader test than the "primary purpose" test because it looks only at causal connection, and not a "primary" reason. *See Visa U.S.A., Inc. v. First Data Corp.*, No. C-02-1786JSW(EMC), 2004 WL 1878209, at *4 (N.D. Cal. Aug. 23, 2004). In the attorney-client privilege context, the "because of" test might thus ask whether a dual-purpose communication was made "because of" the need to give or receive legal advice.

As the *Sanmina* court recently noted, the Ninth Circuit has not explicitly adopted either the "primary purpose" test or the "because of" test in determining whether dual-purpose communications are entitled to attorney-client privilege. *Sanmina*, 968 F.3d at 1118. And *Sanmina* itself declined to resolve this issue because the district court there had made a factual finding that the communications were not dual-purpose. *Id.* at 1119. Without guidance from our court, district courts in this circuit have split, applying both tests for attorney-client privilege claims. *Id.* at 1118 n.5 (summarizing district court cases).

II. The Primary-Purpose Test Applies to Dual-Purpose Communications in the Attorney-Client Privilege Context.

Because this case squarely involves dual-purpose communications, we now answer the question that *Sanmina* left open. We hold that the primary-purpose test applies to attorney-client privilege claims for dual-purpose communications.

To start, the "interpretation of the privilege's scope is guided by 'the principles of the common law . . . as interpreted by the courts . . . in the light of reason and experience.' " *Swidler & Berlin v. United States*, 524 U.S. 399, 403, 118 S.Ct. 2081, 141 L.Ed.2d 379 (1998) (quoting Fed. R. Evid. 501). At common law, the attorney-client privilege extends only to communications made "for the purpose of facilitating the rendition of professional legal services." *See United States v. Rowe*, 96 F.3d 1294, 1296 (9th Cir. 1996) (citation omitted); Restatement (Third) of the Law Governing Lawyers § 68 (Am. L. Inst. 2000) (stating that communication must be "for the purpose of obtaining or providing legal assistance for the client" to qualify for protection under attorney-client privilege). Thus, the "client must consult the lawyer for the purpose of obtaining legal assistance and not predominantly for another purpose." Restatement, *supra*, § 72 cmt. c; *see Swidler & Berlin*, 524 U.S. at 406–07, 118 S.Ct. 2081 (discussing scholarly commentary in describing the contours of privilege at common law). As the Supreme Court has recognized, the attorney-client privilege "protects only those disclosures necessary to obtain informed legal advice which might not have been made absent the privilege." *See Fisher v. United States*, 425 U.S. 391, 403, 96 S.Ct. 1569, 48 L.Ed.2d 39 (1976) (citation omitted). Thus, the scope of the attorney-client privilege is defined by the purpose of the communication consistent with the common law. *See Swidler & Berlin*, 524 U.S. at 410–11, 118 S.Ct. 2081; Fed. R. Evid. 501.

Appellants assert, however, that we should instead borrow the test from the work-product doctrine when a communication has a dual purpose. In Appellants' view, the attorney-client privilege should apply "when it can be fairly said that the document was created because of anticipated litigation and would not have been created in substantially similar form but for the prospect of that litigation." *See In re Grand Jury Subpoena (Mark Torf/Torf Env't Mgmt.)*, 357 F.3d 900, 908 (9th Cir. 2004) (describing when work-product doctrine applies). Appellants thus ask us to depart from the holdings of most courts and adopt a new test for attorney-client privilege—at least in the context of dual-purpose communications. But, as in *Swidler & Berlin*, Appellants offer no persuasive reason to abandon the common-law rule, 524 U.S. at 410–11, 118 S.Ct. 2081, which focuses on the purpose of the communication, not its relation to anticipated litigation. While the dual-purpose nature of Law Firm's representation can complicate the analysis of whether the communication was made to obtain legal advice, we see no reason to tinker with the privilege's scope and deviate from its common-law form to accommodate that concern.

While the attorney-client privilege and work-product doctrine are typically mentioned together, attorney-client privilege and the work-product protection doctrine are animated by different policy goals. It thus makes sense to have different tests for the two. *See id.* at 404–05, 118 S.Ct. 2081 (discussing policy rationale behind common-law scope of privilege in declining to adjust privilege's scope).

In the work-product context, the concern is "to preserve a zone of privacy in which a lawyer can prepare and develop legal theories and strategy with an eye toward litigation, free from unnecessary intrusion by his adversaries." *United States v. Adlman*, 134 F.3d 1194, 1196 (2d Cir. 1998) (cleaned up). In short, the work-product doctrine upholds the fairness of the adversarial process by allowing litigators to creatively develop legal theories and strategies—without their adversaries invoking the discovery process to pry into the litigators' minds and free-ride off them. *See, e.g., Allen v. Chi. Transit Auth.*, 198 F.R.D. 495, 500 (N.D. Ill. 2001) (explaining that the intent of the work-product doctrine "is to protect the adversarial process by providing an environment of privacy" and insure "that the litigator's opponent is unable to ride on the litigator's wits"). Given this goal, it makes sense to have a broader "because of" test that shields lawyers' litigation strategies from their adversaries.

In contrast, the attorney-client privilege encourages "full and frank communication between attorneys and their clients and thereby promote broader public interests in the observance of law and administration of justice." *Upjohn Co. v. United States*, 449 U.S. 383, 389, 101 S.Ct. 677, 66 L.Ed.2d 584 (1981). Unlike the work-product doctrine, the privilege is not necessarily tied to any adversarial process, and it is not so much concerned with the fairness of litigation as it is with providing a sanctuary for candid communication about any legal matter, not just impending litigation. Applying a broader "because of" test to attorney-client privilege might harm our adversarial system if parties try to withhold key documents as privileged by claiming that they were created "because of" litigation concerns. Indeed, it would create perverse incentives for companies to add layers of lawyers to every business decision in hopes of insulating themselves from scrutiny in any future litigation. Because of these different aims, it makes sense to apply different tests for the attorney-client privilege and the work-product doctrine. *See Sanmina*, 968 F.3d at 1120 ("[W]ork-product protection is not as easily waived as the attorney-client privilege based on the distinct purposes of the two privileges." (cleaned up)).

Further, Appellants only point to two district court cases to support their position, but most, if not all, of our sister circuits that have addressed this issue have opted for some version of the "primary purpose" test instead of the "because of" test. *See Swidler & Berlin*, 524 U.S. at 404, 118 S.Ct. 2081 (rejecting invitation to change scope of privilege from its common law form after noting that majority view tracked common law). The great weight of the authority goes against Appellants' position, which counsels against adopting it.

In sum, we reject Appellants' invitation to extend the "because of" test to the attorney-client privilege context, and hold that the "primary purpose" test applies to dual-purpose communications.

III. We Leave Open Whether the "A Primary Purpose Test" Should Apply.

Even if the "primary purpose test" applies here, Appellants argue that we should adopt "*a* primary purpose" as the test instead of "*the* primary purpose," relying on the D.C. Circuit's decision in *In re Kellogg Brown & Root, Inc.*, 756 F.3d 754 (D.C. Cir. 2014). The D.C. Circuit articulated its version of the primary-purpose test: "Was obtaining or providing legal advice a primary purpose of the communication, meaning one of the significant purposes of the communication?" *Id.* at 760. As *Kellogg* explained, "trying to find the one primary purpose for a communication motivated by two sometimes overlapping purposes (one legal and one business, for example) can be an inherently impossible task" because, often, it is "not useful or even feasible to try to determine whether the purpose was A or B when the purpose was A and B." *Id.* at 759.

In the eyes of the *Kellogg* court, "the primary purpose test, sensibly and properly applied, cannot and does not draw a rigid distinction between a legal purpose on the one hand and a business purpose on the other." *Id.* Even though it theoretically sounds easy to isolate "the primary or predominant" purpose of a communication, the exercise can quickly become messy in practice. That was the case in *Kellogg* in which the company conducted an internal investigation for both legal (*e.g.*, to obtain legal advice) *and* business reasons (*e.g.*, to comply with regulatory requirements and corporate policy). A test that focuses on *a* primary purpose instead of *the* primary purpose would save courts the trouble of having to identify a predominate purpose among two (or more) potentially equal purposes.

We see the merits of the reasoning in *Kellogg*. But we see no need to adopt that reasoning in this case. None of our other sister circuits have openly embraced *Kellogg* yet. We also recognize that *Kellogg* dealt with the very specific context of corporate internal investigations, and its reasoning does not apply with equal force in the tax context. Nor are we persuaded that the facts here require us to reach the *Kellogg* question. Moreover, the universe of documents in which the *Kellogg* test would make a difference is limited. The *Kellogg* test would only change the outcome of a privilege analysis in truly close cases, like where the legal purpose is just as significant as a non-legal purpose. Because the district court did not clearly err in finding that *the* predominate purpose of the disputed communications was not to obtain legal advice, they do not fall within the narrow universe where the *Kellogg* test would change the outcome of the privilege analysis. *See Sanmina*, 968 F.3d at 1119 (affirming the district court's finding about the purpose of a communication because it was not clearly erroneous). We thus see no need to adopt or apply the *Kellogg* formulation of the primary-purpose test here.

CONCLUSION

The district court's orders holding Company and Law Firm in contempt are **AFFIRMED**.

SOLUTIONS: THE LAWYER SHOULD HAVE, WOULD HAVE, COULD HAVE. . .

Great care must be taken with the ACP. Once the toothpaste is out of the tube, it cannot be put back in; in other words, once the privileged information is released or the privilege lost, the damage is done and is very difficult to rectify. Know at a minimum that merely cc'ing a lawyer on a communication dealing with a business decision does not make it privileged, regardless of the test being applied.

LEANING INTO PRACTICE

Imagine a potential client, Debbie Debtor, approaches you because she wants help with a debt. She is a single mother, recently unemployed. Her creditor, Larry Loan, is a prominent local politician. He is a member of the city council, and is currently running for mayor. Debbie tells you she signed a promissory note with Larry a few years back, but is having trouble making the payments. This is not her only debt, and bankruptcy may be on the table. But she would like you to try to renegotiate her loan with Larry first. And she mentions two other ideas. She says that she thinks that it might not play well politically for Larry if he is overly harsh to a recently unemployed woman like herself. And she has taken the initiative to follow Larry around time. In the process, she took an unflattering video of him appearing to hit an 8-year-old child while he was coaching a Little League team. She asks if that might help renegotiate the loan.

What strategies can you ethically follow to help Debbie achieve her goals? What would you personally be willing to do?

Becoming a Professional

X-Ray Questions

This article is from an MBA program, about negotiating across cultures. Do you agree with the advice given? Have you seen the principles discussed in your life? Do you see how these issues will play a role into your role as a transactional lawyer?

BEYOND THE CITE

Cross Cultural Negotiation (Business): **What You Need to Know, SMU Cox School of Business, March 10, 2020.**

Negotiation is an essential part of an effective business strategy. Key business decisions may either come to fruition or fall apart, depending on how successfully you negotiate a deal.

When negotiating internationally, cultural differences can make the process even more challenging. You want to ensure that your goals are met, but at the same time, you want to respect others' cultural norms and cultural values. As you begin preparations for an intercultural negotiation, here's what you need to know to make the interaction as successful as possible:

You Can Overcome the Language Barrier with Interpreters

For most people, the language barrier can be the most intimidating cultural difference—after all, if you can't have clear communication with each other, how can you even begin a discussion? Cross cultural communication is important. Therefore, some people choose to use an interpreter so the focus stays on the deal at hand, and not the semantics of language. This also ensures that no caveat, addendum or important detail is lost in translation. Just keep in mind:

- The interpreter doesn't know your business. Help this person by briefing him or her on the deal prior to the meeting. Make sure there is communication about any technical terms or special acronyms that may be used in the discussion. A little bit of context can help the interpreter better understand the full situation.

- The interpreter is an ally, not an opponent. Remain respectful with your interpreter. Don't take your frustrations out on him or her if they tell you what you don't want to hear (i.e., don't shoot the messenger), as it may result in a conflict between you and your interpreter.

An interpreter may not be appropriate for all situations. Although you may feel like the hire is a further effort in due diligence, it could be viewed as impersonal in a different culture. Know that you may be able to successfully navigate the conversation with little knowledge of the language by remembering these guidelines:

- Speak slowly and clearly.

- Keep your words concise and straightforward.

- Don't use too much technical jargon.

- Ask questions to clarify meaning and offer a chance for the negotiators to do the same.

- Remain attentive and listen to understand, not simply to respond.

Above all, don't use words to impress. You may pick up a few words or phrases of the negotiators' native language, but don't throw them in the discussion haphazardly to show that you know something of their culture. This could inadvertently offend someone, and moreover, you could look like you're trying too hard to make a good impression.

Know the Cultural Differences Among Business Standards

The way we do business in America is not necessarily how business is done in Spain, Turkey or Nigeria. Every culture abides by its own set of business standards and it's important to be aware of the different ways each country does business before you even set foot in the boardroom. You must develop international business skills to succeed in global settings:

- Punctuality—In the U.S., timing is everything. If you walk into a meeting or an interview one minute past the start time, you've already started off on the wrong foot and may run into conflict. But in other cultures, tardiness may not be considered offensive at all. In fact, punctuality-or showing up too early-can be seen as uptight and too formal.

- Formality—Along those same lines, some cultures favor an informal negotiation over a formal negotiation. In these situations, the negotiator will invite small talk to first get to know you as a person. Using an interpreter here would likely not be in your best interest.

- Individual vs. group negotiation—In some countries, a group of negotiators (negotiation team) is preferred, whereas in others, a single negotiator is trusted to do the job.

- Negotiation style/Negotiation Strategy—Every culture has a different negotiation process or negotiation behavior. We Americans tend to favor a win-win negotiation where everyone walks away with something. However, in some cultures or another country, the process of negotiating is confrontational, and a win-lose negotiating style is preferred.

- Emotions—Keep your cool, but don't expect others to keep theirs. In some countries, showing emotion during negotiations is acceptable, while in others, participants may remain stoic.

Walk into the meeting with open eyes and take the time to observe the other negotiators. Follow their lead and be open to adapting your style to theirs when necessary. Be open to other communication styles as it will help build a relationship between you and another culture.

WHAT'S NEXT?

The Rules we have studied amount to little unless there is a law firm culture—no matter the size of the firm—that honors the adherence to the Rules both as the proper way to run a justice system and as good business. What follows is a discussion of how these two values intersect in a lawyer's everyday legal practice.

> To assess your understanding of the material in this chapter, click here to take a quiz.

PART VI

The Lawyer as Businessperson
and Entrepreneur

CHAPTER 9

Managing the Law Firm

Coming Attractions

Law is a business as well as a profession. Experiencing professional responsibility as a business is a client centric proposition. This orientation is consistent with the letter of, and the spirit animating, the Rules you learned thus far. Lawyers owe a duty to see that the lawyers in the firm act ethically; partners are likewise charged with that responsibility on an individual basis regardless of if the matter involved is one they are managing. The rules embody a pronounced tilt towards a simple ethic: making money takes a subordinate role to the welfare of the client specifically and to the public generally. For example, lawyers are forbidden from proposing or agreeing to a non-competition agreement if a lawyer leaves a firm because of a client's authority to select the lawyers that they believe are best suited for their needs. Thus, even though non-compete agreements might make business-sense, they would offend the values of the profession. Similarly, capitalism would embrace a lawyer agreeing—as part of a settlement agreement—never to sue the defendant again on behalf of any other client, the Rules forbid such an arrangement. Why? It removes a lawyer from the universe of lawyers that a member of the public can select, often—because of the previous experience in settled lawsuit—the best lawyer for the matter impacting prospective clients.

This chapter also revisits a central tenet of legal ethics; namely, the duty of lawyers to use their unhindered judgment in the best interests s of the client and to remain uninfluenced by other considerations. Accordingly, the Rules prohibit a lawyer from sharing fees, except in very limited circumstances with non-lawyers. This mandate encompasses a prohibition on entering a partnership with non-lawyers when one of the purposes of the partnership is practicing law. Why? The non-lawyers might be driven more by an interest in expanding profits than in serving the clients.

Does this way of doing business still make sense in a complex and interrelated economy? What harm would there be if a law firm and say, an accounting firm or a consulting firm, merged services to provide more expansive and efficient client service? Essentially, a one stop shop. Or should these rules be considered more along the lines of consumer protection rules intended to protect the prospective client, the client, and the public in a variety of ways. Protect from what? Potential overreaching, abuse of persuasion training, prioritizing personal desires ahead of client needs.

Finally, as we study these Rules, frame them as consumer protection rules. Many are intended to protect the prospective client, the client, and the public in a variety of ways. Protect from what you might ask? Lawyer overreaching, misuse of our persuasion training, prioritizing our needs ahead of the client's/public's needs.

Section 1.   The Responsibility of Managing an Ethical Law Firm

A.   Ensuring Adherence to the Rules of Professional Responsibility, Individually/Firmwide

Model Rule 5.1: Responsibilities of Partners, Managers, and Supervisory Lawyers

(a)   A partner in a law firm, and a lawyer who individually or together with other lawyers possesses comparable managerial authority in a law firm, shall make reasonable efforts to ensure that the firm has in effect *measures giving reasonable assurance* that all lawyers in the firm conform to the Rules of Professional Conduct.

(b)   A lawyer having *direct* supervisory authority over another lawyer shall make reasonable efforts to ensure that the other lawyer conforms to the Rules of Professional Conduct.

(c)   A lawyer *shall* be responsible for another lawyer's violation of the Rules of Professional Conduct if:

(1)   the lawyer orders or, with knowledge of the specific conduct, *ratifies* the conduct involved; or

(2)   the lawyer is a partner or has comparable managerial authority in the law firm in which the other lawyer practices, or has direct supervisory authority over the other lawyer, and knows of the conduct at a time when its consequences can be *avoided or mitigated* but fails to take reasonable remedial action.

Deconstruction Exercise/Rule Rationale

This Rule is multilayered in order to ensure that adherence to the rules is given maximum coverage. Note how the rule mandates that a firm ensure that those in charge of a firm ensure that all lawyers adhere to the rules of ethics. This broad charge can be delegated within the partnership ranks, but that delegation must be competently performed by placing qualified partners into this role.

The Rule then drills down to a micro level and holds that supervisory lawyers must likewise ensure that those under their direction act ethically.

These rules are capped off by a requirement (a) that a lawyer cannot act unethically through the acts of another which they direct and (b) that a lawyer who does not correct an unethical act, but later comes to *know* of it, and takes no corrective action, ratifies the conduct and is held to have violated the rules. Likewise, a firm partner—even with no direct supervisory responsibility over another lawyer who acted unethically—must take action to correct the conduct or risk a personal rule violation.

Finally, the rule does have certain guardrails; namely, the last section that provides that action must be taken "at a time when the consequences (of the unethical act) can be avoided or mitigated. . ." This language in (c)(2) is again a decision on competing values: on the one hand the desire to ensure that there is an even playing field and on the other the need for, at some point, an ultimate resolution of a matter. Thus, it is a fair inference that if "consequences" cannot be "avoided" or "mitigated" that the matter has been concluded. If so, the rules place the focus on the value of certainty in a matter's conclusion over fairness in the resolution of a matter.

Let's drill down further into the rule. There are only four instances in which a lawyer is permitted to share legal fees with a nonlawyer. The remainder of the rule specifies the most common instances in which a lawyer might be tempted to share fees with a nonlawyer but in which a lawyer is prohibited from doing so. Note that the common thematic structure in these subsections—(b), (c), and (d)—each focuses on others, who are nonlawyers, possessing the ability to influence a lawyer's judgment on behalf of a client and a lawyer's loyalty to a client As with our discussion on conflicts, the rule focuses on the possibility of the influence being present and not its actual exercise.

LEANING INTO PRACTICE

Scenario No. 1: The Case of the Wayward Associate and the Responsible Partner

Eddie Associate is performing document review in order to respond to a request for production (RFP) provided by the litigant opposite. He comes across a "smoking gun" document that will doom the client's case. The document is responsive to a specific request in the RFP. Eddie does not destroy the document but puts it in a file dealing with hundreds of travel invoices in hopes that counsel opposite will not notice the document. He then sends off the production in that format to counsel opposite. He tells the responsible partner a few days later about his action. What should the partner do? What if Eddie tells the responsible partner after the litigation is concluded?

Scenario No. 2: The Case of the New Partner and the Wayward Associate

Imagine the same facts as Scenario No. 1 but Lola Partner, who was just been admitted to the partnership, learns of Eddie's conduct shortly after sending off the document to counsel opposite. Lola lacks no supervisory responsibility over the case or the file. Same questions as to Lola as above.

Model Rule 5.4: Professional Independence of a Lawyer

(a)   A lawyer or law firm shall not share legal fees with a nonlawyer, except that:

(1)   an agreement by a lawyer with the lawyer's firm, partner, or associate may provide for the payment of money, over a reasonable period of time after the lawyer's death, to the lawyer's estate or to one or more specified persons;

(2)   a lawyer who purchases the practice of a deceased, disabled, or disappeared lawyer may, pursuant to the provisions of Rule 1.17, pay to the estate or other representative of that lawyer the agreed-upon purchase price;

(3)   a lawyer or law firm may include nonlawyer employees in a compensation or retirement plan, even though the plan is based in whole or in part on a profit-sharing arrangement; and

(4)   a lawyer may share court-awarded legal fees with a nonprofit organization that employed, retained or recommended employment of the lawyer in the matter.

(b)   A lawyer shall not form a partnership with a nonlawyer if any of the activities of the partnership consist of the practice of law.

(c)   A lawyer shall not permit a person who recommends, employs, or pays the lawyer to render legal services for another to direct or regulate the lawyer's professional judgment in rendering such legal services.

(d)   A lawyer shall not practice with or in the form of a professional corporation or association authorized to practice law for a profit, if:

> (1)   a nonlawyer owns any interest therein, except that a fiduciary representative of the estate of a lawyer may hold the stock or interest of the lawyer for a reasonable time during administration;

> (2)   a nonlawyer is a corporate director or officer thereof or occupies the position of similar responsibility in any form of association other than a corporation; or

> (3)   a nonlawyer has the right to direct or control the professional judgment of a lawyer.

Deconstruction Exercise/Rule Rationale

Lawyers owe a duty of unqualified loyalty to the client. If that duty is somehow compromised, then the lawyer's judgment, advice, and decision making could conceivably be clouded. And the concept conceivably being clouded takes us back to MR 1.8 in general—it is not so much that the lawyer will commit an ethical breach as that the lawyer is tempted to do so. Once again a prophylactic rule.

Scenario No. 1: The Case of the Staff Bonus

Tony Lawyer is a personal injury lawyer. Tony believes that the happiness of his staff is important because happy staff take good care of clients. And happiness often translates into money for the staff. So, in an effort to improve client satisfaction, Tony announces to the staff that "You all know that our firm is working on a big case involving a contingency fee. So, once we win the case or settle it, I will set aside 20% of the resulting fees for staff bonuses." Brain Paralegal thinks this is great because he goes to law school on a part time basis and will use the money for tuition. But after several months pass, and there is no bonus, because the case is dragging on, he asks Tony "so where is the bonus you promised?!? I have half a mind to report you to the State Bar. And several of my fellow workers think the same thing." Should Tony be concerned? Why or why not? Tony shrugs it off because Brian is always complaining about something. Does it make any difference to your analysis if the bonus is based on overall profit versus profit from a single case?

Scenario No. 2: The Case of the Client Centric Lawyer

Ismir Lawyer owns a bustling family law practice. He generally represents men in their divorces and usually these men are high income individuals, if not downright wealthy. Because there are numerous financial issues that arise in handling the divorces, he retains Esmeralda Finance-Wizard to be an expert witness or simply to counsel and advise clients. She has an M.B.A. from Harvard and is a C.P.A. as well. One day Esmeralda, while working with Ismir on a case, tells him, "Tell you what! Let's go into partnership together. It will be more efficient for us and more importantly will be of immediate benefit to our clients because I am not always available to work with you and them." Ismir agrees and they form the partnership of Lawyer & Finance-Wizard. Is this partnership allowed under the Rules? Why or why not? If you say "no" what can be done, if anything, to achieve the goals of client service that Ismir seeks to achieve?

B. Ensuring Access to the Public's Choice of Lawyer

Model Rule 5.6: Restrictions on Rights to Practice

A lawyer shall not participate in offering or making:

> (a) a partnership, shareholders, operating, employment, or other similar type of agreement that restricts the right of a lawyer to practice after termination of the relationship, except an agreement concerning benefits upon retirement; or

> (b) an agreement in which a restriction on the lawyer's right to practice is part of the settlement of a client controversy.

Deconstruction Exercise/Rule Rationale

Note the use of the mighty "or" which again makes the Rule more expansive, covering the offering of certain deals as well their acceptance. Two types of agreements are covered, each of which restricts the right of a lawyer to practice: one after the lawyer leaves a firm (generally called a non-competition agreement) and the other an agreement (as a condition of a lawsuit settlement) that the plaintiff's lawyer will not ever again sue the defendant (colloquially labeled "Never Darken My Door Again"). Once again, pure capitalism for a lawyer is relegated to a lesser good. But a lesser good compared to what? Here the well-being of the public in being able to select the lawyer of their choice, a lawyer best suited for their needs. And this rationale is in alignment with the hesitancy you learned about earlier in a court granting a DQ motion.

Cases and Materials

X-Ray Questions (*Fearnow*)

As you read the rule consider that one key word is the verb "restricts." Why is this a key word in applying the Rule? A purely textual analysis would mean that an agreement that makes it more challenging to practice law—but that does not forbid same—would pass muster under MR 5.6(a). We see this view articulated in the following case that applies the California interpretation of MR 5.6(a). Other courts disagree, holding that a noncompete is a rule violation if it functionally acts to prohibit a lawyer from leaving a firm by placing obstacles in their way and thereby effectively discouraging them from or, if they do so, restricting client access to them. Which view do you this has a better argument.

William D. Fearnow and Elizabeth Fearnow v. Ridenour, Swenson, Cleere & Evans, P.C.

Supreme Court of Arizona, 2006.
138 P.3d 723.

HURWITZ, JUSTICE.

¶ 1 Ethical Rule ("ER") 5.6(a) of the Arizona Rules of Professional Conduct prohibits an "agreement that restricts the right of a lawyer to practice [law] after termination of [a law firm] relationship." Ariz. R. Sup.Ct. 42 (2006). This case involves the application of ER 5.6(a) to a shareholder agreement requiring a departing lawyer to tender his stock to a professional corporation for no compensation if he thereafter competes with the corporation in the practice of law. We hold that such an agreement does not violate ER 5.6(a), but rather should be evaluated under the well-established law governing similar restrictive covenants in agreements between non-lawyers.

I.

¶ 2 In 1987, William Fearnow paid $33,674.42 for a law firm partnership interest. Four years later, the partners decided to wind down the firm. Several partners, including Fearnow, formed a new firm, Ridenour, Swenson, Cleere & Evans, P.C. ("RSCE"). *See* Ariz.Rev.Stat. ("A.R.S.") §§ 10–2201 to –2249 (2004) (governing professional corporations) (hereinafter "the Professional Corporations Act" or "the Act"). The former partners made no new capital contributions to RSCE; rather, their original partnership contributions were converted to stock. Fearnow was thus deemed to have paid $33,674.42 for one share of RSCE stock.

¶ 3 Fearnow and the other RSCE shareholders signed a Shareholder Agreement ("Agreement"). The Agreement generally provided for the repurchase of a lawyer's stock for the original subscription price upon disability, retirement, withdrawal, or expulsion from the firm. Separate provisions in the Agreement (collectively, the "voluntary withdrawal provisions") required a shareholder voluntarily withdrawing and thereafter competing in the firm's "geographic area for more than ten hours per week" to "tender his or her Share back to the Corporation for no compensation."

¶ 4 In 1998, Fearnow voluntarily left RSCE to join another Phoenix firm. Fearnow demanded $33,674.42 for his RSCE stock. RSCE refused, citing the voluntary withdrawal provisions. Fearnow sued, alleging that the provisions violated ER 5.6(a).

¶ 5 The parties filed cross-motions for summary judgment. The superior court held that the voluntary withdrawal provisions violated ER 5.6(a) and were therefore unenforceable. Because the Agreement had no severability clause, the court held the entire contract invalid. The trial court then found Fearnow to be a "disqualified person" as defined by the Professional Corporations Act, *see* A.R.S. § 10–2201(1), and ordered a valuation of his stock pursuant to A.R.S. § 10–2223. The superior court ordered RSCE to repurchase the stock for $86,500.

¶ 6 The court of appeals affirmed in part and reversed in part. *Fearnow v. Ridenour, Swenson, Cleere & Evans, P.C.*, 210 Ariz. 256, 110 P.3d 357 (App.2005). The court found the voluntary withdrawal provisions unenforceable, but held that Fearnow was not a "disqualified person" entitled to redemption of his stock under the Act. *Id.* at 262 ¶ 32, 110 P.3d at 363.

¶ 7 Fearnow petitioned for review and RSCE filed a conditional cross-petition. We granted review of both petitions because the issues presented are of first impression and statewide importance. We have jurisdiction pursuant to Article 6, Section 5(3), of the Arizona Constitution and A.R.S. § 12–120.24 (2003).

II.

A.

¶ 8 As a general rule, a contract restricting the right of an employee to compete with an employer after termination of employment "which is not unreasonable in its limitations should be upheld in the absence of a showing of bad faith or of contravening public policy." *Lassen v. Benton*, 86 Ariz. 323, 328, 346 P.2d 137, 140 (1959), *modified on other grounds*, 87 Ariz. 72, 347 P.2d 1012 (1959); *see also* 15 *Corbin on Contracts* § 80.15 (2003) (noting that in determining the enforceability of such a provision, "reasonableness is the North Star"). Such a restrictive covenant is unreasonable if "(a) the restraint is greater than is needed to protect the promisee's legitimate interest, or (b) the promisee's need is outweighed by the hardship to the promisor and the likely injury to the public." Restatement (Second) of Contracts § 188 (1981).

¶ 9 The determination of "[r]easonableness is a fact-intensive inquiry that depends on the totality of the circumstances." *Valley Med. Specialists v. Farber*, 194 Ariz. 363, 369 ¶ 20, 982 P.2d 1277, 1283 (1999). "Each case hinges on its own particular facts." *Bryceland v. Northey*, 160 Ariz. 213, 217, 772 P.2d 36, 40 (App.1989). As the court of appeals has noted,

> [w]hat is reasonable depends on the whole subject matter of the contract, the kind and character of the business, its location, the purpose to be accomplished by the restriction, and all the circumstances which show the intention of the parties.

Gann v. Morris, 122 Ariz. 517, 518, 596 P.2d 43, 44 (App.1979).

¶ 10 Most of our cases concerning the enforcement of restrictive covenants deal with "non-compete" agreements, under which an employee is prohibited from competing with the former employer in a geographic area for a period of time. *See, e.g., Farber*, 194 Ariz. at 365 ¶ 3, 982 P.2d at 1279 (finding unreasonable a covenant between physicians forbidding competition within a five-mile radius of any medical office owned by the former employer for three years); *Lassen*, 86 Ariz. at 328, 346 P.2d at 140 (finding reasonable a provision prohibiting competition for five years within a twelve-mile radius of a veterinarian's former employer). We have, however, employed the same fact-based reasonableness analysis to determine the enforceability of agreements under which a departing employee is not entirely forbidden to compete. *See Olliver/Pilcher Ins., Inc. v. Daniels*, 148 Ariz. 530, 715 P.2d 1218 (1986). *Olliver/Pilcher* involved an "anti-piracy" agreement forbidding solicitation of the former employer's customers. *Id.* at 531, 715 P.2d at 1219. While recognizing that such a provision is "less restrictive than a covenant not to compete," *id.* at 531, 715 P.2d at 1218, we reiterated that " 'the test of validity of restrictive covenants is one of reasonableness,' " *id.* at 532, 715 P.2d at 1219 (quoting *Lessner Dental Labs. v. Kidney*, 16 Ariz.App. 159, 160, 492 P.2d 39, 40 (1971)).

B.

¶ 11 Were Fearnow not an attorney, the voluntary withdrawal provisions would be subject to a fact-based reasonableness analysis. This Court, however, has adopted a rule governing the ability of lawyers to enter into certain types of agreements. That rule, ER 5.6, provides:

> A lawyer shall not participate in offering or making:
>
> (a) a partnership or employment agreement that restricts the rights of a lawyer to practice after termination of the relationship, except an agreement concerning benefits upon retirement; or
>
> (b) an agreement in which a restriction on the lawyer's right to practice is part of the settlement of a controversy between private parties.
>
> Such restrictions are prohibited because they limit a lawyer's "professional autonomy" and interfere with "the freedom of clients to choose a lawyer." ER 5.6 cmt.

¶ 12 The Arizona Rules of Professional Conduct, of which ER 5.6 is part, are based on the 1983 Model Rules of Professional Conduct promulgated by the American Bar Association ("ABA"). *See* Ariz. R. Sup.Ct. 42 (providing that the professional conduct of State Bar members shall be governed by the ABA Model Rules, as amended by this Court). But even before the ABA adopted Model Rule 5.6(a), its Committee on Professional Ethics had issued several opinions condemning non-compete agreements among lawyers under previous Canons of Professional Ethics. Those opinions stressed the same themes as the current commentary to ER 5.6—lawyer autonomy and client choice. *See, e.g.,* ABA Comm. on Prof'l Ethics, Formal Op. 300 (1961) (finding a non-compete agreement improper under Canon 7 (forbidding encroachment on the business of another lawyer), Canon 27 (prohibiting solicitation), and Canon 35 (protecting client confidences)); ABA Comm. on Prof'l Ethics, Informal Op. 1072 (1968) (stating that covenants not to compete "interfere with and obstruct the freedom of the client in choosing and dealing with his lawyer" and that an "attorney must remain free to practice when and where he will and to be available to prospective clients who might desire to engage his services"). These opinions led to the adoption in 1969 of Disciplinary Rule ("DR") 2–108 of the Model Code of Professional Responsibility, which in turn was incorporated into Rule 5.6 of the 1983 Model Rules without substantive change.

¶ 13 ER 5.6 categorically forbids lawyers from making an "agreement that restricts the right of a lawyer to practice after the termination of [a law firm] relationship," ER 5.6(a), or a settlement agreement containing "a restriction on a lawyer's right to practice," ER 5.6(b). Neither ER 5.6 nor prior ABA opinions, however, expressly deals with agreements that do not restrict a lawyer's right to practice or compete, but rather impose only some financial disincentive for doing so. Such provisions are before us today.

C.

¶ 14 In analyzing the voluntary withdrawal provisions, we write on a clean slate. No prior opinion of this Court has applied ER 5.6(a). We did, however, discuss ER 5.6 in *Farber,* which involved a covenant not to compete among physicians. In that case, we analogized the importance of a patient's right to choose a doctor to the need for a client to be free to choose an attorney. 194 Ariz. at 368 ¶¶ 16– 17, 982 P.2d at 1282. Citing ER 5.6, we stated that "restrictive covenants are prohibited between attorneys," *id.* at 369 ¶ 18, 982 P.2d at 1283, and that "public policy considerations preclude their applicability," *id. (quoting Dwyer v. Jung,* 133 N.J.Super. 343, 336 A.2d 498, 500 (Ch. Div.1975) (quotation marks omitted)). We concluded that the doctor/patient relationship, like the attorney/client relationship, "is special and entitled to unique protection." *Id.* ¶ 19. We did not, however, find the covenant in *Farber* invalid as a matter of law. Expressly declining the invitation to hold such agreements between physicians "void per se as against public policy," *id.* ¶ 19 n. 1, we instead examined the covenant for reasonableness, *id.* ¶ 19.

¶ 15 The above-quoted dicta from *Farber* support the conclusion that agreements violative of ER 5.6(a) will not be enforced. Cases from other jurisdictions so hold, finding void agreements that expressly forbid attorneys from representing particular clients or competing in a specific geographic area for a specified period of time. *See, e.g., White v. Med. Review Consultants, Inc.,* 831 S.W.2d 662, 664–65 (Mo.Ct.App.1992) (upholding a rule prohibiting the restriction of a lawyer's right to practice); *Dwyer,* 336 A.2d at 501 (finding void as against public policy a covenant prohibiting departing attorneys from working with partnership clients).

¶ 16 The case law is less clear, however, when the covenant does not categorically forbid competition or representation of former clients, but rather provides only a financial disincentive that may discourage the departing lawyer from doing so. Many courts hold such provisions void. For example, in an oft-quoted opinion, the New York Court of Appeals refused to enforce a law firm partnership agreement that conditioned the payment of earned but uncollected partnership revenues upon a withdrawing partner's refraining from competing with the firm. *Cohen v. Lord, Day & Lord,* 75 N.Y.2d 95, 551 N.Y.S.2d 157, 550 N.E.2d 410, 410 (1989). The court reasoned:

> [W]hile the provision in question does not expressly or completely prohibit a withdrawing partner from engaging in the practice of law, the significant monetary penalty it exacts, if the withdrawing partner practices competitively with the former firm, constitutes an impermissible restriction on the practice of law. The forfeiture-for-compensation provision would functionally and realistically discourage and foreclose a withdrawing partner from serving clients who might wish to continue to be represented by the withdrawing lawyer and would thus interfere with the client's choice of counsel.

Id. at 411. Other jurisdictions have reached similar results on similar reasoning.

¶ 17 There is, however, a strong opposing view, articulated principally by the California courts. The seminal case is *Haight, Brown & Bonesteel v. Superior Court,* 234 Cal.App.3d 963, 285 Cal.Rptr. 845 (1991), which involved a provision requiring withdrawing attorneys competing with the law firm to forfeit capital investments and accounts receivable. Construing an ethical rule quite similar to ER 5.6, the court found that the provision was not prohibited because it did "not expressly or completely prohibit the [attorneys] from engaging in the practice of law, or from representing clients." *Id.* at 848. The court noted that the rule "simply provides that an attorney may not enter into an agreement to refrain from the practice of law." *Id.* The rule does not prohibit a withdrawing partner from agreeing to compensate his former partners in the event he chooses to represent clients previously represented by the firm from which he has withdrawn. Such a construction represents a balance between competing interests. On the one hand, it enables departing attorneys to withdraw from a partnership and continue to practice anywhere within the state, and to be able to accept employment should he choose to so do from any client who desires to retain him. On the other hand, the remaining partners remain able to preserve the stability of the law firm by making available the withdrawing partner's share of capital and accounts receivable to replace the loss of the stream of income from the clients taken by the withdrawing partner to support the partnership's debts.

Id. at 848.

¶ 18 Three years later, the California Supreme Court held that "an agreement among law partners imposing a reasonable toll on departing partners who compete with the firm is enforceable." *Howard v. Babcock*, 6 Cal.4th 409, 25 Cal.Rptr.2d 80, 863 P.2d 150, 151 (1994). The provision at issue required departing attorneys who worked with other departing attorneys in competition with the law firm to forfeit all withdrawal benefits; departing attorneys who worked on their own but competed with the law firm were required to forfeit seventy-five percent of their benefits. *Id. Howard* was decided against a backdrop of California statutes favoring non-compete agreements. *Id.* at 154. But the decision did not turn on those statutes; the court expressly noted that it had the "power to impose a higher standard of conduct on lawyers" through ethical rules. *Id.* at 155. The California Supreme Court concluded, however, that its ethical rule was not "intended to . . . prohibit the type of agreement that is at issue here." *Id.* at 155–56. *Howard* found a critical distinction between an agreement imposing disincentives against competition and one forbidding competition:

> An agreement that assesses a reasonable cost against a partner who chooses to compete with his or her former partners does not restrict the practice of law. Rather, it attaches an economic consequence to a departing partner's unrestricted choice to pursue a particular kind of practice.

Id. at 156.

¶ 19 Recognizing that law firms have an obligation to protect their own economic interests and their investments in training and promoting partners, *Howard* found "no legal justification for treating partners in law firms differently in this respect from partners in other business and professions." *Id.* at 157. Such an approach, the court noted, would "have no deleterious effect on the current ability of clients to retain loyal, competent counsel of their choice." *Id.* at 156–57. Thus, *Howard* concluded that a contract provision that did not prevent a departing lawyer from competing was not void on its face, but rather would be evaluated for reasonableness. *Id.* at 160.

D.

¶ 20 We find the reasoning of *Howard* compelling. ER 5.6 prohibits only an agreement "that *restricts the right of a lawyer to practice*" law after termination of employment with a firm. (Emphasis added.) It is one thing for this Court, in its supervisory capacity over the legal profession, to adopt a limited exception to the general rule construing restrictive covenants for reasonableness when confronting a contract the terms of which forbid a lawyer from engaging in practice or representing certain clients. It is quite another, as *Howard* notes, to completely "distinguish lawyers from other professionals such as doctors or accountants, who also owe a high degree of skill and loyalty to their patients and clients." *Howard*, 25 Cal.Rptr 80, 863 P.2d at 160. We are unable to conclude that the interests of a lawyer's clients are so superior to those of a doctor's patients (whose choice of a physician may literally be a life-or-death decision) as to require a unique rule applicable only to attorneys. The language of ER 5.6 does not support such a sweeping special treatment of lawyers, nor does protection of clients mandate such a result.

¶ 21 We therefore decline to read ER 5.6(a) in the expansive fashion suggested by Fearnow. Although the rule prohibits—and we will hold unenforceable—agreements that forbid a lawyer to represent certain clients or engage in practice in certain areas or at certain times, its language should not be stretched to condemn categorically all agreements imposing any disincentive upon lawyers from leaving law firm employment. Such agreements, as is the case with restrictive covenants between other professionals, should be examined under the reasonableness standard.

E.

¶ 22 The Shareholder Agreement requires a withdrawing attorney engaging in "lawyering activity in competition with the Corporation and within the Corporation's geographic area" to forfeit his or her stock in the professional corporation. The provisions do not restrict the lawyer's right to practice law after termination. Rather, they merely provide a lawyer who withdraws and decides to practice elsewhere with less money than others making different decisions.

¶ 23 Because the superior court held that the voluntary withdrawal provisions were void as a matter of law, it did not construe the provisions for reasonableness. The court of appeals, even assuming that the case was governed by the more permissive standard of *Howard*, found the provisions unreasonable as a matter of law because they required Fearnow to forfeit his entire capital contribution even if he took no RSCE clients. *Fearnow*, 210 Ariz. at 259 ¶ 17, 110 P.3d at 360.

¶ 24 As an initial matter, we note that RSCE claims that Fearnow did take clients with him upon his departure; the court of appeals' observation that the voluntary withdrawal provisions might be unreasonable when applied to a lawyer who took none is thus not dispositive. More importantly, because the case was decided on summary judgment under the superior court's view of ER 5.6(a),

RSCE never had the opportunity below to present facts concerning the reasonableness of the provisions. Nor has Fearnow had the opportunity to present evidence that these particular provisions are unreasonable. Because "[e]ach case turns on its own particular facts," *Bryceland*, 160 Ariz. at 217, 772 P.2d at 40, we cannot conclude as a matter of law whether the voluntary withdrawal provisions are reasonable. We remand to allow the superior court to address the reasonableness of the voluntary withdrawal provisions.

III.

¶ 25 The second issue before us is the appropriate remedy if the voluntary withdrawal provisions are found unreasonable. The superior court held that Fearnow was entitled to redemption of his stock under the Professional Corporations Act as a "disqualified person." The court of appeals disagreed, holding that Fearnow has no such statutory remedy as long as he is licensed to practice law. *Fearnow*, 210 Ariz. at 260 ¶ 23, 110 P.3d at 361.

¶ 26 We agree with the court of appeals. Section 10–2201(1) defines a "disqualified" person as "an individual or entity that is not or ceases to be a qualified person"; section 10–2201(7) in turn defines a "qualified person" simply as "a person that is eligible under this chapter to be issued shares by a professional corporation." As the court of appeals correctly noted, section 10–2220(A)(1) allows issuance of shares to "[i]ndividuals who are licensed by law in this or another state to render a professional service described in the corporation's articles of incorporation." At all times relevant to this case, Fearnow was licensed to practice law in Arizona. He therefore is not a "disqualified person."

¶ 27 *Vinall v. Hoffman*, 133 Ariz. 322, 651 P.2d 850 (1982), upon which Fearnow relies, is not to the contrary. That case involved a prior version of the Professional Corporations Act, which required the repurchase of stock after the "resignation" of a shareholder. *Id.* at 323, 651 P.2d at 851 (citing former A.R.S. § 10–909(D) (repealed 1995)). Our holding in *Vinall* that the word "resignation" meant resignation from the corporation, not the profession, is therefore of no aid in interpreting the present version of the Professional Corporations Act, which triggers the right to repurchase upon "disqualification."

¶ 28 But it does not follow, as the court of appeals held, that Fearnow must retain his RSCE stock until his retirement or disqualification to practice law. The Professional Corporations Act provides that "[a] provision for the acquisition of shares contained in a professional corporation's articles of incorporation or bylaws or in a private agreement is enforceable." A.R.S. § 10–2223(A).

Therefore, should the voluntary withdrawal provisions be eventually found unreasonable, the next question is whether the Agreement nonetheless requires the acquisition of Fearnow's shares.

¶ 29 The superior court held that because the Agreement had no severability clause, Fearnow had no contractual remedy. The court of appeals, while disagreeing with the superior court's conclusion that Fearnow was entitled to repurchase of his stock under the Professional Corporations Act, did not address whether the Agreement itself provided a remedy. *Fearnow,* 210 Ariz. at 262 ¶ 29 n. 8, 110 P.3d at 363 n. 8 (stating that "we merely hold that there is not a remedy under the Act that provides for the mandatory repurchase of such shares as long as the departing shareholder remains licensed").

¶ 30 Although the Agreement has no severability clause, we believe that the contract nonetheless requires repurchase of Fearnow's share for his original subscription price if the voluntary withdrawal provisions are deemed unenforceable. Under the Agreement, any shareholder who becomes permanently disabled, retires from the practice of law, is expelled from the law firm, or voluntarily withdraws must tender his or her stock to the corporation. In all cases but one, that tender is made in return for the original subscription price. Only the partner who voluntarily withdraws and competes with the firm in a stated geographic area is forced to tender stock for no compensation.

¶ 31 Although "we will not permit courts to add terms or rewrite provisions" to covenants, *Farber,* 194 Ariz. at 372 ¶ 31, 982 P.2d at 1286, "Arizona courts will 'blue pencil' restrictive covenants, eliminating grammatically severable, unreasonable provisions," *id.* ¶ 30. In this case, the voluntary withdrawal provisions are severable from the balance of the agreement. The contracting parties plainly contemplated that *all* departing shareholders would be required to return their stock to RSCE. The Agreement also provides that all but those choosing to compete would receive their original subscriptions in return for the stock. If the only exceptions to the rule—the voluntary withdrawal provisions— are unenforceable, the severability of those provisions is plainly "evident from the contract itself." *Olliver/Pilcher,* 148 Ariz. at 533, 715 P.2d at 1221.

¶ 32 Therefore, if the superior court concludes on remand that the voluntary withdrawal provisions are unreasonable, it should order RSCE to repurchase Fearnow's share for $33,674.42, his original subscription price.

IV.

¶ 33 For the reasons above, we vacate the opinion of the court of appeals, vacate the judgment of the superior court, and remand to the superior court for further proceedings consistent with this opinion. Because we do not yet know which party will ultimately be successful in this matter, we decline to award either party attorneys' fees either under the Agreement or under A.R.S. § 12–341.01.

SOLUTIONS: THE LAWYER SHOULD HAVE, **WOULD HAVE, COULD HAVE. . .**
Before signing any agreement with your firm do what you tell clients to do—get some legal counsel, know the rules in your jurisdiction, and decide whether agreeing to it is smart legally and practically. Otherwise, you might find yourself entangled in legal claims post-departure. Conversely, if it is a firm you control or manage consider the same considerations in deciding whether to offer such agreements.

LEANING INTO PRACTICE

Once upon a time, lawyers went to work for a firm and stayed for the rest of their careers. As lawyers in a new generation, however, you will likely move firms several times in your career. "In the first 12 years of practice, many lawyers had had four or more jobs. That is a job change on average every three years." https://thepractice.law.harvard.edu/article/legal-careers/.

Nicole Lawyer and Nadda Lawyer were friends in law school. They each go to work for the same firm upon graduation. The firm does mostly family law but also some commercial litigation. They are each overjoyed to have a job after graduation. Karen Lawyer is the founder of the firm as well as its managing partner. She tells them that she hopes they have found a "home" with her and the other firm lawyers. "I want to create a harmonious and fulfilling atmosphere to practice law, so I want you to know that you are always free to leave me and take my clients with you. But if you do so, you need to pay the firm 5% of the fees you generate at your new firm from any clients you take with you. I will be providing training to both of you—gosh, law school really teaches you zip—and the firm needs some return on its investment. You each need to give the firm ninety days' notice of your departure. Plans must be made!" Karen teams Nadda up with Joe Lawyer who is an expert in custody disputes in the family law context and about to retire. For two years Joe mentors Nadda and, as planned, then retires. This leaves Nadda as the only custody expert in the firm. Nadda and Nicole become restless however and want to start their own firm. So Nicole goes to Karen and tells her, "Karen, we owe you a lot. But it is time to leave the nest. Nicole and I will be starting our own firm this coming Monday. Nicole is calling several clients now and letting them know we will be leaving." Karen explodes with rage and is apoplectic. "How dare you! I made you! I will break you! You hear me. And don't forget that you owe me my 5%." Nadda tells Nicole, "Well that did not go so well." But now what?

What are the questions for Nicole and Nadda? How about Karen? The breakup will not be a pleasant one.

Question: What about the 90-day notice period? Is this a violation.

Answer: Yes, but to answer the question presupposes that their agreement is a valid one. All three lawyers are bound to the duty of diligence in MR 1.3 and to expedite litigation seen in MR 3.2. A 90-day period could interfere with the duty to diligently represent the clients. A 90-day period is so long that it would unreasonably delay diligent representation of the clients or unreasonably interfere with a lawyer's departure. Moreover, MR 3.2 mandates that lawyers help expedite litigation. While this rule is normally framed as involving a lawyer seeking a continuance of say, a trial setting, it applies with equal force here. A client's matter cannot be allowed to languish. While there will be transition issues, all three lawyers must keep in mind that the rules are designed to protect their clients and to serve the clients' needs, not their needs.

Question: Who decides which lawyers take or retain which clients?

Answer: ABA Opinion Letter 489 (December 4, 2019) gives a four-word mandate: "Clients are not property." Therefore, the client decides which lawyer it will select. This rule is consistent with the client's right to terminate a lawyer at any time, and for any reason(s), as well as the bedrock principle that the client owns the matter as we discussed in MR 1.2. The opinion letter sets out a sequence of events which sound ideal in theory but which can be messy in execution. "[D]eparting lawyers need not wait to inform clients of the fact of their impending departure, provided that the firm is informed contemporaneously. Law firm management and lawyers remaining at the firm may also contact clients to inform them of the lawyer's impending departure." Then the lawyers must all seek to draft and send a joint communication to clients announcing the departure and asking the client to make an election of which lawyers will represent them. So Nadda and Nicole are, in the view of the Model Rules, good to go. It would be a good idea, however, for them to prepare a draft and present it to Karen.

(Note that some states, such as Florida, eschew the messy approach and mandate that departing lawyers, before contacting any client, *first* tell their current firm of the impending departure and make a good faith effort to negotiate the language of the joint communication.)

Under either rule, the duty of communication, as embodied in MR 1.4, requires that a lawyer inform the client of what is occurring with their matter.

Question: What about the 5% fee sharing? Are Nadda and Nicole on the hook for that?

Answer: The short answer is "no." But why? Well, a firm cannot impose a non-compete upon a lawyer in the firm. This concept is embodied in MR 5.6(a) which forbids imposing restrictions on a lawyer's right to practice after leaving a firm. The rule must be read in a functional manner; that is, a non-compete is forbidden but the functional equivalent of a non-compete is forbidden as well. As one of you authors tells students, "If you can't walk through the front door, you can't crawl through the back window." Or as pout by the ABA in Opinion Letter 489: "Financial disincentives to a competitive departure have routinely been struck down by the courts and criticized in ethics opinions. The Opinion of the highest court in New York, *Cohen v. Lord, Day & Lord*, 550 N.E. 2d 410 (N.Y. 1989), gives you some texture to this important concept. The underlying rationale is that the public and existing clients should be able to select the best lawyers for their needs. The pool of lawyers to accomplish this goal should be as large as possible in order to achieve this goal and restrictions minimize the size of the pool. Note that not all are in agreement, most notably California, where the state's Supreme Court upheld a forfeiture provision in the partnership agreement of an insurance defense firm holding that "(a)n agreement that assesses a reasonable cost against a partner who chooses to compete against his or her former partners does not restrict the practice of law." *Howard v. Babcock*, 863 P. 2d 150 (Calif. 1993).

Question: What duties do Karen and Nadda/Nancy share?

Answer: The more something goes without saying, the more it needs to be said. So here it is: Karen must cooperate fully in getting a file up to date if the client elects to leave with Nadda/Nicole and, conversely, Nadda/Nicole must co-operate with making sure that the files they leave behind are up to date. There will be hurt feelings of the lawyers in this scenario but those feeling must be subordinated to the greater good of the client. Moreover, Karen and her firm must ascertain whether they remain competent, for example, to continue to represent in a matter involving custody. Recall from our discussion of MR 1.1 that the duty of competence is a continuing one and must be constantly reassessed due to changing circumstances. This is merely another example of this important principle.

The Opinion letter provides an actionable summary:

Lawyers have a right to leave a firm and practice at another firm. The ethics rules do not allow non-competition clauses in partnership or employment agreements. Lawyers and law firm management have ethical obligations to assure the orderly transition of client matters when lawyers notify a firm they intend to move to a new firm. Firms may require some period of advance notice of an intended departure to provide sufficient time to select who will represent them, assemble files, adjust staffing at the firm if the firm is to continue as counsel on matters previously handled by the departing attorney. . .

(The opinion letter goes on to make clear in its summary that a "poison pill" of replacing the departing lawyers with new lawyers is prohibited.)

Firms should not, therefore, displace departing lawyers before departure by assigning new lawyers to a (departing) client's matter absent client direction or exigent circumstances requiring protection of clients' interests.

X-Ray Questions (*Golden Rule*)

It is common, though unethical, to propose, as a condition of settlement, that the suing lawyer never again sue your client. This type of language is sometimes referred to as a "never darken my door again" clause. But if the party paying for settlement wants this as a term, why should it be improper? After all, they are the ones paying and the buyer should get what she seeks, right?

BEYOND THE CITE

By: Michael P. Maslanka, *Follow the Golden Rule: Model Rule 5.6, That Is,* **Texas Lawyer, Aug. 1, 2017.**

It's easier to comply with the law than to circumvent it. This summer I am teaching this simple yet profound lesson to the students in our Professional Responsibility class.

A rule in point, Model Rule of Professional Conduct 5.6: "A lawyer shall not participate in offering or making an agreement in which a restriction on the lawyer's right to practice is part of the settlement of a client controversy." So, a defense lawyer is prohibited from offering to pay X amount to a plaintiff's lawyer if she agrees not to sue the defendant in the future. Conversely, a plaintiff's lawyer may not suggest to a defendant that he will not sue the defendant in the future if paid a certain sum of money. Why the rule? As one Judge aptly put it: "(to prohibit) a corporate buyout of plaintiff's attorneys."

Despite the rule's clarity, lawyers continue to cha-cha around the rule. But as I tell my students, "If you can't walk through the front door, then you can't crawl through the back window." What follows are some notable attempts.

Take the case of *In re Conduct of Brandt* from the Oregon Supreme Court. As part of a settlement, the lawyers for the plaintiffs (distributors of machine parts) would provide legal consulting services to the defendant, the manufacturer. The argument as to why no violation: we are not directly foreclosing our ability to represent future plaintiffs oh no, we are merely indirectly doing so because we would be conflicted out of doing so.

The court rejected this dichotomy as a classic front door/back window tactic, noting that the rule does not make such a fine distinction. The result: one lawyer suspended for twelve months, another for thirteen months. (By the way, a 5.6 violation is usually as in this case coupled with other violations such as failure to adequately communicate with the clients).

Yet another law firm tried to waltz around the rule using The Chameleon Approach. In a products liability case, the defense lawyer made a settlement contingent on the plaintiff's lawyer's acceptance of $50,000 to be allocated to reimbursement of costs but which was to be paid back if the plaintiff's lawyer ever sued the company again, either directly or indirectly, on similar claims. In considering the ethics of this proposal, the Philadelphia Bar Association (in an opinion letter) acknowledged that there was a very sizeable settlement proposal on the table, but that the client's right pursuant to Model Rule 1.2 to decide on whether to settle must give way to the policy considerations behind Rule 5.6. Oh, and here is the bonus round: the Bar Association noted that the plaintiff's lawyer must consider reporting the defense lawyer to the Bar pursuant to Model Rule 8.2 involving reporting professional misconduct. And, if you do not report, you may be in violation of the rules of professional conduct as well.

And finally, rounding out this trifecta is *Johnson et al v. Nextel Communications et al*, a 2011 case from the Second Circuit reversing the granting of a Rule 12(b)(6) motion in which the allegations were not of clever distinctions of direct/indirect or of fancy word play but of an out and out client sell out. A law firm signs up 587 potential plaintiffs who sought to bring discrimination claims against Nextel. But Nextel and the law firm for the plaintiffs reach an agreement: we will pay you to convince your clients to agree to ultimately submit all their claims to binding arbitration thereby waiving their right to a jury trial. But wait, as they say on late night infomercials, there's more! Once all the claims are processed, Nextel will hire the law firm as a consultant for a period of two years. Total to be paid to the law firm: $ 7.5 million. And Nextel would pay claimants attorney fees and expenses in consideration for entering into the arbitration agreements.

Well, it all came undone (all it takes is one person of the 587 to get upset) and the law firm was sued for malpractice and breach of fiduciary duty and Nextel for a variety of claims. This story is not so much as someone crawling through the back window as it is one of breaking down the front door. Another example is one in which in-house counsel got embroiled in an offer to buy out plaintiff's lawyers to not represent other employees in future litigation, *Adams v. BellSouth Telecommunications Inc.* Yet another plaintiff's lawyer who entered into a restrictive agreement changed her mind and successfully sued to set it aside. *Cardillo v. Bloomfield 206 Corp.*

It really is both that easy and I guess that hard (as Oscar Wilde remarked, he could resist everything except temptation). But there is a more important point undergirding Model Rule 5.6. To paraphrase Justice Cardozo: The public deserves something to protect them, something much stricter than the morals of the marketplace.

C. Obligations to the Public of Managing an Ancillary Legal Services and the Sale of a Law Firm

Model Rule 5.7: Responsibilities Regarding Law-Related Services

(a)   A lawyer shall be subject to the Rules of Professional Conduct with respect to the provision of law-related services, as defined in paragraph (b), if the law-related services are provided:

(1)   by the lawyer in circumstances that are not distinct from the lawyer's provision of legal services to clients; or

(2)   in other circumstances by an entity controlled by the lawyer individually or with others if the lawyer fails to take reasonable measures to assure that a person obtaining the law-related services knows that the services are not legal services and that the protections of the client-lawyer relationship do not exist.

(b) The term "law-related services" denotes services that might reasonably be performed in conjunction with and in substance are related to the provision of legal services, and that are not prohibited as unauthorized practice of law when provided by a nonlawyer.

Model Rule 1.17: Sale of Practice

A lawyer or a law firm may sell or purchase a law practice, or an area of law practice, including good will, if the following conditions are satisfied:

(a) The seller ceases to engage in the private practice of law, or in the area of practice that has been sold, [in the geographic area] [in the jurisdiction] (a jurisdiction may elect either version) in which the practice has been conducted;

(b) The entire practice, or the entire area of practice, is sold to one or more lawyers or law firms;

(c) The seller gives written notice to each of the seller's clients regarding:

(1) the proposed sale;

(2) the client's right to retain other counsel or to take possession of the file; and

Deconstruction Exercise/Rule Rationale

In these two rules we see the strong bias in the rules towards a client/public centric bias of the Rules. While MR 5.7 allows a lawyer to engage in a business ancillary to the practice of law (such as a bail bond or a title company), the lawyer must nonetheless remain cognizant that there could be client confusion if the business is run as a separate entity from the law firm itself. If so, the client must be made aware that the entity is a separate business and that certain important client protections inherent in the ACR—such as the ACP or maintaining client confidences—are inapplicable to what the client says or does in relation to the entity. This is so because an ancillary service is not the practice of law, in which advice or representation is sought by a company or an individual and given by a lawyer. The ancillary business is, quite simply, a business like any other and therefore these protections cannot be extended.

MR 1.17 concerns itself with the concern of the drafters of the rules that clients not be treated as fungible commodities. Consider this scenario: a plaintiff's lawyer is handling 100 personal injury lawsuits; 50% are valued by the lawyer at over $100,000 while are valued as worth less. The lawyer cannot sell these lesser valued cases. It is the client who selects the lawyer and the client who decides whether to retain or to replace that lawyer. As we've seen this is a fundamental client right.

And speaking of fundamental client rights, the issue of confidentiality arises in this rule with respect to MR 1.17(c)(3) when a client cannot be reached to be informed of the sale of the firm and that the client has the right to remain with the buyer of the firm or to seek other counsel. In that instance there is a detailed procedure to be followed in seeking court permission, but as you see in the Rule, only a limited amount of confidential information may be shared with the court ("to the extent necessary") in obtaining a court order transferring the file to the buyer of the firm.

Section 2. Ethical Marketing Conduct for a Public Profession

Model Rule 7.1: Communications Concerning a Lawyer's Services

A lawyer shall not make a false or misleading communication about the lawyer or the lawyer's services. A communication is false or misleading if it contains a material misrepresentation of fact or law, or omits a fact necessary to make the statement considered as a whole not materially misleading.

Deconstruction Exercise/Rule Rationale

This is a short rule, is it not? But when you consider it closely it packs a big punch. Why? The Rule covers all *communications*. What is the key word in the rule? If you answered "or," you are 100% correct. The word "or" expands the scope of the rule and does not constrict it. Also, make special note of the scope of the rule inasmuch as a violation occurs from the failure to be 100% transparent and candid. Where have we seen this structural concept previously? You saw it in MR 2.1: Advisor; MR 4.1: Truthfulness in Statements to Others; and MR 8.4(c): Conduct. The reason for MR 7.1 is that the public needs to be protected from an outright falsehood or from a misleading statement when they consider selecting a lawyer. Many will only need to hire a lawyer once, and the selection is often over a very important matter to the person or the person's family. Thus, the profession must take steps to, as much as possible, ensure that the selection is not clouded by misinformation or deceit. While a brief or a once in a lifetime contact with the legal system, the memories and experience will be long lasting. In short, what a lawyer takes as just another day at the office can be anything but to a client for whom a legal encounter is a major life event. So, clients must have accurate information to make the right choice for them.

Scenario No. 1: The Case of the Small Print That Makes a Big Difference

A lawyer for injured workers handled several multi-million-dollar cases and advertises to that effect. This is permissible because it is literally true and is not misleading. And if the lawyer won several of the cases, she could advertise that to the public, but she would need a disclaimer to state that every case is different and that results may "vary" depending on the facts. Otherwise, a prospective client could conclude that he too will be awarded a comparable amount. Without the disclaimer, the statement is possibly misleading.

Scenario No. 2: The Case of the Misleading Name

Ed Lawyer decides to practice law in his hometown of Lubbock, Texas. When he establishes the firm, he names it: "The Lubbock Legal Clinic" in order to communicate where he is located (Lubbock) and will provide a variety of legal services (thus, the use of the word "clinic"). What could possibly be wrong? Lawyers must view the name not as they would but rather from the viewpoint of a member of the public. What concepts night the word "clinic" conjure up in the mind of a non-lawyer? People who are familiar with law school or legal aid "clinics" might think the service is free. Thus, Ed should consider a disclaimer so as not to violate MR 7.1.

Model Rule 7.3: Solicitation of Clients

(a)   "Solicitation" or "solicit" denotes a communication initiated by or on behalf of a lawyer or law firm that is directed to a specific person the lawyer knows or reasonably should know needs legal services in a particular matter and that offers to provide, or reasonably can be understood as offering to provide, legal services for that matter.

(b)   A lawyer shall not solicit professional employment by live person-to-person contact when a significant motive for the lawyer's doing so is the lawyer's or law firm's pecuniary gain, unless the contact is with a:

(1)   lawyer;

(2)   person who has a family, close personal, or prior business or professional relationship with the lawyer or law firm; or

(3)   person who routinely uses for business purposes the type of legal services offered by the lawyer.

(c)   A lawyer shall not solicit professional employment even when not otherwise prohibited by paragraph (b), if:

   (1)   the target of the solicitation has made known to the lawyer a desire not to be solicited by the lawyer; or

   (2)   the solicitation involves coercion, duress or harassment.

(d)   This Rule does not prohibit communications authorized by law or ordered by a court or other tribunal.

(e)   Notwithstanding the prohibitions in this Rule, a lawyer may participate with a prepaid or group legal service plan operated by an organization not owned or directed by the lawyer that uses live person-to-person contact to enroll members or sell subscriptions for the plan from persons who are not known to need legal services in a particular matter covered by the plan.

Deconstruction Exercise/Rule Rationale

Once again, we see how the Rules in the later sections of the book lean more towards a Do/Don't orientation. For example: Do not engage in live, in person solicitation. Notice here how it is clear what is permitted and what is not. Essentially a "safe-harbor" provision is included in the Rule and is designed to alert a lawyer as to what is permissible. A group legal service plan can solicit subscribers—but only if they are not known to currently need legal services. The Rule is clearly targeting the despised stereotype of the lawyer-as-ambulance-chaser.

Here, note that the key word is the verb "solicit" which is an active, present tense verb. It was selected because the danger to the public is that of a skilled lawyer, trained in the arts of examination and persuasion, bringing those skills to bear upon a person who needs legal representation. Just as a client is empowered to freely fire a lawyer, so too is a person empowered to select the right lawyer for them without undue harassment or overbearing intrusion in the decision-making process. The rule seeks to provide the person with a calm and deliberate selection process when a lawyer is needed.

Cases and Materials

X-Ray Questions (*Shapero*)

This case reflects the purposes of the Rule. What does the Court mean when it writes that "The relevant inquiry is not whether there exist potential clients whose "condition" makes them susceptible to undie influence, but whether the mode of communication poses a serious danger that lawyers will exploit such susceptibility." How does the Court apply this crucial concept in its holding? How does a targeted solicitation letter differ from an in person direct solicitation? The Court says that it does. Why? How do the First Amendment rights of a lawyer figure into this case?

Richard D. Shapero v. Kentucky Bar Association

Supreme Court of the United States, 1988.
486 U.S. 466.

JUSTICE BRENNAN announced the judgment of the Court and delivered the opinion of the Court as to Parts I and II and an opinion as to Part III in which JUSTICE MARSHALL, JUSTICE BLACKMUN, and JUSTICE KENNEDY join.

This case presents the issue whether a State may, consistent with the First and Fourteenth Amendments, categorically prohibit lawyers from soliciting legal business for pecuniary gain by sending truthful and nondeceptive letters to potential clients known to face particular legal problems.

I

In 1985, petitioner, a member of Kentucky's integrated Bar Association, see Ky.Sup.Ct. Rule 3.030 (1988), applied to the Kentucky Attorneys Advertising Commission1 for approval of a letter that he proposed to send "to potential clients who have had a foreclosure suit filed against them." The proposed letter read as follows:

"It has come to my attention that your home is being foreclosed on. If this is true, you may be about to lose your home. Federal law may allow you to keep your home by *ORDERING* your creditor [*sic*] to *STOP* and give you more time to pay them.

"You may call my office anytime from 8:30 a.m. to 5:00 p.m. for *FREE* information on how you can keep your home.

"Call *NOW*, don't wait. It may surprise you what I may be able to do for you. Just call and tell me that you got this letter. Remember it is *FREE*, there is *NO* charge for calling."

The Commission did not find the letter false or misleading. Nevertheless, it declined to approve petitioner's proposal on the ground that a then-existing Kentucky Supreme Court Rule prohibited the mailing or delivery of written advertisements "precipitated by a specific event or occurrence involving or relating to the addressee or addressees as distinct from the general public."

Ky.Sup.Ct. Rule 3.135(5)(b)(i). The Commission registered its view that Rule 3.135(5)(b)(i)'s ban on targeted, direct-mail advertising violated the First Amendment—specifically the principles enunciated in *Zauderer v. Office of Disciplinary Counsel of Supreme Court of Ohio,* 471 U.S. 626, 105 S.Ct. 2265, 85 L.Ed.2d 652 (1985)—and recommended that the Kentucky Supreme Court amend its Rules. See App. to Pet. for Cert. 11a–15a. Pursuing the Commission's suggestion, petitioner petitioned the Committee on Legal Ethics (Ethics Committee) of the Kentucky Bar Association for an advisory opinion as to the Rule's validity. See Ky.Sup.Ct. Rule 3.530; n. 1, *supra.* Like the Commission, the Ethics Committee, in an opinion formally adopted by the Board of Governors of the Bar Association, did not find the proposed letter false or misleading, but nonetheless upheld Rule 3.135(5)(b)(i) on the ground that it was consistent with Rule 7.3 of the American Bar Association's Model Rules of Professional Conduct (1984). App. to Pet. for Cert. 9a.

On review of the Ethics Committee's advisory opinion, the Kentucky Supreme Court felt "compelled by the decision in *Zauderer* to order [Rule 3.135(5)(b)(i)] deleted," 726 S.W.2d 299, 300 (1987), and replaced it with the ABA's Rule 7.3, which provides in its entirety:

> " 'A lawyer may not solicit professional employment from a prospective client with whom the lawyer has no family or prior professional relationship, by mail, in-person or otherwise, when a significant motive for the lawyer's doing so is the lawyer's pecuniary gain. The term 'solicit' includes contact in person, by telephone or telegraph, by letter or other writing, or by other communication directed to a specific recipient, but does not include letters addressed or advertising circulars distributed generally to persons not known to need legal services of the kind provided by the lawyer in a particular matter, but who are so situated that they might in general find such services useful.' " 726 S.W.2d, at 301 (quoting ABA, Model Rule of Professional Conduct 7.3 (1984)).

The court did not specify either the precise infirmity in Rule 3.135(5)(b)(i) or how Rule 7.3 cured it. Rule 7.3 like its predecessor, prohibits targeted, direct-mail solicitation by lawyers for pecuniary gain, without a particularized finding that the solicitation is false or misleading. We granted certiorari to resolve whether such a blanket prohibition is consistent with the First Amendment, made applicable to the States through the Fourteenth Amendment, 484 U.S. 814, 108 S.Ct. 64, 98 L.Ed.2d 28 (1987), and now reverse.

II

Lawyer advertising is in the category of constitutionally protected commercial speech. See *Bates v. State Bar of Arizona,* 433 U.S. 350, 97 S.Ct. 2691, 53 L.Ed.2d 810 (1977). The First Amendment principles governing state regulation of lawyer solicitations for pecuniary gain are by now familiar: "Commercial speech that is not false or deceptive and does not concern unlawful activities . . . may be restricted only in the service of a substantial governmental interest, and only through means that directly advance that interest." *Zauderer, supra,* 471 U.S., at 638, 105 S.Ct., at 2275 (citing *Central Hudson Gas & Electric Corp. v. Public Service Comm'n of New York,* 447 U.S. 557, 566, 100 S.Ct. 2343, 2531, 65 L.Ed.2d 341 (1980)). Since state regulation of commercial speech "may extend only as far as the interest it serves," *Central Hudson, supra,* at 565, 100 S.Ct., at 2351, state rules that are designed to prevent the "potential for deception and confusion . . . may be no broader than reasonably necessary to prevent the" perceived evil. *In re R.M.J.,* 455 U.S. 191, 203, 102 S.Ct. 929, 937, 71 L.Ed.2d 64 (1982).

In *Zauderer,* application of these principles required that we strike an Ohio rule that categorically prohibited solicitation of legal employment for pecuniary gain through advertisements containing information or advice, even if truthful and nondeceptive, regarding a specific legal problem. We distinguished written advertisements containing such information or advice from in-person solicitation by lawyers for profit, which we held in *Ohralik v. Ohio State Bar Assn.,* 436 U.S. 447, 98 S.Ct. 1912, 56 L.Ed.2d 444 (1978), a State may categorically ban. The "unique features of in-person solicitation by lawyers [that] justified a prophylactic rule prohibiting lawyers from engaging in such solicitation for pecuniary gain," we observed, are "not present" in the context of written advertisements. *Zauderer, supra,* 471 U.S., at 641–642, 105 S.Ct., at 2277.

Our lawyer advertising cases have never distinguished among various modes of written advertising to the general public. See, *e.g., Bates, supra* (newspaper advertising); *id.,* 433 U.S., at 372, n. 26, 97 S.Ct., at 2703, n. 26 (equating advertising in telephone directory with newspaper advertising); *In re R.M.J., supra* (mailed announcement cards treated same as newspaper and telephone directory advertisements). Thus, Ohio could no more prevent Zauderer from mass-mailing to a general population his offer to represent women injured by the Dalkon Shield than it could prohibit his publication of the advertisement in local newspapers. Similarly, if petitioner's letter is neither false nor deceptive, Kentucky could not constitutionally prohibit him from sending at large an identical letter opening with the query, "Is your home being foreclosed on?," rather than his observation to the targeted individuals that "It has come to my attention that your home is being foreclosed on." The drafters of Rule 7.3 apparently appreciated as much, for the Rule exempts from the ban "letters addressed or advertising circulars distributed generally to persons . . . who are so situated that they might in general find such services useful."

The court below disapproved petitioner's proposed letter solely because it targeted only persons who were "known to need [the] legal services" offered in his letter, 726 S.W.2d, at 301, rather than the broader group of persons "so situated that they might in general find such services useful." Generally, unless the advertiser is inept, the latter group would include members of the former. The only reason to disseminate an advertisement of particular legal services among those persons who are "so situated that they might in general find such services useful" is to reach individuals who *actually* "need legal services of the kind provided [and advertised] by the lawyer." But the First Amendment does not permit a ban on certain speech merely because it is more efficient; the State may not constitutionally ban a particular letter on the theory that to mail it only to those whom it would most interest is somehow inherently objectionable.

The court below did not rely on any such theory. See also Brief for Respondent 37 (conceding that "targeted direct mail *advertising*"—as distinguished from "*solicitation*"—"is constitutionally protected") (emphasis in original). Rather, it concluded that the State's blanket ban on all targeted, direct-mail solicitation was permissible because of the "serious potential for abuse inherent in direct solicitation by lawyers of potential clients known to need specific legal services." 726 S.W.2d, at 301. By analogy to *Ohralik,* the court observed:

> "Such solicitation subjects the prospective client to pressure from a trained lawyer in a direct personal way. It is entirely possible that the potential client may feel overwhelmed by the basic situation which caused the need for the specific legal services and may have seriously impaired capacity for good judgment, sound reason and a natural protective self-interest. Such a condition is full of the possibility of undue influence, overreaching and intimidation." 726 S.W.2d, at 301.

Of course, a particular potential client will feel equally "overwhelmed" by his legal troubles and will have the same "impaired capacity for good judgment" regardless of whether a lawyer mails him an untargeted letter or exposes him to a newspaper advertisement—concededly constitutionally protected activities—or instead mails a targeted letter. The relevant inquiry is not whether there exist potential clients whose "condition" makes them susceptible to undue influence, but whether the mode of communication poses a serious danger that lawyers will exploit any such susceptibility. Cf. *Ohralik, supra,* 436 U.S., at 470, 98 S.Ct., at 1926 (MARSHALL, J., concurring in part and concurring in judgment) ("What is objectionable about Ohralik's behavior here is not so much that he solicited business for himself, but rather the circumstances in which he performed that solicitation and the means by which he accomplished it").

Thus, respondent's facile suggestion that this case is merely "*Ohralik* in writing" misses the mark. Brief for Respondent 10. In assessing the potential for overreaching and undue influence, the mode of communication makes all the difference. Our decision in *Ohralik* that a State could categorically ban all in-person solicitation turned on two factors. First was our characterization of face-to-face solicitation as "a practice rife with possibilities for overreaching, invasion of privacy, the exercise of undue influence, and outright fraud." *Zauderer,* 471 U.S., at 641, 105 S.Ct., at 2277. See *Ohralik, supra,* 436 U.S., at 457–458, 464–465, 98 S.Ct., at 1919–1920, 1922–1923. Second, "unique . . . difficulties," *Zauderer, supra,* 471 U.S., at 641, 105 S.Ct., at 2277, would frustrate any attempt at state regulation of in-person solicitation short of an absolute ban because such solicitation is "not visible or otherwise open to public scrutiny." *Ohralik,* 436 U.S., at 466, 98 S.Ct., at 1924. See also *ibid.* ("[I]n-person solicitation would be virtually immune to effective oversight and regulation by the State or by the legal profession") (footnote omitted). Targeted, direct-mail solicitation is distinguishable from the in-person solicitation in each respect.

Like print advertising, petitioner's letter—and targeted, direct-mail solicitation generally—"poses much less risk of overreaching or undue influence" than does in-person solicitation, *Zauderer,* 471 U.S., at 642, 105 S.Ct., at 2277. Neither mode of written communication involves "the coercive force of the personal presence of a trained advocate" or the "pressure on the potential client for an immediate yes-or-no answer to the offer of representation." *Ibid.* Unlike the potential client with a badgering advocate breathing down his neck, the recipient of a letter and the "reader of an advertisement . . . can 'effectively avoid further bombardment of [his] sensibilities simply by averting [his] eyes,' " *Ohralik, supra,* 436 U.S., at 465, n. 25, 98 S.Ct., at 1923, n. 25 (quoting *Cohen v. California,* 403 U.S. 15, 21, 91 S.Ct. 1780, 1786, 29 L.Ed.2d 284 (1971)). A letter, like a printed advertisement (but unlike a lawyer), can readily be put in a drawer to be considered later, ignored, or discarded. In short, both types of written solicitation "conve[y] information about legal services [by means] that [are] more conducive to reflection and the exercise of choice on the part of the consumer than is personal solicitation by an attorney." *Zauderer, supra,* 471 U.S., at 642, 105

S.Ct., at 2277. Nor does a targeted letter invade the recipient's privacy any more than does a substantively identical letter mailed at large. The invasion, if any, occurs when the lawyer discovers the recipient's legal affairs, not when he confronts the recipient with the discovery.

Admittedly, a letter that is personalized (not merely targeted) to the recipient presents an increased risk of deception, intentional or inadvertent. It could, in certain circumstances, lead the recipient to overestimate the lawyer's familiarity with the case or could implicitly suggest that the recipient's legal problem is more dire than it really is. See Brief for ABA as *Amicus Curiae* 9. Similarly, an inaccurately targeted letter could lead the recipient to believe she has a legal problem that she does not actually have or, worse yet, could offer erroneous legal advice. See, *e.g., Leoni v. State Bar of California*, 39 Cal.3d 609, 619–620, 217 Cal.Rptr. 423, 429, 704 P.2d 183, 189 (1985), summarily dism'd, 475 U.S. 1001, 106 S.Ct. 1170, 89 L.Ed.2d 290 (1986).

But merely because targeted, direct-mail solicitation presents lawyers with opportunities for isolated abuses or mistakes does not justify a total ban on that mode of protected commercial speech. See *In re R.M.J.*, 455 U.S., at 203, 102 S.Ct., at 937. The State can regulate such abuses and minimize mistakes through far less restrictive and more precise means, the most obvious of which is to require the lawyer to file any solicitation letter with a state agency, *id.,* at 206, 102 S.Ct., at 939, giving the State ample opportunity to supervise mailings and penalize actual abuses. The "regulatory difficulties" that are "unique" to in-person lawyer solicitation, *Zauderer, supra,* 471 U.S., at 641, 105 S.Ct., at 2277—solicitation that is "not visible or otherwise open to public scrutiny" and for which it is "difficult or impossible to obtain reliable proof of what actually took place," *Ohralik, supra,* 436 U.S., at 466, 98 S.Ct., at 1924—do not apply to written solicitations. The court below offered no basis for its "belie[f] [that] submission of a blank form letter to the Advertising Commission [does not] provid[e] a suitable protection to the public from overreaching, intimidation or misleading private targeted mail solicitation." 726 S.W.2d, at 301. Its concerns were presumably those expressed by the ABA House of Delegates in its comment to Rule 7.3:

> "State lawyer discipline agencies struggle for resources to investigate specific complaints, much less for those necessary to screen lawyers' mail solicitation material. Even if they could examine such materials, agency staff members are unlikely to know anything about the lawyer or about the prospective client's underlying problem. Without such knowledge they cannot determine whether the lawyer's

representations are misleading." ABA, Model Rules of Professional Conduct, pp. 93–94 (1984).

The record before us furnishes no evidence that scrutiny of targeted solicitation letters will be appreciably more burdensome or less reliable than scrutiny of advertisements. See *Bates*, 433 U.S., at 379, 97 S.Ct., at 2706; *id.*, at 387, 97 S.Ct., at 2711 (Burger, C.J., concurring in part and dissenting in part) (objecting to "enormous new regulatory burdens called for by" *Bates*). As a general matter, evaluating a targeted advertisement does not require specific information about the recipient's identity and legal problems any more than evaluating a newspaper advertisement requires like information about all readers. If the targeted letter specifies facts that relate to particular recipients (*e.g.*, "It has come to my attention that your home is being foreclosed on"), the reviewing agency has innumerable options to minimize mistakes. It might, for example, require the lawyer to prove the truth of the fact stated (by supplying copies of the court documents or material that led the lawyer to the fact); it could require the lawyer to explain briefly how he or she discovered the fact and verified its accuracy; or it could require the letter to bear a label identifying it as an advertisement, see *id.*, at 384, 97 S.Ct., at 2709 (dictum); *In re R.M.J.*, *supra*, 455 U.S., at 206, n. 20, 102 S.Ct., at 939, n. 20, or directing the recipient how to report inaccurate or misleading letters. To be sure, a state agency or bar association that reviews solicitation letters might have more work than one that does not. But "[o]ur recent decisions involving commercial speech have been grounded in the faith that the free flow of commercial information is valuable enough to justify imposing on would-be regulators the costs of distinguishing the truthful from the false, the helpful from the misleading, and the harmless from the harmful." *Zauderer, supra*, 471 U.S., at 646, 105 S.Ct., at 2279.

III

The validity of Rule 7.3 does not turn on whether petitioner's letter itself exhibited any of the evils at which Rule 7.3 was directed. See *Ohralik*, 436 U.S., at 463–464, 466, 98 S.Ct., at 1922–1923, 1923. Since, however, the First Amendment overbreadth doctrine does not apply to professional advertising, see *Bates*, 433 U.S., at 379–381, 97 S.Ct., at 2706–2707 we address respondent's contentions that petitioner's letter is particularly overreaching, and therefore unworthy of First Amendment protection. *Id.*, at 381, 97 S.Ct., at 2707. In that regard, respondent identifies two features of the letter before us that, in its view, coalesce to convert the proposed letter into "high pressure solicitation, overbearing solicitation," Brief for Respondent 20, which is not protected. First, respondent asserts that the letter's liberal use of underscored, uppercase letters (*e.g.*, "Call *NOW*, don't wait"; "it is *FREE*, there is *NO* charge for calling") "fairly shouts at the recipient . . . that he should employ Shapero." *Id.*, at 19. See also Brief in Opposition 11 ("Letters of solicitation which shout commands to the individual, targeted recipient in words in underscored capitals are of a different order from advertising and are subject to proscription"). Second, respondent objects that the letter contains assertions (*e.g.*, "It may surprise you what I may be able to do for you") that "stat[e] no affirmative or objective fact," but constitute "pure salesman puffery, enticement for the unsophisticated, which commits Shapero to nothing." Brief for Respondent 20.

The pitch or style of a letter's type and its inclusion of subjective predictions of client satisfaction might catch the recipient's attention more than would a bland statement of purely objective facts in small type. But a truthful and nondeceptive letter, no matter how big its type and how much it speculates can never "shou[t] at the recipient" or "gras[p] him by the lapels," *id.*, at 19, as can a lawyer engaging in face-to-face solicitation. The letter simply presents no comparable risk of overreaching. And so long as the First Amendment protects the right to solicit legal business, the State may claim no substantial interest in restricting truthful and nondeceptive lawyer solicitations to those least likely to be read by the recipient. Moreover, the First Amendment limits the State's authority to dictate what information an attorney may convey in soliciting legal business. "[T]he States may not place an absolute prohibition on certain types of potentially misleading information . . . if the information may also be presented in a way that is not deceptive," unless the State "assert[s] a substantial interest" that such a restriction would directly advance. *In re R.M.J.*, 455 U.S., at 203, 102 S.Ct., at 937. Nor may a State impose a more particularized restriction without a similar showing. Aside from the interests that we have already rejected, respondent offers none.

To be sure, a letter may be misleading if it unduly emphasizes trivial or "relatively uninformative fact[s]," *In re R.M.J.*, *supra*, at 205, 102 S.Ct., at 938 (lawyer's statement, "in large capital letters, that he was a member of the Bar of the Supreme Court of the United States"), or offers overblown assurances of client satisfaction, cf. *In re Von Wiegen*, 63 N.Y.2d 163, 179, 481 N.Y.S.2d 40, 49, 470 N.E.2d 838, 847 (1984) (solicitation letter to victims of massive disaster informs them that "it is [the lawyer's] opinion that the liability of the defendants is clear"), cert. denied, 472 U.S. 1007, 105 S.Ct. 2701, 86 L.Ed.2d 717 (1985); *Bates*, *supra*, 433 U.S., at 383–384, 97 S.Ct., at 2709 ("[A]dvertising claims as to the quality of legal services . . . may be so likely to be misleading as to warrant restriction"). Respondent does not argue before us that petitioner's letter was misleading in those respects. Nor does respondent contend that the letter is false or misleading in any other respect. Of course, respondent is free to raise, and the Kentucky courts are free to consider, any such argument on remand.

The judgment of the Supreme Court of Kentucky is reversed, and the case is remanded for further proceedings not inconsistent with this opinion.

It is so ordered.

SOLUTIONS: THE LAWYER SHOULD HAVE, WOULD HAVE, COULD HAVE. . .

The Rules are permeated with cautions to lawyers not to use undue influence over a client. Here is a famous poem by the poet Robert Burns: "Oh, would some power give us the gift/ To see ourselves as others see us. It would from many a blunder free us." Lawyers see themselves as being decent and good. But the public often sees us as trying to earn a dollar at their expense. Thus, there are rules to protect us from our blindness an how we are perceived.

LEANING INTO PRACTICE

Scenario No. 1: The Case of the Generous Customer

Lou Lawyer is a long time regular at the Queen of Duaminds Lounge. His favorite bartender is Lilli Bartender. One night, Lilli tells him that her former husband is seeking custody of their daughter, has a lawyer and Lilli does not, and she wonders aloud what she can do. Lou is actually a well-respected family lawyer, knows that Lilli is likely financially strapped (despite his history of generous tipping) and says: "Lilli you've been a great bartender to me, and I am grateful. I know this area of the law and will represent you on an 75% discounted basis from my normal hourly rate! What do you say?" Lilli agrees and they enter into an engagement letter. Is Lou in violation of the Rule?

Scenario No. 2: The Case of the Law School Study Group

Inez and Omar are members of the same law school study group throughout all three years of law school. They study for the bar together and they both pass. Inez though decides to go into business for herself instead of practicing law; namely, sales of her mother's homemade hot sauce. Omar sets up his own practice and specializes in representing entrepreneurs. They have not seen one another for a year but then meet once again at a law school happy hour.

They explain to one another the paths they have taken, and Omar says to her "Let me represent you. I am learning all about internet sales and it can be complex. Sort of like getting the band back together. I will charge you fair rates. Maybe even agree to a percentage off your profits as my fee. Come on, what do you say !?!" Has Omar violated any of the Model Rules? Has he set himself up in a posture to do so?

Model Rule 7.2 (excerpts): Paid Endorsements and Referral Services

(a)   A lawyer may communicate information regarding the lawyer's services through any media.

(b)   A lawyer shall not compensate, give or promise anything of value to a person for recommending the lawyer's services except that a lawyer may:

(1)   pay the reasonable costs of advertisements or communications permitted by this Rule;

(2)   pay the usual charges of a legal service plan or a not-for-profit or qualified lawyer referral service;

(3)   pay for a law practice in accordance with Rule 1.17;

(4)   refer clients to another lawyer or a nonlawyer professional pursuant to an agreement not otherwise prohibited under these Rules that provides for the other person to refer clients or customers to the lawyer, if:

(i)   the reciprocal referral agreement is not exclusive; and

(ii)   the client is informed of the existence and nature of the agreement; and

(5)   give nominal gifts as an expression of appreciation that are neither intended nor reasonably expected to be a form of compensation for recommending a lawyer's services.

Deconstruction Exercise/Rule Rationale

This rule is another example of professional norms limiting business strategies that would likely be potent and effective. You have likely heard that "word-of-mouth" is the best marketing strategy. Indeed, it is. A happy former client who refers future clients is probably better advertising than any billboard that a lawyer could ever pay for. Personal recommendations are powerful marketing. But this rule imposes a key limitation: Lawyers may not pay for them.

Our profession does not want endorsements and referrals to be tainted by the influence of money.

If you look at the Rule's structure, it is mostly permissive of most standard forms of advertising. It allows lawyers to communicate about their services. It allows most paid advertising. It really contains one clear prohibition: paying someone "for recommending the lawyer's services."

Broadly, this rule has two applications, both driven by an interest in promoting transparency and avoiding manipulation.

One is that it prohibits a certain kind of lawyer referral service. Lawyers can pay to be part of a listing of attorneys for prospective clients. But they cannot pay to be part of an "exclusive" referral service. That is, a lawyer cannot pay to be the only (or, probably, one of just a few) attorneys who will get precious referrals. The reason is that prospective clients might think that the referral service uses a short list because they believe this one lawyer is the best, or the only one available, when really the lawyer just paid money. Lawyers can form paid arrangements among themselves---another example of the legal profession privileging its own members---to refer clients to each other, but the clients being referred must be informed of the "nature of the agreement." That means lawyers cannot hide from clients the fact that they are being paid for the referral.

The other application of this rule concerns paid celebrity endorsements. Or, for that matter, any paid endorsements. Here, again, you can see the legal profession limiting itself in comparison to routine marketing strategies used throughout business. It is one thing to have a testimonial from a happy client. But it is another to pay for it. Similarly, law firms cannot pay a well-known and trusted person to recommend them. The ABA Comment to the Rule says that any communication with a paid person is a prohibited recommendation "if it endorses or vouches for a lawyer's credentials, abilities, competence, character, or other professional qualities."

These rules likely have newly heightened importance in the internet age – where it fairly easy to set up an online referral service that people entering certain search terms will find. And its limitations are likely extremely important in a social media age in which popular "influencers" are able to reach people with shared niche concerns, and in which the influencer is highly trusted. One of the ways influencers make money is by promoting products and services, but often without disclosing whether they have been paid to do so. Consider the two following scenarios involving a bankruptcy firm.

Scenario No. 1: A Friend Who Can Help

There is a TikTok influencer who goes by the name Julie Checkbook, with 6 million followers. She talks mostly about personal finance, and occasionally about politics and entertainment. She also likes to rant about the way big banks exploit regular people. Every few weeks, she appears in a video with Jenny Edwards, a bankruptcy attorney in Nevada (where Julie Checkbook lives). Julie usually introduces these segments by saying something like, "A lot of you have been writing to me about your own struggles with the banks and with debt. I have a good friend who can help." On Julie's TikTok profile, there is a link to Jenny Edwards' firm website with the line "A friend who can help." Is this arrangement permissible?

Scenario No. 2: A Friend Who Can Help, the Website

Julie Checkbook sets up a website using her celebrity. It includes videos, blog posts about financial managements, links to information about issues being debated in Congress, and advertisements. Most of the paid ads are place there by online ad services, and there are many attorney ads regarding bankruptcy services. Julie does not control these banner ads, as they are called. Anyone who pays for them can have their ad placed on her site. But she also has a link on her website that says, "Where to turn for help." If someone clicks on that page, they seek a picture of Julie with and Jenny Edwards together, with text that says: "I am not a lawyer, and I cannot advise you about your financial situation. But if you are struggling, I have a friend who can help. You know her from my video: Jenny Edwards." The link invites people to give their contact information and to describe their problems on a basic webform that is sent to Jenny Edwards' law firm." And just as in Scenario 1, Jenny Edwards is paying for this, but that fact is not disclosed anywhere on the website. Is this permitted?

Model Rule 7.6: Political Contributions to Obtain Legal Engagements

A lawyer or law firm shall not accept a government legal engagement or an appointment by a judge if the lawyer or law firm makes a political contribution or solicits political contributions for the purpose of obtaining or being considered for that type of legal engagement or appointment.

Editor's Note: Judges are elected in some states while in other they are appointed. Some states use a hybrid system in which a judge is initially appointed and then must be elected in order to retain the position.

Deconstruction Exercise/Rule Rationale

The key to how this Rule works is the causation standard set out in Comment 5.

[5] Political contributions are for the purpose of obtaining or being considered for a government legal engagement or appointment by a judge if, but for the desire to be considered for the legal engagement or appointment, the lawyer or law firm would not have made or solicited the contributions. The purpose may be determined by an examination of the circumstances in which the contributions occur. For example, one or more contributions that in the aggregate are substantial in relation to other contributions by lawyers or law firms, made for the benefit of an official in a position to influence award of a government legal engagement, and followed by an award of the legal engagement to the contributing or soliciting lawyer or the lawyer's firm would support an inference that the purpose of the contributions was to obtain the engagement, absent other factors that weigh against existence of the proscribed purpose. Those factors may include among others that the contribution or solicitation was made to further a political, social, or economic interest or because of an existing personal, family, or professional relationship with a candidate.

This standard seeks to strike a balance between the reality in those states in which judges are elected with the concomitant reality that lawyers will contribute financially to their election campaigns. The standard is essentially "But for causation; that is, the contribution would not have been made but for the desire" to receive appointments. Other causation standards could have been used such as a motivating factor but were not. Why? A motivating factor test would set too low a bar for the finding of a violation and effectively prohibit campaign contributions.

Model Rule 5.5: Unauthorized Practice of Law; Multijurisdictional Practice of Law

(a) A lawyer shall not practice law in a jurisdiction in violation of the regulation of the legal profession in that jurisdiction, or assist another in doing so.

(b) A lawyer who is not admitted to practice in this jurisdiction shall not:

(1)   except as authorized by these Rules or other law, establish an office or other systematic and continuous presence in this jurisdiction for the practice of law; or

(2)   hold out to the public or otherwise represent that the lawyer is admitted to practice law in this jurisdiction.

(c)   A lawyer admitted in another United States jurisdiction, and not disbarred or suspended from practice in any jurisdiction, may provide legal services on a temporary basis in this jurisdiction that:

(1)   are undertaken in association with a lawyer who is admitted to practice in this jurisdiction and who actively participates in the matter;

(2)   are in or reasonably related to a pending or potential proceeding before a tribunal in this or another jurisdiction, if the lawyer, or a person the lawyer is assisting, is authorized by law or order to appear in such proceeding or reasonably expects to be so authorized;

(3)   are in or reasonably related to a pending or potential arbitration, mediation, or other alternative resolution proceeding in this or another jurisdiction, if the services arise out of or are reasonably related to the lawyer's practice in a jurisdiction in which the lawyer is admitted to practice and are not services for which the forum requires pro hac vice admission; or

(4)   are not within paragraphs (c) (2) or (c)(3) and arise out of or are reasonably related to the lawyer's practice in a jurisdiction in which the lawyer is admitted to practice.

(d)   A lawyer admitted in another United States jurisdiction or in a foreign jurisdiction, and not disbarred or suspended from practice in any jurisdiction or the equivalent thereof, or a person otherwise lawfully practicing as an in-house counsel under the laws of a foreign jurisdiction, may provide legal services through an office or other systematic and continuous presence in this jurisdiction that:

(1)   are provided to the lawyer's employer or its organizational affiliates, are not services for which the forum requires pro hac vice admission; and when performed by a foreign lawyer and requires advice on the law of this or another U.S. jurisdiction or of the United States, such advice shall be based upon the advice of a lawyer who is duly licensed and authorized by the jurisdiction to provide such advice; or

(2)   are services that the lawyer is authorized by federal or other law or rule to provide in this jurisdiction.

(e)   For purposes of paragraph (d):

(1)   the foreign lawyer must be a member in good standing of a recognized legal profession in a foreign jurisdiction, the members of which are admitted to practice as lawyers or counselors at law or the equivalent, and subject to effective regulation and discipline by a duly constituted professional body or a public authority; or,

(2)   the person otherwise lawfully practicing as an in-house counsel under the laws of a foreign jurisdiction must be authorized to practice under this Rule by, in the exercise of its discretion, [the highest court of this jurisdiction].

Deconstruction Exercise/Rule Rationale

This is a long rule that stands for a short and simple proposition. Lawyers cannot engage in practice in a state in which they are not licensed except for a variety of exceptions. The tension in values is this: on the one hand, states want to protect the lawyers who are actually based in the state and are dues paying members of the bar versus the reality that lawyers practice in multiple states in order to meet the national needs of their clients.

LEANING INTO PRACTICE

Scenario: The Case of the out of State Lawyer and the Transferred Spouse

Joe Lawyer is a member in good standing of the Texas Bar. His spouse is transferred to her employer's facility in Tulsa, Oklahoma. Joe moves to Tulsa, he is not a member of the Oklahoma Bar, but he finds a job at a law firm in which he practices law under the daily and close supervision of a lawyer barred in Oklahoma. Is Joe in violation of the Rule? How about the supervising lawyer?

Section 3.   Practicing Law as a Public Trust

The goal of a profitmaking business is to turn a profit. But a business is also a citizen and often seeks to burnish their public image: sponsoring the Little League team; raising money for a telethon to cure an illness; offering internships to high school students. A law firm is both the same and different. The former in the sense that the better its overall reputation, the more likely to be retained by incumbent clients as its law firm or to be hired by prospective clients. And the latter in the sense that lawyers have a monopoly on the practice of law; that only a licensed lawyer can do so; and that all lawyers benefit, not just some firms, by strengthening the image of a functional and fair justice system, Rules on the even playing field perform the same role and are mandatory. These rules perform the identical function and—while voluntary—are no less important.

Model Rule 6.1: Voluntary Pro Bono Public Service

Every lawyer has a professional responsibility to provide legal services to those unable to pay. A lawyer should aspire to render at least (50) hours of pro bono public legal services per year. In fulfilling this responsibility, the lawyer should:

(a) provide a substantial majority of the (50) hours of legal services without fee or expectation of fee to:

(1) persons of limited means or

(2) charitable, religious, civic, community, governmental and educational organizations in matters that are designed primarily to address the needs of persons of limited means; and

(b) provide any additional services through:

(1) delivery of legal services at no fee or substantially reduced fee to individuals, groups or organizations seeking to secure or protect civil rights, civil liberties or public rights, or charitable, religious, civic, community, governmental and educational organizations in matters in furtherance of their organizational purposes, where the payment of standard legal fees would significantly deplete the organization's economic resources or would be otherwise inappropriate;

(2) delivery of legal services at a substantially reduced fee to persons of limited means; or

(3) participation in activities for improving the law, the legal system or the legal profession.

In addition, a lawyer should voluntarily contribute financial support to organizations that provide legal services to persons of limited means.

Model Rule 6.3: Membership in Legal Services Organization

A lawyer may serve as a director, officer or member of an organization involved in reform of the law or its administration notwithstanding that the reform may affect the interests of a client of the lawyer. When the lawyer knows that the interests of a client may be materially benefitted by a decision in which the lawyer participates, the lawyer shall disclose that fact but need not identify the client.

Model Rule 6.4: Law Reform Activities Affecting Client Interests

A lawyer may serve as a director, officer or member of an organization involved in reform of the law or its administration notwithstanding that the reform may affect the interests of a client of the lawyer. When the lawyer knows that the interests of a client may be materially benefitted by a decision in which the lawyer participates, the lawyer shall disclose that fact but need not identify the client.

Model Rule 6.5: Nonprofit and Court Annexed Limited Legal Services Programs

(a) A lawyer who, under the auspices of a program sponsored by a nonprofit organization or court, provides short-term limited legal services to a client without expectation by either the lawyer or the client that the lawyer will provide continuing representation in the matter:

(1) is subject to Rules 1.7 and 1.9(a) only if the lawyer knows that the representation of the client involves a conflict of interest; and

(2) is subject to Rule 1.10 only if the lawyer knows that another lawyer associated with the lawyer in a law firm is disqualified by Rule 1.7 or 1.9(a) with respect to the matter.

(b) Except as provided in paragraph (a)(2), Rule 1.10 is inapplicable to a representation governed by this Rule.

Comment on Rule 6.5

[1] Legal services organizations, courts and various nonprofit organizations have established programs through which lawyers provide short-term limited legal services—such as advice or the completion of legal forms—that will assist persons to address their legal problems without further representation by a lawyer. In these programs, such as legal-advice hotlines, advice-only clinics or pro se counseling programs, a client-lawyer relationship is established, but there is no expectation that the lawyer's representation of the client will continue beyond the limited consultation. Such programs are normally operated under circumstances in which it is not feasible for a lawyer to systematically screen for conflicts of interest as

is generally required before undertaking a representation. See, e.g., Rules 1.7, 1.9 and 1.10.

[2] A lawyer who provides short-term limited legal services pursuant to this Rule must secure the client's informed consent to the limited scope of the representation. See Rule 1.2(c). If a short-term limited representation would not be reasonable under the circumstances, the lawyer may offer advice to the client but must also advise the client of the need for further assistance of counsel. Except as provided in this Rule, the Rules of Professional Conduct, including Rules 1.6 and 1.9(c), are applicable to the limited representation.

[3] Because a lawyer who is representing a client in the circumstances addressed by this Rule ordinarily is not able to check systematically for conflicts of interest, paragraph (a) requires compliance with Rules 1.7 or 1.9(a) only if the lawyer knows that the representation presents a conflict of interest for the lawyer, and with Rule 1.10 only if the lawyer knows that another lawyer in the lawyer's firm is disqualified by Rules 1.7 or 1.9(a) in the matter.

[4] Because the limited nature of the services significantly reduces the risk of conflicts of interest with other matters being handled by the lawyer's firm, paragraph (b) provides that Rule 1.10 is inapplicable to a representation governed by this Rule except as provided by paragraph (a)(2). Paragraph (a)(2) requires the participating lawyer to comply with Rule 1.10 when the lawyer knows that the lawyer's firm is disqualified by Rules 1.7 or 1.9(a). By virtue of paragraph (b), however, a lawyer's participation in a short-term limited legal services program will not preclude the lawyer's firm from undertaking or continuing the representation of a client with interests adverse to a client being represented under the program's auspices. Nor will the personal disqualification of a lawyer participating in the program be imputed to other lawyers participating in the program.

[5] If, after commencing a short-term limited representation in accordance with this Rule, a lawyer undertakes to represent the client in the matter on an ongoing basis, Rules 1.7, 1.9(a) and 1.10 become applicable.

Deconstruction Exercise/Rule Rationale

While engaging in the activities listed in these rules are voluntary, the lawyer still must adhere to professional rules while doing so. Thus, under MR 6.1, while the lawyer can be lauded for taking on a pro bono client, the person is still a client, and all the Rules must be adhered to in representing the client. A lawyer can and should, if feasible, became involved in organizations seeking reform of the legal system. Yet, the lawyer must be transparent with the organization if the lawyer's client is interested in decisions made by these organizations. And this duty of *transparency* is in sync with other Rules you have learned: MR 2.3: Evaluation by Third Persons; MR 2.4: Lawyer Serve as Third Party Neutral; MR 3.9: Advocate in Non-adjudicative Proceedings. Different contexts, identical obligation. And with MR 6.5, lawyers—if they volunteer to serve on a legal hotline—must remain attuned to their duties of client loyalty in the conflict context, with a very narrow and surgical exception made to allow for lawyers to work the phones for the good of the profession as a whole.

Becoming a Professional

Thew following advertising clips from the television show "Better Call Saul" are about an ethically challenged lawyer. They are paired with comments from a law review article. Remember that ads for legal services are not about good taste or production values but rather about accurate representations as embodied in MR 7.1.

BEYOND THE CITE

Have you watched the television drama "Better Call Saul? The story line follows a lawyer, James McGill, who passes the bar exam on his fourth attempt, changes his first name to Saul because he believes it will be better for business development, and then launches an ad campaign to bring in clients. The following links are ads from the show.

As to each ask these questions:

➤ Is the ad in violation of any of the Model Rules? Which ones? Why?

➤ Why are ads like these permitted? Is there an ultimate public good that is served by the ads? What is it?

➤ Likely you've seen ads like these on television or radio or social media. Do you think they are effective? Why? Would you engage in this type of client development?

Take 1: **Old Commercial—Better Call Saul Webisode**
https://youtu.be/wqnHtGgVAUE

Take 2: Saul Says: "Sue Em Now"—Better Call Saul Webisode

https://youtu.be/pPd67CEL54E

Take 3: Better Call Saul: The Song,
https://youtu.be/mGsC_LO3oFY

Take 4: Saul Goodman Aviation Disaster Commercial
https://youtu.be/YDZFm4gzTQs

Take 5: Letters To Saul: Did I Murder an Old Man?—Better Call Saul Webisode
https://youtu.be/j3DY1_zijgA

Take 6: Another Satisfied Client of Saul Goodman: Carl—Better Call Saul Webisode
https://youtu.be/nDc-LNW8z18

WHAT'S NEXT?

In Chapter 11, we will look closely at your life and return to what we wrote at the start of this book. One day each of you will reflect on your career and we hope you will say, "What a wonderful way to have spent my life." But because hope is not a strategy, we wanted to give concrete advice to go from aspiration to reality. But first, it is important to appreciate the difficult paths that your predecessor lawyers—especially lawyers of color as well as with consciences—have had to travel to make this a possibility.

To assess your understanding of the material in this chapter,
click here to take a quiz.

PART VII

Your Career As a Lawyer

CHAPTER 10

The Lawyer in Waiting

Coming Attractions

In this chapter we tackle a question sure to be relevant to almost every law student: How does a person get licensed to practice law? The way we admit lawyers to the bar has been evolving for well more than a century, and it continues to evolve. In fact, as we write this in 2023, we may be in a period of particularly rapid change. It is entirely possible that 10 years from now the answer to that question—how does a person get a law license?—will be substantially different than it is today, at least in some states. The COVID-19 pandemic seems to have accelerated interest in major reforms of bar admissions. Or, maybe, not much will change.

There is a very ugly history of bar admission, featuring exclusion of women, African-Americans, and religious, sexual and ideological minorities. Much of that discrimination was accomplished using tools like character and fitness review, which are still part of the process, and which likely have a legitimate and necessary purpose—even if they are vulnerable to abuse. Recently the bar exam has been the target of considerable criticism, and it may be the subject of the most dramatic reforms in the near-term future. But the bar exam was itself a reform, an innovation meant to combat the vices of what came before it. With that background in mind, we offer a summary of the main elements of the admission process, and highlight some of the alternatives and reform proposals that seem to be getting the most attention today.

Section 1.   What Makes a Good Lawyer?

Why should we even require lawyers to be licensed in the first place? A reasonable person, especially with a highly libertarian orientation, might argue that we don't need professional licenses at all. Perhaps the free market would be enough. The authors of this book do not endorse this view, but we can imagine someone arguing that anyone should be able to offer legal services, and the public and the marketplace will figure out who is good and trustworthy and who is not.

There is at least one good reason to be skeptical of professional licensing systems overall. A licensing system creates a barrier to entry to the profession, inherently limiting who can provide the service. This might discriminate against potential members of the profession on illegitimate grounds (more on that very soon). But it also simply shrinks the pool of available service providers, which raises prices for the public. It makes it harder for people to obtain legal services. It renders the profession more elite and potentially elitist, at the expense of the public. Also, remember that bar admissions are controlled by the legal profession itself. When a profession is self-regulating, as the bar is, there is an ever-present risk that decisions about how to select and license lawyers will be made for the interests of the current members of the profession, and not in the interest of the public. For these reasons, it is hardly pointless to scrutinize professional licensing systems. And even if one accepts that lawyers and other professionals should be licensed, it may be healthy to be skeptical about the specific decisions made about how to actually operate that licensing system.

A possible example of such a protectionist approach was struck down by the Supreme Court in the 1985 case of *Supreme Court of New Hampshire v. Piper*, 470 U.S. 274 (1985). In that case, New Hampshire limited bar admissions to people who were actually residents of the state. That excluded people like Kathryn Piper, who lived in Vermont just 400 yards from the state line. But this type of rule would also prevent, say, Boston-based law firms from developing a practice serving their more sparsely populated neighbor. The Supreme Court reasoned that practicing law was a fundamental right protected by the privileges and immunities clause of the Constitution, and that allowing non-residents to practice law in a state served an important purpose: "Out-of-state lawyers may-and often do-represent persons who raise unpopular federal claims. In some cases, representation by nonresident counsel may be the only means available for the vindication of federal rights." 470 U.S. at 281.

Despite this healthy skepticism of protectionist licensing schemes, there is good reason to require licenses of at least some professionals: Consumer protection. The free market might work well when consumers are well placed to assess who is selling the best product or service. But it doesn't work very well when the service is highly technical so that the consumer may not be able to know immediately if they are being served well and may not know what to "shop" for when choosing a provider. Likewise, if most people might only need the service once or twice in their lifetimes, and if the stakes are often extremely high, we cannot count on people to learn through experience and trial and error, the way people learn not to go to restaurants where the food is not good. This is why the government might need to play an essential role in trying to ensure a minimum level of quality by requiring a license. Even if there is reason to think that American states impose licensing requirements on too many professions, there seems to be a very compelling argument to require a license of some professions, like medicine and law.

If the purpose of licensing lawyers is to protect legal consumers from bad lawyers, then a discussion of legal licensing ought to start with a simple but difficult question: What makes a good lawyer? To put that another way, if the State Bar says, "This person is good enough for us to admit her; she is now a licensed attorney." what exactly should that mean?

X-Ray Questions: (*The Competencies of an Attorney*)

There have been multiple efforts to itemize the skills that a good attorney must have. This is one example. Do you think it captures the most important factors? Is it missing anything? Creating a list like this should have implications for both bar admission and legal education. Do you think that bar examiners should try to verify competence in all of these areas, or focus on just a few? Do you think law school has adequately given you and other student the chance to develop all of these skills? As you read this Beyond the Cite correlate the skill sets described with the Rules and concepts we studied. What do you see?

BEYOND THE CITE

By: E. Eugene Clark, Report of the Task Force on Law Schools and the Profession: Narrowing the Gap (*excerpt*), American Bar Association (1992).

INTRODUCTION

This American Bar Association (ABA) Task Force publication is a report of the findings of an in-depth study of the "range of skills and values necessary for a lawyer to assume responsibility for handling a legal matter." The ABA Task Force which prepared the Report was comprised of approximately 40 leading law academics, legal practitioners and members of the judiciary. The project took three years to complete and is commendable for its thoroughness and the manner in which it built upon the foundation laid by earlier studies such as Zemans and Rosenblum, The Making of a Public Profession. The purpose of this review article is twofold: first, to summarise the findings of this ABA Task Force Report which was released in November 1992; and second, to consider what implications this US study may hold for Australian Legal Education which is facing, or in the future will face, many of the same issues.

INTRODUCTION TO THE REPORT

The Report begins by taking issue with the name given to the Task Force which was to examine the "gap" which separates the legal education community from the profession. The image of a "gap" which must be closed is a distorted one. For this reason, the authors chose for its title the word "continuum" as opposed to "gap".

The skills and values of the competent lawyer are developed along a continuum that starts before law school, reaches its most formative and intensive stage during the law school experience, and continues throughout a lawyer's professional career. Legal educators and practicing lawyers should stop viewing themselves as separated by a "gap" and recognize that they are engaged in a common enterprise—the education and professional development of members of a great profession.

PART II.   A VISION OF THE SKILLS AND VALUES NEW LAWYERS SHOULD SEEK TO ACQUIRE

Central to the Task Force's Report was its attempt to formulate a vision of what fundamental lawyering skills and ethical values should be central to legal education. The Committee, however, emphasizes the point that the vision outlined below is not the final word on the subject, but only a starting point for discussion to encourage the profession, legal educators and the judiciary to reconsider in a holistic way what skills and values new lawyers should acquire through the continuum of their legal careers. The Taskforce Report articulated the following vision of the skills and values which new lawyers should seek to acquire:

FUNDAMENTAL LAWYERING SKILLS

Skills 1: Problem Solving

In order to develop and evaluate strategies for solving a problem or accomplishing an objective, a lawyer should be familiar with the skills and concepts involved in:

1.1 Identifying and diagnosing the Problem;

1.2 Generating Alternative Solutions and Strategies;

1.3 Developing a plan of action;

1.4   Implementing the plan;

1.5   Keeping the planning process open to new information and new ideas.

Skills 2: *Legal Analysis and Reasoning*

In order to analyze and apply legal rules and principles, a lawyer should be familiar with the skills and concepts involved in:

2.1   Identifying and formulating legal issues;

2.2   Formulating relevant legal theories;

2.3   Elaborating legal theory;

2.4   Evaluating legal theory;

2.5   Criticizing and synthesizing legal argumentation.

Skills 3: *Legal Research*

In order to identify legal issues and to research them thoroughly and efficiently, a lawyer should have:

3.1   Knowledge of the nature of legal rules and institutions;

3.2   Knowledge of and ability to use the most fundamental tools of legal research;

3.3   Understanding of the process of devising and implementing a coherent and effective research design.

Skills 4: *Factual Investigation*

In order to plan, direct, and (where applicable) participate in factual investigation, a lawyer should be familiar with the skills and concepts involved in:

4.1   Determining the need for factual investigation;

4.2   Planning a factual investigation;

4.3   Implementing the investigative strategy;

4.4   Memorializing and organizing information in an accessible form

4.5   Deciding whether to conclude the process of fact-gathering;

4.6   Evaluating the information that has been gathered.

Skill 5:   Communication

In order to communicate effectively, whether orally or the recipient of in writing, a lawyer should be familiar with the skills and concepts involved in:

5.1 Assessing the perspective of communication;

5.2 Using effective methods of communication.

Skill 6:   Counseling

In order to counsel clients about decisions or courses of action, a lawyer should be familiar with the skill and concepts involved in.

6.1 Establishing a counseling relationship that respects the nature and bounds of a lawyer's role;

6.2 Gathering information relevant to the decision to be made;

6.3 Analyzing the decision to be made;

6.4 Counseling the client about the decision to be made;

6.5 Ascertaining and implementing the client's decision.

Skill 7:   Negotiation

In order to negotiate in either a dispute-resolution or transactional context, a lawyer should be familiar with the skills and concepts involved in:

7.1 Preparing for negotiation;

7.2 Conducting a negotiation session;

7.3 Counseling the client about the terms obtained from the other side in the negotiation and implementing the client's decision.

Skill 8:   Litigation and Alternative Dispute-Resolution Procedures

In order to employ—or to advise a client about—the options of litigation and alternative dispute resolution, a lawyer should understand the potential functions and consequences of these processes and should have a working fundamentals of:

8.1 Litigation at the trial-court level;

8.2 Litigation at the appellate level;

8.3 Advocacy in administrative and executive forums;

8.4   Proceedings in other dispute-resolution forums.

Skill 9:   Organizations and Management of Legal Work

In order to practice effectively, a lawyer should be familiar with the skills and concepts including:

9.1   Formulating goals management; required for efficient management, and principles for effective practice

9.2   Developing systems and procedures to ensure that time, effort and resources are allocated efficiently;

9.3   Developing systems and procedures to ensure that work is performed and completed at the appropriate 'time;

9.4   Developing systems and procedures for effectively working with other people;

9.5   Developing systems and procedures administering a law office.

Skill 10:   Recognizing and Resolving Ethical Dilemmas

In order to represent a client consistently with applicable ethical standards, a lawyer should be familiar with:

10.1 The nature and sources of ethical standards;

10.2 The means by which ethical standards are enforced;

10.3 The processes for recognizing dilemmas.

FUNDAMENTAL VALUES OF THE PROFESSION

Value 1: Provision of Competent Representation

As a member of a profession dedicated to the service of clients, a lawyer should be committed to the values of:

1.1   Attaining a level of competence in one's own field of practice;

1.2   Maintaining a level of competence in one's own field of practice;

1.3   Representing clients in a competent manner.

Value 2: Striving to Promote Justice, Fairness, and Morality

As a member of a profession that bears special responsibilities for the quality of justice, a lawyer should be committed to the values of:

2.1   Promoting justice, fairness, and morality in one's own daily practice;

2.2 Contributing

2.3 Contributing to the profession's responsibility to ensure that adequate legal provided to those who cannot afford to pay for them; to the profession's fulfillment of services fulfillment of its are its responsibility to enhance the capacity of the law and legal institutions to do justice.

Value 3: *Striving to Improve the Profession*

As a member of a self-governing profession, a lawyer should be committed to the values of:

3.1 Participating in activities designed to improve the profession;

3.2 Assisting in the training and preparation of new lawyers;

3.3 Striving to rid the profession of bias based on race, religion, ethnic origin, gender, sexual orientation, or disability, and to rectify the effects of these biases.

Value 4: *Professional Self-development*

As a member of a learned profession, a lawyer should be committed to the values of:

4.1 Seeking out and taking advantage of opportunities to increase his or her knowledge and improve his or her skills;

4.2 Selecting and maintaining employment that will allow the lawyer to develop as a professional and to pursue his or her professional and personal goals.

Section 2. Character and Fitness

Whatever the list of competencies may be, the bar admissions process tends to funnel them into two broad categories. One of them is, roughly speaking, focused on legal knowledge and analysis, which is currently assessed by requiring most lawyers to graduate from an accredited law school and then pass the bar exam. We will look at the bar exam (and its alternatives) a bit later. The other major inquiry is character and fitness.

Given how important judgement, trustworthiness and integrity are to legal practice, ensuring some degree of personal character for lawyers is probably essential. And yet, defining exactly what the necessary character of a lawyer is difficult.

To accomplish this goal, state bars require applicants to consent to an invasive investigation of their lives, including delving into matters that would otherwise be private. Applicants will need to disclose their employment and academic history, and will usually need to have former employers confirm the information separately. They will need, usually, to let the bar review their credit history. And they will need to disclose any criminal history. Some states require the disclosure of even parking citations. And they ask about any history of substance abuse or mental illness.

With regard to criminal records, bar applications typically delve far beyond criminal convictions. Some ask, for instance, if the applicant has ever been granted immunity to testify. Many require disclosure of arrests, not only convictions. The Wisconsin application, for example, says "You must disclose each instance however adjudicated, whether or not the charge and the plea or conviction differ, whether arrest, judgment, conviction, or sentence has been withheld or expunged, or the record sealed."

The financial disclosure requirements are sometimes controversial. Many states specifically ask whether the applicant is behind on any debts. The New York application, for instance, asks "Do you owe any debt for $300 or more, which is past due for over 90 days?" If the answer is "yes," it requires a detailed explanation for each debt. Many state bars ask if the applicant has ever filed for bankruptcy. And even if they don't ask, this information would usually be included on the credit reports that applicants need to disclose.

The controversy with these financial disclosures is that the questions seem to disadvantage people from less privileged backgrounds. If a person lost a job and fell behind on debts, or struggled financially while going through law school, does that say something negative about his or her character or fitness to be a lawyer? Bankruptcy is permitted by law, so why is taking advantage of it an issue?

Similar questions might be asked about criminal records. Is any arrest or conviction history a problem, or are only certain kinds of criminal records important? What if the applicant was arrested for trespass during a political protest? What if they have many speeding tickets? What about a serious crime committed many years in the past, followed by an impressive record of personal rehabilitation, culminating in graduation from law school?

There are few hard and fast rules that anyone can offer to answer these questions, but there are a few things that we can say.

First, the questions on bar applications are just questions. The bar usually wants to solicit as much information as it can about applicants, and thus forces them to surrender their privacy in the process. But just because they ask about something that might be a conceivable blemish on a person's record does not mean that that the applicant's chances are doomed. You have heard that the cover up is often worse than the crime. In bar applications, non-disclosure of an issue is usually worse than the issue itself. We know former students who have histories of alcohol abuse, struggles with mental illness, or significant prison terms in their past who have successfully obtained admission to the bar. But they always disclosed the issue and addressed it head on. When an applicant to the bar knows there is something on his or her record that will worry the bar, the best course of action will be to submit additional evidence and explanations to address the bar's legitimate concerns.

Second, the issues that are most likely to cause a problem, and which are most legitimately of concern to a state bar, are those that bear directly on whether the applicant has the ability to be trustworthy or to handle the pressures of legal practice. Thus, it may not actually matter that an applicant has a history of financial struggles, but a history of fraud or impulsive financial behavior will likely be a red flag. Substance abuse and mental illness are of concern to the bar because they are known to be causes of major ethical lapses by attorneys. But documented recovery and a long period of stability or sobriety can remedy the problem. All that said, the character and fitness inquiry is amorphous, and as a result there is always the possibility of a state bar trying to exclude a person for less legitimate reasons, as we will explore next.

Section 3. Regulating Bar Admission as Discrimination

The notion of character and fitness is vulnerable to ambiguity, subjectivity, abuse and bigotry. Historically this is exactly what has happened. Character and fitness review has been a primary tool of discrimination to keep people out of the profession illegitimately.

A. Discrimination Against Women

X-Ray Questions (*The Supreme Court and Exclusion of Women*)

Among the many offensive Supreme Court decisions upholding discrimination in the 19th Century, the Court in 1872 approved the exclusion of Myra Bradwell from legal practice because she was a married woman. The misogyny and sexism of the decision are hardly surprising for their era. But we can see that even this highly sexist decision may unwittingly say some interesting things about what it means to be a lawyer. Note how in this decision the Court does not think access to joining the bar is a privilege inherent in being a citizen.

Does this seem right to you? How does this compare to the *Piper* decision, which came more than a century later? Note also the concurrence by Justice Bradley, which is even more overtly sexist than the majority opinion. In the process of articulating traits that women supposedly lacked, does Justice Bradley unwittingly articulate any valid understanding of traits that a lawyer must have (even if he is self-evidently wrong about women's competence)?

Bradwell v. State of Illinois

Supreme Court of the United States, 1872.
83 U.S. 130.

MR. JUSTICE MILLER delivered the opinion of the court.

The record in this case is not very perfect, but it may be fairly taken that the plaintiff asserted her right to a license on the grounds, among others, that she was a citizen of the United States, and that having been a citizen of Vermont at one time, she was, in the State of Illinois, entitled to any right granted to citizens of the latter State.

The court having overruled these claims of right founded on the clauses of the Federal Constitution before referred to, those propositions may be considered as properly before this court.

As regards the provision of the Constitution that citizens of each State shall be entitled to all the privileges and immunities of citizens in the several States, the plaintiff in her affidavit has stated very clearly a case to which it is inapplicable.

The protection designed by that clause, as has been repeatedly held, has no application to a citizen of the State whose laws are complained of. If the plaintiff was a citizen of the State of Illinois, that provision of the Constitution gave her no protection against its courts or its legislation.

The plaintiff seems to have seen this difficulty, and attempts to avoid it by stating that she was born in Vermont.

While she remained in Vermont that circumstance made her a citizen of that State. But she states, at the same time, that she is a citizen of the United States, and that she is now, and has been for many years past, a resident of Chicago, in the State of Illinois.

The fourteenth amendment declares that citizens of the United States are citizens of the State within which they reside; therefore the plaintiff was, at the time of making her application, a citizen of the United States and a citizen of the State of Illinois.

We do not here mean to say that there may not be a temporary residence in one State, with intent to return to another, which will not create citizenship in the former. But the plaintiff states nothing to take her case out of the definition of citizenship of a State as defined by the first section of the fourteenth amendment.

In regard to that amendment counsel for the plaintiff in this court truly says that there are certain privileges and immunities which belong to a citizen of the United States as such; otherwise it would be nonsense for the fourteenth amendment to prohibit a State from abridging them, and he proceeds to argue that admission to the bar of a State of a person who possesses the requisite learning and character is one of those which a State may not deny.

In this latter proposition we are not able to concur with counsel. We agree with him that there are privileges and immunities belonging to citizens of the United States, in that relation and character, and that it is these and these alone which a State is forbidden to abridge. But the right to admission to practice in the courts of a State is not one of them. This right in no sense depends on citizenship of the United States. It has not, as far as we know, ever been made in any State, or in any case, to depend on citizenship at all. Certainly many prominent and distinguished lawyers have been admitted to practice, both in the State and Federal courts, who were not citizens of the United States or of any State. But, on whatever basis this right may be placed, so far as it can have any relation to citizenship at all, it would seem that, as to the courts of a State, it would relate to citizenship of the State, and as to Federal courts, it would relate to citizenship of the United States.

The opinion just delivered in the Slaughter-House Cases6 renders elaborate argument in the present case unnecessary; for, unless we are wholly and radically mistaken in the principles on which those cases are decided, the right to control and regulate the granting of license to practice law in the courts of a State is one of those powers which are not transferred for its protection to the Federal government, and its exercise is in no manner governed or controlled by citizenship of the United States in the party seeking such license.

It is unnecessary to repeat the argument on which the judgment in those cases is founded. It is sufficient to say they are conclusive of the present case.

JUDGMENT AFFIRMED.

Mr. Justice Bradley:

I concur in the judgment of the court in this case, by which the judgment of the Supreme Court of Illinois is affirmed, but not for the reasons specified in the opinion just read.

The claim of the plaintiff, who is a married woman, to be admitted to practice as an attorney and counsellor-at-law, is based upon the supposed right of every person, man or woman, to engage in any lawful employment for a livelihood. The Supreme Court of Illinois denied the application on the ground that, by the common law, which is the basis of the laws of Illinois, only men were admitted to the bar, and the legislature had not made any change in this respect, but had simply provided that no person should be admitted to practice as attorney or counsellor without having previously obtained a license for that purpose from two justices of the Supreme Court, and that no person should receive a license without first obtaining a certificate from the court of some county of his good moral character. In other respects it was left to the discretion of the court to establish the rules by which admission to the profession should be determined. The court, however, regarded itself as bound by at least two limitations. One was that it should establish such terms of admission as would promote the proper administration of justice, and the other that it should not admit any persons, or class of persons, not intended by the legislature to be admitted, even though not expressly excluded by statute. In view of this latter limitation the court felt compelled to deny the application of females to be admitted as members of the bar. Being contrary to the rules of the common law and the usages of Westminster Hall from time immemorial, it could not be supposed that the legislature had intended to adopt any different rule.

The claim that, under the fourteenth amendment of the Constitution, which declares that no State shall make or enforce any law which shall abridge the privileges and immunities of citizens of the United States, the statute law of Illinois, or the common law prevailing in that State, can no longer be set up as a barrier against the right of females to pursue any lawful employment for a livelihood (the practice of law included), assumes that it is one of the privileges and immunities of women as citizens to engage in any and every profession, occupation, or employment in civil life.

It certainly cannot be affirmed, as an historical fact, that this has ever been established as one of the fundamental privileges and immunities of the sex. On the contrary, the civil law, as well as nature herself, has always recognized a wide difference in the respective spheres and destinies of man and woman. Man is, or should be, woman's protector and defender. The natural and proper timidity and delicacy which belongs to the female sex evidently unfits it for many of the occupations of civil life. The constitution of the family organization, which is founded in the divine ordinance, as well as in the nature of things, indicates the domestic sphere as that which properly belongs to the domain and functions of womanhood. The harmony, not to say identity, of interest and views which belong, or should belong, to the family institution is repugnant to the idea of a woman adopting a distinct and independent career from that of her husband. So firmly fixed was this sentiment in the founders of the common law that it became a maxim of that system of jurisprudence that a woman had no legal existence separate from her husband, who was regarded as her head and representative in the social state; and, notwithstanding some recent modifications of this civil status, many of the special rules of law flowing from and dependent upon this cardinal principle still exist in full force in most States.

One of these is, that a married woman is incapable, without her husband's consent, of making contracts which shall be binding on her or him. This very incapacity was one circumstance which the Supreme Court of Illinois deemed important in rendering a married woman incompetent fully to perform the duties and trusts that belong to the office of an attorney and counsellor.

It is true that many women are unmarried and not affected by any of the duties, complications, and incapacities arising out of the married state, but these are exceptions to the general rule. The paramount destiny and mission of woman are to fulfil the noble and benign offices of wife and mother. This is the law of the Creator. And the rules of civil society must be adapted to the general constitution of things, and cannot be based upon exceptional cases.

The humane movements of modern society, which have for their object the multiplication of avenues for woman's advancement, and of occupations adapted to her condition and sex, have my heartiest concurrence. But I am not prepared to say that it is one of her fundamental rights and privileges to be admitted into every office and position, including those which require highly special qualifications and demanding special responsibilities. In the nature of things it is not every citizen of every age, sex, and condition that is qualified for every calling and position. It is the prerogative of the legislator to prescribe regulations founded on nature, reason, and experience for the due admission of qualified persons to professions and callings demanding special skill and confidence.

This fairly belongs to the police power of the State; and, in my opinion, in view of the peculiar characteristics, destiny, and mission of woman, it is within the province of the legislature to ordain what offices, positions, and callings shall be filled and discharged by men, and shall receive the benefit of those energies and responsibilities, and that decision and firmness which are presumed to predominate in the sterner sex.

For these reasons I think that the laws of Illinois now complained of are not obnoxious to the charge of abridging any of the privileges and immunities of citizens of the United States.

MR. JUSTICE SWAYNE and MR. JUSTICE FIELD concurred in the foregoing opinion of MR. JUSTICE BRADLEY.

THE CHIEF JUSTICE dissented from the judgment of the court, and from all the opinions.

SOLUTIONS: THE LAWYER SHOULD HAVE, WOULD HAVE, COULD HAVE. . .

We wrote this book in 2022 and 2023. That is 150 years from the date of this decision. But it was not until 2016 that the Rule adopted MR 8.4(g) (mentioned earlier) which provides as follows:

[A lawyer shall not]

(g) engage in conduct that the lawyer knows or reasonably should know is harassment or discrimination on the basis of race, sex, religion, national origin, ethnicity, disability, age, sexual orientation, gender identity, marital status or socioeconomic status in conduct related to the practice of law. This paragraph does not limit the ability of a lawyer to accept, decline or withdraw from a representation in accordance with Rule 1.16. This paragraph does not preclude legitimate advice or advocacy consistent with these Rules.

We will study this rule in greater depth in out last chapter. For now, consider whether we have actually changed out views internally or whether there still exists sexism and racism in the practice of law. And when one sees these traits at a firm and speaks up against them, are they left to later regret being courageous because of retribution, direct and indirect?

A final point. While this case might seem like ancient history, we do well to remember the Faulkner quote: "The past is never dead. It is not even past." As we write this the state Legislature in Missouri is considering mandating that women who appear on the floor with the body wear sleeves and not appear bare armed. Similarly, the United States House of Representatives is considering a similar rule. *Id.*

X-Ray Questions (*The Uses and Abuses of Character and Fitness Review*)

In 1960, there was not a single African-American attorney in the State of Nevada. Nevada in that era was sometimes called "The Mississippi of the West," because of rampant overt discrimination in housing and in the casinos and resorts of Las Vegas and Reno. In that year, Charles Kellar, an African American lawyer and real estate investor from New York moved to Las Vegas. He was an activist in the NAACP, and came west hoping to engage in civil rights work. He took the Nevada State Bar and attained an almost perfect score—and then was initially denied admission to the State Bar on grounds of character and fitness. Mr. Kellar went public with his outrage, accusing the state bar of racial discrimination. He also litigated and eventually prevailed. Clearly stung by the criticism, the state bar admitted two other African American lawyers before Mr. Keller eventually won at the state Supreme Court.

The *Kellar* case is more than just a historical artifact. As you will see reading the decision, especially the dissent, he did not have an entirely unblemished record. Those who wanted to keep him from practicing law in Nevada thus had vulnerabilities that they could point to. The case thus raises a central question. How can we distinguish cases where there is a legitimate character and fitness issue from those where character and fitness are weaponized to carry out racial or other forms of animus?

Application of Charles L. Kellar for Admission to the Bar of the State of Nevada

Supreme Court of Nevada, 1965.
81 Nev. 240.

WINES, DISTRICT JUDGE.

Charles L. Kellar has shown the court 39 years of irreproachable conduct while living in Brooklyn, New York. For some 20 of these years he was engaged in the practice of the law and had an established practice when he left New York to make his home in Las Vegas, Nevada, in the spring of 1960. Lawyers and judges with whom he dealt in his practice, have written letters commending his professional competence, sense of ethics and civility. His affiliations portray him as a communicant who attends his church regularly, a party man active in the affairs of his political party, a Negro man sensitive to the problems of his people and persistent in his efforts to solve these problems. His many civic activities while living in New York mark him as a responsible member of his community. He has always been a shrewd and successful investor. He has raised a family of two boys, though the mother of those children and he are now divorced and he has remarried and has two children by his present wife. That he is a scholar of the law is attested to by his having taken and passed the Nevada Bar examination.

The Board of Bar Examiners recommended that he be not admitted on the ground that he had failed to meet character standards. After reviewing the record supplied us we would not have so recommended. We acknowledge that we have the benefit of hindsight and a record supplemented since the time of the board's recommendation, and the supplementary information favors the petitioner. We apprehend too that the members of the board and of the Local Administrative Committee for District 1 in their investigation of his character were handicapped in their performance and in their duty to this court by a lack of power of subpoena and by a nice observation of our Rule 57. This rule was drafted on the premise that admission to practice in this state is a matter of grace and favor, a notion we are now obliged to discard. Willner v. Committee on Character and Fitness, 373 U.S. 96, 83 S.Ct. 1175, 10 L.Ed.2d 224. Our rule has a function. Confidential reports may properly be used to apprise of but should not be used in the trial of issues as to character.

Here we perceive the mischief of the rule and admit it invites error. When the petitioner could not find his name among the successful applicants of the bar he made inquiry. He was informed that the board had sought and obtained leave to file a supplemental report and a recommendation. Further inquiry elicited from the Secretary of the State Bar that it was the policy of the board to obtain a report on the activities of the applicant if he has practiced in another jurisdiction.

When, several months later, the Local Administrative Committee took up the matter the committee had information that the petitioner had associated with subversive organizations and persons in New York, in several instances practiced law in this state, was guilty of impropriety in a real estate transaction, had attempted submission of spurious items to an adjuster of an insurance claim, and had drafted a letter for another person's signature addressed to Robert Kennedy, Attorney General, charging discrimination in the matter of his application.

At this point we believe the petitioner should have been seasonably and fully advised of these charges, of the intent of the committee to hold a hearing and to take testimony from witnesses and the names of the witnesses should have been endorsed on the notice. Also, at this juncture, counsel should have been appointed to investigate, evaluate, and present the evidence against the petitioner. Having thus removed themselves from the contest the members, not personally involved, could have judiciously ruled upon the issues. At the hearing it is implicit that the petitioner would have been confronted by the witnesses against him, given opportunity to cross-examine, and should have been permitted to call witnesses on his behalf. This is what we read in the text on due process.

Instead, the petitioner was not so noticed nor advised. He was not permitted to confront and cross-examine witnesses against him and did not present any witnesses on his behalf. The committee members interrogated the witnesses and the petitioner and two members were sworn and gave testimony. In this exchange tempers soured and petitioner and the members were soon trading criticisms.

The board and the committees while hearing such issues should adjudicate and not advocate. Advocacy predicates assuming and attempting to sustain a point of view and cannot be reconciled with adjudication.

Confidential reports and the testimony of witnesses taken without confrontation and cross-examination and without notice to the applicant as to the issues cannot prevail against an established good character and the testimony of the petitioner.

Proceedings before the Board of Bar Examiners were conducted in the same manner except that the board heard a number of witnesses who appeared voluntarily to testify on the petitioner's behalf and were cross-examined by the board. The board did not take any evidence against petitioner and apparently relied on that taken by the Administrative Committee.

We do not intend reading the members of the Administrative Committee and the Board of Bar Examiners a lesson on due process. The record reflects their concern with this aspect of the hearings. Nor do we ignore these facts. At the time of the hearing the board did not have power to subpoena and no funds for retention of counsel. We have, in effect, written a new rule and redefined an old rule so as to comply with the ruling in the Willner case.

Before the opinion in the Willner case was handed down, we had denied a preliminary motion by the petitioner Kellar in the instant matter, to disclose the confidential written reports submitted by the National Conference of Bar Examiners and by other persons. Ex parte Kellar, 79 Nev. 28, 377 P.2d 927. At that time the disclosure would have served no purpose. As a practical matter, the hearings before the committee and the board had served to give the petitioner notice of the issues on the subject of his fitness and character.

He was given an opportunity to deny, to explain, and to discuss the charges reflecting on his character and fitness and he did in the course of the hearings. By this court he was granted leave to supplement the record and submit his affidavits and those of other persons having a firsthand knowledge of the facts. This procedure did not afford the petitioner nor the members of the committee and the board opportunity to confront and cross-examine the witnesses. This approach is not tolerable any longer. But we persist in our previous conclusion that we are not required to disclose confidential written reports by the Willner case. That case would require us and other persons acting as arms of the court, if issues result from a study of the confidential reports, to state the charges against the applicant, and if challenged to produce for confrontation and cross-examination, all witnesses on the issues. When the charge is not denied, or when the evidence in support of the charge is of an undisputed documentary character, procedural due process would be complied with if the applicant is given opportunity to reply or explain.

We turn now to two critical events. The information regarding these events came after the report and recommendation of the Board of Bar Examiners. One we learned of by disclosure from the petitioner and the other was a news event and his part in it is admitted by the petitioner. The evidence therefore comes within the exception noted in the Willner case as the facts are known by us from the statements made by the petitioner.

On November the 16th, 1962, the petitioner filed in this court his petition in which he alleged that he was in all respects qualified for admission to the Nevada State Bar and that he had been denied that privilege because of racial prejudice. On that same day the petitioner appeared at a television broadcasting station in Reno, Nevada, and was interviewed regarding this issue.

He was asked what legal action he had taken. He stated that he had filed his petition and then added in answer to that question that he believed he had been discriminated against as a Negro and not because of his law attainments or his character. The single evidential fact reported by him in support of that charge was that in 98 years of this state's existence not a single Negro applicant had been admitted to the bar and he said he thought this was not an accident but 'contrived' and to be 'eradicated' by efforts on the part of those denied 'their just constitutional rights.' In answer to another question he enumerated those courts and agencies he was entitled to practice before, adding that none of these privileges had been withdrawn. The interview closed with this question—if he thought it was 'strictly racial prejudice.' He answered in the affirmative adding that the bar had set out to obtain 'secret affidavits to present their things to the members of the Bar.' All of these complaints had been alleged in his petition which was a public document, except that the Nevada State Bar had not been accused but the Board of Bar Examiners.

We think it apposite to point out that since this interview two Negroes have been admitted to the bar; that prior to Mr. Kellar's application there had been but a single Negro applicant and he had failed in the bar examination. Also that approximately a month later when a reporter for a Las Vegas Newspaper sought an interview from Mr. Kellar he was refused on the ground that the matter was pending in this court.

On or about December the 29th, 1961, the grand jury of Kings County recommended and the district attorney of that county filed informations against Charles L. Kellar, Cornelia Street, Kellars Industrial Limited, Inc., and Adventure Development Corporation charging those defendants with violations of the New York Rent Control Law during the years 1959 and 1960. The two corporations were family corporations and Charles L. Kellar was the major stockholder. Their corporate purpose was to engage in domestic and foreign real property investments. Cornelia Street, in 1959 and 1960, was the petitioner's secretary. Specifically Charles L. Kellar was charged with perjury in the second degree, a misdemeanor, and with having charged excessive rents, also a misdemeanor. Cornelia Street was similarly charged. There were additional charges made against the corporations.

We are concerned about these actions since it was not until May 13th, 1963 that the petitioner disclosed the existence and nature of the actions to this court. It has been argued that the withholding of this information over that period shows a lack of candor.

These things should be said for the petitioner. The petitioner, who was then residing in Nevada, voluntarily appeared in the actions within weeks of the filing. On application of the People the disposition of the actions was continued from time to time until July 11th, 1963, when upon the insistence of the defendants in the cases they were marked ready and set for July 12th, 1963. All of the defendants pleaded not guilty. The defendants were prepared to take issue with the People's evidence against them. Finally on July the 12th they agreed to this disposition of the actions upon the suggestion of the district attorney. The actions would be dismissed as to all defendants except as to Adventure Development Corporation. That corporation would enter a plea of guilty to the charge of demanding and obtaining excessive rents and that defendant Kellar agreed to pay to the tenants any sums found to be owing by either of the corporations. The district attorney stated in open court that the statute of limitations barred civil remedies and he was concerned with getting relief for the aggrieved tenants. On July the 23rd, 1963 this compromise was executed; Adventure Development Corporation pleaded guilty and paid a civil penalty of a $1,000 fine; the district attorney and Mr. Kellar had agreed on the names of those tenants entitled to recover ad a sum sufficient to pay them was handed to the district attorney on that day. The actions against Charles L. Kellar, Cornelia Street, and Kellars Industrial Limited Inc., were dismissed.

The petitioner has offended against the ethic of our Canon and is by that Canon censured. See Canon 20, Canon of Ethics of the American Bar Association. Issues of this kind are not to be tried to the people by means of the news media. The filing fee is the newsworthiness of the litigant's cause, there is not a sifting of the evidence presented and often, as in this instance, the other party is not heard at all. The esteem of some 30 years of seemly endeavor and achievement is now in jeopardy because of this rash appeal. We could readily understand and forgive his impatience with our admission procedures but we have no patience with his percept of the sinister in the conduct and conclusions of the board and of the committee. Our concern here is with the impress the discipline of our profession has made upon him. Years of industry, achievement, good citizenship and honorable conduct are not compurgators; these years testify to his regard for the profession and his obligations as a professional person. We think it harsh then to deny the petitioner admission because of a single offense of this nature, here disciplined according to the Canon.

We are less troubled about his candidness in reporting the charge against him in New York. He did not shirk his responsibility to the people of the State of New York. If he did this in concern with his application in this state he did not as an opportunist, forthwith report to this court. We, in decent respect to a man who meets his private obligations, write this down as a shrewd and in no manner dishonest appraisal of the complainant's demand. His polity in this action was not discreditable and he has not been disciplined by the bar of New York.

The recommendation of the Board of Bar Examiners that Charles L. Kellar be denied admission is rejected, and we conclude that petitioner is entitled to practice law in the State of Nevada. It is so ordered.

BADT, JUSTICE (dissenting):

I dissent.

Although I concur in many of the things said in the majority opinion, I cannot reconcile myself to restricting this court's reaction to a mere reprimand for his broadcast on television and for his failure to disclose the criminal charges that were pending against him in New York. It is true that both of these incidents occurred after the recommendations of the Board of Bar Examiners that admission to practice in Nevada be denied. However, we had given the board permission to file a further supplemental report. These matters then developed.

In his television broadcast he said: 'I believe that I have been discriminated against, and that I am not being admitted to the bar here purely because of my race. It is not because of my qualifications or my inability or my character, as they say, but rather because they do not want a Negro to practice law in this state. In the 98 years that the State of Nevada has been in existence and so far as I have been able to gather, no Negro has ever been admitted to practice law in its courts. This is not just an accident. This is a contrived and a situation which, of course, can be eradicated and changed only by effort on the part of those who are being denied the opportunity to get their just constitutional rights.' Similar statements were made to the Board of Bar Examiners.

First, the statement is misleading with reference to the facts. Only one other Negro had sought admission in Nevada and he failed to pass the bar examination. Since the Kellar application, two Negroes have been admitted in Nevada after passing the 1964 bar examination. No other Negroes, except in the cases mentioned, have ever applied for permission to practice in this state. The same applies to applicants of any other race than Caucations.

At the time Mr. Kellar broadcast his remarks on television a highly emotional situation existed throughout the United States in general and in Nevada in particular. Civil rights legislation or contemplated legislation was pending in the Congress and also in the state legislature. At the time the remarks were made there was pending in this court the applicant's petition for a review of the recommendations of the Board of Bar Examiners. There can be but little doubt that the telecast had as its purpose the raising of social pressure on this court to reverse the action of the board. In oral argument we asked petitioner's counsel if he thought that the telecast was a lawyer-like thing to do. The most counsel would admit was that 'it was in poor taste.' In my opinion it was far worse than simply 'in poor taste.' His statement, 'I am not being admitted to the bar here purely because of my race * * * because THEY do not want a Negro to practice law in this state * * * no Negro HAS EVER BEEN ADMITTED to practice in its courts * * *. This is not just an accident. This is a CONTRIVED * * * situation * * *' was not in effect directed simply to the Board of Bar Examiners. It was a broad wave of his arm which took in the Board of Bar Examiners, the state bar, and this court. (Emphasis supplied.)

The Board of Bar Examiners has often been referred to as an arm of the court. It comprises seven lawyers of high standing in this state. Their task in preparing the bar examinations and, in the case of application for admission by attorneys from foreign jurisdictions, carrying on extensive correspondence with the investigative arm of the National Conference of Bar Examiners, grading the examinations, conducting hearings, is an arduous and difficult one. It is undertaken without compensation. It is a tremendous drain upon the time of the members of the board. It sometimes results, as in the present case, in charges such as those made by Mr. Kellar. As the decision of the board in this case was unanimous, the charge is directed against every member of that board. As to the nature and extent of the character investigation, reference is made to an article by James B. Tippin, Jr., Executive Director, Florida Board of Bar Examiners, entitled 'Technique of Character Investigation—Vigilance with Due process,' published in 1963, Volume 32, Nos. 3–4, of 'The Bar Examiner,' published by the National Conference of Bar Examiners, which is composed of members of law-examining boards and character committees. The article is too long to quote at length, but I may refer to the following part of the author's address to the National Conference of Bar Examiners:

'Those of you who are in the unfortunate position of constantly being designated as respondents in the petitions filed by the disgruntled applicants are not unfamiliar, I am sure, with the applicants' glossary which invariably includes such terms as 'Kangaroo Court,' 'star chamber,' 'inquisition,' 'persecution,' 'oppression,' 'rumor,' and 'innuendo.''

Nor can I overlook Mr. Kellar's lack of candor in failing to report the criminal charges against him in New York. The majority opinion makes light of the criminal proceedings pending against Mr. Kellar apparently because the charge of 'perjury in the second degree' and the charge of having 'charged excessive rents' were both merely misdemeanors. I cannot treat them lightly. They both involve moral turpitude—the making of false affidavits of installation of improvements in the rented premises that would justify increased rentals. These amounted to $3,500 which he in behalf of his corporation (which had pleaded guilty) refunded to the tenants, whereupon the district attorney dismissed the charges. His corporation also paid a $1,000 fine. He reported these proceedings to the board when he must have known that the board had, or was about to receive, knowledge thereof. They were established by introduction of exemplified copies of the court records.

In Willner v. Committee on Character and Fitness, 373 U.S. 96, 83 S.Ct. 1175, 10 L.Ed.2d 224, cited by the majority opinion, reference is made to the concurring opinion by Justice Goldberg, in which Justices Brennan and Stewart joined. It was said: "* * * [W]hen the derogatory matter appears from information supplied or confirmed by the applicant himself, or is of an undisputed documentary character disclosed to the applicant, and it is plain and uncontradicted that the committee's recommendation against admission is predicated thereon and reasonably supported thereby, then neither the committee's informal procedures, its ultimate recommendations, nor a court ruling sustaining the committee's conclusion may be properly challenged on due process grounds, provided the applicant has been informed of the factual basis of the conclusion and has been afforded an adequate opportunity to reply or explain. Of course, if the denial depends upon information supplied by a particular person whose reliability or veracity is brought into question by the applicant, confrontation and the right of cross-examination should be afforded.'

This dissent has nothing to do with due process.

I am in entire disagreement with that part of the majority opinion in which it is stated that the majority is not troubled about his [lack of] candidness in reporting the New York charges against him. I do not agree that 'He did not shirk his responsibility to the people of the State of New York.' I do not agree with the majority's statement as follows: 'If he did this in concern with his application in this state he did not as an opportunist, forthwith report to this court.' This appears to me to be admission of his opportunism, which Webster defines as follows: 'Art, policy, or practice of taking advantage, as in politics, of opportunities or circumstances, or, often of seeking immediate advantage with little regard for principles or ultimate consequences.' I thoroughly disagree with the majority's following conclusion: 'We, in decent respect to a man who meets his private obligations, write this down as a shrewd and in no manner dishonest appraisal of the complainant's demand.' The majority also deems it important that he has not been disciplined by the bar of New York. He may yet be, if he returns to New York to practice.

I should add that there are places in the record of the hearing before the Board of Bar Examiners which sustain the contention that he was at times evasive and that his testimony is in some instances incredible.

Faced with the situation above outlined it is my conclusion, with due respect to the majority opinion, that the unfavorable recommendation of the Board of Bar Examiners should be followed, and the applicant denied admission to the bar of this state.

B. Discrimination by Ideology

Do you think there are certain ideological beliefs that are incompatible with the practice of law? What if someone is a white supremacist? Or a misogynist, like Justice Bradley in the *Bradwell* case? What if someone is against democracy, or has opposed the peaceful transfer of power under the Constitution?

State Bars have often thought that ideology might in a legitimate factor in a character and fitness assessment. But they have not usually used this against sexists and racists. Instead, the most prominent targets historically have been people on the political left—especially during the McCarthy Era.

As of 2022, the Florida bar application contains this question: "Have you ever organized or helped to organize or been a member of any organization or group of persons that, during the period of your membership or association, you knew was advocating or teaching that the government of the United States or any state or any political subdivision thereof should be overthrown or overturned by force, violence, or any unlawful means?" Some other states have similar questions. Is this a legitimate inquiry?

What might you say about the proper place of ideology, if any, in bar admission?

X-Ray Questions (*The Uses and Abuses of Character and Fitness Review, Redux*)

In the *Schware* case, the Supreme Court relied on procedural due process, even though the real issue seems to be ideological. Why didn't the Court look at this as a First Amendment case? And given that the court did not address free speech, what rules (if any) can we actually apply to ideologically-based exclusions from legal practice in the future?

Schware v. Board of Bar Examiners
of the State of New Mexico

Supreme Court of the United States, 1957.
353 U.S. 232.

MR. JUSTICE BLACK delivered the opinion of the Court.

The question presented is whether petitioner, Rudolph Schware, has been denied a license to practice law in New Mexico in violation of the Due Process Clause of the Fourteenth Amendment to the United States Constitution.

New Mexico has a system for the licensing of persons to practice law similar to that in effect in most States. A Board of Bar Examiners determines if candidates for admission to the bar have the necessary qualifications. When the Board concludes that an applicant qualifies it recommends to the State Supreme Court that he be admitted. If the court accepts the recommendation, the applicant is entitled to practice law upon taking an oath to support the constitutions and laws of the United States and New Mexico. An applicant must pass a bar examination before the Board will give him its recommendation. The Board can refuse to permit him to take this examination unless he demonstrates that he has 'good moral character.'

In December 1953, on the eve of his graduation from the University of New Mexico School of Law, Schware filed an application with the Board of Bar Examiners requesting that he be permitted to take the bar examination scheduled for February 1954. His application was submitted on a form prescribed by the Board that required answers to a large number of questions. From the record, it appears that he answered these questions in detail. Among other things, he disclosed that he had used certain aliases between 1933 and 1937 and that he had been arrested on several occasions prior to 1940. When he appeared to take the examination, the Board informed him that he could not do so. He later requested a formal hearing on the denial of his application. The Board granted his request. At the hearing the Board told him for the first time why it had refused to permit him to take the bar examination. It gave him a copy of the minutes of the meeting at which it had voted to deny his application. These minutes read:

'No. 1309, Randolph Schware. It is moved by Board Member Frank Andrews that the application of Rudolph Schware to take the bar examination be denied for the reason that, taking into consideration the use of aliases by the applicant, his former connection with subversive organizations, and his record of arrests, he has failed to satisfy the Board as to the requisite moral character for admission to the Bar of New Mexico. Whereupon said motion is duly seconded by Board Member Ross L. Malone, and unanimously passed.

At the hearing petitioner called his wife, the rabbi of his synagogue, a local attorney and the secretary to the dean of the law school to testify about his character. He took the stand himself and was thoroughly examined under oath by the Board. His counsel introduced a series of letters that petitioner had written his wife from 1944 through 1946 while he was on duty in the Army. Letters were also introduced from every member of petitioner's law school graduating class except one who did not comment. And all of his law school professors who were then available wrote in regard to his moral character. The Board called no witnesses and introduced no evidence.

The record of the formal hearing shows the following facts relevant to Schware's moral character. He was born in a poor section of New York City in 1914 and grew up in a neighborhood inhabited primarily by recent immigrants. His father was an immigrant and like many of his neighbors had a difficult time providing for his family. Schware took a job when he was nine years old and throughout the remainder of school worked to help provide necessary income for his family. After 1929, the economic condition of the Schware family and their neighbors, as well as millions of others, was greatly worsened. Schware was then at a formative stage in high school. He was interested in and enthusiastic for socialism and trade-unionism as was his father. In 1932, despairing at what he considered lack of vigor in the socialist movement at a time when the country was in the depths of the great depression, he joined the Young Communist League. At this time he was 18 years old and in the final year of high school.

From the time he left school until 1940 Schware, like many others, was periodically unemployed. He worked at a great variety of temporary and ill-paying jobs. In 1933, he found work in a glove factory and there he participated in a successful effort to unionize the employees. Since these workers were principally Italian, Schware assumed the name Rudolph Di Caprio to forestall the effects of anti-Jewish prejudice against him, not only in securing and retaining a job but in assisting in the organization of his fellow employees. In 1934 he went to California where he secured work on the docks. He testified that he continued to use the name Rudolph Di Caprio because Jews were discriminated against in employment for this work. Wherever Schware was employed he was an active advocate of labor organization. In 1934 he took part in the great maritime strikes on the west coast which were bitterly fought on both sides. While on strike in San Pedro, California, he was arrested twice on 'suspicion of criminal syndicalism.' He was never formally charged nor tried and was released in each instance after being held for a brief period. He testified that the San Pedro police, in a series of mass arrests jailed large numbers of the strikers.

At the time of his father's death in 1937 Schware left the Communist Party but later he rejoined. In 1940 he was arrested and indicted for violating the Neutrality Act of 1917. He was charged with attempting to induce men to volunteer for duty on the side of the Loyalist Government in the Spanish Civil War. Before his case came to trial the charges were dismissed and he was released. Later in 1940 he quit the Communist Party. The Nazi-Soviet Non-Aggression Pact of 1939 had greatly disillusioned him and this disillusionment was made complete as he came to believe that certain leaders in the Party were acting to advance their own selfish interests rather than the interests of the working class which they purported to represent.

In 1944 Schware entered the armed forces of the United States. While in the service he volunteered for duty as a paratrooper and was sent to New Guinea. While serving in the Army here and abroad he wrote a number of letters to his wife. These letters show a desire to serve his country and demonstrate faith in a free democratic society. They reveal serious thoughts about religion which later led him and his wife to associate themselves with a synagogue when he returned to civilian life. He was honorably discharged from the Army in 1946.

After finishing college, he entered the University of New Mexico law school in 1950. At the beginning he went to the dean and told him of his past activities and his association with the Communist Party during the depression and asked for advice. The dean told him to remain in school and put behind him what had happened years before. While studying law Schware operated a business in order to support his wife and two children and to pay the expenses of a professional education. During his three years at the law school his conduct was exemplary.

At the conclusion of the hearing the Board reaffirmed its decision denying Schware the right to take the bar examination. He appealed to the New Mexico Supreme Court. That court upheld the denial with one justice dissenting. 60 N.M. 304, 291 P.2d 607, 630. In denying a motion for rehearing the court stated that:

'(Schware's membership in the Communist Party), together with his other former actions in the use of aliases and record of arrests, and his present attitude toward those matters, were the considerations upon which (we approved the denial of his application).'

Schware then petitioned this Court to review his case alleging that he had been denied an opportunity to qualify for the practice of law contrary to the Due Process Clause of the Fourteenth Amendment. We granted certiorari. 352 U.S. 821, 77 S.Ct. 34, 1 L.Ed.2d 46. Cf. In re Summers, 325 U.S. 561, 562, 564—569, 65 S.Ct. 1307, 1308, 1309, 1312, 89 L.Ed. 1795. And see Konigsberg v. State Bar of California, 353 U.S. 252, 77 S.Ct. 722.

A State cannot exclude a person from the practice of law or from any other occupation in a manner or for reasons that contravene the Due Process or Equal Protection Clause of the Fourteenth Amendment. Dent v. State of West Virginia, 129 U.S. 114, 9 S.Ct. 231, 32 L.Ed. 623. Cf. Slochower v. Board of Higher Education, 350 U.S. 551, 76 S.Ct. 637, 100 L.Ed. 692; Wieman v. Updegraff, 344 U.S. 183, 73 S.Ct. 215, 97 L.Ed. 216. And see Ex parte Secombe, 19 How. 9, 13, 15 L.Ed. 565. A State can require high standards of qualification, such as good moral character or proficiency in its law, before it admits an applicant to the bar, but any qualification must have a rational connection with the applicant's fitness or capacity to practice law. Douglas v. Noble, 261 U.S. 165, 43 S.Ct. 303, 67 L.Ed. 590; Cummings v. State of Missouri, 4 Wall. 277, 319—320, 18 L.Ed. 356. Cf. Nebbia v. People of State of New York, 291 U.S. 502, 54 S.Ct. 505, 78 L.Ed. 940. Obviously an applicant could not be excluded merely because he was a Republican or a Negro or a member of a particular church. Even in applying permissible standards, officers of a State cannot exclude an applicant when there is no basis for their finding that he fails to meet these standards, or when their action is invidiously discriminatory. Cf. Yick Wo v. Hopkins, 118 U.S. 356, 6 S.Ct. 1064, 30 L.Ed. 220.

Here the State concedes that Schware is fully qualified to take the examination in all respects other than good moral character. Therefore the question is whether the Supreme Court of New Mexico on the record before us could reasonably find that he had not shown good moral character.

There is nothing in the record which suggests that Schware has engaged in any conduct during the past 15 years which reflects adversely on his character. The New Mexico Supreme Court recognized that he 'presently enjoys good repute among his teachers, his fellow students and associates and in his synagogue.' Schware's professors, his fellow students, his business associates and the rabbi of the synagogue of which he and his family are members, all gave testimony that he is a good man, a man who is imbued with a sense of deep responsibility for his family, who is trustworthy, who respects the rights and beliefs of others. From the record it appears he is a man of religious conviction and is training his children in the beliefs and practices of his faith. A solicitude for others is demonstrated by the fact that he regularly read the Bible to an illiterate soldier while in the Army and law to a blind student while at the University of New Mexico law school. His industry is depicted by the fact that he supported his wife and two children and paid for a costly professional education by operating a business separately while studying law. He demonstrated candor by informing the Board of his personal history and by going to the dean of the law school and disclosing his past. The undisputed evidence in the record shows Schware to be a man of high ideals with a deep sense of social justice. Not a single witness testified that he was not a man of good character.

Despite Schware's showing of good character, the Board and court below thought there were certain facts in the record which raised substantial doubts about his moral fitness to practice law.

Aliases.—From 1934 to 1937 Schware used certain aliases. He testified that these aliases were adopted so he could secure a job in businesses which discriminated against Jews in their employment practices and so that he could more effectively organize non-Jewish employees at plants where he worked. Of course it is wrong to use an alias when it is done to cheat or defraud another but it can hardly be said that Schware's attempt to forestall anti-semitism in securing employment or organizing his fellow workers was wrong. He did give an assumed name to police in 1934 when he was picked up in a mass arrest during a labor dispute. He said he did this so he would not be fired as a striker. This is certainly not enough evidence to support an inference that petitioner has bad moral character more than 20 years later.

Arrests.—In response to the questions on the Board's application form Schware stated that he had been arrested on several occasions:

In 1934, while he was participating in a bitter labor dispute in the California shipyards, petitioner was arrested at least two times on 'suspicion of criminal syndicalism.' After being held for a brief period he was released without formal charges being filed against him. He was never indicted nor convicted for any offense in connection with these arrests.

The mere fact that a man has been arrested has very little, if any, probative value in showing that he has engaged in any misconduct. An arrest shows nothing more than that someone probably suspected the person apprehended of an offense. When formal charges are not filed against the arrested person and he is released without trial, whatever probative force the arrest may have had is normally dissipated. Moreover here, the special facts surrounding the 1934 arrests are relevant in shedding light on their present significance. Apparently great numbers of strikers were picked up by police in a series of arrests during the strike at San Pedro and many of these were charged with 'criminal syndicalism.' The California syndicalism statutes in effect in 1934 were very broad and vague. There is nothing in the record which indicates why Schware was arrested on 'suspicion' that he had violated this statute. There is no suggestion that he was using force or violence in an attempt to overthrow the state or national government. Again it should be emphasized that these arrests were made more than 20 years ago and petitioner was never formally charged nor tried for any offense related to them.

In 1940 Schware was arrested for violating the Neutrality Act of 1917 which makes it unlawful for a person within the United States to join or to hire or retain another to join the army of any foreign state. He was indicted but before the case came to trial the prosecution dropped the charges. He had been charged with recruiting persons to go overseas to aid the Loyalists in the Spanish Civil War. Schware testified that he was unaware of this old law at the time. From the facts in the record it is not clear that he was guilty of its violation. But even if it be assumed that the law was violated, it does not seem that such an offense indicated moral turpitude—even in 1940. Many persons in this country actively supported the Spanish Loyalist Government. During the prelude to World War II many idealistic young men volunteered to help causes they believed right. It is commonly known that a number of Americans joined air squadrons and helped defend China and Great Britain prior to this country's entry into the war. There is no record that any of these volunteers were prosecuted under the Neutrality Act. Few Americans would have regarded their conduct as evidence of moral turpitude. In determining whether a person's character is good the nature of the offense which he has committed must be taken into account.

In summary, these arrests are wholly insufficient to support a finding that Schware had bad moral character at the time he applied to take the bar examination. They all occurred many years ago and in no case was he ever tried or convicted for the offense for which he was arrested.

(3) Membership in the Communist Party.—Schware admitted that he was a member of the Communist Party from 1932 to 1940. Apparently the Supreme Court of New Mexico placed heavy emphasis on this part membership in denying his application. It stated:

'We believe one who has knowingly given his loyalties to (the Communist Party) for six to seven years during a period of responsible adulthood is a person of questionable character.' (60 N.M. 319, 291 P.2d 617.)

The court assumed that in the 1930's when petitioner was a member of the Communist Party, it was dominated by a foreign power and was dedicated to the violent overthrow of the Government and that every member was aware of this. It based this assumption primarily on a view of the nature and purposes of the Communist Party as of 1950 expressed in a concurring opinion in American Communications Ass'n v. Douds, 339 U.S. 382, 422, 70 S.Ct. 674, 695, 94 L.Ed. 925. However that view did not purport to be a factual finding in that case and obviously it cannot be used as a substitute for evidence in this case to show that petitioner participated in any illegal activity or did anything morally reprehensible as a member of that Party. During the period when Schware was a member, the Communist Party was a lawful political party with candidates on the ballot in most States. There is nothing in the record that gives any indication that his association with that Party was anything more than a political faith in a political party. That faith may have been unorthodox. But as counsel for New Mexico said in his brief, 'Mere unorthodoxy (in the field of political and social ideas) does not as a matter of fair and logical inference, negative 'good moral character.

Schware joined the Communist Party when he was a young man during the midst of this country's greatest depression. Apparently many thousands of other Americans joined him in this step. During the depression when millions were unemployed and our economic system was paralyzed many turned to the Communist Party out of desperation or hope. It proposed a radical solution to the grave economic crisis. Later the rise of fascism as a menace to democracy spurred others who feared this form of tyranny to align with the Communist Party. After 1935, that Party advocated a 'Popular Front' of 'all democratic parties against fascism.' Its platform and slogans stressed full employment, racial equality and various other political and economic changes.

During the depression Schware was led to believe that drastic changes needed to be made in the existing economic system. There is nothing in the record, however, which indicates that he ever engaged in any actions to overthrow the Government of the United States or of any State by force or violence, or that he even advocated such actions. Assuming that some members of the Communist Party during the period from 1932 to 1940 had illegal aims and engaged in illegal activities, it cannot automatically be inferred that all members shared their evil purposes or participated in their illegal conduct. As this Court declared in Wieman v. Updegraff, 344 U.S. 183, 191, 73 S.Ct. 215, 219, 97 L.Ed. 216: 'Indiscriminate classification of innocent with knowing activity must fall as an assertion of arbitrary power.' Cf. Joint Anti-Fascist Refugee Committee v. McGrath, 341 U.S. 123, 136, 71 S.Ct. 624, 630, 95 L.Ed. 817. And finally, there is no suggestion that Schware was affiliated with the Communist Party after 1940—more than 15 years ago. We conclude that his past membership in the Communist Party does not justify an inference that he presently has bad moral character.

The State contends that even though the use of aliases, the arrests, and the membership in the Communist Party would not justify exclusion of petitioner from the New Mexico bar if each stood alone, when all three are combined his exclusion was not unwarranted. We cannot accept this contention. In the light of petitioner's forceful showing of good moral character, the evidence upon which the State relies—the arrests for offenses for which petitioner was neither tried nor convicted, the use of an assumed name many years ago, and membership in the Communist Party during the 1930's—cannot be said to raise substantial doubts about his present good moral character. There is no evidence in the record which rationally justifies a finding that Schware was morally unfit to practice law.

On the record before us we hold that the State of New Mexico deprived petitioner of due process in denying him the opportunity to qualify for the practice of law. The judgment below is reversed and the case remanded for proceedings not inconsistent with this opinion.

It is so ordered.

Reversed and remanded with directions.

MR. JUSTICE WHITTAKER took no part in the consideration or decision of this case.

MR. JUSTICE FRANKFURTER, whom MR. JUSTICE CLARK and MR. JUSTICE HARLAN join, concurring.

Certainly since the time of Edward I, through all the vicissitudes of seven centuries of Anglo-American history, the legal profession has played a role all its own. The bar has not enjoyed prerogatives; it has been entrusted with anxious responsibilities. One does not have to inhale the self-adulatory bombast of after-dinner speeches to affirm that all the interests of man that are comprised under the constitutional guarantees given to 'life, liberty and property' are in the professional keeping of lawyers. It is a fair characterization of the lawyer's responsibility in our society that he stands 'as a shield,' to quote Devlin, J., in defense of right and to ward off wrong. From a profession charged with such responsibilities there must be exacted those qualities of truth-speaking, of a high sense of honor, of granite discretion, of the strictest observance of fiduciary responsibility, that have, throughout the centuries, been compendiously described as 'moral character.'

From the thirteenth century to this day, in England the profession itself has determined who should enter it. In the United States the courts exercise ultimate control. But while we have nothing comparable to the Inns of Court, with us too the profession itself, through appropriate committees, has long had a vital interest, as a sifting agency, in determining the fitness, and above all the moral fitness, of those who are certified to be entrusted with the fate of clients. With us too the requisite 'moral character' has been the historic unquestioned prerequisite of fitness. Admission to practice in a State and before its courts necessarily belongs to that State. Of course, legislation laying down general conditions of an arbitrary or discriminatory character may, like other legislation, fall afoul of the Fourteenth Amendment. See Cummings v. State of Missouri, 4 Wall. 277, 18 L.Ed. 356. A very different question is presented when this Court is asked to review the exercise of judgment in refusing admission to the bar in an individual case, such as we have here.

It is beyond this Court's function to act as overseer of a particular result of the procedure established by a particular State for admission to its bar. No doubt satisfaction of the requirement of moral character involves an exercise of delicate judgment on the part of those who reach a conclusion, having heard and seen the applicant for admission, a judgment of which it may be said as it was of 'many honest and sensible judgments' in a different context that it expresses 'an intuition of experience which outruns analysis and sums up many unnamed and tangled impressions,—impressions which may lie beneath consciousness without losing their worth.' Chicago, B. & Q.R. Co. v. Babcock, 204 U.S. 585, 598, 27 S.Ct. 326, 329, 51 L.Ed. 636. Especially in this realm it is not our business to substitute our judgment for the State's judgment—for it is the State in all the panoply of its powers that is under review when the action of its Supreme Court is under review.

Nor is the division of power between this Court and that of the States in such matters altered by the fact that the judgment here challenged involves the application of a conception like that of 'moral character,' which has shadowy rather than precise bounds. It cannot be that that conception—moral character—has now been found to be so indefinite, because necessarily implicating what are called subjective factors, that the States may no longer exact it from those who are to carry on 'the public profession of the law.' (See Elihu Root, in 2 A.B.A.J. 736.) To a wide and deep extent, the law depends upon the disciplined standards of the profession and belief in the integrity of the courts. We cannot fail to accord such confidence to the state process, and we must attribute to its courts the exercise of a fair and not a biased judgment in passing upon the applications of those seeking entry into the profession.

But judicial action, even in an individual case, may have been based on avowed considerations that are inadmissible in that they violate the requirements of due process. Refusal to allow a man to qualify himself for the profession on a wholly arbitrary standard or on a consideration that offends the dictates of reason offends the Due Process Clause. Such is the case here.

Living under hard circumstances, the Petitioner, while still in his teens, encountered the confusions and dislocations of the great depression. By one of those chance occurrences that not infrequently determine the action of youth, petitioner joined the Young Communist League to-ward the end of his high-school days. That association led to membership in the Communist Party, which he retained until the Hitler-Stalin Pact began a disaffection that was completed by his break with the Party in 1940. After 1940, the record of his life, including three years of honorable service in the army, establishes that these early associations, and the outlook they reflected, had been entirely left behind. After his war service, three years as a small businessman, and one year at Western Michigan College, petitioner resolved on becoming a lawyer. And so in 1950, at the age of 36, he enrolled in the University of New Mexico Law School and made full disclosure of his early Communist career to its Dean. These are the facts that, taken together with the use of aliases and arrests without conviction or even prosecution, both in his early years, led the Supreme Court of New Mexico, in an original proceeding before it after adverse action by the Board of Bar Examiners, to deny petitioner's application to take the bar examination.

For me, the controlling element in determining whether such denial offended the Due Process Clause is the significance that the New Mexico Supreme Court accorded the early Communist affiliations. In its original opinion and in its opinion on rehearing, the court thus reiterated its legal position:

'We believe one who has knowingly given his loyalties to such a program and belief for six to seven years during a period of responsible adulthood is a person of questionable character.' 60 N.M. 304, 319, 339, 291 P.2d 607, 617, 630.

Since the New Mexico Supreme Court unequivocally held this to be a factor without which, on a fair reading of its opinion, it would not have denied the application, the conclusion that it drew from all the factors in necessary combination must fall if it drew an unwarranted legal conclusion from petitioner's early Communist affiliation. Not unnaturally the New Mexico Supreme Court evidently assumed that use of aliases in the pre-1940 period, several unprosecuted arrests, and what it deemed 'his present attitude toward those matters,' 60 N.M. at page 339, 291 P.2d at page 630 (as drawn from the printed record and not on the basis of having given the petitioner a hearing before the court) precluded denial of his application on these factors alone.

This brings me to the inference that the court drew from petitioner's early, pre-1940 affiliations. To hold, as the court did, that Communist affiliation for six to seven years up to 1940, fifteen years prior to the court's assessment of it, in and of itself made the petitioner 'a person of questionable character' is so dogmatic an inference as to be wholly unwarranted. History overwhelmingly establishes that many youths like the petitioner were drawn by the mirage of communism during the depression era, only to have their eyes later opened to reality. Such experiences no doubt may disclose a woolly mind or naive notions regarding the problems of society. But facts of history that we would be arbitrary in rejecting bar the presumption, let alone an irrebuttable presumption, that response to foolish, baseless hopes regarding the betterment of society made those who had entertained them but who later undoubtedly came to their senses and their sense of responsibility 'questionable characters.' Since the Supreme Court of New Mexico as a matter of law took a contrary view of such a situation in denying petitioner's application, it denied him due process of law.

I therefore concur in the judgment.

Section 4. Contemporary Issues in Bar Admissions

A. Honesty as a Cardinal Virtue

Model Rule 8.1: Bar Admission & Disciplinary Matters

An applicant for admission to the bar, or a lawyer in connection with a bar admission application or in connection with a disciplinary matter, shall not:

(a)　knowingly make a false statement of material fact; or

(b)　fail to disclose a fact necessary to correct a misapprehension known by the person to have arisen in the matter, or knowingly fail to respond to a lawful demand for information from an admissions or disciplinary authority, except that this rule does not require disclosure of information otherwise protected by Rule 1.6.

Rule 8.1 Bar Admission and Disciplinary Matters—Comment

[1]   The duty imposed by this Rule extends to persons seeking admission to the bar as well as to lawyers. Hence, if a person makes a material false statement in connection with an application for admission, it may be the basis for subsequent disciplinary action if the person is admitted, and in any event may be relevant in a subsequent admission application. The duty imposed by this Rule applies to a lawyer's own admission or discipline as well as that of others. Thus, it is a separate professional offense for a lawyer to knowingly make a misrepresentation or omission in connection with a disciplinary investigation of the lawyer's own conduct. Paragraph (b) of this Rule also requires correction of any prior misstatement in the matter that the applicant or lawyer may have made and affirmative clarification of any misunderstanding on the part of the admissions or disciplinary authority of which the person involved becomes aware.

[2]   This Rule is subject to the provisions of the Fifth Amendment of the United States Constitution and corresponding provisions of state constitutions. A person relying on such a provision in response to a question, however, should do so openly and not use the right of nondisclosure as a justification for failure to comply with this Rule.

[3]   A lawyer representing an applicant for admission to the bar, or representing a lawyer who is the subject of a disciplinary inquiry or proceeding, is governed by the rules applicable to the client-lawyer relationship, including Rule 1.6 and, in some cases, Rule 3.3.

Deconstruction Exercise/Rule Rationale

The Model Rules stress a lawyer's obligation to be candid, honest, and transparent. These cardinal values start with this rule, and its mandate that applicants to the bar demonstrate they possess them and that those recommending applicants to the Bar corroborate that they possess them. The rule acts in tandem with MR 8.3 which requires that a lawyer report professional misconduct. These values work in tandem to create the very foundation of a self-regulated profession. By contrast, other professions—plumbers, opticians, homebuilders—are managed by government appointed boards whose members not even need to be a professional in the area regulated. The rule further mandates that those against whom a grievance is filed cooperate with the investigation by fellow lawyers, yes, another feature of self-regulation.

LEANING INTO PRACTICE

Scenario: The Case of the Outstanding Law Student with the Checkered Past

Law Student asks law Professor Smith for a letter of recommendation in the application to the bar. The student tells Professor Smith, "I appreciate you writing the letter, but I want you to know before law school, I engaged in the escort business selling sex. But I promise there is no record of it, and I was never arrested. Promise that you will not mention this." Professor Smith promises. The professor reasons that the student has been outstanding in every way and Professor Smith personally considers the escort business to be a victimless crime. The letter is written and sent. Is Professor Smith in violation of MR 8.1?

Cases and Materials

X-Ray Questions

Here is the opinion, it was a 4–3 vote to allow admission. Summarize the arguments for the majority and the dissents. Who has the more persuasive argument? Why? More directly, do you have an issue with being partners with this applicant? Be suspicious of her conduct if she is counsel opposite?

Matter of Admission of Padlock

Supreme Court of Wisconsin, 2021.
398 Wis.2d 67.

Opinion

PER CURIAM.

¶ 1   We review, pursuant to Supreme Court Rule (SCR) 40.08(7), the final decision of the Board of Bar Examiners (Board) declining to certify that the petitioner, Abby D. Padlock, has satisfied the character and fitness requirements for admission to the Wisconsin bar set forth in SCR 40.06(1). The Board's decision was based primarily on its conclusion that Ms. Padlock was deceptive in her law school application and in her bar application by underreporting, in a misleading manner, the details of an arrest that caused her to be charged with two felony drug charges, which were later dismissed pursuant to a deferred prosecution agreement.

¶ 2   The initial duty to examine an applicant's qualifications for bar admission rests with the Board. In the final analysis, however, this court retains supervisory authority and has the ultimate responsibility for regulating admission to the Wisconsin bar. See In re Bar Admission of Rippl, 2002 WI 15, ¶ 3, 250 Wis. 2d 519, 639 N.W.2d 553, and In re Bar Admission of Vanderperren, 2003 WI 37, ¶ 2, 261 Wis. 2d 150, 661 N.W.2d 27. Here, although Ms. Padlock's disclosures raised significant questions about her fitness to practice law, we conclude that Ms. Padlock may be admitted to the practice of law in this state. Accordingly, we reverse and remand the matter to the Board for further proceedings.

¶ 3   Ms. Padlock was a high school athlete who played Division I volleyball in college and graduated with excellent grades. However, during and after college, sports injuries and serious family issues led to what she describes as a "dark time." When she was 24, Ms. Padlock wanted to work internationally as a language instructor. To acquire money for this venture she and a friend agreed to transport a substantial amount of marijuana across state lines as a means of raising cash.

¶ 4   In October 2015, Ms. Padlock and her friend left the State of Oregon with a shipment of marijuana in her car that they were attempting to deliver to Wisconsin. They were stopped by law enforcement officials in Minnesota. Her friend, who was driving at the time, consented to a K9 search. Officers discovered seventy-six (76) individually sealed packages of marijuana, weighing approximately 114 pounds in the vehicle. They also found three cell phones, $473 in cash, assorted marijuana edibles, other marijuana, and drug paraphernalia. During a follow up search of Ms. Padlock's home, police found $30,120, which was later subject to civil forfeiture.

¶ 5   Ms. Padlock was arrested and charged in Minnesota with two felony counts of a controlled substance crime in the second degree. She was offered a deferred prosecution agreement; the felony charges were later reduced to one count of possession of marijuana in the third degree, a misdemeanor. She received a stay of adjudication, was sentenced to three days in jail, fined $1,000, and placed on probation for two years. When she successfully completed her probation, the charge was dismissed. Ms. Padlock had been paid approximately $30,000 for the attempted delivery; as noted, these funds were subject to a civil forfeiture.

¶ 6   After Ms. Padlock was sentenced, but before she had finished serving that sentence, she applied to the University of Wisconsin Law School.

¶ 7 Ms. Padlock's disclosures on her law school application form the first basis for the Board's decision to deny her admission to the Wisconsin bar. The law school application requires applicants to describe in detail any criminal infractions that occurred prior to admission. Applicants are directed to report instances in which they were cited, arrested, charged, convicted, or sentenced to any criminal, civil, or ordinance violation at the federal, state, or local level. The application also requires applicants to answer whether or not the matter was resolved in a conviction, a dismissal, or was resolved at the same or a different level of seriousness as the original violation. Applicants must answer even if a finding of guilt or sentence was suspended or withheld, or if the record was expunged or sealed.

¶ 8 Ms. Padlock reported that she had been given a stay of adjudication and that the charges against her had been dismissed. This was inaccurate. The charges had not yet been dismissed at the time Ms. Padlock applied to law school. She was still on probation. Moreover, Ms. Padlock did not provide any other details about the 2015 criminal matter. She did not report the amount of marijuana that was discovered, the initial felony charges that she faced, any information about the $1,000 fine, her three days in jail, or her two years of probation. She did not mention the $30,000 civil forfeiture.

¶ 9 Ms. Padlock was admitted to the University of Wisconsin Law School and began her studies. It is not disputed that during law school, Ms. Padlock spoke openly about her conviction in class and with colleagues and faculty. At some point, Ms. Padlock received an offer to participate in a law school program that required a background check. During this background check, the law school learned the details of the underlying criminal offense and determined that Ms. Padlock had "seriously mischaracterized her 2015 criminal matter."

¶ 10 The law school revoked its employment offer and conducted an investigation. Ultimately, the law school imposed no discipline on Ms. Padlock and she was permitted to complete law school, although she was warned that this incident might adversely affect her admission to the bar.

¶ 11 In November 2019, as a third-year law student anticipating graduation, Ms. Padlock applied for admission to the Wisconsin State Bar under the diploma privilege, SCR 40.03. Ms. Padlock's disclosures on her bar application form the second basis for the Board's decision to deny her admission to the Wisconsin bar. In her bar application, Ms. Padlock reported that in October of 2015, she "drove from Oregon to Wisconsin with marijuana in [her] car." She reported that she was charged with possession of marijuana on

December 14, 2015. She indicated that the final disposition of those charges was a stay of adjudication with an ultimate dismissal of the charges.

¶ 12 Following some inquiries by the Board that resulted in Ms. Padlock amending her bar application, the Board informed Ms. Padlock that her bar admission application was at risk of being denied on character and fitness grounds. SCR 40.08(1). Ms. Padlock formally contested the Board's preliminary adverse determination and requested a hearing before the Board.

¶ 13 The Board conducted an evidentiary hearing on September 11, 2020, via videoconference. Ms. Padlock testified about her history and her application materials. Professor Mary Prosser and Professor Greg Wiercioch, both faculty members at the University of Wisconsin Law School, testified in support of Ms. Padlock's application.

¶ 14 The Board issued a written adverse decision and order on October 26, 2020. As relevant, the Board made the following findings about Ms. Padlock's law school application:

11.   In her application for admission to the University of Wisconsin Law School, Ms. Padlock reported that she made a conscious choice to do something that she knew was wrong and illegal. She further reported that she was charged with possession of marijuana on December 14, 2015. She indicated that the final disposition of those charges was a stay of adjudication with an ultimate dismissal of the charges. Ms. Padlock did not provide any additional details about her arrest, including, for instance, the amount of marijuana that was discovered, the initial charges that she faced, or any information about the $30,000.00 forfeiture.

12.   At the time Ms. Padlock made those statements to the University of Wisconsin Law School, her underlying criminal charges had not been dismissed.

* * *

15.   Specifically and with regard to the 2015 criminal matter, Ms. Padlock failed to disclose on her law school application that she was initially charged with multiple counts of a controlled substances crime, that she accepted guilt for one count of a controlled substances crime, that she was sentenced on a count different than the original one and that it was resolved at a different level of seriousness, and that she omitted the details of her sentence including a $1000.00 fine, three days in jail, and two years of probation.

¶ 15 The Board made the following findings about her bar application and her credibility regarding her application disclosures:

18.   In her application for admission to the Wisconsin bar Ms. Padlock reported that on October 27, 2015, she "drove from Oregon to Wisconsin with marijuana in [her] car." She did not reveal that she had been transporting one hundred and fourteen (114) pounds of marijuana, nor did she indicate that she was originally charged with two counts of felony trafficking of controlled substances.

19.   In her testimony before the Board, Ms. Padlock revealed that she had participated in another illegal drug delivery between Oregon and Wisconsin approximately two weeks prior to the October 27th incident. She reported being paid $10,000 for the earlier drug transaction. Ms. Padlock had not previously revealed that information to the Board or to the University of Wisconsin Law School.

* * *

24.   By having repeatedly minimized her criminal conduct surrounding her illegal transportation of marijuana across state lines, Ms. Padlock demonstrated a lack of character and fitness that is essential for admission to the Wisconsin bar.

25.   By engaging in repeated acts of misconduct, including one that she disclosed for the first time during her testimony before the Board, Ms. Padlock has not met her burden of establishing her honesty, diligence, or reliability.

26.   Ms. Padlock has not demonstrated a sufficient effort towards or provided any significant evidence of rehabilitation.

27.   By minimizing her criminal conduct in applying to the University of Wisconsin Law School and on her application for admission to the Wisconsin bar, Ms. Padlock was both dishonest and deceptive. Her explanations about each were neither plausible nor believable. Accordingly, the Board did not find Ms. Padlock to be a credible witness.

¶ 16 In its written decision the Board indicated that Ms. Padlock had failed to provide details about her arrest, including, for instance, the amount of marijuana that was discovered, the initial charges that she faced, or any information about the $30,000 forfeiture. She did not disclose that she had been transporting 114 pounds of marijuana or that she was originally charged with two counts of felony trafficking of controlled substances. The Board found, further, that these omissions and incomplete disclosures were intentional. The Board also emphasized that during the hearing, in response to a question, Ms. Padlock disclosed that she had actually completed another illegal drug delivery between Oregon and Wisconsin approximately two weeks before the October 2015 incident and that she had been paid $10,000 for that drug transaction. Ms. Padlock had not previously revealed that information. The Board found that Ms. Padlock lacked credibility, that her omissions reflected an effort to deceive the law school and the Board, and that she had failed to establish good moral character and fitness to practice law in Wisconsin under SCR 40.06(1) and (3).

¶ 17 Ms. Padlock seeks review. The crux of this appeal is whether Ms. Padlock has established that she has the requisite character and fitness for admission to the bar. When this court reviews an adverse determination of the Board pursuant to SCR 40.08(7), we adopt the Board's findings of fact if they are not clearly erroneous. In re Vanderperren, 261 Wis. 2d 150, ¶ 20, 661 N.W.2d 27. We then determine if the Board's conclusions of law based on those facts are proper. Id.

¶ 18 First, we observe that the Board properly declined to offer Ms. Padlock conditional admission under SCR 40.075. The character and fitness concerns that gave rise to the Board's adverse determination are not amenable to conditional admission. Only applicants who are able to demonstrate a record of documented, ongoing recovery and who are able to meet the competence and the character and fitness requirements may be considered for conditional admission under SCR 40.075. When an applicant appeals an adverse determination, this court may elect to impose post-admission conditions as a condition of admitting the applicant, but this is a distinct procedure from conditional admission under SCR 40.075. In re Bar Admission of Jarrett, 2016 WI 39, 368 Wis. 2d 567, 879 N.W.2d 116.

¶ 19 Next, Ms. Padlock contends that two of the Board's factual findings are clearly erroneous and should be rejected by this court. See In re Bar Admission of Rusch, 171 Wis. 2d 523, 528–29, 492 N.W.2d 153 (1992). She further contends that the Board's legal conclusion regarding her character is not supported by the record evidence, and is inconsistent with other decisions of this court. See Rippl, 250 Wis. 2d 519, ¶ 16, 639 N.W.2d 553; In re Bar Admission of Crowe, 141 Wis. 2d 230, 232, 414 N.W.2d 41 (1987). She suggests that the Board was biased against her and that she did not receive a fair hearing. From her perspective, the Board "has interpreted every word she spoke in the most negative light possible, ignoring some of the evidence favorable to her, and distorting the rest into the portrait of an incorrigible liar." She maintains that she has met her burden of producing information sufficient to affirmatively demonstrate her present character and fitness and she asks this court to order her admission. Alternatively, she suggests that she should be afforded admission with conditions.

¶ 20 The standards for evaluating an applicant's admission to the Wisconsin bar are well-settled. Supreme Court Rule 40.06(1) requires that applicants for bar admission establish good moral character and fitness to practice law. The burden rests with the applicant to establish character and fitness to the satisfaction of the Board. See SCRs 40.06(3) and 40.07. The Appendix to SCR ch. 40 contains the Board's rules that provide additional guidance to the Board and to applicants.

¶ 21 Bar Admission Rule (BA) 6.01 provides that "[a] lawyer should be one whose record of conduct justifies the trust of clients, adversaries, courts and others with respect to the professional duties owed to them." That same section notes that "[a] record manifesting a deficiency in the honesty, diligence or reliability of an applicant may constitute a basis for denial of admission."

¶ 22 Bar Admission Rule 6.02 provides that in determining whether an applicant possesses the necessary character and fitness to practice law, 12 factors "should be treated as cause for further inquiry." BA 6.02 (Relevant Conduct or Condition). As relevant, these factors include a person's unlawful conduct, academic misconduct, false statements by the applicant, including concealment or nondisclosure, and acts involving dishonesty or misrepresentation. See *id.*

¶ 23 Bar Admission Rule 6.03 provides that in assigning weight and significance to the applicant's prior conduct, the following factors are to be considered:

(a) the applicant's age at the time of the conduct;

(b) the recency of the conduct;

(c) the reliability of the information concerning the conduct;

(d) the seriousness of the conduct;

(e) the mitigating or aggravating circumstances;

(f) the evidence of rehabilitation;

(g) the applicant's candor in the admissions process;

(h) the materiality of any omissions or misrepresentations; and

(i) the number of incidents revealing deficiencies.

See SCR ch. 40 App., BA 6.03.

¶ 24 The Board states that its adverse decision is predicated on Ms. Padlock's alleged lack of candor in the application process, BA 6.03(g)–(h), not her underlying misconduct. It is not seriously disputed that the disclosures made on Ms. Padlock's law school application were insufficient. Ms. Padlock essentially concedes this as she admits that her application "set her up for trouble with the Law School." She maintains, however, that she did not intend to deceive the law school and she attributes the admitted shortcomings to having a "lay person's understanding of her legal position" at the time. Ms. Padlock's disclosures on her bar application were less problematic, but still appear to minimize her misconduct. So, the critical question is whether Ms. Padlock's failure to make sufficiently detailed disclosures on her law school and bar applications reflects systematic evasion with an intent to deceive, or simply an error in judgment.

¶ 25 Our case law emphasizes the extreme importance of an applicant's candor with regard to prior misconduct as being as important as the underlying misconduct itself. In In re Bar Admission of Gaylord, 155 Wis. 2d 816, 456 N.W.2d 590 (1990), we affirmed the Board's decision to deny an applicant admission where the applicant failed to disclose having been charged three times with criminal offenses including unlawful possession of a controlled substance with intent to sell, and the possession of a weapon without a permit. Id. at 819, 456 N.W.2d 590. We stated:

> It must be emphasized that the basis of the decision to decline certification of [the applicant's] character and fitness to practice law was not her conduct that led to the three criminal charges and the numerous traffic offenses. Rather, [the Board] determined that [the applicant] did not meet her burden to establish good moral character and fitness to practice law solely by virtue of the inaccuracies and omissions in her admission application.

Id. at 822, 456 N.W.2d 590.

¶ 26 Our analysis in bar admission cases typically begins with an assessment of the Board's factual findings, then proceeds to the de novo review of its legal conclusions. Here, this is complicated, somewhat, by the fact that the Board's credibility determinations are intertwined with its legal conclusion that Ms. Padlock lacks the character and fitness to practice law. We are generally disinclined to second-guess credibility determinations made by factfinders. That said, we are charged with considering the record as a whole when we conduct our de novo review of the Board's legal conclusions. According, we review the evidence.

¶ 27 At the evidentiary hearing, Ms. Padlock acknowledged that her law school application does not explicitly identify the crime she was initially charged with, but points out that it "does reference consequences that bespeak felony penalties." She explains that from her perspective, it seemed as though everyone knew about her arrest. She repeatedly notes that anyone with access to the Internet has only to enter "Abby Padlock" in a search engine to get a detailed account of her arrest, complete with mugshot. She says that she assumed (wrongly, she now agrees) that law schools undertook their own investigations. She reasons that if she had been attempting to cover up her history, she would not have spoken about it openly with peers and professors, and would not have applied for a law school student mentoring program that she knew required a background check. She adds that the law school was ultimately satisfied by her explanations and concluded that there was no need to discipline her or take action against her. Ms. Padlock maintains her oversights were unintentional, that she was not dishonest, that the statements on her applications were not false, and that she wrote what she thought was required of her.

¶ 28 Ms. Padlock also offered, in addition to her own testimony, the character testimony of two of her academic supervisors. Both stated that Ms. Padlock had been forthcoming about her past. Professor Mary Prosser taught her small group class on criminal law, and later supervised Ms. Padlock in the Legal Assistance to Incarcerated People Project (LAIP). Professor Prosser spoke at length about Ms. Padlock's honesty, the fact that she did not shade the truth, the fact that she was forthcoming, her belief that Ms. Padlock had not intended to deceive the admissions department, and her conclusion that Ms. Padlock was a suitable candidate for admission to the bar.

¶ 29 Adjunct Professor Greg Wiercioch also worked closely with Ms. Padlock during her time in LAIP, and spoke about how Ms. Padlock led off her application to the program with a dramatic reference to her criminal case, stating: "Facing a 50-year prison sentence can drastically change one's perspective on life. Exactly one year, three weeks, and six days ago, I was in this exact predicament." Professor Wiercioch stated he had no concerns about her character, her honesty or integrity, or in recommending her for admission to practice.

¶ 30 The Board's factual findings derive from Ms. Padlock's undisputed underlying criminal misconduct, the disclosures on her two applications, and from the Board members' credibility determinations based on the testimony and evidence adduced at the Board's hearing.

¶ 31 Ms. Padlock argues that the Board's factual finding regarding evidence of her rehabilitation is clearly erroneous. Specifically, the Board found that there was "a notable lack of evidence that Ms. Padlock had engaged in any significant rehabilitative efforts to offset her misdeeds." The Board stated that "Padlock has not demonstrated a sufficient effort toward or provided any significant evidence of rehabilitation." In its brief, the Board goes farther, claiming that Ms. Padlock has exhibited effectively no evidence of rehabilitation. This is an important challenge, as a number of our cases reflect the importance of "post-incident" rehabilitative conduct when we evaluate an applicant's character and fitness during an appeal from an adverse determination. See, e.g., In re Bar Admission of Anderson, 2006 WI 57, ¶ 26, 290 Wis. 2d 722, 715 N.W.2d 586 (holding that Anderson's post-incident conduct has reflected a record of good behavior and the establishment of the requisite character and fitness to be admitted to the Wisconsin bar). The Board's finding is not consistent with the record evidence.

¶ 32 The record reflects that Ms. Padlock provided services to incarcerated persons through the LAIP program, citing her own experience with the justice system as a reason for her involvement with the program. She hoped to become a mentor, publicly stating that that her experience fueled her desire to help people, a sentiment her professors confirmed. She joined a group of law students who went to Dilley, Texas, to provide legal assistance to women seeking asylum. She fundraised, organized, and led camps in Kenya staffed by UW students to help disadvantaged children build sustainable futures. She was asked to join the board of the nonprofit that ran the camps, and did so. She regularly volunteered to provide legal assistance to veterans at the Madison Veterans hospital. She started a small business seven months after graduating law school. Based on these undisputed facts of record we conclude there is significant evidence of rehabilitation and we deem Finding 26 clear error.

¶ 33 Ms. Padlock next argues that the Board's factual finding that she was dishonest and deceptive in her applications is clearly erroneous. Finding 27 states:

By minimizing her criminal conduct in applying to the University of Wisconsin Law School and on her application for admission to the Wisconsin bar, Ms. Padlock was both dishonest and deceptive. Her explanations about each were neither plausible nor believable. Accordingly, the Board did not find Ms. Padlock to be a credible witness.

¶ 34 Ms. Padlock faces an uphill battle with this challenge. The Board is brutally disparaging of her credibility, employing rhetoric that seems, at times, unnecessarily scathing. The Board condemns her "repeated and flagrant displays at minimizing and concealing her wrongful conduct." The Board says:

Ms. Padlock has consistently neglected to acknowledge the seriousness and the breadth of her actions to any one body or institution.

* * *

She selectively provides information about her criminal history in dribs and drabs without a complete accounting of the whole story, the whole picture, or the whole truth, to either the University of Wisconsin Law School or to the Board of Bar Examiners.

* * *

Ms. Padlock lies by omission unless and until confronted by it as was the case during her hearing before the Board when she reported, for the first time, that she had been involved in a second illegal drug smuggling operation to import a sizable amount of marijuana to Wisconsin from Oregon for which she supposedly received $10,000.

* * *

She has persistently and consistently demonstrated a lack of candor and seems not to have any real inkling about the importance of fully, completely, and wholly embracing the truth.

* * *

The Board did not find her testimony with regard to either claim to be credible or convincing. By repeatedly minimizing her criminal conduct surrounding the illegal transportation of drugs across state lines, the Board found that Ms. Padlock manifested a deficiency in honesty and integrity both of which are essential characteristics for admission to the bar in this state.

* * *

The Board has concluded that Ms. Padlock is unable to recognize and to understand what it means to be truthful, what constitutes a complete disclosure, or how to be forthright and argues that she cannot be expected to bring those essential skills to the table as a lawyer in this state.

* * *

The Board is not persuaded that she has been anything other than dishonest and deceptive.

¶ 35 One exchange at the hearing was clearly pivotal to the Board's determination that the shortcoming in Ms. Padlock's applications reflect a calculated effort to deceive the law school and the Board. In response to a direct question from a Board member, Ms. Padlock admitted that she had actually successfully made one cross-country marijuana delivery before she was caught, for which she was paid $10,000. For Ms. Padlock, this admission evidences her "complete candor to the Board—she could have kept this fact to herself, and no one would have been the wiser." For the Board, this admission clearly shredded whatever tatters of credibility Ms. Padlock retained. The Board heavily faults Ms. Padlock for not previously disclosing this incident. The Board says "[h]er claim that she has never intentionally concealed her past is simply false as illustrated not only by her failure to include her first illegal drug transaction on her law school application but also on her application for admission to the bar."

¶ 36 We generally accord deference to a factfinder's credibility determinations because the factfinder has the opportunity to observe the witness' demeanor and gauge the testimony's persuasiveness. Here, the Board did not believe Ms. Padlock's explanations for her incomplete disclosures, and we are bound by that finding. However, the Board's disbelief of Ms. Padlock's reasons for her insufficient disclosures does not lead, inexorably, to the conclusion that she lacks the character and fitness to practice law. Were that the case, any effort to appeal an adverse determination predicated on credibility would be a fruitless endeavor.

¶ 37 In our view, the Board gives undue weight to Ms. Padlock's disclosure. Recall that the Board's stated basis for deeming her application at risk was Ms. Padlock's lack of candor on her applications—not her underlying criminal conduct itself. Those charges were dismissed. While in no way condoning her illegal activity, neither the law school application nor the bar application requires an applicant to disclose behavior that was immoral or even unlawful, but that was never formally investigated or prosecuted. Such an expectation would be entirely subjective, would place the honest and forthright candidate at a disadvantage, and would be impossible to administer.

¶ 38 The Board then wholly discounted the character testimony of the two University of Wisconsin law professors who know and worked with Ms. Padlock personally. The Board faults them for apparently not knowing of her first drug delivery for which she was never apprehended, and for not affirmatively indicating they knew all the details of her underlying arrest and prosecution. The Board states that it "is unknown whether either knew about her first marijuana delivery for which she was never apprehended. Regardless, each supported her admission to the bar."

¶ 39 We find the Board's position in this regard somewhat troubling. Both professors had extensive direct contact with Ms. Padlock and both are longtime specialists in criminal law. Moreover, as Ms. Padlock points out, every member of the Board was given the opportunity, individually and by name, to ask them questions. The goal of this proceeding was to evaluate Ms. Padlock's character and fitness. It is perplexing that not a single member of the Board asked a question of these character witnesses. It is somewhat concerning that these witnesses were then discredited for failing to answer questions that were never asked of them.

¶ 40 Moreover, the record before us reflects that each professor did more than merely "allude to having some awareness" of Ms. Padlock's crime. Professor Prosser described the letter she wrote on Ms. Padlock's behalf to the court, seeking to terminate her probation, and she stated that Ms. Padlock was completely forthcoming about her situation. Professor Wiercioch testified that his first introduction to Ms. Padlock was her cover letter that led with an admission of her criminal charge. He testified that she was up-front about her history, which they discussed at length. The record confirms that both witnesses had definite knowledge of Ms. Padlock's criminal case, and believed that she was honest and forthcoming about it. Rather, it seems these professors could not overcome the Board's antipathy for Ms. Padlock.

¶ 41 This court has, on several occasions, certified applicants to the bar despite an adverse determination from the Board. Ms. Padlock points to In re Jarrett, 368 Wis. 2d 567, 879 N.W.2d 116. Mr. Jarrett was admitted to practice law with conditions after several incidents of demonstrated academic misconduct in law school. Mr. Jarrett, unlike Ms. Padlock, was completely forthcoming about his academic misconduct throughout the application process, although he failed to disclose several speeding tickets. Neither the Board nor the court were persuaded by his explanation for doing so, but this court determined that the omission regarding the tickets was insufficient to preclude his admission.

¶ 42 Also relevant to our analysis is In re Vanderperren, 261 Wis. 2d 150, 661 N.W.2d 27, where the Board's refusal to certify Ms. Vanderperren was based primarily on her "less than forthright and complete responses" to questions on her application for admission to Hamline University School of Law, and on her subsequent Wisconsin bar application. Her underlying issues were not criminal, but involved a series of alcohol-related incidents, obnoxious behavior, and argumentative run-ins with police and university authorities. The Vanderperren case reflects the importance of post-conduct rehabilitation because, by the time this court considered her bar application, Ms. Vanderperren had been admitted to practice law in Minnesota, had passed the Wisconsin bar exam, had voluntarily corrected her bar application, and several years had elapsed since her last reported incident involving excessive alcohol consumption. Vanderperren, 261 Wis. 2d 150, ¶ 65, 661 N.W.2d 27; see also Rippl, 250 Wis. 2d 519, ¶ 3, 639 N.W.2d 553. She had undergone an AODA evaluation and had attended AA meetings and changed her drinking habits. Accordingly, this court opted to admit her to the practice of law.

¶ 43 Ms. Padlock reminds the court that here, more than six years have elapsed since her criminal misconduct. We have determined there is evidence of her rehabilitation on this record and we accord more weight to the testimony of her faculty supervisors than did the Board, and less weight to her disclosure of information that—while unsavory—she was not required to disclose.

¶ 44 This was not an easy case. Ms. Padlock would have done better to be exceedingly forthcoming on her law school and her bar applications. That said, we have concluded that the shortcomings in her applications are not sufficient to preclude her admission to the bar in light of the record as a whole. Denying Ms. Padlock admission to the bar because of the shortcomings, even factoring in the Board's perception that she minimized her misconduct, is simply too harsh a penalty under the circumstances presented. Her goal of becoming a lawyer has already been delayed, and her prospect of obtaining bar admission has been uncertain. Her own actions—and the manner in which she disclosed them—have caused her significant obstacles, embarrassment, and had financial consequences. The language of a much cited concurrence written by Justice Prosser is apt here. He observed:

> All in all, I believe the applicant deserves the benefit of the doubt. She should have the opportunity to begin the practice law with a clean slate-with the understanding of the importance that courts attach to character and ethics and a warning that this court has a long memory.

Vanderperren, 261 Wis. 2d 150, ¶ 65, 661 N.W.2d 27. We again choose to exercise our prerogative and afford this applicant the benefit of the doubt.

¶ 45 Accordingly, we reverse the Board's conclusion of law regarding Ms. Padlock's character and fitness to practice law, and we direct the Board to certify Ms. Padlock's admission to practice law in Wisconsin and her enrollment with the State Bar of Wisconsin pursuant to SCR 10.03(2). The Board did not identify any conditions that should be imposed on Ms. Padlock in the event we elected to admit her, and we impose no conditions upon her practice of law.

¶ 46 IT IS ORDERED that the decision of the Board of Bar Examiners declining to certify that Abby D. Padlock has satisfied the requirements for admission to the practice of law in Wisconsin is reversed and the matter is remanded to the Board for further action consistent with this order.

¶ 47 IT IS FURTHER ORDERED that the documents submitted under seal are deemed confidential and shall remain under seal until further order of the court.

ANNETTE KINGSLAND ZIEGLER, C.J. (dissenting).

¶ 48 I would affirm the final decision of the Board of Bar Examiners (Board) declining to certify Abby Padlock's character and fitness for admission to the Wisconsin bar. The Board found that Ms. Padlock underreported, in a misleading manner, the details of a 2015 interstate drug trafficking incident that caused her to be charged in Minnesota with two felony counts of a Controlled Substance Crime in the Second Degree. I agree.

¶ 49 The inadequacy of the disclosures on her law school application later caused the law school to determine that Ms. Padlock had "seriously mischaracterized her 2015 criminal matter." In fact, she was paid $10,000 to illegally transport drugs cross country before being caught. With respect to the underreported charges, Ms. Padlock failed to report the amount of marijuana that was discovered: 114 pounds. She failed to report that she faced felony charges. She failed to report that she spent three days in jail, or that she was subject to a $30,000 civil forfeiture. She inaccurately claimed that the charges against her had already been dismissed when, in fact, she was still on probation at the time she applied to law school.

¶ 50 Ms. Padlock was warned that the insufficient disclosures on her law school application might adversely affect her admission to the bar. Nonetheless, Ms. Padlock again underreported her criminal conduct in her application seeking bar admission.

¶ 51 Ms. Padlock's inadequate disclosures reflect dishonest and deceptive behavior, which demonstrates that Ms. Padlock has acted in a manner that is not honest, diligent, or reliable. Coupled with the Board's finding that Ms. Padlock was not credible nor convincing at the evidentiary hearing before the Board, I conclude that there are simply too many incidents in which, despite being previously warned, Ms. Padlock considered candid disclosure optional.

¶ 52 Our cases emphasize the extreme importance of an applicant's candor with regard to prior misconduct as being as, if not more, important as the underlying misconduct itself. See, e.g., In re Bar Admission of Gaylord, 155 Wis. 2d 816, 819, 456 N.W.2d 590 (1990) (affirming the Board's decision to deny certification of bar applicant where the applicant failed to disclose having been charged three times with criminal offenses). The applicant in Gaylord did not meet her burden to establish good moral character and fitness to practice law due to the inaccuracies and omissions in her admission application. Id. at 822, 456 N.W.2d 590. I conclude the same is true of Ms. Padlock. By repeatedly minimizing her criminal conduct surrounding the illegal transportation of drugs across state lines, Ms. Padlock manifested a deficiency in honesty and integrity, both of which are essential characteristics for admission to the bar in this state.

¶ 53 Based on the record before this court, I am not persuaded that Ms. Padlock has yet demonstrated the requisite moral character and fitness "needed to assure to a reasonable degree of certainty the integrity and the competence of services performed for clients and the maintenance of high standards in the administration of justice." SCR 40.06. I would affirm the Board's decision.

¶ 54 For the foregoing reasons, I respectfully dissent.

¶ 55 I am authorized to state that JUSTICES PATIENCE DRAKE ROGGENSACK and BRIAN HAGEDORN join this dissent.

SOLUTIONS: THE LAWYER SHOULD HAVE, WOULD HAVE, COULD HAVE. . .

It is always better to be transparent in your application to take the bar exam. Even if you fail to disclose or minimize your background issues and pass the bar, you will still be held to account if later discovered. Lawyers must be honest with others, with their clients, and with the tribunals before which they appear. And lawyers must also be honest with themselves.

B. Mental Health Issues as a Disqualification to Admission

Cases and Materials

X-Ray Questions

The Judge in this case is not using the phrase "Bar Bureaucracy" as a descriptive phrase but rather as a pejorative one. He is enraged that this applicant had to go through so many painful obstacles to finally become a lawyer in

Kentucky. He draws a lesson between the actions of the "Bureaucracy" and mounting and growing mental health crises among lawyers in the state. What is the lesson he draws? Do you agree? What accounts for the reported hostility of the "Bureaucracy?" Would an applicant with a broken arm who is having difficulty healing be treated as this was the applicant? Can you see the arguments against admission.

Doe v. Supreme Court of Kentucky

United States District Court, W.D. Kentucky, 2020.
482 F.Supp.3d 571.

MEMORANDUM OPINION

Courts, journalists, and scholars have extensively documented the mental health issues that afflict lawyers. The problems begin in law school, where "law students have disproportionate levels of stress, anxiety, and mental health concerns compared with other populations." After graduation, lawyers suffer from depression at higher rates than non-lawyers. Not long ago, the Kentucky Bar Association President described a spike in Kentucky lawyers dying by suicide as "disproportionate" and "disconcerting."

Jane Doe was a lawyer in Florida. She moved to Kentucky. She wanted to practice law here. Bureaucrats didn't want her to. They thought her mental disability made her unfit. For over two years, they stopped her. But she didn't give up. And they eventually relented.

Then Doe sued them, alleging they had illegally asked about her mental health history and treatment, illegally forced her to turn over her medical records and her therapists' notes from their counseling sessions, and illegally treated her like a criminal because of her disability.

This case is not only about Jane Doe. It's also about the lawyers who decide who else can be a lawyer.

Under the Kentucky Constitution, that power belongs to the Supreme Court of Kentucky. The court, in turn, delegates that job to its Bar Bureaucracy:

- The Character and Fitness Committee and Board of Bar Examiners comprise the Office of Bar Admissions.

- The Character and Fitness Committee prohibits people from practicing law if the committee thinks they are immoral or unfit.

- The Board of Bar Examiners prohibits people from practicing law if they can't pass a timed exam that tests their ability to memorize whole areas of the law they will never again need to know anything about.

- The Kentucky Bar Association decides who gets to stay a lawyer.

- The Kentucky Lawyer Assistance Program keeps tabs on lawyers and aspiring lawyers who have mental health issues by monitoring their medications, counseling, where they live, and where they travel.

Anyone with any power in this Bar Bureaucracy is a lawyer. So, just like an oil or drug cartel, those who are already selling something get to decide who else may sell that same thing. Of course, unlike most cartels, this one is legal. In fact, the Kentucky Constitution requires it.

If Doe had sued the Bar Bureaucracy back when it stopped her from entering the market, she would have had standing to ask the Court to block it from treating her like it did. But you can't blame Doe for waiting to sue. If your goal is to persuade the Bar Bureaucracy's lawyers to let you join their club, it isn't a good strategy to poke them in the eye with a lawsuit that accuses them of violating the Americans with Disabilities Act and the United States Constitution.

Because the Bar Bureaucracy (finally) allowed Doe to practice law, she lacks standing for prospective relief. And because legislative and judicial immunity protect Bar Bureaucracies from money damages arising from the promulgation of bar rules and the adjudication of bar applications, the Court will dismiss Doe's federal claims. In addition, the Court declines to exercise supplemental jurisdiction over Doe's state-law claims.

The Bar Bureaucracy won this round against an applicant it deemed suspect and undesirable. But there will be more applicants—and more lawsuits. Some of those plaintiffs will have standing to seek prospective relief. And when they do, the Bar Bureaucracy will have to answer for a medieval approach to mental health that is as cruel as it is counterproductive.

I.

A.

Several federal and state courts have held that the Americans with Disabilities Act prohibits Bar Bureaucracies from unnecessarily interrogating applicants about their mental health. So too did the Department of Justice. In 2014, it concluded that questions about applicants' mental health do "*not* provide an accurate basis for predicting future misconduct." Instead, they likely "deter applicants from seeking counseling and treatment for mental health concerns, which fails to serve the Court's interest in ensuring the fitness of licensed attorneys." In other words, according to the Department of Justice, a Bar Bureaucracy's decision to ask applicants about their mental health status makes aspiring lawyers *less* fit to practice law.

B.

Jane Doe was born and raised in Kentucky. She earned her Florida law license in 2006 and worked there in government and private practice. After a 2014 diagnosis for Bipolar I Disorder, Doe entered a monitoring program run by the Florida Lawyers' Assistance Program. She was, and remains, in good standing with the Florida bar.

In December 2015, Doe applied for a Kentucky law license. The application required her to disclose her history of depression and Bipolar I Disorder and that she had undergone treatment. And so began her 994-day tale of bureaucratic woe.

Doe disclosed everything Kentucky's Bar Bureaucracy required her to disclose. That included two required releases giving the Bar Bureaucracy "complete access to her personal and private medical records, including treatment notes" and a third for her monitoring records from Florida. In January 2016, Doe's doctor told the Bar Bureaucracy that Doe had "compli[ed] with medical advice, prescription instructions," and what the Florida bar required of her. Doe's doctors have always said she should "continue practicing law without concerns for her or the public's safety."

The Bar Bureaucracy pressed on. So Doe sent in yet another form. This fourth medical records release granted "access to inpatient records, outpatient records, and treatment notes."

The next month, shortly before Doe took the February 2016 bar exam, the Character and Fitness Committee refused to approve her application. Instead, in March, the Bar Bureaucracy proposed, and Doe signed, a "consent agreement" for conditional admission. It required 1) a Kentucky Contract (more on that later); 2) compliance with Florida's rules and Kentucky's rules and reporting requirements; and 3) "residency in Kentucky . . . unless" Doe was relocating for work and the Bar Bureaucracy approved.

The consent agreement did not provide details about the Kentucky Contract. Yvette Hourigan, Director of the Kentucky Lawyer Assistance

Program, said the contract would mirror the monitoring arrangement Doe had with the Florida Lawyers' Assistance Program, which was tailored to Doe's diagnosis.

Doe passed the bar exam. She paid the dues and swearing-in fee.

C.

Although Hourigan had promised to send a proposed contract, she didn't. Instead, she arranged to meet with Doe the morning of the new lawyers' swearing-in ceremony at the State Capitol. That day, Hourigan "texted that she was running late and they would meet on the steps of the Capitol" minutes before the swearing-in.

At this point, you might be thinking that a public place with many of Doe's peers isn't an ideal place to discuss private medical issues. (It isn't.)

You might also wonder if other bar applicants could overhear their discussion. (They could.)

Instead of the personalized contract Hourigan had promised, she presented a boilerplate contract. It included a host of medically unnecessary requirements, including random drug and alcohol testing. When Doe told Hourigan she had never had drug or alcohol problems, Hourigan told her the provisions were standard. Hourigan, who is not a doctor but plays one on the Capitol steps, also said Doe's medications required abstinence from alcohol. (They don't.)

Doe refused to sign the contract. She told Hourigan it violated the Americans with Disabilities Act, and "the ADA does not permit the disabled to be treated like criminals." (It doesn't.)

D.

Later in 2016, after Doe provided yet another medical-records release, Doe's doctor advised Hourigan that Doe could drink alcohol on her medication.

Hourigan partially relented. She removed the alcohol provisions from the Kentucky Contract. But other intrusive and unnecessary requirements remained. For example, Doe had to tell Hourigan if she was leaving town for longer than a week.

Unable to practice law, Doe taught civics, safety, and sewing to refugees. Meanwhile, the Bar Bureaucracy ordered her to appear for a formal hearing, at Doe's expense, to show cause for allegedly violating the consent agreement. The Bar Bureaucracy's lawyer, Elizabeth Feamster, demanded even more documents, as well as the contact information for Doe's employer.

Doe asked Feamster if they could "discuss the ADA issues and how the parties could resolve concerns on both sides," rather than having a hearing. But Feamster demanded that Doe prove she wasn't practicing law. In December 2016, Doe received in-patient treatment for her disability.

Doe's formal hearing was on April 27, 2017. She again expressed her concerns about violations of the Americans with Disabilities Act. Feamster relied solely on Doe's disability in denying Doe a full law license. Soon after, the Character and Fitness Committee recommended that the Supreme Court of Kentucky permanently revoke Doe's conditional license. Recall that on the record before us, Doe had been licensed by Florida for the past eleven years— and had practiced there for the first nine of those years—and remained in good standing that whole time.

E.

A year later, in 2018, Doe successfully completed Florida's monitoring program. Her doctor wrote yet another letter to the Bar Bureaucracy saying he still "had no concerns regarding her mental health and encouraged her to continue practicing law."

In July 2018, the Bar Bureaucracy held another hearing. Again, they interrogated Doe about her disability. After the hearing, Feamster demanded still more information about Doe's medical treatment. And yet again, Doe told the Bar Bureaucracy that they were violating the Americans with Disabilities Act.

Finally, in August 2018, Doe was unconditionally admitted to practice law in Kentucky.

Her bar file still contains protected health information and show cause orders suggesting that "her disability and treatment [are] character and professional flaws."

In 2019, Doe filed this suit against the Bar Bureaucracy for violating the Americans with Disabilities Act, the Rehabilitation Act, and the Equal Protection Clause. She also sued under Kentucky law for defamation and intentional infliction of emotional distress.

F.

The Bar Bureaucracy moves to dismiss for lack of subject-matter jurisdiction and for failure to state a claim. In addition, some defendants object to Doe's use of a pseudonym.

As for the pseudonym, Kentucky law explicitly protects the confidentiality of those who receive help (or hindrance) from the Kentucky Lawyer Assistance Program. Kentucky law also protects Doe's character and fitness results from public disclosure. And Doe's prior conditional admission status is confidential.

The Bar Bureaucracy knows who Doe is. Opposing her pseudonym does little for its credibility. But ultimately that motion is moot because Doe's suit will be dismissed.

II.

A.

Article III of the Constitution limits the Court's jurisdiction to only "Cases" and "Controversies. Doe asks for injunctive relief, damages, and attorneys' fees. She must have standing for each claim "and for each form of relief that is sought."

1.

For injunctive relief, Doe wants the Bar Bureaucracy "to remove show cause orders and medical information and records from [her] file." But Doe has not alleged any harm that may result from the allegedly tainted file, much less that an injury is "certainly impending."

Although it took years to get there, Doe is now a full-fledged Kentucky lawyer. And if she avoids any disciplinary issues here in Kentucky—just as she remained in good standing in Florida—the file may never come into play. It's conceivable that her file could be used at some point for some other purpose. But any future injury is "speculative or tenuous," so Doe has "no standing to seek injunctive relief."

2.

Doe also lacks standing for the federal claims she brings against the Office of Bar Admissions, the Kentucky Board of Bar Examiners, the Kentucky Bar Association, the Kentucky Lawyer Assistance Program entities, and Yvette Hourigan in her official capacity. There is no "causal connection" between Doe's injuries and these defendants. They didn't block her from practicing law, if only because they didn't have that power.

Dissecting this byzantine Bar Bureaucracy takes a little digging. It turns out that none of those entities have any authority in the character and fitness process. Instead, the Character and Fitness Committee makes its own rules, which the Supreme Court of Kentucky approves. Likewise, the Character and

Fitness Committee decides who has the "character and fitness" to practice law, and only the Supreme Court of Kentucky can review that decision. The same is true for deciding who is conditionally admitted: Only the Character and Fitness Committee makes that call, and only the Supreme Court can overrule it. Thus, although the Character and Fitness Committee is a division of the Office of Bar Admissions, the Office of Bar Admissions doesn't actually make any final decisions—at least not for our purposes.

3.

Doe does, however, have standing for her federal-law damages claims against the Supreme Court of Kentucky and the Character and Fitness Committee. They had the power to (and did) decide to ask her about her mental health. They had the power to (and did) put her through the ringer based on her honest answers. They had the power to (and did) deny her an unconditional license for over two years. They had the power to (and did) impose administrative and financial burdens on her that they didn't impose on other applicants.

All these injuries are "fairly traceable" to the Kentucky Supreme Court and the Character and Fitness Committee. And a damages decision in Doe's favor would redress these injuries.

Doe also has standing to sue both Hourigan and Feamster personally for defamation and intentional infliction of emotional distress. The remaining claims and defendants are:

- The Supreme Court of Kentucky (federal-law claims);

- The Character and Fitness Committee (federal-law claims); and

- Hourigan and Feamster (state-law claims).

B.

The second jurisdictional question concerns the *Rooker-Feldman* doctrine. Some of the defendants rely on it in asking for dismissal. But *Feldman* explicitly says the Court has "subject matter jurisdiction over general challenges to state bar rules, promulgated by state courts in nonjudicial proceedings, which do not require review of a final state court judgment in a particular case." Here, Doe challenges Kentucky's bar rules, including its "licensing and bar admission system. The *Rooker-Feldman* argument fails

C.

The third jurisdictional question is straight out of a Fed Courts exam. Is state sovereign immunity the type of jurisdictional issue the Court must decide before it considers non-jurisdictional issues (like judicial and legislative immunity)?

Let's start with the argument for "yes." The Sixth Circuit has said, repeatedly and as recently as last week, that state sovereign immunity is "jurisdictional." Also, the Eleventh Amendment talks about the "Judicial power of the United States" and where it "shall not be construed to extend," which sure sounds jurisdictional.

But here's why, in this case, the answer is "no." Unlike subject-matter jurisdiction, which can never be waived, a state can waive its sovereign immunity. In the same vein, while the party invoking jurisdiction has the burden of establishing jurisdiction, a defendant invoking sovereign immunity has the burden to show it applies. That's because the Eleventh Amendment "enacts a sovereign immunity from suit, rather than a nonwaivable limit on the Federal Judiciary's subject-matter jurisdiction. It "does not automatically destroy original jurisdiction."

Under *Nair v. Oakland County Community Mental Health Authority*, "a State that has authority to waive the broader question (of whether it is amenable to suit at all) has authority to waive the narrower question (of whether a court must address a sovereign-immunity defense before the merits)." And that's what happened here: Although the defendants raised sovereign immunity in their motions to dismiss, at oral argument, they expressly declined to raise it as a threshold defense, and they specifically cited *Nair* in doing so. Thus, under *Nair*, the Court may address judicial and legislative immunity before state sovereign immunity.

This conclusion doesn't contravene the precedents of this circuit that at most imply otherwise. Even *Russell v. Lundergan-Grimes*, which held that Eleventh Amendment immunity is "jurisdictional," said that courts are "not required" to raise Eleventh Amendment immunity if the defendant doesn't. In contrast, the Court must always consider issues of subject-matter jurisdiction, even if the parties don't raise them.

In this case, the sovereign immunity question is complex. Congress has abrogated sovereign immunity when a state violates the Americans with Disabilities Act and also the Fourteenth Amendment. Courts have split on whether systems similar to Kentucky's violate the Americans with Disabilities

Act. The issue "has been the subject of intense controversy." And if the Bar Bureaucracy violated only the Americans with Disabilities Act and not the Fourteenth Amendment, then the Court would decide "whether Congress's purported abrogation of sovereign immunity as to that class of conduct is nevertheless valid."

Those issues can and should be avoided by first answering the question of judicial and legislative immunity—a question on which there is binding precedent directly on point.

D.

In *Sparks v. Character & Fitness Committee of Kentucky*, the Bar Bureaucracy refused to admit Gerald Sparks to the bar. He sued for damages. The Sixth Circuit held that "the nature of the function involved in determining qualifications for admission to the bar" is "a judicial act." Therefore, "absolute immunity" shielded both the Supreme Court of Kentucky and the Character and Fitness Committee.

The Sixth Circuit reached the same result in *Mayfield v. Francks*. And again in *Thomas v. Michigan State Board of Law Examiners*. And once again in *Lawrence v. Welch*. In each instance, judicial immunity protected a Bar Bureaucracy when plaintiffs sought damages for how it adjudicated their bar applications.

Another immunity, legislative immunity, protects the Supreme Court of Kentucky from a challenge to its promulgation of bar admission rules, including the rules requiring the Character and Fitness Committee to interrogate applicants about their mental health. In *Supreme Court of Virginia v. Consumers Union of the United States*, the U.S. Supreme Court held that the Bar Bureaucracy's "members are the State's legislators for the purpose of issuing the Bar Code," so they "are immune from suit when acting in their legislative capacity." Likewise, the Sixth Circuit has applied legislative immunity to block suits challenging how a state supreme court and its delegates promulgated rules about who gets to become a lawyer.

By this point, you might be wondering how a plaintiff could ever challenge the way a Bar Bureaucracy asks applicants about their mental health and puts them through the ringer if they truthfully disclose a mental disability. The answer is that a plaintiff could sue for prospective relief—a declaration that the questions violate federal law and an injunction prohibiting the Bar Bureaucracy from asking them. To have standing, the plaintiff would need to be a bar applicant, not an unconditionally licensed lawyer like Doe was when she filed this suit.

E.

Let's recap. For her federal-law claims, Doe lacks standing for prospective relief. She also lacks standing to sue the institutional defendants other than the Supreme Court of Kentucky and the Character and Fitness Committee because the others didn't cause her injuries. Judicial immunity and legislative immunity shield the Supreme Court of Kentucky and Character and Fitness Committee from damages.

Doe's federal claims must therefore be dismissed. And the Court declines to exercise jurisdiction over her state-law claims.

* * *

Law school is hard. The stress, rigor, and competition can lead to depression, anxiety, and substance abuse. Many students who start school healthy are far from it by the time they graduate. Some kill themselves.

Aspiring lawyers should seek the health care they need. But if Kentucky continues to punish people who get help, many won't. And one day, a law student will die after choosing self-help over medical care because he worried a Character and Fitness Committee would use that medical treatment against him—as Kentucky's did against Jane Doe.

It is not a matter of if, but when.

**SOLUTIONS: THE LAWYER SHOULD HAVE,
WOULD HAVE, COULD HAVE. . .**

Mental impairments are no different than physical impairments. Yet the first are stigmatized while the second are normalized. Lawyers should seek to normalize mental impairments and deal with them like any other impairments. We must be candid with ourselves and start with pre-conceptions we have as individuals and as a society. Where do these beliefs originate? How can they be reframed?

X-Ray Questions

This petition for cert was denied by the Supreme Court but it sets out clearly urgent issues on mental health and bar admission. A law school graduate sought admission to the Bar. While in law school he became depressed. Ultimately, he was diagnosed with delusional disorder. His condition caused him to send 40 inappropriate emails to the board of law examiners. He was denied admission. Should the Americans with Disabilities Act apply to bar admissions? Was it fair, given his acknowledgment of his misconduct, to deny admission? How long should a bar applicant's past be considered?

Thomas J. Skelton v. Illinois Supreme Court, Illinois Board of Admissions to the Bar, and Committee on Character and Fitness for the First Judicial District

Supreme Court of the United States, 2020.
2020 WL 3104087.

INTRODUCTION

This case presents a narrow, frequently presented and yet unresolved question regarding the applicability of the ADA to bar admissions cases: May a state bar regulatory authority deny an applicant certification to practice law in its jurisdiction by using the applicant's disability as a factor in finding the applicant's lack of fitness to practice, without providing reasonable accommodations? In the absence of review by the federal courts due to the Rooker-Feldman doctrine, and despite a seemingly straight-forward application, this question has instead resulted in a patchwork of varying state regulations and thresholds. See Rooker v. Fid. Trust Co., 263 U.S. 413, 44 S.Ct. 149, 68 L.Ed.2d 362 (1923), and D.C. Court of Appeals v. Feldman, 460 U.S. 462, 103 S.Ct. 1303, 75 L.Ed.2d 206 (1983). This Court should grant review to decide both the applicability of the ADA in state bar admissions cases, as well as the extent to which an applicant's disability, and any resulting reasonable accommodations, may be considered factors in bar admissions decisions.

After both graduating from law school and passing the Illinois bar in 2017, Thomas Skelton faced one last procedural hurdle to gaining admission to the Illinois bar: certification by the Committee, an entity under the Illinois Board of Admissions to the Bar charged with certifying the fitness of bar applicants to practice law in Illinois. Following a certification hearing before a hearing panel of the Committee, the panel issued a written decision declining to certify Mr. Skelton, without providing reasonable accommodations. For example, rules promulgated by the Illinois Supreme Court and the Committee, and applicable to proceedings before the Committee, set forth the circumstances under which an applicant would be eligible for conditional admission to the bar, in which an applicant is awarded a license subject to probationary conditions, compliance with which is monitored by the Illinois Attorney Registration and Disciplinary

Commission. Mr. Skelton met the qualifications for conditional admission and argued, at hearing, that it was appropriate. Nevertheless, the Hearing Panel majority disregarded that option, and instead simply declined to certify Mr. Skelton for admission. In its written decision, the panel cited findings related to Mr. Skelton's mental health history and diagnosis, including their unsupported opinions of his self-reported internal thoughts, ongoing symptoms of mental illness, and facets of his social and support network. These findings unquestionably placed a burden on Mr. Skelton which would not have been placed on an applicant without his mental health history.

Although the ADA prohibits public entities from discriminating against individuals with disabilities, which includes a prohibition against the administration of a licensing or certification program by subjecting those with disabilities to discrimination, the hearing panel majority engaged in exactly that type of discrimination against Mr. Skelton. By making findings related to Mr. Skelton's mental health history and diagnosis, without offering reasonable accommodations, the majority cited findings which would not have been raised for applicants without his diagnosis. In so doing, the panel majority not only discriminated against Mr. Skelton, but also acted in contravention of the ADA and its protections for individuals with disabilities.

Further, by denying Mr. Skelton relief on these and other grounds, the Illinois Supreme Court's three-sentence denial effectively affirmed the rationale of the hearing panel majority and allowed Mr. Skelton's mental health diagnosis to play a significant factor in denying his certification, again in contravention of the ADA.

States are granted wide latitude in the administration of their bar admissions practices and procedures. However, in combination with a significant lack of recourse before the federal courts when considering ADA applicability and relief, and an ever-increasing need to address lawyer well-being, mental health, and the stigma associated with mental illness, the denial to certify Mr. Skelton creates harmful precedent by allowing the Committee, Illinois, and other jurisdictions to improperly use mental health as a justification to deny applicants admission to their bar. Accordingly, certiorari is warranted to resolve this increasingly recurring and consequential issue.

STATEMENT OF THE CASE

A. Factual Background

Mr. Skelton is a native of Oak Park, Illinois who graduated from St. Louis University in 2010 with degrees in history and philosophy. App. 26. After working for AmeriCorps and in construction for a few years, he attended The John Marshall Law School in Chicago, Illinois ("JMLS"). App. 27.

While he was in college, Mr. Skelton experienced depression, requiring 5 days of inpatient treatment in 2009. App. 26. He sought that treatment voluntarily. Id. The treatment was helpful, but it did not end his feelings of depression. Id. Mr. Skelton met with a social worker for counseling regularly during the remainder of his college career, and he took anti-psychotic and anti-depressant medications as prescribed by a doctor, although the anti-psychotic was at a low dosage. App. 26, 220.

Returning to Oak Park before law school, Mr. Skelton began seeing a psychiatrist. App. 27. She prescribed him Wellbutrin, which he took. App. 220.

1. Conduct at JMLS

Mr. Skelton began attending JMLS in 2014, and he found the experience of law school to be stressful. App. 35. He began to perceive that he was being persecuted, and that others were inappropriately accessing information related to him. Id.

Despite his difficulties, Mr. Skelton had friends at JMLS. App. 28. However, he did not feel comfortable confiding in them concerning his mental health struggles. Id. Generally, when dealing with his feelings, he would leave the JMLS campus, and that would help him avoid having an outburst. Id. On four occasions, he caused disturbances that were brought to the attention of school staff and administrators. App. 204–05. Those incidents included:

a.   April 16, 2015—A student overheard Mr. Skelton in the JMLS library being loud and vulgar. She asked him to quiet down, but he did not. A security officer asked Mr. Skelton to leave the building until class began, which he did.

b.   October 13, 2015—While at JMLS, Mr. Skelton was heard yelling at himself at various times throughout the day. When a security officer went to ask him to leave, Mr. Skelton was already preparing to do so and admitted he had been yelling.

c.   February 18, 2016—As Mr. Skelton was exiting through a turnstile of the law school lobby, a security officer observed him acknowledge the presence of an administrator in a nearby office and yell profanity at the administrator. Mr. Skelton then exited the building.

d.   April 8, 2016—Student heard Mr. Skelton yelling and swearing in the JMLS library and asked if he was all right. He ignored her and left the building.

During his attendance at JMLS, Mr. Skelton sought and obtained some mental health counseling through the school. App. 29. JMLS did not take any disciplinary action against Mr. Skelton, although a dean discussed three of the above incidents with him in February 2016. App. 206. Mr. Skelton did not engage in any similar behavior during his third year in law school between April 2016 and May 2017. Id.

2.   Emails During the Character and Fitness Process

Mr. Skelton graduated from JMLS in June 2017. App. 222. He passed the July 2017 Illinois bar examination. Id. During the Board's review of his application, the Board alerted him to his omission to report certain college-era alcohol violations to JMLS. App. 30. Mr. Skelton had forgotten about those violations when he applied to JMLS. Id. He disclosed the incidents to JMLS in 2017. JMLS allowed him to amend his application to the school retroactively in order to include those disclosures, and it otherwise took no action following Mr. Skelton's report. App. 30, 222.

In September 2017, Mr. Skelton applied for, and obtained, the position of Freedom of Information Act ("FOIA") Officer at the City of Chicago Law Department in September 2017. App. 30.

Between approximately mid-October 2017 and mid-March 2018, Mr. Skelton began experiencing delusional thoughts about the Committee's review of his application. App. 222. He came to have paranoid thoughts and beliefs concerning the Committee's review of the JMLS incidents, and he began to feel that he would be denied admission as a result of it. Id. He sent approximately 40 emails to several recipients, including Ellen Mulaney (the member of the Committee assigned to review his case) and the staff of the Board. App. 4. In the emails, Mr. Skelton suggested that JMLS, the Board, the Committee, and the legal system were biased against him, and that they lacked integrity. He used charged language, including political rhetoric and themes of persecution, in some of the emails. Id. Excerpts of some of the emails are set forth at App. 4–7.

On March 20, 2018, Mr. Skelton met with Ms. Mulaney and two other members of an inquiry panel of the Committee. App. 207. In its subsequent report, the inquiry panel commended Mr. Skelton for the honesty he exhibited in discussing his conduct and mental state, and for demonstrating responsibility in his work as a FOIA officer for the City of Chicago. Id. The Inquiry Panel also noted that Mr. Skelton had recently met with a new psychiatrist, that he had just begun asking an anti-psychotic medication, and that he was seeking a psychotherapist. Id. However, the inquiry panel also noted that Mr. Skelton had not then clearly or convincingly demonstrated present fitness to practice law. *Id.*

Mr. Skelton's meeting with the inquiry panel helped him to realize that he was not being persecuted. App. 33. He understood the inquiry panel's declination to certify him for admission, and he understood that the emails must have struck them as frightening and offensive. Id. He is embarrassed and remorseful about having written and sent the emails. App. 33, 223. He apologized to the inquiry panel and to JMLS for his conduct. App. 223.

Shortly after the inquiry panel meeting, in April 2018, Mr. Skelton began therapy with Dr. Leslie Wolowitz. App. 33. He also sought treatment from a psychiatrist who prescribed the medication Seroquel. App. 32–33. Seroquel is an anti-psychotic which helps to organize the personality, ensure stability, and suppress symptoms, including the hearing of voices. App. 11. Dr. Wolowitz eventually referred Mr. Skelton to another psychiatrist, Dr. Charles Turk, who continued to prescribe Seroquel and monitor Mr. Skelton's use of that medication. App. 10.

Shortly after he began seeing Mr. Skelton, Dr. Turk diagnosed him with delusional disorder. App. 11. Delusional disorder involves an elaborate construction of thought departing from reality and that accounts for disturbed feelings, fears, and behaviors. Id. The disorder also involves a patient having paranoid thoughts. Id. Dr. Turk observed paranoid thoughts in Mr. Skelton, as well as a sense of being personally selected as the target of a conspiracy. App. 11–12. Dr. Turk testified that in his opinion, the isolated incidents involving Mr. Skelton at JMLS and the emails he sent to the Board were caused by Mr. Skelton's delusional disorder. App. 15.

At his July 15, 2019 hearing before the Committee, Mr. Skelton admitted that those emails were inappropriate, grandiose and deranged. App. 31. He also acknowledged that they were not spontaneous, and that they resembled arguments. App. 32. He explained that he was feeling unhinged during that time, and that his fears as expressed in the emails were not based in reality. Id. As he composed the emails, he did not think about how the recipients would react, but by the time of the hearing, he understood why they would have reacted negatively. App. 223. He took responsibility for his misperceptions and failure to take his delusional thoughts seriously. App. 223.

Dr. Turk opined at the hearing that Mr. Skelton was undertreated at the time he sent the emails. App. 209. But he further stated that in light of his treatment since that time, including his continued use of Seroquel or other medication, Mr. Skelton would be able to practice law. App. 16.

Dr. Wolowitz agreed with Dr. Turk's diagnosis of Mr. Skelton. App. 16. She described Mr. Skelton's conduct at JMLS as acting out inappropriately, with high sensitivity, emotional reactivity, some paranoid ideation, and a history of some depression and anxiety as well. App. 18. Paranoid ideation is a delusional reference involving thinking that something is aimed at the individual which, in reality, is not. Id.

Mr. Skelton told Dr. Wolowitz that the emails he sent to Board staff and the inquiry panel were motivated by feelings of not being understood and of persecution, and that he inappropriately spoke his thoughts in the emails. App. 18, 213. During his early consultations with Dr. Wolowitz, Mr. Skelton expressed some confusion about some aspects of the inquiry panel process, and he occasionally expressed a question about what made sense to him. App. 213. In general, though, he was able to understand why his behavior had given rise to concern and alarm. Id.

Mr. Skelton has been extremely cooperative and communicative during therapy, which has continued on a regular weekly basis. App. 19. Since beginning treatment with Dr. Wolowitz, Mr. Skelton has not acted out, as he did at JMLS or in the emails, but instead has demonstrated insight and self-reflection. App. 19, 214. He has support from a long-standing group of friends outside the workplace—some from high school, some from previous jobs, some from college, and some from law school. App. 214.

Mr. Skelton has had therapeutic conversations with both Dr. Turk and Dr. Wolowitz in which he mentioned incidents in which he questioned his perception conduct at JMLS as acting out inappropriately, with high sensitivity, emotional reactivity, some paranoid ideation, and a history of some depression and anxiety as well. App. 18. Paranoid ideation is a delusional reference involving thinking that something is aimed at the individual which, in reality, is not. Id.

Mr. Skelton told Dr. Wolowitz that the emails he sent to Board staff and the inquiry panel were motivated by feelings of not being understood and of persecution, and that he inappropriately spoke his thoughts in the emails. App. 18, 213. During his early consultations with Dr. Wolowitz, Mr. Skelton expressed some confusion about some aspects of the inquiry panel process, and he occasionally expressed a question about what made sense to him. App. 213. In general, though, he was able to understand why his behavior had given rise to concern and alarm. Id.

Mr. Skelton has been extremely cooperative and communicative during therapy, which has continued on a regular weekly basis. App. 19. Since beginning treatment with Dr. Wolowitz, Mr. Skelton has not acted out, as he did at JMLS or in the emails, but instead has demonstrated insight and self-reflection. App. 19, 214. He has support from a long-standing group of friends outside the workplace—some from high school, some from previous jobs, some from college, and some from law school. App. 214.

Mr. Skelton has had therapeutic conversations with both Dr. Turk and Dr. Wolowitz in which he mentioned incidents in which he questioned his perception some patients with delusional disorder are unable to refrain from telling others about their condition or their specific delusions, and that Mr. Skelton's ability to refrain from doing so was "evidence of Affiant's good judgment and his positive response to treatment." App. 198.

No evidence was introduced at the hearing that contradicted the information or opinions presented by Drs. Turk or Wolowitz. The attorney appointed by the Board for the purpose of presenting matters adverse to Mr. Skelton did not seek to admit any evidence into the record, instead only cross-examining the testifying witnesses.

At the time of the hearing, Mr. Skelton worked as a FOIA officer in the City of Chicago Law Department. App. 23. His supervisor, Amber Ritter, never saw Mr. Skelton have any problem with the stress of the job, which involves short turnaround times and frequent interactions with lawyers, the media and the public. App. 24. She was never aware of any incident in which Mr. Skelton acted inappropriately toward anyone in the course of his work. App. 25, 218. She would "absolutely" be comfortable with Mr. Skelton's admission to the Bar of Illinois. App. 219. She would "certainly" recommend Mr. Skelton for a job in the City's litigation division. Id.

B. Proceedings Below

Mr. Skelton applied for admission to the Illinois bar on March 19, 2017. App. 1. His application included a Character and Fitness Questionnaire, which is used by the Committees to determine the fitness of applicants by asking wide-ranging questions regarding the applicant's background. See App. 1. Although the Board had not yet certified Mr. Skelton for admission to the bar, Mr. Skelton received his Juris Doctor from The John Marshall Law School on June 11, 2017, and subsequently took and passed the July 2017 Illinois Bar Exam. App. 1–2.

On March 20, 2018, an inquiry panel of the Committee voted against recommending that Mr. Skelton be certified for admission, citing specific emails sent by Mr. Skelton as evidence that he had not clearly and convincingly demonstrated his fitness to practice law. App. 2, 9. Based on their vote to deny his recommendation, Mr. Skelton sought review of the inquiry panel's decision before a hearing panel of the same Committee. App. 9. The hearing panel granted Mr. Skelton's request, and held a hearing on July 15, 2019 regarding Mr. Skelton's application and certification to the Illinois bar. App. 9.

At the July 15, 2019 hearing before the hearing panel, Mr. Skelton presented three witnesses, in addition to himself, who testified on his behalf: Dr. Charles Turk, Dr. Leslie Wolowitz, and Amber Ritter. See App. 208, 212, 216. Dr. Turk and Dr. Wolowitz, as Mr. Skelton's treating therapists, testified as to their evaluations, diagnoses, ongoing treatment, and prognoses of Mr. Skelton's treatment. See App. 208–16. Both also testified in their professional opinions as to the success of Mr. Skelton's treatment, and the positive prognosis as a result of his ongoing and future treatment, which, in time, would allow him to competently practice law. App. 13–16, 19–23.

Ms. Ritter, as Mr. Skelton's immediate supervisor within the City of Chicago's Law Department, testified as to her professional and managerial knowledge of and relationship with Mr. Skelton. See App. 23. She testified that, in the course of reviewing his work as a FOIA officer for the City of Chicago, she believed him to handle the highly stressful nature of his work responsibly, complete tasks timely and successfully, create positive relationships with FOIA requesters, and called him "one of the best" FOIA officers the City of Chicago employs. App. 24–25.

After Mr. Skelton's July 15, 2019 hearing before a hearing panel of the Committee, the hearing panel requested additional information concerning Mr. Skelton's support network. App. 37. He provided that information along with affidavits from both Dr. Turk and Dr. Wolowitz. Id. The hearing panel issued its Findings and Conclusions on October 9, 2019. See App. 1. In a 3–2 vote, the majority of the panel declined to certify Mr. Skelton for admission. App. 47.

The hearing panel majority declined to find that Mr. Skelton had proved, clearly or convincingly, his present character and fitness to practice law. App. 47. It found that Mr. Skelton's five-month course of conduct in sending the emails to the Board and the inquiry panel constituted multiple individual acts of misconduct, and that although he could have reconsidered and changed course, he did not do so. App. 41. The majority further found that "[o]n denial by the inquiry panel, Mr. Skelton acknowledged his inappropriate conduct, but still could not understand why that conduct was alarming to the Inquiry Panel." App. 41–42.

The majority further found that while Ms. Ritter provided positive testimony concerning Mr. Skelton's job performance, her testimony was diminished by the fact that "just before Hearing . . . she was unaware of the incidents at JMLS and Mr. Skelton's emails." App. 42. The majority also found that for Mr. Skelton to have sent some of the emails during work hours undermined Ms. Ritter's ability to "clearly and convincingly corroborate his abilities either to take responsibility for his misconduct or use good judgment in a professional setting." Id.

While it considered Mr. Skelton's doctor's testimony "link[ing] his misconduct to a medical condition," the majority focused on the testimony of Dr. Turk, Dr. Wolowitz, and Mr. Skelton concerning therapeutic discussions in which he described to his doctors incidents in which he compared his initial perceptions to reality, and avoided acting out or experiencing paranoid thoughts. App. 42–43. The majority termed those "recent instances of delusional thought during non-stressful circumstances." App. 43. The majority also cited the doctors' "recommendation of long-term treatment" as a reason for concern. Id. It found that there had been an "insufficient passage of time clearly and convincingly corroborative of his acceptance of responsibility and demonstrative of rehabilitation." Id. The majority further faulted Mr. Skelton for not having produced the testimony of his parents to corroborate his testimony that they have been supportive of him. Id. The majority found that "evidence failed to demonstrate a robust support network" for Mr. Skelton in general, which "remain[ed] a serious concern." App. 44. In concluding its findings, the majority stated its expectation that "going forward Mr. Skelton will conduct himself as set forth in the essential eligibility requirements . . . and demonstrate rehabilitation from misconduct." Id.

The two dissenting members of the hearing panel found that Mr. Skelton had been "extremely candid" and had "demonstrated full acceptance of responsibility and sincere remorse for disturbing or offending the recipients of his email correspondence." App. 44. The dissent credited Ms. Ritter's testimony as "persuasive ... that Mr. Skelton has conducted himself properly and respectfully of others in the context of his two-year employment and that he would be able to do so in a stressful environment as a practicing attorney." App. 45. The dissent also gave weight to the testimony of Mr. Skelton's doctors, and it noted the effectiveness of the treatment they provided. App. 45–46.

The dissenting members found that Mr. Skelton had demonstrated the essential eligibility requirements necessary for admission to the bar, and would have recommended that he be conditionally admitted, with a monitoring period extending beyond the normal two-year period. App. 46.

Mr. Skelton thereafter petitioned the Illinois Supreme Court for review of the hearing panel's decision. See App. 201. In a three-sentence order, the Court denied Mr. Skelton's petition, effectively affirming the underlying hearing panel decision. App. 48–49.

REASONS FOR GRANTING THE PETITION

A. The Majority's Decision Below Discriminates Against Mr. Skelton Based on a Disability.

1. The Illinois Board of Licensing is Subject to the Americans with Disability Act.

The ADA prohibits public entities from discriminating against individuals with disabilities. The Act provides:

> [N]o qualified individual with a disability shall, by reason of such disability be excluded from participation in or be denied the benefits of the services, programs, or activities of a public entity, or be subjected to discrimination by any such entity.

42 U.S.C. § 12132. Public entities include "any department, agency, special purpose district or other instrumentality of a State or States or local government." 42 U.S.C. § 12131(1)(B).

Significantly, a public entity may not "administer a licensing or certification program in a manner that subjects qualified individuals with disabilities to discrimination on the basis of a disability." *Id.* § 35.130(b)(6). Additionally, a public entity may not impose or apply "eligibility criteria that screen out or tend to screen out an individual with a disability or any class of individuals with disabilities from fully and equally enjoying any service, program, or activity, unless such criteria can be shown to be necessary" for the provision of the service, program, or activity. *Id.* § 35.130(b)(8). A public entity may not "unnecessarily impose requirements or burdens on individuals with disabilities that are not placed on others." 28 C.F.R. pt. 35, App. B at 673. The Board is a public entity under the ADA because it is a public licensing scheme. *Hanson v. Medical Bd. of California*, 279 F.3d 1167, 1172 (9th Cir. 2002).

In order to establish that the majority's decision contravened the ADA, Mr. Skelton must prove that he is a qualified individual with a disability. The ADA defines a disability as:

(A)   a physical or mental impairment that substantially limits one or more major life activities of an individual;

(B)   record of such an impairment; or

(C)   being regarded as having such an impairment.

42 U.S.C. § 12102(1). The evidence in this matter establishes that Mr. Skelton's delusional disorder is a disability under the Act: it substantially limited his ability to participate in one or more major life activities.

Next, Mr. Skelton must prove that he is a qualified individual and that the Board has discriminated against him because of a disability.

2.   Mr. Skelton is a qualified individual because he meets the essential eligibility requirements for admission to the Bar.

By the time Mr. Skelton presented evidence to the hearing panel, it was clear that he met the essential eligibility requirements for admission to the bar, as set forth by the Illinois Supreme Court. Pursuant to Rule 6.3, those elements are:

(1)   the ability to learn, to recall what has been learned, to reason, and to analyze;

(2)   the ability to communicate clearly and logically with clients, attorneys, courts, and others;

(3)   the ability to exercise good judgment in conducting one's professional business;

(4)   the ability to conduct oneself with a high degree of honesty, integrity, and trustworthiness in all professional relationships and with respect to all legal obligations;

(5)   the ability to conduct oneself with respect for and in accordance with the law and the Illinois Rules of Professional Conduct;

(6)   the ability to avoid acts that exhibit disregard for the health, safety, and welfare of others;

(7)   the ability to conduct oneself diligently and reliably in fulfilling all obligations to clients, attorneys, courts, creditors, and others;

(8)   the ability to use honesty and good judgment in financial dealings on behalf of oneself, clients, and others;

(9)   the ability to comply with deadlines and time constraints; and

(10) the ability to conduct oneself properly and in a manner that engenders respect for the law and the profession.

The testimony of all of the witnesses in the hearing below establishes that Mr. Skelton meets the above criteria. Ms. Ritter's detailed, specific, and unimpeached testimony concerning Mr. Skelton's conscientious and skillful performance of his duties as a FOIA officer establishes elements (1), (2), (3), (4), (7), (9), and (10). Dr. Turk three times described Mr. Skelton as "forthright," which establishes element (4), as does Mr. Skelton's own truthful and open conduct and testimony throughout the Character and Fitness process. Even the inquiry panel, toward which he had behaved improperly as a result of his disorder, noted Mr. Skelton's honesty, and commended him for it. No evidence was presented that Mr. Skelton does not meet elements (5), (6), or (8), and no facts appear from any materials compiled by the Board that would indicate that those elements are somehow not satisfied.

Moreover, other than discriminatory presumptions and inferences made by the hearing panel majority, it was undisputed that at the time of the hearing and the panel's decision, Mr. Skelton's psychiatric treatment was working and he satisfied all essential eligibility requirements. *See Hason v. Med. Bd.*, 279 F.3d 1167, 1173 (9th Cir. 2002) (reversing dismissal of plaintiff 's ADA claim based on improper denial of his application for a medical license due to a history of mental health impairment because allegations that "by the time of the Medical Board's decision" the plaintiff "had received treatment for his [mental health] disability and was capable of practicing medicine" established that plaintiff was a qualified individual with a disability); *In re Petition and Questionnaire for Admission to Rhode Island Bar*, 683 A.2d 1333, 1337 (R.I. 1996) (holding character and fitness questionnaire was ADA compliant because it asked only whether the applicant was "currently" suffering from a disorder that impaired his or her judgment). To the extent Mr. Skelton's mental health history posed a risk of relapse, such risk was not evidence that Mr. Skelton actually failed to meet the eligibility requirements at the time of the panel's decision. Rather, a risk of relapse merely entitled Mr. Skelton to the reasonable accommodation of conditional approval.

3.   The Majority's Decision Discriminates Against Mr. Skelton Based on a Disability.

The majority's decision discriminates against Mr. Skelton based on a disability, in a manner inconsistent with the ADA. The Seventh Circuit has held that discrimination under Title II of the ADA [m]ay be established by evidence that (1) the defendant intentionally acted on the basis of the disability, (2) the defendant refused to provide a reasonable modification, or (3) the defendant's rule disproportionally impacts disabled people. *Washington v. Indiana High Sch. Athletic Assoc.*, 181 F.3d 840, 847 (7th Cir. 1999). The majority's decision intentionally discriminates against Mr. Skelton based on his disability, the majority refused to provide a reasonable accommodation, and its approach to the issues raised by Mr. Skelton's disability disproportionally impacts disabled people.

i.   The Majority's Decision Intentionally Discriminates Against Mr. Skelton Based on a Disability.

In its decision, the panel majority made findings adverse to Mr. Skelton based on criteria that would not have been applicable to non-disabled applicants without a similar mental health history. For example, the majority made reference to testimony elicited from Mr. Skelton's treatment providers not concerning his past conduct, but in reference to wholly unrelated incidents that Mr. Skelton had discussed with them over the course of his treatment. The majority characterized those incidents as involving "delusional thoughts," and gave them the same adverse weight as the other, more serious incidents that gave rise to the proceedings before the inquiry and hearing panels.

The hearing panel unfairly scrutinized the implications of Mr. Skelton's treatment evidence. The doctors themselves did not describe the incidents as serious, instead noting that the incidents only involved passing thoughts that Mr. Skelton had, which he then reported to them. They resulted in no conduct of any kind, much less conduct that harmed anyone. In one case, the thoughts in question involved Mr. Skelton's quibble – contained entirely within his own mind – regarding a grade in a graduate school class. No applicant without Mr. Skelton's mental health history would find such an incident the subject of a finding in a character and fitness decision. That it arose in this case is evidence both of discrimination against Mr. Skelton based on his disability, and of the disparate impact the majority's reasoning has on people with disabilities.

The majority's suggestion that Mr. Skelton needed to prove the existence of his support network also contravenes the ADA. In point of fact, affidavits from various members of Mr. Skelton's network of friends and colleagues were in evidence, as part of the Committee file; but the majority ignored them. Instead, it suggested that the absence of other affidavits from Mr. Skelton's family corroborating his testimony indicated that Mr. Skelton was socially isolated, which it termed a matter of "serious concern." It would not be a matter of "serious concern" in any case not involving the mental health issues presented here. All applicants to the Illinois bar submit character affidavits of the same kind that Mr. Skelton submitted, and they are routinely determined to be sufficient proof of an applicant's character and of the relationship that forms the basis for the affiant's knowledge of the applicant. The majority, however, wrongly disregarded Mr. Skelton's affidavits and created a "serious concern" where there was none, due to its discriminatory misconstruction of Mr. Skelton's condition. The majority skewed the evidence to justify a finding that Mr. Skelton is socially isolated and then used that finding in its final determination. But evidence of "social isolation" is not a criterion that a non-impaired applicant would face. Thus, Mr. Skelton's disability forms the entire basis for the "serious concern," and it was based on a criterion not applicable to non-impaired applicants. Under the ADA, that places a burden on Mr. Skelton that other applicants would not have, in a manner inconsistent with 28 C.F.R. pt. 35, App. B at 673, which "prohibits policies that unnecessarily impose requirements or burdens on individuals with disabilities that are not placed on others" and which prohibits the imposition of criteria that "tend[s] to" screen out an individual with a disability.

ii.   The Majority Refused to Provide a Reasonable Accommodation.

In addition to declining to recommend certification of Mr. Skelton to the bar, the panel majority also refused to provide Mr. Skelton with reasonable accommodations or modifications in certifying his admission. Under the ADA, a public entity is required to reasonably accommodate a qualified individual with a disability when necessary to avoid discrimination on the basis of a disability. *See Dadian v. Village of Wilmette*, 269 F.3d 831 (7th Cir. 2001); 42 U.S.C. § 12131(2); 28 C.F.R. § 35.130(b)(7)(i). Those accommodations may include making changes to its rules, policies, practices or services. *See Oconomowoc Residential Programs v. City of Milwaukee*, 300 F.3d 775 (7th Cir. 2002).

The reasonable accommodation requested by Mr. Skelton, and rejected by the majority, was Mr. Skelton's admission to the bar on a conditional basis. App. 37, 40. More specifically, Mr. Skelton's request for conditional admission proposed for his continued and supervised treatment for an agreed-upon period of time, to be supervised by the agency responsible for the registration and discipline of attorneys in Illinois, the Illinois Attorney Registration and Disciplinary Commission ("ARDC"). *See* App. 211, 216. Mr. Skelton's request for conditional admission as a reasonable accommodation was supported by several factors, which included qualification under a plain reading of the Committee's own rules, and the professional opinions testified to by Dr. Turk and Dr. Wolowitz. App. 211, 216, 270–71.

Under Rule 7 of the Board Rules of Procedure, a panel may consider conditional admission, if, among other requirements, the applicant is engaged in sustained and effective course of treatment for or remediation of "... a diagnosed mental or physical impairment that, should it reoccur, would likely impair the applicant's ability to practice law or pose a threat to the public. . . ." App. 270–71. The rule further states that conditional admission may be recommended in order to allow an applicant to practice law while their ongoing course of treatment or remediation for prior misconduct is monitored, in order to protect the public. *Id.* The Rule also provides that conditional admission is appropriate when an applicant has already engaged in "sustained and effective" treatment for a time period demonstrating the applicant's commitment and progress "but not yet sufficient to render unlikely a recurrence of the misconduct or unfitness." *Id.*

In addition, the testimony of both Dr. Turk and Dr. Wolowitz corroborated the propriety of conditional admission. Dr. Turk opined that Mr. Skelton would remain fit to practice law assuming he continued treatment during the course of any recommended conditional admission. *See* App. 211. Further support for the effectiveness of ongoing treatment came from Dr. Wolowitz, who also opined that three to five years of additional therapy would result in additional progress of Mr. Skelton's self-awareness with a low likelihood of reverting to his prior conduct. App. 216.

Based on the eligibility provisions, Mr. Skelton met not only the baseline requirements but also the purpose of the conditional admission process. As testified to by Mr. Skelton, Dr. Turk and Dr. Wolowitz, Mr. Skelton was engaged in ongoing treatment for his disability, with demonstrative positive effects on his disability and mental health, but for which additional treatment was still necessary.

Despite Mr. Skelton's two treating therapists providing their uncontested opinions as to the effectiveness of Mr. Skelton's current treatment, the positive effects of his future treatment, the relation to conditional admission, and Mr. Skelton meeting both the baseline requirements and purpose of the conditional admission process under the Board's rules, the panel majority nonetheless disregarded the evidence. In its report, the majority not only rejected Mr. Skelton's request for a reasonable accommodation or modification through conditional admission, but also failed to recommend or provide any other reasonable accommodation required to avoid discrimination against Mr. Skelton on the basis of his disability. As a result, the majority's findings and decision with respect to their failure to provide or recommend any reasonable modifications were also in contravention of the ADA.

iii. The Majority's Decision Disproportionately Impacts Disabled People.

The majority's decision disparately impacts not just Mr. Skelton himself, but disabled people generally. Mr. Skelton candidly provided evidence and responsive information to the hearing panel at every turn, even discussing and allowing his treatment providers to discuss the most intimate details of his counseling sessions. That evidence was then used to further stigmatize Mr. Skelton. To encounter that stigma in this kind of proceeding is discouraging to those who would seek to obtain professional help in an effort to demonstrate competency and fitness.

The American Bar Association National Task Force on Lawyer Well-Being recently published a report addressing lawyer well-being, mental illness, and addiction in the legal profession. National Task Force on Lawyer Well-Bring, *The Path to Lawyer Well-Being: Practical Recommendations for Positive Change* (2017). The report repeatedly emphasized that lawyers and law students often avoid seeking assistance for mental health or addiction issues because of fear that seeking help will impact their licensure. Lawyers and law students avoid seeking help to the point that their illness impacts their daily function in addition to their ability to practice law competently. The majority's decision contributes to the stigma that results in lawyers and law students avoiding mental health treatment by grounding its finding of unfitness in Mr. Skelton's mental health status. Disabled people are concerned with the impact of that stigma upon them in a direct way that non-disabled people are not; thus, the majority's decision has a disproportionate impact on disabled people.

B. This Court Should Grant Review to Provide Guidance on the ADA's Applicability to Admissions Cases.

Admissions cases are creatures of state proceedings and as a result, will not typically be reviewed in federal courts. Indeed, the *Rooker-Feldman* doctrine specifically provides that lower federal courts do not have subject matter jurisdiction to review state court civil decisions. *See Rooker v. Fid. Trust Co.*, 263 U.S. 413, 44 S.Ct. 149, 68 L.Ed.2d 362 (1923), and *D.C. Court of Appeals v. Feldman*, 460 U.S. 462, 103 S.Ct. 1303, 75 L.Ed.2d 206 (1983); *Young v. Murphy*, 90 F.3d 1225, 1230 (7th Cir. 1996). An applicant therefore can seek review through the state court system and then, if necessary, petition the United States Supreme Court for a writ of certiorari. *See Young*, 90 F.3d at 1230.

This complicates an applicant's ability to have a federal court review an admission board's decisions and specifically, whether such decisions violate the ADA. For example, consider *Edwards v. Illinois Bd. of Admissions to Bar*, 261 F.3d 723 (7th Cir. 2001). There, an applicant to the Illinois bar brought an action against the Illinois Board of Admissions to the Bar, the bar president, and others, seeking a declaratory judgment that the defendants' conduct violated the ADA. *Edwards*, 261 F.3d at 725. After a thorough review of the *Rooker-Feldman* doctrine, the Seventh Circuit concluded "that the district court lack[ed] subject matter jurisdiction to review [the applicant's] ADA claims and that dismissal was appropriate." *Id.* at 731. Thus, the applicant's "only avenue for federal relief was through the United States Supreme Court." *Id.* at 729. *See also Feldman*, 460 U.S. at 486, 103 S.Ct. 1303; *see also Dale v. Moore*, 121 F.3d 624, 627 (11th Cir. 1997) (holding that plaintiff's ADA claim was "inextricably intertwined with the state's judicial proceedings relating to his bar admission"); *Campbell v. Greisberger*, 80 F.3d 703 (2d Cir. 1996) (finding that *Rooker-Feldman* barred the district court from reviewing whether the New York state court violated the ADA when it required the applicant to provide medical information as a precondition to renewal of his bar application).

In *Schware v. Board of Bar Exam. of State of N.M.*, 353 U.S. 232, 249 (1957), this Court held that "a state cannot exclude an applicant from the practice of law when there is no basis for finding that the applicant fails to meet the standards of qualification or when the state action is invidiously discriminatory." *Id.* Therefore, under *Schware*, a state can have and enforce requirements and qualifications for admission to its bar; however, those qualifications must bear a rational relationship to fitness to practice, and determinations of whether those qualifications are met must not be made in arbitrary or discriminatory ways.

Here, the State's application of its admission criteria, juxtaposed with its consideration of Mr. Skelton's mental health and refusal to apply reasonable accommodations, violates the ADA. In denying Mr. Skelton admission, the majority relied principally on isolated conduct at JMLS and emails to the inquiry panel. In doing so, the State failed to properly apply the ADA. Consider the following:

(a)   Shortly after the emails sent to the inquiry panel, Mr. Skelton began therapy with Dr. Wolowitz.

(b)   Mr. Skelton began taking Seroquel.

(c)   Mr. Skelton began seeing Dr. Turk, who diagnosed him with delusional disorder and continued to prescribe Seroquel.

(d)   Both doctors who testified provided medical evidence that Mr. Skelton's alleged misconduct at JMLS and in sending the emails was the result of his delusion disorder.

(e)   Both doctors who testified provided medical evidence that Mr. Skelton's medication and therapy were appropriate treatment for his delusion disorder and would address any concerns regarding his practice of law.

(f)   The evidence presented unquestionably demonstrated that Mr. Skelton was skilled and qualified to become a lawyer, meeting the essential eligibility requirements.

Thus, pursuant to the medical evidence provided, Mr. Skelton had a disability, it was being properly addressed, and as long as he was accommodated by allowing treatment, it did not limit his ability to practice law. Without presenting any evidence to the contrary, the State made quasi-psychological conclusions adverse to the presented medical testimony and did not provide any explanation why reasonable accommodations could not be provided.

CONCLUSION

This petition for a writ of certiorari should be granted.

WHAT'S NEXT?

In the final chapter we talk about matters that will concern you directly and personally when you become sister and brother lawyers. Personal integrity.

Ethical choices you must make. The temptations that will confront you—that confront all of us—and dealing with them effectively.

> To assess your understanding of the material in this chapter, click here to take a quiz.

CHAPTER 11

Experiencing PR: Up Close and in Person

Coming Attractions

We start with MR 5.2(a) and (b) and a new lawyer's duty not to just blindly follow orders of a more senior lawyer. These rules plays an important role in a new lawyer's professional life. New lawyers should know their core values and not become distracted or give in easily to their senior lawyer's requests or demands. You are still bound by rules of professional responsibilities, and you will not be immune from malpractice claims. It is your bar license at stake.

Another issue you will have with the legal professional is the systemic tendency to steer lawyers toward becoming overworked, lonely, and miserable. The toxic expectations of workaholics seem often to be baked into the professional culture. The implicit assumption seems to be that overworked lawyers are good lawyers. Have you ever heard a lawyer basically bragging about how late she is working? It shouldn't be something to be proud of—but if the highest rewards go to the lawyers who bill the most hours, then a form of misery may be redefined as professional success.

We need to change this. We shouldn't praise any attorneys losing control of their own life. Instead, we should encourage work-life balance and self-care so there can be longevity in the profession. Lawyers should focus on a strong mind set and mental health. And, when you think about it, making ourselves mentally and physically healthy is a client-centric goal as well; after all, an effective lawyer is a lawyer that can be fully engaged. Law firms and legal employers need to play a lead role here. But you as a new lawyer will have a key role in this new reality.

Still, while this chapter points out the perils in experiencing PR, it also offers concrete counsel and actionable suggestions on avoiding them. We offer them to help fulfill our aspiration stated at the commencement of the book—to enable you to look back on your professional life and say, "What a wonderful way to have lived my life!"

Section 1.   Your Career as a Lawyer

This section introduces you to what you may confront as a new lawyer as you face ethical challenges. It is not always easy to determine the right thing to do. It is even harder if a more senior lawyer in your firm tells you to do something about which you have reservations. MR 5.2(a) and (b) deal with this part of your practice. You will observe, once again, that you will be called upon to use your judgment and discretion in deciding whether to carry out the instruction. You may decide to research the legitimacy of the instruction or ask questions of the more senior lawyer about it, or, in some circumstances, refuse to carry out the instruction. There might be times when you are called upon to say, "No, I won't."

A.   Using Your Own Ethical Judgment

Model Rule 5.2: Responsibilities of A Subordinate Lawyer

(a)   A lawyer is bound by the Rules of Professional Conduct notwithstanding that the lawyer acted at the direction of another person.

(b)   A subordinate lawyer does not violate the Rules of Professional Conduct if that lawyer acts in accordance with a supervisory lawyer's reasonable resolution of an arguable question of professional duty.

Deconstruction Exercise/Rule Rationale

Note how subsection (a) of the Rule is written. Why does it state, "another person" and not "another lawyer"? Why make the rule broader than narrow? The underlying principle is that a lawyer's judgment must be independently exercised. More importantly, this subsection makes clear that you, as a subordinate lawyer, are accountable for your own ethical violations and cannot "punt" clear ethical issues to a more senior lawyer, a client, or even a judge.

Now, subsection (b) deals with whether a narrow class of ethical problems, namely when there is an "arguable" case for more than one course of action. In that situation—and only in that situation—a subordinate lawyer is not accountable for following the directions of a senior lawyer. Essentially (b) is a defense for the subordinate lawyer. But note the crucial modifying words of "reasonable" before "resolution" and "arguable" before "question." Why were these modifiers used? What other words could have been used instead? Why were they not used? The purpose of these word selections is to provide sufficient bandwidth for a subordinate lawyer to claim that there was a sufficient factual and legal basis for the lawyer to adhere to the senior lawyer's instructions although the subordinate lawyer disagrees with them from a strategic viewpoint. While not used here, an apt word we saw previously in a different context is "abide."

Cases and Materials

X-Ray Questions (*Beverly Hills Concepts, Inc.*)

This case deals with a malpractice claim bought against a firm and one of its associates by a former client. Like *Orr*, the firm undertook to represent the client in drafting franchise documents that were to be used in the sale of franchises. A partner in the firm represented to the client that the firm was experienced in franchise matters and that he would be personally involved in managing the file. The statements were made in the presence of a junior associate lawyer, Jane Seidl. Neither statement was accurate and Seidel was tasked with managing the entire file. The matter went awry and the firm as well as Seidel—in her individual capacity, not in her firm capacity—were sued for malpractice, breach of fiduciary duty, and negligent misrepresentation. The Supreme Court of Connecticut held that she could be sued for malpractice as an individual lawyer. Ask yourself: what does it mean that a lawyer was sued in an *individual* capacity, in addition to the firm being sued? (Consider what you learned in *Baldwin*).

Now, a malpractice claim is a type of tort claim. As you learned in 1L torts, a tort requires the undertaking of a duty owed and a breach of that duty. What is that duty here and how did Ms. Seidel arguably breach that duty? Crucially for your understanding of this rule and for experiencing professional responsibility, what was her defense to the malpractice claim and why was it rejected? Be sure to grasp the interrelationship between MR 1.1 and MR 5.2 in answering this question.

Beverly Hills Concepts, Inc. v. Schatz & Schatz, Ribicoff & Kotkin

Supreme Court of Connecticut., 1998.
247 Conn. 48.

KATZ, ASSOCIATE JUSTICE.

The principal issue in this appeal is the proper method for calculating damages for the destruction of a nascent business. We conclude that: (1) unestablished enterprises must be permitted to recover damages for legal malpractice and that a flexible approach in determining those damages generally is appropriate; (2) lost profits for a reasonable period of time may serve as an appropriate measure of damages under certain circumstances; and (3) the plaintiff bears the burden of proving lost profits to a reasonable certainty. As applied to the facts of this case, however, we conclude that the plaintiff has not sustained its burden of proof regarding damages.

This appeal arises from a malpractice action brought by Beverly Hills Concepts, Inc. (plaintiff) against the named defendant, the law firm, Schatz and Schatz, Ribicoff and Kotkin (Schatz & Schatz), and the individual defendants, attorneys Stanford Goldman, Ira Dansky and Jane Seidl. In its complaint, dated November 2, 1989, the plaintiff alleged legal malpractice (first count), breach of contract (second count), intentional misrepresentation (third and fifth counts), negligent misrepresentation (fourth count), breach of fiduciary duty (sixth count), breach of the covenant of good faith and fair dealing (seventh count), and violation of the Connecticut Unfair Trade Practices Act (CUTPA), General Statutes § 42–110a et seq. (eighth count). On January 27, 1997, following a trial to the court, Hon. Robert J. Hale, judge trial referee, rendered judgment for the plaintiff on the first, second, fourth, sixth and seventh counts, and for the defendants on the third, fifth and eighth counts. The trial court awarded the plaintiff damages in the amount of $15,931,289.

On February 6, 1997, the defendants filed a motion to reargue and/or open or set aside the judgment, for a new trial, and/or for judgment, which the trial court denied. The defendants also filed, on June 17, 1997, a motion for articulation, which the trial court, likewise, denied.

The defendants appealed the judgment to the Appellate Court. The plaintiff filed a cross appeal, challenging the trial court's rejection of the CUTPA claim. We transferred the appeal and the cross appeal to this court pursuant to Practice Book (Rev.1998) § 65–1, formerly § 4023, and General Statutes § 51–199(c).

The trier of fact reasonably could have found the following facts. Charles Remington, Wayne Steidle, and Jeannie Leitao, incorporated the plaintiff as a Massachusetts corporation in April, 1987. They sold fitness equipment with a distinctive color scheme and logo, as well as a plan for operating a fitness club for women. The plaintiff's system included everything an owner would need to run a club, including equipment, training, sales and marketing support, and advertising and promotional materials. The plaintiff incorporated in Connecticut on August 17, 1987, and opened a corporate headquarters in Rocky Hill. From its Rocky Hill headquarters, the plaintiff licensed purchasers to use its concept, and sold distributorships to investors who gained the exclusive right to sell the plaintiff's products and to sublicense its name within a regional territory.

In October 1987, prompted by a legal problem regarding the plaintiff's trademark in California, Leitao contacted the law firm of Schatz & Schatz. On October 28, 1987, the plaintiff met with Goldman, a partner at Schatz & Schatz, and Seidl, an associate in the firm. Leitao advised them that she recently had filed a trademark application for the name "Beverly Hills Concepts" in Washington, D.C. Goldman assumed incorrectly that this meant that the plaintiff had a "federally registered trademark," which would have alleviated the need to register as a "business opportunity" pursuant to the Connecticut Business Opportunity Investment Act (act). General Statutes (Rev. to 1987) § 36–503 et seq. He told Leitao that Schatz & Schatz possessed expertise in the field of franchising, and that the firm was well qualified to handle the plaintiff's legal affairs. Goldman also said that he would be involved personally in the firm's representation of the plaintiff.

In fact, beginning in late 1987, Goldman turned the plaintiff's file over to Seidl, a junior associate, and Ira Dansky, a "contract" lawyer not yet admitted to the Connecticut bar. Neither Seidl nor Dansky possessed expertise in the law of franchising and business opportunities. Schatz & Schatz billing records revealed that Goldman spent only about two hours on the plaintiff's matter between December, 1987, and June, 1988.

Before turning the plaintiff's file over to Seidl, Goldman visited the plaintiff's headquarters in Rocky Hill and examined its distributorship and licensing agreements and promotional materials. Despite the plaintiff's request for guidelines regarding the sale of its equipment and "system" pending its franchise registration, Schatz & Schatz failed to advise the plaintiff that it was violating the act by selling fitness club packages without first registering with the state banking commissioner. Rather, after analyzing the plaintiff's documents, Goldman told Remington that the question of whether the plaintiff was offering business opportunities within the meaning of the act was a "gray area" of the law.

Recognizing that the plaintiff would need financial statements in order to file its franchise documents, Schatz & Schatz referred the plaintiff to the accounting firm of Coopers and Lybrand (Coopers). Schatz & Schatz advised Coopers, however, only of the financial statements required under federal law. It failed to inform Coopers of the requirements of the act.

In the winter of 1987–88, Seidl began drafting the plaintiff's franchise documents. On February 8, 1988, another Schatz & Schatz associate, who had been assigned the task of researching the franchise registration requirements of fourteen states, including Connecticut, informed Seidl that the plaintiff was not exempt from the registration requirements of the act. That same day, Schatz & Schatz contacted the plaintiff's Washington, D.C., trademark attorney, who confirmed that the plaintiff's trademark application was pending, and that no federal registration had been issued. Under these circumstances, Schatz & Schatz lawyers should have realized that the plaintiff was not exempt from the filing requirements of the act. Yet no one from the defendant law firm apprised the plaintiff of that fact.

In June, 1988, Dansky terminated Schatz & Schatz's representation of the plaintiff, stating that he was concerned that the plaintiff's franchise offering documents overstated its financial position. Shortly afterwards, the plaintiff retained Martin Clayman, an attorney with the firm of Clayman, Markowitz and Tapper, to complete the plaintiff's franchise registration. Within a few weeks, Clayman and his partner, Holly Abery-Wetstone, had prepared an application for the plaintiff to register as a business opportunity in Connecticut. The plaintiff decided not to file the registration documents, however, until its trademark had been approved, an event that its Washington, D.C., attorney had estimated would occur within a few months.

On September 15, 1988, an official acting for the banking commissioner notified the plaintiff that its marketing of franchises violated the act. The plaintiff contacted Clayman and Abery-Wetstone, who began preparing a postsale registration for the plaintiff's previous sales. The plaintiff complied immediately with advice from Abery-Wetstone that it should stop advertising and selling franchises. The plaintiff filed a postsale registration application on December 7, 1988, in an effort to comply with the act. Nevertheless, on June 28, 1989, the banking commissioner issued a cease and desist order and a notice of intent to fine the plaintiff up to $10,000 for each sale made in violation of the act. The commissioner further issued a stop order invalidating the plaintiff's postsale registration. On June 26, 1991, following hearings in September and November of 1989 and May of 1990, the commissioner issued a final cease and desist order, stating that the plaintiff had violated the act repeatedly by selling unregistered business opportunities in Connecticut. This malpractice action followed.

For purposes of this appeal, the defendants do not challenge the trial court's determination that they breached the applicable professional standard of care. Rather, they raise claims regarding the issues of causation and damages. Specifically, the defendants argue that the trial court improperly: (1) rendered judgment against Seidl on the negligent misrepresentation and breach of fiduciary duty claims based on the same conduct underlying the judgment of malpractice; (2) concluded that the defendants' failure to advise the plaintiff of its violation of the act caused its demise; (3) awarded damages based on lost profits rather than the going concern value of the business at the date of destruction; (4) awarded the plaintiff approximately $15.9 million in lost profits calculated over a period of twelve years; and (5) included prejudgment interest in the damages award.

We agree with the defendants' first and fourth claims. Accordingly, we reverse the judgment of the trial court and render judgment for the defendants.

I

We first examine whether the trial court improperly found Seidl liable for the negligent misrepresentation and breach of fiduciary duty counts. We conclude that the trial court should not have held Seidl, a junior associate at Schatz & Schatz, liable on these counts.

The trial court did not distinguish between the defendants in finding for the plaintiff on the claims of legal malpractice, breach of contract, negligent misrepresentation, breach of fiduciary duty, and breach of the covenant of good faith and fair dealing. The defendants now argue that Seidl, a junior associate playing a lesser role in the events that gave rise to the action, should not have been found liable on the negligent misrepresentation and breach of fiduciary duty counts. We agree.

We note first that the defendants do not challenge on appeal the trial court's determination that their failure to register the plaintiff with the banking commission constituted legal malpractice. Seidl shares the blame for that lapse.

The trial court also reasonably could have found that Seidl had engaged in legal malpractice because, in her position as a junior associate, she failed to seek appropriate supervision. Rule 1.1 of the Rules of Professional Conduct provides that: "A lawyer shall provide competent representation to a client. Competent representation requires the legal knowledge, skill, thoroughness and preparation reasonably necessary for the representation." The commentary to rule 1.1 provides in part that a lawyer who lacks relevant experience may "associate or consult with, a lawyer of established competence in the field in question. . . ." Having little experience in franchising, Seidl, therefore, could have rendered competent representation by seeking appropriate supervision. She failed to do so. She testified that she had sent both Goldman and Dansky copies of her work product. Seidl's pursuit of supervision, however, went no further. She stated that she had "assume[d] somebody was . . . watching, taking care of looking at my work." The trial court reasonably concluded that this passivity departed from the applicable standard of care.

Professional negligence alone, however, does not give rise automatically to a claim for breach of fiduciary duty. Although an attorney-client relationship imposes a fiduciary duty on the attorney; see *Matza v. Matza*, 226 Conn. 166, 183–84, 627 A.2d 414 (1993); not every instance of professional negligence results in a breach of that fiduciary duty. "[A] fiduciary or confidential relationship is characterized by a unique degree of trust and confidence between the parties, one of whom has superior knowledge, skill or expertise and is under a duty to represent the interests of the other." (Internal quotation marks omitted.) *Konover Development Corp. v. Zeller*, 228 Conn. 206, 219, 635 A.2d 798 (1994). Professional negligence implicates a duty of care, while breach of a fiduciary duty implicates a duty of loyalty and honesty. See *Edwards v. Thorpe*, 876 F.Supp. 693, 694 (E.D.Pa.1995); *Bukoskey v. Walter W. Shuham, CPA, P.C.*, 666 F.Supp. 181, 184 (D.Alaska 1987).

Goldman, a partner in Schatz & Schatz, represented to the plaintiff that the firm possessed the necessary franchising experience to handle its legal affairs. Goldman and Dansky, who, although not admitted in Connecticut, held himself out as a partner of the firm, managed the relationship with the plaintiff. Seidl, by contrast, was a junior associate to whom Goldman and Danksy delegated research and drafting responsibilities. Because it cannot be said that Seidl represented that she had superior knowledge, skill or expertise in the field of franchising, nor that she sought the plaintiff's special trust, it was improper for the trial court to conclude that her professional negligence rose to the level of a breach of fiduciary duty.

For similar reasons, the trial court should not have held Seidl liable for negligent misrepresentation. This court has stated: "One who, in the course of his [or her] business, profession or employment. . . supplies false information for the guidance of others in their business transactions, is subject to liability for pecuniary loss caused to them by their justifiable reliance upon the information, if he [or she] fails to exercise reasonable care or competence in obtaining or communicating the information." (Internal quotation marks omitted.) *D'Ulisse-Cupo v. Board of Directors of Notre Dame High School*, 202 Conn. 206, 218, 520 A.2d 217 (1987). At oral argument, however, the plaintiff conceded that Seidl herself had made no false statement of fact. Her presence at a time when a senior attorney made such an inaccurate statement does not suffice to render her liable for negligent misrepresentation.

We conclude, therefore, that the trial court improperly found Seidl liable for negligent misrepresentation and breach of a fiduciary duty. Accordingly, we reverse the trial court's conclusions holding Seidl liable on these two counts.

SOLUTIONS: THE LAWYER SHOULD HAVE, WOULD HAVE, COULD HAVE. . .

Subordinate lawyers are in the best position to know their level of competence. And while malpractice insurance likely covered this claim, it is nonetheless hard for any lawyer (especially a new lawyer) to be sued for malpractice and engage in the litigation process. Try to persuade the managing lawyer of your views on your competence on the matter. Consider framing the argument in the context of what is best for the client and optimal fit the partner, not what is best or optimal for you.

Cases and Materials

X-Ray Questions (*Shaffer Equipment Co.*)

This case posed a dilemma for the subordinate lawyer. He wanted to please his superiors and win the case but was trying to balance these desires with his oath-based obligations of candor and truthfulness. As you read the case, create a timeline with "exit ramps"; the ramps will be those moments when the lawyer could have changed course and avoided, well, disaster. Think about what other exit points he could have taken; what could he have said at those points as well as the more obvious ones. Would you have availed yourself of the exit opportunities? Why do you think he didn't do so? How did MR 3.3 and MR 3.4 factor into the dynamics of the ethical breaches here? Note too, the court's discussion of the import of a "knowing "violation and the court's rejection of the DOJ's cramped reading of "knowing." What was the court's basis for the rejection of the argument? What was the source of the court's authority to impose sanctions? What did the court say about the "integrity of the judicial process "and why was that a crucial factor in its reasoning? Finally, compare this case to *Capital Title* in which the court declined to impose the equivalent of the litigation death penalty as did the court here.

United States of America v. Shaffer Equipment Company; Anna Shaffer; Berwind Land Company; Berwind Corporation; The Johns Hopkins University, United States of America v. Berwind Land Company; Berwind Corporation, and Shaffer Equipment Company; Anna Shaffer; The Johns Hopkins University

United States Court of Appeals, Fourth Circuit, 1993.
11 F.3d 450.

NIEMEYER, CIRCUIT JUDGE:

In an action brought by the United States Environmental Protection Agency ("EPA") under the Comprehensive Environmental Response, Compensation, and Liability Act ("CERCLA"), 42 U.S.C. § 9601 et seq., to recover over $5 million in costs incurred in cleaning up a hazardous waste site in Minden, West Virginia, the district court found that the government's attorneys deliberately and in bad faith breached their duty of candor owed to the court during the course of proceedings. The court found that Robert E. Caron, the EPA's on-scene coordinator for the cleanup, had misrepresented his academic achievements and credentials in this and in other cases and that the government's attorneys wrongfully obstructed the defendants' efforts to root out the discrepancies and failed to reveal them once they learned of them. Finding the breaches "most egregious and disturbing," the court dismissed the action with prejudice, concluding that dismissal was "the only sanction available that is consistent with the duty of candor violations." The court also awarded the defendants attorney's fees.

On appeal, the government contends that the district court adopted an overly broad interpretation of the applicable rules of lawyer conduct and abused its discretion in imposing the most severe sanction by dismissing the action.

Having reviewed the record carefully, we affirm the district court's detailed findings of fact and its conclusion that the government attorneys violated their duty of candor. In light of the strong policy that cases be decided on their merits, however, we believe that outright dismissal is not required to punish and deter effectively the misconduct in question and to repair the wrongs done to the defendants. We therefore vacate the judgment and remand solely for the purpose of entering a sanction short of dismissal.

I

Shaffer Equipment Company, a firm in Minden, West Virginia, was engaged in the business of rebuilding electrical substations for the local coal mining industry, which involved the storing and disposing of transformers and capacitators on its property. Shaffer Equipment also modified transformers for customers, which often involved disposing of residual transformer fluid. Evidence revealed that while some of the fluid was simply poured onto the ground, the predominant practice was to store the fluid in drums and containers at the site, some of which later deteriorated and leaked fluid onto the ground. In response to a complaint, West Virginia authorities and the EPA tested soil samples from the site and discovered that the soil at the site was contaminated with polychlorinated biphenyls ("PCB's"). Because of the risk to persons in the area, the EPA regarded the site as hazardous and in need of remediation.

The EPA approached Anna Shaffer, the sole proprietor of Shaffer Equipment, and Berwind Land Corporation, the owners of the contaminated land, requesting that they undertake a cleanup of their land. Shaffer indicated that she did not have the resources to undertake a cleanup, and Berwind Land Corporation denied responsibility. The EPA accordingly undertook to clean up the site beginning in December 1984. It designated Robert E. Caron as the "On-Scene Coordinator."

The methodology initially chosen by the EPA to remedy the site's contamination was a new technology recommended by Caron, described as a "solvent extraction method," by which contaminated soil is washed on site in methanol to extract the PCB's. The method is designed to avoid transportation of contaminated soil to a remote landfill for disposal. Although the EPA expended over $1 million in implementing its solvent extraction plan at the site, the technique failed to achieve sufficient success to justify its continued use, and Caron directed abandonment of the method about a year after it was begun. Ultimately, the EPA removed 4,735 tons of contaminated soil to a hazardous waste dump in Alabama, as well as 23 drums of capacitators, 24 drums of transformer fluid, 32 drums of transformer flush, and 31 transformers. Over 200 truckloads were required for the transportation. The site and the Shaffer Equipment office building were thereafter restored, cleanup facilities were destroyed, and excavations were backfilled and graded. The entire cleanup was completed by December 1987, and the total cost, including the expenses incurred for the failed solvent extraction method, was ultimately reported by the EPA to be over $5 million.

In December 1990, the United States commenced this action under CERCLA to recover its response costs from the defendants. Following discovery, the district court established a schedule for filing summary judgment motions and for trial. After all summary judgment motions were filed, but before trial, the court received a letter dated January 31, 1992, from the Assistant United States Attorney whose appearance had been entered for the United States in the case, which stated:

A serious problem has arisen with regard to the testimony of a material EPA witness in the above-referenced action. The United States Attorney's Office has been advised that an investigation has been commenced by the appropriate governmental authorities. As a result of the pendency of those investigations and information provided to the United States by counsel for the defendants the United States is unable to proceed in good faith with the litigation of this action until further inquiry is made. We are, therefore, filing the attached Motion for a Stay of all proceedings in this action and respectfully request that the Court allow us a period of sixty days to evaluate this case in light of this information.

As it was later disclosed to the court, the EPA On-Scene Coordinator, Caron, had misrepresented his academic credentials and qualifications in this case and others, and this information had not been brought promptly to the attention of counsel for the defendants and the court.

The court granted the stay and directed the United States to conduct its investigation and to report by March 13, 1992, whether the United States wished to continue prosecuting the case. When the government reported that it would continue with the case, counsel for defendants filed a motion to dismiss the action for bad faith conduct.

After receiving the relevant documents about the charges, the district court conducted a two-day hearing directed largely to receiving the testimony of the attorneys involved. Based on conduct that began in September 1991 and which continued through January 1992, the court found that the government's attorneys repeatedly and deliberately violated their duty of candor to the court by failing to disclose Caron's misrepresentations, by obstructing defendants' efforts to discover them, and by continuing the litigation and filing court papers dependent on an administrative record developed largely by Caron. The district court's findings of fact relevant to government misconduct are reported fully at *United States v. Shaffer Equipment Company*, 796 F.Supp. 938, 942–49 (S.D.W.Va.1992), and therefore we repeat only those necessary to our discussion.

When the defendants first scheduled the deposition of Caron for September 12, 1991, an EPA assistant regional counsel, Charles Hayden, reviewed Caron's academic credentials. Caron was unable to produce his college diploma (allegedly because his mother failed to mail it to him), but he stated that he had received an undergraduate degree from Rutgers University in 1978 and had taken courses at Drexel University, Trenton State College, and Brookdale Community College. As it was later discovered, Caron in fact did not complete his class work for a degree from Rutgers and never attended any classes at any of the other schools.

On the morning of September 12, prior to the deposition, Hayden learned that Caron had not formally received a degree from Rutgers and so advised J. Jared Snyder, a Department of Justice attorney representing the government at the deposition. At the deposition, however, Caron testified, in the presence of Snyder, that he had completed all of the requirements for a degree at Rutgers and that the only reason he had not received his diploma was a question of paperwork. Caron also testified that he had continued taking courses at Drexel for a masters degree. He stated that his bachelors degree work was in environmental science and that his masters degree work was in organic chemistry.

When the deposition was resumed about two months later, on November 27, 1991, Caron was shown a copy of a professional resume on which he had claimed to have received a B.S. degree in environmental science from Rutgers and an M.S. degree in organic chemistry from Drexel. At that point, Snyder directed the witness not to answer any questions about the resume, claiming that the inquiry was not relevant, despite defense counsel's assertion that Caron's credibility was at issue. When counsel for the defendants suggested that the parties obtain a court ruling, Snyder took a recess from the deposition and consulted with the Assistant United States Attorney who recommended that Snyder state his objections on the record but allow Caron to answer the questions. Snyder then called his superior at the Department of Justice, William A. Hutchins, who called his superior, Bruce Gelber, who called the Deputy Regional Counsel of the EPA, Michael Vaccaro. Following the various calls, Hutchins eventually called Snyder back and instructed him to advise Caron of the option to refuse giving further testimony until Caron obtained his own attorney. In addition, Hutchins advised Snyder to permit Caron to answer if Caron so elected and to place any objections on the record. When the deposition resumed, Snyder followed Hutchins' instructions, but he continued to maintain that the questioning was irrelevant: "There is no foundation to any questions relating to his [Caron's] credibility. In fact, I don't even think his credibility is an issue in any way." Defense counsel agreed not to proceed on the issue of Caron's credentials further because, as the court found, counsel concluded that to do so would create the appearance of taking advantage of Caron by questioning him without his having first consulted an attorney.

Two days after the deposition, Snyder researched the question of whether Caron's credibility was relevant to the litigation and concluded that it was relevant as a matter of law. Snyder nonetheless did not supplement the government's response to an earlier interrogatory directed to Caron's credentials (to which the government had objected on the basis of irrelevance) and did not withdraw the relevancy objection to the discovery, despite his conclusion that the inquiry was relevant under current law.

In early December 1991, Vaccaro began an EPA civil investigation into Caron's credentials, advising Hutchins of the investigation and directing him not to advise anyone about it. Vaccaro also told Hutchins that a discrepancy had appeared in Caron's employment application with the EPA and that Caron had testified under oath in another case that he had earned a masters degree. On December 19, 1991, after Vaccaro told the EPA Office of the Inspector General about "the Caron problem," the Inspector General began a criminal investigation. Vaccaro advised Hutchins that he had contacted the Inspector General's office; Hutchins did not learn until later, in early January, that the Inspector General had commenced the criminal investigation.

Hutchins learned in December, during the course of his own investigation, that of the Superfund sites on which Caron had worked six were in litigation. Hutchins then instructed the government attorneys on each of those six cases that the government was not to rely on Caron's testimony. Hutchins also directed the attorneys not to disclose the existence of any investigation because to do so might prejudice the investigation and might also violate Caron's privacy rights.

As the attorney on this case, Snyder received Hutchins' instructions and followed them. Thus, in December 1991, when Snyder prepared the government's motion for summary judgment, he did not cite any testimony from Caron, nor did he include any affidavits executed by Caron. But Snyder did base the summary judgment motion on the administrative record compiled under Caron's direction as the On-Scene Coordinator during the cleanup. The district court found that "Caron [had] played a significant role in the preparation of documents contained in the administrative record."

On January 7, 1992, the defendants, in an effort to learn more facts about Caron's qualifications and credentials, subpoenaed records from the various colleges identified by Caron during his deposition. When Snyder learned of this, he telephoned counsel for the defendants to object because the subpoena was served after December 31, 1991, the discovery cutoff date. Snyder followed up with a letter requesting that the subpoena be withdrawn and that the documents be returned to the various institutions. Drexel University later reported that it had no record of Caron's attendance there, and Snyder was so advised by defense counsel. In response, Snyder wrote a letter of thanks dated January 17, 1992, stating that "we are looking into the matter and will let you know if Mr. Caron's testimony requires correction." While Snyder had also intended, in that letter, to disclose the existence of the criminal investigation and had so drafted the letter, Hutchins and Gelber directed him to delete the reference, and Snyder followed the instruction.

On January 17, 1992, Snyder filed the government's motion for summary judgment which he had started preparing in December. He made no mention of the EPA investigation, the criminal investigation, or the misstatements or misrepresentations of Caron's credentials.

Still attempting to discover the extent of the Caron problem after the government filed its summary judgment motion, defense counsel discovered in late January 1992, through independent means, that Caron had testified falsely in another case. Defense counsel decided to bring this evidence to the attention of the Assistant United States Attorney on the case who, following consultation with Snyder and Hutchins, then advised the court for the first time in a letter dated January 31, 1992, of the Caron problem and requested a stay.

Based on these facts, the district court concluded that Snyder and Hutchins violated their general duty of candor to the court as well as the particular duties imposed by West Virginia Rule of Professional Conduct 3.3 (describing the lawyer's duty of candor toward the tribunal) and Federal Rule of Civil Procedure 26(e)(2) (obliging counsel to supplement discovery requests). With respect to Snyder's conduct, the court found that even though Snyder knew, as of September 12, 1991, that Caron had no college degree, he obstructed efforts by defense counsel to discover this at the November 27 deposition by instructing Caron not to answer questions about his resume which claimed that Caron had two college degrees. The court also found that Snyder failed to withdraw his objections to interrogatories submitted earlier and to modify the positions taken in the deposition, or to advise the court or opposing counsel when he concluded two days later, through his own independent legal research, that Caron's credibility in this case was relevant. The court found that despite discovering the discrepancies in Caron's employment application with the EPA, the commencement of an investigation by the EPA, and the commencement of a criminal investigation, Snyder "continued to litigate the matter unabated without disclosing the investigations to the Court."

With respect to Hutchins, Snyder's superior, the district court found that his actions were "egregious" and constituted more severe violations. Hutchins had learned on November 27, 1991, that Caron had no college degree even though Caron's resume stated otherwise. In early December, Hutchins had learned of (1) the EPA civil investigation, (2) the false testimony given by Caron in another litigation claiming that he had a masters degree, and (3) Vaccaro's referral of the matter to the EPA's Office of Inspector General. Shortly thereafter, in January, Hutchins had learned that an actual criminal investigation had been commenced. The district court found that Hutchins improperly continued the litigation without disclosing to the court the existence of the ongoing investigations, and that Hutchins had prevented Snyder from disclosing the facts when Snyder had proposed to do so in a letter to opposing counsel. Finally, the court also found that Hutchins improperly concealed his knowledge that Caron had testified falsely in other cases and in affidavits sent to the EPA Office of Inspector General.

Concluding its findings regarding the conduct of the government's attorneys, the district court stated,

> [C]ounsel for the United States has deliberately placed its loyalty and allegiance to its agency client (EPA) and client's servant (Robert Caron) far and above the unending duty of candor owed to this Court. Such conduct is reprehensible and lies in bad faith.

796 F.Supp. at 951–52. Stating that the only sanction appropriate to address the violation was dismissal, the court dismissed the action under its inherent powers and awarded the defendants their attorney's fees incurred in responding to the government's misconduct, under the Equal Access to Justice Act, 28 U.S.C. § 2412.

This appeal followed.

II

The underlying factual findings of the district court are not contested and, based on our review of the record, we conclude that they are not clearly erroneous. The government does advance additional facts that tend to provide explanations about why certain actions were taken, focusing particularly on the issue of whether Caron's credentials were material and what information government counsel were entitled to credit as the problem emerged. The heart of the government's position, however, is its contention that the district court misunderstood and misapplied West Virginia Rule of Professional Conduct 3.3 (describing the lawyer's duty of candor toward the tribunal). This is a question of law and we review it *de novo*.

The government contends that a proper application of Rule 3.3 requires "close adherence" to the specific provisions of the rule which mandate disclosure only when an attorney has *actual knowledge* of a *material fact* which, if not disclosed, will assist *a client's* criminal or fraudulent act. The government argues that even if its attorneys are imputed with *actual* knowledge of Caron's discrepancies, which it denies, Caron's veracity was not material to the government's case to recover response costs under CERCLA because proof of that case does not rely on Caron's testimony but instead on the administrative record, subject to review on an arbitrary and capricious standard. *See* 42 U.S.C. § 9613(j). In addition, the government argues that Rule 3.3 is not violated because its lawyers were not assisting a *client's* fraudulent act. The government maintains that the United States could not be defrauding the court since its claim relied only on the administrative record which has not been shown to be false. Finally, the government argues that opposing counsel already had impeachment information about Caron to use in response to the motion for summary judgment, and that even if the information were inadequate, the government made full disclosure before the defendants were called upon to respond to the motion.

It appears that the district court, in finding that the government's attorneys violated a duty of candor to the court, applied the general duty of candor imposed on all attorneys as officers of the court, as well as the duty of candor defined by Rule 3.3. Although the court referred to Rule 3.3, it also described the duty of candor more broadly as that duty attendant to the attorney's role as an officer of the court with a "continuing duty to inform the Court of any development which may conceivably affect the outcome of litigation." 796 F.Supp. at 950. It concluded, "Thus, attorneys are expected to bring directly before the Court all those conditions and circumstances which are relevant in a given case." *Id.* In its brief, the government did not address the existence, nature, and scope of any general duty of candor and whether its attorneys violated that duty. Nevertheless, we are confident that a general duty of candor to the court exists in connection with an attorney's role as an officer of the court.

Our adversary system for the resolution of disputes rests on the unshakable foundation that truth is the object of the system's process which is designed for the purpose of dispensing justice. However, because no one has an exclusive insight into truth, the process depends on the adversarial presentation of evidence, precedent and custom, and argument to reasoned conclusions—all directed with unwavering effort to what, in good faith, is believed to be true on matters material to the disposition. Even the slightest accommodation of deceit or a lack of candor in any material respect quickly erodes the validity of the process. As soon as the process falters in that respect, the people are then justified in abandoning support for the system in favor of one where honesty is preeminent.

While no one would want to disagree with these generalities about the obvious, it is important to reaffirm, on a general basis, the principle that lawyers, who serve as officers of the court, have the first line task of assuring the integrity of the process. Each lawyer undoubtedly has an important duty of confidentiality to his client and must surely advocate his client's position vigorously, but only if it is truth which the client seeks to advance. The system can provide no harbor for clever devices to divert the search, mislead opposing counsel or the court, or cover up that which is necessary for justice in the end. It is without note, therefore, that we recognize that the lawyer's duties to maintain the confidences of a client and advocate vigorously are trumped ultimately by a duty to guard against the corruption that justice will be dispensed on an act of deceit. *See* 1 Geoffrey C. Hazard, Jr. and W. William Hodes, *The Law of Lawyering* 575–76 (1990) ("[W]here there is danger that the tribunal will be misled, a litigating lawyer must forsake his client's immediate and narrow interests in favor of the interests of the administration of justice itself.").

While Rule 3.3 articulates the duty of candor to the tribunal as a necessary protection of the decision-making process, *see Hazard* at 575, and Rule 3.4 articulates an analogous duty to opposing lawyers, neither of these rules nor the entire Code of Professional Responsibility displaces the broader general duty of candor and good faith required to protect the integrity of the entire judicial process. The Supreme Court addressed this issue most recently in *Chambers v. NASCO, Inc.,* 501 U.S. 32, 111 S.Ct. 2123, 115 L.Ed.2d 27 (1991). There, an attorney had taken steps to place certain property at issue beyond the jurisdiction of the district court and had filed numerous motions in bad faith, simply to delay the judicial process. The district court, the court of appeals, and the Supreme Court all agreed that neither Federal Rule of Civil Procedure 11 (subjecting to sanction anyone who signs a pleading in violation of the standards imposed by the rule) nor 28 U.S.C. § 1927 (subjecting to sanction anyone who "multiplies the proceedings . . . unreasonably and vexatiously") could reach the conduct. However, the Supreme Court accepted the district court's reliance on the inherent power to impose sanctions, rejecting arguments that Rule 11 and § 1927 reflect a legislative intent to displace a court's power to vacate a judgment upon proof that a fraud has been perpetrated upon the court:

> *We discern no basis for holding that the sanctioning scheme of the statute [28 U.S.C. § 1927] and the rules displaces the inherent power to impose sanctions for the bad faith conduct* described above. These other mechanisms, taken alone or together, are not substitutes for the inherent power, for that power is both broader and narrower than other means of imposing sanctions. First, whereas each of the other mechanisms reaches only certain individuals or conduct, the inherent power extends *to a full range of litigation abuses.* At the very least, the inherent power must continue to exist to fill in the interstices.

501 U.S. at ___, 111 S.Ct. at 2134 (emphasis added).

The general duty of candor and truth thus takes its shape from the larger object of preserving the integrity of the judicial system. For example, in *Tiverton Board of License Commissioners v. Pastore*, 469 U.S. 238, 105 S.Ct. 685, 83 L.Ed.2d 618 (1985), counsel failed to apprise the Supreme Court that during the appeal process, one of the respondents, a liquor store challenging the admission of evidence at a Rhode Island liquor license revocation proceeding, had gone out of business, rendering the case moot. Rebuking counsel for failing to comply with a duty of candor broader than Rule 3.3, the Supreme Court stated, "It is appropriate to remind counsel that they have a '*continuing duty to inform the Court* of any development *which may conceivably affect the outcome*' of the litigation." *Id.* at 240, 105 S.Ct. at 686 (quoting *Fusari v. Steinberg*, 419 U.S. 379, 391, 95 S.Ct. 533, 540, 42 L.Ed.2d 521 (1975) (Burger, C.J. concurring)) (emphasis added).

The general duty to preserve the integrity of the judicial process was similarly identified in *Hazel-Atlas Glass Co. v. Hartford-Empire Co.,* 322 U.S. 238, 64 S.Ct. 997, 88 L.Ed. 1250 (1944). Without the support of any rule, the Court opened up a long-standing judgment because one of the litigants had introduced a document at trial which was later discovered to be fraudulent. The Supreme Court stated,

> *It is a wrong against the institutions* set up to protect and safeguard the public, institutions in which fraud cannot complacently be tolerated consistently with the good order of society. Surely it cannot

be that *preservation of the integrity of the judicial process* must always wait upon the diligence of litigants. The public welfare demands that the agencies of public justice be not so impotent that they must always be mute and helpless victims of deception and fraud.

Id. at 246, 64 S.Ct. at 1001 (emphasis added).

In this case, the district court found that both Snyder and Hutchins repeatedly failed to advise the court of the Caron problem and the civil and criminal investigations relating to it, continuing "to litigate the matter unabated." Without repeating the factual findings which support the court's conclusion, we are satisfied that these are matters involving deceit that, when not disclosed, undermine the integrity of the process. Moreover, their disclosure could conceivably have affected the outcome of the litigation, as we discuss more fully, below. Accordingly, the conduct violates the general duty of candor that attorneys owe as officers of the court. *See Pastore*, 469 U.S. at 240, 105 S.Ct. at 686.

Even limiting our consideration to the provisions of Rule 3.3 which, the government argues, define a lawyer's duty of candor more restrictively, we are nevertheless satisfied that the district court was justified in finding that the government's attorneys breached their duty of candor under that rule.

Rule 3.3 of Professional Conduct, which defines the duty of candor to the tribunal, states in pertinent part, "A lawyer shall not knowingly . . . fail to disclose a material fact to a tribunal when disclosure is necessary to avoid assisting a criminal or fraudulent act by the client." The government argues that the defendants failed in this case to establish three critical elements of the rule: (1) that the government's attorneys had actual knowledge of Caron's misrepresentations, (2) that Caron's credentials were material, and (3) that the attorney's conduct in failing to disclose the Caron problem assisted the EPA in a fraudulent act. We will address these contentions in order.

Addressing first the "actual knowledge" requirement of Rule 3.3, the government contends that, while it may have had suspicions about Caron's misstatements, it did not fully appreciate their falsity until the investigation was completed. While it is true that a mere suspicion of perjury by a client does not carry with it the obligation to reveal that suspicion to the court under Rule 3.3, *see In re Grievance Comm. of the United States Dist. Court*, 847 F.2d 57, 63 (2d Cir.1988), the government's attorneys in this case cannot find shelter behind any such doubt. Caron admitted to Snyder as early as September 1991 that he did not have a college degree. By December 1991, when an EPA investigation was under way and EPA regional counsel had referred the matter to the Office of Inspector General, the lawyers for the United States had actual knowledge of the discrepancy in Caron's sworn testimony in which he said, on the one hand, that he had no college degree and, on the other, that he had both a bachelor of science degree and a masters degree. At that time, the government's lawyers also had had conversations with Rutgers University which confirmed that no degree had been issued, were aware of misrepresentations on Caron's employment application, and actually possessed a copy of Caron's fraudulent resume. Against this evidence, the government's claim to have held only a suspicion rings hollow.

We move to the government's principal argument under Rule 3.3, that the information which Caron falsified in his credentials was not material to the proceeding. First of all, we find the sincerity of the position undermined because Snyder, the Justice Department attorney in this case, reached the exact opposite conclusion during the course of his independent research in November 1991. Moreover, when the Assistant United States Attorney for the Southern District of West Virginia was presented with an example of Caron's perjury by counsel for the defendants, he promptly wrote a letter to the court asking for a stay in which he stated, "A serious problem has arisen with regard to the testimony *of a material EPA witness*" (emphasis added). But it is principally an analysis of the record which leads us to the conclusion that the information is material.

The issue before the district court in this case was whether the defendants are liable to the EPA for costs incurred in cleaning up a hazardous waste site. To establish its case, the government must demonstrate that the release or the threatened release of hazardous wastes caused the EPA to incur "response costs." 42 U.S.C. § 9607(a). One method for challenging the appropriateness of the response costs is for the defendant to demonstrate that the methods of cleaning up are not consistent with the National Contingency Plan established by CERCLA, 42 U.S.C. § 9601 *et seq*. Procedurally, the government relies on the administrative record developed during the cleanup, and the defendant bears the burden of demonstrating that this reliance is arbitrary and capricious. *See* 42 U.S.C. § 9613(j). Because this method for establishing its case relies on the administrative record and not testimony, the government argues that Caron's credibility and credentials are not material. This position, however, ignores the fact that the *integrity* of the administrative record *is* relevant to inquiries about both the propriety of costs and the EPA's response selection. It is undisputed that Caron was responsible for making that record.

The administrative record in this case is large, consisting of volumes of bills, communications, and authorizations developed primarily from on-site activity. The person placed in overall charge of the site was Robert Caron. While Caron's decisions were subject to approval by superiors, as On-Scene Coordinator he made most of the decisions and, when he sought the approval of superiors, his recommendations were adopted in virtually all of the cases. It was Caron who recommended and obtained approval for the solvent extraction method, side-stepping the traditional method of physically removing the contaminated soil. As it turned out, the pilot process proved unsatisfactory and the traditional method of removing the soil was ultimately utilized. However, the experimental process was abandoned only after over $1 million in costs were incurred, which the EPA now seeks to impose on the defendants. While Caron's role in this litigation relates primarily to supporting response selection, he also had a major role in approving project-related expenditures. Thus, Caron's credentials, capability and credibility are relevant to the examination of the administrative record in this case.

Even where review of a case is confined to the evidence contained in the administrative record, the Supreme Court has concluded that evidence of bad faith or improper behavior by an administrative agency's official in compiling that record justifies inquiry beyond the record compiled. *See Citizens to Preserve Overton Park v. Volpe,* 401 U.S. 402, 420, 91 S.Ct. 814, 825–26, 28 L.Ed.2d 136 (1971). The fact that the government's agent in charge of monitoring expenses and selecting responses filed fraudulent documents with the federal government and perjured himself repeatedly in connection with his federal employment is, we think, of primary relevance to an examination of the integrity and reliability of the administrative record.

It is obviously difficult to assess the impact that Caron's fraud may have had on the development of the record, particularly on the selection of the solvent extraction method, an issue hotly debated by the parties. Would Caron have been given the responsibility for initiating a pilot program if his credentials had not been misrepresented to the EPA in his employment application? Would his recommendations have carried the same weight on review by superiors? To what extent are the defendants saddled in this case with decisions in the administrative record tainted by questions of competence and integrity? While it may never be possible to find answers to these questions and therefore accurately assess the full impact of the fraud, that inability must not, by default, cause the administrative record to be accepted as is and the fraud to be deemed immaterial. *See Hazel-Atlas Co.,* 322 U.S. at 247, 64 S.Ct. at 1001–02. Given the great possibility that Caron's deception affected administrative decisions in this case and disguised a weakness in his capabilities, we cannot agree with the government that the sole relevance of the "Caron problem" is with regard to impeachment of Caron's testimony. That approach is too narrow. *See Citizens to Preserve Overton Park*, 401 U.S. at 420, 91 S.Ct. at 825–26. Moreover, the significance of impeaching the principal EPA witness, who was largely responsible for developing the record, renders impeachment information material. We thus reject the government's position that the court is essentially stuck with an unimpeachable administrative record. We conclude that the district court did not err in finding this issue to be material.

Once we find the government's attorneys had actual knowledge of Caron's deception and that the deception was material under Rule 3.3, we move to a review of whether Caron's conduct amounted to a fraudulent act of the EPA. The government's attorneys argue that no fraud was attempted *by their client,* the EPA, and that in the absence of such an attempt, they had no responsibility to reveal Caron's perjury under the duty of candor under Rule 3.3. Again, we disagree. Caron's perjury in an attempt to cover up his earlier deception was certainly a fraudulent act. Since Caron was involved in the case as an important agent of the EPA and his misrepresentation was made in the course of his employment with the EPA with the effect of disguising a weakness in the EPA's case, his action is fairly characterized as an act of the EPA.

Distilling the district court's findings, this case reduces to an effort by an important EPA witness to cover up or minimize his long history of fraud. The government's attorneys compounded the problem by obstructing the defendants' efforts to uncover this perjury and in failing themselves to reveal it. When the government's attorneys filed a motion for summary judgment dependent on the administrative record made by Caron and requested a favorable resolution of the case prior to a full documentation of the perjury, these attorneys overstepped the bounds of zealous advocacy, exposing themselves and their employer to sanctions. While this violation was effectively brought to light by opposing counsel, this was not done until after the expenditure of significant time and money.

III

The district court, exercising its inherent power, imposed the most severe sanction and dismissed the government's CERCLA action against the defendants, concluding that dismissal with prejudice is "the only sanction available that is commensurate with the duty of candor violations by counsel" and that dismissal not only penalizes the improper conduct but also deters others. The court added, "Today we will send a message to all counsel who appear before this Court that the duty of candor will be upheld and preserved at all times irrespective of the identity of the parties and the monetary stakes in the litigation." 796 F.Supp. at 953.

The government contends that, in dismissing its case outright, the district court "erroneously weighed the public and private interests." In particular, the government argues that the district court failed to give adequate consideration to lesser sanctions that could deter and rectify the unethical conduct while at the same time vindicate the public interest in having the defendants pay for cleaning up their hazardous waste. Before addressing specifically the government's argument, it is helpful to review the scope of the court's inherent powers.

Due to the very nature of the court as an institution, it must and does have an inherent power to impose order, respect, decorum, silence, and compliance with lawful mandates. This power is organic, without need of a statute or rule for its definition, and it is necessary to the exercise of all other powers. *See Chambers,* 501 U.S. at ____, 111 S.Ct. at 2132. Because the inherent power is not regulated by Congress or the people and is particularly subject to abuse, it must be exercised with the greatest restraint and caution, and then only to the extent necessary. *See id.; Roadway Express, Inc. v. Piper,* 447 U.S. 752, 764, 100 S.Ct. 2455, 2463, 65 L.Ed.2d 488 (1980) (restraint required because the inherent powers of a court are "shielded from direct democratic controls"). Under the inherent power, a court may issue orders, punish for contempt, vacate judgments obtained by fraud, conduct investigations as necessary to exercise the power, bar persons from the courtroom, assess attorney's fees, and dismiss actions. Since orders dismissing actions are the most severe, such orders must be entered with the greatest caution.

The Supreme Court has held that a judgment obtained by fraud may be vacated under a court's inherent power, *see Hazel-Atlas Co.,* 322 U.S. at 248, 64 S.Ct. at 1002; that an action not prosecuted may be dismissed, *see Link v. Wabash Railroad Co.,* 370 U.S. 626, 629–30, 82 S.Ct. 1386, 1388, 8 L.Ed.2d 734 (1962); and that bad faith or abuse can form a basis for a realignment of attorney's fees, *see Chambers,* 501 U.S. at ____, 111 S.Ct. at 2133. While we have not published on the subject, the inherent power to dismiss a case for the misconduct of counsel is undoubtedly clear. In *Hazel-Atlas Co.,* the Supreme Court observed that the court of appeals could have dismissed that case where it was discovered that counsel had suppressed the truth about the authorship of an important article offered into evidence. 322 U.S. at 250, 64 S.Ct. at 1003. The power has been recognized also by courts of appeals. *See Aoude v. Mobil Oil Corp.,* 892 F.2d 1115, 1118 (1st Cir.1989) (recognizing the inherent power to dismiss where a party "defiles the judicial system in committing a fraud on the court"); *Halaco Engineering Co. v. Costle*, 843 F.2d 376, 380 (9th Cir.1988) (recognizing the inherent power to dismiss EPA case for discovery abuses, but reversing dismissal order as excessive in the circumstances); *United States v. National Medical Enterprises, Inc.*, 792 F.2d 906, 912 (9th Cir.1986) (recognizing the inherent power to dismiss for government's improper influencing of trial witnesses, but reversing dismissal order for district court to reconsider pursuant to the "appropriate legal standard"). In *National Medical Enterprises*, the court confirmed its standard that dismissals under the inherent power are justified if "a party has willfully deceived the court and engaged in conduct utterly inconsistent with the orderly administration of justice." 792 F.2d at 912 (quoting *Fjelstad v. American Honda Motor Co.*, 762 F.2d 1334, 1338 (9th Cir.1985)).

Accordingly, we recognize here that when a party deceives a court or abuses the process at a level that is utterly inconsistent with the orderly administration of justice or undermines the integrity of the process, the court has the inherent power to dismiss the action. Our review of the use of that power on appeal is for an abuse of discretion.

Mindful of the strong policy that cases be decided on the merits, and that dismissal without deciding the merits is the most extreme sanction, a court must not only exercise its inherent power to dismiss with restraint, but it may do so only after considering several factors, which we have detailed under other circumstances. *See Hillig v. Commissioner*, 916 F.2d 171, 173–74 (4th Cir.1990) (dismissal under Fed.R.Civ.P. 41(b)); *Wilson v. Volkswagen of America, Inc.*, 561 F.2d 494, 504 (4th Cir.1977) (dismissal under Fed.R.Civ.P. 37(b)), *cert. denied*, 434 U.S. 1020, 98 S.Ct. 744, 54 L.Ed.2d 768 (1978); *Davis v. Williams*, 588 F.2d 69, 70 (4th Cir.1978) (dismissal under Fed.R.Civ.P. 41(b)). Thus, before exercising the inherent power to dismiss a case, a court must consider the following factors: (1) the degree of the wrongdoer's culpability; (2) the extent of the client's blameworthiness if the wrongful conduct is committed by its attorney, recognizing that we seldom dismiss claims against blameless clients; (3) the prejudice to the judicial process and the administration of justice; (4) the prejudice to the victim; (5) the availability of other sanctions to rectify the wrong by punishing culpable persons, compensating harmed persons, and deterring similar conduct in the future; and (6) the public interest.

In this case, the government proposed to the district court a lesser sanction to be imposed if a breach of the duty of candor were to be found. It suggested (1) opening for *de novo* review the administrative record with respect to the selection of the solvent extraction method; (2) allowing discovery by defendants on the EPA's selection of the solvent extraction method; and (3) allowing discovery on any and all matters involving Caron. The district court rejected this offer as a "rather slight sanction." Because it found the conduct in this case to be "most egregious and disturbing," the court concluded that dismissal with prejudice was "the only sanction available that is commensurate with the duty of candor violations." 796 F.Supp. at 953. The court also observed that the duty of candor is "priceless" and must be enforced "without reservation." *Id.*

In doing so, we believe that the district court did not adequately address the broad policies of deciding the case on the merits where the orderly administration of justice and the integrity of the process have not been permanently frustrated, and of exercising the necessary restraint when dismissal is based on the inherent power. Thus, we reverse its dismissal order. We are confident that the district court's objective of punishing the wrongdoers, deterring similar future conduct, and compensating the defendant can be achieved by a sanction, short of dismissal, tailored more directly to those goals. *See Halaco Engineering Co.,* 843 F.2d at 380–82.

The occasion to consider the disciplining of members of the bar is not a happy one, and the district court's response was understandably stern. We are in full agreement with the district court's expressed concern, and we repeat that our adversary system depends on a most jealous safeguarding of truth and candor. But we also observe that through an outright dismissal, the defendants receive the benefit of a total release from their obligations under the environmental protection laws. This would provide the defendants relief far beyond the harm caused by the government attorneys' improper conduct and would frustrate the resolution on the merits of a case which itself has strong policy implications. Unfortunately, these factors were not adequately considered.

Without suggesting a sanction which is appropriate, we point out that in considering the proper role of the administrative record in this case and the respective burdens of proof, the district court may deny the government the benefit of any portion of the record or the right to claim any expense, which may have been tainted by Caron's misconduct, even if it becomes impossible to assess accurately the extent of that taint. Because of the government's misconduct, the benefit of any doubt must be resolved in the defendants' favor. In *Hazel-Atlas Co.,* for example, where the effect on a judgment of the admission of a fraudulent document could not be accurately assessed, the Court resolved the question against the wrongdoer and vacated the entire judgment. It stated:

Doubtless it is wholly impossible accurately to appraise the influence that the article exerted on the judges. But we do not think the circumstances call for such an attempted appraisal. Hartford's officials and lawyers ... are in no position now to dispute its effectiveness.

322 U.S. at 247, 64 S.Ct. at 1001–02.

Accordingly, we affirm the district court's finding that a breach of ethical conduct occurred, but we vacate the judgment of the district court dismissing the case and remand for the imposition of a sanction short of outright dismissal. Since an award of attorney's fees may be part of the district court's overall calculus in selecting a sanction after further proceedings, we leave for later review, if necessary, any question on whether attorney's fees were appropriately awarded.

AFFIRMED IN PART, REVERSED IN PART, VACATED AND REMANDED.

SOLUTIONS: THE LAWYER SHOULD HAVE, WOULD HAVE, COULD HAVE. . .

We selected this case because the subordinate lawyer knew that the course of conduct was unethical yet stayed essentially silent. This could happen to any new lawyer—even a more experienced one. How do you raise the issue when you might be concerned about losing your job or falling into disfavor with your employer? You can use prospective hindsight ("Let's image we do XYZ or fail to do ABC" and describe the consequences as we discuss in the following Beyond the Cite) or you can focus on protecting the image of the partner (ego is not an unknown trait in the legal profession) "I want you to look your best and this could blow up in our faces"). Or use MR 1.6 (b)(4) and seek advice from an outside lawyer on ethical compliance.

X-Ray Questions

Cognitive science and psychology can offer insights on how lawyers can avoid behaving unethically under the influence of errant authority figures.

BEYOND THE CITE

In their insightful new book, "Beyond the Rules: Behavioral Legal Ethics and Professional Responsibility," Professor Catherine Gage O'Grady and Professor Tigran W. Eldred discuss the "wrongful obedience" experiment of cognitive theorist Stanley Milgram conducted in the early 1970s. Here were its elements:

➤ Milgram's student confederates sought subjects for the experiment. They were told the experiment would deal with memory and learning. The subjects would be paid.

➤ Participants included subjects from both blue-collar backgrounds as well as professional ones. The subjects met the researchers, who were dressed in official looking lab coats, at a research facility.

➤ The job of the subjects were to administer electric shocks to an actor in the next room that the subject could not see but could hear. The shock would be given when the actor gave an incorrect answer on a memory test. The voltage went from 15 volts (described as a "slight shock") to 450 volts (described as a "severe shock").

➤ The researchers would tell the subjects, if they resisted giving further shocks that the subject promised to participate. The actor would cry out for the test at various points. From time to time the unseen actor in the next room would cryout in fabricated pain.

➤ Here though was the key as described in the book: "At 300 volts, (the actor) stopped responding all together and was silent. A session ended only when a participant expressed resistance to four (verbal) prods by the (researcher) or when the subject had pressed the highest switch on the generator, 450 volts, three times."

➤ The factual question: what percentage of the subjects went to 450 volts? Amazingly, 63%. The same results were obtained in numerous replications of the experiment in various parts of the country. But what is really interesting is the huge statistical gap between the ultimate result and those who beforehand said that they would *never* go that far. The lesson: we all, including your authors, very likely underestimate the rate of wrongful obedience. Each of us can do wrong and, well, we do. This is why we inoculate ourselves against wrong doing by courses like PR and by continuing legal education requirements that we study legal ethics on a yearly basis.

Answer these questions the experiments:

(1) Do you think there is a tendency among people to please authority? If so, why? Have you felt that way? What were the situations?

(2) How can new and subordinate lawyers protect themselves from suspending their ethical and moral compass in order not to defer to authority?

(3) Think about which is worse: the subordinate lawyer cannot even see the ethical issue at hand or the lawyer sees the issue but fears speaking up to the boss for fear of losing her job? How can the senior lawyer (which will be the role you will fill someday) make it easier for the subordinate to speak out?

(4) On the Ariely experiments, do you think people, as a whole, think they are more ethical and moral then they truly are? Explain your reasoning.

X-Ray Questions

Do you think it is a valuable trait for a lawyer to be able to question authority? Why or why not? Is it in our nature to not question authority? Why or why not? When was the last time you did it? Or when was the last time you wanted to but decided against it? Why did you make that decision?

BEYOND THE CITE

By: Michael P. Maslanka, *Questioning Authority: How It Can Be Done Effectively*, Texas Lawyer, July 27, 2022.

What is the single hardest concept to teach a law student, a new lawyer, or even a seasoned veteran? Teaching the mindset brave enough to question authority and adept enough to do so effectively. To that end, here are five suggestions.

Riddle me this: What is the single hardest concept to teach a law student, a new lawyer, or even a seasoned veteran? Cross-examination? The Rule Against Perpetuities? How to think like a practicing lawyer, not a tenured professor? No. Here's the answer: teaching the mindset brave enough to question authority and adept enough to do so effectively. To that end, here are five suggestions.

The Socratic Method as Socrates Intended

Whether at a law school or at a firm, a cultural icon that has inflicted incalculable damage on teaching a questioning authority mindset—and continues to do so—is the movie, "The Paper Chase." Recall the establishing shot with Mr. Hart, the student, who is unprepared for class; Professor Kingsfield mocks him; a so-called Socratic dialogue ensues. Professor Kingsfield explains that through this teaching method, he will be "probing" their minds and transforming their "skulls (now) full of mush" into a skull full of legal acumen. But Socrates, in the Apology, envisioned the method as being a two-way dialogue, not a one-way interrogation, with a teacher questioning a student, and a student, in turn, questioning the teacher. Questioning the teacher not merely on holdings and legal conclusions but also, crucially, on the validity and viability of those holdings and conclusions. As Joshua Krook perceptively writes, legal education fails all of us "(by focusing) solely on the reasoning of judges; students learn that a decision is always justified by reference to another decision. Never is the 'end point' or the original conception of (the legal principle), in terms of its derivation from politics, society, morality, (or) social values allowed to be questioned." A self-referential and closed-off loop.

The Real Socratic Method: Law Schools Fail to Understand Why Socrates Asked So Many Questions.

Questioning Mindset Toolbox: All teachers of law—professors, mentors, law firm partners—should use the original Socratic method by asking: what is the rationale undergirding this rule or legal proposition? Does it help fulfill its avowed purpose? What is the result if the rule or proposition is abolished? And should we have a different rule or, perhaps, even a different value sought to be achieved? The Socratic method, as now deployed, is sadly misused for self-aggrandizement or as a bully pulpit (not in a good way), or as a time filler. The legal profession can do better.

Demonstrate Openness to the Questioning Mindset

Walk the talk. Here is one method I used when working with a new and less-experienced lawyer. Cut away to my office.

Me: "So, in working with me, you need to understand the answer to one question: Why do airplanes crash?"

New Lawyer: Silence. Uncomfortable looks. An expression that radiates, "Oh gee."

Me: "I'll tell you. The copilot sees a blinking red light on the console. The less-experienced copilot thinks, 'if something were wrong, the experienced captain would surely know, so I will not ruin my career by saying something.'" And that is why planes crash. You will never be punished for speaking your mind or made to feel small, despite what some of your law school professors did to you, or some senior partner. "Come to me, tell me you see the blinking red light, and we will talk then or make an appointment to do so soon."

Questioning Mindset Toolbox: Why pose this question or something similar? You are investing in our colleagues' ability to think for themselves, and that investment, I promise, will deliver outsized returns.

Engage Others in a Transcendent Purpose

The Stanley Milgram experiments from the 1960s supposedly found that we have a strong tendency to blindly obey authority. Recall the set-up: participants are given the role of "Teacher" who must administer electric shocks to an unseen "Learner" at the direction of a white-coated "Experimenter" whenever the "Learner" errs in an answer to a question. The Teacher, under the direction of the Experimenter, ups the voltage for every incorrect answer. The Experimenter tells the Teacher that the test is a very important study designed to measure memory in the Learner and that the Teacher is making an important contribution to the study of humanity; and that the Teacher plays an integral role in this advancement in education. The result: 65% of the Teachers give the maximum shock despite screams and pleas from behind a wall from the Learner (actually an actor) to please stop. But recent scholarship unearthed Milgram's research notes, and scholars now come to a different lesson. Milgram induced loyalty in the Teachers to the Experimenters through articulating these noble, albeit made-up, goals. As a result, the Learners became "engaged followers," not mindless and cowed drones. (Haslam et al, "Questioning Authority: New Perspectives on

Milgram's 'Obedience' Research and Its Implications for Intergroup Relations," ScienceDirect, 2016).

Questioning Mindset Toolbox: The converse should thus be applicable as well; engaged followers can be developed if the better angels of our nature are tapped into, and that questioning authority is seen not as subversive but rather as a normative value; not as pointless rebellion but rather as productive liberation; not as necessary conformity but rather as useful autonomy.

Truly Understand 'Questioning' and 'Authority'

What does "questioning" mean? It does not mean that you reject outright the teaching of others, which accomplishes nothing of value. Instead, to question authority presupposes that you are seeking an answer, and sometimes you will agree with that answer, and sometimes you will reject it. But you will be thinking for yourself in the process. As Dean Steve Nowicki of Duke University writes, "To question something is to be skeptical. . .Don't believe what you are told simply because someone with presumed authority has told it to you, whether in a lecture or a casebook. . . ." Or, I would add, because a partner in a law firm tells you. We, as lawyers, have an independent duty under our Rules of Professional Conduct to question an instruction that we believe to be ethically wrong. Here is the rule in all of its simplicity: "A lawyer is bound by the Rules of Professional Conduct notwithstanding that the lawyer acted at the direction of another person."

And what is authority? A law firm partner? Check. A law school professor? Check. Cultural authority? You bet. Huckleberry Finn and Jim, a runaway slave, befriended one another. Huck's aunt admonishes him to turn Jim into the authorities. If not, Huck's punishment will be severe: "everlasting fire." (People actually believed this in the 1800s.). Huck struggles with his choice but reflects on friendship and morality. This leads him to question authority in the form of his aunt and society in general. Huck ultimately says to himself, "All right, then, I'll go to hell." Huckleberry Finn would be a credit to the legal profession.

Questioning Mindset Toolbox: Transmit the value of thinking for oneself and explain why it is a value to be cherished, not a burden to be ignored. Recently the head coach of the Baylor Bears football team, Dave Aranda, spoke of the value of this mindset in building a championship program: "(Players say, coach) why are we doing this? Why do we do it this way? We used to do it this way. . . (I just think this type of questioning) allowed the players to take ownership . . . and allowed them to express in games who they had become." There is power in questioning. Sic 'em Bears!

The Absolute 'No' Is for the Absolute End

Questioning authority is not a suicide pact: Say nothing and lose your integrity; say something and lose your job. Here are some nuanced techniques. Use a positive/negative sentence: "While I appreciate the desire to win for the client, we must nevertheless consider the possibility of sanctions for our proposed course of conduct." First, the acknowledgment, "I hear you," then the warning. Or think about using prospective hindsight: "If we now destroy the document as you suggest, we must imagine ourselves standing in front of a federal judge and explaining our action." Or the technique of naming the game with a non-accusatory tone: "Let me see if I understand your request. You want me to bill for time we did not work and then send that bill into the United States mail. Do I understand this correctly?"

Questioning Authority Toolbox: Note that none of these approaches engages in the dead-end proposition of accusing a person of unethical conduct. Only when these forms of questioning authority are unavailing should you resort to the final "no way, no how."

I teach students to "show me, don't tell me." So, here is a time when I failed to question authority. A senior lawyer and myself are representing eight plaintiffs in an age discrimination trial. We are discussing whether to strike a manager at a large company who came to jury selection in a coat and tie. He had been promoted through the blue-collar ranks. I said that we should; the senior lawyer responded to me—rudely and condescendingly—"no, even though he is a manager, he will never forget where he came from." But I know human nature is not that idealized, and the newly minted manager wants to forget his origins and live his new reality. And what did I then say? Not a thing. Crickets. I remained silent. Guess who became the foreperson of the jury? I still profoundly regret my failure to question authority. I put my reluctance to undergo further criticism above my duty to the clients. The lesson: have a bias towards the principled questioning of authority. We owe it to our profession and, on reflection, to ourselves. Your Role If a Judicial Clerk.

Section 2. Your Life Beyond Being a Professional

X-Ray Questions

A famous line of poetry states, "The mind is its own place and in itself can make a heaven of hell or a hell of heaven." Awareness of our mindset can assist a lawyer in developing mental resilience; not merely to bounce back from a setback, but to come back even stronger.

BEYOND THE CITE

By: Michael P. Maslanka, *Mindsets and Mental Health,* Texas Lawyer, July 18, 2021.

Law practice is the loneliest profession; having the right mindset can head off lots of trouble, says Michael P. Maslanka, an associate professor of law at the University of North Texas at Dallas College of Law.

Mental health challenges are on par with physical ones, although the fix is harder to detect and fix because itis often unseen or unrecognized or—if apparent—stigmatized. What to do? The following are not designed to turn the reader into a therapist. They are not designed to help a seriously troubled lawyer or law student needing specialized assistance. Instead, these mindsets are offered as prophylactics, vaccines of a sort, inoculating us all upfront from incipient troubles. Cures and remediations are fine; prevention and avoidance are better.

And know that the latter is needed and needed now. In March 2018, researchers published in the Harvard Business Review that law practice is the loneliest profession, calling the result "not surprising given the known high prevalence of depression among lawyers." The result:" loneliness has the same effect as 15cigarettes a day "on overall health. And that is our future as well, as Professor Tiffany D. Atkins reports in *"#For the Culture: Gen Z and the Future of Legal Education,"* Volume 26, Michigan Journal of Race and Law, (2020) depicts a stark future for Gen Z students (born between 1995 and 2010)—especially students of color—now filling up law school seats and already "suffering from insecurity, depression, (and) anxiety." Why? The life promised to them in social media and the life delivered to them by reality. This cognitive conflict flows over into the practice of law.

Here, then, are the Five Mindsets. So, roll up your metaphorical sleeve for a painless jab.

Mindset No.1: *Eschew Comparison*

I am a teenager watching a golf tournament on our black and white TV. (Yes, much is lost in translation.) The winner—I think was Tom Watson—says at a press conference that his competition is not the other golfers. Oh no. "When I'm out there, it's just me versus the course." I tell this story to students who despair of becoming the good ole girl lawyer, or the money-making rainmaker, or the fabulously articulate trial lawyer. Yes, learn from others but do not compare yourself to others. Our job as senior lawyers and thus teachers, by the way, is not to create mini-mes but rather to facilitate them into becoming better versions of themselves. (Reminds us of Oscar Wilde, does it not? "Be yourself. Everybody else is already taken."

Mindset No. 2: *Reframe, 24/7*

Unlike the movie line, "always be closing," this message is positive, not exploitive. It is about the power of adaptability. It is a message of liberation. Professor Heidi K. Brown nails these concepts in *"Law School Grades Are Not Your Story—You Are Your Story."* (ABA, "Student Lawyer," March 2020) Poor grade? Reframe from defeat to opportunity, from damning judgment to useful intelligence. Perhaps what the student thought would be their life work is, well, just not their true calling or mission. If so, there is time to recalibrate and reorient. Thoreau was right, "it's not what you look at that matters. . . ." Why? Because what matters is what "you see." Embrace perspective, hold it close.

Mindset No. 3: *Values, Not Drives*

WW II leaves the world devastated. A brave voice speaks out against the prevailing wisdom that man is pushed by drives. The voice is Viktor Frankel's. Having survived three concentration camps, he comes to believe that man—to be fulfilled—needs a transcendent meaning to life. In short, we are pulled by values, and those values must be centered not on our needs but on the needs of others. (Of course, there are limits. One of my well-meaning doctors suggested that I get a pet which, well, is not a good concept for me and, more importantly, the pet.) We pick whether we are pushed by our drives or pulled by our values. Here is Frankel: "Between stimulus and response, there is a space. In that space is our power to choose our response. In our response lies our growth and our freedom." Utilizing that space lifts us out of depression, feelings of helplessness, and lack of self-worth.

Mindset No. 4: *Trust planning, not plans*

That's General Eisenhower and his insight that plans go askew, but that the knowledge they generate illuminates our way. Planning is based on studying and reading and reflecting. In short, on deliberation. Law schools can be at the forefront, as we see with Professor Bridgette A. Carr whose course at the University of Michigan Law School, "Designing a Fulfilling Life in Law," was launched last year. Medical students learn by acronyms, and so should law students. Here is one of hers in order to remember to live a FULL life:" F: Find your joy, purpose, values, energy; U: Build an Umbrella to protect you from life's storms; L: Create high-quality Linkages to sustain you; L: Develop your Lane to move forward. Stanford Law does likewise, as you can read in "Designing a Legal Career" by Sharon Driscoll, Stanford Lawyer (November 22, 2019), where the message is to have a bias towards action in your career; if you do, good things will happen; if not, well, then they won't. And for solos read a book by Texas lawyer, Mike Whelan, Jr., "Lawyer Forward: Finding Your Place in the Future of Law," in which he attributes lawyer depression to the structure of the practice (the "churn" which is based on endless billable hour after billable hour until lawyer life ends) and proposes two better replacements. Change your practice's structure, change your life's outcomes.

Mindset No 5: *Resilience, not Resignation*

The final mindset is, in a way, the most crucial. It is summed up by Seneca, the Roman thinker, who taught us that each day is a lifetime. Each and every day for our entire lives, the universe gives us a wonderful gift: the chance today to be a better person; to aspire differently; to extend help to others, than we were the day before. Knowing this we can summon up our resilience, not to bounce back like we were before, but better than we were before.

Mindsets are small candles. Think about lighting one.

X-Ray Questions

The following article states that a mere 4.7% of lawyers are black. Why? Do you agree with the author's view that the notion of "professionalism" is part of the problem? Why or why not? Consider, as she does, the new MR 8.4(g) which provides that a lawyer should not:

(g)   engage in conduct that the lawyer knows or reasonably should know is harassment or discrimination on the basis of race, sex, religion, national origin, ethnicity, disability, age, sexual orientation, gender identity, marital status or socioeconomic status in conduct related to the practice of law. This paragraph does not limit the ability of a lawyer to accept, decline or withdraw from a representation in accordance with Rule 1.16. This paragraph does not preclude legitimate advice or advocacy consistent with these Rules.

How does this this Rule fit into the way that she views the world? The rule, in theory, prohibits discriminatory conduct by lawyers, including toward other lawyers. But in reality, can it stop all problematic conduct? The author notes (among other things) that there is a cost to expecting people to endure repeated microaggressions and to nevertheless remain "professional" at all times.

BEYOND THE CITE

By: Leah Goodridge, *Professionalism as a Racial Construct*, originally printed in 69 UCLA L. REV. DISC. (Law Meets World) 38 (2022).

Introduction

On a Friday afternoon, I appeared with a colleague in New York City Housing Court on behalf of a client in an eviction proceeding. Aside from the unfortunate nature of the case, it was supposed to be a routine court appearance. But Housing Court is known to be unpredictable, and that afternoon, it lived up to its reputation. While appearing before the judge, opposing counsel—a white woman—yelled at me, interrupted me, talked over me, sighed and rolled her eyes when I spoke. Before this appearance, we had only seen each other in passing. Dumbfounded, I spent half of the time making legal arguments and the other half wondering whether my presence in court, as a Black woman, was the main factor in the attorney's scorn. Curiosity inched closer to certainty when I learned that my junior colleague, who is white, appeared by herself on the same case just weeks before. We danced around it—"That was ridiculous!" "Oh man, Housing Court"—until we finally made our way to: "She wasn't like that with me. She treated me with respect."

That weekend, still reeling from humiliation, I reimagined the court appearance. Would I have appeared too sensitive if I said that opposing counsel's conduct is racist? Is it professional to use the court's time to address racism and misogynoir when the negotiations for my client are still in progress? The answers were unclear, but what was certain was that if I had behaved like opposing counsel, I would have been seen as unprofessional and aggressive, and likely admonished by the judge. Professionalism was a one way street—it applied to me but not my opposing counsel.

I wanted to scream. I wanted to tell both the judge and opposing counsel that they upheld systems of racial hierarchy. I did not. Instead, I shouted words on paper.

These words are my screams.

I am one of the 4.7 percent of Black attorneys in the United States and have been practicing law for the past decade. In this Essay, I question whether professionalism is a tool to subjugate people of color in the legal field. Professionalism encompasses: (1) communication style, (2) interpersonal skills, (3) appearance, (4) how well a person adheres to the standards of their field and employer, and (5) efficacy at the job. Through this analysis, professionalism is revealed to be a racial construct.

The canon of Critical Race Theory shifted the understanding of racism from intentional hatred by individual actors to a set of systems and institutions that produce racial inequality and subordination. Criminal justice is a system of laws and individuals who enforce them. While everyone is beholden to the laws, the criminal justice system disproportionately ensnares people of color within its grasp, resulting in harsher punishment. Similarly, professionalism is a standard with a set of beliefs about how one should operate in the workplace. While professionalism seemingly applies to everyone, it is used to widely police and regulate people of color in various ways including hair, tone, and food scents. Thus, it is not merely that there is a double standard in how professionalism applies; it is that the standard itself is based on a set of beliefs grounded in racial subordination and white supremacy.

In Part I, I examine three main aspects of legal professionalism: (1) threshold to withstand bias and discrimination, (2) selective offense, and (3) the reasonable person standard. Each Subpart starts with a day in my life as an attorney to illustrate how these elements play out. Professionalism in the legal industry often carries the silent expectation that people of color, women, people with disabilities and people who identify as LGBTQIA have a high threshold to withstand discrimination. Professionalism as a racial construct is not limited to attorneys and paralegals—it also extends to individuals participating in the legal process. For example, Black people have been excluded from serving on a jury because they "failed to make eye contact, lived in a poor part of town, had served in the military, had a hyphenated last name, displayed bad posture, were sullen, disrespectful or talkative, had long hair, wore a beard"—many of which are under the guise of professionalism.[7] In addition, I discuss how harmful and racist behavior in the legal profession are normalized to the point that challenges to such conduct are seen as unprofessional. Lastly, I analyze how the law functions in a colorblind fashion, having the effect of making any emphasis or focus on race seem impolite or—unprofessional. In Part II, I explore recommendations of how to deconstruct professionalism as a tool of white supremacy.

I.   Constructing the Concept of Professionalism in the Legal Profession

A.   Bias and Discrimination Threshold

In June 2018, a group of legal service organizations sent a letter to the Supervising and Administrative Judges of Housing Court. Typewritten words on paper laid bare the experiences that many tenant attorneys and paralegals endured for years: over eighty examples of alleged bias, microaggressions and incivility which took place in Bronx Housing Court by landlord attorneys, court clerks, officers and judges. The purpose of the letter was to demand accountability. As a result, the Supervising Judge convened a meeting for tenant and landlord attorneys to discuss bias and incivility.

More than anything, this meeting revealed that there were at least two perceptions of what it meant to be a professional attorney. In one view, an attorney's inability to laugh and move along from microaggressions indicated that they were too unpolished or hypersensitive for the field. In the other, an attorney was race and equity conscious and when those norms were eschewed, readily called for accountability to create a workable and inclusive environment. During the meeting, it became clear that the former had been the standard for many years.

Professionalism was based on the notion that one withstood microaggressions and bias with grace and lightheartedness. The higher the threshold one had to tolerate bias, the more polished the attorney or paralegal appeared. This was particularly the case for women, people of color, LGBTQIA people, and people with disabilities. Professionalism as a racial construct manifests itself in two ways. First, that professionalism is measured by how well a person adapts to a hostile work environment is in of itself a racial construct because that system is built for people of color to fail. Second, that professionalism incorporates the ideology to have a thick skin manifests as a racial construct because even the definition of thick skin aligns with who holds the most power. For example, if attorneys on the receiving end of microaggressions, bias, and racism are considered sensitive for not laughing along, why are the attorneys who engage in harmful behavior not also considered sensitive for their inability to handle criticism about their conduct? Thus, even in defining tolerance, whose feelings are prioritized and validated and whose are minimized within the context of professionalism shapes the narrative that people of color—not their white peers—need to develop thicker skin.

It was not coincidental that this meeting took place almost a year after the passage of the right to counsel law, which provides low-income tenants the right to free legal representation. With the city's investment, there was a new legion of attorneys and paralegals of color in court that stood apart from the mostly white male landlord bar, many of whom had practiced in housing court for a decade of more prior to the demographic shift.

These views on professionalism were not neatly cut along landlord and tenant attorney lines, or even by race. There were larger issues at play here. In the American capitalist economy, enduring a toxic and abusive work environment can be a rite of passage in some workplaces. Even in the sphere of public interest law, a gripe about the astronomical case dockets could be met with quips that "back in my day, I had two times as many cases." In both the nonprofit industrial complex and law firms, the measure of a good attorney was not only how much of an impact they had on their clients' lives, but also the quantity of cases they were able to handle at once. In fact, some would say that a high number of cases is the impact. Beyond enduring microaggressions, racism and other discriminatory behavior, there seemed to be a wider expectation to tolerate abusive practices that was woven into the fabric of the American workforce.

In an attempt to navigate Housing Court better, I sought guidance from Black attorneys whom I admired and revered. They all practiced in different areas of law for over a decade. Their advice all started with "Don't let them make you look unprofessional." I spoke with at least ten Black attorneys with decades of experience in courtrooms and every single one understood and iterated that despite white opposing counsels or peers acting in the most inappropriate and unprofessional manner, I was the one who would look unprofessional if I came close to or matched their behavior. Professionalism did not apply to them, but it applied to me. Moreover, since racism permeated the profession, consistently complaining or challenging it would not necessarily indicate that it was pervasive; instead it would likely reflect that I was not cut out to be an attorney.

None of these attorneys advised me to file grievances. Racism is a reality and dealing with it meant survival. Survival meant avoiding direct challenges to racism which could lead to negative career consequences. Reflecting on their words, it became clear to me that they began their legal careers at a time when there were even fewer Black attorneys, and in the aftermath of the Civil Rights Act and other laws. There had been so much fight to get their foot in the door that appearing unnerved was not an option. Most advised indirect ways to challenge macro- or microaggressions—speedy, humorous comebacks in response to certain situations to assert dominance and show I was impermeable to anyone's discomfort of my existence. If I was mistaken for my client or any other Black person, a response could be, "Well, I can tell you apart from Brad Pitt. Now, where's the rent breakdown, Charles?"

I followed their approach, but its effectiveness quickly wore off. At the time, I was a new staff attorney making $50,000 with a docket of nearly forty eviction cases. I was navigating my own emotions of sometimes overhearing in Spanish in court "I'm getting evicted but at least I'm not Black," and dealing with helping many of those same tenants navigate the bureaucratic maze of government agencies. The job presented a rude awakening that the role of staff attorney also included hidden duties such as social worker, government agency advocate, and case administrative coordinator. Given the breadth of the position, I did not have the energy or bandwidth to engage in witty banter with opposing counsel during routine negotiations—it felt like playing the sassy Black woman and providing a form of entertainment where I was not the one amused.

Moreover, the societal expectation of Black forgiveness seemed to be endemic to having a thick skin in the workplace. Fear of Black rage spurred vagrancy and loitering laws, after all.[15] Black forgiveness soothed anxiety that there was not any rage, thus hug your brother's murderer, proclaim a church bomber has been forgiven—be gracious and dignified. The question remained: Why did I have to build my tolerance threshold to acclimate to a hostile environment but the people creating that environment could remain the same?

Perhaps the greatest irony is that the threshold standard is seen in the remedy for discrimination itself. The American Bar Association adopted a rule that incorporated discrimination as misconduct. Under 8.4(g), it is professional misconduct for a lawyer to:

> [E]ngage in conduct that the lawyer knows or reasonably should know is harassment or discrimination on the basis of race, sex, religion, national origin, ethnicity, disability, age, sexual orientation, gender identity, marital status or socioeconomic status in conduct related to the practice of law.

Most states have adopted the ABA's rules on professional conduct, thereby incorporating a measure for disciplinary procedures. The Chair of the Committee on Standards of Attorney Conduct of the New York State Bar Association stated: "Although Rule 8.4(g) does not expressly state that a complainant must exhaust administrative and judicial remedies before filing a discrimination complaint with a grievance committee, that is how the rule operates on a practical level." The expectation to exhaust all remedies before filing a complaint under the rule effectively operates to force individuals to withstand bias and discrimination for a longer period of time than they would if they immediately sought relief. The abusive conduct is deprioritized, and the burden is placed on the complainant to prove that they tolerated a sufficient amount of it.

One of the main mistakes of the legal profession is to approach bias and discrimination complaints as personality conflicts. For example, sexual harassment in a legal office may be seen as two attorneys who do not get along rather than one lawyer harassing the other. Since attorneys, particularly from a marginalized group, are expected to have a high threshold to absorb bias, the imbalance of power in these situations may be ignored. The same happens in the courtroom. In my case when opposing counsel yelled and talked over me, the judge kindly asked her at least eight times to allow me to finish my sentence. There was no admonishment: "If you do not stop, I will hold you accountable, hold you in contempt, or stop the proceeding." Instead, it appeared as two attorneys sparring during a case rather than abusive and unprofessional behavior that should be addressed to prevent further disruption. Treating racist, misogynistic, transphobic, or other discriminatory behavior as two people in disagreement equalizes behavior where there is often an imbalance of power. The effect is that it allows the decisionmaker—whether it be a judge or head of a legal office—to avoid taking responsibility for stopping the unprofessional conduct.

B.   Selective Offense: Constructing What Is Unprofessional

In a meeting, a white male colleague called me derogatory names. I reacted the way many do during an attack: I froze. This behavior was not new for him and as it wore on, my bias threshold reached its capacity. Later that day, I challenged his behavior openly as misogynistic and racist. He was clearly unprofessional—or so I thought. As I sat in various conversations processing while simultaneously explaining what happened, reality slowly sunk in that his behavior was not offensive to everyone. Lips moved, but I only heard garbled words in twos: "team player," "get along," "minor bump," "take personally," "right approach." These words pieced together an ugly truth—one that my elders long warned. Some are more offended by a Black woman challenging racism than by a white person perpetuating it.

Selective offense is the normalization of racist, misogynistic, ableist or otherwise discriminatory behavior while the denunciation of said behavior is seen as disruptive. For example, this is seen when employees sit in meetings for months or years with a known problematic colleague who engages in harmful racist, misogynistic, or transphobic behavior and take no action to meaningfully admonish or halt the behavior; yet the same employees are suddenly—or selectively—offended when someone from a marginalized group challenges the problematic employee's behavior. This manifests professionalism as a racial construct because the problematic employee who engages in racist, misogynistic, or transphobic behavior is not deemed unprofessional, yet the tone, approach, and timing of the person who challenges said behavior is so scrutinized.

There are four stages to selective offense. First, people minimize and fail to admonish the harmful behavior. Second, people impute charm or innocence to the harmful behavior. Even the most clear-cut inappropriate behavior could be likened to humor or quirk. Not deemed harmful, it is instead attributed to the personality of the person perpetuating the harm. The distinction between personality and behavior is crucial because many believe a person can correct another's behavior—but not their personality. Third, people accept the harmful behavior. Fourth, any challenges to the harmful behavior are seen as a personal character attack rather than rectifying harm.

During my tenure in the legal field, I have observed how these four stages unfold, particularly when the person engaging in harmful conduct is a white male. Once in conversation with attorneys, one mentioned a white male judge who was known to have a moody disposition. He remarked with a chuckle, "We call him Grumpy Grandpa." The judge's disgruntled disposition was transformed into a charming quirk that humanized him. For all intents and purposes, his behavior was unprofessional. A judge's demeanor is essential to the role, especially when interfacing with litigants who are traumatized or stressed by the eviction process. Yet not only was the harmful effect ignored, it was turned into an attribute of his personality. There is also another layer as to why this harmful behavior is attributed to charm or humor. The act of humiliating, regulating, or rebuking people of color, especially in a public setting, has historically been a form of entertainment. From lynching as an American pastime to interactions with the police to degrading interactions in the workplace, inflicting pain on people of color is a public sport. Thus, when a person perpetuates this harm, they are seen as humorous because their actions are amusing for some to watch.

This begged the question: If a person of color or woman judge came in every day for years with a grouchy disposition, would they also be likened to charming or would they be perceived as unprofessional and temperamental? Conversely, I have also observed some judges of color attempt to implement order in their courtrooms by chiding attorneys who engage in conduct that is racist, misogynistic, or otherwise discriminatory. In response, their judicial temperament and bias threshold are scrutinized as much or more than the attorneys' harmful conduct. It is yet another example of how inappropriate behavior is normalized.

An additional contributing factor to selective offense is the use of public interest work as cover for racism or bias. Why challenge a person's harmful behavior when they are supposedly doing the work of social or racial justice? The "my best friend is Black" defense to allegations of racism becomes "my clients are Black," "my staff is Black," or "my courtroom litigants are Black." Proximity to people of color or any marginalized group is weaponized to inoculate the person engaging in harmful conduct. And so it becomes offensive and even unprofessional when a person identifies racism against such a person. The spoken truth: "I'm not like the virulent racists on our TV screen." The unspoken truth: "I could be like them thus I deserve recognition for even moderately attempting to be racially aware."

C.   Justice Is Blind and the Reasonable Person Is White

On June 1, 2020, I learned that police officers killed a Black man in Minneapolis. Against my better judgment, I watched the video of the murder circulating on social media. The video depicted hatred, violence, and a visual display of antiblackness.

During the first days after George Floyd's murder, I questioned whether everyone watched the same video. There was unusual silence in the American workplace, including the legal sector. I am part of many different communities in the legal profession such as working groups, boards, and coalitions. Routine business emails continued. Since I spent years internalizing the bias threshold discussed in Subpart I.A, I began to wonder whether I was unprofessional for my inability to complete work due to trauma. I was jarred back to reality in an unexpected way. A former client of mine, a Black woman, emailed me: "Ms. Goodridge, with all that's going on, I just wanted to see if you were okay." I had been operating on the lie that I was justified in ignoring the pangs of anxiety quietly roaring inside of me while I continued working to protect my clients. In five words—"with all that's going on"—my client forced me to confront the underbelly of American racism. In that moment of vulnerability, I replied that I was not okay. She responded with a lengthy Bible passage and words of encouragement that we will get through this.

I called Black colleagues and friends who also worked in public interest law in various positions to inquire if they were experiencing the same silence. I was not alone. One friend said, "I just saw a Black man get lynched on television and people are sending emails about service and motions. What is going on?" In almost all instances that I knew of, legal organizations were mostly silent until a person of color raised that the murder of George Floyd required more than a cursory mention—this was a racial reckoning.

Many people adhere to the axiom that discussion of politics in the workplace must be avoided in order to maintain a harmonious environment. In the legal profession, however, it goes beyond politics. Lawyers have been taught for centuries that thinking like a lawyer means putting all emotions aside. Divesting of emotion for the sake of legal reasoning in and of itself is an exercise of privilege. For example, law students have been forced to complete exam questions that reenact situations such as Michael Brown's murder in Ferguson, Missouri. Even the way law students are taught to view defendants and their circumstances is through the narrow prism of the reasonable person standard. The reasonable person is supposedly a raceless and genderless blank slate which parallels with the ideology that justice is blind. However, stripping identity from the reasonable person means that whiteness becomes the norm and lens which legal advocates look through. Though fictional and imaginary, the reasonable person in "its present manifestation, applied within the trappings of the past, becomes less reflective of the population that will soon become the majority, becomes less legitimate if law's purpose is to serve the People."

Even in antiracist, progressive spaces, I observed how the law was envisioned as motion-writing, research, and oral arguments while racial and social justice were ancillary. Activities such as attending a protest related to the attorney's field or engaging in racial justice learning were seen as additional tasks to the legal work—even though they helped an attorney to have cultural competency to better understand their clients. I also observed that courts often inferred a dichotomy between the fields of housing and fair housing. Housing denotes Housing Court, which typically handles eviction and repair cases. Fair housing applies to cases pertaining to antidiscrimination laws such as the Fair Housing Act. In my experience, housing operates in a more colorblind fashion than fair housing. Some legal organizations have a racial justice best practice to name the client's race in legal motions. Other than the mention of a client's race in a motion, race or the role it plays is rarely emphasized in housing cases, even in a practice where people of color comprise the majority of tenants facing eviction, the effects of gentrification and systemic racism. In contrast, a client's disability, income and contours of reasonable accommodation are more readily understood. I noticed that the actual teaching of race discrimination was not common and often referred to as a fair housing issue, even if the legal claims pertaining to race were squarely in legal codes related to eviction. This, of course, is a function of how the law and the reasonable person centers whiteness.

This occurs in other areas as well. After the murder of George Floyd, many legal institutions such as law firms, courts, and legal service organizations provided ongoing antiracism initiatives for their employees. Though there are multiple ways to discuss antiracism, equity, and inclusion, I noticed that in many instances, the framing focused almost entirely on white allyship. This meant that there were only rudimentary discussions of racism, (centering questions like: What does racism look like?) which did not allow for a more nuanced understanding of concepts like colorism, featurism, intraracial violence, and intersectional identities. In addition, the tailoring of racial justice education for a white audience often resulted in examining race only through a Black and white binary. This excluded other racial groups such as Asian American and Pacific Islander and Native American. As a result, the only way for people of color in those rooms to participate was to be of service to the learning experience of their white peers rather than to process their own pain or even learn themselves. This functions to make the purpose of the presence of marginalized groups to be useful to the education of their white peers.

In fact, when I later asked non-Black people why there was stifling silence when the news first showed the murder, the responses were: "I did not know what to say," "I did not feel I had license to speak because I am not Black," "I thought it might be impolite to raise this topic at work," and "I did not think it was related to our work of eviction." Attorneys who represent people of color everyday still felt they did not have license to talk about race. This is a systemic reflection of how legal practice functions in a largely colorblind fashion.

II. Accountability: Deconstructing Professionalism as a Racial Construct

After laying out my experiences and thoughts on professionalism as a racial construct, it is time for you to take action. The first step is to absorb this Essay in its entirety and identify what your role has been: target, bystander, accomplice, challenger, or perpetuator of professionalism as a racial construct. If it is difficult to identify your role, ask yourself how you are reacting to this Essay. Are you defensive? Ready to share it privately to an individual colleague? Ready to share it publicly to all of your colleagues? Or are you reticent about sharing this Essay with colleagues because you believe it will negatively impact your career? Will you ignore this Essay entirely? How you react to this Essay—the experiences of a Black woman attorney speaking on professionalism as a tool for white supremacy—may correlate with the role you play in challenging it within your own institution.

Next, send the Essay to family or friends to discuss ways that you can (further) challenge professionalism as a racial construct. The basis of professionalism as a racial construct is the belief that the racial hierarchy which produces the phenomenon will remain the same and that practitioners will adapt to it rather than challenge it. Since it has been deeply inculcated into the legal practice and American workforce, these conversations may prove difficult and enlightening because fear of change undergirds much of the perpetuation of professionalism as a racial construct.

The next step is to send this Essay to your colleagues for a discussion at the next staff meeting. You can discuss the Essay generally or discuss the Subparts over multiple meetings. The main question should be: How does professionalism as a racial construct manifest at this institution?

Moving forward, in order to disrupt professionalism as a racial construct, you must name it by using the framework in this Essay to identify the conduct as it happens. For example, you can say:

Why are you so bothered that Jane, a Black woman, called out an attorney for his racist conduct but you do not have this same reaction towards John, a white man, who still cannot correctly pronounce the names of people of color after ten years of working here? This seems like selective offense.

Your Honor, opposing counsel has interrupted me several times and there has been no warning of contempt or forcing them to leave the courtroom. Are my client and I expected to silently endure this—a high bias threshold—during this proceeding?

Respondent is Chinese American and lives in the Soho section of New York. The area has historically been comprised of 70 percent Asian American and Pacific Islanders; however in the last decade, that population has drastically declined due to gentrification, redlining and displacement. This eviction case is not divorced from that. Respondent would like to remain in her community.

In writing this Essay, I had an internal tug of war in speaking about my experiences and those of many people of color in the legal profession. I struggled with the reality that some will be more offended by reading the truth of professionalism as a racial construct on these pages than the fact that it exists in the halls of courthouses, law firms and legal organizations. I almost quelled my own voice and the fire within. Then I remembered the court appearance in 2020, after George Floyd's murder, where the Black judge and I both had weary eyes which met, for a moment, as opposing counsel rattled on about the eviction moratorium. I remembered brunch with friends when they spoke about being the first generation of Black, Latinx, and Asian immigrant parents and internalizing the bias threshold—sacrifices their parents made to come to this country meant ignoring and tolerating racism at work. I remembered the many times I watched people of color shy away from staunch racially progressive positions under a belief that disassociation would help them appear more professional. I remembered the conversations with relatives, friends, and colleagues of color, venting and processing a racist incident and in determining how to respond, the pendulum swinging between comfort of white peers, self-respect, and rage. And I remembered using chemicals to destroy and straighten my natural hair during job interviews in law school in the hopes of increasing my chances of securing employment. I remembered all of these contours of professionalism as a racial construct. And I remembered my own duty to disrupt the system and get in good trouble.

X-Ray Questions

A lawyer can have a rewarding career and a fulfilling personal life. Here is a farewell to a lawyer who did both. You can do it, too.

BEYOND THE CITE

By: Neil Genzlinger, *Susan Rosenblatt, Who Took On Big Tobacco, Dies at 70*, N.Y. Times, Dec. 4, 2021.

Susan Rosenblatt, who with her husband and law partner, Stanley Rosenblatt, took on Big Tobacco in a Florida case that seemed an absurd mismatch for their small firm, but that resulted in a record $144.8 billion jury award in favor of people sickened by cigarettes, died on Nov. 14 in Houston. She was 70.

Her death, at MD Anderson Cancer Center, was confirmed by her son David Rosenblatt, who said the cause was acute myeloid leukemia.

Ms. Rosenblatt, who lived in Miami Beach, was the quieter side of the Rosenblatt firm; in the headline-making tobacco case and other prominent lawsuits, Stanley Rosenblatt did much of the in-court presenting and after-court news conferencing. But it was Ms. Rosenblatt's legal scholarship—the research she did, the briefs she wrote—that provided the ammunition that made their successes possible.

"I always would say I didn't have a dream team, I had Susan," Mr. Rosenblatt said in a phone interview.

That dream team (which also included a small support staff) was never more challenged than by the case the Rosenblatts filed in 1994 against R.J. Reynolds and other tobacco companies on behalf of seven smokers—one of whom, Dr. Howard A. Engle, was the pediatrician for most of the

Rosenblatts' nine children and became the lead plaintiff. The case was certified as a class action representing all Florida smokers, a group that encompassed hundreds of thousands of people.

The case, one of a number being pursued at the time against the industry by states and individuals, dragged on for years. In 1996, when the biggest of those cases, a national class-action suit, was thrown out by a federal appellate panel in New Orleans, Mr. Rosenblatt told The New York Times, "Now it's up to Ma and Pa Kettle."

He and his wife pressed on with the Engle case, arguing that the industry had knowingly addicted smokers and failed to warn them adequately about the dangers of their products.

In 2000, a jury awarded several representative plaintiffs $12.7 million in compensatory damages, then followed that up with a stunning award of punitive damages to the whole class: almost $145 billion, the largest such award in history.

The award didn't stand; in 2003 a Florida appeals panel threw it out, finding, among other things, that the case should not have been declared a class action because each smoker's case is unique. But the Rosenblatts' efforts weren't wasted: In 2006 the Florida Supreme Court ruled that individuals who wanted to pursue cases could invoke some of the original jury's findings, including that smoking causes lung cancer, that nicotine in cigarettes is addictive and that the cigarette companies concealed information about smoking's health effects.

Individual suits, known as the Engle progeny cases, have been working through the Florida courts ever since, some successfully and some not. Mr. Rosenblatt said the legacy of his and his wife's work was the precedent.

"The fraud, the conspiracy—there's a record now of just how evil the tobacco industry had been all those years," he said.

Susan Goldman was born on Jan. 5, 1951, in Brooklyn. Her parents, Sol and Shirley (Kaslow) Goldman, operated a real estate business together.

When Susan was about 10, the family moved to Miami Beach. Academically, she was a prodigy, enrolling at the University of Miami at 13 and graduating in 1968 with a bachelor's degree in economics. She graduated from the university's law school in 1972. She received a master of laws degree in 1978.

She and Mr. Rosenblatt married in 1980. She maintained her own appellate practice until her growing family took precedence.

"But after three children, I really was bored," she told The Miami Herald in 1996. "I'm not the type to go out with girlfriends to lunch."

So she began working with her husband, even as their family continued to grow.

"I was very fortunate to have easy pregnancies," she told The Herald. "And the kind of work I do is reading cases, reading depositions, preparing briefs, which I could do at home in bed."

Although the Ma and Pa Kettle self-description was apt in some ways, the Rosenblatts were hardly neophytes when they took on the tobacco companies. They had won significant awards for plaintiffs in a number of cases. Most notably, they had already taken on the tobacco industry in another case, representing airline flight attendants who argued that their health had been damaged by secondhand smoke in the days when smoking was allowed on airplanes. That case, filed in 1991, ended in 1997 with a settlement in which the cigarette companies agreed to pay$300 million for the study of tobacco-related diseases.

Ms. Rosenblatt said that she had been reluctant to take on Big Tobacco—"I thought it was chasing windmills," she told The Times in 2000. But, her husband said, she came around and nudged him ahead, knowing he'd get a kick out of deposing the tobacco executives he had come to revile.

"I think she was humoring me," he said. " 'Take the depositions of these guys and have some fun, and it's not going to go anywhere.' And it took over our life."

When the Engle case went ahead, the tobacco industry, as it had in other cases, tried to bury its opponents in motions and challenges, hoping to exhaust the lawyers and the plaintiffs. During the trial itself, which stretched for almost two years, the companies would sometimes bring in skilled lawyers just to examine a single witness or argue single motion, Mr. Rosenblatt said, while he relied on his wife.

"Sometimes, the only thing I'd use to cross-examine those witnesses was what Susan would have prepared for me," he said. And while he was cross-examining, she would be working on what he needed the next day.

If Mr. Rosenblatt drew most of the attention, Ms. Rosenblatt was, as The Chicago Sun-Times described her in 2000, "the expert on the law balancing his expertise in front of the jury, the worrier compared with his slouching nonchalance, the detail person balancing his big-picture view."

In addition to her husband and their son David, Ms. Rosenblatt is survived by two other sons, Joshua and Moshe; six daughters, Miriam Hoffman, Rachel Gdanski, Rebecca Assaraf, Jaclyn Richter, Rina Kleiner and Sharon Franco; a brother, Alan Goldman; a sister, Ruth Schwager; and 30 grandchildren.

Busy as they were, the Rosenblatts, who were Orthodox Jews, never worked on the Sabbath, yet Ms. Rosenblatt sometimes lamented that she spent so much time on cases at the expense of home life. Mr. Rosenblatt, though, said there was a philosophy behind their domestic madness.

"Susan felt, and I agreed with her, that the most important thing parents can do is set an example," he said.

Ms. Hoffman, the couple's eldest daughter, said one bit of family lore merged Ms. Rosenblatt's legal expertise and parenting skills. At one point, she said, her mother acquired a used mini-school bus—yellow, of course— to transport the brood here and there. A Miami Beach neighbor complained that parking a yellow school bus in a residential neighborhood was a violation of city code. Ms. Rosenblatt, Ms. Hoffman said, convinced an administrative judge that if the bus weren't yellow, it would be in compliance. So she had the thing painted green.

"That was my mom," Ms. Hoffman said by email. "She always had a special way of doing things. Unlike anyone else."

Section 3.   Losing Your Way/Finding Your Way

Cases and Materials

X-Ray Questions (*Gellene*)

The defendant was a famous bankruptcy lawyer who went to federal prison. What crimes did he commit? What was his motive? How was he blinded to basic rules of ethics? Often the issue of an ethics violation is not about complex and convoluted schemes of a shady nature but rather about violating the basic ethical norms of business behavior (think of Enron and how the crime was taking losses and placing them in an offshore account in order to inflate Enron's profits and thus to inflate its stock price). Consider what the court says regarding the integrity of the judicial system and the importance of maintaining the same. Finally, note how the falsification of his bar admissions played out in his trial. What lesson do you take from this?

United States of America v. John G. Gellene

United States Court of Appeals, Seventh Circuit, 1999.
182 F.3d 578.

RIPPLE, CIRCUIT JUDGE.

John G. Gellene, a partner at the law firm of Milbank Tweed Hadley & McCloy ("Milbank") in New York, represented the Bucyrus-Erie Company ("Bucyrus") in its Chapter 11 bankruptcy. Mr. Gellene filed in the bankruptcy court a sworn declaration that was to include all of his firm's connections to the debtor, creditors, and any other parties in interest. The declaration failed to list the senior secured creditor and related parties. Mr. Gellene was charged with two counts of knowingly and fraudulently making a false material declaration in the Bucyrus bankruptcy case, in violation of 18 U.S.C. § 152, and one count of using a document while under oath, knowing that it contained a false material declaration, in violation of 18 U.S.C. § 1623. Although Mr. Gellene admitted that he had used bad judgment in concluding that the representations did not need to be disclosed, he asserted that he had no fraudulent intent. After a six-day trial, on March 3, 1998, the jury returned guilty verdicts against Mr. Gellene on all three counts. Mr. Gellene was sentenced to 15 months of imprisonment on each count, to run concurrently, and was fined $15,000.

I

BACKGROUND

A.   The Bucyrus Bankruptcy Proceedings

Bucyrus, a manufacturer of mining equipment based in South Milwaukee, Wisconsin, had retained Milbank to represent it in general corporate matters in the 1980s. Between 1988 and 1992, Bucyrus' financial transactions, including a leveraged buy-out, left the company with more than $200 million in debt. During that time, the head of Milbank's Mergers and Acquisitions Department, Lawrence Lederman, managed the Bucyrus account. In 1993, Lederman brought in Mr. Gellene, a bankruptcy attorney at Milbank, to work on the financial restructuring of Bucyrus.

At that time, the major parties with an interest in Bucyrus included Goldman Sachs & Co., Bucyrus' largest equity shareholder, which held 49% of the Bucyrus stock; Jackson National Life Insurance Company ("JNL"), Bucyrus largest creditor, which held approximately $60 million in unsecured notes; and South Street Funds, a group of investment entities, which held approximately $35 million in senior secured notes and leasehold interests. South Street Funds was managed and directed by Greycliff Partners, an investment entity which consisted of financial advisers Mikael Salovaara and Alfred Eckert, former employees of Goldman Sachs.

On February 18, 1994, Bucyrus filed its Chapter 11 bankruptcy petition in the Eastern District of Wisconsin. Because the legal representation of a debtor is subject to court approval, Bucyrus submitted an application requesting that Milbank be appointed to represent it in the bankruptcy. Pursuant to Bankruptcy Rule 2014, the application included the required sworn declaration disclosing "any connection" that Milbank had with "the Debtors, their creditors, or any other party in interest." Ex. 22, ¶ 5. Mr. Gellene, Milbank's lead attorney in the Bucyrus bankruptcy, under oath disclosed that his firm had previously represented Goldman Sachs and JNL in "unrelated" matters and would continue to represent Goldman Sachs in non-Bucyrus proceedings. *See id.* at ¶ 6. Mr. Gellene did not disclose any of Milbank's representations of South Street, Greycliff Partners or Salovaara.

The United States Trustee and JNL filed objections to Mr. Gellene's Rule 2014 declaration. They sought additional information regarding Milbank's representation of Goldman Sachs and questioned whether there was a sufficient conflict of interest to bar Milbank's retention as counsel for the debtor.

On March 23, 1994, the bankruptcy court conducted a hearing on the issue. It requested that Mr. Gellene submit a second declaration containing more detail about possible conflicts of interest. The court specifically commented: "If you represent them [Goldman Sachs] in other matters, then I think it's important to state precisely what arrangements have been made internally to separate what you're doing in this matter with the recommendation in other matters." Tr. 917–18.

On March 28, 1994, Mr. Gellene signed a second sworn Rule 2014 statement providing details about Milbank's representation of Goldman Sachs and the "Chinese wall" that the firm planned to put in place. It also disclosed its prior representation of two other creditors, Cowen & Co. and Mitsubishi International. The declaration then stated:

> Besides the representations disclosed in my declaration dated February 18, 1994, after due inquiry I am unaware of any other current

representation by Milbank of an equity security holder or institutional creditor of [Bucyrus].

Ex. 27, ¶ 7. Mr. Gellene again did not disclose any representation by Milbank of South Street, Greycliff Partners or Salovaara. However, at the time of both declarations, Milbank was doing their legal work, including the representation of Salovaara when his partner, Alfred Eckert, sued him.

At Milbank, one partner recognized that there might be a conflict of interest between Milbank's representation of Salovaara in the Salovaara-Eckert dispute and its representation of Bucyrus in its bankruptcy proceedings. At a meeting on December 22, 1993, with Mr. Gellene, Lederman and Milbank partner Toni Lichstein, all of whom were working on the Bucyrus bankruptcy and the Salovaara-Eckert dispute, Lichstein raised the possibility of conflict. Both Lederman and Mr. Gellene stated it was not a problem. Lichstein raised the issue again in March 1994 after she, representing Salovaara, had attended a South Street investors' meeting at which South Street's investment in Bucyrus was discussed. At that time, Mr. Gellene responded that Salovaara was not a creditor of Bucyrus and that all disclosure obligations had been satisfied. However, Lederman suggested that, if Lichstein had further concerns, Salovaara should obtain other counsel. After that, Milbank's representation of Salovaara in his dispute with Eckert slowed and eventually ended. By December 1994, Lederman had resigned his representation of South Street/Greycliff and had written off the billings generated in a tangential matter, a Colorado bankruptcy (about $16,000), and in the Salovaara-Eckert dispute (more than $300,000). Mr. Gellene also wrote off $13,000 in fees and expenses on the Bucyrus bankruptcy billings. Mr. Gellene never informed anyone at Bucyrus of the other Milbank representations.

Meanwhile, the Bucyrus bankruptcy creditors' committee worked through the summer and fall of 1994 to see if it could formulate a plan that would satisfy the major creditors. By late fall, a compromise was reached and all the parties to the Bucyrus bankruptcy agreed to the new plan of reorganization.

Thereafter, Milbank filed a petition requesting compensation for its work on the bankruptcy case. In November 1995, a hearing was held on Milbank's application for more than $2 million in legal fees and expenses. The United States Trustee and JNL both opposed the application. Mr. Gellene was lead attorney for Milbank at those hearings. However, when he testified in support of his firm's request for fees, Milbank partner David Gelfand was the attorney who put on Mr. Gellene's testimony. Gelfand presented Mr. Gellene's sworn declarations to him on the stand. Mr. Gellene testified that the supplemental

Rule 2014 declaration had disclosed Milbank's relationship with Goldman Sachs and thus that the court had been fully aware of that relationship. However, Mr. Gellene did not testify that his firm had represented and was continuing to represent South Street and Greycliff. The United States Trustee did not learn of that representation until the late fall of 1996. The court ultimately awarded Milbank approximately $1.8 million in fees and expenses.

In late 1996, JNL discovered that Milbank had represented Salovaara in his dispute with Eckert at the same time it was representing Bucyrus. JNL then filed a motion in the bankruptcy court in December 1996 seeking disgorgement of Milbank's fees. Mr. Gellene did not respond to the motion. On February 24, 1997, when his partners became aware of the motion and asked him about it, Mr. Gellene responded falsely that the answer was due in a few days. Mr. Gellene even altered the JNL filing to conceal the date it had been signed. When that deception was uncovered, however, Mr. Gellene admitted to Lichstein and Gelfand that he had lied about the response due date.

In March 1997, Mr. Gellene filed a third declaration with the bankruptcy court. In it, he explained that he had made an error in legal judgment by omitting Milbank's representations of South Street and of Salovaara and took "full personal responsibility for failing to disclose these matters to the court." Tr. 1247.

B.   The Federal Criminal Charges

On December 9, 1997, a federal grand jury returned a three-count indictment against Mr. Gellene, charging him with two counts of bankruptcy fraud and with one count of perjury. It alleged that Mr. Gellene had lied three times in the course of a bankruptcy case: twice when he filed the Rule 2014 declarations knowing that they were false and once when he used the supplemental declaration, while under oath at a bankruptcy hearing, knowing that it contained a false material declaration.

At Mr. Gellene's trial, the government produced evidence of other false representations by the defendant, evidence that was admitted under Rule 404(b) of the Federal Rules of Evidence. The first concerned Mr. Gellene's bar status. He joined the New York State Bar in 1990; however, between 1981 and 1990 he represented himself to be a member of that bar in court filings and in legal publications. Mr. Gellene also represented himself to be a member of the federal bar in the Southern District of New York, both by repeatedly appearing in that court and by claiming that membership when applying for membership in the

Eastern District of Wisconsin to represent Bucyrus in its bankruptcy proceedings.

The second category of evidence admitted at trial concerned Milbank's relationship with Lotus Cab Company: Mr. Gellene had included his charges to the cab company in the itemized expenses of the Milbank fee request but had failed to disclose to the court the ownership interest of some law firm partners in that company. The third false representation admitted at Mr. Gellene's trial under Rule 404(b) was made to the Colorado bankruptcy court. After South Street, Milbank's client, failed to produce discovery documents in the bankruptcy case of George Gillett, the bankruptcy court dismissed the South Street claim. Mr. Gellene moved for reconsideration; he stated that the delay in producing the documents was caused by the winding-up of South Street and by the ongoing dispute between Eckert, the managing partner of South Street, and the Funds' portfolio advisor, Greycliff Partners, regarding control of the funds. At Mr. Gellene's trial, however, Eckert testified that Mr. Gellene's explanation was not true and that he had produced the documents shortly after Mr. Gellene had requested them—which was after the deadline for production of the documents.

Mr. Gellene testified as the only defense witness at his trial. He stated that he began work at Milbank in 1980 and developed a bankruptcy practice. He testified that Lederman gave him the Bucyrus work and the South Street/Greycliff representation. He also admitted being aware in December 1993 of his firm's representation of Salovaara in the Eckert dispute. He testified that he failed to disclose these representations in the Bucyrus bankruptcy because he did not consider Salovaara to be a creditor, did not distinguish South Street/Greycliff from Salovaara, and thus did not think the representations needed to be disclosed. He also testified that the matters involving Salovaara, South Street and Greycliff were unrelated to the Bucyrus matter and that an agreement with Salovaara had already been reached. He called these conclusions "bad judgment" and "stupid, but not criminal." The jury did not agree; it convicted him on all three counts.

II

DISCUSSION

A.   Bankruptcy Fraud under 18 U.S.C. § 152(3)

1.

Mr. Gellene was found guilty of two counts of making false oaths in a bankruptcy proceeding, in violation of 18 U.S.C. § 152(3). He was convicted specifically of "knowingly and fraudulently" making false declarations under oath in two Rule 2014 bankruptcy applications. Twice he applied for an order approving his employment as attorney for the debtor; first, on February 18, 1994, the day he filed Bucyrus' Chapter 11 bankruptcy, and second, on March 28, 1994, after the hearing on his application, when he elaborated on potential conflicts of interest, as the bankruptcy court had requested. Those applications failed to list the senior secured creditor and related parties.

At trial, the district court instructed the jury on the elements of bankruptcy fraud and specifically instructed that "[a] statement is fraudulent if known to be untrue and made with intent to deceive." Jury Instructions at 18. Mr. Gellene submits that the court's definition of "fraudulent" as "with intent to deceive" is erroneous. In his view, the statute requires that the statement be made not simply with the intent to deceive but with the intent to defraud. He further claims that, because the government misapprehended the statutory requirement, it failed to present evidence that he made his declarations with an intent to defraud because it believed it needed to prove merely an intent to deceive. He submits that the distinction between the two terms is significant: To deceive is to cause to believe the false or to mislead; to defraud is to deprive of some right, interest or property by deceit. Therefore, under § 152 of the Bankruptcy Code, he contends, the defendant must have a specific intent to alter or to impact the distribution of a debtor's assets and not merely to impact the integrity of the legal system, as the government argued.

We cannot accept Mr. Gellene's narrowly circumscribed definition of "intent to defraud" or "fraudulently." Mr. Gellene would limit exclusively the statute's scope to false statements that deprive the debtor of his property or the bankruptcy estate of its assets. In our view, such a parsimonious interpretation was not intended by Congress.

First, the plain wording of the statute suggests no such limited scope. Rather, the plain wording of the statute punishes making a false statement "knowingly and fraudulently." The common understanding of the term "fraudulently" includes the intent to deceive. Indeed, our case law has long acknowledged a broader scope for the statutory language than Mr. Gellene suggests. We have held that the section is designed to reach statements made "with intent to defraud the bankruptcy court." *United States v. Key*, 859 F.2d 1257, 1260 (7th Cir.1988). In *United States v. Ellis*, 50 F.3d 419 (7th Cir.), *cert. denied*, 516 U.S. 849, 116 S.Ct. 143, 133 L.Ed.2d 89 (1995), we commented that § 152 has long been recognized as the Congress' attempt to criminalize all the possible methods by which a debtor or any other person may attempt to defeat the intent and effect of the Bankruptcy Code and that the expansive scope of the statute "reaches beyond the wrongful sequestration of a debtor's property and also encompasses the knowing and fraudulent making of false oaths or declarations in the context of a bankruptcy proceeding." *Id.* at 423 (citing *Key*, 859 F.2d at 1259–60).

In addition, *Ellis* commented that the omission of material information in a bankruptcy filing "impedes a bankruptcy court's fulfilling of its responsibilities just as much as an explicitly false statement." *Id.* (affirming § 152 conviction of debtor for omission of prior bankruptcies from petition); *see also United States v. Cherek*, 734 F.2d 1248, 1254 (7th Cir.1984) (holding that failure by corporation president to list asset on corporation's bankruptcy petition was omission of material information supporting a § 152 conviction), *cert. denied*, 471 U.S. 1014, 105 S.Ct. 2016, 85 L.Ed.2d 299 (1985); *United States v. Lindholm*, 24 F.3d 1078, 1083 (9th Cir.1994) (affirming § 152 conviction of debtor for omission of prior bankruptcy filings). Thus, whether the deception at issue is aimed at thwarting the bankruptcy court or the parties to the bankruptcy, § 152 is designed to protect the integrity of the administration of a bankruptcy case. As one commentator has put it:

> The orientation of title 11 toward debtors' rehabilitation and equitable distribution to creditors relies heavily upon the participants' honesty. When honesty is absent, the goals of the civil side of the system become more expensive and more illusive. To protect the civil system, bankruptcy crimes are not concerned with individual loss or even whether certain acts caused anyone particularized harm. *Instead, the statutes establishing the federal bankruptcy crimes seek to prevent and redress abuses of the bankruptcy system.* Thus, most of the crimes do not require that the acts proscribed be material in the grand scheme of things, that the defendant benefit in any way nor that any creditor be injured.

1 *Collier on Bankruptcy,* ¶ 7.01[1][a] at 7–15 (Lawrence P. King ed., 15th ed. rev.1999) (emphasis added).

2.

Mr. Gellene's narrow reading of the statute leads him to take a narrow view of the provision's materiality requirement. In his view, the statute criminalizes only fraud that is intended to frustrate the equitable distribution of assets in the bankruptcy estate. As counsel explained at oral argument, the fraud ought to be considered material only when it is related to the estate's assets, to pecuniary and property distribution issues. Under this narrow interpretation, his failure to divulge his representation of a major secured creditor of the debtor was not material, he asserts, because it was not intended to impact on the equitable distribution of assets in the bankruptcy.

We agree that § 152 requires that materiality be an element of the crime of bankruptcy fraud and, indeed, we have incorporated such a requirement in our analysis of § 152 fraud. *See Key*, 859 F.2d at 1261. The statute is therefore construed to require that the false oath be in relation to some material matter. *See United States v. Jackson*, 836 F.2d 324, 329 (7th Cir.1987) (citing cases). That material matter about which the misrepresentation was made could of course be the debtor's business transactions, the debtor's estate assets, the discovery of those assets, or the history of the debtor's financial transactions. *See id.* (holding that the debtor's false statements about the location of assets of the estate were material to the proceedings). However, we have never accepted Mr. Gellene's view that only misrepresentations that relate to the assets of the bankruptcy estate are material. Indeed, we, like other circuits, have rejected expressly such a reading. *See Key*, 859 F.2d at 1261 (stating that materiality does not require showing that creditors were harmed by the false statements). The same commentator, addressing the materiality element, likewise has explained why a broader view of materiality than the one urged by Mr. Gellene is compatible with the purpose of the bankruptcy laws:

> Materiality in this context does not require harm to or adverse reliance by a creditor, nor does it require a realization of a gain by the defendant. Rather, it requires that the false oath or account relate to some significant aspect of the bankruptcy case or proceeding in which it was given, or that it pertain to the discovery of assets or to the debtor's financial transactions. Just what is significant is difficult to say for the general case: failing to disclose ownership of a ream of paper in a multi-million dollar bankruptcy is probably not material, but in many cases a false social security number or a false prior address may be. Statements given by individuals in order to secure a particular adjudication carry their own reliable index of materiality; the person

giving the statement believed it sufficiently important—and hence, material—to the goal of obtaining the desired action.

Collier on Bankruptcy, ¶ 7.02[2][a][iv] at 7–46 to 7–47. We conclude that the materiality element does not require proof of the potential impact on the disposition of assets.

We have no doubt that a misstatement in a Rule 2014 statement by an attorney about other affiliations constitutes a material misstatement. The Bankruptcy Code requires that attorneys who seek to be employed as counsel for a debtor apply for the bankruptcy court's approval of that employment. *See In re Crivello*, 134 F.3d 831, 835–36 (7th Cir.1998). Bankruptcy Rule 2014 requires the potential attorney for the debtor to set forth under oath any "connections with the debtor, creditors, [and] any other party in interest." Fed. R. Bankr.P. 2014(a). The disclosure requirements apply to all professionals and are not discretionary. The professionals "cannot pick and choose which connections are irrelevant or trivial." *In re EWC, Inc.*, 138 B.R. 276, 280 (Bankr.W.D.Okl.1992). "[C]ounsel who fail to disclose timely and completely their connections proceed at their own risk because failure to disclose is sufficient grounds to revoke an employment order and deny compensation." *Crivello*, 134 F.3d at 836; *see also Rome v. Braunstein*, 19 F.3d 54, 59 (1st Cir.1994). As Judge Kanne pointed out in *Crivello*, this procedure is designed to ensure that a "disinterested person" is chosen to represent the debtor. This requirement goes to the heart of the integrity of the administration of the bankruptcy estate. The Code reflects Congress' concern that any person who might possess or assert an interest or have a predisposition that would reduce the value of the estate or delay its administration ought not have a professional relationship with the estate. *See Crivello*, 134 F.3d at 835.

3.

We now consider whether there was sufficient evidence of Mr. Gellene's guilt. We therefore must determine, after viewing the evidence in the light most favorable to the government, whether a rational trier of fact could have found the essential elements of the offense of bankruptcy fraud beyond a reasonable doubt. *See United States v. Webster*, 125 F.3d 1024, 1034 (7th Cir.1997), *cert. denied*, 522 U.S. 1051, 118 S.Ct. 698, 139 L.Ed.2d 642 (1998). "Circumstantial evidence is sufficient to prove fraudulent intent and to support a conviction." *Id.*

Our review of the record verifies that the government established Mr. Gellene's knowledge of his duty to disclose. It set forth Mr. Gellene's expertise in bankruptcy and the bankruptcy court's statements alerting him to the importance of full disclosures. Mr. Gellene was fully apprised of the importance of the information that had been excluded. He had been questioned by his law partner, Toni Lichstein, several times about whether there might be a conflict of interest and whether all necessary disclosures had been made. Yet Mr. Gellene continued to withhold the information over a two-year period; he simultaneously worked on the Bucyrus bankruptcy and represented South Street, Greycliff and Salovaara without informing his client Bucyrus of the other representations.

In addition to the direct evidence of Mr. Gellene's intentional fraudulent omission of information from the Rule 2014 applications, the government offered evidence that he had committed deceptions on the bankruptcy court and other courts with respect to (1) his failure to disclose his law firm partners' interest in the Lotus Cab Company, from whom he had submitted a bill; (2) his failure to file documents in a Colorado bankruptcy court; and (3) the status of his bar memberships. Moreover, Mr. Gellene himself testified regarding his mental state; therefore, the jury had an opportunity to judge in detail his innocent explanations regarding his conduct. After viewing the evidence in the light most favorable to the government, we conclude that there was evidence from which a jury reasonably could have found beyond a reasonable doubt that Mr. Gellene knowingly and fraudulently made two false material declarations in the Bucyrus bankruptcy case.

4.

Mr. Gellene claims that the court's definition of "fraudulent," which was set forth in the instructions, was erroneous. We therefore have considered the jury instructions, viewing them as a whole and acknowledging that we may overturn Mr. Gellene's conviction only if those instructions failed to treat the contested issues fairly and adequately. *See United States v. Lerch*, 996 F.2d 158, 161 (7th Cir.1993), *cert. denied*, 510 U.S. 1047, 114 S.Ct. 697, 126 L.Ed.2d 664 (1994).

The district court instructed the jury that a "statement or representation is fraudulent if known to be untrue, and made with intent to deceive." This instruction, given the facts of the case, adequately presented the issue to the jury. The defendant's conduct was to make a fraudulent statement. Because he is the attorney for the debtor rather than the debtor, his use of false statements defrauded the entire bankruptcy process when he withheld the name of a client that was the debtor's major secured creditor and of other related entities. We conclude that the instruction given in this case, which notably was given along with an instruction stating the elements of § 152 that must be proven beyond a reasonable doubt, adequately addressed the issue of intent. We hold that the district court treated all elements of the offense fairly and accurately, and accordingly we affirm the use of the jury instruction defining "fraudulent."

B. Perjury under 18 U.S.C. § 1623

1.

Mr. Gellene was convicted on Count 3 of using a document, while under oath, knowing that it contained a material falsehood, in violation of 18 U.S.C. § 1623.16 This charge arose from the bankruptcy court's hearing in November 1995 to consider Milbank's fee application. JNL opposed the application on the ground that Milbank had conflicts of interest in its representation of the debtor Bucyrus. Specifically, JNL challenged Milbank's relationship with Goldman Sachs.

At the fee hearing, Mr. Gellene testified on direct examination that he previously had disclosed to the bankruptcy court Milbank's representation of Goldman Sachs; in the course of his testimony, he referred to the two sworn declarations as exhibits to establish that disclosure. The second declaration in particular demonstrated that Milbank had divulged its relationship with Goldman Sachs and had put in place a "Chinese wall" to keep separate the Goldman Sachs legal representation and the Bucyrus bankruptcy work. That second declaration then made this concluding statement, alleged to be false in Count 3:

> Besides the representations disclosed in my declaration dated February 18, 1994, after due inquiry, I am unaware of any other current representation by Milbank of an equity security holder or institutional creditor of the Debtors.

Indictment, Count 3, ¶ 2.

However, when Mr. Gellene drafted this Rule 2014 disclosure statement (around March 28, 1994) and when he used it at the fee hearing (November 29, 1995), he and his firm were actively representing South Street and Greycliff. Notably, Milbank's representation of those entities was not known at the time of the fee hearing to anyone involved in the Bucyrus bankruptcy.

2.

Section 1623(a), often called the "false swearing statute" to distinguish it from its older sibling, the general federal perjury statute, *see United States v. Sherman*, 150 F.3d 306, 310 (3d Cir.1998), punishes anyone who "knowingly makes any false material declaration" under oath in a court proceeding. 18 U.S.C. § 1623(a). A material statement is one that has "a natural tendency to influence, or was capable of influencing, the decision of" the decisionmaker to which the statement was addressed. *Kungys v. United States*, 485 U.S. 759, 770, 108 S.Ct. 1537, 99 L.Ed.2d 839 (1988) (citing cases as examples). Materiality is an element of the offense; it must be proven by the government and decided by the jury. *See United States v. Gaudin*, 515 U.S. 506, 509, 115 S.Ct. 2310, 132 L.Ed.2d 444 (1995); *United States v. Akram*, 152 F.3d 698, 700 (7th Cir.1998) ("Since *Johnson v. United States*, 520 U.S. 461, 117 S.Ct. 1544, 137 L.Ed.2d 718 (1997), it has been clear that materiality under § 1623(a) is an element of the prosecution's case and must therefore be submitted to the jury and proven beyond a reasonable doubt.").

Mr. Gellene challenges his conviction on several grounds. First, he claims that the evidence was not sufficient to prove his guilt beyond a reasonable doubt because his testimony at the fee hearing did not constitute a knowing "use" of a "false material" document. Second, he asserts (for the first time on appeal) that, because the document was literally true, his statement based on the declaration cannot form the basis for a perjury conviction. And, third, he submits that the district court should have granted the motion for judgment of acquittal. We shall address the first two contentions in some detail and, in the course of our analysis, also discuss the sufficiency of the evidence.

a.

The false swearing statute, as the government seeks to apply it here, requires the "use" of a false statement. Mr. Gellene claims that his testimony at the fee hearing was entirely and historically accurate. In his view, the focus of the inquiry was on another paragraph of his March 1994 declaration, the paragraph that disclosed his relationship with Goldman Sachs. Mr. Gellene contends that he did not "use" the paragraph mentioned in the indictment because he never referred to that paragraph or used that paragraph to bolster his testimony; the inquiry was limited to Milbank's relationship with Goldman Sachs, and he made no mention at the fee hearing of the paragraph set forth in the indictment.

We cannot accept this argument. The thrust of JNL's challenge to the fee petition was a challenge to Milbank's divided loyalty. Although its allegation was limited to Milbank's association with Goldman Sachs, a fair interpretation of the record—and one the jury was certainly entitled to accept—was that JNL's foundational concern was that Milbank's divided loyalties might jeopardize the position of the creditors. The statement at issue in the indictment informed, and assured, the bankruptcy court that, beyond the area of acknowledged concern (Milbank's relationship with Goldman Sachs), there were no other areas of representation of which Mr. Gellene was aware. The statement conveyed the message that, once he met JNL's concern about Goldman Sachs, there was no other cause for concern about Milbank's divided loyalties and the fee petition could be approved.

We believe that the district court was correct in its determination that Mr. Gellene "used" the designated paragraph of the supplemental statement in his 2014 application during his testimony. His reference to—and his reliance upon—the application allowed him to demonstrate not only that he had disclosed the representation of Goldman Sachs but also that he had examined other possible areas of concern and had determined that there were no other similar representations that warranted the court's scrutiny before awarding fees.

For essentially the same reasons, we believe that the use of the application was material. The district court noted that a document "is material if it has a natural tendency to influence or is capable of influencing the decision of the person to whom it was addressed." R.50 at 6 (citing *United States v. Gaudin*, 515 U.S. 506, 509, 115 S.Ct. 2310, 132 L.Ed.2d 444 (1995), and *United States v. Ross*, 77 F.3d 1525, 1545 (7th Cir.1996)). According to the district court, the testimony of David Gelfand, Mr. Gellene's partner at Milbank who examined Mr. Gellene at the fee hearing, was sufficient evidence of materiality; Mr. Gelfand testified that the document was introduced to convince the bankruptcy court to award attorney's fees.

Our study of the record convinces us of the correctness of the district court's ruling. The jury was entitled to believe that the statement was designed to lull the bankruptcy court and the parties into believing that there were no other Milbank relationships deserving of scrutiny before the award of fees. The jury was entitled to conclude that the sequence of events established that Mr. Gellene had knowingly used the document to convey such an impression to the bankruptcy court. Indeed, Mr. Gellene stated prior to the hearing that he intended to use the declarations in response to JNL's allegation that Milbank had conflicts of interest. David Gelfand, who examined Mr. Gellene at that hearing, later testified that Mr. Gellene had chosen to proffer his sworn declarations as exhibits and had orchestrated the subsequent questioning of his own sworn testimony. According to Gelfand, the purpose in presenting the documents was to establish that Milbank was entitled to the $2 million in fees because all potential conflicts had been disclosed and considered by the bankruptcy court. There is no question that his proffer of the statement constituted use of a material document under § 1623.

The record permitted the jury to conclude that Mr. Gellene knowingly introduced the false document in order to gain approval of Milbank's $2 million fee request. Evaluating the testimony presented to it, the jury was entitled to conclude that Mr. Gellene had virtually bragged about the forthrightness of Milbank's disclosure of its representation of Goldman Sachs, all the while knowing that no one involved in the bankruptcy proceedings was aware of Milbank's undisclosed representations of South Street and the other entities. It was not until the next year that the falsity of that disclosure information was discovered. Only then could the United States Trustee seek return of the fees and an order of sanctions against Milbank.

Accordingly, we believe that sufficient evidence existed for the district court to find that materiality has been established.

b.

Mr. Gellene contends that his conviction under § 1623 cannot stand because the statement made in the paragraph set forth in the indictment is literally true. The government made no effort to prove, he contends, that Milbank's undisclosed clients—South Street, Greycliff and Salovaara—were "institutional creditors" or "equity security holders" of Bucyrus. Because there was nothing "materially false" about that paragraph of Mr. Gellene's declaration, he claims, the government could not have proven those necessary elements of the crime of perjury under § 1623. Therefore, he submits, his perjury conviction cannot be sustained.

The government points out that, because Mr. Gellene has raised this issue for the first time on appeal, he may obtain a reversal only if he can demonstrate a "manifest miscarriage of justice." *United States v. Hickok,* 77 F.3d 992, 1002 (7th Cir.), *cert. denied,* 517 U.S. 1200, 116 S.Ct. 1701, 134 L.Ed.2d 800 (1996). It further argues that a reviewing court should uphold the conviction as long as the falsity is established by a "common sense reading" of the language used. *United States v. Yasak,* 884 F.2d 996, 1001 (7th Cir.1989). The government then submits that South Street and Greycliff were "institutional creditors" and that Mr. Gellene was fully aware that these entities were represented by Milbank at the time he stated that he was "unaware" of such creditors.

The jury was entitled to credit the testimony of Alfred Eckert, partner of Mikael Salovaara and half-owner of South Street and Greycliff, who stated that South Street's first investment was a secured loan to Bucyrus in the summer of

1992. As Eckert explained, South Street had loaned $35 million to Bucyrus "and we were collateralized by all the assets of the company so that . . . we would be paid off first if there was a problem." Tr. 573. Eckert also testified that the interest of South Street certainly was affected by the Bucyrus bankruptcy. It is obvious from this testimony that, whether or not Mr. Gellene defines it as an "institutional creditor," South Street was a party in interest in the Bucyrus bankruptcy, one that should have been identified and disclosed by Mr. Gellene on his Rule 2014 declaration as long as he or his firm had any connection with it.

Because it is clear that South Street and Greycliff were institutions that had lent to and were owed millions of dollars by Bucyrus, we believe that the jury had sufficient information from the trial testimony of Eckert and others to determine that South Street and Greycliff were institutional creditors of the debtor Bucyrus. Accordingly, it was not a miscarriage of justice for the jury to find that South Street and Greycliff fit the term "institutional creditor" and then to conclude that Mr. Gellene's supplemental declaration was false.

C. Admissibility of Rule 404(b) Evidence

1.

Mr. Gellene next submits that the district court abused its discretion in admitting evidence, pursuant to Rule 404(b) of the Federal Rules of Evidence, of certain other events on the ground that they were relevant and probative on the issue of intent.

During the course of trial, the court admitted evidence that Mr. Gellene had misrepresented his status as a member of the bar when applying to become a member of the bar of the Eastern District of Wisconsin: He stated that he was a member of the bar of the Southern District of New York and had been a member since 1981, but in fact he has never been a member of that bar, despite repeated appearances in that court over the years. In addition, Mr. Gellene practiced law in New York State between 1981 and 1990 without ever joining that bar. During that time, he represented himself to be a member of the New York bar in legal publications and court filings. The court also admitted evidence of (1) Mr. Gellene's misrepresentation to the Colorado bankruptcy court concerning his failure to produce discovery documents, and (2) Mr. Gellene's misrepresentation to the Wisconsin bankruptcy court in this case concerning his law firm's relationship with Lotus Cab Company.

Mr. Gellene explained that he had passed the bar but had neglected to complete the requisite paperwork to be licensed. He also admitted that he did not tell his law firm that he was not a member of the bar and, as a result, practiced law for almost nine years without a proper license. Nevertheless, he contends that the government sought to admit this irrelevant evidence to prove his propensity to make misrepresentations, thereby allowing the jury to infer that he must have been untruthful and even must have fraudulently intended the charged conduct. In his view, stating that he was a licensed attorney when he only had passed the bar exam, although not commendable conduct, is not equivalent to the state of mind involved with providing false testimony as to a material issue under litigation.

In admitting the evidence, the district court reasoned that, by denying that he had the requisite fraudulent intent for the charged crimes, Mr. Gellene had made intent an issue in the case; therefore, the court concluded, the government was entitled to rebut that contention with evidence of other bad acts that tended to undermine the defendant's innocent explanations for his act. Concerning Mr. Gellene's bar status, the court determined that there was clear evidence of (1) his knowledge that he was not a member of the New York state bar and (2) "his continuing intent for a period of almost nine years to deceive anyone who would have an interest [in] believing that indeed he was a member of the New York bar." Tr. 1480. The court then determined that this intent to deceive concerning his bar status was similar to his intent to defraud, to deceive and to perjure himself under Counts 1, 2 and 3 of the indictment. It noted Mr. Gellene's status as an officer of the court—in the bankruptcy court in Milwaukee, a federal court in New York, a bankruptcy court in Denver, or elsewhere—and then found that his conduct in those courts was similar and "appropriate to consider on the very narrow issue of this defendant's intent in his candor with the United States Bankruptcy Court in the Eastern District of Wisconsin." Tr. 1482.

2.

We review the district court's determinations concerning the admissibility of evidence under the abuse of discretion standard. *See United States v. Lerch*, 996 F.2d 158, 162 (7th Cir.1993). Our circuit's traditional four-part test to determine the admissibility of evidence under Rule 404(b) permits the admission of prior acts when:

(1) the evidence is directed toward establishing a matter in issue other than the defendant's propensity to commit the crime charged, (2) the evidence shows that the other act is similar enough and close enough

in time to be relevant to the matter in issue, (3) the evidence is sufficient to support a jury finding that the defendant committed the similar act, and (4) the probative value of the evidence is not substantially outweighed by the danger of unfair prejudice.

United States v. Asher, No. 98–1700, 178 F.3d 486, 491 (7th Cir.1999). Our review, on appeal, of the district court's application of Rule 404(b) requires us to "ascertain whether the tendered evidence is directed toward establishing a matter in issue *other than* the defendant's propensity to commit the charged crime." *United States v. Allison,* 120 F.3d 71, 74 (7th Cir.), *cert. denied,* 522 U.S. 987, 118 S.Ct. 455, 139 L.Ed.2d 389 (1997) (emphasis added). When the defendant is charged with a specific intent crime, as Mr. Gellene is, "the government may present other acts evidence to prove intent." *United States v. Lewis,* 110 F.3d 417, 420 (7th Cir.) (quoting *United States v. Long,* 86 F.3d 81, 84 (7th Cir.1996)) (citations and internal quotation marks omitted), *cert. denied,* 522 U.S. 854, 118 S.Ct. 149, 139 L.Ed.2d 95 (1997). The admission of evidence of other crimes for that limited purpose is proper.

We cannot say that the district court abused its discretion in admitting the evidence. The district court was correct in its determination that Mr. Gellene had placed his intent in issue. It was clear from the parties' opening statements that the facts were basically not in dispute and that the focus of the trial would be on the intention underlying Mr. Gellene's conduct. On this record, we also think that the district court was entitled to conclude that Mr. Gellene's false representations regarding his bar status and his other misrepresentations were similar enough in nature to the charged offenses to be relevant. Both the charged conduct and these other misrepresentations involve intentional misrepresentations before a court. The evidence admitted by the district court, like the offenses of conviction, tended to show intentional dishonesty, absence of mistake, and a cavalier disregard for the truth in his dealings with tribunals. For instance, Mr. Gellene's intentional deception in falsely representing to various courts (including the United States District Court for the Eastern District of Wisconsin) that he was a member of the bars of other courts, when he was not, is not dissimilar to his intentional deception in falsely representing to the bankruptcy court that he had no connection with other parties in interest in the bankruptcy, when in fact he was representing the major secured creditor. Certainly, his attempt to treat the earlier conduct as de minimis, trivial, a matter of neglect, a matter of embarrassment but not a knowing deception—when the circumstances evince knowing deception—is similar to the dishonesty reflected in his filings of the two fraudulent disclosure statements and the perjurious statement he made subsequent to the filing of those documents in order to win the requested $2 million fee award.

Even when such evidence has a slight tendency to show Mr. Gellene's propensity to commit wrongs, "its predominant effect pertained to the legitimate purpose of proving [the defendant's] intent." *United States v. Sinclair*, 74 F.3d 753, 761 (7th Cir.1996) (affirming district court's discretionary decision to admit evidence that the defendant had signed certificates affirming that he complied with the bank's code of conduct but had not obtained permission to serve as an officer of another corporation, as the code required). We note, moreover, that the district court instructed the jury that Mr. Gellene was "not on trial for any act or conduct not alleged in the indictment" and that the jury was allowed to consider "evidence of acts of the defendant other than those charged in the indictment . . . only on the question of the defendant's intent." Jury Instructions at 4, 9. Given these limiting instructions, we cannot say that the danger of prejudice outweighed the probity of the evidence. The district court did not abuse its discretion in admitting evidence of Mr. Gellene's false representations and omissions concerning his bar status with respect to the "narrow issue" of his intent.

D. The Court's Sentencing Determinations

1. U.S.S.G. § 3B1.3

Mr. Gellene contends that the district court erroneously enhanced his conviction on Count 3, the perjury charge, under U.S.S.G. § 3B1.3 for abuse of a position of trust. According to Mr. Gellene, he does not occupy a position of trust with respect to his client Bucyrus, the bankruptcy court, the creditors, or his law partners.

We review a district court's interpretation of "position of trust" de novo. However, because the question whether the defendant occupied a position of trust is a factual one, we review that determination for clear error. *See United States v. Bhagavan*, 116 F.3d 189, 192 (7th Cir.1997). The § 3B1.3 adjustment is appropriate if (a) the defendant occupied a position of trust, and (b) his abuse of the position of trust significantly facilitated the offense. *See United States v. Emerson*, 128 F.3d 557, 562 (7th Cir.1997). Whether a defendant holds a position of trust depends on the amount of professional managerial discretion he has been given, *see* § 3B1.3, or on his "access or authority over things of value." *United States v. Lamb*, 6 F.3d 415, 419 (7th Cir.1993). When a person is given a great deal of autonomy by his employer, for example, and is in a position to steal or to do other harm without being caught, that person, if he abuses that trust, may be punished more heavily. *See United States v. Deal*, 147 F.3d 562, 563 (7th Cir.1998).

Mr. Gellene was a bankruptcy lawyer representing a large corporate client in bankruptcy. He held a position of considerable professional discretion. *See* § 3B1.3 n. 1 (giving the example that a lawyer who embezzles from his client abuses a position of trust). In our view, Mr. Gellene, as lead Milbank lawyer in the Bucyrus bankruptcy, occupied a position of trust.

We next ask, therefore, whether Mr. Gellene's abuse of his role as attorney for the debtor significantly facilitated the commission of the perjury. The district court determined that it did; Mr. Gellene, as counsel for Bucyrus, abused that position of trust by concealing critical information from his client, namely his representation of the senior secured creditor, South Street. Mr. Gellene's offense was lying about those representations in the Rule 2014 disclosure statements, at the bankruptcy fees hearing, and over a two-year period during which Bucyrus was never told of the conflicting representation. As the district court stated, such nondisclosure constituted a serious breach of trust and of "the ethical obligations that one owes to his client to be free from all the intrusions that surround potential conflicts of interest." Sent. Tr. 103.

We believe there was no error in the district court's imposition of the enhancement. Mr. Gellene's position representing the debtor brought with it fiduciary duties to act in the debtor's interest throughout the bankruptcy proceeding. *See Bhagavan*, 116 F.3d at 193 (concluding that the president/majority shareholder, with fiduciary duties to act in the interests of minority shareholders, occupied a position of trust). His undisclosed representation of the senior secured creditor of the debtor certainly created a potential if not actual conflict of interest and thus was a breach of his position of trust with the debtor. Mr. Gellene also abused his position of trust as an officer of the bankruptcy court by using his fraudulent sworn document to verify his perjurious sworn testimony.

2. Imposition of fine

Mr. Gellene claims that the district court did not properly consider his inability to pay the $15,000 fine imposed on him at sentencing. He asserts that the government miscalculated his net worth at $360,131.50 and that he actually is insolvent with three daughters dependent upon him for financial support. According to Mr. Gellene, the fine was imposed in disregard of the applicable sentencing standards and must be set aside.

Section 5E1.2 mandates that a district court impose a fine on a defendant unless he "establishes that he is unable to pay and is not likely to become able to pay any fine." U.S.S.G. § 5E1.2(a). It is the defendant's burden to demonstrate that he lacks the ability to pay. It is the court's duty to consider the factors for imposition of a fine found in U.S.S.G. § 5E1.2(d) and 18 U.S.C. § 3572.24 *See United States v. Young*, 66 F.3d 830, 838 (7th Cir.1995). We do not require that the sentencing court make specific findings regarding each of the relevant factors, however; in fact, the articulation of findings may be satisfied by adopting the PSR findings. *See United States v. Bauer*, 129 F.3d 962, 966 (7th Cir.1997). "[T]he sentencing court must consider the relevant factors and provide a reasoned and reviewable basis for its decision to impose a fine." *Id.* at 968.

In this case, the record makes clear that the district court spent considerable time properly considering the relevant factors. The court followed the PSR's factual findings, questioned Mr. Gellene concerning his current financial situation, and then asked Mr. Gellene and his attorney to meet over lunch with the probation officer who prepared the presentence report in order to provide to the court "a little detail about where all this money went in the last six years." Sent. Tr. 69. The probation officer's notes from that discussion became a supplement to the PSR—a supplement created by both parties. *See Bauer, 129 F.3d at 969* (recognizing that the defendant approved the supplement to the PSR). The court reviewed the material and questioned Mr. Gellene further concerning the estimated unpaid taxes and life insurance. He noted the high cost of living in New York and costs involved in schools for his daughters. After assessing Mr. Gellene's financial situation along with the nature of his conduct, the court believed that "the interests of justice and the interests of society" required some fine within the guideline range. Sent. Tr. 146. It determined that $15,000 was the appropriate fine within the guideline fine range of $4,000 to $40,000 for his offense level.

In our view, the district court gave Mr. Gellene the opportunity to prove his inability to pay a fine when it asked him to meet again with the probation officer over lunch. It carefully reviewed Mr. Gellene's claim of insolvency during the sentencing hearing before rejecting it. Mr. Gellene has given us no grounds for re-evaluating the district court's decision on this matter. The district court was within its discretion, and committed no error, when it fined Mr. Gellene. Moreover, " 'we have no authority to inquire into the precise amount of the fine the district judge specified,' because claims 'that the judge should have made a greater departure ... [are] outside our jurisdiction.' " *United States v. Sanchez Estrada*, 62 F.3d 981, 995 (7th Cir.1995) (quoting *United States v. Gomez*, 24 F.3d

924, 927 (7th Cir.), *cert. denied,* 513 U.S. 909, 115 S.Ct. 280, 130 L.Ed.2d 196 (1994) (citation omitted)); *see also Young,* 66 F.3d at 839–40 (concluding that we are without authority to depart below the minimum fine level).

Conclusion

For the foregoing reasons, we affirm the judgment of the district court.

AFFIRMED.

SOLUTIONS: THE LAWYER SHOULD HAVE, WOULD HAVE, COULD HAVE. . .

Mr. Gellene's ethical and criminal breaches seemed to snowball, but he always thought he had an argument. He claimed he did not have intent to defraud when he omitted key facts. He split hairs about whether disclosure was required. But the core problem, the original sin, was failing to be fully transparent and honest, and then failing to promptly correct his first mistake.

LEANING INTO PRACTICE

The photos below are a paperweight. It is from the now defunct Enron Company that bankrupted itself, with some of its executives going to federal prison, because of shady business practices. It sits at the desk of one of your authors. The most recent changes to MR 1.13 were made because of the scandal. In the photo look carefully at the values that Enron purported to hold dear. What strikes you about them? What lessons can you draw from such self-professed values?

Photos are courtesy of Research Assistant, Carmen Coreas.

INTEGRITY

INTEGRITY
WE WORK WITH CUSTOMERS
AND PROSPECTS OPENLY,
HONESTLY, AND SINCERELY.
WHEN WE SAY WE WILL DO
SOMETHING, WE WILL DO IT;
WHEN WE SAY WE CANNOT
OR WILL NOT DO SOMETHING,
THEN WE WON'T DO IT.

X-Ray Questions

The late Vincent W. Foster Jr. was a distinguished member of the Arkansas bar. He left his lucrative practice to join the administration of newly inaugurated President Bill Clinton. He gave the 1993 commencement talk at his law school alma mater, the University of Arkansas Law School, shortly thereafter. He suggests that the law graduates adhere to certain core values. In your own words, what are they? Would the lawyer in the previous case have benefitted from his counsel?

BEYOND THE CITE

By: Vincent W. Foster, Jr., *Roads We Should Travel,* **Commencement Address at the Law School, University of Arkansas, Fayetteville, Arkansas (May 8, 1993)** *reprinted by* **The Arkansas Bar Association.**

Dean Strickman, Dr. Leflar, honored faculty of the University of Arkansas School of Law, class of 1993, family and friends, I cannot tell you what a thrill it is to return to these beautiful hills and celebrate with you the completion of your law school career.

It is humbling for me to deliver this message from a stage shared by so many outstanding teachers, many of whom taught me well. What a challenge it is for many commencement speaker, let alone this one, to attempt to develop and convey to you an uplifting message with any staying power whatsoever, knowing full well the wide range of emotions which are preoccupying you at this moment: Your senses of achievement, appreciation, satisfaction, relief, survival and perhaps apprehension; and particularly some sense of impatience for this speaker to get on with it, deliver his remarks so that you may receive congratulations from your family and friends.

Governor Cuomo reports that when he was first asked to speak at a graduation he sought advice out from Father Flynn, then the president of St. John's University. Commencement speakers, said Father Flynn, should think of themselves as the body at an old-fashioned Irish wake. They need to have you there in order to have the party but they don't expect you to say much.

When Dean Strickman, in Washington a few weeks ago, conveyed to me the invitation, I protested that I was not only unworthy of the honor but unprepared for the experience.

You see, I skipped my commencement ceremonies some 22 years ago. This is the first law school exercise that I have ever attended.

The law school commencement at the time was a mass joint enterprise with all the other schools on campus, and since I had not been much on ceremony, and since I felt I knew everything there was to know, I rationalized that I should rush to Little Rock to assume my new job and save on the rental gown. My wife, Lisa, who put me through law school with much personal, professional and financial sacrifice, would have been relegated to the balcony and did not object.

Maturity and experience have taught us that we were wrong. We had much to learn and time to spare. We would have benefited from one last celebration with our professors and our friends and families, and we would have profited by pausing one more time to think about where we had come from and where we were going and what roads we should travel.

This invitation has caused me to stop this hectic and challenge adventure I am on in Washington to think about the roads I have traveled to get there and the roads I wish I had traveled. This reflection has focused me on some turmoil on the roads before you-the choices and opportunities and challenges you will have as lawyers of this time and place in history.

I congratulate you on this achievement. You have sacrificed a considerable amount of your time on earth. You have mastered a strange new language. You have postponed the start of your vocation. You've been swept up in rapid rumors in job opportunities and job conditions. You've changed your daily worth ethics, and you have forgone many of life's simple pleasures. Some of you have earned special recognition this afternoon, and we all congratulate you.

But, tomorrow, my friends, the slate is wiped clean again. Prospective clients don't inquire about class rank. The local bar association you will join does not have a special class of membership for law review staffs. Judges and jurors will not ask to see your resume.

You will be evaluated instead by your product, your energy, your temperament and your backbone. The reputation you develop for intellectual and ethical integrity will be your greatest asset or your worst enemy. You will be judged by your judgment.

The practice of law you've already learned does not lend itself to true-and-false analysis. If the problem is black or white, the client does not need a lawyer.

Instead, your challenge will be to use your education and all your life's experiences to exercise good judgment to select from among the shades of gray.

Practice law with excellence, with pride in your product. Treat every pleading, every brief, every contract, every letter, every daily task as if your career will be judged on it.

Each client is entitled to your best effort. Practice law with a heart. The clients you represent will remember you long after you have forgotten their names. While routine for you, what you are doing for them may be the most important thing in their lives.

For most, you'll be the only lawyer they will ever come into contact with, and they form their perceptions of our justice system and your profession on how you treat them as a person and the quality of your work.

Practice law with consideration and courtesy. No matter how righteous the cause or clear your victory, assure that your adversary with his or her client leaves with dignity.

As Judge Perry Whitmore in Little Rock used to tell us, you can disagree without being disagreeable. Besides, your adversary today may be your judge tomorrow.

Following the bar exam, your most difficult test will not be of what you know but what is your character. Some of you will fail.

The class of 1971 had many distinguished members who also went on to achieve high public office. But it also had several who forfeited their license to practice law. Blinded by greed, some served time in prison.

I cannot make this point to you too strongly. There is no victory, no advantage, no fee, no favor which is worth even a blemish on your reputation for intellect and integrity.

Nothing travels faster than an accusation that another lawyer's word is no good. A judge who catches you in a disingenuous argument or a mischaracterization of a case will turn hard of hearing when you next show up to argue.

Dents to the reputation in the legal profession are irreparable. Every lawyer I know carries around a mental black book which is recorded in indelible ink the names of his adversaries who breached the presumption of good-faith dealing.

Each of you, I hope, will strive always to set your professional goals and your personal goals out there just barely at the end of your reach. Stretch your talents, grasp beyond the closest branch, take a risk, stick your neck out, speak your mind, challenge the status quo and conventional wisdom. Do not just accept responsibility. Chase it down.

You will have failures and disappointments. Take comfort in knowing that opinions of those who really matter will never be as forgiving of your failures or as admiring of your victories as they are at this stage of your career.

Sometimes doing the right thing will be very unpopular with your other clients and with the pundits at the local coffee shop. When the head of controversy swarms around you, the conviction that you did the right thing will be the best salve and the best sleeping medicine.

Listen to each other; listen to older lawyers. If I could have one wish for each of you, it would be to find a mentor who will bring you along, and whose values will be the ones you admire and absorb. In my experience, that is the critical key to professional success and happiness.

Even with such a mentor you will go home some nights feeling like you never want to practice again-the way you've done here after an exam or a Moot Court argument went badly.

But you will go home other days anxious to get back again and slay the dragon. In a few short years you will be a mentor to some new lawyer. Start preparing now to be a good one, to be the kind of mentor that you would want for yourself. Strive to be a lawyer whom other lawyers admire.

Along the way you will receive recognition for achievement, a complimentary newspaper article, an award, a plaque, and if the gods are with you, maybe even a commencement address. When you smile for the camera and bask in the applause and take your bow, pause and reflect and recognize who helped you get there. Your spouse, your law partner, your parents, your friends.

Because there will also be failures, and criticisms and bad press and lies, stormy days and cloudy days, and you will not survive them without the support of those same spouses, law partners and friends. Sit it is.

I pause: Three weeks ago my wife, Lisa, and I celebrated our 25th anniversary, and it was here in Fayetteville in law school where we celebrated our first. Like many in this audience, she began by putting me through law school. For 22 years she always encouraged me to persevere and aim higher. She has been my editor, my jury consultant and my best friend. I wish for all you a Lisa.

A word about family: You have amply demonstrated that you are achievers willing to work hard, long hours, to set aside your personal lives. It reminds me of that observation that no one was ever heard to say on their death bed, I wish I had spent more time at the office.

Balance wisely your professional life and your family life. If you are fortunate to have children, your parents will warn you that your children will grow up and be gone before you know it. I can testify that it is true. God only allows us so many opportunities with our children to read a story, go fishing, play catch, say our prayers together. Try not to miss a one of them. The office can wait. It will still be there when your children are gone.

This ceremony is called a commencement because it's a new journey. Your law school studies are completed, but your education is just under way. Continue to study, but don't limit your studies to the law. If you strive to become a great lawyer, you must be more than a lawyer.

We are defined as persons and lawyers by the depth and variety of our experiences. Continue to broaden your horizons. Read religiously-works other than law.

Travel. By all means travel every chance, everywhere you can. Travel the back roads, not the interstates. Mingle with those of different background and culture and ages.

Quietly observe your fellow man. Sit still and listen to those who are different from you. Look and listen for the values that you share, which you have in common. Tolerance does not come naturally to any of us. You must work at it. We all must work harder at it.

Take time out for yourself. Have some fun, go fishing, every once in a while take a walk in the woods by yourself. Learn to relax, watch more sunsets. Those of you who do not have your life planned out, don't worry. It wouldn't turn out the way you planned it in any event.

Having waited 22 years to make my first career change, as satisfying and successful as that first career was, today I would travel a number of different routes instead.

I hope you will consider trying the wide variety of professional opportunities that the practice of law will over you. Spend some time in public service, whether as an assistant to the prosecutor or a public defender, or a legal service program. Or got to Washington and work for a congressional delegation or one of the federal agencies. Or go to your state capitol and work for a state agency or state commission. Or run for the legislature, school board, city council, or teach at your community college.

But whatever you do, choose a professional life that satisfies you and helps others. If you find yourself getting burned out or unfulfilled, unappreciated or the profits become more important than your work, then have the courage to make a change.

Public service, even volunteer service, presents difficult choices for you, I know. Those of you who have student loans, have deferred buying homes, and deferred other material objects, and you are anxious about the debt, you are anxious about the job market. I understand. But there will be ample time and opportunity for you to make a good living.

But it won't be enough for you to make all the money you can. No matter how successful you are financially, your professional lives will be unhappy if you do not devote some measure of your task to improving your profession and your community. You can do good and still do well.

The First Lady said it best recently. She said service means you get as well as you give. Your life is changed as you change the life of others. It is the way we find meaning in our lives.

Now, I am not under any illusion about why I was invited here today. I know that 48-year-old commercial trial lawyers are not on the short list of graduation speakers. It must have something to do with my recent job change.

That job change has either added credibility to my voice or made me somewhat of a curiosity. And some would ask what motivates one with a comfortable practice in a prominent law firm, to dislodge his family for a new job with longer hours, with half the pay, in a city that costs twice as much to live.

But the reason I am on this new adventure in Washington is because our country is in transition. The people, the citizens, have demanded a change in our government. They are talking back to it in record numbers. The President receives almost a million letters a month. The White House phones are jammed.

Middle-aged Americans all over this country are volunteering to join the administration, to leave lucrative practices and businesses, and to participate in changing our government. Washington is teeming with young people just like you, from all over this country, from all wails of life, who have a sense of a common purpose and desire to be involved.

When we leave work at night, we pull up to a large heavy gate that surrounds the White House complex. While the Secret Service guards slowly open that gate, I always look to my right, and inevitably there are dozens of people aligned along that iron fence that runs along Pennsylvania Avenue, holding on the bars, peering through intently at the White House lit in the background.

When I look into their faces, I can tell that each has hope for something from their government. It is a wonderful reminder of why we are there. I am more encouraged than I have ever been that the pendulum has begun to swing back; that there is a renewed spirit of our common purpose; that Americans, particularly your generation, are again acknowledging that it is the duty of all of us to use all that we have been given to make this a better world, not just for ourselves or our families, but for everyone on earth.

In my job I have now found myself surrounded by young people just like you, who have energized me with their vigor, their optimism, their ideas. I sense that same spirit in this auditorium today, this auditorium made for optimists and doers.

I have the feeling that you are believers and doers who will make something better of what we have handed you. You are the reason for hope because you can be the agents for change-change of your community and change of your legal profession.

The President last week addressed a group just like you. And he said, "Our country needs you. We need your knowledge, your initiative and your energy. We need you because you are still free of the cynicism that has paralyzed too long your parents and your grandparents who led us to spend too much time talking about what we can't do, instead of seizing what we can do."

Like those people along the iron fence on Pennsylvania Avenue, I look into your faces and I see your potential to restore responsibility to our profession and to our society. I see your potential to restore a sense of community, to use your talents to help others and to be fulfilled. God bless you and good luck to you.

Section 4. The Commencement of Your Ethical Career

Ryan Holiday, in his new book, *Discipline is Destiny: The Power of Self-Control* writes:

Aristotle described virtue as a kind of craft, something to pursue just as one pursues the mastery of any profession or skill. "We become builders by building and we become harpists by playing the harp," he

wrote. Similarly, then, we become just by doing just actions, temperate
by doing temperate actions, brave by doing brave actions.

We agree. So, we close this book by stating this single most important rule: If you want to be an ethical and professional lawyer, act ethically and professionally.

Go forth, and relish careers that are fulfilling, challenging, and a contribution to a just society.

BEYOND THE CITE

By: Robert Gottfried, *The Anatomy of Our Oath as Lawyers,* **January 01, 2022.**

The road to becoming a practicing attorney is a long and arduous one. After years of law school and months of studying for the bar exam, one more step remains before we're officially licensed to practice: Every lawyer in the country must be sworn in and take their state's oath of attorney.

This ceremony may seem traditional and mundane, but it has never been more important. This oath binds each attorney to certain professional obligations and requires us, as lawyers, to faithfully uphold and support the laws of our state and our country.

What does it mean to take an oath?

Merriam-Webster defines an oath as: "a solemn attestation of the truth or inviolability of one's words." We ask new attorneys to take an oath on the day they receive their license and as a condition of that license.

The words in that oath are a mandate to all attorneys that they practice with professionalism, integrity, and respect. Each state's oath varies in its wording, but they all require of us the same three duties: to support the Constitution of the United States, to faithfully discharge the duties of an attorney, and to conduct oneself with integrity and civility.

Here's what each means.

1. "I solemnly swear that I will support the Constitution of the United States, . . ." As officers of the courts, lawyers are sworn to support the Constitution not just of the state in which they seek to practice, but above all, to support the Constitution of the United States. This promise is included first in every state's attorney oath, and it's the most important promise a new attorney will make.

This promise commands an attorney to take action to ensure the supreme law of the land is followed and upheld. It's a burden on all lawyers—every lawyer must defend the U.S. Constitution, in all ways, at all times.

Current events have caused us to look closer at this promise. Are we obligated to defend the Constitution if a client is paying us to do the opposite? Are we required to support the Constitution when our desired outcome justifies its subversion? Without question or qualification, the answer to both questions is yes.

A prerequisite of your license is your inviolable promise that you'll always support and defend the Constitution in all situations. Lawyers may not take actions, advocate for positions, or demand relief that would cause them to do otherwise; this is, above all, our most sacred promise.

2.   "... that I will faithfully discharge the duties of the office of attorney, ..." Next, new attorneys are asked to "faithfully discharge the duties of the office of attorney." Every state has its own code of professional conduct, and many are based on the ABA's own Model Rules.

These rules define the nature of an attorney's personal and professional life, prescribing exactly what an attorney must do outside and inside the courtroom or in practice. We're required to take these rules seriously, to work and live by the rules defining the duties of our office. They require us to maintain our client's confidence, execute our professional functions competently and diligently, conform to the law's requirements in our business and personal affairs, uphold the legal process, and seek improvement in the law and access to legal systems.

Herein is another burden imposed by our oaths: Even when we think no one is watching, even when our client's position would cause us to advocate for the opposite, even when we're engaging in business outside the practice of law, our oaths require us to remain honest and diligent and to uphold the rule of law even when it's difficult or adverse to our personal or professional objectives.

3.   "... and that I will conduct myself at all times with integrity and civility." This last promise isn't explicitly requested of attorneys in every state. However, integrity and civility are written into the codes of professional conduct in each state, and maintaining those qualities is a component of faithfully discharging the duties of our office.

That said, many states explicitly call out the need for attorneys to maintain integrity, civility, honesty, dignity, and courteousness. Turn on the news, and you'll find that attorney dishonesty, incivility, and lack of integrity are omnipresent in our society. In our adversarial system, it has become common to attack opposing parties rather than work with them. Vitriol and stubbornness prevail more often than not.

This final promise in our oaths reminds us that we have a duty to comport ourselves oppositely. We have a duty to be civil, personify the values of honesty and integrity, and build up the reputation of the profession. This promise requires us to work together to achieve a fairer system—a system that represents the needs of our clients first and foremost, not the wants of their attorneys.

In that sense, we see what the oath of attorney is about—it's about devoting ourselves to the betterment of the profession and our communities, to ensuring that the rule of law is upheld, to advocating honestly and with integrity, and to making the system a fairer, more representative, and more just place for all.

Oaths of Admission for All 50 States

Alabama

I do solemnly swear (or affirm) that I will demean myself as an attorney, according to the best of my learning and ability, and with all good fidelity, as well to the court as to the client; that I will use no falsehood or delay any person's cause for lucre or malice, and that I will support the Constitution of the State of Alabama and of the United States, so long as I continue a citizen(or legal resident) thereof, so help me God.

Alaska

I do affirm:

I will support the Constitution of the United States and the Constitution of the State of Alaska;

I will adhere to the Rules of Professional Conduct in my dealings with clients, judicial officers, attorneys, and all other persons;

I will maintain the respect due to courts of justice and judicial officers;

I will not counsel or maintain any proceedings that I believe are taken in bad faith or any defense that I do not believe is honestly debatable under the law of the land;

I will be truthful and honorable in the causes entrusted to me, and will never seek to mislead the judge or jury by an artifice or false statement of fact or law;

I will maintain the confidences and preserve inviolate the secrets of my client, and will not accept compensation in connection with my client's business except from my client or with my client's knowledge or approval;

I will be candid, fair, and courteous before the court and with other attorneys, and will advance no fact prejudicial to the honor or reputation of a party or witness, unless I am required to do so in order to obtain justice for my client;

I will uphold the honor and maintain the dignity of the profession, and will strive to improve both the law and the administration of justice.

Arizona

I, (state your name), do solemnly swear that I will support the Constitution of the United States and the Constitution of the State of Arizona;

I will maintain the respect due to courts of justice and judicial officers;

I will not counsel or maintain any suit or proceeding that shall appear to me to be without merit or to be unjust;

I will not assert any defense except such as I honestly believe to be debatable under the law of the land;

I will employ for the purpose of maintaining the causes confided to me such means only as are consistent with truth and honor; I will never seek to mislead the judge or jury by any misstatement or false statement of fact or law;

I will maintain the confidence and preserve inviolate the secrets of my client; I will accept no compensation in connection with my client's business except from my client or with my client's knowledge and approval;

I will abstain from all offensive conduct; I will not advance any fact prejudicial to the honor or reputation of a party or witness, unless required by the justice of the cause with which I am charged;

I will never reject, from any consideration personal to myself, the cause of the defenseless or oppressed, nor will I delay any person's cause for greed or malice;

I will at all times faithfully and diligently adhere to the rules of professional responsibility and a lawyer's creed of professionalism of the State Bar of Arizona.

Arkansas

I DO SOLEMNLY SWEAR OR AFFIRM:

I will support the Constitution of the United States and the Constitution of the State of Arkansas, and I will faithfully perform the duties of attorney at law.

I will maintain the respect and courtesy due to courts of justice, judicial officers, and those who assist them.

I will, to the best of my ability, abide by the Arkansas Rules of Professional Conduct and any other standards of ethics proclaimed by the courts, and in doubtful cases I will attempt to abide by the spirit of those ethical rules and precepts of honor and fair play.

To opposing parties and their counsel, I pledge fairness, integrity, and civility, not only in court, but also in all written and oral communications.

I will not reject, from any consideration personal to myself, the cause of the impoverished, the defenseless, or the oppressed.

I will endeavor always to advance the cause of justice and to defend and to keep inviolate the rights of all persons whose trust is conferred upon me as an attorney at law.

California

I solemnly swear (or affirm) that I will support the Constitution of the United States and the Constitution of the State of California, and that I will faithfully discharge the duties of an attorney and counsel or at law to the best of my knowledge and ability.

Colorado

I DO SOLEMNLY SWEAR by the Everliving God (OR AFFIRM) that:

I will support the Constitution of the United States and the Constitution of the State of Colorado; I will maintain the respect due to Courts and judicial officers; I will employ only such means as are consistent with truth and honor; I will treat all persons whom I encounter through my practice of law with fairness, courtesy, respect and honesty; I will use my knowledge of the law for the betterment of society and the improvement of the legal system; I will never reject, from any consideration personal to myself, the cause of the defenseless or oppressed; I will at all times faithfully and diligently adhere to the Colorado Rules of Professional Conduct.

Connecticut

You solemnly swear or solemnly and sincerely affirm, as the case may be, that you will do nothing dishonest, and will not knowingly allow anything dishonest to be done in court, and that you will inform the court of any dishonesty of which you have knowledge; that you will not knowingly maintain or assist in maintaining any cause of action that is false or unlawful; that you will not obstruct any cause of action for personal gain or malice; but that you will exercise the office of attorney, in any court in which you may practice, according to the best of your learning and judgment, faithfully, to both your client and the court; so help you God or upon penalty of perjury.

Delaware

I do solemnly swear (or affirm) that I will support the Constitution of the United States and the Constitution of the State of Delaware; that I will behave myself in the office of an attorney within the Court according to the best of my learning and ability and with all good fidelity, as well to the Court as to the client; that I will use no falsehood, nor delay any person's cause through lucre and malice.

Florida

I do solemnly swear: I will support the Constitution of the United States and the Constitution of the State of Florida; I will maintain the respect due to courts of justice and judicial officers; I will not counsel or maintain any suit or proceedings which shall appear to me to be unjust, nor any defense except such as I believe to be honestly debatable under the law of the land; I will employ, for the purpose of maintaining the causes confided in me such means only as are consistent with truth and honor, and will never seek to mislead the judge or jury by any artifice or false statement of fact or law; I will maintain the confidence and preserve inviolate the secrets of my clients, and will accept no compensation in connection with their business except from them or with their knowledge and approval; To opposing parties and their counsel, I pledge fairness, integrity, and civility, not only in court, but also in all written and oral communications; I will abstain from all offensive personality and advance no fact prejudicial to the honor or reputation of a party or witness, unless required by the justice of the cause with which I am charged; I will never reject, from any consideration personal to myself, the cause of the defenseless or oppressed, or delay anyone's cause for lucre or malice. So help me God.

Georgia

I do solemnly swear that I will conduct myself as an attorney or counselor of the Supreme Court of Georgia, truly and honestly, justly and uprightly, and according to law; and that I will support the Constitution of the State of Georgia and the Constitution of the United States. So help me God.

Hawaii

I do solemnly swear (or affirm) that I will support and defend the Constitution of the United States and the Constitution and laws of the State of Hawaii, and that I will at all times conduct myself in accordance with the Hawaii Rules of Professional Conduct.

As an officer of the courts to which I am admitted to practice, I will conduct myself with dignity and civility towards judicial officers, court staff, and my fellow professionals.

I will faithfully discharge my duties as attorney, counselor, and solicitor in the courts of the state to the best of my ability, giving due consideration to the legal needs of those without access to justice.

Idaho

I DO SOLEMNLY SWEAR THAT: (I do solemnly affirm that:)

I will support the Constitution of the United States and the Constitution of the State of Idaho. I will abide by the rules of professional conduct adopted by the Idaho Supreme Court.

I will respect courts and judicial officers in keeping with my role as an officer of the court.

I will represent my clients with vigor and zeal, and will preserve inviolate their confidences and secrets.

I will never seek to mislead a court or opposing party by false statement of fact or law, and will scrupulously honor promises and commitments made.

I will attempt to resolve matters expeditiously and without unnecessary expense.

I will contribute time and resources to public service, and will never reject, for any consideration personal to myself, the cause of the defenseless or oppressed.

I will conduct myself personally and professionally in conformity with the high standards of my profession.

SO HELP ME GOD. (I hereby affirm.)

Illinois

I do solemnly swear (or affirm, as the case may be), that I will support the constitution of the United States and the constitution of the state of Illinois, and that I will faithfully discharge the duties of the office of attorney and counselor at law to the best of my ability.

Indiana

I do solemnly swear or affirm that: I will support the Constitution of the United States and the Constitution of the State of Indiana; I will maintain the respect due to courts of justice and judicial officers; I will not counsel or maintain any action, proceeding, or defense which shall appear to me to be unjust, but this obligation shall not prevent me from defending a person charged with crime in any case; I will employ for the purpose of maintaining the causes confided to me, such means only as are consistent with truth, and never seek to mislead the court or jury by any artifice or false statement of fact or law; I will maintain the confidence and preserve inviolate the secrets of my client at every peril to myself; I will abstain from offensive personality and advance no fact prejudicial to the honor or reputation of a party or witness, unless required by the justice of the cause with which I am charged; I will not encourage either the commencement or the continuance of any action or proceeding from any motive of passion or interest; I will never reject, from any consideration personal to myself, the cause of the defenseless, the oppressed or those who cannot afford adequate legal assistance; so help me God.

Iowa

I do solemnly swear:

I will support the Constitution of the United States and the Constitution of the State of Iowa; I will maintain the respect due to courts of justice and judicial officers;

I will not counsel or maintain any suit or proceeding which shall appear to me to be unjust, nor any defense except the defense of a person charged with a public offense;

I will employ for the purpose of maintaining the causes confided to me such means only as are consistent with truth, and will never seek to mislead the judges by any artifice or false statement of fact or law;

I will maintain the confidence, and, at any peril to myself, will preserve the secret of my client;

I will abstain from all offensive personality, and advance no fact prejudicial to the honor or reputation of a party or witness, unless required by the justice of the cause with which I am charged;

I will refuse to encourage either the commencement or continuance of an action proceeding from any motive of passion or interest;

I will never reject, from any consideration personal to myself, the cause of the defenseless or oppressed; and

I will faithfully discharge the duties of an attorney and counselor at law to the best of my ability and in accordance with the ethics of my profession, So Help Me God.

Kansas

You do solemnly swear or affirm that you will support and bear true allegiance to the Constitution of the United States and the Constitution of the State of Kansas; that you will neither delay nor deny the rights of any person through malice, for lucre, or from any unworthy desire; that you will not knowingly foster or promote, or give your assent to any fraudulent, groundless or unjust suit; that you will neither do, nor consent to the doing of any falsehood in court; and that you will discharge your duties as an attorney and counselor of the Supreme Court and all other courts of the State of Kansas with fidelity both to the Court and to your cause, and to the best of your knowledge and ability. So help you God.

Kentucky

I do solemnly swear (or affirm, as the case may be) that I will support the Constitution of the United States and the Constitution of this Commonwealth, and be faithful and true to the Commonwealth of Kentucky so long as I continue a citizen thereof, and that I will faithfully execute, to the best of my ability, the office of . . . . according to law; and I do further solemnly swear (or affirm) that since the adoption of the present Constitution, I, being a citizen of this State, have not fought a duel with deadly weapons within this State nor out of it, nor have I sent or accepted a challenge to fight a duel with deadly weapons, nor have I acted as second in carrying a challenge, nor aided or assisted any person thus offending, so help me God.

Louisiana

I, SOLEMNLY SWEAR OR AFFIRM

I will support the Constitution of the United States and the Constitution of the State of Louisiana;

I will maintain the respect due to courts of justice and judicial officers; I will not counsel or maintain any suit or proceeding which shall appear to me to be unjust nor any defense except such as I believe to be honestly debatable under the law of the land;

I will employ for the purpose of maintaining the causes confided to me such means only as are consistent with truth and honor and will never seek to mislead the judge or jury by any artifice or false statement of fact or law;

I will maintain the confidence and preserve inviolate the secrets of my client and will accept no compensation in connection with a client's business except from the client or with the client's knowledge and approval;

To opposing parties and their counsel, I pledge fairness, integrity, and civility, not only in court, but also in all written and oral communications;

I will abstain from all offensive personality and advance no fact prejudicial to the honor or reputation of a party or witness unless required by the justice of the cause with which I am charged;

I will never reject from any consideration personal to myself the cause of the defenseless or oppressed or delay any person's cause for lucre or malice.

SO HELP ME GOD!

Maine

You solemnly swear that you will do no falsehood nor consent to the doing of any in court, and that if you know of an intention to commit any, you will give knowledge thereof to the justices of the court or some of them that it may be prevented; you will not wittingly or willingly promote or sue any false, groundless or unlawful suit nor give aid or consent to the same; that you will delay no man for lucre or malice, but will conduct yourself in the office of an attorney within the courts according to the best of your knowledge and discretion, and with all good fidelity, as well as to the courts, as to your clients. So help you God.

Maryland

I do solemnly (swear) (affirm) that I will at all times demean myself fairly and honorably as an attorney and practitioner at law; that I will bear true allegiance to the State of Maryland, and support the laws and Constitution thereof, and that I will bear true allegiance to the United States, and that I will support, protect and defend the Constitution, laws and government thereof as the supreme law of the land; any law, or ordinance of this or any state to the contrary notwithstanding.

Massachusetts

I (repeat the name) solemnly swear that I will do no falsehood, nor consent to the doing of any in court; I will not wittingly or willingly promote or sue any false, groundless or unlawful suit, nor give aid or consent to the same; I will delay no man for lucre or malice; but I will conduct myself in the office of an attorney within the courts according to the best of my knowledge and discretion, and with all good fidelity as well to the courts as my clients. So help me God.

Michigan

I do solemnly swear (or affirm):

I will support the Constitution of the United States and the Constitution of the State of Michigan; I will maintain the respect due to courts of justice and judicial officers;

I will not counsel or maintain any suit or proceeding which shall appear to me to be unjust, nor any defense except such as I believe to be honestly debatable under the law of the land;

I will employ for the purpose of maintaining the causes confided to me such means only as are consistent with truth and honor, and will never seek to mislead the judge or jury by any artifice or false statement of fact or law;

I will maintain the confidence and preserve inviolate the secrets of my client, and will accept no compensation in connection with my client's business except with my client's knowledge and approval;

I will abstain from all offensive personality, and advance no fact prejudicial to the honor or reputation of a party or witness, unless required by the justice of the cause with which I am charged;

I will never reject, from any consideration personal to myself, the cause of the defenseless or oppressed, or delay any cause for lucre or malice;

I will in all other respects conduct myself personally and professionally in conformity with the high standards of conduct imposed upon members of the bar as conditions for the privilege to practice law in this State.

Minnesota

You do swear that you will support the Constitution of the United States and that of the state of Minnesota, and will conduct yourself as an attorney and counselor at law in an upright and courteous manner, to the best of your learning and ability, with all good fidelity as well to the court as to the client, and that you will use no falsehood or deceit, nor delay any person's cause for lucre or malice. So help you God.

Mississippi

I do solemnly swear (or affirm) that I will demean myself, as an attorney and counselor of this court, according to the best of my learning and ability, and with all good fidelity as well to the court as to the client; that I will use no falsehood nor delay any person's cause for lucre or malice, and that I will support the Constitution of the State of Mississippi so long as I continue a citizen thereof. So help me God.

Missouri

I do solemnly swear that I will support the Constitution of the United States and the Constitution of the State of Missouri;

That I will maintain the respect due courts of justice, judicial officers and members of my profession and will at all times conduct myself with dignity becoming of an officer of the court in which I appear;

That I will never seek to mislead the judge or jury by any artifice or false statement of fact or law; That I will at all times conduct myself in accordance with the Rules of Professional Conduct; and,

That I will practice law to the best of my knowledge and ability and with consideration for the defenseless and oppressed.

So help me God.

Montana

I do solemnly swear (or affirm) that I will support, protect and defend the Constitution of the United States, and the Constitution of the State of Montana, and that I will discharge the duties of my office with fidelity (so help me God).

Nebraska

You do solemnly swear that you will support the Constitution of the United States, and the Constitution of this state, and that you will faithfully discharge the duties of an attorney and counselor, according to the best of your ability.

Nevada

I, _____, do solemnly affirm that I will support, protect and defend the Constitution and Government of the United States, and the Constitution and government of the State of Nevada, against all enemies, whether domestic or foreign, and that I will bear true faith, allegiance and loyalty to the same, any ordinance, resolution or law of any state notwithstanding, and that I will well and faithfully perform all the duties of the office of attorney, on which I am about to enter; under the pains and penalties of perjury.

New Hampshire

You solemnly swear or affirm that you will do no falsehood, nor consent that any be done in the court, and if you know of any, that you will give knowledge thereof to the justices of the court, or some of them, that it may be reformed; that you will not wittingly or willingly promote, sue or procure to be sued any false or unlawful suit, nor consent to the same; that you will delay no person for lucre or malice, and will act in the office of an attorney within the court according to the best of your learning and discretion, and with all good fidelity as well to the court as to your client. So help you God or under the pains and penalty of perjury.

New Mexico

I, _____, do solemnly swear or affirm:

I will support the Constitution of the United States and the Constitution of the State of New Mexico; I will maintain the respect due to courts of justice and judicial officers;

I will comply with the Rules of Professional Conduct adopted by the New Mexico Supreme Court;

I will not counsel or maintain any suit or proceeding which shall appear to me to be unjust, nor any defense except such as I believe to be honestly debatable under the law of the land;

I will employ for the purpose of maintaining the causes confided to me such means only as are consistent with truth and honor, and will never seek to mislead the judge or jury by any artifice or false statement of fact or law;

I will maintain the confidence and preserve inviolate the secrets of my clients, and will accept no compensation in connection with their business except from them or with their knowledge and approval;

I will maintain civility at all times, abstain from all offensive personality, and advance no fact prejudicial to the honor or reputation of a party or witness unless required by the justice of the cause with which I am charged;

I will never reject from any consideration personal to myself the cause of the defenseless or oppressed, or delay any person's cause for lucre or malice.

New Jersey

I do solemnly swear (or affirm) that, to the best of my knowledge and ability, I will support and defend the Constitution of the United States against all enemies, foreign and domestic, and that I will bear true faith and allegiance to the same; that I take this obligation freely, without any mental reservation or purpose of evasion; and that I demean myself as an Attorney At Law of this Court, uprightly and according to law. So help me God.

New York

I do solemnly swear (or affirm) that I will support the constitution of the United States, and the constitution of the State of New York, and that I will faithfully discharge the duties of the office of [attorney and counselor-at-law], according to the best of my ability.

North Carolina

I, _____, do solemnly swear that I will support the Constitution of the United States; so help me God.

I, _____, do solemnly and sincerely swear that I will be faithful and bear true allegiance to the State of North Carolina and to the Constitutional powers and authorities which are or may be established for the government thereof; and that I will endeavor to support, maintain and defend the Constitution of said state, not inconsistent with the Constitution of the United States, to the best of my knowledge and ability; so help me God.

I, _____, do swear that I will truly and honestly demean myself in the practice of an Attorney, according to the best of my knowledge and ability, so help me God.

North Dakota

I do solemnly swear (or affirm as the case may be) that I will support the Constitution of the United States and the Constitution of the State of North Dakota; and that I will faithfully discharge the duties of the office of _____ according to the best of my ability, so help me God (if an oath), (under pains and penalties of perjury) if an affirmation, and any other oath, declaration, or test may not be required as a qualification for any office or public trust.

Ohio

I Do Solemnly Swear:

I will support the Constitution of the United States and the Constitution of the State of Ohio; I will maintain the respect due to courts of justice and judicial officers;

I will not counsel or maintain any suit or proceeding which shall appear to me to be unjust, nor any defense except such as I believe to be honestly debatable under the law of the land;

I will employ for the sole purposes of maintaining the causes confined to me such means only as are consistent with truth and honor, and will never seek to mislead the judge or jury by any artifice or false statement of fact or law;

I will maintain the confidence and preserve inviolate the secrets of my client, and will accept no compensation in connection with his business except from him or his knowledge and approval;

I will abstain from all offensive personality, and advance no fact prejudicial to the honor or reputation of a part or witness, unless required by the justice of the cause with which I am charged;

I will never reject, from any consideration person to myself, the cause of the defenseless or oppressed, or delay any man's cause for lucre or malice.

So Help Me God.

Oklahoma

You do solemnly swear that you will support, protect and defend the Constitution of the United States, and the Constitution of the State of Oklahoma; that you will do no falsehood or consent that any be done in court, and if you know of any you will give knowledge thereof to the judges of the court, or some one of them, that it may be reformed; you will not wittingly, willingly or knowingly promote, sue, or procure to be sued, any false or unlawful suit, or give aid or consent to the same; you will delay no man for lucre or malice, but will act in the office of attorney in this court according to your best learning and discretion, with all good fidelity as well to the court as to your client, so help you God.

Oregon

I ____ swear or affirm

That I will faithfully and honestly conduct myself in the office of an attorney in the courts of the State of Oregon; that I will observe and abide by the Rules of Professional Conduct approved by the Supreme Court of the State of Oregon; and that I will support the Constitution and laws of the United States and of the State of Oregon.

Pennsylvania

I do solemnly swear (or affirm) that I will support, obey and defend the Constitution of the United States and the Constitution of this Commonwealth and that I will discharge the duties of my office with fidelity, as well to the court as to the client, that I will use no falsehood, nor delay the cause of any person for lucre or malice.

Rhode Island

You solemnly swear that in the exercise of the office of attorney and counselor you will do no falsehood, nor consent to any being done; you will not wittingly or willingly promote, sue or cause to be sued any false or unlawful suit; or give aid, or consent to the same; you will delay no man's cause for lucre or malice; you will in all respects demean yourself as an attorney and counselor of this court and of all other courts before which you may practice uprightly and ac-cording to law, with fidelity as well to the court as to your client; and that you will support the constitution and laws of this state and the constitution and laws of the United States. So help you God.

South Carolina

I do solemnly swear (or affirm) that:

I am duly qualified, according to the Constitution of this State, to exercise the duties of the office to which I have been appointed, and that I will, to the best of my ability, discharge those duties and will preserve, protect and defend the Constitution of this State and of the United States;

I will maintain the respect and courtesy due to courts of justice, judicial officers, and those who assist them;

To my clients, I pledge faithfulness, competence, diligence, good judgment and prompt communication;

To opposing parties and their counsel, I pledge fairness, integrity, and civility, not only in court, but also in all written and oral communications;

I will not pursue or maintain any suit or proceeding which appears to me to be unjust nor maintain any defenses except those I believe to be honestly debatable under the law of the land, but this obligation shall not prevent me from defending a person charged with a crime;

I will employ for the purpose of maintaining the causes confided to me only such means as are consistent with trust and honor and the principles of professionalism, and will never seek to mislead an opposing party, the judge or jury by a false statement of fact or law;

I will respect and preserve inviolate the confidences of my clients, and will accept no compensation in connection with a client's business except from the client or with the client's knowledge and approval;

I will maintain the dignity of the legal system and advance no fact prejudicial to the honor or reputation of a party or witness, unless required by the justice of the cause with which I am charged;

I will assist the defenseless or oppressed by ensuring that justice is available to all citizens and will not delay any person's cause for profit or malice;

[So help me God.]

South Dakota

I do solemnly swear, or affirm, that:

I will support the Constitution of the United States and the Constitution of the State of South Dakota; I will maintain the respect due to courts of justice and judicial officers;

I will not counsel or maintain any suit or proceeding which shall appear to me to be unjust, nor any defense except such as I believe to be honestly debatable under the law of the land;

I will employ for the purpose of maintaining the causes confided to me such means only as are consistent with truth and honor, and will never seek to mislead the judge or jury by any artifice or false statement of fact or law;

I will maintain the confidence and preserve inviolate the secrets of my client, and will accept no compensation in connection with a client's business except from that client or with the client's knowledge or approval;

I will abstain from all offensive personality, and advance no fact prejudicial to the honor or reputation of a party or witness, unless required by the justice of the cause with which I am charged;

I will never reject, from any consideration personal to myself, the cause of the defenseless or oppressed, or delay any person's cause for lucre or malice.

Tennessee

I, _____, do solemnly swear or affirm that I will support the Constitution of the United States and the Constitution of the State of Tennessee, and that I will truly and honestly demean myself in the practice of my profession to the best of my skill and abilities, so help me God.

Texas

I, _____, do solemnly swear that I will support the constitution of the United States, and of State; that I will honestly demean myself in the practice of the law, and will discharge my duties to my clients to the best of my ability. So help me God.

Utah

I DO SOLEMNLY SWEAR that I will support, obey and defend the Constitution of the United States and the Constitution of Utah; that I will discharge the duties of attorney and counselor at law as an officer of the courts with honesty, fidelity, professionalism, and civility; and that I will faithfully observe the Rules of Professional Conduct and the Standards of

Professionalism and Civility promulgated by the Supreme Court of the State of Utah.

Vermont

You do solemnly swear (or affirm) that you will do no falsehood, nor consent that any be done in court, and if you know of any, you will give knowledge thereof to the judges of the court or some of them, that it may be reformed; that you will not wittingly, willingly or knowingly promote, sue or procure to be sued, any false or unlawful suit, or give aid or consent to the same; that you will delay no person for lucre or malice, but will act in the office of attorney within the court, according to your best learning and discretion, with all good fidelity as well to the court as to your client. (If an oath) So help you God. (If an affirmation) Under the pains and penalties of perjury. [I do.]

You do solemnly swear (or affirm) that you will be true and faithful to the State of Vermont, and that you will not, directly or indirectly, do any act or thing injurious to the Constitution or Government thereof. (if an oath) So help you God. (If an affirmation) Under the pains and penalties of perjury. [I do.]

You do solemnly swear (or affirm) that you will be true and faithful to the United States of America and that you will not, directly or indirectly, do any act or thing injurious to the Constitution or Government thereof. (If an oath) So help you God. (If an affirmation) Under the pains and penalties of perjury. [I do.]

Virginia

Do you solemnly swear or affirm that you will support the Constitution of the United States and the Constitution of the Commonwealth of Virginia, and that you will faithfully, honestly, professionally, and courteously demean yourself in the practice of law and execute your office of attorney at law to the best of your ability, so help you God?

Washington

I, _____, do solemnly declare:

1. I am fully subject to the laws of the State of Washington and the laws of the United States and will abide by the same.

2. I will support the Constitution of the State of Washington and the Constitution of the United States.

3. I will abide by the Rules of Professional Conduct approved by the Supreme Court of the State of Washington.

4. I will maintain the respect due to the courts of justice and judicial officers.

5. I will not counsel or maintain any suit or proceeding which shall appear to me to be unjust, or any defense except as I believe to be honestly debatable under the law, unless it is in defense of a person charged with a public offense. I will employ, for the purpose of maintaining the causes confided to me, only those means consistent with truth and honor. I will never seek to mislead the judge or jury by any artifice or false statement.

6. I will maintain the confidence and preserve inviolate the secrets of my client and will accept no compensation in connection with the business of my client, unless this compensation is from or with the knowledge and approval of the client or with the approval of the court.

7. I will abstain from all offensive personalities and advance no fact prejudicial to the honor or reputation of a party or witness unless required by the justice of the cause with which I am charged.

8. I will never reject, from any consideration personal to myself, the cause of the defenseless or oppressed, or delay unjustly the cause of any person.

West Virginia

I do solemnly swear or affirm that: I will support the Constitution of the United States and the Constitution of the State of West Virginia; that I will honestly demean myself in the practice of law; and, to the best of my ability, execute my office of attorney-at-law; so help me God.

Wisconsin

I will support the constitution of the United States and the constitution of the state of Wisconsin; I will maintain the respect due to courts of justice and judicial officers;

I will not counsel or maintain any suit or proceeding which shall appear to me to be unjust, or any defense, except such as I believe to be honestly debatable under the law of the land;

I will employ, for the purpose of maintaining the causes confided to me, such means only as are consistent with truth and honor, and will never seek to mislead the judge or jury by any artifice or false statement of fact or law;

I will maintain the confidence and preserve inviolate the secrets of my client and will accept no compensation in connection with my client's business except from my client or with my client's knowledge and approval;

I will abstain from all offensive personality and advance no fact prejudicial to the honor or reputation of a party or witness, unless required by the justice of the cause with which I am charged;

I will never reject, from any consideration personal to myself, the cause of the defenseless or oppressed, or delay any person's cause for lucre or malice. So help me God.

Wyoming

I _____, do solemnly swear that I will support, obey and defend the Constitution of the United States and the Constitution and laws of the State of Wyoming, and that I will faithfully and honestly and to the best of my ability discharge the duties of an Attorney and Counselor at Law.

To assess your understanding of the material in this chapter, click here to take a quiz.

Index

References are to Pages

EVIDENCE